LET'S GO

Australia

▓ Let's Go writers travel on your budget.

"Guides that penetrate the veneer of the holiday brochures and mine the grit of real life."
—*The Economist*

"The writers seem to have experienced every rooster-packed bus and lunar-surfaced mattress about which they write."
—*The New York Times*

"All the dirt, dirt cheap."
—*People*

▓ Great for independent travelers.

"The guides are aimed not only at young budget travelers but at the independent traveler, a sort of streetwise cookbook for traveling alone."
—*The New York Times*

"Flush with candor and irreverence, chock full of budget travel advice."
—*The Des Moines Register*

"An indispensable resource. *Let's Go*'s practical information can be used by every traveler."
—*The Chattanooga Free Press*

▓ Let's Go is completely revised each year.

"Only *Let's Go* has the zeal to annually update every title on its list."
—*The Boston Globe*

"Unbeatable: good sight-seeing advice; up-to-date info on restaurants, hotels, and inns; a commitment to money-saving travel; and a wry style that brightens nearly every page."
—*The Washington Post*

▓ All the important information you need.

"*Let's Go* authors provide a comedic element while still providing concise information and thorough coverage of the country. Anything you need to know about budget traveling is detailed in this book."
—*The Chicago Sun-Times*

"Value-packed, unbeatable, accurate, and comprehensive."
—*Los Angeles Times*

Let's Go Publications

Let's Go: Alaska & the Pacific Northwest 1999
Let's Go: Australia 1999
Let's Go: Austria & Switzerland 1999
Let's Go: Britain & Ireland 1999
Let's Go: California 1999
Let's Go: Central America 1999
Let's Go: Eastern Europe 1999
Let's Go: Ecuador & the Galápagos Islands 1999
Let's Go: Europe 1999
Let's Go: France 1999
Let's Go: Germany 1999
Let's Go: Greece 1999 **New title!**
Let's Go: India & Nepal 1999
Let's Go: Ireland 1999
Let's Go: Israel & Egypt 1999
Let's Go: Italy 1999
Let's Go: London 1999
Let's Go: Mexico 1999
Let's Go: New York City 1999
Let's Go: New Zealand 1999
Let's Go: Paris 1999
Let's Go: Rome 1999
Let's Go: South Africa 1999 **New title!**
Let's Go: Southeast Asia 1999
Let's Go: Spain & Portugal 1999
Let's Go: Turkey 1999 **New title!**
Let's Go: USA 1999
Let's Go: Washington, D.C. 1999

Let's Go Map Guides

Amsterdam	Madrid
Berlin	New Orleans
Boston	New York City
Chicago	Paris
Florence	Rome
London	San Francisco
Los Angeles	Washington, D.C.

Coming Soon: Prague, Seattle

Let's Go
Publications

Let's Go
Australia
1999

Sonja B. Starr
Editor

Eli Ceryak
Kristin C. Gore
Associate Editors

Researcher-Writers:

David Collins	Bryan Leach
David Fagundes	Kathleen Peggar
Robert Fuller	Amy Piper
Derek Glanz	Sarah Thomas
Lillian Gutwein	Georgia Young

St. Martin's Press ❧ New York

HELPING LET'S GO

If you want to share your discoveries, suggestions, or corrections, please drop us a line. We read every piece of correspondence, whether a postcard, a 10-page email, or a coconut. Please note that mail received after May 1999 may be too late for the 2000 book, but will be kept for future editions. **Address mail to:**

**Let's Go: Australia
67 Mount Auburn Street
Cambridge, MA 02138
USA**

Visit Let's Go at **http://www.letsgo.com**, or send email to:

**feedback@letsgo.com
Subject: "Let's Go: Australia"**

In addition to the invaluable travel advice our readers share with us, many are kind enough to offer their services as researchers or editors. Unfortunately, our charter enables us to employ only currently enrolled Harvard-Radcliffe students.

About Let's Go

THIRTY-NINE YEARS OF WISDOM

Back in 1960, a few students at Harvard University banded together to produce a 20-page pamphlet offering a collection of tips on budget travel in Europe. This modest, mimeographed packet, offered as an extra to passengers on student charter flights to Europe, met with instant popularity. The following year, students traveling to Europe researched the first, full-fledged edition of *Let's Go: Europe,* a pocket-sized book featuring honest, irreverent writing and a decidedly youthful outlook on the world. Throughout the 60s, our guides reflected the times; the 1969 guide to America led off by inviting travelers to "dig the scene" at San Francisco's Haight-Ashbury. During the 70s and 80s, we gradually added regional guides and expanded coverage into the Middle East and Central America. With the addition of our in-depth city guides, handy map guides, and extensive coverage of Asia and Australia, the 90s are also proving to be a time of explosive growth for Let's Go, and there's certainly no end in sight. The maiden edition of *Let's Go: South Africa,* our pioneer guide to sub-Saharan Africa, hits the shelves this year, along with the first editions of *Let's Go: Greece* and *Let's Go: Turkey.*

We've seen a lot in 39 years. *Let's Go: Europe* is now the world's bestselling international guide, translated into seven languages. And our new guides bring Let's Go's total number of titles, with their spirit of adventure and their reputation for honesty, accuracy, and editorial integrity, to 44. But some things never change: our guides are still researched, written, and produced entirely by students who know first-hand how to see the world on the cheap.

HOW WE DO IT

The series is completely revised and thoroughly updated every year by a well-traveled set of over 200 students. Every winter, we recruit over 160 researchers and 70 editors to write the books anew. After several months of training, researcher-writers hit the road for seven weeks of exploration, from Anchorage to Adelaide, Estonia to El Salvador, Iceland to Indonesia. Hired for their rare combination of budget travel sense, writing ability, stamina, and courage, these adventurous travelers know that train strikes, stolen luggage, food poisoning, and marriage proposals are all part of a day's work. Back at our offices, editors work from spring to fall, massaging copy written on Himalayan bus rides into witty yet informative prose. A student staff of typesetters, cartographers, publicists, and managers keeps our lively team together. In September, the collected efforts of the summer are delivered to our printer, who turns them into books in record time, so that you have the most up-to-date information available for your vacation. Even as you read this, work on next year's editions is well underway.

WHY WE DO IT

We don't think of budget travel as the last recourse of the destitute; we believe that it's the only way to travel. Living cheaply and simply brings you closer to the people and places you've been saving up to visit. Our books will ease your anxieties and answer your questions about the basics—so you can get off the beaten track and explore. Once you learn the ropes, we encourage you to put *Let's Go* down now and then to strike out on your own. You know as well as we that the best discoveries are often those you make yourself. When you find something worth sharing, please drop us a line. We're Let's Go Publications, 67 Mount Auburn St., Cambridge, MA 02138, USA (email: feedback@letsgo.com). For more info, visit our website, http://www.letsgo.com.

v

Contents

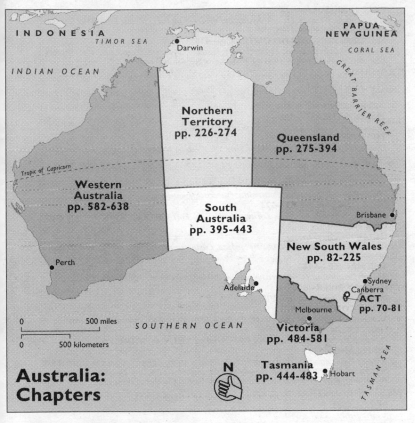

INDONESIA
TIMOR SEA
INDIAN OCEAN

PAPUA
NEW GUINEA
CORAL SEA

Darwin

GREAT BARRIER REEF

Tropic of Capricorn

Northern Territory
pp. 226-274

Queensland
pp. 275-394

Western Australia
pp. 582-638

South Australia
pp. 395-443

Brisbane ●

Perth ●

New South Wales
pp. 82-225

● Sydney
Canberra ●
ACT
pp. 70-81

Adelaide ●

Melbourne ●

0   500 miles
0   500 kilometers

SOUTHERN OCEAN

Victoria
pp. 484-581

Australia: Chapters

N

Tasmania
pp. 444-483   Hobart

TASMAN SEA

Let's Go Picks

BEST NATURAL ATTRACTIONS Scuba diving in the marine splendor of the **Great Barrier Reef** (p. 275). Camping in the sandy wonderland of **Fraser Island** (p. 318). Starlight sailing around the **Whitsunday Islands** (p. 336). Wading in the dark at **Tunnel Creek** in the Kimberley (p. 633). Canoeing along the quiet river in beautiful **Katherine Gorge** (p. 255). Hiking between the giant, unearthly red mounds of the **Olgas** (p. 272). The scenic drive along **Bells Line of Road** (p. 133). Exploring the caves in the western fringe of the **Atherton Tablelands** (p. 368). The awesome sight of **Ayers Rock** at sunset (p. 271). The spectacular **12 Apostles** (p. 527). The granite peaks and still water of **Wineglass Bay** (p. 470). The windsurfing mecca of **Geraldton** (p. 614). Hiking the spectacular ridges of the world famous **Overland Track** in Tasmania (p. 482).

BEST CULTURAL ATTRACTIONS Aboriginal rock art and emerald vistas at **Ubirr** in Kakadu (p. 241). Sneak-previewing the **Olympic site** at Homebush Bay (p. 116). Browsing through the busy **Mindil Beach Sunset Market** in Darwin (p. 237). Catching the wild spectacle of **Question Time** in the House of Representatives (p. 78). Dancing, didgeridoo music, and Aboriginal narratives at **Tjapukai** (p. 356). Spooky night tours of the **Old Melbourne Gaol** (p. 508). A cultivated night of acoustic pleasure at the **Opera House** (p. 111). The salacious **Mardi Gras Festival** in the gay and lesbian mecca of Sydney (p. 115). The hourly **Waltzing Matilda** display in Melbourne Central's glass atrium (p. 506).

BEST ACCOMMODATIONS A day or a lifetime at **Taggerty Bush Settlement** for a first-hand experience with Australian fauna, pioneer history, and Aboriginal culture (p. 558). The **Moreton Bay Lodge** in Manly (p. 294). The **Samurai Beach Bungalows Backpackers** in Port Stephen (p. 148). **Jolly Swagman Backpackers** in Kings Cross (p. 97). Sleep in teepees or island bungalows at **Byron Bay's Arts Factory Backpackers Lodge** (p. 178). Relax at the **Sunset Strip Budget Resort** in Coolangatta (p. 298). Unconventional accommodations at **Fuzzies Farm,** a post-industrial collective microsociety in the Adelaide Hills (p. 409).

BEST FOOD, WINERIES, AND PUBS Authentic outback cuisine at the sizzling **Red Ochre Grill** in Alice (p. 235). Dinner and an evening of stargazing at the **Stromlo Observatory** in Canberra (p. 81). Pure herbivore heaven at Adelaide's **Vego and Lovin' It!** (p. 405). **Govinda's** in Kings Cross for can't miss Indian food and cinema (p. 103). A delicious dining experience at Brisbane's **Garuva** (p. 289). **Betty's Burgers** in Noosa, with burgers from a buck (p. 311). The sweet taste of sinfulness at the **Cadbury Chocolate Factory** in Hobart (p. 450). Savoring the bouquet of **McLaren Vale's** rich wines (p. 412). The youthful cafe scene in **Glebe** and **Newtown** (p. 100).

BEST WILDLIFE Prowling croc-filled waters on a **Yellow Water Cruise** in Kakadu (p. 241). Swimming with whale sharks at **Ningaloo Reef**, Exmouth (p. 620). Spying on dolphins from the wind-beaten cliffs of **Rottnest Island** (p. 595). Watching the wild koalas lounging in treetops on **Magnetic Island** (p. 345) and little penguins stumbling home on **Kangaroo Island** (p. 416). Sunset camel rides down miles of sand on **Cable Beach,** Broome (p. 628). Fossils of megafauna at **Naracoorte** (p. 422). An afternoon visit to the **Habitat Wildlife Center** in Port Douglas to observe crocs, 'roos, emus, and more (p. 372).

List of Maps

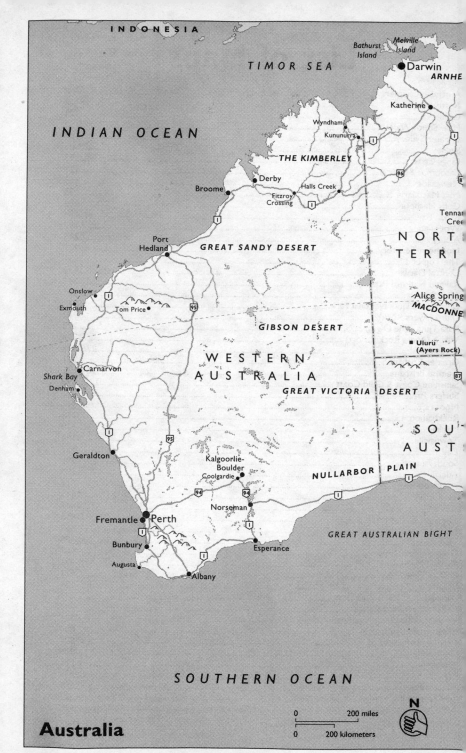

Australia

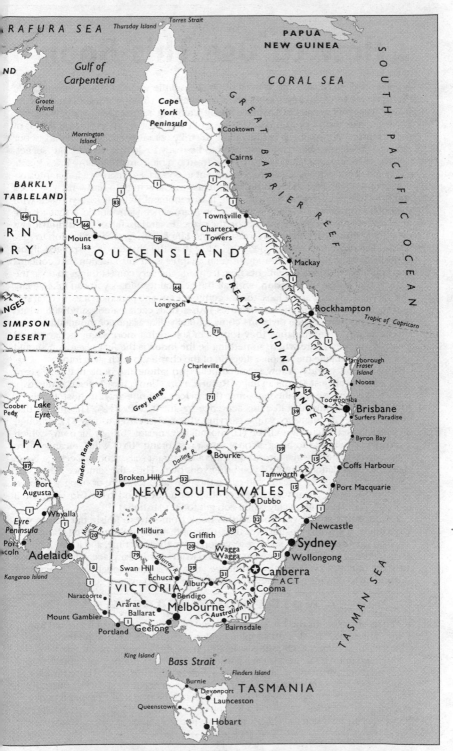

ARAFURA SEA

Thursday Island   Torres Strait

PAPUA
NEW GUINEA

Gulf of
Carpenteria

CORAL SEA

SOUTH PACIFIC OCEAN

ND

Groote
Eyland

Mornington
Island

Cape
York
Peninsula

Cooktown

GREAT BARRIER REEF

Cairns

BARKLY
TABLELAND

Townsville
Charters
Towers

Mount
Isa

QUEENSLAND

Mackay

RN
RY

Longreach

Rockhampton

Tropic of Capricorn

NGES

SIMPSON
DESERT

GREAT DIVIDING RANGE

Charleville

Maryborough
Fraser
Island

Noosa

Coober
Pedy

Lake
Eyre

Grey Range

Toowoomba

Brisbane
Surfers Paradise

LIA

Flinders Range

Darling R.

Bourke

Byron Bay

Coffs Harbour

Broken Hill

Tamworth

Port Macquarie

Port
Augusta

NEW SOUTH WALES

Dubbo

Whyalla

Newcastle

Eyre
Peninsula

Murray R.

Mildura

Griffith

Sydney

Port
acoln

Adelaide

Swan Hill

Murray R.

Wagga
Wagga

Wollongong

Kangaroo Island

Echuca

Albury

Canberra
ACT

Cooma

Naracoorte

VICTORIA

Bendigo

Australian Alps

Mount Gambier

Ararat

Ballarat

Melbourne

Portland

Geelong

Bairnsdale

King Island

Bass Strait

Flinders Island

Burnie

Devonport

TASMANIA

Queenstown

Launceston

Hobart

How to Use This Book

A good travel guide, like the Wizard of Oz, has a little something for everyone. We can't provide you with a heart or a brain, but we hope to provide useful guidance no matter what your agenda in Australia: hiking, clubbing, sightseeing, diving, you name it. As much as we'd like to, however, we can't take your vacation for you. Much of the adventure of traveling is being willing to strike out on your own, and part of our job is to provide the basic info you need to be ready to do that. So take our suggestions as starting points, and don't be afraid to stray a bit from the Yellow Brick Road.

This book encompasses an entire continent in 658 pages. There is a lot of information crammed in here, and it's important that you know how to find what you need and how to interpret what we say. First, take a moment to familiarize yourself with the book's organization. The first two chapters are general introductions that are definitely worth reading before you get on the plane: **Essentials,** full of "hard" info about everything from plane flights to farmstays; and **Life & Times,** an introduction to Australian history, culture, and biodiversity. After that, the chapters are arranged alphabetically by state. At the beginning of each chapter is an introduction that contains two important features: a **highlights box,** featuring the very coolest things to do in the state; and **practical information,** with all the general resources you can take advantage of statewide, like auto clubs, tourist commissions, and parks services. (You'll also find highlights boxes in the major cities.) After that, each state is subdivided into regions. Sometimes region divisions come naturally, like islands or mountain ranges, and other times, unavoidably, they represent somewhat more vague geographical areas. If you're not sure where something is, the **index** is the first place you should look. We also outline the regional division of the chapter in each state intro.

Now, the nitty gritty. A few terms appear throughout the book that may seem unclear; many are just Australian lingo. **Return,** as in "1km return," means round-trip. If it's not otherwise specified, assume that **prices are one-way.** In hostel listings, you'll often see something like this sentence fragment: **VIP, YHA.** This means that the hostel gives discounts to people carrying VIP or YHA cards (usually $1), although they usually aren't actually a VIP or YHA hostel. BYO means "bring your own," which means you're allowed to bring alcohol into a restaurant; "BYO wine" means you're only allowed to bring wine. **Licensed** means a restaurant sells alcohol. **Corkage** is the charge some restaurants apply if you bring your own. Thus, the sentence "Licensed; BYO wine, corkage $1" means you can either buy alcohol there or bring your own wine; for the latter, you pay $1. A host of other terms are found in the **Glossary;** you'll probably pick them up quickly when you get to Oz (Australia).

You probably won't want to read this book from start to finish, but before you leave home, it's worth looking over the towns and states you're thinking about visiting. You may need to make some reservations way ahead of time, and it also helps to have a sense of how long you'll want to spend in any particular place. Once you're on the road, of course, you can always change your plans. But enough talk—you've got a continent to conquer. Let's draw the curtain on the wizard and go…

A NOTE TO OUR READERS

The information for this book was gathered by *Let's Go*'s researchers from May through August 1998, with supplementary seasonal research done during the Australian summer. Each listing is derived from the assigned researcher's opinion based upon his or her visit at a particular time. The opinions are expressed in a candid and forthright manner. Other travelers might disagree. Those traveling at a different time may have different experiences since prices, dates, hours, and conditions are always subject to change. Check beforehand to avoid inconvenience and surprises. Travel always involves a certain degree of risk, especially in low-cost areas. When traveling, always take particular care to ensure your safety.

Essentials

PLANNING YOUR TRIP

While we all idealize the spontaneous getaway, the reality of modern travel is that escapes are not made without prior planning. Budget travel tends to require even more preparation—you pay for ease, after all. You can eliminate a lot of surprises by setting aside the time to read through this chapter before you jump into anything. With a little more research you may find better and cheaper ways of doing things. Before you get on the plane, it is a good idea to have at least a tentative itinerary, to read through *Let's Go*'s listings of those towns, and to make reservations where necessary. Don't be afraid to change your plans, though; just remember: the more knowledge you have, the more prepared you will be to be spontaneous.

■ When to Go

Australia is big. Really big. When to travel depends on where you're going and what you're doing. Most of the country is in a temperate climate zone, with the **seasons** reversed from those in the northern hemisphere. Summer lasts from December to February, autumn from March to May, winter from June to August, and spring from September to November. For the most part, Australian winters are mild, comparable to the southern U.S. or southern Europe; snow is infrequent except in the mountains, but it's definitely too cold to have much fun at the beach. The north is an entirely different story—many people forget that over one-third of Australia is in the tropics, where it's always, always hot. Seasons there are defined not by the almost-constant temperature but by the wildly swinging precipitation. **"The Wet"** lasts from November to April, and **"the Dry"** is from May to October. Traveling in the Wet is not recommended for the faint of heart; not only will you be rained on, but unsealed roads tend to get washed out, making driving a huge challenge in non-urban areas.

A countervailing consideration is that the price and crowdedness of everything from flights to hostel bunks tend to be directly proportional to the pleasantness of the weather. If you're traveling in the high season, start planning your trip and booking accommodations months ahead of time if possible. As a general rule, tourism peaks when school is out of session. Summer holidays for primary and secondary schools generally include December and January; for universities, they're from the end of November to the end of February. From Christmas to New Year's is ultra-peak season. Winter break runs from the end of June through early July.

January and February are the rainy months on the **Great Barrier Reef;** the water is clearest between April and October. The toxic **box jellyfish** is most common near the east coast between October and April. Ski season in New South Wales and Victoria runs between June and September, and the famous wildflowers of Western Australia bloom from September to December. The charts below have useful temperature and rainfall data, while the **Appendix** (see p. 639) has a list of public and school holidays.

CLIMATE CHARTS

To convert from °C to °F, multiply by 1.8 and add 32. For a rough approximation, double the Celsius and add 25. To convert from °F to °C, subtract 32 and multiply by 0.55. For a rough approximation, subtract 25 and cut it in half.

°C	-5	0	5	10	15	20	25	30	35	40
°F	23	32	41	50	59	68	77	86	95	104

Average Temp. Low-High	January °C	°F	April °C	°F	July °C	°F	October °C	°F
Adelaide	17-29	63-84	12-22	54-72	8-15	46-59	14-22	57-72
Alice Springs	21-36	70-97	13-28	55-82	4-19	39-66	15-31	59-88
Brisbane	21-29	70-84	17-26	63-79	10-20	50-68	16-26	61-79
Cairns	24-31	75-88	22-29	72-84	17-26	63-79	20-29	68-84
Canberra	13-28	55-82	7-20	45-68	0-11	32-52	6-19	43-66
Darwin	25-32	77-90	25-32	77-90	20-30	68-86	25-32	77-90
Hobart	12-22	54-72	9-17	48-63	4-12	39-54	8-17	46-63
Melbourne	14-26	57-79	11-20	52-68	6-13	43-55	9-20	48-68
Perth	18-30	64-86	14-25	57-77	9-18	48-64	12-22	54-72
Sydney	19-26	66-79	15-22	59-72	8-16	46-61	13-22	55-72

Average Rain (mm)	Jan	Feb	Mar	Apr	May	June	July	Aug	Sep	Oct	Nov	Dec
Adelaide	19	6	35	52	57	70	83	74	62	45	32	21
Alice Springs	38	45	34	14	17	15	17	12	10	22	25	36
Brisbane	163	158	141	87	73	68	56	47	47	77	98	134
Cairns	424	441	449	190	94	47	28	27	34	38	87	173
Canberra	60	57	54	49	48	37	39	48	52	69	61	51
Darwin	404	430	349	63	35	8	1	2	19	73	116	313
Hobart	48	40	47	53	49	57	53	52	53	63	56	57
Melbourne	48	48	52	58	58	49	48	51	59	68	59	58
Perth	8	12	19	45	123	183	173	137	80	54	21	14
Sydney	102	113	135	124	121	131	100	80	69	78	81	78

■ Useful Information

GOVERNMENT INFORMATION OFFICES

The government-sponsored **Australian Tourist Commission** promotes tourism internationally (but not within Australia), distributing literature and sponsoring helplines. The ATC carries specific books, magazines, and fact sheets for backpackers, younger people, disabled travelers, and others with special interests or concerns. Check out their fairly comprehensive web page at http://www.aussie.net.au. Requests for information should be directed to the addresses and phone numbers below.

Australia (Head Office): Level 4/80 William St, Wolloomooloo, Sydney 2011, NSW (tel. (02) 9360 1111; fax (02) 9331 2538).

Europe: Fax or phone London office for country-specific helpline phone numbers (dial country code 44, then the number listed below).

Ireland: Helpline (tel. (01) 402 9896); send faxes to London office, below.

New Zealand: 22 Centre St, Auckland 1. Helpline (tel. (0800) 65 0303 or (09) 527 1629; fax (09) 377 9562).

U.K.: Gemini House, 10-18 Putney Hill, London SW156AA. (tel. (0891) 07 07 07; fax 171 940 5221; brochure orders only tel. (0891) 633 235).

U.S./Canada: 27911 W. Franklin Parkway, Valencia, CA 91355. Helpline tel. (805) 775-2000; fax (805) 775-4448. General information tel. (800) 333-4305.

INTERNET RESOURCES

While virtual travel will probably never replace real travel (we hope), the Internet can certainly make real travel a whole lot easier. You can request loads of information, and can make airline, hotel, hostel, or car rental reservations online. **Search engines** (services that search for web pages under specific subjects) are an essential tool for browsing the Web. **Lycos** (http://a2z.lycos.com), **Alta Vista** (www. altavista.digital.com), and **Excite** (http://www.excite.com) are among the most popular. **Yahoo!** is a slightly more organized search engine; its travel links are at http://www.yahoo.com/Recreation/Travel. Even better is the **Australia-specific Yahoo!,** at http://www.yahoo.com.au. The most popular Australian search engine is **AAA Matilda** (http://www.aaa.com.au/). Another good way to explore is to find a site with a good list of links and surf from there. Check out *Let's Go*'s own page (http://www.letsgo.com) for starters.

Another popular info source are **newsgroups**, forums for discussion of specific topics. There are thousands of different newsgroups on almost every imaginable topic. Be warned, however, that newsgroups have no quality control—any idiot can post what they want, and many do. **Usenet,** the name for the family of newsgroups, can be accessed easily from most Internet gateways. The "rec" (recreation) hierarchy is especially good for travelers, with newsgroups such as **rec.travel.air** or **rec.travel.australia+nz.**

Let's Go lists relevant web sites throughout this and other chapters, but web sites can be ephemeral, so please bear with us. Some general Australia sites to get you started are:

Charles Sturt University's Guide to Australia (http://www.csu.edu.au/australia/ozguide.html) aims to be the ultimate index to Australia-related web sites, and does a damn good job. Tourist information is only part of what it offers.

Walkabout: The Australian Travel Guide (http://www.walkabout.fairfax.com.au), by the *Sydney Morning Herald,* is simply superb. It covers over 1400 towns, and while its accommodation and restaurant listings have only facts, not reviews, its history and sights writeups offer insight that's rare on the web.

G'Day, Mate! (http://www.ozemail.com.au/~gdaymate/) is an excellent tourist resource, with accommodations, cybercafes, festivals, holiday dates, and more.

Australian Yellow Pages and White Pages (http://www.yellowpages.com.au and http://www.whitepages.com.au) are the official Telstra phone book—on-line. You can search by business or private name, state, or type of service. The white pages take into account which country you are calling from and provide access codes, as well as a nifty time converter. This service is incredibly valuable since **you can't phone Australian directory assistance from abroad.**

Australian Tourist Commission (http://www.aussie.net.au) is targeted specifically at international travelers and is quite comprehensive.

Telstra Springboard to Australia (http://springboard.telstra.com.au/australia/) provides links for travel, business, arts, entertainment, and maps.

City.Net Travel (http://city.net/countries/australia) provides current weather reports in big cities and links to city and town info. Sometimes slow, though.

About Australia (http://www.about-australia.com/about.html) Sometimes plagued by slow or broken links, this nevertheless has a broad list of travel resources.

Australian Recipe Collection (http://www.wsnet.com/~ang/recipe) is your source for pavlovas, lamingtons, and meat pies. It's a private web page whose owner will respond to queries.

To keep up with daily events in Oz, read the **Sydney Morning Herald** online at (http://www.smh.com.au) or Melbourne's **The Age** at (http://www.theage.com.au). The official Sydney **Olympics** home page is at (http://www.sydney.olympic.org).

■ Documents and Formalities

ESSENTIALS

Having all of your paperwork in order before departing for Australia and upon returning home can make the difference between a smooth transition and a bureaucratic nightmare. If the information listed below does not apply to your individual situation, please contact the nearest Consulate General and make sure you have everything you need. Make sure to apply for passports or long-term visas several weeks or months ahead of time, especially between January and August, when demand is highest in most Northern Hemisphere countries. A backlog in processing can spoil your plans.

When you travel, always carry on your person two or more forms of identification, including at least one photo ID. A passport combined with a driver's license or birth certificate is usually adequate. Many establishments, especially banks, require several IDs before cashing traveler's checks. Never carry all your forms of ID together, however; you risk being left entirely without ID or funds in case of theft or loss. A good safety measure is leaving photocopies of all your important papers with friends or family at home. Also carry several extra passport-size photos that you can attach to the sundry IDs you may eventually acquire. If you plan an extended stay, register your passport with the nearest embassy or consulate.

AUSTRALIAN EMBASSIES AND CONSULATES

Canada: All visa applications should go to Ottawa.
Australian High Commission, 50 O'Connor St #710, Ottawa, ON K1P 6L2 (visa tel. (613) 783 7665; general tel. 236-0841; all faxes 236-4376).
Australian Consulate, Suite 1255, 888 Dunsmuir St, Vancouver, BC V6C 3K4 (tel. (604) 684-1177; fax 684-1856).
Australian Consulate General, 175 Bloor St East, #316, Toronto, ON M4W 3R8 (tel. (416) 323-1155; fax 323-3910).
Ireland: Fitzwilton House, Wilton Terrace, Dublin 2 (tel. (01) 676 1517; fax 678 5185).
New Zealand: 72-78 Hobson St, Thorndon, Wellington (tel. (04) 473 6411; fax 498 7118). Union House, 32-38 Quay St., Auckland 1 (tel. (09) 303 2429; fax 377 0798). Visa requests should be sent to Auckland.
South Africa: 292 Orient St, Arcadia, Pretoria 0083 (tel. (012) 342 3740; fax 342 4222).
United Kingdom: Australia House, The Strand, London WC2B 4LA (tel. (0171) 379 4334; fax 465 8210), also in Edinburgh and Manchester.
United States of America: Visa requests should go to Washington or Los Angeles.
Australian Embassy, 1601 Massachusetts Ave NW, Washington, D.C. 20036-2273 (tel. (202) 797-3000; fax 797-3100).
Australian Consulate General, 150 E. 42nd St, 34th Floor, New York, NY 10017-5612 (tel. (212) 351-6500; fax 351-6501).
Australian Consulate General, 1 Bush St, #700, San Francisco, CA 94104 (tel. (415) 362-6160; fax 986-2775).
Australian Consulate General, 1000 Bishop St, Penthouse, Honolulu, HI 96813 (tel. (808) 524-5050; fax 531-5142).
Australian Consulate General, Century Plaza Towers, 19th floor, 2049 Century Park East, Los Angeles, CA 90067 (tel. (310) 229-4800, visa office direct tel. 229-4840; fax 277 5620).

ENTRANCE REQUIREMENTS

Citizens of Canada, Ireland, New Zealand, South Africa, the U.K., and the U.S. all need valid **passports** to enter Australia, and to re-enter their own country. Some countries do not allow entrance if the holder's passport expires in under six months; returning home with an expired passport is illegal, and may result in a fine. **Australia also requires all visitors to have a visa.** New Zealand nationals will receive a "special category" visa upon arrival in Australia; all other visitors need to procure a visa before arriving. If your home country requires children to carry their own passports, they also need their own visas. For more information, please see **Visas,** p. 7.

Upon entering a country, you must declare certain items from abroad and pay a duty on the value of those articles that exceed the allowance established by that country's **customs** service. Keeping receipts for purchases made abroad will help establish values when you return. It is wise to make a list, including serial numbers, of any valuables that you bring from home; if you register this list with customs before your departure and have an official stamp it, you'll avoid import duty charges and ensure an easy passage upon your return. Be especially careful to document items manufactured abroad.

When you enter Australia, dress neatly and carry **proof of your financial independence,** such as a visa to the next country on your itinerary, an airplane ticket to depart, enough money to cover the cost of your living expenses, etc. Admission as a tourist does not include the right to work, which is authorized only by a work permit. If you are studying in Australia, immigration officers may also want to see proof of acceptance from a school and proof that the course of study will take up most of your time in the country, as well as proof that you can support yourself.

No vaccinations are required to enter the country unless you have been in an area with **yellow fever** within the last six days. No other health certificate is required.

PASSPORTS

Before you leave, photocopy the page of your passport that contains your photograph, passport number, and other identifying information. Carry one photocopy in a safe place apart from your passport, and leave another copy at home. These measures will help prove your citizenship and facilitate the issuing of a new passport if you lose the original document. You should also carry an expired passport or an official copy of your birth certificate in a part of your baggage separate from other documents.

If you do lose your passport, immediately notify the local police and the nearest embassy or consulate of your home government. To expedite its replacement, you will need to know all information previously recorded and show identification and proof of citizenship. A replacement may take weeks to process, and it may be valid only for a limited time. Some consulates can issue new passports within 24 hours if you give them proof of citizenship. Any visas stamped in your old passport will be irretrievably lost. In an emergency, ask for immediate temporary traveling papers that will permit you to reenter your home country.

Your passport is a public document belonging to your nation's government. You may have to surrender it to a foreign government official, but if you don't get it back in a reasonable amount of time, inform the nearest mission of your home country.

Canada

Application forms in English and French are available at all passport offices, Canadian missions, many travel agencies, and Northern Stores in northern communities. Citizens may apply in person at any of 28 regional Passport Offices across Canada. Canadian citizens residing abroad should contact the nearest Canadian embassy or consulate. Children under 16 may be included on a parent's passport. Passports cost CDN$60, plus a CDN$25 consular fee, are valid for 5 years, and are not renewable. Processing takes approximately 5 business days for applications in person or three weeks for mail delivery. For additional info, contact the Canadian Passport Office, Department of Foreign Affairs and International Trade, Ottawa, ON, K1A 0G3 (tel. (613) 994-3500; http://www.dfait-maeci.gc.ca/passport). Travelers may also call (800) 567-6868 (24hr.); in Toronto (416) 973-3251; in Vancouver (604) 775-6250; in Montréal (514) 283-2152. Refer to the booklet *Bon Voyage, But...,* free at any passport office or by calling Info-Centre at (800) 267-8376 (within Canada), for further help and a list of Canadian embassies and consulates abroad. You may also find entry and background information for various countries by contacting the Consular Affairs Bureau in Ottawa (24hr. tel. (800) 267-6788 (24hr.) or (613) 944-6788).

Ireland

Citizens can apply for a passport by mail to either the Department of Foreign Affairs, Passport Office, Setanta Centre, Molesworth St, Dublin 2 (tel. (01) 671 1633; fax (01)

671 1092), or the Passport Office, Irish Life Building, 1A South Mall, Cork (tel. (021) 272 525; fax (021) 275 770). Obtain an application at a local Garda station or request one from a passport office. The new Passport Express Service, available through post offices, allows citizens to get a passport in 2 weeks for an extra IR£3. Passports cost IR£45 and are valid for 5 years. Citizens under 18 or over 65 can request a 3-year passport that costs IR£10.

New Zealand

Passport applications are available in New Zealand from travel agents and Department of Internal Affairs Link Centres in the main cities and towns. Overseas, contact New Zealand embassies, high commissions, and consulates. Applications may also be forwarded to the Passport Office, P.O. Box 10526, Wellington. Standard processing time is 10 working days. The fees are adult NZ$80, and child NZ$40. An urgent passport service is also available from New Zealand and some foreign locations for an extra NZ$80. Fees are higher if applying from overseas. Under a recent change, children require their own passport, valid for 5 years. Adult passports are valid for 10 years. More information is available on the Internet at http://www.emb.com/nzemb or http://www.undp.org/missions/newzealand.

South Africa

Citizens can apply for a passport at any **Home Affairs Office** or **South African Mission.** Tourist passports, valid for 10 years, cost SAR80. Children under 16 must be issued their own passports, valid for 5 years, which cost SAR60. Allow at least 3 months for processing. If a passport is needed in a hurry, an **emergency passport** may be issued for SAR50. An application for a permanent passport must accompany the emergency passport application. Current passports less than 10 years old (counting from date of issuance) may be **renewed** until December 31, 1999; every citizen whose passport's validity does not extend far beyond this date is urged to renew it as soon as possible, to avoid the expected premillennial glut of applications. Renewal is free, and turnaround time is usually 2 weeks. For further information, contact the nearest Department of Home Affairs Office.

United Kingdom

British citizens, British Dependent Territories citizens, British Nationals (overseas), British subjects, and British Overseas citizens may apply for a **full passport,** valid for 10 years (5 years if under 16). Applications are available at passport offices, main post offices, many travel agents, and branches of Lloyds Bank and Artac World Choice. Apply by mail or in person (for an additional UK£10) to one of the passport offices, located in London, Liverpool, Newport, Peterborough, Glasgow, or Belfast. The fee is UK£31, UK£11 for children. As of October 1998, children under 16 need their own passports. The London office offers same-day, walk-in rush service; arrive early. The British Visitor's Passport has been abolished; travelers over 16 now need standard 10-year passports. The U.K. Passport Agency can be reached by phone at (0990) 21 04 10.

United States

Citizens may apply for a passport at any federal or state **courthouse** or **post office** authorized to accept passport applications, or at the nearest **U.S. Passport Agency.** Refer to the "U.S. Government, State Department" section of the telephone directory or the local post office for addresses. Parents must apply in person for children under age 13. You must apply in person if this is your first passport, if you're under age 18, or if your current passport is more than 12 years old or was issued before your 18th birthday. Passports are valid for 10 years (5 years if under 18) and cost US$65 (under 18 US$40). Passports may be **renewed** by mail or in person for US$55. Processing takes 3-4 weeks. **Rush service** is available for a surcharge of US$30 with proof of departure within 10 working days (e.g. an airplane ticket or itinerary), or for travelers leaving in 2-3 weeks who require visas. Given proof of citizenship, a U.S. embassy or consulate abroad can usually issue a new passport. For more info, contact the U.S. Passport Information's **24-hour recorded message** (tel. (202) 647-0518). U.S. citizens abroad should contact any passport agency, U.S. embassy, or consulate; or send information requests along with a self-addressed stamped envelope to: Overseas Citizens Services, Room 4811, Department of State, Washington, D.C. 20520-4818 (tel. (202) 647-5225; fax 647-3000). Additional information is available through the Bureau of Consular Affairs homepage at http://travel.state.gov, or through the State Department site at http://www.state.gov.

VISAS

A **visa** is an endorsement that a foreign government stamps into a passport which allows the bearer to stay in that country for a specified purpose and period of time. Australian **tourist visas** are free and allow you to spend three months in the country, within one year from the date of issue. **Work visas** vary according to your plans; contact the Australian embassy or consulate in your home country with questions. **All visitors, except New Zealand nationals, need a visa before arriving in Australia.** The easiest way to acquire a tourist visa is through the new **Electronic Travel Authority (ETA)** service, for which citizens of 25 countries are eligible, including the U.S., Canada, U.K., and Ireland. The ETA can be acquired instantly through most travel agents and airlines; you don't have to be in your country of residence to apply. For stays of over three months or work permits, you have to apply the old-fashioned way. Visas can be acquired in person or by mail from the Australian embassies and consulates in your home country (see p. 4), and airlines and travel agents sometimes have copies of the application forms. Applications can be downloaded from the web at http://www.anzac.com/aust/visa.htm. If you apply in person, tourist visas can generally be issued while you wait; allow at least three weeks if you apply by mail. If you need a visa good for multiple visits or for more than three months, the fee is US$21.

For more information, send for *Foreign Entry Requirements* (US$0.50) from the **Consumer Information Center,** Department 365E, Pueblo, CO 81009, or contact the Center for **International Business and Travel (CIBT),** 25 West 43rd St. #1420, New York, NY 10036 (tel. (800) 925-2428 or (212) 575-2811 from NYC), which secures visas for travel to and from all countries for a variable service charge.

CUSTOMS: ENTERING

Because of its isolation as an island nation, Australia has been able to avoid some of the pests and diseases that plague other countries. But with increased tourism, there is an increased risk of contamination from imported goods. Customs is therefore taken extremely seriously. Australia expressly forbids the entry of drugs, steroids, and weapons. Articles subject to quarantine may include live animals, food, animal products, plants, plant products, and protected wildlife. These articles are not automatically forbidden, but they will undergo a **quarantine inspection.** Don't risk large fines or hassles when entering Australia—throw out questionable items in the big customs bins as you leave the plane and declare anything about which you have the slightest suspicion. The beagles in orange smocks know their stuff, and they WILL find you out. If you are planning to stay for a while and must bring your **pets** with you, contact the **Australian Quarantine and Inspections Service,** GPO Box 858, Canberra, ACT 2601 (tel. (02) 6272 4454; fax 6272 3110) to obtain a permit. Pick up a **Customs Information for Travellers** pamphlet at an Australian consulate or any travel agency for more information. If you wish to enter or leave Australia with more than AUS$10,000 or the equivalent in foreign currency, you must first inform the Australian Customs Office (within Australia 1300 363 263; from abroad dial (61) 2 9213 2000). It is a good idea to declare valuables you have brought from home as well.

CUSTOMS: GOING HOME

Upon returning home, you must declare all articles you acquired abroad and pay a **duty** on the value of those articles that exceed the allowance established by your country's customs service. Goods and gifts purchased at **duty-free** shops abroad are not exempt from duty or sales tax at your point of return; you must declare these items as well. "Duty-free" merely means no tax in the country of purchase.

Canada

Citizens who remain abroad for at least 1 week may bring back up to CDN$500 worth of goods duty-free any time, including tobacco and alcohol. You are permitted to ship goods except tobacco and alcohol home under this exemption as long as you declare them when you arrive. Citizens of legal age (which varies by province) may import in-person up to 200 cigarettes, 50 cigars or cigarillos, 200g loose tobacco, 1.14L wine or alcohol, and 24 355mL cans/bottles of beer; the value of these products is included in the CDN$200 or CDN$500. For more information, write to Canadian Customs, 2265 St. Laurent Blvd, Ottawa, Ontario K1G 4K3 (tel. (613) 993 0534), phone the 24hr. Automated Customs Information Service at (800) 461 9999, or visit Revenue Canada at http://www.revcan.ca.

Ireland

Citizens must declare everything in excess of IR£142 (IR£73 for travelers under 15 years of age) obtained outside the EU or duty- and tax-free in the EU above the following allowances: 200 cigarettes, 100 cigarillos, 50 cigars, or 250g tobacco; 1L liquor or 2L wine; 2L still wine; 50g perfume; and 250mL toilet water. Goods obtained duty and tax paid in another EU country up to a value of IR£460 (IR£115 per traveler under 15) are not subject to customs duties. Travelers under 17 may not import tobacco or alcohol. For more info, contact The Revenue Commissioners, Dublin Castle (tel. (01) 679 27 77; fax 671 20 21; email taxes@iol.ie; http://www.revenue.ie) or The Collector of Customs and Excise, The Custom House, Dublin 1.

New Zealand

Citizens may import up to NZ$700 worth of goods duty-free if they are intended for personal use or are unsolicited gifts. The concession is 200 cigarettes (1 carton) or 250g tobacco or 50 cigars or a combination of all 3 not to exceed 250g. You may also bring in 4.5L of beer or wine and 1.125L of liquor. Only travelers over 17 may import tobacco or alcohol. For more information, contact New Zealand Customs, 50 Anzac Ave, Box 29, Auckland (tel. (09) 377 35 20; fax 309 29 78).

South Africa

Citizens may import duty-free: 400 cigarettes, 50 cigars, 250g tobacco, 2L wine, 1L of spirits, 250mL toilet water, and 50mL perfume, and other consumable items up to a value of SAR500. Goods up to a value of SAR10,000 above this duty-free allowance are dutiable at 20%; such goods are also exempted from payment of VAT. Items acquired abroad and sent home as unaccompanied baggage do not qualify for any allowances. You may not export or import South African bank notes in excess of SAR25000. For more info, consult the free pamphlet *South African Customs Information,* available in airports or from the Commissioner for Customs and Excise, Private Bag X47, Pretoria 0001 (tel. (12) 314 99 11; fax 328 64 78).

United Kingdom

Citizens or visitors arriving in the U.K. from outside the EU must declare goods in excess of the following allowances: 200 cigarettes or 100 cigarillos or 50 cigars or 250g tobacco; still table wine (2L); strong liqueurs over 22% volume (1L), or fortified or sparkling wine, other liqueurs (2L); perfume (60 cc/mL); toilet water (250 cc/mL); and UK£145 worth of all other goods including gifts and souvenirs. You must be over 17 to import liquor or tobacco. These allowances also apply to duty-free purchases within the EU, except for the last category, other goods, which then has an allowance of UK£75. Goods obtained duty and tax paid for personal use (regulated according to set guide levels) within the EU do not require any further customs duty. For info contact Her Majesty's Customs and Excise, Custom House, Nettleton Road, Heathrow Airport, Hounslow, Middlesex TW6 2LA (tel. (0181) 910-3602/3566; fax 910-3765) or check the web (http://www.open.gov.uk).

United States

Citizens may import US$400 worth of accompanying goods duty-free and must pay a 10% tax on the next US$1000. You must declare all purchases, so have sales slips ready. The US$400 personal exemption covers goods purchased for personal or household use (this includes gifts) and cannot include more than 100 cigars, 200 cigarettes (1 carton), and 1L of wine or liquor. You must be at least 21 to bring liquor into the U.S. If you mail home personal goods of U.S. origin, you can avoid duty charges by marking the package "American goods returned." For more information, consult the brochure *Know Before You Go,* available from the U.S. Customs Service, Box 7407, Washington D.C. 20044 (tel. (202) 927-6724), or visit the Web (http://www.customs.ustreas.gov).

YOUTH, STUDENT, & TEACHER IDENTIFICATION

The **International Student Identity Card (ISIC)** is the most widely accepted form of student identification. Flashing this card can procure you discounts ("concessions") for entertainment, accommodation, transport, and other services. Present the card wherever you go, and ask about discounts even when none are advertised. It also provides insurance benefits, including US$100 per day of in-hospital sickness for a maximum of 60 days, and US$3000 accident-related medical reimbursement for each accident (see **Insurance,** p. 19). In addition, cardholders have access to a toll-free 24-hour ISIC helpline whose multilingual staff can provide assistance in medical, legal, and financial emergencies overseas (tel. (800) 626-2427 in the U.S. and Canada; elsewhere call collect to the UK office (44) 181 666 9025).

Many student travel agencies around the world issue ISICs, including STA Travel in Australia and New Zealand; Travel CUTS and via the web (http://www.isic-canada.org) in Canada; USIT in Ireland and Northern Ireland; SASTS in South Africa; Campus Travel and STA Travel in the U.K.; Council Travel, Let's Go Travel, STA Travel, and via the web (http://www.ciee.org/idcards/index.htm) in the U.S. When you apply for the card, request a copy of the *International Student Identity Card Handbook,* which lists by country some of the available discounts. The card is valid from September to December of the following year and costs US$20, CDN$15 or AUS$15. Applicants must be at least 12 years old and degree-seeking students of a secondary or post-secondary school. Because of the proliferation of phony ISICs, many airlines and some other services require other proof of student identity, such as a signed letter from the registrar attesting to your student status and stamped with the school seal or your school ID card. The **International Teacher Identity Card (ITIC)** offers the same insurance coverage, and similar but limited discounts The fee is US$20, UK£5, or AUS$13. For more information on these cards, consult the organization's web site (http://www.istc.org; email isicinfo@istc.org).

Federation of International Youth Travel Organizations (FIYTO) issues a discount card to travelers who are under 26 but not students. Known as the **GO25 Card,** this one-year card offers many of the same benefits as the ISIC, and most organizations that sell the ISIC also sell the GO25 Card. A brochure that lists discounts is free when you purchase the card. To apply, you will need a passport, valid driver's license, or copy of a birth certificate; and a passport-sized photo with your name printed on the back. The fee is US$20. Information is available on the web at http://www.ciee.org.

INTERNATIONAL DRIVING PERMIT

You probably won't need the **International Driving Permit (IDP)** in Australia, as long as you have a current license from your own country. A few car rental agencies do require the IDP, however, and it can serve as an additional piece of ID in a tough situation. An IDP, valid for one year, must be issued in your own country before you depart and must be accompanied by a valid driver's license from your home country. Contact the national automobile association in your home country for details.

■ Money

CDN$1=AUS$1.31	AUS$1=CDN$0.88
IR£1=AUS$2.51	AUS$1=IR£0.40
NZ$1=AUS$0.87	AUS$1=NZ$1.15
SAR1=AUS$0.27	AUS$1=SAR3.68
UK£1=AUS$2.95	AUS$1=UK£0.34
US$1=AUS$1.76	AUS$1=US$0.57

Exchange rates listed above are current as of this printing. Note, however, that for the past year or so the rates have been in flux as a result of spillover from the Asian currency crisis, and you can expect more changes. For updates on all world exchange rates, check the website http://www.oanda.com/cgi-bin/ncc. The Aussie dollar has fallen versus most currencies, and that's great news for travelers; the U.S. dollar buys about 30% more in Australia now than it did a year ago. On the other hand, the effect on the Australian economy can be expected to be inflationary, so don't be surprised if the prices listed in this guide rise somewhat to compensate.

If you stay in hostels and prepare your own food, expect to spend at least A$30-$40 per person per day in Australia, depending on the local cost of living and your needs. Transportation will increase these figures, as will activities fees and restaurant meals. Don't sacrifice your health or safety for a cheaper tab. No matter how low your budget, you will need to keep handy a larger amount of cash than usual. Carrying it around with you is risky but necessary; personal checks from home are seldom accepted no matter how many forms of identification you have, and even traveler's checks may not be accepted in some locations.

CURRENCY AND EXCHANGE

It is cheaper to buy domestic currency than to buy foreign, so as a rule you should convert money after arriving. However, converting some money before you go will allow you to zip through the airport while others languish in exchange lines. It's a good idea to bring enough foreign currency to last for the first 24-72 hours of a trip, to avoid getting stuck with no money after banking hours or on a holiday. Americans can get foreign currency from the comfort of home; contact **Capital Foreign Exchange** on the East Coast (toll-free (888) 842-0880; fax (202) 842-8008), or on the West Coast, **International Currency Express** (toll-free (888) 278-6628; fax (310) 278-6410). These organizations will deliver foreign currency or traveler's checks overnight (US$15) or second-day (US$12) at competitive exchange rates.

Watch out for commission rates and check newspapers to get the standard rate of exchange. Banks generally have the best rates, but not always; sometimes tourist offices or exchange kiosks have better deals. A good rule of thumb is to only go to banks or bureaux de change which have only a 5% margin between their buy and sell prices. Anything more, and they are making too much profit. Be sure that both prices are listed. Since you lose money with every transaction, convert in large sums (unless the currency is depreciating rapidly), but don't convert more than you need, because it may be difficult to change it back to your home currency, or to a new one.

If you are using traveler's checks or bills, be sure to carry some in small denominations (A$80 or less), especially for times when you are forced to exchange money at disadvantageous rates. However, it is a good idea to carry a range of denominations since charges may be levied per check cashed, depending on location.

TRAVELER'S CHECKS

Traveler's checks are one of the safest means of carrying funds, as they can be refunded if stolen. Several agencies and many banks sell them, usually charging a small commission. **American Express** and **Visa** are the most widely recognized, though other major checks are sold, exchanged, cashed, and refunded with almost equal ease. In small towns, traveler's checks are less readily accepted than in cities. Nonetheless, there will probably be at least one place in every town where you can exchange them for local currency. If you're ordering checks, do so well in advance, especially for large sums.

Each agency provides refunds **if your checks are lost or stolen,** and many provide additional services. You may need a police report verifying the loss or theft. Inquire about toll-free refund hotlines in Australia, emergency message relay services, and stolen credit card assistance when you purchase your checks. You should expect a fair amount of red tape and delay in the refund process. To expedite matters, keep your check receipts separate from your checks and store them in a safe place or with a traveling companion, record check numbers when you cash them and leave a list of check numbers with someone at home, and ask for a list of refund centers when you buy your checks. Keep a separate supply of cash or traveler's checks for emergencies. Never countersign your checks until you're prepared to cash them, and always bring your passport with you when you plan to use the checks.

American Express: Call (800) 25 19 02 in Australia; in New Zealand (0800) 44 10 68; in the U.K. (0800) 52 13 13; in the U.S. and Canada (800) 221-7282). Elsewhere, call U.S. collect (801) 964-6665. American Express traveler's checks are now available in currencies including Australian, British, Canadian, U.S., and soon South African. They are the most widely recognized worldwide and the easiest to replace if lost or stolen. Checks can be purchased for a small fee (1-4%) at American Express Travel Service Offices, banks, and American Automobile Association offices (AAA members can buy the checks commission-free). Cardmembers can also buy checks at American Express Dispensers at Travel Service Offices at airports, or order them by phone (tel. (800) ORDER-TC (673-3782). American Express offices cash their checks commission-free (except where prohibited by national governments), although they often offer slightly worse rates than banks. You can also buy *Cheques for Two* which can be signed by either of two people travelling together. Visit their online travel offices (http://www.aexp.com).

Citicorp: Call (800) 645-6556 in the U.S. and Canada; in Europe, the Middle East, or Africa (44) 171 508 7007; from elsewhere call U.S. collect (813) 623-1709. Sells both Citicorp and Citicorp Visa traveler's checks in currencies including U.S., Australian, and Canadian dollars and British pounds. Commission is 1-2% on check purchases. Citicorp's World Courier Service guarantees hand-delivery of traveler's checks when a refund location is not convenient.

Thomas Cook MasterCard: For 24-hr. cashing or refund assistance: from the U.S., Canada, or Caribbean call (800) 223-7373; from the U.K. call (0800) 622 101 free or (1733) 318 950 collect; from anywhere else call (44) 1733 318 950 collect. Offers checks in currencies including U.S., Canadian, Australian, British, South African, and ECUs. Commission 2% for purchases. Thomas Cook offices will cash checks commission-free; banks will make a commission charge. Thomas Cook MasterCard Traveler's Checks are also available from **Capital Foreign Exchange** (see **Currency and Exchange**) in currencies including U.S., Canadian, British.

Visa: Call (800) 227-6811 in the U.S.; in the U.K. (0800) 895 078; from anywhere else in the world call (44) 1733 318 949 and reverse the charges. Any of the above numbers can tell you the location of their nearest office. Any type of Visa traveler's checks can be reported lost at the Visa number.

CREDIT CARDS

Credit cards are generally accepted in all but the smallest businesses. Major credit cards like **MasterCard** and **Visa** can be used to extract cash advances from associated banks and ATMs throughout the country. Credit card companies get the wholesale exchange rate, which is generally 5% better than the retail rate used by banks and even better than that used by other currency exchange establishments. **American Express** cards also work in some ATMs, as well as at AmEx offices and major airports. All such machines require a **Personal Identification Number (PIN),** which credit cards in the United States do not usually carry. You must ask your credit card company to assign you a PIN before you leave; without it, you will be unable to withdraw cash with your credit card outside the U.S.

Credit cards are also invaluable in an emergency—an unexpected hospital bill or ticket home or the loss of traveler's checks—which may leave you temporarily without other resources. Furthermore, credit cards offer an array of other services, from insurance to emergency assistance, which depend completely on the issuer.

American Express (tel. (800) 843-2273) has a hefty annual fee (US$55) but offers a number of services. Cardholders can cash personal checks at AmEx offices, and U.S. Assist, a 24-hour hotline offering medical and legal assistance in emergencies, is also available (from abroad call U.S. collect (202) 554-2639). Australia hotlines are also available: to report loss of cards call 1800 230 100), and in emergencies, call 1800 644 379. The card also offers extensive travel related services, including holding your mail at AmEx offices. **MasterCard** (tel. (800) 999-0454) and **Visa** (tel. (800) 336-8472) are issued in cooperation with individual banks and other organizations; ask the issuer about services provided.

ATM (CASH) CARDS

ATMs (Automated Teller Machines) are widespread in Australia, and are in all but the smallest of towns. ANZ and National Australia Bank, among others, normally have the machine. Depending on which system your bank at home uses, you will probably be able to access your bank account whenever you want. Look on the back of your ATM card to see which systems the card can tap into (or call your bank). **Cirrus** is the most widespread ATM network in Australia; **Plus** is almost as good, and **Visa** is probably third best. **Mastercard** and **American Express** are found less often, but are possibilities. **NYCE** is not found in Australia. ATMs are scarce in northern Western Australia.

Happily, ATMs get the same wholesale exchange rate as credit cards, and spit out Aussie dollars. However, there is often a limit on the amount of money you can withdraw per day (usually about US $500, depending on the type of card and account), and computer network failures are not uncommon. Be sure to memorize your PIN code in numeral form, since machines in Australia don't always have letters on the keys. Also, if your PIN is longer than four digits, ask your bank whether the first four digits will work, or whether you need a new number. Many ATMs are outdoors; be cautious and aware of your surroundings. Finally, keep all of your receipts—even if a misbehaving ATM won't give you your cash, it may register a withdrawal. You will probably be charged US$1-5 each time you withdraw abroad, depending on your bank's policy, but the better exchange rate usually makes up for the fee.

American Express allows green-card holders to draw cash from their checking accounts at any of its major offices and many of its representatives' offices, up to US$1000 every 21 days (no service charge, no interest). AmEx also offers Express Cash from ATMs. Green-card holders may withdraw up to US$1000 in a seven-day period. There is a 2% transaction fee for each withdrawal, with a US$2.50 minimum/$20 max. To enroll in Express Cash, U.S. cardholders may call (800) CASH NOW (227-4669). Outside the U.S. call collect (336) 668-5041. Unless using the AmEx service, avoid cashing checks in foreign currencies; they usually take weeks and a US$30 fee to clear.

EFTPOS (Electronic Funds Transfer at Point Of Sale) is an extremely common way for Australians to pay for goods. ATM cards (from Australian banks only) swiped at the register work as debit cards, withdrawing money directly from your bank account. This means that people can carry less cash, without worrying about credit card bills. If you'll be in Australia for a while, the convenience of this service, among other reasons, may justify opening an Australian bank account.

GETTING MONEY FROM HOME

Money can be wired abroad from the U.S. through international money transfer services operated by **Western Union** (tel. 800 325-6000). Friends in the U.S. can call Western Union any time at (800) CALL-CASH (225-5227) to cable you money, using a Visa, Discover, or MasterCard. The rates for sending cash are generally US$10 more than with a credit card, and the money is available in Australia in 13-15 hours.

In extremely dire emergencies, for a US$15 fee, U.S. citizens can have money sent to the nearest consular office via the State Department's **Overseas Citizens Service, American Citizens Services,** Consular Affairs, Room 4811, U.S. Department of State, Washington, D.C. 20520 (business hours tel. (202) 647-5225, other times (202) 647-4000; http://travel.state.gov). **Non-American travelers** should contact their embassies or consulates for information on wiring cash.

TIPPING

Tipping is not required at restaurants or bars, in taxis, or hotels—service workers are fully salaried and do not rely on tips for income. Tips are occasionally left at more expensive restaurants, if you think the service was exceptionally good. In this case, 10% is more than sufficient.

DISCOUNTS

"Concessions" is the Australian catch-all phrase for discounts always given to specific groups, most often students, senior citizens, and youth. However, it may include any combination of these or be limited to holders of specific Australian concession cards. "Pensioners" are Australian senior citizens, and discounts for pensioners may or may not apply to non-Australians who otherwise fit the bill. Student discounts often require that you show an ID, and may only apply to Australian University students, or even to university students within the particular state. Discounts on accommodations are regularly given to VIP, YHA, ISIC, or Nomads card holders. Play it safe and carry a couple forms of ID with you at all times.

OPENING A BANK ACCOUNT

Banks are generally open from 9:30am to 4pm Monday through Thursday, and from 9:30am to 5pm on Friday. Larger cities may mean longer hours. Multiple forms of ID are necessary to open an account; passports, driver's licenses, birth certificates or other "major ID" are best, though non-photo IDs like credit cards help as supplements. Visitors who apply within six weeks of arrival to the country, however, need only show a passport. If you open an account, be sure to obtain an Australian Tax File Number, so that your interest is not taxed at the highest rate. This Tax File Number will also let you claim lower deduction rates if you get a job.

■ Safety and Security

PERSONAL SAFETY

Although Australia is a relatively safe country, it is always important to keep personal safety in mind. Tourists are particularly vulnerable to crime for two reasons: they often carry large amounts of cash and they are not as street savvy as locals. To avoid unwanted attention, try to **blend in** as much as possible. The gawking camera-toter is a more obvious target than the low-profile traveler. Walking directly into a cafe or shop to check a map beats checking it on a street corner. Better yet, look over your map before setting out. Muggings are more often impromptu than planned; nervous, over-the-shoulder glances can be a tip that you have something valuable to protect.

When exploring a new **city,** extra vigilance is wise, but no city should force you to turn precautions into panic. Find out about unsafe areas from tourist information, from the manager of your hotel or hostel, or from a local whom you trust. Especially if you travel alone, be sure that someone at home knows your itinerary. Never say that you're traveling alone. You may want to carry a small **whistle** to scare off attackers or attract attention. Anywhere in Australia, **dial 000 for emergency medical help, police, or fire.**

Whenever possible, *Let's Go* warns of unsafe neighborhoods and areas, but you should exercise your own judgment about the safety of your environs. A district can change character drastically between blocks.

ESSENTIALS

There is no sure-fire set of precautions that will protect you from all of the situations you might encounter when you travel. A good **self-defense course** will give you more concrete ways to react to different types of aggression, but it often carries a steep price tag. **Impact/Model Mugging** can refer you to local self-defense courses in the United States (tel. (800) 345-KICK). Course prices vary from $50-400. Women's and men's courses are offered. Community colleges frequently offer inexpensive self-defense courses.

Sleeping in your car is one of the most dangerous (and often illegal) ways to get your rest. If your car breaks down, wait for the police to assist you. Do not wander away from your car looking for assistance—your car is easier to find than you are. If you must sleep in your car, do so as close to a police station or a 24-hour service station as possible. Sleeping out in the open can be even more dangerous—camping is recommended only in official, supervised campsites or in wilderness back country.

The **Australian Department of Foreign Affairs and Trade** (tel. (2) 6261 9111) offers travel information and advisories at their website (http://www.dfat.gov.au).

DANGEROUS WILDLIFE

When Gondwanaland split up into continents ages ago, Australia ended up with more than her fair share of extremely dangerous animal life. With a few precautions, travelers should be able to avoid the nastiest creatures out there, but hospitals do stock anti-venoms and if you get bitten or stung, it is best to take the offending creature to the hospital with you (if you are not in danger of being bitten or stung again) so that doctors can administer the right anti-venom.

Sea life can be deadly during certain times of year, and warnings to stay out of the water should be strictly observed. The most notorious of these beasts is the **box jellyfish,** which inhabits the waters of northern Australia from November to April. Swimming on beaches north of Rockhampton, Queensland during these months is forbidden. The sting is potentially lethal to adults, and almost certainly lethal to children. Box jellyfish that have washed up on shore are still dangerous, so walking barefoot at the water's edge is discouraged. The **stonefish** and **blue-ringed octopus** also present danger at the beach. Sharks are common to some Australian shores, but lifeguards at heavily visited beaches keep a good look out—don't swim outside the red and yellow flagged areas.

Fresh and saltwater **crocodiles** present another water and water's-edge hazard in north and northwest Australia. "Salties" are the more dangerous of the two. They can be found in fresh and salt water, are hard to see, and attack without provocation. Heed local warning signs, don't swim or paddle in streams, lakes, the ocean, or other natural waterways, and keep kids and dogs away from the waters edge. "Freshies" are found in fresh water and will not attack unless provoked, but they are also hard to see and you may provoke one without knowing it's there.

Several Australian **snakes** are venomous and thus very dangerous. Most snakes attack if threatened or alarmed, so watch where you walk in the bush. Wear boots, socks, and long pants to minimize the danger.

Of the two most dangerous **spiders** in Australia, the funnel-web is found in and around Sydney, and the redback is common throughout Australia. Stinging **insects** abound in Australia, including the bull-ant, wasp, bee, and bush-tick, and although these may hurt a lot, they are not life-threatening. If you know that you are allergic to bee stings or other insect bites, you should carry your own epinephrine kit. After a period of time in the bush, check for lumps on your skin to find and remove bush-ticks. For a friendlier description of Australia's wildlife, see **Biodiversity,** p. 66.

FINANCIAL SECURITY

Don't put a wallet with money in your back pocket. Never count your money in public and carry as little as possible. If you carry a purse, buy a sturdy one with a secure clasp, and carry it slung across your body, away from the street with the clasp against you. Secure your packs with small combination padlocks which slip through the two zippers. A **money belt** is the best way to carry cash; you can buy one at most camping supply stores. A nylon, zippered pouch with belt that sits inside the waist of your pants or skirt combines convenience and security. Avoid keeping anything precious in a "fanny-pack" (even if it's worn on your stomach): your valuables will be highly visible and easy to steal. (In Australia, the word "fanny" refers to female genitalia, so if you must carry one of these packs, it's best to find a new name for it.)

Be particularly careful on **buses** (for example, carry your backpack in front of you where you can see it), don't check baggage on trains, and don't trust anyone to "watch your bag for a second." *Let's Go* lists locker availability in hostels and train stations, but you may need your own padlock. Lockers are useful if you plan on sleeping outdoors or don't want to lug everything with you, but don't store valuables in them. Try never to leave your belongings unattended; crime occurs in even the most demure-looking hostel or hotel. If you feel unsafe, look for places with either a curfew or a night attendant. When possible, keep valuables or anything you couldn't bear to lose at home.

If you travel by **car**, try not to leave valuable possessions—such as radios or luggage—in it while you're off rambling. Radios are especially tempting. If your tape deck or radio is removable, hide it in the trunk or take it with you. If it isn't, at least conceal it under a lot of junk. Similarly, hide baggage in the trunk—although savvy thieves can tell if a car is heavily loaded by the way it sits on its tires.

DRUGS AND ALCOHOL

Australia has fairly strict drug laws, and **illegal drugs** are best avoided altogether. Australia does not differentiate between "hard" drugs and more mainstream ones such as marijuana, all of which are illegal to possess in any quantity. If you carry **prescription drugs** while you travel, take the prescription with you to show at customs.

Very strict **drunk-driving** (or "drink-driving" as they say in Australia) laws apply and most states operate frequent random breath-testing. The maximum legal blood-alcohol limit for drivers in Australia is .05%. Although alcohol consumption laws vary slightly by state, you must be 18 years old to purchase or consume alcohol in public.

Smoking is prohibited in government buildings and on most public transportation in Australia, including domestic flights. Some international airlines even prohibit smoking while flying in Australian airspace.

■ Health

In the event of a serious illness or emergency, **call 000 from any phone**—this is a free call—to connect to police, ambulance, or the fire department.

Common sense is the simplest prescription for good health while you travel: eat well, drink and sleep enough, and don't overexert yourself. Travelers complain most often about their feet and their stomach, so take precautionary measures. Drinking lots of fluids can often prevent dehydration and constipation, and wearing sturdy shoes and clean socks, and using talcum powder can help keep your feet dry. To minimize the effects of jet lag, reset your body's clock by adopting the time of your destination immediately upon arrival. Most travelers feel acclimatized after two or three days.

BEFORE YOU GO

Australia is generally a safe and healthy country in which to travel. If you haven't come from or visited a yellow-fever infected country or zone in the past 6 days, no **vaccinations** or health certificates are necessary to enter Australia. Although no amount of planning can guarantee an accident-free trip, preparation can help minimize the likelihood of contracting a disease and maximize the chances of receiving effective health-care in the event of an emergency. Good medical care is widely available in Australia, but hospitals and doctors may expect immediate cash payment of around $3. Foreign medical insurance is not always valid abroad (see **Insurance,** p. 19 for details).

Citizens of New Zealand, the United Kingdom, Ireland, Malta, Sweden, Italy, Finland, and the Netherlands are covered by **Medicare,** Australia's national health insurance plan, while traveling in Australia. Medicare will cover any immediately necessary treatment (but not elective treatments, ambulance service, etc.). You can register at any Medicare office, but check with the health insurance plan of your home country before heading to Australia to make sure you have the proper documents. In the event of illness, your embassy, high commission, or consulate will usually offer you a list of approved doctors upon request.

For minor health problems on the road, bring a compact **first-aid kit,** including bandages, aspirin, or other pain killer, antibiotic cream, a thermometer, a Swiss Army knife with tweezers, moleskin, a decongestant for colds, motion sickness remedy, medicine for diarrhea or stomach problems, sunscreen, insect repellent, and burn ointment.

In your passport, write the names of any people you wish to be contacted in case of a medical emergency, and also list any allergies or medical conditions of which you would want doctors to be aware. If you wear glasses or contact lenses, carry an extra prescription and pair of glasses or arrange to have your doctor or a family member send a replacement pair in an emergency. Allergy sufferers should find out if their conditions are likely to be aggravated in the regions they plan to visit, and obtain a full supply of any necessary medication before the trip, since matching a prescription to a foreign equivalent is not always possible. Carry up-to-date, legible prescriptions or a statement from your doctor, especially if you use insulin, a syringe, or a narcotic. While traveling, be sure to keep all medication with you in carry-on luggage. Australian pharmacies, called chemists, can fill most prescriptions written by an Australian doctor.

Those with medical conditions (e.g. diabetes, allergies to antibiotics, epilepsy, heart conditions) may want to obtain a stainless steel **Medic Alert** identification tag (US$35 the first year, and $15 annually thereafter), which identifies the disease and gives a 24-hour collect-call info number. Contact Medic Alert at (800) 825-3785, or write to Medic Alert Foundation, 2323 Colorado Ave, Turlock, CA 95382. In South Australia, the Medic Alert number is 61 88 274 0361. In West Australia, it's 61 9 334 1222. Diabetics can contact the **American Diabetes Association,** 1660 Duke St, Alexandria, VA 22314 (tel. (800) 232-3472) to receive copies of the article "Travel and Diabetes" and a diabetic ID card, which carries messages in 18 languages explaining the carrier's diabetic status. Also, one of the best diabetic research and treatment facilities in the world is located in Victoria, Australia. Contact the **International Diabetes Institute,** 260 Kooyong Rd, Caulfield, VIC 3162 (tel. 03 9258 5050), if you want consultation on the continent. Check out their website with the latest info on diabetes at http://www.idi.org.au.

PREVENTING DISEASE

You can minimize the chances of contracting a disease while traveling by taking a few precautionary measures. Australia is officially free of **rabies,** but there have been reports of a rabies-like disease among indigenous bats. If you are bitten, clean your wound thoroughly and seek medical help immediately to find out whether you need treatment.

Dengue fever is an "urban viral infection" transmitted by Aedes mosquitoes, which bite during the day rather than at night. Dengue has flu-like symptoms and is often indicated by a rash three to four days after the onset of fever. There is no vaccine; the only prevention is to avoid mosquito bites. If you experience symptoms, see a doctor immediately. To treat the symptoms, rest, drink lots of water, and take fever-reducing medication such as acetaminophen (but avoid aspirin). The risk is present but low in the Pacific Islands, and even lower in Northern Queensland and the Torres Strait Islands.

From Carnarvon north in Western Australia, certain species of mosquito can transmit the Ross River and Barmah Forest viruses, as well as encephalitis. See **Mosquito-Borne Diseases,** p. 619, for more specific information. The Health Department of Western Australia recommends wearing long, loose clothing and using topical DEET to fend off bites. Try to avoid long periods outdoors at dawn and at dusk.

Australia sometimes requires that the passenger compartments of incoming aircraft be sprayed with insecticide while passengers are present. Called **disinsection,** this practice is used to prevent the importation of insects such as mosquitoes. The World Health Organization has determined that disinsection is safe, but it may aggravate allergies and other medical conditions. Call the airlines and ask your doctor for more information.

...But We Play One on TV

It's useful, especially if you're going to be out in the wilderness or outback, to have a general idea of how to prevent and treat various health problems. Still, if you experience symptoms of serious illness, remember that Let's Go is not a doctor, and unless you are, you should consult a physician.

Parasites (tapeworms, etc.) hide in unsafe water and food. *Giardia,* for example, is acquired by drinking untreated water from streams or lakes all over the world, including Australia. It can stay with you for years. Symptoms of parasitic infections in general include swollen glands or lymph nodes, fever, rashes or itchiness, digestive problems, eye problems, and anemia. Boil your water if it comes from a questionable source, wear shoes, avoid bugs, eat cooked food, and see a doctor if you experience symptoms. See the camping section below for more specific precautions while in the outback.

Hepatitis A (distinct from B and C) is a low risk in Australia. Hepatitis A is a viral infection of the liver acquired primarily through contaminated water, ice, shellfish, or unpeeled fruits and vegetables (as well as from sexual contact). Symptoms include fatigue, fever, loss of appetite, nausea, dark urine, jaundice, vomiting, aches and pains, and light stools. Ask your doctor about a new vaccine called "Harvix," or ask to get an injection of immune globulin (IG; formerly called Gamma Globulin). Risk is highest in rural areas and the countryside, but is also present in urban areas.

HOT AND COLD

It pays to be extra careful regarding sunblock. The ozone's thinner down under, and Australians have the highest rate of **skin cancer** in the world. Be sure to wear the highest SPF level sunblock at all times, a hat, and some form of upper body cover during the hottest times of the day. And drink *lots* of water.

Common sense goes a long way toward preventing **heat exhaustion,** characterized by profuse sweating, flushed skin, dizziness, and nausea. Relax in hot weather, drink lots of non-alcoholic fluids, and lie down out of the sun if you feel awful. Continuous heat stress can eventually lead to **heatstroke,** characterized by rising body temperature, severe headache, and cessation of sweating. Wear a hat, sunglasses, and a lightweight longsleeve shirt to avoid heatstroke. Victims must be cooled off with wet towels and taken to a doctor as soon as possible.

Always drink enough liquids to keep your urine clear. Alcohol and caffeine won't help—they're dehydrating. If you'll be sweating a lot, be sure to eat enough salty food to prevent electrolyte depletion, which causes severe headaches. Be especially careful up north during the Dry, which is called that for a reason.

Extreme cold is just as dangerous as heat—overexposure to cold brings the risk of **hypothermia,** a lowering of the body's core temperature that can lead to coma and death. It is caused by exposure to cold (even temperatures around 45°F/7°C) and accelerated by wind, moisture, dehydration, and fatigue, all common in Australia's mountains. It is important to detect the condition at an early stage and to get victims to a doctor as soon as possible. Symptoms include pale skin, shivering, poor coordination, disorientation, and poor judgment. Advanced symptoms include a decrease in shivering, slurred speech, hallucinations, and collapse leading to death. Before this happens, take action. If hiking, stop immediately and seek shelter from wind and rain. Remove the victim's wet clothing, and get him or her into a sleeping bag if available. Give warm, sweet liquids in moderation. Do not give caffeine or alcohol, which cause dehydration, increase the rate of heat loss, and decrease the body's ability to regulate temperature. To avoid hypothermia, stay hydrated and well-fed, keep dry, and stay out of the wind.

When the temperature is below freezing, dress in layers and watch for **frostbite.** Look for skin that has turned white, waxy, and cold, and if you find frostbite do not rub the skin. Drink warm beverages, get dry, and slowly warm the area with dry fabric or steady body contact. Take serious cases to a doctor as soon as possible; skin that has been frostbitten once is more likely to become so a second time.

WOMEN'S HEALTH

Women traveling in unsanitary conditions are vulnerable to urinary tract and bladder infections, common and severely uncomfortable bacterial diseases that cause a burning sensation and painful and sometimes frequent urination. To try to avoid these infections, drink tons of vitamin-C-rich juice and plenty of clean water, and urinate frequently, especially right after intercourse. Untreated, these infections can lead to kidney infections, sterility, and even death. If symptoms persist, see a doctor. If you often develop vaginal yeast infections, take along enough over-the-counter medicine, as treatments may not be readily available in Central America. Women may also be more susceptible to vaginal thrush and cystitis, two treatable but uncomfortable illnesses that are likely to flare up in hot and humid climates. Wearing loosely fitting trousers or a skirt and cotton underwear may help. Tampons and pads are sometimes hard to find when traveling; certainly your preferred brands may not be available, so it may be advisable to take supplies along. Refer to the *Handbook for Women Travellers* by Maggie and Gemma Moss (published by Piatkus Books) or to the women's health guide *Our Bodies, Our Selves* (published by the Boston Women's Health Collective) for more extensive information specific to women's health on the road.

BIRTH CONTROL

Reliable contraceptive devices can be difficult to find while traveling. Women on the pill should bring enough to allow for possible loss or extended stays. Bring a copy of your prescription—forms of the pill vary a good deal but with that information you will probably be able to match yours. Women who use a diaphragm should have enough contraceptive jelly on hand. Though condoms are widely available, you might want to stock up on your favorite national brand before you go; availability and quality vary.

Although abortion laws differ by state, abortion is in general not available on request, but only to protect the mental or physical health of the mother. Parental consent is required for minors in some states. Women who want an abortion should contact the **National Abortion Federation Hotline** in the U.S. For information on contraception, condoms, and abortion in Australia and worldwide, contact the **International Planned Parenthood Federation (IPEF)**. The western hemisphere regional office is in New York (tel. (212) 248-6400). The European regional office is at Regent's College Inner Circle, Regent's Park, London NW1 4NS (tel. (0171) 487 7900; fax 487 7950). The IPPF affiliate in Australia is **Family Planning Australia, Inc. (FPA)**, located at 9/114 Maitland St, Hackett, ACT 2602 (tel. 2 6230 5255; fax 6230 5344; http://actonline.com.au/fpa; email fpa@actonline.com.au). The website contains links to the different state planning associations. Planned Parenthood is not a referral service.

AIDS, HIV, STDS

Acquired Immune Deficiency Syndrome (AIDS) is a growing problem around the world. The World Health Organization estimates that there are around 30 million people infected with the HIV virus, and women now represent 40% of all new HIV infections. The easiest mode of HIV transmission is through direct blood to blood contact with an HIV+ person; *never* share intravenous drug, tattooing, or other needles. The most common mode of transmission is sexual intercourse. Health professionals recommend the use of latex condoms, readily available in Australia. Council's brochure, *Travel Safe: AIDS and International Travel*, is available at all Council Travel offices.

Hepatitis B is a viral infection of the liver transmitted by sharing needles, having unprotected sex, or coming into direct contact with an infected person's lesioned skin. If you think you may be sexually active while traveling or if you are working or living in rural areas, you are typically advised to get the vaccination for Hepatitis B. Vaccination should begin six months before traveling. **Sexually transmitted diseases (STDs)** such as gonorrhea, chlamydia, genital warts, syphilis, and herpes are a lot easier to catch than HIV, and can also be very serious. Condoms may protect you from certain STDs, but oral or even tactile contact can lead to transmission.

■ Insurance

Beware of buying unnecessary travel coverage—your regular insurance policies may well extend to many travel-related accidents. **Medical insurance** (especially university policies) often cover costs incurred abroad; check with your provider. **Medicare's** "foreign travel" coverage for U.S. residents is valid only in Canada and Mexico, not in Australia. Canadians are protected by their home province's health insurance plan for up to 90 days after leaving the country. Australia has Reciprocal Health Care Agreements (RHCAs) with Finland, Italy, Malta, the Netherlands, New Zealand, Sweden, and the U.K.,; when traveling in Australia citizens of these nations are entitled to many of the services that they would receive at home, and vice versa. For those who are interested in purchasing insurance coverage for a foreign visit, check out **Medibank** at http://www.medibank.com.au. Your **homeowners' insurance** (or your family's coverage) often covers theft during travel. Homeowners are generally covered against loss of travel documents (passport, plane ticket, railpass, etc.) up to US$500.

ISIC and **ITIC** provide basic insurance benefits (see **Youth, Student, and Teacher Identification,** p. 9), and access to a toll-free 24-hour helpline whose multilingual staff can provide assistance in medical, legal, and financial emergencies overseas (tel. (800) 626-2427 in the U.S. and Canada; elsewhere call the U.S. collect (713) 267-2525). **Council** and **STA** offer a range of plans that can supplement your basic insurance coverage, with options covering medical treatment and hospitalization, accidents, baggage loss, and even charter flights missed due to illness. **American Express** cardholders receive automatic travel accident coverage (US$100,000 in life insurance) on flight purchases made with the card; call Customer Service (tel. (800) 528-4800). YHA travel insurance gives a 10% discount on Australian and overseas travel insurance policies.

Other private travel insurance providers include **The Berkely Group/Carefree Travel Insurance,** 100 Garden City Plaza, P.O. Box 9366, Garden City, NY 11530-9366 (24hr. tel. (800) 323-3149 or (516) 294-0220; fax 294-1095; http://www.berkely.com; email info@berkely.com); and **Globalcare Travel Insurance,** 220 Broadway, Lynnfield, MA 01940 (tel. (800) 821-2488; fax (617) 592-7720; email global@nebc.mv.com; http://www.nebc.mv.com/globalcare).

■ Alternatives to Tourism

STUDY

Foreign study programs vary tremendously in expense, academic quality, living conditions, degree of contact with local students, and exposure to local culture and languages. There is a plethora of exchange programs for high school students. Most American undergraduates enroll in programs sponsored by U.S. universities, and many colleges have offices that give advice and information on study abroad. Ask for the names of recent participants in these programs, and contact them for the real scoop.

American Field Service (AFS), 310 SW 4th Ave, Suite 630, Portland, OR 97204-2608 (tel. (800) 237-4636; fax (503) 241-1653; email afsinfo@afs.org; http//www.afs.org/usa). AFS offers summer, semester, and year-long homestay international exchange programs with Australia for high school students and graduating high school seniors.

American Institute for Foreign Study, College Division, 102 Greenwich Ave, Greenwich, CT 06830 (tel. (800) 727-2437 ext. 6084; http://www.aifs.com). Organizes programs for high school and college study in universities in Australia. Summer, fall, spring, and year-long programs offered. Scholarships available.

Butler University Institute for Study Abroad, 4600 Sunset Ave, Indianapolis, IN 46208 (tel. (800) 858-0229; http://www.butler.edu/www/isa), offers 14 different programs in various locations in Australia. The ISA-Butler Sydney office is located at 118 Darlington Rd, Sydney, NSW 2008.

School for International Training, Kipling Rd., P.O. Box 676, Brattleboro, VT 05302-0676 (tel. (800) 336-1616; fax (802) 258-3500; email info@sit.edu). Offers extensive

College Semester Abroad programs in Oceania. Programs cost US$9300-11,500, including tuition, room and board, and airfare. Scholarships are available and federal financial aid is usually transferable from home college or university. Write for a brochure. At the same address, the **Experiment in International Living** runs 3-5 week summer programs offering cross-cultural, educational homestays, community service, and ecological adventure in Australia (tel. (800) 345-2929; fax (802) 258-3428; email eil@worldlearning.org; http://www.worldlearning.org). Positions as group leaders are available world-wide if you are a college graduate, have previous in-country experience, and have experience with high school students.

International Association for the Exchange of Students for Technical Experience (IAESTE), 10400 Little Patuxent Pkwy #250, Columbia, MD 21044-3510 (tel. (410) 997-3068; fax 997-5186; email iaeste@aipt.org; http://www.aipt.org). Operates 8- to 12-week programs in over 50 countries for college students who have completed 2 years of study in a technical field. Non-refundable US$50 application fee; apply by Dec. 16 for summer placement.

Youth For Understanding International Exchange (YFU), 3501 Newark St. NW, Washington, D.C. 20016 (tel. (800) TEENAGE (833-6243) or (202) 966-6800; fax 895-1104; http://www.yfu.org). Places U.S. high school students worldwide for year, semester, summer, and sport homestays.

WORK

There's no better way to immerse yourself in a foreign culture than to become part of its economy. Call the Consulate or Embassy of Australia to get more information about work permits. It is often easier to find work in large cities than smaller towns, and some work, like fruit picking, is necessarily seasonal. Check newspapers under "Situations Vacant," especially on Saturdays and Wednesdays. The **Commonwealth Employment Service's** many offices provide information, and backpacker magazines or hostels usually have info on seasonal work. If you are planning to work for an extended period of time or want to open a bank account in Australia, you should apply for a Tax File Number. These are not required, but without one, tax will be withheld at the highest rate. Contact a local branch of the Australian Taxation Office.

If you are a **U.S. citizen** and a full-time student at a U.S. university, the simplest way to get a job abroad is through work permit programs run by **Council on International Educational Exchange (Council)** and its member organizations. For a US$225 application fee, Council can procure three- to six-month work permits (and a handbook to help you find work and housing) for Australia and New Zealand. Peterson's publishes *Work Your Way Around the World* (US $16.95) to help you along the way.

VOLUNTEERING

Volunteer jobs are available almost everywhere. You may receive room and board in exchange for your labor, and the work can be fascinating (or stultifying). You can sometimes avoid the high application fees charged by the organizations that arrange placement by contacting the individual workcamps directly; check with the organizations. Listings in Vacation Work Publications's *International Directory of Voluntary Work* (UK£10; postage UK£2.50, £1.50 within the U.K.) can be helpful (see above).

Willing Workers on Organic Farms (WWOOF), Mt. Murrindal Co-op, Gelantipy Rd., Buchan Vic 3885 (tel. (03) 5155 0218; email BuchanNH@b150.aone.net. au). This Australian subset of the world-wide organization distributes a list of names of farmers who offer room and board in exchange for help on the farm. WWOOF has about 200 sites in Australia, mainly in Victoria, New South Wales, and Queensland. To join, send AUS$15 (or AUS$20 from overseas) and you'll get a membership number and booklet listing sites all over the country.

Australian Trust for Conservation Volunteers (tel. (03) 5333 1483). Does conservation projects including tree planting, track construction, sand dune restoration, and heritage programs. Volunteers pay AUS$20 per day for food and lodging while working on projects throughout the country. Long term packages also available.

■ Specific Concerns

WOMEN TRAVELERS

Women exploring on their own inevitably face additional safety concerns, but these warnings and suggestions should not discourage women from traveling alone. Be adventurous, but avoid unnecessary risks. Trust your instincts: if you'd feel better somewhere else, move on. Always carry extra money for a phone call, bus, or taxi. You might consider staying in hostels which offer single rooms that lock from the inside or in religious organizations that offer rooms for women only. Communal showers in some hostels are safer than others; check them before settling in. Stick to centrally-located accommodations and avoid solitary late-night treks or metro rides. **Hitching** is never safe for lone women, or even for two women traveling together.

Don't hesitate to seek out a police officer or a passerby if you are being harassed. *Let's Go* lists emergency numbers (including rape crisis lines) in the Practical Information listings of most cities. See **Safety and Security**, p. 13, for additional tips. The following resources may be helpful if you want more information:

Australia for Women: Travel and Culture by Susan Hawthorne and Renate Klein presents tales and advice in the form of fiction, poetry, and essays from 57 Australian women reflecting on their country and their experiences as women traveling within it. Published by The Feminist Press and available in bookstores and from http://www.Amazon.com (US$17.95).

Travelers Tales: Gutsy Women, Travel Tips, and Wisdom for the Road by Marybeth Bond is a handy pocket guide with travel tips that also address traveling with your mother or your children. Published by Traveler's Tales Inc. and available in bookstores (US$7.95).

A Foxy Old Woman's Guide to Traveling Alone by Jay Ben-Lesser encompasses practically every specific concern, offering anecdotes and tips for anyone interested in solitary adventure. Available in bookstores and from Crossing Press in Freedom, CA (tel. (800) 777-1048), US$11.

A Journey of One's Own: Uncommon Advice for the Independent Woman Traveler by Thalia Zepatos offers advice on safety and health concerns along with stories of cross-cultural encounters. Published by Eighth Mountain Press (US$16.95).

OLDER TRAVELERS

Senior citizens are eligible for a wide range of discounts on transportation, museums, movies, theaters, concerts, restaurants, and accommodations. If you don't see a senior citizen (or "pensioner") price listed, ask; you may be delightfully surprised. Agencies for senior group travel include the following.

Elderhostel, 75 Federal St, 3rd Fl., Boston, MA 02110-1941 (tel. (617) 426-7788; email Cadyg@elderhostel.org; http://www.elderhostel.org). For those 55 or over (spouse of any age). Programs at colleges, universities, and other learning centers in over 70 countries on varied subjects lasting 1-4 weeks.

Eldertreks, 597 Markham St, Toronto, Ontario, Canada M6G 2L7 (tel. (800) 741-7956 or (416) 588-5000; fax 588-9839; email passages@inforamp.net).

No Problem! Worldwise Tips for Mature Adventurers, by Janice Kenyon. Advice and info on insurance, finances, security, health, packing. Useful appendices. US$16 from Orca Book Publishers, P.O. Box 468, Custer, WA 98240-0468.

Unbelievably Good Deals and Great Adventures That You Absolutely Can't Get Unless You're Over 50, by Joan Rattner Heilman. After you finish reading the title page, check inside for some great tips on senior discounts. US$10 from Contemporary Books or online at http://www.amazon.com.

BISEXUAL, GAY, AND LESBIAN TRAVELERS

The profile of bisexual, gay, and lesbian people in Australia has risen in recent years, most notably in the popularity of the **gay and lesbian Mardi Gras** in Sydney each year. The east coast is especially gay-friendly—Sydney would probably rank in the top five most gay-friendly cities on earth. The farther into the country you get, the more homophobia you may encounter. Homosexual acts are now legal in all states.

The **Australian Gay and Lesbian Tourist Association (AGLTA)** is a nonprofit nationwide network of tourism industry professionals who are dedicated to the welfare and satisfaction of all gay and lesbian travelers. They can be reached at P.O. Box 2174, Fitzroy BC, VIC, or take a look at their web site at ⟨http://aglta.asn.au/index.htm⟩. Listed below are relevant contact organizations and publishers.

Ferrari Guides, P.O. Box 37887, Phoenix, AZ 85069 (tel. (602) 863-2408; fax 439-3952; email ferrari@q-net.com; http://www.q-net.com). Gay and lesbian travel guides: *Ferrari Guides' Gay Travel A to Z* (US$16), *Ferrari Guides' Men's Travel in Your Pocket* (US$16), *Ferrari Guides' Women's Travel in Your Pocket* (US$14), *Ferrari Guides' Inn Places* (US$16). Available in bookstores or by mail order.

International Gay and Lesbian Travel Association, 4331 N. Federal Hwy, Suite 304, Fort Lauderdale, FL 33308 (tel. (954) 776-2626 or (800) 448-8550; fax (954) 776-3303; email IGLTA@aol.com; http://www.iglta.org). An organization of over 1350 companies serving gay and lesbian travelers worldwide. Call for lists of travel agents, accommodations, and events.

Spartacus International Gay Guides (US$32.95), published by Bruno Gmunder, Verlag GMBH, Leuschnerdamm 31, 10999 Berlin, Germany (tel. (49) 030 615 0030; fax (49) 030 615 9007; email bgvtravel@aol.com). Lists bars, restaurants, hotels, and bookstores around the world catering to gays. Also lists hotlines for gays in various countries and homosexuality laws for each country. Available in bookstores and in the U.S. by mail from Lambda Rising, 1625 Connecticut Ave NW, Washington D.C., 20009-1013 (tel. (202) 462-6969).

TRAVELERS WITH DISABILITIES

Hotels and hostels have recently become more accessible to disabled persons, and many attractions are trying to make exploring the outdoors more feasible. Call ahead to restaurants, hotels, parks, and other facilities to find out about the existence of ramps, the widths of doors, the dimensions of elevators, etc. Establishments that are not wheelchair accessible are usually willing to do whatever they can to accommodate special needs. However, public transportation is lagging a bit behind; arrange transportation well in advance to ensure a smooth trip. If you give sufficient notice, some major car rental agencies offer hand-controlled vehicles at select locations. Wheelchair-accessible taxis are available in most large cities.

For information on accessible transport, accommodation, and venues, contact the **National Information Communication Awareness Network (NICAN),** P.O. Box 407, Curtin, ACT 2605 (tel. (02) 6285 3713; fax 6285 3714; email nican@spirit.com. au). Another resource for state-based assistance organizations and tour operators for people with disabilities is the **Australian Council for the Rehabilitation of the Disabled (ACROD),** P.O. Box 60, Curtin, ACT 2605 (tel. (02) 6282 4333). The **Australian Association of the Deaf,** 225 Clarence St, Sydney, NSW 2000 (tel. (02) 9262 3506), can provide resources for deaf travelers on services available including telephone relay systems, interpreting services, and specially designed items such as hearing aid batteries, vibrating alarm clocks, or TTYs.

There are a number of general books helpful to travelers with disabilities. The following organizations provide information or publications that might be of assistance:

Mobility International USA (MIUSA), P.O. Box 10767, Eugene, OR 97440 (tel. (514) 343-1284 voice and TDD; fax 343-6812; email info@miusa.org; http://www.miusa.org). Sells the 3rd Edition of *A World of Options: A Guide to Interna-*

tional Educational Exchange, Community Service, and Travel for Persons with Disabilities (individuals US$35; organizations US$45).

Society for the Advancement of Travel for the Handicapped (SATH), 347 Fifth Ave, #610, New York, NY 10016 (tel. (212) 447-1928; fax 725-8253; email sath-travel@aol.com; http://www.sath.org). Advocacy group publishes a quarterly color travel magazine *OPEN WORLD* free for members or on subscription (US$13 for non-members). Also publishes a wide range of info sheets on disability travel facilitation and accessible destinations. Annual membership US$45, students and seniors US$30.

Directions Unlimited, 720 N. Bedford Rd, Bedford Hills, NY 10507 (tel. (800) 533-5343, in NY (914) 241-1700; fax 241-0243). Specializes in arranging vacations, tours, and cruises for the physically disabled. Group tours for blind travelers.

MINORITY TRAVELERS

Australia is a generally tolerant and diverse country, but a fear of losing jobs to **Asian** immigrants has inflamed racism in some areas. This may well extend to Asian travelers. White Australians are often described as racist in their attitudes toward the **Aboriginals,** and this assessment is not unfounded. However, the political-correctness craze has not really struck Australia yet, and the use of labels like "blackfella" and "abo" do not necessarily imply a derogatory attitude. Blacks of African descent are likely to get a few stares in smaller towns, and may encounter some hostility in outback areas, but will probably not be discriminated against in cities. As always, cities tend to be more tolerant than small towns, but don't let this dissuade you from venturing off the beaten track. *Let's Go* asks that its researchers exclude from the guides establishments that discriminate. Please let us know by mailing us a letter if you encounter discrimination in any establishment we list (see **Helping Let's Go,** in the very front of this guide).

TRAVELERS WITH CHILDREN

Family vacations can be extraordinary experiences, if you slow your pace and plan ahead. If you rent a car, make sure the rental company provides a car seat for younger children. Consider using a backpack-style device to carry your baby on walking trips. Be sure that your child carries some sort of ID in case of an emergency or in case she gets lost. The following publications offer tips for adults traveling with children or distractions for the kids themselves.

Backpacking with Babies and Small Children (US$9.95). Published by Wilderness Press, 2440 Bancroft Way, Berkeley, CA 94704 (tel. (800) 443-7227 or (510) 843-8080; fax 548-1355; email wpress@ix.netcom.com).

Travel with Children by Maureen Wheeler (US$12, postage US$2.50). Published by Lonely Planet Publications, 150 Linden St., Oakland, CA 94607 (tel. (800) 275-8555 or (510) 893-8555; fax 893-8563; email info@lonelyplanet.com; http://www.lonely-planet.com). Also at P.O. Box 617, Hawthorn, Victoria 3122, Australia.

DIETARY CONCERNS

Vegetarians should have little problem finding suitable cuisine in Australia, despite the prevalence of meat pies. Most restaurants have vegetarian selections on their menus, and some cater specifically to vegetarians. *Let's Go* often notes restaurants with good vegetarian selections in city listings. Small towns may present more of a problem. Travelers who keep **kosher** should contact synagogues in larger cities for information on kosher restaurants. Kosher meats are much more difficult to find than vegetarian fare in Australia. If you are strict in your observance, consider preparing your own food on the road or sticking to vegetarian food. **The Jewish Travel Guide** lists synagogues, kosher restaurants, and Jewish institutions in over 80 countries, including Australia. It is available in the U.K. from Vallantine-Mitchell Publishers, Newbury House 890-900, Eastern Ave, Newbury Park, Ilford, Essex, U.K. IG2 7HH (tel. (0181) 599 88 66; fax 599 09 84). It is available in the U.S. ($15 plus $3 shipping) from Sepher-Hermon Press, 1265 46th St, Brooklyn, NY 11219 (tel. and fax (718) 972-9010; contact person Samuel Gross).

■ Packing

Plan your packing according to the type of travel you'll be doing and the area's high and low temperatures. If you don't pack lightly, your back will suffer. Before you leave, pack your bag, strap it on, and imagine yourself walking uphill on hot asphalt for the next three hours. A good rule is to lay out only what you absolutely need, then take half the clothes and twice the money. If you're traveling by foot, a sturdy backpack is unbeatable; get one with a strong, padded hip belt to transfer weight from your shoulders to your hips. Good packs cost anywhere from US$150-420; anything lower is likely to be poor quality. Bringing a smaller daypack in addition to your pack increases your flexibility. Suitcases are fine if you're traveling by car or staying in one or two cities, but a hassle otherwise. If you're planning to hike, invest in a good pair of boots and prepare for rain. Gore-Tex® is a miracle fabric that's both waterproof and breathable; it's all but mandatory if you plan on hiking. Avoid cotton—it's useless and even dangerous when wet. In addition to the obvious, here are a few items not to forget:

Sleepsacks: If you plan to stay in **youth hostels,** don't pay the linen charge; make the requisite sleepsack yourself. Fold a full size sheet in half the long way, then sew it closed along the open long side and one of the short sides. For those less handy with a needle, sleepsacks can be bought at any HI outlet store. Many hostels will not allow sleeping bags as a substitute.

Electric current: In Australia, as in most European countries, electricity is 240V AC, enough to fry any 120V North American appliance. Australian outlets are made for 3 pronged plugs with the top 2 prongs angled in. Visit a hardware store for an adapter (which changes the shape of the plug) and a converter (which changes the voltage). Don't make the mistake of using only an adapter (unless appliance instructions explicitly state otherwise), or you'll melt your radio.

Film: Despite disclaimers, airport security X-rays *can* fog film, so either buy a lead-lined pouch, sold at camera stores, or ask the security to hand inspect it. Always pack it in your carry-on, since higher-intensity X-rays are used on checked bags.

Some more valuable items: **sunscreen,** sun hat, sunglasses, **first-aid kit** including moleskin (for blisters), garbage bags (for lining your pack, covering your pack), sealable **plastic bags** (for damp clothes, soap, food, shampoo, and other spillables), alarm clock, waterproof matches, **needle and thread,** safety pins, pocketknife, plastic water bottle, compass, string (makeshift clothesline and lashing material), clothespins, towel, padlock, **flashlight,** whistle, rubber bands, toilet paper, earplugs, **insect repellent,** duct tape (for patching tears), maps, tweezers, and vitamins.

GETTING THERE

■ Budget Travel Agencies

Students and people under 26 ("youth") with proper ID qualify for enticing reduced airfares. These are rarely available from airlines or travel agents, but instead from student travel agencies which negotiate special reduced-rate bulk purchase with the airlines, then resell them to the youth market. Return-date change fees also tend to be low (around US$35 per segment through Council or Let's Go Travel). Most flights are on major airlines, although in peak season some agencies may sell seats on less reliable chartered aircraft. Student travel agencies can also help non-students and people over 26, but probably won't be able to get the same low fares.

Austravel, 51 East 42nd St, Suite 616, New York, New York (http://australia-online.com/austravel.html; email austravel@australia-online.com). Specializes in flights through Los Angeles from the continental U.S. to Sydney. Packages available. To book by phone: (800) 633-3404; in New York call (212) 972-6880.

Campus Travel, 52 Grosvenor Gardens, London SW1W 0AG (http://www.campus-travel.co.uk). Forty-six branches in the U.K. Student and youth fares on plane, train, boat, and bus travel. Skytrekker, flexible airline tickets. Discount and ID cards for students and youths, travel insurance for students and those under 35, and maps and guides. Puts out travel suggestion booklets. Telephone booking service: in Europe (0171) 730 34 02; in North America (0171) 730 21 01; worldwide (0171) 730 81 11; in Manchester (0161) 273 17 21; in Scotland (0131) 668 33 03.

Council Travel (http://www.ciee.org/travel/index.htm), the travel division of Council, is a full-service travel agency specializing in youth and budget travel. They offer discount airfares on scheduled airlines, railpasses, hosteling cards, low-cost accommodations, guidebooks, budget tours, travel gear, and international student (ISIC), youth (GO 25), and teacher (ITIC) identity cards. In the **U.S.,** call 800-2-COUNCIL (226-8624) for the agency nearest you. The **London** office is located at 28A Poland St (Oxford Circus), London, W1V 3DB (tel. (0171) 287 3357). Visit the web site at http://www.ciee.org/cts/ctshome.htm.

Let's Go Travel, Harvard Student Agencies, 17 Holyoke St, Cambridge, MA 02138 (tel. (617) 495-9649; fax 495-7956; email travel@hsa.net; http://hsa.net/travel). Railpasses, HI-AYH memberships, ISICs, ITICs, FIYTO cards, guidebooks (including every *Let's Go* at a substantial discount), maps, bargain flights, and a complete line of budget travel gear. All items available by mail; call or write for a catalogue (or see the catalogue in the center of this publication).

Journeys International, Inc., 4011 Jackson Rd, Ann Arbor, MI 48103 (tel. (800) 255-8735; fax (313) 665-2945; email info@journeys-intl.com; http://www.journeys-intl.com). Offers small-group, guided explorations of 45 different countries in Asia, Africa, the Americas, and the Pacific. Call or email to obtain their free 74-page color catalogue, *The Global Expedition Catalogue.*

STA Travel, 6560 Scottsdale Rd #F100, Scottsdale, AZ 85253 (tel. (800) 777-0112 nationwide; fax (602) 922-0793; http://sta-travel.com). A student and youth travel organization with over 150 offices worldwide offering discount airfares for young travelers, railpasses, accommodations, tours, insurance, and ISICs. Sixteen offices in the U.S. Call for the one nearest you. In New Zealand, 10 High St, **Auckland** (tel. (09) 309 97 23). There are STA offices throughout Australia; to list a few: 224 Faraday St, **Melbourne** Vic 3000 (tel. (03) 9347 6911); and **Canberra** ACT (tel. (02) 6247 0800, fast fares 1300 360 960; email traveller@statravelaus.com.au; http://www.statravelaus.com.au/). Specializes in discounted fares and packages for students and young travelers. Open M-F 9am-5pm.

Travel CUTS (Canadian Universities Travel Services Limited), 187 College St, Toronto, ON M5T 1P7 (tel. (416) 979-2406; fax 979-8167; email mail@travelcuts). Canada's national student travel bureau and equivalent of Council, with 40 offices across Canada. Also in the U.K., 295-A Regent St., **London** W1R 7YA (tel. (0171) 637 31 61). Discounted domestic and international airfares open to all; special student fares to all destinations with valid ISIC. Issues ISIC, FIYTO, GO25, and HI hostel cards, as well as railpasses. Offers the free *Student Traveller* magazine, as well as information on the Student Work Abroad Program (SWAP).

Usit Youth and Student Travel, 19-21 Aston Quay, O'Connell Bridge, Dublin 2 (tel. (01) 677 8117; fax 679 8833). In the U.S.: New York Student Center, 895 Amsterdam Ave, New York, NY, 10025 (tel. (212) 663-5435; email usitny@aol.com). Additional offices in Cork, Galway, Limerick, Waterford, Maynooth, Coleraine, Derry, Athlone, Jordanstown, Belfast, and Greece. Specializes in youth and student travel. Offers low-cost tickets and flexible travel arrangements all over the world. Supplies ISIC and FIYTO-GO 25 cards in Ireland only.

■ By Plane

The privilege of spending up to 24 hours on an airplane doesn't come cheap. Full-price fares to Australia from the eastern United States usually run between US$1300 and $1800, although if you fly from Los Angeles, you may be able to find flights as low as

$850. Special deals can knock that price down even more. Flights from the United Kingdom are usually even pricier; a London to Sydney link usually runs £800-925.

The **airline industry** seems to squeeze every dollar from customers; finding a cheap airfare will be easier if you understand the airlines' systems. Call every toll-free number and don't be afraid to ask about discounts; if you don't ask, it's unlikely they'll be volunteered. Have knowledgeable **travel agents** guide you; better yet, have an agent who specializes in the region(s) you will be traveling to guide you. Travel agents may not want to spend time finding the cheapest fares (for which they receive the lowest commissions), but if you travel often, find an agent who will cater to your needs and track down deals in exchange for your frequent business.

Students and others under 26 should never need to pay full price for a ticket. Seniors can also get great deals; many airlines offer senior traveler clubs or airline passes with few restrictions and discounts for their companions as well. Sunday newspapers often have travel sections that list bargain fares from the local airport. The Saturday travel section of the *Sydney Morning Herald* is worth consulting at a library or on-line. Outsmart airline reps with the phone-book-sized *Official Airline Guide* (check your local library; at US$359 per yr., the tome costs as much as some flights), a monthly guide listing nearly every scheduled flight in the world (with fares, US$479) and toll-free phone numbers for all the airlines which allow you to call in reservations directly. More accessible is Michael McColl's *The Worldwide Guide to Cheap Airfare* (US$15), an incredibly useful guide for finding cheap airfare.

To obtain the **cheapest fare,** buy a round-trip ticket and stay over at least one Saturday. Midweek round-trip flights run about US$40-50 cheaper than on weekends; weekend flights, however, are generally less crowded. Traveling from hub to hub (for example, Los Angeles to Sydney) will win a more competitive fare than from smaller cities. Return-date flexibility is usually not an option for the budget traveler; traveling with an "open return" ticket can be pricier than fixing a return date and paying to change it. When dealing with any commercial airline, buying in advance is best. Periodic **price wars** may lower prices in spring and early summer months, but they're unpredictable; don't delay your purchase in hopes of catching one. Most airlines allow children under two to fly free (on the lap of an adult).

It is not wise to buy **frequent flyer tickets** from others—it is standard policy on all commercial airlines to check a photo ID, and you could find yourself paying for a new, full-fare ticket. Make sure to open a frequent flyer account ahead of time and use it—it's many kilometers to Australia, no matter where you're coming from.

Whenever flying internationally, pick up your ticket well in advance of the departure date, have the flight confirmed within 72 hours of departure, and arrive at the airport at least three hours before your flight to ensure you have a seat; airlines often overbook. (Of course, being "bumped" from a flight doesn't spell doom if your travel plans are flexible—you will probably leave on the next flight and receive a free ticket or cash bonus. If you would like to be bumped to win a free ticket, check in early and let the airline officials know.)

Many airlines are now offering ticketing and reservations over the internet, and some award discounts to web reservers. Free worldwide flight schedules are available at http://www.travelocity.com. **TravelHUB** (http://www.travelhub.com) will help you search for travel agencies on the web. The **Air Traveler's Handbook** (http://www.cs.cmu.edu/afs/cs.cmu.edu/user/mkant/Public/Travel/airfare.html) is an excellent source of general information on air travel. Edward Hasbrouck maintains a **Consolidators FAQ** (http://www.travel-library.com/air-travel/consolidators.html) that provides great background on finding cheap international flights. Groups such as the **Air Courier Association** (http://www.aircourier.org) offer information about traveling as a courier and provide up-to-date listings of last minute opportunities. **Travelocity** (http://www.travelocity.com) operates a searchable online database of published airfares, which you can reserve online.

The following programs, services, and fares may be helpful for planning a reasonably-priced air trip, but always be wary of deals that seem too good to be true.

COMMERCIAL AIRLINES

The commercial airlines' lowest regular offer is the **Advance Purchase Excursion Fare** (APEX); specials advertised in newspapers may be cheaper, but have more restrictions and fewer available seats. APEX fares provide you with confirmed reservations and allow "open-jaw" tickets (landing in and returning from different cities). Generally, reservations must be made seven to 21 days in advance, with seven- to 14-day minimum and up to 90-day maximum stay limits, and hefty cancellation and change penalties (fees rise in summer). Book APEX fares early during peak seasons. Look into flights to less-popular destinations or on smaller carriers. Even if you pay an airline's lowest published fare, you may waste hundreds of dollars. Before shopping for secret discounts, you should find out the average commercial price in order to measure just how great a "bargain" you are being offered.

TICKET CONSOLIDATORS

Ticket consolidators resell unsold tickets on commercial and charter airlines at unpublished fares. The consolidator market is mostly international; domestic flights, if they do exist, are typically for cross-country flights. Consolidator flights are a great deal for expensive destinations like Australia, especially on short notice, since you bypass advance purchase requirements. Fares sold by consolidators are generally much cheaper; a 30-40% price reduction is not uncommon. There are rarely age constraints or stay limitations, but unlike tickets bought through an airline, you won't be able to use your tickets on another flight if you miss yours, and you will have to go back to the consolidator to get a refund, rather than the airline. Keep in mind that these tickets are often for coach seats on connecting (not direct) flights on foreign airlines, and that frequent-flyer miles may not be credited.

Not all consolidators deal with the general public; many only sell tickets through travel agents. **Bucket shops** are retail agencies that specialize in getting cheap tickets. Although ticket prices are marked up slightly, bucket shops generally have access to a larger market than would be available to the public and can also get tickets from wholesale consolidators. Generally, a dealer specializing in travel to the country of your destination will provide more options and cheaper tickets. The **Association of Special Fares Agents (ASFA)** maintains a database of specialized dealers for particular regions (http://www.ntsltd.com/asfa). One of the dealers listed for Australia is **Cyber Air Broker** (http://www.airdiscounter.com; email philt@world.net). Look for bucket shops' tiny ads in the travel section of weekend papers; in the U.S., the Sunday *New York Times* is a good source. In Australia, these ads often pop up in the *Sydney Times*. Kelly Monaghan's *Consolidators: Air Travel's Bargain Basement* (US$8 plus $3.50 shipping) from the Intrepid Traveler, P.O. Box 438, New York, NY 10034 (email info@intrepidtraveler.com), is an invaluable source for more information and lists of consolidators by location and destination.

Be a smart shopper; check out the competition. Among the many reputable and trustworthy companies are, unfortunately, some shady wheeler-dealers. Contact the local Better Business Bureau to find out how long the company has been in business and its track record. Although not necessary, it is preferable to deal with consolidators close to home so you can visit in person, if necessary. Ask to receive your tickets as quickly as possible so you have time to fix any problems. Get the company's policy in writing: insist on a **receipt** that gives full details about the tickets, refunds, and restrictions, and record who you talked to and when. It may be worth paying with a credit card (despite the 2-5% fee) so you can stop payment if you never receive your tickets. Beware the "bait and switch" gag: shyster firms will advertise a super-low fare and then tell a caller that it has been sold. Although this is a viable excuse, if they can't offer you a price near the advertised fare on *any* date, it is a scam to lure in customers—report them to the Better Business Bureau. Also ask about accommodations and car rental discounts; some consolidators have fingers in many pies.

For destinations **worldwide,** try **Airfare Busters,** offices in Washington, D.C. (tel. (202) 776-0478), Boca Raton, FL (tel. (561) 994-9590), and Houston, TX (tel. (800) 232-

783); **Pennsylvania Travel,** Paoli, PA (tel. (800) 331-0947); **Cheap Tickets,** offices in os Angeles, CA, San Francisco, CA, Honolulu, HI, Seattle, WA, and New York, NY (tel. 800) 377-1000); or **Moment's Notice,** 7301 New Utrecht Ave, Brooklyn, NY (tel. (718) :34-6295; fax 234-6450; http://www.moments-notice.com) offers air tickets, tours, and otels; US$25 annual fee. **NOW Voyager,** 74 Varick St #307, New York, NY 10013 (tel. 212) 431-1616; fax 334-5243; email info@nowvoyagertravel.com; http://www.now- oyagertravel.com), acts as a consolidator and books discounted international flights, nostly from New York, as well as courier flights (see **Courier Companies,** below), for registration fee of US$50. For a processing fee, depending on the number of travelers nd the itinerary, **Travel Avenue,** Chicago, IL (tel. (800) 333-3335; fax (312) 876-1254; ttp://www.travelavenue.com), searches for the lowest international airfare available, ncluding consolidated prices, and gives a 5% rebate on fares over US$350.

CHARTER FLIGHTS

Charters are flights a tour operator contracts with an airline (usually one specializing in charters) to fly extra loads of passengers to peak-season destinations. Charters are often cheaper than regular flights, especially during peak seasons. Some operate nonstop, and their restrictions on minimum advance-purchase and minimum stay are more enient. However, charter flights fly less frequently than major airlines, make refunds particularly difficult, and are almost always fully booked. Schedules and itineraries may change or be cancelled at the last moment (as late as 48hr. before the trip, without a full refund), and check-in, boarding, and baggage claim are often much slower. As always, pay with a credit card if you can; consider traveler's insurance against trip interruption.

Eleventh-hour **discount clubs** and **fare brokers** offer members savings, including charter flights and tour packages. Research your options carefully. **Last Minute Travel Service,** 100 Sylvan Rd, Woburn, MA 01801 (tel. (800) 527-8646 or (617) 267-9800); and **Travel Avenue** (tel. (800) 333-3335; see **Ticket Consolidators,** above) are both options. Study these organizations' contracts closely; you don't want to end up with an unwanted overnight layover.

COURIER COMPANIES AND FREIGHTERS

Those who travel light should consider flying to Australia as a **courier.** The company hiring you will use your checked luggage space for freight; you're only allowed to bring carry-ons. You are responsible for the safe delivery of the baggage claim slips (given to you by a courier company representative) to the representative waiting for you when you arrive—don't screw up or you will be blacklisted as a courier. You will probably never see the cargo you are transporting—the company handles it all—and airport offi- cials know that couriers are not responsible for the baggage checked for them. Restric- tions to watch for: you must be over 21 (18 in some cases), have a valid passport, and procure your own visa (if necessary); most flights are round-trip only with short fixed- length stays (usually two weeks in Australia); only single tickets are issued (but a com- panion may be able to get a next-day flight). Many companies charge a one-time regis- tration fee of approximately $50 when you first purchase a ticket.

Air-Tech.Com, 588 Broadway #204, New York, NY 10012 (tel. (212) 219-7000; fax 219-0066), offers courier flights to Australia. For approximately US$700 from Los Ange- les, you can get a plane ticket good for a two-week stay in Australia. The only other departure point is New York, and although you can stay three months and fly on Qan- tas, the ticket will likely cost US$1200. Contact the company at least a month in advance for details. Air-Tech also arranges confirmed seats at discount rates.

NOW Voyager, 74 Varick St. #307, New York, NY 10013 (tel. (212) 431-1616; fax 334-5243; email info@nowvoyagertravel.com; http://www.nowvoyagertravel.com), acts as an agent for many courier flights worldwide. Flights to Australia leave from Los Angeles and New York, and prices are similar to Air-Tech prices, although the New York fares may be slightly cheaper. (They also act as a consolidator; see **Ticket Consol- idators,** above.) Other agents with flights to Australia are **Halbart Express,** 1000 W.

Hillcrest Blvd., Inglewood, CA 90301 (tel. (310) 417-3048; fax 417-9792); and **Discount Travel International** (tel. (212) 362-3636; see **Ticket Consolidators,** above).

For an annual fee of $45, the **International Association of Air Travel Couriers,** 8 South J St, P.O. Box 1349, Lake Worth, FL 33460 (tel. (561) 582-8320), informs travelers (via computer, fax, and mailings) of courier opportunities worldwide. For a practical guide to the air courier scene, check out Kelly Monaghan's **Air Courier Bargains** (US$14.95 plus $3 shipping), available from Upper Access Publishing (UAP), P.O. Box 457, Hinesburg, VT 05461 (tel. (800) 356-9315; fax 242-0036; email upperaccess@aol.com or info@upperaccess.com for entry into their website), or consult the **Courier Air Travel Handbook** (US$9.95 plus $3.50 shipping), published by Bookmasters, Inc., P.O. Box 388, Ashland, OH 44805 (tel. (800) 507-2665; fax (419) 281-6883).

■ By Boat

If you really have travel time and cash to spare, **Ford's Travel Guides,** 19448 Londelius St, Northridge, CA 91324 (tel. (818) 701-7414; fax 701-7415), lists **freighter companies** that will take passengers to Australia. Boats depart from many points in the United States, especially along the East Coast, and arrive in Melbourne, Sydney, and Brisbane. Trips cost between US$81-108 per person, per day, and the trip takes between 23 and 42 days one-way. You can also travel from many points in Europe, although be warned: a trip by sea from Italy to Australia takes 81 days. Ask for their *Freighter Travel Guide and Waterways of the World* (US$16, plus $2.50 postage if mailed outside the U.S.).

ONCE THERE

■ Embassies and Consulates

Canada: The High Commission on Commonwealth Ave., **Canberra** ACT 2600 (tel. (02) 6273 3844; fax 6273 3285). Consulate General at Level 5, Quay West Building, 111 Harrington St, **Sydney** NSW 2000 (tel. (02) 9364 3000; fax 9364 3098). Consulate near **Melbourne** at 123 Camberwell Rd, East Hawthorn, Vic 3123 (tel. (03) 9811 9999; fax 9811 9969). Consulate at 267 St George's Tce, 3rd Fl., **Perth** WA 6000 (tel. (08) 9322 7930; fax 9261 7700).

Ireland: Embassy in **Canberra** at 20 Arkana St, Yarralumla ACT 2600 (tel. (02) 6273 3022; fax 6273 3741). Honorary Consul General at P.O. Box 20 (Aberdeen St in the Northbridge district), **Perth** WA 6865 (tel. (08) 9385 8247; fax 9385 8247).

New Zealand: High Commission on Commonwealth Ave, **Canberra** ACT 2600 (tel. (02) 6270 4211; fax 6273 3194). Consulate-General at GPO Box 62 (Watkins Pl. Building, 288 Edward St), **Brisbane** QLD 4001 (tel. (07) 3221 9933; fax 3229 7495). Consulate-General at 60 Albert Rd, South **Melbourne** Vic 3205 (tel. (03) 9696 0501, immigration tel. 9696 0445; fax 9696 0391). Consulate-General at GPO Box 365 (level 14, Gold Fields Building, 1 Alfred St, Circular Quay), **Sydney** NSW 2000 (tel. (02) 9247 1999, customs police tel. 9247 8567; fax 9247 1754).

South Africa: High Commission in **Canberra** at State Circle, Yarralumla ACT 2600 (tel. (02) 6273 2424).

U.K.: The British High Commission in **Canberra,** Commonwealth Ave, Yarralumla ACT 2600 (tel. (02) 6270 6666, recorded info tel. 0055 63220; fax 6273 3236). Consul-General on level 26, Waterfront Pl, 1 Eagle St., **Brisbane** QLD 4000 (tel. (07) 3236 2575; fax 3236 2576). Consul-General on 17th Fl., 90 Collins St, **Melbourne** Vic 3000 (tel. (03) 9650 3699; fax 9650 2990). Consul-General on level 26, "Allendale Square," 77 St Georges Tce, **Perth** WA 6000 (tel. (08) 9221 5400; fax 9221 2344). Consul-General on level 16, The Gateway, 1 Macquarie Pl, **Sydney Cove** NSW 2000 (tel. (02) 9247 7521; fax 9251 6201). Consul on level 22, Grenfell Centre, 25 Grenfell St, **Adelaide** SA 5000 (tel. (08) 8212 7280; fax 8212 7282). Honourary Consul on 39 Murray St, **Hobart** Tas 7000 (tel. (03) 6230 4647; fax 6223 2279).

United States: Embassy in **Canberra,** 21 Moonah St, Yarralumla ACT 2600 (tel. (02) 6270 5000; fax 6273 3191). Consulate at Level 59, MLC Centre, 19-29 Martin Pl, **Sydney** NSW 2000 (tel. (02) 9373 9200; fax 9373 9184); Consulate at 553 St Kilda Rd, P.O. Box 6722, **Melbourne** Vic 3004 (tel. (03) 9526 5900; fax 9510 4646). Consulate on 13th Fl., 16 St. Georges Tce, **Perth** WA 6000 (tel. (08) 9231 9400; fax 9231 9444). The U.S. Consulate in **Brisbane** closed in March, 1996.

■ Getting Around

BY PLANE

Because Australia is so large, many travelers, even budget travelers, take a domestic flight at some point while touring the country. Qantas and Ansett Australia are the two major domestic carriers. Oz Experience and Qantas offer an Air-Bus Pass with which travelers can fly one way, and bus back (or vice versa) around Australia. Passes are valid for 6 months with unlimited stops. Airbus reservations can be made by calling (02) 9221 4711 in Sydney or 1300 301 359 anywhere else.

Qantas: Reservations tel. 13 13 13; http://www.qantas.com.au. Qantas allows travellers to change flight dates free of charge on domestic flights; cities can be changed for $50. For international travellers (with the exception New Zealand and Fiji, who are not eligible), a boomerang pass may be the best domestic flight option. One-way passes within zones are AUS$175, between zones are AUS$220. Zones are roughly broken down into east (including Sydney, Melbourne, Brisbane, Cairns, and Ade-

laide), middle (including Ayers Rock, Alice Springs, and Darwin) and west (including Perth). The $220 travel pass can also be used for travel to New Zealand and Fiji.

Ansett Airlines: Reservations tel. 13 13 00; http://www.ansett.com.au. Offers a domestic flight option similar to the boomerang pass. Specializes in domestic routes in Australia and New Zealand, although it flies internationally to Japan, Hong Kong, and Bali, Indonesia. Major port cities include Adelaide, Cairns, Denpasar (Bali), Hong Kong (China), Melbourne, Osaka (Japan), Perth, Sydney, Canberra, and Darwin.

BY TRAIN

Each state runs its own rail service, and transfers between services may require a bus trip to the next station. The main rail companies are **CountryLink,** based in New South Wales, **V/Line** in Victoria, **Queensland Rail** in Queensland, **Westrail** in Western Australia, and **Great Southern Railways** (http://www.gsr.com.au) in South Australia and the

On the Right Track

The history of Australia's rail system is a classic case of colonial confusion. In the 19th century, when the country's original six colonies started building railroad tracks, each individual colony conferred with London instead of its neighbors. The result: by 1901 (the year of Australian federation), the six areas of the country had tracks of six different widths. Australians have been standardizing the system ever since, and travelers can now visit all of the state capitals with the exception of Darwin (and Hobart, of course) on a train. Lines also run up to Cairns and into outback Queensland, and a track runs south to Adelaide from Alice Springs. But track and operator discrepancies linger, and these differences can make rail travel slow, inefficient, and not particularly cheap. It is, however, a comfortable way to see the country, and a good option if you don't have wheels of your own.

Northern Territory. For reservations in New South Wales, Queensland, Victoria, and the ACT, telephone 13 23 32, in South Australia, the Northern Territory, Tasmania, and Western Australia telephone 13 21 47. For reservations and ticketing from the U.S., call 1 (800) 423 2880. Wheelchair access on interstate trains is generally poor, since the corridors are too narrow for most wheelchairs. Some of the larger stations provide collapsible wheelchairs, but not all do.

The **Austrail Pass** allows travel over consecutive days within a given period; contact the railroad for specific rates. The **Austrail Flexipass** allows you to purchase 8, 15, 22, or 29 non-consecutive traveling days over a six-month period and is slightly more expensive. The **East Coast Discovery Pass**, for travel between Melbourne and Cairns, allows unlimited stops on the Eastern Seaboard.

BY BUS

People travel by bus (coach) in Australia much more frequently than they travel by train. Buses run regularly to major cities, but journeys off the beaten track may require a wait of a few days. **Major express routes** run daily: Sydney-Adelaide (24hr.); Sydney-Canberra (4½hr.); Sydney-Melbourne (14½hr.); Canberra-Melbourne (9½hr.); Melbourne-Adelaide (9½hr.); Adelaide-Alice Springs (20hr.); Adelaide-Perth (35hr.); Adelaide-Brisbane (33½hr.); Darwin-Alice Springs (19hr.); Darwin-Kakadu (3½hr.); Alice Springs-Ayers Rock (6hr.); Cairns-Brisbane (25hr.); Cairns-Darwin (42hr.); Brisbane-Sydney (17hr.); Brisbane-Melbourne (25hr.); and Perth-Darwin (33hr.).

Greyhound Pioneer (tel. 13 20 30) covers the whole country, including Western Australia. Greyhound has dozens of travelpass options. Seven to 21-day passes allow you to travel on any Greyhound route within 30 to 60 days, depending on the length of your pass; days of travel do not have to be consecutive. These passes cost between AUS$499 and $982. The **Aussie Explorer Pass** allows you to predetermine a route and take up to 12 months to get there, while an **Aussie Kilometer Pass** lets you choose a number of kilometers which can be used on any Greyhound route. The **All-Australian Pass** allows unlimited travel across the continent for $1555. All of these passes can be used to take one or more of the **Greyhound Pioneer Tours,** which offer combinations of tours for National Parks and scenic spots in Central Australia, Western Australia, and the Top End. A 10% discount is available for YHA, VIP, Euro26, ISIC, and Nomads card holders; possibly more if bookings are made overseas.

McCafferty's Coachlines (tel. 13 14 99) runs through most of the country. The buses can't take you into Western Australia, but they can arrange for you to connect to the Indian Pacific train from Adelaide to Perth, and can get you almost anywhere else. **Travel Australia passes** are valid for three to 12 months, and let travelers ride with unlimited stops one-way along any of eight predetermined routes. These passes can be purchased from a local travel agent or at any McCafferty's terminal; a 10% discount is available for international students and pensioners, and backpacker cardholders, the discount is 15% if the purchase is made outside of Australia. A 12-month pass is $820; and for $950 travellers also receive three day-tours with AAT Kings along the route. McCafferty's recently introduced an **Aussie Roamer** pass, which allows for long-distance travelers to pay by the kilometer. McCafferty's also offers two kinds of **day passes for international travelers** only; these must be purchased before arrival in Australia. These **Discover Australia** day passes allow unlimited unrestricted travel on the McCafferty's network for a set number of days within a longer period, or for a set number of consecutive days. A pass good for any seven days of travel within a 90-day period costs AUS$495. Ten, 15, 21, 30, 60, and 90-day consecutive and within-period passes are all available. For the within-period passes, overnight segments are allowed to equal one day, since a day is defined as a 24hr. period.

Other popular bus companies include **Oz Experience,** 3 Orwell St, Kings Cross, NSW 2011 (tel. (02) 9368 1766 in Sydney, 1300 300 038 elsewhere; fax 9368 0908; email backpack@world.net; http://www.ozex.com.au/), which offers backpacker tour packages with a lot of flexibility, and drivers who double as tour guides. **Wayward Bus** (tel. (08) 8232 6646; fax 8232 1455; email wayward@usa.net; www.wayward.bus.com.au)

runs similar trips with a natural focus between Alice Springs, Adelaide, Melbourne, and Sydney, appealing to backpackers of all ages.

BY CAR

Some regions of Australia are virtually inaccessible without a car, and in many areas, public transportation options are simply inadequate. One of the major dilemmas of traveling in Australia, at least beyond the main coastal cities, is that the road system is in many areas astonishingly primitive and poorly maintained. To travel on most outback roads and in many national parks, you will need a **four wheel drive (4WD),** which unfortunately can double the cost of renting or buying. Shopping around well ahead of time is advisable.

Renting

Although the cost of renting a car can be prohibitive for an individual traveler, when traveling with a group rentals can become cost-efficient. **Car rental agencies** fall into two categories: national companies with hundreds of branches, and local agencies which serve only one city or region. Budget, Hertz, Avis, and Thrifty are Australia's largest national companies. These complement dozens of smaller local agencies, which usually have lower prices. The big companies are multinational; you can generally make reservations before you leave by calling their offices in your home country. However, occasionally the price and availability information they give doesn't jive with what the local offices in Australia will tell you. Try checking with both numbers to make sure you get the best price and accurate information. Local desk numbers are included in town listings; for home-country numbers, call your toll-free directory or check the web. Australia numbers and web addresses are listed below:

Avis (tel. in Sydney (02) 9353 9000, toll-free outside of Sydney 1800 225 533; http://www.avis.com). YHA member discounts available; quote No. P081600 when making reservations.

Budget (tel. in Sydney (02) 9669 1467, outside of Sydney (03) 9206 3222; http://budgetrentacar.com). YHA discounts are sometimes available; call the National Reservations area (tel. 13 38 48) and give the code 113.

Hertz (tel. in Australia 13 30 39 or (03) 9698 2555; fax (03) 9698 2295; http://www.hertz.com). Renters must be 25, but if a member of AAA (RACV, etc.) can be between 21 and 24.

Thrifty (tel. 1800 652 008, in Tasmania 1800 030 7309; http://www.thrifty.com).

To rent a car from most establishments in Australia, you need to be at least **21 years old.** Some agencies require renters to be 25, and many charge those aged 21-24 an additional insurance fee. Policies and prices vary from agency to agency. Small local operations occasionally rent to people under 21, but be sure to ask about the insurance coverage and deductible, and check the fine print of your agreement.

Rental car prices start at around AUS$45 a day from national companies, $30 from local agencies. Expect to pay more for larger cars and for 4WD. Long-term rentals are always cheaper. Cars with **automatic transmission** can cost up to $15 a day more than standard (stick shift), and in Western Australia, Northern Territory, and more remote areas of the eastern states, automatic transmission is hard to find in the first place. It is virtually impossible, no matter where you are, to find an automatic 4WD.

Some rental packages offer unlimited kilometers, while others offer 100-200km/day with a surcharge of approximately $0.25 per kilometer after that. Quoted rates do not include petrol or tax, so ask for the total cost before handing over the credit card; airport surcharges are another possibility. Return the car with a full tank of petrol to avoid high fuel charges at the end. Be sure to ask whether the price includes **insurance** against theft and collision. Every registered car automatically carries a green slip that provides no-fault insurance, but not necessarily anything more. Remember that if you are driving a conventional vehicle on an **unsealed road** (Australian for unpaved) in a rental car, you are almost never covered by insurance; ask about this before leaving the rental agency. Cars rented on an **American Express** card in Australia do *not* carry the automatic insurance that they would in some other countries. Insurance plans almost come with an **excess** (or deductible) of around $750 for conventional vehicles; excess ranges up to around $2500 for younger drivers and for 4WD. This means you pay for all damages up to that sum, unless they are the fault of another vehicle. The excess you will be quoted applies to collisions with another moving object; collisions with stationary objects ("single-vehicle collisions") will cost you even more. The excess can often be reduced or waived entirely if you pay an additional charge, between $5-20 per day.

If you rent, lease, or borrow a car, you will need to get a **green card,** or **International Insurance Certificate,** to prove that you have liability insurance. These can be obtained through the car rental agency; most include coverage in their prices. If you lease a car, you can obtain a green card from the dealer. Even if your auto insurance applies abroad, you will need a green card to certify this to foreign officials.

National chains sometimes allow cars to be picked up in one city and dropped off in another, although **one-way rentals** are not usually allowed into or out of Western Australia or the Northern Territory. There is usually a minimum hire period and sometimes an extra charge.

On the Road

Australians drive on the **left side** of the road. In unmarked intersections, a driver must yield to vehicles entering the intersection from his or her right. By law, **seat belts** must be worn. The speed limit in most areas of Australia is 60kph (35mph), while on highways it's 100 or 110kph (62 to 68mph). Speed radar guns are sometimes used to patrol well-traveled roads. **Petrol (gasoline)** costs about 70¢ per liter in cities and 80¢ per liter in outlying areas, but prices vary according to state gasoline taxes.

When traveling in the summer or in the outback, bring 20 liters (5 gallons) of **water** per person for drinking and for the radiator. For long outback drives, travelers should register with the police before beginning the trek and again upon arrival at the destination. Check with the local automobile club for details. In the north, **four-wheel-drive (4WD)** is essential for seeing the parks, particularly in the Wet, when dirt roads turn to mud. When traveling in the outback or for long distances, tune up the car before you leave, make sure the tires are in good repair and have enough air, and get good maps. A **compass** and a **car manual** can also be very useful. You should always carry a **spare tire** and **jack, jumper cables, extra oil, flares, a torch (flashlight),** and **blankets** (in case your car breaks down at night or in the winter). If you don't know how to **change a tire,** learn before heading into the outback. Blowouts on dirt roads are exceedingly common. If you do have a breakdown, **stay with your car.**

Unsealed roads dominate rural Australia, ranging from smooth, hard-packed sand to an eroded mixture of mud, sand, and stones. Locals are a good source of information on the road conditions in the immediate vicinity. If you're planning longer-range driving, ask at tourist bureaus. One can skid on gravel almost as badly as on ice. **Parking** is safest in garages or well-traveled areas. Children under 40 lbs. should ride only in a specially-designed carseat, available for a small fee from most car rental agencies.

Remember: Australia's highway system is much worse than you probably expect. Find out ahead of time whether roads are sealed, especially if you're driving a conventional vehicle. **Kangaroos are a serious danger** to drivers as well; they are huge animals that can destroy cars, and, however cute they seem, they're stupid and will jump in front of your car. They may cross at any time, but around dusk is a particular danger period. When driving on unsealed roads, call regional tourist boards ahead of time for road conditions, especially in the North, as the wet season sometimes makes roads impassible for months after the rains stop. Furthermore, you should allow at least twice as much time as you would for travel on paved roads.

The **Australian Automobile Association (AAA)** is the national organization that encompasses all of the local automobile organizations. You won't often see it called the AAA, though; in most states, the local organization is called the **Royal Automobile Club (RAC).** In New South Wales and the ACT, it's the **National Royal Motorist Association (NRMA).** Services—from breakdown assistance to map provision—are similar to those offered by automobile associations in other countries. If you are a member of one of these overseas organizations and bring proof of your membership to Australia, you'll be able to use AAA facilities free of charge, since they all operate on a reciprocal basis within the country. To join in the US, dial (800) 222-4357. **AAA roadside assistance** can be reached at tel. 13 11 11, except in the Northern Territory, where it's (08) 8941 0611. It's possible to join AAA through any state's organization. *Let's Go* lists the location of the state automobile organization in each state introduction.

Buying and Selling Used Cars

Buying used cars and then reselling them is popular among long-term travelers or those too young to rent. Automotive independence can be yours for AUS$1600-5000. In addition to the commercial used-car lots, capital cities and large towns often have **used car lots** filled with backpackers and others trying to **buy and sell used cars.** Lot owners charge people trying to sell cars a fixed rate to park their cars and sit by them; buyers stroll around and haggle. Hostel or university bulletin boards are another good bet. In Sydney, check the *Weekly Trading Post* on Thursdays for used car advertisements, and the *Daily Telegraph Mirror* and *Sydney Morning Herald* on Fridays and weekends. It's always easiest to sell a car for the best price when demand is high; consider the high tourist season for the region you're in. Vehicles are also easier to sell if they are registered in the state where they are being sold—new owners need to register the car, and some states don't allow registration transfer by mail. If you buy a car privately, check the registration papers against the license of the person who is selling the car.

Because many people buy (or rent) cars and sleep in them while traveling (definitely not recommended from a safety standpoint), station wagons and campervans are favorites. The **Ford Falcon, Holden Kingswood,** and **Holden Commodore** are among the most popular large cars, while the **Toyota Corolla** and **Mazda 626** have cornered much of the small-car market. Those who buy campervans report having the most luck with **Toyota.** Buying popular automobiles can pay off if you end up needing parts in the middle of nowhere. Holden, Ford, Nissan, Toyota, Mazda, and Mitsubishi are all fairly safe bets. Keep in mind the low resale value of used cars—you probably won't turn a profit or finance your ticket home at the end of your trip. Another option is to purchase a car from a dealer who guarantees to buy the car back at the end of your trip. Be especially wary of small print when contemplating these **buy-back deals.**

Before buying a used car, check in with the local branch of the AAA, because states have varying requirements for a transfer of ownership, and local organizations can advise you on how to get your money's worth. For example, the NRMA in New South Wales publishes brochures entitled *International Tourists Car Buying Advice* and *Worry-free Guide to Buying a Car.* In Victoria, all cars are required to carry a Road Worthiness Certificate, and it's probably unwise to purchase a car without one. Local auto clubs also do mechanical inspections (NRMA vehicle inspections tel. 13 21 32).

When considering buying a car, call the **Register of Encumbered Vehicles** to confirm that a vehicle is unencumbered—that it has not been reported as stolen, and has no outstanding traffic warrants. For cars registered in ACT, Qld, or NT, dial (02) 9600 0022 or 1800 424 988. For cars registered in Vic, dial (03) 9348 1222. For cars registered in Tas, dial 13 11 05. For cars registered in SA, dial (08) 8232 0800. For cars registered in WA, dial (08) 9222 0711. You'll need to provide the registration number, engine number, and VIN/chassis numbers of the vehicle. In New South Wales, a car must have a pink inspection certificate to guarantee that it is roadworthy. It is valid for 20 days, and is available at most service stations.

Insurance and Registration

Third-party personal injury insurance, sometimes called a green slip, is automatically included with every registered vehicle. In the event of an accident, this covers any person who may be injured except the driver at fault, but does not cover damage or repairs to any cars or property. Even travelers trying to save money should consider purchasing additional insurance. **Third-party property damage insurance** covers the cost of repair to other people's cars or property if you're responsible for an accident. **Full compre-**

hensive insurance, which covers damage to all vehicles, including your own, is more expensive, but provides more peace of mind.

Within two weeks after purchase, you'll need to **register** the car in your name at the Motor Vehicle Registry. Although requirements vary from state to state, re-registration costs about AUS$15, and must be completed within about two weeks. Again, turn to the local automobile organization for help in this area.

BY BICYCLE

Australia has many **bike tracks** to attract cyclers and few cars to distract them. Much of the country is flat, and road bikers can travel long distances without needing to huff and puff excessively. In theory, bicycles can go on **buses and trains,** but most major bus companies require you to disassemble your bike and pay a flat AUS$15 fee. You may not be allowed to bring your bike into the train compartment with you.

The **Bicycle Federation of Australia (BFA),** GPO Box 792, Adelaide 5001 (tel. (02) 6355 1724; fax 6355 1724; email bicycle@lisp.com.au; http://www.ozemail.com.au/ ~bicycle), a nonprofit bicycle advocacy group, publishes *Australia Cyclist* magazine and has a list of regional bicycling organizations on its web page. Member groups include the **Bicycle Institute of South Australia** (tel. (08) 8271 5824), the **Western Australia Cyclists' Action Group** (tel. (08) 9384 7409), **Western Australia Bicycle Transportation Alliance** (tel. (09) 470 4007), **Bicycle Tasmania** (tel. (002) 33 6619), **Bicycle New South Wales** (tel. (02) 9283 5200; fax 9283 5246), **Bicycle Victoria** (tel. (03) 9328 3000; fax 9328 2000), and the **Bicycle Institute of Queensland** (tel. (07) 3844 1144; fax 3844 1144). Some cyclists say that some of these organizations focus more on resources for daytrips and short excursions than on long-distance riding, but they are definitely the place to begin.

Safe and secure cycling requires a quality helmet and lock. A good **helmet** costs about $40—much cheaper than critical head surgery. Helmets are required in Australia. Cyclists recommend traveling with **maps** from the state Automobile Associations.

BY MOTORCYCLE

Motorcycles (or motorbikes, as they're sometimes known in Australia) remain a popular way to travel the long stretches of highway. You are required by Australian law to have a **license and a helmet.** See the section on cars (above), since many of the same suggestions apply. It may be cheaper than car travel, but it takes a tenacious soul to endure a motorcycle tour. If you must carry a load, keep it low and forward where it won't disturb the cycle's center of gravity. Fasten it either to the seat or over the rear axle in saddle or tank bags. Of course, **safety** should be your primary concern. Motorcycles are incredibly vulnerable to crosswinds, drunk drivers, the blind spots of cars and trucks, and wandering wildlife. *Always ride defensively.* Dangers skyrocket at night; travel in the daytime. For **trail bike riding** info, contact the **Australian Motorcycle Trail Riders Association** (AMTRA) at P.O. Box 8, Ringwood Vic 3134 (tel. (03) 9434 1039).

BY THUMB

Let's Go strongly urges you to seriously consider the risks before you choose to hitch. We do not recommend hitching as a safe means of transportation and none of the information printed here is intended to do so.

Given the infrequency of public transportation to several popular destinations, travelers often need to find other ways to get where they're going. Hostels frequently have message boards where those seeking rides and those seeking to share the cost of gas can meet up. If you are looking to travel with a stranger, car-less travelers report having a good deal of luck meeting willing drivers in roadhouses or cafes. This arrangement gives them an opportunity to size up potential lifts before accepting a ride. On the east coast, backpacker traffic moves from Sydney to Brisbane, and those who go with the flow are sure to make friends who have wheels.

Standing on the side of the highway with your thumb out is much more dangerous than making a new friend at your hostel. Safety issues are always imperative, even when you're traveling with another person. Hitching means entrusting your life to a random person who happens to stop beside you on the road and risking assault, sexual harassment, and unsafe driving. If you're a woman traveling alone, don't hitch. It's just too dangerous. A man and a woman are a safer combination; two men will have a harder time finding a ride. Avoid getting in the back of a two-door car, and never let go of your backpack. Hitchhiking at night can be particularly dangerous. Don't accept a ride that you are not entirely comfortable with. If you ever feel threatened, insist on being let off, but keep in mind that the vast distances between towns on some stretches of highway increase your chance of being left literally in the middle of nowhere, without food, water, or the possibility of another ride for days.

If you decide to hitch, choose a spot on the side of the road with ample space for a car to pull over, where traffic is not moving too fast. The edges of town are ideal as people have not yet accelerated to highway speed. Dress nicely and keep your backpack in full view, as it tells people you're a backpacker and justifies your reason for hitching.

■ Accommodations

While hotels in large cities are typical of hotels in large cities around the world, **"hotels" in rural Australia,** particularly in Victoria and New South Wales, are actually simple furnished rooms above local pubs. Some smack of fancy Victorian-era lodging with grand back staircases, high tin ceilings, and wrap-around verandas. Others have been converted to long-term worker housing, and are thus less conducive to brief overnight stays. Singles in these hotels usually cost AUS$15-30. This generally includes a towel, a common (shared) bathroom, and a private bedroom (no bunks, usually). A simple breakfast may be included, and there's usually a common kitchen. The pubs are fully functional downstairs, so it's a good idea to choose a quieter one if you're fond of tucking in early. **Motels** in Australia are accommodations with parking.

HOSTELS

For tight budgets and those lonesome traveling blues, hostels can't be beat. Hostels are generally dorm-style accommodations, often in single-sex large rooms with bunk beds, although some hostels do offer private rooms for families and couples. They sometimes have kitchens and utensils for your use, bike or moped rentals, storage areas, and laundry facilities. There can be drawbacks: a very few Australian hostels close during certain daytime "lock-out" hours, have a curfew, impose a maximum stay, or, less frequently, require that you do chores. But most, especially in backpacker-heavy coastal Queensland, are so anxious to court budget travelers that they have swimming pools, free local transportation, and even free weekly barbecues. Fees generally range from AUS$10-20 per night and hostels associated with one of the large hostel associations often have lower rates for members. Check out the **Internet Guide to Hostelling** (http://hostels.com), which includes details on hostels from around the world in addition to oodles of information about hostelling and backpacking worldwide.

Australia's **YHA** is a member of the international youth hostel federation **Hostelling International.** Australia's other main hosteling organization is **Backpackers Resorts International,** which is often abbreviated BRI. Discounts from BRI are usually designated **VIP.** If a hostel gives VIP discounts, it means that guests get AUS$1 off per night. **Nomads Backpackers** is a third major hosteling chain in Australia.

Reservations for over 300 **Hostelling International (HI)** hostels (see listing below) may be made via the International Booking Network (IBN), a computerized system which allows you make hostels reservations months in advance for a nominal fee (U.S. tel. (202) 783 6161). Overseas visitors who join HI in their own countries are able to stay in HI/YHA hostels worldwide (see below). If you do not join before arriving, however, you can buy a one-year HI Card in Australia. This costs AUS$44 and is available

from state membership and travel centers or directly from any YHA hostels. In Sydney, the office to pick up cards is at 422 Kent St (tel. 9261 1111).

Australian Youth Hostels Association (AYHA), Level 3, 10 Mallett St, Camperdown NSW 2050 (tel. (02) 9565 1699; fax 9565 1325; email YHA@yha.org.au; http://www.yha.org.au). Memberships $44, renewal $27; under 18 $13.

Hostelling International-American Youth Hostels (HI-AYH), 733 15th St. NW, Suite 840, Washington, D.C. 20005 (tel. (202) 783-6161; fax 783-6171; email hiayhserv@hiayh.org; http://www.hiayh.org). Memberships can be purchased at many travel agencies or at the national office in Washington, D.C. One-year membership US$25, under 18 $10, over 54 $15, family cards $35.

Hostelling International-Canada (HI-C), 400-205 Catherine St., Ottawa, ON K2P 1C3 (tel. (613) 237 7884; fax 237 7868, email info@hostellingintl.ca; http://www.hostellingintl.ca). IBN booking centers in Edmonton, Montreal, Ottawa, and Vancouver. Membership packages: 1yr. under 18 CDN$12; 1yr. over 18 $25; 2yr. over 18 $35; lifetime $175.

An Óige (Irish Youth Hostel Association), 61 Mountjoy St., Dublin 7 (tel. (353) 1 830 4555; fax 830 5808; anoige@iol.ie; http://www.irelandyha.org). One-year membership is IR£7.50, under 18 £4, family £7.50 for each adult with children, under 16 free.

Scottish Youth Hostels Association (SYHA), 7 Glebe Crescent, Stirling FK8 2JA (tel. (01786) 89 14 00; fax 89 13 33; email syha@syha.org.uk; http://www.syha.org.uk). Membership UK£6, under 18 £2.50.

Youth Hostels Association of England and Wales (YHA), Trevelyan House, 8 St. Stephen's Hill, St. Albans, Hertfordshire AL1 2DY, England (tel. (01727) 855215; fax 844126; email yhacustomerservices@compuserve.com; http://www.yha.org.uk). Enrollment fees: UK£10; under 18 £5; £20 per parent with children under 18 free; £10 for 1 parent with children under 18 enrolled free; £140 lifetime membership.

Hostelling International Northern Ireland (HINI), 22-32 Donegall Rd., Belfast BT12 5JN (tel. (01232) 32 47 33 or 31 54 35; fax 43 96 99; email info@hini.org.uk; http://www.hini.org.uk). Annual memberships UK£7, under 18 £3, family £14 for up to 6 children, lifetime £50.

Youth Hostels Association of New Zealand (YHANZ), P.O. Box 436, 173 Cashel St., Christchurch 1 (tel. (643) 379 9970; fax 365 4476; email info@yha.org.nz; http://www.yha.org.nz). Annual membership fee NZ$24.

Hostel International South Africa, P.O. Box 4402, Cape Town 8000 (tel. (021) 24 2511; fax 24 4119; email info@hisa.org.za; http://www.hisa.org.za). Membership SAR50, group SAR120, family SAR100, lifetime SAR250.

BED AND BREAKFASTS

For a cozy alternative to impersonal hotel rooms, B&Bs (private homes with rooms available to travelers) range from the acceptable to the sublime. Hosts will sometimes go out of their way to be accommodating by accepting travelers with pets, giving personalized tours, or offering home-cooked meals. On the other hand, many B&Bs do not provide phones, TVs, or private bathrooms.

Several travel guides and reservation services specialize in B&Bs. **Travel-Link International** has a website at http://www.travel-link.org/index2.html with over 2000 B&B listings in Australia. Run in partnership with HomeLink International, Travel-Link uses its extensive network to help travelers plan their itineraries. *The Complete Guide to Bed and Breakfasts, Inns and Guesthouses in the U.S., Canada, and Worldwide* (US$17) lists over 11,000 B&Bs and inns, and includes Australia locations (available through Lanier Publications, P.O. Box D, Petaluma, CA 94953 (tel. (707) 763 0271; fax 763 5762; email lanier@travelguides.com; http://www.travelguides. com). If you can stand the name, **Nerd World's Bed and Breakfasts by Region** (http://www.nerdworld.com/users/dstein/nw854.html) offers an excellent listing of international B&Bs, including accommodations in Australia. **Bed and Breakfast Australia,** P.O. Box 48, Gordon, NSW 2072 (tel. (02) 9498 5344; fax 9498 6438; email bnb@bnba.com.au), can help groups and individuals plan itineraries and make advance bookings.

UNIVERSITY RESIDENCE HALLS

Many Australian **universities** open their residence halls to travelers when school is not in session, typically for quite low rates. Because they are in student areas, the dormitories are often good sources of information for things to do, places to stay, and possible rides out of town. The typical summer break at the university level is from late November to late February. Easter break lasts for two weeks over Easter, while winter break encompasses the first two weeks of July. The Universities of Canberra, Sydney, and Queensland, as well as Flinders University of South Australia, Melbourne University, and Monash University in Melbourne are among those occasionally offering accommodation. No one policy covers all of these institutions. Contact the universities directly, or request the *Campus Accommodation* **information sheet** from the Australian Tourist Commission (http://www.aussie.net.au). Demand is high, so book ahead.

HOMESTAYS AND FARMSTAYS

Homestays and farmstays are a phenomenal way to get in touch with Australian culture firsthand. Homestay Associations are usually near public transportation and guests can usually stay anywhere from a few days to six months or more. Prices vary with length of stay and type of accommodation. The Australian Tourist Commission publishes a *Homestay Information* sheet.

Rule's ECOLE/Homes Across The Sea, 11 Murphy St, Ipswich Qld 4305 (tel. (07) 3812 0211; fax 3812 2188; arule@gil.com.au). Over 410 host families with a range of accommodations, concentrated in SE Queensland but scattered throughout Australia. Offers programs for those with special interests, including flower cultivation, horse-racing, government, history, Aboriginal culture, and computers.

Homestay Network, 5 Locksley St, Killara NSW 2071 (tel. (02) 9498 4400; fax 9498 8324). Over 1400 homes on Sydney's north shore and eastern suburbs, as well as farm stays in Cooma and Benambra, which can accommodate stays ranging from a few days to two years.

Unique Australian Holidays Pty Ltd., 67 Rathowen Parade, Killarney Heights NSW 2086 (tel. (02) 9975 4550; fax 9975 1655), can help arrange accommodation and study tours around Sydney, the Gold Coast, Perth, and Melbourne.

Agritours Australia, 126 Barney St, Armidale NSW 2350 (tel. (02) 6772 9230; fax 6772 2244). Arranges farmstays, generally on cattle or sheep stations. Can tailor itineraries to specific group needs.

Host Farms Association, 6th Fl., 230 Collins St, Melbourne Vic 3000 (tel. (03) 9650 2922; fax 9650 9434). Arranges farm stays on 155 Victorian host farms. Book in advance, particularly during summer and school holidays.

HOME EXCHANGE AND RENTALS

Home exchange offers the traveler with a home the opportunity to live like a native, and to dramatically cut down on accommodation fees—usually only an administration fee is paid to the matching service. Once the introductions are made, the choice is left to the two hopeful partners. Most companies have pictures of members' homes and information about the owners (some will even ask for your photo). A great web site that lists many exchange companies can be found at http://www.aitec.edu.au/~bwechner/Documents/Travel/Lists/HomeExchangeClubs.html. Renting a home may also be a good deal for some: this will depend on the length of stay and the desired services.

HomeLink International, P.O. Box 260, Maldon Vic 3463 (tel. (03) 5475 2829; fax 5475 1078; http://www.homelink.org). 25 offices worldwide; contact the office in your home country to facilitate home exchange. Listing of 11,000 homes worldwide, and 600 homes throughout Australia. Paid subscribers have access to a comprehensive webpage; on-line registration available.

International Travel and Home Exchange, 43 James St., Guildford WA 6055 (tel. (08) 9279 2366; fax 9279 1451). Australian-based organization matches up international home exchanges. Publishes a directory for participants.

Latitudes Home Exchange, P.O. Box 436., South Perth WA 6951 (tel. (08) 9367 9412; fax 9367 9576; http://www.iinet.net.au/~homeswap). Offers temporary home exchange for 1-24 months. Computerized matching service ($50 lifetime membership; $250 fee when the member approves a match) or directory listings ($100 for 3 publications per year).

■ Camping and the Outdoors

If your travels take you to Australia when the weather is agreeable, camping is by far the cheapest way to go. Many hostels have camping facilities or at least allow guests to pitch tents in the yard, and the ubiquitous caravan parks offer sites without power for tent campers. Apart from being a sound financial decision, the flexibility of camping allows you to access the more remote corners of the country's numerous wilderness areas, including any of the 11 World Heritage Sites.

Every World Heritage Site has been determined to have significant ecological or cultural value for the world, and most countries have only a handful. Some of the other World Heritage Sites are the Acropolis, Stonehenge, the Serengeti, and Yellowstone. Australia's include **The Great Barrier Reef** and **Fraser Island** in Queensland; **Kakadu National Park** and **Uluru** (Ayers Rock in Kata-Tjuta National Park) in Northern Territory; **Lord Howe Island** and **Willandra Lakes** in New South Wales; **Shark Bay** in Western Australia; and **Naracoorte Conservation Park** in South Australia, as well as Tasmanian wilderness, fossil sites in Queensland and South Australia, and the wet tropics of Queensland. For more information on World Heritage Sites, check out http://www.cco.caltech.edu/~salmon/world.heritage.html.

USEFUL RESOURCES

Australia is full of agencies that protect and administer national parks and wilderness areas. These can be useful in supplying information or camping permits to prospective

bushwalkers, or in providing boating information. In addition, a variety of publishing companies offer hiking guidebooks to meet the educational needs of novice or expert. See the special-interest publications listed above for some options. For **topographical maps of Australia,** contact the Australian Surveying & Land Information Group at (02) 6201 4201 or http://www.auslig.gov.au. Or write to AUSLIG, P.O. Box 2, Belconnen, ACT 2616. AUSLIG publishes over 500 maps; most run $7.50 (plus $5 shipping).

National Parks and Wildlife Service Head Office: 43 Bridge St., Hurstville NSW 2220 (tel. (03) 9585 6333). Open M-F 9am-5pm.

Bushwalking in Australia This website (http://bushwalking.hightide.net.au) focuses on—yes—bushwalking.

Australia Outdoor Connection A website (http://flinders.com.au/home.htm) sponsored by Flinders Camping in Adelaide that provides camping and environmental information and links.

Adventurous Traveler Bookstore, P.O. Box 64769, Burlington, VT 05406-4769 (tel. (800) 282-3963; fax (800) 677-1821; email books@atbook.com; http://www.AdventurousTraveler.com). Free 40-page catalogue upon request. Many outdoor adventure travel books, including titles like *100 Walks in New South Wales* (US$16) or *Bushwalking in Australia* (US$18). Good web site, too.

The Mountaineers Books, 1001 SW Klickitat Way, #201, Seattle, WA 98134 (tel. (800) 553-4453 or (206) 223-6303; fax 223-6306; email mbooks@mountaineers.org). Many titles on hiking (the *100 Hikes* series), biking, mountaineering, natural history, and conservation.

CAMPING AND HIKING EQUIPMENT

Purchase **equipment** before you leave. This way you'll know exactly what you have and how much it weighs. Spend some time examining catalogues and talking to knowledgeable salespeople. Whether buying or renting, finding sturdy, light, and inexpensive equipment is a must.

Sleeping bags: Most good **sleeping bags** are rated by "season," or the lowest outdoor temperature at which they will keep you warm ("summer" means 30-40°F, "three-season" usually means 0°F, and "four-season" or "winter" often means below -50°F and are rarely necessary). Sleeping bags are made either of down (warmer and lighter, but more expensive, and miserable when wet) or of synthetic material (heavier, more durable, and warmer when wet). Prices vary, but might range from US$65-100 for a summer synthetic to US$250-550 for a good down winter bag. **Sleeping bag pads,** including foam pads (US$15 and up) and air mattresses (US$25-50) cushion your back and neck and insulate you from the ground. Another good alternative is the **Therm-A-Rest,** which is part foam and part air-mattress and inflates to full padding when you unroll it.

Tents: The best **tents** are free-standing, with their own frames and suspension systems; they set up quickly and require no staking (except in high winds). Tents are also classified by season, which should be taken into account to avoid baking in a winter tent in the middle of the summer. Low profile dome tents are the best all-around. When pitched their internal space is almost entirely usable, which means little unnecessary bulk. Tent sizes can be somewhat misleading: two people *can* fit in a two-person tent, but will find life more pleasant in a four-person. If you're traveling by car, go for the bigger tent; if you're hiking, stick with a smaller tent that weighs no more than 3-4 lbs. Good two-person tents start at US$150, four-person tents at US$400, but you can sometimes find last year's model for half the price. Seal the seams of your tent with waterproofer, and make sure it has a rain fly.

Backpacks: If you intend to do a lot of hiking, you should have a **frame backpack. Internal-frame packs** mold better to your back, keep a lower center of gravity, and can flex adequately to allow you to hike difficult trails that require a lot of bending and maneuvering. **External-frame packs** are more comfortable for long hikes over even terrain since they keep the weight higher and distribute it more evenly. Whichever you choose, make sure your pack has a strong, padded hip belt, which transfers the weight from the shoulders to the legs. Any serious backpacking requires a pack of at least 4000 cubic inches. Allow an additional 500 cubic inches for your sleeping bag in internal-frame packs. Sturdy backpacks cost anywhere from US$125-500. This is one area where it doesn't pay to economize—cheaper packs may be less comfortable, and the straps are more likely to fray or rip. Before you buy any pack, try it on and imagine carrying it, full, a few miles up a rocky incline.

Boots: Be sure to wear hiking boots with good **ankle support** which are appropriate for the terrain you are hiking. Your boots should fit snugly and comfortably over one or two wool socks and a thin liner sock. Be sure that the boots are broken in—a bad blister will ruin your hiking for days.

Other necessities: Rain gear should come in two pieces, a top and pants, rather than a poncho. **Synthetics,** like polypropylene tops, socks, and long underwear, along with a pile jacket, will keep you warm even when wet. When camping in autumn, winter, or spring, bring along a **"space blanket,"** which helps you to retain your body heat and doubles as a groundcloth (US$5-15). Plastic **canteens** or water bottles keep water cooler than metal ones do, and are virtually shatter- and leak-proof. Large, collapsible **water sacks** will significantly improve your lot in primitive campgrounds and weigh practically nothing when empty, though they can get bulky. Bring **water-purification tablets** for when you can't boil water. Though most campgrounds provide campfire sites, you may want to bring a small **metal grate** or **grill** of your own. For those places that forbid fires or the gathering of firewood (this includes virtually every organized campground in Europe), you'll need a **camp stove.** A **first aid kit, Swiss army knife, insect repellent, calamine lotion,** and **waterproof matches** or a **lighter** are essential camping items. Other items include: a **battery-operated lantern,** a **plastic groundcloth,** a **nylon tarp,** a **waterproof backpack cover** (although you can also store your belongings in plastic bags inside your backpack), and a **"stuff sack"** or plastic bag to keep your sleeping bag dry.

The mail-order firms listed below offer lower prices than those you'll find in many stores, but shop around locally first in order to determine what items actually look like and weigh. Keep in mind that camping equipment is generally more expensive in Australia, New Zealand, and the U.K. than in North America.

Campmor, P.O. Box 700, Saddle River, NJ 07458-0700 (tel. (888) 226-7667, outside the U.S. call (201) 825-8300; email customer-service@campmor.com; http://www.campmor.com), has a wide selection of name brand equipment at low prices. One-year guarantee for unused or defective merchandise.

Eastern Mountain Sports (EMS), One Vose Farm Rd, Peterborough, NH 03458 (tel. (603) 924-7231; email emsmail@emsonline.com; http://www.emsonline.com) has stores throughout the U.S. Though slightly higher-priced, they provide excellent service and guaranteed customer satisfaction on most items sold. They don't have a catalogue, and they generally don't take mail or phone orders; call for the branch nearest you.

Recreational Equipment, Inc. (REI), (tel. (800) 426-4840); http://www.rei.com) stocks a comprehensive selection of REI brand and other equipment, clothing, and footwear for travel, camping, cycling, paddling, climbing, and winter sports. In addition to mail order and an Internet commerce site, REI has 49 retail stores.

L.L. Bean, Freeport, ME 04033-0001 (tel. (800) 441-5713 in Canada or the U.S.; (0800) 962 954 in the U.K.; (207) 552-6878 elsewhere; fax (207) 552-4080; http://www.llbean.com). This monolithic equipment and outdoor clothing supplier offers high quality and loads of info. Call or write for their free catalogue.

Mountain Designs, P.O. Box 1472, Fortitude Valley Qld 4006 (tel. (07) 3252 8894; fax 3252 4569) is a leading Australian manufacturer and mail order retailer of camping and climbing gear.

YHA Adventure Shop, 14 Southampton St, London, WC2E 7HY (tel. (01718) 36 85 41). Main branch of one of Britain's largest outdoor equipment suppliers.

CARAVANNING

Many North American campers harbor a suspicion that traveling with a camper or caravan is not "real camping." No such stigma exists in Australia, where caravanning is popular. Many campgrounds double as caravan parks, consisting of both tent sites and powered sites for caravans. On-site caravans (also called on-site vans) are a frequent feature at caravan parks, and save those on holiday the expense and hassle of renting a caravan by anchoring one permanently to the site and renting it out. "Cabins" at caravan parks are often analogous to an on-site van, with a toilet inside.

There is a distinction between **caravans** and **campervans.** The former needs to be pulled as a trailer, while the latter has its own cab. Renting a caravan will always be more expensive than tenting or hosteling, but cheaper than renting a car and staying in hotels. The convenience of bringing along your own bedroom, bathroom, and kitchen makes it an attractive option for some, especially older travelers and families.

It's not difficult to arrange a campervan rental from overseas, although you will want to begin gathering information several months before your departure. Rates vary widely by region, season (Dec., Jan., and Feb. are the most expensive months), and type of van. It always pays to contact several different companies to compare vehicles and prices. **Avis** (tel. (800) 331 1084) and **Hertz** (tel. (800) 654 3001) are U.S. firms which can arrange caravan rentals in Australia. **Maui Rentals** (tel. (02) 9597 6155; fax 9556 3900) rents campervans in Australia and New Zealand.

WILDERNESS AND SAFETY CONCERNS

Stay warm, stay dry, and **stay hydrated.** The vast majority of life-threatening wilderness problems stem from a failure to follow this advice. On any hike, however brief, you should pack enough equipment to keep you alive should disaster befall. This includes **rain gear, hat** and **mittens, a first-aid kit, high energy food,** and **water.** Dress in warm layers of **wool** or **synthetic materials** designed for the outdoors. Pile fleece jackets and Gore-Tex® raingear are excellent choices (see **"camping and hiking equipment" on page 45**). *Never* rely on **cotton** for warmth. This "death cloth" will be absolutely useless should it get wet. When camping, be sure to bring a proper tent with rainfly and warm sleeping bags.

Check **weather forecasts** and pay attention to the skies when hiking. Weather patterns can change instantly. If the weather turns nasty, turn back; if you're on an overnight trip, start looking immediately for shelter. If you can, notify someone of your travel plans, either a friend, your hostel, a park ranger, or a local hiking organization. Do not attempt a hike beyond your ability—you may be endangering your life.

See **Health,** p. 15, for info about environmental dangers, basic medical concerns and first-aid, and outdoor ailments such as giardia, rabies, and insects. A good guide to outdoor survival is *How to Stay Alive in the Woods,* by Bradford Angier (Macmillan, US$8).

ENVIRONMENTALLY RESPONSIBLE TOURISM

While protecting yourself from the elements, also make an effort to protect the wilderness from you. At the very least, a responsible traveler practices **"minimum impact camping"** techniques. Leave no trace of your presence when you leave a site. Don't cut vegetation or clear new campsites. A campstove is the safer (and more efficient) way to cook, but if you must, make small fires using only dead branches or brush. Never do this on a Total Fire Ban Day, however; you don't want to be responsible for starting a bushfire. Make sure your campsite is at least 75m from water supplies or bodies of water. If there are no toilet facilities, bury human waste (but not paper) at least 10cm deep and above the high-water line 75m or more from any water supplies and campsites. Always pack your trash in a plastic bag and carry it until you reach the next trash can.

Responsible tourism means more than picking up your litter, however. Growing numbers of "ecotourists" are asking hard questions of resort owners and tour operators about how their policies affect local ecologies and local economies. Some try to give something back to the regions they enjoy by volunteering for environmental organizations at home or abroad. Above all, responsible tourism means being aware of your impact on the places you visit, and taking responsibility for your own actions.

For more information, contact the **Ecotourism Association of Australia,** P.O. Box 26, Paddington Qld 4064 (tel. (07) 3369 6099).

ORGANIZED ADVENTURE

Organized adventure tours offer another way of exploring the wild. Activities include hiking, biking, skiing, canoeing, kayaking, rafting, climbing, photo safaris, and archaeological digs, and go *everywhere*. Begin by consulting tourism bureaus, which can suggest parks, trails, and outfitters as well as answer more general questions. The **Specialty Travel Index,** 305 San Anselmo Ave, Suite 313, San Anselmo, CA 94960 (tel. (800) 442 4922 or (415) 459 4900; fax 459 4974; email spectrav@ix.netcom.com; http://www.specialtytravel.com) is a directory listing hundreds of tour operators worldwide. **Roadrunner International**, Quincy, MA, 02169 (tel. (800) TREK USA (873 5782) in North America; (01892) 51 27 00 in Europe and the U.K.; fax (617) 984 2045), offers hostel tour packages to Australia and New Zealand.

■ Keeping In Touch

TIME DIFFERENCES

Calculating time differences is more confusing than it might seem. Hemisphere differences, daylight savings time, and large time differences all combine to create chaos. Australia stretches across three time zones. The three most northern states (WA, NT, and Qld) do not observe **daylight savings time,** but the other states do. Confusingly, border towns sometimes take the time zone of a neighboring state. There is a comprehensive chart of time conversions by state and season in the **appendix,** p. 639.

MAIL

Sending Mail to Australia

When sending mail to Australia, make sure to include the name, street address or P.O. box, city name or post office of delivery, state or territory abbreviation (ACT, NSW, NT, Qld, SA, Tas, Vic, WA), and postal code. The bottom line should say AUSTRALIA in all capitals. *Let's Go* lists postal codes in the **Practical Information** section for cities and towns. All of Australia's **postal codes** are at http://www.auspost.com.au.

Mail can be sent internationally through *Poste Restante* (the international phrase for Hold Mail) to any city or town; it's well worth using, generally has no surcharges, and is much more reliable than you might think. Mark the envelope "HOLD," add the regular required postage to Australia, and address it with the last name capitalized and underlined followed by the appropriate city, state, and postal code; GPO stands for general post office, and is almost always the best destination choice. For example: Dave COLLINS, Poste Restante, GPO Melbourne, Melbourne Vic 3550, AUSTRALIA. The mail will go to a special desk in the central post office, and Dave Collins can arrive in person, show the clerk his passport, and pick up his package free of charge. *Poste Restante* mail is generally held for only 30 days. If the clerks insist that there is nothing for you, have them check under your first name as well.

American Express travel offices throughout the world will act as a mail service for cardholders if you contact them in advance. Under this free **"Client Letter Service,"** they will hold mail for 30 days, forward upon request, and accept telegrams. Some offices offer these services to non-cardholders (especially those who have purchased AmEx Travellers' Cheques), but call ahead to make sure. Check the **Practical Information** section of the cities you plan to visit; *Let's Go* lists AmEx office locations for most large cities. A complete list is available free from AmEx (Australian tel. (800) 25 19 02; U.S. tel. (800) 528 4800), in the booklet *Traveler's Companion,* or online at http://www.americanexpress.com/shared/cgi-bin/tsoserve.cgi?travel/index.

Sending Mail from Australia

General post offices (GPO) are usually **open** from 9am to 5pm Monday through Friday. Larger branches also open on Saturday mornings. Visa, Mastercard, and American Express are often accepted, but a minimum purchase may be required.

Air mail to the United States and Canada takes approximately seven to 10 business days. **Economy air mail,** which is slightly cheaper, takes anywhere from two to six weeks. **Sea mail** is by far the cheapest and slowest way to send mail, although letters and postcards can not be sent by sea mail from Australia. It can take up to three months for sea mail packages to cross the ocean—appropriate for sending large quantities of items you won't need to see for a while. It is vital, therefore, to distinguish your air mail from surface mail by explicitly labeling all letters and packages "air mail." If regular airmail is too slow, ask about more expensive options.

Postcards and letters sent within Australia cost 45¢. Postcards to Canada or the USA cost 95¢ air mail or 80¢ economy air mail. Small letters cost $1.05/90¢. Postcards to the U.K., Ireland, South Africa, and Europe cost $1/85¢. Small letters cost $1.20/$1. Postcards to New Zealand cost 70¢/65¢. Small letters cost 75¢/70¢.

Aerograms, printed sheets that fold into envelopes and travel via airmail, are available at post offices and cost 75¢ to any destination worldwide. When ordering books and materials from abroad, always include one or two **International Reply Coupons (IRCs)**—a way of providing the postage to cover delivery. IRCs should be available from your local post office as well as abroad.

TELEPHONES

Public phones are easy to find nearly everywhere you go in Australia. Some phone booths in Australia are coin-operated, some are phone-card operated, and some accept either coins or phone cards. Local calls from phone booths cost 40¢. In addition to phone booths, public phones can sometimes be found in bars and hotels, and local calls on these often cost 50¢. Residential phone services (like in a home or business) do not provide free local calls, which cost 25¢.

Australia has two telecommunications companies: Optus and Telstra. Telstra **prepaid phonecards** are available in AUS$5, $10, $20, and $50 denominations from many newsagents and pharmacies. They are accepted in over 75% of Australia's phones. The time is measured in minutes or "talk units," and the card usually has a toll-free access telephone number and a personal identification number (PIN). Cards that must be inserted into phones are also available. As phone cards have grown in popularity, so have the number of booths accepting cards only. Telstra telephones are often bright orange. Phones in motels and restaurants are sometimes small blue boxes which don't take phone cards. Most phones accept coins only larger than 10¢, and you sometimes can't put in an initial combination of over five coins.

For **directory assistance,** you can call 013 from any public phone at no charge. A table of other directory assistance numbers is on the inside back cover. Six-digit phone numbers beginning with **13** are information numbers that can be dialed from anywhere in Australia for the price of a local call. Numbers beginning with 1300 operate very similarly. Unfortunately, Phone Away cards cannot be used for 13 calls (normal pre-paid phone cards are fine). Phone numbers beginning with **1800** are toll-free.

Nine-digit phone numbers beginning with 018, 019, or similar combinations indicate **mobile phones** and require all nine digits when being dialed. Mobile phones are everywhere in urban Australia; people walk down the street talking on the phone, and some hotel owners routinely ask guests to register their mobile phones when they check in. Usually the caller picks up the charges when calling a mobile phone, and charges run about 80¢ per minute.

Long-distance calls within Australia use STD (Subscriber Trunk Dialing) services. You have to dial a **phone code** before the eight-digit number. You'll get the cheapest rates if you call between 6pm Saturday and 8am Monday, or at night during the week. Long-distance calls overseas use international direct dialing (IDD) services.

Calling Australia

You can place **international calls** from most telephones. To call direct, dial the universal international access code for the country you're calling from (see the inside back cover) followed by the country code (61 for Australia), the state telephone code (one digits—see the beginning of each chapter or the appendix—don't dial the initial zero), and the local number (usually eight digits). Numbers beginning with 1800 and most numbers beginning with 13 or 1300 cannot be dialed from outside Australia. If you're abroad and need to find a local phone number, check out Telstra's online directory (see **Internet Resources,** p. 3). Local tourist offices may also be able to help. Wherever possible, use a calling card (see **calling cards,** below) for international phone calls, as the long-distance rates for national phone services are unpredictable and often exorbitant.

Calling Home

To **dial overseas direct,** press 0011, then the country code, the city code, dropping the initial zero (e.g. 171 for London, 212 for New York) and the telephone number. See the inside back cover for country codes. A Telstra call to Britain or the U.S. costs $1.35 per minute ($1.03 off-peak). A call to New Zealand costs $1.09 a minute (72¢ off-peak).

You can usually make direct international calls from **pay phones,** but you may need to drop your coins as quickly as your words if you're not using a phone card or credit card. Be wary of more expensive, private pay phones and the insidious in-room hotel phone call. Although incredibly convenient, these calls invariably include an arbitrary and sky-high surcharge (as much as $10 in some establishments).

Operators will place **collect calls** for you. It's cheaper to find a pay phone and deposit just enough money to be able to say "Call me" and give your number (although some pay phones can't receive calls). Some companies, seizing upon this "call-me-back" concept, have created **callback phone services.** Under these plans, you call a specified number, ring once, and hang up. The company's computer calls back and gives you a dial tone. You can then make as many calls as you want, at rates about 20-60% lower than you'd pay using credit cards or pay phones. This option is most economical for loquacious travelers, as services may include a US$10-25 minimum billing per month. For information, call **America Tele-Fone** (US tel. (800) 321 5817) and **Telegroup** (U.S. tel. (800) 338 0225).

A **calling card** is probably your best and cheapest bet; your local long-distance service provider will have a number for you to dial while traveling (either toll-free or charged as a local call) to connect instantly to an operator in your home country. The calls (plus a small surcharge) are then billed either collect or to the calling card. See the inside back cover for access numbers from Australia. MCI's WorldPhone also provides access to MCI's **Traveler's Assist,** which gives legal and medical advice, exchange rate information, and translation services. Many other long distance carriers and phone companies provide such travel information; contact your phone service provider.

EMAIL

The wave of the future, **electronic mail (email)** is an attractive option, and increasingly easy to access world-wide. With a minimum of computer knowledge and a little planning, you can beam messages anywhere and instantly for no per-message charges. **Traveltales.com** (http://traveltales.com) provides free, web-based email for travelers and maintains a list of over 500 cybercafes throughout the world, travel links, and a travelers' chat room. Other free, web-based email providers include **Hotmail** (http://www.hotmail.com) and **USANET** (http://www.usa.net). Search through http://www.cyberiacafe.net/cyberia/guide/ccafe.htm to find a list of **cybercafes** around the world from which you can drink a cup of joe and email him too. For information on internet access world-wide, http://www.nsrc.org has a host of connections to sites supplying further internet information on any country. Most big cities in Australia have cybercafes; *Let's Go* lists them under individual cities' **practical information** sections.

If you're already hooked up to the infobahn at home, you should be able to find access numbers for your destination country; check with your internet provider before leaving. Travelers who have the luxury of a laptop with them can use a **modem** to call an Internet service provider. Long-distance phone cards specifically intended for such calls can defray normally high phone charges. Check with your long-distance phone provider to see if they offer this option; otherwise, try a **C.COM Internet PhoneCard** (US tel. (888) 464-2266), which offers Internet connection calls for 15¢ per minute, minimum initial purchase of US$5.

Life & Times

Oz: It's no place like home.

—Popular tourist slogan.

■ History

Australia Before the Europeans

According to recent estimates, the ancestors of the **Aboriginal** people of Australia have inhabited the island continent for as long as 60,000 to 100,000 years. Fossil records suggest that migration to Australia may have occurred in waves that predated the advent of agriculture in Asia and the Middle East. Estimates of the Aboriginal population of the continent just prior to European colonization vary widely, from 300,000 to over a million. It has been estimated that there were more than 250 distinct languages with up to 600 dialect groups. The Aboriginal people were foragers, living in even the driest areas of the country and migrating seasonally in search of food. Although they did not farm, they did increase the land's productivity by burning large tracts each year. Fire replaced necessary nutrients in the soil and allowed the germination of plants with seed pods that open only under intense heat.

Because Aboriginals lived in such interdependence with the land, complex relationships developed among their kinship structures, the land, and its resources. These relationships evolved into a complicated system of joint ownership and stewardship of particular areas of land by members of different family groups. The relationships also formed the basis and focus of Aboriginal spiritual life and the land was thus the most important factor in determining a person's spiritual and secular identity. For information on present-day Aboriginal issues, see p. 57.

Early European Settlement

Although Australia's history is inextricably linked with England's, the British were not the first outsiders to lay claim to the land. **Chinese** explorers were almost certainly the first non-Aboriginals to arrive, and 15th-century **Portuguese** and **French** sailors knew details about the existence of *Terra Australis* (southern land). On 16th-century maps, a misshapen Australia is labeled New Netherlands, since the western and northernmost coasts had been explored and mapped by the **Dutch,** who concluded that the continent contained very little of value and never established a settlement. **Abel Tasman,** the explorer after whom Tasmania was eventually named, was an early Dutch explorer under the commission of Governor General Anthony van Diemen of the Dutch Indies. Tasmania was called Van Diemen's Land for many years. As

---

The Dreaming

The concept of the Dreaming is one of the most famous ideas associated with the Australian Aboriginals. It is not a single story or idea, but one that arose in different forms in various tribes. Once called the Dreamtime, the name was changed in the 1950s to reflect the ever-presentness of the Dreaming within the cyclical Aboriginal understanding of time. It describes the basis of the Aboriginal relationship with the land, which they believe to be a spiritual phenomenon, created by spiritual forces that once emerged from a formless earth. These forces took forms that frequently combined features of humans, animals, plants, and other forces—serpent-women, bush fig-men, wind—and moved over the surface of the landscape. As they moved, they and their activities, tracks, and artifacts were transformed into the features of the land and the heavens. The whole of the land was therefore sacred to the Aboriginals, dotted with sites significant to the Dreaming stories and tied to the origins of the people themselves.

early as 1573, occasional English documents suggested exploring the southern hemisphere although few raised the prospect of settling.

English Exploration and Settlement

In 1770, on a scientific mission to observe the transit of Venus across the sun, the English captain **James Cook** explored the eastern coast of what would become Australia. The other sides of the island continent had all been explored and mapped, but the Great Barrier Reef had previously deterred explorers from the east. Cook and his crew of astronomers and scientists discovered and named **Botany Bay,** and returned to England with stories of strange animals and plants.

In the wake of the American Revolution, England could no longer dispose of convicts by transporting them to America to serve their sentences. A doctor who had been on Cook's voyage testified before Parliament that the unclaimed southern lands might serve the purpose. The prisons in London were full, and Australia, by all accounts, was remarkably empty. Preparations for a convict settlement began in 1785. But full prisons were not the only justification for such expense. The English government wanted a base for its global navy in the eastern seas, and anticipated finding natural resources, particularly timber, for its fleet.

The 11 ships of the **First Fleet** sailed from England with their unwilling cargo on May 13, 1787. **Lord Sydney** (less formally known as Thomas Townshend) was the secretary of state for home affairs, and appointed Arthur Phillip commander of the fleet. About 730 convicts—570 men and 160 women—were on board, along with more than 250 guards, officers, wives, and children. Over the course of the eight-month voyage 36 men and four women died, and seven children were born. The fleet arrived at Botany Bay on January 19 or 20, 1788. But when the harbor, soil, and water were all found to be lacking, Commander Phillip headed north to Port Jackson. The English flag was finally planted on January 26, and a colony was born in the spot where Sydney stands today.

The Early Convict Years

Upon arrival in Australia, the convicts and their guards faced a land foreign and unyielding. The first years of the colony went even more poorly than many had feared. Half of the potential labor was used up guarding the other half. The livestock escaped into the bush, relations with the Aboriginals rapidly deteriorated, most of the follow-up supply ships wrecked, and the land itself seemed supremely inhospitable. According to plan, the convicts were put to work on government-sponsored farms, but since most of them came from the slums of London, they had no agricultural experience. In addition, the English seeds and cuttings that the fleet had so carefully carried across the sea did not thrive in the strange soil and new climate. In the first six months, the First Fleeters managed to build only four huts (for officers); everyone else lived in tents. Captain Phillip's grandiose plans for streets 200 feet wide in Sydney had to be scrapped, since the colony had no power source other than the inhabitants' own labor; no mill or team of cattle was available for over eight years.

While the convict colony struggled on in Sydney, an English naval officer named **Matthew Flinders** headed an 1801 expedition to circumnavigate and chart the southern land. At the end of three years, he declared it one mass and argued that the name New Holland or New Netherlands should be replaced with a different moniker: Australia. This suggestion sat well with the leaders of the English government, who considered the land England's anyway, but the term "Australia" was not used on a regular basis to describe the continent until 1817.

The End of the Convict Era

In 1809, **Colonel Lachlan Macquarie** granted full citizenship rights to convicts who had served their seven years but remained in Australia. Meanwhile, the upkeep costs for the convicts became an increasingly onerous economic burden on England, since the colony was not self-supporting. After 1815, as ever more convicts arrived on Australia's shores, the government began to assign convicts to private employers to

When Something Goes Missing

In the late 18th and early 19th centuries, it didn't take much to win a free trip to Australia, as long as you didn't mind traveling aboard a convict ship. Most of the convicts were guilty of petty thievery—and of being poor, ill-connected, and often Irish. Many had originally been sentenced to death, with those sentences commuted to "transportation beyond the seas" and seven years' service upon arrival. Records show that the disappearance of one coffee pot, one guinea, 28 lb. of hair powder, six live turkeys, five woolen blankets, one piece of yellow canvas, three petticoats, 11 yards of printed cotton, 8 lb. of cheese, or one sheep was enough to send one convict or another to Australia. One man was convicted of destroying 12 cucumber plants, while another "unlawfully cut down one maiden ash timber tree." One woman was convicted of "spoiling, burning, and defacing the garment of a female." Another woman received a sentence of death, commuted to Australian transportation, for stealing two linen aprons. A boy, age 11, was shipped out for stealing one pair of silk stockings.

lighten the strain on the Crown's purse. By 1830, a total of about 50,000 male convicts and 8000 female convicts had arrived in Australia, and many had worked on private farms and in private workshops. But after the abolitionist crusades in the 1830s, some Brits began to argue that the Australian practice of assigning convicts to private employers smelled suspiciously of **slavery.** In 1840, the practice was abolished, and suddenly, Australians thought that more convicts seemed like less of a good idea. In response to protests, the Crown virtually stopped sending convicts to eastern Australia by 1852. Western Australia and Tasmania continued to receive convicts until January 10, 1868, when the last convict ship arrived in Australia. In all, a total of approximately 160,500 convicts had been sent to Australia.

Gold and Expansion

In addition to sending convicts, England encouraged free settler migration with **land grants** until 1831 and offered inexpensive passage to women to remedy the gender imbalance. **Wool** was Australia's major export beginning in the mid-1830s. By 1845, sheep farming was the most profitable business in the country. But despite the land grant incentives and economic improvements, the population remained stagnant.

The discovery of Australian **gold** in 1851 accomplished what the promise of land could not. Two years after the great California gold rush, wealth and immigrants flooded Australia, and by the end of 1851, the non-Aboriginal population numbered around 450,000, eight times that of a quarter-century earlier. Ten years later, the number was 1,150,000. Competition for gold inevitably led to conflict, and the 1854 Eureka Stockade Rebellion marked Australia's closest brush with civil war. Miners in Ballarat, Victoria, formed a collective and built a stockade in protest of the government's licensing fees for miners. Government forces crushed the uprising in a 15-minute clash that cost about two dozen miners their lives.

The three decades between 1829 and 1859 marked an important period of growth. Four of the six states (the Northern Territory is not a state) were formed during this time. The English Parliament first ratified New South Wales's and Victoria's constitutions in 1855—bringing **self-government** to Australia for the first time. Throughout the second half of the 19th century, however, each individual colony had very little formal relation with the other colonies, communicating directly with London (see **On the Right Track,** p. 32). The **University of Sydney** was founded in 1850, and the **University of Melbourne** in 1853.

White Australia Policies

At the end of the convict era, race-based immigration restrictions were adopted. Australia's main source of labor dried up in the 1840s when convicts stopped arriving in New South Wales, and Europeans subsequently began importing Chinese laborers. But as more **Chinese immigrants** came to the country, and particularly when they started working the goldfields, many English colonists wanted to keep Asian immigration to a minimum. The laws were couched in political language. An 1855 "Act to Make Provision for Certain Immigrants" was passed in Victoria. The act put a tax on each Chinese arrival and stipulated that only one Chinese person would be granted entrance for every 10 tons of shipping. In 1879, an Intercolonial Trades Union Congress, one of the first national meetings with representatives from all of the states, published a warning that Chinese immigration "supplanted white labour, and would leave no work or hope for the rising generation, who would fill the jails in consequence." By 1888, the "Chinese question" had emerged onto the political front stage, and a Queensland journal first coined the rallying cry **"White Australia."** Increasing racism led to the 1896 extension of the anti-Chinese legislation to all non-whites.

In another attempt to exclude Asian immigrants, the new government passed the **Immigration Restriction Act of 1901,** which required immigrants to pass, at the discretion of the immigration officer, a 50-word dictation test in a European language. In 1905, responding to complaints from New Zealand, Australia's prime minister ruled that the Maori, New Zealand's indigenous people, could have European status.

Federation and Women's Suffrage

By 1901, Australia's non-Aboriginal population had reached 3,370,000, 64.5% of whom had been born in Australia. The Commonwealth of Australia was founded on January 1, 1901. On September 3, 1901, the first **Australian flag** flew over the Exhibition Building in Melbourne, the winner of a design contest that had attracted 32,823 entries from all over the world. The blue flag has the Union Jack in the upper left corner, with the star of Australia underneath, today with seven points, one for each state or territory in the federation. The Southern Cross star formation is to the right.

The very next year, Australia became only the second country in the world, after New Zealand, to grant federal suffrage to women. (The statute that had barred women was not the only law that seems archaic today. In the same year, police arrested a man at Manly, outside Sydney, for swimming during the day, in direct defiance of the law prohibiting daylight swimming.) In 1921, **Edith Dircksey Cowan** of Western Australia became the first female in a state parliament.

The new national government gradually consolidated its power over the states. As a compromise between the urban centers of Sydney and Melbourne, the capital was located in a brand-new city between the two. **Canberra** formally became the capital in 1927. In 1922, **Qantas** (Queensland And Northern Territory Air Service), the government-sponsored outback air-mail service, began passenger service in outback Queensland. An 85-year-old man, Alexander Kennedy, was the first passenger, chosen because he had been the first to make the eight-month mail trek by wagon, decades earlier.

The World Wars

At the outset of **World War I,** Australia's Prime Minister declared support for the mother country, saying: "Our duty is quite clear—to gird up our loins and remember that we are Britons." About 330,000 Australians girded up and 60,000 lost their lives. While these figures pale in comparison to the casualties from other countries, they are a shocking percentage of the country's relatively small population. The worst single day of battle was April 25, 1915, when 2000 members of the **Australia and New Zealand Army Corps** (ANZAC) were killed at Gallipoli, Turkey, initiating a campaign that eventually took 8500 Australian lives and resulted in the evacuation of Gallipoli. Australia celebrates **Anzac Day** (April 25) each year to remember the heroism of these troops.

A generation later, **World War II** struck closer to home. After the Japanese attack on the United States' Pearl Harbor (Dec. 7, 1941), Australian citizens became increasingly concerned about the safety of their own shores. The concern brought a shift in geopolitical outlook, as the U.S. became Australia's ally in the Pacific, while Britain seemed far away and less relevant. In December 1941, Prime Minister Curtin pronounced, "Australia looks to America, free from any pangs about our traditional links of friendship to Britain." When Singapore fell on February 15, 1942, 15,000 Australians became prisoners of war. **Darwin,** the capital of the Northern Territory, suffered the first of a series of destructive bombings at the hands of the Japanese just four days later. Over the course of the war, about 30,000 Australian soldiers died while fighting with the Allies.

The Last Half-Century

From 1948, when the **Holden,** the first domestically manufactured car, rolled out of the factory, until the first domestic television broadcast in 1956, the country enjoyed a time of relative peace and prosperity marked by rapid immigration. In the thirty years following the end of the war, the population grew from 7 million to 13.5 million. In the meantime, Australian-American relations were formalized in 1951 with the signing of the **Australia-New Zealand-United States (ANZUS)** pact.

Consequently, when the United States became embroiled in the **Vietnam** conflict, Australians were conscripted to serve, touching off a slowly gathering storm of anti-war protest. Violent protests in Sydney and Melbourne in 1968 led to a call to expel students from university who disobeyed conscription laws. Dissent culminated in 1969, when Australian students stormed the U.S. Consulate in Melbourne.

In 1965, the **White Australia** clauses, added early this century to discourage Asian immigration, were finally erased from the books. In 1967, Australia broke its currency link with Britain in deciding not to devalue the pound sterling. In that same year, **Japan** replaced the United Kingdom as the primary recipient of Australian exports. In 1984, Japan passed the United States as Australia's largest supplier of imports. Australia today is a member of the **Asia Pacific Economic Cooperation (APEC).**

Echoing movements the world over, the 1970s also saw the beginnings of **environmental activism** in Australia. The first case to create a nationwide impact was a disagreement over **Lake Pedder** in Tasmania. Despite environmentalists' protests, a hydroelectric dam was erected in 1973, making Lake Pedder a lake no more. The loss galvanized environmentalists to organize and protest, and eventually to put the Green political party in power in Tasmania in 1989.

The Last Four Years

In 1995, after French President Jacques Chirac decided to sponsor **nuclear weapon testing** in the South Pacific, the French consulate in Perth was fire-bombed, and demonstrations were held all over the country. On April 28, 1996, at **Port Arthur, Tasmania,** deranged citizen Martin Bryant shot and killed 35 strangers. This tragedy fueled Australia's gun-control movement, and led to a much-touted plan to ban rapid-fire weapons. In recent years, the government **privatized** several of its large corporations, including **Qantas.** In May of 1997, the Australian government funded a $1.3 billion project to clean up the Murray and Darling Rivers, by selling **Telstra,** the previously state-owned telecommunications company.

Pauline Hanson, a Queensland member of federal Parliament, has received a great deal of negative press for her inflammatory political platform. Hanson, a reactionary conservative, is a leader of the **One Nation Party,** and the most controversial figure in Australian politics today. The One Nation Party supports isolationist policies, charges that Asian interests have corrupted Australian business, and calls for strict limits on immigration. Hanson's views may be hurting Australia's economy: in July 1997, Chinese investors who were angered by the tide of anti-Asian racism halted a multi-million dollar industrial project in Ballarat. The party also challenges the government's social programs for Aboriginals, arguing that they represent unfair preferences.

Such xenophobia is a recurring theme in Australia's history, from the first white-Aboriginal contact to the strained relations between English and Chinese gold diggers in the 19th century. Still, most Australians today cringe at many of Hanson's beliefs and are embarrassed at the image of national politics she presents internationally. In July and August 1998, tens of thousands of students joined a series of peaceful demonstrations against racism in cities across Australia; some of the protesters burned posters with Hanson's picture. Some of the protests addressed the recent, controversial **uranium mining** project on Aboriginal lands in Kakadu National Park (see **Beneath the Surface,** p. 249), showing a nexus between two of the most important themes in contemporary Australian politics, race and the environment. The nation's response to the collision of cultures will continue to shape Australia, as debate persists over what exactly defines an Australian—and who has the power to change that definition.

Despite these currents of xenophobia, for the most part Australia has increasingly emphasized its role as a member of the Pacific economic and security community. As a member of the **ASEAN Regional Forum (ARF),** it has increased military dialogue with its Southeast Asian neighbors. International trade is vital to Australia's economy, particularly within the region; hence, the continuing **Asian currency crisis** that began in the summer of 1997 has had damaging spillover effects. While Australia's economy has not collapsed, its dollar's value has spiraled downward and exports to Asia have declined. The political fallout may endanger the leadership of **Prime Minister John Howard.** In August 1998, Howard scheduled a new election in response to public demand, to be held (as of this printing) on October 3, 1998. For Northern Territorians, these elections will include a referendum on the territory becoming **Australia's seventh state,** a move approved by the Canberra government in August and expected to meet strong public support. If approved, statehood will take effect in January 2001, bringing with it increased parliamentary representation and the likely new name **State of the Northern Territory.**

Finally, another phase in Australia's history may soon be underway, as the country contemplates severing its ties with the British monarchy. See **Government,** below.

■ Government

Since federation in 1901, Australia has been a democracy under a federal system, in which power is divided between the federal and state levels. The heart of the government is the **Commonwealth Parliament,** which consists of the Senate, the House of Representatives, and the Governor-General as representative of the Queen of England. These three elements make Australia a constitutional monarchy, a federation, and a parliamentary democracy all at once. State government is particularly strong and active, and laws can vary widely between states. Australia established universal suffrage for whites in 1902; Aboriginals were given the vote in 1962 and did not gain full citizenship rights until 1967. **Compulsory voting** was introduced in 1925, and since then voter participation has risen to nearly 90%, partly because anyone eligible to vote who does not can be fined. Voting is **preferential,** meaning that a voter must rank all the candidates in order of preference.

There are two main political parties, the **Liberal Party** (the conservatives) and the **Labor Party** (often referred to as the social democrats; more liberal, in the left-wing sense, than the Liberals themselves, but becoming increasingly moderate). Several other strong parties influence the outcome of voting in Parliament. The **Green Party** (the ecologists), the farthest left, began to win Senate seats in the 80s, and became a powerful force in Tasmanian state politics. The independent **Democrats** (the social-liberals) have held the balance of power in the Senate in recent years. The **National Party** (also called the Conservatives), formerly the Country Party, usually votes in coalition with the Liberals. Independent candidates can also win seats in Parliament, and often have a significant effect on policy and debate. The One Nation Party has recently increased its influence (see **The Last Four Years,** above). In the federal government there are two houses of Parliament: the **Senate** and the **House of Representatives.** The **Prime Minister** is not elected directly but rather is the head of the party that holds a parliamentary majority in the House of Representatives. The **Australian Head of State** is the British monarch, currently Queen Elizabeth II. Her representative, the **Governor General,** is theoretically the highest authority in Australia, though traditionally this post has been largely symbolic.

Australians are often stereotyped as uninterested in politics. This may have been the case in the nation's early history, but was clearly disproven on November 11,

1975, when the Governor General, acting in response to a deadlock over government finances, exercised his right to **dissolve Parliament** in times of crisis. The deadlock had occurred after two states replaced outgoing Labor members of Parliament with Liberals, swaying the Parliamentary balance in favor of the Liberals. The Governor General responded by dismissing the Labor Prime Minister, Edward Gough Whitlam, and appointing Malcolm Fraser, a Liberal, to lead a caretaker government. This act shocked the Australian people and raised popular support for **republicanism,** a movement geared toward gaining full Australian independence from the British Commonwealth. Nevertheless, in elections held a year after the dissolution, the Liberals under Fraser were indeed voted into power and remained there for eight years.

In 1983, Labor once again took control of Parliament under **Bob Hawke,** who retained power through four terms. He was succeeded by **Paul Keating,** also a member of the Labor Party, who fought for Mabo legislation, tried to improve economic relations with Asia, and sought to transform Australia into a republic by the Sydney Olympics in 2000. In 1996, after 13 years of uninterrupted Labor rule, the Liberals regained control of Parliament under **John Howard,** whose platform includes industrial relations reform and privatization. A social conservative and a constitutional monarchist, he has sought to reverse some of the more liberal policies of the previous Labor administration. **Sir William Deane** is the current Governor General.

Despite Prime Minister John Howard's constitutional monarchist leanings, the government has recently been compelled to readdress the issue of Australian republicanism. On February 13, 1998, a constitutional convention voted overwhelmingly in favor of severing Australia's 210-year-old links to the British monarchy and making the country a republic by January 1, 2001. Many republicans who had favored election of a president by popular ballot compromised and accepted a proposal by the Australian Republican Movement to have the president elected by parliament. A **public referendum** to decide the issue definitely is planned for the coming year. As of the time of this printing, a date for the referendum had not yet been set.

■ Aboriginal Rights

LAND RIGHTS

As in most non-European lands, the history of white settlement is, at least in part, a history of genocide. When the British landed in Australia and claimed the land for the Crown, they did so under a doctrine of *terra nullius,* or empty land. *Terra nullius* meant, either that the previous inhabitants did not own the land, or that there were no people on the continent, depending on one's interpretation. However rationalized, this doctrine gave the British free rein to take what land they wished, without the hassle of treaties or agreements. The Northern Territory was set aside as land primarily for the Aboriginal people, but large numbers of Aboriginals were killed and most groups were displaced, if not eradicated. The history of Aboriginal and white interaction in Tasmania, where the Aboriginals had remained isolated for over 12,000 years, is particularly horrid; systematic genocide of the Aboriginal population caused their near-complete extinction within 70 years of first contact.

In 1933, the Aboriginal population of Australia hit a low of 73,828. By 1981 this had risen to just over 171,000, and the most recent census (1996) counted 353,000 Aboriginals, making up two percent of the total population. The Australian Bureau of Statistics points to many people's increased willingness to answer "yes" to the Census question: "Do you have Aboriginal or Torres Strait Islander origin?" as a partial explanation for the rising numbers.

The land rights issue has become a hot topic in Australia during the last few decades, as Aboriginal peoples demand land rights and compensation for the abuse they have endured. Many Australians of European descent—particularly those with mining and other industry interests—vehemently defend their control of the land. The courts and the government have taken up the issue, but recent legal developments and legislation have simply fueled the controversy.

In 1966, the **Gurindji** Aboriginal people from the northwest Northern Territory formed the first Aboriginal-owned and -operated cattle station, Daguragu. Although it took a long and difficult 20 years, the Gurindji were officially given permanent title to the land in a 1986 court decision. This Aboriginal legal success paved the way for the controversial **Mabo** decision in 1992. The Mabo case originated with a claim by Koiki (Eddie) Mabo, a Torres Straits Islander who argued for the return of Murray Island to the Mer people (its original inhabitants) through the Australian legal system. The bid was successful. The High Court struck down the legal fiction of *terra nullius*, recognizing that the principle of **native title** had existed before the arrival of the British. Native title is defined as the traditional Aboriginal right of access, use, or occupation of the land. These rights are based on traditional laws and customs, and do not necessarily exclude other title rights.

The Mabo decision left ambiguities as to where and to whom native title was applicable, and as to what exactly it meant. The **Native Title Act of 1993** sought to clarify the decision with legislation. The Act laid out guidelines to reassure farmers, miners, and conservatives who fear that the Aboriginals will attempt to claim Native Title to the whole of the continent. It also set out a means of compensating Aboriginals whose Native Title was lost, placed limitations on future acts affecting Native Title land and waters, and created a **Land Fund** to help Aboriginal and Torres Strait Islander peoples acquire and manage land.

The effectiveness of the Act is still in doubt, as many believe that it was tokenism, granting few substantial new rights to Aboriginals and leaving many of the ambiguities in place. As a result, several amendments have been proposed, partly in response to the issues emerging from the 1993 **Wik** case. In June of 1993, the Wik and Thayorre peoples of western Cape York managed to obtain a ruling that the granting of **pastoral lease** by the government (the Crown rents its land to a farmer for a long, long time) does not necessarily mean that the Aboriginals who live on that land have to leave. In fact, both the farmer and the Aboriginal people can claim rights to the same land, and live peacefully within the fabric of Australian law; pastoral leases can co-exist with Native Title. In the case of a conflict, however, the former takes precedence, which limits the significance of Native Title throughout the 42% of Australia that is under pastoral lease. Wik remains a theoretical decision, not yet having been applied to the lands in question.

In a further setback for Aboriginal rights following the Court's decision, the government developed a **10-point plan on Native Title** that eliminated Native Title in certain circumstances. The **Native Title Amendment Bill of 1997** incorporates this plan and has been resoundingly condemned by Aboriginal leaders and their supporters. The erosion of native title rights could spark an international backlash, and Aboriginal leaders have already threatened boycotts of beef products and the Sydney Olympics. Currently, other new bills related to Aboriginal land issues are under consideration and several new cases have recently come before the High Court. As each bill addresses more complications, and each case heard by the High Court sets a new precedent, it is clear that the Aboriginals' struggle for land rights is far from over. For updated information on Aboriginal political events and Native Title claims, check out the web site of the Aboriginal and Torres Strait Islander Commission at http:\\www.atsic.gov.au, or that of the Australian Institute for Australian and Torres Strait Islander Studies at http:\\www.aiatsis.gov.au.

ABORIGINAL ASSIMILATION: STOLEN CHILDREN

As early as 1837, the **Select Committee on Aborigines in the British Settlements** published a report suggesting that British action toward Aboriginals in Australia had led to the destruction of Aboriginal society. "Europeans have entered [the Aboriginal] borders uninvited," the document read, "and, when there, have not only acted as if they were undoubted lords of the soil, but have punished the natives…They are driven back into the interior as if they were dogs or kangaroos." The report suggested that the way to repair the damage was to invest in more missionaries and pay for additional Christianizing programs. Since the early 1800s, some missionaries had tried to make Aboriginals "employable" by converting them to Christianity and teaching them European skills and customs. Some of the program leaders decided that this was impossible if Aboriginal children were raised by Aboriginal parents, and the children were moved out of their homes to live with European families. This removal became state policy in New South Wales in 1883 and, astonishingly, was not officially discontinued until 1969. Aboriginals refer to these children as "taken" or "stolen," and it is estimated that there may be 100,000 people of Aboriginal descent today who do not know their families or the communities of their birth. Many are still seeking restitution or merely an overdue government apology.

■ The People

According to the most recent census (1996), the Commonwealth of Australia is home to **17.9 million people**. The census showed that 22% of the population was **born overseas**. Nearly 1.1 million of these 3.9 million foreign-born people came from the U.K. The next largest source was New Zealand (291,000), then Italy, Vietnam, Greece, China, Germany, the Philippines, and the Netherlands. More than half of the overseas-born lived in Sydney or Melbourne. **English** was the only language spoken at home in 81% of Australian homes. Just over 70% of Australians (approximately 12.6 million) declared themselves **Christians** in the 1996 census. Roman Catholics made up 38% of the population, while Anglicans accounted for 31%. The census showed that 5% of Australians (about 616,000) belong to **non-Christian** religions, with Buddhism, Islam, Judaism, and Hinduism leading the list. Roughly a quarter of all Australians rejected organized religion.

Australia's **population density** is 15 people per square kilometer; in comparison, an average square kilometer squeezes in 192 people in the United States and 1590 people in the United Kingdom. Eighty-five percent of Australians live in urban areas, and the suburbs are still growing. The vast majority live on or relatively near the coasts, particularly the east. The coasts of Queensland and northern New South Wales boast the fastest-growing populations of Australia.

In 1996, Australians earned a median weekly **income** of $292. Residents of the ACT reported the highest median income, at $430 per week, while residents of Tasmania reported the lowest, at $257. The median **age** was 33 years for men and 34 years for women, and approximately 12% of the population was over 65. Females outnumbered males in every state except the Northern Territory.

■ The Arts

Australia is a young nation, relatively speaking, and its artistic identity is still continuing to define itself. Historically, European arts exerted a strong influence on non-Aboriginal Australian artists and writers, and the artists responded by seeking to create an Australian identity and to define the Australian experience. Many focused particularly on Australians' relationship with their unique landscape and climate. Australian artists today are moving into a variety of styles. At the same time, the most popular national arts are still those that depict traditional themes, sustain an Australian mythology, or explore some facet of the nation's cultural and natural heritage.

LITERATURE

Australian literature truly got its start with the advent of **The Bulletin,** founded in Sydney in 1880. This literary journal, thought to be the most famous and significant of its kind, started a tradition of publishing new and original works with an emphasis on Australian content, encouraging local artists and writers by providing a regular outlet for their work. *The Bulletin*'s contributions to literature continued through the 20th century, but as its politics became increasingly conservative and anachronistic, sales fell. The journal became *The Bulletin with Newsweek* after coming under new ownership, and its significance has faded in the past three decades. However, numerous other literary magazines have emerged, catering to a variety of tastes and genres.

Bush Ballads and Poetry

Possibly the first uniquely Australian literature was the **bush ballad,** a form of poetry frequently published in *The Bulletin* that celebrated the workingman and the superiority of life in the bush to urban life. The most famous of these ballads is Banjo Patterson's **Waltzing Matilda,** often thought of as the Australian national anthem (see p. 137). Patterson also wrote the popular poem *The Man from Snowy River.* Despite the popularity of the ballad, a strong division existed between popular and intellectual **poetry;** intellectual poets were often seen as too pseudo-European. This has changed in recent decades, as writers have rejected defining their Australian identities as exiles in a historical vacuum. **Judith Wright** has led a movement towards a reexamination of colonial literature, establishing a continuity of identity with the poets of the past. A good example of this continuity is **A.D. Hope's** "Australia" which, while condemning Australia's insularity, is an affirmation of faith in its future.

Short Stories

The **short story** was popularized with stories of life in the bush as well. **Henry Lawson** and **Barbara Baynton** are two writers who captured the essence of this experience. Many short story writers still strive to define the relationship between person and landscape, and their work represents a search for cultural identity and historical continuity. In recent years the prose style has diversified with increased overseas influences, and short stories today explore social issues and express the realities of urban life.

Novels

The Australian **novel** has a complicated history, in part because many of the early novelists spent most of their adult lives outside Australia. Like artists of other genres, early novelists focused on the search for Australian identity, providing the definitions that allow contemporary writers to branch out with great diversity. Among the better-known early writers is **Miles Franklin,** author of *My Brilliant Career.* Franklin rejected the traditional female role of wife and mother to work as a journalist and feminist in Sydney, bequeathing her estate to establish a prestigious annual literary award in her name. One of the most famous works of Australian literature is *Voss,* by Nobel Prize-winning author **Patrick White.** Focusing on the uniqueness of Australia—the vacancy at the center, life on the perimeter, urban residents' obsession with the bush—*Voss* has been the basis for a play and an opera of the same name.

The strong tradition of mateship and misogyny that was apparent in early bush ballads and short stories provoked a sort of war between male and female writers earlier in this century, but the contribution of female writers has grown steadily, as has the attention given to "ethnic" writing, Aboriginal literature, and song-cycles. Today's names in literature continue to broadly examine the meaning of being Australian, but the meat of their work is increasingly varied. **Peter Carey** is best known as the author of *Bliss,* a humorous exploration of the Australian national character. **Tim Winton,** Western Australian short-story writer and novelist, writes about the everyday lives of the Westralians. The work of **Elizabeth Jolley,** who emigrated to Australia as an adult, explores the lives of refugees and foreigners. **David Malouf's** background as a poet comes through in his fiction, which explores the relationships between past and present on the changing face of Australia.

A growing number of **Aboriginal writers** are gaining recognition on a national scale. For samplings of contemporary Aboriginal literature, check out the anthology *Paperbark.* However, many of these artists continue to encounter racism and difficulties with mainstream acceptance, and most Australians still encounter Aboriginals primarily at staged "Aboriginal Culture Shows" of questionable authenticity.

POPULAR MUSIC

Australia's early colonial music was British folk music, with lively fiddle and drum reels of Irish immigrants playing for bushdances in cleared-out sheep-shearing sheds. Like the society in general, though, popular music has grown rich, with imports from America and Europe starting in the 50s and 60s, and more recently with Aboriginal sounds. You can now find almost any sound you want in Sydney or Melbourne, all at locally grown prices. Australia's youth radio, **JJJ (Triple J),** plays a lot of contemporary local music, and is always promoting new acts.

The Australian pop of the late 50s was epitomized by rocker **Johnny O'Keefe** whose sound, inspired by the musical blend emerging from the American south, took the country by storm. Television hit Australia at the same time as rock and roll, creating a booming youth culture based around shows like **Australian Bandstand.** The Beatles rolled into town in the early 60s, before their American tour, shaping the next decade of Australian music and spawning dozens of Beatles-esque bands, like the Easybeats, a one-hit wonder on the British music scene. At the same time, a lively folk music scene, heavily influenced by groups like Peter, Paul, and Mary, thrived in the 50s and 60s, but few names gained international recognition. **The Seekers,** a wholesome quartet with hits in England and America, were the great exception.

In the late 70s, **AC/DC** hit the charts with blues-influenced heavy metal grown out of pub culture. But after making it big, the group moved its headquarters to Europe and is no longer considered truly Australian. **The Skyhooks** were a local hit and were heavily promoted on television. Refusing to simply emulate American and English sounds, **Cold Chisel, Goanna,** and **Australian Crawl** gained similar local fame and influence; their Aussie-themed hits are still perennial radio favorites.

The 80s saw the advent of politically aware bands like **Midnight Oil,** another group born out of hard rock pub culture, which became popular for its enthusiastic live shows, and then used the fame and influence to promote social causes. While most popular Australian bands never managed to sell their sound outside of Australia, a few notable exceptions exist. **Men At Work** broke into the American music scene with a couple of huge hits before fading out of the limelight. **Crowded House** followed in their footsteps and became a well-known international band. **INXS** became one of the most successful Australian bands, but a recent planned comeback tour was cut short by the suicide of lead singer Michael Hutchence.

Today's Australian music is very diverse, influenced by grunge and world music. Aboriginal groups have entered the mainstream music culture, particularly **Yothu Yindi,** a band out of Arnhem Land in the Northern Territory that has combined traditional Aboriginal musical styles and themes with dance music and rock, and continues Midnight Oil's tradition of using the spotlight to further political causes. Other similarly politicized Aboriginal "bush rock" groups are the **Coloured Stones** and the **Warumpi Band. Archie Roach,** whose country-influenced tunes reflect on his background as a "stolen child" and the problems of Aboriginals in urban Australia, has recently become popular as well.

Country music is big, and is celebrated at an annual **Country Music Festival** in Tamworth, the "country capital" of Australia. The music takes its cues from its American counterpart, but is strongly influenced by the peculiarities of Australian rural life. **Slim Dusty** is the style's founding father, having sold over three million albums since he began songwriting at age 12.

U.S. soldiers brought big band **jazz** to Australia during WWI, and the American music has found increasingly firm footing. **Don Burrows** and **Graeme Bell** were inspired leaders of big and small groups in the 60s, establishing an Australian jazz scene that gained mainstream attention with the likes of too-hip singer **Vince Jones,** instrumental wizard **James Morrison,** and genius pianist **Paul Gabowsky** in the 80s. Each capital city has a flourishing live scene, nourished by intensively creative jazz programs in the conservatories of Perth and Sydney and the Victorian College of the Arts in Melbourne, all excellent places to look for music and musicians.

VISUAL ARTS

The visual arts of the modern era began, like other arts, with a search for Australian identity. This trend is seen clearly in the work of early Australian impressionists such as **Tom Roberts** (1856-1931), whose *Break Away* depicts the red, dry, dusty land of the cattle station, and **Frederick McCubbin** (1850-1917), whose *Lost Child* shows the thin forests of smoky green gum trees. Later landscape paintings by artists like **Hans Heysen, Robert Juniper,** and **Russell Drysdale** continue to focus on similar natural features, with a greater variety of style, color, and mood.

The themes and images of Australia have lent themselves particularly well to series painting. Possibly the most famous series of Australian paintings is the **Sidney Nolan** paintings of Ned Kelly, which tell of the folk hero's exploits, final capture, and execution. Completed in 1945 and 1954, these pieces appear in Australia's National Galleries today. Nolan has also done series on the Eureka Stockade, Gallipoli, and images of drought, among others. Other prominent contemporary artists include **John Perceval,** the expressionist **Albert Tucjer,** the abstract artist **John Colburn,** and **Arthur Boyd,** who depicts popular figures of Australian legend. Younger Australian painters (**Mandy Martin, Susan Norrie,** and **Neil Taylor**) are flooding the scene, often with difficult-to-categorize images and explorations of post-industrial Australia.

Aboriginal painting is, of course, the nation's original visual art, although its origin was not exclusively artistic, but educational, spiritual, and functional. Before the 1970s, public perception of Aboriginal art was restricted to "bark paintings"—paintings on strips of eucalyptus traditionally created as part of a ritual and generally destroyed during or after the ceremony. After becoming collector's items in the 1940s, these bark paintings have since been widely reproduced. During the 1970s, other forms of Aboriginal art were rediscovered. Art forms such as mural art, body painting, and rock painting became popularized throughout Australia, encouraged by new interest and government support. Among Aboriginal artists today, there exists a division between **contemporary traditional art,** which focuses primarily on themes connected to the Dreaming and Aboriginal culture, and **urban Aboriginal art,** which focuses on themes connected to general life experience, using western art techniques and avoiding images that have ritual significance. In the 80s and 90s, contemporary traditional art has achieved more international popularity, probably because it appears more "authentically Aboriginal" to the rest of the world.

FILM

The world's first feature length film, *The Story of the Kelly Gang,* was screened in Australia in 1901. Thus began a long tradition of originality in Australian film. The rest of the world began paying attention to Australian talent in the film industry in the 70s. The **Australian Film School** opened in 1973 and began training the likes of **Gillian Armstrong, Paul Cox,** and **Bruce Beresford.** In 1976, **Peter Weir's** acclaimed *Picnic at Hanging Rock* hit the international scene, followed by his *Gallipoli* in 1980 (which starred Australian-born and bred superstar **Mel Gibson**). Other popularly recognized and appreciated Australian films of this time period include Phillip Noyce's *Newsfront* and Gillian Armstrong's *My Brilliant Career.* The 80s brought the *Mad Max* trilogy and *The Year of Living Dangerously.* More recent hits from the land down under include *Strictly Ballroom, Death in Brunswick, Muriel's Wedding, Adventures of Priscilla, Queen of the Desert,* and *Shine.* The same Australian creative team that produced *Strictly Ballroom* also produced the well-received modern interpretation of *Romeo and Juliet.* Besides these international hits, many smaller Australian films have been honored with awards at the Cannes Film Festival. Though most of these independently-made films remain unseen by the rest of the world, they continue the Australian tradition of producing quirky, offbeat films.

■ Food and Drink

Australians eat three meals a day: breakfast, lunch, and dinner. Aussies hardly ever eat their **"brekkie"** out, and most restaurants don't open till noon. The evening meal is sometimes called **"tea,"** but shouldn't be confused with the diminutive British version; it's the largest meal of the day. Beware of ordering only an **"entree,"** which is an appetizer in Australia. A **"cuppa"**—tea or coffee—should tide you over between meals. **Tipping** in Australian restaurants and pubs is rare and never expected.

The diet of most Australians is largely shaped by their ethnicity, but tourists will find an abundance of flavors to choose from in the more cosmopolitan cities. Food courts generally present a balance of Asian, fish and chips, and fast food. **Kosher** meats are unknown in much of the country, but **vegetarians** shouldn't go hungry despite Australia's meat-hungry reputation. Trendy urban eateries will frequently cater to special diets, but traditional establishments rarely will. Restaurants may offer to remove meat from dishes, but won't necessarily prepare them separately.

IMPORTED CUISINES

Australia's origin as a humble convict colony didn't exactly endow the country with a subtle palate. Australia still suffers from a reputation of having a notoriously dull national cuisine, but it has been remarkably successful at adding layers of flavor with each wave of immigration. As is to be expected from the island-continent, **seafood** is a highlight. From the British come cholesterol-heavy **pub meals,** such as steak and eggs, and the Aussie institution of **fish and chips.** A popular meal for families on Friday nights, the fish is fried, battered, rolled in newspaper, and served with British-style chips (thick french fries). "Chippers" are the quintessential Aussie eating establishment, the equivalent of the American pizzeria. Most specialize in **takeaway** (take-out). **Chook** (chicken) is often substituted for fish to create much-needed variety. **Meat pies** are the epitome of unimaginative Australian fare. Inexplicably popular, these square, doughy shells contain meat of dubious origin and frequently a mushy vegetable filling. Most consumers douse them in **tomato sauce** (a sweet ketchup-like concoction) to disguise the taste. Use Australian condiments sparingly until you are familiar with them. Aussie mustard delivers a horseradishy kick to the unwary, and the infamous **Vegemite,** a dark, yeasty by-product of the beer-brewing process, should be scraped thinly rather than spread liberally.

Recent European and Middle Eastern arrivals have spiced up Australian menus with Greek souvlaki, Italian pasta, and Lebanese tabouleh. The cheapest way to sample these flavors is at any of numerous takeaway joints. Influxes of immigrants from Asian and Pacific countries have added further variety. Chinese dishes first arrived with Chinese gold prospectors in the 1850s and have so infiltrated the menu that even their names have taken a uniquely Australian twist: **"dim sims"** are Australian dim sum. Still, the Chinese food reliably contains a standard array of vegetables and predictable sauces. Japanese, Thai, Malay, and Vietnamese restaurants also are abundant, particularly in Darwin and cosmopolitan centers in the southeast.

Australia has plentiful pickings when it comes to **fruit;** its tropical north supports fruit industries that other western countries can only fantasize about. Travelers from fruit-deprived countries will encounter exotic offerings such as custard apples, lychees, passion fruit, star fruit, coconuts, mangoes, and pineapples. Queensland is the main fruit-producing region, although Tasmania ships its apples to the mainland. Of the typical prepared desserts: the ubiquitous **lamington** is a coconut-covered chunk of pound cake dipped in chocolate, and the festive **pavlova** is a chewy meringue covered in whipped cream and fresh fruit.

BUSH TUCKER

Coastal Aboriginals have eaten crayfish, **yabbies** (freshwater shrimp), and fish for centuries, and the first English settlers rapidly followed suit. But in the harsh environments of the bush, Aboriginal foragers exploited food resources that early colonists

LIFE & TIMES

> ### On Eating a Country's Fauna
>
> Kangaroo has a tangy slam to it, not unlike grilled liver. The meat is tough and demands a thick peanut sauce. Crocodile is indifferent: bleached and as tasteless as virgin sand, it must be regarded from a respectful distance. Buffalo, with its wandering edges of gristle and chewy texture, is sanguine and can only be penetrated under the spell of soy sauce. Emu has a curious flavor that becomes clear to the tongue when presented with pineapple, or better, a more vigorous fruit, like the mango. The meat otherwise is tasteless and gray.

found a little too unorthodox to stomach. **Witchetty grubs** are the most well-known of the bush foods that make first-timers recoil in horror. Yet some bush tucker, particularly indigenous sources of meat, has made it on to hip urban menus. **Kangaroo** steaks are growing in popularity and **crocodile** meat is highly regarded; a few restaurants serve **emu.** If you want to sample **goanna** or **ants,** however, you might have to catch dinner yourself or join one of the Red Centre tours that feature bush tucker.

BEER AND WINE

For many, a close associate exists between Australia and **beer,** and with good reason. Australians produce some of the world's best brew and consume it readily. Darwin in particular claims fame as Australia's thirstiest city. Some Australians display scorn for **Fosters,** which owes its international name-recognition to saturation advertising. Instead, loyalty is expected to the state brew. **Victoria Bitter** (VB), **Toohey's,** and **XXXX** ("four-ex") hail from Victoria, New South Wales, and Queensland, respectively. While many beers have a relatively high alcoholic percentage (around 5%), there has been a recent trend towards "light" beers, which have less alcohol (not fewer calories). **Strongbow,** Australia's favorite cider, is quietly gaining popularity in pubs as a potent and tasty alternative, but beer unequivocally prevails. The favorite place to share a coldie with your mates is the omnipresent Aussie **pub.** Traditional payment etiquette is the **shout,** in which drinking mates alternate rounds. If the beach is more your style, throw a slab (24 containers of beer) in the Esky (ice chest). For more beer terminology, consult the **appendix,** p. 641.

Australian **wines** rival those the world over. Overseas export started soon after the first vineyards began to produce wine in the early 1800s, and the industry has gained renown after a post-WWII influx of European talent. The **Hunter Valley** (in New South Wales), the **Barossa** and **Clare Valleys** (in South Australia), the **Swan** and **Margaret Rivers** (in Western Australia), and the **Derwent** and **Tamar Valleys** (in Tasmania), possess some of the best Aussie vineyards. Many cafes and low-end restaurants advertise that they are **BYO,** or "bring your own." Though typically not licensed to serve alcohol, these establishments permit patrons to furnish their own bottle of wine with the meal and charge only a small **corkage fee,** if anything. The **cask** of wine, another Australian innovation, is ideal for picnics.

■ Sport

Australians, spectators and participants alike, take sport very seriously. The 1956 Melbourne Olympics inaugurated national television broadcasting in Australia, and televisions in public places have, more or less, been tuned to sporting events ever since. While the big event on everyone's calendar these days is the Sydney Olympics in summer 2000, the national team-sports melodrama extends year-round, year in and year out. In winter, Western Australia, South Australia, and Victoria catch **footy fever** for **Australian Rules Football,** while New South Wales and Queensland traditionally follow **rugby.** In summer, **cricket** is the spectator sport of choice across the nation. Throughout the year, star Aussie Rules football players and top cricketers enjoy hero status similar to that accorded basketball players in the U.S. or soccer players in Europe. For good insight into Australian sport culture, tune in to H. G. Nelson and Roy Slaven's Saturday morning Triple-J radio show, *This Sporting Life.*

CRICKET

The uninitiated may have trouble making sense of a sport where people can "bowl a maiden over of five flippers and a googly," but visitors won't be able to avoid match enthusiasm. In cricket, two teams of 11 players face off in a contest that can last anywhere from an afternoon to five days. At the national level, cricket teams compete throughout the summer for the **Sheffield Shield,** culminating in the March finals.

Each summer, the national Shield competition is supplanted by international cricket. A "test match" is not just a scrimmage; rather it is the most lengthy and serious form of international cricket. In 1877, Australia's cricket team headed to England for its first international Test against the mother country. Surprisingly, the colonials won. The Australians, as a shocked English reporter wrote, had "taken off with the ashes" of English cricket. Ever since that first match, the England and Australian Test teams have been in noble competition for **"the Ashes"** (the trophy is actually a small, symbolic urn). In the summers when the England team does not come to Australia, a different international team arrives for a **full tour,** which consists of five test matches, one each in Melbourne, Sydney, Perth, Adelaide, and Brisbane. These five-day matches are supplemented by smaller, titillating one-day matches. The tour takes place in December and January; check out any cricket magazine in a newsagency for a summer cricket schedule. When watching a Test, where all players wear white, you can distinguish Australian players by their baggy green caps. Earning the right to wear such a cap is the highest privilege for an Australian cricket player. The international tour is over by February, and the country then turns its attention to national cricket just in time for the Sheffield Shield finals.

AUSTRALIAN RULES FOOTBALL

In Victoria, South Australia, and West Australia in winter, the **Australian Football League (AFL)** teams fill the void that the end of the cricket season might otherwise leave. The game was originally designed to keep cricket players in shape during the winter, and is played on cricket ovals. Aussie Rules is actually a fairly simple game with a few basic rules. Essentially, teams just need to get the red leather ball from one end of the field to the other and kick it through the opposing team's posts to score. Each team of 18 players defends three sets of posts for four 20-minute quarters: six points are earned for scoring in the middle goal, and one point for reaching either side goal. The basic move in AFL is the **punt,** used for both passing and scoring; good players can punt the ball over 70m. The most spectacular move, though, is the **mark.** If a player can catch the ball on the kick before it bounces, he is entitled to unobstructed possession of that ball. Consequently, just after a kick, the players all pack together and run, jump, and soar under and over each other, in a heroic effort to snatch the ball from the sky.

In the last decade, the Victorian football league expanded to become a national league. The AFL is still composed mainly of Victorian teams with a few regional teams thrown in, explaining why regions as large as the West Coast compete against obscure Melbourne suburbs. The AFL grand final, in early September, is a marvelous spectacle at the home of Australian sport, the **MCG (Melbourne Cricket Ground).** A good AFL **website** is at http://www.odyssey.com.au/sports/afl/links.html.

OTHER SPORT

But all in Australia is not cricket shots or footy marks. On Boxing Day, even as the Melbourne cricket Test gets underway, half of Australia's amateur sailing community fills Sydney Harbour with billowing white sails to begin the **Sydney-to-Hobart yacht race,** the highlight in a full calendar of water sports. Melbourne hosts one of tennis' Grand Slam events, the **Australian Open,** each January. Grassy tennis courts, bowling greens, and golf courses pepper the cities coast-to-coast. Every town also has a race track, and on the first Tuesday in November, the entire country stops to watch jockeys jockey for the prestigious **Melbourne Cup.** Australia is, of course, famous for its surfing, which for some is a competitive sport in addition to a great way to spend a summer morning. Finally, as Sydney anticipates hosting the **2000 Summer Olympics,** the world's largest celebration of sport, the city is already a blur of preparation and pride. See **The Olympics,** p. 83, for more information.

Even if you'll miss the Olympics, cricket seems eternally confusing, or Aussie Rules football is still incomprehensible, just join in the crowds, cheer for the home team, and remember the old adage that many an Australian sports fan takes to heart: **It's all fun and games until somebody loses an eye—then it's sport.**

■ Biodiversity

The one who stands apart often proves to have something special to offer. Such is the case with Australia's wildlife, which has benefited from millions of years of isolation on a very large island. This sheltered existence has bred one of the world's most distinctive arrays of plants and animals. When the first immigrant species landed on a continent with an abundance of habitats, many found themselves in a nursery for biological variation, nearly devoid of competition. The consequence was a series of adaptive radiations that produced a multiplicity of plants and animals from a limited number of ancestral taxa.

Much of this variety is currently threatened. Australia's inevitable contact with outside species presented enormous challenges to its unique biology. The colonization of the continent by human hunters introduced a new and dangerous predator, and both Aboriginals and Europeans brought species that upset Australia's delicate ecology. In recent years, Australian environmental policy has begun to recognize the importance of protecting the continent's precious biodiversity.

INDIGENOUS FAUNA

Marsupials are the stars of the Australian menagerie. Because marsupials, which bear immature young and nurse them in a pouch, had few mammalian competitors on the continent, they radiated into many different niches. The common names that early naturalists have applied to many of these animals reflect the families of other ecosystems, not any phylogenetic relationship. Thus, the koala is not a bear; the marsupial "rat" is not a rat; and the marsupial "cat" and "mole" are more closely related to each other than to their namesakes. Images of **kangaroos** bounding across the landscape are virtually synonymous with Australia. In fact, there's a serious overpopulation of 'roos, and kangaroo-culling programs have been enacted.. The kangaroo's look-alike cousin, the **wallaby,** is another common outback critter. Other distinctive marsupials include **wombats, possums, bandicoots,** and **quolls.**

Australia's other most-beloved marsupial, the **koala** lives on and among the leaves of certain eucalypt trees. Sleeping, on average, 18 of every 24 hours and existing on a diet made up exclusively of the intoxicating and semi-toxic eucalyptus leaves, the koala hasn't much energy for hunting, gathering, or even moving. Seeing a koala is often just a matter of being patient enough to scan the treetops for a familiar furball or impatient enough to find the nearest zoo or nature preserve.

Still more fantastic, giant marsupials once roamed the landscape of prehistoric Australia. Now extinct, these **megafauna** included towering relatives of kangaroos called diprotodons. The megafauna died off soon after the arrival of humans on the continent, due either to hunting or to climatic changes (see **Cenozoic Megafauna,** p. 225). The **thylacine,** or Tasmanian tiger, is a more recent loss. Resembling a large wolf with stripes, this predator was driven to the edge of extinction by competition with dingoes, then hunted by white settlers who feared for their livestock. One infamous marsupial carnivore has survived, however. Fierce in temperament, **Tasmanian devils** are nocturnal scavengers. They also hunt small prey and have been known to take livestock with their powerful jaws (see **Marsupials from Hell,** p. 477).

Australia's list of peculiar mammals does not end with marsupials. There are just two families of **monotremes,** or egg-laying mammals. **Echidnas** are small ant-eaters

Boing!

Let no one say that the cover of *Let's Go: Australia* panders to kitschy stereotypes about the region. The fact is that "Kangaroo Crossing" road signs just like the one pictured on our cover are ubiquitous in Australia. As you careen down the highway, you'll probably notice crows feasting on the result of some other driver's failure to heed the warnings. Kangaroos travel in groups known as mobs, which can have over 20 members. Several dozen species can be categorized into two groups: red kangaroos are generally larger and a bit more aggressive than grey. Male red kangaroos can grow to be 3m long, nose to tail, and are capable of propelling themselves nearly 9m at a single bound.

Kangaroos, like most indigenous Australian mammals, are marsupials; after approximately 33 days of gestation, an embryo emerges from the uterus and follows a trail of saliva, lain by the mother, from her pudenda to her pouch. At any one time after the age of two, a female kangaroo is likely to have one offspring in the womb, one living in the pouch, and one making occasional visits to the pouch. This productivity accounts for the female's markedly shorter lifespan. This style of reproduction, combined with the kangaroo's unique ability to suspend embryonic gestation in a state of dormancy for up to two years, ensures survival in harsh desert environments. Kangaroos have thrived on the fringes of human communities since colonization, leading the Australian government to conduct an annual program of kangaroo culling. Contrary to popular myth, kangaroos do not feed marmalade sandwiches to small bears or send their young out to play with tree-dwelling pigs and tail-bouncing tigers.

that resemble porcupines with protruding snouts. When threatened, the echidna buries itself in the ground, leaving only long spines exposed. Strangest of all, the **platypus** sports a melange of zoological features: the bill of a duck, the fur of an otter, the tail of a beaver, and webbed claws. So outrageous did this anatomy seem to European colonists that early British naturalists refused to consider stuffed specimens real.

Outshining Australia's mammals in vividness of color, if not in biological singularity, is a tremendous diversity of **birds.** The **emu** is related to other flightless birds such as the African ostrich and the extinct moa of New Zealand. Also flightless, hordes of **little** (or **fairy**) **penguins** can be spotted at sites on the south coast, where they wade ashore each night. Australia's flight-endowed birds include noisy flocks of **galahs,** colorful **rainbow lorikeets,** and unreasonably large **cassowaries** (see p. 351). Songs and poems have immortalized the unmistakable laugh of the **kookaburra.** Both **crimson rosellas** and **cockatoos** are common in the southeast.

The most fearsome of Australia's **reptiles,** saltwater crocodiles (**salties**) actually live in both brine and freshwater and grow to lengths of 7m. For a primer on discriminating between the salty and its less threatening freshwater relative—and avoiding becoming croc fodder—take a look at **Freshies and Salties,** p. 239. In addition to its crocodiles, Australia's reptiles include aggressive **goannas** and a wide array of **snakes.**

INTRODUCED FAUNA

Humans have been responsible for the introduction of animals to Australia since prehistoric times. The **dingo,** a lithe, wild canine with a bite but no bark, crossed the Timor Sea with ancestors of Aboriginal populations several thousand years ago. The creatures mainly hunt small, wild prey, but may also menace livestock. Although dingoes pose no threat to adult humans, ranchers detest them and kill those they encounter near their flocks. They've even gone so far as to build a "Dingo Fence" over 3300km long to keep the beasts away from cattle and sheep.

More recent arrivals accompanied European colonists. Domesticated **cattle** and **sheep** are of tremendous economic importance in Australia, with stations (ranches) across the continent. These species have had a dramatic impact on the landscape and ecological balance of the nation; vast tracts have been converted to pasture to support the meat industry. Many animals that are now considered pests have also been introduced, whether intentionally or accidentally. The massive overpopulation of **rabbits,** purportedly introduced to Australia to provide practice targets for marksman, has become one of Australia's gravest wildlife problems. Accidental introductions such as European **rats** also represent serious threats to native fauna.

MARINE LIFE AND THE GREAT BARRIER REEF

Fur seals, elephant seals, and **sea lions** populate Australia's southern shores during their summer breeding seasons, but it's the **Great Barrier Reef** that makes Australia's sea life unique. It's also one of Australia's biggest tourist draws, a diving wonderland. A comprehensive overview on **diving and snorkeling** the reef is in the introduction to the Queensland chapter (see **Experiencing the Great Barrier Reef,** p. 275).

The longest coral formation in the world, the reef is actually a series of many reefs that stretches more than 2000km along the eastern coast of Queensland from the Tropic of Capricorn to Papua New Guinea. Although adult **coral polyps** are sedentary, corals actually belong to the animal kingdom. Thus, the Great Barrier Reef is the only community of animals visible to the eye from space. Corals rely on sunlight filtering down from the ocean surface and cannot grow at depths greater than 50m. Reef accumulates whenever a coral polyp dies and leaves behind its skeletal legacy of calcium carbonate. As layers of **limestone** build, the reef rises toward the surface. Once the coral reaches the top of the waves, the surf pounds it into sand-size bits. Add some more years and the bits form a little mound that sticks out of the water, which is called a **cay.** Birds come along, land on the cay, and ingloriously deposit seeds from the mainland, and vegetation turns the cay into an island. Sea turtles and birds come to nest, and soon a whole ecosystem has literally risen from the water.

Colonies of coral grow by asexual reproduction, but new colonies propagate by **sexual reproduction**—quite a feat for creatures fixed to one spot. Using the moon for synchronization, all of the corals along the whole reef release their gametes at once so as to maximize the chance of fertilization. On a single night each October, the water fills with an impenetrable fog of reproductive cells.

Coral reefs take a number of different forms. Closest to the shore are **patch reefs,** comprised of patches of both **hard** and **soft coral.** The former is often dried, bleached and sold to tourists in shops (but beware of national marine park rules against removing living creatures from the sea). Soft corals, however, lose their shape and turn to sludge when taken out of water. Long, slender **sea whips** and delicate, intricate **fan corals** are some of the most plentiful and beautiful of the soft corals. Hard corals can come in hues ranging from purple to emerald to red, and are mostly categorized as either branched, boulder, or plate coral. The fast-growing **branched coral** is named for its appearance; its most common varieties are the thin, brittly **needle coral,** the antler-like **stag coral,** and **finger coral,** also appropriately named. **Boulder coral** is sturdier and slower-growing, including the **honey-comb, golfball** and **brain boulders;** in areas where cyclones are frequent, these are the species that tend to survive. **Plate corals,** such as **sheet** and **table corals,** also look like they sound.

Further out than the patch reefs are the **fringe reefs,** which contain all of the same types of coral. Their arrangement in circular patterns deeply entrenched in the sea floor means that they frequently fill with silt, which spells bad visibility for divers. The far outer reef is made up of 710km of **ribbon reef;** this includes some of Australia's best diving, but is accessible only to boats that venture out for four days or longer.

The reef also houses a spectacular variety of colorful, sometimes otherworldly **fish,** from the enormous **potato cod** to the **fusaleres,** a family of fish that change color at night. The **parrotfish** eats bits of coral by cracking it in its beak-like mouth, and at night envelops itself in a protective mucus sac, a phenomenon that might be a highlight of a night dive. If you're diving, taking a **briefing course** on marine life is an excellent way to familiarize yourself with what you'll see. While it's impossible to memorize every species, many shops sell **fish identification cards** that you can take down with you. A few terms to know: **damsel fish** are your ordinary fish-shaped fish; the **wrasse** is a long, slender, cigar-like fish; **angel** and **surgeon fish** have similar oblong shapes, but the surgeon has a razor-sharp barb close to its tail; the **butterfly** and **bat fish** are round, but the latter is a larger and has a black stripe across the eye. **Sharks** make occasional appearances, but are rarely a threat to divers. Besides fish, the reef houses **turtles, porpoises, dolphins,** and **whales,** as well as **echinoderms:** sea cucumbers, sea stars, feather stars, and brittle stars. The more dangerous reef denizens are outlined in the **Safety** secion of the diving overview.

FLORA

Dominating Australia's forests virtually from coast to coast, the **eucalypts,** or **gum trees,** demonstrate the extent to which biological taxa can successfully adapt to diverse environments. Gums have taken on many different shapes and sizes across the continent. The majestic **karri** soars over 50m skyward in ancient stands along well-watered valleys, while the **mallee** gum grows in stunted copses across scrubland such as that of western Victoria. The characteristically bulging trunk and splayed branches of the **boab** mark the horizon of the Kimberley in Western Australia.

In addition to gums, other regulars appearing in the bush and coastal thickets include **banksias, ti trees,** and **grevillias.** Feathery and almost pine-like in appearance, **casuarinas** also exist in multiple habitats. In temperate, rain-fed stretches of Victoria and Tasmania, valleys of tall, dinosaur-era **tree ferns** are dwarfed by towering **mountain ash,** the tallest flowering plant in the natural kingdom (and yet another gum). Most of Australia's large trees have trunks that are lighter in color than their leaves, and the leaves themselves usually grow high above the ground. The effect created is quite different than that of most European and North American forests. Here bushwalkers find themselves surrounded by white and gray in place of brown and green.

A remarkable feature found along parts of Australia's tropical coasts, the **mangrove** has adapted readily to its unfavorable environment, and stilt-like trunks cling tenaciously to the briny mud of alluvial swamps. Meanwhile, Australia has wide swaths of land that grow nary a tree. The arid outback is dominated by **spinifex** grasses, which grow in dense tufts across the vast interior of the world's flattest continent. Another common plant is the **saltbush,** a hearty shrub that grows in soil too salty for other plants and that has been pivotal in converting harsh habitats to livestock pastures.

In more fertile areas, **wildflowers** are abundant. Western Australia is home to **swamp bottlebrush, kangaroo paw,** and **Ashby's banksia,** along with nearly 10,000 other species. Expansive fields of yellow and pink **everlastings** cover fields across the country, to the delight of casual wildflower viewers, but rare **spider orchids** hidden in the forests reveal themselves only to the most dogged of investigators. The **Sturt pea** adds a distinctive splash of red and black to the inland deserts of South Australia and WA. Acacia trees also contribute to Australia's floral colors; one common species in the drier areas of the southeast is the **golden wattle.** Elsewhere in the country, **orchids** and **begonias** provide additional visual garnish.

Australian Capital Territory

■ Canberra

The site selected in 1908 to be the capital of the newly federated nation of Australia was not a thriving center for national affairs. Rather, it was the result of a compromise between the rival poles of Sydney and Melbourne, acceptable to both because of its midway location. The Australian Capital Territory (ACT), including Canberra, suburbs, and parkland, was thus carved out of southeastern New South Wales, but is not governed by that state. Life in Canberra has picked up its pace a bit, but even today, many newcomers to Australia are surprised to learn that Sydney isn't the capital. Canberra maintains a low profile and a refined, unhurried lifestyle to match.

Yet regardless of its reputation as a dull city, the city serves as both a national exhibition and the international face of the political body of Australia. Canberra's revolutionary design was the outcome of an international competition, won by an American, Walter Burley Griffin. Construction began in 1913, and the first Canberra Parliament convened in 1927. Today, Canberra supports a metropolitan population of nearly 310,000. Despite the downtown area's daily hubbub, the streets for the most part remain amazingly quiet. From its unique traffic pattern to its roster of national centers, memorials, and museums, a sense of purposeful order pervades life in this city. The physical beauty surrounding Canberra makes a full day of sight-seeing enjoyable and convenient. It's not Sydney, nor does it try to be. Still, Canberra's blend of culture and class may qualify it as one of Australia's more underrated destinations.

🏛 CANBERRA HIGHLIGHTS

- Getting caught in the crossfire of **Question Time,** a spectacle of wit, persuasion, and political antics in the House of Representatives (see p. 78).
- Interactive learning at the **National Science and Technology Centre** (see p. 78).
- Biking on a spring day along the paths around Parliamentary Triangle (see p. 72).
- Canberra Festival's **hot air balloon** extravaganza (see p. 80).
- View from **Mt. Ainslie** down ANZAC Pde toward Parliament House (see p. 77).
- Dinner and an evening of stargazing at the **Mt. Stromlo Observatory** (see p. 81).
- Art and remembrance at the elegant **Australian War Memorial** (see p. 78).

ARRIVAL AND DEPARTURE

By Plane

Located in Pialligo, 7km east of the city center, the **Canberra International Airport** (tel. 6209 3333) is an easy target by car. From Commonwealth Ave, take Parkes Way east past the roundabout at Kings Ave. The road changes its name first to Morshead Dr, then to Pialligo Ave, en route to the airport. ACTION Bus #80 runs along Northbourne Ave, through the bus interchange in Civic, and to the airport (M-F 6:30am-10pm). For weekend transit, a **taxi** ($12-15 from the city center) is your best bet.

The misnamed airport only handles domestic flights at present; international transport requires a stop in nearby Sydney. Both **Qantas** (tel. 6250 8211 or 13 13 13) and **Ansett** (tel. 6249 7641 or 13 13 00) connect Canberra to Sydney (50min., $163), Melbourne (1hr., $232), Brisbane (1hr. 50min., $341), and Adelaide (90min., $337) and offer discounts for students, seniors, and advance reservations.

By Bus

Intercity **buses** through Canberra are based at **Jolimont Tourist Centre,** 65-7 Northbourne Ave, just north of Alinga St in Civic. (Open daily 6am-10:30pm; in winter 5am-

10:30pm. Public showers available. Lockers $4 per day, overnight storage available by prior arrangement.) Several bus companies, both major domestic airlines, and **Countrylink** (tel. 6257 1576; open M-F 7am-5:30pm) have desks in the building.

Greyhound Pioneer (tel. 13 20 30) provides frequent service to Sydney (4-5hr., 4-6 per day, $28), Melbourne (8-10hr., 2 per day, $45-54), Adelaide (17hr., 2 per day, $96), Goulburn (1hr., 3 per day, $20), and to Thredbo via Jindabyne (3½hr., June-Oct. 2 per day, $40). **Murray's** (tel. 13 22 51) also runs to Sydney (4hr., 3 per day, $28). Extensive coverage of New South Wales' south coast is their specialty (to Bateman's Bay 2½hr., 1-2 per day, $22). During school holidays, **Sid Fogg's** (tel. 1800 045 952) sends three buses per week to Newcastle (6½hr., M, W, and F 7:30am, $45). **Transborder Express** (tel. 6241 0033) makes the trip to Yass (1hr., 5 per day, $10). Always ask about **student and senior discounts** when buying bus tickets.

By Train

The **Canberra Railway Station,** on Wentworth Ave in Kingston, 6km from the city center, is on ACTION bus route #39 (station open daily 5am-11:30pm). Driving from Civic, follow Commonwealth Ave south to State Circle and exit on Brisbane Ave. Wentworth Ave continues southeast where Brisbane Ave ends, four blocks from State Circle. The station houses little more than a **Countrylink office** (tel. 6239 7039 or 13 22 32; open M-Sa 6:20am-5:30pm, Su 10:30am-5:30pm). Trains leave for Sydney (4hr., 3 per day, $42), Melbourne (8½hr., daily, $79), Brisbane (23hr., daily, $112), and Adelaide (22hr., daily, $135). Advance purchase can yield up to a 40% discount.

By Car

The **NRMA automobile club,** 92 Northbourne Ave (tel. 6240 4620), is the place to turn for road service or car problems (open M-F 9am-5pm). For 24-hour **emergency road service,** call 13 21 32. **Budget** (tel. 13 27 27; open M-F 7am-9pm, Sa 8am-5pm), on the corner of Mort St and Girrahween St, **Avis,** 17 Lawnsdale St (tel. 6249 6088 or 1800 225 411; open M-F 8am-6pm, Sa 8am-1pm, Su 9am-12noon), **Hertz,** 32 Mort St (tel. 6257 4877; open M-F 8am-6pm, Sa 8am-noon), and **Thrifty,** 29 Lawnsdale St (tel. 6247 7422 or 1800 652 008; open M-F 8am-5:30pm, Sa-Su 8am-5pm), all have offices in Braddon and at the airport. Local outfits **Value Rent-a-Car** (tel. 6295 6155; open daily 8am-6pm), in the Regis Capital Hill Hotel at Canberra Ave and National Circuit, and **Oz Drive,** 13 Yallourn St (tel. 6239 2639; call ahead to book M-F 9am-6pm), each charge about $40 per day with rates decreasing over longer rentals. **Noss Car and Van Rentals,** 41 Whyalla St (tel. 6280 0320), in Fyshwick, rents used cars from $25 per day or $160 per week (open M-F 8:30am-5pm, Sa 9am-noon).

ORIENTATION

Lake Burley Griffin, formed by the damming of the Molonglo River, splits Canberra in two. The area known as the Parliamentary Triangle spans the lake with one point at **Capital Hill** on the south shore. From Capital Circle, running around Capital Hill, **Commonwealth Ave** stretches north to **Vernon Circle,** known as the city center, and **King's Ave** crosses the lake heading northeast to the government offices in Russell and ending at the Australian-American Memorial. **Parkes Way** connects the two avenues on the north shore. These boundaries encircle most of the city's museums and government-related attractions. The area around Vernon Circle, known as **Civic,** houses the main city bus interchange (1 block north on Mort St), as well as a series of shopping centers organized around **City Walk,** a pedestrian mall with travel agencies, currency exchange offices, nightclubs, and skateboarders galore. **Northbourne Ave,** leading north from Vernon Circle, is the major axis of the city's northern half.

There are two distinct features that help one understand the Canberra city plan. First, to avoid the unpleasant appearance of sprawling suburbs creeping up the hills, construction in the city is restricted to the valleys; it must not extend above a certain altitude. Street signs therefore often direct one to a valley rather than to a specific street. Second, the city is based on a system of roundabouts surrounded by concentrically ringed streets and wheel-spoke off-shoots, which can be very confusing. The easiest way to navigate it is to travel by bus and avoid the issue. If you do drive, a good map is invaluable. Many budget accommodations hand out free street maps to guests, or ask the Canberra Visitors Centre for a free *Canberra Holiday Guide*, which contains an excellent map. Do familiarize yourself with the city's named districts.

Canberra's roundabouts are well-marked, but signs often refer to districts rather than streets. **Kingston,** southeast of Capital Hill, is home to the railway station and budget lodging. The embassies populate **Yarralumla,** just west of Capital Hill. **Dickson,** northeast of Civic via Northbourne Ave and Antill St, and **Manuka** (MA-nik-uh), southeast of Capital Hill, both include clusters of reasonably priced restaurants.

Thanks to a superb system of **bicycle paths,** the capital's relatively long distances can also be covered easily on a bike. A ride along the shores of Lake Burley Griffin is an excellent way to take in Parliamentary Triangle without having to find parking.

GETTING AROUND

Canberra's public transit system, **ACTION (ACT Internal Omnibus Network)** (tel. 6207 7600, route and fare information tel. 13 17 10; TTY 6207 7689; http://www.netinfo.com.au/action), centers on the city bus interchange, on East Row at Alinga St, one block south of the Jolimont Tourist Centre. All tickets can be purchased on the bus or at the sales desk in the city bus interchange. Buses cover Canberra and the inner suburbs, with connections to the greater ACTION network that covers the entire populated area of the ACT. The invaluable *Bus Pack* ($2) is available at the bus interchange, at the Canberra Visitors Centre, and from newsagents. Route maps are posted at the city bus interchange. (Approximate service hours M-F 6:30am-11:30pm, Sa 7:30am-11pm, Su 8:30am-6pm; some routes have more limited hours.) Certain marked ACTION buses accommodate wheelchairs and guide dogs.

ACTION bus fares are based on a zone system which divides the greater Canberra area into north, central, and south zones. The vast majority of the city's tourist attractions and budget accommodations and the airport fall within the central zone, so you'll probably only need the **one-zone fare** ($2; concessions and children ages 5-15 $1). **Fare-saver tickets** are available for 10 one-zone rides ($17, $6, $8.50). **Weekly** ($17, $8.50) and **monthly** ($55, $27.50) tickets provide for unlimited travel over the allotted period of time. All-zone tickets are about twice as expensive.

Murray's Canberra Explorer (tel. 13 22 51) makes 19 stops over a 25km route, allows passengers to get on and off as many times as they like, and the ride includes a full running commentary. (Tickets $18, seniors $16, ages 3-14 $8; discounted tickets available at YHA and Victor Lodge $10.) Buses set off each hour from Jolimont Centre (daily 10:15am and 4:15pm). A one-hour, no-stop pass gives you a look at the city for $7 (seniors $6, ages 3-14 $5). VIP, Nomads, and YHA discounts are available.

Aerial Taxi Cab (tel. 6285 9222) covers the city and suburbs at all hours. For **bike rental,** try **Mr. Spokes Bike Hire and Cafe** (tel. 6257 1188), on Barrine Dr in Acton Park, near the Ferry Terminal (from $7 per hr.; open W-Su and public holidays 9:30am-6pm, in winter 9am-5pm). Another option is **Dial-a-Bicycle** (tel. 6294 3171; $30 per day, 2 days $40; delivery, helmet, and lock included; call daily 8am-6pm).

PRACTICAL INFORMATION

Tourist and Travel Information

Tourist Office: Canberra Visitors Centre (tel. 6205 0044 or 1800 026 166; fax 6205 0776; http://www.canberratourism.com.au), on Northbourne Ave, about 3km north of Vernon Cir. Take bus #30, 31, 32, 39, 50, 80. Overflows with helpful staff and free brochures on many attractions. Pocket-sized map and the ever-useful *Bus Pack* for sale, $2 each. Free accommodations booking. Wheelchair accessible. Open M-F 9am-5:30pm, weekends 9am-5pm. **Canberra Tourism Booth** (tel. 6247 5611), inside Jolimont Tourist Centre, 2 blocks from the city bus interchange on City Walk, has a somewhat smaller selection. Open M-F 8:30-11:30am, 2:30-5:30pm, Sa-Su 11am-3pm.

N

Canberra
ACCOMMODATIONS
A Burton and Garran Hall
B City Walk Hotel
C Fenner Hall
D Kingston Hotel
  Backpackers
E Motel Monaro
F Victor Lodge Bed and
  Breakfast

TURNER

Haig Park

Masson St.

Frogatt St.

Barry Drive

BRADDON

Girrahween St.

Cluines Ross St.

Daley Rd.

North Rd.

University Ave.

Moore St.

Northbourne Ave.

Mort St.

Rugby Park

Cooyong St.

Donaldson St.

Australian National Botanic Gardens

ACTON

A

Childers St.

Marcus Clarke St.

Ellery Cres.

Rudd St.

Alinga St.

B

London Circuit

Petrie Pl.

Petrie St.

Ballumbir St.

Bunda St.

City Walk

Akuna St.

Ainslie Ave.

REID

Limestone Ave.

Australian War Memorial

Park

Australian National University

National Film and Sound Archive

Gordon St.

McCoy Cct.

Edinburgh

CITY

VERNON CIRCLE

Glebe Park

Coranderrk St.

Euree St.

Reid

Anzac Pde.

Balmain Cct.

London Circuit

Allara St.

footbridge

London

Parkes Way

Archbishop's Residence

Constitution Ave.

St. John the Baptist

Parkes Way

Commonwealth Park

Captain Cook Memorial Water Jet

Blundells' Cottage

Lake Burley Griffin

Commonwealth Ave.

Flynn Dr.

National Library

National Science and Technology Centre

PARKES

High Court

RUSSELL

National Carillon

Alexandrina Dr.

STIRLING PARK

Coronation Dr.

National Rose Garden

Parkes Place

King Edward Tce.

King George Tce.

National Gallery of Australia

Kings Park

Forster Cr.

Queen Victoria Tce.

Old Parliament House

Kings Ave.

Lake Burley Griffin

Perth Ave.

State Circle

Capital Circle

Federation Mall

Bowen Dr.

Arkana St.

BARTON

Adelaide Ave.

CAPITAL HILL

Prime Minister's Lodge

Parliament House

Brisbane Ave.

State Circle

Sydney Ave.

DEAKIN

Empire Circuit

Melbourne Ave.

FORREST

Hobart Ave.

National Circuit

Canberra Ave.

Telopea Park

Wentworth Ave.

Dominion Circuit

Empire Circuit

Collins Park

Tasmania Circle

MANUKA

Manuka Park

Manuka Circle

Giles St.

Eyre St.

Dawes St.

E

F

KINGSTON

Train Station

D

Captain Cook Cr.

Mugga Way

Arthur Circle

GRIFFITH

Canberra Ave.

HUME PLACE

Gowrie Dr.

0   300 yards

0   300 meters

Budget Travel Office: STA Travel, 13-15 Garema Place (tel. 6247 8633; Fast Fares tel. 1300 360 960; email traveller@statravelaus.com.au; http://www.statrave-laus.com.au), on the corner of City Walk. Open M-F 9am-5pm, Sa 10am-4pm.

Financial Services

Currency Exchange: Thomas Cook (tel. 6247 9984; fax 6249 7469), Canberra Centre shopping mall, Bunda St, corner of Petrie Plaza. 1% fee on non-Thomas Cook traveler's checks and currency exchange. Open M-F 9am-5pm, Sa 9:30am-12:30pm.

American Express: Shop 1, Centrepoint, 185 City Walk (tel. 6247 2333), on the corner of Petrie Plaza. Cardholders and Traveller's Cheque users can have mail held for 3 weeks at no charge. Send mail ATTN: Client Mail, P.O. Box 153, Civic Square ACT 2608. No fee for AMEX Traveller's Cheque transactions. Currency exchange incurs a 1% fee, $3 minimum. Open M-F 8:30am-5pm, Sa 9am-noon.

Local Business Hours and Holidays: Usually M-F 9am-5pm, but shopping centers stay open until 9pm on Friday. In addition, most stores are open Sa 9am-4pm and Su 10am-4pm. Many local banks close at 4pm M-F and are open Saturday mornings.

Embassies and Consulates

Unless specified as south of the lake or in Forrest, all locations are in Yarralumla.

Britain (tel. 6270 6666, visas 6257 1982, passports 6257 2434; fax 6257 5857), on Commonwealth Ave. Open M-F 9am-4:30pm. Phone inquiries taken M-F 10am-4:30pm. **Canada** (tel. 6273 3844; fax 6273 3285), on Commonwealth Ave, south of the lake. Open for consular services M-F 8:30am-12:30pm and 1-4:30pm. **France,** 6 Perth Ave (tel. 6216 0100). For personal passport or visa matters, contact the consulate in Sydney. **Germany,** 119 Empire Circuit (tel. 6270 1911; fax 6270 1951). Open M and W-Th 8am-noon, Tu 2-4pm, F noon-2pm. **Indonesia,** 8 Darwin Ave (tel. 6250 8600; fax 6273 3545). Open M-Th 9am-12:30pm and 2-5pm, F 9am-4:30pm. **Ireland,** 20 Arkana St (tel. 6273 3022; fax 6273 3741). Open M-F 9:30am-12:45pm and 2-5pm. **Japan,** 112 Empire Circuit (tel. 6273 3244; fax 6273 1848). Open M-F 9am-12:30pm and 2-5pm. **New Zealand** (tel. 62704211; fax 6273 3194), on Commonwealth Ave, south of the lake. For consular services, contact the consulate in Sydney. **South Africa** (tel. 6273 2424; fax 6273 3543), on the corner of State Circle and Rhodes Pl. Open M-F 8:30am-5pm. **Switzerland,** 7 Melbourne Ave. (tel. 6273 3977), in Forrest. Passport and visa matters handled in Sydney. **Thailand,** 111 Empire Circuit (tel. 6273 1149; fax 6273 1518). Open M-F 9am-12:30pm, 1:30-4pm. **USA,** Moonah Place (tel. 6214 5600). Open M, W, and F 8:30-11:30am. For visa inquiries, call M-F 2-4pm.

Emergency, Health, and Social Services

Public Markets: Gorman House Markets (tel. 6249 7377), on Ainslie Ave between Currong and Doonkuma St (Sa 10am-4pm), the **Hall Markets** (tel. 6282 4411), at the Hall Showground (Feb.-Dec. 1st Su of the month, 10am-3pm) and the **Old Bus Depot Markets,** 49 Wentworth Ave (tel. 6292 8391; Su 10am-4pm).

Library: ACT Library Service (tel. 6207 5155; fax 6207 5052), inside the Civic shopfront, on East Row between Alinga St and London Circuit. Open M-Th 10am-5pm, F 10am-7pm, Sa 9:30am-5pm. (See also National Library of Australia, p. 78)

Bookstores: Travelers Maps and Guides (tel. 6249 6006), inside the Jolimont Tourist Centre. Open M-F 8am-6pm, Sa 9am-5pm, Su 10am-5pm.

Ticket Agencies: Ticketek (tel. 6248 7666; http://www.ticketek.com.au), GIO building, Akuna St, Civic. Open M-F 9am-5pm, Sa 9am-noon.

Late-Night Pharmacy: Day and Night Chemist, 7 Sargood St (tel. 6248 7050 or 6249 1919), in the O'Connor Shopping Centre. Open daily 9am-11pm. **Urgent Prescription Service** (tel. 6249 1919) operates after 11pm for emergencies.

Hotlines: Lifeline (general depression counseling; 24hr. tel. 6257 1111). **Drug and Alcohol Crisis Line** (24hr. tel. 6205 4545). **Poison Information Centre** (24hr. tel. 13 11 26). **Gay/Lesbian Line** (tel. 6247 2726), M-F 6-10pm. **Women's Information and Referral Service** (tel. 6205 1075), M-F 9am-5pm.

Hospital/Medical Services: Canberra Hospital (tel. 6244 2222; 24hr. emergency line 6244 2324), on Yamba Dr, Garren. Follow signs to Woden heading southwest from Capital Hill. **Travelers Medical and Vaccination Centre** (tel. 6257 7156),

inside City Walk Arcade on the second level. Advice and vaccinations for tropical diseases. Consultations $35-52. Open M-W and F 8:30am-5pm, Th 8:30am-8pm.
Police: (tel. 6256 7777), on London Circuit opposite University Ave.
Emergency: Dial 000.

Post and Communications

Internet Access: The **ACT Library Service** (see above) and the National Library (see **Sights,** below) offer free 30min. sessions. **Cyberchino**, 33 Kennedy St (tel. 6295 7844; http://www.cyberchino.com.au), in Kingston has full-service access and delicious hot cocoa. $6 for 30min., $10 for 1hr. with $3 minimum charge; Mondays ½ price. Open daily 8:30am-midnight. The kiosk at the **Jolimont Tourist Centre** costs $2 per 10min.
Post Office: General Post Office (GPO), 53-73 Alinga St (tel. 6209 1680). Open M-F 8:30am-5:30pm. **Australia Post** at Civic Square, outside Canberra Centre mall, has stamps and counter service. Open M-F 8:30am-5:30pm, Sa 10am-1:30pm.
Postal Code: 2601.
Phone Code: 02.

ACCOMMODATIONS AND CAMPING

Book ahead during public holidays. Check-out is generally at 10am.

Hostels and Dorms

◉**Victor Lodge Bed and Breakfast,** 29 Dawes St (tel./fax 6295 7777), 6km south of the city center in Kingston. Free pick-up in Civic at Jolimont Tourist Centre daily 7am-8pm. Bus #38 or 39 from the city bus interchange stops 2 blocks away on Eyre St. So clean and accommodating that the staff actually washes up after hostelers in the kitchen. TV, no smoking. Within biking distance of Parliamentary Triangle (bikes $12 full day, $8 half day). Reception open daily 7:30am-10pm. Check-out 10am. Dorms $18; singles $36; doubles $46. Weekly: singles $185. VIP. Linen and breakfast included. Laundry $2.40 to wash, $1.60 to dry. Key deposit $10.
Canberra YHA Hostel (YHA), 191 Dryandra St (tel. 6248 9155; fax 6249 1731; email yha@yhansw.com.au), 5km northwest of the city center in O'Connor. Take bus #35 from the city interchange, and follow the signs from the stop at the corner of Miller and Scrivener St. By car, follow Northbourne Ave north from city center. Take a left on MacArthur, go 2km, and turn right on Dryandra. Pretty Refreshingly communal feel, with large kitchen, TV/pool rooms. Cinderblock dorms are less than cozy. Reception open daily 7am-10pm. Travel desk, bike rental (half day $11, full day $16), off-street parking, small store, laundry. Internet kiosk $2 for 20min. Dorms $16, under 18 $8; twins $21-23, $11. Linen $2. Key deposit $10.
Kingston Hotel Backpackers, 73 Canberra Ave (tel. 6295 0123; fax 6295 7871), on the corner of Giles St in Kingston, about 7km from Civic. Take bus #38 or 39. Canberra's least expensive, most basic pub accommodation, the "Kingo" provides clean dorms with sinks and a popular downstairs bar and restaurant combo. The mattresses and shared bathrooms could use an upgrade, but for the price, no one's complaining. 1- to 4-bed dorms $12 per person. Linen $4. Key deposit $10.
Australian National University (housing tel. 6249 3454) offers accommodation in several residence halls. **Toad Hall** (tel. 6267 4999), on Kingsley St on campus, 3 blocks west of Northbourne Ave via Barry Dr, is the only one offering term-time lodging for travelers. Singles $16. Office open M-F 9am-5pm. The much nicer, recently refurbished **Fenner Hall,** 210 Northbourne Ave (tel. 6279 9000, after-hours warden 6279 9017), is located closer to Civic, but generally has rooms only during uni holidays; it's worth calling during term-time just in case. Singles $25, students $18. Open M, W, F 8:30am-12:30pm and 1:30-5pm; Tu, Th 8:30am-12:30pm and 2-7:30pm. Other holiday-only housing in **Burton and Garran Hall** (tel. 6267 4700), on Daley Rd on campus. Singles $31, students $22.50. (Open M-F 8:30am-12:30pm and 1:30-5pm.) All 3 halls have ample kitchens and shared baths.
City Walk Hotel, 2 Mort St (tel. 6257 0124; fax 6257 0116; email citywalk@ozemail.com.au), visible from the city bus interchange. Privacy is scarce in the 14-bed dorms; still, this is the only budget accommodation in the city center, within walking distance of the bus interchange and much of the town's nightlife. Kitchen, TV

room, laundry. Dorms $18-20; singles $38, with bath $52; doubles $47, with bath $57. Reception open M-Sa 7:30am-10pm, Su 7:30am-7pm. Wheelchair accessible, though elevator runs only 7:30am-10pm. Weekly: 7th night free. Linen included.

Camping

Canberra Motor Village (tel. 6247 5466 or 1800 026 199; fax 6249 6138), 4km northwest of the City Center, on Kunzea St, O'Connor. Take Bus #35 to Miller and Macarthur Ave. By car, follow Northbourne Ave north from Civic, turn left on Macarthur, go 2km and turn right on Dryandra, and take an immediate left on Kunzea. Toilets, showers, laundry, tennis courts, barbecue, pool, store, restaurant, playground. Sites $10; for 2 $11; family of 4 $18. With power and water $16; $20; $25. Each extra person $2. Reception 24hr. Wheelchair-accessible facilities available.

Canberra Carotel (tel. 6241 1377; fax 6241 6674), 6km north of the city center, on Federal Hwy in Watson and the #39 bus line. By car, follow Northbourne Ave out of town until it becomes Federal Hwy. Restaurant, store, swimming pool, playground, barbecue, toilets, showers, and laundry. Reception open M-F 7am-9pm, Sa-Su 7am-8pm. Tent sites for 2 $10, powered $12; each extra person $2. On-site caravans with cooking facilities for 1 person $30; each additional person up to 4 $3. Cabins for 2 people (no cooking facilities) $45; cabins with cooking facilities for up to 5 people (wheelchair accessible) $90, but much higher during public holidays.

Motels and Guesthouses

⊕**Blue and White Lodge,** 524 Northbourne Ave, and the affiliated **Blue Sky Lodge,** 528 Northbourne Ave (tel. for both 6248 0498; fax 6248 8277), Downer, 4km north of the city center. Bus #50 passes out front. Canberra's next step up from hostel lodging is a big one. It's hard to differentiate between the string of B&Bs on Northbourne, but these two identical guesthouses offer TVs, fridges, and kettles in all rooms. Full cooked breakfast served daily 7:30am-8:30am. Reception open daily 7am-8:30pm. Singles $55, with ensuite bath $70; doubles $70, $80.

Northbourne Lodge, 522 Northbourne Ave (tel. 6257 2599), next door to the Blue and White. Slightly more upscale; all rooms have ensuite bathrooms and full amenities. Cooked English breakfasts served each morning between 7:30am and 9am. Reception open daily 7:30am-midnight. Owner always reachable via courtesy phone. Singles $69; doubles $85. Skip breakfast and all prices drop around $10. Weekly rates available, as are special standby rates on non-busy nights.

Motel Monaro, 27 Dawes St (tel. 6295 2111; fax 6295 2466), in Kingston, 6km from Civic. Take bus #38 or 39. A standard Best Western, with TV, fridge, toaster, hair dryer, and other electrical goodies in each room. Family units are a good deal with the per-person pricing system. Rooms for one $62-70; each additional person $10.

FOOD

In a city populated by government officials, cheap food is never easy to find. Cafes in the city center and the food court at Canberra Centre provide welcome exceptions. For many medium-price restaurants with excellent, primarily Asian cuisines, visit Woolley St in Dickson, off Northbourne Ave on Bunda St across from Canberra Centre. The **City Market** complex packs in fruit stands, butcher shops, and prepared food stalls in a variety of flavors and prices. At the heart of the complex lies the **Supabarn** supermarket (tel. 6257 4055), the biggest grocery outpost in the city center (open M-Th 8am-9pm, F 8am-10pm, Sa-Su 8am-8pm). **Woolworths** has locations in Manuka (tel. 6295 0738) on Flinders Way, and in Dickson (tel. 6249 6809). Both stores are open daily 7am-midnight.

⊕**Dickson Asian Noodle House,** 29 Woolley St (tel. 6247 6380), in Dickson. Take bus #38 or #35 on weekends. Succulent platefuls of stir-fry noodles and a variety of spicy Thai dishes ($8.50-11) make this the kind of restaurant where locals keep coming back to try every item on the menu. Vegetable dishes $7-8. Dine in or take advantage of speedy takeaway service. Open daily 11:30am-11pm. BYO.

Fisho Cafe, 48 Giles St (tel. 6295 3153), across from Tench St. Take bus #38 or #39. Amid the bustle of the Kingston Shops, this cafe quietly earns rave reviews for fresh fish and elegant preparation. Mussels marinara $9.50; pastas $12, risottos $13. Licensed and BYO, bottles only. Corkage $4.50. Open daily 10am-10pm.

Sizzle City (tel. 6248 5399), on Bunda St at the entrance to the City Market. A Japanese hole-in-the-wall serving tasty, fresh sushi at great prices. Construct your own combo from individual pieces or take a ready-made lunch ($6-9). Vegetarian lunch $7.50. Open M-Th and Sa 11am-5pm, F 9am-9pm. Another branch, called **Sizzle Bento,** is located on City Walk across from Garema Place, and is open on Sundays.

Tu Tu Tango, 124 Bunda St (tel. 6257 7100; fax 6257 7288), between Petrie Plaza and Garema Place, offers Southwestern American (Santa Fe style) cuisine with a gourmet twist. Classy decor and outdoor seating. Wood-fired pizzas $13.90, wraps $10.50. Licensed and BYO, bottled wine only. Corkage $4. Open daily 10am-late.

The Pancake Parlor, downstairs on the corner of East Row and Alinga St in Civic (tel. 6247 2982, fax 6248 5743). Booths and a blazing hearth make the Parlor a great place for group gatherings, especially for the Wednesday night 5-course, all-you-can-eat pancake and crepe feast ($13). Mains range from $10-13, loading everything from steak to fish onto pancakes. Open daily 7am-10:30pm, F-Sa 24hr.

La Capanna, 32 Giles St in Kingston (tel. 6239 6712). The lines at this trendy pizza and pasta restaurant are long at dinnertime, probably because the prices for their big portions blow away their neighboring competitors (most dishes under $12). Grilled foccacias ($6.50) and a range of tasty pizzas are especially good value. BYO wine only. $1 corkage per head. Open daily 12noon-2:30pm, 6pm-10:30pm.

SIGHTS

Lookouts

A stop at one of the city's lookouts is an appropriate start to a sight-seeing tour of the capital. From a hill in Commonwealth Park, at Regatta Point on the north shore of Lake Burley Griffin, the **National Capital Exhibition** (tel. 6257 1068; fax 6247 1875) includes not just a vista but exhibits on the planning, construction, and growth of Canberra. *(Open in summer daily 9am-6pm; in winter 9am-5pm. Free. Wheelchair accessible.)* Farther back from the city's center, **Mt. Ainslie** and **Black Mountain** offer broader views of the city. Located north of Lake Burley Griffin and east of the city center, Mt. Ainslie rises to a height of 845m to overlook the lake, the Parliamentary Triangle, and the Australian War Memorial, providing the classic postcard view down Anzac Pde. To reach the summit by car, take Fairbairn Ave east from the end of Anzac Pde to Mt. Ainslie Dr. Trails lead to the top from behind the War Memorial. The two lookout points on Black Mountain look down on the city in different directions. The first, on Black Mountain Dr, accessible by taking Barry Dr to Clunies Ross St and heading southwest, faces southeast and takes in the Parliamentary Triangle and Lake Burley Griffin. The second viewpoint faces north toward the surrounding countryside and the Australian Institute of Sport. From the peak of Black Mountain, **Telstra Tower** (tel. 6248 1911 or 1800 806 718; fax 6257 6600) climbs an additional 195m to ensure an unobstructed view in every direction. *(Tower open daily 9am-10pm. Admission $3, seniors and ages 4-16 $1, under 4 free.)* Exhibits in the tower treat the history of Australian telecommunications, and the cafe at the top is much more affordable (sandwiches around $9) than the revolving restaurant below it.

Parliamentary Triangle

A showpiece of grand architecture and cultural attractions, Canberra's Parliamentary Triangle is the center of the capital. **Parliament House** (tel. 6277 5399; fax 6277 5068), the focal point of the triangle, takes the ideal of unifying architecture with the landscape to a new level. The building is actually built into Capital Hill so that its two sides seem to jut out of the earth, leaving the grassy hilltop on its roof undisturbed and open to the public 24 hours a day. Perched atop this landmark is a four-pronged stainless steel flagpole visible from nearly every part of Canberra. Inside, the free guided tours conducted every half hour give a good overview of both the unique features of the building and the workings of the government housed inside. *(Open daily 9am-5pm. Free. Wheelchair accessible.)* Visitors can also observe both houses of Parliament from galleries. The House of Representatives, which fills up more often then the Senate, allows people to book seats in advance by calling ahead (tel. 6277 4889). The televised **Question Time** provides particularly viewer-friendly acrimony.

Old Parliament House (tel. 6270 8222; fax 6270 8111) served as Australia's seat of government from 1927 until 1988, when the current Parliament House was completed. *(Open daily 9am-4pm. $2, students, seniors, and ages 4-16 $1, families $5. Wheelchair accessible.)* The building is aligned with the front of Parliament House, 500m closer to the lake, and now serves as a political history museum and home to the **National Portrait Gallery** (tel. 6270 8210; fax 6270 8181). Daily tours occur on the half hour. Admission to Old Parliament House covers the National Portrait Gallery and any current exhibits.

The third tier of the Parliamentary Triangle is comprised of the four large modern building on Parkes Place, just off King Edward Tce. On the southeastern end, nearest Kings Ave, the **National Gallery of Australia** (tel. 6240 6411; fax 6240 6529; http://www.nga.gov.au) displays an extensive Australian collection, including Aboriginal works and a good contemporary collection. *(Open daily 10am-5pm. Free 1hr. guided tours daily 11am and 2pm. Aboriginal art tour Th, Su 11am. Admission $3; pensioners, students and age 4-16 free; separate fees for special exhibits. Wheelchair accessible.)* The surrounding sculpture garden is free and open 24 hours. Next door, the **High Court of Australia** (tel. 6270 6811 or 6270 6850; fax 6273 3025) presents a seven-story wall of glass and steel on the outside of its grand public hall. *(Open M-F 9:45am-4:30pm; free. Wheelchair accessible.)* When court is in session, visitors may watch the proceedings in Australia's highest court from public galleries in the three court rooms.

The **National Science and Technology Centre,** also known as **Questacon** (tel. 6270 2800; fax 6270 2808), is on the court's northwest side and is a several-hour experience. *(Open daily 10am-5pm. Admission $8, students and seniors $5, ages 4-16 $4. Wheelchair accessible.)* Interactive devices mete out entertaining science lessons to people of all ages. Free displays at the entrance let you sample before you pay. The final stop on Parkes Place, the **National Library of Australia** (tel. 6262 1111; fax 6257 1703) is open for research and for casual visitation. *(Open M-Th 9am-9pm, F-Sa 9am-5pm, Su 1:30-5pm. Tours Tu-Th 12:30pm. Wheelchair accessible.)* The nation's largest library (6 million books) mounts excellent exhibitions (call 6262 1156 for program) and provides free Internet access.

The last two attractions in the Parliamentary Triangle are actually located *in* Lake Burley Griffin. The **Captain Cook Memorial Jet** blows a six-ton column of water to heights of up to 147m to commemorate Captain James Cook's arrival at the east coast of Australia. Hey, why not? The bell tower of the **National Carillon** (tel. 6257 1068) is located on Aspen Island at the other end of the lake's central basin. A gift from Britain on Canberra's 50th birthday in 1963, the Carillon is played several times per week for 45-minute concerts. *(M-F 12-45pm, Sa-Su 2-45pm; in summer also Th 5:45pm.)*

Northeast

Anzac Pde extends northeast from Parkes Way, continuing the line formed by the old and new Parliament Houses across the lake toward the crucifix-shaped **Australian War Memorial** (tel. 6243 4211; fax 6243 4325), on bus route #33 from Civic. *(Open daily 10am-5pm. Tours daily 10, 10:30, 11am, 1:30, and 2pm. Free. Wheelchair accessible.)* The war-related artifacts and photos, as well as depictions of life in wartime by major Australian artists, make the Memorial a moving, popular tribute. Exhibitions are organized according to military campaign. The Hall of Memory holds the tomb of an unknown Australian soldier underneath a beautiful handmade mosaic dome.

The nearby **St. John the Baptist Church** (tel. 6248 8399; fax 6247 5481), on the corner of Anzac Pde and Constitution Ave, has given services since 1845, long before the current city rose up around it. *(Open daily 9am-5pm; museum open W 10am-noon, Sa-Su. 2-4pm.)* The church's former schoolhouse is now a museum of pioneer life in Canberra. **Blundells' Cottage** (tel. 6273 2667), on Wendouree Dr off Constitution Ave, is an 1860 house built as lodging for the people who once farmed the land where Lake Burley Griffin is today. *(Open Tu-Su 10am-4pm, last entry 3:30pm; admission $2, students, seniors, and ages 5-14 $1, families $5.)* Blundells' has a "please touch" philosophy regarding its relics. From this area, the 79m-tall **Australian-American Memorial,** a simple column topped by an eagle to commemorate Australian and American cooperation in WWII, is hard to miss. The base stems from the eastern end of Kings Ave.

Northwest

One of Canberra's least-sung and most enjoyable attractions, the **National Film and Sound Archive** (tel. 6209 3035; fax 6209 3165), on McCoy Circuit in Acton, is a bonanza of sight and sound relics of Australia's radio, film, and television industries, from the 1800s to today. *(Open daily 9am-5pm. Admission varies. Wheelchair accessible.)* Just behind the archive sits **Australian National University** (tel. 6249 0794; fax 6249 5568), and both are best reached by bus #34 to Liversedge St. The contemporary art exhibits at the uni's **Drill Hall Gallery** (tel. 6249 5832), on Kingsley St, justify a visit. *(Open W-Su 12noon-5pm; free.)* The **Australian National Botanic Gardens** (tel. 6250 9540; fax 6250 9599) run along the northwestern border of the campus on Clunies Ross St at the foot of Black Mountain. *(Open daily 9am-5pm; free; wheelchairs available. Free concerts Sa evenings in Jan. Guided walks daily 11am.)* Bus #34 stops nearby on Daley Rd, leaving a 15-minute walk towards the lake along Clunies Ross Rd. Its flora include 30% of all Australian species and a rainforest that's well outside the norm for the middle of Canberra.

From Parkes Way, heading out of the city to the west, Lady Denman Dr branches south toward the **National Aquarium and Australian Wildlife Sanctuary** (tel. 6287 1211; fax 6288 0477) at Scrivener Dam. *(Open daily 9am-5:30pm. Admission $10, students, seniors, ages 4-16 $6, under 4 free, families $32. Wheelchair accessible.)* The trip from the city center is made worthwhile by the aquarium's diving tanks and underwater tunnel exhibit, and the nearly 7-hectare sanctuary for native Australian fauna.

The **Australian Institute of Sport (AIS)** (tel. 6252 1444 or 6252 1010; http://www.ausport.gov.au/aistours.html), on Leverrier Circle just northwest of O'Connor, was established in 1981 as a training facility for the nation's top athletes. *(Reservations tel. 6252 1281. Pool use $3.50. Outside courts $8 per hr. Admission with 1½hr. tour $8, ages 5-15 $4, families $20. Take bus #80 from Civic. Open M-F 8:30am-4:45pm, Sa-Su 9:45am-4:15pm.)* Tours led by athletes working at the institute take regular humans through the world of the aerobically, nutritionally, and electronically conditioned. If you're inspired to work out, there's public access to the pool and tennis courts.

Southwest

West of Capital Hill on the south side of the lake, **Yarralumla** is peppered with the **embassies** of over 70 nations, displaying a multicultural melange of architectural styles. The **Lodge,** home to the Australian Prime Minister, is on Adelaide Ave, but it's closed to the public. Farther west pm Adelaide, the **Royal Australian Mint** (tel. 6202 6999 or 6202 6819; email ramint@netinfo.com.au), on Denison St in Deakin allows you to watch coins being produced. *(Open M-F 9am-4pm, Sa-Su 10am-3pm; coin production M-F 9am-noon and 12:40-4pm. Free. Wheelchair accessible.)*

NIGHTLIFE AND ENTERTAINMENT

Though Sydneysiders with a superiority complex sometimes scoff at it, Canberra's after-hours scene is surprisingly vibrant. The student population supports a solid range of bars and clubs, while relaxed licensing allows boozing to continue till 4am. Most places claim to close "late," meaning midnight on slow nights and until people stop raging on busier nights. Canberra has fewer pub-style watering holes than most Australian cities, tending toward dance clubs and sleeker bars. The Thursday *Good Times* supplement in the *Canberra Times* has a full roster of entertainment options.

Clubs

Mooseheads, 105 Condon Circuit (tel. 6257 6496), is a rare Canadian pub, though without the maple leaf flags everywhere it might be difficult to tell. Lively throughout the week in the downstairs pub; the upstairs nightclub gyrates with techno and top-40 until 5am on Thursdays and Saturdays. Open M-Sa 11am-late.

ACT

Pandora's, on the corner of Alinga and Bunda St, near the bus interchange (tel. 6248 7405), is worth braving the queues for. Thursdays 9pm-midnight are "Jolly Jug" time (jugs of beer $5.50; jugs of spirits $8.50); Saturdays 9-11pm schooners of beer are $2. You can tell the place has seen some wild parties by the stickiness of the dance floor; the nearby balcony provides a fresh air escape for those who no longer want to bust a move. $4 cover Th and Sa. Open M-Sa 11am-late.

Heaven Nite Club (tel. 6257 6180), on Bunda St, in the center of Canberra's shopping and eating district. Largely gay male crowd, with techno beats so persistent they sometimes outlast the dark hours. Open Tu-F 9pm-late, Sa 10pm-Su 7am.

Pubs

Gypsy Bar (tel. 6247 7300), City Walk, has superb live music acts (Tu-Sa) that run the gamut from acoustic to heavy stuff, from local performers to big name Australian artists. Cover varies ($5-20) but the setting is always jovial enough to merit a visit. Open Tu-F 4:30pm-late, Sa 6:30pm-late, Su (blues night) 3pm-midnight.

ANU Student Uni Bar (tel. 6249 0786), on the corner of North Rd and University Ave in the student union building, is the big student hangout. Happy hour M-F 5-6pm (schooner of VB $1.90; normally $2.40). Hands down the cheapest pub in Canberra, with cover only for big live acts. Open M-Sa 12noon-late year-round.

La Grange Boutique Bar and Brasserie (tel. 6295 8866), on Franklin St in Manuka (bus routes #35, 39, or 84), caters to Canberra's thirty-somethings. Weekdays, the mellow bar scene spills over from dinner into the late hours. Becomes a dance club Th-Sa nights, with a noticeably younger crowd. Cover Sa $5. Open daily 2pm-late.

Other Entertainment

Casino Canberra, 21 Binara St (tel. 6257 7074) can help you strike it rich or lose it all, and the upstairs nightclub **Déjà Vu** lets people lounge around or get down on weekends. (Cover F $5, Sa $4; open F-Sa 9pm-late; casino open daily 12noon-6am.) In addition to the usual first-run cineplex theaters, Canberra has some artsy alternatives for the black-wearing set, including **Electric Shadows** (tel. 6247 5060), on Akuna St near City Walk (tickets $12, students $8). The **National Gallery** (tel. 6240 6502) offers free Friday matinees of videos and films on art and artists (12:45pm). The Gallery calendar has details, and occasionally features concerts and film festivals (tickets around $7).

Housing several venues in varying shapes and sizes, the **Canberra Theatre** (tel. 6257 1077 or 1800 802 025) is the best place to start looking for live entertainment. For information on the theater and other presentations at the **Australian National University** call *What's On Next Week* at 6249 0742.

Canberra's calendar is packed with minor **festivals,** but there are two annual events that temporarily transform the city. For 10 days in March (March 6-15 in 1999), **Canberra Festival** brings the capital to life with musical productions, a hot-air balloon show, and street parties. The last day of the festival is a public holiday, Canberra Day. Mid-September to mid-October ushers in **The Floriade** (tel. 1800 020 141), which paints the shores of Lake Burley Griffin with thousands of springtime blooms.

■ Sights South of Canberra

Bushland pushes in on Canberra's borders to offer a constant reminder of the city's youth and an easy retreat from its refinement. Most notably, **Tidbinbilla Nature Reserve** and **Namadgi National Park,** south of the city, together cover nearly half of the entire area of the ACT. *(Park open daily 9am-6pm. Admission $8 per car. Bring your own food. Several paths and visitors centre have wheelchair access.)* The **Tidbinbilla Visitor Centre** (tel. 6205 1233; fax 6205 1232), off Paddy's River Rd, a 40-minute drive southwest of Civic, has information on bushwalks and ranger-led activities throughout the 500-hectare park. *(Open daily 9am-6pm, 9am-9pm during summer.)* Dedicated to preserving the natural gum forest habitat of the kangaroos, wallabies, koalas, emus, and other animals who roam the area, the reserve loosely encloses its residents to better your chances of encountering them. Bushwalks in the park range from 30-minute strolls to day-long outings. The walk to Gibraltar rock (3hr. return) rewards easy hiking or not-so-easy rock climbing with stupendous views.

The expansive **Namadgi National Park** forms the western border of Tidbinbilla Nature Reserve, and fills almost all of the southern arm of the ACT with preserved alpine wilderness for bushwalkers of all expertise levels. Traversed by only one major road, Naas/Bobayan Rd, the park is noted for its untrammeled recesses accessible only to more serious hikers. The **Yankee Hat Trail** (3hr. return), signposted from the Bobayan Rd in the southern part of the park, is an excellent moderate hike which leads to an Aboriginal art site. The **Namadgi Visitor Centre** (tel. 6207 2900; fax 6207 2901), on the Naas/Bobayan Rd 3km south of **Tharwa**, distributes topographical maps and information on Aboriginal rock painting and camping in the park. *(Open daily 9am-4:30pm.)* **Campsites** at Orroral River and Mt. Clear, each with parking nearby, have firewood and toilets but little else and must be booked in advance ($2 per person). The water at the sites should be boiled before drinking.

Between Canberra and the parks, two attractions direct visitors' attention skyward. Off Cotter Rd, west of Canberra, about 15min. from New Parliament House (17km), lies the **Mt. Stromlo Exploratory** (tel. 6249 0276). *(Open daily 9:30am-4:30pm; admission $5, students, seniors, and ages 5-15 $3, family of 4 $12.)* This visitors center for **Mt. Stromlo Observatory** gives visitors a look at the work of professional astronomers through hands-on exhibits. On Wednesday nights (beginning around 7pm), visitors can pay $8 to take in the exhibitions, and can also stargaze through the powerful telescopes with the staff's guidance. One of the three most powerful antenna centers in the world, **Canberra Deep Space Communications Complex,** off Paddy's River Rd, is for serious space junkies. The 70m radio dish tracks and records signals from orbiting spacecraft, and the visitors info center, known as the **Canberra Space Centre** (tel. 6201 7800), has displays on the history of space exploration. *(Open daily 9am-8pm; in winter 9am-5pm.)*

Built in several stages over the course of the 1800s, the buildings at **Lanyon Homestead** (tel. 6237 5136; fax 6237 5202), on Tharwa Dr 30km south of the city, comprise a survey of Canberra's European history from the days of convict labor through the elegant colonial era. Meanwhile, an Aboriginal canoe tree on the grounds gives evidence of earlier habitation at the same site. Lanyon's greatest draw may be the **Nolan Gallery** (tel. 6237 5192; fax 6237 5794), located on the grounds. *(Open Tu-Su 10am-4pm; grounds open until 5pm. Admission to homestead buildings $5, students, seniors, and ages 5-15 $2.50, families $12. Gallery admission $2, $1, $5. Wheelchair accessible.)* The works at the gallery include several of Sidney Nolan's paintings of bushranger Ned Kelly.

■ Sights North of Canberra

The privately run **National Dinosaur Museum** (tel. 6230 2655; fax 6230 2357; email natdinom@interact.net.au), on the Barton Hwy at the corner of Gold Creek Rd, includes 10 full-sized dinosaur skeletons and three reconstructions complete with skin and teeth. *(Open daily 10am-5pm. Admission $8, students and seniors $6, ages 4-16 $5, families $23.)* Also off Barton Hwy at O'Hanlon Pl, **Cockington Green** (tel. 6230 2273 or 1800 627 273; fax 6230 2490) transports travelers to a Kingdom far, far away, with miniature reproductions of buildings from Britain and elsewhere set among winding garden paths and sculptured bushes. *(Open daily 9:30am-4:30pm. Admission $7.95, seniors $5.95, children $3.95, families $22.50.)* **Murray's** (tel. 13 22 51) runs a daily tour to Cockington Green which covers travel and admission, and allows for approximately two hours there. *($18, seniors $13, children $5; departs Jolimont Centre daily 10am.)*

Just over the New South Wales border on the Murrumbidgee River, **Ginninderra Falls** sits at the center of a park bearing the same name (tel. 6237 5160). *(Open daily 10am-5:30pm. Admission $5, students and seniors $2, children $1.)* The falls themselves spill down the 200m **Ginninderra Ravine** and provide spectacular views from several bushwalking trails. The park is also known for its rock climbing faces.

A
C
T

New South Wales

From a historical perspective, there's no disputing that New South Wales is Australia's premier state. It was here that British convicts lived through the first bitter years of colonization, dreaming of what might lie beyond the impassable Blue Mountains, and here that explorers first broke through the Great Dividing Range, opening the interior of the country for settlement and ensuring the stability of the colony. In the central plains and on the rich land of the Riverina, Merino wool and agricultural success provided the state with its first glimpses of prosperity. Then, in 1851, prospectors struck gold just west of the mountains, and Australia's history changed forever. No longer the desolate prison of exiled convicts, New South Wales became a place that promised new life and a chance to strike it rich. Although the gold rush days are over, New South Wales has continued to grow. Today, it's the most populous state and the well-touristed, diverse, and sophisticated center of modern Australia.

The country's biggest and flashiest city, capital Sydney sits midway down the New South Wales coast. All along the coast, sandy beaches string together in an almost unbroken scenic strip. Many are great for surfing and swimming, and most are open to the public. The trip up the coast from Sydney is the be-all-end-all of backpacker party routes, while the south coast is colder and far less touristy but every bit as beautiful. Directly west of Sydney's suburban reaches and just 100km inland, the Blue Mountains separate the coastal strip and its hinterlands from the expansive Central West and outback regions. Once an insurmountable obstacle, the mountains now encompass some of the state's favorite getaways. The New England Plateau, along the Great Dividing Range north of the wineries of the Hunter Valley, achieves an unusually lush and high-altitude setting for a cozy collection of small Australian towns. Just below the carved-out enclave of the Australian Capital Territory, the Snowy Mountains offer winter skiing and superb summer hiking. The attractions of New South Wales are as varied as the terrain. Whether it's challenging bushwalks, laid-back surf culture, cosmopolitan fun, or the simplicity of the outback, most visitors find something to write home about.

🦘 NEW SOUTH WALES HIGHLIGHTS

- The bumpin' nightlife in **Sydney's** King Cross and Oxford St (see p. 112).
- Living the unexamined life in **Byron Bay** (see p. 178).
- Sweet, sweet sand and sun on the copious beaches in **Sydney** (see p. 83).
- Escaping Sydney to the great outdoors of the **Blue Mountains** (see p. 124).
- Sampling the fine wines of the **Hunter Valley** (see p. 185).
- Exploring the underwater world of **Jervis Bay** (see p. 198).
- Skiing at **Thredbo** (see p. 205), one of the top slopes down under.
- Exploring ancient archaeology on a **Mungo National Park** tour (see p. 224).
- **Nimbin** (see p. 175), where the only culture is counterculture.

PRACTICAL INFORMATION

For general assistance in planning a trip to New South Wales the **New South Wales Holiday Information** (tel. 13 20 77) is a good start. You can arrange accommodation directly through the **Tourism NSW** website (http://www.tourism.nsw.gov.au). For those who want to visit Australia one watering hole at a time, the free **Pubstays** booklet has a listing of over 50 participating NSW pubs. Pick it up at any tourist office, or call 1800 807 772. For the hostel-inclined, **YHA NSW**, 422 Kent St, Sydney (tel. 9261 1111; fax 9261 1969; http://www.yha.org.au; email yha@yhansw.org.au), can give you a full list of budget hostels at over 30 locations, tell you about how to become a YHA member, and sell you vouchers for use at any YHA. Smaller backpackers' places band together in a quasi-official group called "Small, Clean, and Friendly Accommodation." Their brochure, with a list of members, is available at member hostels, of which the **Wattle House** (tel. 9552 4997) in Sydney and **Blue Mountains Backpackers** (tel. 4782 4226) are two of the most prominent. The **Bed and Breakfast Council of New South Wales** (tel. 9918 6932) lists over 100 B&Bs.

The **National Parks and Wildlife Services** have offices throughout the state. The branch offices that administer particular campgrounds are listed throughout the chapter. For general info, check their website (http://www.npws.gov.au) or ask at the office in the Rocks in Sydney (tel. 9247 5033).

For camping or other outside activity planning, contact the **State Forests of NSW**, Building 2, 423 Pennant Hills Rd, Pennant Hills NSW 2120 (tel. (03) 9980 4296). Other helpful contacts are the **NSW Confederation of Bushwalking Clubs**, GPO Box 2090, Sydney NSW 2001 (recorded information tel. (02) 9548 1228; http://www.bushwalking.org.au), the **Yachting Association of NSW**, P.O. Box 537, Glebe NSW 2037 (tel. (02) 9660 1266; fax 9552 6159; http://www.yachting.nsw.org.au), and the **NSW Canoe Association** (tel. 9660 4597; fax 9518 7859).

New South Wales has an excellent **public transportation** system, especially in the eastern part of the state. For timetables or route info regarding bus, rail, or ferries in Sydney and throughout the state, call **Cityrail** (tel. 13 15 00) or **Countrylink** (tel. 13 22 32). NSW's AAA affiliate is the **National Roads and Motorists Association (NRMA)**, whose main office is at 151 Clarence St, Sydney (tel. 13 11 22 or 9892 0355; open M-F 9am-5pm, Sa 9am-noon), in the block between King and Barrack St. NRMA publishes maps of Sydney and New South Wales, free to members and members of affiliated national autoclubs. Mechanical inspections cost $105, or $125 for nonmembers. Members, and members of affiliated national auto clubs (see **Essentials**, p. 34), can also call for roadside assistance. (Membership $84 for the first year, $44 per additional year.)

If you decide to move on from New South Wales, there are several tourist bureaus in Sydney which can be of assistance. The **Queensland Travel Centre** has offices at 327 George St (tel. 9246 7000; fax 9246 7046) and 75 Castlereagh St (tel. 9209 8600; fax 9209 8686). (Open M-W, F 8am-6pm, Th 8am-7pm, Sa 9am-4pm, George St office also open Su 11am-3pm.) The office for **Tourism Victoria** (tel. 9299 2288 or 13 28 42; fax 9299 2288) is at 403 George St (open M-F 9am-5pm). **Australian Holiday Center**, 247 Pitt St, mezzanine (tel. 9264 3374; fax 9264 2279), is the best bet for South Australian info (open M-F 9am-5pm). **Tasmanian Tourism**, 149 King St (tel. 9202 2055 or 1800 806 846; fax 9202 2055), is open M-F 9am-5pm and Sa 10am-2pm. The **Northern Territory Tourist Commission** can be reached at 1800 621 336. For tourism info on the **ACT** call 1800 026 166 or fax 6205 0076. Call the **Western Australian Tourism Commission** (tel. 1300 361 351 or (08) 9483 1111) for info on Western Australia. The **New Zealand Tourism Board** (tel. 1902 260 558; fax 9241 1136) is at 35 Pitt St, level 8.

Phone numbers in New South Wales have recently changed. Regional phone codes are now **almost all** 02, followed by eight-digit numbers. If you have trouble making a call, try adding a zero at the beginning, which was the old system. Conversely, if you happen upon an outdated number with a three-digit regional code and a six-digit number, try dropping the zero and dialing the remaining eight digits. Border towns may take the Queensland or South Australia phone codes.

SYDNEY

Sometimes elegant, sometimes wacked-out, and always amazing, Sydney pulses with energy and swaggers with the self-assurance that comes from being one of the world's great cities. This is where it all goes down, where most international travelers first touch Australian soil and find themselves in a cosmopolitan whirlwind set against a backdrop of concrete, bright lights, and gorgeous waterfront. It isn't quite as overwhelmingly fast-paced as some cities of equal size; this is Australia, after all, famous for its no-worries attitude. Everyday life here hums along to an exciting but manageable beat. Diversity is to be expected in a huge city, and Sydney (pop. 3,775,000,

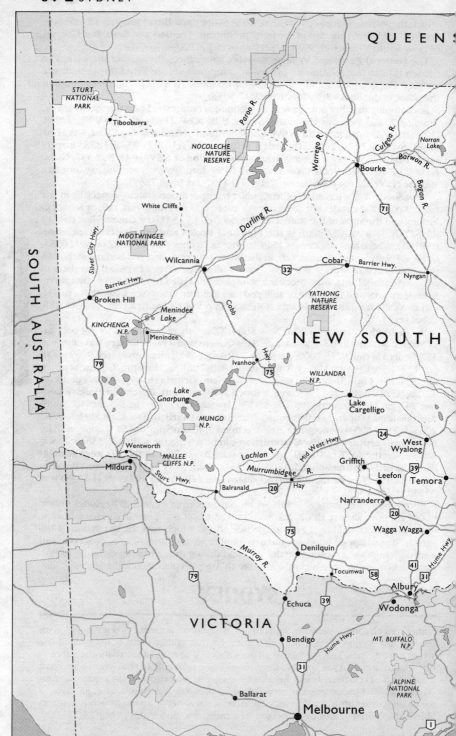

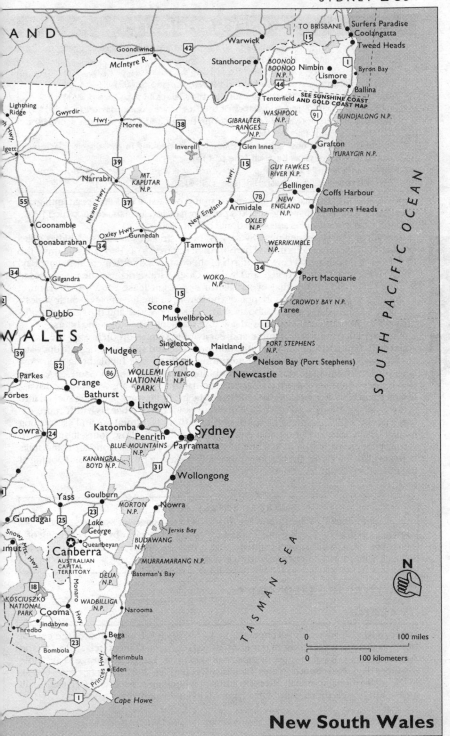

New South Wales

🐨 *SYDNEY HIGHLIGHTS*

- World-famous **Bondi Beach** (see p. 111), where beachgoers are as pretty as the crystal waters and pristine beaches.
- Unending parties on Darlinghurst Rd in **King's Cross** (see p. 112).
- The youthful cafe scene in **Glebe** and **Newtown** (see p. 103).
- A cultivated night of acoustic pleasure at the **Opera House** (see p. 111).
- The lively crowds, music, and wares of the **Rocks weekend market** (see p. 115).
- The postcard-quality view of the Harbour Bridge and Opera House from **Mrs. Macquarie's Point** (see p. 107).
- One of the world's best gay and lesbian scenes, peaking in the all-out salaciousness of the **Mardi Gras Festival** (see p. 115).
- **Manly** and **Taronga Zoo** (see p. 110)—both scenic ferry rides from downtown.
- **Olympic tours** of Homebush Bay (see p. 116).

---

about 20% of the national total) is home to numerous Asian and European immigrant enclaves as well as perhaps the world's premier gay and lesbian scene, which peaks at Mardi Gras in a salacious and sensational celebration.

Beneath all this shiny newness, Sydney is, by Australian standards, as old as cities get. In 1788, its stupendous natural harbor, then referred to as Port Jackson, drew the First Fleet of colonists and convicts north of their intended settlement at Botany Bay. Today, the iconic Harbour Bridge and Sydney Opera House occupy the foreshores of Sydney Cove and ensure that every visitor spends at least a few photo-framing moments recognizing the importance of the harbor in the life of New South Wales's capital. On sunny days, when sailboats skim across the water and the sidewalk cafes buzz with a hundred conversations, those few moments easily become hours.

With the 2000 Summer Olympic and Paralympic Games on their way, the city is abuzz with construction and beautification projects, and spirits are high. Sydney-siders are eager to show off their ever-mounting skyline while highlighting their concern for environmental conservation, dubbing theirs the "Green Games." As if to prove their point, several surprisingly serene national parks are within easy driving distance and allow for weekend escapes into the bush. Be wary of getting sucked into Sydney forever, though; as Aussies are quick to point out, life here is hardly representative of the typical Australian experience, and there's cultural life and astonishing natural beauty throughout the vast continent beyond. Still, allow yourself the time to savor Sydney's many flavors. It's one of the friendliest big cities on Earth, and folks here are glad you came; after raging at the clubs, relaxing by the water, and oohing at the historic and cultural attractions, you will be too.

Water Safety Alert

As of September 1998, reports were mixed as to the safety of Sydney's water following a giardia outbreak. Some expect the water to be clear by the beginning of October 1998, while others estimate that it may be unsafe for up to two years. Check with tourist offices to determine water drinkability.

■ Arrival and Departure

BY PLANE

Sydney's **Kingsford-Smith Airport** (tel. 9667 6058), 10km southwest of the central business district, serves most major international carriers. **Qantas** (tel. 13 13 13) and **Ansett** (13 13 00) cover most domestic destinations. **Luggage storage** is available ($4-6 per day). **New South Wales Tourism Centre** (tel. 9667 6050; fax 9667 6057), in the international terminal, offers brochures, a booking service, and free calls to all area youth hostels (open daily 5am-11pm, midnight in summer).

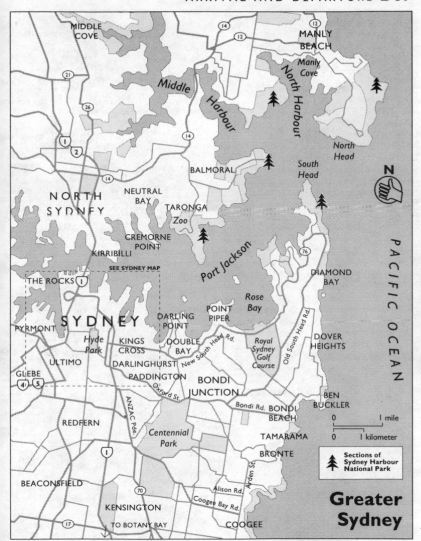

Greater Sydney

Local bus #100 goes to the city center, but officials discourage use of the bus by travelers with luggage (every 30min. M-F 6:30am-6:30pm; $2.50, students half-price). **Airport Express** (tel. 13 15 00) runs to the city center (#300) or Kings Cross (#350). (Service daily 5am-11pm. $6, ages 4-14 $4, under 4 free.) **Kingsford Smith Transport** (tel. 9667 3221) runs to accommodations in the city or the inner suburbs (every 20min. daily 5am-11pm; $6). From International Arrivals, exit Gate B to bus bay 1 or 2. Most hostels offer free pick-up with a one- or two- night booking. A **taxi** to the city center costs about $20 from the domestic terminal, $25 from the international area; the drive takes between 20 and 45 minutes, depending on traffic.

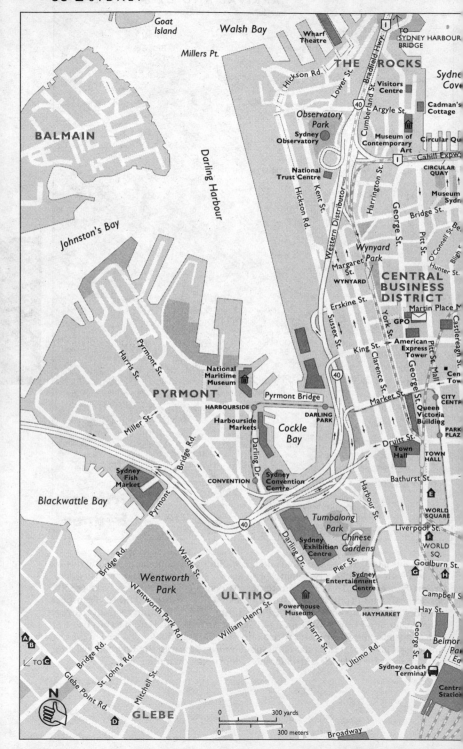

Goat Island

Walsh Bay

Millers Pt.

Wharf Theatre

THE ROCKS

TO SYDNEY HARBOUR BRIDGE

Sydney Cove

Hickson Rd.

Lower St.

Bradfield Hwy.

Visitors Centre

Cadman's Cottage

Cumberland St.

Argyle St.

Circular Qu

BALMAIN

Observatory Park

Sydney Observatory

Museum of Contemporary Art

Circular Quay

Cahill Expwy

CIRCULAR QUAY

National Trust Centre

Kent St.

Harrington St.

George St.

Bridge St.

Museum Sydn

Darling Harbour

Hickson Rd.

Western Distributor

Margaret St.

Wynyard Park

O'Connell St.

Be.

Johnston's Bay

WYNYARD

CENTRAL BUSINESS DISTRICT

Hunter St.

Bligh

Erskine St.

Martin Place M

Castlereagh St.

Pyrmont St.

Harris St.

York St.

GPO

American Express Tower

King St.

Clarence St.

Sussex St.

George St.

Pitt St. Mall

Cen Tow

National Maritime Museum

PYRMONT

Pyrmont Bridge

Market St.

CITY CENTR

Miller St.

HARBOURSIDE

DARLING PARK

Queen Victoria Building

PARK PLAZ

Harbourside Markets

Cockle Bay

Druitt St.

Town Hall

TOWN HALL

Bridge Rd.

Darling Dr.

CONVENTION

Sydney Convention Centre

Bathurst St.

Sydney Fish Market

Pyrmont

WORLD SQUARE

Blackwattle Bay

Harbour St.

Tumbalong Park

Liverpool St.

WORLD SQ.

Wattle St.

Sydney Exhibition Centre

Chinese Gardens

Pier St.

Goulburn St.

Wentworth Park

ULTIMO

William Henry St.

Powerhouse Museum

Sydney Entertainment Centre

HAYMARKET

Campbell S

Hay St.

Harris St.

George St.

Belmor Pa Ea

Bridge Rd.

A
B

TO C

Glebe Point Rd.

St. John's Rd.

Mitchell St.

Ultimo Rd.

Sydney Coach Terminal

Centra Statio

N

GLEBE

D

0 ————— 300 yards

0 ————— 300 meters

Broadway

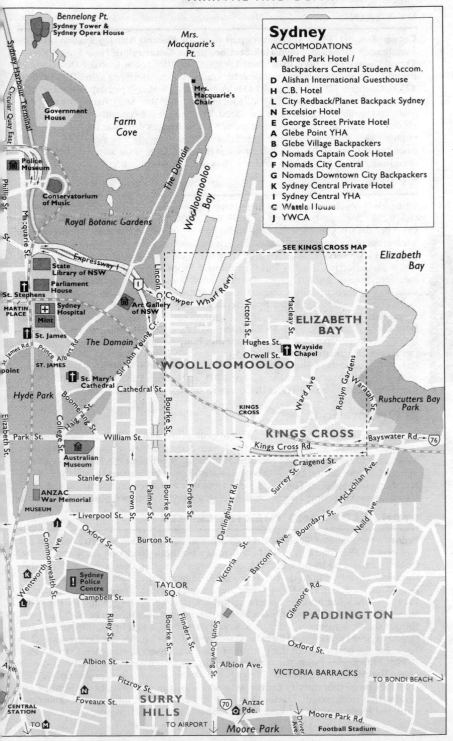

Sydney

ACCOMMODATIONS

M Alfred Park Hotel /
Backpackers Central Student Accom.
D Alishan International Guesthouse
H C.B. Hotel
L City Redback/Planet Backpack Sydney
N Excelsior Hotel
E George Street Private Hotel
A Glebe Point YHA
B Glebe Village Backpackers
O Nomads Captain Cook Hotel
F Nomads City Central
G Nomads Downtown City Backpackers
K Sydney Central Private Hotel
I Sydney Central YHA
C Wattle House
J YWCA

BY TRAIN

Countrylink (tel. 13 22 32) trains depart from the **Central Railway Station** on Eddy Ave. Branch offices at **Town Hall Station,** in the **Countrylink New South Wales Travel Centre** next door to Wynyard Station, on Alfred St at Circular Quay, and in **Bondi Junction Station** also sell tickets. Trains run to Adelaide (27hr., 2 per week, $152), Canberra (4hr., 3 per day, $41), Melbourne (10½hr., 2 per day, $93), and Brisbane (14-15½hr., 2 per day, $93), via Coffs Harbour (8½hr., $65), Byron Bay (12½hr., $82), and Surfer's Paradise (13-15hr., $88). Trains go less frequently to Perth, Cairns, Mount Isa, and Alice Springs. For trips in NSW, kids ages 4-16 ride for half price and younger kids are free. Interstate travel discounts are slightly less. Ages 4-16 pay half-price on trips within NSW and slightly less discounted rates on interstate travel; children under 4 ride free in NSW and at a discount on interstate trips.

BY BUS

Fifteen bus companies operate from the **Sydney Coach Terminal,** Central Station (tel. 9281 9366), on the corner of Eddy Ave at Pitt St. **Luggage storage** is available ($4-8 per day). Because special rates and concessions vary, it is always wise to consult a travel agent for the lowest rate on any given itinerary. The two major national companies, **McCafferty's** (tel. 13 14 99; email infomcc@mccaffertys.com.au; http://www.mccaffertys.com.au) and **Greyhound Pioneer** (tel. 13 20 30; email passinfo@greyhound.com.au), generally offer more frequent trips to major destinations than do the smaller regional carriers, but their rates are not always the best. **McCafferty's** runs to Adelaide (22hr., 1 per day, $96), Brisbane (15-17hr., 3-4 per day, $71), Byron Bay (12-13hr., 1-2 per day, $69), Canberra (4½-5hr., 2 per day, $28), Coffs Harbour (11hr., 2 per day, $57), Melbourne (13½hr., 2 per day, $50), and Surfers Paradise (14-16hr., 2-3 per day, $71). **Greyhound Pioneer** runs to Adelaide (23-24hr., 2-3 per day, $105), Brisbane (15-16hr., 4-5 per day, $79), Byron Bay (12½-13½hr., 3 per day, $77), Canberra (4-5hr., 5-6 per day, $33), Coffs Harbour (9-10hr., 3 per day, $65), Melbourne (12-20hr., 4 per day, $60 or $70), and Surfers Paradise (13½-15hr., 3 per day, $79). Both companies offer discounts to students, seniors, and children.

■ Orientation

In its broadest definition, the Sydney metropolitan area is huge and contained only by the forces of nature, with Ku-Ring-Gai Chase National Park in the north, the Blue Mountains to the west, Royal National Park in the south, and the Pacific Ocean and Sydney Harbour on the east. Much of this area, however, is made up of largely uninteresting outer suburbs. For a bird's eye view that will give you a sense for the city's layout, ascend the **AMP Tower Centrepoint,** located downtown near the Pitt St Mall.

SYDNEY COVE AND THE CITY CENTER

Sydney's most famous sights lie on the harbor at **Sydney Cove,** directly north of the city center. The southern end of the **Sydney Harbour Bridge** is anchored in **The Rocks,** surrounded by upscale boutiques. Drivers entering downtown Sydney from the north have two options, the **Harbour Bridge** and the **Harbour Tunnel** (southbound toll for either $2). Though less scenic, the tunnel is a more convenient route for anyone heading into the eastern suburbs. Opposite the bridge and on the other side of the cove, the **Sydney Opera House** perches prominently on Bennelong Point, though the view from Circular Quay is now partially blocked by a controversial construction project. The **Royal Botanic Gardens** and a park called **the Domain** are at its back. For the best views of the Harbour Bridge and Opera House, take a stroll down to **Mrs. Macquaries Point,** the tip of the peninsula which forms the northeast corner of the Botanic Gardens. Or take a ferry ride from the wharves at **Circular Quay.**

Sydney proper, or the **city center,** is bounded by Circular Quay to the north, **Central Station** to the south, **Darling Harbour** to the west and the **Royal Botanic Gardens** and **Hyde Park** to the east. **George St** and **Pitt St** are major avenues that run parallel from Circular Quay straight down through the heart of the city to Central Station in the south. Street numbers begin at the water and increase as you proceed from the Rocks down to Central. The **central business district** centers on Martin Place, a pedestrian mall spanning the five blocks between George and Macquarie St. Moving south, the next major center of activity is **Town Hall,** located on Druitt St between George and Kent St. The area around **Central Station** supports several backpacker accommodations and a good number of cheap restaurants. Sydney's fast-growing **Chinatown** can be found just northwest of the station, radiating from the intersection of Hay, Sussex, and George St; this area is also known as **Haymarket.**

INNER SUBURBS

Many tiny municipalities known as the **inner suburbs** populate the rest of Sydney's central urban area. Despite their proximity, the suburbs do maintain distinct characters and special attractions. Many areas overlap, however, and some are known by more than one name. West of the city center, **Pyrmont** covers the point of land between Darling Harbour and Blackwattle Bay. The waterside part of this area is also called **Darling Harbour** and is serviced by the Sydney Monorail. South of Pyrmont, **Ultimo** approaches the west side of Central Station and reaches up to the Chinatown area. **Glebe,** southwest of Ultimo and just north of the University of Sydney, benefits from the presence of students in all of the usual ways: casual cafes, cheap food, fun pubs, and good bookstores. Glebe Point Rd is the center of activity in this district. **Newtown,** on the southern side of the uni, feels the student influence, but is a bit rougher around the edges.

The infamous inner suburb of **Kings Cross,** east of the city center at the far end of William St, reigns as the undisputed center of Sydney backpacker culture. Lively, crowded hostels and cafes line Victoria St north of William St, while busy nightclubs and pubs are packed in along Bayswater Rd. The XXX theaters on Darlinghurst Rd demonstrate the neighborhood's seamier side. Travelers should watch all belongings in the Cross and take caution walking alone at night.

Near Kings Cross, **Woolloomooloo** gets down to the business of shipping while **Potts Point** and **Elizabeth Bay** house and feed some of Sydney's wealthier denizens. Here again, suburban borders get fuzzy; a Potts Point address may be across the street from your Kings Cross hostel. To the south of Kings Cross, **Victoria St** goes chic with some of the city's coolest cafes lining the way to **Darlinghurst.** Along with **Surry Hills** to the south and **Paddington** to the east, Darlinghurst provides fashionable housing for young, creative types. Much of Sydney's nightlife revolves around the outrageous clubs along **Oxford St,** the main road through Darlinghurst, Paddington, and Woollahra to the east. Just south of the army's stately Victoria Barracks, **Moore Park** and **Centennial Park** to its east form the city's largest swath of greenery. Here you'll find Sydney's major athletic facilities, including **Sydney Football Stadium** and **Sydney Cricket Ground. Redfern,** south of Central Station, may be unsafe at night.

FAR EAST AND SOUTHERN BEACHES

Outside of these central areas, surroundings get less urban. East of Paddington, **Woollahra's** terrace houses provide a nice change of scenery. To the north, **Double Bay** and **Rose Bay** are among Sydney's most expensive residential areas. **Bondi Junction,** south of Woollahra, is the last train stop on the eastern end of the subway system. Ten minutes east of here by bus is famous **Bondi** (BOND-eye) **Beach,** after which many a surf movie has been modeled. Farther south, the beaches of **Tamarama, Clovelly,** and **Bronte** offer low-key alternatives for families and quieter sunbathers. **Coogee Beach** lies farthest south and rivals Bondi with its wicked waves and young residents. Decide for yourself by taking the hour-long walk along the coastline between Bondi and Coogee Beaches, sampling all the beaches in between.

NORTH SHORE

The second half of Sydney's professional district fronts the **north shore** of Sydney Harbour at the other end of Harbour Bridge. Tourist attractions on the north shore are essentially limited to **Taronga Park Zoo** in Mosman and the beach community of **Manly,** both accessible by ferry. The rides are scenic enough to justify a trip, though, and Manly complements its natural beauty with galleries and other attractions.

■ Getting Around

Sydney is nothing if not navigable. The standard city map, with its many boldfaced suburban labels, creates the impression that Sydney's central area is far larger than it actually is. In truth, the areas that Sydney-siders call suburbs most other people would call neighborhoods, and small ones at that. The walk from Central Station to Circular Quay along Pitt St takes less than 30 minutes, and from Kings Cross 15 minutes.

Comprised of **Sydney Buses, CityRail** trains, and **Sydney Ferries,** the **Sydney Transit Authority (STA)** network stops just about anywhere. For **information** or route advice on any part of the STA system, call 13 15 00. Circular Quay also has a **bus information kiosk** (open M-F 8am-8pm, Sa-Su 9am-2pm) at the corner of Alfred and Loftus St, and a **ferry kiosk** (open M-F 7am-5:45pm, Sa-Su 8am-5:45pm) on the wharf. There's a **train kiosk** at Central Station (open daily 6am-10pm). Additional **bus kiosks** are located in Wynyard Station (open daily 8am-6pm) and the Queen Victoria Building on York St near the junction with Market St (open M-F 8am-6pm, Sa-Su 8:30am-4:30pm). Check out the various forms of passes available rather than paying individual fares. The one-week **TravelPass** for the four centermost zones includes unlimited seven-day access to buses, trains, and ferries for just $21.

Although the STA does not distribute **maps,** the free brochure *Sydney: The Official Book of Maps,* available from all CountryLink offices and most tourist info outlets, contains detailed route maps. Similar information is available in the seasonal *Sydney Visitors Guide* and the *Sydney Map guide: CITY HOST.*

BY BUS

Drivers don't automatically stop at bus stops; hail them like a taxi. (Fares $1.25-4.60, depending on distance. Kids half-price, seniors $1-3. Pay when boarding.) Color-coded **TravelTen** passes cover 10 bus trips at a significant discount, and can be purchased from most news agencies. The **Bus Tripper** ($7.80) covers one day of unlimited bus travel. Most buses circulate between 5am and 11:30pm, but there is 24-hour service between the city center, Kings Cross, and other central locales. The STA info line (tel. 13 15 00) has schedule details.

In addition to local commuter bus service, the STA operates two sight-seeing buses, the **Sydney Explorer** and the **Bondi & Bay Explorer,** which allow passengers to get on and off at major attractions along their designated routes. The Explorer service is expensive, at $25 for a one-day pass for either route (ages 4-16 $18, family $68), but it can be an excellent way to do concentrated touring. The Sydney Explorer takes in sights between the harbor and Central Station, moving as far east as Woolloomooloo Bay and as far west as Darling Harbour, at 15-minute intervals from 8:40am to 6:50pm. Bondi & Bay Explorer service visits the eastern bays and southern beaches, down to Coogee, from 9:15am to 5:55pm every 25 minutes. Start early to get your money's worth.

The **Sydney Pass** includes unlimited bus, train, and ferry use within the basic TravelPass zone, round-trip Airport Express service, access to both Explorer Buses, and passage on Sydney Harbour cruises and the higher-speed ferries to Manly and Parramatta. The Sydney Pass can be purchased for use on three, five, or seven days within any seven-day period (3-day pass $70, ages 4-16 $60, families $200; 5-day pass $95, $80, and $270; 7-day pass $110, $95, and $315).

BY SUBWAY

Sydney's **CityRail** subway system rumbles under the city from Bondi Junction in the east to the most distant corners of the suburban sprawl in the north, west, and south. Service is fast, frequent, and easy to navigate. CityRail's lowest one-way fare is 80¢, but most trips cost a bit more. During peak hours (before 9am on weekdays) return fares are double the one-way price. At all other times, purchase of a round-trip "off-peak return" ticket gets you a sizable discount. The combined service **TravelPass** detailed above generally works out to a bargain for regular subway users. CityRail trains hug the rails daily from 3:55am to 1:30 or 2:30am.

BY FERRY

Providing an excellent view of the harbor, a ferry ride can be seen as both transport and entertainment. Aimless cruising is highly recommended. Ferries embark from the **Circular Quay** wharves between the Opera House and the Harbour Bridge. The **information office** (tel. 9207 3170) is opposite Wharf 4. Short trips in the harbor cost $3.20 one-way; a **FerryTen** pass for the same area, much like the TravelTen bus pass described above, costs $19. The fare for high-speed JetCat cruises to Manly is $5.20 (FerryTen pass $44). The STA's fastest and longest commuter ferry service is the RiverCat to Parramatta ($5; FerryTen $35). For $12, **DayPass** affords you unlimited use of the full range of Sydney Ferries and local buses for one day. Children ages 4-16 ride all these ferries for half-price. Ferries set out daily 5am to midnight.

STA administers several daily **Sydney Ferries Harbour Cruises;** the one-hour Morning Cruise ($12, ages 4-16 $8, families with up to 3 kids $32), the two-and-a-half hour Afternoon Cruise ($16, $12, $44) and the 90-minute after-dark Harbour Lights Cruise ($14, $10, $38). The Sydney Ferries information line (tel. 9207 3172; open M-F 7am-5:15pm) has details. **Quayside Booking Centre** (see **Practical Information,** below) has brochures for private companies that offer more deluxe ferry cruise services.

BY CAR

The **NRMA** is headquartered at 151 Clarence St (tel. 13 11 22 or 9892 0355; open M-F 9am-5pm, Sa 9am-noon) and is a comprehensive driver's resource (see p. 82). All major **car rental** companies have desks in Kingsford-Smith Airport, and most appear again on William St near Kings Cross. The big names include **Avis,** 214 William St (tel. 9353 9000), **Budget,** 76 Anzac Parade (tel. 13 27 27), **Hertz** (tel. 13 30 39), on the corner of William and Riley St, **Thrifty,** 78 William St (tel. 9380 5399), and **Dollar** (tel. 9223 1444 or 1800 358 008) on Sir John Young Crescent. Dollar cuts a little lower than the others with small, manual transmission cars for $55 per day (with unlimited km) and automatic transmission cars for $65 per day, with no surcharge for 21-25 year olds. However, it is a smaller chain, which can make interstate travel and drop-off more difficult.

In general, local or regional outfits offer much better deals than the big companies. **Delta Car Rentals,** 77 William St (tel. 9380 6288), has small, manual cars for $39 per day and automatics for $59 (open M-F 8am-6pm, Sa-Su 8am-5pm). **Ascot,** 113 William St (tel. 9317 2111), starts at $49 per day but has great monthly rates (open daily 7am-7pm.) **Bayswater Car Rental,** 120 Darlinghurst Rd in Kings Cross (tel. 9360 3622; fax 9331 4072), is cheap and has the lowest age limit (20). All companies offer reduced long-term rental rates, and most offer free pick-up from the airport or Central Station.

Hostel noticeboards overflow with fliers for privately-owned cars, campers, and motorcycles **selling** for as little as several hundred dollars. See **Essentials,** p. 34, for more information on car sales. **Kings Cross Car Market** (tel. 9358 5000 or 1800 808 188; fax 9358 5102), on the second level of the Kings Cross Car Park on the corner of Ward Ave and Elizabeth Bay Rd, brings buyers and cars together daily from 9am to 6pm. (Weekly charge $35. Required vehicle inspection $23.) **Travellers Auto Barn,** 177 William St (tel. 9360 1500; fax 9360 1977), offers guaranteed buy-back agreements on cars from $3000. Minimum buy-back rates range from 40 to 50% of pur-

NEW SOUTH WALES

chase price depending on the length of time you take the car. (Warranties, free NRMA Service membership. Open M-Sa 9am-6pm, Su 10:30am-4pm.) **Boomerang Car Market,** 30 Ewan St (planning to move soon; tel. 9700 8595; fax 9567 6872), in the southern suburb of Mascot, guarantees buy-back at 30-40% on cars from $2000 (call ahead for free pick-up; open M-F 8am-5pm, Sa till 4pm, Su by appointment). Both provide full auto maintenance before you go. When it comes time to sell, try the car market before collecting on your guaranteed buy-back price. People often lose less than they expected to.

BY BICYCLE

Bicycle rental shops are less common than you might expect in a backpacker-friendly city, although several are located south of Centennial Park, on Clovelly Rd (bus #339 from Central Station). **Australian Cycle Company,** 28 Clovelly Rd (tel. 9399 3475), across from the bus stop on Earl St, has 18-speed mountain bikes (open daily 9am-5pm). Closer to the center of town, **Inner City Cycles,** 31 Glebe Point Rd (tel. 9660 6605), 50m from the Broadway St end of the road on the right, rents similar bikes (open M and W-F 9am-6pm, Tu 9am-5pm, Sa 9am-4pm, Su 11am-3pm). For a coastal ride, visit **Manly Cycle Centre,** 36 Pittwater Rd (tel. 9977 1189), at Denison St in Manly (open M-W and F 9am-6pm, Th 9am-7pm, Sa 9am-4:30pm, Su 11am-3pm.) Market prices are around $8-10 per hour, $25 per day, or $60-80 per week. All of these shops require a credit card or a prohibitive cash deposit.

■ Practical Information

TOURIST AND TRAVEL INFORMATION

Tourist Office: The **Sydney Visitors Centre,** 106 George St (tel. 9255 1788 or 1800 067 676; fax 9241 5010) in the Rocks. The 17min. presentation on The Rocks area is an entertaining introduction to the city's history. Open 9am-6pm daily. Located more towards the center of the city, the **Sydney Information Kiosk** (tel. 9235 2424), atop the Martin Place subway station between Castlereagh and Elizabeth St, has basic though less comprehensive info. Open M-F 9am-5pm.

Travel Offices: Australian Travel Specialists, Jetty 6 and Jetty 2, Circular Quay (24hr. tel. 9555 2700; fax 9555 2701; email quayside@ozemail.com.au), on the waterfront. Open daily 8am-6:30pm. **Student Uni Travel,** 92 Pitt St, on level 8 (tel. 9232 8444; fax 9231 1254; email sydney@backpackers.net; http://www.backpackers.net), near Martin Place. Free email and Internet access. Mail forwarding. Luggage storage $1 per day. Open M-F 8:30am-6pm, Sa 10am-2pm. YHA, VIP, student discounts. **Travellers Contact Point,** 428 George St, level 7 (tel. 9221 8744; fax 9221 3746; email sydney@travellers-contact.com.au), between King and Market St. Internet access $5 per 30min.; free Internet access 15min. per day with purchase of $35 email account package, good for 1 year. Word processing $5 per hr. Mail forwarding and holding in Australia $40 per year. Employment board with recruiting officers for travelers with work visas. Open M-F 9am-6pm, Sa 10am-4pm. **YHA Membership and Travel Center,** 422 Kent St (tel. 9261 1111; fax 9261 1969; email yha@yhansw.org.au; http://www.yha.org.au), behind Town Hall, between Market and Druitt St. Open M-F 9am-5pm, Sa 10am-2pm.

Consulates: Canada, 111 Harrington St, level 5 (tel. 9364 3000; fax 9364 3098). Open M-F 8:30am-4:30pm. **France,** 31 Market St (tel. 9261 5779; fax 9364 3098). Offices open M-F 9am-12:30pm, phones answered 9am-4pm. **Germany,** 13 Trelawney St (tel. 9328 7733; fax 9327 9649), off Ocean St in Woollahra. Open M-F 9am-noon, W 2-3pm. **New Zealand,** 1 Alfred St, Goldfields Bldg., level 14 (tel. 9247 1344), on the corner of George St. at Circular Quay. Passport office open M-F 9am-4pm (tel. 9247 7500). Visa office (tel. 9247 1511, phones answered M-F 10am-1pm) open M-F 10am-4pm. **Switzerland,** 500 Oxford St., level 23 Plaza Tower #2 (tel. 9369 4244; fax 9369 1334), in Bondi Junction over the Westfield Shopping Centre. Open M-F 9am-2pm. **U.K.,** 1 Macquarie Pl, level 16 (tel. 9247 7521; fax 9233 1826). Open M-F 10am-4:30pm. **U.S.,** 19-29 Martin Pl, #59 (tel. 9373 9200), in the MLC Centre. Open M-F 8am-12:30pm, phones answered 8am-5pm.

FINANCIAL SERVICES

Banks and exchange offices abound (generally open M-F 9am-5pm), as do **ATMs**, which usually take Plus and Visa; Cirrus is less common.

Thomas Cook (tel. 9317 2100) has several locations in the international terminal of Kingsford-Smith Airport. Service charge 2%; minimum of $4 on currency, $10 on traveller's checks. Open daily 5:30am-10:30pm. There are also offices at 175 Pitt St (tel. 131 771), open daily 8:45am-5:15pm; and on the lowest level of the Queen Victoria Building on George St (tel. 9264 1267), open 9am-6pm.

Singapore Money Exchange, 67A Darlinghurst Rd (tel. 9368 0972/fax 9368 1372), in Kings Cross, exchanges at competitive rates. $5 charge per $100 to cash traveler's checks. Other offices at 304-308 George St (tel. 9223 6361), opposite Wynyard Station; in Chinatown, 401 Sussex St (tel. 9281 0663); on Eddy Ave near Central Station, Shop #10 by the Greyhound office (tel. 9281 4118) and on the Castlereagh St level of Centrepoint Tower (tel. 9223 9222). All offices open M-Sa 9am-6pm, Su 9am-5pm.

Money Change, on the mall at Darlinghurst Rd and Springfield Ave, Kings Cross. 5% commission for traveler's checks. Open Su-F 8am-11:30pm, Sa 8am-1am.

American Express Office, 92 Pitt St (tel. 9239 0666; fax 9236 9240), around the corner from Martin Pl. Traveler's checks cashed and currency exchanged for a 1% commission. Mail held for up to a month. Open M-F 8:30am-5:30pm, Sa 9am-noon.

EMERGENCY AND SOCIAL SERVICES

Library: Sydney City Library, Town Hall House (tel. 9265 9470; 24hr. recorded info 9265 9053), corner of Kent and Druitt St. From Town Hall Station, walk through the arcade and enter off Sydney Square. Open M-F 8am-7pm, Sa 9am-noon. Other locations are at 744 George St (tel. 9281 9491), with an extensive Asian languages section, and at 40 William Henry St, Ultimo (tel. 9660 6187), with web access ($4 per hr., $8 per hr. nonmembers; open M-F 11am-7pm, Sa-Su noon-4pm).

Bookstores: Dymocks Booksellers, 424-430 George St (tel. 9235 0155) is the southern hemisphere's largest bookshop. Open M-W and F 9am-6pm, Th 9am-9pm, Sa 9am-5pm, Su 10am-5pm. **Abbey's Bookshops,** 131 York St (tel. 9264 3111), opposite the Queen Victoria Building. Open M-F 8:30am-6pm, Sa 9am-5pm, Su 10am-5pm. **Berkelouw Books,** 19 Oxford St (tel. 9360 3200). Open daily 10am-midnight. Both are independent stores and local favorites for selection, atmosphere, and pricing. **Gleebooks,** 49 Glebe Point Rd (tel. 9660 2333), off Parramatta Rd, is open M-Sa 8am-9pm, Su 9am-9pm. Its huge collection of used books and children's literature are at its 191 Glebe Point Rd location (tel. 9552 2526; open Su-F 10am-9pm, Sa 9am-9pm).

Gyms: University of Sydney Sports Union (tel. 9660 0220), at Cordington and Darlington St. 50m swimming pool; basketball, tennis, and squash courts; aerobics classes; weight room. At $2.20, it's the best deal in town. Open Su-F 6am-10pm, Sa 6am-8pm. **City Gym,** 107 Crown St, East Sydney (tel. 9360 6247), is central and open 24hr ($10). **Al's Sydney Gym and Fitness,** 213 Bronte Rd, Bondi (tel. 9369 2290), is no-frills and affordable ($6). For more info, check http://sydney.sidewalk.com.au.

Ticket Agencies: Ticketek (tel. 9266 4800; fax 9267 4460; http://www.ticketek.com.au) has offices in retail stores and in the Sydney Information kiosk between Castlereagh and Elizabeth St. Full-price advance booking for music, theater, sports, and selected museums. Phone lines are open for credit card purchases M-Sa 7:30am-10pm, Su 9am-8pm. **Halftix** (tel. 00552 6655) sells half-priced sameday tickets for a less extensive slate of events and discounted admission to major museums. The daily roster of available tickets is posted on the Sydney Information kiosk at noon and can be accessed by phone from 11am. Open M-F 9am-5pm, Sa 12pm-4pm. **Ticketmaster** (24hr. tel. 9320 9000) covers many theatrical venues. Open M-Sa 9am-6pm.

Taxis: Legion Cabs (tel. 13 14 51), RSL Cabs (tel. 9581 1111), Taxis Combined (tel. 9332 8888). Initial fare $3 ($4 with call-in request), plus $1.07 per km.

Weather: For conditions 24hr., dial 1196.

Hotlines: Alcohol and Drug Information Service: tel. 9361 2111. Crisis counseling 24hr. **Rape Crisis Centre:** 24hr. tel. 9819 6565, outside of Sydney tel. 1800 424 017. **HIV/AIDS Information Line:** tel. 9332 4000 or 9332 1090.

Late-Night Pharmacy (Chemist): Crest Hotel Pharmacy, 60A Darlinghurst Rd in King's Cross (tel. 9358 1822), opposite the rail station. Open Tu-Sa 8am-2am, Su-M 8am-midnight. **Wu's Pharmacy,** 629 George St, Chinatown (tel. 9211 1805). Open M-Sa 9am-9pm, Su 9am-7pm. **24-hour Prescription Service:** tel. 9235 0333.

Medical Services: Sydney Hospital (tel. 9382 7111, vaccinations 9361 2685, emergency 9382 7009), on Macquarie St opposite the Martin Pl station. **Traveller's Medical and Vaccination Centre,** 428 George St, level 7 (tel. 9221 7133). Consultation fee $38. Open M-W and F 9am-6pm, Th 9am-8pm, Sa 9am-1pm. **Kings Cross Travellers' Clinic,** 13 Springfield Ave (tel. 9358 3066). Consultation fee $35. Open M-F 9:30am-6pm, Sa 10am-noon. Full complement of vaccinations for traveling in tropical regions runs $150 at either place. **Contraceptive Services,** 195 Macquarie St, level 3 (tel. 9221 1933). Open M-F 8:30am-4:30pm, Sa 8am-noon.

Police: Sydney Police Centre, 151 Goulbourn St (24hr. tel. 9265 4144), at the corner of Riley St in Surry Hills.

Emergency: Dial 000.

POST AND COMMUNICATIONS

Internet Access: Coin-op kiosks throughout the city, including at many hostels and the airport, usually include web browsers but no telnet and cost about $2 per 10min. By far the best comprehensive Internet service provider in the city is **Global Gossip,** with locations at 770 George St near Sydney Central YHA (tel. 9212 1466) and 111 Darlinghurst Rd in King's Cross (tel. 9326 9777). $10 per hr. ($12 in Kings Cross), $2 for 10min. They also offer super-cheap international call rates in their on-site phone booths. Open daily 8am-midnight. The Internet Cafe at **Hotel Sweeney,** 236 Clarence St (tel. 9261 5666), has 11 terminals charging $2 per 10min. Open M-F. 9am-9pm, Sa noon-11pm. **Student Uni Travel** currently offers free access but has only a couple of terminals (see **Travel Offices,** p. 94). **Digi.Kaf,** 174 St. John's Rd, Glebe (tel. 9660 3509; fax 9660 6405; email info@digikaf.com.au), has word processing, telnet, and web access. $2 per 15min. Open M-Th 8am-6pm, F 8am-4pm, 7pm-11pm, Sa-Su 9am-6pm.

Post Office: Sydney General Post Office (GPO), 159-171 Pitt St (tel. 13 13 17), on Martin Pl, is being renovated. Stamps, boxes, and other supplies can be purchased at 130 Pitt St. Open M-F 8:15am-5:30pm, Sa 9am-1pm. *Poste Restante* awaits at 310 George St, inside Hunter Connection across from Wynyard Station. Enter under the "Through to Pitt Street" sign. Computers allow you to check whether you've received anything. Open M-F 8:30am-5:30pm. **Postal Codes:** 2000 for city center, 2001 for *Poste Restante.* Suburbs have their own post offices and postal codes.

Phone Code: 02.

WORKING IN SYDNEY

Sydney is riddled with backpackers seeking jobs, especially young Britons taking advantage of easy visa agreements. (See **Documents and Formalities,** p. 4, for information on **work permits.**) Fortunately, there's plenty of work available, and those who arrive without prior arrangements report a 10-20 day lag before finding semi-permanent employment. It pays to start preparing before leaving your home. Have a resumé typed and saved on a PC floppy; you can print it using Microsoft Word at most Internet shops. Don't get stuck shelling out a lot to prepare a shabby document in a public facility.

The best way to prepare yourself for job hunting in Sydney is to do your research and establish contacts before departing. Spend time searching the web. Qualified applicants in computer fields enjoy the most success in landing high quality positions. If you haven't the opportunity to set up house before your job search commences, it is advisable not to list hostel specs as contact information. Use a friend, get yourself a cellular phone, or set up a mailbox at **Global Gossip,** 770 George St (tel.

9212 1466; fax 9212 1499; email globalgossip@hotmail.com), which is a source of job search ideas and allows you to receive incoming faxes (see **Internet Access,** above). The **news classifieds site** (http://www.newsclassified.com.au) is a comprehensive site and a great place to start. It posts job ads from all publications owned by Rupert Murdoch—nearly every newspaper on the continent. **Cowley's Job Centre** (http://www.cowleys.com.au) allows you to advertise yourself, and provides a link to the **Australian Resume Server,** with its full list of links to job banks and search information. Also try the **Monster Board** (http://www.monsterboard.com.au), where you can post your resume and search a list of employers. IT professionals might look to **ACP** (Australian Computer Professionals, tel. 9744 3888; fax 9744 7188; acp@mpx.com.au). Newspapers are always an essential resource. The *Sydney Morning Herald* is stuffed with job classifieds on Wednesday and Saturday. *The Australian* is especially strong for computer opportunities in its Tuesday listings.

Visa holders can consult the **Job Referral Centre,** 770 George St (open 8:45am-10pm). There are computers with job info and a *Seasonal Work Guide* pamphlet. The information desk operators answer questions regarding taxes and schedule interviews with job placement advisers. These meetings are held by walk-in appointment between 8:45 and 10:45am; you may check into a maximum of two jobs. Arrive early. For tax information, visit the **Australian Taxation Office,** 100 Market St, GPO Box 9990 (tel. 13 28 61; http://www.ato.gov.au), at the Centrepoint shopping plaza in the CBD. There you can grab the annual *TaxPack* (open M-F 8:30am-4:35pm). The helpful officers at this office report that the biggest misunderstanding for foreigners is that they will be charged the 47% income tax while their tax number is still being processed by immigration. In fact, you are allowed a 28-day grace period.

■ Accommodations

As most travelers' gateway to Australia, Sydney supports a thriving budget accommodation market with little seasonal variation in pricing. Prices listed are **winter rates,** but most dorm beds increase in price by only $2 during peak season (Nov.-Feb.).

The first question most travelers must answer when finding a bed in Sydney is whether or not to stay in Kings Cross. Well-located, traveler-friendly, and party-ready, Kings Cross has become an established backpacker mecca, and the high concentration of steadily improving hostels ensures that beds are almost always available. However, the omnipresence of prostitutes and the profusion of go-go bars make many travelers uncomfortable. In addition, tales of regular theft are rampant. If you do opt to stay in the Cross, be sure you feel comfortable with your hostel's security measures before letting your valuables out of your sight.

While staying in the city center brings the benefit of convenient transportation, many travelers sing the praises of more remote suburbs. While Bondi is Sydney's high-profile beach, the accommodations at Coogee Beach are nicer on the whole and worthy of an extended stay. Sydney's **camping** areas have been banished to the outskirts of the metropolitan area by haphazard urban growth. The two listed (see p. 103) are accessible by public transportation, but the cost of repeated bus and train trips makes most sites less economical than hostel beds in the city center.

Unless stated otherwise, hostels accept major credit cards, and have a common room with a TV, hall bathrooms, 24-hour access, a $10 key deposit, and free pick-up from airport, bus, and train stations. Laundry, when available, is $2 per wash or dry.

KINGS CROSS AND AROUND

◎**Jolly Swagman Backpackers,** 27 Orwell St (tel. 9358 6400; http://www.backpackers-world.com.au/jolly); 16 Orwell St (tel. 9358 6600), under the Sydney Central Backpackers sign; and 144 Victoria St (tel./fax 9357 4733 or 1800 805 870). Offers everything: travel agency, frequent bus trips to nearby beaches, roof-top dining on Victoria St, cafe with cheap eats (meals $5), Internet access ($2 per 10min.) at 27 Orwell St, and a respite from the relative craziness of the Cross at 16 Orwell St. Clean, bright rooms with fridges, lockers, sinks. Ample, lively lounges and kitchens. Group activities such as videos and pub crawls fill the calendar. 27 Orwell St has a 24hr. security attendant and valuables storage. Coin-op laundry at the Orwell St locations. Reception open M-F 8am-6pm; Sa 8am-1pm; 24hr. daily at 27 Orwell St. Check-out 9am. 4-bed dorms $18; doubles $44. Weekly: $108; $264. Linen included. Key deposit $20.

◉**Eva's Backpackers,** 6-8 Orwell St (tel. 9358 2185; fax 9358 3259). Cozy, homey feel, with tidy rooms and agreeable management. Picnic tables in kitchen and rooftop garden provide great meeting places. Laundry, safe for valuables. Hourly security patrols. Reception open daily 7am-1pm and 5-8pm. Check-out 10am. Bunks in 4- to 10-bed dorms with or without bath $18; doubles and twins $42. 7th night free during winter. Key deposit $5. Laundry $3 wash/dry. Book ahead.

The Pink House, 6-8 Barncleuth Sq (tel. 9358 1689 or 1800 806 384) off Ward Ave. Unlike most other Kings Cross hostels, the Pink House feels like a house—a big, fun, very pink house. Nice wooden beds, big bathrooms. Brick kitchen opens onto garden terrace. Events include trivia nights and sausage sizzles. Laundry facilities. Free email and word-processing. Web access $8 per hr. Dorms $16-18; doubles and twins $40; garden flats $42. Weekly: $95-105; $240; $250. VIP, YHA. Book ahead.

Highfield Private Hotel, 166 Victoria St (tel. 9326 9539; fax 9358 1552). A backpacker might not appreciate the long hallways and lack of common space, but it's ideal for less hectic, comfortable longer-term stays. Pristine bathrooms, small kitchen and TV room, security-coded lock and a safe for valuables. Reception open M-F 7:30am-7pm, Sa-Su 8am-noon and 5-7pm. Check-out 10am. 3-bed dorms $18; doubles $38 or $50. Weekly: $105; $220 or $300. Linen $2.50.

Potts Point House, 154 Victoria St (tel. 9368 0733). Unappealing exterior hides perhaps the most spacious, well-equipped dorms in the Cross, complete with big TVs, fans, wardrobes, and bedside tables. Kitchen and dining area are small. Lock on front door and owner on call are the extent of night security. Laundry ($2.40 wash/dry). Reception daily 8am-7pm. Dorms $15; doubles $40. Weekly $90; $240.

Original Backpackers, 160-162 Victoria St (tel. 9356 3232; fax 9368 1435). The kitchen and dining area comprise the most spacious hostel common area in the Cross, but the rooms and bathrooms still need improvement to match that standard. Cable TV, Internet access ($2 for 12 min), 24hr. night managers, safe for valuables, security patrols, laundry. Reception open daily 7am-11pm. Dorms $17; doubles $44. Weekly $105; $260. VIP. Deposits: blankets $20, key $20.

Travellers Rest, 156 Victoria St (tel. 9358 4606). Less lively than the bigger Kings Cross hostels, but with a good balance of quiet and camaraderie. Caters to working travelers by providing contacts and lists of potential employers. Rooms have phones, TVs, fridges, basins, and kettles. Small kitchen and dining area open daily 6am-10:30pm. Laundry ($1.40 wash/dry). Reception daily 8am-noon and 4:30-6pm. Check-out 9am. 3- to 4-bed dorms $17; singles $35; twins $38, with private bath $45. Weekly: $105; $155; $220, $240. Linen included. No advance booking.

Funk House Backpackers, 23 Darlinghurst Rd (tel. 9358 6455; fax 9358 3506; email funkhouse@bigpond.com), above Hungry Jack's. Enter via Llankelly Pl, an alley off the main drag. In the middle of all the action, with an interior as bizarre as its surroundings. Cozy 3- to 4-bed dorms. Laundry. No smoking in rooms. Reception daily 7am-10pm. Check-out 10am. Dorms $18; twins $42. Weekly: $108; $252. VIP.

Rucksack Rest, 9 MacDonald St (tel. 9358 2348, mobile tel. 04 1246 7892), off MacLeay St, a few blocks north of Kings Cross proper, in Potts Point. Quiet and homey. Fridge and sink in room. Fully-equipped kitchen. Check-out around 11am. Dorm beds $17, twins $38, large doubles $40. 7th night free. No key deposit. Foreign travelers only. No guaranteed booking.

NEAR CENTRAL STATION AND SOUTH

◉**Sydney Central YHA** (tel. 9281 9111; fax 9281 9199), on the corner of Pitt St and Rawson Pl, visible from the Pitt St exit of Central station. The mothership has landed. The world's largest hostel, with 532 beds and every possible service: pool (open daily 7:30am-10:30pm), game room, employment and travel desks, TV/video room, Internet access ($2 per 10min.), parking ($7 per night), multiple kitchens, arranged activities, attached bar and bistro, and on and on. It's size is both amazing

Kings Cross

ACCOMMODATIONS
- **B** Eva's Backpackers
- **H** Funk House Backpackers
- **C** Jolly Swagman
- **G** Highfield House
- **F** Original Backpackers
- **I** Pink House
- **D** Potts Point House
- **A** Rucksack Rest
- **E** Travellers Rest

and a little alienating, and not necessarily warm and personal. 14-day max. stay. Reception open 24hr. Check-out 10am. Check-in noon. 4-bed dorms $21, 6-bed dorms $18, 8-bed dorms $17; twins $52, with bath $56. Under 18 half-price. YHA nonmembers $3 more. Wheelchair accessible. Linen $2, towels $1, lockers $3.

Y on the Park (YWCA), 5-11 Wentworth Ave (tel. 9264 2451, reservations 1800 294 124; fax 9285 6288; http://www.ywca.org.au/travel). From Museum Station, exit onto Liverpool St and turn right to get to Wentworth St. Recently renovated, the newly sophisticated and sleek foyer is connected to a cheap cafe with Internet access (open daily 7am-8pm). Rooms with four single beds (no bunks) are more like barracks à la Martha Stewart—loads of carpeting, closet space, and pastels. Everything's sparkling and spacious, with A/C and heat. Linens and towels provided. No kitchen. Reception open 24hr; check-out 10am. 4-bed dorms $24, under age 4 free; singles $60, with bath $90; twins $80, $110; triples $90, $120. Discount for YWCA members 10%. Laundry $1 per wash or dry. Wheelchair accessible.

Alfred Park Private Hotel, 207 Cleveland St (tel. 9319 4031; fax 9318 1306; email hotels@g-day.aust.com; http://www.g-day.aust.com/~hotels), behind the railyard end of Central Station. Former home of a family with 14 children. Hotel atmosphere. Terraced dining space, medium-size kitchen. Average-size rooms feature TVs, fridges, fans, and armoires. Laundry. Reception open daily 8am-10pm. Free pick-up 7am-10pm. Shuttle to airport $5. Check-out 9am. Dorms $18; weekly discounts. Winter special $20 for 2 nights. Single or twin $50, with bath $60; double with bath $100. All prices increase by $10 during school holidays. Linen included.

Nomads City Central Backpackers, 752 George St (tel. 9212 4833 or 1800 249 910; fax 9212 5753). Exit Central Station on Pitt St and take Rawson Pl from the north corner of the station to George St. The hostel's entrance is a hall with a bright mural, across from Commonwealth Bank. Freshly painted, with TV/VCR lounge and clean kitchen. Small, reasonably clean bathrooms on each floor. Dorm rooms are large and carpeted, with A/C and fans. Dorms $18, with Nomads card $17; weekly $126, $108.

Excelsior Hotel/City-Side Backpackers (VIP Backpackers), 64 Foveaux St (tel. 9211 4945; fax 9211 8499). Exit Central Station on Chalmers St; Foveaux intersects Chalmers at the north corner of the station. A clean, friendly place made brighter by good windows. Lively pub downstairs has a bistro and live bands daily. Laundry. Pick-up available. Reception open daily 6:30am-midnight. Check-out 10am. Dorms $17, weekly $100. Twins and doubles $45, weekly $230. VIP. Linen included.

Nomads Captain Cook Hotel, 162 Flinders St (tel. 9331 6487 or 1800 655 536; fax 9331 7746) in Darlinghurst. A 20min. walk from Central Station down Foveaux St into Fitzroy St, and another block beyond South Dowling St. Call for free pick-up or take bus #373, 374, or 377 from Wynyard or #339, 391, or 393 from Central Station. Small, relaxed pubstay; not the brightest or best-equipped of Sydney's hostels, but relaxed and fun. Mail holding and incoming calls. Free lockers, storage, and 1800. Free tea and coffee. Laundry. Reception open daily 7am-midnight. Check-out 10am. Dorms $15-16. Singles with double beds, doubles, and twins $44. Weekly: $7 less. Nomads cardholders $1 off. Linen and key deposit $20.

Backpackers Central Student Accommodation, 243-247 Cleveland St (tel. 9698 8839 or 0418 248 862; fax 9310 3752; email bpstudent@viper.net.au; http://www.viper.net.au/~bpstudent). Exit Central Station onto Chalmers St, head right (south); the hostel is at the intersection of Chalmers and Cleveland St, at the boundary of Prince Alfred Park. Dorm rooms have shelves, desks, dressers, hanging space, and carpeting. Courtyard barbecue. Internet $2 for 15min. Office hours 7am-noon and 5-8:30pm daily. Dorms $16, weekly $85; twins $36. Doubles $20 per person, weekly $120; $10 more nightly and weekly during summer.

Nomads Downtown City Backpackers, 611 George St (tel. 9211 8801 or 1800 248 815; fax 9211 8803), on the corner of Goulburn and George St. Take the airport bus to the Chinatown stop. Party hostel, a bit messy but with good common space and Internet access ($2 per 10min.). Max. stay generally 2 weeks. Reception open 7am-10pm. Luggage storage and use of facilities free on day of departure. Dorms $18-20. Lockers and linen free. Bookings with credit card only.

City Redbacks/Planet Backpack Sydney, 198 Elizabeth St (tel. 9211 4200 or 1800 774 545; email backpackplant@hotmail.com). Exit Central Station onto Chalmers St, head north to the intersection with Elizabeth St. From the airport take local bus #100 or 305, the Express Bus, or the Airport Shuttle Bus. Small, carpeted dorms. Caters to short-term and European guests. Bathroom floors could be cleaner, but you might not notice after the weekly night of 2-for-1 beers at the 24hr. bar downstairs. Internet $3 for 15min. Checkout 9:30am. Office hours 8am-9pm daily. Linen and blankets included. Free airport pick-up and luggage storage on day of departure. Safety box $3 per day, $20 deposit. Dorms $18; doubles $45. 7th night free.

GLEBE

To get to Glebe Point Rd, take bus #431, #432, #433, or #434 from anywhere on the eastern side of George St. By car, follow George St south towards Central Station until it feeds into Broadway, then turn right onto Glebe Pt Rd opposite Victoria Park.

Wattle House, 44 Hereford St (tel. 9552 4997; fax 9660 2528), a 5min. walk from Glebe Point Rd. A hostel with a B&B feel. Country home decor includes lace curtains, brick kitchen, manicured backyard garden. Plush bean bags fill the small TV room, where guests get acquainted over long-term stays. Laundry. Reception open M-F 9am-noon and 6-7pm, Sa 10am-noon, Su 10am-noon. 3- to 4-bed dorms $19; doubles $50. Weekly: $122; $322-350. A $20 deposit covers key, linen, and cutlery.

Glebe Point YHA, 262 Glebe Point Rd (tel. 9692 8418; fax 9660 0431). With long narrow halls and boxy rooms, the hostel feels like a university dorm with cleaner bathrooms. Guests hang out on the roof and in the subterranean lounge. It's worth paying a bit extra over the place next door for the spacious kitchen and dining area, in-room sinks, and frequent pub outings. Internet access $2 per 10min.

Reception open daily 7am-11pm. Laundry open 7am-10pm. Dorms $19-21; twins $50; doubles $50. YHA nonmembers $3 more. Linen $2. Towel $1.

Glebe Village Backpackers, 256 Glebe Point Rd (tel. 9660 8133 or 1800 801 983; fax 9552 3707). If this place achieves half of its intended renovations it will rapidly overtake the nearby YHA as the most happening place for the younger crowd in Glebe. As is, its many activities don't make up for less impressive dorm rooms and bathrooms. Still, it's the cheapest place in town. Laundry. Internet access $2 per 12min. Reception open daily 8am-8pm. Check-out 9:30am. Dorms $16-18. Weekly: $100-119. VIP. Work exchanges for rent possible on longer stays. Linen included.

Alishan International Guest House, 100 Glebe Point Rd (tel. 9566 4048; fax 9525 4686; email kevin@alishan.com.au). Neat Victorian house features new rooms with TVs and refrigerators. The dorms are a bit shabbier than the sparkling private rooms, which are ideal for couples and families. On-site parking. Reception daily 8am-11pm. Dorms $20; singles with bath $75; doubles with bath $85. Weekly: $126; $490; $560. Family room with bath $95. Wheelchair-accessible room available. Linen included.

BONDI BEACH

Take bus #380 or #382 from Circular Quay or drive east along Oxford St.

Indy's Bondi Beach Backpackers, 35A Hall St (tel. 9365 4900; fax 9365 4994), just beyond the Commonwealth Bank, set back from the street, 1½ blocks inland from Campbell Pde. Free breakfast, tea, and coffee, open video library, complimentary use of bikes, surf and boogie boards, and in-line skates. Dorm partitions available for improvised privacy. Laundry. Internet access $2 for 12min. Reception open M-Sa 7:30-11am and 4-8pm, Su 8-11am. Check-out 10:30am. Large dorms $16, weekly $95. Doubles at beachfront location $18 per person. Book through main office, and inquire about family room setups as well. $20 key deposit.

The Biltmore Private Hotel, 110 Campbell Pde (tel. 9130 4660; fax 9365 0195; email biltmore@magna.com.au). As close as you can get to Bondi's waves without sleeping on the beach. Tidiest rooms in town for the lowest price around. Kitchen, comfy common room with big TV, laundry. Downstairs reception 7:30am-6pm, manager on premises 24hr. Dorms $15, weekly $95; singles $30, $170.

Bondi Lodge, 63 Fletcher St (tel. 9365 2088 or 9130 3685; fax 9365 2177). Take Sandridge St from the south end of Campbell Pde and turn west on Fletcher St. Classy budget digs. Room rates include buffet-style cooked breakfasts and 3-course dinners to make up for the lack of a common kitchen. Fans and fridges in rooms. Rooftop sundeck with spa. Laundry facilities. TV rental $5 per night, $15 per week, students $10 per week. 4-6 bed dorms $30, space in a 2-bed dorm $40; singles $60. Weekly: $150; $210; $280. Linen included. Key deposit $50.

Nomads on Bondi Beach, 2-8 Campbell Pde (tel. 9130 1366 or 1800 814 885; fax 9130 1377). Great common space includes game room, kitchen, rooftop patio. Rooms have lockers, basins, TVs, and fridges, but many could use new paint and new furniture. Reception daily 8am-11pm. Dorms $15, weekly $90; singles $35, $180; doubles $35, $150. Check-out 11am (casual). Book ahead in summer.

COOGEE BEACH

Take bus #373 or #374 from Circular Quay or #372 from Central Station.

Surfside Backpackers, 186 Arden St (tel. 9315 7888 or 1800 807 872; fax 9315 7892; email surfside@enternet.com.au), above the McDonald's, overlooking the beach. You couldn't ask for a better location, with the shops of Coogee Bay Rd to one side, professional athletic fields to the other, and the beach right out in front. Sunlight streams into the rooms and long balconies connect them, making the setup particularly open for socializing. The bigger dorms, especially the 16-bed dinosaur, are somewhat cramped, but that's par for the course at the beachside hostels. Internet access $2 per 10min. Laundry. Female-only dorm available. Reception open daily 8am-12:30pm and 5-8pm. Check-out 9:30am. Dorms $16-18; doubles $40. Weekly: $85-105; $240. VIP. Key, kitchen, and linen deposit $20.

Original Coogee Beach Backpackers, 94 Beach St (tel. 9315 8000 or 9665 7735; fax 9664 1258; email milkrist@webmail.com.au), high atop the steep hill at the north end of the beach. Surfside cottage with a view that's worth the hike. Two common rooms with TVs, 3 kitchens, big windows, and good vibes. Laundry. Reception open daily 8am-1pm and 5-8pm. Check-out 9:30am. Dorms $17-18; doubles and twins $45. Weekly: $85-95; $260. VIP. Key deposit $20.

Aegean Coogee Bay Road Backpackers, 40 Coogee Bay Rd (tel. 9314 5324), 3 blocks inland from the beach. Brims with amenities: 5 full kitchens (open daily 8am-10pm), heated outdoor pool, sauna, rooftop balcony. A bit crowded, but with a relaxed communal feel. Free airport pick-up with 2-night stay. Internet kiosk $12 for 10min. Laundry. Reception daily 8am-10pm, in winter 8am-noon and 5-10pm but check-in is 24hr. Check-out 10am. Dorms $16; weekly $90. Twin rooms with bunks $40. Linen $2 in summer. Key deposit $20. Luggage storage $10 per week.

Indy's Coogee Beach Backpackers, 302 Arden St (tel. 9315 7644), 5min. walk south from the central beach area. Quiet and homey, with a comfy common room and a busy kitchen. Caters to long-term travelers. Free cereal, tea, coffee, and use of bikes and boards. Laundry. Reception open daily 7:30-10:30am and 4:30-7pm. Check-out 10:30am, casual. Dorms $16, weekly $95. Key and linen deposit $20.

KIRRIBILLI

Kirribilli Court Private Hotel, 45 Carabella St (tel. 9955 4344), in Kirribilli. Take the Neutral Bay ferry from Circular Quay to Kirribilli. Walk up Holbrook St, which is straight ahead from the ferry, exit and turn right onto Carabella St. Quiet residential neighborhood. The big white house would benefit from a little more indoor upkeep, but facilities are ample. Big, messy dorm rooms have wood floors, 2-4 beds; some have TVs and fridges. 3 kitchens, laundry. 24hr reception. Dorms $15; singles $20; doubles and twins $30. Weekly: $80; $120; $160. Linen included.

MANLY

Manly Backpackers Beachside, 28 Raglan St (tel. 9977 3411; fax 9977 4379). Take the ferry to Manly, cross the Esplanade to Belgrave St, which becomes Pittwater St, and turn right on Raglan. Despite the blank, narrow hallways, the hostel manages to have an open, friendly atmosphere and clean, cozy dorms. Picnic tables bring guests together over meals in the kitchen and on the patio dining area. Small, sparse TV room. Free use of body boards. Laundry. Reception open M-F 9am-1pm and 4-8pm, Sa-Su 9am-1pm and 4-7pm, holidays 9am-noon only. Check-out 9:30am, $5 for late check-out. Dorms $15-16. Weekly $90-95. Doubles and twins $40, with bath $45. VIP. Linen and blankets $2, free for multi-night stays.

Manly Bunkhouse, 46 Malvern Ave (tel. 1800 657 122 or 9976 0472). Cross the Esplanade to Whistler St, follow Whistler to Pine St, make a left and a quick right on to Malvern Ave. This small and quiet hostel is one of the best-kept in Manly. No common room, but each 4-bed dorm has its own kitchenette, bathroom, color TV, heaters, lockers, and closet space. There's an outdoor courtyard and eating area, plus a rooftop perfect for contemplative nights. Free pick-up from wharf. Check out 9:30am. One-time $2 linen fee. Dorms $18, weekly $119; twins $50. VIP. Wheelchair accessible rooms, but there is one small step to access the kitchen.

Manly Astra Backpackers, 68-70 Pittwater Rd (tel. 9977 2092). From the ferry, cross the Esplanade to Belgrave St, which becomes Pittwater St. Feels like Grandma's house. Reception open daily 9am-noon and 6-7pm, but the live-in manager often answers the bell outside these hours. Check-out 9:30am. Kitchen open daily 5am-9:30pm. Dorms $17; doubles $38. Weekly $90; $190. VIP. $20 deposit covers key, linen, colorful Mexican blankets, and dishes.

Manly Boarding House/Manly Travellers Hostel, 56 Whistler St (tel. 9977 1299), between Belgrave and the Corso. This tiny, surf-friendly hostel has large-ish rooms with desks, bureaus, fridges, and closets. No TV room. Outdoor courtyard, neat kitchen, 2 little bathrooms. Reception M-F 9-11am, 4-6pm; Sa-Su 9:30-11am, 4:30-6pm. Dorms $15, weekly $90; twins $33, $200. Linen included.

Steyne Hotel (tel. 9977 4977), on Steyne St at the end of the Corso. Rooms at the Steyne outclass average pub accommodation for singles and doubles, although dorms are merely average. Rooms are nicely furnished, dorms have sinks, desks, and lockers, and shared bathrooms are vigorously scrubbed. Linen and hot breakfast included. Check-in daily 11am-late. Check-out 10am. 4-bed dorms $25. Singles $40; doubles with shared bath $70. Key deposit $100 or credit card slip.

CAMPING

Sheralee Tourist Caravan Park, 88 Bryant St (tel. 9567 7161), in Rockdale. Take the Cityrail train to Rockdale, and walk down Bryant St toward the water (15min.). None-too-scenic camping in an open grassy patch comes with toilets, hot showers, a kitchen area, and a TV room. Laundry. Reception open 24hr. Sites for 1-2 people $15, powered $20, extra person $4. Basic caravans $40 for 2, extra person $10.

Lakeside Van Park (tel. 9913 7845), on Lake Park Rd, in Narrabeen. Take bus #190 from Wynyard Station toward Palm Beach; it's the 3rd stop after Narrabeen Lake. The caravan park setting is uninspiring, but the tent camping area lies close to the beach and has both the wind and the view to show for it. Toilets, showers, common kitchen area. Reception daily 8am-6pm. Sites for 2 people $17, powered $20. Each additional adult $5, children $2. Cabins from $70. Deposit for gate card $25.

■ Food

Sydney's streets overflow with eateries of every flavor for any budget. Asian options, most notably Thai and Chinese cuisine, rank highly among the international selections. Though the neighborhoods vary in their offerings, no area disappoints.

KINGS CROSS

◉**Govinda's,** 112 Darlinghurst Rd (tel. 9380 5162). A unique, can't-miss restaurant and cinema, Govinda's serves a mostly-Indian, wholly vegetarian all-you-can-eat buffet. The $14 cost includes a movie in the upstairs theater, which features cushy, reclining sofas for total viewing bliss or dark room flirtation. Open daily 6pm-11pm, last movie starts at 9:30pm. Call movie hotline (tel. 9360 7853) for showtimes.

Harry's Cafe de Wheels, Cowper Wharf Rdwy (tel. 9357 3074), Woolloomooloo, northeast of Kings Cross proper. Easy late-night stagger down Brougham St for a post-party pie. The house special, meat pie and peas ($2-3), reflects Harry's half-century of pie-making expertise. Open Su-Th 7am-2am, F-Sa 7am-4am.

Roys Famous, 176 Victoria St (tel. 9357 3579). The walls' copper glow attracts the stalwarts of urban chic for coffee and lunch. The people-watching is as interesting as the food. Lunch from $7.50. Breakfast until 5pm from $2.50. Licensed, BYO wine only. Corkage $3 per bottle. Open daily 9am-midnight. Service stops at 11pm.

Mamma Maria Cafe, 230 William St (tel. 9357 2097), has a superb breakfast deal of eggs, bacon, ham, grilled tomato, and toast for $3.90. Good-sized portions of fresh ravioli, penne, and other pastas $6.90. Open daily 6:30am-11pm.

SURRY HILLS

Prasits Northside Thai Take Away, 395 Crown St (tel. 9332 1792), several blocks south of Oxford St. Hot, fresh, hot, creative, hot dishes for sit-down dining or takeaway. Unusual, tasty spring rolls ($1.50 each). The green peppercorn stir-fry might be used to melt iron if it weren't so yummy ($10.50). Limited seating available. BYO, corkage $1 per person. Open Tu-Su noon-3:00pm and 5:30-10pm.

Mehrey Da Dhaba Indian Street Restaurant, 466 Cleveland St (tel. 9319 6260). Named for the roadside foodstalls of north India, the Dhaba brings a tradition of hearty, inexpensive, and filling food across the ocean without losing any of the flavor. Whole tandoori chicken $8. Vegetarian meals $6-9. Meat dishes $8-12. Naan or roti 90¢. BYO. Open for dinner daily from 5:30pm, for lunch W-Su noon-3pm.

DARLINGHURST

Burgerman, 116 Surry St (tel. 9361 0268), just off Victoria St, is a 50s-style American burger joint with a metallic techno hip identity crisis. The black, orange, and silver decor goes as well with the electronic soundtrack as the french fries ($2-3.50) go with the tomato-shaped ketchup bottles. Scrumptious veggie burger $7.20. Open daily noon-10:30pm. Licensed and BYO corkage $1 per person or $4 for the bottle.

Green Chillies, 113-115 Oxford St (tel. 9361 3717). Despite the address, the entrance is around the corner on Crown St. Serves traditional Thai dishes with far more style than you pay for. Dishes are flavored liberally with chili, lime, mint, and coriander. Mains $9-10. Takeaway lunch specials M-F. 11:30am-3:30pm ($7). BYO wine only, corkage $2 per person. Open Su-Th 11:30am-10:30pm, F-Sa 11:30am-midnight.

Flicks Cafe, 3 Oxford St (tel. 9331 7412) between Flinders St and Greens Rd. Plastered with posters, this movie-themed cafe goes the whole nine yards. The tables for two are perfect for a slow weekend morning, especially with the delicious banana cinnamon pancakes ($5). Pastas, salads, and crepes $9. Surcharge of 50¢ per person on weekends and public holidays. Open S-Th 10am-11pm, F 10am-1am, Sa 10am-2am.

Metro Cafe, 26 Burton St (tel. 9361 5356). A favorite of Sydney vegetarians and anyone who doesn't need to have meat at *every* meal. The wooden booths and fan-shaped wall mirrors lend an Art Deco European flair. Stuffed peppers with potatoes and cheese have a tasty, nutty twist ($8.50). Mains $8.50. Half meals $6.50. Entrées $5.50. BYO, no corkage. Open daily 6-10:30pm, sometimes later.

CHINATOWN

Dixon House Food Court, 80 Dixon St, downstairs on the corner of Little Hay St. Filling East Asian meals, consistently better than their bland pictorial representations. Meals $6-10. Open daily 10:30am-8:30pm.

B.B.Q. King, 18-20 Goulburn St (tel. 9267 2433), near the corner of Sussex St. Spare, dingy decor and plastic dishes from your childhood tea set leave only the food to plead this restaurant's case. After a meal of fresh, crispy, well-prepared Chinese vegetables and perfectly cooked meats, the royal moniker makes a lot more sense. Braised chicken with cashew nuts $10.50. Spring rolls $3.50 for 4. BYO corkage $2 per person. Open daily 11:30am-2am.

GLEBE

Cafe Otto, 79 Glebe Point Rd (tel. 9552 1519; fax 9552 3813). Elegant, high-ceilinged diner with an insulated outdoor courtyard, serving everything from pizza and pastas to pricier meat dishes and wine. Separate kids menu. For dessert, try the local fave: sticky date pudding ($7). Open Su-Th 9am-11pm, F-Sa 9am-midnight.

Perry's Wood Fire Gourmet Pizza, 381 Glebe Pt Rd (tel. 9660 8440 or 9660 8094). The name pretty much says it all. Watch as your pizza is cooked to perfection in the wood fire and then spend the rest of the meal wondering how you ever settled for pizza cooked another way. Traditional medium pizza $8.

Badde Manors, 37 Glebe Pt Rd (tel. 9660 3797). World music plays in the background and the scent of freshly ground coffees permeates the air at this all vegetarian cafe. Gourmet coffee, fresh sorbet and smoothies. Lentil burger $7.50. Open M-Th 8am-midnight, F 8am-1am, Sa 9am-1am, Su 9am-midnight.

NEWTOWN

Tamana's North Indian Diner, 196 King St (tel. 519 2035), with a smaller location at 236 King St. It's rare to find a fast food restaurant with such a faithful following, but Tamana's keeps locals coming back for more with its generous portions of meat and vegetarian curries, all for under $6. Open daily 11:30am-10:30pm.

Kilimanjaro African Eatery, 280 King St (tel. 9557 4565). Re-creates the flavors of several African nations, with dishes cooked in glazed clay pots and served in a simple dark-wood setting. Couscous replaces the usual noodles or rice. Filling mains $8.50. Entrees and sides $5. BYO, no corkage. Open for lunch during week noon-3pm, Sa-Su noon-5pm. Open for dinner Su-Th 6-10pm, F-Sa 6-11pm.

Old Saigon, 107 King St (tel. 9519 5931). Old Saigon serves some of Sydney's most beloved Vietnamese and Thai food. The *kan keow wan,* Thai-style green curry chicken ($13), earns repeat visits from locals. Mains cost $10-17. Lychees with ice cream are fresh, fruity, and $5. Licensed and BYO corkage $1.50 per person. Open Tu and Sa-Su 6-10:30pm, W-F noon-2pm and 6-10:30pm.

INNER EAST AND WATSON'S BAY

Spice Market, 340 New South Head Rd (tel. 9328 7499), Double Bay. Primarily a takeaway counter, with a few wooden tables. Delightfully flavorful dishes range from sweet to spicy. Spring rolls have a peppery kick ($1.50). The pumpkin and tofu stir-fry is a masterpiece ($8.50). Meals with rice feed 2 people easily. Lunch specials M-F noon-4pm $5.50. BYO, no corkage. Open M-F noon-4pm and 5-10pm, Sa-Su 5-10pm.

Doyle's Take-out (tel. 9337 1572), on the wharf at Marine Pde in Watsons Bay. Take bus #324 or 325. Doyle's dominates the wharf, with 3 restaurants within a stone's throw of the water. The takeaway counter, located closest to the Wharf Restaurant, provides the cheapest taste of Sydney's best fish and chips (huge portions $8). If your arteries just can't take it, try the sushi ($7). Open daily 10am-5pm.

Tak's Thai, 462 Oxford St. (tel. 9332 1380), in Paddington, at the Centennial Park end of Oxford St. Sydney-siders would walk a mile for the filling meals in this and black-and-white tile establishment. Heaping chicken Thai noodles $5.80. Main dishes $6-12. BYO. Open Su-F 6pm-midnight, Sa 12:30pm-midnight.

BONDI AND COOGEE BEACHES

Noodle King, 126 Campbell Pde (tel. 9130 8822). Big bowls of noodles, rice dishes and coconut milk-based laksa dishes summon you from the beach. Flavorful Chinese, Thai, and Malaysian meals. Open daily 11:30am-10:30pm.

The * Bite, 164 Russel St (tel. 9130 1908), a walkway that runs off Campbell Pde. Much like the artist formerly known as Prince: goofy name, but fabulous anyway. A baked potato bar that's a hit with backpackers, * Bite (pronounced "Star Bite") goes crazy with a dazzling array of combos, from baked beans and cheese ($4) to Mexi-veggie ($4.90).Open in summer daily 10:30am-3am, during winter daily 10:30am-10pm.

Barzura (tel. 9665 5546), on the end of Carr St, at the south end of the beach. Outdoor seating. Berry flapjacks $6.50. Meals with eggs and toast $7.50. Licensed, BYO wine only. Corkage $2 per person. Open daily 7am-11pm. Breakfast till 1pm.

Erciyes 2, 240 Coogee Bay Rd (tel. 9664 1913). Near Arden St and the beach, Erciyes serves piping hot Turkish pizzas and less filling but equally popular kebabs. Veggie pizzas ($7.50-$8.50) are particularly tasty. BYO. Open daily 10:30am-midnight.

Coogee Bay Hotel (tel. 9665 0000), on the corner of Coogee Bay Rd and Arden St. An entertainment complex with a nightclub, a full size concert hall, three separate bars, and a restaurant. Cook your own juicy T-bone steak or chicken breast for $10, including salad and a roll. Kids meals of chicken nuggets or fish and chips are $6. Open for lunch noon-3pm, dinner 6-9:30pm.

NORTH SHORE

Billi's Cafe, 31a Fitzroy St (tel. 9955 7211), in Kirribilli, just east of Harbour Bridge. Fresh baked goods, quiche ($9.50), and coffee ($2.30) are house staples. The stir-fry ($8.50-$9.50) and chicken satay ($9.50) are amazing. BYO, corkage $1 per bottle. Open M-F 7am-10:30pm, Sa 8am-10:30pm; no service after 9pm M-F, 10pm Sa.

Blues Point Cafe, 135 Blues Point Rd (tel. 9922 2064), on McMahon's Point. Speedy service in a light atmosphere with patio seating. Herb omelets $6, dinner specials $8.50, breakfast specials $5. Licensed, BYO, no corkage. Open M-F 8am-11pm.

Witham's Coffee Shop, 97 Bay Rd (tel. 9955 4762), in Waverton. Discerning coffee drinkers say that Witham's daily brew, roasted on-site and served piping hot, is Sydney's best cup of joe. The much-hailed flat white is $2.50. Lunches range from the huge leg of ham sandwich ($6) to the toasted bagel laden with salmon, cream cheese, and capers ($9). Open daily 7:30am-6pm.

NEW SOUTH WALES

MANLY

Green's Eatery, 1-3 Sydney Rd (tel. 9977 1904), on the pedestrian stretch of Sydney Rd near the Corso. Sunny, mostly vegetarian cafe serves amazingly hearty meals with rice and interesting vegetable combos for $3-6. A medium serving ($5) makes a fine full dinner. Try the chick pea casserole or the sauteed vegetables with tofu. Baseball-sized tuna rissoles $2.80. BYO, no corkage. Open daily 8am-6:30pm.

Bluewater Cafe, 28 South Steyne St, shop 2 (tel. 9976 2051), on the water between Wentworth St and the Corso. Beautiful breakfast setting, with a surf-gone-stylish feel. Bowl of fruit, yogurt, muesli, and milk $6.50. Later in the day, mains go for $8-17. Open daily 7:30am-late, breakfast till 11:30am. Su and holidays 10% surcharge.

■ Sights

Sydney's sights range from architectural landmarks to beaches, from museum tours to neighborhood strolls. Because of the city center's manageable size, many cultural attractions can be seen in a few days of serious sight-seeing. Exploring the tasty cafes, interesting stores, and nooks and crannies of the suburbs will take much longer.

THE HARBOR

Sydney Harbour National Park (tel. 9337 5511) preserves four harbor islands, several south shore beaches, and a few green patches on the northern headlands, providing plenty of space for recreation (see **Water Activities,** p. 110). *(Office open M-F 8:30am-4:30pm.)* Visits to the harbor islands must be arranged in advance through the **National Park Information Centre,** 110 George St (tel. 9247 5033), in Cadman's Cottage, in the Rocks. The early colony's most troublesome convicts were once isolated on Pinchgut Island, off Mrs. Macquarie's Point. Now called **Fort Denison,** the island supports a fort that was built to protect the city from a feared Russian invasion. West of the city center, near the shore at Balmain, the sandstone gunpowder station and barracks of **Goat Island** were the site of cruel punishments for the convicts who built them. Tours departing from Cadman's Cottage offer the only opportunities to stop on either island. *(2hr. Goat Island tours F, Sa, M 1pm, Su 11:30am. $11, concessions and kids $7.50, family $29.50. Reservations required. Call for info about Fort Denison tours.)*

The park's south shore beaches, **Nielson Park, Camp Cove,** and the nude, gay beach of **Lady Bay,** are situated on Vaucluse Bay and Watsons Bay, accessible by bus route #325 to Watsons Bay. Popular north shore harbor beaches include **Balmoral Beach,** on the north side of Middle Head, a 15-minute walk from Military Rd; **Chinaman's Beach,** north of Balmoral, a seven-minute walk from Spit Rd; and **Manly Cove,** surrounding the ferry port at Manly Wharf. To get to Balmoral Beach, take bus #178, 180, or 182 to Spit Junction, then take #257 or 229 to Balmoral. To get to Manly Cove, take #143 or 144 from Spit Junction to Manly.

THE ROCKS AND CIRCULAR QUAY

The arching steel latticework of **Harbour Bridge** spans the harbor from the northern tip of Dawes Point to the southern tip of Milson's Point. Opened in 1932, the bridge is a visual symbol of the city and the best place to get a look at the harbor and the cityscape. Pedestrians can enter the bridge walkway from a set of stairs on Cumberland St just south of Argyle St in the Rocks. The bridge's southern pylon has an entry on the walkway leading to a 200-step stairway and spectacular views. The **Harbour Bridge Museum** (tel. 9247 3408), inside the pylon, tells the story of the bridge's construction. *(Open daily 10am-5pm. Admission to lookout and museum $2, seniors and kids $1.)*

On Bennelong Point, opposite the base of Harbour Bridge, the striking **Sydney Opera House** (tel. 9250 7250) stands like a fleet of sailboats beating into the wind (or, perhaps, like the monster clams of a Godzilla-era Japanese horror film). *(1hr. tours every ½hr. Th-Tu 9am-4pm, W 9:15-noon. $10, students $7.)* Designed by Danish architect Jørn Utzon, Sydney's pride and joy took 14 years to construct. A saga of bureaucracy and broken budgets (planned at $7 million, the building cost $102 million by the time it was finished) surrounded the construction and eventually led the architect to divorce himself from the project prior to its completion. In 1973, the queen of England opened the building, despite strong winds, a false fire alarm, and 1400 spectator seats initially set up facing the wrong way. Today, in addition to starring in thousands of tourist photographs every day, the Opera House stages operas, ballets, classical concerts, plays, and films (see **Entertainment**, p. 111, for box office info).

At the base of the bridge, the Rocks is the site of the original Sydney Town settlement. Built during the lean years of the colony's founding, the area remained quite rough well into this century. In the 1970s, when plans to finally raze the slums were developed, a movement to restore the area to its historic potential began. Today the Rocks bustles with tourists wandering from historic cafe to historic storefront. The **Sydney Visitors Centre** (tel. 9255 1788 or 1800 067 676; open daily 9am-6pm) and the **Rocks Walking Co.** (tel. 9247 6678) share the white, three-story Sailor's Home at 106 George St. The former has brochures on local attractions and displays on the history of the Rocks, and the latter conducts informative walking tours of the neighborhood (80min. tours depart M-F 10:30am, 12:30pm, and 2:30pm, Sa-Su 11:30am and 2pm. $11, ages 10-16 $7.50, under 10 free.) Built in 1816, **Cadman's Cottage,** 110 George St (tel. 9247 5033), next door to the Sailor's Home, is the oldest standing house in Sydney and the current home of the Sydney Harbour National Park Information Centre. (Open daily 9am-5pm. Contact the cottage for tour schedule. Admission $11-15, children $7-9.)

The huge, sandstone **Sydney Observatory** (tel. 9217 0485), on Watson Rd at the top of Observatory Hill, caters to the starry-eyed. It's on Miller's Point, a quick walk west of George St via Argyle St. Guided tours of the heavens (through the telescopes, that is) take place every night at 6:15pm and 8:15pm. ($8, children and students $3, families $18. Book in advance.) In the daytime, the observatory functions as a museum of astronomy with displays, films, talks, and simulated skyscapes. (Open daily 10am-5pm. $5, children and students $2, families $12.) Also on Observatory Hill, the **National Trust Centre** (tel. 9258 0123) and **S.H. Ervin Gallery** (tel. 9258 0150) has information on Sydney's historical sights and changing shows of both recent and historic Australian art. (Open Tu-F 11am-5pm, Sa-Su noon-5pm. Admission $5, children, students, and seniors $3.)

The **Museum of Contemporary Art,** 140 George St (tel. 9252 4033; recorded info 9241 5892; fax 9252 4361; http://www.mca.com.au), injects a little life into an area largely concerned with what has come and gone. Exhibits showcasing the museum's extensive collection of Aboriginal work are consistently worthwhile, but the museum is a bit too small to justify the admission price. (Open daily 10am-6pm, in winter 10am-5pm. $9, students, seniors, YHA members, backpackers, and ages 5-16 $6, families $18.)

Inland from the Opera House, the plants, flowers, and trees of the 30-hectare **Royal Botanic Gardens** fill the area around Farm Cove. Daily guided walks begin at the Visitors Centre (tel. 9231 8125), located in the southeast corner of the park near Art Gallery Rd. (Open daily 7am-5pm. 2hr. walks 10:30am; free.) Within the gardens, attractions such as the Aboriginal plant trail and the formal rose garden are free, but the **Tropical House,** a pair of shapely glass greenhouses housing plants from Australia and around the South Pacific, charges admission. (Open daily 10am-4pm. $5, concessions and kids $2.) **Government House** (tel. 9931 5222), in the northeast corner of the Botanic Gardens, served as the home of the governor of New South Wales as recently as 1996. (Grounds open daily 10am-4pm, house open F-Su 10am-3pm. Free.) On the eastern headland of Farm Cove, the Royal Botanic Gardens end at **Mrs. Macquarie's chair.** The chair, carved from the stone at the end of the point, was fashioned for the wife of Governor Lachlan Macquarie and is now another classic Sydney photo op.

Circular Quay, between Dawes Point and Bennelong Point, is the departure point for both the city ferry system and numerous private cruise companies, becomes a lively hub of tourist activity on the weekends, with street performers, souvenir shops, and easy access to many of the city's major sights. Directly inland from the southeastern corner of Circular Quay, the **Justice and Police Museum** (tel. 9252 1144), at the corner of Albert and Phillip St, indulges Sydney's outlaw past. (Open Jan. Su-Th10am-5pm; Feb.-Dec. Sa-Su 10am-5pm. Admission $6, students, seniors, and ages 5-18 $3, families

NEW SOUTH WALES

$15.) The new, stylish **Museum of Sydney** (tel. 9251 5988), on the corner of Phillip and Bridge St, celebrates the history of the city through films and high-tech exhibitions. *(Open daily 10am-5pm. Admission $6, students, seniors, and ages 5-18 $3, families $15.)*

CITY CENTER AND THE DOMAIN

Sydney's age insures that architecture in the center of town is far from being uniformly modern. The French Renaissance **Town Hall** (tel. 9265 9189) fronts George St between Park and Bathurst St (open M-F 9am-5pm). Built during the prosperity of the late 1800s, the building's outrageous excess merits at least a passing look. The wood-lined concert hall boasts an 8000-pipe organ. The imposing statue of Queen Victoria, visible from the north corner of Town Hall, guards the entrance to the lavish **Queen Victoria Building,** 455 George St. The Byzantine edifice was constructed in 1898 as a home for the city markets, but recent renovations have brought in ritzier shopping venues. Still, a stroll through the shopping center's fantastic wood and brass interior doesn't cost a cent.

Around the corner at the end of the Pitt St pedestrian mall, the **Sydney Centre-point Tower,** 100 Market St (tel. 9229 7444), rises 325m above sea level for a stunning, panoramic view of the city and the surrounding areas. *(Open Su-F 9am-10:30pm, Sa 9am-11:30pm. $10, concessions $8, ages 5-16 $4.50, families $22.)* The 40-second ride to the top is steep in grade and price, so don't waste a trip on a cloudy day. When the sky is clear, views extend as far as the Blue Mountains to the west, the New South Wales central coast to the north, and Wollongong to the south.

Set aside in 1810 by Governor Lachlan Macquarie, **Hyde Park,** between Elizabeth and College St at the eastern edge of the city center, is Sydney's most structured public green space, complete with fountains and stately trees. A buzzing urban oasis during the day, the park warrants some caution when walking through at night. In the southern half of the park, below Park St, the **ANZAC Memorial** (tel. 9267 7668) commemorates the service of the Australia and New Zealand Army Corps in WWI, as well as that of the Australians who have fought in the nation's nine overseas conflicts. *(Open daily 9am-4:35pm. Free tours by arrangement.)* The **Australian Museum** (tel. 9320 6000), on the corner of College and William St at the east side of Hyde Park, achieves an interesting mix of natural and cultural history. *(Open daily 9:30am-5pm. Admission $5, students $3, ages 5-12 $2, seniors and under 5 free, families of 4 $12. Special exhibits cost extra.)* Stuffed re-creations of prehistoric Australian megafauna cast shadows over popular Aussie animals such as the koala and kangaroo. Though the science exhibits are fun for kids only, the museum's treatment of the cultures of indigenous Australian peoples, both historically and as part of Australian society today, is superb.

Macquarie St runs from the north end of Hyde Park to Circular Quay and defines the eastern edge of the central business district. **Sydney Hospital** (built 1814) faces Macquarie St at the end of Martin Pl and is a landmark of colonial architecture. The central section of the building is still Sydney's main medical facility, while the **NSW Parliament House** (tel. 9230 2111) occupies the former north wing. Visitors are welcome in the building, which has both daily free tours and open access to public viewing galleries during parliamentary sessions. *(Open M-F 9:30am-4pm. Tours M-F 10, 11am, and 2pm, during parliamentary session Tu only.)* In 1854, with new wealth coming in from the recent gold rush, Sydney Hospital's south wing became a branch of the Royal Mint. Next door at Queens Sq, the 1819 **Hyde Park Barracks** (tel. 9223 8922) now house a museum devoted to the daily lives of the convicts who once inhabited the building. *(Open daily 9:30am-5pm. Admission $6, students, seniors, and ages 5-18 $3, families $15.)* Beside the north end of the former hospital complex, the **State Library of New South Wales** (tel. 9273 1414) houses galleries and research facilities. *(Open M-F 9am-9pm, Sa-Su 11am-5pm.)*

Behind the buildings on Macquarie St, the unmanicured, grassy expanse of **the Domain** stretches east along the south edge of the Royal Botanic Gardens. Concerts fill the open area during January's **Sydney Festival** (see p. 115). During the rest of the year, the park is most popular for weekday lunch breaks from downtown offices and for Sunday-morning rabble-rousing at Speakers' Corner. Located in the northeast corner of the park, the **Art Gallery of New South Wales** (tel. 9225 1744; recorded info 9225 1790; http://www.artgallery.nsw.gov.au), on Art Gallery Rd, is Sydney's major metropolitan art museum. *(Open daily 10am-5pm. Free, except special exhibits. Free guided tours M 1, 2pm; T, F 11am, noon, 1pm, 2pm; check for info on weekends and public holidays.)* The collection's strength lies in its modern Australian paintings and its Aboriginal gallery, which is the largest permanent exhibition of such work.

DARLING HARBOUR

Darling Harbour, on the west side of the city center, is developed enough to be both upmarket and tacky. Still, the concentration of tourist attractions in this small area makes it a perfect outing for afternoon sight-seeing and a popular spot for families. On foot, Darling Harbour lies only 10 minutes from Town Hall Station. Follow George St north to Market St and Market St west to Pyrmont Bridge. Bus #456 approaches Darling Harbour from Circular Quay by way of Town Hall, and ferries run from Circular Quay to the Aquarium steps. For transportation as tourist-oriented as the destination, hop on the **monorail** from Pitt St, at Park or Market St in the city center. *($2.50, seniors $1.80, under 6 free; day pass $7, family day pass $19.)*

Fish from Australia's many aquatic regions inhabit the tanks at **Sydney Aquarium** (tel. 9262 2300; fax 9290 3553), on the pier at Darling Harbour's east shore. *(Open daily 9:30am-10pm, last admission at 9pm. $15.90, students $10, seniors $12, ages 3-15 $8.90, under 3 free; families $37. Aquariumpass covers admission and round-trip ferry transport from Circular Quay: $18, ages 3-15 $9, families around $47. Wheelchair accessible.)* If you need more evidence that Australia has the weirdest fauna on earth, stop at the mudskipper containment. These freaks of the fish world display their ability to live out of water by absorbing moisture from the air. More conventional attractions include the seal pool and a small touching pool. The underwater Oceanarium, a plexiglass walking tunnel through a huge fish enclosure, makes the pricey admission less bothersome.

The massive Soviet submarine docked opposite the aquarium belongs to the **National Maritime Museum** (tel. 9552 7777; recorded info 0055 62002). *(Open daily 9:30am-5pm. Admission including one special exhibit $9, students, seniors, and ages 5-15 $4.50, families $19.50. Museum and all special exhibits $15, $9, $59; special exhibits only $13, $8, $34. Wheelchair accessible.)* The museum provides a fascinating survey of Australian history from the times of early Aboriginal trading to the present.

Australia's largest museum, the **Powerhouse Museum,** 500 Harris St (tel. 9217 0111; recorded info 9217 0444; fax 9217 0333), just south of Darling Harbour between Ultimo and Haymarket, explores the breadth of human enterprise and ingenuity through exhibits, interactive displays, and demos. *(Open daily 10am-5pm. Admission $8, students $3, ages 5-15 $2, seniors and under 5 free, families $18. Wheelchair accessible.)* With subject matter ranging from decorative arts to space exploration, the museum's astounding variety makes it popular with visitors of all ages.

The serene **Chinese Garden** (tel. 9281 6334; fax 9281 1052), at the corner of Harbour and Pier St, was a bicentennial gift to New South Wales from her sister province in China, Guangdong. *(Open daily 9:30am-5:30pm. Admission $4, students, seniors, and children $2, families $8, wheelchair-bound persons free.)* In traditional southern Chinese style, the delicately manicured garden provides a break from the hubbub of the city.

INNER EAST

The suburbs just east of the city center are some of Sydney's most vibrant areas for shopping, eating, and meandering. Although Kings Cross tends to be a bit seedy, the neighborhood is not without a certain vibrance and charm. Oxford St slides through Surry Hills, Darlinghurst, and Paddington in an endless string of cafes, clothing shops, and hip homewares outlets. Sydney's large, outgoing gay community calls this strip home for much of its length. **Moore Park** contains **Sydney Football Stadium** and the city's professional cricket oval. For a tour of the two facilities and a small museum of Australian sports history, call **Sportspace** (tel. 9380 0383). *(Tours M-Sa 10am, 1, and 3pm during non-game days. Admission $18, seniors and under 19 $12.)* Until this year, Moore

Park was also the home of the Royal Agricultural Society's **Easter Show.** Now that the RAS has moved their event to the Homebush Bay Olympic Site, the park stands poised to take on a new carnival, a 20th Century Fox studio, and an entertainment center slated to open in 1999. **Centennial Park,** the city's largest park, abuts Moore Park's east side and stretches north to meet Oxford St between Paddington and Woolahra. The park includes eight small lakes, a bird sanctuary, athletic fields, and tracks set aside for walking, cycling, and horseback riding. Buses #378, 380, and 382 run the length of Oxford St from the city center connecting to the inner eastern suburbs.

NORTH SHORE

Koalas, kangaroos, and tigers live with million-dollar harbor views in the **Taronga Park Zoo** (tel. 9969 2777; recorded info 1900 920 218; http://www.zoo.nsw.gov.au), at the end of Bradley's Head Rd in Mosman. *(Open daily 9am-5pm. $16, students $11.50, seniors $10, ages 4-15 $8.50, under 4 free. A Zoopass can be purchased at Circular Quay and covers admission, ferry and bus transport, and the cable car ride inside the zoo: $21, students $14, ages 4-15 $10.50.)* To reach the zoo, you'll need to take a 12-minute ferry ride from Circular Quay then a short jaunt on a bus. The zoo's impressive collection includes animals from all over Australia and the world, but some visitors come away disappointed by the animals' crowded conditions. The cable car is widely considered the best part of the visit.

Coastal amusements at the northern beach resort of **Manly** have a tacky boardwalk feel unusual for an Australian beach. **Ocean World** (tel. 9949 2644; fax 9949 7950), on the West Esplanade at Manly Cove, earns rave reviews for the strange, rare specimens in its large tropical fish collection. *(Open daily 10am-5:30pm. $14.50, concessions $7.50, families $34.)* Experienced divers should ask about swimming with sharks in the huge tank surrounding the underwater tunnel view area.

■ Activities and Entertainment

Let the Games begin! But until they do, you've got a few options.

SPECTATOR SPORTS

Sailboat races in the harbor provide a picturesque and sporting distraction on winter Sundays and summer Saturdays. Views from the bridge give a good perspective on most of the course. In Moore Park, the **Sydney Football Stadium** (tel. 9360 6601) draws crowds for rugby league action throughout winter and for the Wynfield Cup finals in September. It's home for the **South Sydney** team (tickets $12, children $3) and the **Sydney City Side** ($15, children free). Call 9389 1011 for tickets. The **Sydney Swans,** of the Australian Rules Football League play here, and have begun to generate huge home crowds since their 1995 Grand Finals appearance. Tickets are sold through Ticketek (tel. 9266 4800). The **Sydney Cricket Ground** (tel. 9360 6601), also in Moore Park, fields a number of matches and Tests, including the one-day World Series matches.

WATER ACTIVITIES

Sydney's most popular pastimes take advantage of the harbor and coastline's natural playgrounds. On any sunny day, white sails can be seen clipping across the waters. **Sydney by Sail** (tel. 0419 367 180) conducts 90-minute hands-on introductory sailing lessons from the National Maritime Museum. *(Trips daily depending on weather and demand; 12-person max. $49 per person. Call ahead to book.)* **Elizabeth Bay Marina,** 1 Ithaca Rd (tel. 9358 2977), in Elizabeth Bay, allows you to test the waters of Watson's Bay and the Harbour Bridge for yourself with rental boats. *(Open daily 8am-5pm. 17-foot launches for up to 6 people $65 for a half day, full day $110, deposit $50.)* The Marina is a short walk from Kings Cross. Follow MacLeay St to Greenknowe St, take a right, and then take the second left at Ithaca Rd. **East Sail Sailing School** (tel. 9327 1166) caters to all experience levels. *(Open daily 8am-6pm. Lessons 9:30am-12:30pm and 1-4pm. Beginning sailing course $380 per person, $350 with 2 or more, trial lesson $85.)*

Sydney's rocky shores include several worthwhile spots for both shore diving and boat diving. **ProDive,** with locations in the city center, 428 George St (tel. 9264 6177; open M-W and F 9am-5:30pm, Th 9am-8:30pm, Sa 9am-5pm, Su 11am-4pm) and at Coogee, 27 Afreda St (tel. 9665 6333; open M-F 9am-5:30pm, Sa-Su 8:30am-5pm), has excellent advice on local diving spots and all the gear you'll ever need. *(Boats and gear for a full day of diving $95, depending on day, season, and specials; gear alone $45.)*

Surfing at **Bondi Beach** makes all the postcards, but Sydney has other beaches with equally appealing waves and smaller crowds. On the south ocean shore, try Bondi, Tamarama, and Coogee. Bronte and Narubra are also popular, and Clovelly is recommended for more experienced surfers. Heading north, the hot spots are Manly, Curl Curl, Dee Why, North Narrabeen, Newport Reef, and Palm Beach. **Bondi Surf Co.,** 72 Campbell Pde (tel. 9365 0870), rents bodyboards with wetsuits for $30 per day. *(3hr. $20; credit card or passport required. Open F-W 9:30am-6pm, Th 9am-6:30pm.)* At Manly, try **Aloha Surf,** 44 Pittwater Rd (tel. 9977 3777). *(Open M-W and F-Sa 9am-7pm, Th 9am-9pm, Su 9am-6pm. Full day $25, half-day $15, wetsuit included.)* To rent **in-line skates,** visit **Bondi Boards and Blades,** 148 Curlewis St (tel. 9365 6555; open daily 10am-6pm) in Bondi, or **Manly Blades,** 49 North Steyne St (tel. 9976 3833; open F-W 9am-7pm, Th 9am-9pm), in Manly. Both rent skates and pads (1st hr. $10, $5 per hr. thereafter).

To explore the area's inland waterways or to get a more in-depth look at the harbor coast, call **Balmoral Marine** (tel. 9969 6006), on Awaba St at Balmoral Beach. *(Open daily 8am-5pm. Canoes $10 per hr.; kayaks $15 per hr., kayaks $20 per hr., half- and full-day rates negotiable.)* Take bus #244 or 247 toward Mosman from Wynyard Station.

PERFORMING ARTS

Sydney's prized **Opera House** (box office tel. 9250 7777; open M-Sa 9am-8:30pm and before Su shows) has four auditoriums and a wide variety of cultural endeavors. Reserved opera seats range from $75-132 and often sell out quickly. Restricted view seats vary in quality, and mean that you'll see less, and possibly none, of the stage. *(In advance $33-38; limit of 2 tickets per person.)* Tickets for standing room go on sale at 9am the morning of a performance ($20, limit 2 per person). Any tickets left unsold 30 minutes prior to a performance are sold at student rush rates ($25). People often line up before tickets become available, so it is wise to get to the Opera House before the 30-minute window. The resident theater company, **Drama Theatre,** presents works from well outside the canon, and tickets are both less expensive and less sought-after than those for opera. *($47 flat rate. Standing room tickets sold 1hr. before the show $25, limit 2. Student rush tickets sold 30min. before showtime, $25.)* The **Sydney Dance Company,** the city's best, also performs in the Opera House.

The **Sydney Symphony Orchestra** (24hr. tel. 9334 4600) performs at the Sydney Opera House and at **Eugene Goosens Hall,** 700 Harris St (tel. 9333 1500; calls taken M-F 9am-5pm), in Ultimo, from February through November. Ticketing is handled by the Symphony and, for Opera House performances only, by the Sydney Opera House box office. Student rush tickets, when available, must be purchased on the day of the concert at that evening's venue ($12). Concerts in Sydney's **Town Hall Auditorium** (tel. 9265 9333) are booked by Ticketek (tel. 9266 4800). The **Sydney Conservatorium of Music** (tel. 9230 1263), in the Royal Botanic Gardens, stages free concerts during school terms, which range from jazz to classical (W and F 1:10pm).

The **Sydney Theatre Company,** performs at the **Wharf Theatre** (tel. 9250 1777; open M-Sa 9am-8:30pm), at Pier 4, on Walsh Bay and at the Drama Theatre at the Opera House. For tickets call the Wharf theater box office. Other First Call theater venues include the **Capitol Theatre** (tel. 9230 9122), at George and Campbell St, just north of Central Station, the **Theatre Royal** (tel. 9320 9122), on King St, in the MLC Center, and the fabulously ornate and ostentatious **State Theatre,** 49 Market St (tel. 9373 6655), between George and Pitt St. For more unusual fare, try the **Belvoir Street Theatre,** 25 Belvoir St, Surry Hills (tel. 9699 3444).

CINEMAS

Sydney doesn't have a great film scene, but has its share of arthouse and mainstream cinemas. Arrive early on discount days for blockbusters. **Standard prices** are $12 for adults, $9 for concessions, and $7.50 for children. Seniors often get discounts before 5pm. Large theaters offer a reduced $7.50 fare on Tuesdays (all day), and smaller theaters do so on Mondays. For show times at all theaters, call **Moviefone** (tel. 13 37 77). The biggest mainstream theater is **Hoyt's Centre,** 505 George St (tel. 13 77 00), midway between China Town and the CBD. Others include the **Village George Street,** 545-551 George St (tel. 9264 6701, movie info tel. 1300 655 601), the **Greater Union Cinemas,** 525 George St (tel. 9273 7373, ticket tel. 12 34 56), and **Pitt Centre,** 232 Pitt Ctr (9264 6701), opposite the Hilton, all of which also host occasional artsy and foreign fare. The **Panasonic IMAX Theatre** (tel. 13 34 62), on the Southern Promenade at Darling Harbour, blasts viewers with a screen 10 times the size of one in a normal movie house (tickets $14, students and seniors $11, children $10).

For indie, art-house, and un-dubbed foreign films, try **Chauvel Cinema** (tel. 9361 5398), an intimate theater in the Paddington Town Hall at Oxford and Oatley St. The **Valhalla,** 166D Glebe Point Rd, Glebe (tel. 9660 8050), caters to the young and the grungy, showing documentaries, recent favorites *(Trainspotting),* retro favorites *(A Clockwork Orange, One Flew Over the Cuckoo's Nest),* and foreign language films. The fringe of the fringe are screened on Sunday matinees and late-night Friday and Saturday. **The Third Eye,** 112 Darlinghurst Rd, Darlinghurst (tel. 9360 7853), reaps cult, classic, and contemporary films. Other quasi-artsy cinemas like the **Academy Twin** (tel. 9331 3457) and the **Verona** (tel. 9360 6099), both in Paddington, and the three **Dendy Cinemas** (King St tel. 9550 5699) are scattered about the city.

■ Nightlife

Whether they're out on the town for drinks and dancing or huddling around a TV for the latest crucial sports telecast, many Sydney-siders hit the pub and club scene four or five times per week. Different neighborhoods have distinctly different scenes, and they vary from night to night as well. Bars in Kings Cross attract a large, straight male crowd which quickly spills over from the strip joints into the pubs and dance clubs. Backpackers round out the mix in this neighborhood, giving several spots an unexpectedly international feel. Outside Kings Cross, travelers generally congregate in pubs to avoid the high cover charges and inflated drink prices of Sydney's high-profile dance venues. **Gay Sydney** struts its stuff on Oxford St in Darlinghurst and Paddington, where some establishments are specifically gay or lesbian and many others are mixed and comfortable. Because the gay clubs provide much of the city's best dance music, flocks of young, beautiful club scenesters of all persuasions fill any extra space on their vibrant, vampy dance floors. Taylor Sq, at the intersection of Oxford, Flinders, and Bourke St, is the heart of this district. Suits clog the bars in the Central Business District, and night spots in the Rocks tend toward the expensive. For more casual pub crawling, wander on Bourke and Flinders St in Surry Hills. Large student populations in Glebe and Newtown make for a younger crowd and cheaper drinks on special nights at pubs in these areas.

Aside from the major concerts in the **Sydney Entertainment Centre** (tel. 1900 957 333; box office open M-F 9am-5pm, Sa 10am-1pm), on Harbour St in Haymarket, the **Hordern Pavillion** (tel. 9380 8038), or the **Enmore Theatre,** 130 Enmore Rd, Newtown (tel. 9550 3666; fax 9550 2990), Sydney's **live music** scene consists largely of local bands casting their pearls before pub crowds. The *Metro* section of the Friday *Sydney Morning Herald* and free weeklies such as *Beat* and *Sydney City Hub* contain listings for upcoming shows, along with info on art showings, movies, theater, and DJ appearances city-wide. The bible of the Sydney clubber is *3-D World,* a free publication that comes out on Tuesdays and can be found in music stores, trendy clothes stores, and hostel. It gives the lowdown on what special events are on each night of the week. *Capital Q Weekly* (free) focuses on the gay community, while *Drum Media* covers music.

BARS AND PUBS

⊛Durty Nelly's, 9-11 Glenmore Rd, Paddington (tel. 9360 4467), just off Oxford St at Gipps St. Sydney's best traditional Irish pub takes its Guinness very seriously, and those in the know claim it's hands-down the best around (schooner $3.20). Even on weekends when it's packed, the dark wood decor coupled with the jovial staff creates a relaxing refuge from the nearby Oxford St melee. Sunday nights feature a musical contest with traditional Irish singalongs. Open daily 11am-midnight.

⊛Hopetoun Hotel (tel. 9361 5257), in Surry Hills, at the corner of Bourke and Fitzroy St. Features live music that ranges from acoustic to rock. The crowd is usually young and lively, though few travelers make the trek down Bourke St. Occasional cover about $5. Schooners $3. Open M-Sa noon-midnight, Su noon-10pm.

⊛Friend In Hand Pub, 58 Cowper St, Glebe (tel. 9660 2326), off Glebe Pt Rd. Wednesday nights crab races and eating contests are legendary. The pub shows its character throughout the week with Trivia nights (Thursdays) and poetry competitions (Tuesdays), all promising "absolutely pathetic prizes." Somewhat tamer weekend nights. Open M-Sa 10am-midnight, Su noon-10pm.

O'Malley's Hotel, 228 William St (tel. 9357 2211), in Kings Cross, at the corner of Brougham St. Upscale style in a casual pub atmosphere. The row of TVs makes O'Malley's into something of an Irish sports bar, but its nightly live music is the best in the Cross. Eclectic crowd proves that backpackers, business-types, and locals can indeed mix well. Schooners of Toohey's $3. Mixed drinks $4. Open daily 11am-2:30am.

The Lord Nelson, 19 Kent St (tel. 9251 4044), on the corner of Argyle St in the Rocks. Six house beers include the award-winning Old Admiral ($5.30). Young crowd contrasts with the setting of Sydney's oldest hotel and pub, first licensed in 1841 to a former convict landlord. Open M-Th 10am-11pm, F-Sa 11am-11pm, Su noon-6pm.

Baron's, 5 Roslyn St (tel. 9385 6131), off Darlinghurst Rd in Kings Cross. The kind of place where other bartenders go to hang out after they're done for the night. Groups gather around the fireplace for a drink or play backgammon into the wee hours. Dark and crowded on the weekends, and just far enough out of the way to prevent it from becoming a backpacker haunt. Open daily 6:30pm-6:30am.

Mansions, 18 Bayswater Rd (tel. 9358 6677) in Kings Cross on the corner of Kellett St. Big, open bar area, hardwood floors, and bright, contemporary decor create a classy haven in the Cross. Familiar 80s and early 90s tunes fill the air, and crowds flood in after midnight to get down on the small dance floor or just to chill and have a drink in relative peace. Sa $5 cover. Open Su-Th noon-2am, F noon-3:30am, Sa noon-4am.

Toxteth Hotel, 345 Glebe Pt Rd, Glebe (tel. 9660 2370), on the corner of Ferry Rd. Lively atmosphere, right near all Glebe's hostels. Schooners of VB $2.80. Open M-Sa 11:30am-midnight, Su noon-midnight.

Orient Hotel 87 George St (tel. 9251 1255), in the Rocks, at the corner with Argyle St. Free live entertainment every night. Drink 10 beers from around the world and they'll throw in a free T-shirt. Schooners from $3. Open M-Th 10am-1 or 2am, F-Sa 10am-3am, Su 10am-2am.

Coogee Bay Hotel (tel. 9665 0000), on Campbell Pde at Coogee Beach. Large and swanky, supplying the juice for the Coogee scene. Backpackers swarm to the cheap drinks (schooners $3; house spirits $3.50) like killer bees to their helpless victims. Selina's Entertainment Center, in the hotel, is one of Sydney's more popular concert venues and sometimes gets international acts. Three bars open M-W 9am-Midnight, Th-Sa 9am-3am, Su 9am-midnight.

The Comedy Hotel, 115 Wigram Rd, Glebe (tel. 9552 2999) off Glebe Pt Rd. Laughs aplenty every night. Before, during, and after the performance the Hotel doubles as a full bar with the usual pool and pokies. Open M-F noon-midnight, Sa 11am-midnight, Su noon-10pm. Ticket reservations by phone or in person.

Taxi Club, 40 Flinders St, Darlinghurst (tel. 9331 4256). Waves of intrigue emanate from one of Sydney's most notorious alternative bars. From transvestites to musclebound bouncers, the 24hr. Taxi Club guarantees a wild time. Dance club open F-Sa 11pm until 5 or 6am (cover $10). Check it out post-party for one last, cheap drink.

Scruffy Murphy's, 43-44 Goulburn St (tel. 9211 2002 or 9281 5296), in the city center on the corner of George St. It may not be the most authentic Irish pub, but it's reputed to be the best live music venue in the city center. Backpackers flock to the $6 jug nights on Mondays and special promotions for the nearby Sydney Central YHA. Schooners of VB $3.50. Open M-Th 11am-2am, F-Sa 11am-4am, Su 11am-3am.

The Fringe Bar, 106 Oxford St, Paddington (tel. 9360 3554). Upscale bar housing a nice mix of young execs, sports fans, and locals. Monday is comedy night (cover $4) and Sundays are set aside for pool competitions. On other nights, people groove to hip-hop beats. Restaurant-style booths for lounging. Open M-W 11am-1am, Th until 2am, F-Sa until 3am, Su noon-midnight; DJs Th-Sa.

Kuletos Cocktail Bar, 157 King St, Newtown (tel. 9519 6369). Deliciously fruity liqueurs go down smooth during Kuletos' daily happy hour from 6-7:30pm, with 2-for-1 drinks. The mixed drinks are pricey during normal hours ($9-$10.50). The Toblerone, Red Corvette, and Peach Passion are the house favorites. Open M-Sa 4pm-late; extra happy hour Th 9:30-10:30pm.

The New Brighton Hotel, 71-73 The Corso, Manly (tel. 9977 3722). The downstairs area of this lively 2-part bar is more for workers, but the upstairs is far more youth-oriented. Free pool upstairs on Mondays after 8pm and Sundays from noon-4pm. DJ upstairs on Wednesday. Open M-Sa until 3am, Su until 11:30pm.

City of Sydney RSL Club, 565 George St (tel. 9264 6281), between Goulburn and Liverpool St. Minor dress code—males must wear collared shirts and no thongs—but with extremely cheap drinks (most beers $1.10-$3.40, jugs $7.50, wines and spirits under $3), it's the perfect place for pre-partying revelry. A photo ID is required as proof of residence 5km or more outside of Sydney. Open M-Th 9am-6am, F-Sa 9am-2:30am.

DANCE CLUBS

◉**Q-Bar,** 44 Oxford St, level 2 (tel. 9360 1375). Entering Q-Bar is a bit like navigating your way into the BatCave—before you can find the club, you'll need to locate the "Synergy Hair" sign, proceed underneath it through an unmarked corridor, and hop onto an old elevator which will take you to the party upstairs. Fortunately, the stealthy entrance gives way to a head-spinning, body-thumping dance floor where the tightly clad bounce to techno beats. Thursday's "Prom Nights" are the exception—rock sing-alongs own the night. A massive pool hall sits next to the dance area ($10 per hr., plus $10 deposit) as does a small bar and lounge area. Open daily 4pm-4am or later, but the dance floor action rarely heats up until midnight.

◉**Midnight Shift,** 85 Oxford St, Darlinghurst (tel. 9360 4319). The boy-toy pictures downstairs come to life on the video screens up above, where DJs spin hot dance tunes for an almost exclusively gay male audience. The showy, sexual atmosphere, enhanced by a catwalk and dancing stands, gets deeper and dirtier on Friday's His and Hercules Night (cover $5). Thursday is Fantasia Night, aimed primarily at an Asian clientele, while Sunday is the designated retro day. Sa cover $15. Draft beers $3.00-3.80. Open M-F noon-3am or later, Sa 6am-noon Su, Su 2pm-noon M.

◉**Imperial Hotel,** 35 Erskineville Rd (tel. 9519 9899). Take a train to Erskineville, take a taxi, make the hike. The costumes at the outrageously fabulous weekend drag shows make it worth it. The "Priscilla Queen of the Imperial" show adds one more layer to the parody and homage surrounding Swedish super-group Abba; scenes from the *Priscilla* movie were filmed here. Get there early; the crowd is straight, gay, lesbian, and huge by showtime. Schooners of VB $3.30. No cover. Shows F-Sa 11:30pm (Priscilla) and 2:15am (changing themes). Open M 2pm-10pm, Tu 2pm-2:30am, W 2pm-3:30am, Th 2pm-7am, F-Sa 2pm-8am, and Su 2pm-midnight.

The Burdekin Hotel, 2 Oxford St (tel. 9331 3066) on the Hyde Park end of Oxford St. Part bar and part upscale nightclub, the Burdekin's 5 levels each have a slightly different feel, from the chill-out level, featuring sofas and the original Space Invaders, to the dance-crazy main level. Open M-Sa 11am-3am. Wheelchair accessible.

Rhino Bar, 24 Bayswater Rd, Kings Cross (tel. 9357 7700). The subdued African safari lodge theme makes weekend dance parties a little incongruous, but that's the last thing on anyone's mind. Colored lights flash throughout the small and smoky dance area as DJs work their magic Th-Sa. Jugs $8 (usually $5 on Th). Drinks $2 F 9pm-midnight, Sa 5pm-6am. Cover F-Sa $5. Open M-Th 3pm-late, F-Sa 3pm-6am.

Mr. Goodbar, 11A Oxford St, Paddington (tel. 9360 6747). Combines a trendy and exclusive bar that caters to the artsy crowd with a vibrant downstairs dance area. DJs rarely disappoint, with Wednesday night techno and weekend hip-hop and house. Open M 7:30pm-3am, W 10pm-3am, Th-Sa 10pm-3am or later.

DCM, 33 Oxford St, Darlinghurst (tel. 9267 7380). You can't miss the glowing rainbow rings and huge glittery letters. The dancing is fast and showy and the crowd young and beautiful. Avoid Saturday nights unless you have time to waste standing on the sidewalk. Otherwise, it's great, sweaty fun for all. Cover Th $5, F and Su $10, Sa $20 with invite. Open Th-Su 11pm-early morning.

Albury Hotel, 6 Oxford St, Paddington (tel. 9361 6555). Two large rooms provide separation between the drag show entertainment and dancing and the less-energized bar scene. Together, these halves comprise a fully functioning meat market. Gay men and straight women place bets on which of the bartenders will go shirtless next. Shows change all the time; check the lineup on posters outside. Happy hour 2-8pm. Open daily 2pm-2am.

The Globe, corner of Elizabeth and Park St (tel. 9264 4844), overlooking Hyde Park in the city centre. The big Saturday event at the Globe is called "Lick," drawing over 700 people into the two floors of this otherwise spacious venue (Sa cover $12). On other nights, the Globe is a bit too posh and pricey, but during the week, they do have $10 jugs of cocktails during happy hour 5:30-6:30pm M-F. Open M-W noon-11pm, Th noon-1am, F noon-4am, Sa noon-7am, Su noon-midnight.

■ Markets and Festivals

Sydney has numerous year-round weekend markets, all of which tend more toward arts, crafts, and gifts than toward fresh produce. Still, the scene is fun, the food is reasonably priced, and there's generally at least one cart selling fresh fruit. **Paddington Bazaar,** 395 Oxford St (tel. 9331 2646) is Sydney's best known and most lively market, featuring entertainment, food, and a variety of crafts (open Sa 10am-4pm; Sa 10am-5pm in summer). **Balmain Markets** (tel. 9818 2674 or 0418 765 736), at St. Andrew's Church on the corner of Darling St and Curtis Rd, can be reached by taking a ferry to Balmain and then a bus up Darling St, or by taking any Balmain bus from the city (open Sa 8am-4pm). **Glebe Markets,** at Glebe Public School, on the corner of Glebe Point Rd and Derby Pl, sells new and second-hand crafts on pleasant Saturdays from 10am to 4pm. On Sundays, the hip **Bondi Beach Market** (tel. 9315 8988), at Bondi Beach Public School on Campbell Pde, features locally-made arts and crafts (open 10am-4pm). **Paddy's Markets** (tel. 1900 957 202), on Ultimo Rd at Hay St, are enclosed and a bit more commercial. They're also the only market in Sydney with a wide array of produce and cheap toiletries. (Open Sa-Su 9am-4:30pm, rain or shine.) **The Rocks Market** (tel. 9255 1717), at the north end of George St under the bridge, takes the market concept upmarket with antiques, jewelry, and collectibles (open Sa-Su 9am-5pm, rain or shine).

Sydney Festival kicks off the year's calendar with arts and entertainment events throughout the month of January. Check the newspaper for details on free concerts in the Domain, street theater in the Rocks, and fireworks in Darling Harbour. February brings the rip-roaring, no-holds-barred festivities of **Gay Mardi Gras.** A huge international event, the festival reaches its climax on the last Saturday of the month (Feb. 27, 1999), with a parade attended annually by over half a million people, and a gala party at the RAS Show Ground in Moore Park. Though the party is restricted and the guest list fills up way ahead of time, gay and lesbian travelers can get on the list by contacting the organizing committee (tel. 9557 4332) and becoming "International Members of Mardi Gras" well in advance (membership $40, tickets around $75).

The **Royal Agricultural Society's Easter Show** (RAS tel. 9704 1111) is held at the Homebush Olympic Site (April 4-18 in 1999). The carnival atmosphere surrounding the show makes it fun for everyone, not just those with an interest in farming. The ornate State Theatre, 49 Market St, between George and Pitt St, comes alive with the **Sydney Film Festival** (tel. 9373 9050) each June. The festival showcases documentaries, retrospectives, and art films from around the world. Tickets begin at $20 for three daytime films. The **City to Surf Run** (tel. 1800 555 514 or 9282 3606), held on the second Sunday in August, draws over 30,000 contestants for a semi-serious trot from Park St. to the beach at Bondi. Entries are accepted up to the day of the race for a fee of $18 (under 18 $12). Falling on even years, the **Sydney Biennale** (tel. 9368 1411) will reappear in the winter of 2000, and bring special showings of art from 40 countries to the Art Gallery of New South Wales, Pier 23, Goat Island, and other gallery spaces citywide.

Spring festivals include the **Manly Jazz Festival** over Labor Day weekend and the **Kings Cross Carnival** at the end of October. At **Christmas,** Bondi sets the pace for debauchery up and down the coast as travelers from around the world gather for one foot-stomping beach party. The Boxing Day **Sydney to Hobart Yacht Race** brings the city's attention back to civilized entertainment for a brief interlude before end-of-the-year festivities reclaim the harbor on **New Year's Eve.**

■ Olympics

The countdown to the 2000 Summer Olympic and Paralympic Games is well under-way as proud Sydney-siders prepare for their city to strut its stuff before the rest of the world. Australia and Greece are the only two countries that have participated in every Summer Olympics since 1896, the beginning of the modern games, and the Sydney Olympics will mark the second time Australia has hosted the games (the first was in Melbourne, 1956). The **Sydney Millennium Olympics** will run from Friday, September 15 to Sunday, October 1, 2000, and the **mascots** will be a platypus named Syd, an echidna named Millie, and a kookaburra named Olly (representing sea, land, and air). The **Paralympic Games** will follow, beginning October 18 and closing October 29, 2000. The S**ydney Organizing Committee for the Olympic Games** (SOCOG) handles ticketing and marketing of the games (http://www.sydney.olympic.org) while the **Olympic Coordination Authority** (OCA) manages tours of the venues before the fortnight of fun begins (http://www.nsw.gov.au).

Construction is progressing according to schedule at the **Homebush Bay Olympic Site,** the area where the majority of events will take place and the self-proclaimed "new heart of Sydney," 14km west of the city centre along the Parramatta River. Nearly half of the venues are already complete and open for public visits, with the remainder slated to be ready by September 1999, a full year before the Games begin.

At Homebush Bay, the world's largest mobile crane has been brought in to help assemble the granddaddy of Olympic stadiums. **Stadium Australia** will seat a record 110,000 spectators for the star-studded opening and closing ceremonies, the marathon and track and field competitions, and the soccer final. Next to the stadium, the **Multi-Use Arena** will host Olympic and Paralympic basketball as well as Olympic artistic gymnastics events in a fully enclosed, air conditioned setting with a capacity of 18,000. On the opposite side of Stadium Australia, across Dawn Fraser Ave, the **Sydney International Aquatic Centre** is by far the most visitor-friendly venue at Homebush Bay, containing three pools, all open to the public (M-F 5am-9:45pm, Sa-Su 6am-7:45pm, until 6:45pm in winter). The first has a waterpark-style tubular slide and sprinklers; the second has an adjustable floor so that pool depth constantly varies; and the third is a regulation-size lap pool. (General admission $2.50; pool entry $4, students and ages 4-15 $3.50, seniors and handicapped $3.) The Aquatic Centre will serve as the venue for both swimming and diving. **The Olympic Tennis Centre** sits at the head of Olympic Boulevard, a 1.5km street that bisects the Homebush site and links the major sporting venues with the **Olympic Village,** which will accommodate over 15,000 athletes and officials. Between the tennis and aquatic centers just off Olympic Blvd, the **State Sports Centre** is the unglamorous venue for tae kwon do and table tennis, while the nearby **Hockey Centre** will house field hockey.

Any tour of the Homebush Bay site should begin with a trip to the OCA's **Information Centre,** 1 Herb Elliot Ave (tel. 9735 4800; fax 9735 4346; open daily 9am-5pm). Bus tours of the site depart from the centre every half hour beginning at 10am through 1pm during the week, and every hour from 11:30am through 2:30pm on weekends ($5 adults, concessions $2.50). Housed within the information centre, a walk-through exhibit on the site's plans and progress leads to a short video presentation on the various venues (free). An alternative tour begins at Circular Quay, proceeding by ferry to the wharf at Homebush, where the same bus tour then begins. ($15. Tours depart M-F 10am, 11am, noon, 1pm, and 1:30pm; Sa-Su 10:35am and 12:25pm. For further info, call 9207 3170.) While this offers more scenic transport, this tour does not allow time for exploring the venues since you must return on a specific ferry. The best way to reach the site is by **train** to the brand new **Olympic Park Station** (caution: do not take the train to "Homebush"!). Until the Olympics draw nearer, direct train service runs only 4 times a day during the week from Central Station to Olympic Park and back. Weekend service is on the half hour, but even when direct service is unavailable, a free bus will zip you from the Strathfield Station to Homebush Bay. By **car,** take the Homebush Bay Drive exit off the M4 Motorway— during the games, however, no parking will be available. Instead, several park-and-ride stations will be established, delivering you into Homebush by bus. Finally, **bicycles** can enter the site from the eastern side via Victoria Avenue near the Concord West train station, where a scenic path carves through the surrounding wetlands of Bicentennial park and on into the heart of Homebush Bay.

Several events will be held in towns near Homebush. **Sydney International Regatta Centre**, a few km north of Penrith, is already complete and will hold all rowing events, including kayaking at the nearby Whitewater Stadium. Back in Sydney proper, boxing, wrestling, weightlifting, and judo are currently set to take place in the **Exhibition Halls** at Darling Harbour, world-famous **Bondi Beach** will host beach volleyball, and Rushcutter's Bay in the Harbor will be the scenic locale for Olympic Sailing. For information on other events and venues, contact OCA at 9735 4800 or visit them at Homebush Bay. **Red Terra Tours** runs tours of the Olympic site from Circular Quay (Jetty 2) twice daily (8am and 1pm) and includes tours of the Aquatic Centre and Bicentennial Park ($48.50, children $28.50; bookings through Australian Travel Specialists at 9555 2700).

AROUND SYDNEY

▓ Royal National Park

Just 30km south of Sydney's city center, **Royal National Park** is an easy and glorious escape from city life. The park, Australia's oldest and the world's second-oldest (after the United States' Yellowstone), covers 14,969 hectares of beach, heath, rainforest, swamp, and woodland. Eucalypt variety is particularly attractive. The range of activities available in the park is as broad as the diversity of habitat would suggest. Bushwalkers, birdwatchers, swimmers, and surfers all find favorite getaways in different corners of the park, while an extensive network of trails and driving routes allows everyone to spread out during the busy summer weekends. Across the Princes Hwy on the west side of the park, the smaller, often-forgotten **Heathcote National Park** contributes another 2000 hectares of heathland to the cause of travelers and Sydneysiders trying to lose themselves in the green.

GETTING THERE **CityRail trains** from Sydney come to Loftus in the northwest ($2.80, off-peak return $3.40), Waterfall in the west ($3.80, $4.40), or Otford at the park's southern point ($4.40, $5.20). From Waterfall or Otford, walk east to enter the park. To approach the northeast corner, take CityRail to Cronulla ($3.20; 3.80 from Central Station) and then catch a **Cronulla National Park Ferries** (tel. 9523 2990) boat to Bundeena, home of **Bonnie Vale campground** and the **Coastal Track** trailhead. (To Bundeena M-F 5:30am-7pm, hourly on the half hr., Sa-Su 8:30am-5:30pm; no 12:30pm departure. To Cronulla M-F 6am-7pm hourly on the hr., Sa-Su 9am-6pm; no 1pm departure. $2.40, ages 4-15 and seniors

$1.20.) **By car,** the Princes Hwy. provides easy access to the park from Sydney. Follow the signs to head east on Farnell Ave. south of Loftus and the Princes Hwy to Airport and Wollongong.

PRACTICAL INFORMATION The **Audley Visitor Centre** (tel. 9542 0648, open daily 8:30am-4:30pm), 2km inside the park's entrance and 4km south of Loftus, distributes information on walking trails, ranger-led activities, and camping in the park. The main park road, running from the northwest entrance to Otford, stays open 24 hours, but turn-offs have locked gates from 7:30pm to 7am. Toilet kiosks are located at Audley (wheelchair accessible), Wattamella, and Garie Beach. Entrance to the park costs $9 per car (pedestrians and cyclists free).

CAMPING AND ACCOMMODATIONS The National Parks and Wildlife Service (NPWS) administers one car-accessible serviced camping area in Royal National Park, **Bonnie Vale,** just inside the park at Bundeena. From Audley, take the main park road to Bundeena Rd. and follow the signs to Bonnie Vale. Sites have access to parking, toilets, showers, water, laundry facilities, pay phones, and trash bins and cost $10 for the first two people (each additional person $2, children under 5 free; no electrical hook-ups or individual water supplies). No open fires are permitted anywhere in the park. The gates on Bundeena Rd open from 6am to 9:30pm, but keys may be borrowed from the Audley Visitors Centre or from the camp manager (deposit $25). The NPWS also oversees 150 free, **campsites** in six locations throughout Royal National Park and at the popular Kingfisher Pool camping area in nearby Heathcote National Park. Required permits for any of these areas can be obtained at the Audley Visitors Centre or by mail. For bushcamping permits or to put in an application for a Bonnie Vale lottery periods (conducted for sites during school holidays), write to NPWS South Metropolitan District, P.O. Box 44, Sutherland NSW 2232.

Royal National Park's only public accommodation with a roof is the **Garie Beach YHA Hostel** is a three-room house overlooking Garie Beach. In the right mood, it's idyllic. The view is fabulous (12 beds; $6, under 18 $3). Reservations and key pick-up must be arranged in advance through the YHA Travel and Membership Centre, 422 Kent St., Sydney (tel. 9261 1111), or at either of the Sydney YHA hostels.

SIGHTS AND ACTIVITIES The breathtaking 26km **Coastal Track** tops Royal National Park's list of bushwalking trails. Running along the sandstone cliff line between Bundeena and Otford, the trail is generally approached as a two-day affair, allowing time to enjoy the wildflowers of the heath, the depths of the coastal caves, and the sheer expanse of the ocean views. Hikers with less time often hike a piece of the trail from one of the park roads and then return to their starting point. The park's only **wheelchair-accessible trail** runs up to Bungoona Lookout from the Audley Visitors Centre (1km round-trip). The short **Aboriginal rock engravings** walk begins at Jibbon Beach, on Port Hacking, east of Bundeena. The engravings, believed to be between 800 and 5000 years old, depict animals that were important to the local tribe's diet. Although Aboriginal carvings appear on rocks throughout the park, officials only direct tourists to the Jibbon site. Defacement at the site makes their reasoning obvious. From Otford Lookout, at the park's southern tip, the 1km **Werrong (Hellhole) Track** leads to the only **nude swimming beach** in Royal National Park. When the wind is right, Werrong is also an excellent surf spot (wetsuit recommended). The park visitors' center has maps and directions to other walking trails, many of which lead to swimming holes, waterfalls, or secluded beaches.

Most **surfers** favor the beaches at Garie, North and South Era, or the secluded Burning Palms area. Surf Life Saving Clubs overlook the beaches at both Garie and Burning Palms. Wattamolla is a fun area 15min into the park and just off the main artery. It has a lagoon and cove beach. A long headland keeps the waters calm; the sea is a bit chilly. A kiosk sells refreshments beside a large parking area. Although visitors are prohibited from touching animals inside the park, **fishing** off the shore is quite all right, and Jibbon Point, Wattamolla, Garie, and Burning Palms are all popular spots for casting a line. The **Audley Boatshed** (tel. 9545 4967), off Farnell Ave, about 2km beyond the Audley Visitors Centre, rents rowboats, canoes, kayaks (1hr. $10, 2hr. $16, half-day $16-18, full day $20), **mountain bikes** (1hr. $10, full day $24), **tandem bicycles** (1hr. $12, full day $44), and **aqua bikes** ($10 per half hr.). All rentals require a $10 deposit. (Open daily 8:30am-before sundown, roughly 7pm in summer and 4:30pm in winter.)

The water off of Bonnie Vale, Jibbon Beach, Wattamolla, and Little Marley is safe for **swimming.** Marley Beach, just north of Little Marley, is considered unsafe. Inland, freshwater swimming holes, such as Deer Pool, near Marley Beach, and the Kangaroo Creek, southwest of Audley, offer more placid and secluded settings for a dip.

■ Ku-Ring-Gai Chase National Park

Seven years old when the Australian colonies federated in 1901, the country's second-oldest national park, Ku-Ring-Gai Chase, came close to gaining a far more central role in the new nation's development, as the site of the capital city. However, the proposal to build the city on the park land in medieval English style—as a moated fortress capital to be called Pacivica—was eventually passed over in favor of the plan which led to the creation of Canberra. The park, located 24km north of downtown Sydney, has remained the preserve it was intended to be from the outset and has since grown to include over 15,000 hectares covering most of the southern headlands of Broken Bay. Waterways leading out to the ocean carve their way through the park's sandstone rock landscape and giving the park a rugged beauty. Many Sydney-siders come for the numerous Aboriginal rock engravings and the exotic wildflowers that bloom early in winter.

The volunteer-run **Kalkari Visitors Centre** (tel. 9457 9853; fax 9457 9054) on Ku-Ring-Gai Chase Rd, 4km inside the park gates, distributes free hiking maps. Volunteers from the center run a program of mostly free **guided walks** highlighting Aboriginal engraving sites and the park's scenic gems (open daily 9am-5pm). Drivers should be sure to note that park gates close at 6pm during winter, 8:30pm in summer, and reopen at 6am. **Bobbin Head Information Centre** (tel. 9457 1049), inside the Wildlife Shop, at the bottom of the hill at Bobbin Head, is the official National Parks and Wildlife Service information outlet for the park (open daily 9am-4pm). Four roads provide vehicle access to the park: Ku-Ring-Gai Chase Rd from the Pacific Hwy and Bobbin Head Rd from Turramurra, both in the southwest corner of the park, and Coal and Candle Dr and Pittwater Rd, which branch from Mona Vale Rd to enter the southeast section of the park (park entry $9 per car). Ferries come into the park from **Palm Beach Ferry Service** (tel. 9918 2747 or 9974 5235), stopping at the Basin (hourly beginning at 9am $3.50), Bobbin Head (daily at 11am, $14), and Patonga (daily at 9, 11am, and 3:45pm, $6). Sydney Bus #90 goes from Central Station to Palm Beach near the wharf from which the ferries set out. Public transportation for other destinations within the park is explained below.

The park's **camping area** and **hostel** can be approached by car from the east side of the park, but each requires that you leave the car behind somewhere along West Head Rd. The campground at the Basin (tel. 9451 8124) is accessible by ferry from Palm Beach or by a 2.5km hike on the Basin track from West Head Rd. The site has cold showers, toilets, wood barbecues, and a public phone, but all supplies must be carried in. (Sites for 2 $10, each additional person $2; during school holidays $15, $3; children under 5 free.) Bookings must be arranged through the NPWS office (tel. 9972 7378; open M-F 9am-4pm), but payment can be made at the site.

Possibly the most refreshingly remote hostel in the greater Sydney area, the **Pittwater YHA Hostel** (tel. 9999 2196; fax 9997 4296), accessible by ferry from Church Point (round-trip $6), enjoys lush green scenery from its lofty terraced perch over Pittwater. Take bus #156 from Manly or bus #E86 from Wynyard, or follow Pittwater Rd to reach the Church Point wharf. The open, outdoorsy hostel provides a retreat without the distraction of TV or radio. Hosts encourage guests to get out and use any of the 16 walking trails which start in the immediate area or to partake of a summer swim in the nearby bay. You can unwind by the fire at day's end or recline in the hostel's hammock. (Dorms $16, under 18 $8; twins $40. Sa $21, $11; $50; YHA non-members pay $3 more. Linen $2-3. Canoe rental $6 for length of stay. Bike rentals $15 per day. Reception open daily 8-11am and 5-8pm. Bookings required.)

Ku-Ring-Gai Chase has a number of bushwalks for any level of expertise. The 20-minute discovery walk just outside the Kalkari Visitors Centre is a quick, easy way to see the local animal life (wheelchair accessible). The circuit created by linking the Bobbin Head Track and the Sphinx Track, between the Bobbin Head Rd. entrance to the park and Bobbin Head, covers almost 10km, passing through mangroves, along a creek, and near an Aboriginal engraving site. For the best views of the Hawkesbury River as it feeds out into the Pacific Ocean at Broken Bay, proceed as far north as possible along West Head Rd until you reach a picnic lookout area. Take **Shorelink Bus Company** (tel. 9457 8888) bus #577 from Turramurra Railway Station (from Central Station $2.80, off-peak return $3.40) to the park entrance gates (M-Sa every hr., limited service on Su, $2.10 each way). There are no patrolled swimming **beaches** in the park, but the protected coves of **Pittwater** and **West Head,** in particular at the **Basin,** are less turbulent than the open waters of **Broken Bay. Halvorsen Boats** (tel. 9457 9011), at Bobbin Head near the Wildlife Shop, rents motorboats (1st hr. $30, each additional hr. $8; deposit $30) and rowboats ($10, $4, $10). Sundays are often busy, but reservations are not accepted; call ahead to check availability, and get there early. (Open M-F 8:30am-4pm, Sa-Su 8:30am-4:30pm.)

■ Botany Bay National Park

The two sections of Botany Bay National Park, located on the outermost reaches of land surrounding Botany Bay, have been preserved more for their historical significance than for their scenic beauty. The two sites, designated together as a National Park in 1988, memorialize the voyages of Captain James Cook and French explorer Jean-Françoise de Galaup, Count de Laperouse. Cook's landing at Kurnell on the southern headland of the bay was the origin of British colonization. The Laperouse expedition, to which the northern half of the park is dedicated, ended less successfully with the mysterious disappearance of two ships and scores of men. Despite popular impressions of Botany Bay as either sleepy and suburban or ugly and industrial, visitors often remember best the ocean views and beaches.

The **Discovery Centre** (tel. 9668 9111), 450m beyond the toll gate inside the park's southern section, has a fine exhibit on the eight-day landing of Cook's ship the *Endeavour.* Exhibits are also devoted to the indigenous people and their use of the surrounding wetlands. (Open M-F 11am-3pm, Sa-Su 10am-4pm.) Nearby, a short walking trail passes several monuments and historical markers related to Cook's landing. Most of the park's ocean-front shoreline is considered dangerous for water activities, but **swimming, fishing,** and **diving** are possible on the Botany Bay shore near the Discovery Center. **Surfers** should move down the beach to **Cronulla.** To access the park's southern section from Sydney, take the **train** from Town Hall or Central Station to Cronulla ($5.80). From Central Station, **Sydney bus** #309 or #391, which runs every 15 minutes, can be taken to the Port Botany stop ($2.50, $1.20 children). **Kurnell Bus Company** (tel. 9524 8977) has regular service from Cronulla Railway Station to the park on Route 987 (M-F 11 per day, Sa 8 per day, Su 3 per day; $2.80, students, seniors, and ages 4-18 $1.40). By **car,** follow the Princes Hwy south and branch left at Taren Point Rd. Turn left on Captain Cook Dr, which heads directly to the park. (Gates open daily 7am-7:30pm. Park entry $5 per car, collected only Sa-Su and holidays. Pedestrians free.)

The northern half of the Botany Bay National Park charges no entrance fee. Here, the **Laperouse Museum** (tel. 9311 3379), at the end of Anzac Pde, recounts the tale of Laperouse and his mysterious last voyage. The mystery's not huge—the poor guy sank—but the museum does an excellent job of building suspense. (Open W-Su 10am-4:30pm. $5, concessions and kids $3.) The French government's **monument** to Laperouse, erected in 1828, stands near the current museum. Across a short footbridge, **Bare Island Fort** once guarded Sydney's southern approach from the none-

> ### It Might've Been "L'Australie"
>
> On January 26, 1788, members of the British First Fleet were surprised to see two ships approach the shore at Botany Bay. The French Laperouse expedition arrived just six days after the British brought the first convicts to the planned penal colony. Three years into an around-the-world exploratory mission, the French crew needed time to rest and repair their vessels. The British Captain Phillip moved north to Port Jackson, later renamed Sydney, while Laperouse stayed at Botany Bay for six weeks. Despite national rivalry, the two groups interacted regularly and were on friendly terms throughout the stay of the French. On March 10, Laperouse and his party set sail and cruised into the South Pacific, never to be seen again. The French government sent out a search party in 1791, and Louis XVI's last request before his death in 1793 was "any news of Monsieur de Laperouse?" Forty years passed before any trace of his wreck was found.

too-likely threat of attack. Today the fort is accessible via guided tours booked by the Laperouse Museum (40min; Sa-Su 12:30, 1:30, 2:30, and 3:30pm; $5, concessions and kids $3). The **Boatshed Cafe** (tel. 9661 9315), on the water near the museum, is a convenient spot to grab lunch and watch the windsurfers and ships on Botany Bay. (Fish and chips $4.50, chicken burger $3.50. Open Tu-F 10am-5pm, Sa-Su 10am-6pm; longer in summer.) The surrounding rocks are perfect for a takeaway picnic. When you're tired of watching, rent a boat from **First Fleet Marine** (tel. 9661 9315), inside the Boatshed Cafe Building (motor boats $25 per hr., $15 each additional hr.; paddle boats $10 per hr) Fisherfolk will find bait and tackle for sale, but there's no equipment to rent. The beach below the cafe is clean, sandy, and suitable for swimming. Sydney bus #393 from Railway Square and #394 from Circular Quay make the trip to this end of Botany Bay regularly. Drivers need only take Anzac Pde until it ends at the Laperouse Museum.

■ Parramatta to Penrith

In April 1788, Governor Phillip led an expedition west to see what lay up the river from the new settlement of Sydney. Australia's second town was established as a result of that mission in November of the same year. Then called Rose Hill, the settlement grew into the present-day town of Parramatta, a 20-minute drive from Sydney along Parramatta Rd. Before reaching Parramatta, the road becomes the M4 Tollway, at Strathfield, the most direct route to the Blue Mountains (toll $1.50).

■ Parramatta

The village whose fertile farmland once fed the starving Sydney colony is now a suburban extension of the nearby city. Parramatta does, however, maintain several buildings from the early days of colonization which rank high on many history-minded tourists' must-see lists. The most notable of these buildings is **Old Government House** (tel. 9635 8149; fax 9891 4102), in Parramatta Park at the west end of town. Originally a plaster cottage built by Governor Phillip in 1790, the house grew into its current Georgian grandeur through renovations made by Governor Lachlan Macquarie between 1812 and 1818. In addition to its primary claim to fame as the oldest remaining public building in Australia, Old Government House contains the country's most extensive collection of pre-1855 colonial furniture. The National Trust now administers the building and offers tours whenever people gather. (Open Tu-F 10am-4pm, Sa-Su 11am-4:00pm, last admission 30min. before closing; admission $5, students, seniors, and under 16 $3, families of 4 $12; combined admission ticket with Experiment Farm Cottage $8, concessions $6.)

Elizabeth Farm, 70 Alice St (tel. 9635 9488; fax 9891 3740), in Rosehill, east of the town center, was the home of John and Elizabeth Macarthur, founders of the Australian Merino wool industry. A bungalow-style home exemplary of early Australian architecture, the farm house features furnishings in the style of the late 1700s and early 1800s and a large number of historical replicas made to fit descriptions of pieces owned by the MacArthurs. Visitors are allowed to wander through the house at their own pace, and afterwards, can enjoy lunch or tea at the adjacent cafe. (Cafe open daily 10am-4pm; house open daily 10am-5pm. Admission $6; students, seniors, and ages 5-15 $3; under 5 free; families of 4 $15.)

John Macarthur built **Hambleton Cottage** (tel. 9635 6924), on the corner of Hassall St. and Gregory Pl, in 1824 as a home for his son Edward. (Open W-Th and Sa-Su 11am-4pm. Admission $3, seniors $2.50, ages 5-12 $1.50.) In 1789, the colonial government made its first land grant in the Australian colony to the convict James Ruse at the site of **Experiment Farm Cottage**, 9 Ruse St (tel. 9635 5655). (Open Tu-Th 10am-4pm, Su 11am-4pm. Admission $5, students, seniors, and under 15 $3; combined admission ticket with Old Government House $8, $6 concession.)

The **Parramatta Visitors Centre** (tel. 9630 3703; fax 9630 3243; email parrinfo@magna.com.au), on the corner of Church and Market St, distributes information on sights in the Parramatta area (open M-F 10am-4pm, Sa 9am-1pm, Su 10:30am-3pm). From Sydney, trains (from Central Station $2.80, off-peak return $3.40) and ferries both make the trip to Parramatta. The ferry ride ($5), an hour long cruise on a sleek, new RiverCat pontoon boat, is far preferable to the 30-minute train ride.

West of Parramatta, in Doonside, **Featherdale Wildlife Park,** 217 Kildare Rd (tel. 9622 1644; recorded info 9671 4984; fax 9671 4140), provides interactive animal fun, allowing visitors to feed kangaroos and interact with the country's largest collection of native Australian animals (open daily 9am-5pm; admission $12, students $10, seniors $8, ages 4-14 $6, families of 4 $30). Forty minutes from Sydney by car, the park is also accessible by bus #725 from the Blacktown train station (from Central Station $3.20, daily off-peak return $4). Attractions at **Australia's Wonderland** (tel. 9830 9100 or 1800 252 198; recorded info 9830 1777; fax 9675 2002) run the gamut from wombats to waterslides and roller coasters galore. (Open 10am-5pm. Admission $37, seniors and ages 4-12 $26, under 4 free.) To reach this carnival paradise, take the Wallgrove Rd exit from the M4, or catch **Busways** bus #738 (round-trip $4.20) from the Rooty Hill train station (from Central Station $3.80, off-peak return $4.60).

■ Penrith

The town of **Penrith,** 35km west of Parramatta along the Great Western Hwy, hovers at the edge of Sydney's sphere of suburban influence, at the base of the Blue Mountains. Running through the west half of town, the **Nepean River** is one of Penrith's best features, a wide, placid corridor. Although no one in town rents boats for casual use, you can enjoy the river with a cruise on the **Nepean Belle** (tel. 4733 1274 or 4733 1888), a paddlewheel riverboat which makes leisurely trips through the dramatic Nepean Gorge in **Blue Mountains National Park.** The double-decker boat departs **Tench Reserve Park,** off Tench Ave, on an irregular schedule (shortest cruise 90min.; $15, ages 3-11 $6). Just 5km north of town along Castlereagh Rd, the **Sydney International Regatta Centre** and **Whitewater Stadium** are being constructed and will serve as the **Olympic** venues for all rowing and kayaking events.

Closer to the center of town, the **Museum of Fire** (tel. 4731 3000), on Castlereagh Rd. one block north of the Great Western Hwy, educates and amuses with entertaining films and more serious displays on the fire safety and the history of fire-fighting in New South Wales. The exhibit on bushfire and the simulation of a home fire are important additions to what might otherwise be just a collection of gadgetry. (Open M-Sa 10am-3pm, Su 10am-5pm. Admission $5, concessions $3, families of 5 $12.50.) Devoted to the development of modernism in Australian art, the **Penrith Regional Gallery and the Lewers Bequest,** 86 River Rd. (tel. 4735 1100; fax 4735 5663), west of town in Emu Plains, mounts changing exhibitions to augment the modest standing collection in a riverside house surrounded by a sculpture garden. (Open Tu-Su 11am-5pm. Admission $2, students, seniors, ages 7-15 $1, under 7 free.)

The **Penrith Visitors Centre** (tel. 4732 7671; fax 4732 7690), on Mulgoa Rd., inside the Panther's World Entertainment Complex, covers Penrith and carries additional information on the Blue Mountains. The **Nepean River Caravan Park** (tel. 4735 4425; fax 4735 6301) provides excellent, inexpensive sleeping arrangements. Tent sites lie at the bottom of a steep hill, secluded from the rest of the park and surrounded by trees. (Reception open daily 8am-6pm. Sites $10; with power $17.50; cozy 4-bed dorms $14 per person, standard cabins for 2 $39, each additional person up to 6 $7. Amenities key and gate card deposit $10. Laundry facilities). **CityRail** trains to Penrith and Emu Plains, the end of the suburban line, take approximately one hour from Central Station (to either station $5.40, off-peak return $6.40).

■ The Upper Hawkesbury

The fertile farmland of the Upper Hawkesbury has been cultivated since the first decade of Australian colonial inhabitancy, but it was not until 1810 that towns were established in the area. Governor Lachlan Macquarie selected sites for five towns, naming them **Windsor, Richmond, Wilberforce, Castlereagh,** and **Pitt Town.** Today, these towns, collectively known as the **Macquarie Towns,** lie at the east end of Bells Line of Road (see p. 133), a scenic alternative to the freeway between the outskirts of Sydney and the Blue Mountains. **Tourism Hawkesbury** (tel. 4588 5895; fax 4588 5896), on Richmond Rd. between Windsor and Richmond, has information on the entire area, including the helpful booklet *Richmond and Windsor Walks* ($1; office open M-F 9am-5pm, Sa 9am-3pm, Su 9am-1pm).

Clifton Cottage, 22 Richmond Rd (tel. 4587 7135), just outside Windsor, offers bed and breakfast in an antique-laden garden setting for reasonable rates. (Singles $45; doubles $65. Reception open daily 8am-8pm. Check-out 10am.) The town of Windsor is particularly well-preserved, and the refurbished center at Thompson Square features several historical buildings. On the square, the Daniel O'Connell Inn houses the **Hawkesbury Museum of Local History** (tel. 4577 2310) and a small tourist information office (both open daily 10am-4pm; museum admission $2.50, students, concessions, and ages 5-15 $1.50, under 5 free). The 1815 **Macquarie Arms Hotel** (tel. 4577 2206) claims to be "the oldest pub in Australia" and the owner is fond of leading ghost tours into the cellar beneath the building, where smuggling often took place. A plaque on the building's front wall marks the height of the flood of 1867, the greatest of many floods which have plagued the region. **St. Matthew's Anglican Church** on Moss St at the corner of Greenway Crescent (tel. 4577 3193), built between 1817 and 1822, is considered to be one of the greatest achievements of ex-convict architect Francis Greenway (open daily dawn-dusk). The church cemetery contains stones dating from 1810.

Windsor River Cruises (tel. 9831 6630) conducts informative cruises up the Hawkesbury River with coffee and commentary. Trips depart Windsor Wharf Wednesdays at 10:30am and Sundays at 1:30pm barring weather difficulties (2½hr., $15, ages 5-15 $7.50, families of 4 $35). Sights along the route include the 1809 **Ebenezer Church** (tel. 4579 9350), 5km outside Wilberforce on Coromandel Rd, Australia's oldest church that's still used for public worship. The grounds of the sandstone building, which seats about 80, include a cemetery with the graves of several of the areas earliest European inhabitants (open daily 10am-3:30pm). **Hawkesbury Heritage Farm** (tel. 4575 1457), on Rose St in Wilberforce, 6km northeast of Windsor off Putty Rd, recreates early colonial life in a collection of historical buildings and antiques. (Open Th-Su 10am-5pm. Admission $10, students, seniors, and ages 5-15 $6, under 5 free, families of 5 $25.) Richmond, 10km northwest of Windsor via Richmond Rd, has a nice collection of 1800s homes and churches, as well as a **National Parks and Wildlife Service** office (tel. 4588 5247; fax 4588 5335; open M-F 9:30am-12:30pm and 1:30-5pm). CityRail trains from Sydney's Central Station reach both Windsor (one-way $4.60, off-peak return $5.60) and Richmond ($5.40, $6.40).

NEW SOUTH WALES

BLUE MOUNTAINS

For the first 25 years of British colonization, the unscalable walls of the Blue Mountains, just 100km from the coast, contained the growth of the new colony and the exploration of Australia. Numerous expeditions approached the mountains only to come away stumped. Because the so-called mountains are actually a series of canyons separated by several high plateaus, the explorers found cliffs at the edges of the valleys instead of hills. A successful route was not found until 1813, when Blaxland, Lawson, and Wentworth, assisted by local Aboriginal know-how, attempted to cross the mountains along the ridges. Today, the mountains are the first stop on most trips west from Sydney and an easy year-round getaway for Sydney-siders. The short trip inland, just a 90-minute drive or a two-hour train ride, grants summertime visitors a reprieve from the oppressive heat that hangs over the coast. In winter, crisp sunny days, occasional snowfalls, and holiday festivities continue to draw travelers.

Although a variety of adventure activities such as abseiling (rappelling) and canyon rafting have become popular in recent years, the Blue Mountains' major draws remain their excellent hiking trails and lookouts. Sunlight filtering through eucalyptus oil suspended in the air gives the forest its tint. From the lookout points, the earth falls away into an endless sea of blue foliage speckled with white bark and bordered by distant sandstone cliffs. Whether you have a hankering for gorgeous waterfalls, serene rainforest, or jaw-dropping panoramic views, you'll find it all here.

Three national parks divide the wild stretches of the region. **Blue Mountains National Park,** the largest and most accessible of the three, spans most of the Jamison Valley (south of the Great Western Hwy between Glenbrook and Katoomba), as well as the Megalong Valley (south of the Great Western Hwy west of Katoomba) and the Grose Valley (north of the Great Western Hwy and east of Blackheath). The Grose and Jamison Valleys appeal primarily to hikers, while horseback riders tend to favor the Megalong Valley (see **Blackheath,** below, for more information on horse-riding). **Kanangra-Boyd National Park,** tucked between two sections of Blue Mountains National Park in the southwest reaches of the mountains, is reserved for skilled bushwalkers. The park, accessible by partially paved roads from Oberon and from Jenolan Caves, has only one 2WD road. **Wollemi National Park** contains the state's largest preserved wilderness area. It's a place so unspoiled and untrafficked that a species of pine tree only before seen in fossil form was found here, alive and well, in 1994. Access to the park, the south edge of which abuts the north side of **Bells Line of Road,** is possible at Bilpin and at several points north of the central Blue Mountains.

The national parks of the Blue Mountains are divided into regions and administered by different branches of the **National Parks and Wildlife Services (NPWS).** If you are planning to bushcamp or even to drive into these parks, it is always advisable to contact the appropriate NPWS office (see specific park listings) a few days in advance to ensure that roads are drivable and that no bushfire bans are in place.

GETTING THERE AND AROUND

The Blue Mountains are an easy 90-minute drive west of Sydney. Take Parramatta Rd west from the city to the Western Motor Tollway (M4; toll $1.50). The tollway passes through Penrith to become the **Great Western Hwy,** the main route through the mountains. The area's major service centers and attractions lie on or near this path. Alternatively, the northern route, **Bells Line of Road,** stretches west from Windsor, northeast of Parramatta, providing a more beautiful and less developed passage.

CityRail makes stops throughout the Blue Mountains at most of the towns along the Great Western Hwy, offering the least expensive option for travelers who are willing to walk from rail stations and bus stops to trailheads. Within the towns, most distances are walkable, and local bus companies cover those that aren't (see **Katoomba,** p. 127, for bus info). There is no public transportation to Kanangra-Boyd National Park or Wollemi National Park.

There are two above-par smaller bus tour companies. **Wonderbus** (tel. 9555 9800; fax 9555 1345; http://www.wonderbus.com.au), offers a basic tour (daily 7:45am-5pm; $60, $48 seniors, students, YHA members) including stops at Euroha Clearing Campground, Wentworth Falls, Katoomba's Echo point, and Blackheath's Govett's Leap. The aim is to allow time for wilderness bushwalks with the experienced advice of the driver-guide, and if you want to stay the night, you can call to get a ride home on a later bus. **Wildframe Ecotours** (tel. 9314 0658; email wildframe@5054.aoue.net.au) provides an exclusive trip into the challenging Grand Canyon, a rainforest walk in Blackheath. ($55, students/VIP/YHA $49, children under 15 $40.) Both companies offer other trips as well, including caving and abseiling.

Several companies run bus tours to the mountains from Sydney. A common one-day package includes stops at Katoomba's Echo Point, the Scenic Railway and Skyway, and at Govett's Leap in Blackheath, and some throw in visits to the Edge Maxvision Cinema in Katoomba and the Australian Wildlife Park at Australia's Wonderland. Trips focus on bushwalking with stops at Echo Point, the Wentworth Falls Conservation Hut, and Govett's Leap. **AAT Kings,** Jetty 6 at Circular Quay (tel. 9252 2788), has the best basic Blue Mountains tour along the Great Western Hwy. (Departs 9am, returns 5:45pm. $71, concessions $67, under 15 $36. Bushwalking package $75, $68, $28. Third package available. YHA 15% discount.) **Great Sights** (tel. 9241 2294), on Circular Quay, offers a more scenic round-trip down Bells Line of Road with longer bushwalks ($80, $73, $40).

■ Glenbrook to Leura

Located on the Great Western Hwy outside the easternmost section of **Blue Mountains National Park,** the **Blue Mountains Tourist Authority,** Glenbrook office (tel. 4739 6266; fax 4739 6787), serves as the gateway to the Blue Mountains from Sydney, with extensive info on accommodations, attractions, and hiking (open M-Sa 8:30am-5pm, Su 8:30am-4:30pm). The **NPWS Glenbrook Office,** south of Glenbrook on Bruce Rd, is the nearest entrance to the park. (Car entrance fee $5, motorcycles $3, cyclists and pedestrians free.) From the highway take Ross St until it dead-ends, then turn left on Burfitt Pde, which becomes Bruce Rd and leads to the park.

Inside the park, 4km over partially unpaved roads beyond the Bruce Rd entrance, is the **Euroka Clearing Campground.** The site has pit toilets, but no water or cooking facilities. Wallabies congregate close by in the fall and winter. The entrance is locked between 6pm and 8:30am, and campers are advised to bring ample firewood and food. You must call the NPWS in Richmond (tel. 4588 5247) to arrange permits in advance. (Fees for 1-2 people $5 per night, for 3 people $7 per night; plus park entrance fee.) Bushcamping is free. The **Red Hands Cave trail** from the Glenbrook Visitors Centre runs an easy 8km circuit through patches of rainforest to an Aboriginal rock engraving site and the **Jellybean Pools** (named for their shape, not their contents) are popular swimming holes near the park's entrance. **CityRail** runs from Sydney's Central Station to Glenbrook ($6, off-peak return $7.20).

At **Blaxland,** less than 1km west of Glenbrook, Layton Ave turns off toward **Lennox Bridge,** constructed between 1832 and 1833. The **oldest bridge** on the Australian mainland, it's a pleasant 2km detour. As you approach the bridge, take note of the **Glenbrook Lagoon,** which marks the spot where the team of Blaxland, Lawson, and Wentworth set up their first camp before tackling the peaks. The National Trust-owned **Norman Lindsay Gallery,** 14 Lindsay Cr (tel. 4751 1067), in **Faulconbridge,** houses a large collection of work by the artist who once inhabited the house. (Open W-M 10am-4pm; admission $6, students and seniors $4, under 15 $2.) The turn-off for the gallery, Grose Rd, is just east of Faulconbridge in Springwood. A second **NPWS campsite** can be found at **Murphy's Glen,** 10km south of the Great Western Hwy outside of Woodford. Take Park Rd from the highway to Railway Pde, turn left and proceed less than 1km, then turn right onto Bedford Rd. The road is unpaved for most of the way, and the campground, located in a thick eucalypt forest, has only pit toilets (free camping; no permits required). **CityRail** trains stop in Blaxland ($6), Springwood ($6.80), Faulconbridge ($6.80), and Woodford ($7.60).

   Wentworth Falls, renowned for its picturesque waterfall walks, hugs the highway 4km beyond Woodford. To find the starting points of the walks, turn off the highway at Falls Rd, and proceed south through the town's center. For the most direct access to the falls, continue along Falls Rd until you reach a trailhead area which offers short paths (under 1hr. return) to the smaller upper falls, more challenging trails leading to the base of the falls, and a short walk to **Princes Rock Lookout,** which provides an excellent vantage point for appreciating the full scale of the drop. If you're willing to devote half a day to a walk in this area, turn right off Falls Rd, following signs to the **National Park Conservation Hut** (tel. 4757 3827). Perched on the rim of the Jamison Valley, the hut is primarily a tea house with a killer view (tea or coffee $2.50), but it also distributes pamphlets on tourist facilities and walking tracks in the Blue Mountains (open daily 9am-5pm).

   From the hut, try the **Valley of the Waters walk,** (4km; 3hr.), which provides stunning views of several nearby waterfalls and connects to the longer, more difficult **National Pass circuit** (6km; 3½hr.), a gorgeous walk hewn into the side of the cliff line. The return trail offers some of the best possible views of Wentworth Falls, although it involves an extremely steep ascent.

   Yester Grange (tel. 4757 1110), at the east edge of town on Yester Rd just off the highway via Tableland Rd, commands a spectacular panoramic view of the central mountains. The house, built in 1888, contains beautifully restored rooms filled with period furniture and paintings, as suitable a setting for Devonshire tea ($7) as the mountains have to offer. An incongruous downstairs gallery displays and sells work by local artists. (Open M-F 10am-4pm, Sa-Su 10am-5pm. Admission to house and gallery $5, concessions $4, high school students $2.50, under 12 $1.)

   For camping in Wentworth Falls, the **Ingar Campground** is 13km farther southeast along Tableland Rd and the unsealed Queen Elizabeth Dr. The campground has "bush toilets," no water, and no cooking facilities (free; no permits required). Nearby, a small mountain pond makes the spot popular for picnics as well as camping. The **CityRail** train from Sydney to Wentworth costs $8 (off-peak return $9.60).

   The likeable town of **Leura,** 3km west of Wentworth Falls and adjacent to Katoomba, offers shops, cafes, and galleries along its central street, Leura Mall. **Everglades Gardens,** 37 Everglades Ave (tel. 4784 1938), is a lush example of the floral cultivation for which the town is known. (Open Sept.-Feb. 10am-5pm; Mar.-Aug. 10am-4pm. Admission $5, concessions $3, ages 6-12 $1, under 6 free.) Nearby, Fitzroy St leads east to Watkins Rd which soon turns into Sublime Point Rd and ends at the breathtaking overlook at **Sublime Point.** Coming south down Leura Mall from the highway, turn left on Craigend St, right onto Everglades Ave, then left onto Fitzroy St, proceeding from there as explained above. CityRail runs from Sydney to Leura ($8.80, $10.60 off-peak return). For travelers continuing west, the 8km **Cliff Drive,** beginning at Gordon Rd near the south end of Leura Mall, provides a scenic escape from the highway. The loop skirts the south edge of Katoomba passing many lookouts and a handful of trailheads. The views from Leura Cascades and Katoomba's Echo Point (see below) are stand-outs.

▨ Katoomba

Throughout the world, the image most widely associated with the Blue Mountains is that of the **Three Sisters,** a towering three-pronged rock formation that brings tourists from miles around to the otherwise small mountain town of Katoomba. In addition to its physical beauty, Katoomba offers excellent hiking, climbing, and biking opportunities and a convenient rail-accessible location, and the result is a backpacker's and lay-mountaineer's dream. Though it's touristy, the town retains a distinctively liberal flavor, replete with VW vans, vegetarian eateries, and dread-locked 'dos.

ORIENTATION AND PRACTICAL INFORMATION

Katoomba sits just south of the Great Western Hwy, 2km west of Leura and 109km from Sydney. The town's main drag, **Katoomba St,** runs south from the **Katoomba Railway Station** through town toward **Echo Point.** Echo Point Rd brings visitors to the Blue Mountains' most famous view, the **Three Sisters.** In the downtown area, Katoomba St is flanked by **Lurline St** to the east and **Parke St** to the west. **Pioneer Place** occupies the area between Katoomba and Parke St, and can be reached via narrow alleys off either street. At the north end of town, **Main St** runs parallel to the Great Western Hwy, becoming **Gang Gang St** east of the railway station and **Bathurst Rd** to the west.

Tourist Office: Blue Mountains Tourism Authority (tel. 4739 6266; fax 4739 6787), on Echo Point at the end of Echo Point Rd. Take Lurline St south from the middle of town and veer left onto Echo Rd when Lurline St ends. The center has an amazing clifftop view and tons of info, but the staff's too busy to give much hiking advice. Try NPWS in Blackheath (see p. 131) instead.

Budget Travel Office: Fantastic Aussie Tours, 283 Main St (24hr. tel. 4782 1866; fax 4782 1860), next to the railway station. Books all of the bus tours listed below and distributes info on area attractions. Offers a variety of discounts to VIP, YHA, Nomad's cardholders. Tour buses pick up outside of Katoomba train station on Main St. Open M-F 9am-5pm, Sa 9am-2:30pm, Su 9am-1:30pm.

Trains: Katoomba Railway Station, on Main St (tel. 4751 5444), at the north end of Katoomba St, is part of the **CityRail** network. Trains run at least every hr. to Sydney, Glenbrook, Blackheath, and Lithgow (fares vary $2-9). **Countrylink** (tel. 13 22 32) also services the area (open daily 7am-8pm).

Buses: Greyhound Pioneer (tel. 13 20 30) stops opposite the Gearins Hotel once daily on the way from Sydney to Adelaide. To: Bathurst (2hr., $24), Dubbo (4¾hr., $42), and Broken Hill (14hr., $105). Student and backpacker discounts available. For casual day-touring at your own pace, the **Blue Mountains Explorer Bus** (24hr. tel. 4782 1866) runs an 18-stop circuit and allows passengers to get on and off as often as they choose. Stops include Echo Point, the Scenic Railway and Scenic Skyway, Leura Cascades, Gordon Falls, Everglades Gardens, and the Edge Maxvision Cinema. Buses run Sa-Su and public holidays every hr. 9:30am-4:30pm. $18, seniors $16, ages 5-15 $9, family of 4 $45.

Local Public Transportation: Blue Mountains Bus Company (tel. 4782 4213) runs between Katoomba and Woodford with stops at Katoomba Station, near Echo Point, at the Edge Cinema, on Leura Mall, at the Valley of the Waters trailhead, the scenic skyway, and in Wentworth Falls. Fares $1.60-3; students and ages 5-18 half off. Regular service approximately 7:30am-6pm. Buses pick up outside Carrington Hotel on Main St. **Mountainlink** (tel. 4782 3333) includes Leura, Blackheath, and Mt. Victoria. Fares from $1.20; students, seniors, and ages 5-15 half off. Service times vary by route. Timetables for both services are available at the Blue Mountains Tourism Authority center on Echo Point.

Taxis: Katoomba Leura Radio Cars (tel. 4782 1311) picks up anywhere between Wentworth Falls and Mt. Victoria 24hr. Initial fare $4, plus $1.07 per km.

Car Rental: Cales Car Rentals, 136 Bathurst Rd (tel. 4782 2917), has cars from $55 per day. Ages 21 and up only. Open M-Sa 8:30am-5pm, Su 8-9am and 5-6pm.

Automobile Clubs: NRMA (tel. 13 21 32; road service tel. 13 11 11).

Bike Rental: Cycletech, 3 Gang Gang St (tel. 4782 2800; fax 4782 4550), across from the railway station, rents excellent mountain bikes. Half-day $25, full day $45. Non-front suspension bikes half-day $15, full day $25. Helmets, locks, and repair kits included. Credit card, passport, or cash deposit required. 10% YHA and backpackers discount. Open M-F 8:30am-5:30pm, Sa 8:30am-4pm, Su 9am-4pm.

Hotlines: Lifeline (24hr. tel. 13 11 14); **Poison Information Centre** (24hr. tel. 13 11 26); local: **Wentworth Sexual Assault Clinic** (tel. 4724 2512); **Rape Crisis Centre** (24hr. tel. 1800 424 017).

Hospital: Blue Mountains District Anzac Memorial Hospital (tel. 4780 6000), on the Great Western Hwy, 1km east of the railway station.

Emergency: Dial 000.

NEW SOUTH WALES

Post office: Shops 4-5, Pioneer Pl (tel. 13 13 18). Open M-F 9am-5pm. **Postal code:** 2780.

Internet Access: The **Katoomba Library**, Town Centre Arcade, Katoomba St (tel. 4782 0750), has two terminals—one bookable and the other first-come first-served. **Internet Explorer** allows web access but no telnet. Open M-F 10am-5:30pm, Sa 9am-4pm. Full access at **The Escape Hatch**, 166a Katoomba St (tel. 4782 2080). 30min. $4, 1hr. $6. Open daily 9:30am-9:30pm.

Phone Code: 02.

ACCOMMODATIONS AND CAMPING

Blue Mountains Katoomba YHA (tel. 4782 1416), on the corner of Lurline and Waratah St. Tons of common space, clean facilities, ample dorms. From train station, go down Katoomba St, turn left on Wenatah St, and look for YHA sign. Convenient location down the street from Echo Point. Book ahead for private rooms. Kitchen open 7am-9:30pm. VCR, game room, lockers ($1), and great security. Bike rental $24 per day. Key deposit $10. Linen $2; blankets provided. Check-out 10am, late fee $5. Reception daily 7am-10pm. Dorms $12-16. YHA non members $3 more.

Blue Mountains Backpackers, 190 Bathurst Rd (tel. 4782 4226; fax 4782 4236; email bluemountains@hotmail.com), a 5min. walk west of the railway station. Fun, friendly accommodation aimed at younger crew. Arrangements range from mattresses on the floor to doubles. Small kitchen and dining area, common room with VCR, rides to trailheads, safe for valuables. Less than stellar bathrooms. Reception daily 9am-noon and 6-9pm (winter 5-8pm). Check-out 10am. Dorms $15-$18; floor mattresses $14; doubles or twins $40; tent sites $10. Weekly: $84-$98; $84; $210; $63 (summer rates slightly higher). VIP, YHA discount $1-2. Bike rentals $20 per day. Abseiling and canyon rafting (from $69) trips. Linen $1. Key deposit $10.

Gearins Hotel, 273 Great Western Hwy (tel. 4782 4395), behind the train station, above Katoomba's most raucous and lively pub. Free linen, lockers, and thick blankets. Comforters for cold mountain nights. Reception open daily 8am-6pm. Check-out 10am. Dorms $15; singles $25; doubles $50.

Katoomba Falls Caravan Park (tel. 4782 1835), on Katoomba Falls Rd, south of town via Katoomba St, is well-positioned for several bushwalks and the Scenic Skyway and Scenic Railway. Toilets, hot showers, indoor barbecue area. No linens and blankets. Reception daily 8am-6pm. Check-out 10am. Tent sites $7 per person, families of 4 $18; with power $10, families $25; additional person $5. Cabins with bath for 2 people $51; each additional person $10. On-site caravans for 1 person $31, each additional person up to 6 $5. Key deposit $5 for campers, $10 for caravan or cabin occupants. Plan ahead 3-4 weeks for cabin bookings.

Number 14, 14 Lovel St (tel. 4782 7104), 5min. east of station via Gang Gang St. Luxurious, quiet homestyle pad. Outstanding kitchen, hardwood floors, central heating. Reception open daily 7:30am-9:30pm. Singles $20 during summer, $25 during winter, doubles $40; $45, ensuite room with 3 beds $50, each child over 2 half price, 2 or under free.

FOOD AND ENTERTAINMENT

Katoomba's two largest grocery stores stand to either side of the K-Mart on Parke St.: the **Jewel Food Barn** (tel. 4782 1819; open M-F 7am-10pm, Sa 7am-8pm, Su 9am-6pm), and **Coles** (tel. 4782 6133; open M 6am to Sa midnight, Su 8am to midnight). The **Katoomba Village Fruit Market,** 170 Bathurst Rd (tel. 4782 4972), a five-minute walk west of the train station, carries a warehouse full of high-quality produce at great prices (open M-F 8am-6pm, Sa-Su 8am-5pm).

The **Blues Cafe,** 55-7 Katoomba St (tel. 4782 2347), serves primarily veggie cuisine for sit down or take-away. (Open Su-W 9am-9pm, M-Tu 9am to 5pm.) Although it's not much to look at, **Tom's Eats,** 200 Katoomba St (tel. 4782 3182), is another solid choice, serving specialty milkshakes, burgers, spicy chicken dishes, and pastas. Tom's will deliver dinner anywhere in town every day except Tuesday and delivers all day on the weekends. (Open Su-Th 11am-9pm, F-Sa 11am-10pm.) **Siam Cuisine,** 172 Katoomba St (tel. 4782 5671), has spicy, delicious food. (Lunch specials $6, din-

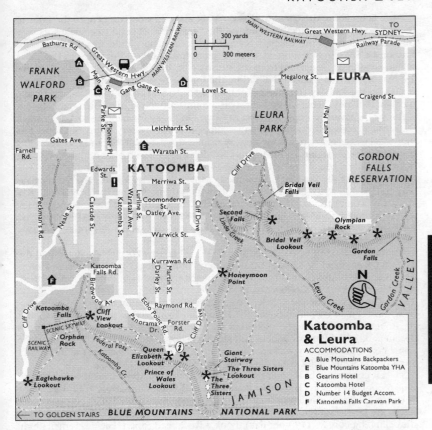

Katoomba & Leura

ACCOMMODATIONS

A Blue Mountains Backpackers
E Blue Mountains Katoomba YHA
B Gearins Hotel
C Katoomba Hotel
D Number 14 Budget Accom.
F Katoomba Falls Caravan Park

ner mains $14.50, spring rolls 4 for $5. BYO, no corkage. Open Tu-Su 11:30am-2:30pm and 5:30-10pm.)

Katoomba's nightlife revolves around two main downtown pubs. The **Gearins Hotel,** 273 Great Western Hwy (tel. 4782 6028), can get rowdy, especially on the ever-popular Wednesday "Jam Nights." The tamer, more yuppie alternative is the **Carrington Hotel,** Main St across from the station (tel. 4782 1111 or 4782 6666), which has pool tables and two separate bars (pints of Guinness $4.50). On Saturday nights, the upstairs nightclub keeps rolling until 4 am (cover $5).

The **Edge Maxvision Cinema,** 225 Great Western Hwy (tel. 4782 8900), projects a 38-minute film on the Blue Mountains, called The Edge, onto a six-story screen for the closest possible cinematic approximation of actual exploration. Just in case the draw of a seat more comfortable than an abseiling harness doesn't grab you, the movie goes to several places in the mountains which cannot be accessed by visitors, including the secret grove where the recently-discovered Wollemi pine species grows. (6 shows daily between 10am and 5:15pm; tickets $12, concessions $10, ages 3-14 $8.) The cinema also shows other giant-format films and screens recent feature films every evening (tickets $10, $9, $7.50; call for programs and showtimes).

WALKS AND LOOKOUTS

Nearly everyone ventures out to Echo Point on the southernmost tip of town to take in the romantic view of the **Three Sisters.** Between dusk and 10:30pm, strategically placed floodlights lend new brilliance to these three golden dames.

From Echo Point, the **Giant Stairway Walk** makes a steep descent to the floor of the Jamison Valley to meet the **Federal Pass trail.** The Federal Pass snakes its way through the trees in the valley, passing Cook's Crossing picnic area at the base of **Katoomba Falls** and continuing on to **Orphan Rock,** a beautiful free-standing pillar which erosion has separated from the nearby cliff. Just beyond Orphan Rock, there are two ways to get back to civilization, the **Furber Steps** (moderate climb, 30min.) or the **Scenic Railway** (tel. 4782 2699; $3, ages 3-13 $1; total trip 5km, 2.5 hours, medium difficulty). The Scenic Railway is a tourist attraction in its own right since it is the **world's most steeply inclined railway.** Originally for hauling coal, it's now a short roller-coaster through spectacular Jamison Valley scenery. Many bus tours and individual travelers approach the railway from Katoomba Falls Rd and take the short trip just for kicks (10min. round-trip; $4.50 adults, $2 children), but for hikers coming from either the Federal Pass or the Ruined Castle Track (see below), the ride is a restful way to cover the last 250 vertical meters after a long day's walk. The **Scenic Skyway** (tel. 4782 2699), is a cable gondola which departs from the Scenic Railway station for a quick trip out over Katoomba Falls Gorge and back (7min.; $4.50, ages 3-13 $2). Although waiting in line for the Scenic Railway and Skyway can be a long ride for a short glide (each lasts under 4min.), the views are worth it. (Both open daily 9am-5pm; last rides 4:50 pm.)

On the west side of town, the easy walk along **Narrow Neck Plateau** beyond the gate on Glenraphael Dr leads to fabulous views of the Megalong and Jamison Valleys on either side of the clifftop trail. Before the gate, about 1km out onto the plateau from the Cliff Dr, the **Golden Stairs** run down the cliff face to the Ruined Castle Track. The walk to **Ruined Castle,** a distinctive rock formation reminiscent of crumbling turrets, makes a difficult 8km, five-hour round-trip via the Golden Stairs. Once at the Ruined Castle, try the short climb to the top and look straight across the valley to distant parts of the Blue Mountains and Kanangra-Boyd National Parks. Because of the stairs' taxing grade, many walkers tack on an extra hour and walk east to the Furber Steps or the Scenic Railway on the return trip.

Several companies in Katoomba organize adventure activity trips throughout the Blue Mountains region. The **Australian School of Mountaineering,** 166b Katoomba St (tel. 4782 2014; email asm@pnc.com.au), inside the Paddy Pallin outdoor shop, offers the best resources and conducts introductory rappelling ($79 per day) and rock-climbing courses ($90 per day). Book a day ahead (open daily 8:15am-5:30pm; YHA, Nomads, VIP, student discounts). The **Blue Mountains Highlights tour** (24hr. tel. 4782 1866), covers the area's star attractions (3hr.; 3 per day; $32, VIP, YHA $25, seniors $28, students age 5-15 $16, families of 4 $80). Tours to the **Jenolan Caves** (see p. 132; 24hr. tel. 4782 1866) include views of Echo Point and Govett's Leap and take about three hours to explore the caves or the surrounding area ($52, $48, $44, $26, $140). Overnight trips to the caves, not including accommodation or cave tours, cost $34 each way (seniors $30, ages 5-15 $17, families of 4 $90). A one-way ticket combined with two to three days of walking and camping on the **Six Foot Track,** a 42km trail from Nellies Glen Rd, off the Great Western Hwy at the west end of town, to Jenolan Caves, makes an affordable and adventurous outing for serious hikers.

■ Blackheath

The Great Western Hwy snakes 11km west and north from Katoomba to the town of Blackheath on the way to Mount Victoria and Lithgow. To the northeast of this plateau-top town lies the beautiful **Grose Valley,** which offers many of the area's best lookout points and most challenging walks. The **Megalong Valley,** to the south of the town, is a farmland area popular for horseback riding and other ranch entertainments. Given its prime position between these two areas and its easy accessibility, Blackheath is a natural choice as a Blue Mountains base; unfortunately, its services and budget accommodation are more limited than Katoomba's.

PRACTICAL INFORMATION The **Blue Mountains Heritage Centre** (tel. 4787 8877), on Govett's Leap Rd just inside the national park, is the main NPWS visitors center for the Blue Mountains and carries detailed trail guidebooks ($2-$4), as well as park officials who know their stuff. A small exhibit inside the center presents the history of Aboriginal and European peoples in the mountains and also explains the geology of the region (open daily 9am-4:30pm). **Mountainlink** (tel. 4782 3333) runs buses from Katoomba to Mt Victoria by way of Blackheath, coming as close as possible to the town's major trailheads (fares from $3.20, concessions and kids from 70¢; from Blackheath Railway Station to Blue Mountains Heritage Centre $4.80; service M-F 7:30am-6pm, Sa 6:30am-4:30pm). **CityRail** runs to Blackheath from Sydney's Central Station via Katoomba ($10.60, off-peak return $12.80).

ACCOMMODATIONS AND FOOD The clean, almost frilly rooms in the Art Deco **Gardner's Inn Hotel,** 255 Great Western Hwy (tel. 4787 8347), set a high standard for pub accommodation. (Cushy lounge with piano, no kitchen. Reception at the bar open daily 9am-late; check-out 10:30am. Singles, doubles, and twins Su-Th $20 per person, F-Sa $25. Family rooms available: ages under 8 free, 8 or over discounted.) The tent camping area at **Blackheath Caravan Park** (tel. 4787 8101), on Prince Edward St, off Govett's Leap Rd, lies in a tree-covered grove secluded from the rest of the park and down a steep hill. It can get chilly in the shade. (Toilets, showers, barbecues. Reception daily 8am-6pm. Check-out 10am. Sites $7 per person, families of 4 $18; with power for 2 $10, each additional person $5, families $25. Key deposit $5.)

The nearest **free national park camping areas** can be found at **Perry's Lookdown,** on the sometimes paved Hat Hill Rd, 8km from the Great Western Hwy, and at **Acacia Flat,** on the floor of the Grose Valley, a hefty two-hour hike from Govett's Leap. Both sites have pit toilets and no other facilities. Water from Govett's Creek is available at Acacia Flat, but it must be treated before use. Blackheath's limited food and services line the Great Western Hwy and the first few blocks of Govett's Leap Rd leading away from the highway, forming a tiny town center. Among the small eateries, the **Wattle Cafe,** 240 Great Western Hwy (tel. 4787 8153), is a cozy place for a sandwich (burgers of all kinds $3; breakfast served all day; open daily 7:30am-7pm).

SIGHTS AND ACTIVITIES Walks in the Blackheath area vary widely in length and level of difficulty. The **Fairfax Heritage Walk** is a one-hour (2km), wheelchair-ready alternative to the 350m drive between the Blue Mountains Heritage Centre and **Govett's Leap,** one of the most magnificent lookouts in the national park. From Govett's Leap, the moderate walk to the lookout at **Pulpit Rock** (3hr. return; 5km) follows the cliff line northward for an almost non-stop display of breathtaking views out over the Grose Valley. Following the cliffs in the other direction leads you to **Evans Lookout** (2hr. one way; 3km; moderate) by way of **Bridal Veil Falls,** a majestically thin and wispy stream whose water takes nearly ten seconds to tumble to the valley below. Since most of the Blackheath walks originate at either Govett's Leap or Evans Lookout, this walk allows you to connect to others, thereby sampling Blackheath's best hiking in under a day.

One of two possible trailheads for the popular **Grand Canyon** hike, Evans Lookout gives way to a manageable descent to the canyon floor. The trail then runs alongside Greaves Creek through the wet, forested clime of the narrow canyon and up again at **Neates Glen,** the other possible entry point. A short walk on the unpaved portion of Evans Lookout Rd completes the moderate four-hour (5km) circuit back to Evans Lookout. From the Great Western Hwy, Hat Hill Rd runs parallel to Govett's Leap Rd, leading north of town to **Perry's Lookdown,** then branches off to the superb lookout at **Anvil Rock** nearby. Perry's Lookdown provides the steepest descent into the valley 600m below. From Perry's Lookdown, a trail leads into the valley to the beautiful **Blue Gum Forest** (2hr.; 2.5km). Returning along the same route makes the trip to the forest a difficult five-hour trek. The other option is to turn toward Govett's Leap and make a full day of walking through the forest along Govett's Creek, although this strenuous walk is generally reserved for summer when the days are longer. *(Circuit using cliff-top track and Hat Hill Rd.: 10hr., difficult.)*

The **scenic drive** into the Megalong Valley begins on Shipley Rd, across the Great Western Hwy from Govett's Leap Rd. Megalong Rd, a left from Shipley Rd just after Centennial Glen Rd, leads down into a picturesque farmland area that contrasts nicely with the wilderness of its surroundings. In the valley, outfitters conduct guided trail rides or supply horses for hourly use. **Werriberri Trail Rides** (tel. 4787 9171), on Megalong Rd near Werriberri Lodge, offers rides from 30-minute walks ($15) to three-hour outings with more opportunities to get up some speed *(1st ride 9am, last ride 3:30pm. $48; open for reservation calls daily 7:30am-8:30pm.)* The **Megalong Australian Heritage Centre** (tel. 4787 8188), a bit farther south on Megalong Rd, has longer guided rides and allows riders to make unguided outings. *(Rides daily 10am-4pm; office open daily 8:30am-6pm. Full day ride with lunch $95; 3hr. ride with lunch $65; horses alone $25 for 1st hr., each additional hr. $22.)* Megalong also offers daily livestock lassoing shows, horse and cart rides and 4WD forays into the surrounding bush.

Seven kilometers beyond Blackheath on the Great Western Hwy, **Mount Victoria** is a quiet village that can serve as an alternate Blue Mountains base. It has several historical buildings, including **Manor** (built 1876), on Montgomery St, the former summer home of John Fairfax, and the **Toll Keeper's Cottage** (built 1849), 1km east of town off the Great Western Hwy. For accommodation in Mount Victoria, try the **Victoria and Albert Guesthouse,** 19 Station St (tel. 4787 1241), which has a lavish lobby and charming rooms. (Pool, spa, sauna, tea and coffee lounge. Reception open daily 24hr. with advance call. Check-out 10am. B&B with shared bath Su-Th $45 per person, F-Sa $60.) Nearby, the 19th-century administrative center of **Hartley** houses some old buildings now operated as a historical site by the NPWS (tel. 6355 2117).

▓ Jenolan Caves

The amazing limestone and crystal formations of Jenolan (Je-NO-lan) Caves, on Jenolan Caves Rd, 45km south of the Great Western Hwy from Hartley, have beguiled visitors since they were first introduced to the general public in 1838. One can reach the caves by bus from Katoomba (see p. 126). The cave system, overseen by the **Jenolan Caves Reserve Trust** (tel. 6359 3311; fax 6359 3307; email jencaves@jenolan.org.au), contains nine open caves, accessible through the trust's extensive program of **guided tours,** and many more unexplored recesses (13 tours per day during week, 21 on weekends1-2hr.; $12-20, seniors and ages 5-15 $8-20, families of 4 $32-50; ticket office open daily 9am-5pm). Because it displays a broad range of the features seen throughout the caves, **Lucas Cave** is generally presented as the place to start (1½hr. tour, $12, $8, $32). Large group sizes detract from the experience, however. **Orient Cave** and **Imperial Cave** both have a more tolerable flow of visitors as well as several noteworthy rock formations. (Orient 1½hr.; $16, $10, $42. Imperial 1 $12, $8, $32.) **Adventure tours** take small groups (limited to 8-12) through some of the cave system's less accessible areas—the hard way. These tours, organized primarily for bus touring companies, involve moderate to strenuous climbing, some crawling, and a healthy dose of darkness. Ask at the ticket office about open spaces (2-8hr., from $40). Three arches are open for unguided viewing as well; ask for a map of the area from the tour ticket office. The minimum age for adventure tours is generally 16, although age 10 and up can adventure in Elder Cave. Two caves, Orient Cave and Chifley Cave, are partially wheelchair accessible.

▓ Kanangra-Boyd National Park

Kanangra-Boyd National Park comprises 68,000 hectares of stark wilderness punctuated by pure rivers and creeks, still-developing caves, and the dramatic sandstone cliffs that mark the edges of the Boyd Plateau. The park's remote location and rugged terrain attract serious bushwalkers with a hankering for long-term solitude. The park is nonetheless worthwhile for the more casual visitors who follow its only 2WD road across the Boyd Plateau to the famous lookouts at Kanangra Walls.

Sandwiched between sections of Blue Mountains National Park to the east and south, Kanangra-Boyd National Park extends one small arm north to nearly surround Jenolan Caves. A dirt road continues from the end of Jenolan Caves Rd and enters the park only 5km past the caves. This path, through Jenolan Caves from the Great Western Hwy, is the only car-accessible eastern approach to the park. From the west, another road also called Jenolan Caves Rd and paved for only half its length, comes in from the town of Oberon. These roads meet at the edge of the park to become Kanangra Walls Rd, the direct 26km route to the cliff-top lookout of the same name. The **National Parks and Wildlife Service** office, 38 Ross St (tel. 6336 1972), in Oberon, has details on the park's longer tracks. You must get necessary cave exploration permits at least four weeks in advance. (Open M-F 9am-4:30pm.)

The **Boyd River Campground,** on Kanangra Walls Rd 5km before Kanangra Walls, has the park's only car-accessible camping. There are pit toilets, potable water from the Boyd River (boil before drinking), and fireplaces, but you should bring in your own wood and fuel. Bushcamping in the rest of the park is free but two rules must be followed: stay 500m from any major path, and always minimize your impact.

Three **scenic walks** begin at the **Kanangra Walls** car park. **Lookout Walk** (10min. one-way, easy) is a wheelchair-accessible path leading first to the lookout over the Kanagra Creek gorge and then to the view over the eight-tiered 400m **Kanangra Falls.** The **Waterfall Walk** (20min. one-way with steep return) leads from the second lookout to the deep pool at the bottom of **Kalang Falls.** The **Plateau Walk** (2hr. return, moderate), which branches from the Lookout Walk between the parking lot and the first lookout, descends briefly from the plateau before ascending to Kanangra Tops for views of Kanangra Walls. Along the way, **Dance Floor Cave** contains indented floors and other signs of old-time recreation in the park. A water container placed in the cave in 1940 catches pure, drinkable water which drips from the cave ceiling. Longer walks, such as the overnight trip to **Batsch Camp** (pit toilets, no water), on the park's southern border, should be planned in advance with help of the Oberon NPWS office.

■ Bells Line of Road

The difference between taking the Great Western Hwy and taking Bells Line of Road through the Blue Mountains is similar to the difference between setting out to get drunk with a tumbler of straight gin and doing so with a bottle of fine wine. You wind up in the same place, but one route allows you to savor the experience a bit more along the way. This 87km drive between Windsor and Lithgow provides rambling, scenic passage through the mountains, perfect if you have a car and a little extra time.

At the top of Kurrajong Heights, 16km west of Richmond, the **Kurrajong Heights Grass Karts and Ski Park** (tel. 4567 7184 or 4567 7260) rents specially designed "grass karts" (made of little more than a board, four rubber wheels and a hand brake) and grass skis, both of which allow you to careen down a mountainside regardless of the weather or season. An uphill lift ensures that visitors get the most out of their time. (Must be 130cm tall. 1st hr. $10, each additional hr. $6. Open weekends and public holidays 9am-5pm.) Even if breakneck speeds aren't for you, stop by for the spectacular panoramic views of the Hawkesburg River valley from the **Old Fruit Shop Cafe** (tel. 4567 7498) perched atop the race course (open daily 10am-late afternoon, except Wednesday).

The town of **Bilpin,** 5km west of Kurrajong Heights, has several active **orchards,** and roadside fruit stands sell fresh-picked produce most of the year. The **Pines Orchard** (tel. 4567 1195) allows travelers to pick their own fruit, in season, at the going rate with no additional bag charges. (Peaches, plums, and nectarines late Dec. to late Feb., apples late Jan. to mid-May. Open daily 8am-5pm.)

A couple kilometers west of Berambing, **Mt. Tomah Botanic Garden** (tel. 4567 2154) is the cool-climate and high-altitude plant collection of the Royal Botanic Garden in Sydney. The plants, most from the southern hemisphere, thrive on the rich volcanic soil and grow in naturalistic arrangements with the exception of the herbs and roses in the formal terrace garden. The garden's best moments are in spring, when the large collection of rhododendrons and other flowers bloom (Sept.-Nov.), and in fall, when the deciduous forest areas change their colors (Mar.-May). Volunteers conduct free tours of the grounds during the week, and on weekends for large groups only. Tours depart the visitors center. (Garden open Mar.-Sept. daily 10am-4pm; Oct.-Feb. 10am-5pm. Entrance fee $5 per car, $2 per pedestrian or cyclist.)

People come from far and wide to see the formal, European-style gardens and unspoiled rainforest of the small town of **Mt. Wilson**, 8km north of Bells Line of Road between Mt. Tomah and Bell. For a sample of the fern-laden rainforest, turn right onto Waterfall Rd off the main road through town, and proceed about 500m until you reach a park area on the left. From there, follow signs to a 45-minute circular walk of medium difficulty (steep steps) which leads to the base of two small waterfalls and provides a splendid sample of the sounds of the rainforest. Three gardens stay open throughout the year: **Sefton Cottage** (tel. 4756 2034), on Church Ln (open daily 10am-6pm; admission $2, under 15 free), **Merry Garth** (tel. 4756 2121) on Davies Ln 500m from Mt. Irvine Rd (open daily 9am-6pm; admission $3, under 15 free), and **Lindfield Park** (tel. 4756 2148), on Mt. Irvine Rd, 6km northeast of Mt. Wilson (open daily 10am-6pm; admission $3, under 14 free).

The **Zig Zag Railway** (tel. 6353 1795, recorded info 6351 4826), 10km east of Lithgow at Clarence, is a piece of the 1869 track that first made regular travel across the Blue Mountains and down into the Lithgow Valley possible. Trains make the 1½-hour trip to the bottom and back three to four times per day. (Trains leave 11am, 1pm and 3pm during week; 10:30am, 12:15pm, 2pm and 3:45pm on weekends and public holidays. All tickets round-trip: $12, concessions $10, ages 5-18 $6.) By request, **CityRail** trains from Sydney's Central Station will stop near the bottom of the track ($12.40, off-peak return $14.80).

■ Wollemi National Park

Wollemi (WO-lem-eye) National Park sprawls from the Blue Mountains in the south to the Hunter and Goulburn River valleys in the north, containing New South Wales's largest remaining wilderness area. With limited vehicle access and a largely undeveloped interior, the park has many pockets which remain unscrutinized to this day. One such area yielded an amazing find in 1994, when scientists recognized a species of pine tree whose closest relatives had only previously been seen in fossil form. Although the location of the **Wollemi Pine** is a closely-guarded secret, most visitors find the park's deep forests, sandstone gorges, and mountain rainforests sufficiently unique and awe-inspiring. Entrance is free, though there are small fees at campgrounds. Those who wish to bushcamp outside of designated sites should have some familiarity with the landscape and should be well-trained in wilderness survival.

The park's southernmost entrance point is at Bilpin on Bells Line of Road. In this corner of the park, also accessible from Putty Rd north of Windsor. The **Colo River** slices the landscape along the 30km Colo Gorge. The car-accessible **camping area** at **Wheeny Creek** lies near good walking tracks and recommended swimming holes. The nearest **National Parks and Wildlife Service office,** 370 Windsor Rd (tel. 4588 5247; fax 4588 5335), in Richmond, has information on camping and walking in the southeast corner of the park (open M-F 9:30am-12:30pm and 1:30-5pm).

Farther west, roads from Lithgow and Wallerawang enter the park at **Newnes**, where a one-time industrial village now lies dormant since its desertion in the 1940s. The **Newnes Historic Ruins Track** (5km, medium difficulty) tours the remains of the village along the banks of the Wolgan River. The large, unserviced camping area and the striking rocky faces which surround the Wolgan Valley make Newnes one of Wollemi's more popular stops. Ten kilometers south of town, hundreds of tiny **bioluminescent worms** in an abandoned railway tunnel happily provide hours of free semi-psychedelic entertainment; be sure to bring a flashlight. Keep in mind that what you're looking at is not a beautiful constellation but a wall plastered with shining excrement. **Glow Worm Tunnel** can be reached by following a walking track from Newnes (11km) or by a half-hour walk from a carpark on the road from Lithgow. Maps are available at the **Lithgow Visitors Centre,** 1 Cooerwull Rd (tel. 6353 1859; fax 6553 1851), off the Great Western Hwy in Lithgow (open M-F, Sa-Su 9am-4pm).

The **Mudgee NPWS office,** 160 Church St (tel. 6372 7199; fax 6372 7850; email mudgee@npws.nsw.gov.au), administers the northwest section of the park, including the campground at **Dunn's Swamp,** and distributes trail maps for the area (open M-F 8:30am-4:30pm). Known for its canoeing and bushwalking, Dunn's Swamp, 90 minutes from Mudgee by way of Rylstone, is also an excellent place to look for Aboriginal engravings and paintings. The area's mammoth sandstone pagodas provide beautiful views of the surrounding wilderness, and the watery environment draws a variety of wildlife from kangaroos to rare birds.

From Mudgee, a series of sometimes paved roads makes an arc along the park's north edge to Bulga in the northeast. Along the way, roads dip into the park, providing access to breathtaking views in the **Widden Valley** and to the creeks which lace the region. These routes often pass through private property, however, so it is advisable to inquire at the **Bulga NPWS office** (tel. 6574 5275; fax 6574 5274) on Putty Rd before venturing into this part of the park (open Tu-Th 8:30am-4pm). There are no marked trails in the northern section of Wollemi National Park; bushwalkers should be certain to carry a compass and a small-scale topographic map, available at the Bulga NPWS office. South of Bulga, Putty Rd traces the east edge of the park with 4WD access to the wilderness at several points along the way.

▓ Lithgow

The Great Western Hwy and Bells Line of Road meet on the west side of the Blue Mountains at Lithgow, a medium-sized industrial city two hours' drive from Sydney, at the end of the CityRail train line. A one-time center for steel production and still largely supported by coal mining, the town has little inherent charm beyond its utility as a base for exploring nearby wilderness areas such as **Wollemi National Park** to the north and **Jenolan Caves** and **Kanangra-Boyd National Park** to the south. Still, the small downtown area, organized around Main St, provides enough entertainment for a short stay.

Lithgow lies 40km west of Katoomba and 61km east of Bathurst on the Great Western Hwy. The **Greater Lithgow Visitor's Centre,** 1 Cooerwull Rd (tel. 6353 1859; fax 6353 1851; email lithtour@lisp.com.au) occupies the old Bowenfels Railway Station, off the Great Western Hwy on the Bathurst end of town. Their free map is extremely helpful. (Open M-F 9am-5pm, Sa-Su 9am-4pm.) Trains stop on Main St; **CityRail** runs to Sydney ($14.20). **CountryLink** (tel. 13 22 32) coach service heads to Bathurst (1hr., 2-6 per day, $9) and Mudgee (2½hr., 1-2 per day, $18, reservations required). **Greyhound Pioneer** buses (tel. 13 20 30) between Adelaide and Sydney stop across from the McDonald's on the Great Western Hwy; they also run to Broken Hill (13hr., 1 per day, $105). Lithgow's **post office** (tel. 6351 3562), on Main St across from the train station, is brought to you by the **postal code** 2790 (open M-F 9am-5pm).

The **Grand Central Hotel,** 69 Main St (tel. 6351 3050; fax 6351 3109), is the pick of the Lithgow litter with its spacious singles and refurbished hallway showers. Take a left out of the train station and walk two blocks. (Singles $18, doubles $36, triples $54. Linen included.) The pub downstairs is pleasant, as is the adjacent bistro (open daily noon-2pm and 6-9pm; not wheelchair accessible). For a slightly older crowd, pay a visit to the **Lansdowne Hotel,** 137 Main St (tel. 6351 3045). Turn right out of the train station. (Singles $18, doubles $30; weekly $85 per person; book ahead in summer.) For camping space, try **Lithgow Caravan Park,** 58 Cooerwull Rd (tel. 6351 4350). The park includes big, clean bathrooms and showers and laundry. (Reception open daily 8:30am-8:30pm. Check-out 10am. Sites $10, powered sites for 2 $14; each additional person $3.) **Coles** grocery store (tel. 6352 1966) is on Hassan St. From the train station, turn right on Main St, left at traffic light onto Lithgow St and look for

Coles straight ahead in shopping complex. (Open nonstop M 6am-Sa 10pm and Su 8am-8pm.) The **Blue Bird Cafe,** 118 Main St (tel. 6353 1520), prepares huge cheese omelets ($5) and great milkshakes (open daily 6:30am-7:30pm).

CENTRAL WEST

The cities and towns of the Central West lie between the rugged plateaus of the Blue Mountains and the stark dryness of outback New South Wales. The major route into the region from the east is the **Great Western Hwy,** which crosses through the Blue Mountains to Bathurst. From Bathurst, the **Mitchell Hwy** heads northwest to Dubbo, Bourke, and beyond, and the **Mid Western Hwy** runs southwest to Cowra and eventually Hay. Both of these roads intersect the **Newell Hwy,** the major route between Melbourne and Brisbane, which cuts a long path across the Central West. Most towns of the Central West are regarded as waystations between grander destinations, though several have enough interesting sights to fill an afternoon between buses. Even in a short stay in this region, you'll notice an extraordinary degree of hospitality from locals who have chosen to live the less hectic life. To get to know this area, however, takes a longer stay with time to appreciate the individual towns' agricultural or industrial significance.

■ Bathurst

Bathurst's wide avenues and large, ornate lampposts suggest that it was once slated for greatness, but it is an unadorned route on the southwest corner of town which has brought the city notoriety. Originally built as a scenic drive in 1938, the 6km circular road up Mt. Panorama and back down does double duty as both a public road and the track for the annual **AMP Bathurst 1000** and **Australian 1000 Classic touring car races** held in early October and mid-November, events which draw crowds of over 40,000 to this otherwise low-profile town. Year-round, however, Bathurst has a certain vibrance that lacks in the purely industrial towns of the region, largely thanks to the large population of students at **Charles Sturt University.**

PRACTICAL INFORMATION Bathurst is located 101km west of Katoomba at the end of the Great Western Hwy. The **Bathurst Visitors Centre,** 28 William St (tel. 6332 1444; fax 6332 2333), has brochures and free maps (open daily 9am-5pm). **Bathurst Railway Station** receives trains and buses at the intersection of Keppel St and Havannah St, three blocks from the town center. The **CountryLink** office (tel. 6332 4844 or 13 22 32; open M-F 8am-5:30pm, Sa 8:30am-12:15pm and 1:15-5:15pm) books buses to Lithgow (1hr., 2-6 per day, $9), Orange (1hr., 2-6 per day, $8), Cowra (1½hr., 12 per week, $15), Dubbo (3½hr., 2 per day, $28), and Sydney (3½hr., daily, $31). **Greyhound Pioneer** (tel. 13 20 30) passes through on its runs between Sydney and Adelaide (1 per day in each direction). The Bathurst **post office** is at 230 Howick St (tel. 6331 3133; open M-F 9am-5pm; postal code 2795).

ACCOMMODATIONS, CAMPING, AND FOOD Bathurst has a number of pubstays downtown. The **Victoria Hotel**, 3 Keppel St (tel. 6331 5777), on the corner of Havannah St directly across from the train station, offers clean rooms with bedwarmers. (Free tea and coffee. Downstairs bar open M-Sa 10am-late, Su 11am-10:30pm. Check-out 10am. Singles $20; twins $35. Light breakfast $3.50.) Bathurst's only year-round camping area, **East's Bathurst Holiday Park** (tel. 6331 8286; fax 6332 6439), on Sydney Rd (the Great Western Hwy) 4km east of the town center, provides a hilly, tree-strewn tent camping area more appealing than most. (Barbecue, toilets, showers, laundry facilities, games, TV room. Reception open daily 8am-8pm. Check-out 10am. Two-person sites $12, powered $14; each additional adult $6, child $3.) Ask at the visitors center for more options, especially on race weekends.

Waltzing Matilda

Some song that no one could care less about is Australia's official national anthem, but none is as deeply ingrained in the hearts of Aussies as *Waltzing Matilda*. While many assume the song is about a kangaroo, the folk ballad actually has its origins in the social upheaval created by the shearing disputes between unionist woolworkers and their wealthy landowners during the late 19th century. This conflict erupted in September 1894 at Dagworth Station, when laborers and police fired at each other and a shed containing 100 "jumbucks" (colloquial for sheep, derived from an Aboriginal term) and hundreds of bales of wool were burned to the ground. Banjo Patterson, a wealthy man who sided with the workers, adapted an old Scottish folk song to commemorate the event. The result, completed in 1895, still strikes a chord in the Australian psyche, displaying the tough frontier spirit of the bushmen and shearers (who were defeated handily by the police forces at Dagworth). It's best expressed in the final stanza, where the swagman (the song's hero) finds himself cornered and facing certain capture at the hands of the squatter (rich landowner), chooses death rather than surrender: "But the swagman, he up and he jumped into the waterhole/Drowning himself by the Coolabah tree/and his ghost may be heard as it sings in the Billabong/'Who'll come a-waltzing Matilda with me?'"

Coles grocery store, 47 William St (tel. 6332 9566; open nonstop M 7am-Sa 10pm and Su 8am-8pm), has a deli with cheap sandwiches and pizza ($1-3; open 8am-3:30pm). **Ziegler's Cafe,** 52 Keppel St (tel. 6332 1565), offers a range of salads, grilled veggie dishes, and burgers. By night, Ziegler's has a coffeehouse feel, attracting everyone from students to older couples with its hardwood floors and open-air patio. (Open M-Sa 9am-late, Su 10am-5pm. Wheelchair accessible.)

SIGHTS A trip to Bathurst would be incomplete without a spin round the **Mount Panorama circuit.** As you twist and turn your way up and down the steep hill, you'll gain a newfound appreciation for the pros who take turns in excess of 200kph. Head southwest on William St until it becomes Panorama Ave; large banners mark the track. The **National Motor Racing Museum** (tel. 6332 1872), near the starting line, keeps the thrill of the race alive year round with cars, photos, and trophies. *(Open daily 9am-4:30pm. $5, concessions $3, ages 5-15 $1.50, families of 4 $12.)* Once you've followed the course to the peak, aside from the spectacular views below, take time to enjoy the **Sir Joseph Banks Nature Park** (tel. 6333 6286), with Aussie animals in a 41-hectare enclosure criss-crossed by walking tracks. *(Open daily 9am-4:15pm. $3, children under 12 $1, concessions $2, family $8.)* The **Bathurst Goldfields** (tel. 6332 2022), also off the track at the end of the Conrod Straight, remembers the city's gold rush days through exhibits and antique equipment. *(Admission through tours only $8, families of 5 $20. Call the Bathurst Visitors Centre for tour days and times.)* Tours include panning for gold.

The **courthouse** on Russell St was considered so grand when it was built in 1880 that residents of the town thought there must have been a mistake in building the structure in Bathurst. *(Open M-F 9:30am-1pm and 2-4pm.)* Rumors circulated that the building was meant either for a more prominent colonial outpost in India or for a location in Africa where the massive railings encircling the building might have been necessary for keeping out elephants. The east wing houses a museum with Bathurst artifacts ranging from Aboriginal weapons to penny-farthing bicycles. *(Open Tu-W and Su 10am-4pm, Sa 9:30am-4:30pm. Admission $1, ages 5-18 50¢, under 5 free.)*

■ Cowra

On August 5, 1944, over 1000 Japanese soldiers staged a daring escape at the Prisoner of War camp in Cowra. Their attempt failed, and as the escapees were rounded up, 231 perished, some through suicide and some through the violence of the breakout. Through its sensitive handling of the event, Cowra has since earned a reputation as a promoter of amnesty and cross-cultural awareness. Cowra has formed strong ties, including a regular exchange of gifts and visits, with the government of Japan, the latter being grateful for Cowra's help in looking after the graves of Japanese servicemen. Today, three monuments commemorate the **Cowra Breakout** and bring an international focus to what would otherwise be a charming but isolated country town.

Cowra sits in the Lachlan Valley 109km southwest of Bathurst on the banks of the Lachlan River. The Mid Western Hwy cuts through town toward Grenfell and parts west, while Rte 81 heads north to meet the Mitchell Hwy. For free maps, brochures, and good advice, see the jovial people at **Cowra Tourism** (tel. 6342 4333; email tourism@cowra.nsw.gov.au), on the corner of Boorowa Rd and the Mid Western Hwy (open daily 9am-5pm). Transportation arrangements for Sydney-bound **CountryLink** (tel. 13 22 32) and **Greyhound Pioneer** (tel. 13 20 30) buses through Cowra can be made at **Harvey World Travel**, 89 Kendal St (tel. 6342 1288; open M-F 8:30am-5:30pm). Greyhound Pioneer runs buses to Forbes (1½hr.; daily; $41), while **Rendell's** (tel. 1800 023 328) makes stops in Orange (1½hr.; 2 per week; $25, concessions $20) and Canberra (3hr.; 2 per week; $30, concessions $25).

The **Imperial Hotel,** 16-18 Kendal St (tel. 6341 2588; fax 6341 3970), offers newly refurbished rooms and a classy, wood-paneled dining area and pub. (Singles $25, doubles $45, family rooms $55. Continental breakfast included. Reception at the bar daily 10am-midnight. Reservations recommended.) The **Lachlan Hotel**, 66 Kendal St (tel. 6342 2355), rents good, clean pub rooms with decent bathrooms and throws in a light breakfast. (Reception at the bar Su-Th 10am-10pm, F-Sa 10am-2am. Singles $20, doubles $35.) Just under the Kendal St bridge, **Cowra Van Park** (tel. 6342 1058) on Lachlan St provides riverside camping right in the center of town. (Toilets, showers, laundry. Wheelchair-accessible bathrooms. Reception open daily 8am-10pm. Checkout 10am. Sites for 2 $11, powered $15; each additional person $4.) The **Bi-Lo Supermarket** (tel. 6342 3283) is at the corner of Macquarie and Kendal St (open M-W and F 7am-9pm, Th 7am-10pm, Sa 7am-7:30pm, Su 8am-5pm).

The first of Cowra's memorials is a **monument at the site of the breakout,** on Sakura Ave at the corner of Farm St. The foundations of the POW camp's buildings still divide the field into barracks and lanes, and a photograph shows how the camp looked in 1944. Two kilometers north of the actual memorial on Doncaster Dr, the adjoining **Japanese and Australian War Cemeteries** make a powerful statement of common mourning. The **Japanese Gardens and Cultural Centre** (tel. 6341 2233) on Scenic Dr, a continuation of Brisbane St just north of the downtown area, was opened in 1979 as a statement of peace and friendship between Australia and Japan. The serene gardens, designed in traditional Japanese style, are punctuated by ponds, gigantic rock gardens, and low benches for quiet contemplation. Don't miss the authentic Japanese cottage, newly built on the site. (Open daily 8:30am-5pm. Admission $7, students and seniors $6.50, ages 5-18 $5, families $16.50.)

■ Forbes

The former stomping grounds of famed bushranger **Ben Hall,** Forbes today shows little evidence of its checkered past. Still, an overall feeling of timelessness and a handful of good pubs compensate somewhat for its lack of compelling sights and make it a solid base for a trip around the Central West.

The **Newell Hwy** runs through Forbes, with Dubbo 153km to the northeast. There are also reasonably direct routes east to Orange (93km) and southeast to Cowra (70km). The downtown area is surrounded by the flood-prone **Lake Forbes,** which looks suspiciously like a river to the untrained eye. The old railway station on Union St has been converted into the **Forbes Railway Arts and Tourist Centre** (tel. 6852 4155; fax 6852 2347) now that passenger trains no longer service the town (open daily 9am-5pm). **Harvey World Travel,** 6 Templar St (tel. 6852 2344), sells tickets for all inter-city buses from Forbes (open M-F 9am-5pm, Sa 9am-noon). **CountryLink** (tel. 13 22 32) runs to Orange (2hr., 13 per week, $13) and Parkes (30min., 3 per week, $4), from the railway station, and **Greyhound Pioneer** (tel. 13 20 30) handles service to Cowra (1hr., daily, $41) from the Cal-Tex 24 Roadhouse, 1km north of town on the Newell Hwy.

Pub accommodations in Forbes are some of the best in the Central West and can be had for insanely low prices. Everything's huge at the **Albion Hotel,** 135 Lachlan St (tel. 6851 1881), at the head of Court St, from the clean rooms which come with in-room kettle, toaster, and complimentary cookies, to the showers which could house a town meeting. At $15 per person, it's highway robbery, Ben Hall-style. (Reception at the bar open M-Sa 10am-midnight or later, Su noon-10pm.) Alternatively, the **Vandenberg Hotel** (tel. 6852 2015), on Court St across from Victoria Park, provides rooms with high ceilings, mini-fridges, toasters, kettles, and bibles. Ask for a room with a balcony overlooking Forbes' downtown park and enjoy the comfortable TV lounge. (Singles $20, doubles $32, each additional under 12 $10. Ask at the bar daily 10am-10:30pm.)

The riverbank location of the **Apex Caravan Park,** 86 Reymond St (tel. 6851 1929), 2km south of the town center via Bridge St and Flint St, is well worth the drive. (Toilets, showers, laundry and barbecue facilities, small pool, store. Live-in owners will receive visitors anytime. Sites for 2 $11; with power $14, $4 per additional person, children under 5 free.) Groceries can be found at **Woolworths** (tel. 6852 2421), at the corner of Rankin St and Grenfell St (open M-Sa 7am-9pm, Su 9am-6pm).

The **Forbes Museum** (tel. 6852 2635), on Cross St, has a small collection of local artifacts and displays on the town's most notorious resident, Ben Hall (open Oct.-May daily 2-4pm, June-Sept. 3-5pm; admission $2, ages 5-15 $1).

■ Near Forbes: Parkes Radio Telescope

The **64m dish** visible from the Newell Hwy 55km northeast of Forbes on the road to Dubbo belongs to the **Parkes Radio Telescope.** A major contributor to international understanding of astronomy since its opening in 1961, the Parkes Telescope has participated in such high-profile projects as the televising of the first moon walks and the rescue of NASA's Apollo 13. More recently, the telescope has been involved in the quest to understand the mysterious **dark matter** which populates the cosmos. The **Visitors Discovery Centre** (tel. 6361 1777) is a surprisingly low-tech facility housing displays on the telescope and its accomplishments. The knowledgeable and talkative staff and a 30-minute film make the whole thing interesting even for non-scientists. (Center open daily 8:30am-4:30pm. Free. Film for a modest cost.)

■ Mudgee

A land of wine and honey cradled in the foothills of the Great Dividing Range, Mudgee (from the Aboriginal "nest in the hills") features over 20 vineyards serving up free samples. Tourism is growing, and locals proudly proclaim that Mudgee is "tasting better each year."Although only a 3½-hour drive from Sydney, Mudgee, between Lithgow (159km) and Dubbo (109km) on Hwy 86, feels pleasantly remote.

Armed with maps and good advice, the **Mudgee Visitors Centre,** 84 Market St (tel. 6372 5875; fax 6372 2853; email tourist@mudgee.nsw.gov.au; open M-F 9am-5pm, Sa 9am-3:30pm, Su 9:30am-2pm), is a fine first stop and one of two spots where **CountryLink** coaches (tel. 13 22 32) pause on the way through town. Buses between Sydney (5hr., $38) and Coonabarabaran (3hr., $64) come through Mudgee once or twice a day in each direction stopping in Lithgow (2½hr., $18) and Gulgong (30min., $5) as well. **Harvey World Travel**, Shop 12, Town Centre, Church St (tel. 6372 6077), can help with booking (open M-F 8:30am-5:30pm, Sa 9am-noon). The **NPWS office,** 160 Church St (tel. 6372 7199; fax 6372 7850; email mudgee@npws.nsw.gov.au), administers the northwest section of Wollemi National Park (see p. 134) and now offers 4WD "tag-along" tours of the park (follow a certified driver in your own car). (Open M-F 8:30am-4:30pm.) Mudgee's **post office**, 80 Market St (tel. 6372 2071) has postal code 2850. (Open M-F 9am-5pm.)

There's one inexpensive hotel near each of the two inter-city bus stops. To get to the **Federal Hotel,** 34 Inglis St (tel. 6372 2150; fax 6372 6393), near the old train station, follow Church St down past McDonald's, and turn left on Inglis before railway crossing. The hotel has all the perks (bedwarmers, TV lounge and free tea) at perky prices. (Singles $20, doubles $35. Reception open daily 10am-11pm or midnight. Check-out 10am but flexible.) Cheaper but less snazzy, the **Woolpack Hotel,** 67 Market St (tel. 6372 1908), is near the visitors center (turn left and go one block) and provides free tea and coffee and a communal fridge. (Singles $15; reception open daily 8:30am-midnight; check-out 10am.) The slightly dreary **Mudgee Riverside Caravan and Tourist Park,** 22 Short St (tel. 6372 2531), is just behind the visitors center near the Cudgegong River. (Toilets, showers, laundry facilities. Sites for 2 $10, with power $13, each additional person $4. Reception open daily 8am-10pm, check-out 10am.) The light and open **Lawson Park Hotel Bistro,** 1 Church St (tel. 6372 2183), is a great spot for good grub. (Steak dinner $9.50. Local wine by the glass from $3.50, by the bottle from $9. Open Su-Th noon-2:30pm and 6-9pm, F-Sa noon-2:30pm and 6-9:30pm.) The bar stays active later. Get your groceries at **BI-LO Supermarket,** (tel. 6372 7155) on Church St (open M-Sa 7am-10pm, Su 9am-6pm).

Mudgee's **wineries and vineyards** range from small vineyards that share their wine-making facilities to large, self-sufficient ones. Visits to the larger wineries, such as **Craigmoor Winery** (tel. 6372 2208; open M-Sa 10am-4:30pm, Su 10am-4pm), on Craigmoor Rd, and **Huntington Estate Wines** (tel. 6373 3825; open M-F 9am-5pm, Sa 10am-5pm, Su 10am-3pm), on Cassilis Rd, which offers a self-guided tour, tend to be most interesting. **Botobolar,** 89 Botobolar Rd (tel. 6373 3840), is one of Mudgee's **organic wineries,** and the 40-minute self-guided tour leads out into the vineyards, an unusual feature for most tours (open M-Sa 10am-5pm, Su 10am-3pm). The historic **Fairview winery** has recently been reopened by **Platt's Wines** (tel. 6372 7041), on the corner of Cassilis Rd and Henry Lawson Dr. With an art exhibition and the reasonably-priced **Cafe Fairview** (tel. 6372 7040; open daily 8am-5pm) on the premises of the old winery, Platt's is a nice place for a longer stop among the tours (open daily 9:30am-5pm). Travelers passing through in September will find the streets hopping with the **Mudgee Wine Festival**.

■ Near Mudgee: Gulgong

The narrow streets and wooden buildings of Gulgong, 30km northwest of Mudgee off the road from Dubbo, harken to the days of the frontier when the discovery of gold at Red Hill made the town a bustling center. For a town of its size, Gulgong has a surprising number of fascinating museums, beginning with the labyrinthine old **Gulgong Pioneers Museum,** 73 Herbert St (tel. 6374 1513), which keeps an amazing collection of pictures, personal items, furniture, buildings, vehicles, and music on over an acre of land. The volunteer-run museum is expertly organized and worth a full afternoon (open daily 9am-5pm; admission $4, seniors $3, students, and ages 5-15 $2). The **Henry Lawson Centre,** 147 Mayne St (tel. 6374 2049), celebrates the wit and style of the famous writer who grew up in nearby Eurunderee. (Open Su-F 10am-noon, Sa 10am-3pm. Admission $2, seniors $1, ages 5-15 50¢.) Rounding out Gulgong's list of historical attractions, the **Prince of Wales Opera House** (tel. 6374 1162), on the corner of Mayne St and Herbert St, claims to be the oldest opera house in Australia. Originally made of bark and dirt floors, the opera house housed Dame Nellie Melba in her early career and famous boxer Les Darcy in his last exhibition fight on Australian soil in 1916. A must-see for theatre enthusiasts—all visitors should request access at the adjacent gift shop (open M-Sa 9am-5pm, Su 9am-1pm during summer; M-Sa 9:30am-4:30pm, Su 9am-1pm during winter).

The **Gulgong Tourist Information Centre,** 109 Herbert St (tel. 6374 1202; fax 6374 2229), has additional info on the town's history (open M-F 8am-4:30pm, Sa 9am-3pm, Su 9:30am-2pm). The bus from Mudgee arrives and departs from the **tourist office** (30min., 1-2 per day, $5) and booking is handled by the **post office,** 90 Herbert St (tel. 6374 1292). For lodging, try the **Commercial Hotel,** on the corner of Mayne

St and Medley St (reception at the bar M-Sa 10am-midnight, Su 10am-10pm; $20 per person). The **Red Hill Field Studies Centre** (tel. 6374 2558), on Tom Saunders Ave off White St, is an educational center for primary school children but welcomes travelers whenever there are free beds. No linen or pillows are provided, but there are large cooking rooms and spacious "teacher rooms" perfect for families (office open M-F 8:30am-3:30pm; $10).

▓ Dubbo

The hub of the Central West, Dubbo sits at the intersection of the Newell Hwy (39) between Melbourne and Brisbane, and the Mitchell Hwy (32), leading from Sydney and Bathurst to points west. Headlined by the Western Plains Zoo, Dubbo's roster of attractions makes it a worthwhile one-night stop along these routes.

PRACTICAL INFORMATION Dubbo's sprawling layout makes life difficult for those without a car. **Talbragar St** runs east-west, parallel to the two major highways which sandwich the town. The intersection of Talbragar and **Macquarie St** marks the town center. The **Dubbo Visitors Centre** (tel. 6884 1422), at the corner of Erskine and Brisbane St, is at the northwest corner of the small downtown area (open daily 9am-5pm). Dubbo is accessible via public transportation from Sydney, Canberra, and other towns in the Central West. **CountryLink** trains and buses (tel. 6884 2511 or 13 22 32) depart from the railway station on Talbragar St. The **Inter-city Coach Terminal,** at Erskine and Darling St, is the drop-off point for both **Greyhound Pioneer** (tel. 13 20 30 or 6882 2033) and **Rendell Coaches** (tel. 6884 2411). Flights from Sydney (1hr., 3-7 per day, $15) come to **Dubbo Airport,** northwest of town off the Mitchell Hwy, on **Hazelton Airlines** (tel. 13 17 13). Dubbo's **post office** (tel. 6882 2022) is on Talbragar St between Macquarie and Brisbane St (open M-F 9am-5pm; postal code 2830). A stellar Olympic **swimming pool** (tel. 6882 2485) is across Talbragar St from the train station.

ACCOMMODATIONS AND FOOD The cheapest beds are at the **Dubbo YHA Hostel,** 87 Brisbane St (tel. 6882 0922), 500m from the bus station, with a TV room, kitchen, and two porches. The owners rent bikes ($6 per day) and sometimes arrange trips to the zoo and local stockyard. (Bunks $14; twins and doubles $28.) For pub accommodation at the center of town, stay at **The Imperial** (tel. 6882 4455; fax 6882 7638), at Talbragar and Dalby St, where Montmarte prints add a touch of class to the bistro and bar. (Singles $25; twins and doubles $45. Breakfast included. Counter meals $5-7.) The excellent **Dubbo City Caravan Park** (tel. 6882 4820; fax 6884 2062), on Whylandra St just before it becomes the Newell Hwy southwest of the city center, has shady campsites overlooking the Macquarie River. (Sites from $11; powered $14-18. Reception open daily 8am-7pm.) There are plenty of hotels in the city center, clustered around Talbragar St. All charge $20 or more for singles, sometimes including breakfast.

Sandwich shops and bakeries are plentiful in the city center, and both **Coles** and **Woolworths** have huge grocery stores inside the plazas on Macquarie St. The **Dubbo Markets** (tel. 6882 6699), on the corner of Darling and Erskine St, are in a small, covered marketplace. (Open M-W 8:30am-6pm, Th 8:30am-8pm, F 8:30am-6:30pm, Sa-Su 8:30am-4pm.) The **Bus Stop Cafe** (tel. 6884 4677), in the Inter-city Coach Terminal on Erskine St, is surprisingly good, clean, and friendly, without greasy spoon chaos (hamburgers $3.50, steak sandwiches $4.95, full breakfast $8.95; open 24hr.).

SIGHTS Dubbo's premier tourist attraction is the **Western Plains Zoo** (tel. 6882 5888), on Obley Rd, off the Newell Hwy south of the city center. In addition to Australian native species, the zoo houses Bengal tigers, black rhinoceri, and Australia's only African elephants. Many of the animals wander unrestrained through loose enclosures. Although the sealed road is suitable for cars, it's a lot more fun if you walk or bike. *(Open daily 9am-5pm, no entry after 3:30pm. $15, students $10.50, seniors $9, ages 4-16 $7.50, families of 5 $38. Bike rental $8 for 4hr.)* On Obley Rd 2km before the zoo,

Dundullimal Homestead (tel. 6884 9984) is a National Trust-registered slab house dating from the 1830s and boasting a saddlery workshop and petting zoo. *(Open daily 9am-5pm. $5, students $3, seniors $4, under 17 $2.)* The dough-faced animatronic models of **Old Dubbo Gaol** (tel. 6882 8122), on Macquarie St, tell the bygone convicts' sad and macabre stories in a way that proves any subject can be funny when you add enough goofy talking mannequins. *(Open daily 9am-5pm, last entry 4:30pm. $5, concessions $3.50, ages 5-16 $1.)* Down the street, the **Dubbo Museum** (tel. 6882 5359) presents local history with a straighter face. *(Open daily 9am-4:30pm. $5, concessions $3.50, ages 5-16 $1, families $11.)*

NORTH COAST OF NEW SOUTH WALES

Often called the Holiday Coast by Sydney-siders, this sand-strewn fantasyland of the northern NSW coast caters equally to leisurely backpackers, die-hard surfers, and hordes of families. Newcastle and Port Macquarie, with urban shores only a day from Sydney, draw holiday-makers itching to sunbathe, water-ski, or wet their surfboards. At the other end of the spectrum, inland eco-activist centers Lismore and Bellingen thrive on highly productive agricultural land punctuated by scenic national parks and fast-flowing rivers. With virtual cult status, Byron Bay synthesizes these two distinct flavors and seems to have a magnetic pull for all kinds of travelers, luring sunburned and party-ready hordes up the coast and detaining them for a while before they progress toward the Queensland border and the clutch of beaches beyond. For coverage of Tweed Heads, see **Tweed Heads and Coolangatta,** p. 298.

■ Newcastle

Newcastle (pop. 265,000) is trying hard to shake its reputation as a smokestack-ridden industrial metropolis. It's New South Wales' second largest city, but a building code that limits construction to eight stories keeps man's work from overwhelming nature's. Newcastle is still the world's largest coal exporter, shipping out one million tons each week aboard the long, lean cargo ships that glide through the harbor. But since the recent massive scaleback of the steelworks, **Broken Hill Proprietor** (BHP), tourism has become a major focus of Newcastle's economic agenda. The city has long been a mecca for surfers eager to share a wave with world champion Mark Richards. Newcastle has other attractions too: easy access to the Hunter Valley wineries and nearby wilderness and wetness reserves, picnic-perfect parks, fascinating historical sites, and plenty of watery fun on its gorgeous shores.

ORIENTATION

Newcastle's commercial district is on **Hunter Street,** which runs parallel through the city to both the waterfront (Wharf Rd) and King St. Hunter St becomes Scott St before Newcastle Station, down Wharf Rd, as the land stretches east in a long, thin strip. At the tip of Nobby's Head is Nobby's Lighthouse, surrounded by **Nobby's Beach,** a terrific surfing spot. Also on the peninsula is **Fort Scratchley,** high on the hill, and the **Harbour Foreshore Park. Queen's Wharf** begins with the **Tourist Centre** at 92 Scott St, across the street from the park and beyond the railway station and long-distance bus depot. The tall **Queen's Wharf Tower,** open for 360° views of the city and harbor, stands in the center of a group of harborside cafes and upscale pubs. A passenger **ferry** runs across Newcastle Harbor to **Stockton,** a mostly residential suburb whose shores show the remnants of the area's history of fatal shipwrecks.

Newcastle's shore is lined with white sand beaches, tidal pools, and green parks. Walking clockwise around the peninsula from Nobby's Beach leads to a surf pavilion and public beaches, then to **Bogey Hole,** a historic convict-built ocean bath at the edge of lovely **King Edward Park.** Further along, you'll see a cliff walk leading to the **Susan Gilmore** nude beach; further still, the large **Bar Beach,** popular with surfers.

To the east, Hunter St becomes the highway to **Hexham,** where the Pacific and New England Hwy fork; the former heads north up the coast and the latter branches west to the Hunter Valley wineries and the New England region.

PRACTICAL INFORMATION

Tourist Office: 92 Scott St (tel. 4929 9299), in the Old Stationmaster's Cottage. As you stand in front of the railroad station with the wharf at your back, the tourist office is on your left. The free map of the Newcastle/Hunter region is especially good. Open M-F 9am-5pm, Sa-Su 10am-3:30pm.

Trains: Newcastle Railway Station information line for trains, buses, and ferries (tel. 13 15 00). Open daily 6am-10pm. **CityRail** travels locally throughout Newcastle and to the Hunter Valley region; trains to Maitland ($3.20) and Sydney ($14.20) leave several times daily from the station. Luggage storage available.

Buses run along Hunter St every 15min. during the day, less frequently at night (info tel. 49 61 89 33). Some run as late as 4am. Tickets allow unlimited travel for a specified length of time; a 1hr. ticket costs $2. Some senior citizen discounts available. **Rover Motors** (tel. 4990 1699) runs between Newcastle's Watt St terminal and Cessnock's Vincent St (M-F 6 per day, Sa 3 per day; $8.30).

Ferries: Passenger ferry (tel. 4929 2106) departs the front of the tower every 30min. or less and crosses Newcastle Harbor to Stockton. Buy tickets on board. (M-Th 5:15am-11pm, F 5:15am-midnight, Su 8:30am-10pm; $1.30, children 65¢.)

Taxis: Newcastle Taxi Services (tel. 4962 2622 or 4969 6333) provides local taxi service, airport shuttles, and private sight-seeing tours of Newcastle ($30 per hr.).

Car Rental: ARA, 86 Lawson St, Hamilton (tel. 4962 2488), rents sedans from $49 and 2-door hatches from $44. **Thrifty** (tel. 4942 2266), 13 Parry St, is a bit pricier.

Bicycles: The Bicycle Center (tel. 4929 6933), at the corner of King and Darby St. Bikes available for $20 per day; long term cheaper. **Trike Hires** (tel. 4958 7582), on the foreshore, rents tricycles built for 3. Open Sa-Su and public holidays 11am-4:30pm. $6 per 30min. **Harley Davidson Motorcycle Rentals** (tel. 4962 2488), at ARA on the corner of Lawson and Tudor, start at $150 for 8hr., with 400km free.

Currency Exchange: The Hunter Mall, in the city center on Hunter St between Newcomen St and Perkins St, has several **banks** (open M Th 9:30am-4pm, F 9:30am-5pm) and 24hr. **ATMs,** as does Beaumont St north of Tudor St.

Hospital: On Shortland Esplanade. In an **emergency,** dial 000.

Police: At the corner of Church St and Watt St (tel. 4929 0999).

Public Markets: Six, each open on Sa or Su. Ask the tourist office for info.

Public Toilets, Baths, and Showers: The nearby library has a cleaner alternative to Civic Park's icky toilets. Free showers are at Ocean Baths on the shore.

Library: (tel. 4925 8342), on Laman St behind Civic Park, in the Newcastle Memorial Cultural Centre. Open M-F 9:30am-8pm, Sa 9:30am-2pm.

Pharmacy: Newcastle DayNight Chemist, 707 Hunter St (tel. 4929 4999) is open 8:30am-11pm daily.

Post Office: 96 Hunter St, Hunter Street Mall. It ain't just postage anymore in this kitsch-filled haven, where you can finally find that elusive Mr. Bean lunchbox. Open M-F 9am-5pm. **Postal Code: 2300.**

Internet Access: Internet Cyber Cafe, 538 Hunter St, Newcastle West (tel. 4929 7601). Web or email access $10 per hr. Open 9am-9pm.

Telephone Code: 02.

ACCOMMODATIONS

There are tons of year-round great values in Newcastle's accommodation scene, many with negotiable long-term rates, especially in winter. Book ahead in summer and on weekends. The tourist office has a listing of cushier digs.

West End Guest House, 775 Hunter St (tel. 4961 4446), at the intersection of Stewart St (Pacific Hwy), is a 15min. walk from the city center and a world away from an average backpackers. Immaculate and cheerful rooms filled with artwork and potpourri, kitchen access, a lounge with TV, books and games, friendly ownership. Shared bathrooms. Free pick-up from Newcastle Station. Bicycle loans available.

Reception 24hr. Dorms $18; singles $32; doubles $42; twins $44; family rooms $60. Weekly rates cheaper. Discounts for any backpackers card.

ⓦHarbourside Motel Newcastle (Hotel Terminus), 107 Scott St (tel. 4926 3244), across from Newcastle Station. Prime location near the wharf, gorgeous beach, the city center, and bus service. The tidy rooms have TVs, refrigerators, private bath. Reception 7am-9pm. Check-out 10am. Superb deal for families or groups; suites with a double adjoining a triple are $79. Singles $50; doubles $55; twins $63; triples $71. $10 key deposit. Long-term rates lower. Free laundry.

Backpackers Newcastle, 42-44 Denison St, Hamilton (tel. 4969 3436; fax 4940 8726), has free pick-up and drop-off in town and, most tellingly, free surf lessons year-round. 25min. walk from the city center with bus access, 5min. from happening Beaumont St. Owner keeps guests informed about events and will book hostels up north or winery tours. Two kitchens, TV area, reading room, coin-op laundry, linen, plates, safe for valuables, and co-ed bathrooms. No lockout time; no check-in midnight till 8am. Photo ID required for check-in. Check-out 10am. Dorms $16; singles $26; doubles $36-38. Long-term rates cheaper. Small children free. The building at 44 Denison St (same prices, doubles only) is much more elegant.

The Grand Hotel (tel. 4929 3489; fax 4929 7301) is an upmarket pub hotel on the corner of Church and Bolton St. Away from the noisy wharf, but within the city center and close to the shore. The pub is fun but noisy. TV, coffee, and tea in relatively clean rooms; restaurant, billiards room, and nightclub (free M and Sa) downstairs. Reception 7:30am-10pm or at the bar. Check-out 10am. Large doubles or singles $40, with bath $50; triples $55. Laundry free. Long-term rates negotiable.

The Crown and Anchor Hotel, 189 Hunter St (tel. 4929 1027; fax 4927 0161), on the corner of Perkins St and King St, is the cheapest hotel in the city. Great location by Queen's Wharf, above a relaxed pub with frequent live music. Small but clean rooms, sinks, free laundry. No TV, no kitchen. Shared single-sex bath. Reception 7:30am on; book ahead, especially on weekends. Check-out 10:30am. Smoking allowed. Singles $30; doubles $40; twins $45; negotiable. Extra person $15.

Commonwealth Hotel (tel. 4929 3463; fax 4929 5151), corner of Union and Bull St. Mellow pubstay with no laundry or kitchen, but plenty of TVs downstairs. Single $35, double $50, twin $60; weekly $130, $150, $180. Co-ed bathrooms. Student, senior discounts. 10min. walk from city center. Reception 10am-midnight.

Stockton Beach Caravan and Tourist Park, Pitt St, Stockton (tel. 4928 1393), across the harbor. A bit dank and compact, but spectacular waterfront location. Campsites $10-13; van sites $13-16. Prices depend on season and electricity access. Budget cabins with TVs, kitchens, and shared bath $30-55. Bigger cabins with private bath $50-75. Rates cover 2 adults. Weekly rates cheaper. Max. stay 2 months. Kitchenware supplied; no linen. All cabins non-smoking. Check-out 10am.

FOOD

For the cheapest eats, search out the huge and bargain-filled **Bi-Lo** supermarket (tel. 4926 4494) in Newcastle West at the West End Marketown (open 24hr.). **Nina Clancy's,** 73 Beaumont St (tel. 4961 2184), is good for cheap groceries (open M-F 8am-10pm, Sa-Su 8am-8pm). **Hunter Street** has numerous hot bread shops, takeaways, and small ethnic restaurants, most with $5-6 lunch specials, many with sandwiches under $3. If you're trying to sneak a cheap dinner, go early—most close around 6pm. One of the less greasy lunch options is the **Pure and Healthy Bar,** 315 Hunter St (tel. 4926 4226), where you can create your own sandwich on fresh bread baked daily; no item on the menu costs more than $4.50.

Many cafes throughout the city specialize in super-cheap meals in the early part of the week. Hamilton's **Beaumont St,** a 25-minute walk from the city, is filled with good, cheap Italian restaurants. **The Oasis,** on the corner of Beaumont and Cleary St, has a variety of food stands and an outdoor patio. Perhaps the best deal in Hamilton is the student **TAFE** restaurant, 19 Parry St (tel. 4969 9411), in the Hunter Institute of Technology Block A, with mains for $3.50 and salads and desserts for $1. (Open M-F noon-1:15pm, plus W 2:45-5:30pm. Call ahead to confirm hours.)

Darby St welcomes you with **Benvenuti Restaurant,** 88 Darby St (tel. 4926 4798), and the **Black and White Cafe,** 150 Darby St (tel. 4925 2151), both with $5 pastas (at

NEW SOUTH WALES

Newcastle

ACCOMMODATIONS
A Backpackers Newcastle
C The Crown and Anchor Hotel
D The Grand Hotel
B Hunter-on-Hunter

PACIFIC OCEAN

STOCKTON

King St.
Pitt St.
Mitchell St.
Fullerton St.

Nobby's Lighthouse
Nobby's Beach
Nobby's Rd.

Fort Scratchley
Wharf Rd.
Scott St.

Railway Station
Queen's Wharf

Court House
Watt St.
Newcomen St.
King St.
Wolfe St.
Church St.
Brown St.
Ordnance St.
King Edward Park
Bogey Hole
Newcastle Beach

CENTRAL NEWCASTLE

Port Hunter (Hunter River)

CARRINGTON

Bourke St.
Cowper St.

Hunter St.
Lee Wharf Rd.
Tyrrell St.
King St.
Laman St.

Newcastle Regional Art Gallery

Brooks St.
Darby St.
Dawson St.
Bruce St.
Corlette St.
Bull St.
Parry St.
Union St.
National Park St.

National Park

Throsby Basin

Throsby Creek

WICKHAM

Hannell St.
Hannell St.
Albert St.
Hunter St.

Newcastle Regional Museum

Denison St.

Pacific Hwy. (Stewart Ave.)

Downie St.
Lewis St.
Pacific Hwy.
Donald St.
Lindsay St.
Tudor St.
Everton St.
Dumaresq St.

HAMILTON

Gordon Ave.
Lawson St.
Beaumont St.

Newcastle Racecourse

400 yards
400 meters
0
0

the Black and White, M-W only). **Taters,** 78 Darby St (tel. 4929 2730), is a takeaway with baked potatoes and low-fat fare. **Mucho's Mexican Restaurant,** 52 Glebe Rd (tel. 4969 2060), in the Junction, has $7 specials on Mondays. **Arrivederci Restaurant,** 53 Glebe Rd (tel. 4963 1036), lets you choose from 10 belly-filling pastas (M-Tu $5).

Queen's Wharf has many waterfront cafes, but you can't beat the combination of views and prices at **Scratchley's,** 200 Wharf Rd (tel. 4929 1111), right on the water. Award-winning main courses, including seafood, cost $9-20. The cafe is BYO, but a local store will deliver alcohol within 10 minutes. (Open M-Sa 10am-3pm and 5:30-9pm, Su 10am-9pm. Book ahead on weekends.) **The Harbourview Takeaway** is the cheapest place on the wharf, good for quickie fish and chips.

SIGHTS

Even in days long gone, Newcastle suffered from image problems: the city was established in 1804 as a convict settlement, dubbed "Sydney's Siberia." Many of its gorgeous **heritage buildings** were built by convicts, and 80% survived until a disastrous 1989 earthquake. Many have since been reconstructed. **Newcastle's Famous Tram** (tel. 4929 1822) offers a delightful, informative overview of the city. *(45min.; departs from Newcastle Railway Station daily on the hour from 10am to 3pm. Tours $8, $10 with unlimited stops, children $5, concessions $7, families of 4 $20.)* The excellent weekday tours focus more on architecture, while the weekend tours specialize in history.

Fort Scratchley is a must-see. It has a great view of the city and harbor, two museums, and an important history. The fort was originally constructed during the 1880s as a strategic defense against the Russians, but it rose to dubious glory as the only fort used against the Japanese during WWII. The skirmish was a comical failure. The Japanese fired 27 shells in an effort to blow up BHP Steelworks and missed every time. The Australians returned six shells and managed only to blow off a roof in nearby Stockton. The fort has been an inactive military site since 1972, but now houses the **Military Museum.** *(Open Sa-Su and public holidays noon-4pm, or by appointment. Free, but tours of the underground tunnel system are $1.50.)* Next door, the **Maritime Museum** (tel. 4929 2588) provides detailed historical information. *(Open Tu-Su noon-4pm.)*

The **Newcastle Regional Museum,** 787 Hunter St, Newcastle West (tel. 4962 2001; http://www.nma.gov.au/sites/newcastle), is a wonderful three-level collection of hands-on science exhibits and heritage displays. *(Open Tu-Su 10am-5pm. Free.)* There is a fee for the traveling exhibits; 1999's are "Gargantuans of the Garden" (an insect exhibit) and a dinosaur display. *(Children under 5 free. Student and family rates available.)* The **Newcastle Region Art Gallery** (tel. 4929 3263), on Laman St off Darby St behind Civic Park, has Australian and international art. *(Open Tu-Su 10am-5pm. Free.)* For morbid fascination, try **Newcastle Police Station Museum,** 90 Hunter St, located in a 120-year-old station. *(Open M-F 9am-1pm, Sa-Su 11am-4pm. $1.)* Exhibits include a hand-stitched padded leather cell streaked with fingernail scratches.

The **Blackbutt Reserve** (tel. 4952 1449) is a lovely 200-acre tree sanctuary with walking trails, small caves, and many animals. *(Open daily 9am-5pm. Free.)* There's a koala enclosure and kangaroo and emu reserves. Bring your own food for a picnic or barbecue; no food is available at the reserves. Catch bus #232 or #363 in the city center to Lookout Road Cardiff Heights (35min.).

The **Wetlands Centre** (tel. 4951 6466) offers sanctuary to birds, reptiles, and humans, with walking and cycling paths and a creek and swamp for canoeing. *(Open daily 9am-5pm. Donation $2.)* The center rents canoes and sponsors a monthly "Breakfast with the Birds," as well as twilight guided walks each Sunday. Take the CityTrain to Sandgate, in the suburb of Shortland, and then walk 10 minutes to the Wetlands Centre. **Cafe Jacuna,** the gift shop, sells light refreshments.

ENTERTAINMENT

The *Newcastle Herald* publishes an entertainment guide with Thursday's paper. Extra copies are available at the info center and motels. The **Civic Theatre,** 375 Hunter St (tel. 4929 1977), has excellent productions of familiar plays, large musicals,

> ### Third Time's the Charm
> The windmill on Nobby's Point was built in 1820 as a landmark for the many ships which were turning into nearby Lake Macquarie, thinking it was Newcastle Harbor. The 1989 earthquake ruined the landmark, and it took 47 men four months and ten days to repair it. Ten days later, lightning struck the new structure and catapulted it 3m into the air.

and children's shows. **Showcase Cinemas** (tel. 4929 5019), on Wolfe St off the Hunter St Mall, specializes in foreign and art films. More mainstream fare is offered at the **Greater Union Tower Cinemas,** 183 King St (tel. 4926 2233), with a special Tuesday rate ($6). The **King Street Fair** (tel. 4926 4000), the **Newcastle Jazz Festival** (tel. 4982 1264), and **Oktoberfest** (tel. 4954 6136) are three of the livelier yearly fairs. The **Wog Rock,** 12-14 Beaumont St (tel. 4961 6200), at the intersection with Hudson, is an award-winning dinner theater for a hefty price ($25-30). **SJ's** on Beaumont St is a gaming room and pub that gets swamped on weekend nights.

The **Northern Star Hotel,** 112 Beaumont (tel. 4961 1087) and the **Kent Hotel,** 59-61 Beaumont (tel. 4961 3303), are popular jazz spots. **The Castle** nightclub, at the intersection of King and Steel St, is loud, large, and lively, especially Wednesday and Thursday evenings. **Jack's,** on King St, has $2 drinks on Friday retro night from 8 to 10pm. Fanny's on Wharf Rd is also popular. **The Newcastle Workers Club** (tel. 4926 2700), at the corner of King and Union St, is a huge facility with gaming and sometimes live music; it's dead on Friday nights, but Saturdays sizzle with the "World's Biggest Disco" till 3am ($2; free for travelers). **The Barracks,** 139 Maitland St (Hunter St) in Islington, is gay- and lesbian-oriented but straight-friendly. (Drag shows F 12:30am. Free entry F and Sa before 11pm, free drinks after.) For more upscale and refined fun, try **The Brewery,** on Queen's Wharf, a pub that brews its own and often gives coupons to hotel and hostel owners. For other clubs and pubs, look at the free local guide *TE (That's Entertainment),* or check http://www.nnp.com.au.

■ Near Newcastle

Fifteen minutes south of Newcastle is **Lake Macquarie,** Australia's largest coastal saltwater lake (four times the size of Sydney Harbour) and a holiday hotspot. The shore is popular with surfers and families alike, with great waves, caverns at **Caves Beach,** and an old mining village at **Catherine Hill Bay.** Spelunkers must go at **low tide** so as not to get caught in the caves. Tide tables are at the info center. The district has many caravan parks and motels. It's also convenient to stay in Belmont or Charlestown, suburbs of Newcastle. The **Lake Macquarie information center** (tel. 4972 1172) is at 72 Pacific Hwy in the Blacksmiths (open M-F 9am-5pm, Sa-Su 9am-4pm).

The mountainous **Watagan State Forests** separate Lake Macquarie from the Hunter River. An hour from Newcastle and the Hunter Valley, they're ideal for hikes, picnics, or camping. There are six campsites, most with firewood, barbecues, toilets, and water. Call the **State Forests of NSW** office (tel. 4973 3733) for more info.

■ Myall Lakes National Park

If you're motivated and crafty enough to evade the noisy motorboats and littered caravan parks that plague parts of Myall Lakes National Park, you'll find yourself in a rugged, peaceful refuge, surrounded by over 10,000 hectares of lakes, 40km of beaches, and walking tracks traversing coastal rainforest, heath, and paperbark swamp. To find seclusion, pick up the park notes in nearby tourist information centers, and explore the various ways to access the park from The Lakes Way. Most people enter via **Buladelah,** 83km north of Newcastle and 78km south of Taree along the Pacific Hwy, and 60km southwest of Forster by The Lakes Way. From Buladelah, take the Myall Road, a.k.a. Lakes Road, a one-lane paved road with an absurd 100kph speed limit. Beware the cars, caravans, and boat tugs barreling along.

The road finishes at **Bombah Point,** a center of activity for both the Myall Lake and Bombah Broadwater. Here, the office and kiosk of **Myall Shores Tourist Area** (tel. 4997 4495; fax 4997 4600) distributes maps and an excellent brochure on the Mungo Brush Rainforest Walking Track. They also rent canoes ($7.50 per hr.) and outboards ($25 per 2hr.), and sell petrol. The facilities within the campground include electric and wood barbecues, laundry, a store, and a restaurant. (Campsites $13.50, powered $16.50, $2 extra on weekends.) A **toll ferry** carries vehicles over to the Mungo Brush area of the park (every 30min. 9am-6pm, $3). The paved **Mungo Brush Road** extends 25km along the coast to the southern edge of the park. There are various entrances to the usually-crowded Mungo Brush **campgrounds** on the lake side of the road. The far campgrounds seem to be the semi-permanent homestead to campervanners. At these sites you'll find tap water, toilets, sporadic electric barbecues, and close access to the shallow lake in which you can swim. Access points all along the road lead to the beach. The abundant and fearsome goannas shouldn't bother you unless you leave food scraps around. Arachnophobes, beware of terrifyingly large webs; carry a flashlight at night to inspect gaps between trees. From the northern end of Mungo Brush begins the **Mungo Brush Rainforest Walking Track,** a 1.5km loop through a littoral rainforest whose fertility is unusual for this stretch of coast.

■ Port Stephens

North of Newcastle, Port Stephens is a lovely bay and collection of townships surrounded by clear blue water and the **Tomaree National Park.** During the summer, surfing beaches and luxury resorts draw backpackers and families alike, clogging central shopping areas with traffic. Sea life of the cute and fuzzy kind can be seen year-round: 80 bottlenose **dolphins** are visible from October to mid-June, while **whale-watching** season runs from early June to October. On the coastal edge of the national park, abandoned Australian-American forts are left over from WWII training camps.

ORIENTATION

Nelson Bay Road leads from Newcastle into Port Stephens, which is comprised of four residential townships on the spit of land south of the port. The road then forks onto **Gan Gan Road,** which leads to the first township of **Anna Bay,** home to **Stockton Bight,** the largest sand dune area in Australia, and close to the popular surfing destination of **One Mile Beach.** Gan Gan and Nelson Bay Rd rejoin en route to the other three townships: **Nelson Bay** (the largest), **Shoal Bay,** and finally **Fingal Bay.** The marina, shopping complex, and cafes are located on **Victoria's Parade** in Nelson Bay. The **Salamander Shopping Center** is nearby. Shoal Bay is surrounded by beaches and the Tomaree National Park, and Fingal Bay is quite rural and out of the way.

PRACTICAL INFORMATION

Tourist Office: (tel. 4981 1579 or 1800 808 900; http://www.portstephens.org.au), on Victoria's Pde, Nelson Bay.

Buses: Port Stephens Buses (tel. 4982 2940) runs from Sydney (3½hr.; daily at 2pm; $22 one-way, $36 return) and Newcastle (1½hr.; M-F 12 per day, Sa-Su and holidays 3 per day; $8) to the four townships. Local buses hourly (around $2; 1-day unlimited travel $10). The main stop in Nelson Bay is at the Bi-Lo on Stockton St.

Ferries: The **Myall Lady and Ferry** (tel. 018 682 117) makes occasional trips to **Tea Garden,** just across the water from Nelson Bay. Schedule varies seasonally.

Taxis: Call 4913 1008, or on a mobile phone 4984 6699.

Money: Many **banks** with **ATMs** are near the tourist office on Stockton and Magnus St. ATMs are also at the Salamander Shopping Center.

Police: On Government Rd, Nelson Bay (tel. 4981 1244). In an **emergency,** dial 000.

Post Office: Corner of Stockton and Magnus St (tel. 4981 1240), or in the Salamander Shopping Center.

Phone Code: 02.

ACCOMMODATIONS AND FOOD

Like most resort areas, Port Stephens has many lodgings, but beds go quickly and prices shoot up in the summer and during holidays, though there are often great deals during winter. All of the following are on the Port Stephens bus route.

Samurai Beach Bungalows Backpackers (tel. 4982 1921 or 018 682 2710), on Robert Connell Circle, off Frost Rd, which is off Nelson Bay Rd right outside Anna Bay. An ecotourist's dream, with small cabins encircling an open green. There's a kitchen, volleyball court, and a campfire where guests share stories and play the owner's drum. In summer, koalas can be seen from the balconies. TV, pool table, free bikes, surfboards, boogie boards. Beaches and bus stop nearby. Rooms with TV, bath, mini-kitchen $60. Family room with shared bath $50. Sparse dorms $15. VIP. Linen included. Off-season special: 2 nights in twins plus dolphin cruise $47.

Sandy Point Motor Lodge, 19-21 Sandy Point Rd, Corlette (tel. 4981 1744), on the route of the daily Sydney Coach from Central Station. Extremely clean rooms all have a private bathroom, TV, fan, toaster, coffee pot, and mini-fridge. Peak season rates vary; singles around $40, doubles $55. Off-season: singles $30, doubles $45, family rooms $50; midweek 3 nights in a double $99. Bargains on whale- and dolphin-watching cruises and long-term rates are also available.

Shoal Bay YHA, 59-61 Shoal Bay Beachfront Rd (tel. 4981 1744; fax 4984 1052), in the Shoal Bay Motel, directly across from the beach and a 15min. walk from the Tomaree National Park. Clean, well-lit rooms have heat and A/C. The 8-bed women's dorm has an attached bathroom, while the 6-bed men's dorm is separated from the common room by a sheet. Kitchen, comfortable TV lounge, sauna, barbecue. Dorms $15, YHA nonmembers $17. Linen rental $2.

Shoal Bay Holiday Park (tel. 4981 1427), on Shoal Bay Rd on the way to Fingal Bay, within hearing distance of the ocean. Ensuite cabins for 5 $40-58. Powered tent and caravan sites $15.50 or $18, depending on season. 7th night free. Prices and minimum stay vary during school holidays. Book ahead in summer.

Nelson Bay is the best place to find cheap eats, although prices tend to be higher here than in larger cities. **Fish and Chips** on Stockton St has cheap hamburgers and good deals on its namesake. Further up the street in the **Twin Cinema Mall,** there are some well-priced choices at **Chez Jules** (tel. 4981 4500) and great breakfast deals at the **Tin Shed** (under $5; open M-Sa; breakfast 8am-11am). Trusty supermarket **Bi-Lo** has locations on the corner of Stockton and Donald St (tel. 4981 1666) and in the Salamander Shopping Center. There's also a **Woolworths** in Salamander.

ACTIVITIES

Dolphin and **whale-watching cruises** usually depart twice daily in the summer and once daily in the winter. The cheapest of the lot is the large *Tamboi Queen* (tel. 4982 0707 or 018 494 509). *(2hr. cruise $9, children $7.)* The *M.S. Waywind* (tel. 4982 2777) is a small, beautiful, no-motor sailing vessel with a boom net. *(2hr. summer dolphin cruise approximately $16; 3-4hr. winter whale cruise $35. Check for child and student rates.)*

There are several **sports rental** stores in the area. **Nelson Bay Sports,** 77 Victoria Pde (tel./fax 4981 2333), opposite the tourist office, rents equipment for outdoor activities: cycles ($15 for 2hr., $25 for 8hr. day), snorkeling gear ($10 for 4hr., $15 per day), body boards ($10 for 4hr., $20 per day), roller blades ($12 for 2hr., $25 per day), and fishing gear ($6 per day). *(Open daily 8:30am-5pm.)* **Shoal Bay Bike Hire,** 63 Shoal Bay Rd (tel. 4981 4360), near the YHA, is a somewhat cheaper bike option. *($10 for 2hr.; $20 for 24hr. Open 9am-5pm; hours vary during winter, closed Tu.)*

Sahara Trails (tel. 4981 9077 or 015 290 340) offers two-hour horse rides on the Blue Lagoon Trail for $30 and spectacular two-hour coastal dune and beach rides for $40. *(Open Sa-Su and school and public holidays, M-F by appointment only.)* **Toboggan Hill Park** (tel. 4984 1022), at Salamander Way on Nelson Bay, is a big theme park with a 700m downhill toboggan run, a 19-hole mini golf course, and indoor rock climbing.

NEW SOUTH WALES

■ Forster

Forster and its inconsequential twin town Tuncurry are neither picturesque nor charming, but Forster boasts heaps of activities offered at reasonable prices, a great pub, and access to the Great Lakes region. To get around Forster, you need only know three streets. **Head Street,** the continuation of the bridge, runs north-south along the seashore. **Wharf Street,** which originates by the lake a block over from Head St, is home to **ATMs,** the butcher, the baker, but no candlestick-maker. The shoreline drive begins by Wharf St, first calling itself **Memorial Drive** and then **Little Street.** They lead onto **The Lakes Way,** which takes you to **Booti Booti National Park** and **Myall Lakes National Park** (see p. 147). The **Great Lakes Visitors Centre** (tel. 6554 8799) is on Little St by the wharf, and is also the **coach terminal.** The center has all the usual maps and info, and is an obligatory stop if you wish to book tours, rentals, or lessons (open daily 9am-5pm). **Great Lakes Coaches** (tel. 1800 043 263) connects Forster to Sydney. (5½hr., M-F 4 per day, Sa-Su 2 per day. $38, students $26.50.) The **post office** (tel. 6554 6144) is on Wallace St at the end of Wharf St (postal code 2428; open M-F 9am-5pm).

Do you like nice people? Meet the owner of the **Dolphin Lodge (YHA),** 43 Head St (tel./fax 6555 8155), who treats you to bikes, boogie boards, a kitchen, TV lounge with VCR, and patio picnic tables. A January 1998 TV special highlighted **Smugglers Cove Holiday Village,** 45 The Lakes Way (tel. 6554 6666), which has top notch facilities (sites $12-16). For foodstuffs, try the small market on Wharf St, or for selection, go to the Forster Shopping Village (tel. 6554 5044), which has a **Coles Supermarket.** At the Tuncurry end of Wharf St, the **Mexican Cantina** (tel. 6554 5573) serves a Beer 'n' Beef Special ($13), chili prawns ($14.50), and has live music on Thursdays (open W-M 5-10pm). As soon as work gets out on Friday afternoon, the **Lakes and Ocean Hotel** gets its taps running full volume. In this pub at Little and Lake St, Shannon Lee wrote her locally famed novel *The Dog House.* Live bands play on weekends.

Tobwabba, 10 Breckenridge St (tel. 6554 5755), means "place of clay" to the Worimi Aboriginals who welcome visitors to this studio and art gallery (open daily 10am-4:30pm). At the north end of **Forster Beach,** at the end of West St off Head St, there are changing rooms, a gas barbecue, a saltwater swimming pool, and a beach. For stunt skiing, seaplane flights, fishing cruises, or diving, consult the tourist bureau. The **Amaroo Coffee Cruise** (tel. 0419 333 445) is an inexpensive two-hour jaunt departing daily in summer ($18). Boat and tackle rental sheds line the lake shore.

■ Near Forster: Great Lakes Region

Booti Booti National Park

Following The Lakes Way south of town, you follow the coastline of Elizabeth Bay. The forest and shrubland between the road and beach, the hinterland on the road's other side, and Wallis Lake comprise **Booti Booti National Park.** Aww, yeah. **Tiona Park** (tel. 6555 0291; fax 6554 0711), less than 10 minutes from Forster, rents sites on both the lake and beach sides of the road (sites $12-26; cabins $30-43; vans $26-34). On the lake side, a one-hour walk around the lake through cabbage tree palms and eucalypts will lead you to the ocean and **Elizabeth Beach.** You can camp with less clutter at **The Ruins Camping Area,** known as the "Bull Ring" to locals, by the soft white sand of Seven-Mile Beach next to a mangrove forest. Good surfers should travel 1km north to Janice's Corner. Pay camping fees in slots at the entrance to the Bull Ring. (Barbecue, toilets, and showers. $17.50 for 1 night, longer stays cheaper.)

Bluey's Beach and Pacific Palms

Approximately 20 minutes drive along The Lakes Way south of Forster, there appears a sign for Bluey's Beach. The road, Boomerang Drive, passes several excellent beaches and continues through the small town of Pacific Palms before rejoining with The Lakes Way a few kilometers south. **Elizabeth's Beach** is the first turn-off on the left. The waves usually die down in summer, making the surf ideal for swimmers, although it's unpatrolled. Further along Boomerang Dr is **Shelly's Beach,** a calm stretch patrolled by pelicans and lifeguards. **Boomerang Beach,** home of myriad surfer dudes, is just a couple minutes further. Here you can crash at **Moby Dick** (tel. 6554 0292), a plain caravan park with a little kiosk and hot junk food (sites $12, powered $15, cabins $35-55). From here, Boomerang Dr loops through **Pacific Palms,** which has a small strip of shops selling junk food, sundries, and magazines, but no ATM, although EFTPOS is available. At its end is the **info center** (tel. 6554 0123; open daily 9am-4pm). A bit farther on you can camp in style at the **Oasis Caravan Park** (tel. 4997 4495; fax 4997 4600). There's petrol, a market, and a small swimming pool on the premises. (Office open daily 8am-8pm, in winter 9am-7pm. Cabins $80, campsites $15-17; off-season $60, $12-14.)

Sandbar

A kilometer south of the southern end of Boomerang Dr along The Lakes Way is the turn-off for a dirt road that takes you 2km to a parking lot for **Celito Beach.** Wow. The 300m boardwalk leads through dry littoral forest to a beach to drool over, whether you're a surfer or a sun lover. On a good day, surfers marvel at the sunset peaks that break here, and there's always ample room to sunbathe or swim. Leave the beach area and go left back on the main dirt road to the **Sandbar Caravan Park** (tel 6554 4095; fax 6554 4253), a wilderness site on **Smith's Lake** (sites $12-19, cabins $32-53; prices depend on season). Canoeing, boating, swimming, and fishing are popular.

Seal Rocks

South of Pacific Palms and Bluey's Beach, The Lakes Way turns westward to skirt **Myall Lakes National Park** on its way to rejoining the Pacific Hwy at Buladelah. Between Smiths Lake and Myall Lake, there is an easterly turn-off from The Lakes Way onto **Seal Rocks Road.** The community of Seal Rocks has insisted that much of this road (15km) remains unpaved in order to preserve its seclusion from mass tourism. Just past the roadhouse, there's a small carpark near the long **Number One Beach.** Beyond this, a narrow dirt track leads to **Boat Beach.** Swimmers, windsurfers, and surf fishermen share this spot, and you can snorkel and dive between sharks and strange offshore rock formations. The **Seal Rocks Camping Reserve** (tel./fax 4997 6250), near Number One Beach, offers accommodations. (Unpowered sites $10.50, vans $32-39, cabins $42-49. Prices cover up to 4 people.)

Gloucester and Barrington Tops

Gloucester floats in a no-man's land, neither on the coast nor in the New England region. Not much goes on there; travelers use it to pick up info on Barrington Tops (1hr.) and supplies for camping trips and barbecues. Take The Lakes Way north out of Forster, head to the Pacific Hwy at the first opportunity, then turn south, and in a couple kilometers a sign will point you to Gloucester. Expect a journey of at least an hour. The **Tourist Information Centre** (tel. 6558 1408) is on Denison St (open daily 9:30am-4:30pm). **Country Link** (tel. 13 22 32) travels to Newcastle (1½ hr., 1 per day, $15). The only **ATM** is at **Commonwealth Bank,** Church St. For a bed, see the **Ann Valley Inn,** 82 Church St (tel. 6558 1016), on the main road (singles $20, doubles $30). Contact the **Barrington Outdoor Adventure Centre** (tel. 6558 2093) to rent bikes, canoes, or kayaks, or to arrange 4WD tours. Their materials are detailed but disorganized, describing bike trails, horse trails, fishing spots, walks, and canoe routes. The **Williams River Area** is the most accessible spot, with easy and difficult walks, short (1½hr.) and long walks (5-8hr.), barbecues and toilets, but no campsites. **Gloucester River** is the nearest campsite. Camping away from official grounds is permitted.

■ Taree

Taree (pop. 1800), located on the Manning River and the Pacific Highway, is small and run-of-the-mill. It is, however, a great base for daytrips to nearby beaches, state parks and forests. The many budget hotels, motels and caravan parks that line the

Pacific Hwy in Taree and the surrounding areas provide another argument for spending a day or two before heading to more expensive pastures.

PRACTICAL INFORMATION Taree's main street, **Victoria St,** overlaps the Pacific Hwy, but must be turned onto; going straight will lead off the Pacific Hwy and to nearby **Wingham.** Most shops and restaurants are on Victoria St or the offshoots between Pulteney and Macquarie St. The **tourist office** (tel. 1800 801 522 or 6552 1900) is on the Pacific Hwy 3km north of town, between the Manning Entertainment Centre and McDonald's, just past the Big Oyster (open daily 9am-5pm). **Tourist radio** is 88.0 FM, and is surprisingly interesting. The **post office** (tel. 6552 1139) is on Albert St; look for the sign on Victoria St and go through the mall to the back parking lot (open M-F 8:30am-5pm; postal code 2430). **Banks** with **ATMs** can be found on Victoria and Manning St. Taree has **police** (tel. 6551 1044), **firefighters** (tel. 6551 5246), and a **hospital,** 105 High St (tel. 6551 1511). In an **emergency,** dial 000.

Greyhound Pioneer (tel. 13 20 30) coaches run daily from Sydney's Central Station and from Brisbane, as do **Countrylink** (tel. 6552 0609) trains and coaches. **Eggins Comfort Coaches** (tel. 6552 2700) go from Taree to Diamond Beach (M-F 9:50am) and Old Bar (M, W, F 2 per day; Tu, Th 4 per day). **Taxis** can be reached at 6551 3855.

ACCOMMODATIONS AND FOOD Accommodations in Taree are cheap and plentiful, with more upmarket possibilities mixed in. The tourist office has a full listing. By far the cheapest option is **The Exchange Hotel** (tel. 6552 1160), on the corner of Victoria and Manning St. A pub hotel in the center of Taree, it can be a bit noisy. The very basic rooms are clean (apart from the occasional roach) and decorated with beautiful wood dressers and bureaus, sinks. (Singles $12, doubles $25, twins $24).

A bit further up the ladder are a series of inexpensive motels. **The Chatham Motel,** 39 Chatham Ave (tel. 6552 1659), off the Pacific Hwy just before the tourist office, has pretty small rooms, but they come with refrigerators, heating, fans, TVs, and private bathrooms. Breakfast is cheap and a toaster can be rented for $1. (Singles and doubles $30, $5 more during peak periods. Family rooms for 5, $55-75.) Down the road towards the tourist office is the **Arlite Motor Inn.** The pool is a bit dingy, but the rooms have lots of amenities (phone, fridge, A/C, coffeemaker, TV, private bathroom) plus stylin' wood paneling and cheesy ocean paintings. (Economy singles $32-35; doubles $32-38, depending on season.) On the way back to the center of Taree is the **Aquatic Motor Inn** (tel. 6551 2822). This place is so clean it smells like detergent. The average-size rooms have TVs and coffeemakers, and there's a pool with a barbecue. (Singles $28, doubles $30; noisier front units $2 less. Family room around $48.)

Two caravan parks are on the Pacific Hwy: **Taree Caravan Park** (tel. 6552 1751), near the tourist office, and **Twilight Caravan Park** (tel. 6552 2857 or 015 354 442), closer to the beaches. Taree has a pool, carwash, laundry, color TV, and wheelchair access. (For 2 people, ensuite cabin $36-$42; standard cabin $30-$35, depending on season. $4 per extra person. Two-person powered sites $12; unpowered $6 for 1; $2 per extra person; higher during holidays.) Twilight has partial wheelchair access, a behind-the-counter convenience store, a saltwater pool, barbecue area, and kitchens in all units. Pets allowed. (Ensuite cabins $34-38 regularly; standard cabins $25-28. Sites $10-12, powered $14. Rates slightly higher during holidays, lower by the week.)

Woolworths (tel. 6551 7067) is in the Triple Cee Mall on Albert St, between Pulteney St and Manning St. In Manning Mall across the street, there is a **Bi-Lo** (tel 6552 5578). There are many cheap eateries on Pulteney and Manning St near Victoria St. **Bert's Place Cafe,** on Manning St, has sandwiches and hamburgers.

BEACHES The beaches near Taree are gorgeous and inviting, but have unexpected currents; swim only where patrolled. The closest is **Old Bar Beach** in the little village of Old Bar, a 15-minute drive from the town center. **Wallabi Point,** to the south, has a swimming lagoon. **Diamond Beach** and **Hallidays Point,** two well-known beaches further south, both have **camping.** To the north is Crowdy Head, site of a lighthouse lookout. Crowdy Head, Hallidays, and Old Bar Beaches are all patrolled in season.

■ Between Taree and Port Macquarie

Crowdy Bay National Park, home to some of the areas most popular beaches, bush-walks, and picnic areas, and a year-round supply of kangaroos, has something for every visitor. The southern entrance is at Moorland on the Pacific Hwy. Coralville Rd leads into the park. Wild eastern grey **kangaroos** live at all three of the **camping sites: Diamond Head, Indian Head,** and **Kylie's Rest Area** (named for Australian author Kylie Tennant). All the sites have restrooms, though the showers are erratic at best.

While groups of kangaroos hop within feet of astounded visitors, and whales can be spotted of the headlands, it often takes an expert to spot more elusive **koalas** at Indian Head and Kylie's Hut. The best time for **wildflowers** is October. There are 3 reasonably tame bushwalks in the park. The shortest walk is along the base of the cliff of the headland, accessible at low tide form Diamond Head. A second walk links Diamond Head and Indian Head, while the third goes from Kylie's Hut to the beach at Crowdy Bay. Visitors must bring their own fresh water into the park. The roads are 2WD-accessible dirt tracks; watch out for animals. (One-time camping charge $7.50, plus $5 a night for 2 people and $2 per extra person.)

Bulga State Forest is the site of a 99km tourist drive (No. 8), a 190km, full day trip from Taree. The Bulga Forests are actually four separate forests: the Bulga, Doyles River, Dingo and Knorrit. The Bulga is home to the **Tirrill Creek Flora Reserve,** with walking trails, picnic areas, and the **Blue Knob Lookout,** from which even Taree is sometimes visible. **Maxwells Flat,** with toilet and barbecue facilities, has **camping.**

Perhaps the most spectacular sight of the Bulga drive is **Ellenborough Falls,** at 160m the largest single drop in the Southern hemisphere. It was created by a major fault line 30 million years ago, and the surrounding gorge contains rocks up to 550 million years old. There are multiple walking tracks, the most difficult of which leads to the bottom of the gorge but has rest benches along the way. At the top of the Falls, there are picnic tables and restrooms. There is a **refreshment kiosk** (tel. 6550 3329; open weekends and school holidays 10am-4pm). The falls can be reached without the Bulga drive, through an east-west trip through **Comboyne,** with beautiful pastoral and mountain scenery. This route also gives access to the **Boorganna Nature Reserve.** Both this drive and the Bulga drive are along rough unsealed roads. For more information, call the **State Forests Office** in Taree at 6551 0249 or 6551 0266.

An alternative coastal drive runs through **Laurieton,** rather than taking the Pacific Hwy, a change that adds negligible time. Driving north through Crowdy Bay National Park leads to Laurieton A quick drive through **Dooragan National Park** leads to the amazing lookout at **North Brother** mountain, with a panorama of the surrounding valley and bodies of water. There are also walking trails in Dooragan.

East of the Pacific Hwy en route from Taree to Port Macquarie there's another series of drives and parks. The **Middle Brother State Forest** (tourist drive #5) and **Coopernook Forest** (drive #7) are accessible from Moorland. Middle Brother, near **Kendall,** contains many trails, lookouts, the two largest blackbutt trees in the state, and the equally huge **Big Fella Gum Tree.** The Coopernook drive, 25km northeast of Taree, goes through the **Landsdowne** and **Comboyne State Forests** as well. Along with walks and lookouts, there is the **Big Nellie** volcanic plug, a 20-minute climb to the top, and the swimming spot of **Waitui Falls.** Forestry offices in Taree (tel. 6551 0249), Kendall (tel. 6559 4108), and Port Macquarie (tel. 6583 7100) have info.

■ Port Macquarie

Unless you're an aficionado of Australia's convict history, the biggest draws of Port Macquarie are its sand, surf, and nearby nature reserves. Once a remote lock-up for Sydney's worst offenders, this easily accessible coastal town (pop. 33,000) is now a popular stopover on a trip up the coast. The town sometimes feels quiet, but comes alive during summer, when water sports abound. The less athletically inclined should note that the small, tight rips at the breaks that create great boogie boarding and surf-ing conditions are rough on leisurely swimmers, while wind often makes sunbathing unpleasant. Furthermore, the geography requires a car or developed quads for running, walking, or biking to beaches. Fortunately, however, adventure companies here offer fun at cheaper prices than at Coffs Harbour and points north.

ORIENTATION AND GETTING THERE

Port Macquarie's town center is bordered on the north by the Hastings River and on the west by a small bridged creek. **Horton St,** parallel to **Hay St,** is the main commercial street, and the streets in the surrounding 1-2 block radius comprise the central business district. Perpendicular to Hay, running along the water to the Marina, is **Clarence St,** which houses the tourist office and many restaurants to the west, and accommodations to the east. To the northwest, across the bridge, is **Settlement City,** an upmarket residential district with its own shopping center. The marina is opposite the tourist office; parks and picnic tables run parallel to this section of the bay.

The nearby town of **Wauchope,** pronounced "WAR-hope," is the closest that **trains** get to Port Macquarie. **McCafferty's** and **Greyhound buses** both run through Port Macquarie daily. **Port Macquarie Bus Service** (tel. 6583 2161) provides local transportation. The stop is at Ritz Corner across from the tourist office. Local buses run to Wauchope (4 per day, $6.60) and Kempsey (M-F 3 per day). **Sonters Travelways** (tel. 6559 8989) travels between Dunbogan, Laurieton, and Port Macquarie.

PRACTICAL INFORMATION

The **Visitor Information Centre** (tel. 6583 1077, bookings 1800 025 935) is at the corner of Clarence and Hay St (open M-F 8:30am-5pm, Sa-Su and public holidays 9am-4pm). Look for Vicki—she's a whiz with a homing instinct for pamphlets. **Banks** with **ATMS** line Horton St, and there are also ATMs in the Port Central Mall. **Bicycles** can be rented from **Graham Seers Cyclery** (tel. 6583 2333) in the marina. ($6 for the 1st hour ranging down to $2 for the 4th; $20 per day, $50 per week.) **Cars** are available through **Budget** (tel. 6583 5144, reservations 13 27 27), at the corner of Gordon and Hollingsworth St, **Hertz,** 102 Gordon St (24hr. tel. 6583 6599), or **Thrifty** (tel. 6584 2122), at the corner of Horton and Hayward St. **Port Macquarie Taxi Cabs** are at 6581 0081. The **post office** is at the corner of Horton and Clarence St (open M-F 9am-5pm; postal code 2444). The cheapest **Internet access** is at the **library,** on Clarence St just right of the tourist office. ($4 per hour; open M-F 9:30am-6pm, Sa 9am-noon.) The **Police Station** (tel. 6583 0199) is located on the corner of Hay St, by the water.

For beach adventures, there are a few **surf shops. Hydro-Surf,** 53 Pacific Dr (tel. 6584 1777), opposite Flynn's Beach, rents surfboards ($15 for 4hr., $25 per day) and wetsuits ($10 for 4hr., $15 per day). They usually have a blue trailer set up at Town Beach. **Gypsy Boat Hire,** 52 Settlement Point Rd (tel. 6583 2353), rents fishing boats ($16 for 2hr.) and cabin cruisers ($30 for 2hr., $50 for 5hr.). **Settlement Point Boatshed** (tel. 6583 6300), on the river next to Settlement Point Ferry, rents fishing boats ($20 for 2hr.) and canopy runabouts ($25 for 2hr.). They also rent picnic and barbecue boats, which hold 10-12 people (1hr. $35, 2hr. $50).

ACCOMMODATIONS

Port Macquarie has a wide range of accommodation options. Most offer winter specials of 3 nights for $30 and 7th night free. Peak season is during summer holidays and Easter; motel and caravan park prices can double, and booking ahead is essential.

Ozzie Pozzie Backpackers (Nomads), 36 Waugh St (tel. 6583 8133 or 0417 285 593), off Gore St between Buller and Bridge St. The newest hostel in town, and the closest to the town center, centers around a courtyard with comfy hammocks. Bedrooms have cheery matching comforters and security lockers ($1). Coin-op Internet access will be installed in 1999. The smallish common room has a VCR (movies free with $5 deposit). The friendly owners will give you a tour of the town's sights and bargains. Wheelchair accessible. Coin-op laundry. Common room closes

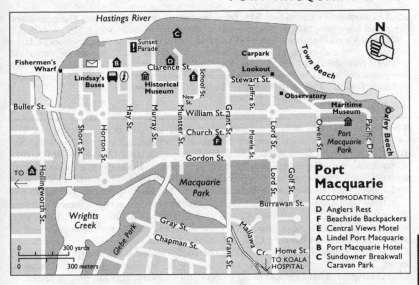

Port Macquarie

ACCOMMODATIONS

D Anglers Rest
F Beachside Backpackers
E Central Views Motel
A Lindel Port Macquarie
B Port Macquarie Hotel
C Sundowner Breakwall Caravan Park

11pm, other facilities midnight. Free boogie boards, bikes and fishing gear. Dorms $13 with any backpackers card, $14 in summer. ($15, $16 without).

Lindel Port Macquarie (tel. 6583 1791), at the corner of Hastings River Dr and Gordon St, 5-10min. from the town center. Inside this lovely Heritage-listed house, the facilities are modern. Pool, barbecue, picnic tables, TV room, billiards room, small bookshelf, and sunny kitchen give a wonderfully relaxed, social feel. Super-friendly owners organize not-to-be-missed 10km morning beach walks. Free use of bikes and boogie boards. Quiet time at 11pm but kitchen and common room remain open 24hr. Dorms $16; twins or doubles $38. VIP, YHA. Linen included.

Anglers Rest, 15 Clarence St (tel. 6583 5032), two blocks from the tourist office on the opposite side of the street, is an amazing deal, especially if you've had enough of hostels. Two-bedroom suites have a lounge/TV room, kitchen, dining area and private bathroom (some with bathtubs). Laundry is free, linen is provided, plus quick access to the town center and beaches. Double $35; $45 for 3; family $50. Rates go to about $80 for 3 weeks around Christmas. Long term rates cheaper.

Beachside Backpackers (YHA), 40 Church St (tel. 6583 5512), is the closest hostel to the beaches and a 5-10min. walk from the town center. Clean and very quiet but friendly, with a large kitchen and TV lounge. Most bathrooms are in a separate building behind the hostel. You're welcome to join the owner on his daily swimming/surfing trips at 7:30am. Free use of surfboards, bikes, boogie boards, and fishing rods. Lockers available. Linen provided. 11pm lights-out in common area. Dorms $13, YHA non-members $16; twins $17 (usually more for non-members).

Limeburners (tel. 6583 3381), on Shoreline Dr, is in a house on a lagoon, nearly 10km and a ferry-ride away from the town center. For those who make it there, there are many rewards. A comfy lounge with TV and a large kitchen are downstairs. Outside is a barbecue, stone pool, 35 acres of land and wandering peacocks. Free pick-up and drop-off. Caters to groups and families more than backpackers. Rooms hold 5-8 or 14. $16 per person. Coin-op laundry. Wheelchair accessible.

Sundowner Breakwall Tourist Park, 1 Munster St (tel. 6583 2755), is an enormous waterfront caravan park near Town Beach. It has a large pool, barbecue facilities, convenience store, bait and tackle shop, and food stand. Tent sites $15, during Easter and Christmas $26; powered $17, $29. Caravans $38, during school holidays $53, during Easter and Christmas $69. 7th night free. Each additional person $5. Book far in advance in summer. No pets. Linen not supplied.

Hotel Macquarie (tel. 6583 1011), at the corner of Horton and Clarence St, is the cheapest and most centrally located pub hotel. Very basic singles $25, with bath

$30; doubles $40, with bath $45. Breakfast included. 7th night free. The connected motel has triples ($80 off-season) and quads ($95). Holiday prices $10-15 more.

Central Views Motel (tel. 6583 1171), at the corner of Clarence and School St, has a small pool and excellent views of the water from the deck. Rooms are clean and well furnished with televisions, kitchen, private bathrooms, dining areas, and patios or balconies. Shared barbecue area. Twins $45, $100 during summer holidays. Doubles $50, $110. Family room for 2-5 $65 off-season.

FOOD

Clarence St has many restaurants with worthwhile specials or daily low prices. The best bet for fresh seafood takeaway is **Macquarie Seafood** (tel. 6583 8476), at the corner of Clarence and Short St (fish and chips $4.30; open daily 11am-9pm). If you plan to cook for yourself, visit the **Fish Market,** (tel. 6583 8348) at the marina on the bottom of Clarence St, where the catch comes straight off the boat (open daily). **Cafe 66** (tel. 6583 2484) has two-for-one pasta dinners on Tuesdays. **Contasia,** 14 Clarence St (tel. 6584 9638), on the corner of Clarence and Munster St, serves a huge $5 all-you-can-eat lunch buffet with continental and Asian foods. They charge for water. Another buffet for the same price but with fewer choices (free water, though) is available at the **Westport Bowling Club** (tel. 6583 1499) on Buller St.

The **Port Central Mall** to the left of the tourist office has a cheap, typical food court. The **Ritz Center**, at Horton and Clarence St, houses the popular and reasonable **Duangluck Thai Restaurant,** (tel. 6584 1847; open lunch and dinner Tu-Su), as well as **Delicious and Nutritious** (tel. 6584 0480), an inexpensive eatery that lives up to its name (open M-Sa). If for some reason you prefer Australian food, there's **Ridgey Didge Pies** (tel. 6584 0720) with meaty concoctions baked fresh every 20 minutes (open daily 8am-6pm). **Cafe Margo** (tel. 6583 5145) on Clarence St, is a local favorite and has an outside eating area (main courses $7.50-14.50, open 3 meals a day).

There are some other spots popular amongst the locals which are not in the city center. **Flynn's Beach Pasta Place** 53 Pacific Drive (tel. 6583 2679), across from Flynn's Beach, features homemade pastas for $7-9 that are often big enough for 2. (Indoor and outdoor dining. BYO, no corkage. Open Su-Th 5pm-8:30pm, F-Sa 5pm-9pm. Closed Su in winter.) **Lotus at Lighthouse** 42 Watonga St (tel. 6582 3233), off of Riverside Dr near Lighthouse Beach, serves Chinese and Malaysian food. Main courses begin at $7.80. Huge, delicious laksas are worth a splurge ($14.50 and up). (Open for lunch noon-2pm, dinner from 5pm. Closed M.) Downstairs in the same building is the inexpensive **Lighthouse Beach Takeaway** (open 8am-8pm daily).

SIGHTS AND ACTIVITIES

Many companies offer **boat cruises** up the Hastings River and to the Everglades. **M.V. Port Venture,** 3174 Clarence St (tel. 6583 3058 or 018 656 522), has the largest boat, and Thursday through Tuesday runs two-hour Devonshire tea and dolphin spotting cruises. *($17, children 6-14 years $7, families $42.)* Every Wednesday at 10am is a five-hour barbecue cruise to a private park. *($32, children $15, families $80.)* **Sunshine Jet** (tel. 6585 1168), at the town wharf, is a small, very mobile jet boat that travels sideways quickly. Rides are guaranteed to get you wet. *($30 for 20min.; book in advance.)*

The **NPWS** (tel. 6584 2203) sponsors tours to the otherwise unrecognizable **Innes ruins,** the badly neglected site of a colonial mansion. *(First and second Sundays of each month; 9am-noon; children $5, family of 4 $30. Bookings essential.)* One monument to Port Macquarie's past is the beautiful **St. Thomas Church** (tel. 6584 1033), built by convicts between 1824 and 1828. *(Open to public M-F 9:30am-noon and 2-4pm. Admission $2, children $1.)* The jail's former superintendent is buried under one of the pews. As the story goes, he feared that his body would have been exhumed by vengeful convicts had he been buried in the church cemetery. Evening services are Sunday at 5pm.

The **Historical Museum,** 22 Clarence St (tel. 6583 1108), has a huge and well-catalogued collection of photos, clothing, military weapons, and other Port Macquarie paraphernalia. *(Open M-Sa 9:30am-4:30pm, Sunday 1pm-4:30pm. Admission $4, children $1, $8 for a family of 4.)* On clear starry nights, consider heading to the small **Observatory** (tel. 6583 1933), at the top of Clarence St in Rotary Park. *(Open W, Su only; in summer 8:15-9:30pm; in winter 7:30-9pm. Admission $2, children $1.)* You'll get a quick lesson on telescopes and astronomy that will teach you to pick out the Southern Cross.

You're in luck if you like **koalas:** the Port Macquarie area has the biggest urban population in the country and many opportunities to see them. One of Australia's few **Koala Hospitals** (tel. 6584 1522) is located a 20-minute walk out of the town center on Lord St. *(Open daily 9am-4:30pm; it's best to go during feeding times: 7:30am, winter 3pm, summer 3:30pm. Free, but $2 donation requested.)* There are usually four or more injured or sick koalas on site (more during summer's breeding time), which volunteers nurse back to health, along with two permanent residents, Pebbles and Cloud. Koalas can also often be seen in the trees surrounding the hospital. There's a small gift shop. The Koala Hospital is behind **Roto House,** (tel. 6584 2203), a 19th century homestead. *(Open daily 9am-4pm.)* Finally, the **Billabong Koala Breeding Centre,** 61 Billabong Drive (tel. 6585 1060), is on the way to Kempsey. *(Admission $7.50, children $4.)* Here, you can touch not just koalas but wallabies, kangaroos, and wombats.

Unbelievably tacky but surprisingly entertaining is **The Big Bull** (tel. 6585 2044), a dairy farm park 15 minutes from Port Macquarie off the Oxley Hwy. *(Open daily 9am-5pm. Admission $5, children $4.)* The park's main feature is an eyesore: **the world's largest fiberglass bull,** five stories tall. Other features include a hayride, complete with Farmer John's wacky commentary, a farm animal nursery, and tours of a working dairy farm. Over 70 hectares of the last subtropical rainforest on the coast is preserved at **Sea Acres Rainforest Center** (tel. 6582 3355), a few minutes out of town at Miner's Beach. *(Open daily 9am-4:30pm. Admission $8.50, children $4.50, VIP $7.)* A 1.3km boardwalk circles through the forest with guided tours available. There's also a cafe. The last walk leaves around 3pm.

Port Macquarie Camel Safaris (tel. 6583 7650) offers even more unusual jaunts at Lighthouse Beach. *($12 for 20min., children $8; $22 for 1hr.; 1hr. tours must be booked in advance.)* X-Games fans can have their own moments of glory at **Watersports World** (tel. 6583 9777) on the wharf, including **parawhaling** (parasailing while whale-watching) for $50, and riding a Thunder Dux in excess of 100kph ($25 for 15min.). Area extreme sports vendors have formed the association **A Total Adventure** (tel. 1800 063 648; http://www.Oznetcity.com.au/atotaladventure), which offers land, air, and water thrills and can be booked through the tourist office (tel. 1800 025 935). A gentler introduction to the world of water sports is available through **Round House Surfing Tours** (tel. 041 747 9972). *(All equipment supplied. 2hr. lessons $25.)*

BEACHES AND PARKS

Port Macquarie specializes in beaches (it has nine) and nature walks. While the beaches can be crowded, walks down the sand are pleasant year-round. A 10km walk which includes all the area's beaches begins at the **Lighthouse Beach** lookout (Lindel Backpackers will drop you here). Head down Lighthouse Beach Rd (5-10min.) to the **"Miner's Beach"** sign on the right; an entrance by a subtropical forest path leads to the beach and up sometimes-hard-to-locate cliff paths. Three kilometers down is **Shelly's Beach,** said by some to be Port Macquarie's best. If you're only doing part of the walk, try to hit Miner's and Shelly's. Shelly's has barbecue and toilet facilities, and is also the place to meet Harry, the Port's living legend who has camped in a small caravan on the beach since 1960, keeps an autograph and souvenir book, and is a delight to talk to. His contributions to the area are a "thong tree" and a more respected and spectacular railed footpath up to **Harry's Lookout,** which offers a view so gorgeous that it's been the site of more than 100 weddings.

Nobby's Beach, the next to the north, is easily identified by the adjacent Nobby's Headland. The obelisk on the headland stands in memory of people who have died while swimming in the dangerous blowhole in the headland's base (don't even think about it). Continuing north, **Flynn's Beach** is most popular with surfers. The southern end of **Town Beach** is good for swimming, sunbathing, and fishing and provides showers, toilets, and fast food. At the end of Horton St is the entrance to the peaceful bushland of **Kooloonbung Creek Nature Park,** where several kilometers of footpaths wind through mangroves and rainforest.

A short trip across the bay leads to **Point Plomer and Limeburner Creek Nature Reserve,** the site of Aboriginal artifacts and the Big Hill walking track. From Settlement Point, a vehicle ferry runs across the river. The 16km coastal road to Point Plomer is unsealed and rough, but bikeable. There are **campsites** at Barries Bay and Point Plomer; book ahead in summer (tel. 6583 8805). The tourist office has a list of nearby national parks and nature reserves.

ENTERTAINMENT

There are three nightclubs in Port Macquarie. **Lachlans** (tel. 6583 1011), in the Hotel Macquarie on Horton St opposite the post office, has free entry every night and free pizza Fridays from 8-11pm. There's free live music on Saturdays and sometimes other nights, though for some well-known performers there's a small fee. There's also a busy pub **Port Bar** in the hotel. **TC's** (tel. 6583 5466), on William St upstairs in the Galleria Building, has no cover before 11pm. It rages on Fridays, and has Retro Night on Thursdays and Dance Party Night on Saturday. **Downunder** (tel. 6583 4018) is on Short St next to Coles Supermarket and has karaoke on Wednesday, games night Thursday, and free pasta on Friday (6-9pm, plus free entry to 11pm). The free weekly entertainment guide, *Hastings Happenings,* is published on Wednesdays.

The Ritz Center, at Horton and Clarence St, also has playtime options. **Twin Cinemas** (tel. 6583 8400) has a daily student rate of $6 (children under 12 $4; W, F, Su all shows $5). Upstairs, **Port Zone Amusements** (tel. 6584 3545) has billiards, table hockey, foosball and video games, plus Sunday specials. (One hour unlimited play on all games $4, 10am-5pm. Open M-Th 9am-7pm, F-Sa 9am-midnight; Su 10am-6pm.)

■ South West Rocks

South West Rocks is as yet way off the backpacker trail. Until the 1970s, the region's virtues—perhaps the best year-round climate, beachside scenery, and variety of beach type on the north coast of NSW—were known only to locals. Within manageable distances you can find long waveless stretches of sand and sea, tumultuous but safe swimming coves, and surfing waves in places with no buildings in sight.

Coming from the south, the turn-off for South West Rocks and Hat Head National Park is about 10km after Kempsey. You approach town by way of **Gregory St.** At its end, go left to find the **tourist information center** (tel. 6566 7099) on Ocean St in old Boatman's Cottage. The volunteers know the area's trails, beaches, and history inside and out (open daily 10am-4pm). In this part of town you'll find the food shops, an **ATM,** the **post office** (postal code 2431), and a **dive center,** 100 Gregory St (tel. 6566 6959). Just below the tourist office is **Horseshoe Bay Beach Park** (tel. 6566 6370; fax 6566 6302), a caravan park a couple of paces from a surf and swim beach. (Office open daily 8am-6pm; powered sites $16.50, vans $35, cabins $47.) The best **surfing** waves break beyond the tourist office at **Back Beach.**

Even better than this western area is the eastern cape of South West Rocks. Take Philip Dr 5km till it turns into Wilson St after the Lagoon View Caravan Park. Soon afterwards, turn left at the juncture of Wilson and Caldwell Streets toward the Trial Bay Gaol (see below), or follow signs to **Little Bay.** A narrow opening guarded by two cliffs on either side opens to rushing waves and deep water. Gas barbecues and toilets are by the carpark. From here, you can enter **Hat Head National Park** via **Gap Beach Track** (1km to Gap Beach; 5km to **Smoky Beach**). Also, beyond the toilets and barbecues, a stairway leads to walking tracks toward the gaol (40min.).

In 1887, the New South Wales government shipped convicts to South West Rocks to build themselves a prison as well as a break wall so that sea captains could moor in Trial Bay instead of wrecking. In a classic example of British colonial governance, planners ordered the break wall built at a 90° angle to the northwest swell. When the wall was half-built, the first swell it encountered destroyed it. The **Trial Bay Gaol** (tel.

6566 6168) remains one of the best-maintained and most interesting convict historical sites in the country, also serving as a park service office. The government last used the granite building to hold potential dissidents—German immigrants and a few Buddhist monks—during WWI (Open daily 10am-4pm; admission $4). Down below the Gaol, you can enjoy the **Akaroon Recreation Area** day or night. **Front Beach** curves around Trial Bay, whose warm water makes for a placid and pleasant swimmin' hole (campsites $10, Dec.-Jan. and Easter $12-25).

■ Nambucca Heads

For the traveler in need of a break from relentless tourist attractions and constant activities, peaceful Nambucca Heads (nam-BUH-kuh; pop. 6,000) is a welcome stop. Nambucca's allure is its natural attributes, most especially its dazzling beaches. Residents often refer to it as "our paradise," and, with more days of sunshine per year than any other town in New South Wales, you can understand why. Surfing, fishing, and strolling along strips of isolated beach are all favorite pastimes in the summer, when parents bring their families back to this vacation spot they enjoyed as children.

ORIENTATION AND PRACTICAL INFORMATION

The tiny **Nambucca Valley Visitor Information Centre** (tel. 6568 6954; open daily 9am-5pm) and nearby **long-distance bus terminal** are on the Pacific Hwy, just south of the turn-off into the town. Behind the terminal is a shopping center with a supermarket and a movie theater. The Pacific Hwy splits off to the right to **Riverside Dr,** the main road. Riverside has more names than the artist formerly known as Prince: when it inclines steeply at the RSL club it becomes **Fraser St,** at the town center it becomes **Bowra St,** and on the way back out to the Pacific Hwy, it's **Mann St. Shelly Beach** and **Beilby's Beach** are to the east of town. **Ridge St** forks as it leaves town. **Liston St,** to the left, leads to the **Headland** and **Main Beach. Parkes St,** to the right, leads to **Shelly Beach.** The **post office** (postal code 2448), **police station,** and a **bank** are in the town center on Bowra St. The **railway station** is just out of town; from Mann St, bear right at the roundabout to Railway Rd.

 Newman's Coaches (tel. 6568 1296) has service between Nambucca Heads, Bowraville, Macksville, and Coffs Harbour (M-F 4 per day, less frequently during school holidays; $6 to Coffs). **Pell's** (tel. 6568 6106) connects Nambucca Heads, Macksville, and Valla Beach (M-F 6 per day, during school holidays 4 per day, no service on public holidays). **Joyce's** (tel. 6655 6330) links Urunga, Bellingen, and Nambucca (M-F 4 per day, during school holidays 3 per day). One day of unlimited travel costs $10, or $8 for backpackers. Both **Greyhound** (13 20 30) and **McCafferty's** (13 14 99) serve Nambucca Heads daily on their Sydney-Brisbane route (to Brisbane $46, students $41; Sydney $53, $48). **Radio Cabs** (tel. 6568 6855) has 24-hour service. For an email fix, go to **Cafe Internet,** 2-3 Mann St, at the end of the main strip of shops on Bowra St (tel. 6568 9030; email info@NVI.NET.AU; $7.50 per hr. for email or web access).

 A 16km beach separates Nambucca Heads and **Scotts Head,** an excellent surfing beach and small residential town to the south. **Bowraville,** 25 minutes west, and Macksville, 20 minutes southwest along the Pacific Hwy, are both small residential townships with limited accommodations. **Taylors Arm,** home of the misleadingly-named **Pub With No Beer** (tel. 6564 2101), is a 40-minute drive from Nambucca Heads, and west of Macksville. The tavern stars in the hit country song by Slim Dusty.

ACCOMMODATIONS AND FOOD

Nambucca and the surrounding townships of Bowraville, Scotts Heads, and Valla Beach are chock-full of places to sleep. To be safe, though, book ahead for summer holidays. There are few lodgings in the town center, but a solid mass around the beaches, and a full line of cheap motels along the Pacific Hwy near the tourist office.

Nambucca Heads Backpackers, 3 Newman St (tel. 6568 6360). After the third speed bump on Bowra St, turn right onto Rosedale St, continue 2 long blocks to Newman St, and turn right again; the hostel is on your left. Two kitchen areas, 2 common rooms with television, one for movies only. The helpful owners offer orientation tours and great advice on local bushwalks. 10am check-out strictly enforced. 24hr. courtesy pick-up, meaning at night they'll pay for your cab fare for stays over 2 days (otherwise they pay half). Call ahead to arrange pick-up. Dorms $15, off-peak 3-night special $39; doubles and twins $32. VIP. Linen included.

White Albatross Holiday Resort (tel. 6568 6468; fax 6568 7067), at the ocean end of Wellington Dr. A glorified caravan park with a gorgeous setting near a swimming lagoon and the Nambucca River. Picnic and barbecue areas, small game room, convenience store, takeaway cafe. All prices based on 2 people per site. Tent and caravan sites $16; on-site caravans with mini-kitchen and no bathroom $25-28; more modern 1-bedroom flat with kitchen and bathroom $48. Weekly: $80; $120-140; $280. Extra adult $8, child $4. Weekly: $40, $25, $20. Easter and Sept.-Oct. school holidays, tent and caravan sites $21, weekly $126; mid-Dec. to late Jan. tent and caravan sites $22, weekly $154. Linen $5. Book well in advance for summer.

Max Motel (tel. 6568 6138), on Fraser St, just past the RSL. Standard motel fare but near the beach and town. Though a bit run-down, the rooms are spacious, with kitchenettes, TVs, and private bath. Shared patio overlooking the ocean. Doubles $35-45 ($45-60 during holidays), $10 ($14 during holidays) per extra person.

Scott's Guesthouse, 4 Wellington Dr (tel. 6568 6386), at the town end of Wellington Dr. Built in the 1880s and beautifully restored, this B&B is one of the area's oldest buildings, and worth a splurge. All the thoughtful details one could want, including comfy bedrooms with TV, fridge, private balcony, and private bath. The breakfast room downstairs has lace-covered tables. Covered parking (no lace). Doubles $60, with water view $80; extra person $10, $20.

Bowra Hotel, 33 High St (tel. 6564 7041; fax 6564 8471), on the main street of Bowraville at the intersection with Conan St, is a Heritage building constructed around 1910 but recently renovated. Located above a popular local pub, the basic rooms have beautiful wood furniture, high ceilings, private verandas, and down comforters. Shared bathrooms complete with tub. Singles, doubles, twins or triples $15 per person. Dorms $10. All-you-can-eat breakfast included.

FOOD AND ENTERTAINMENT

Bowra St has an assortment of quick, cheap food. **Zippy's** is one that's open late. Nambucca Plaza, just south of the tourist office on the Pacific Hwy, has some cheap options as well, like the **Plaza Cafe** (tel. 6568 9620). The Plaza is also home to **Nambucca Plaza Cinemas** (tel. 6568 6677), where all shows are $5 every day. The **RSL Club,** at the bottom of Back St, has game rooms and a gorgeous view of the river (meals $6-10). The **V-Wall Tavern** (tel. 6568 6344), at the mouth of the Nambucca River on Wellington Dr, also has unbeatable views. It also has a monopoly on the night scene, with discos on some Fridays and a cocktail bar upstairs in summer. (Meals $6-10; open 10am-midnight daily.) The **Bluewater Brasserie** (tel. 6568 6394), the tavern's restaurant, is pricier ($7-18), but worth it, while the **White Albatross Kiosk,** the holiday park's takeaway in the same building, is the cheapest by far of the three.

SIGHTS AND ACTIVITIES

Nambucca is full of delightful and spontaneous artwork. Don't miss the **mosaic wall** in front of the police station on Bowra St, a glittering, 3D, 60m-long sea serpent scene made completely of broken crockery, including a toilet. Many of the town's lampposts are painted with colorful underwater scenes. Hundreds of rocks along the breakwater wall, called the V-Wall because of its shape, are painted and inscribed with dates and rhyming ditties from years of tourists, honeymooners, and families.

The **Headland Historical Museum** (tel. 6568 6380), beside the Headland parking area at the Main Beach off Liston St, covers local and Australian history. *(Open W and Sa-Su 2-4pm and by appointment; admission $1.)* **Nambucca Heads Island Golf Club** (tel. 6569 4111) is an inexpensive 18-hole course on Stuart Island, connected to Riverside

Dr by a bridge. *(Nine holes $12, 18 holes $17. Children under 18 $3, $6. Weekly price $60.)* The club also has squash courts, barbecue facilities, picnic tables, and a restaurant.

The **Nambucca Boatshed,** 1 Wellington Dr (tel. 6568 5550), has a good selection of fishing gear and boats. *(Boat rentals start at $22 for 2hr. Canoes $7 per hr. Kayaks and fishing rods $5 per hr. Fishing equipment free with boat rental. Open daily 8am-5pm.)* **Beachcomber Marine** (tel. 6568 6432), on Riverside Dr, also rents boats and fishing gear. *(Boats $14 for the first hr., $8 per hr. after, $30 per day including equipment, petrol and maps.)* **Nambucca Dive Centre,** 3 Bowra St (tel. 6569 4422 or 0419 695781), in the Mobil Service Station at the intersection with Wellington Dr, rents equipment and conducts diving courses. *(Dives $60-80, intro course $120. Deals are available through the hostel.)*

There are also a number of walks of varying difficulty levels through the beach and bush, many of which begin at the backpackers on Newman St. You can park your car at the end of Wellington Dr and walk along the boardwalk to the V-Wall and then onto Wellington Rock and the beaches as far as you care to go. For more passive enjoyment, there are three gorgeous lookouts: **Rotary, Captain Cook,** and **Lions.**

■ Bellingen

Bellingen (pop. 2350) is a calm, scenic town between Coffs Harbour and Nambucca Heads, 30 minutes from **Dorrigo National Park** (see p. 192). Although its heyday was 50 years ago, when it was the financial and commercial center for the Coffs Harbour region, Bellingen has recently earned a reputation as an artsy community. Craft shops and organic cafes abound, and the annual jazz festival draws many visitors.

ORIENTATION AND PRACTICAL INFORMATION **Hyde St** forms the city center, and leads in one direction to Urunga (20min. away), Coffs Harbour, and the ocean. Dorrigo and Armidale are close by in the other direction. **Tourist information** is available at **Traveland**, 42 Hyde St. They book seats on various bus services. The **buses** stop at Hyde and Church St, the next corner up from Traveland. **Jessups** (tel. 6653 4552) services Coffs Harbor (1hr., 3 per day M-F). **Kearns** (tel. 1800 043 339) travels to Armidale ($23) through Dorrigo (3hr., 1 per day Tu, Th, and Su only). The nearest train station is in Urunga. Hail a cab from **Bellingen Valley Taxi** (tel. 018 653 535). The **post office,** 41 Hyde St, (tel. 6655 1020), is across the street from the tourist office. (Open M-F 9am-5pm; postal code 2454.) To hook into the **Internet,** visit the **library** (tel. 6655 1744), in the park across from the post office.

ACCOMMODATIONS AND FOOD **Bellingen Backpackers,** 2 Short St (tel. 6655 1116), is in a gorgeous two-story house a block and a half off Hyde St. The floors are polished wood and the downstairs lounge/kitchen has oversized floor pillows, a TV, free tea and coffee, and magazines. Owners provide pick-up from the Urunga train or bus stations (return $5), and will arrange group trips to Dorrigo National Park ($10 per person). You may be treated to fresh eggs from the resident hens and seasonal fresh fruit. They also rent bikes ($5 per day) and canoes ($30 per ½day). The gregarious owners can sometimes help find work in the surrounding farmlands. (Dorms $15, weekly $95. Doubles or twins $32. Tent sites $8 solo, $12 per couple.)

Church St has a row of cafes, eateries, and coffee shops, some with outdoor seating. **Cool Creek Cafe,** 5 Church St (tel. 6655 1886), seats you in soft lighting under the glow of orange snapdragon wall paint and old photos of a 20s women's jazz band. Live music plays every couple weeks. (Cajun chicken burrito $7.50. YHA discount. Open Th-Tu 11am-10pm.) The **Old Butter Factory Cafe** (tel. 6655 2150), opposite the high school playing fields on Hyde St, has outdoor seating and scrumptious snacks and meals, including scones with jam and cream ($3.30).

SIGHTS AND ACTIVITIES The **Sweetwater Gallery** (tel. 6655 6199), on Hyde St upstairs from the posh Kakadu Clothing, is the bee's knees. *(Open M-Sa 9am-5pm, Su 10am-5pm.)* They display a rotating exhibition of fine painting and crafts. Behind the Bellingen Caravan Park, across the river, is the entrance to **Bellingen Island,** summer home to an active colony of "flying foxes," or fruit bats. A walking trail loops through the subtropical rainforest around the peninsular "island."

The **Promised Land** and the **Never Never River,** lovely spots with barbecue facilities and excellent **swimming holes,** are easier to reach than their names imply. Both are an easy 10-15km bike ride from town. Cross the Bellingen Bridge and take a left at the first rotary. Continue straight until you see a sign for Glennifer; bear right at this sign and continue for 6km. The river is behind the church. Cross the bridge and take the first right turn to the Promised Land. Platypuses live in the river; it's possible to see them in the early morning or late afternoon.

On the Wallaby (tel. 6655 2171) provides 4WD tours through the valley and Dorrigo Plateau ($25 per ½day). Half-day tours of local sites with an Aboriginal guide are offered through **Gambaarri Tours** (tel. 6655 4195). *(Tours Sa-Su and school holidays. Admission $45, children $25.)* Also see the **Bellingen YHA** for equipment hire and canoe outings. The **Jazz Festival** (info tel. 6655 9345; email belljazz@midcoast.com.au), with ticketed performances and street performers, is in mid-August. The **Global Carnival** features world music on Labor Day weekend in October.

■ Coffs Harbour

A water sports haven in a sub-tropical climate, Coffs Harbour basks in its own natural beauty. It's a regular town of 58,000 which just happens to be situated along a gorgeous coastline, backed by hills covered in lush banana plantations, and located a boat ride away from a nationally recognized marine reserve. Much of the town's tourism industry today aims to please adrenaline-seekers with cash to spare, though there are plenty of opportunities for fun on a budget as well.

ORIENTATION AND PRACTICAL INFORMATION

The **Pacific Highway** is Coffs Harbour's main street and roughly divides the town in two; the majority of the commercial buildings and lodgings lie along the highway or to the east. Many of the area's attractions lie just south and north of the town on the highway; Coffs' famed resorts are to the north. The highway is called **Grafton Street** as it passes through the center of town, and then becomes **Woolgoolga Rd** north of the showgrounds. Three large shopping centers divide the focus of the town: the **Palm Centre Mall** on Grafton St in the center of town, the **Jetty Village Shopping Centre** by the water, and the **Palm Beach Plaza** on the Pacific Hwy in the northern part of town. **High St** is the main east-west thoroughfare. Interrupted by the pedestrian **City Centre Mall,** it continues east past the **Botanic Gardens** and all the way to the **jetty,** a narrow strip of land with fish stores, markets, and a marina. **Muttonbird Island Nature Reserve** is accessible by walking down the marina boardwalk.

Tourist Office: Visitor Information Centre (tel. 6652 1522; bookings tel. 1800 025 650). As you head north through town, it's to the right just off Woolgoolga Rd, at the corner of Rose Ave and Marcia St. Open daily 9am-5pm.

Airport: South of the city off Hogbin Dr. Serviced by **Ansett Express** (tel. 6652 2299) and **Eastern Airlines** (tel. 6651 1966).

Trains: The **railway station** is at the end of Angus McLeod St by the jetty. From High St, turn right on Camperdown St and take your first left. **Countrylink** (tel. 6651 2757 or 13 22 32) passes through Coffs several times daily.

Buses: Both **McCafferty's** (tel. 13 14 99) and **Greyhound** (tel. 13 20 30) stop at least 3 times per day in Coffs. The long distance bus stop is at 34 Moonee St, near the corner of High and Grafton St; hostel owners meet nearly all arrivals. **Premier Motor Service** (tel. 1300 368 100) travels through Coffs on its Sydney-Brisbane run (3 per day; to Sydney $47, students $38; Byron Bay $36, $29). **Jessup's** (tel. 6653 4552) operates between Coffs, Urunga, and Bellingen (M-F 3 per day; $4.50). **Watson's City Link** (tel. 6654 1063) runs from Coffs Harbor to Woolgoolga to Grafton.

Car Rental: Coffs Harbour Rent-A-Car (tel. 6652 5022), at the Shell Roadhouse, corner of Pacific Hwy and Marcia St, rents from $39. Free pick-up within 15km.

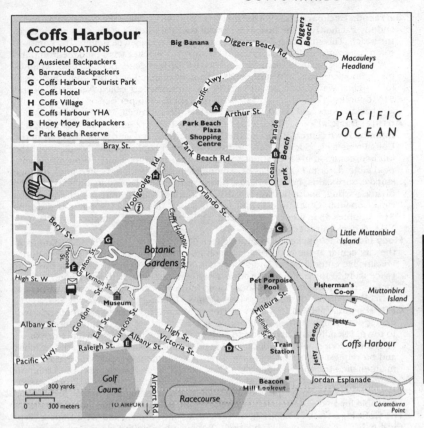

Coffs Harbour

ACCOMMODATIONS

D Aussietel Backpackers
A Barracuda Backpackers
G Coffs Harbour Tourist Park
F Coffs Hotel
H Coffs Village
E Coffs Harbour YHA
B Hoey Moey Backpackers
C Park Beach Reserve

Budget (tel. 13 27 27) has free delivery and rents from $39; $18 per day surcharge for under 25yr.-olds. **Hertz,** 45 Grafton St (tel. 6651 1899), rents from $48 (3-day minimum; free delivery within 10km). **Thrifty,** at the corner of the Pacific Hwy and Marcia St (tel. 6652 8622), rents from $45 (4-day minimum). **A Little Car and Truck Hire,** 32 Alison St (tel. 6651 3004), rents cars from $29; 4WD from $70.

Currency Exchange: ANZ bank, corner of Moonee and High St. Other banks with 24hr. international **ATMs** are in the Palm Centre Mall and the Park Beach Plaza.

Police: 16 Moonee St (tel. 6652 0299). **Water Police** (tel. 6652 0257), on the wharf.

Emergency: Dial 000. **Ambulance:** Dial 6613 1233. **Fire:** Dial 6651 6891.

Post Office: (tel. 6652 2022), in the Palm Centre. Open M-F 8:30am-5pm, Sa 8:30am-noon. Other branches are at the Palm Beach Plaza and in Coffs Promenade at the jetty. **Postal Code:** 2450.

Internet Access: Happy Planet, 84 City Centre Mall, 2nd Fl. (tel. 6651 7520; email hpcafe@happyplanet.com.au). $2 per 10min., $10 per hr., $6 after first 2hr. Serves Italian coffee and cake. Open M-W and F 9am-5pm, Th 9am-8pm, Sa 9am-2pm.

Phone Code: 02.

ACCOMMODATIONS

All four hostels in Coffs Harbour are pretty good and offer 24-hour courtesy pick-up, winter discounts, and good laundry and kitchen facilities. Dozens of motels are clustered along the highway just outside of town, along Grafton St and Woolgoolga Rd, and along Park Beach Rd. Coffs has three central caravan parks.

Barracuda Backpackers, 19 Arthur St (tel. 6651 3514), near the corner of Arthur St and the Pacific Hwy; the first street north past Park Beach Plaza. 5-10min. walk to the beach. This small hostel is immaculate and amazingly welcoming. The common room has comfy leather couches and 10 movies a week. Each 4-bunk bedroom has colorful linen, lockers, and a fridge. Free use of barbecue, pool, jacuzzi, weights, bikes, boogie boards, and surfboards. Frequent planned activities and bus rides to local sights. Watch for a new hostel by the same owners called **Aardvark.** Dorms $15; doubles $17 per person, $19 with bath; twins $16 per person. Discount with any backpackers card. Wheelchair accessible. Pets allowed.

Aussitel Backpackers, 312 High St (tel. 6651 1871), 25min. walk down High St from the town center, 10min. to the jetty's marinas, and across the street from the Coffs Promenade. Social, clean, and wholesome. People constantly mill about the kitchen/common area, complete with coin-op Internet connection, ping-pong, pool table, darts and video games. Amenities include outdoor heated pool, luggage storage, surfboards, boogie boards, bikes, and canoes. Discounts on activities like diving, surfing, and whitewater rafting. Courtesy van to transportation stations runs 6am-9pm. Quiet time 11pm; facilities shut down at 11:30pm. 6-bed dorms $15, doubles $34. Weekly $80, $180. Off-season special: 3 nights for $40. VIP, YHA. Wheelchair accessible.

Hoey Moey Backpackers, Ocean Pde (tel. 6651 7966 or 1800 683 322), 3km from the city center at the end of Park Beach Rd, 50m from the beach. Lively pub has weekly live entertainment and a beer garden. "Booze Cruizer" courtesy bus runs twice daily to town. Four-bed rooms are functional with bath and fridge, but the motel arrangement minimizes socializing. Internet access, picnic tables, barbecue. Free bikes, surfboards, boogie boards. Dorms $14; doubles $32. Weekly $84, $192.

Coffs Harbour YHA, 110 Albany St (tel. 6652 6462), 15min. walk from the town center down High St, then right onto Curacoa St and left on Albany. Closest hostel to town. Friendly staff advises on local bargains. Everything's clean and everyone's active. Outdoor pool, billiards, and ping-pong. Bus runs twice daily to the beaches and on request to local attractions. Tons of equipment is available for use for $5 maintenance fee and $15 deposit. The kitchen, large dining area, and common room are open 24hr. year-round. Dorms $15, twins and doubles $17 per person, family rooms for 4-6 people $40-70. Winter special: 3 nights for $35. Breakfast is available for $3-6 and some food items are sold. Backpacker and student discounts.

The Coffs Hotel (tel. 6652 3817), on the corner of Grafton St and West High St. Typical pubstay above a popular hangout. Rooms are basic but clean. Large common room has tables and an old TV. Singles $20, doubles $25. Weekly rates cheaper.

Camping

Coffs Harbour Tourist Park (tel. 6652 1694) and **Coffs Village** (tel. 6652 4633) are both on the Pacific Hwy near the tourist office. **Park Beach Reserve** (tel. 6652 3204), near the Surf Club on Ocean Pde, is a five-minute walk from the beach. (Unpowered tent sites $10 for 1 person, $12 for 2 year-round. Powered sites $12, on-site caravans $23, cabins $32; in summer and holidays $15, $25, $35. $3 per additional person.)

FOOD

The **City Centre Mall** and **Palm Beach Plaza** each offer supermarkets, plentiful cheap takeaways, and sit-down cafes. Near Coffs Promenade along High St is a series of inexpensive restaurants. A local favorite is **Tahruah Thai Kitchen,** 366 High St (tel. 6651 5992), where filling mains run $6-15. Nearby is **Laddy's Pier Hotel Bistro,** which offers $6 lunches (M-Sa 12-2pm). Across the street in the Jetty Village Shopping Center is **The Chippy Factory** (tel. 6652 6518), which has $5 fish and chips and cheap hamburgers, and the **Hog's Breath Cafe** (tel. 6652 5646) which offers a beer and a burger for $7.95.

The **Fisherman's Co-op** (tel. 6625 2811) at the end of the jetty, makes fresh, delicious seafood that's so popular that it can take 30 minutes to get fish and chips in the summer. (Fresh fish and sushi counters open daily 8:30am-5pm; cooked counter open M-Th 10:30am-6:30pm, F-Su 10:30am-7pm; in summer open ½hr. later.) For another jetty seafood option, try **The Iguana Beach Cafe** (tel. 6652 5725), at the

Yacht Club on Marina Dr. The outdoor deck has a somewhat obscured view of the bay. Lunch specials (noon-3pm) are $5.50; dinner specials (from 7pm) start at $9.

The pub at the **Plantation Hotel** has an all-you-can-eat pasta and salad bar (Th 6-9pm). The **Catholic Club** (tel. 6652 1477), on West High St off the Pacific Hwy, offers cheap and hearty meals. The gorgeous **Rainforest Bar** in the **Greenhouse Tavern** (tel. 6651 5400) across from the Park Plaza Mall has a huge rainforest mural with hidden fairies and elves (lunch $5 or less; open daily noon-2:30pm and 6-8:30pm).

SIGHTS

The Coffs Harbour **jetty** was built in 1890 and was the center of a busy marine industry in the first years of this century. Nowadays, pleasure boats and charter boats predominate. At the end of the marina is **Muttonbird Island,** a high-elevation nature reserve that houses several species of birds and is a terrific lookout for spotting **whales.** The jetty foreshore has barbecue facilities and is an easy walk from **Jetty Beach,** popular with families. **Park Beach** and the beach on the other side of the marina are also popular, but have dangerous currents. The best **surfing** is at **Diggers Beach,** north of Macauleys Headland and accessible off the Pacific Hwy by Diggers Beach Rd, opposite the Big Banana.

The **Botanic Gardens** (tel. 6648 4188) are about 1km east down High St from the City Centre Mall; park at the end of Hardacre St. *(Info centre open M-F 10am-2pm, Sa-Su 9am-5pm. Gardens open daily 9am-5pm. Orchid house open W, F, and Su 10am-2pm. Admission by donation.)* The lovely 20-hectare gardens make for great self-guided walks through mangroves, rainforests, and international flora. For 20¢ you can buy food to throw to the carp in the pond of the beautiful Japanese Garden. The Gardens can also be visited via a detour off the **Coffs Creek Walk,** which leads from Rotary Park at Coff St in the city center out 5.4km past the marina to Muttonbird Island (2hr.).

On Orlando St by Coffs Creek, water animals star at the **Pet Porpoise Pool** (tel. 6652 2164), also known as the **Oceanarium.** *(Open daily 9am-5pm. Admission $11, backpackers $10, students and seniors $8.50, children $5, family of 5 $33.50.)* Dolphins and seals perform tricks daily in the Sea Circus (10:30am-noon and 2·15-4pm). You can also pet dolphins, talk to cockatoos, watch kangaroos, and see peacocks strut their stuff. Eighty species of mammals live at the **Coffs Zoo** (tel. 6656 1330), 12km north of Coffs just past Moonee Beach. *(Open daily 8:30am-5pm; in winter 8:30am-4pmr. $12, students and seniors $9, children 3-14yr. $6, family of 4 $30.)* The zoo has a talk on rainforest birds at 10am, koala shows at 11am and 3pm, and a reptile presentation at 1:15pm.

The **Coffs Harbour Historical Museum,** 191 High St (tel. 6652 5794), documents the history of the area with a model banana plantation and other displays. *(Open Tu-Th and Su 1:30-4pm.)* Others may prefer the **Bunker Cartoon Gallery** (tel. 6651 7343), at the corner of Hogbin Dr and Albany St near the airport. *(Open daily 10am-2pm; school holidays 10am-4pm. Admission $2, children $1.)* It's Australia's first and only collection of contemporary and classic original cartoons. Meanwhile, the **Big Banana** (tel. 6652 4355), on the Pacific Hwy north of town, is quintessential kitsch. *(Open daily 9am-4pm. Free admission; monorail tour $9.50, children $5.50.)* Zoom around the plantation on a space shuttle-like monorail and learn more than you need to know about banana cultivation methods, or just stare at the boat-sized banana out front.

In Bonville, 14km from Coffs, the **Kiwi Down Under Farm** (tel. 6653 4449) is a 25-acre commercial organic fruit farm that produces 30 tons of kiwis a year and houses a wide variety of tropical trees. Their tours are unexpectedly interesting and allow visitors to feed the resident animals. *(Open W-Su and public holidays noon-5pm. Feedings Sa-Su and holidays 2, 3, and 4pm.)* The farm also runs a retail store which sells organic produce. A bit closer to town is another child-friendly attraction. Don't swat or you'll destroy the main exhibit at the **Butterfly House** (tel. 6653 4766) in Bonville on the Pacific Hwy south of Coffs. *(Open Tu-Su, Nov.-Mar. 9am-4:30pm, Apr.-Oct 9am-3:30pm.)* It's one of the largest displays of live butterflies in Australia, and there's a tearoom, giftshop, and a large outdoor maze with a treasure hunt for children. The why-would-you-want-to-go-there prize goes to the **Big Fat Worm Farm** (tel. 6669 5297), 45km south of Coffs Harbour on Valla Rd. *(Open daily 10am-4pm. Guided tours on the hr. Admission $5, families $12.)* You can pick, pack, and race the worms, or just watch.

ACTIVITIES

There's no shortage of things to do in Coffs, and the field is ever-increasing. Hostels can offer good rates on diving courses and skydiving lessons, but don't hesitate to call companies directly and ask about commission-free fun.

Diving

Now that Coffs Harbour's **Solitary Islands** have been declared a national marine park, they are becoming increasingly respected as a top diving spot; with both tropical and cold-water fish and less crowding, it even has advantages over the Great Barrier Reef. The Islands are composed of at least 19 protected beaches, headlands, creeks, and rocks. For more info contact the **Marine Reserve Office** (tel. 6652 3977), on the jetty. Visibility is often better during the winter, but the water is chilly. You can swim with harmless gray nurse sharks year-round; they breed from June to September. Coffs has three dive shops, all of which rent equipment and conduct lessons and trips to the Solitary Islands Marine Park. Diving requires a medical certification which typically costs $40-70. A PADI course or open-water course is a requirement for independent diving. A "resort" or introductory dive is done one-on-one with an instructor and does not result in any certification for later dives. For an overview on diving, see p. 275.

Divers Depot (tel. 6652 2033; or 0417 201 223; email diversd@omcs.com.au), on the jetty, offers an unbeatable deal on PADI certification: for backpackers staying at any Coffs Hostel, the 4-day course, including off-shore dives, costs $150. Manuals are not included, minimum class size is 4, and the company is known to give extra practice dives until it deems beginners ready. Two dives with gear supplied $80, intro dives $120. Open Tu-F 9am-5pm, Sa-Su 8am-1pm.

The Jetty Dive Centre, 398 High St (tel. 6651 1611). Weekend dive packages with 4 dives and 2 nights accommodation $160. PADI course with 2 free dives $255, $345 if you keep the manuals. Two dives with gear start at $90; intro dives $99 or $125 for 2; snorkeling charters $45.

Pacific Blue Dive Center, 321 High St (tel. 6652 2759; email BLUE@CHC.NET.AU), in the Coffs Promenade. Their equipment is new, though limited. They offer pickup and will copy a tape of your dive. Two dives with gear $85; intro dive $115. PADI courses $280 for 7 days, $220 with a backpackers card.

Water Sports and Adrenaline Activities

The region's rivers offer some of the best whitewater rafting in New South Wales. Most tour companies pick up from both Coffs and Byron, but the drive from Byron can be three times as long. The **Nymboida River,** about an hour west of Coffs, is the most popular. The rapids are mainly grade 3 to 4 (on a scale where grade 6 is "waterfall"), with sections of grade 5, and pass through dense rainforest. The **Gwydir River** flows only November through February; the release of cotton irrigation water from the Coperton Dam creates a nearly constant grade 4 to 5 river which runs through granite country. The **Goolang River** is actually a man-made concrete kayaking course at a steady grade 3. Full-day trips offer superior value to half-day specials.

A few tour companies offer trips with courtesy shuttles from Coffs and big lunches included. **Rapid Rafting** (tel. 6652 1741) has full-day ($99), half-day ($70), and one-hour ($40, transportation not provided) trips on the Nymboida or Goolang River. They have backpacker discounts on Tuesdays and Thursdays.

WOW Rafting Professionals (tel. 6654 4066) does a 12-hour trip with tea, lunch, barbecue dinner, and a break for rope swinging for $135; a two-day trip is $285. Backpackers get $5 discounts. **Wildwater Adventures** (tel. 6653 4469) conducts daytrips for $125 and two-day trips for $265 (Sa-Su $280). The two-day Gwydir River trip includes accommodation and leaves from Inverell (available mid-Oct. to Feb.). **Endless Summer Adventures** (tel. 6658 0590) runs three-hour sea kayaking trips from Charlesworth Bay to Park Beach. The $29 cost includes breakfast and leaves at 8am.

Coopers Surf Centres, 380 High St (tel. 6652 1782), at the Coffs Harbour jetty, rents surfboards by the day. *(Malibus $25, surfboards $15, bodyboards $10. Open M-W and F 9am-5:30pm, Th 9am-8pm, Sa 9am-2:30pm, Su 9am-2pm.)* **East Coast Surf School** (tel. 6651 5515) has two-hour lessons and private one-hour lessons (both $25). Although there's no guarantee you'll be standing by the end, the instructors do a great job teaching the basics. They also have classes for more advanced surfers.

Absolute Adrenaline, 396B High St (tel. 6651 9100), at Coffs Harbour jetty, is a private bookings center that has good displays, including videos, of selected "action activites." **Soaring Adventures** (tel. 0412 305 799) conducts 20-minute glider flights from 900m over Coffs and the region for $75; 10-15 minute flights are $65. **Coffs City Skydivers** (tel. 6651 1167) offers tandem skydiving from 3000m. A 40-second free fall followed by about five minutes of parachuting costs $270. *(Backpacker special rate $195, minimum 2 people. Video $75, 24 pictures $60; both $110.)*

Bikes, Horses, Rocks, and Racing

Mud, Sweat and Gears (tel. 6653 4577), 20km south of Coffs in Valery, has mountain bike tours of the Pine Creek State Forest. *($30 for 2hr., half-day $55.)* **Bob Wallis Bicycle Centre** (tel. 6652 5102), at the corner of Collingwood and Orlando St. at Coffs Harbour jetty, rents mountain bikes, locks, and helmets. *($15 per day, $50 deposit; open M-F 8:30am-5pm, Sa 8:30am-1pm; Oct.-Dec. on Su 9am-1pm.)* **Valery Trails** (tel. 6653 4301), in Valery, offers two-hour horseback rides with tea, but no transport to Valery. *(Sa-Th 10am and 2pm, school holidays daily; $30.)* A good rainy day activity is **Coffs Rock** indoor rock climbing (tel. 6651 6688 or 0419 275 632), at GDT Seccombe, off Orland St. *(Open W-Th 1-8pm, F 1-5pm, Sa-Su noon-5pm. $10 per hr., $12 for 4hr. Harness and safety instructions included. Shoes $3.50, chalkbags $1.)* The staff recommends climbing in pairs. **Raleigh Racing Kart Hire** (tel. 6655 4017 or 0411 377 017), on Valery Rd off the Pacific Hwy south of Coffs, is an international standard track over 1km long. *(Open daily 9am-5pm, 9am-6pm during daylight savings. $12 for 5 laps; $20 for 10. Must be 12 yrs. old to drive, 4 yrs. old to ride. Disabled-access special kart available.)*

Tours

The double-decker **Coffs Explorer bus** (tel. 6653 7115) has full-day trips to area sights Tuesdays and Thursdays, lunch and tea included, for $30. Trips are also offered to the Bellingen Market and Dorrigo National Park, but the bus doesn't run during school vacation weeks. Personalized mini-bus tours aimed at backpackers are offered by **Blue Tongue Tours** (tel. 6651 4411), a brand new company with trips to Dorrigo, Bellingen, wineries, rainforests, and national parks. Barbecue lunch included. **Coffs Harbour Mountain Trails 4WD Tours** (tel. 6658 3333) has full day tours through rainforests and past waterfalls for $72 (occasionally $58 off-peak). **Phil and Margaret's Motorcycle Tours** (tel. 6653 7725) is run by a couple who practically grew up on Harleys. *(30min. city circuit tour $30. 1hr. coastal and country circuit tour $50.)*

Whales swim by Coffs from June to July and again (in the other direction) from September to November. Many chartered boats convert to whale-watching cruisers during these times. The most adventurous can try "parawhaling," or parasailing 100m above the ocean off of a chartered boat. The parasailing cruise is $58; book through the **Marina Booking Office** (tel. 6651 4612).

ENTERTAINMENT

Coffs has grown faster than its slowly-improving nightlife scene, which is centered around Grafton St and the Pacific Hwy. Hostels usually organize trips on the weekends. The *Coffs Harbour Advocate* publishes an entertainment guide.

Some of the cheapest drinks in town can be found at the **Ex-Serviceman's Club,** on the corner of Grafton and Vernon St, although you'll need a passport to get in. Along with the **RSL Club,** on the corner of Vernon St and Pacific Hwy, which has cheap meals and cheaper drinks, it's where many people start their evenings before heading to more lively pastures. Across the street is the **Plantation Hotel,** with live rock music on Thursdays, Fridays, and Saturdays (no cover before 11pm) and a relaxed sports bar. The **Coffs Harbour Hotel** and the **Fitzroy Hotel** also have live music on weekends; the Fitzroy has a 24-hour license, and often waits to close until the last person leaves. The **Hoey Moey Backpackers pub** has live entertainment a few nights a week, usually hard rock. It's also got a beer garden, pool, gaming room, and tons of space.

A great developing place for travelers is the **Greenhouse Tavern** (tel. 6651 5400) across from the Palm Beach Plaza. It has two bars, live music weekly, pool tables, and full gambling facilities, and offers free drink vouchers through Barracuda Backpackers. In the same lot is one of the two **Coffs Harbour Cinemas** (tel. 6651 6444). The other is on Vernon St opposite the Ex-Serviceman's Club. The cinemas are usually showing about eight different movies between the two, and are only $5 on Tuesdays (otherwise adults $8.50, children and seniors $6, students $7). For games, try the **Replay Family Entertainment Center** arcade in the City Palm Centre Mall ($10 for 2hr. unlimited play on Su 9am-11am or 6pm-8pm).

■ Woolgoola

Don't be deterred by the two large, tacky, artificial elephants at the north entrance to town: Woolgoola has a gorgeous coastline and weather that allows you to enjoy it all year. After your senses have been tricked by these tusked monuments (advertising an Indian restaurant), trick them again by heading straight to the **Woolgoola Headland.** This spot is bird's eye for viewing the **Solitary Islands Marine Reserve,** a smattering of small islands with marine biodiversity approaching that of the Great Barrier Reef. Dolphin and whale sightings are common from May to October, too. Two **beaches** flank the headland. The surfing- and fishing-friendly **Back Beach** stretches to your right when facing the ocean; **Front Beach** is a patrolled area off to the left. If you have a hankering to stroll in the rainforest, leave town past the elephants and cross the highway onto Woolgoola Creek Road; a picnic area 3km down marks the beginning of a short walk toward a waterfall.

Call us if you find a more endearing staff than the people at the **Tourist Information Centre** (tel. 6654 8080), in the Neighborhood Centre at the corner of Boundary Rd and Beach St, the main drag. They hand out fun, detailed, artist-designed maps (open daily 10am-3pm). **Ryan's buses** (tel. 6652 3201) run between Coffs Harbour and Woolgoola, where they stop at the shopping center (40min.; M-F 5 per day, Sa 2 per day). **CityLink** (tel. 6654 1063) services Grafton (1½hr.; 3 per day). The **post office** is at Woolgoola Plaza on Beach St, as are **phones** and an **ATM.**

To sleep in the bush—or near it, anyway—curve left when entering town by car; at the end of the road you'll arrive at the **Lakeside Holiday Park** (tel. 6654 1210), which allows direct access to the beach and a lake. (Sites $9.50-13.50. Onsite vans $20-28.) The **Raj Mahal** (tel. 6654 1149), behind the elephants on the Pacific Hwy at the north end of town serves up nan ($2.90-4.50), tandoori chicken ($13-$17), and vindaloo ($13). (Open Tu-Su noon-3pm; dinner begins 6pm.)

■ Ballina

Ballina is a peaceful port, quiet beach town, and thriving retirement community three hours north of Coffs Harbour, known to backpackers primarily as a transport hub for trips to Lennox Head or Lismore. There's not a whole lot to do here, but details on dolphin watching, cycling, and walking tracks are available at the unbelievably organized **Information Centre** (tel. 6686 3484; fax 6686 0136; email balinfo@om.com.au; open daily 9am-5pm). It's at the north end of town on the corner of Las Balsa Plaza and the main drag, the Pacific Hwy, known as **River St** in the town center.

McCafferty's and **Greyhound** stop in Ballina on their Sydney-Brisbane runs. **Kirkland's** (tel. 6686 7124) also runs to Lismore ($9, students $7, children $4.40) and Brisbane twice daily ($26, students $20, children $13). **Blanch's Coaches** (tel. 6686 2144) leaves Ballina's River St stop outside Jetset Travel for Lennox Head ($4) and Byron Bay (M-F 6 per day, Sa 5 per day, Su and holidays 3 per day to both destinations;

$7). The **Transit Centre** is a good 5km from the center, in a large building complex known affectionately as **The Big Prawn** for the enormous pink shrimp nailed to the roof. The only way to get to town from here is by taxi; the **Ballina Taxi Service** (tel. 6686 9999) will take you for about $10.

Ballina Travelers Lodge, 36-38 Tamar St (tel. 6686 6737), is a motel and YHA hostel. Go two blocks up Norton St from the tourist office, then turn left. The owners are friendly and intent on keeping their lodge quiet and meticulously clean. The YHA half has a large communal kitchen, barbecue area, laundry, and lots of showers. Larger motel rooms with TVs and lots of amenities. There's a small pool, free bikes and surfboards, and courtesy pick-up from the Transit Centre. (4-bed dorms $14, YHA nonmembers $16; doubles $32, $36. Linen included. Motel singles $46; doubles $47, up to $85 at Christmas.) It's wheelchair accessible.

Forgotten Country (tel. 6687 7845) offers half-day ($50), full-day ($95), and 2- or 3-day ($275-$425) tours to nearby rainforests, waterfalls, and an ancient volcano shield. (10% discount for students, half-price for children.) For self-guided exploring, **Jack Ransom Cycles,** 16 Cherry St (tel. 6686 3485), rents bikes by the half-day ($8), full-day ($12), or week ($30); helmet and lock are included.

■ Near Ballina: Broadwater and Evans Head

The best time to visit **Broadwater National Park** is in springtime, when wildflowers burst into bloom in pinks, blues, whites, yellows, and reds. The park is permanently interesting because of thick vegetation that has survived the harsh conditions and poor soils of the coastline. Most of the park is beach and heath growing atop windswept dunes, speckled with the distinctive red and orange flowers of the wedding bush banksia. The beach can be accessed at several points along the **Broadwater-Evans Head Road,** which runs the 8km length of the park. A couple kilometers into the park from the north end is the **Broadwater Lookout,** the best place for surveying the park. Drive 4km south to the start of the **Salty Lagoon Track,** a 3km flat path that ends at a lagoon and is colorful in springtime.

To reach the park from the north, take Broadwater-Evans Head Rd from the Princes Hwy in Broadwater, about 20km south of Ballina. From the south, take Woodburn-Evans Head Rd 11km east to **Evans Head,** between Broadwater and Bundjalong National Parks. **Country Link** buses (tel. 13 22 32) pass through daily. **Pub accommodation** is available, or stay at the tidy beachside **Koinina** recreation park (tel. 6682 4329), on Terrace St at the edge of the Broadwater-Evans Head Rd and Broadwater National Park (sites $8).

At Evans Head is a little known entrance to **Bundjalong National Park;** cross the Evans River Bridge and turn right. The road narrows into dirt track, and several turn-offs lead to rest stops and boat launches on the estuary. Continue 2km to the road's end at the **Gamma Garra Picnic Area.** Three walks begin across the foot bridge next to the park and finish at an Aboriginal midden. The **Dirrawong Track** hugs the river and passes through swamp and dry littoral forest. The **Jenna Jenna Track** crosses a

---

Keeping Kids from Getting Stoned

Six kilometers south of Byron Bay is Broken Head, a beach and rainforest preserve. Popular for fishing, rainforest walks, and the clifftop "Two Sisters" walking track, it is also home to **Whites Beach,** claimed by some Aussies to be the most beautiful beach in the world (and a 10-minute walk down to the shore). The Cocked Hat Rocks outcrops, visible from the walking paths in Broken Head, didn't just serve as a warning to ships, but to the children of the Bundjalong people as well. Local Aboriginal mythology tells a Dreamtime story of two sisters bathing in the waters off the headlands. When one became caught in the current, the other swam to save her but was swept away, too. The rocks formed in their place, and children were told that to avoid the same stony fate, they must not swim off the headlands. That's one way to avoid needing a lifeguard!

hill campsite of the Aboriginals, and the **Guweean** leads past a barbecue area and through a dry forest. Camping is forbidden in these sections of the park.

■ Lennox Head

Lennox Head (pop. 2300) lies between Ballina and Byron Bay. It's renowned for its excellent surf—it's one of the top ten areas in the world from June to August, and is home to **Grumfest,** a national surfing competition for under-16s, in early July. The highway enters the town on Tourist Rd, from which the "town center" (really barely a village) is accessible by taking the roundabout to Ballina St, which becomes Pacific Pde and runs along **Seven Mile Beach,** a prime lookout for dolphin-spotting. Tea-dyed **Lake Ainsworth** is at the north end of Pacific Pde. Two kilometers in the opposite direction along the beach is **Lennox Point,** an excellent but crowded surf area. **All Above Board,** 68 Ballina St (tel. 6887 7522), next to the chemist, rents surfboards ($12), Malibus ($15), and body boards ($8). Nearby **Beach Life Surf Centre,** 71 Ballina St (tel. 6887 7038), charges slightly more but also rents snorkel equipment for $8. **Lennox Cycle Hire** (tel. 6687 7210) rents bikes ($12 per half-day, $18 per day). **Blanch's Coaches** runs through Lennox Head and will pick up on request.

The **Lennox Head Beach House** (tel. 6687 7636) is at 3 Ross St, 100m from Seven Mile Beach and a short walk from Lake Ainsworth. The friendly owners offer free use of surfboards, boogie-boards, bicycles, and fishing rods; unlimited use of windsurfers and catamarans is just $5, and lessons are free. Aspiring gourmets can help themselves to the herb garden and dine in the open courtyard. Once a week, enjoy a massage from their "natural healing center." Bedrooms are small but tidy. (Dorms $16; doubles $36. VIP. 10% off weekly.) **Lake Ainsworth Caravan Park** (tel. 6687 7249) has tent sites ($11) and cabins ($28, $33 with bath) next to the lake.

■ Murwillumbah

Murwillumbah (more-WOOL-um-bah) is a small country town whose name has several suggested meanings, including "place of high mountain which catches sun" and "place of many possums and people." The residents have seized on the second definition and have begun to paint possum murals on their Art Deco public buildings, creating a cohesive, if strange, motif. There are four national parks near Murwillumbah: **Nightcap** (30km southwest), **Border Ranges, Lamington,** and **Mt. Cougal.** It's also a handy base for exploring the enormous, spectacular volcanic rim of **Mt. Warning.**

ORIENTATION AND PRACTICAL INFORMATION

Murwillumbah is halfway between Byron Bay and Tweed Heads. The **Tweed River** runs through the east side of town, and the Pacific Hwy and the **railway station** are on the east bank. The stop for **Greyhound** and **McCafferty's** is opposite the railway station. In Budd Park at the corner of the highway and Alma St is the **tourist information center** for the region, located in the **World Heritage Rainforest Centre** (tel. 6672 1340; fax 6672 5948; open M-Sa 9am-4pm, Su 9am-3pm).

The town centers on the west bank of the Tweed River, which is crossed by the **Alma St bridge** behind Tweed Tavern. Alma St crosses Commercial St and becomes **Wollumbin St** (also known as Main St), which has several eateries and a shopping center with a 24-hour **Coles** supermarket at the end of the block on the left. The crossroad is **Brisbane St,** which goes one block to the right to **Murwillumbah St.** The **post office** is at Brisbane and Murwillumbah St (postal code 2484). The **Pioneer Motor Services** and **Kirkland's bus** depot are on Murwillumbah St, across from **National Bank.**

ACCOMMODATIONS AND FOOD

The **Mt. Warning/Murwillumbah YHA,** 1 Tumbulgum Rd (tel. 6672 3763), is the second oldest YHA in NSW, and a well-kept, family-oriented lodge decorated with a mural. It's most popular as a base for people making a trip up Mt. Warning. From the railway station, cross the Alma St bridge, turn right on Commercial St, and follow the river bank. Set right on the Tweed River, the YHA offers free use of rowboats, canoes, surfskis, fishing gear, and, in the summer, inner tubes for lazing in the river. There's free ice cream in the evening, a courtyard, and resident parakeets. Bike rental is available. (Dorms $14; twins and doubles $16 per person.)

Main St has several inexpensive ethnic restaurants. At the corner of Wollumbin St and Commercial Rd, **South of the Border** (tel. 6672 1694) serves up Mexican cuisine, steaks, and seafood ($6-16; open for dinner W-Su and lunch on F). **Austral Cafe**, 88 Main St, is large, simple, and friendly (lunches $2-5; open M-F 7:30am-5:30pm, Sa 7:30am-12:30pm). Across the street is **Margherita's Cantina** (tel. 6672 6767), which serves breakfasts all day for under $6, sandwiches for under $3, and buffet plates for under $7 (open M-F 7:30am-5pm, Sa 7:30am-3pm).

SIGHTS

The area's main attraction is the splendid **Mt. Warning** (see below). In town, the small **Art Gallery** (tel. 6672 0409), which awards the **world's biggest art prize** ($100,000 for portraiture), is down Tumbulgum Rd. *(Open W-Su 10am-5pm.)* Murwillumbah holds two **markets**, one on the second Sunday of the month near the Coles, and a larger market on the fourth Sunday of the month at the showgrounds off Queensland Rd.

Chillingham Trail Rides (tel. 6679 1369), 20 minutes from Murwillumbah, conducts horse rides through the Chillingham Valley bush, waterfall, and creek twice daily at 8:30am and 1:30pm. Book ahead for weekends ($40).

■ Mt. Warning and Border Ranges

The spire that caps **Mt. Warning**, which catches the sun's rays before any other spot on the coast, is the centerpiece of a bowl-shaped landform born of an eroded, extinct volcano that once stood twice its current height. The climb to the peak offers a fantastic 360° view of the coast and surrounding forest. This moderately strenuous walk, called the **Summit Track**, covers 8.8km round-trip and takes four to five hours. It passes through subtropical and temperate rainforest, wet sclerophyll forest, and heath scrub. Don't commence after 2pm in the winter, lest you get caught in the dark. Bring your own water; there are toilets at the **Breakfast Creek** picnic area at the start of the walk. To reach the Summit Track from Murwillumbah, take Kyogle Rd 12km west, turn on Mt. Warning Rd, and go about 6km to Breakfast Creek. A **cab** (tel. 6672 1344) costs around $20, and you can even catch a ride on a **school bus**, which departs Knox Park at 7:10am and drops off at the national park entrance 6km from the carpark ($2).

If you find Mt. Warning too touristed, the gorgeous **Border Ranges National Park** is an ideal getaway. It takes some work to get there, but its seclusion rewards you with the shade of a lush canopy and a great vantage point for viewing the volcano region. Take the Kyogle Rd west from Murwillumbah for 44km; the Barker Vale turn-off leads 15km along gravel road to the park entrance. Inside the park, the road becomes the **Tweed Range Scenic Drive** (60km, 4-5hr.). It's steep in places, but not very windy. The drive exits the park at **Wiangaree**, 13km from Kyogle and 66km from Murwillumbah.

The first picnic area in the park is **Bar Mountain,** with toilets and a lovely beech glade. Less than 1km farther is the more remarkable **Blackbutts** picnic area, with striking views of Mt. Warning and the basin. If heights don't scare you, try the **Pinnacle Lookout,** another 8km north. For the **Forest Tops** camping area, go another 4km and turn left, then go 4km and turn left again. Here, a right turn leads to the **Brindle Creek** picnic area, the departure point for a three-hour walk among rainforests and waterfalls galore that ends at the **Antarctic Beech** picnic area.

■ Whian Whian and Mullumbimby

Adjoined to Nightcap National Park to the east, **Whian Whian State Forest** is another rainforest and waterfall showcase, accessible through Dunoon, Mullumbimby, or some of the villages around Lismore. The best way to see the park is the **Forest Drive,** a 30km, two-hour trip beginning at **Minyon Falls** or Gibbergunyah Range Rd. **Minyon Grass** is a picnic area with many walking trails and toilets, 2km before Minyon Falls. **Rummery Park** is a popular camping spot, with access to the 16km Nightcap track which ends at **Mt. Nardi.** The next stop along that trail, **Peates Mountain Lookout,** is a five- to 10-minute walk up. Along with blackbutt and flooded gum plantations, the drive passes through **Gibbergunyah** and **Big Scrub Flora Reserves** before reaching **Rocky Creek Dam,** a favorite family picnic stop.

The town of **Mullumbimby** (pop. 2700) is so small and tranquil it doesn't even have a tourist office. **Dalley St** is the main thoroughfare and **Burringbar St** has most of the shops. A convenient stopping place for trips to Whian Whian as well as the **Border Ranges National Park,** Mullumbimby has a string of motels on Dalley St. **Mullumbimby Motel,** 121 Dalley St (tel. 6684 2387), is a bit less expensive than the average, with rather large $40 singles, doubles, or twins ($10 per extra person), with TV, fan, heating, and laundry. The cheapest option is **Maca's Camping Ground** (tel. 6684 5211); from Dalley St head to the Pacific Hwy and turn left onto Main Arm Rd. Follow it 12km out and Maca's will be on your right. It costs $6 per person and has a kitchen, dining area, laundry, showers, and general store. Tents can be hired. **Brunswick Valley Coaches** (tel. 6685 1385) runs to **Byron Bay** and **Murwillumbah** daily.

■ Lismore

Lismore (pop. 45,500) is a large industrial town with a strong Aboriginal presence. Emphasis on environmental protection follows naturally from its surroundings: three world heritage rainforests, volcanic remains, and a disproportionately high number of rainbows (due to the position of valleys), earning it the nickname **Rainbow Region.** The students at nearby **Southern Cross University** inject palpable activist energy and help to sustain Lismore's cultural venues.

ORIENTATION AND PRACTICAL INFORMATION

In the hinterlands west of Ballina, Lismore lies off the Bruxner Hwy (called **Ballina St** in town) just east of the **Wilson** (or **Richmond) River.** Approaching the river from the east, Ballina St crosses **Dawson, Keen,** and **Molesworth St,** the busiest part of town. Perpendicular to these streets in the town center are small **Conway** and **Magellan St** and the main thoroughfare **Woodlark St,** accessible from the Dawson St roundabout and leading across the river to **Bridge St** and **Nimbin.** At the corner of Molesworth and Ballina St, the **tourist office** (tel. 6622 0122; fax 6622 0193; email tourism@nor.com.au; http://www.liscity.nsw.gov.au) is worth seeing, with a small indoor tropical rainforest (admission $1) and a handy topographical map of the national parks. (Open daily 9am-4:30pm.) The **post office** (tel. 6622 1855) is on Conway St between Molesworth and Keen St at the top of a big ramp (open M-F 8:30am-5pm). The **police** (tel. 6621 9699) are on Molesworth St. For an **ambulance** dial 6621 2408, for **fire** 6621 5660.

The brand new **Transit Centre** is on the corner of Molesworth and Magellan St and has toilets and a baby changing room for 50¢, showers for $2. It's the stop for **Hall's Bus Service** (tel. 6628 4101), running to Whian Whian; **Beaumont's** (tel. 015 257 355 or 0416 216 231), to Mullumbimby; **Justice Bus Service** (tel. 6686 7324 or 018 664 410), to Murwillumbah, Nimbin, and Lismore; **Marsh's** (tel. 6689 1220), to Nimbin. (All services M-F 1 per day.) The **Nimbin Shuttle Bus** (tel. 6687 2007) has free pick-up and is $20 round-trip from Lismore daily.

Greyhound Pioneer buses stop at the **Ampol Roadhouse,** 136 Woodlark St (open 24hr.). Greyhound includes Lismore on its coastal Brisbane-Sydney service (1 per day to Brisbane $29, students $24; Sydney $67, $54). The **Kirklands** buses terminal (tel. 6622 1499) is at the end of Magellan St, just past Molesworth St. Kirklands runs to Byron Bay ($11), Brisbane (several times per day, $28), Surfers Paradise ($26), Tweed Heads ($18), Lennox Head ($10), and Ballina ($9); backpackers and YHA members pay 25% less. Kirklands also stops in some of Lismore's nearby villages, although the best way to get around might be to rent a car. Options include **Hertz,** 49 Dawson St (tel. 6621 8855), **Budget,** 32 Keen St (tel. 6681 4036), and **Thrifty,** 113 Dawson St (tel. 6622 2266). **Countrylink** has several services daily through Lismore. The railway station is on Union St, right across the river. For a **taxi** call 13 10 08. **ATMs** can be found on Conway, Magellan, Woodlark, and Molesworth St. **Internet access** is at **NRG** (tel. 6622 3488; email admin@nrg.com.au), on Molesworth St (minimum charge $5 for 30min.).

ACCOMMODATIONS

More like a home than a hostel, **Currendina Lodge/Lismore Backpackers,** 14 Ewing St (tel. 6621 6118), offers clean rooms with all the little amenities to make you feel welcome. From the information center, take a left on Ballina, cross Molesworth and Keen St, and turn left on Dawson St. Ewing is halfway down Dawson St. The well-equipped kitchen (with a sandwich-maker!) has free tea and coffee and opens to a sunny eating area. Guests enjoy a comfy TV lounge and laundry facilities. (Dorms $15; singles $20-22; doubles and twins $32-35. Weekly: $90; $105-140; $150. Additional person $10. VIP, YHA, ISIC. Group bookings available.)

Gollan Hotel (tel. 6621 2295), on the corner of Keen and Magellan St, is a pubstay. From the information center, go up Molesworth St and take a right on Magellan; Keen is two blocks ahead. The rooms are surprisingly nice, freshly painted, and have sinks and carpeting. (Singles $20, with bathroom $30; doubles $30, with bathroom $35-40. Weekly: $80-100; $90-110; $110-150. There is one triple for $15 per person.)

The **Lismore Palms Caravan Park,** 42-58 Brunswick St (tel. 6621 7067), is basic and cheap. Follow Dawson north and make a right onto Brunswick. (For 2 people, cabins with bathroom $32; caravans $25-28; tent sites $10, powered $12. Prices lower by the week, slightly higher during long weekends, Christmas, and Easter. $4 extra adult, $2 extra child. Check for student rates.)

FOOD

Lismore's students' demand for vegetarian cheap eats has turned out some terrifically funky cafes. Shop for yourself at the cheapest grocery in town, **Woolworths** on Keen St (back entrance on Carrington St; open M-Sa 7am-10pm, Su 9am-4pm). **Fundamental Foods Store,** 140 Keen St (tel. 6622 2199), is a moderately priced supermarket specializing in organic food, vegetables, and vitamins (open M-W and F 9am-5:30pm, Th 9am-7pm, Sa 8:30am-noon). Many pubs offer cheap lunch and dinner meals.

Dr. Juice Bar (tel. 6622 4440), on Keen St, is an all-vegetarian student haunt, with a few long wooden booths and a wall plastered with community notices. The Doctor prescribes marvelous smoothies ($3), veggie burgers ($4), and wildly popular apricot tofu cheesecake ($2.80). $6 meal specials. Open M-F 9am-6pm, Sa 9am-1pm.

Caddies Coffee, 20 Carrington St (tel. 6621 7709), tees off with an indoor split-level deck, an outdoor patio, and beautiful stained glass. Fresh sandwiches, bagels, pasta, and focaccia ($2-9.50). Open M-F 8am-6pm, Sa 8am-1:30pm.

Northern Rivers Hotel (tel. 6621 5797), at the corner of Bridges and Terania St. Follow Woodlark St to the bridge, cross it, and turn left on Bridges St. The best deal in town is a choice of about 10 dishes, including lasagna, steak, and roast chicken with vegetables or salad for lunch ($2) or dinner ($3). You can also cook your own T-bone for $7, and there's a leafy courtyard and a supervised children's playroom.

20,000 Cows, 58 Bridge St (tel. 6622 2517 or 0418 610 879), across from the hotel. No cows are served (interpret that in either sense) at this vegetarian restaurant, with mismatched, wildly patterned tablecloths pinned down with tall candlesticks, and a delightful assortment of chairs. Unbelievably fresh pasta, and Indian and Middle Eastern food ($5-20). Open W-Su from 6pm.

Lismore Workers Club, 231 Keen St (tel. 6621 7401), at the end of Keen St, has meals for $2-8 and is open daily for lunch and dinner.

SIGHTS AND FESTIVALS

Almost two blocks up Molesworth St from Ballina St is the **Lismore Regional Art Museum** (the white building), 131 Molesworth St (tel. 6622 2209). *(Open Tu-Sa 10am-4pm. Donation requested.)* It houses a two-floor collection of paintings, sculpture, and photographs. Visiting exhibitions make it especially worth a look, and the monthly special displays for 1999 include Aboriginal pottery in March and a North Coast portrait prize in July. Farther along the street is the fabulous **Richmond River Historical Society,** 165 Molesworth St (tel. 6622 9993), in the Municipal Building. *(Open M-F 10am-4pm. $2, students 50¢.)* There's a pioneer room, a shipping room, a natural history room with preserved baby crocs and mummified tropical birds, and a hallway with Aboriginal boomerangs and tools.

For a breath of fresh air, there are many parks nearby. Behind the visitors center on Molesworth St is **Rotary Park,** six hectares of hoop pine and giant fig tree rainforest equipped with an easy boardwalk. The **Boatharbour Nature Reserve,** 6km northeast of Lismore on Bangalow Rd, sports 17 hectares of rainforest trees, the remnants of the "Big Scrub Forest." The original 75,000 hectares of lowland forest throughout northern New South Wales has been almost completely deforested. The **Tucki Tucki Nature Reserve,** which doubles as a koala sanctuary, is 15 minutes from Lismore on Wyrallah Rd. Lismore's water supply comes from the **Rocky Creek Dam,** home to a waterfront boardwalk and a platypus lagoon.

Lismore comes alive during the **Northern Rivers Folk Festival** (tel. 6621 7537) held the first weekend in October. In late May, a **Lantern Festival** brings hundreds of hand-crafted, flickering, colorful paper lanterns to the city streets at twilight.

ENTERTAINMENT

Like any hard-working industrial town, Lismore knows how to kick back and have a few. The town's nightlife centers around the hotel pubs in the town center. There are two nightclubs, both in pubs and open only Thursday through Saturday. The **Legends Night Club** is in the **Oakes Hotel** (tel. 6621 7964), on the corner of Woodlark and Keen St at the roundabout, attached to the Ruins Cafe. Upscale and clean, it has live music Thursdays and Saturdays and some outrageous decorations. (Open until 2am. Wheelchair accessible.) **Powerhouse** in the **Canberra Hotel,** 77 Molesworth St (tel. 6622 4736), has live music Thursday through Saturday, pool tables, and the **Main St Bar** and **Main St Vegas** gaming room (open Th until 3am, F 3:30am, Sa 4am).

On Keen St, the **Lismore Workers Club** (open F and Sa till midnight) has gambling and cheap drinks as does the **Lismore RSL,** 1 Market St. The **New Tattersalls Hotel** (tel. 6621 2284) on Keen St is open until around 2am on weekends and has live music Thursday and Saturday. On the corner of Woodlark and Keen St is the **Gollan Hotel** (tel. 6621 2295) whose yellow and blue pub features jam sessions by university students on Mondays, retro or techno on Wednesdays, and bands Thursday through Saturday. Further down the street on the corner of Zadoc and Keen St is the **Rous Hotel,** which occasionally has unplugged music sessions of local artists. The **Lismore Four Cinema** (tel. 6621 2361) is on the corner of Keen and Zadoc St in the Star Court Arc.

■ Around Lismore: The Villages

Each of the 10 small villages within the Lismore region boasts some unique feature to draw visitors, if only for an afternoon. **Bexhill's** main attraction is an open-air cathedral and periodic organ recitals. **Dunoon,** near the Whian Whian State Forest, has rows of macademia nut factories, some with free samples. Scenic **Rosebank** is particularly beautiful in late October when the jacarandas are in bloom.

The Channon, 20 minutes from Lismore, is home every second Sunday to the **Channon Markets,** the largest in the region, with spectacular displays of music and homemade food. It's also the closest village to the lovely **Protestor's Falls,** named for a group of activists who, in 1979, were determined to prevent logging of the Terania Creek Forests. They arrived for a one-day demonstration and stayed for six weeks. Their efforts paid off: the tall, elegant stands of intertwined limbs were declared a national park in 1983, and the powerful falls still empty into a shaded swimming hole.

■ Nimbin

At the climax of Nimbin's 1995 Mardi Grass Festival (organized by HEMP: Help End Marijuana Prohibition), 200 protesters rolled joints, blazed up, headed to the police station, and demanded to be arrested. Marijuana use is a criminal offense in Nimbin, as throughout New South Wales, but the police were helpless, with only enough cells to arrest two people. This kind of event reinforces the image of Nimbin as a haven for hippies. The area houses more than 350 communes, some open to the public. Don't get too judgmental, though. In a region so full of natural beauty, you too may soon be longing to let your hair down, kick your shoes off, and chill among the flowers and trees.

PRACTICAL INFORMATION Nimbin's commercial district and center is on Cullen St between the police station and the corner hotel. You'll know you're there by the vivid murals, wild storefront displays, and thin wisps of smoke. Nimbin has no tourist center, just a self-appointed tourist official hell-bent on promoting Nimbin's "straight" side. He works in **The Nimbin Tourist Connexion** (tel. 6689 1764; also a transportation booking agency) at the end of Cullen St. (Open M-F noon-5pm, Sa-Su noon-2pm.) Limited tourist information is also available from **Perceptio Books** (tel. 6689 1766) on Cullen St in the center of town, also the source for **Internet access.** ($2 for 7min., progressively cheaper thereafter. Open M-Sa 10am-5pm.) The **Nimbin Shuttle Bus** (tel. 6687 2007) departs daily to Nimbin from Byron Bay at 10am, returning at 1:30pm ($13). For visitors who just want a glimpse of this spectacle, Byron-based tours to nearby national parks often stop in town for an hour or two. **Jim's Alternative Tours** (tel. 6685 7720) and **Bay to Bush** (tel. 6685 6889) have $30 full-day tours of the region leaving from Byron Bay. The **Nimbin Explorer Eco-Tours** (tel. 6689 1557) runs daily two-hour tours of the sacred rocks, Permaculture Education Center, and Rainbow Power Company ($15).

ACCOMMODATIONS AND FOOD Granny's Farm (YHA) (tel. 6689 1333) is a five- to 10-minute walk from the town center north on Cullen St. Turn left just before the bridge. The creekside lodge has two pools, showers, a kitchen, frequent barbecues, and laundry facilities. Don't expect to stay long; they like turnover. (Dorms or train car $13; doubles $30; extra person $10; tent sites $8 per person.) **The Rainbow Retreat,** 75 Thorburn St (tel. 6689 1262), is 10 minutes from the town center. Take a left onto Thorburn from Cullen St just across a bridge; the hostel is up a rocky driveway on your left. This cozy hostel has a campfire, hippie decorations, and horses eating dinner while you do. A bed in the guest house, a teepee, or van costs any international backpacker $10 (non-backpackers $15), and the gypsy wagon double is $30. **The Nimbin Caravan Park** (tel. 6689 1402) is on Sibley St, next to the turn-off for the Rainbow Power Company; take a right at the bowling club. The **community pool,** closed in the winter, is on site. There are laundry and barbecue facilities but no kitchen. (2-person tent sites $12; caravan sites $15. Weekly $60; $70.)

Many of the area communes are part of **WWOOF** (tel. (03) 5155 0218), in which **W**illing **W**orkers exchange their labor for homestays **O**n **O**rganic Farms (see p. 19). The Nimbin Connection sells directories for $25. Nimbin has a few good eateries, all on Cullen St. **Rick's Cafe** (tel. 6689 1296) makes terrific big veggie burgers ($4), and has tons of under-$5 choices. The nearby **Nimbin Emporium** (tel. 6689 1205) sells health and bulk foods (open M-F 8:30am-6:15pm, Sa-Su 9am-6pm).

NEW SOUTH WALES

SIGHTS AND ACTIVITIES The mural-covered **Nimbin Museum** on Cullen St redefines creativity and historical interpretation. *($2 donation requested.)* Party vans burst through the front facade, and the 3D tangle of cobwebs, clocks, psychedelic fans, tree branches, and kitchen appliances lend credence to Einstein's quote, found in the second room: "Imagination is more important than knowledge." The rooms relate the museum founders' version of regional history: the first room is about Aboriginals, the second about European settlers, and the next five about the hippies. This last group is illustrated by dollhouses, fluorescent-lit cave rooms, melted skeletons (presumably illustrating nuclear meltdown), and marijuana legalization propaganda.

In 1973, the Australian Union of Students created the **Aquarius Festival** as a forum for creating a new future. The most direct outcome of the festival, and a major employer in Nimbin, is the **Rainbow Power Company** (tel. 6689 1430), a 10-minute walk from the city center down Cullen St to Alternative Way, on the right. The building, made of mud bricks, is a remarkable achievement in energy production; they even sell their excess generated power to the electricity grid for general consumption. One-hour factory tours are available with advance booking. *(Tours $2 and up depending on group size. Open M-F 9am-5pm, Sa 9-noon.)*

■ Near Nimbin: Nightcap National Park

A 4000-hectare park with the highest rainfall in the state and containing the southern rim of the 20-million-year-old **Mt. Warning** volcano crater, Nightcap has two main areas: **Mt. Nardi,** 12km out of Nimbin, and the **Terania Creek/Protestors Falls** area, 15km out of **The Channon** (20km from Nimbin). Mt. Nardi, one of the highest peaks, is accessible on sealed roads and has barbecue and picnic facilities. The viewing platform has info on the 1km walk to nearby **Mt. Matheson;** the 2km **Pholi's Walk,** with a lookout to the **Tweed Valley; Googarna Track,** which starts 500m before the summit and traipses through rainforest; and **Nightcap Track,** a 9km graded walk.

Terania Creek Rd, mostly gravel, leads to Protestors Falls in the Terania Creek basin and to a picnic area with barbecue, toilets, wood, and covered shelter. **Camping** is limited to one night. The 1.4km return track to Protestors Falls (see **The Villages,** p. 174) passes **Waterfall Creek** on the way to the falls. **Tuntable Falls** in the Tuntable Falls commune is a 120m waterfall, a three- to four-hour round-trip walk from the parking lot. From Nimbin, the turn-off is 6km down Sibley St; then go another 6km. The sacred **Nimbin Rocks** are the other way out of town, towards Lismore

■ Clarence Valley

Hard-core partiers may see the Clarence Valley as an interruption on the coastal backpacker fiesta route. Those who don't mind kicking off their dancing shoes for a brief respite in this cluster of small towns and national parks, however, may appreciate getting a taste of how the rest of Australia lives. **Grafton** is relatively boring, though it offers acceptable accommodations. **MacLean** is smaller and more pleasant; it's a fairly typical village with a couple of good sandwich shops and a river where prep school rowers scull. It's worth a coffee and lunch stop, or even a night of relaxation. The **Lower Tourist Visitor's Centre** (tel. 6645 4121) is off the Pacific Hwy in Ferry Park (open daily 9am-5pm). **CountryLink buses** (13 22 32) go to Sydney and Brisbane daily. The Route 380 private bus runs local service (M-F 3-5 per day, Sa 2 per day, Su 1 per day). For fares and schedules, contact **Riverland Travel** (tel. 6645 2017), at the north end of River St (open M-F 9am-5pm, Sa 9am-noon). A **bank** and an **ATM** are at 219 River St. There's a **pharmacy** at 253 River St (tel. 6645 2004). **Web access** is available at **Big River Internet,** behind River St on Stanley St (tel. 6645 1133; open M-F 9am-5pm). The **post office** is at 44 River St (open M-F 9am-5pm, postal code 2463).

The **MacLean Hotel,** 28 River St, (tel./fax 6645 2412), a basic pub with local flavor always offers a special $5 counter meal (singles $15, doubles $25). **Rissole's Coffee Lounge,** 243 River St (tel. 6645 3599), serves up mountainous sandwiches (open M-F 8:30am-5pm, Sa 9am-noon).

■ Yamba and Northern Yuragyir

The raw earth and sea of this 43km stretch of the Princes Hwy are quite simply fasci-nating. The Iluka Road takes you 3km east off the Pacific Hwy and through a spooky forest. Two roads diverge in this wood, and you'll probably want to take the one more traveled by: southeast to Yamba (7km).

Yamba is a hick-meets-surfer town, with the feel of a small village that wants to be big business. **The Pacific Hotel** (tel. 6646 2466; fax 6646 2662) sits atop the cliff overlooking the ocean. Between the atmosphere inside and the atmosphere outside, it probably is the most interesting spot in Yamba. (Rooms $17.50 per person, Dec-Jan $25. Office open daily 9am-midnight. Bar hosts bands and stays open late Th-Sa. Cover $3; free for guests.) The most alluring activity in Yamba is simply a short drive or long walk beginning at the Pacific Parade. There's a **post office** on Yamba St (tel. 6646 2402), and the BP station rents outboards ($30 per 5hr., $20 deposit).

A road running south along the coast brings you to a 3-way dead end into the bush: **Angourie.** Only hard-core surfers venture into this desolate terrain. In Angourie's front yard are two **natural pools** and a surf beach. The Green Pool and the Blue Pool (more popular for no apparent reason) are side by side. A merciless shore of square rocks leads to **Spooky Beach,** where the wise wear wetsuits. Nearly next door in northern **Yuragyir National Park** are swimming beaches. There is no camping allowed in this area. You must hike 3km on the **Angourie Walk** to **Shelley Head** to camp. Predatory fauna of the spider, bird, and reptile categories abound—beware.

The other road at the aforementioned Iluka Rd fork heads toward **Iluka;** the main reason to turn here is the **Woody Head Camping Area** (tel. 6646 6143) in **Bundja-long National Park.** Approximately 3km from Iluka, it fills quickly in summer and Easter and takes advanced bookings. **Campervans** are allowed, and there are hot showers, a large kitchen, barbecues, laundry facilities, and a kiosk. Visitors take advantage of surf and swim beaches and swamp forest and littoral rainforest for bush-walking. (Open M-F 8:30am-5pm. Sites $10, high season $13, 2-8 person cabins $7.50-15 per person, depending on group size.)

■ Minnie Water

The **Wooli Road** branches off the Pacific Hwy and passes through the raw **Glenngie State Forest.** A fork in the road gives you the options of heading for Wooli or Minnie Water, both set in central **Yuragyir National Park.** The area is uncommercialized and you could spend weeks exploring the bush coastal area. In the village of Minnie Water, there's a beach, a general store, and a few houses. The **BP General Store** (tel. 6649 7586) sells gas and basic groceries and has a pay phone. (Open M-F 6:30am-7:30pm, Sa-Su 6:30am-7pm; in winter M-F 7am-6pm, Sa-Su 6:30am-6:30pm.) You can walk along the beach to the **Minnie Water Lagoon** or take the Hyawath Rd (just out-side of town) and take the second left to the parking area. Here you can swim or hike the **Headlands Walking Track.**

To enter Yuragyir National Park, continue past the BP store and climb onto the 2WD-friendly dirt track. You can flop down less than a kilometer into the park at the **Ilaroo Camping Area.** There's fresh water at the entrance, it's on the beach, and it accesses the **Angaphora Grove** trail. From here you can walk to the secluded **Rocky Point Camp.** Continuing into the park will take you to **Wilson's Headland,** a 500m walk across dunes to the beach, and, 2km farther along, to the recommended **Boork-room Rest Area.** The **Wilson's Headland Walking Track** (2km each way) takes in ocean blue, intertidal rock platforms, and coastal banks. You can examine tidal pools for sea urchins, starfish, and other echinoderms. Robins and eagles are plentiful, but beware of large **spiders that prey on small birds.** We're serious—these guys are nasty, and so are their enormous webs. **Diggers Camp Village** is buried at the end of the park road; camping here costs $10 per night. At campsites throughout the park, firewood is provided, but you should bring your own water.

■ Byron Bay

The "come for a day, stay for a week" coastal malaise that infects many a wandering traveler on the Holiday Coast of Australia hits its peak in Byron Bay, one of the most popular stops on the Sydney-to-Cairns route. Here, *everyone* stays longer than they had planned. With Byron's excellent family and surfing beaches (champion Denny Wills grew up one block from the beach) and pulsating tourism industry, it's not hard to see why. While Byron boasts palm reading, massage classes, and bead shops, it's more than just commercialized karma. The relaxed, rejuvenating coastal town with a famously "alternative" attitude is nirvana for its diverse devotees: aged hippies, dred-locked backpackers, bleached surfing devotees, punks, ravers, young families, sharp businessmen, and yoga gurus. It seems that Byron's lighthouse, the first in Australia to see the sunrise, is a beacon for travelers the world over.

ORIENTATION

Byron is not on the Pacific Hwy, but is accessible from it from the west or through nearby Bangalow. From the latter, **Bangalow Rd** enters Byron Bay from the south. A turn off a roundabout onto Browning St leads to **Jonson St**, whose six blocks leading north to **Main Beach** constitute the city center, along with the perpendicular streets: **Carlyle, Marvell, Byron, Lawson,** and **Bay St. Fletcher** and **Middleton St** run parallel to Jonson one and two blocks east, respectively. To the east, Lawson St becomes **Lighthouse Rd,** running past **Clarkes Beach, The Pass** surfing spot, **Wategos Beach,** the **lighthouse,** and the Cape Byron lookout. To the west, Lawson becomes **Shirley St** and curves off to **Belongil Beach.** Further west it becomes **Ewingsdale Rd** and passes the **Arts and Industrial Estate** before reaching the Pacific Hwy.

PRACTICAL INFORMATION

Tourist Office: Tourist Information Centre (tel. 6685 8050), by the railway station on Jonson St. Not very helpful. Luggage storage $2 per day. Open daily 10am-4pm.

Buses: Greyhound (tel. 13 20 30) and **McCafferty's** pass through 1-3 times daily on their Sydney-Brisbane route (Sydney 14hr., Brisbane 4hr.). **Kirklands** (tel. 6622 1499) stops in Byron between Brisbane and Lismore (each way M-F 4 per day, Sa-Su 2 per day). **Blanch's Coaches** runs between Byron, Ballina, and Lennox.

Car Rental: Earth Car Rentals (tel. 6685 7472) and **JetSet Travel** (tel. 6685 6554) have the cheapest car rentals in the area, from $35 per day. Earth delivers cars to accommodations within 5km of Byron.

Budget Travel: Byron Bus and Backpacker Centre (tel. 6685 5517), behind the long-distance bus stop, is a booking agency ($3 per-call charge) for transportation, tours, and accommodation. Backpack storage $3 per day. Open daily 7am-7pm. **Backpackers World** (tel. 6685 8858) on Byron St, another booking agency, works on commission and bills itself as the backpacker travel specialist. **Byron Bay Bunk-house** (tel. 6685 8311) also does booking and has great deals on trips up the coast.

Currency and Exchange: ANZ (tel. 6685 6502), 57 Jonson St; **National** (tel. 6613 2265), 33 Jonson St; **Westpac** (tel. 6685 7407), 73 Jonson St. All open M-Th 9:30am-4pm, F 9:30am-5pm. Other **ATMs** across the street from the tourist office.

Taxis: Byron Bay Taxis (tel. 6685 6290 or 855 008) operates 24hr.

Emergency: Dial 000.

Hospital: Byron District Hospital (24hr. tel. 6685 6200) on Wordsworth St.

Police: 24hr. tel. 6685 6300.

Post Office: Located diagonally across from the bus zone toward the beach and next to the community center. Open M-F 9am-5pm. **Postal code:** 2481.

Internet Access: The Internet Cafe and Public Telephone Centre (tel. 6680 8574; fax 6680 8573; email hellobb@norex.com.au), on Byron St between Fletcher and Middleton St. Email $2 for 10min., $10 for 1hr. Cheap phone rates too. Open daily 9:30am-11pm. **Backpackers World** (tel. 6685 8858; email travel@backpackers-world.com.au), also on Byron St. Same rates for the web, but no telnet. **Koo's Cafe** (tel. 6685 5711) on Marvell St has only 1 computer and lots of waiting. $2 for 10min., $11 per hr. Open M-F 7:30am-5pm, Sa 7:30am-3pm.

Phone Code: 02.

If you're stuck for cash on your travels, don't panic. Millions of people trust Western Union to transfer money in minutes to 153 countries and over 45,000 locations worldwide. Our record of safety and reliability is second to none. So when you need money in a hurry, call Western Union.

WESTERN UNION | MONEY TRANSFER®

The fastest way to send money worldwide.®

MCI Spoken Here

Worldwide Calling Made Simple

International Calling As Easy As Possible.

The MCI Card with WorldPhone Service is designed specifically to keep you in touch with the people that matter the most to you.

The MCI Card with WorldPhone Service....

- Provides access to the US and other countries worldwide.
- Gives you customer service 24 hours a day
- Connects you to operators who speak your language
- Provides you with MCI's low rates and no sign-up fees

For more information or to apply for a Card call:
1-800-955-0925

Outside the U.S., call MCI collect (reverse charge) at:
1-916-567-5151

Pick Up the Phone, Pick Up the Miles.

Please cut out and save this reference guide for convenient U.S. and worldwide calling with the MCI Card with WorldPhone Service.

You earn frequent flyer miles when you travel internationally, why not when you call internationally? Callers can earn frequent flyer miles if they sign up with one of MCI's airline partners:

- American Airlines
- Continental Airlines
- Delta Airlines
- Hawaiian Airlines
- Midwest Express Airlines
- Northwest Airlines
- Southwest Airlines
- United Airlines
- USAirways

Your MCI Worldphone Access Numbers

COUNTRY	WORLDPHONE TOLL-FREE ACCESS #
#Singapore	8000-112-112
#Slovak Republic (CC)	00421-00112
#Slovenia	080-8808
#South Africa (CC)	0800-99-0011
#Spain (CC)	900-99-0014
#Sri Lanka (Outside of Colombo, dial 01 first)	440100
#St. Lucia ⋄	1-800-888-8000
#St. Vincent	1-800-888-8000
#Sweden (CC) ♦	020-795-922
#Switzerland (CC) ♦	0800-89-0222
#Syria	0800
#Taiwan (CC) ♦	0080-13-4567
#Thailand ★	001-999-1-2001
#Trinidad & Tobago ⋰	1-800-888-8000
#Turkey (CC) ♦	00-8001-1177
#Turks and Caicos ⋰	1-800-888-8000
#Ukraine (CC) ⋰ ♦	8▼10-013
#United Arab Emirates ♦	800-111
#United Kingdom (CC) To call using BT ■	0800-89-0222
To call using C&W ■	0500-89-0222
#United States (CC)	1-800-888-8000
#Uruguay	000-412
#U.S. Virgin Islands (CC)	1-800-888-8000
#Vatican City (CC)	172-1022
#Venezuela (CC) ⋰ ♦	800-1114-0
Vietnam ●	1201-1022
Yemen	008-00-102

■ Automation available from most locations.
(CC) Country-to-country calling available to/from most international locations.
⋰ Limited availability.
▼ Wait for second dial tone.
► When calling from public phones, use phones marked LADATEL.
■ International communications carrier.
★ Not available from public pay phones.
♦ Public phones may require deposit of coin or phone card for dial tone.
● Local service fee in U.S. currency required to complete call.
▲ Regulation does not permit intra-Japan calls.
⋄ Available from most major cities

And, it's simple to call home.

1. Dial the WorldPhone toll-free access number of the country you're calling from (listed inside).

2. Follow the voice instructions in your language of choice or hold for a WorldPhone operator.
   - Enter or give the operator your MCI Card number or call collect.

3. Enter or give the WorldPhone operator your home number.

4. Share your adventures with your family!

The MCI Card with WorldPhone Service... The easy way to call when traveling worldwide.

MCI Calling Card
123 456 7890 1234
J.D. SMITH
WorldPhone

For more information or to apply for a Card call:
1-800-955-0925

Outside the U.S., call MCI collect (reverse charge) at:
1-916-567-5151

Please cut out and save this reference guide for convenient U.S. and worldwide calling with the MCI Card with WorldPhone Service.

COUNTRY		WORLDPHONE TOLL-FREE ACCESS #
American Samoa		633-2MCI (633-2624)
#Antigua	(available from public card phones only)	#2
		1-800-888-8000
#Argentina (CC)		0800-5-1002
#Aruba ÷		800-888-8
#Australia (CC) ♦	To call using OPTUS ■	1-800-551-111
	To call using TELSTRA ■	1-800-881-100
#Austria (CC) ♦		022-903-012
#Bahamas		1-800-888-8000
#Bahrain		800-002
#Barbados		1-800-888-8000
#Belarus (CC) From Brest, Vitebsk, Grodno, Minsk		8-800-103
From Gomel and Mogilev		8-10-800-103
#Belgium (CC) ♦		0800-100-12
#Belize	From Hotels	815
	From Payphones	817
# Bermuda ÷		1-800-888-8000
# Bolivia (CC) ♦		0-800-2222
#Brazil (CC)		000-8012
#British Virgin Islands ÷		1-800-888-8000
#Brunei		800-011
#Bulgaria		00800-0001
# Canada (CC)		1-800-888-8000
# Cayman Islands		1-800-888-8000
#Chile (CC)	To call using CTC ♦	800-207-300
	To call using ENTEL ■	800-360-180
#China ❖		108-12
	For a Mandarin-speaking Operator	108-17
#Colombia (CC) ♦		980-16-0001
#Costa Rica ♦	Collect Access in Spanish	0800-012-2222
#Cote D'Ivoire		980-16-1000
#Croatia (CC) ★		0800-22-0112
#Cyprus ♦		080-90000
#Czech Republic (CC) ♦		00-42-000112
#Denmark (CC) ♦		8001-0022
#Dominica		1-800-888-8000
#Dominican Republic	Collect Access	1-800-888-8000
	Collect Access in Spanish	1-800-888-1120
#Ecuador (CC) ÷		999-170
#Egypt (CC) ✦		355-5770
El Salvador	(Outside of Cairo, dial 02 first)	800-1767

COUNTRY		WORLDPHONE TOLL-FREE ACCESS #
#Federated States of Micronesia		624
#Fiji		004-890-1002
#Finland (CC) ♦		08001-102-80
#France (CC) ♦		0800-99-0019
French Antilles (CC) (includes Martinique, Guadeloupe)		0800-99-0019
French Guiana (CC)		0-800-99-0019
#Gabon		00-005
#Gambia ♦		00-1-99
#Germany (CC)		0-800-888-8000
#Greece (CC) ♦		00-800-1211
#Grenada ÷		1-800-888-8000
#Guam (CC)		1-800-888-8000
Guatemala (CC) ♦		99-99-189
Guyana		177
#Haiti ÷	Collect Access in French/Creole	193
#Honduras ÷		190
#Hong Kong (CC)		800-96-1121
#Hungary (CC) ♦		00▼800-01411
#Iceland (CC) ♦		800-9002
#India (CC) ❖	Collect Access	000-127
		000-126
#Indonesia (CC) ♦		001-801-11
Iran ÷	(SPECIAL PHONES ONLY)	800-888-8000
#Ireland (CC)		1-800-55-1001
#Israel (CC)		1-800-940-2727
#Italy (CC) ♦		172-1022
#Jamaica ÷		1-800-888-8000
	Collect Access	873
#Japan (CC) ♦	(From Special Hotels only)	
	(From public phones)	
	To call using KDD ■	0039-121▼
	To call using IDC ■	0066-55-121
	To call using ITJ ■	0044-11-121
#Jordan		18-800-001
#Kazakhstan (CC)		8-800-131-4321
#Kenya ❖		080011
#Korea (CC)	To call using KT ■	009-14
	To call using DACOM ■	0309-12
	Phone Booth+÷	0369-14
	Military Bases	Press red button, 03, then *
#Kuwait		800-MCI (800-624)

COUNTRY		WORLDPHONE TOLL-FREE ACCESS #
Lebanon	Collect Access	600-MCI (600-624)
#Liechtenstein (CC) ♦		0800-89-0222
#Luxembourg (CC)		0800-0112
#Macao		0800-131
Macedonia (CC)		99800-4266
#Malaysia (CC) ♦		1-800-80-0012
#Malta		0800-89-0120
#Marshall Islands		1-800-888-8000
#Mexico (CC)	Avantel	01-800-021-8000
	Telmex ▲	001-800-674-7000
	Collect Access in Spanish	01-800-021-1000
#Monaco (CC) ♦		800-90-019
#Montserrat		1-800-888-8000
#Morocco		00-211-0012
#Netherlands (CC) ♦		0800-022-9122
#Netherlands Antilles (CC) ÷		001-800-888-8000
#New Zealand (CC)		000-912
Nicaragua (CC)	Collect Access in Spanish	166
	(Outside of Managua, dial 02 first)	
	From any public payphone ♦	
#Norway (CC) ♦		800-19912
Pakistan		00-800-12-001
#Panama		108
	Military Bases	2810-108
#Papua New Guinea (CC)		05-07-19140
#Paraguay ÷		00-812-800
#Peru		0-800-500-10
#Philippines (CC) ♦	To call using PLDT ■	105-14
	To call using PHILCOM ■	1026-14
	Collect Access via PLDT in Filipino	105-15
	Collect Access via ICC in Filipino	1237-77
#Poland (CC) ÷		00-800-111-21-22
#Portugal (CC) ÷		05-017-1234
#Puerto Rico (CC)		1-800-888-8000
#Qatar ★		0800-012-77
#Romania (CC) ÷		01-800-1800
#Russia (CC) ♦ ÷	To call using ROSTELCOM ■	747-3322
	(For Russian speaking operator)	747-3320
	To call using SOVINTEL ■	960-2222
#Saipan (CC) ÷		950-1022
#San Marino (CC) ♦		172-1022
Saudi Arabia (CC) ÷		1-800-11

FOLD

ACCOMMODATIONS

In summer, especially around Christmas, Byron floods with thousands of tourists; hostels, motels, apartments, and camping grounds are packed, and some non-hostel accommodation prices go up 150-200%. The best advice is to book early, but demand is so high that many hostels do not take reservations in summer. Many unlucky would-be Byron dwellers make do with accommodation in Ballina or Lennox Head.

Hostels

Byron has 11 hostels, and the standard of quality is amazingly high. Price wars have been nasty in recent years, but rates seem to be stabilizing. Most of the hostels have strict 11pm lights-out in the common room, and all have 10am check-out.

Arts Factory Backpackers Lodge, Skinners Shoot Rd (tel. 6685 7709 or 6685 7276; fax 6685 8534; email artsfact@om.com.au; http://www.omcs.com.au/arts-factory). Cross the railroad tracks behind the bus stop and take a right on Burns St to Skinners Shoot Rd. It's worth the 15min. walk from the city center. Weirdly wonderful sleeping options from teepees to island bungalows in a swamp. Daily activities include didgeridoo-making, yoga, and drum workshops. Weekly talent shows and barbecue. Free use of bikes and scooters, volleyball courts, pool, spa. Dorms $16. Cowboy wagon, teepee, or women-only pentagon tent $20. Doubles on island or in bungalows, or twins or doubles in wooden log room $50. Camping $10. VIP, YHA. Discounts for 3-night stays, students, and in the off-season.

Aquarius Backpackers Resort, 16 Lawson St (tel. 6685 7663 or 1800 028 909; fax 6685 7439; email aquarius@om.com.au), at intersection with Middleton St, 2 blocks off Jonson St. Many of the luxurious rooms have two levels, porches, sinks, and fridges; all have beautiful rosewood beds. Pool, kitchen, cafe (everything under $6.50; open daily 8am-noon and 5:30-8pm), 2 bars, and Internet access ($2 for 8min.). Free boogie boards, bikes (for 3hr.), and shuttle bus. Dorms with bath $20; doubles $45, with shared bath and TV $55. Summer $25, $55, $65. VIP, YHA.

Nomads Main Beach Backpackers (tel. 6685 8695; fax 6685 8609), on the corner of Lawson and Fletcher St. Take a right on Lawson from the beach end of Jonson St. A true beauty, with high ceilings and wood lining. Fireplace for winter, rooftop deck for summer. Friendly but surfer-centric and usually quiet. Patio, saltwater pool, secured parking, barbecue, comfortable common room with TV and pool table. Internet access $2 for 10min. Clean bedrooms with individual lockers. Dorms $10-25, with wide seasonal variation. Doubles $45, with bath $60; higher during Christmas. VIP, YHA. Wheelchair accessible.

Cape Byron Hostel (YHA) (tel. 6685 8788 or 1800 652 627; fax 6685 8814), at the corner of Middleton and Byron St. From the tourist office, go 2 blocks down Marvell St and take a left on Middleton. Great owners give this place a homey atmosphere, except there aren't pinball machines, a pool table, and video games in the living room at home. Internet access $2 for 10min. Loft kitchen, nice TV room with VCR, solar-heated pool, outdoor deck and eating area. All-you-can-consume barbecue and wine twice a week ($9). Family-suitable and disabled-accessible rooms are available (no wheelchair access to kitchen). Secured parking. Dorms $15 in winter, $18 in summer, $14 per day weekly winter rate. Doubles and twins $46, $48, $42. Double with bath $55, $60, $50. Extra person $13. "Supplemental" linens $1. YHA.

The Blue Iguana Beachouse, 14 Bay St (tel. 6685 5298), opposite the Surf Club on the corner of Bay and Fletcher St. Lovely, small, and intimate house across from the beach. Sundeck and screen front porch with couches and TV; porch and kitchen open 24hr. High-ceilinged dorms with bath, bureaus, fans, and lockers $18; doubles $60. Winter: $16; $50. 7th night free. Off-street parking. Linens provided.

J's Bay Hostel (YHA), 7 Carlyle St (tel. 6685 8853 or 1800 678 195; email jbay@nor.com.au), across from the Woolworths on Jonson St. Clean, colorful, and cozy, J's has one of the best all-you-can-eat-and-drink barbecue deals with live music and lots of wine for $6 on Tu and F. Game rooms, pool, Internet access ($2 for 10min.). Family-friendly; you can rent a separate building in the courtyard ($55). Free use of bikes, boogie boards, and surfboards. Dorms $10-18 depending on room size; doubles and twins $42, with bath $45-48; $98 weekly per person. YHA. Disabled accessible. "Supplemental" linens $1.

Backpackers Inn on the Beach, 29 Shirley St (tel. 6685 8231; fax 6685 5708). Follow Jonson St, veer left onto Lawson St, cross the railroad tracks and continue on Shirley to the corner of Milton St. Great access to surfing beach. Large, functional, and social. Loft kitchen, common area with Internet access, volleyball, heated pool, barbecue area, pool table. Basic, clean rooms with shelves and ceiling fans. Free bikes and boogie boards. Weekly party and barbecue. Small cafe sells food for under $6. Dorms $17, in summer $18. Doubles $38-45 (seasonal). Wheelchair accessible. YHA, VIP, ISIC, ITC, Nomads. Discounts for 3 or more nights.

Holiday Village Backpackers, 116 Jonson St (tel. 6685 8888; fax 6685 8777), 2 blocks from the tourist center. Motel-style, with large courtyard, picnic tables, pool, spa, TV and video room. Internet access $3 for 15min. Free use of bikes, surfboards, boogie boards, volleyballs, and basketballs. 4-bed dorms $17; doubles $40 ($1 discount with VIP, YHA). Self-contained apartments next door $19 per person. Weekly prices lower; summer rates vary. All-you-can-eat barbecue M and F ($9).

Byron Bay Bunkhouse, 1 Carlyle St (tel. 6685 8311 or 1800 241 600; fax 6685 8258; email byronbay@nrg.com.au), across from the Jonson St Woolworths. Crowded and loud, but it's the cheapest hostel in town. No TV. $1.50-2 dinners every night which can be eaten on the beautiful, often candle-lit terrace. Free pancakes every morning. Live entertainment on weekends. Free bikes and boogie boards. 6- and 8-bed dorms $10 first night, $15 after. $90 weekly.

Belongil Beachhouse, Childe Rd (tel. 6685 7868; fax 6685 7445). 15min. beach walk to Belongil Beach, or 25min. walk from the town center. Cross the railroad tracks to Shirley St and take a right on Kendall St. Belongil is past the Epicentre Club. Gorgeous high-ceilinged wooden lodges, with an earthy, therapeutic feel created by incense-filled walkways and a massage center. The fantastic Belongil Cafe is next door, and the sometimes-nude beach is across the street. Free breakfast 8am. Free bikes, boogie boards, and volleyball. Courtesy bus to town center 5-6 times daily. Dorms $16, in summer $1; doubles $38, $42-45. 7th night free. Motel-style rooms with kitchenette $55-65. Small, beautiful cottages with 2 double beds $80, in summer $120. VIP, YHA.

Cape Byron Lodge, 78 Bangalow Rd (tel. 6685 6445 or 1800 247 070), 15-20min. from the town center down Jonson St. Free bikes, surfboards, boogie boards. Several courtesy buses per day run to town, and the hostel has its own nightlife in the summer. Decor is quirky and jungle-themed. Bathrooms, especially sinks, are small. Common area has a pool table and even older TV, and opens to a courtyard and the small kitchen. Free pancakes the first morning. Dorms $10 the first night in winter, $12 after; up to $18 in summer. Doubles $30; up to $65 in summer. 7th night free.

Other Accommodations

Aussie Way Homestay, 6 Julian Rocks Dr (tel. 6685 6895 or 018 740 963). From Bayshore Dr at the Arts and Industrial Estate, turn right onto Sunrise Blvd and left onto Julian Rocks, 30-40min. walk from town center. Rooms with kitchen $25.

Gumtrees, 5 Burns St (tel. 6685 7842), behind the railway station, has a more central location, laundry, a kitchen, and common room. Rooms $25.

Byron Bayside New Motel, 14 Middleton St (tel. 6685 6004; fax 6685 8552). Take Byron St from Jonson St. Great location near town center and beaches. Large, clean rooms with new furniture, full kitchen, TVs, washer/dryer, dining area phone, and sparkling private bathroom. Off-season single $60; doubles and twins $65; $15 per person after. Price increases $5 for weekends, $20 for holidays and long weekends, $60 Christmas and Easter. Weekly rates cheaper. Wheelchair accessible.

Byron Central Apartments (tel. 6685 8800; fax 6685 8802), on Byron St. Small, spotless rooms with bath, TV, kitchenettes, phones, and tables surround a courtyard pool. Good deal for groups; apartments house 2-4. Daily $65-145, weekly $415-950. Weekends with 2 night min. stay $75 per night (1 night $90), winter $65. Extra child $15. Wheelchair accessible.

First Sun Caravan Park, Lawson St (tel. 6685 6544), near the railroad tracks between Jonson and Butler St. On the main beach; popular with backpackers. Kitchen, barbecue, laundry. Public pool next door. Tent sites for 2 $15 off season,

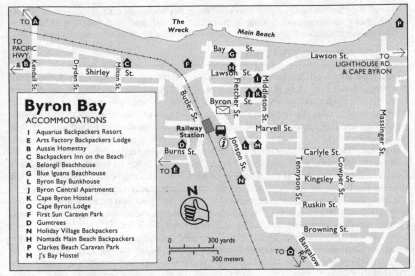

Byron Bay
ACCOMMODATIONS

I	Aquarius Backpackers Resort
E	Arts Factory Backpackers Lodge
B	Aussie Homestay
C	Backpackers Inn on the Beach
A	Belongil Beachhouse
G	Blue Iguana Beachhouse
L	Byron Bay Bunkhouse
J	Byron Central Apartments
K	Cape Byron Hostel
O	Cape Byron Lodge
F	First Sun Caravan Park
D	Gumtrees
N	Holiday Village Backpackers
H	Nomads Main Beach Backpackers
P	Clarkes Beach Caravan Park
M	J's Bay Hostel

$18.50 holidays, $25 Christmas and Easter. Additional person $3.50-6. Cabins $44, $50, $57.50; with toilet $50, $55, $75. Extra person $3.50-8. Linen and TV rental available. $40 deposit for bookings. Wheelchair accessible.

Clarkes Beach Caravan Park (tel. 6685 6496), off Lighthouse Rd on Clarkes Beach. Pretty, well-kept sites. Covered-deck barbecue area with tables. Lights out 9:30pm. Book 1 year ahead for holidays; $40 deposit. Tent sites for 2 $15.50 off-season, $16.50 holidays, $22 Christmas and Easter; weekly $92, $99, $154. Additional person $5-6.50. Cabins with bath $53, $59, $85; weekly $317, $407, $594.

FOOD

Thai Lucy (tel. 6680 8083), Bay Lane, in the alley opposite Hog's Breath Cafe on Jonson St. You'll have to wait to get in, but the food is fantastic. Indoor and outdoor seating. Prices are medium range (main dishes $8-14) but worth it for every savory bite. Takeaway available. BYO. Open Tu-Su noon-3pm and 5:30-10pm.

Supernatural Foods (tel. 6685 5833), at the Arts Factory. Hare Krishna staff prepares delicious, fabulously popular vegetarian dinners ($4-12). Candles and lights hang from ropes suspended from the lofty ceiling. Long wooden tables and booths are surrounded by stone statues, sculptures, and a splashing waterfall.

The Ark (tel. 6685 5880), in the Woolworths parking lot next to the Carpark nightclub on Jonson St. Middle Eastern and Indian specialty restaurant with great tasting and very popular dishes ($3-12). BYO wine. Open Tu-Sa from 6pm.

Belongil Cafe (tel. 6685 7144), next to Belongil Beachhouse. Trendy, high-brow, literary atmosphere. Nightly specials and super-cheap, great-tasting "backpacker specials" (meals $3.50-10). Guests can sit inside at elegant wooden tables or out on the patio. Live entertainment most Su nights. Open daily 8am-late.

Hog's Breath Cafe (tel. 6685 5320), at the beach end of Jonson St, is lively and backpacker-friendly with tons of choices. Aussie meat pie, curly fries, and peas lunch special $5. Burger, beer, and fries or dinner salad $8. Open daily from 11:30am.

Bay Kebabs (tel. 6685 5596), at the corner of Jonson and Lawson St. Unassuming shop serves up delicious takeaway foot-long toasted kebabs for $4.80. Lamb, barbecued chicken, and falafel are all tasty. Open daily 10am-late.

Ringo's Cafe (tel. 6685 6433), Jonson St. Plastered with posters and funky memorabilia, Byron's trendy, intellectual spot has a small secondhand bookshop with occasional poetry and literature readings. At night, the lights go dim, the music's turned up, and candles appear on the tables. Winter dinner specials $7. Burgers $4.50-9. Breakfast $3-9.50. Open daily 8:30am-9pm.

Byron Bay Services Club (tel. 6685 6878), at the southern end of Johnson St. $3.50 lunches daily noon-2pm. Six menu choices, with fish and chips, roast, and frequent $6 dinner specials. W night 2-for-1 specials ($11). Cheap drinks; six-packs $8.

SIGHTS AND ACTIVITIES

The **Byron Bay Lighthouse** is Cape Byron's crowning glory. *(Tours only during school holidays. Grounds open daily year-round 8am-5:30pm.)* A steadily rotating beam pierces through 40km of darkness every night, as it has since first constructed in 1901. The interior is red cedar, the outside concrete. The last lighthouse keeper left in 1988, long after the lighthouse become fully automated. The keepers' cottages are still standing, however. One is a small museum and the other is available for private holiday rental. The site is at the end of Lighthouse Rd, which starts at the east end of Lawson Rd. It can also be reached via a boardwalk that leads to the right along Main Beach to Clarks Beach and the **Captain Cook Lookout.** From here, a walking circuit follows the beach to The Pass, and winds up a steep gradient past Wategos Beach to the **Headland Lookout,** the easternmost point in Australia and an excellent place for spotting dolphins and whales. The lighthouse is just a short distance further; the track then heads through forest and back to Captain Cook Lookout.

Byron's artistic community is flourishing and growing; the best example is the **Michael Commerford Gallery,** 9 Fletcher St (tel. 6680 8433), across from Main Beach Backpackers (open daily 11am-6pm). Many artists have studios around town. To visit them, start at the **Waywood Gallery,** 3 Centennial Circuit (tel. 6685 5808); cross the railroad tracks going north and follow the signs to the Art and Industrial Area. West of town, the **Arts and Industrial Estate,** off Ewingsdale Rd (called Shirley Rd in town), houses paintings, sculptures, and crafts, and sells shoes cheap. Colin Heaney's famous **glassblowing studio,** 6 Acacia St (tel. 6685 7044), is open daily.

Surfing, Kayaking, and Rafting

Boards slung over shoulders, herds of bleach-blond surfers trudge dutifully to Byron's beaches every morning at sunrise. Surf schools entice novices by providing all equipment and soliciting through hostels. A recent and exuberant start-up is **Swell Surf Co.** (tel. 6685 5352 or 018 970 804, after-hours 6685 8250). *(1½hr. group lessons at 12:45pm, $12, 12 people max. 3hr. at 10am or 2pm, $25. 1hr. private lessons $30; for 2 people $50. 1hr. family lessons $60. Board rental $15 for 15hr.)* **Byron Surf School** (tel. 6685 7536 or 1800 707 274) is in the Byron Surf Shop at the corner of Lawson and Fletcher St. *(3hr. group lessons daily 11am and 1pm; also 9am and 3pm in summer; 1st lesson $20, 2nd $18. Surfboard rental $12 half-day, $20 full-day. Wetsuits $5 per day.)* The **East Coast Surf School** (tel. 6685 5989) has group lessons (2½hr., $20) while its agent, **Bay Action,** 14 Jonson St (tel. 6685 7819), also rents equipment. *(Surfboards $5 per hr., $20 per day, $60 per week. Wetsuits $3, $10, $40. Boogie boards $4, $15, $45. Flippers $2, $5, $15.)*

Byron is famous for its excellent surfing spots, located around the bay so that there are good waves no matter what the wind conditions. A crowded spot off Main Beach, **The Wreck** is known for fast waves that break close to the beach. Working down the beach toward the lighthouse, **The Pass** is great for long, challenging rides, but dangerous because of overcrowding, sharp rocks, and boats. The water off **Wategos Beach,** close to The Pass, is best for longer surfboards since the waves are slow and rolling. Again, though, the rocks can be dangerous. **Cosy Corner,** on the other side of the headland from Wategos, is great for northern-wind surfing. On the other side of Main Beach, southern winds bring **Broken Head** and **Belongil Beach** alive.

Ocean kayaking is a great way to see the dolphins, and **Ocean Kayaking Byron Bay** (tel. 6685 7651) runs daily half-day trips past the area's wrecks and reefs to a snorkeling site (equipment provided) and ends with surfing. *($25 if booked directly, pick-up and drop-off included.)* **Byron Bay Sea Kayaks** (tel. 6685 5830) offers $30 trips which include breakfast. Whitewater rafting on the Nymboida River, official training ground for the 2000 Olympics, is possible through **Rapid Rafting Co.** (tel. 6685 8687 or 1800 629 797; email rafting@midcoast.com.au; http://www.qaiadrenaline). *(Full-day trips $99 for backpackers with any card or a picture of your mom. We kid you not. Regular $110.)*

Diving

Most diving is done at **Julian Rocks Marine Park,** 2.5km off Main Beach, widely considered one of the 10 best dive sites in Australia. Julian Rocks has both warm and cold currents and is home to 400 species of fish, including the occasional grey nurse shark. Required medical clearances are $35-50. The dive certification courses go up by $70-100 or more during the summer.

Sundive (tel. 6685 7755), on Middleton St next to the YHA, has an on-site pool and offers five-day PADI certification courses. *($395, in winter $325; required medical check $40. Intro dives $95. Snorkeling trips with equipment $35.)* Courses usually start on Mondays, but weekend certification courses are sometimes offered. The other two dive shops, **Byron Bay Dive and Adventure Centre** (tel. 6685 7149), 111 Jonson St, and smaller **Bayside Scuba** (tel. 6685 8333), at the corner of Lawson and Fletcher St, recently merged and are working out the details. *(4-day SSI certification courses $325, at Christmas $395; medical check $40. Intro dives $110; snorkeling $40.)*

Indoors, Outdoors, and Falling Out of the Sky

Samadhi Flotation Centre (tel. 6685 6905), opposite Woolworths on Jonson St, has massages and cheap, great-value massage classes. *(1hr. float, 1hr. massage $60. Backpacker special $45. Cash only. Must supply own towel. Intro massage classes W, Su and on demand; $30. Book a week ahead in summer. Open daily 9am-6pm.)* Classes include hands-on training, a manual, a certificate, and morning and afternoon tea. The other major massage center, **Relax Haven** (tel. 6685 8304), at the rear of Belongil Beachhouse, 2km from town, is much smaller. *(1hr. float, 1hr. massage $40, including tea.)*

Cabin fever victims might enjoy the small but wildly colored **Wave Rock** (tel. 6680 8777), on Centennial Circuit at the Arts and Industrial Estate. *($10 for unlimited climbing, plus safety instructions, including harness. Boot rental $5. Chalk bag $1. Open daily 10am-10pm, but call if you plan to go after 8:30pm.)* It's a well-plotted indoor rock climbing room with over 50 different climbs. A more unusual option is the **Byron Bay Beach Club Flying Trapeze and Circus School** (tel. 6685 8000), on Bay Shore Dr, with trapeze classes that also squeeze in some tumbling, juggling, trampoline jumping, and more. *(1hr. $14, 2hr. $20. Free pick-up for backpackers.)*

There are two horseback riding companies in the area. **Spirit of Equus** (tel. 6684 7499), 10 minutes from Byron in Tyagarah, has daily two-hour rides at 9am and 2pm on isolated beaches. *($40, pick-up included.)* **Pegasus Park Equestrian Centre** (tel. 6687 1446), about 15 minutes west of Byron, leads rides along Byron Creek. *($30-35; three-hour sunset rides $45.)* In late July, Byron holds a huge **kite festival** on its beaches.

Byron Bay Hang-gliding School (tel. 015 257 699) has flights from the cliffs west of the lighthouse (30min., $95 with pick-up), as does **Flight Zone** (tel. 6685 8768). **Skylimit** (tel. 6684 3711) offers hang-gliding and motorized ultralight tours from $55. For tandem skydiving, **Skydive** (tel. 6684 1323) costs $230-310 depending on height; it's cheaper if paid in cash and booked directly.

Tours

Three companies offer good-value tours of neighboring areas. **Big Day Out** (tel. 1800 629 797), by the Rapid Rafting Co., is perhaps the most elaborate: a full-day trip to Minyon Falls, the Mt. Warning volcanic crater, Nimbin, Border Ranges National Park, and area rainforests, with a $5 pub lunch, is capped off with a 45m (150ft.) bungee jump. *($75, $45 without bungee jump.)* A glass of champagne to celebrate is followed by cold beer for the ride home. For $30, **Jim's Alternative Tours** (tel. 6685 7720) runs a great nine-hour trip through Minyon Falls, Nimbin, Protestor's Falls, and the half-crazy but entirely delightful **Fruit Spirit botanical gardens.** The gardens are cultivated by Dr. Paul Recher, a New York City "environmental refugee" and a first-class character. He walks visitors through his estate and slices open some of his hundreds of fruit species for sampling, all the while explaining the importance of energy conservation. **Bay to Bush** (tel. 6685 6889 or 0418 662 684; email bush@mullum.com.au; http://www.byrontobush.com.au) has similar $30 day tours through Nimbin, Minyon Falls, and the rainforest, that include a stop at a swimming hole and tea. Both companies

---

Maybe It's the Name

The North Coast Steam Navigation Company's 2240-ton vessel *T.S.S. Wollongbar* was once the fastest ship on the east coast of Australia. It ran bi-weekly to Sydney and could hold up to 300 passengers. On May 14th, 1921, however, it became a permanent part of Byron Bay, now known simply as **The Wreck.** On that day, the ship was docked at the now long-gone jetty when a gale sprang up. The ship's captain decided to lift anchor and go to sea. Bad timing: six waves in rapid succession knocked the ship sideways onto the shore and split its back while it was grounded. Hoping to recover some of their losses, the owners sold off whatever they could; some of the ship's furniture is on display around town. The unmoved ship has itself become a Byron landmark, with the stern still visible at low tide. Perhaps it's just an unlucky name: the second *Wollongbar* was torpedoed near Kempsey by a Japanese oceangoing submarine during World War II.

---

also provide shuttle service to the **Channon** ($10 return) and **Bangalow** ($5 return) markets. **The Pioneering Spirit** (tel. 6685 7721 or 014 048 135) offers a full-day guided climb of Mt. Warning. *($20; pick-up, transportation, and light snack included.)*

ENTERTAINMENT

Byron Bay nightlife is crowded but limited. There are two nightclubs that both advertise heavily through hostels and are open until 3am. The **Carpark Nightclub,** in the Woolworths parking lot on Jonson St, is hot, sweaty, loud, and heavy on techno. Expect a haze of smoke both manufactured and secondhand, bright lights, and a raver atmosphere. Wednesdays are backpackers nights with $1.50 sangria, and the popular Martini Night is held some Thursdays. **Cocomangas,** 32 Jonson St (tel. 6685 843), has a slightly calmer and smaller dance floor and tons of drink specials. Monday is 70s night, Tuesday is industrial and techno, Wednesday is ladies' night, and Thursdays feature three DJs. Backpacker party night rotates.

The **Railway Friendly Bar** (tel. 6685 7662), next to the railway station on Jonson St, has meals and live music nightly. It's usually packed with eager, loud backpackers and local twenty-somethings who spill out onto the outdoor patio. The **Great Northern Hotel** (tel. 6685 6454), on the corner of Jonson and Byron St, draws a marginally more mellow crowd and has live music Monday through Wednesday in the front bar, Wednesday through Saturday in the back room. (Cover free or up to $20, depending on the band. Open till 1:15am daily.)

The **Hog's Breath Cafe** (see **Food,** p. 181) is a great place to start the night, with excellent margaritas. Across the street on the corner of Bay St is the gorgeous and relaxed **Beach Hotel** (tel. 6685 6402), a favorite of slightly older drinkers, with a garden bar and huge patio that is uncovered when weather permits but refreshing regardless. Live entertainment plays on one of the best sound systems in Byron Wednesday through Sunday, almost always for free. There's also a backpackers special of $2 burgers and $1 soft drinks on Tuesday nights. (Open till midnight.)

Out of the town center on the way to the Arts and Industrial Estate is the enormous **Epicentre** studio complex (tel. 6685 6979), home once or twice a month to wild 9pm to 9am no-alcohol raves which attract 1500 or more partiers ($15-20). It's also sometimes used as a concert venue ($15-50). **Pighouse Flicks** (tel. 6685 5828 after 4:30pm), at the Piggery on Skinners Shoot Rd next to the Arts Factory, shows art and foreign (read: American) films three times nightly (4 times on Sa; $8.50, $7.50 concession). The theater features a black-lit foyer, large, comfy seats, and room to stretch out in the first couple of rows. You can take off your shoes, so BYO socks. There's a movie/dinner deal (from $11.50) at the nearby vegetarian restaurant.

NEW ENGLAND

A lovely, scenic alternative to the coast, with rustic beauty and a cooler year-round climate, the New England Highway begins in Sydney, continues along Hwy 15 to Brisbane, and is serviced by most major bus lines. Most of this 380km stretch of road is dotted with inviting country towns. The highway traverses the **Hunter Valley,** with scenery transforming from Newcastle's industrial machines and coal ships, along Maitland's vineyards, past Singleton's army base and mines, and through Muswellbrook's coal mines and Scone's horse stud farms. It then begins the dramatic climb up the Dividing Range from Tamworth to Armidale, in New England proper.

The **national parks** in the New England region (clustered in southern Queensland and northern New South Wales) are worth re-routing an itinerary for. There are absolutely no entrance fees, and almost all of the parks have picnic areas, camping sites, toilets, fireplaces, and spectacular views. Unfortunately, most are accessible only by vehicle (some only by 4WD), although there are companies attempting to start cheap shuttle service; call the Armidale Visitors Centre (see p. 190) for an update.

■ Hunter Valley

Though not actually part of New England, the Hunter Valley marks the beginning of the New England Hwy and is an excellent daytrip from Newcastle or Sydney or a pleasant stop on the way north. It's home to 77 wineries, many of which have an international reputation for producing high quality wines at reasonable prices. The region specializes in *shiraz,* a spicy, peppery number, and the dry *semillon.* Most of the wineries are in the lower Hunter Valley, clustered northwest of Cessnock; seven are in the upper Hunter area, centered in Denman, one hour north. The best time to visit wine country is mid-week, when population and prices are lower than on weekends. **Keans Travel Express** (1800 043 339; fax 4990 6186) runs through the Hunter Valley twice daily during the week and once daily on weekends en route between Sydney and Tamworth. (Sydney to Scone $37, students $30, children $19; to Muswellbrook $31, $25, $16; to Singleton $28, $23, $14; to Cessnock $24, $19, $12.) Most Hunter Valley accommodations raise their prices from 10 to 100% on Friday and Saturday; some require that you take two-night B&B packages. Book ahead.

■ Cessnock and Towns in the Lower Valley

From Newcastle, the Valley's closest town is Cessnock, 10 to 15 minutes away from the vineyards. The **Cessnock Visitors Centre** (tel. 4990 4477; fax 4991 4518), 1.2km off Vincent St on Abeudare Rd in Turner Park, has information on the wineries and weekly specials on accommodations and meals (open M-F 9am-5pm, Sa 9:30am-5pm, Su and public holidays 9:30am-3:30pm). The *Hunter Valley Wine Country* visitor information booklet is indispensable. **Amico's,** 138 Wollombi Rd (tel. 4911 1995) specializes in Italian, Mediterranean, and Mexican food; its huge servings of pasta on Monday are the best deal in town (open daily 7pm-late). At the **Tallawanta Hotel and Motel** (tel. 4998 7854), on Broke Rd, you can cook your own meat for $8.50-$14 including an unlimited salad and pasta bar ($7.50 for salad and pasta bar only; open daily 11:30am-3pm, Su-Th 6-8:30pm, F-Sa 6-9:30pm).

The **Chardonnay Sky Motel** (tel. 4991 4812), on Allandale Rd, about a 10-minute drive out of town, has backpacker accommodations with private baths for $20, including continental breakfast (motel doubles $49, on weekends $95). **Cessnock Caravan Park** (tel. 4990 5819) on the corner of Allandale and Branxton Rd, 2km north of town, has a pool, laundry facilities, and backpackers accommodations ($15, $20 on weekends), cabins ($48, $65), on-site caravans ($30, $40), and campsites ($6 per person, powered $7). Discounts are offered for extended stays. There is no public transportation to the park on the weekends; taxis from town cost $6-8 (wheelchair accessible). The **Royal Oak Hotel** (tel. 4990 2366), at the corner of Vincent St and Aberdare Rd about 500m from the bus station, has large bedrooms, a TV lounge, and a modern, fully equipped kitchen. (Singles $25, twins and doubles $40; $5 less for 2 nights or more; $5 more per person on weekends; light breakfast included.) Across Vincent St is the **Black Opal Hotel** (tel. 4990 1070), a surprisingly nice lodging with an outside beer garden (4-bed dorms and singles $20, weekend $25; doubles and twins $40, $50). Closer to the vineyards at 136 Wollombi Rd is the **Australia Hotel** (tel. 4990 1256) with singles, doubles, triples and quads for $15-$20 per person, and $25 with full cooked breakfast.

Maitland is 30 minutes east of Cessnock along the Hunter River. A historic city, it once rivaled Sydney as a potential state capital. Its 150-year-old buildings continue to earn it architectural praise, and are the stars of the town's Heritage Walk. Artistic, cultural, and vintage train exhibitions are among the main objects of attention during Maitland's **Heritage Month Celebrations** every April. The **Visitor's Information Centre** (tel. 4933 2611) is in Ministers Park, near the junction of High St and the New England Hwy (open daily 9am-5pm). The **Imperial Hotel** (tel. 4933 6566) on High St offers singles over a pub for $30 (doubles and twins $50) with breakfast.

Morpeth is a five-minute drive north of Maitland. It has many tearooms, art collections, and antique shops, as well as a "weird and wonderful teapot exhibition" each August. Its biggest event is the two-day **Jazz Festival** (tel. 4933 6240) held in May.

■ Towns in the Upper Hunter Valley

Well northwest of Cessnock, **Scone** (pop. 9375) is a small but pretty town which prides itself on being the horse capital of Australia. The distinction is owed to the annual week-long **Scone Horse Festival** in mid-May (May 9-17, 1999), which includes an air show featuring WWII fighter jets. The week culminates in three days of thoroughbred racing for the Scone Cup. The racecourse is five minutes from the town center. Large thoroughbred stud farms sprawl alongside the New England Hwy near the town, and many are open for tours. The **tourist information center** (tel. 6545 1526), at the corner of Kelly (New England Hwy) and Susan St, across from Elizabeth Park, has a **Countrylink** office (tel. 13 22 32). (Open daily 9am-5pm.) The **Scone YHA** (tel. 6545 2072), on Segenhoe Rd, is 8km off the highway in a converted country school house near horse stud farms. It has a kitchen, barbecue, and campfires (dorms $14, in summer $17; doubles $30, $36). The **Highway Caravan Park,** 248 New England Hwy (tel. 6545 1078), is a place to pitch a tent (sites for 2 $8, powered $10; caravans $20; extra person $5). **The Station Cafe** (tel. 6545 2144), in the railroad station, makes tomato soup to die for (open M-F 11am-4pm, Sa-Su 10am-4pm).

Twenty-five kilometers and a scenic tourist drive away from Scone, **Muswellbrook** is most proud of its abundance of historical buildings, many of them visible on the 4.5km Muswellbrook Heritage walk which begins at the Old Tea House on Bridge St (New England Hwy). The highway is also the site of a living **Vietnam Memorial,** a grove of 519 trees that represent each the Australian casualties of that conflict. The **tourist office,** 87 Hill St (tel. 6541 4050), just off Bridge St, shares a building with the Upper Hunter Wine Centre (open daily 9am-5pm). **Eatons Hotel** (tel. 6543 2403), on Bridge St, has basic singles ($20), and doubles and twins ($30). **Pinaroo Caravan Park** (tel. 6543 3905), on the New England Hwy, has tent sites for two ($10; powered $13) and basic cabins ($30). Forty-five kilometers southwest of Muswellbrook, **Singleton** (pop. 18,000) is the home of the **world's largest sundial.**

■ Wineries and Tours

Most wineries are open daily for free tastings and occasional tours from 10am to 5pm, although some are only open on weekends. If you're able, the best time to tour is during the week, since the wineries can become very crowded on weekends. Of the 77 wineries, the largest are **McGuigans** (which also has a cheese outlet with free tastings), **McWilliams, Mt. Pleasant, Lindemans, Tyrrells,** and **Rothbury Estate.** The smaller ones are not as glitzy, but are generally more relaxed. Check with the tourist office about free tours of individual wineries.

Unless you have a car, you'll need to arrange some kind of tour to see the wineries. The **Vineyard Shuttle Service** (tel. 4991 3655, mobile 019 327 193) makes pick-ups at accommodations and shuttles folks to designated wineries from 10am to 5pm for $20 (every 20min.). A one-day tour with unlimited stops and an evening restaurant shuttle costs $28. **Hunter Vineyard Tours** (tel. 4991 1659, mobile tel. 018 497 451) has pick-ups from Newcastle and Maitland for $34 (with lunch $50). Pick-ups from Cessnock and the vineyards are $29 (with lunch $45). **Shadows** (tel. 4990 7002, mobile tel. 019 459 307) also offers full-day tours for $30 ($45 with lunch). **Jump Up Creek Vineyard Tours,** based in Sydney (tel. 6574 7252, mobile tel. 0417 416 297), specializes in the smaller wineries and offers small, personalized tours, with pick-ups from Cessnock, Colburn, Singleton, sometimes Maitland and Newcastle, and the vineyards ($27.50; Sa $30). **Wonderbus** (tel. 9555 9800) offers special deals for backpackers on daytrips from Sydney ($65). **Grapemobile** (tel. 4991 2339, mobile tel. 0418 404 039) has day bicycle tours, including lunch, for $98. Bicycle rental is available from the Hermitage Lodge (tel. 4998 7639) in Pokolbin ($15 per half-day, $25 per full-day). Horse-drawn carriage tours are available through **Paxton Brown** (tel. 4998 7362) and **Brokenback Trail Tour** (tel. 4998 7305) and range from $48. If you'd like a running start on wine tasting, **Hunter Cellars School of Wine** (tel. 4998 7466) has daily lessons from 10am to 12:30pm ($20, book ahead). You can also see take a somewhat quicker and higher-adrenaline tour of the wineries with **NSW Skydiving Centre** (tel. 4990 1000) at the Chardonnay Sky Motel, 210 Allendale Rd (tandem jump plus two nights accommodation $45).

Springtime brings additional entertainment to the wineries. **Opera in the Vineyards,** October 16-17, 1999, offers opera, wine and cheese tastings, and fireworks (Sa night tickets $39, Su afternoon $29). For more information, call 1800 675 875 or, for bookings, 9266 4811. Another winery, Tyrell's Long Flat paddok in Pokolbin, northwest of Cessnock, hosts **Jazz in the Vines,** a full-day music extravaganza that will fall on October 30, 1999 (tickets $22; call 4938 1345 to order).

■ Tamworth

Tamworth (pop. 50,000) calls itself the country music capital of Australia, largely on the basis of its **Country Music Festival,** which brings famous crooners and hordes of people to town each January. For the rest of the year country music is scarce, save for cheesy tourist attractions including a giant golden guitar and a concrete slab with handprints of country artists. Up until the mid-1980s, Tamworth was a big dairy region, but when the government-regulated industry collapsed, many farmers started to plant olive trees instead. The tourist office, perhaps sensing a better souvenir market, prefers to embrace Tamworth's musical side, and the building is fashioned in the shape of a guitar. An olive would have been too easy.

ORIENTATION AND PRACTICAL INFORMATION Tamworth is 380km north of Sydney on the New England Hwy (which enters the town from the east and departs south) and is a convenient rest stop on a journey to Brisbane. The town center lies along eight blocks of **Peel St** between Kable St and Bicentennial Park, on the bank of the Peel River. Peel St is parallel to and one block southwest of the highway. The **Macquarie St** rotary and **Viaduct Park** are on the northwest side of Peel St. **Marius St,** which houses the **railway station** between Bourke and Brisbane St, runs parallel to Peel St. **Brisbane St** continues west across the Peel River, becomes **Bridge St** in West Tamworth, and leads to the turn-off to the westward-leading Oxley Hwy.

The **information center** (tel. 6766 9422; email tour_ism@tamworth.nsw.gov.au) is at the corner of Peel and Murray St (open M-F 8:45am-4:35pm, Sa-Su 9am-5pm). Several **banks** and international **ATMs** are in the center of Peel St, and the **police station** and **post office** are on Fitzroy St. Around the corner on the New England Hwy, **Internet access** is available at the **library** (tel. 6755 4457; email tcclib@tamworth.nsw.gov.au; 30min. $2; open M-Th 10am-8pm, F 10am-6pm, Sa 9am-noon).

ACCOMMODATIONS AND FOOD Most rooms for January's Country Music Festival are gone by the previous March, but throughout the rest of the year, beds are plentiful. The centrally located hotels are a better option than the more expensive motels. The only hostel in town is **Country Backpackers,** 169 Marius St (tel. 6761 2600), opposite the railway station. Brand-new and impeccably clean, it boasts an **art gallery** including reproductions of time-honored masterpieces with an Australian country twist. (Dorms $15-18; doubles $35. Breakfast included.) **Tamworth Hotel,** 147 Mapilus St (tel. 6766 2923), opposite the railway station, is the most upscale pub of the lot; its tiny rooms have a bureau, sink, and dresser (singles $25; doubles $35). **Tattersall's Hotel** (tel. 6766 2114) is at the east end of Peel St, a 15-minute walk from the city center. The rooms are large and nicely furnished, but the real reason to stay is the **Noses of Fame** (a spoof on Tamworth's Hands of Fame), which ingloriously line a small patch of pavement out back. (Singles or twins $15 per person.) **Paradise Caravan Park** (tel. 6766 3120) is next to the info center bordering the creek, and has laundry, barbecue facilities, and a playground.(Tent sites $11.50 for 2 people, with power $16. Cabins for 2 with bath $50; on-site caravans $31. 7th night free. Additional person $5. Surcharge of 25% on long weekends and during the festival.)

There is a **Coles** Supermarket on Peel St and a **Woolworths** on Bridge St. Pub bistros cluster around Peel St. Lunch (noon–2pm) costs around $5, while dinner (from 6pm) runs $6-12. **Brumby's Homestead Cafe** (tel. 6766 4512), in the Shearer Arcade at Fitzroy and Peel St, serves good lunches for around $7. The **Inland Cafe,** 407 Peel St (tel. 6761 2882), is a local fave, with tasty sandwiches ($5-6) and meaty or veggie mains ($6.50-14.50; open M-W 7am-6pm, Th-Sa 7am-11pm, Su 9am-5pm).

SIGHTS AND ENTERTAINMENT You don't have to be a country music fan to enjoy Tamworth—you just need a high tolerance for kitsch. The turn-off for **The Country Collection** (tel. 6765 2688) is marked on the New England Hwy by a gaudy 12m golden guitar. *(Gift shop open daily 9am-5pm, museum closes a bit earlier. $5, children $2, family of 5 $12.)* The complex features a wax "Gallery of Stars" museum and a gem and mineral display. The popular **Hands of Fame Cornerstone** is on the corner of the New England Hwy and Kable Ave; make sure to check out Tattersall's Hotel's Noses of Fame as well (see above).

Parallel to Peel St is **Bicentennial Park,** a quiet, reclusive stretch of greenery, ponds, and picnic tables with a delightful bit of masonry on its rocks. *(Open daily 8am-4:45pm.)* If you look closely, you'll find more than a dozen reliefs of animals jutting off the stones near the water fountain. A 90-minute, 4.7km **Heritage Walk** loops through the town. The tourist office has guides. For a more rigorous walk, try the **Kamilaroi Walking Track,** a three-hour scenic tour beginning with a bird's eye view at **Oxley Scenic Lookout** at the top of White St. The track passes by **Endeavor Drive Marsupial Park,** at the top of Brisbane St. The **Tamworth City Gallery** (tel. 6755 4459) shares a building on Marius St with the library and houses Australian and European art. *(Open M-F 10am-5pm, Sa 9am-noon, Su 1-4pm.)* **Phil's Adventure Tours** (tel. 6767 0200) has paragliding ($65), tandem skydiving ($250), and gliding ($30).

Bring out the cowgirl inside at one of the **"Jackaroo and Jillaroo schools"** in the Tamworth area, with crash courses on how to ride horses, pen sheep, train dogs, milk cows, lasso, and operate farm equipment. Certificates and, often, help finding jobs are received upon completion. **Leconfield** (tel. 6769 4230) has highly recommended 11-day camps. *($495; free pick-up and drop-off from Tamworth. Shorter courses $60 per day, 3 day minimum.)* **Echo Hills Station** (tel. 6769 4217 or 1800 810 242) offers a six-day course. *($349, YHA/VIP $339; breakfast included.)* **Oakey Creek** (tel. 6766 1698 or 1300 300 043) has the same prices; an additional week costs $229.

Outside of the January festival, don't expect to find much actual country music here. Most of the time, the **RSL Club** (tel. 6766 4661), behind Peel St on Kable Ave, is the only music venue. *(Free shows downstairs Th-Sa 8pm.)* On the third Saturday of each month, the **Tamworth Country Theater** in the RSL (tel. 1800 803 561) hosts a lively evening of country singing ($12). The **Tamworth Regional Entertainment Centre,** opening in fall 1998, will feature touring events and exhibitions. The **Impe-**

rial pub draws a young crowd and, in October, even a few celebrities, during its month-long outdoor beach-theme party. *(Live rock music Th-Sa nights.)*

■ Oxley Highway

The New England Hwy (15) reaches a juncture at **Bendemeer,** 41km north of Tamworth. Here, you can head coastward along the **Oxley Hwy** (follow signs to Walcha), a stretch of raw and remote national parks that are nothing short of spectacular. From Armidale, follow the New England Hwy south for 22km to Uralla where a tourist route takes a shortcut directly to Walcha along the Oxley Hwy. The Oxley meets Port Macquarie at the coast, 178km east from Walcha.

■ Walcha

Small and unexciting, Walcha is nevertheless a useful jumping-off point for **Oxley Wild Rivers National Park** (see **Apsley and Tia Gorges,** below, and p. 191). Relevant pamphlets and wisdom abound at the **tourist information center** (tel. 6777 1075) in the Old School Art Gallery on the Oxley Hwy. There's also an exhibition room with Aboriginal art and artifacts (open M-F 9am-4:30pm). For lodging or a hearty meal, try the **Commercial Hotel** (tel. 6777 2551), on Oxley Lane off the Oxley Hwy ($20 per person, breakfast included). The diminutive **Aboriginal Museum and Cultural Center,** 38 Derby St, is worth a few spare moments (open M-F 9am-4:30pm).

■ Apsley and Tia Gorges

Crashing cascades carving cliffs are the reason behind the moniker for **Oxley Wild Rivers National Park.** The highlights of the eastern end of this park are these must-see waterfalls, which are most easily accessed from the Oxley Hwy. The larger part of the park is usually accessed from Waterfall Way, closer to Armidale; see p. 191. About 15km south of Walcha and 83km from Armidale is the turn-off for the **Apsley Gorge,** just a kilometer off the highway. This mighty gorge will take your breath away. At the far carpark (2min.) is a stairway leading partway into the gorge, with a good view of the falls. In order to swim in the pool below, you must go bush at your own risk. Beware of sometimes-submerged boulder just in front of the falls. The 2km **Oxley Walk** (45min.) takes you around the rim of the gorge and across a bridge over the Oxley River. Camping and fresh water are available. Nineteen kilometers south of the Apsley Falls entrance is the small picnic and camping area of **Tia Falls.** A rim walk shows off the **Tia Gorge.**

■ Werrikimbe National Park

Remoteness and the cruddiness of access roads have preserved the rugged wilderness of Werrikimbe National Park. This is a camper's paradise, and many of them choose to stay for days and weeks, gleefully veering from the paths into the depths of temperate and subtropical rainforest, eucalypt forest, and snow gum woodlands. Consult District Managers in Armidale (tel. 6773 7211; fax 6771 1894; email armidale@npws.gov.au) or Port Macquarie (tel. 6583 5518) to discuss expeditions beyond the western section of the park, discussed here. Look closely for the road signposted Werrikimbe National Park and Moorback Rd, which appears 40km south of Walcha. The first 15km of this track isn't bad, but the twisting, climbing, and loose gravel may wear on conventional vehicles. Inside the park, the tracks crumble but remain flat and direct. You can either go left a few kilometers to Moorback Rest Area or right to Cobcroft's Rest Area. **Moorback** is set amidst snow gum woodlands and by the Moorback Creek. You can commence walks along the creek or go deeper into the forest. Campsites at **Cobcroft** are set in open eucalypt forest with a few tree ferns for seasoning. The **Carrabeen Walk** passes through an adjacent warm temperate rainforest. The vivid passage crosses through gullies of Antarctic Beeches whose gnarled, web-like bases take astounding shapes. In places, strangler vines have taken over the beeches and eucalypts. This one-hour walk can be extended by connecting with other paths. The campsites have pit toilets, campfire grates, and firewood.

■ Armidale

Armidale (pop. 22,000) is a secure, comfortable, country town laced with creeklands and hilly sidestreets. Two cathedrals complement the many historical and architecturally significant buildings decorating its streets. The town supports various small museums and galleries, although shopping centers are the most popular attractions. The **University of New England's** campus, 5km from Armidale's center, brings energy and business for a healthy number of pubs. The transitions between the brisk winters and dry, hot summers bring life and color, from the spring-green awakening from winter's hibernation to the vibrant reds and yellows of autumn that welcome the annual infusion of students. Conveniently positioned at the beginning of "Waterfall Way" (see p. 191), Armidale is a base for many surrounding national parks.

ORIENTATION AND PRACTICAL INFORMATION Armidale's main drag is **Marsh St.** The **Visitors Centre** (tel. 6772 4655 or 1800 627 736; fax 6771 4486; email armvisit@northnet.com.au; http://www.com.au/neiss/armitour) and **bus terminal** are at 82 Marsh St, behind the Pizza Hut. (Visitors Centre open M-F 9am-5pm, Sa 9am-4pm, Su 10am-4pm. Luggage storage $1 per day.) **McCafferty's, Greyhound,** and **Countrylink** all offer buses to Brisbane, Sydney, and Melbourne, but McCafferty's boasts the best deals. McCafferty's buses travel to Brisbane (6½hr.; $48, $38 student) and Sydney (9hr.; $53, $42 student). Greyhound offers a Melbourne trip (20hr.; $118, $95 student). The travel agency in town is **Harvey World Travel** (tel. 6772 1177 or 1800 620 318) at Beardy and Dangar St, by the end of the Beardy St Mall. (Open M-F 9am-5:30pm, Sa 9:30am-12:30pm). One block up Marsh St is the start of the **Beardy St Mall,** Armidale's cluster of upscale shops and cafes. A supermarket, KMart complex, and **Woolworths** are at the far end of the Mall, and **banks** and the **post office** are at the center. **Commonwealth Bank** (tel. 6772 9555) sits on the mall and sports an **ATM** (open M-Th 9:30am-4pm, F 9:30am-5pm). Also on the Beardy St Mall is the **Ancal Pharmacy** (tel. 6772 2317. Open M-F 8:45am-6pm, Sa 8:45am-1pm).

ACCOMMODATIONS, FOOD, AND ENTERTAINMENT All accommodations can be booked through the visitors center. The **Wicklow Hotel** (tel. 6772 2421; fax 6772 2316) is directly opposite the tourist office on the corner of Marsh and Dumaresq St. Referred to as the "pink pub" for its unusual facade, it's friendly and family-oriented. (Singles $26; doubles $36; showers $2.) Two kilometers east of town on Grafton Rd., past the racecourse, is the **Pembroke Caravan Park** (tel. 6772 6470). The adjoining **YHA hostel** is packed with bunks. The grounds have a swimming pool, tennis courts, and a gorgeous hilly backdrop. The entire park is clean, comfortable, and well organized. (Dorms $14; tent sites $12; caravan sites $14.50. Cabins and on-site caravans available. Arrive before 9pm. Price depends on season.)

Many of the pubs have bistros with cheap or all-you-can-eat meals. The **Wicklow's** $10 dinners are delicious; they also have $2 cappuccino and freshly squeezed orange juice. In the winter, you can eat in front of a log fire. The historic **New England Hotel,** on the corner of Faulkner and Beardy St, has great steak dinners and has been serving beer since it opened in 1857. **Rumors** (tel. 6772 3084) is the most popular cafe on the mall, though loaded with the pretentious erudite. The cafe window displays advertisements for concerts, raves, and temporary employment. Salads, pastas, and sandwiches cost around $7 (open M-F 8am-5:30pm, Sa 8am-2pm). For a cup of coffee with a country feel, nothing beats the **Walnut Tree** at 130 Marsh St. Housed in a Hansel-and-Gretel-like cottage, it has mobiles hanging from the rafters and small pottery bowls on each table (open daily).

Students hang out at the campus bistro, and they also frequent pubs in town. **Sevens,** on the east mall, is a popular student night spot. **Tattersall's Hotel,** "Tatt's" (tel. 6772 2247), is owned by the student union. Live bands play there on weekends. The

New England Hotel (tel. 6772 7622) has a nightclub upstairs that's open till 3am Saturday and Sunday. The **Ex-Serviceman's Club** is popular for its cheap drinks. The **Belgrave Twin Cinema** (tel. 6772 2856) screens recent releases and art films daily. Armidale's biggest festival is the annual **Wool Expo,** a one-week event in early May.

SIGHTS AND ACTIVITIES The visitors center has guides for the 3km or 6.2km **Heritage Walking Tours,** covering 35 National Trust buildings in the city, and the two-hour **Heritage Drive,** a 25km tour of many of the same buildings, and more. Following Marsh St south and up the hill, to the corner of Kentucky St, leads to the much-praised **New England Regional Art Museum** (tel. 6772 5255). *(Open daily 10am-5pm. Free.)* The museum has over 3000 paintings, but limited display space, so exhibits rotate every six weeks. As you come out of the art museum, on your right is the **Aboriginal Cultural Centre and Keeping Place** (tel. 6771 1249). *(Open M-F 9am-5pm, Sa-Su 2-5pm. Admission $3, concessions $1.50.)* The **Folk Museum** on the corner of Faulkner and Rusden St stores a small collection of cultural and architectural objects, including a reproduction of a colonial house and a room devoted to Aboriginal art. *(Open daily 1-4pm. Free.)*

Horseback riding tours can be arranged through **Harlow Park** (tel. 6778 4631) or **Beambolong** (tel. 6771 2019). **Wilderness Rides** (tel. 6778 4631) offers overnight tours for experienced riders through the New England Blue Mountain Gorge. The visitors center has information and maps on New England fishing. **Fly Fish New England** (tel. 6772 5085) or **Matt's Sport Safari** (tel. 6772 8689) offer tours.

A 5.7km cycleway runs along Dumaresq Creek to the **University of New England.** By car, follow signs from Marsh St and you'll reach Madgwick Dr and Trevenna Rd within five minutes. To reach the **Sports Union** (tel. 6773 2316), follow signs which should take you left·off Trevenna Rd before reaching the academic campus. *(Open M-F 7am-10pm, Sa-Su 8am-7pm.)* Visitors can play squash ($8), tennis ($6, under lights $7), swim indoors ($2), use the gym ($6), play basketball (free), and rent mountain bikes ($17 per day, $35 per week).

▓ Waterfall Way

Waterfall Way (Rte 78) runs east-west between Armidale and the north coast of New South Wales. Along the way, the aptly named tourist route passes four excellent national parks with accessible campgrounds, several small towns with pub accommodation, and the charming town of **Bellingen** (see p. 161). The 169km route is well worth the trip, but beware the steep winding of the highway in some places. In addition to the parks listed below, the **Ebor Falls,** approximately 42km west of Dorrigo and just 600m off the highway, are a killer photo op. A walk of 600m from the car park leads to a most scintillating vantage point.

■ Oxley Wild Rivers National Park

Oxley is an extensive park of rough, rocky terrain with a network of gorges, campsites, bushwalks, and appropriately wild rivers. The Armidale District maintains park facilities. Useful pamphlets with photos and maps can help you choose a site to camp or picnic; contact the Armidale **NPWS** (tel. 6773 7211; fax 6771 1894; email armidale@npws.nsw.gov) or **Armidale Visitors Centre** (tel. 1800 627 736; email visit@northnet.com.au). See also p. 189 for information on **Apsley and Tia Gorges** at the more remote eastern end of the park.

Dangars Gorge is an easy trip from Armidale. With the 120m Dangars Falls as the centerpiece, the rest area is equipped with barbecue facilities, firewood, pit toilets, and a series of walks ranging from the **Gorge Lookout** path (100m) to 10-14km half-day walks. An eroding, unofficial path leads down to the Gorge riverbed and a deep pool. The trail zigzags along a steep gradient; allow two hours for the return climb. Take Gangarsleigh Rd (Kennedy St) from Armidale for about 11km, then go left at the Perrott's War Memorial; 10km of gravel lead to the Gorge. **Long Point** is a secluded wilderness area with campsites in an open eucalypt forest adjacent to rare **dry rain-forest.** It has earned World Heritage status as one of the few world spots with this vegetation. Dry rainforest sounds oxymoronic, but the main criterion for rainforest classification is a closed canopy forest ceiling. The turn-off for Long Point appears 40km east of Armidale along Waterfall Way. Seven kilometers of sealed track passes through the two-horse town of Hillgrove where a left turn skips onto an adequate dirt track that reaches the park 20km later. There are pit toilets, picnic tables, and fresh water at the site. Here also begins an easy 1.5km walk and the 5km **Chandler Walk** (2-2½hr.). The excellent Chandler Walk takes you through a tunneled grove of mosses, vines, and the yellow-spotted Hillgrove Gums, which are only found in this area. A tremendous lookout along the walk surveys the valley and Chandler River.

The **Wollombi Falls** are just 2km off the highway by bitumen after a turn-off 40km east of Armidale. This gorge is severe and the surrounding forest rugged and dry. A medium to strenuous 1.2km walk leads to the river, and a 700m path to a gorge look-out. The strenuous 5.6km **Chandler River Track** takes nearly four hours to complete. A bush camping site near the entrance to the gorge area is equipped with basic facilities and fire pits.

■ New England National Park

New England National Park offers some fabulous bushwalking trails. Its densely vegetated basalt cliffs formed from several lava flows from the Ebor volcano over 18 million years ago. Even in summer the park gets chilly, and in winter expect cold. Near the park entrance, 85km from Armidale and 75km from Dorrigo, is the **Thungutti Campground.** Nearby begin the Wright's Lookout Walk (2½hr.) and Cascades Walk (3½hr.). Most people skip these outskirts to head for the **Point Lookout Picnic Area,** the park's hub. Point Lookout Rd heads up to the area; about 11km is gravel, 2.5km sealed. There are toilets and fire pits there, as well as ample parking. Point Lookout marks the start of 9 walks ranging from 5min. to 3½hrs., and these can be linked up for nearly a full day of walking. The Point Lookout, a vertical escarpment rising 1564m from sea level, surveys dense forest which is often shrouded in mist. **Eagles Nest Track** (2hrs.) passes straight down and along the steep cliffside. It takes some ingenuity to negotiate rocky areas through moss-covered beeches, water sprays which turn to icicles in winter, and snow gum woodland. Life spills out from all sides, especially birds; you may spot a lyrebird. The difficult **Lyrebird Walk** links with the Eagles Nest Track and can be made a 2km (1hr.) route or a 7km (3½hr.) circuit through cool temperate rainforest.

■ Cathedral Rock National Park

The area 70km east of Armidale off the Armidale-Grafton Rd is best known for its granite boulders, wildflowers, and eucalypt forests. Park residents include grey kangaroos, wallabies, cockatoos, and wedge-tailed eagles. It is generally regarded as less interesting than Dorrigo and New England National Parks. Three walking tracks range from 1km to 10.4km. Picnic and camping facilities are available at Barokee and Native Dog Creek Rest Areas. Contact the Dorrigo Park ranger (tel. 6657 2309).

■ Dorrigo National Park

Dorrigo is one of these marquee National Parks that's close enough to a prosperous town (Bellingen) to set up and support a **Rainforest Centre** (tel. 6657 2309), complete with educational displays and audiovisuals, and a gift shop staffed by rangers in fatigues (open daily 9am-5pm). Allow 45 minutes to drive from Bellingen, 42km east. Dorrigo is lush rainforest, with sections of multi-layered canopy and wet eucalypt forest. When the rain makes things sloppy, the leeches have a field day. Pick them off, rub them with salt, or ask the rangers for cream stick that repels them. Adjacent to the Centre, the well-known 100m **Skywalk** boardwalk allows an aerial view of the forest canopy. The **Wonga Walk** (5.8km return) is a more satisfying journey through the subtropical rainforest. It passes a couple falls and is likely to soak your shoes. To get deeper into the park and flee the center area, take the well-maintained gravel **Dome Rd** (10km) to **Never Never Picnic Area,** the origin of several walks that wind among loping vines and yellow clay soils. The **Blackbutt Trail** (6.4km one-way) just might be named for an explorer's assistant who fell asleep at the beach.

■ Tenterfield and Nearby Parks

It was in Tenterfield in 1889 that Sir Henry Parkes made his "one nation" speech that foresaw Australian federation. Though it clings to its history with some preserved buildings, travelers today know Tenterfield as a base for exploring nearby parks and a stop on the way into Queensland's Darling Downs region. The New England Hwy becomes **Rouse St** in town, and along it you'll find the **tourist office,** 157 Rouse St (tel. 6736 1082), with a broad range of park info (open M-F 9am-5pm, Sa 9am-4pm, Su 9am-3:30pm). **Countrylink** (tel. 13 22 32), **Greyhound Pioneer** (tel. 13 20 30), and **McCafferty's** (tel. 7690 9888) all run to Sydney (11hr.; $60); Greyhound, McCafferty's, and **Crisp's** (tel. 7661 8333) also serve Brisbane (4hr.; $30-40). **Kirkland's** (tel. 1800 150 467) services Byron Bay (4hr.; $30, students $18). **Commonwealth Bank,** at the north end of Rouse St, has an **ATM** (bank open M-Th 9:30am-4pm, F 9:30am-5pm). The **post office** is at 225 Rouse St (open M-F 9am-5pm; postal code 2372).

Book ahead for dorm space at the YHA-affiliated **Tenterfield Lodge** (tel. 6736 1477), reached from the tourist office by turning left off Rouse onto Manners St and turning right at its end onto Railway St (dorms $15; doubles $35; campsites $12). There's a **supermarket** on High St, off Rouse (open M-F 8;30am-6pm, Sa 8am-1pm). The **Famous Pie Shop** (tel. 6736 3556) on Rouse St has hot pies ($2-3), thick milkshakes ($2.30), and fresh bread, with eat-in or takeaway (open M-F 7:30am-5pm, Sa-Su 7:30am-noon).

Near Tenterfield lie two interesting but unspectacular national parks. **Bonoo Bonoo National Park** (pronounced, inexplicably, "Bunner Bernoo") is 27km away; take Rouse St south and go right on Nas St, then quickly bear left on Mt. Lindesay Rd. The next 27km to the park entrance is mostly unsealed; then 14km of gravel leads to **Boonoo Bonnoo Falls,** the park hub and overnight camping area (no water; $5). The park is dominated by eucalypts and has a few rock pools. There's a swimming hole 5km back from the falls toward the park entrance. If you can't reach Ayers Rock, you'll have to make do with **Bald Rock National Park,** featuring the largest exposed granite rock in Australia. To reach it, take the Mt. Lindesay road 29km to a gravel road that runs 5km to the parks camping area. The 5km **Burgoona Walk** takes you to the 1277m summit, with a view of the McPherson Ranges and the Clarence River.

SOUTH COAST OF NEW SOUTH WALES

The coastal towns south of Sydney, strung together by the Princes Hwy, are far less touristed than their northern counterparts. While industry dominates many of the larger towns such as Wollongong and Bega, the smaller coastal towns in between are some of New South Wales' undiscovered treasures. With a string of beautiful beaches on one side and mountainous escarpment on the other, the South Coast is certainly worth a visit. Cool winters cause the area to be particularly deserted between June and August; still the windy coastline retains a certain charm.

■ Wollongong

Directly down the coastline about 80km from Sydney, Wollongong (WOOLEN-gong) suffers from the same city-versus-town identity crisis that plagues many mid-sized cities. New South Wales's third largest metropolitan area, Wollongong has a city center small enough to be walkable yet urban enough to be unattractive. The mall at the center of town is less than charming but a handful of decent pubs, many frequented by university students, redeems the downtown area somewhat. The proximity of Port Kembla's steel, copper, coal, electricity, and grain plants compounds Wollongong's image problems. Still, Wollongong's location between the green peaks of the Illawarra Escarpment and the foamy blue of the Pacific Ocean creates diversions enough to fill a short stay with outdoor entertainment.

ORIENTATION AND PRACTICAL INFORMATION

The Princes Hwy leads directly into Wollongong, becoming **Flinders St** just north of the city center and merging into **Keira St** downtown. The north-south streets to remember in this area are Keira St furthest inland, and Church, Kembla, and Corrimal St closest to the coast. The cross streets Campbell, Smith, Market, Crown, and Burelli St form a fairly neat grid. The **pedestrian shopping mall** on Crown St, between Keira and Kembla St, constitutes the city's commercial heart. **Buses** arrive at the Wollongong City Coach Terminus (tel. 4226 1022; fax 4228 9090), on the corner of Keira and Campbell St. (Open M-F 7:30am-5:30pm, Sa 7:30am-2:30pm; Sunday buses meet passengers outside the station.) **Premier Motor Service** (tel. 1300 368 100) conducts daily buses north to Sydney (2hr., 2-3 per day, $11) and south to Nowra (1¼hr., 2-3per day, $11), while **Greyhound Pioneer** (tel. 13 20 30) sends one more expensive bus to Sydney daily ($19) except Sunday and another to Nowra daily ($19) except Saturday. **Murray's** (tel. 13 22 51) covers the road to Canberra (3½hr., daily, $28). **CityRail trains** stop at Wollongong City Station on Station St, and continue on to many stops including Berry ($5.40, $6.40) and Bombaderry, the closest stop to Nowra ($6.40, $7.60). Heading north, stops include Corrimal ($1.80, $2.20), Bulli ($2.20, $2.60), Coal Cliff ($2.80, $3.40), and Sydney's Central Station ($7.20, $8.60). Check the City Rail information line (tel. 13 15 00) for train times before setting out; trains come to these more distant stops only every one to two hours.

The corner of Keira and Burelli St, at the south end of the Gateway Shopping Center, figures into most **local bus routes.** Two companies, **Rutty's** (tel. 4271 1322; open M-Sa 7:30am-1pm) and **John J. Hill** (tel. 4229 4911; open M-F 8:30am-4:30pm), split the local area, so there's no central info line or standard fare. Timetables are displayed at the Gateway stop and can be picked up at Tourism Wollongong.

The staff at **Tourism Wollongong,** 93 Crown St (tel. 4227 5545 or 1800 240 737; fax 4228 0344), on the corner of Kembla St, offers good advice for travelers with varied interests (open M-F 9am-5pm, Sa 9am-4pm, Su 10am-4pm). The **post office** (tel. 4228 9322) is in the Gateway Shopping Center, on Keira St between Crown and Burelli St (open M-F 9am-5pm). **Internet access** is at **Hot Key Internet,** 67 Kembla St (tel. 4225 8677; fax 4225 8133, email manager@wollongong.hotkey.net.au), a full-service provider with five terminals and few frills ($12 per hr. or $1 per 5min; open M-Sa 9-5pm). **Cyberelectric** is the town's Internet cafe, 105 Crown St on the Mall (tel./fax 4227 1624), with the same rates and slightly better hours (open M-Sa 9am-7pm).

ACCOMMODATIONS AND CAMPING

Keiraleagh House, 60 Kembla St (tel. 4228 6765 or 0415 163 368), between Market and Smith St, is the cheapest and friendliest option. The big green house shows its age, but there's a kitchen, dining area, TV lounge, laundry, and a friendly dog. Check-out 10am. Live-in owners can be reached on mobile phones if not around the house. 3-bed dorms $15; singles $20. Cold breakfast included. Key deposit $10.

Hotel Illawarra (tel. 4229 5411), on the corner of Market and Keira St. Rooms are less swanky than the bar and nightclub downstairs, but they're spacious and tidy. The bartender can direct you to the reception. Sinks in every room, hallway bathrooms. Noisy in the evenings. Check-out 9am. Singles $30; doubles $60. Laundry $2 per wash or dry. Key deposit $20.

Dicey Riley's, 333 Crown St (tel. 4229 1952). Although the wallpaper needs replacing, the rooms are decent and there's a comfy TV lounge with leather couches. Typical pub accommodation with sinks, baths, and downstairs revelry. Ask at the bar. Singles $25; doubles $35. Key deposit $10. Free laundry. Check-out 10am.

Wollongong Surf Leisure Resort, on Pioneer Rd in Fairy Meadow (tel. 4283 6999; fax 4285 1620), 4.5km north of downtown Wollongong, is the nearest campground. Travelers with cars should follow the Princes Hwy north to Elliot's Rd, take a right, and then go left on Pioneer Rd after crossing the bridge. It's a 10min. walk from the Fairy Meadow CityRail. Pool, spa, and indoor tennis courts. Office, pool area, and game room open M-Sa 8am-9pm, Su 8am-6pm. Tent sites for 2 people vary seasonally $15-26, powered $18-30. Each additional person $5 per night. Hot water 10¢ per 5min. Laundry $2 per wash or dry. Bicycle rental $4 per hr. Wheelchair-accessible. Key deposit for toilet and shower blocks $10.

FOOD AND NIGHTLIFE

Downtown Wollongong has a plethora of cheap eateries. **Woolworths,** on the corner of Kembla and Burelli St (tel. 4228 8066), provides the grocery option and some of the city's most convenient serving hours (open M-F 7:30am-midnight, Sa 7:30am-9pm, Su 8am-8pm). The restaurants lining Keira St north of Market St cover a wide variety of cuisines with main dishes averaging $9-12. The most affordable, **Food World Gourmet Cafe,** 148 Keira St (tel. 4225 9655), serves healthy platefuls of tasty Chinese dishes for $5.50-7.50 (open Su-W 11am-8pm, Th-Sa 11:30am-9pm). Farther north, **Benny's Place,** 108 Keira St (tel. 4227 3755), has a nicer decor and a "student menu" with over 30 choices, most for under $7 (open daily 11:30am-3pm and 5-10pm). **Tannous,** 120-3 Corrimel St (tel. 4228 3213), gives you as much tabouli as you can safely wrap a pita around for $3. The baklava ($1) makes an excellent after-dinner gift to yourself or a loved one (BYO; open daily 8:30am-late). For a picnic lunch at North Beach, stop in at **North Beach Coffee Cove** (tel. 4229 7876), on Bourke St half a block from the beach, and pick up sandwiches ($2.50-4.50) or fresh fruit salad ($2.50; open daily 7am-4pm).

The **Illawara Hotel** and **Dicey Riley's** (see **Accommodations and Camping,** above) draw crowds throughout the week. Illawara draws a twentysomething crowd in the early evenings for cocktails and conversation, but on Fridays and Saturdays loud music makes this a happening dance spot. (Open M-Th 10am-1am, F-Sa noon-3am, Su noon-midnight.) The Irish theme at Dicey Riley's is enlivened by Wednesday night trivia, pool competitions, cover bands on Friday and Saturday nights, and occasional Irish performers. Up-and-coming rock bands play at the student-dominated **Oxford Tavern,** 47 Crown St (tel. 4228 3892; fax 4226 9755), every Wednesday, Friday, and Saturday (open M-Sa 10am-3am, Su 10am-10pm).

SIGHTS AND ACTIVITIES

The **Wollongong City Gallery** (tel. 4228 7500; fax 4226 5530), on the corner of Kembla and Burelli St, displays regional and widely known art. *(Open Tu-F 10am-5pm, Sa-Su noon-4pm. Free.)* The **Illawarra Museum,** 11 Market St (tel. 4229 8225, 4228 0158, or 4228 7770), east of Corrimal St, covers the history of Wollongong and the surrounding area with exhibits and period room recreations from the late 1800s. *(Open Th noon-3pm, Sa-Su 1-4pm. Admission $2, students and pensioners $1, children 50¢.)*

Wollongong's **harbor** is its nicest feature. The small, sandy cove shelters both sailboats and the fishing fleet that docks in Belmore Basin. The old lighthouse, visible from the beach, adds an air of old-time nautical charm absent from the rest of the city. Just north, **surfers** wait for waves at **North Beach. Stuart Park,** at the end of Cliff Rd, inland from North Beach, has a cricket oval, and plenty of open spaces.

South of Port Kembla, **Lake Illawarra** draws crowds from Wollongong when the weather is good. **Windang Boat Shed,** 1 Judbooley Pde (tel. 4296 2015), on the lake in Windang, rents motor boats and rowboats. *(Open M-F 7am-sunset, Sa-Su 7:30am-5pm.)* Train service runs to the Port Kembla CityRail Station ($1.80, off-peak return $2.20), a short walk from the lake. Otherwise, John J. Hill buses #50 and 51 run from the Wollongong City Station or the Gateway Shopping Center to Windang Bridge (fare approximately $3), also a short walk to the lake. From Port Kembla Station, the ocean beaches of **Port Beach** (patrolled at least Oct.-Apr.) and **MM Beach** are nearby.

■ Near Wollongong

The **Bulli Pass** takes the Princes Hwy inland to the Southern Freeway, 12km north of Wollongong, and provides an excellent view of the area from its crest. Down at sea level, **Bulli Point,** also know as Sandon Point, and farther north **Austinmer Beach** have some of the area's best **surfing** (take CityRail to Bulli or Thirroul; from Wollongong $2, off-peak return $2.60). **Thirroul,** between Bulli and Austinmer, was the temporary home of English writer **D.H. Lawrence** for several months in 1922, and descriptions of the area feature recognizably in his novel *Kangaroo*. The home is privately owned, inaccessible to the public, but the beach is open for strolling and literary speculation. Lawrence Hargrave Dr winds along the coast north of Bulli Pass, providing tantalizing glimpses of the shore below before reaching the lookout at **Bald Hill,** north of Stanwell Park, perhaps the best of all the views on this stretch of coast. It was here that **Lawrence Hargrave** contributed to the development of aviation by experimenting with box kites. Today, the hill continues its service as an aeronautical jumping-off point in the employ of skilled **hang gliders.**

The **Illawarra Escarpment** defines Wollongong's inland border. The nearest peak, **Mt. Keira,** is a short drive from town on Mt. Keira Rd., but cannot be reached by bus or train (taxi fare $7-8 from city center). At the top, bushwalking trails and a panoramic overlook await. In the southern suburb of **Berkeley** on the north shore of Lake Illawarra, the largest Buddhist Temple in the southern hemisphere, **Nan Tien Temple** (tel. 4272 0600), on Berkeley Rd, towers above the horizon and welcomes visitors. (Open Tu-Su 9am-5pm. Museum admission $1. Wheelchair accessible.) Rutty's bus #34 goes right to the temple from the Gateway Shopping Center ($2.40. $1.20 concession).

■ Kiama and Around

Under the right conditions, when the wind is high and the seas are running from the southeast, water washing into a rock cave in Kiama is forced upward through a hole in the rocks to heights of 20-35m. The awesome spray at **Kiama's Blowhole** draws visitors for miles around. But even if the wind doesn't comply, Kiama and the surrounding area make for a pleasant stop. Forty kilometers south of Wollongong via the Princes Hwy or the F6 Freeway, Kiama and the nearby beaches at **Gerringong** and **Gerroa** lie conveniently within Sydney's CityRail daytrip territory.

PRACTICAL INFORMATION The center of tourist life in Kiama is **Blowhole Point,** which can be reached by following Terralong St from Princes Hwy towards the coast. Nearby is the **Kiama Visitors Center** (tel. 4232 3322 or 1800 803 897; open daily 9am-5pm). The **CityRail station** is located on Bong Bong St, just west of Blowhole Pt (to Sydney $10.80, off-peak return $13; Wollongong $3.80, $4.60; Gerringong $1.80, $2.20; Bombaderry $3.40, $4). Daily **Premier Motor Service** (tel. 1300 368 100) buses depart for Sydney via Wollongong from the Kiama Leagues Club, on the corner of Terralong and Colling St (to Sydney 2½hr., 2-3 per day, $16). The **post office** (tel. 4232 1389) is on the corner of Terralong and Manning St (postal code 2533).

ACCOMMODATIONS AND FOOD The **Kiama Backpackers Hostel,** 31 Bong Bong St (tel. 4233 1881), a few steps from the CityRail Station, has the feel of an unexciting brick office building, but manages to preserve the hostel spirit. The knowledgeable owner provides all the necessary services. (Key deposit $10. Kitchen, TV/video, internet access, parking, free use of bikes, fishing reels, and surfboards. Reception open daily 8am-late evening. Dorms $15; doubles and twins $35; singles $20. Weekends and public holidays, twins $40, singles $22. 7th night free. Wheelchair accessible.) Twelve kilometers south, a short walk from Werri Beach, in Gerringong, the **Nestor House YHA Hostel,** 28 Fern St (tel. 4234 1249), occupies a small building on the grounds of a church. The rooms are clean and comfortable but spare. (6-bed dorms $15, under 12 $7.50. Big new kitchen. No TV. Linen available. Reception open daily 5-8pm. No check-ins after 10pm without prior agreement.)

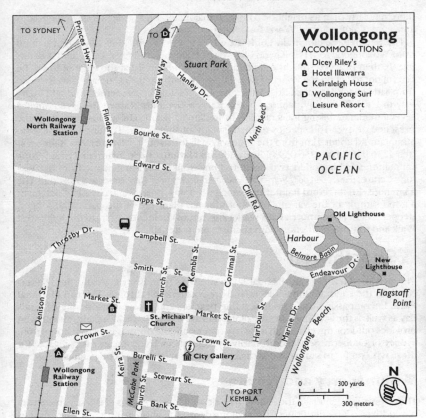

Behind the visitors center on Blowhole Point, the **Blowhole Point Caravan Park** (tel./fax 4232 2707) rents tent or caravan sites perched over the ocean. (Two-person sites $15, powered $18; peak season $20, $23; seniors $12. Backpackers $9, or $14 powered in off-season only. Each extra person $5.) Other parks with slightly different fees include **Surf Beach** (tel. 4232 1791), on Bourroul St near Kendalls Point, **Kendalls Beach** (tel. 4232 1790; wheelchair-accessible sites and restrooms available), on Bonaira St. For a tasty coastal treat, locals recommend **Kiama Harbour Take Away** (tel. 4232 1138), at the front of the beige building nearest the mainland as you head onto Blowhole Point. (Fish and chips $5.50, pelican food $2; open daily 10am-5pm.)

SIGHTS Every visitor to Kiama should give the **Blowhole** a chance to do its trick. But if the wind and the waves just won't comply, there are plenty of other places to go. The **natural rock pool** on the northern face of Blowhole Point is a good swimming spot for both children and adults. A second rock pool, across Kiama Harbour from Blowhole Point and nestled in the rocks of Pheasant Point, is deeper and more suitable for serious swimmers. On the other side of Pheasant Point, experienced **surfers** brave the riptides at **Bombo Beach**. The protected area inside the next headland to the north goes by two names. Sightseers interested in the striking rock formations which mark the spot call it **Cathedral Rock**. Surfers know it as the **Boneyard,** and, despite the menacing nickname, it's a popular spot for catching waves although no place for neophytes. To the south, surfers and swimmers frequent the patrolled **Surf Beach** at Kendalls Point. **Little Blowhole,** on Marsden Head at the end of Tingira Crescent, is often the redemption of disappointed Blowhole-watchers since it erupts more regularly than its neighbor. The next major stop on a surfer's tour of the Kiama area comes 5km south at **Werri Beach** in Gerringong.

The **Saddleback Mountain Lookout** offers travelers with cars views that extend from Wollongong to Jervis Bay on clear days. Follow Manning St south until it bends inland, then proceed straight onto Saddleback Mountain Rd at the edge of town. Be careful not to get on the Princes Hwy. The steep path up the mountain is well signed from Saddleback Mountain Rd. Farther west, accessible by Jamberoo Mountain Rd by way of Hwy 48 through Jamberoo, the **Barren Grounds Nature Reserve** contains several moderate hiking trails ranging from 2km to 19km. The area is known for the presence of over 160 species of birds, many of them rare. Turning off Jamberoo Mountain Rd about 1km from the highway will lead you to **Minnamurra Rainforest** (tel. 4236 0469; fax 4236 0393), in **Budderoo National Park,** a rare tract of subtropical rainforest which offers two delightful bushwalks, both originating from the Visitor's Centre. *(Park open daily 9am-5pm, rainforest access until 4pm; entrance $9 per car.)* The 45-minute, 1.6km return **Rainforest walk** is a looping, boardwalked track which gives a good sample of the various types of unusual plant life in the park. The longer, steeper 2.6km **Minnamurra Falls walk** (2hr. return) branches off from the Rainforest Walk and rewards your effort with picturesque waterfalls.

■ Shoalhaven

The area known as the City of Shoalhaven stretches from Berry in the north to Durras North in the south and includes inland areas extending through **Morton National Park.** Encompassing the sparkling white beaches and unusual marine life of Jervis Bay as well as the acclaimed bushwalking trail at Pigeon House Mountain, Shoalhaven provides outdoor travelers with a variety of outstanding options only two hours from Sydney or Canberra. Serviced primarily by the Princes Hwy, the area is navigable for those who prefer to sample more than one town on their weekend getaway.

■ Bomaderry and Nowra

The population centers of the Shoalhaven sit on opposite shores of the sizeable Shoalhaven River, along the Princes Hwy. Bomaderry, the smaller of the two towns, lies just north of Nowra and is home to the **Shoalhaven Visitors Centre,** 254 Princes Hwy (tel. 4421 0778 or 1800 024 261; open daily 9am-4:30pm). The **National Parks and Wildlife Service (NP.WS),** 55 Graham St (tel. 4423 2170), has an office in Nowra, with information on parks throughout the Shoalhaven (open M-F 8:30am-5pm). Because it is close to both Berry and Kangaroo Valley in the north and the Jervis Bay area to the south, many people choose to stay in Nowra when exploring the area. **M&M's Guesthouse,** 1a Scenic Drive (tel. 4422 8007; fax 4422 8007), on the grounds of the Riverhaven Motel, off to the right just across the bridge from Bomaderry, is run by a friendly older couple with a passion for motorcycles. Don't worry—they do welcome bikers, but they're no Hell's Angels. (Internet access $12 for 10min., TV, pool table, fireplace, laundry. No kitchen. Reception open daily 8am-evening. Dorm beds or private rooms with hall bathrooms and a light brekkie for $20 per person.) Overlooking the Shoalhaven River, tent camping sites at the **Nowra Animal Park** (tel. 4421 3949), on Rockhill Rd, are the area's cheapest and most scenic. (Sites for 2 $19, in winter $11. Each additional person $3. Rock climbers pay $5 per person year-round. Toilets, hot showers, picnic tables. Reception open daily 8am-5pm.) Take a right on Illaroo Rd, just before the bridge to Nowra. Follow McMahon's Rd. left from the roundabout, and take a left on Rockhill Rd. The park houses unusual Australian fauna in a natural setting. (Open daily 8am-5pm. Admission $6, seniors $5, children $3; campers pay once and get unlimited access.) The owner can direct you to the best local **rock climbing** areas. **CityRail** stops in Bomaderry on Railway St, a 15-minute walk from the tourist center by way of Bunberra St. (To Sydney $12.80, off-peak return $15.40; Wollongong $6.40, $7.60.) Heading south from Nowra, the **Australian Naval Aviation Museum** (tel. 4421 1920), 8km southwest of Nowra on Albatross Rd, makes an interesting stop for flight enthusiasts and history buffs (adults $6, pensioners $4, students $2; open daily 10am-4pm).

■ Kangaroo Valley

Nestled between Cambewarra Mountain and Barrengarry Mountain, Kangaroo Valley is far enough off the main highway to make it a pleasantly remote village in the hills, popular for B&B retreats and camping excursions alike. To get there, avoid the steep and winding Kangaroo Valley Rd leading west from Berry and instead opt for the Moss Vale Rd which leads northwest from Bomaderry, of the Princes Hwy. At the northwest end of town, the sandstone **Hampden Bridge** spans the Kangaroo River. The bridge, built in 1898, is Australia's oldest suspension bridge. Located at the south side of the bridge, **Kangaroo Valley Safaris,** 2210 Moss Vale Rd (tel. 0418 221 169; after hours 4465 1502; fax 4465 1636), on the corner of Jenanter Dr, organizes canoe camping trips on the river and rents canoes, kayaks, and camping gear for personalized excursions (open dawn till dusk). Kangaroo Valley is the land of the B&B, but **Glenmack Caravan Park and Camping** (tel. 4465 1372), on the main road just east of town, provides a less expensive option. (Tent sites on an open, grassy area $9 per person, in winter, powered sites $3 more per person. Standard cabins for 2 people $40 in winter. Each additional person $6. Toilets, showers. Reception open daily 8am-6pm.) Eighteen kilometers beyond Kangaroo Valley on Moss Vale Rd, **Fitzroy Falls** is a spectacular sight and one of the few places where Morton National Park can be entered on its eastern side. The **Fitzroy Falls Visitor Centre** (tel. 4887 7270) has maps for local and regional bushwalking trails (open daily 8:30am-5pm).

■ Jervis Bay

Almost entirely enclosed by its northern headland, the Beecroft Peninsula, Jervis Bay is a serene body of water surrounded by striking white beaches, whose marine life and rock formations make for arguably the best diving in Australia outside of the Great Barrier Reef. To take in the Bay, stop at any of the little towns along the shore and wander down the sand until the scenery suits your taste. **Huskisson,** 24km southeast of Nowra, is a good base for a stay. For tourist information, visit the **Huskisson Trading Post** (tel. 4441 5241), on the corner of Tomerong and Dent St. **Leisure Haven Caravan Park** (tel. 4441 5046; fax 4441 5198), 1km outside of town on Woollamia Rd, charges $10 for two-person tent sites in a wooded area on Currambene Creek. (Sites with electricity $12; each additional person $3; key deposit $20; laundry facilities; reception open daily 8am-evening.) The **Husky Pub** (tel. 4441 5001), on Owen St overlooking the Bay, is the town's social center and the source of an excellent all-you-can-eat lunch-time salad bar ($4) (Burger with fries $5. Open for lunch M-Sa noon-2pm, Su noon-2:30pm; bar open daily 11am-late.) The pub also provides standard upstairs **accommodation** with sinks and wardrobes in all the rooms, plus a large balcony overlooking Owen St and part of the bay. (Singles $35, doubles $60. Reception at the bar. Check-out 10am.)

Underwater, Jervis Bay is exquisite. The bay is a natural meeting place for tropical marine life coming down from the north as well as a variety of southern species not found at the Great Barrier Reef. Divers also rave about the massive archways and rock shelves which characterize the aquatic scenery. **Prodive,** 64 Owen St (tel. 4441 5255; fax 4441 7113; email prodive@shoal.net.au) will take certified divers to all the best spots and provide the equipment for one 3hr. dive for $60. Less experienced divers can go out with an instructor and still see plenty, including seals, at a lesser depth for $75 per dive. The water is warmer and visibility better between the months of February and June, but winter is best for viewing a diversity of species. (Open daily dawn to dusk. Bookings essential, at least 1 week in advance in summer.)

For those content to enjoy marine life from a drier vantage point, **Dolphin Watch Cruises,** 50 Owen St (tel. 4441 6311; fax 4441 5885; email cruises@dolphin-watch.com.au), runs two- to three-hour trips to spy on dolphins and winter migratory whales in their natural habitats. Fishermen try their luck at nearby Curramberry

Creek, and **Husky Hire-a-Boat** (tel. 4441 6200) will rent you an aluminum boat, deliver it to a local boat ramp, and lend you a rod if you want to give it a go ($20 per hr.; calls taken daily dawn-5pm). On the southern end of the bay, **Booderee National Park,** formerly Jervis Bay National Park, has three **camping** areas: Greenpatch and Bristol Point on Jervis Bay (toilets, waters, hot showers, tent sites for up to 5 people $10, in winter $8), and Cave Beach near Wreck Bay to the south (cold showers, no electricity, same rates). The **Visitors Centre** (tel. 4443 0977), just beyond the park entry gates, accepts campsite bookings and inquiries Monday through Friday between 10am and 4pm. (Entrance $5 per car.) The park's recent name change stems from a shift to joint management between the Commonwealth Government and the Wreck Bay Aboriginal community. The traditional Aboriginal name "Booderee" for the area means "bay of plenty." and applies to the **Botanic Gardens** (tel. 4442 1122) inside the park as well (open M-F 8am-4pm, Su 10am-5pm; free).

■ Ulladulla

The next major service center moving south through the Shoalhaven is Ulladulla. The **Ulladulla Visitors Centre** (tel. 4455 1269) is on the Princes Hwy in the Civic Centre complex (open M-F 10am-5pm, Sa-Su 9am-5pm). **Internet access** is available here for a low $1 per half hour. **Premier Motor Service** (tel. 1300 368 100) buses stop at the Marlin Hotel on the way south to Bateman's Bay (45min., 2-3 per day, $9) and Bega (3-4hr., $25). Northbound buses to Nowra (1hr., 2-3 per day, $12) and Sydney (4½hr., $24) pause at the Traveland Travel Agency. **Greyhound Pioneer** (tel. 13 20 30) runs the same routes once per day for more money.

The local hostel, **South Coast Backpackers,** 63 Princes Hwy (tel. 4454 0500), between Nurrawallee and North St, is a small operation with an unexciting roadside location, but a nice sundeck and kitchen area and clean facilities to make up for it. (Dorms $16; doubles and twins $37. Check-out 10am. Key deposit $5. VIP. TV, laundry, off-street parking. Reception open daily 8am-8pm.) At the end of South St, **Holiday Haven Tourist Park** (tel./fax 4455 2457) has ample oceanfront camping space. Extras include hot showers, toilets, gas barbecues, laundry facilities, a pool, and access to a secluded beach nearby. (Reception open daily 8am-9pm. Check-out 10am. Sites for two $22, powered $25; in winter $13, $16. Each additional person over 5 years old $5.)

The people at the **Ulladulla Dive Shop,** 10 Wason St (tel. 4455 5303), can give advice on diving in the area or take you out themselves. (Gear rental $50 per day. Trips for certified divers, with gear $60 for 1 dive, $90 for 2. One intro dive $85. Open daily 7am-7pm; in winter M-F 9am-5pm, Sa-Su 8am-5pm.) Bushwalkers generally stop in Ulladulla on the way out to the **Pigeon House Walk.** Turn off the Princes Hwy onto Wheelbarrow Rd 3km south of Burrill Lake. The trailhead is located at a picnic area 27km farther on. The walk, which involves some ladder climbing, is a strenuous 5km round-trip affair, but the view at the top is a knock-out. The nearby lakes, **Burrill** and **Conjola**, have nice swimming beaches, and **Mollymook Beach,** just north of town, is good for surfing.

■ Murramarang National Park

The last piece of Shoalhaven coastline is located within Murramarang National Park, tucked away from the Princes Hwy at the far end of a 15-minute drive over mostly unpaved roads. **Pebbly Beach** is a superb spot where amazingly tame kangaroos congregate on the sand and occasionally take a dip in the ocean. Tent **camping** is cheapest at the Pebbly Beach camping area. (Call 4478 6006 to book for summer use; in winter, first-come first-served. Sites for 2 cost $10, each additional person up to 6 people is $2, plus a one-time park usage fee of $7.50.) A number of worthy campgrounds and caravan parks are spotted throughout other locations in the park, including the NPWS-administered campground at **Depot Beach** (tel. 4478 6582) which has the same fees but features hot shower facilities (office open daily 9am-9pm). At the southernmost point in the Shoalhaven half of Murramarang Park, **Durras North** looks onto

Durras Lake and a beautiful windswept ocean beach. **Durras Lake North Caravan Park** (tel. 4478 6072), the first of several caravan parks at the end of Durras Rd, is clean and quite a kangaroo gathering place in its own right. (Tent sites $7. Caravan for 1-3 $45. Store and reception open daily 8:30am-5pm, but check-in until 10:30pm.)

■ South from Bateman's Bay

Bateman's Bay, about 10km south of Durras Lake on the Princes Hwy and just inland from Murramarang National Park, marks a change in the NSW coast. On the way out of Shoalhaven and into the Eurobodalla shire, the larger towns feel less touristy and more focused on industries such as fishing or dairy farming; the town of **Bega,** famed for its cheese, is otherwise utterly dull. The smaller historic villages nestled in the countryside, such as Mogo and Central Tilba, provide the most compelling reasons to follow the Princes Hwy along the coast instead of the less exciting inland routes.

■ Bateman's Bay

Where the Kings Hwy from Canberra (152km inland) meets the Princes Hwy at the coast, **Bateman's Bay** begins. The town, situated just south of this junction at the mouth of the Clyde River, caters to upmarket tourists on holiday from the capital, but has enough amenities to make it suitable for budget travelers too. The staff at the **Bateman's Bay Tourist Information Centre** (tel. 4472 6900 or 1800 802 528), on the Princes Hwy at Beach Rd, can outfit you with brochures and give good advice about local beaches for swimming or surfing (open M-Sa 9am-5pm, Su 9am-4pm). For award-winning hostel accommodation, stay with the friendly crew at the YHA-affiliated **Bateman's Bay Backpackers** (tel. 4472 4972), located inside a caravan park, on the corner of Old Princes Hwy and South St, just off the new Princes Hwy. The hostel runs daily trips to Pebbly Beach ($10) and Mogo ($3) and rents bikes and surfboards ($10 per day for either). (6-bed dorms $15-20; doubles and twins $38-40. Nonmembers pay a surcharge. Linen included. TV, VCR, stereo, fully equipped kitchen, laundry. Free pick-up. Reception open daily late. Check-out 10am.)

Buses come and go from Bateman's Bay outside the Promenade Plaza on Orient St. **Premier Motor Service** (tel. 1300 368 100) goes north to Wollongong (3½hr., 2-3 per day, $28) and on to Sydney (5½hr., $30). Canberra (2½hr., 1-2 per day, $21.75) is **Murray's** territory (tel. 13 22 57). **Greyhound Pioneer** (13 20 30) makes trips to Melbourne (12hr., daily, $70) or Bega (2hr., daily, $32) every day except Saturday.

Traveling south on the coastal road, you'll find good **surf** at Surf Beach, Malua Bay, and Broulee. The inland route leads to **Mogo,** 10km south of Bateman's Bay, an 1850s gold rush town currently riding the craft craze. **Mogo Zoo,** Tomakin Rd, off Princes Hwy at Mogo (tel. 4474 4930; fax 4474 4855) houses endangered and exotic animals such as snow leopards, red pandas, and the last Siberian tiger in Australia. (Open daily 9am-5pm. Adults $10, pensioners 48, children $5, family of 4 $28.)

■ Narooma

With a **National Parks and Wildlife Service** office (tel. 4476 2888; open M-F 9am-5pm), on the Princes Hwy at Field St, and several free parks within an hour's drive, the town of **Narooma** provides an excellent base for outdoor exploration. One popular 2WD-accessible park is **Eurobodalla National Park,** which conserves patches of coastline along a 30km stretch from Moruya Head in the north to Tilba Tilba Lake in the south and contains one campground at **Coastal Congo,** near the town of Moruya. The picnic area at **Mystery Bay,** 5km off Princes Hwy south of Narooma, is a nice spot for a day of snorkeling in the bay. (No fees; no camping.) Just 7km off-shore, the **Montague Island Nature Reserve** is home to Australian and New Zealand **fur seals,** crested terns, and some 10,000 pairs of **fairy penguins.** Since only 70 people are allowed to visit each day, the reserve is accessible only on official NPWS-sanctioned tours (3½hr.; 1 per day, depending on weather and demand; $50, kids 15 and under

$35, family of 4 $150), for which most people say the thrill outweighs the cost. Tours can be booked at the **Narooma Visitors Centre** (tel. 4476 2881; fax 4476 1690), one block beyond the NPWS office on the Princes Hwy (open daily 9am-5pm).

On Wagonga Head at one end of the golf course, ocean waves and coastal winds have left one rock, known as **Australia Rock,** with a familiar marking: a hole in the shape of Australia. Whether or not you see the resemblance, the area is pretty. Golf enthusiasts should discreetly dart in and admire the famous third hole, which features views of an oceanfront cave and is now known as "Hogan's Hole" ever since Paul "Dundee" Hogan filmed an advertisement there. **Glasshouse Rocks,** another locally famous rock formation named by Captain Cook, lies at the south end of Narooma Beach. **Pioneer Motor Service** (tel. 1300 368 100) stops in Narooma, outside the St. George Bank (northbound) and the Westpac Bank (southbound), and runs to Sydney (6½-7½hr., 2-3 per day, $40) and Bega (1½hr., 2-3 per day, $13). **Murray's** (tel. 13 22 51) travels from Narooma Plaza to Canberra (4½hr., 1-2 per day, $33).

Bluewater Lodge (YHA), 11-13 Riverside Dr (tel. 4476 4440; fax 4476 3492), signposted from just across the Narooma Bridge, is a fair deal. The house has hardwood floors, heat, laundry, a view of the Wagonga Inlet, and use of bikes and canoes for $5 per day. (Check-out 10am. Dorm beds $15 and family suites $46. Nonmembers pay $2 more per night. Reception open daily 8-10am, 4-9pm. Linen included. Internet access $12 for 15min.) Right between the Narooma Golf Course and Narooma Beach, **Surfbeach Caravan Park** (tel. 4476 2275), on Ballingala St, has amazing ocean views and easy beach access. (Sites for 2 $19, powered $22; weekly $119, $154. Winter: $14, $16; weekly $82, $97. Senior discounts in winter. Each additional adult $6, $3 in winter; ages 5-16 $3, $2 in winter. Reception open daily 9am-5pm, later in summer.)

The historic town of **Central Tilba** sits 15km south of Narooma off the Princes Hwy. Built in the 1890s and partially rebuilt in the 1980s, the town has enough turn-of-the-century charm to make it well worth a short detour. Its arts and crafts and antiques stores often draw visitors for longer stays in the relaxed pastoral setting. Information about the Tilba area can be found at **Bates General Store,** just off the highway on Bates St (tel./fax 4473 7290; open M-Sa 8am-5pm, Su 8:30am-5pm). The only pub in Central Tilba, **The Dromedary Hotel,** on Bates St (tel./fax 4473 7223) also has reasonably priced accommodation with a common TV room and laundry and linen included. (Singles $30, doubles $50; reception at bar 9am-9pm.) **Mount Dromedary,** named by Captain Cook for its resemblance to that hump-backed animal, overlooks Central Tilba and **Tilba Tilba,** the neighboring village with an 11km return walking trail up the mountain.

■ Bermagui

You wouldn't want to go to **Bermagui** unless you like to fish. If you do, though, this town on the sapphire coast southeast of Tilba Tilba, 30 minutes from the Princes Hwy, will make for a satisfying afternoon. For tourist information, stop at the **BP Automotive Centre** (tel. 6493 4174; open daily 7am-7pm), on Coluga St just before town. **Blue Pacific Flats,** 73 Murrah St (tel. 6493 4921), opens its splendid cabins—laundry, kitchens, and all—to backpackers for $15 per head, including bikes and fishing equipment. If you're itching to spend the day hauling in marlin and yellowfin tuna, visit the **Bermagui Ocean Hut,** 4 Cutajo St (tel. 6493 4688), where they can organize a day of game fishing with all gear provided. (8hr., $110-150 per head depending on group size. Open daylight-dark during season, 9am-5pm otherwise.) Book ahead. The catch is best between November and May.

You can sample the town's pride and joy at the **Bermagui Fish Co-Op** (tel. 6493 4239), on the waterfront on Cutajo St. (Fish and chips $7.80. Dozen open oysters $7.50. M-Th 9am-6pm, F-Sa 9am-6:45pm, Su 9am-6:30pm.) Those who prefer **swimming** to fishing cluster at Horseshoe Bay between Bermagui Point and Shelly Beach or at the natural rock pool known as **Blue Pool** on Scenic Dr.

SNOWY MOUNTAINS

Australia's highest mountains, the Snowies are a winter wonderland for skiers and snowboarders. Too low to maintain year-round snow, the mountains attract hikers in the warm months. Kosciuszko National Park, home of Mt. Kosciuszko (2228m; Australia's highest peak) and nine other mountains reaching over 2100m, covers much of the area. Car entrance fees for the park are a steep $12 per day (motorcycles $3.50); take advantage, when possible, of winter bus service. The Snowy Mountains Hwy and the Alpine Way, major routes through the area, feature rambling, boulder-strewn countryside and clear passage for most of the year.

■ Cooma

The friendly town of Cooma sits at the eastern edge of the Snowy Mountains region, 113km from Canberra on the Monaro Hwy. Although it's a one-hour drive from the slopes, Cooma fills up during ski season (early June to early October) with snow-seekers looking for bargain accommodations. In the spring, summer, and fall, the town attracts backpackers who find work harvesting fruit and vegetables nearby.

PRACTICAL INFORMATION The **Cooma Visitors Centre**, 119 Sharp St (tel. 6450 1742 or 1800 636 525; fax 6450 1798), is in the center of the village (free accommodation booking service; open mid-Oct. to May daily 9am-5pm; early June to early Oct. 7am-6pm). **Impulse Airlines** (tel. 13 13 81) flies into town from Sydney (1hr., in summer 2 per day, more in winter, $235). **Buses** come through twice a day during ski season, but service is severely curtailed the rest of the year. **Greyhound Pioneer** (tel. 13 20 30) covers Jindabyne (1hr., $36) and Thredbo (2hr., $36) during winter and Sydney (7hr., $47) and Canberra (1½hr., $17) year-round. **Countrylink** (tel. 13 22 32) works on a similar schedule and comes in slightly cheaper for trips to Sydney and Canberra. See the staff at **Harvey World Travel**, 114 Sharp St (tel. 6452 4677; fax 6452 1121), across the street from the visitors center, for reservations or further information (open M-F 9am-5pm, Sa 9am-noon). **Harvest Helpers** (tel. 6452 2172; fax 6452 5536) arranges harvest-related work in New South Wales and Victoria throughout much of the year. The company has a special focus on work in the Cooma area during the summer and fall. (One-time consulting fee $50.)

ACCOMMODATIONS AND FOOD **Cooma Bunkhouse Backpackers,** 28-30 Soho St (tel. 6452 2983), on the corner of Commissioner St, has great year-round hostel accommodation with bathrooms, kitchens, TVs, and most importantly, central heat in each of the self-contained dorms. (Dorms $15, singles in adjacent motel $25, doubles $35; family of 3 $50, with each additional child $10. VIP. Free linen and blankets. Reception open 24hr., call ahead for later arrivals.)

Backpackers often choose **Dodd's Hotel,** 94-98 Commissioner St (tel. 6452 2011), whose basic, neat rooms are pleasant if you can tune out the noise of the pub below. (4-bed dorms $15; singles $22; doubles $40. Key deposit $6. Heaters, electric blankets, common room with TV and books. Reception at the bar daily 11am-2am.) **Alpine Country Guest House,** 32 Massie St (tel. 6452 1414), is ideal for larger groups or families since the well-heated rooms are clean and quiet, and feature ensuite bathrooms. Light breakfast is included in the price. ($30 per person, children 14 and under $15 each. Doubles, singles, and family rooms available. TV, alarm clocks in rooms.)

On the Snowy Mountains Hwy 6km west of Cooma, **Mountain View Caravan Park** (tel. 6452 4513; fax 6452 3500), provides a semi-equipped campers' kitchen along with its basic campsites. (Sites $10, powered $15. Toilets, showers; laundry facilities. Reception open daily 7am-10pm. Check-out 10am.)

Mystic Munchies, 164 Sharp St (tel. 6452 1684), just down from the visitors center, offers a unique decor with a gallery of mystic items and trinkets for sale in display cases surrounding the restaurant seating. Owner and head chef Shane specializes in vegetarian and vegan dishes (veggie nut burger $4.50) but has tasty meat meals on hand as well (foccacias $6.50). Wash it down with one of their popular fruit smoothies (all-fruit crush $3). (BYO, no corkage. Open M-F 8:30am-6pm, so make it an early dinner.) Across the street, **Terry's** (tel. 6452 1002) is another wise choice with sandwiches ($5-10), an all-day breakfast special with bacon, eggs, and toast ($8.50), and the best hot chocolate in town ($2.50; open M-Th 7am-6pm, F-Su 6am-7pm). **Woolworths** (tel. 6452 3638) is on Vale St at Massie St (open daily 7am-10pm).

SKIING AND SIGHTS Ski and snowboard rental shops clutter the village streets, evidence of the area's most popular pastimes. Rates are comparable to those closer to the mountains, so the only advantage to renting in Cooma may be availability. For skis, socks, and boots, you can generally expect to pay $30 the first day and $10-15 each day thereafter. The **Snowy Mountains Hydro-Electric Scheme,** carried out between 1949 and 1974, was responsible for nearly every body of standing water in the Snowy Mountains, included the construction of 16 large dams and involved workers from over 30 countries. The **Snowy Mountains Hydro-Electric Authority Visitors Centre** (tel. 6453 2004 or 1800 623 776; fax 6453 2048), on the Monaro Hwy just north of town, has models, brochures, and a 15-minute film explaining the grand plan, which supplies water to the dry regions west of the mountains and creates energy for the entire southeast corner of Australia (open M-F 8am-5pm, Sa-Su and holidays 8am-1pm; free).

■ Jindabyne

On the scenic shores of man-made **Lake Jindabyne,** the mountain town of Jindabyne is a logical stopping point for those who can't afford to sleep at the foot of the Thredbo chairlifts. To get to the slopes from Jindabyne, buses and cars take the **Alpine Way,** which leads to the SkiTube station (23km) that services the Perisher Blue resorts, then continues onto Thredbo (30km). From there it extends its curvaceous and sometimes treacherous path through the mountains to Khancoban, a full-service town on the western edge of **Kosciuszko National Park.**

PRACTICAL INFORMATION The **Snowy Region Visitors Centre** (tel. 6450 5600; fax 6456 1249), on the Alpine Way at the east end of town, combines an office of the NPWS and an impressive, multi-million-dollar local tourist information center. Entrance passes for trips into the National Park can be purchased here as well ($12 per car per 24hr., motorcycles $3.50; open daily 8am-6pm, except 7am-7pm on ski season weekends). During winter, all vehicles entering the National Park must carry snow chains (fines $200). Chains can be rented at stores and gas stations throughout Jindabyne, but only the **Shell Service Station** (tel. 6456 2270), at the west end of town right across from the turn-off to Thredbo, will rent chains ($20) for the drive west to Khancoban, where you can return them to another Shell station (open 7am-7pm daily). For road conditions dial 6450 5551, and for snow reports dial 6450 5553.

Both **Deane's Buslines** (tel. 6299 3722; fax 6299 3828) and **Jindabyne Coaches** (tel. 041 927 9552) run shuttles from Jindabyne to Thredbo ($12) and to the Skitube train station for Perisher Blue ($6) throughout the ski season. The Snowy Region Visitors Centre has timetables. Transportation into Jindabyne from the northeast passes through Cooma (see p. 203) and operates only during the ski season. **Internet access** is hard to find in the Snowies, but Jindabyne's **Kosciuszko Computer Support,** upstairs in the Snowy Mountains Plaza (tel. 6457 2001; email justin@kos.com.au), offers full services at reasonable rates. ($4 for 15min. or $20 for 6 installments of 15min. Open M-F 9am-5pm, in winter also Sa 10am-4pm and Su 10am-2pm.)

ACCOMMODATIONS AND FOOD Even in the height of ski madness, affordable accommodation in Jindabyne does exist, but availability may be a problem; book well in advance. **The Jindy Inn,** 18 Clyde St (tel. 6456 1957; fax 6456 2057), has dorms with bathrooms, a large, well-equipped kitchen, and a nice adjoining restaurant with special discounts for guests. (Reception open 24hr. daily. Check-out 10am. Dorms $20, June-Oct. $25; doubles $40, $80; family rooms $50, $100.) Down the street, **Kookaburra Lodge,** 10 Clyde St (tel. 6456 2897; fax 6456 2747), suffers from a bad case of faux wood paneling, but rents otherwise palatable singles for reasonable rates that include a hot breakfast. There's a game room, TV room, and heated pool. (Bunk rooms without ensuite bath $30, private rooms with bath $50 per person in summer, $55 during peak winter midweek, $120 during peak weekend nights.)

Jindabyne Holiday Park (tel. 6456 2249; fax 6456 2302), in the center of town on a choice stretch of Lake Jindabyne shoreline, provides easy access to the town shopping area and plentiful space for lakeside camping. Spotless toilet, shower, and laundry facilities all have wheelchair access. The holiday park also has one of the lowest daily ski rental rates in town. (Top-line carving skis, stocks, and boots $33, snowboard and boots $35. Unpowered sites for 1 $10 in summer, each additional person $3; ranges up to $17, $5 in peak season. Key deposit $20.) Jindabyne has a gaggle of agencies which charge small fees for arranging lodge or apartment rentals, one of the cheapest ways for groups to stay in town or for travelers to find more permanent arrangements. **Kosciusko Accommodation** (tel. 6456 2022 or 1800 026 354) and **Alpine Resort and Travel Centre** (tel. 6456 2999 or 1800 802 315), both in the Nuggets Crossing Shopping Center, rank high among the recommended companies.

ACTIVITIES In the winter, skiers and snowboarders populate Jindabyne, but the development of summer adventure activities in the area has made the town a fun place to go year-round. **Paddy Pallin** (tel. 6456 2922 or 1800 623 459; fax 6456 2836) organizes abseiling outings (half-day $59, accompanied child ages 10-15 $45; full day with lunch $100, $75), rents mountain bikes ($10 per hour, half-day $24, full day $35), and canoes and kayaks for individual paddling trips ($30 for half-day, $42 full day; kayaks $30, $44; river-use canoes for 2 people, half-day $38). For a more organized thrill ride rafting down the Murray River, contact **Upper Murray White Water Rafting** (tel. 1800 677 179 or 6457 2002). A one-day adventure with food costs $120 per person. Cross-country skiing adventures are handled by the experts at **Wilderness Sports** (tel. 6456 2966), Nuggets Crossing. (Half-day lesson and tour $35, children 8-15 $25; full-day $54, $35. Open daily 8am-8pm, 9am-6pm in summer.)

In the evenings, people relax at the **Lake Jindabyne Hotel** (tel. 6456 2203), on Kosciuszko Rd in the center of town, where entertainment ranges from good-old-fashioned drinking to concerts by top-notch rock bands. (Schooners of VB $3.10, basic mixed drinks $4.20. Open M-Sa 10am-2am or later, Su 10am-midnight.)

▓ Kosciuszko National Park

Named after the heroic Polish nationalist, but horribly mispronounced, "Kah-zee-AH-sko" National Park marches along the New South Wales and Victoria border. Within the park, Australia's highest peaks loom over some of the country's largest power and irrigation projects. Skiers and hikers traipse about the mountaintops oblivious to the hydroelectric activity under their feet. While Kosciuszko National Park may forever be associated with premier ski resorts, tourists have begun to appreciate the year-round beauty of natural attractions such as Yarrongobilly Caves and the park's wildflower-strewn hikes leading to the rooftop of Australia.

■ Thredbo

Home of the country's longest ski runs, Thredbo is still considered by many to be *the* place to go for Australian snow. With a busy schedule of outdoor events and activities, the resort village has established itself as an entertainment venue rather than just a set of slopes. The **Kosciuszko National Park** entry fee ($12 per car per day, motorcycles $3.50) applies to all vehicles heading into Thredbo on the Alpine Way, whether from Khancoban (82km northwest) or Jindabyne (34km northeast). Thredbo has a total of 12 lifts and a healthy number of challenging blue and black runs to complement the easier slopes on the right side of the mountain. As with any resort in the Snowies, abundant snowmaking can't compensate for unfavorable weather; it's wise to call ahead to see how many lifts are open and what conditions are like. The **Thredbo Information Centre** is at 6 Friday Dr (tel. 6459 4198; fax 6459 4195; open 8am-6pm, in summer 9am-3pm). Their web page (http://www.thredbo.com.au) has weather reports and lift info.

From early June to early October, the entire ski season, two companies, **Deane's Buslines** (tel. 6299 3722; fax 6299 3828) and **Jindabyne Coaches** (tel. 041 927 9552) conduct shuttles between Thredbo and Jindabyne ($8). During these months, **Greyhound Pioneer** (tel. 13 20 30) runs regular bus service from Cooma as well.

Accommodations at most lodges can be booked through the **Thredbo Resort Centre** (tel. 6459 4294 or 1800 020 589. Open during winter daily 9am-6pm; off-season M-F 9am-5pm). People at the center will know which of the lodges is least expensive at any given time. The **Thredbo YHA Lodge,** 8 Jack Adams Path (tel. 6457 6376; fax 6457 6043), is the best deal in town. Though less luxurious than its neighbors, the lodge has a comfortable chalet feel and features ample common space, a big kitchen, and a balcony that looks out onto the slopes. Five minutes of morning chores expected of guests to keep costs down. Reservations for the ski season are made by lottery in late April. Applications must be submitted through the YHA Travel Centre, 422 Kent St, Sydney (tel. 9261 1111). Call the travel center for details. For more impromptu visits, contact the manager at the lodge about single night openings resulting from cancellations. (Reception opens daily 7-10am and 4:30-9:30pm. During ski season (early June-early Oct.) dorms cost $38, accompanied child under 18 $25. Su-Su 7-night package costs $283, under18 $187. Su-F 5-night package $190, $126. F-Sa weekend package $93, $62. During summer adults $16, children $8.)

During the 1998 ski season, **lift tickets** cost $62 per day (under 15 $36), and group ski lessons went for $34. Charges for ski and snowboard rentals at **Thredbo Sports** (tel. 6459 4100 and 6456 2000), at the base of the Crackenback Chairlift and at the east end of the village near the Friday Flat lift, were higher than in Jindabyne or Cooma (mid-range skis, stocks, and boots $42), so it makes sense to rent equipment before arriving in Thredbo. For the use of hikers and ganderers, the **Crackenback**

The Thredbo Landslide

Shortly before midnight on Wednesday, July 30, 1997, the tiny community at Australia's premier ski resort awoke in shock as a landslide loosed the foundations of two Thredbo ski lodges and sent them tumbling down the mountainside in the middle of the village. Over the next week, rescue volunteers worked almost without pause to move piece by piece the pile of concrete, glass, steel, and personal belongings that remained of the lodges in search of the 19 people trapped inside. Two days into the ordeal, a voice called out from the wreckage, and the miraculous rescue of ski instructor Stuart Diver began. The disaster's only survivor, Mr. Diver was carried free of the rubble some 12 hours later. He had lain in a concrete pocket for a total of 56 hours and suffered only frostbite and minor lacerations. The Thredbo landslide claimed the lives of 18 people, almost all of whom were employees of the resort and members of the village's tiny year-round population. Although the matter is still under investigation, experts believe that the landslide was caused by the collapse of the Alpine Way embankment, not by a spontaneous natural disaster, and therefore measures have been taken to reroute the highway. While the rest of the lodges in Thredbo have been judged structurally sound, the tragedy has caused widespread reconsideration of the level of development which is safe and sustainable in such precarious locales. Understandably, it has also profoundly affected the people who live and work here. Over a year after the tragedy the people of Thredbo are pleased to see that tourists have not been scared away, and are eager to preserve the community that the landslide victims had loved.

Gondola Chairlift runs year-round ($18 all-day summer pass; early Oct. to early June, $17 return ticket; hours 8:30am-4:30pm). Several excellent walks depart from the top of the mountain for sweeping views of Kosciuszko National Park. From the top of the chairlift, the **Mt. Kosciuszko Walk** is a 12km return if you want to reach the summit of Australia's tallest mountain, but only 4km return to reach a fantastic lookout point. Because of quick-changing weather conditions, the walk is much more advisable during summer. At the village level, spring opens the way for mountain biking as well as walking. Free maps of all local trails are available throughout the village.

For indoor sports, the Thredbo **Alpine Training Centre** (tel. 6459 4138; fax 6459 4139) has a complex of training facilities open both to elite athletes and to health-conscious visitors. (Swimming pool use $6, under 15 $3; squash court rental $12 per hr. Open daily 10am-8pm.) Thredbo's annual **Blues Festival** (Jan. 15-17 in 1999) and **Jazz Festival** (April 29-May 2 in 1999) bring the hills alive in the summer and fall.

■ Perisher Blue

New South Wales' other premier ski resort, Perisher Blue (tel. 1300 655 822; http://www/perisherblue.com.au) is actually four resorts in one. One lift ticket buys entry to the slopes leading down to the **Perisher Valley, Blue Cow, Smiggins,** and **Guthega** alpine villages. While the runs aren't quite as long as those at Thredbo, they're more plentiful, and the total skiing area is much larger.

Unlike Thredbo, Perisher Blue is not a full-service village, and has no budget accommodation or overnight parking. The **Skitube** (tel. 6456 2010) is an all-weather train that makes the 8km journey from **Bullocks Flat,** located on the Alpine Way, into the Perisher Valley Alpine Village. You can either start your adventures here, or keep riding the skitube halfway up the mountain to the Blue Cow terminal. Here, lifts take more advanced skiers and boarders to the blue and black runs atop **Guthega Peak** and **Mt. Blue Cow.** To get to the Skitube station at Bullocks Flat, take **Deane's Bus-lines** (tel. 6299 3722) or **Jindabyne Coaches** (tel. 041 927 9552), both of which run shuttles from Jindabyne starting around 7am (6 per day, $6). By **car,** drive along the Alpine Way from Jindabyne until you reach the station; there's plenty of parking.

Lift tickets cost $62 per day (under 15 $33) during the 1998 ski season, but you must add $10 to these costs for the Skitube same-day return ticket. If you plan to stay overnight in one of the mountain's already-pricey lodges, you must pay $15 each way for the shuttle. Tickets can be purchased at Bullocks Flat or at the **Perisher Blue Jindabyne Ticket Office** (tel. 6456 1659; fax 6456 1514) in the **Snowy Mountains Plaza** shopping center (open daily 7am-7pm). Two-hour group lessons cost $32. Day care is available; costs vary with age of child. Perisher Blue offers **night skiing,** rare in Australia (Tu, Sa 6:30-10pm; adults $16, children $10 in 1998). Night skiing is restricted to the basic slopes directly in front of the Perisher Centre in Perisher Valley.

■ Yarrangobilly Caves

Nestled in the northern edge of the Kosciusko National Park, 77km south of Tumut and 109km northwest of Cooma, the Yarrangobilly Caves attract curious visitors and hard-core spelunkers alike. Located just off the Snowy Mountains Hwy (Hwy 18), the **Yarrangobilly River** runs through a 12km-long stretch of limestone, riddled with caves. Marked walking trails help tourists better understand the beauty of the caves and the surrounding canopies. The **visitors center** (tel. 6454 9597; fax 6454 5998) at the caves is an essential first stop. Guided tours are the only way to see the caves (daily 11am, 1, and 3pm, or other times with advance scheduling).

Jillabenan is the smallest, shortest (1hr.) and only wheelchair-accessible cave. Its array of fascinating stalactite and stalagmite formations amid pools and crystal-lined nooks is spectacular. The slightly longer **Jersey Caves** tour requires about an hour and a half to see equally stellar sights. (Entrance and tours $10, children $7.) After wandering around the caves, take a load off and relax in the 27°C thermal pools.

The park is 6.5km from the highway and open daily from 9am to 5pm. Fill up your tank before you leave. The nearest **petrol stations** are 43km north in Talbingo or 47km south in Cabramurra. There is **no camping** or **food** available in the area.

■ Mt. Selwyn

Along the Snowy Mountains Highway between Cooma and Tumut, and less than 100km from either, the **Selwyn Snowfields** (tel. 6454 9488; fax 6454 9482; http://selwynsnow.com.au) offer beginner budget skiing steals. Promoted as a family resort, Selwyn has few advanced runs (only 12%). Elevation at the base is 1492m; the summit is 122m higher. Selwyn advertises 12 **lifts,** but only one of these is a standard double chairlift: the others include T-bars, rope-tows, and even a toboggan lift. Accordingly, **lift tickets** are inexpensive: a one-day ticket costs $32 (under 15 $18; valid 8:30am-4:30pm). **Half-day passes** are also available ($21, under 15 $15; valid 8:30am-12:45pm or 12:45-4:30pm). People over 65 and children under 6 ski free. Forty-five marked trails make **cross-country skiing** another attractive option. A shelter, toilets, and a carpark are located at the entrance to the cross-country trails.

Ski hire for alpine or cross-country skis costs $23 for a full day and $16 for a half-day, and (under 15 $19; $14). **Ski wear** can also be hired (pants or parka $14 per day; half-day $10). **Snowboard hire** costs $40 for a full day and $30 for a half-day. **Toboggans** are also available ($7 for the day). Or try out a **lift and lesson** package (1½hr. lesson with a day-long lift ticket; $50; under 15 $36). A credit card or deposit with identification is necessary to hire any equipment.

To save money on accommodations, spend the night in Tumut or Cooma and commute by car. Use tire chains and exercise caution on the often icy roads. **Lever Coachlines** (tel. 6297 3133) also offers a daytrip skiing package from Canberra (round-trip bus, park entry, lift ticket, lesson, and ski hire $75).

HUME CORRIDOR

As the major route between Australia's two largest cities, the Hume Highway provides fast travel without too much in the way of scenery. Upgrades are slowly making the road into a divided freeway for the entire route, but at present some stretches are still two-lane and heavily trafficked. It takes nine to ten hours to cover the 872km between Sydney and Melbourne along the highway, but taking scenic detours along stretches of the Old Hume Hwy where it parts from the new can help spruce up the monotony with some beautiful historic villages tucked away in the countryside. For coverage of towns in the Hume Corridor in Victoria, please see p. 557.

■ Sydney to Goulburn

As the state capital recedes in the rearview mirror, the Hume Hwy leads into an area known as the Cow-pastures, a name given for its use as grazing land outside the young colony at Sydney. Now divided into the towns of **Liverpool, Campbelltown, Camden,** and **Narellan,** this area was the site of some of Australia's first colonial land grants, including the 1805 grant to John Macarthur, whose family's wildly successful investment in wool and wine is popularly considered the starting point of the nation's wealth. Housed at **Mt. Annan Botanic Garden** (tel. 4648 2477), off the F5 freeway between Campbelltown and Camden along Tourist Drive 18, the native plants collection of Sydney's **Royal Botanic Garden** includes specimens collected throughout Australia on over 410 hectares. (Open daily Apr.-Sept. 10am-4pm; Oct.-Mar. 10am-6pm. Entrance $5 per car, $2 per cyclist or pedestrian. Wheelchair accessible.) For a day of Australiana, **Gledswood** (tel. 2606 5111), on Camden Valley Way closer to Camden, entertains visitors through a variety of farm activities including sheep-shearing, boomerang-throwing, and wine-tasting. (Open daily 10am-4pm. Shows begin at 11am. $16, seniors $12.50, ages 5-12 $9. Wheelchair accessible.)

Two budget accommodations are available in the town of **Mittagong,** 40 minutes south of Campbelltown. There's a **caravan park** (tel. 4871 1574), with standard facilities and rates, and comfortable pub accommodation at the **Lion Rampant Hotel** (tel. 4871 1090; fax 4871 1990), whose rooms are clean and comfy (singles $25, doubles $35; inquire at the bar daily 10am-11pm). **Bowral,** 3km further south, was the childhood home of Australia's legendary cricketer, **Sir Donald Bradman.** The **Bradman Museum** (tel. 4862 1247), on Saint Jude St next to the Bradman Oval, documents the history of Australian cricket in sporting club luxury (open daily 10am-4pm; admission $7, ages 5-18 $3, families of 4 $17). Between the two towns, a westward turn-off from the Hume Hwy leads to **Wombeyan Caves** (tel. 4843 5976), a series of five caves open for public exploration. It's a long detour (2hr. each way), but the depth and beauty of the caves make it worthwhile. (Open daily 8:30am-5pm, last tour 4:30pm. $10, ages 5-15 $5, families $25; guided tour $12, $6, $30.)

Thirty kilometers south of Mittagong lies the turn-off for **Morton National Park,** off the Hume Hwy by way of the Bundanoon/Exeter exit. Thick forests stretch toward the sandstone cliffs at the park's interior, carved by excellent walking tracks. At the park's edge, the town of Bundanoon has one lovely accommodation: the **Bundanoon YHA Hostel** (tel./fax 4883 6010), a spacious old guesthouse on Railway Ave on the north end of town. The hostel combines warm management with facilities including a fully-equipped kitchen and a game room. The bedrooms have no heat but lots of blankets. (Reception open daily 8-10am and 5-9:30pm. Dorms $14, under 18 $7; twins $33; doubles $36; family rooms $39. YHA nonmembers $3 more.) From the hostel, a short walking trail leads to the bioluminescent bliss of the **Glow Worm Glen,** best seen at night (1hr. round-trip). Trails from the glen cross into Morton National Park, and hiking maps available at the hostel cover the entire area. **CityRail trains** from Sydney's Central Station stop at Bundanoon's railway station daily ($12.80, off-peak return $15.40).

■ Goulburn

Settled in the early 1830s, Goulburn (pop. 22,000) has long been a regional center: once of agriculture and the judicial system, now of the Merino wool industry. A plethora of public and private buildings that date from the 1800s are still in use. This day-to-day connection with its history gives Goulburn a feeling of continuity unusual among the historical towns of New South Wales.

ORIENTATION AND PRACTICAL INFORMATION Goulburn is on the Hume Hwy between Yass (87km) and Sydney (195km)and 10km east of the junction with the Federal Hwy. **Countrylink** (tel. 4827 1485), **CityRail** (tel. 13 15 00), **Fearnes Coaches** (tel. 1800 029 918), **Greyhound Pioneer** (tel. 13 20 30), and **McCafferty's** (tel. 13 14 99) all run service to area towns and major destinations such as Sydney and Canberra. Trains and buses arrive at the **Goulburn Railway Station** on Sloane St. Across from Belmore Park, the **Goulburn Visitors Centre,** 6 Montague St (tel. 4823 0492; fax 4822 2692; email visitor@gis.net.au; open daily 9am-5pm), distributes heaps of good advice and brochures, including the free *Historic Two Foot Tour* guide to the city's historic buildings. A Victorian-era building doubles as the **post office,** 165 Auburn St (tel. 4821 1422), and the local historic walking tour (open M-F 8:30am-5pm; postal code 2580). **Internet access** is available at the **Southern Tablelands Regional Library** (tel. 4823 0435) in the Civic Centre on Bourke St ($5 per hr.; open M-Sa 10am-5pm, Su 2pm-5pm).

ACCOMMODATIONS AND SIGHTS While the pubs along Sloane St across from the railway station are convenient, cheaper digs can be found at the **Goulburn Gateway Service Station** (tel. 4821 9811), on the corner of Common St and the Hume Hwy, at the north end of town where the owners have converted the defunct bus depot behind their gas station, store, and restaurant complex into a small **dormitory.** The location is disconcerting, but the bedrooms are clean, well-lit, and livable. (Bathrooms, showers, no kitchen, no blankets. Reception open 24hr. at gas station counter. Beds $13. Linen $3.) There's also a typical **caravan park** (tel. 4821 3233) at the opposite end of town.

An enduring, if tacky, monument to the city's livelihood, the 97-ton **Big Merino** (tel. 4821 8800), a three-story Merino Ram, stands next to the Hume Hwy at the southwest end of town. Climb up into his head and look out over Goulburn through the eyes of the Big Merino; enlightenment will come. Postcards to commemorate the moment can be purchased downstairs in the gift shop. (Open daily 8am-8pm. Free.)

The high points of the historic walking tour lie on Montague St in the center of town. On one end, near Sloane St, across from Belmore Park, the dome of the **1887 Court House** (tel. 4821 9522) towers over stately grounds and a magnificent interior (open M-F 9:30am-4pm; free). Two blocks up the street is **St. Saviour's Cathedral** (tel. 4821 2206), built between 1874 and 1884 (open M-Sa 10am-4pm; small donation requested with guided tour). The **Goulburn Brewery** (tel. 4821 6071), on Bungonia Rd, southeast of the city center, doesn't appear on the walking tour but deserves a stop nonetheless. The buildings are open daily for visitation, but guided tours and tastings happen only on Sundays. The restaurant and bar on the premises serve tea, lunch, dinner, and, of course, beer. (Buildings, restaurants, and upstairs exhibits open M-Th 11am-7pm, F-Sa 11am-7pm or later, Su 11am-5pm. Tours Su 11am and 3pm, 40min., $5, under 18 free.)

■ Yass

If you're wondering just what dead white guy the Hume Corridor was named for (hint: not the British philosopher), you can find out in Yass, one hour northwest of Canberra near the junction with the Barton Hwy. The former home of famous Australian explorer Hamilton Hume, Yass lies one hour northwest of Canberra, just west of the Barton Hwy's junction with the Hume Hwy, and one hour west of Goulburn. Next door to the information center, The **Hamilton Hume Museum** (tel. 6226 2557) on Comur St is named after the famous explorer who forged the path from Sydney to Melbourne, and houses a small collection of artifacts from his life and expeditions. (Open Sa-Su, holidays, most Fridays, and some weekdays 10am-4pm. Admission $2, ages 5-15 50¢.) East of town, between Yass and the Barton Hwy on Yass Valley Way, **Cooma Cottage** (tel. 6226 1470) is Hume's home. (Open W-M 10am-4pm; $4, students, seniors, and ages 5-15 $2, families of 4 $10.) For travelers with cars, **Carey's Caves** (tel. 6227 9622), at Wee Jasper, an hour (42km) southwest of Yass, make an excellent daytrip, boasting seven main chambers of limestone and crystal formations. (Tours M and F noon, 1, and 2pm, Sa Su noon, 1, 2 and 3pm. $8, ages 5-15 $4.)

Transborder Express (tel. 6241 0033) connects Yass to Canberra (1hr., 5 per day, $10), and **Greyhound Pioneer** (tel. 13 20 30) passes through on its way from Sydney to Adelaide (6hr., 7 per week, $30). **Fearnes Coaches** (tel. 1800 029 918) has service to Sydney (5hr., 1 per day, $35). The **Australian Hotel Motel** (tel. 6226 1744), 180 Comur St, is a clean and reasonably quiet pubstay (singles $12, doubles $20).

■ Gundagai

Tucked between the Murrumbidgee River and the Hume Hwy, Gundagai's (GUN-dah-GUY) idiosyncratic appeal breaks the monotonous efficiency of a Hume commute. The **Gundagai Tourist and Travel Centre** (tel. 6944 1341; fax 6944 1409) on **Sheridan St** east of the Hume Hwy provides tourist information, and operates transportation from Gundagai via **V/Line, McCafferty's, Firefly, Fearnes,** and **Greyhound.** The center houses a stunning tribute to craftwork and neurosis: **Frank Rusconi's Marble Masterpiece,** a miniature marble cathedral composed of 20,948 pieces of handcrafted marble and constructed between 1910 and 1938. (Office open M-F 8am-5pm, Sa-Su 9am-5pm. Admission to the marble masterpiece $1, children 50¢, family $3). Also of interest are Gundagai's **Historic Bridges,** just south of Sheridan St's eastern end. South of Sheridan, the **Gundagai Historical Museum** (tel. 6944 1995) on

Homer St houses a hodgepodge of old machinery, farm equipment, and even a Model T ($3, children $1, concessions $2). The bridges and surrounding areas offer numerous striking vistas. A final sight to catch is the **Dog on the Tuckerbox** (tel. 6944 1450), immortalized in poetry and song and mercilessly milked by the surrounding tourist complex 5km north of Gundagai.

The **Criterion Hotel** (tel. 6944 1048), on the corner of Sheridan and Byron St, provides excellent pub lodging with complimentary continental brekkie. The pub has some funky nude paintings, but the rooms stick to the practical amenities. (Electric blankets, basins, lounge room. Singles $20; doubles $38. Reception at the bar 10am-10pm daily.) There's also a pleasant enough **caravan park** (tel. 6944 1057) on Junee Rd. The **restaurant** scene is basically just pub grub. The **Foodtown market** is at 152 Sheridan St (tel. 6944 1499; open M-F 8am-6pm, Sa 8am-12:30pm).

■ Albury-Wodonga

Spanning the westward-flowing Murray River, which marks the border between New South Wales and Victoria, the Albury-Wodonga metropolitan area (pop. 90,000) belongs to both states. Right on the Hume Hwy, it breaks the transit between Sydney and Melbourne and provides an excellent base for daytrips into the neighboring Riverina, Murray country, wineries, and alpine retreats. The preponderance of quality budget accommodations and cheap eats make the twin cities the most backpacker-friendly pitstop along the Hume. Many choose to linger a while, especially during the summer months when the river is high and ripe for outdoors excursions.

New South Wales' Albury dominates its sibling, housing high culture art galleries, museums, a movie theatre, and a nightclub. Albury's newly refurbished main street, Dean St, showcases an eclectic array of building styles and serves as a lively shopping and idling boulevard. Wodonga is more discreet and mostly residential. Following WWII, Wodonga became a new home for many displaced persons and refugees from war-torn Europe, endowing Albury-Wodonga with a bit of cosmopolitan ambiance.

ORIENTATION

The **Hume Hwy** (Hwy 31) enters Albury from the northeast before turning sharply west to bypass Wodonga. The **Murray Valley Hwy** (Hwy 16) runs along the Victorian side and enters Wodonga from the southeast, where it runs through town before uniting with the Hume Hwy. Running along the Murray River on the New South Wales side, the **Riverina Hwy** (Hwy 58) goes from Corowa, west of Albury, straight through towards Khancoban in the east. In Albury, **Dean St** forms the central east-west artery, beginning at the railroad tracks and crossed by **Young St** (Hume Hwy) farthest east, then Macauley, David, Olive, Kiewa, and Townsend St. **Smollett St** runs parallel to Dean St one block south. In Wodonga, **High St** defines the small city center, with major cross streets Elgin and Lawrence feeding into it just south of the railroad tracks. Take Elgin St west to rejoin the Hume Hwy.

PRACTICAL INFORMATION

Airport: Albury Airport (tel. 6041 1241) is northeast of the city center on Burella Rd in the direction of Lake Hume. Signs from Hume Hwy point the way. Hazleton and Kendell fly from Albury to Sydney (from $110) and to Melbourne (from $85), but tickets are bookable through Ansett (13 13 00). Prices fluctuate seasonally.

Trains and Buses: Albury Travel Centre (tel. 6041 9555), on Railway St north of the Hume Hwy, 1 block east of Dean St. **CountryLink** (13 22 32) train service to Sydney (7½hr., 11:36am and 11:10pm, $75) and Canberra (by train 11:30am, $45). **McCafferty's** and **Greyhound Pioneer** coach service to Melbourne (3-4hr., 4-5 per day, $37.80), Echuca (Tu, Th, and Sa, 3:30am, $32), Mildura (Tu, Th, and Sa, 7:20am, $54), Adelaide (12hr., 4:25am, $54), and Canberra (3:40pm, $25). Open for bookings M-F 8:30am-5pm, Sa-Su 9:30am-4:30pm.

Tourist Office: Gateway Visitors Information Centre (tel. 6041 3875 or 1800 800 743; fax 6021 0322), in the Gateway Village no-man's land between Albury and

Wodonga on the east (Melbourne-bound) side of the Hume Hwy. Open daily 9am-5pm. Tune in to 88 FM for tourist information.

American Express Office: 574 Dean St (tel. 6041 3333, 24hr. tel. 0419 244 989; fax 6021 1139), in Albury Travel. No mail-holding service. Wheelchair accessible. Open M-F 9am-5:30pm, Sa 9am-noon.

Currency Exchange: Westpac Bank, 613 Dean St (tel. 6041 1111), charges a $7 flat fee to change travelers' checks and no commission for cash exchanges. Open M-Th 9:30am-4pm, F 9:30am-5pm. **ATMs** line Dean St.

Supermarket: Coles (tel. 6041 5377), Kiewa and Smollett St. Open 7am-midnight.

Laundry: (tel. 6041 4050) on the corner of Smollett and David St, across from Albury Backpackers. Open daily 5:30am-10:30pm.

Police: (tel. 6023 9299), on Olive St near Dean St.

Emergency: Dial 000.

Post Office: At the corner of Dean and Kiewa St (tel. 6021 1755). Open M-F 9am-5pm. **Postal Code:** 2640. Branch in the **Big W Shopping Centre,** Lavington (tel. 6025 1357), open M-F 9am-5:30pm, Sa 9am-noon.

Phone code: 02.

ACCOMMODATIONS

Albury offers hostels, pub hotels, and myriad motels and caravan parks. Stay in Wodonga and you'll have to commute to get to the heart of the happenings and the best eateries. But you won't have to worry about fruit flies (see signs along river).

Albury Backpackers, 459 David St (tel. 6041 1822; fax 6031 6335), corner of Smollett St. The spirit of backpacking is alive and well at this comfy hostel near the train station. Travelers bond through the popular overnight canoe trips ($49 for 2-day Murray trip), pub crawls, karaoke nights, or just lounging in the common space. Tidy, well-stocked kitchen, free bike use. Linen included. Check-out 11am. Dorms $13 (1st night $14), weekly $70; doubles and twins $29 (1st night $30). VIP.

Albury Motor Village (YHA), 372 Wagga Rd (Hume Hwy) (tel. 6040 2999; fax 6040 3160), 5km north of the city center in Lavington across from the KFC and Cal-Tex. Pool, kitchenette, TV lounge provide plenty of space for unwinding. Laundry, parking. Quiet, family-friendly. Reception open daily 7:30am-10:30pm. Dorms $14, YHA nonmembers $17. Powered sites $17 for 2 people. Cabins for 2 $43-82. All but deluxe cabins are BYO linens and towels. Book ahead in summer.

Brady's Railway Hotel, 450 Smollett St (tel. 6021 4700; fax 6021 2604), 2 blocks from the railway station. Unbeatable location, accommodating owner, and a downstairs pub clientele a bit more inviting to outsiders than at some of the neighboring pubstays. Check-out 10am. Reception at bar M-Sa 7am-midnight, Su 7am-8pm. Singles $18, doubles $30; ask about backpacker rate. $10 key deposit.

FOOD AND ENTERTAINMENT

Dean St proffers a fine collection of international cuisine ranging from Thai and Indian to Mexican and Lebanese. The **Commercial Club,** 618 Dean St (tel. 6021 1133) serves an all-you-can-eat lunch and dinner with a rich variety of vegetables, meat dishes and surprisingly gourmet desserts, all for $7.70. Provided you don't get lured into the casino next door, it's the best deal in town. (Open daily for lunch noon-2pm, dinner 5:30pm-9pm. Neat casual dress code.) **Za Porchetta,** 460 Dean St (tel. 6021 0755) offers super Italian fare at even better prices. (Open Su-Th 11am-midnight, F-Sa 11am-1am. BYO wine only. Corkage $2 per bottle.) For a funky change of pace, try **Cafe Gryphon,** 468 Dean St (tel. 6041 5899), with a Formica-meets-mismatched-dinette-set decor and a fun, lively mood. You can wolf down $5.80 foccacias or $7-12 dinner entrees, but some swear by the luscious mud cake. (Open daily 10:30am-late.) For those staying in Lavington near the YHA, **Dragon Castle,** 324 Wagga Rd (tel. 6025 5177), opposite McDonalds, is a great Chinese choice (mains $9; open daily noon-2pm and 5pm-10pm).

Albury's one and only nightclub, **The Ritz Tavern Nightclub,** 480 Dean St (tel. 6041 4484), is a high-budget, high-class dance venue. It's always a mad party on

Wednesday Uni Nights, when $2 basic spirits and middies of beer suck CSU students in like a black hole. Thursdays are notoriously silent, but Friday and Saturday nights kick off around midnight to the latest dance music. Strict neat casual dress code applies. (Cover $5 W-F, $8 on Sa. Open W-Th 4pm-4am, F-Sa 4pm-5am.)

SIGHTS AND ACTIVITIES

The **Albury Regional Art Gallery,** 546 Dean St (tel. 6023 8187), presents an array of contemporary art exhibitions, including a collection of works by famous Australian artist Russell Drysdale. **Hothouse Theatre** (tel. 6021 7433) does local drama in a performance space located in the Gateway Village on the Hume Hwy, next to the visitors center. Pick up a schedule of shows and times in the Art Gallery. *(Tickets $9-19, concessions $6-13.)* On Wodonga Pl between Smollett and Dean St, the **Albury Botanic Gardens** (tel. 6023 8241) rest in green splendor. Among the diverse arboreal displays, there's plenty of grassy picnic space. To take in a sweeping view of the region, climb to the top of the **Monument Hill Bushlands** and gaze out on Albury-Wodonga from the Deco obelisk Albury War Memorial. You can walk directly uphill from Dean St, or follow the street up and around the back of the hill.

Departing from Norieul Park on the Murray River, the paddlesteamer **P.S. Cumberoona** (tel. 6041 5558) paddles along the river during spring, summer, and autumn. *(1hr. cruises $8, children ages 4-15 $4.50; 1½hr. $9.50, children $4.50. Cruises depart W, Sa, and Su 10am, noon, and 2pm; Th-F 2pm.)* On the Riverina Hwy 14km east of Albury, the **Hume Weir Trout Farm** (tel. 6026 4334) raises Rainbow Trout for commercial and recreational purposes. You can pet baby trout (if you really, really miss your puppy), catch trout (rods $1, free bait, fish cost $8.50/kg, cleaning 20¢ per fish) and sample smoked trout. *(Open daily 9am-dusk. Admission $5.50, students $4.50, children $2.50, trout free.)* Nearby, massive **Lake Hume** offers fishing, boating, and waterfront picnic areas—inquire at the general store just beyond the turn-off for the trout farm.

■ Near Albury-Wodonga: Ettamogah Pub

Just 15km north of Albury along the Hume Hwy, the Ettamogah Pub explodes in goofy fun as it caters to gawking tourists and satirizes and stereotypes all things Aussie. Based on the work of cartoonist **Ken Maynard,** this amusement-park-style village is composed of eye-popping, off-kilter buildings decorated with a running stream of witticisms. The centerpiece is the hilariously constructed Ettamogah Pub, capped with a vintage Fosters beer truck and filled with business-card-slathered walls. Other sites include a hollowed-out tree ensconced in bars and dubbed Lock Out, a police "offise" covered in corny cop punnery, a real pottery studio, and Dodgie Bros. Auto Repairs and Fire Brigade, which houses vintage autos. The **Ettamogah Winery** at the rear of the complex has free tastings and wine sales (daily 10am-4pm). There's no admission to tour the site, and signs will clearly direct you from the highway.

RIVERINA

Dry, brown, and flat, much of the Riverina's terrain doesn't look like a land suited for farming, yet heavy irrigation has turned the soil into fertile plains. Although not a prime sight-seeing destination, the Riverina attracts budget travelers seeking seasonal farm or fruit-picking labor in order to save up for more exciting destinations. Two rivers fertilize the system; the **Murrumbidgee** starts as a trickle in the Snowy Mountains and then widens into a major waterway that eventually joins the **Murray.**

▓ Wagga Wagga

New South Wales' largest inland city (pop. 58,000), sprawling Wagga Wagga (mercifully abbreviated and pronounced WAU-guh) is more of a commercial and residential center and uni town (housing Charles Sturt University's main campus) than a tourist destination. The **post office** is in the **Wagga Wagga Marketplace** mall on Baylis St between Forsyth and Morgan St (open M-F 8:30am-5pm, Th 8:30am-7pm, Sa 9am-noon; postal code 2650). Find free **Internet access** at the **Wagga Wagga City Library** (tel. 6921 5244), 40 Coorwood St (open M 11am-7pm, Tu-F 10am-7pm, Sa 10am-5pm). For rooms, try the pubs on Fitzmaurice St. A range of cuisine lines Baylis St. There's a **Coles supermarket** (tel. 6921 5377) at Baylis and Forsyth St.

The **Wagga Wagga City Art Gallery**, 40 Gurwood St (tel. 6923 5419), but moving in 1999 into the Wagga Wagga Civic Centre on the corner of Baylis St and Morgan St, houses the **National Art Glass Collection** and the **Carnegie Print Collection.** (Open Tu-F 11am-5pm, Sa 10am-5pm, Su and public holidays noon-4pm. Free. Wheelchair accessible.) South of the city (in the direction of the big hill) is the **Wagga Wagga Botanic Gardens** (tel. 6923 5451) and the neighboring **Wagga Wagga Historical Museum** (tel. 6925 2934). To reach them, you'll have to earn it—turn left out of the railway station onto Edward St, left again immediately onto Edmonson St, follow that up a hill and down to a roundabout, then turn left onto Lord Baden Powell Dr The museum displays 19th-century tools, clothes, and community relics, and includes a hollowed-tree canoe built by the Wiradjuri Aboriginals. (Open Tu-W, Sa-Su, and public holidays 2-5pm. $3, children $1.) Next door, an attractive botanical garden is arranged across nine hectares. A beautiful **aviary** envelops visitors in native birdlife, and pathways wind pleasantly among the brooks and trees. There's also a native-animal **petting zoo.** (Park open daily from dawn to dusk; free).

■ Narrandera

Narrandera blends the convenience of a transportation hub with a peppering of unique attractions, making it the most worthwhile tourist stop in the Riverina. Some come for a quick meander through Narrandera's koala sanctuary, heritage buildings, and water park; others are attracted by the prospect of seasonal agricultural work in nearby Leeton and Griffith. Part of its character is that the town doesn't trip over itself to nab tourists and has kept its small-town intimacy. Situated about halfway between Adelaide and Sydney, off the Sturt Hwy, the town provides excellent budget beds for commuters. It is also about a day's drive from Melbourne en route to Brisbane along the Newell Hwy.

ORIENTATION AND PRACTICAL INFORMATION Narrandera's streets are shaded by large, leafy canopies and are beautiful to drive or stroll along. The town's main road, **East St,** runs north-south one block east of Cadell St. Most accommodations, restaurants, and services lie along East St. The **Narrandera Tourist Information Centre** (tel. 1800 672 392 or 6959 1766), located on Cadell St within the large park, provides excellent maps and accommodation and restaurant listings. It also houses the **world's second largest playable guitar**—Bristol, England, reclaimed the title last year with a slightly larger one. The tourist center operates the **Tiger Moth Memorial** next

---

How to Spot a Koala

If you're expecting to see koalas on the roadside or catch glimpses of them in the trees as you drive by, you may be disappointed. There are relatively few left (unlike the omnipresent kangaroos and wombats), and they spend nearly 20 hours of each day dozing high up in the tree tops, doped up on slightly-toxic but oh-so-yummy-and-spiritually-enlightening (to them) eucalyptus leaves. During the summer, koalas tend to be found lower in the trees and are easier to spot, but the experienced looker can find them any time of the year by carefully searching for fresh droppings resembling elongated, dark brown jellybeans, spread out around the base of the trees. The other trick is to memorize which trees tend to house koalas, since males are often territorial. If watching trees and inspecting marsupial crap isn't your ballgame, well, that's why God made zoos. (Just kidding.)

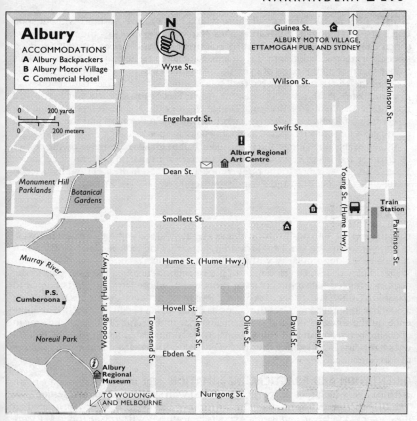

Albury

ACCOMMODATIONS
A Albury Backpackers
B Albury Motor Village
C Commercial Hotel

Guinea St.
TO
ALBURY MOTOR VILLAGE,
ETTAMOGAH PUB, AND SYDNEY

Wyse St.

Wilson St.

Engelhardt St.

Swift St.

Albury Regional
Art Centre

Dean St.

Monument Hill
Parklands

Botanical
Gardens

Smollett St.

Hume St. (Hume Hwy.)

Murray River

Hovell St.

P.S.
Cumberoona

Noreuil Park

Ebden St.

Albury
Regional
Museum

TO WODONGA
AND MELBOURNE

Nurigong St.

Parkinson St.

Young St. (Hume Hwy.)

Parkinson St.

Train
Station

Wodonga Pl. (Hume Hwy.)

Townsend St.

Kiewa St.

Olive St.

David St.

Macauley St.

NEW SOUTH WALES

door, which houses a WWII aircraft and serves as a reminder of Narrandera's role as a training site for the Royal Australian Air Force (both tourist office and Tiger Moth open daily 9am-5pm). Two blocks east of East St's north end is the **railway station** (tel. 6959 3424), basically a snack shop for motor coach passengers (open daily 7:30am-5pm). **Harvey World Travel** (tel. 6959 3330; fax 6959 3325) provides info and can help arrange local transport (open M-F 9am-5pm, Sa 9am-12noon). The **post office** is at the corner of Twynam and East St (open M-F 9am-5pm; postal code 2700).

ACCOMMODATIONS AND FOOD   Across from the railway station, the **Historic Star Lodge** 64 Whittou St (tel. 6959 1768; fax 6959 4164), provides B&B and hostel-style accommodations. Registered with the National Trust, the well-maintained guest-house preserves elegant high ceilings, arches, and ample verandas in their early 20th-century flavor. Dorms sleep four; B&B rooms are a tad fancier. All rooms are climate-controlled and have linens, and bathrooms are immaculate. Downstairs, a TV lounge, sitting room with fireplace, dining room, laundry, and guest kitchen provide additional conveniences. (Reception open daily 8am-10pm. Dorms $17; singles $35; doubles $55. YHA.) For even cheaper lodging, try the **Royal Mail Hotel** (tel. 6959 2007; fax 6959 1059), a pubstay that's a bargain (singles $10, doubles $20; linen included).

For good Chinese food, sample an item from the never-ending menu of **Hing Wah** (tel. 6959 2059), downtown on East St. The large dining room is bedecked in lanterns and has a strange orange painting of a sunset over Hong Kong. (Open Su-Th 5pm-9pm, F-Sa 5pm-10pm. Takeaway available.) For staples, hit **Foodworks** (tel. 6959 2388) on East St (open M-W 8am-6:30pm, Th-F 8am-7pm, Sa 8am-3pm, Su 9am-2pm).

SIGHTS AND ACTIVITIES For all those who'd hate to leave Australia without spotting a koala in the wild, the **Narrandera Nature Reserve** is just the place for you (open daily dawn to dusk). A healthy colony of koalas has been steadily growing since their reintroduction into the area in 1972, and one Sunday each spring locals gather together all the pairs of eyes they can muster to partake in the great koala count in the woods of the reserve (call tourist office for the precise date if you wish to participate). From town, drive south down East St towards the canal until you reach Lake Dr, then cross the canal bridge to enter the Nature Reserve. Within the reserve, two **beaches** are clearly marked off the main dirt road and these provide great places for sunny relaxation as well as wildlife spotting.

Also enjoyable for summer fun is the **Lake Talbot Holiday Complex** on the corner of Broad St and Lake Dr, which borders the creek just past the Narrandera Nature Reserve bridge. Entrance to the **pool** complex costs $2 (children $1) and has a steep **water slide** (30¢ per ride) and a winding water flume (20¢ per ride).

■ Griffith

Griffith (pop. 22,500) positively bustles as a residential and commercial center—well, in comparison to the farmland around it, anyway. One look at a map of the town reveals its striking similarity with the layout of Canberra; both were designed by Walter Burley Griffin. Development of the irrigation scheme in the early part of the century attracted Italian miners from Broken Hill, whose farming efforts helped to transform Griffith and its once-barren soil into the agricultural center it is today. With a 60% Italian population, Griffith retains its cosmopolitan edge, and the Italian influence on the town's food and drink means that dining cheaply doesn't just mean choosing between fish and chips shops. To accommodate its fruit pickers, Griffith does have dirt-cheap lodging, but it is very basic and perhaps not as comfortable as that in Narrandera.

ORIENTATION AND PRACTICAL INFORMATION The main axis through Griffith is Banna Ave, which runs east-west and is lined with strip-mall shops and restaurants. The **Griffith Visitors Information Centre** (tel. 6962 4145; fax 6962 7319), located on the corner of Jondaryan and Banna Ave, sits beneath a WWII airplane (open M-F 9am-5pm, Sa 9am-3pm, Su 10am-2pm). The **post office** is at 245-263 Banna Ave (open M-F 9am-5pm, postal code 2680). Griffith is a stop on most major inter-city bus routes, though often in the middle of the night. Inside the Mobil service station at 121 Banna Ave, **Griffith Travel & Transit** (tel. 6962 7199; fax 6962 4496) handles service for **McCafferty's, Greyhound Pioneer,** and **Countrylink** (tickets sold M-F 9am-5:30pm, Sa 9am-12pm, Su 1:30-2:30pm). **Internet access** is surprisingly as plentiful as the harvest. Try the **Western Riviera Public Library**, 233-7 Banna Ave (tel. 6962 2515; $3 per 30min.; open M-F 9am-5:30pm, Sa 9am-12:30pm), or **Galaxy Gateway Internet Cafe** (tel. 6964 2151; $4 for 30 min; open M-Th 9am-8pm, F 9am-5pm, Sa 10am-4pm). To find **work,** ask the local hostel manager, or call **Pickers Plus,** 200 Olympic St (tel. 6964 0080; fax 6964 2409), which provides training and links growers with laborers.

ACCOMMODATIONS AND FOOD The place to be if you're seeking harvesting work is the **Griffith International Hostel,** 112 Binya St (tel. 6964 4236 or mobile 0418 601 932; fax 6964 4236). The unheated rooms are cramped, but the kitchen and dining areas are spacious, and the price unbeatable for those trying to put away some cash. The catch is that you must have an overseas passport and **work visa,** since their goal is to attract foreign labor to the area. Call ahead and the manager will arrange work in advance and he'll even drop you off at work in the mornings. ($14 nightly, $84 weekly. $5 key deposit, linen included.YHA, VIP. Open daily 7-11am and 4-6pm.) Downtown on Banna Ave, the **Area Hotel** (tel. 6962 3122) offers pub lodging in a recently decorated modern facility (singles $30, with breakfast $35; twins $40, with breakfast $45). The **Griffith Tourism Caravan Park** (tel. 6964 2144), four blocks south of the info center on the corner of Jondaryan St and Willandra Ave, offers the usual prices and range of accommodations. For flavorful cuisine, try any of the Italian restaurants or cafes along Banna Ave. Among the best is **J.D.'s Pizza** (tel. 6962 7777), 188 Banna Ave, where a huge range of saucy pastas are $8 (lunch focaccias $5; open daily 11am-2pm, 5pm-late).

SIGHTS AND ACTIVITIES Griffith's attractions are clustered around the **bush reserve,** located on the town's northern bluffs. The aptly named **Scenic Drive** heading east offers two lookouts over the surroundings. travelers can scope out the surrounding area from two lookouts. Although Griffith's **wineries** produce an incredibly high volume of wine, they are in general slightly less geared for tourists than wineries in other regions. **DeBortoli Winery** (tel. 6964 9444), off Yenda Rd northeast of the town center, has several generations of tradition, a guided tour through the modern facilities Tuesdays at 2pm, and a restaurant for lunch (open M-Sa 9am-5pm, Su 9am-4pm). **Rosetto Wines** (tel. 6963 5214), on Rosetto Rd off Yenda Rd, sells wine in its cellar door and has a guided tour Thursdays at 2pm (open M-Sa 8:30am-5:30pm). The region is particularly noted for its botrytis semillon, which has a divine marmalade sweetness.

Back in town, the **Griffith Regional Theatre** (tel. 6962 7466) shows productions suitable for all audiences (box office open M-F 10am-5pm, Sa 9am-noon). Just down from the post office at 167-185 Banna Ave, an eye-catching pastel building houses the **Griffith Regional Art Gallery** (tel. 6962 5991), which has a collection of contemporary Australian jewelry (temporary exhibitions Tu-Sa 10:30am-4:30pm).

NORTHWEST AND BACK O' BOURKE

The empty stretches of northwest and far west New South Wales couldn't be more antithetical to the state's urbane capital. Although it encompasses the watershed of the Murray and Darling Rivers, the continent's largest river system, the region's arid climate has discouraged widespread settlement. So remote is the image Bourke (pronounced "Burke") evokes in the minds of Sydney siders, that dubbing the state's outback as "back o' Bourke" is tantamount to declaring it the end of the earth. Cotton agriculture supports a modest economy, bolstered by the lead and silver mines at Broken Hill. Sprinkled across this lesser-known half of New South Wales are some of Australia's most remote national parks, including Lake Mungo, which has yielded evidence of human occupation in Australia many tens of thousands of years ago.

■ Coonabarabran

The town of Coonabarabran (coon-a-BAR-a-brin), 159km northeast of Dubbo on the Newell Hwy, is a base town for nearby **Warrumbungle National Park** and a center for astronomical observation. It's also accessible from the northeast through Gunnedah on the Oxley Hwy, which joins the Newell and enters from the north. Warrumbungle and the observatories are both east of town. The main drag is **John St** (the Newell Hwy), home to a number of motels and crossed by Dalgarno, Cassilis, and Edwards St.

PRACTICAL INFORMATION The **Coonabarabran Visitors Centre** (tel. 6842 1441; fax 6842 2766) has an intriguing display on **Australian megafauna,** including the skeleton of a giant Diprotodon, the largest marsupial ever to roam the earth, as well as an exhibit about the catastrophic bushfire that struck the nearby Pilliga Scrub in late 1997. (Open daily 9am-5pm.) It's on John St at the south end of town, along with several **ATMs** and a **post office** (tel. 6842 1193; open M-F 9am-5pm). **Countrylink** (tel. 13 22 32) carries passengers to and from Sydney (8hr.; M-F 1 per day; $66), stopping at the visitors center. **McCafferty's** (tel. 13 14 99) makes twice-daily trips to Narrabri (80min.; $40, students $36) and Dubbo (2hr.; $33, $30). **Greyhound Pioneer** (tel. 13 20 30) has similar trips but its rates tend to be somewhat cheaper. **Harvey**

World Travel, 35A Dalgarno St (tel. 6842 1566; fax 6842 1936), can book seats on any of these buses (open M-F 9am-5pm, Sa 9am-noon). No bus company runs to Warrumbungle National Park.

ACCOMMODATIONS AND FOOD Book ahead for accommodations during school holidays. The **Imperial Hotel** (tel. 6842 1023), on the corner of John and Dalgarno St, is a YHA hostel over a pub with a narrow kitchen, glassed-in dining room terrace, and comfy TV lounge. Rooms have heating, bureaus, and sinks. (Bunks in 3-bed dorm $14, singles or doubles $28, twins $34, family $63. With bath singles $30, doubles $37, triples $40. Linen included.) The **John Oxley Caravan Park** (tel. 6842 1635) is on Chappell Ave just before the Newell Hwy. There's a shop, playground, and gas barbecue. (Reception open daily 8am-noon and 2-9pm. Tent sites $7.50, for 2 $9.50, each additional person $2.50; with power $11, $12, $3; on-site caravans $20, $25, $3. Cabins for 1 or 2 $29.50 with bath $39; each extra person $5; linen not included.) The **Festival IGA Supermarket** (tel. 6842 1179) is on Dalgarno St (open M-F 8:30am-6pm, Th till 6:30pm, Sa 9am-4pm, Su 9am-1pm). There are plenty of lunch counters on John St. The **Jolly Cauli Coffee Shop,** 30 John St (tel. 6842 2021), is a fine choice (pasties $2, Devonshire tea and focaccia $4; open M-F 8am-5:30pm, Sa 9:30am-2pm).

SIGHTS Australia's largest optical telescope resides at **Siding Spring Observatory** (tel. 6842 6211), 28km from Coonabarabran on the road to Warrumbungle National Park. *(Open daily 9:30am-4pm. Admission $5, children and students $3, families $12. Tours are given during school holidays and include admission to the center; $8, $6, $21.)* The observatory's visitors center offers an interactive, multimedia window onto the work of the resident astronomers, though no view of the night sky. Nearby **Skywatch Night and Day Observatory** (tel. 6842 2506), on the road to Warrumbungle National Park 2km from Coonabarabran, has guided night viewing sessions and a planetarium. *(Open daily 2-5pm and 6:30-9pm. 1hr. viewing sessions at 7 and 8pm. $10, ages 5-16 and students $6, seniors $8, families of 4 $26; day exhibit only $6, $4, $5, $16.)* You'll probably have more fun here than at Siding Spring, though you won't be seeing ground-breaking research.

    Warrumbungle Light (tel. 6843 4446) has day-long Aboriginal Culture and Ecological Tours that visit recently rediscovered Aboriginal paintings, carvings, and 200- to 2000-year-old campsites. *(Minimum charge $150 for 2 people, additional persons $60, children free to $50 depending on age, family $180. Morning tea and lunch provided. Book ahead.)*
    Warrumbungle Scenic Flights Coonabarabran (tel. 6842 3560 or 0186 34028) runs half-hour guided flights over the nearby national park. *($50-55; kids under 5 free; family rates and pick-up available.)* **Coona Country Tours** (tel./fax 6842 8245) runs ground trips to the Warrambungles and local attractions. *(Minimum group size 8. $120 per day, not including meals or admission prices. Pick-up from Tamworth or Dubbo available.)*

■ Warrumbungle National Park

The jagged spires and rambling peaks of the Warrumbungle Mountains are the result of volcanic activity millions of years ago. As the softer sandstone has worn away under the hardened lava rock, unusual shapes have been left to slice into the sky above the forested hills. Botanically, the mountains sit at the juncture of the lush east and the barren west. Kangaroos and wallabies have long called the area home, while hikers, rock-climbers, and campers have more recently discovered its splendor.

    A 75km **scenic drive** branches off from the Newell Hwy 39km north of Gilgandra and runs through the park, circling back to the highway at Coonabarabran. The road is paved only between Coonabarabran and the park's western edge. The park entry fee ($5 per car, 2-day pass $8, motorcycles $3, cyclists and pedestrians free) should be paid at the **Warrumbungle National Park Visitors Centre** (tel. 6825 4364), on the park road 33km west of Coonabarabran. The center provides detailed info on facilities and walking tracks in the park and distributes permits for rock-climbing (free) and bush camping ($2, students $1, under 6 free). A great light-up map inside highlights some of the park's unusual rock formations. (Open daily 8:30am-4pm.)

Of the park's serviced camping areas, only four are open to individual travelers (at all areas unpowered sites for 2 $10, each additional person $2). **Camp Blackman** has toilets, water, showers, a public payphone, and car-accessible sites (powered $15, $3; wheelchair accessible). **Camp Pincham** lies a short walk from the nearest car park, while **Burbie Camp** requires a 4km hike from the park road (both areas have toilets and showers). **Gunneemooroo** can be reached by a much longer hike from Burbie Camp or by car over the unsealed road from **Tooraweenah** (toilets, water).

The **Gurianawa Track** runs in an easy circle around the visitors center (15min.) and gives a quick introduction to the park environment, including views of the Siding Spring Observatory and the area's extinct volcanoes. The short walk to **Whitegum Lookout** (1km return), 27km from Coonabarabran at the east end of the park, provides striking views of the surrounding mountains. Both of these trails are wheelchair accessible. The most popular of the park's longer walks, the hike to **Grand High Tops** starts at a carpark 1km south of the main park road and 500m west of the turnoff for the visitors center. The steep 12.5km circuit through the southern half of the park passes stunning views of **Breadknife,** an imposing 90m stone tower, and turnoffs for most of the park's other major sights. The walk back via West Spiney adds 2km to the route and provides a chance to see the eagles that often fly around **Bluff Mountain.** Allow five to six hours for the entire trip, plus two more hours if you climb Bluff Mountain (2.4km).

■ Narrabri

Equidistant from Sydney and Brisbane (560km), the prosperous cotton-growing center of Narrabri (nar-uh-BRYE) has two major attractions: the six-dish **Australia Telescope** complex and the beautifully rugged scenery of **Mount Kaputar National Park.** Located 118km northeast of Coonabarabran on the Newell Hwy, it's the type of small town where everyone knows everyone's name. It was hit hard by flooding in July 1998, with at least $70 million of damage and half the year's crop wiped out.

The **Narrabri Visitors Centre** (tel. 6792 3583) lies on the Newell Hwy (Tibbereena St), which veers north in town along Narrabri Creek (open daily 8.30am-5pm). **Greyhound Pioneer** (tel. 13 20 30) buses stop daily in Narrabri on the way between Melbourne (16hr.; $96, students $77) and Brisbane (7½hr.; $50, $40), with service to Coonabarabran on the southern leg (1½hr.; $40, $32). The main drag is **Maitland St,** which runs parallel to Tibbereena one street further from the creek. Services here include the **NPWS office,** 100 Maitland St, level 1 (tel. 6799 1740; open M-F 8:30am-4:30pm), the **post office** (tel. 6782 2199), on the corner of Doyle St (open M-F 9am-5pm), **police** (tel. 6792 1444), on the corner of Bowen, and **banks** with **ATMs.**

All seven pubs along the central three-block stretch of Maitland St offer inexpensive accommodation, and there are a number of motels on the highway. The best of the bunch is **Tattersall's Hotel** (tel. 6792 2007), with a basic kitchen area and comfortable TV room (reception at the bar daily 10am-midnight; rooms $15, weekly $65). The cheapest motel and camping are both at the **Narrabri Motel and Caravan Park,** 92 Cooma Rd (tel. 6792 2593) on the Newell Hwy towards Coonabarabran. (Singles $36, doubles $43, $8 each additional person. Tent sites $10 for 2, powered $12, each additional person $2. Cabins $33-43, $6 each extra person.) For food, there are several lunch counters and bakeries on Maitland St, or try **Woolworths,** across the street from the tourist office on Tibbereena St (open M-F 8am-9pm, Sa-Su 8am-5pm).

Signs on the Newell Hwy heading toward Coonabarabran lead to the **Australia Telescope,** 20km west of Narrabri, a set of six large radio dishes which comprise the largest, most powerful telescope array in the southern hemisphere. The **Australia Telescope Visitors Centre** (tel. 6790 4070; http://wwwnar.atnf.csiro.au) has a helpful staff, videos, and displays (open daily 8am-4pm, staffed M-F; free).

East of Narrabri, the peaks of the **Nandewar Range** beckon travelers to leave the paved road behind and scale the summit of **Mt. Kaputar,** which boasts a view of onetenth of New South Wales. The entrance to the central section of **Mount Kaputar National Park** lies 31km east of Narrabri via Maitland St and Old Gunnedah Rd. **Bark**

Hut Camping Area is 14km inside the park, and **Dawsons Spring Camping Area** is 21km inside near the Mt. Kaputar summit. Both have hot showers, toilets, electricity, and barbecues, but neither is equipped for caravans. (No reservations; sites $15.) The park's most famous attraction is the amazing basalt rock formation known as **Sawn Rocks,** located in the northern section, accessible from the Newell Hwy north of Narrabri. The excellent *Park Guide* pamphlet available from the NPWS office in Narrabri has more hiking info ($3). A copy is posted at the Dawson Spring ranger's cabin.

■ Bourke

On a blistering hot day, Bourke (BURK) can be an eerie place. It is dead quiet. Haze covering the unusually wide, naked streets distorts distance. At one end of the main drag, Oxley St, white office workers stroll past the orderly, immaculately restored Federation style Courthouse, post office, and banks. At the other end, Aboriginal kids in worn clothing loiter beside the pub, convenience store, and public housing office. Bourke is a study in racial division of the sort that is often hidden beneath the surface of Australian society. That shouldn't scare you away; visiting Bourke is an educational experience in this and many other ways. An important inland port town in the late 19th century, Bourke is rich with history, and today it's both a symbolic (as per the idiom "back o' Bourke") and a very real gateway to the outback.

ORIENTATION AND PRACTICAL INFORMATION Bourke lies on the **Mitchell Hwy** (32), 367km northwest of Dubbo and 142km south of the Queensland/NSW border. The Darling River flows through on its way to the Murray River, Bourke's link to Victoria and the sea. **Richard St** branches off **Anson St,** which is the continuation of the Mitchell Hwy through town, and runs all the way to the **Darling River. Oxley St** runs off Richard St to the left, and should be avoided at night. At the corner of Richard and Oxley is the **police station. Mitchell St** crosses Richard St a half block from Oxley St.

The **tourist office** (tel. 6872 1222) is on Anson St, and has a small in-house museum legendizing Bourke's most industrious tough guys. Officials give **historical and farm tours** in winter (2-3hr.; M,W,and F; $10). They can also refer you to farms for **year-round work.** (Office open M-Sa 9am-5pm, Su 12:30-5pm.) The **Bourke Bowling Club** (tel. 6872 2190), on Mitchell St near Richard St, has an **EFTPOS** machine that will dispense a maximum of $200. For **buses** to Dubbo (5hr.; M, W, F, and Sa), purchase tickets at **Lachlan Travel** (tel. 6872 2092), on Oxley St. The **post office,** 47 Oxley St (tel. 6872 2017), occupies the postal code 2840 (open M-F 9am-5pm).

ACCOMMODATIONS AND FOOD The **Bourke Riverside Motel,** 3 Mitchell St (tel. 6872 2539), is to the left off Richard St and rents comfortable yellow rooms with A/C and TV (singles $40, doubles $50, breakfast $5-8; office open daily 6am-10pm). **Port of Bourke Hotel,** 32 Mitchell St (tel. 6872 2544; fax 6872 2687) often displays Aboriginal art and has bar, bistro, and garden dining (singles $31, twins $52, doubles $46). For a "real outback" experience, contact **Ursino Station** (tel. 6874 7540), Wanaaring, in the red desert back o' Bourke. You need 4WD to reach the outpost, a self-contained area where you can bushcamp, take a camel safari, or stay in cottages (from $45 per couple).

In the outback, "cuisine" means anything hot and on the table. For basic pub food, try the **Port of Bourke Hotel.** The superb **Morall's Cappuccino Bakery** (tel. 6872 2086) has sandwiches named after bush poets ($5; open M-F 7am-4pm, Sa 8am-1pm). The **Rite-Way Supermarket** (tel. 6872 2613) is on Warraweena St off Mitchell St.

SIGHTS A few historical buildings around town merit a peek. The **Court House** at Oxley and Richard St, dates to 1900 and can be visited when it's out of session. The **Post Office** and **London Bank** on Oxley St were also built during Bourke's heyday. The **Darling River Run** is billed as "the last of the Great 4WD Adventures." The 439km route follows the Darling all the way to its conjunction with the Murray at Wentworth. It passes famous bush pubs, camping locations and fishing spots. For a free kit, call 1800 247 221. For other adventures beyond the town's borders, ask at the tourist office for **Back o' Bourke Map Tours,** a leaflet containing 11 mudmaps of historical and bush tours that range from 40 minutes to two months.

■ Broken Hill

Broken Hill sits at the extreme western end of New South Wales and right on the edge of nowhere. It would take either insanity or the prospect of untold riches to convince people to live way the hell out here, and a healthy dose of each gave rise to Broken Hill. In 1883, Charles Rasp, a German-born boundary rider employed on the lonesome Mt. Gipps sheep station, discovered that the misshapen hill known locally as the "hog's back" was in fact one of the biggest lodes of silver-lead ore in the world. Rasp and his associates opened the soon fabulously wealthy Broken Hill Proprietary (BHP), which in turn attracted thousands of people, transforming worthless scrubland into a booming city almost overnight. Some of Australia's most important labor history was forged here. The Amalgamated Miners' Association, one of the country's earliest unions, was founded in 1886, and went on to stage a series of highly charged strikes.

Broken Hill's mining continues to this day, on the same giant lode discovered by Rasp. However, known reserves of ore are projected to run out in less than 20 years, and the town is expected to lose half of its population when the mines close, since there is little else to hold people in this harsh land. For the time being, though, the town remains a classically desolate outback outpost, with a quirky mineral obsession and a typically Australian sense of gritty independence.

ORIENTATION

Rather than use the points of the compass, Broken Hill's streets are aligned with the line of lode that is the city's lifeblood. Most shops and services congregate in the pedestrian-manageable rectangle bounded by **Iodide, Bromide, Crystal,** and **Mica Streets.** A short mall connects to **Argent Street,** which becomes the **Barrier Hwy** at its northeast end and strikes eastward across 1157km of wasteland to Sydney. Parallel to Argent, 1km to the northwest, **Williams Street** is also called the Barrier Hwy as it runs out of town toward Adelaide, 512km distant. Several outlying attractions require motorized transport (particularly **Silverton, Mungo National Park,** and the **Living Desert**), but rental cars are extremely expensive. Organized tours are a reasonable option for seeing all of the sights if you don't drive into town.

PRACTICAL INFORMATION

Tourist Office: Broken Hill Tourist Centre (tel. 8087 6077; fax 8088 5209; http://www.murrayoutback.org.au) on the corner of Blende and Bromide St. From the railway station, turn left onto Crystal and walk 2 blocks west, then turn right onto Bromide; the office is 2 blocks down on the left. Local tours can be booked. Public showers $3. Open daily 8:30am-5pm.

Airplanes: Broken Hill Airport (tel. 8087 1969 or 8087 4128), 7km southeast of town, houses Kendell (one-way to Adelaide $120) and Hazleton (one-way to Sydney $215).

Trains: The **train station** (tel. 8087 1400, after hours 13 22 32) is on Crystal St near the intersection with Chloride St. The **Indian-Pacific** runs to Sydney (18hr.; W, Su 3:20pm; $100); Adelaide (7hr.; Tu, F 9am; $52); and Perth (22hr; $300). **Countrylink** trains go to Sydney (17hr.; daily 4am and Th 7:30pm, $99).

Buses: The **bus depot** (tel. 8087 2735 or 8088 4040; for 24hr. info. 13 20 30) is in the same building as the visitor center, at the corner of Blende and Bromide St. Daily **Greyhound** buses go to Adelaide (7hr.; $66, $56 for YHA members), Dubbo (8½hr.; $90, $84 for YHA), and Sydney (overnight; $105, $84 for YHA). **Sunraysia Bus Lines** (tel. 5021 4424) hauls out to Melbourne (15hr.; W, F 3:45pm; $89), stopping in Mildura (4¼hr.; $37), Ballarat (13hr.; $83), and Geelong (14hr.; $87). Bus depot office open M-F 9:15am-4pm, Sa 9:15-11am.

Taxi: tel. 8013 1008.

Car Rental: Thrifty, 190 Argent St (tel. 8088 1928), $75 per day, plus 25¢ per km over 100. 21- to 23-year-olds pay an $8 per day surcharge. **Holmes,** 475 Argent St (tel. 8087 2210), charges $50 per day, plus 20¢ per km over 100km. Must be 25.

Bike Rental: Johnny Windham, 195B Argent St (tel. 8087 3707). $5 per day, $25 per week; deposit $50. Open M-F 9am-5pm. Same prices at the YHA (see below).

National Parks Information: NSWNP&WS, 183 Argent St (tel. 8088 5933).

Road Conditions: tel. 8091 5155 or 8087 0660.

Bank: ANZ, 357 Argent St (tel. 8088 4288). Open M-Th 9:30am-4pm, F 9:30am-5pm. 24hr. **ATMs** line Argent St.

Library: Broken Hill Library (tel. 8080 2229; fax 8087 8055), on Blende St. Free **Internet access.** Open M-W 10am-8pm, Th-F 10am-6pm, Sa 10am-1pm, Su 1-5pm.

Emergency: Dial 000. **Ambulance:** 8013 1233.

Police: (tel. 8087 02999), on the corner of Comstock and Patton St.

Post Office: 260 Argent St (tel. 8088 1991). Open M-F 9am-5pm. **Postal Code:** 2880.

Phone Code: 08. Broken Hill has adopted the phone code of South Australia, as well as its **time zone,** Central Standard Time (CST), ½hr. behind the rest of NSW.

ACCOMMODATIONS

If the establishments below are full, check out the rest of the budget-range pub hotels that line Argent St.

The Tourist Lodge (YHA), 100 Argent St (tel. 8088 2086; fax 8087 9511). This hostel is huge, and boasts an industrial kitchen and large wooden dining room tables. Nevertheless, the place often fills completely, especially during school holidays. Most rooms are twin share, and there's A/C and a swimming pool to beat the desert heat. The tourist center and bus depot are right at the back door. $14 per person; singles $18; guest house rooms $22.

West Darling Hotel, 400 Argent St (tel. 8087 2691). The hotel of choice for ore magnates back in the day, now a budget pub accommodation, the West D provides plain, neat rooms overlooking the town center. Each room has tea/coffee facilities, fridge, A/C, veranda, heater, and washbasin, and the aging, tiled bathrooms are clean enough. Single $30, includes continental breakfast. Downstairs pub has the best counter fare in town. Meals served noon-2pm and 6pm-7:30pm. Massive breakfast $5.

The Grand Guest House, 313 Argent St (tel. 8087 5305). Slightly more upmarket digs right in the center of town. Rooms are bigger and a touch cleaner than standard budget fare, and include TV, fridge, tea service, and well-kept shared baths. Cozy common room with books and a roaring fireplace for cold desert nights. Continental breakfast included. Singles $45, doubles $52.

FOOD

Grizzled miners aren't known for their delicate palates, so most of Broken Hill's restaurants serve up what the scruffy-bearded pick-wielders want: meat, with a side of meat and some meat juice to wash it all down. Want something else? Then you must be spoilin' for a tussle, stranger. There are numerous takeaway joints along Argent St. **Schinella's Food and Liquor,** on Argent St. across from the YHA hostel, has a solid variety of groceries and hooch; the Schinella family also operates **Fruit Villa,** down the street at 338 Argent, so you don't catch scurvy.

Al Fresco's (tel. 8087 5599), across from the West Darling at the corner of Argent and Oxide St. A little pricier, but worth it for delectable modern Italian fare, including all kinds of funky pizza. Sidewalk dining for those who prefer their meals, well, al fresco. Open 11:30am-9pm.

Stope Cafe, 343 Argent St (tel. 8087 2637). A startlingly slick oasis of hipness, with Kandinsky all over the walls and Spice Girls blasting from the P.A. juxtaposing high and low culture. The food is good, too. Tasty steak diane ($11.80) and prawn kebobs ($11.50), as well as veggie fare. Don't miss the scrumptious fruit smoothies. Open M-W 5:30pm-10pm, Th-Sa 5:30-11pm. BYO.

Ruby's Coffee Lounge, 393 Argent St (tel. 8087 1188). "Lunchtime," they promise, "is yumtime." So it is. Purveyors of the veggie-friendliest food in town, the break-fast and soup-and-sandwich lunch fare comes in under $6. Try the rich pumpkin soup. Open daily 8am-3pm.

Brumby's Hot Bread and Pastries, 413 Argent St (tel. 8088 5533). Bakers of marvel-ous loaves and delectable rich sweets. Ask for something fresh from the oven. Open M-F 7am-6pm, Sa 7am-5pm, Su 7am-3pm.

The Pussy Cat Restaurant, 425 Argent St (tel. 8087 4354). The Pussy is in fact a fam-ily restaurant, with a diverse menu that runs the gamut from beef to pork. Very hearty meals around $10. BYO. Open M-Sa 5:30-9:30pm, Su 5:30-9pm.

SIGHTS AND ENTERTAINMENT

Mining is Broken Hill, and Broken Hill is mining. Gain insight into this complex sym-biosis with a tour of the original **Broken Hill Proprietary Mine** (tel. 8088 1604, after-hours 8087 4905) through Delprat's Mine Tours. The two-hour trip, all 200m under-ground, features equipment demonstrations and a thorough explanation of the mod-ern mining labor system. Tours leave at 10:30am and 2pm from the BHP mine site on top of the Broken Hill ($23; call to book). The **Albert Kersten GeoCentre** (tel./fax 8087 6538; http://www.pcpro.net.au/~geocentre/), on the corner of Bromide and Crystal St, offers a more scientific look at mining, concentrating on geological history and metallurgical techniques. *(Open M-F 10am-5pm, Sa-Su 1-5pm. Admission $3, conces-sions and ages 5-15 $2, under 5 free.)* There is also an extensive display of very beautiful mineral specimens. Diagonally across from the tourist center, on the corner of Blende and Bromide St, the **Sulphide Street Station Railway and Historical Museum** is housed in the old narrow-gauge tramway building that serviced a privately owned rail link to Cockburn in South Australia between 1888 and 1970. The museum's relics include mineral displays and the **Silver City Comet,** an old-fashioned train. *(Open 10am-3pm. Admission $2.)* Broken Hill serves as a hub for the surrounding outback. The **School of the Air** provides remote education for distant schoolchildren. Visitors can observe the proceedings on weekdays but must book at the tourist office the day before and be seated by 8:20am (demerits for tardiness). The **Royal Flying Doctor Service** (tel. 8080 1714), at the Broken Hill Airport, provides health care to outback residents. A museum and brief, exciting film (imagine an airborne, Aussie *ER*) detail the history and workings of this noble institution. *(Open daily 9am-noon; also M-F 3-5pm. $2 admission supports the RFDS.)*

The **Broken Hill City Art Gallery,** on the corner of Blende and Chloride St (tel. 8088 5491; fax 8087 1411), has an interesting variety of excellent local work and a strong collection of 20th-century Australian painting. *(Open M-F 10am-4pm Sa-Su 1-5pm. Admission $3, concessions $2.)* Works of note include the **Silver Tree,** a delicately wrought arboreal centerpiece commissioned by Charles Rasp, and a mural donated by the Communist Party of Australia. Broken Hill is also home to numerous private commercial galleries, most specializing in expansive landscapes inspired by the local terrain. They're all good, but one of the best is **Minchin Gallery,** 105 Morgan St (tel. 8087 5853), which features photo canvases of outback scenes. *(Open 9:30am-4:30pm.)* Art of a different sort has been set up 5km north of town in the **Living Desert Reserve.** In 1993, the **Broken Hill Sculpture Symposium** commissioned a group of sculptors to create stone works atop a hill. Head north along Kaolin Rd. You can drive all the way by obtaining a gate key from the tourist office for $5 (with $10 deposit), but the hike from a nearby car park is more fun and absolutely free.

The **Broken Hill Heritage Trail** is a loop around Argent and Blende Streets that's marked with informational signs; you can do it yourself if you miss the guided tours. *(M, W, F, Sa 10am; donation optional; depart from tourist center.)* Many private tour opera-tors offer trips into the outback, to the sights near Broken Hill, or to the area's national parks. Ask at the **Visitor Information Centre.** Few are particularly cheap, but they offer valuable insight. The slyly-monikered **Goanna Safari** (tel. 8087 6057) offers a panoply of one- to four-day tours starting at $95.

Entertainment in Broken Hill consists of pubs and the rough-and-tumble crowd that gets blind drunk in them. Many are private clubs, but will generally welcome a well-behaved and –dressed outsider. Beware the demon Gamblor, for he stalks the intemperate fortune-seeker here in the form of "Pokies," video poker machines in which you compete against a computer that is very efficiently programmed to kick your ass.

■ Near Broken Hill: Silverton

Diminutive Silverton makes Broken Hill, 25km to the south, look like a metropolis. It came to be as a result of the silver, zinc, and lead ore discovered at Thackaringa in 1876. Prospectors arrived in numbers, and the population peaked at around 3000 in 1885. Unfortunately for Silverton, most of the ore was gone by this point, just as Broken Hill's lode was revealing its precious potential. This combination of circumstances rendered Silverton a ghost town, today home to fewer than 100 hermits. Silverton revels in its emptiness and has been used in numerous bleak films and television spots (including the classic *Mad Max*). But don't let concern over post-nuclear desert mutants keep you away from Silverton; it is an experience like no other.

Silverton's handful of buildings ranges from old brick ruins that have stood abandoned since the 1800s to some good art galleries specializing in outback naturalism. The **Silverton Gaol,** erected in 1889, was used infrequently after the evaporation of Silverton's population and was converted to a boys' reformatory in the 1930s. The buildings were closed in 1943 and then reopened as a museum in 1968, and the former cells are now packed with old-tyme geegaws, including a great array of daguerreotypes from the mining days (open M-F 9:30am-4:30pm; admission $2, concessions $1, children 50¢). The main social activity round this parts is getting sloshed, making the legendary **Silverton Hotel** the most important building in town. Filled to the rafters with a huge diversity of beer cans and signs with naughty sayings, the hotel serves simple food and drink until 9 or 10 in the evening. Don't leave before taking "The Test." **Penrose Park** (tel. 8088 5307), just north of town, offers scandalously cheap accommodation: primitive campsites ($2.50 per person) and three dusty but livable bunkhouses which sleep 6-8 and include shared kitchen, barbecue, A/C, and fridge ($20 per bunkhouse; bring your own linen). The adjacent farm features bizarre yet lovable emus.

During the last Ice Age, glaciers scraped the plains west of Silverton until they were as level as a freshly zambonied ice rink. If you still doubt that the world is round, drive 6km west to **Mundi Mundi Scenic Lookout.** The curvature of the planet is clearly visible. *Let's Go* does not recommend the Mundi Mundi plain to agoraphobics.

■ National Parks of the Far West

MUNGO NATIONAL PARK

Ages ago, before the pyramids at Giza were even a sparkle in the eye of world history, hunter-gatherer communities flourished on the banks of Lake Mungo, in the extreme southwest corner of present-day New South Wales. Forty thousand years and 1600 Aboriginal generations later, life continues at **Mungo National Park,** perhaps the oldest continually inhabited site in the world. Today the lake is dry, and Mungo has undergone some spectacular weathering. Sand dunes on the edges of the lake bed have been sculpted into strange, otherworldly landforms over the course of the past hundred years by erosion created when settlers unwittingly introduced harmful foreign species. Known as the **Walls of China,** their erosion has revealed countless fossils and artifacts, including **Mungo Three,** a skeleton of a human male that is, at an estimated 40,000 years, the oldest remaining Homo sapiens relic in the world. (The skeleton was buried again in a secret location so that it wouldn't be plundered.) The archaeological information uncovered here has earned the **Willandra Lakes** region status as a **World Heritage Site.** On a less grandiose note, the shearing house, next to

Cenozoic Megafauna

Evidence collected throughout Australia strongly suggests that the early Aboriginals shared the continent with some fearsome beasts: giant mammals now termed megafauna. One of the more novel species, Zygomaturus trilobus, was sized like a buffalo, built much like a wombat, and possessed either a horn similar to a rhinoceros's or a short, flexible trunk. Long-dead marsupial carnivores have been found, super-sized ancestors of the almost extinct Tasmanian tiger. Strangest of all is Procoptodon goliah, a kangaroo twice as big as the largest red 'roos which climbed trees and ate leaves. Its skull was flattened and its eyes were set forward in the head, giving it a snub-nosed, eerily humanoid visage. Unlike regular kangaroos, goliah's arms and shoulders allowed it to manipulate objects and even reach overhead, much like the ancestors of human beings. If primates hadn't beaten out marsupials in the race toward human sentience, we might all be hopping today.

the **Visitors Centre,** dates only to the mid-1800s but still contains some of the original sheep-shearing equipment, and much of its odor.

Mungo is 110km northeast of Mildura, Vic on the **Acumpo-Ivanhoe Rd.** Roads within and around the park are unsealed but accessible for 2WD vehicles in good weather. Road conditions can be checked with the NPWS (tel. 8091 5155 or 8087 0660). There is an excellent 60km driving tour that skirts the Walls of China and encompasses all of the best features of the park; maps are available from the Visitors Centre. The **Visitors Centre** near the park entrance has displays on megafauna and Aboriginal life in the area, and collects camping and lodging fees; a 1½hr. nature walk through the Mallee scrub begins just outside the center. The shepherd's quarters next to the Visitors Centre have been converted into several musty guest rooms with bare-bones bunk accommodation and surprisingly clean bathrooms with showers. **Camping** is allowed near the Arump Rd entrance and at Belah Camp on the driving tour; visitors must bring drinking water and firewood. (Campsites 1-2 people $5, each additional person $2.) All fees operate on an honor system, but park rangers perform frequent spot checks..

MOOTWINGEE NATIONAL PARK

Mootwingee, from the Aboriginal term for the area ("Mutawintji"), lies 130km northeast of Broken Hill. It's most famed for Aboriginal paintings and rock carvings, though these cultural artifacts are spiritually significant to the modern Aboriginal community, and are closed to the general public. They can only be viewed through organized guided tours, given at regular intervals by knowledgeable park staff. In addition to these relics, Mootwingee's deep, twisting gorges lined with river redgums harbor abundant animal life, which can be accessed via several scenic walks and drives. Be careful—the unsealed tracks become impassable after a rain. Campsites equipped with tables, toilets, and barbecues are available ($10 per couple, $2 per additional person). The day use fee is $7.50 per vehicle; call the Broken Hill NPWS office for more information.

NEW SOUTH WALES

Northern Territory

Wild, remote, and enormous, the Northern Territory is Australia's true outback, sparsely populated by people as rugged as its wide range of alternately lush and harsh ecosystems. If you saw *Crocodile Dundee* or *Priscilla*, then went to Sydney and wondered where the "real" Australia was, it's probably here, nestled in some dusty pub somewhere between the croc-infested tropical rainforests of the north and the sun-scorched earth of the Red Centre. But the NT is more than kitschy stereotypes. It is heterogeneous in every aspect–biology, geology, climate, and culture—and the rich patchwork that emerges provides a true adventure for the traveler with gusto and an independent spirit.

Dutch explorers were the first Europeans to infiltrate the region in the 17th century. Discoveries of gold along the Finniss River in 1865 brought more settlers composed mainly of zealous miners and occasionally equally zealous missionaries. No permanent settlement was established until 1924, and it wasn't until 1978 that Canberra granted the fledgling territory self-government. The fragile nature of this autonomy was revealed in summer 1998, when the Canberra government simply invalidated a new Territory law legalizing medical euthanasia. The resulting Territorian anger gave strength to a movement for statehood, which John Howard's government seized upon as an opportunity to revitalize the Australian federation. Pending approval by its citizens in a referendum scheduled for October 1998, the NT will become Australia's seventh state in January 2001. While new to white settlers, the region contains some of the oldest land formations as well as the longest surviving cultures in the world. Million-year-old sandstone formations (like Australia's most famous image, the vivid red Ayers Rock), gorges, and plateaus imbue an ancient grace to the raw land. Closely linked with these natural wonders, Aboriginal communities possess complex histories that date back up to 50,000 years as well as rich cultural and spiritual ties to the land. Today, one quarter of Territorians are Aboriginal, by far the highest proportion in the country.

The Northern Territory encompasses nearly one-fifth of Australia's land—1.3 million square kilometers—but barely more than one percent of its people. Furthermore, the vast majority of its less than 200,000 hearty inhabitants cling to two centers: Darwin, the cosmopolitan capital, gateway to Asia, and mecca for backpackers; and Alice Springs, an isolated desert outpost that clings to its rough-and-ready image despite the influx of cappuccino-drinking tourists. Between the two are stretches of land so astonishingly empty as to bring post-apocalyptic visions to the minds of the brave but lonely drivers who venture across. At the same time, the luxuriant tropics are a paradise forgotten by those who think "outback" is synonymous with barren desert. The Top End's dramatic gorges, winding rivers, and pristine plunge pools teem with wildlife, highlighted by world-famous Kakadu National Park, the not-to-be-overlooked Litchfield National Park, and the huge Arnhem Land. For travelers who don't mind being far from bright lights and big cities, the NT offers

🖐 NORTHERN TERRITORY HIGHLIGHTS

- Prowling croc-filled waters on a **Yellow Water Cruise** in Kakadu (see p. 249).
- Hiking between the giant, unearthly red mounds of the **Olgas** (see p. 270).
- Swimming in a crystal plunge pool beneath the spectacular **Wangi Falls** in Litchfield National Park, with goannas and kookaburras meters away (see p. 251).
- The multicultural jubilee of **Mindil Beach Sunset Market**, Darwin (see p. 237).
- **Canoeing** along the quiet river in beautiful Katherine Gorge (see p. 255).
- Serpentine trails among gorges, dunes, rock pools, and orange cliffs in the **West MacDonnell Ranges** (see p. 266).
- Aboriginal **rock art** and emerald vistas at Ubirr in Kakadu (see p. 246).
- **Uluru.** That's one hell of a big rock. (See the cover; it's even better at sunset.)

226

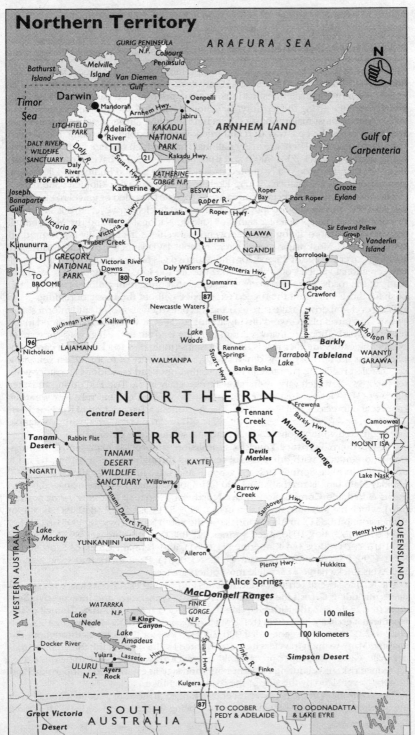

Northern Territory

worlds to explore. And one thing's certain across Australia's last frontier: you'll see spectacular sunsets and more stars than almost anywhere else on earth.

PRACTICAL INFORMATION

The NT's vast expanses of land make transportation a significant issue. Darwin, Alice Springs, and Yulara (Ayers Rock Resort) are most commonly reached by air. Smaller planes often fly to smaller destinations, but the price can be daunting. There is **no train** system traversing the territory. **Greyhound** and **McCafferty's** buses offer extensive service to most major tourist centers but not to the farther reaches of the parks. **Renting a car** is the best way to retain freedom and flexibility traveling, but it's also the most expensive. There are many national chains which operate in the NT; **Territory Rent-a-Car** (tel. 8924 0000) and **Budget** (tel. 13 27 27) have territory specials. Be aware that the price you're quoted usually includes a fixed number of kilometers; because of the large distances, you're likely to have to pay a per-kilometer surcharge.

The major tourist centers in the area are accessible by sealed or gravel roads. You'll need a 4WD only to venture into the bush on dirt tracks; however, this is necessary to see many of the spectacular sights of Kakadu National Park and the MacDonnell Ranges. Furthermore, if you rent a conventional vehicle, it's typically not insured on unsealed roads. Most major agencies rent reliable 4WD vehicles, though usually only to drivers over the age of 25. Ask for one with two gas tanks and high carriage; trendier recreational vehicles often have 4WD but are too low to the ground to navigate many of the roads. There are many safari tours that operate in national parks and the bush for those who want the rugged experience without the hassle of renting.

Wherever you drive, make sure to bring lots of extra water, food, and inform someone of your travel plans. Avoid driving at dusk and dawn when kangaroos tend to loiter by the road. There are many sections of ranch land along the highways; beware of wandering cattle. Another risk is the road trains (multi-part trucks) which carry supplies across the territory. Slow down and give them plenty of room. When venturing on unsealed roads, be sure to call ahead to find out **road conditions** (territory-wide tel. 8922 3394), which vary tremendously, especially in the Top End during and after the Wet (May-Oct.), when some tracks may be washed out entirely. For **weather reports** and forecasts, dial 8982 2826. The **Automobile Association of the Northern Territory, or AANT** (road service tel. 8941 0611) can provide invaluable assistance, and is affiliated with national and international services (see **Essentials,** p. 3).

The **Northern Territory Tourist Commission** can provide maps, ample information, and contacts with other useful resources throughout the territory. Its main offices are in Alice Springs (tel. 8951 8550) and Darwin (tel. 8999 3900). The **NT Holiday Help Line** is reachable at 1800 621 336. National parks are managed by the **Parks & Wildlife Commission of the Northern Territory (http://www.nt.gov.au/paw),** which has locations near Darwin (tel. 8999 5511; fax 8932 3849; P.O. Box 496, Palmerston, NT 0831), in Alice Springs (on the South Stuart Hwy; tel. 8951 8211; fax 8951 8268; P.O. Box 1046, Alice Springs, NT 0871), Katherine (tel. 8972 1886; fax 8971 0702; P.O. Box 344 Katherine NT 0851), and Tennant Creek (2 Scott St; tel. 8962 4599; P.O. Box 394, Tennant Creek NT 0861). **Park entry fees** vary; Kakadu and Ayers Rock charge $15, while most others are free.

The NT has several territory-wide hotlines and resources for travelers with special needs, including **Crisis Line** (tel. 1800 019 116), **Translating and Interpretive Services** (tel. 13 14 50), the **Kids Helpline** (tel. 1800 551 800), the **AIDS Council of the Northern Territory** in Darwin (tel. 8941 1711), and the **AIDS Helpline** in Alice (tel. 8922 8122). In an **emergency,** dial 000. *Let's Go* lists local resources throughout the chapter. Many women travelers here are daunted by the myth of the threatening frontier male. Given the proper precautions, however, traveling alone can be quite safe. To reduce risk, travel during daylight hours and stay in established campground and hostels. Never sleep by the side of the road or hitchhike.

Phone numbers in the NT have recently changed. Instead of a six-digit number following the regional code 089, numbers now being with regional code 08, then have eight digits beginning with 89. If you have trouble making a call, try the corresponding old number instead.

THE TOP END

A lush tropical crown atop a vast interior desert, the winterless Top End enjoys perpetually warm weather; seasons here are divided only into the Wet and the Dry. During the May-to-October dry season, backpack-toting pilgrims descend on the city of Darwin to worship its twin deities: a cloudless sky and a shirtless culture. While enjoying the budding metropolis itself, travelers also use this oasis of civilization as a base from which to explore the region's prime natural wonder—Kakadu National Park. A spectacular rainforest reserve crawling with exotic antipodean wildlife, Kakadu is Australia's largest national park and is best explored in the dry season, when the roads are more likely to be intact. The wetlands teem with the saltwater crocodiles that have captured the popular imagination. Crocodile Dundee's nemesis may become convincing reality on a tour of the park or a visit to a croc farm.

From November to April, the monsoonal Wet drenches parched hills and stony escarpments. Awesome thunderstorms dump over a meter of rain in unbelievably thick sheets. The Wet can be cruelly restrictive, as riverbeds fill like the Red Sea and roads become impassable torrents, yet the seasonal pulse of the monsoon is the heartbeat which sustains the Top End's luxuriant array of life.

■ Darwin

Doused by rain for half the year, flooded by visitors for the rest, Darwin (pop. 80,000) is a remote outpost in a tropical paradise. As the capital of the rugged Northern Territory and gateway to the rich cultures of Southeast Asia, Darwin blends raw Australian grit with the eclectic flair of an international community. Barefoot and barely clad backpackers swarm thicker than the mosquitoes, soaking up the dry season's incessant sunshine. They aren't the only transient population, as young Aussies often come to Darwin for a while to "give it a go." Darwin serves both as a springboard to nearby destinations such as Bali and East Timor and as the front door to Australia; its large immigrant and Aboriginal populations combine to produce one of Australia's newest, fastest-growing, and most diverse cities.

Darwin's character has not always been so footloose and fancy-free. Once the homeland of the Larrakia Aboriginals, it was first settled by Europeans during construction of the Overland Telegraph Line, which ran from Adelaide to Europe via Indonesia. The gold rush and the pearling industry brought more migration. In WWII, Darwin suffered nearly two years of intense Japanese bombing as Australia's hardest hit target. In 1974 Darwin sustained another bombardment—this time at the hands of Mother Nature. On Christmas Eve, Cyclone Tracy decimated the town. With characteristic Territorian determination (and financial support from Canberra), Darwin rebuilt, creating the convenient city center, manicured parks, and a refreshing outdoor mall that exist today.

A prosperous mining industry and booming tourist trade contribute to the city's current fortunes, with scores of new hostels luring backpackers. Still, visitors don't

NORTHERN TERRITORY

🐊 DARWIN HIGHLIGHTS

- Arts, crafts, fruit, and people at **Mindil Beach Sunset Market** (see p. 237).
- **Deck Chair Cinema:** avant-garde films in an avant-ceilings setting (see p. 238).
- Aboriginal art, Sweetheart the croc, and a spooky gaol all rolled into one at the **Museum and Art Gallery of the Northern Territory** (see p. 237).
- Strangely intelligent, yet delectable vegetables at the **Mental Lentil** (see p. 235).
- The friendly fish at **Aquascene.** Well, hungry. They're just fish. (See p. 236.)

come to Darwin looking for refined, urban pleasures. Folks here are distinctly more outdoorsy and independent than those in Sydney or Melbourne. They're on their way to explore the natural splendors of the Top End, including Kakadu and Litchfield National Parks. In the end, Darwin's not so much a final destination as a base camp for a visit to paradise—but one well worth a stop along the way.

GETTING THERE AND AWAY

By Plane

Darwin International Airport (tel. 8920 1850), is about 10km northeast of the city center on McMillans Rd. Take Bagot Rd off the Stuart Hwy. Most hostels offer free airport pick-up for arrivals. Other options for transport between the city and the airport include **shuttle buses** (tel. 8981 5066 or 1800 358 945; $6; call 3-4hr. in advance) and **taxis** (tel. 8981 2222 or 13 10 08; $14-15). **Qantas** and **Ansett** have domestic service to Adelaide ($580), Alice Springs ($389), Ayers Rock-Yulara ($500), Broome ($370), Cairns ($430), Melbourne ($710), and Sydney ($710). Both offer 25% student discounts. Numerous airlines offer international service to Southeast Asian and transoceanic destinations. Flights to Singapore on Singapore Airlines are about $760; flights to Bali on Garuda Indonesia range from $470-520. Currency exchange, lockers, and public showers are all available at the airport.

Airline offices include **Ansett Australia,** in the Mall (tel. 8941 3666 or 13 13 00), **Qantas,** 16 Bennett St (tel. 8982 3316), **Singapore Airlines** in the Mall above the plaza (tel. 8941 1799), and **Garuda Indonesia,** 9 Cavanagh St (tel. 8981 6422). **Airnorth** (tel. 8945 2866 or 1800 627 474) is a local carrier with an airport office.

By Bus

The **Transit Centre** at 69 Mitchell St is the locus of intercity bus travel. Passes for regional travel or a fixed distance (in multiples of 1000km) offer substantial savings. **Greyhound Pioneer** (tel. 13 20 30) runs daily service to Alice Springs (20hr.; 10am, 1pm; $131) via Katherine (4hr.; 10am, 1pm; $36) and Tennant Creek (12hr.; 10am, 1pm; $91). (Transit center counter staffed M-Sa 6am-6pm, Su 6am-2:30pm. All fares assume 10% discount for YHA or VIP cards; ISIC receives 20% off.) **McCafferty's,** 71 Smith St (tel. 8941 0911; reservations tel. 13 14 99), also runs daily to Alice Springs (20hr.; 9am; $131 with YHA) and Adelaide ($252). (Open daily 8am-6pm.)

ORIENTATION

Darwin has a conveniently small city center. Most activity takes place in the grid of blocks created by the intersections of **Mitchell St** and the parallel **Cavanah St** with **Daly and Knuckey Streets. The Mall,** occupying the block of Smith between Knuckey and Bennett St, is closed to traffic. **Stokes Hill Wharf,** at the south side of Darwin Harbor, is a popular entertainment location. As it exits the town to the northeast, Daly St becomes the **Stuart Hwy.** It then curves south toward the **Darwin International Airport.** Lambell Tce, which hugs the coast, becomes Gilruth Ave and then East Point Rd on its way to the **MGM casino, Mindil Beach,** and **Vestey Beach.** The road ends at the **East Point Reserve,** 6km from the city center.

GETTING AROUND

Local buses (fare $1.40) covering Darwin's suburban sprawl depart from the bus terminal (tel. 8924 7666) between Bennett St and Harry Chan Ave. Destinations not on the bus routes can be reached by **taxi** (tel. 8981 8777 or 13 10 08). **Bicycles** can be rented from most hostels for $3 per hour or $15 per day.

Cars, especially 4WD, are a great way to see the Top End, but the vast distances, lousy roads, and seasonally wet climate drive up rates. Sharing costs with a group of friends helps a lot. **Territory Rent-a-Car** (tel. 8924 0000) has locations all over the NT, including Darwin airport (open 4:30am-10:30pm) and 64 Stuart Hwy, a 25-minute walk from Mitchell St (open 8am-5pm). Their cars start at about $74 per day

NORTHERN TERRITORY

Darwin

Beagle Gulf
(Timor Sea)

CASUARINA

Casuarina Beach

Vanderlin Rd.
Lee Point Rd.
McMillans Rd.
Marrara Swamp
Rapid Cr.
Casuarina Dr.
Progress Dr.
Bagot Rd.
Dick Ward Dr.

DARWIN AIRPORT

Stuart Hwy.
Tiger Brennan Dr.

East Point Recreation Reserve
East Point Rd.
Fannie Bay
Vestey's Beach
Mindil Beach
Botanic Gardens
Gilruth Ave.
DARWIN
McMinn St.
Mitchell St.
SEE CENTRAL DARWIN MAP
PARAP

mangroves
mangroves
Frances Bay

TIMOR SEA

ABORIGINAL LAND

N

The Top End

The Top End (regional map)

ARNHEM LAND
Cooper Cr.
E. Alligator R.
Ubirr
Jabiru
Nourlangie Rock
Mt. Gilruth

KAKADU NATIONAL PARK

Jim Jim Cr.
Jim Jim Falls
Twin Falls
Mt. Evelyn

21
36
Arnhem Hwy.
S. Kakadu Holiday Village
Cooinda
S. Alligator R.
Alligator R.
W. Alligator R.
Wildman
Guntom R. Falls
Mary River Road House
Mt. Davis
Two Sisters

20 miles
20 kilometers
0

SEE KAKADU NATIONAL PARK MAP

Van Dieman Gulf

TO THE TIWI ISLANDS

Beagle Gulf
Lee Point

Darwin
Palmerston
Crocodile Farm
Territory Wildlife Park
Howard Springs
Humpty Doo
Berry Springs
Egg/Dam Conservation Reserve
Adelaide River Queen
Annaburroo
Mary R.
Margaret R.
Adelaide River
Adelaide R.
Mt. Douglas
Hayes Creek
Butterfly Gorge Nature Park
Pine Creek
Douglas Hot Springs
Douglas R.
Fish R.
Daly River
Daly R.

Kakadu Hwy.
TO KATHERINE

14
1
21
28
27
1

Batchelor
Darwin River
Litchfield Park
Stuart Hwy.

Who's Fittest Now?

Charles Darwin was not aboard the HMS Beagle in 1839 when it sailed into the harbor that his former shipmates named in his honor. He had been down under three years previously, but disembarked near modern-day Sydney. Darwin's tour of Australia consisted of a trip to the Blue Mountains in New South Wales, which he described as having a "desolate and untidy appearance." In his journal, he wrote of the continent, "Nothing but rather sharp necessity should compel me to emigrate." The biologist might find Australia a more intriguing species today.

---

with the first 100km free, although 4WD vehicles are substantially costlier. **Nifty,** 89 Mitchell St (tel. 8981 2999; fax 8941 0662), is also a good budget choice and offers a one-day special rate of $89 with 400km free. **Avis,** 145 Stuart Hwy (tel. 8981 9922), and **Hertz,** Smith and Daly St (tel. 8941 0944), are reliable, if more expensive. Most agencies require that drivers be over 21. Avis is the only company that rents 4WD to drivers under 25; for longer rentals, ask for the monthly lease plan.

If you are looking to **purchase a car,** or sell one off, you'll have company in Darwin. Check out the **Backpackers Car Market** at Peel and Mitchell St. Sellers pay $30 per week to cram into the lot, but buyers browse for free (open 8am-4pm daily). Cars sell fastest between May and October. There are also useful bulletin boards in hostels. Newly purchased cars must be registered at the **Motor Vehicle Registry** (tel. 8999 3145) on Goyder Rd (turn off the Stuart Hwy at Tom's Tyres). Transferring registration costs $12 and must be done within 14 days of purchase. Stamp duty and registration fee may also apply.

PRACTICAL INFORMATION

Tourist Office: Darwin Region Tourism Association (DRTA) (tel. 8981 4300; fax 8981 0653), in Beagle House Bldg. at Mitchell and Knuckey St, ground floor. Leaving the transit center, walk a block to the right on Mitchell. Wheelchair accessible. Open M-F 8:30am-6pm, Sa 9am-3pm, Su and public holidays 10am-2pm. The airport also has a DRTA kiosk.

Travel Office: STA, Shop T-17 in Galleria, Smith St Mall (tel. 8941 2955; fax 8941 2386). From the transit center take Mitchell St to the right. Turn left on Knuckey St and right on Smith St, then right at the second indoor court. Sells ISIC cards ($15; bring passport photo and proof of student enrollment) and VIP cards ($25). Wheelchair accessible. Open M-F 9am-5pm, Sa 9am-2pm.

Consulates: France, 47 Knuckey St (tel. 8981 3411); **Germany,** P.O. Box 38995, Winnellie (tel. 8984 3770); **Indonesia,** 18 Harry Chan Ave (tel 8941 0048); **Japan,** P.O. Box 1616 (tel. 8981 8722); **Philippines** (tel. 8984 4411).

Currency Exchange: ANZ Bank (tel. 13 13 14), on Knuckey St by the Smith St Mall, processes bank cards and traveler's checks. Open M-Th 9:30am-4pm, F 9:30am-5pm. **Interforex** (tel. 8981 0511), on Mitchell St next to the transit center. Open daily 8am-9pm. Location in the mall (tel. 8941 0511) is open daily 8am-7:30pm.

American Express: Travelers World, 18 Knuckey St, (tel. 8981 4699; fax 8981 1462). Holds mail for card holders or traveler's check holders. Mail should be addressed: ATTN: Client Mail, GPO Box 3728, Darwin NT 0801. Held for 30 days, longer by request. Open M-F 8:30am-5pm, Sa 9am-noon.

Backpacking Supplies: NT General Store, 42 Cavanagh St (tel. 8981 8242; fax 8981 6737). Open M-W 8:30am-5:30pm, Th-F 8:30am-6pm, Sa 8:30am-1pm.

Bookstores: Planet Oz, Transit Centre, 69 Mitchell St (tel. 8981 0690), carries travel guides and a little fiction. Open daily 10am-10pm; 10% discount for YHA and VIP. To buy or sell used books try **Read Back Book Exchange** (tel. 8981 8885), in the Mall. Open M-F 9am-6pm, Sa 9am-2:30pm. **Dusty Jackets,** 29 Cavanagh St, shop 3 (tel. 8981 6772) also buys and sells books. Open M-F 10:30am-5pm, Sa 9am-noon.

Library: Northern Territory Library (tel. 8999 7177), at the corner of Mitchell and Bennett St, inside the Parliament building. Open M-F 10am-6pm, Sa-Su 1-5pm.

Hotlines: Crisis Line (tel. 8981 9227), **AIDS Hotline** (tel. 1800 011 180), **Sexually Transmitted Diseases Line** (tel. 8922 8077).

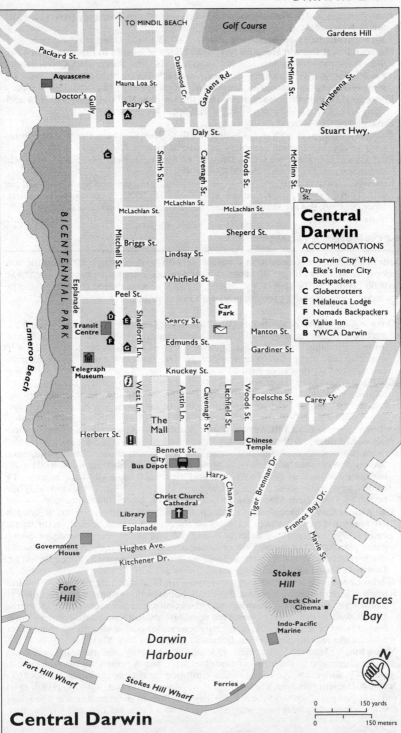

TO MINDIL BEACH

Golf Course

Gardens Hill

Packard St.

Aquascene

Doctor's Gully

Mauna Loa St.

Dashwood Cr.

Gardens Rd.

McMinn St.

Mirabeena St.

Peary St.

B A

Daly St.

Stuart Hwy.

C

Smith St.

Cavenagh St.

Woods St.

McMinn St.

Day St.

McLachlan St.

McLachlan St.

McLachlan St.

Sheperd St.

Central Darwin

ACCOMMODATIONS

D Darwin City YHA
A Elke's Inner City Backpackers
C Globetrotters
E Melaleuca Lodge
F Nomads Backpackers
G Value Inn
B YWCA Darwin

BICENTENNIAL PARK

Mitchell St.

Briggs St.

Lindsay St.

Whitfield St.

Peel St.

Shadforth Ln.

Car Park

Esplanade

Transit Centre

D

E

F

G

Searcy St.

Manton St.

Edmunds St.

Gardiner St.

Telegraph Museum

i

West Ln.

Knuckey St.

Lameroo Beach

Austin Ln.

Cavenagh St.

Litchfield St.

Woods St.

Foelsche St.

Carey St.

The Mall

Herbert St.

Chinese Temple

Bennett St.

City Bus Depot

Harry Chan Ave.

Tiger Brennan Dr.

Christ Church Cathedral

Library

Esplanade

Frances Bay Dr.

Mavie St.

Hughes Ave.

Government House

Kitchener Dr.

Stokes Hill

Fort Hill

Frances Bay

Deck Chair Cinema ■

Indo-Pacific Marine

Darwin Harbour

Fort Hill Wharf

Stokes Hill Wharf

Ferries

N

0   150 yards

0   150 meters

Central Darwin

NORTHERN TERRITORY

Auto Assistance: The **Auto Association of the Northern Territory (AANT),** 79-81 Smith St (tel. 8981 3837; open M-F 8am-5pm).

Police: On Mitchell near Bennett St (24hr tel. 8922 3344). Open M-F 8am-5pm.

Medical: Royal Darwin Hospital (tel. 8922 8888) is located in the suburb of Tiwi, 9km from the city center. For vaccinations, visit the **Australian Government Health Service,** 43 Cavanagh, 1st floor, Cavanagh Centre Bldg. (tel. 8981 7492; fax 8981 6027). Appointments recommended. Open M-F 8:30-11:30am, 1:30-3:30pm.

Pharmacy: Darwin Pharmacy, store 46 in the Smith St Mall (tel. 8981 9202). Wheelchair access. Open M-Sa 9am-8pm, Su 9am-5pm. MC, Visa.

Emergency: Dial 000.

Publications: Papers with event listings include *The NT News,* the free bimonthly paper *Pulse,* and Darwin's monthly calendar of events, *The Daily Plan-It.*

Post Office: General Post Office Darwin, 48 Cavanagh (tel. 8980 8226). Mail held Poste Restante for 30 days. **Postal Code:** 0801.

Internet Access: Several hostels have access for $2 per 10min., $5 per ½hr., $10 per 1hr. **Multigamer,** 20 Knuckey St (tel. 8941 7522; email games@multigamer.com.au), has the same prices and more computers. Surf daily noon-late.

Phone Code: 08.

ACCOMMODATIONS

Darwin's budget accommodation scene centers on hostels, which thrive on the sunseeking backpacker culture. Most are clumped near the transit center on Mitchell St. Beds fill up during the Dry, so call ahead. If you show up during the Wet, you'll be rewarded for your bravery (or insanity) with lower prices.

❀**Darwin City YHA,** 69 Mitchell St (tel. 8981 3995; fax 8981 6674; email yhant@ozemail.com.au), in the same building as transit center. Friendly, clean, and efficient, with a swimming pool, TV room, laundry, kitchen, A/C, Internet access ($2 for 10 minutes), and inexpensive luggage storage. Free airport shuttle. One week max. Dorm beds $16; double or twin $18; single $26; linen $2. Nonmembers pay more.

❀**Chilli's Backpackers (Nomads),** 69A Mitchell St (tel. 8941 9722; fax 8941-9835), adjacent to transit center. Mmm...Chilli's. Friendly staff and swanky new facilities (kitchen, TV room, spa, $1 video rental, A/C, sinks, laundry) account for its popularity. With YHA or VIP, dorms $14; twins $36; doubles $40 or $42 with individual shower. Key deposit $20. Airport shuttle reimbursed. Reservations recommended.

Melaleuca Lodge, 50 Mitchell St. (tel. 8941 3395 or 1800 623 543; fax 8941 3368; email nttours@ozemail.com.au), across from the transit center. Shady patio, pool, and garden create a relaxing environment despite the bustling location. Female, male, or coed rooms come with A/C and lockers. Pool, 2 kitchens, laundry, TV rooms, free airport shuttle. Free pancake breakfast 8:30-9:30am. Twice-weekly barbecue $4. Dorm beds $15; twins $40; doubles $44. Wheelchair accessible.

Elke's Inner City Backpackers, 112 Mitchell St (tel. 8981 8399 or 1800 808 365; elkest@dayworld.net.au), just past Daly St on the right. A 10min. walk from the transit center, Elke's offers facilities as bold and colorful as the reception decor. Shady patio, pool, spa, 2 kitchens, TV room, Internet access, and free evening meals with drink purchase at Globetrotters. Laundry, luggage storage ($2), free breakfast. Dorms $15 with YHA or VIP; singles $37; doubles $39.

Gecko Lodge, 146 Mitchell St (tel. 8981 5569; for bookings only 1800 811 250). In a town where mellowness reigns, this small, conscientious outfit takes relaxation to a new level. Cozy pool and garden, quiet balconies, and airy rooms make up for the 15min. walk to the transit center. Free breakfast, cable TV, kitchen. Courtesy buses from airport or transit center, or reimbursement for cost of shuttle. All rooms have A/C, fridges and supplied linens. Dorms $15, doubles $45. YHA.

Value Inn, 50 Mitchell St (tel. 8981 4733; fax 8981 4730), near the transit center. A quiet alternative to the rowdier hostels. Clean, airy 3-person rooms with private bath, TV, fridge, and A/C. Two rooms equipped for disabled persons. Rooms $67.

YWCA Darwin "Banyan View Lodge," 119 Mitchell St (tel. 8981 8644; fax 8981 6104), just past Daly St on the left. A 10min. walk from the transit center, the Lodge offers clean, simple, if somewhat spartan rooms. Large kitchen and spa, laundry,

TV lounges, and caretaker for extra security. All rooms with shared bath. Dorms $15; singles with fan $30, with A/C $32; twins with fan $40, with A/C $45.

Globetrotters, 97 Mitchell St (tel. 8981 5385; fax 8981 9096), a 5min. walk from the transit center, just before Daly St. Globetrotters lures innocent backpackers with nightly feasts: buy a drink and get dinner free. Rooms are worn and more crowded than most hostels. Pool, kitchen, laundry, and in-house bar. Bunks $15; twins and doubles $44. Key deposit $20. VIP.

Camping options leave something to be desired. With unfriendly weather half the year and no campgrounds in central Darwin, diehard campers will need to head out of town on the Stuart Hwy. **Lee Point Resort** (tel. 8945 0535) is on Lee Point Rd, off MacMillans Rd, which is off Stuart Hwy. (Tent sites $14, campervan sites $18. Weekly: $75, $80.) **Shady Glen** (tel. 8984 3330) is just off the highway about 10km from central Darwin. (Tents $8 per person, campervan sites $19 per night.) Call ahead for conditions and availability. A few kilometers on, Overlander Park, also visible from the highway, has tent and campervan sites for $14.

FOOD

Darwin has evolved a variety of restaurants to feed the onslaught of travelers with big stomachs but small pocketbooks. Luckily, Darwin's food has been influenced more by its Asian neighbors than by the outback. The food stalls that crowds inside the transit center offer hot, relatively cheap, mostly Asian cuisine. Food counters in the Smith St Mall also reflect Darwin's heterogeneous makeup.

For a really cheap meal, line up with hordes of fellow backpackers at the nightly trough established by **Globetrotters Hostel.** Buy a drink at the bar and eat for free. Or buy groceries at **Woolworths** (tel. 8981 2864) at the corner of Knuckey and Smith St (open M-Sa 6:30am-midnight; Su 8am-9pm). All hostels have kitchens and loan out cutlery. For succulent food and atmosphere, visit the **Mindil Beach Sunset Market** (see p. 237) on Thursday nights, where different Asian and European compete for the favor of Darwin's palate (a full meal is usually $6-8).

The Mental Lentil, Transit Center (tel. 8981 1377). Vegetarians rejoice—you have reached the promised land of scrumptious, creative cuisine. Picnic tables available. Try a soya smoothie ($3.00) or a pita sandwich ($4.00). Open 11am-9pm daily.

Coyotes Cantina, 69 Mitchell St (tel. 8941 3676), in the transit center. Santa Ana may never have set foot in Australia, but his spirit lives on in this excellent open-air Mexican restaurant. A wide variety of Mexican cuisine, festive decorations, and (sometimes live) music transport patrons to the other side of the globe. Prices are a little hefty (burritos $9) but justified. Margaritas $3 on Tuesdays. Wednesday all-you-can-eat backpacker special $5. Open M-F noon-late; weekends 6pm-late.

Crepe Expectations, on Mitchell St across from the transit center. Crepes made on the spot all day, with fresh ingredients of your choice. All crepes and breakfast specials $6. Open M-Sa 9am-2pm and 6pm-midnight, Su 10am-2pm and 6-10pm.

Salvatore's Extraordinary Coffee (tel. 8941 9823), intersection of Knuckey and Smith St. This bright modern cafe's outdoor seating and wide windows make it ideal for people-watching and sipping coffee ($2.30) with Darwin's yuppies. Have breakfast ($5-8), or enjoy pasta ($7.50) later in the day. Open daily 7am-midnight.

Pee Wee's at the Point (tel. 8981 6868), at East Point Reserve, 4km from Darwin city. Spectacular views of the turquoise ocean and classy, relaxed outdoor dining. Ideal for a special evening. Mains $20; pastas a more manageable $9.50. "Trail dust fajitas" $10.50. Open M-Sa 6pm-midnight, Su 11am-10pm.

Cafe Capri, 36 Knuckey St (tel. 8981 0010; fax 22781 4942), between Smith and Cavenagh St. Closer to the Riviera than the outback, Capri offers an elegant Mediterranean respite from the rowdy Mitchell St scene. Pastas $10 and up. Excellent veggie options. The enticing desserts ("Death by Strawberries" $5.70) and espresso ($2.70) are a cheaper way to enjoy the atmosphere. Open daily 10am-midnight.

The Magic Wok (tel. 8981 3332), GPO Center on Cavenagh St. China dishes, mirrors, and hanging plants cast a rich spell over this quiet, upscale restaurant. Excellent Asian fare with an Australian twist. The lunch buffet ($13) will leave you stuffed all day, with choice of vegetables, meat (kangaroo, camel, poultry, fish, and deer), and sauce. Open for lunch M-F 11:30am-2:30pm; dinner daily 6-10:30pm.

SIGHTS

Darwin's own attractions justify a diversion here even for travelers who are rarin' to hit Kakadu and Litchfield. For the tourism officials' latest recommendation, pick up a copy of *Darwin & The Top End Today* at any hostel or the tourist office. This brochure includes a guide to historical strolls around Darwin. Most sights are clustered around Darwin's center, and even the more distant points are accessible by foot or by bike. The less industrious can take the **Tour Tub** (tel. 8981 5233). This inanely named trolley, popular with seniors, rounds up passengers at major accommodations or at the corner of Smith and Knuckey, and herds them to 10 popular sights. An $18 pass allows you to ride all day, getting on and off at different sights from Stokes Hill Wharf to the East Point Reserve. *(Children under 12 $9.00. Runs daily 9am-4 pm.)*

Central Darwin and Stokes Hill Wharf

Lonely? Darwin's most unusual sight, **Aquascene** (tel. 8981 7837; fax 8941 8844), at the end of Doctors Gully Rd, lets you snuggle up to a warm and friendly...fish. *(Admission $4.50, under 15 $2.50.)* From the Esplanade, with the water on your left, turn right on Daly St and then left immediately on Doctors Gully Rd. Each high tide, families and backpackers gather here to hand-feed bread to an enormous horde. Call ahead for the feeding schedule. Watch those fingers! More watery fun is available at the **Indo Pacific Marine** (tel. 8981 1294), on Stokes Hill Wharf. *(Admission $12, concessions $11, under-14 $4; 2 adults, 2 kids get $28 family rate. Free talks every half-hour. Open daily 10am-5pm in the Dry; 9am-1pm in the Wet.)* Displays on plate tectonics, the composition of sea water, and the structure of coral encircle a pool containing an ecosystem that is self-sustained (no feeding, no filters) and has twice as many animals as the United States has people. Next door lies the **Australian Pearling Exhibition** (tel. 8999 6573) with exhibits ranging from pearl culturing techniques to historic hard-hat diving. *(Open daily 10am-5pm. Admission $6, children $3, family $15.)*

The Wharf itself is a pylon-supported strip of concrete that curves out into the harbor and ends in the **Wharf Arcade,** a corrugated-metal building containing restaurants and shops. The Arcade is a popular sunset dining spot where parents dine at tables by the water and kids feed unwanted vegetables to the fish. Close to the Wharf on Kitchener Dr, you can see the **WWII storage tunnels** along Darwin Harbour. *(Open for self-guided tours May-Oct. daily 9am-5pm; Nov.-Apr. Tu-Su 10am-2pm.)* Another nearby landmark is the historic **Lyons Cottage,** at the corner of Knuckey St and the Esplanade. *(Open daily 10am-5pm.)* This survivor of Japanese bombs and tropical cyclones was the 1925 headquarters for the construction of Australia-to-Britain telegraph. Its photo history of Darwin is only moderately interesting, but hey, it's free.

NT's Closeted History

The rugged, beer-swilling, macho Northern Territory doesn't exactly seem like a haven for gay culture—or does it? Dino Hodge's study *Did You Meet Any Malagas?* uses oral and written sources to out over a century of Top End culture, starting with Aboriginal communities, where homosexual relationships were once common, sometimes between young boys and elder tribesman. After several generations of white homophobia living next door, the stigma gradually set into Aboriginal communities. But European households were more tolerant than one might think: with 172 males and 29 females in the NT in 1871, the land was not the only thing the pioneersmen were exploring. WWII crackdowns drove this scene behind closed doors, but even after the war ended, some of the beat (or "cruising") areas from that era retained their earlier function. Nevertheless, it was 1970 before gay liberation hit Darwin, and homosexuality was only decriminalized in the NT in the late 1970s.

East Point Road and Beyond

Mindil Beach and **Vestey's Beach,** off Gilruth Ave, are prime locales for soaking in UV rays. Walk north on Smith St past Daly and turn right on Gilruth Ave at the traffic circle. Mindil Beach is on the left behind the Casino, and Vestey's Beach is a few hundred meters on. Shuttles to and from the city center ($4) will save you a half-hour walk. The **Mindil Beach Sunset Market,** a jubilee of arts, crafts, and food, is the gem of Darwin's market scene. Outback goods, pottery, and clothes from Bali comprise many of the sold goods. Make a dinner of dim sims, fresh-squeezed juice, and ice cream for about $7 and watch the sunset with the rest of Darwin. Activity lasts from around 5 to 10pm on Thursdays and Sundays during the Dry.

Just past Mindil Beach, on the opposite side of Gilruth Ave, are the **Darwin Botanic Gardens** (tel. 8989 5535), which have another entrance on Geranium St off the Stuart Hwy. *(Open daily 7am-7pm. Free. Wheelchair accessible.)* Shaded paths wind through different sections of Australian ecosytems: rainforest, mangroves, and dunes. The gardens are old enough to have survived cyclones in 1897, 1937, and 1974. This peaceful, uncrowded park is an ideal picnic spot.

The Museum and Art Gallery of the Northern Territory (tel. 8999 8201) is situated along the shore heading toward Vestey's Beach. *(Open M-F 9am-5pm, Sa-Su 10am-5pm; free; wheelchair accessible.)* Pass the high school on Gilruth Ave and turn left on Conacher St. If you only have time to visit one Darwin museum, this should be the one. The seaside building contains comprehensive exhibits of Aboriginal artwork and Territorial wildlife, including "Sweetheart," a 5m croc famous for sinking fishing boats. Another highlight is the Cyclone Tracy room, with videos, photos, and scary recorded sounds capturing the devastation. A maritime annex to the museum includes a boatyard and the partial skeleton of a 20m blue whale. Also part of the museum, the **Fannie Bay Gaol** opened in 1883 and served as Darwin's main jail until 1979. The marked self-tour leads through eerie, empty rooms where prisoners once slept and died. The Infirmary, built in 1887, was the site of a pair of executions in 1952. Guards and prisoners now claim the building is haunted.

To the north of the Gaol, East Point Rd enters the beautiful peninsular park called **East Point Reserve.** The Reserve itself has picnic areas and predator-free swimming in Lake Alexander. You can often spot wallabies, especially in the evening. Admission is free. East Point Rd becomes Alec Fong Lim Dr, which leads to the **East Point Military Museum** (tel. 8981 9702), located at the site of a WWII anti-aircraft station built to fend off Japanese attacks. *(Open daily 9:30am-5pm. Admission $6, children $3. 45min. bike ride from downtown.)* The huge 25cm diameter guns attest to Darwin's efforts, but photos and a video reveal the decimation ultimately wrought upon the city.

Several inland sights are scattered farther from central Darwin. These include **Crocodylus Park** (tel. 8947 2510), one of several crocodile theme parks in the Top End. *(Open daily 9am-5pm, feedings at 10am, noon, and 2pm; admission $15, under 16 $7.50, senior $12.)* Local bus #5 departs the bus depot on Bennett St and stops a 10-minutes walk from the park. Crocodylus doubles as an "educational adventure" and a research center. "Educational adventure" apparently means letting tourists hold baby crocs and look on as the adults devour hunks of meat. Also removed from the city center is the **Australian Aviation Heritage Centre** (tel. 8947 2145) on the Stuart Hwy in the suburb of Winnellie, whose highlight is an old American B-52 bomber. *(Open daily 9am-5pm. Admission $8, children $4, students $5, families $20.)*

ACTIVITIES AND FESTIVALS

Darwin, at least in the Dry, basks between sunny skies and blue waters. **Scuba diving** is possible; you can rent equipment to explore sunken vessels in the harbor. Bear in mind, coastal waters are unsafe for swimming in large portions of the year: deadly box jellyfish cruise the ocean during the wet season, and saltwater crocs refuse to share their habitat with humans at all. See **Dangerous Wildlife,** p. 14, for more details. Always check with the locals before taking a dip. **Biking** is a convenient way to explore Darwin. A one-hour bike path extends from Darwin City all the way to

East Point Reserve. Take Mitchell St away from town; the bike path starts around the other side of the roundabout. Many hostels rent bikes ($15 per day).

For a vertical challenge, visit **The Rock** (tel. 8941 0747), on Doctor's Gully Rd next to Aquascene. *(Unlimited-length sessions $8; harness and shoe rental $3. Open M-Th 3:30-9:30pm, F 3:30-8pm, Sa-Su 10am-9:30pm.)* In the bowels of an old oil tanker, this climbing gym has an impressive variety of straight wall climbs, cracks, and overhangs for climbing connoisseurs. Beginners get a free lesson. The truly wild at heart can go **skydiving;** a surprising number of backpackers are willing to shell out the $265 a jump. **Pete's Parachuting** (tel. 1800 641 114) offers tandem jumps.

Darwin celebrates the dry season with a number of festivals. The **Darwin Beer Can Regatta** is held off Mindil Beach in early August. Teams of devout beer-chuggers use their empties to construct vessels fit for America's Cup competition and race them across the harbor. In alternating Mays, the **Arafura Sports Festival** brings athletes from all over the Pacific Rim to compete in 26 sports. The annual **Cannonball Run** is a 4000km road race from Darwin to Ayers Rock and back. The Greek population of Darwin stages the **Glenti Festival,** a musical and culinary event, on the second Sunday of June on the Esplanade. Inquire at the tourist office about catching a match of **Aussie rules football;** several important competitions are held in March.

ENTERTAINMENT AND NIGHTLIFE

For a quiet evening, check out the night market at the intersection of Mitchell and Peel St. each evening from 5 to 11pm. The shops along the **Smith Street Mall** sell merchandise of Aboriginal design and are a good place to spend any money you haven't lost at the **MGM Grand Casino** (at the top of Mindil Beach). The **Darwin Cinema Centre,** 76 Mitchell St (tel. 8981 5999), screens recent mainstream flicks. *(After 6pm $11.50; matinees $9; slight discounts for kids, students, and seniors; Tuesday special $7.50.)* The less conventional **Deckchair Cinema** (tel. 8981 0700) shows offbeat, artsy films (many foreign) under the stars in a sunken amphitheater. *(W-Su 7:30pm, additional shows F-Sa around 9:30; $10, concessions $8, kids 5-15 $5.)* Heading away from Darwin Harbor on Bennett St, turn right on McMinn and left on Frances Bay Dr. The driveway to the cinema is 100m down on the right. Walking takes 20 minutes, but at night walk in groups or take a taxi.

Darwin has several venues for **theater.** The **Darwin Entertainment Center** (tel. 9891 1222), the imposing coral facade on Mitchell St halfway between Peel and Daly St, hosts the noteworthy events. Call box office as some shows are free. The **Botanic Gardens Amphitheatre** presents open-air theater in the midst of the lush gardens. **Brown's Mart,** on Smith St near Bennett St, features local productions in one of Darwin's oldest buildings. For the buzz on all this biz, flip through the *NT News* or *Pulse.*

Pubs

Shenannigans Irish Pub, 69 Mitchell St (tel. 8981 2100). Live music and a lively, mostly male clientele draw in locals and backpackers. Drink "Guinness for strength" ($5.00). Irish music 2 nights a week. Open M-Sa 10am-2am, Su noon-2am.
Kiddy O'Shays (tel. 8941 7947), on the corner of Mitchell and Herbert. The Emerald Isle may be thousands of miles away, but the spirit of the Irish lives on here. Friendly staff serves draft beer ($4) and imports ($5). Open 10am-4am daily.
Rorke's (tel. 8941 7171), on Mitchell just past the Value Inn. Rich wood furniture and assortment of beers draw mostly a rich, professional crowd. Outside seating available. Drafts $4. Open 10am-2am daily.

Clubs

The nightlife scene caters both to locals and the backpacker set. Clubs are required by law to charge a cover of $5 after midnight on Friday and Saturday nights. Few exceed that or charge a cover on any other night.

Rattle n' Hum, 14 Cavanagh (tel. 8981 4011), next to the Don Hotel. The atmosphere and beer are mediocre, but hordes of backpackers and locals come anyway for the techno music and pool tables. Raffles (prizes include free body piercing),

500 complimentary beers, and generous drinks ($6 for a jug) keep visitors happy, drunk, and coming back for more. Open daily 9pm-4am.

Time (tel. 8981 9761), near the corner of Smith and Edmunds, behind Woolworths. Darwin's only dance club swings with a lively assortment of techno and 80s. Gay- and straight-friendly. Drafts $4, basic spirits $4. Open M-Sa 8pm-4am.

The Victoria Hotel (tel. 8981 4011) in the Smith St Mall. Welcome to the outback, mate. At the Vic, a handful of travelers attempt to elbow their way into a dense crowd of Territorians. **Settlers** pub downstairs serves beer ($3.50) in rough and rustic atmosphere. Live music every night. Open M-Sa 1am-4am, Su noon-4am. Upstairs, at **Banjo's,** dancing and pool tables draw more of a backpacker crowd, especially on weekends. Lines can be long. Upstairs is open 11:30am-4am.

■ Off the Coast of Darwin: The Tiwi Islands

In the Timor Sea, 80km north of Darwin, lie the Tiwi Islands, **Melville** and **Bathurst.** Melville, the larger, ranks behind only Tasmania among Australia's largest islands. Together, the Tiwis represent 8000 square kilometers of Aboriginal-owned tropics whose main attractions are remoteness, contemporary Aboriginal communities, and relaxing beaches. Budget travel it isn't, though. You can't visit except with a pricey tour (one day rate: $240 adult, $190 children). For bookings call **Tiwi Tours** (tel. 8981 1633) or the **Darwin Region Tourism Association** (tel. 8981 4300)

■ The Stuart Highway out of Darwin

The Stuart Hwy swings east and south out of Darwin through the town of **Palmer- ston,** which has been titled the "fastest-growing city in Australia." The highway con- nects Darwin to Adelaide and divides the continent in two. The first important junction is with the **Arnhem Highway,** 33km south of Darwin. From here, the Arn- hem Hwy heads east into some of the wildest, most memorable wetlands in Australia (see **Kakadu,** below). The Stuart Hwy continues south, "down the track" toward the towns of **Adelaide River** and **Katherine** (see p. 252) and the outback beyond.

A short drive south of Darwin on the Stuart Highway lies **Howard Springs Nature Park.** Popular among locals, the springs offer swimming and a short 45-minute nature hike. (Open daily 8am-8pm.) The **Darwin Crocodile Farm** (tel. 8988 1450) is 40km south of Darwin on the right side of the Stuart Hwy, soon after the Arnhem Hwy junc- tion, on the road to Litchfield. Crocodiles are indeed farmed here, raised for giftshop wallets, belts and snack bar croc burgers ($5). In their pre-burger form, you can see the fierce, formidable creatures be fed in a dramatic fashion. (Feedings daily 2pm and Sa-Su and public holidays at noon. Admission $9.50, children 3-16 $5. Open daily 10am-4pm. Guided tours M-F.) **Darwin Day Tours** (tel. 8981 8696) runs to the farm.

Further south, off the Stuart Hwy onto **Cox Peninsula Rd,** which eventually leads to **Litchfield National Park** (see p. 251), is **Territory Wildlife Park** (tel. 8988 7200; fax 8988 7201). A cross between a large zoo and Jurassic Park, this wildlife complex, encompasses 400 hectares of Top End bush. You can walk directly past wallabies laz- ing in the sun, feast your eyes on the enclosed tunnel aquarium with its barramundi

---

Freshies and Salties

The Top End has two different kinds of crocodiles. The freshwater crocodile, *Crocodylus johnstoni,* lives only in fresh water, while the saltwater crocodile, *Crocodylus porosus,* lives in fresh or salt water. It is easiest to learn the differ- ence between "freshies" and "salties" through association. Salties are signifi- cantly larger than freshies and have rounded snouts, while freshies have narrow snouts. When you see a sign about freshies, it will probably refer to minimum risk and warn you merely to be cautious, since freshies nip only when provoked. When you see a sign about salties, it will most likely refer to death or danger and tell you to stay out. This is because salties eat humans. Freshies have to mind this distinction themselves, because salties eat freshies, too. That's why many areas inhabited by salties don't have freshies. Or swimmers.

and sting rays, and admire local birds' wingspans in the Birds of Prey exhibit. There's also the requisite reptile pavilion and a house for nocturnal critters. The park recommends 4 hours for a visit. (Admission $12, students and pensioners $6, families $30; open daily 8:30am-6pm, last admission at 4pm.) After generating a sweat watching the animals, chill out next door at the **Berry Springs Nature Park.** A popular spot among locals, the springs offer shaded picnic spots, a 30-minute walk through monsoon forests, and natural soaking grounds. (Open daily 8am-6:30pm; free.)

About 80km south of Darwin lies **Lake Bennett Resort** (tel. 8976 0960; fax 8976 0256), which juxtaposes placid seclusion with the amenities and comfort of a modern city. This recently refurbished resort lies 80km south of Darwin and provides immaculate facilities next to Lake Bennett. Swim, canoe, or windsurf in the crystal water, and afterward take in the splendid sunsets. Rooms include fridge, A/C, and TV. (Double $95, quad $135.) The cheaper option is the "camp-o-tel," a tent with a platform ($15 per person; linen charge $5), or you can pitch your own tent ($7 per person, $20 per family; powered sites $20). There are barbecue and laundry facilities. (Canoe rental $15 per hour, $40 per half-day; windsurfing $40 half-day.) Take Stuart Highway south from Darwin for 80km, then turn left on a gravel road (6km before the Batchelor Rd turn) and travel 7km. The affable staff will meet Greyhound bus travelers at the Stuart Hwy.

■ Mary River Wetlands

The **Arnhem Highway,** which leads to **Kakadu National Park,** passes through the **Mary River Wetlands,** a tremendous expanse of wetland sanctuary. In the Dry, the area features a meandering river and floodplains that are home to thousands of birds. Water floods the area in the Wet, transforming the area into a virtual lake. The **Fogg Dam Conservation Reserve,** located 60km east of Darwin and several kilometers north of the Arnhem Highway, is an excellent spot to view the winged inhabitants of the area, especially in the early morning and in the late afternoon. Twenty-eight kilometers from the junction of the Arnhem Hwy and Stuart Hwy lies the **Window on the Wetlands Visitor Centre.** Despite its out-of-place space-age design, this building houses a variety of creative, educational displays on the natural and human history of the Mary River Wetlands. From the lookout deck, the Adelaide River and much of the surrounding area is visible. (Open daily 7:30am-7:30pm. Free.)

Jumping crocodiles, batman! Three kilometers further east on the Arnhem highway you can embark one of the Top End's classic tourist experiences, the **Adelaide River Queen Jumping Crocodile Cruise** (tel. 8988 8144; fax 8988 8130). Giving new meaning to takeaway cuisine, boat attendants dangle chunks of raw pork over the water, provoking voracious crocs to breach the surface. Patrons can ogle at these beasts gnashing their teeth in front of your eyes or enjoy the meandering float down the Adelaide river on the lower deck (with A/C and glass windows) or the second-level viewing deck. Hold onto those kiddies. (90min.; May-Aug. at 9, 11am, 1, and 3pm; Sept.-Apr. at 9, 11am, 2:30pm. Adults $26, children $15. Raw flesh not included.) **AAT King's** (tel. 8941 3844) and **Darwin Day Tours** (tel. 8981 8696) run **buses** to the cruise site from Darwin. At **Annaburroo Billabong,** 35km from the entrance to Kakadu, you can safely enjoy the wetlands area, inhabited only by freshies. The billabong, 1.4km off the highway, has swimming and canoeing in the cool oasis, as well as camping, a lodge, and small cabins (tel. 8978 8971). There is a $2 day fee to enter the billabong. Canoes can be rented ($5 per hour, $15 half-day, $25 full-day), and shady green campsites are available ($6 per person, $15 for families). The lodge offers plain, rustic accommodations ($15, plus $3 linen fee). Small huts are also available, with kitchen facilities and showers ($35-55).

The **Shady Camp Billabong,** 25km down an access road from the highway, has the world's highest concentration of saltwater crocodiles. The **Bark Tree Inn,** a historical homestead supported by huge tree trunks, offers last-minute supplies, a quick snack, or petrol for those heading into Kakadu (open daily from around 6am-9pm).

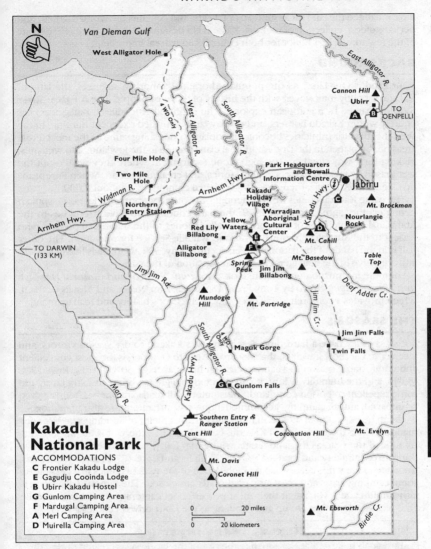

Kakadu
National Park
ACCOMMODATIONS
C Frontier Kakadu Lodge
E Gagudju Cooinda Lodge
B Ubirr Kakadu Hostel
G Gunlom Camping Area
F Mardugal Camping Area
A Merl Camping Area
D Muirella Camping Area

NORTHERN TERRITORY

■ Kakadu National Park

Stretching prominently over 19,804 square kilometers of the Top End, Kakadu National Park is the largest national park on the continent and one of the most dynamic parks in the world. Within its expansive boundaries lie an impressive range of habitats: savannah woodlands, monsoon forests, floodplains, and billabongs, and tidal flats. The dramatic stone escarpment that borders the east side of the park contains some of the oldest geological formations on earth, as well as dramatic waterfalls and gorges. The younger, low-lying woodlands and wetlands provide a sanctuary for hundreds of bird species.

Despite the awe-inspiring breadth and diversity of Kakadu's wilderness, it's the rich interplay between natural beauty and cultural history that gives Kakadu its distinctive charm. The park is permeated by the cultural influence of the Aboriginal groups who have inhabited the land for around 50,000 years, and contains the world's largest, and perhaps oldest, collection of rock art. Kakadu is a designated World Heritage site, one of the few to win that honor for both cultural and natural importance.

BACKGROUND

"Our Land is Our Life." As the popular Aboriginal aphorism suggests, the land of Kakadu is tightly interwoven with the history of the local people. The **Alligator River System** (named by a European explorer who confused crocodiles for alligators) lies entirely within Kakadu borders, and the lowlands provided excellent hunting. In the Wet, the Alligator tributaries become floodplains, nourishing some of the most fertile areas on the planet. In the Dry, Aboriginal clans hunted in the lowlands and wetlands, making their way slowly to the high stone escarpment where they waited out the wet season by making baskets, telling stories, and creating rock art. When Europeans first landed in Australia, there was an Aboriginal community of about 2,000.

The name Kakadu comes from "Gagudju," the primary Aboriginal language spoken here a century ago. Created in 1979, the park continues to have strong ties to the Aboriginal people; 50% of the park officially belongs to the traditional owners who lease it to the Australian National Parks and Wildlife Service for operation. The other half is in the hands of the national government. Today, 300 Aboriginals live in Kakadu and are active in the management and preservation of the park.

For more information on Kakadu, look at *Kakadu Natural and Cultural Heritage and Management,* edited by Tony Press, David Lea, Ann Webb, and Alistair Graham, which provides a comprehensive overview of the Park's history and management.

THE SEASONS

Locals say they have a hard time describing wet Kakadu to dry season visitors, and vice versa. For most travelers, **the Dry,** from April to October, is the most convenient and comfortable season to visit. Dry season highs average 30°C (86°F), lows 17°C (59°F), and the humidity is low. It can get cold at night, so bring an extra layer, and some repellent to poison commando mosquitoes. All roads are open whether paved or unpaved, and all camping, accommodations, and attractions are also operating.

As can be expected of monsoon rains and at least a meter of flooding, **the Wet** dramatically alters the landscape of Kakadu. Locals insist that the Wet is the most beautiful time of the year, as the land teems with green foliage and flowers. Still, with the oppressive humidity and heat—35°C (95°F) highs and 25°C (77°F) lows—and bugs, the price to view this beauty can be high. Much of the park becomes inaccessible, as some camping areas and most unpaved roads are closed. The famous falls, particularly Jim Jim and Twin, are at their most powerful but can only be seen from the air. One plus—boat cruises are up and running, as the Ubirr drive becomes a river.

Kakadu in the Dreaming

Aboriginals believe that Kakadu, like the rest of the world, was created during the Dreaming, the spiritual time when the acts and deeds of powerful ancestral beings shaped the land. A triangular rock at Nourlangie, for instance, is the stolen feather of a powerful spirit, and another slanted slate atop a mountain near Ubirr is the ill-fated raft of a bushwoman who challenged the Rainbow Serpent, one of many ancestors important in the formation of Kakadu. Because the features of the land are linked to the ancestors, the land is not an inherited possession, but a sacred site. Aboriginals discriminate between three classes: ceremonial sites, *djang,* and *djang andjamun.* The ceremonial sites are presently used for burials, rites of passage, and other such events. At *djang* sites, a creator passed through, took shape, or entered or exited the Earth, but is now gone, leaving the site safe to visit. At *djang andjamun* sites, however, the ancestor still lingers, and the sites are considered spiritual hazard zones. Laws prohibit entry to the last group of sites.

The Aboriginals, long acquainted with the climatic patterns, break the year into six seasons of dramatic change. **Gunumeleng,** from mid-October to late December, is the "whisper of the wet," which comes in the form of drenching afternoon thundershowers punctuated by the greatest frequency of lightning strikes on the planet (an average 10,000 per month Nov.-Jan.). Landscape burned brown by the dry months turns green again, amid high temperatures and oppressive humidity. From January to March, the "real" wet season—**Gudjewg**—brings monsoon rains to Kakadu. Enormous amounts of water pour down, humidity hits its peak, the land is green and overflowing, and the waterfalls gush. While the ubiquitous spear grass shoots up 3m, the animals that live on the ground can get trapped in the swollen waterways. April comes, and with it **Banggerreng,** the first glimpse of sunny skies. A handful of storms late in the month interrupt the clear weather, flattening the towering spear grass. The beginning of dry times is the cool **Yegge,** May to mid-June, when the wetlands begin to recede, leaving fields of waterlilies in their wake. The coldest weather comes in **Wurrgeng,** from mid-June to mid-August. With no rains to replenish the floodplains, the land dries out and turns brown. This season slips into **Gunung,** a time of dry heat and very little water, whose end is signaled in October by the return of the thunderclouds of Gunumeleng.

ORIENTATION AND GETTING AROUND

Kakadu National Park has a roughly rectangular shape, the straightest side being the eastern border along the Arnhem escarpment. There are only two ways to drive into the park: the **Arnhem Highway** in the north and the **Kakadu Highway** in the south. These two roads are paved for their entire length and eventually converge in the park's northeastern interior, near the township of **Jabiru.** They remain open year-round, except during the most severe (usually cyclonic) flooding conditions.

Kakadu's north gate is on the Arnhem Hwy, 120km from its junction with the Stuart Hwy. The Arnhem runs eastward through the **South Alligator Region,** which sprawls around the mighty South Alligator River and includes the **Kakadu Holiday Village.** After 81km, the highway enters the **East Alligator Region,** and arrives at **Ubirr Rd,** the turn-off to the rock art sight and lookout of Ubirr Rock, 39km to the north. Ubirr is the only paved road in the park that is routinely closed in the wet season, when it becomes a virtual river crossing. The junction of the Arnhem and Kakadu Hwy is about 1km past Ubirr Rd, in the **Jabiru Region.** Located just 2km from the junction, Jabiru is the primary town in Kakadu Park, with a post office, bank, medical center, pharmacy, supermarket, and police. The Arnhem Hwy ends 5km past Jabiru, and a secondary road goes 1km farther to the **Jabiru Airport.**

Many of the park's tourist hotspots are situated off the Kakadu Highway. Starting from the junction with the Arnhem, the **Bowali Visitor Centre** is just 2km down the Kakadu Highway on the right. The turn-off for the **Nourlangie rock art site** and **Nourlangie Region** is 19km farther, on the left. The **Nourlangie Road** itself is 12km long, paved, and generally open in any season. Continuing another 19km, the **Jim Jim/Twin Falls Road** makes a gravelly left toward the waterfalls of the same names. This 4WD-only route (impassable in the Wet) runs 60km to the Jim Jim camping area and 10km more to Twin. Its opening day in the dry season, eagerly awaited by tourists and tour guides alike, can be frustratingly uncertain. Nine kilometers past the Jim Jim/Twin Falls Road, the road to Cooinda/Yellow Water (paved 500m) turns off to the right of the Kakadu Hwy. The **Yellow Water and Jim Jim Region** surrounds the Cooinda area and the two waterfalls. It is 99km farther on the Kakadu Hwy through the **Mary River Region** to the south gate of Kakadu, and an additional 59km to Pine Creek on the Stuart Hwy. The total length of the loop from the Arnhem Hwy to the Stuart Hwy along the Kakadu Hwy is 207km, and comes out at **Pine Creek,** 90km north of Katherine. The best distance map is in the **Kakadu Air/Kakadu Parklink** brochure, available in most of the lodges in the park.

With a park map and a thorough guidebook, it's easily possible to do Kakadu in your own vehicle. Remember that many areas are open only to 4WD vehicles, and some may not be open at all. Posted signs will fill in most of the gaps. One popular way of visiting the park without a vehicle is by two-day **tour** from Darwin with **Greyhound Pioneer** (tel. 13 20 30), which can be expanded to three or more days. This is an especially economical option for those with a Greyhound kilometer pass. The conductor doubles as a knowledgeable, witty tour guide, and although the visit compresses the main sights, it does give a memorable dose of Kakadu. (Round-trip from Darwin $100. Buses arrive daily from Darwin at 10am and leave for Darwin at 4pm.)

If you're looking for a more rugged outback experience and have some extra time and money, plenty of **tour companies** offer packages. Almost all 4WD operations work out of Darwin. Some rely on lodge accommodations, others camp under the stars, but all encourage more than two to three days to really see the park. **Wilderness 4WD Adventures** (tel. 1800 808 288 or 1800 063 886) is a highly recommended company that specializes in 4-5 day tours geared toward nature lovers who will appreciate the biology-trained guides. **Kakadu Dreams** offers three and five day 4WD "Ecotours" with a maximum of nine people per group (tel. 1800 813 266; fax 8981 3655; email kakadudm@topend.com.au). **Gondwana Kakadu Plus** (tel. 1800 658 378) gets kudos for making a side trip to the **Shady Camp Billabong** (see **Mary River Wetlands,** p. 240). These tours are for fit travelers who don't mind a lot of hiking and hot sun.

PRACTICAL INFORMATION

Airport: The Jabiru Airport, 6.5km east of Jabiru, is the base for aerial tours of Kakadu. Airport buses run by **Kakadu Parklink** depart Jabiru at 7:45, 9:45, 10:45am, 12:45, and 3:45pm, and leave the airport for Jabiru at 8:30am, noon, 3, and 4:30pm ($5 one-way). **Kakadu Air** offers bird's-eye **tours** of Kakadu ($60 ½hr. flights, $100 1hr.). Flights during the Wet are quite popular, as many sites are inaccessible by road. The airport, Kakadu Parklink, and Kakadu Air can all be reached at tel. 1800 089 113 or tel. 8979 2411; fax 8979 2302; or email kakair@kakair.com.au.

Car Rental: Territory Rent-a-Car (8979 2552) has a desk in the lobby of the Gagudja Croc Hotel. Small sedans $55 and up per day. 4WD $99-204 per day.

Hitchhiking: Kakadu has some extremely desolate roads, so hitching often becomes walking, and is strongly discouraged.

Auto Services: Diesel and unleaded **fuel stations** are to be found at the Kakadu Holiday Village (on the Arnhem, 42km east of the north entrance), Jabiru, Cooinda, the Border Store near Ubirr, and the Mary River Roadhouse at the south entrance. The Mobile Station in Jabiru (8979 2001) has **auto repair.** For-up-to-date road conditions, call the Bowali Visitors Centre (tel. 8938 1120).

Entrance Fee: National Park admission $15, under 16 free, good for 14 days. Ticket may be requested at any time to prove you've paid. Seasonal passes are available for $60; these passes apply to a vehicle, so anyone traveling in your car can be admitted with that pass. With the purchase of the park pass, you will receive the thoroughly detailed and immensely informative brochure *Kakadu National Park.*

Ranger Stations: Ranger stations can relay information to the police and clinic from more remote areas, but aren't always open. **South Alligator Ranger Station** (tel. 8979 0194), 40km west of Bowali Center near Kakadu Holiday Village; **East Alligator Ranger Station** (tel. 8979 2291), 40km north of Bowali Center toward Ubirr; **Jim Jim Ranger Station** (tel. 8979 2038), down a 2.5km road that turns off the Kakadu Hwy 45km south of Bowali; **Mary River Ranger Station** (tel. 8975 4578), 1km from the south entry station.

Tourist Information: A stop at the **Bowali Visitor Centre** (tel. 8938 1121; 8938 1115), 2km west of Jabiru on the Kakadu Highway, is both an excellent source of information and a site unto itself. Rangers give weekly talks and guided walks at different sites in the park. Open 8am-5pm daily. Wheelchair accessible. The park manager is at Jabiru, P.O. Box 71, NT 0886. Outside the park, contact Parks Australia North (tel. 8946 4300; fax 8981 3497), at GPO Box 1260, Darwin, NT 0801.

Potable water: At Bowali, Jabiru, Cooinda, Kakadu Holiday Village, and Merl and Gunlom camping areas.

NORTHERN TERRITORY

Wheelchair Access: At Bowali Visitor Center, and at the Merl, Mardugal, Muirella Park, and Gunlom camping areas. Also along the Ubirr and Nourlangie walking tracks, plus the path from Cooinda to the **Warradjan Cultural Centre.**

Travel Agency: Jabiru Tourist Centre (tel. 8979 2548) in Jabiru plaza. Open M-F 9:30am-5:30pm, Sa-Su 9am-noon and 3:30-4:30pm.

Money: Westpac Bank (tel. 8979 2432) in Jabiru Plaza, has **ATMs.** Open M-Th. 9:30am-4pm, F 9:30am-5pm. Cooinda Lodge also has an ATM.

Police: Jabiru Police (tel. 8979 23122), across the street from **Jaiburu Plaza.**

Health Clinic: Jabiru Community Health Clinic (24hr. tel. 8979 2018) in Jaiburu Plaza. Open M, Tu, Th, F 8am-noon and 1pm-4pm; W 8am-noon and 1pm-2:30pm.

Post Office: (tel. 8979 2727) in Jabiru News Agency, in the Plaza. Open M-F 9am-5:30pm, Sa 9am-2pm, Su 10am-2pm.

Internet Access: Library (tel. 8979 2097), in the Plaza. $2.50 per ½hr., $5 per hr. Open M-F 9am-5pm, Sa 9am-noon.

ACCOMMODATIONS AND CAMPING

One of the best and cheapest ways to enjoy the beauty of Kakadu is to camp. The park runs four large campgrounds with facilities ($5 per person) and bush campgrounds (free). **Merl Campground,** 4km from Ubirr, has spacious and shady lots made somewhat private by vegetation. Check about wet season access—much of the road to Ubirr is completely closed in the Wet. (Fees collected on site. Has facilities.) The quiet, fully-equipped **Muirella Park Campground** is located down a 6km gravel track from the Kakadu Hwy; the turn-off is 21.5km from the intersection with the Arnhem Hwy. Another 5km down a 4WD track is the Sandy Billabong. (Fees paid onsite in the Dry, at the Visitor Centre in the Wet.) **Mardugal Campground,** 2km south of Cooinda turn-off on the Kakadu Highway, is well-placed near Yellow Water and the road to Jim Jim and Twin Falls. (Showers, toilets. Fees collected on site in the Dry, at the Visitor Centre in the Wet.) The fully-equipped **Gunlom Campground** is 11km from the Southern entrance of the park, and 37km further on a gravel road. It's a popular site due to its close access to the Gunlom Plunge Pool. (Fees collected on site.)

For private, more expensive full-facilities campgrounds, go to the Gagudju Lodge Cooinda or the Frontier Kakadu Lodge (both listed below), or try the **Frontier Kakadu Village** (tel. 8979 0166), 40km west of Jabiru on the Arnhem Hwy (sites $10, powered $14; pool, spa, tennis courts). The park also contains **free camping areas,** with the most basic facilities or none at all. Travelers should bring their own water. (In the South Alligator area: Two Mile Hole, Four Mile Hole, West Alligator Head, Red Lily Billabong, and Alligator Billabong. In the Nourlangie area: Malabanjbandju, Burdulba, and Sandy Billabong. In the Jim Jim/Cooinda area: Black Jungle Spring, Jim Jim Falls, Jim Jim Billabong, and Magule. In the Mary River area: Kabolgie.)

Of course, there are also more expensive options with four walls and real beds.

Frontier Kakadu Lodge (tel. 8979 2422; fax 8979 2422), in Jabiru. The Frontier never looked like this, mate. What it lacks in personality, it makes up for in comfort and cleanliness. Spacious, concrete dorm rooms with four beds, shared bath, kitchen facilites, barbecue $25. Self-contained trailer cabins, each with a double bed and 3 singles, private bath, and kitchen, $165. All rooms have A/C, linen, towels. Swimming pool, laundry. Two cabins wheelchair accessible. Campsites with access to amenities $10 per person, powered $12. Book ahead.

Gagudju Lodge Cooinda (tel. 8979 0145; fax 8979 0148). Offers pricey motel rooms ($140 plus 5% tax), crowded campgrounds ($8 per person, powered $10), and budget rooms in a cul-de-sac of trailers. The budget rooms are compact but spotless 2-bed arrangements with good A/C. Shared bath, fridge, laundry, and coin-operated BBQ facility. Sheet and pillow provided. Reception open daily 6am-10:30pm. Check-in for budget rooms by noon. Check-out 10am. Budget beds $15, YHA non-members $25. Linen included. Reservations required.

Kakadu Hostel (tel. 8979 2232), 2km south of Ubirr. The only redeeming feature of this dingy hostel is its close access to Ubirr. Cramped dorm rooms in worn-down building. Above-ground pool, laundry, and kitchen facilities. Push bikes available for hire $2. Doubles and twins have fans; dorm rooms have A/C. All beds $15.

FOOD

Kakadu is known for the game in the bush, not on your plate. Dining options are both sparse and expensive, so it is strongly recommended to bring your own food into the park. However, there are **quarantines** on the highways into Kakadu to prevent the spread of the fruit fly. If you are bringing fresh fruits or vegetables into the park, you'll need your grocery receipt and a certificate from the store. The **supermarket** in Jabiru plaza (tel. 8979 2077) has a wide range of groceries as well as a pharmacy, deli, and bakery. (Open M-F 9am-5:30pm, Sa 9am-5pm, Su 10am-2pm.) Simple groceries can also be bought (for an arm and a leg) at the **Border Store** (tel. 8979 2474) next to the **Ubirr hostel** (open daily 8:30am-5:30pm) or at the store in the **Gagudju Lodge Cooinda** (open 6am-9pm in the Dry; 6am-7:15pm in the Wet).

Cafes at the lodges offer a modest range of generic food. The **Barra Bistro** at Cooinda serves up sandwiches for about $3.50. If you're tired of barramundi and kangaroo, try the salad buffet for $7.50 (open 6:30am-9:30pm). Both the **Frontier Kakadu Lodge** and the **Frontier Kakadu Village** have cafes. The poolside bistro at the lodge serves breakfast (7-9am), lunch (noon-2pm), and dinner (5-9pm). At the Village, the cafe is open 9am-5pm. Generally, food is found near accommodations, and snack stands are the most economical ready-made food option. The Border Store sells $3 sandwiches and burgers, or $4 specialty burgers made from buffalo, croc, or barramundi. The snack bar at the Cooinda lodge serves up ham sandwiches for $3.50, but a burger will cost you $11.50. Food stores always sell abundant liquids, as staying hydrated is critical in this hot, often dry, environment. For finer, bug-free dining try **Mimi's Restaurant** at Cooinda, where mouth-watering dinners start at $19; a warm avocado salad costs $10.50 (open 11:30am-2:30pm and 6:30-9:30pm).

SIGHTS AND SHORT WALKS

A natural and cultural wonderland, Kakadu offers a variety of sites for both nature lovers and history buffs. A variety of well-marked short walking trails leave from the major sites; several are wheelchair accessible. **Carry water** wherever you go, and ask before swimming anywhere—salties don't like sharing their jacuzzis.

South Alligator Region

Mamukala Wetlands, 8km east of the South Alligator River crossing, is a floodplain and birdwatching area off the Arnhem Hwy. A short, wheelchair-accessible path leads to a hut where patient ornithologists can observe snowy egrets and jabiru in their hunt for food. In late August and September, the plain literally comes to life as 25,000 magpie geese descend on it. A birdhide lies 600m from the carpark. A 3km circular trail leads around the wetplains, and is occasionally closed in the Wet.

East Alligator Region

Because of the flooding of the Magela Creek, this remarkable area becomes restricted in the wet season. **Ubirr** is a collection of sandstone outliers on which Aboriginal ancestors created rock art; it's the gem of the East Alligator region. Rock art at the base of the Ubirr dates back thousands of years. A wheelchair-accessible 1km circuit passes significant sites such as the **Namarrgarn Sisters,** which tells the story of the appearance of crocodiles, and the **Main Gallery,** which displays several different layers of rock art. A steep, rocky, 250m climb leads to the top of Ubirr, with a spectacular vista of the distant stone escarpment and the emerald expanse of floodplains. Sunsets on top of Ubirr are magic, but be prepared to share the experience with chattering tourists. Ubirr is open daily during the Dry (8:30am-sunset) and conditionally during the Wet (2pm-sunset).

There are several walks along the East Alligator River nearby. The **Manngarre Monsoon Rainforest Walk** departs from the downstream boat ramp for a primarily flat 1.6km circular walk (1hr.). The trail comes close to the river banks here and there,

The Writing on the Wall

Over 5000 sites of Aboriginal rock art have been noted in Kakadu, most on the escarpment wall, and an estimated 10,000 sites remain undiscovered. The age of the art is difficult to determine, partly because pictures dating back thousands of years sit side-by-side with paintings done in the 1980s. Certain works have been "repainted" by descendants who are familiar enough with the old stories to "retell" them by the brush. Some recovered painting materials date to 50,000 years ago, some depicting extinct animals. Corresponding to the climatic changes that affected prehistoric Aboriginals, there are three general styles identified in the rock art. The pre-estuarine period (50,000-8000 BC) corresponds to a wooded Kakadu with an overall uniform style suggesting a small regional population. The estuarine period (8000-2000 BC), during the bountiful hunting era when the ocean was rising, shows previously unknown animals in an "X-ray" art style, which depicts the insides as well as outlines of animals. Booming wildlife meant growing communities, reflected in a rise in artistic diversity. In the freshwater period (2000 BC-present), Aboriginals captured an even greater variety of species with more complex x-ray images, eventually adding their own renditions of first contact with the white colonists. Aboriginals look to the rock art as a window into the past, and as a written history, some of which was painted in the Dreaming.

and crocs can be spotted at low tide. The **Bardedjilidji Sandstone Walk** is a fascinating 2.5km walk that meanders through weathered sandstone pillars, arches, and caves; some of the sandstone cliffs are believed to have been formed over 1,500 million years ago. From the base of the formations, you can see the roots of trees extending 20m down the jagged cliffs to the ground. The second half of the walk passes a small billabong and river. The **Cahills Crossing** spans the river and is the only road access from Kakadu into **Arnhem Land** (see p. 227). There's a safely raised platform for viewing the crocs and other animals that hang out along the river.

The popular **Guyluyjambi Aboriginal Culture Cruise** (tel. 1800 089 113) journeys down the river and into some interesting aspects of Aboriginal life. The tour (part of Kakadu Parklink) runs from the upstream boat ramp (May-Oct. daily 9, 11am, 1, 3pm; 1¾hr.; $25). A free shuttle connects to the Border Store and Merl Camping Area. Call for wet season tour times and bookings.

Jabiru Region

The **Bowali Visitor Centre** is a good place to start a tour of the park, but in this, the most developed region of Kakadu, most sights are man-made. **Gagudju Crocodile Hotel** has a quirky, croc-shaped design that is best appreciated from the air. Far to the east, past the airport, the **Ranger uranium mine** is the most active such mine on Kakadu land. Tours explore this operation daily, leaving from the Jabiru Airport at 10:30am and 1:30pm (May-Oct.), or by sufficient demand ($15 per adult, $7 per child). Reservations (tel. 1800 089 113) are essential.

Nourlangie Region

The principal pull of this part of the park is **Nourlangie** itself, a huge rock outlier used as a shelter and an art studio by earlier Aboriginals. A 1.5km walking track passes the Main Gallery. Part of the track is wheelchair-accessible. Many mystical images are painted on the walls of Nourlangie, including Nabulwinj-bulwinj, a dangerous spirit who eats females after striking them with a yam. The farthest point on the loop is **Gunwarrdehwarrde Lookout,** a craggy climb that affords a surreal view of the distant escarpment, where Aboriginals believe Lightning Man Namarrgon lives.

The serene but buggy **Anbangbang Billabong,** close to Nourlangie Rock, has picnic tables, barbecues, and an easy 2.5km walk circling the water, but is only open in the Dry. Delicate waterlilies and jagged cliffs create an interesting landscape. **Nawurlandja,** a rock outlier next to Nourlangie, is accessible by a road branching off Nourlangie Rd. A short, steep hike to Mirrai Lookout (1.8km) leads to impressive views of the stone escarpment, Nourlangie rock, and surrounding lowlands.

Yellow Water and Jim Jim Region

Yellow Water, part of Jim Jim Creek, is the most popular billabong in Kakadu—not to swim in, but to cruise past meters-long crocodiles, sunning themselves on the banks or floating ominously on the surface of the water. Yellow Water is also famous for its abundant birdlife, visible on a 1.5km circular walk. There's also a wheelchair-accessible platform to view the billabong. But the most popular way to do Yellow Water—a sort of a Kakadu rite—is on a **Yellow Water Cruise** (see **Cruises,** p. 249).

Perhaps the best-loved, and surely the most elusive, sites in the park lie deep in this region. Fifty-nine kilometers up a tough, corrugate road, **Jim Jim Falls** cascade 150m down into a crystal clear plunge pool. A shy waterfall, Jim Jim is not visible for much of the year. By late June its waters have decreased to a hesitant trickle; in the Wet, the falls rush with roaring intensity. However, the same rains that cause the awesome spectacle also prevent road access to it—the only way to see the falls during the Wet is by air. There is a lookout 20 minutes from the carpark. A 1km walk will take you to the **Jim Jim Plunge Pool,** where a dip in the cool water will help ease the memory (and the back pain) of the sojourn to the Falls. Over the river (literally) and 10km through the woods, is **Twin Falls.** The falls are spectacular—two roaring falls cascade down a steep cliff—but you'll have to earn the view; it is a 400m walk and a 500m swim or paddle up a narrow gorge to the plunge pool. Sadly, towards the end of the Dry, the rushing cascade of Twin Falls turns into a modest fall.

The **Warradjan Aboriginal Cultural Centre** (tel. 8979 0051), 1km from the Cooinda Lodge, shows visitors the Aboriginal culture of Kakadu and complements Bowali's focus on wildlife. Built in the shape of a warradjan (turtle), the center contains outstanding displays of Aboriginal culture ranging from tools and rock art to biographies of significant local figures. The exhibit concludes with powerful statements by local Aboriginals on the future of their land and culture. Daily videos screen on a host of topics including Aboriginal dance and the Call of Kakadu. There is a small gift shop (open 9am-5pm daily). **Maguk,** or **Barramundi Falls,** is a smaller cascade in the region. It flows during both seasons, and has a 2km hike through monsoon forest. The falls are located 92km from the Visitor Centre, up a 12km 4WD road.

Mary River Region

This is the land where the rivers begin. In the headwaters of the South Alligator River, a series of falls called **Gunlom** flow rapidly from December to May, but cease almost completely in the Dry. A wheelchair-accessible footbridge leads to the plunge pool, and a steep 2km circuit walk travels to the top of the falls and back for a view of the South Alligator valley (about 1hr.). Gunlom, on the 2WD-accessible Gunlom Rd, is the only escarpment cascade that conventional vehicles can reach in the dry season.

Remember those *djang andjamun* areas that bring catastrophic consequences if entered? **Jarrangbarnmi** is such a site. This series of pools on **Koolpin Creek** is home to **Bula** and **Bolung,** two creation ancestors. No one can enter the area without a permit. **Yurmikmik,** however, the land between the Marrawal Plateau and the South Alligator River, is a popular hiking area. Paths head off in various directions from the parking lot off the Gunlom access road. They lead through the hilly southern landscape, where, in the wet season, several waterfalls plunge from the plateau.

LONGER TRACKS AND BUSHWALKING

While many travelers are content to view Kakadu from the short walks circling the main sites, a number of excellent, longer walks will reward those who venture further out into the bush. Several established, well-marked tracks exist in each region. Bring lots of water (at least 4-8 liters per day), insect repellent, sunscreen, and sturdy shoes. Snakes and spiders live in these areas; long trousers and thick socks will help protect against bites. Saltwater crocodiles are also common in Kakadu. Never swim or wade in water sources and, whenever possible, stay away from the water's edge. Look for posted signs on croc safety. For more detailed descriptions of these walks, check out *Kakadu By Foot,* available for $3 in the Bowali Visitor gallery.

Beneath the Surface: Uranium Mining in Kakadu

Kakadu is renowned worldwide for its tremendous natural splendor and rich cultural heritage. It is surprising to many visitors, then, that the park also harbors the seeming antithesis of this serenity: two uranium mines. Technically its own region but enclosed within Kakadu, the Ranger uranium mine was established at the same time as the national park and became operational in 1981. Its environmental impact and cultural effect on local Aboriginals has long been a hotbed of controversy, especially in the past several years with the proposal of opening a second mine in Jabiluka, 20km from Ranger. The history is complicated, the politics even more so. Permission to build the mine was technically ceded by its traditional owners in the 1970s, but back then the concept of native title was new and ill-defined (see **Aboriginal Rights,** p. 57), and many people today feel that the Aboriginals were the victims of legal and economic coercion. Hence, the protests today center on a complex range of concerns: the mines' environmental effects, land rights issues, and the ultimate use of the uranium. With the backing of many Aboriginal leaders, international and Australian activists have flocked to Kakadu to oppose the new mine. Meanwhile, defenders of the mine argue that it is economically vital for the region. The social and political battle will no doubt continue to rage for some time, although for many travelers, the groups of young people sitting on the road to Kakadu are the only sign that something is remiss beneath the surface of this seemingly untrammeled wilderness.

In the South Alligator region, the **Gungaree Walk** leaves from the Frontier Kakadu Village and extends 3.6km through monsoon forests and skirts the side of a billabong. In the Bowali region, the **Illigadjarr Walk** leaves from the Malabanjbanjdju or Burdulba Camping Areas. This 3.8km flat trail extends past two grassy floodplains and alone the side of the Burdulba Billabong. Beware—bugs abound. In the Mary River region, the **Yurmikmik Walking Tracks** saunter past wet-season waterfalls. There are four different circular tracks (2km, 5km, 7.5km, and 11.5km)

The Nourlangie area offers several good hikes. The **Gubara Pools Walk** is a 6km walk that passes dramatic rock outcroppings and peaceful forest pools. Ideal for hot afternoons, much of the track goes through shady monsoon forests. To get to the trailhead, leave the Nourlangie car park, taking the first road on the right. Drive 9km to the trailhead. The **Barrk Sandstone Bushwalk,** one of the longest and most dramatic established walks in the park, makes a 12km loop past the sandstone cliffs of the Nourlangie region. Impressive views of surrounding lowlands, a variety of ecosystems, and rock art make it an excellent walk for the curious and fit traveler. This untouristed walk allows quiet appreciation of rock sites and natural wonders. Allow 6-8 hours. The shorter **Nanguluwur walk** is a 3.4km on the western side of Nourlangie rock. It passes several galleries of impressive ancient and modern rock art. Leave from the Nanguluwur carpark.

Bushwalking and overnight camping is allowed in the park by **permit.** To attain a permit, call or write the **Bowali Visitor Centre** (P.O. Box 71 Jabiru NT 0886) or apply in person. Permits are free and can be issued overnight. The Visitor Centre also sells detailed topographic maps ($8) of the park for those travelers heading into the bush.

CRUISES

Several **cruises** offer excellent ways to view the park's rivers. The **Yellow Water Cruises** leave from Yellow Water, 1km from Cooinda. These narrated pontoon voyages pass through wetlands. Knowledgeable guides will point out the variety of birds and the occasional croc. Tours last either 90 minutes (daily 11:15am, 1, 2:45pm; adults $23.50, children $12.50) or two hours (daily 6:45, 9am, 4:30pm). The cruise can be booked by calling 8979 0111 or through the **Gagudju Lodge Cooinda** (tel. 8979 0145) where a courtesy bus picks up passengers 20 minutes before departure.

The popular **Guluyambi Aboriginal Culture Cruise** (tel. 8979 2411 or 1899 089 113) provides insight into Aboriginal culture as well as tranquil views of the East Alligator River and the stony cliffs beyond. (Departs at 9, 11am, 1, and 3pm from the upstream boat ramp on the East Alligator River. Adults $25, children 4-14 $11.)

■ Arnhem Land

Although only a few short kilometers from the eastern boundaries of Kakadu, Arnhem Land can feel like another world. An Aboriginal homeland that covers the entire eastern portion of the Top End, rugged Arnhem most likely takes its name from a Dutch ship that skimmed past the coast in 1623. The area's inland borders are cut square, but the expansive coastline takes a wild, jagged path from the **Cobourg Peninsula** in the west (location of **Gurig National Park**) to the **Gove Peninsula** in the east. Arnhem also includes the **Goote** and **Elcho islands** offshore. If you've got the vehicular capacity and patience for red tape to navigate both the roads and the permitting system to enter Arnhem, you'll be rewarded. The land itself is beautiful and untamed, while the local culture is rich, uncommercialized, and enchanting.

By law, Arnhem Land is off-limits to non-Aboriginals, except by **permit** issued by the **Northern Land Council.** These permits admit visitors to three areas: the arts and crafts center, Sandy Creek, and Wunyo Beach (Gurig National Park has a separate permit system). The **Injalak Arts & Crafts Centre** (tel. 8979 0190; fax 8979 0119) located in Oenpelli (Gunbalanya), a short 16km drive from the road to Ubirr, is a recommended stop for travelers seeking Aboriginal art as well as a glimpse of Arnhem Land. The intricate baskets, bark and paper paintings, screen paintings, and didgeridoos are distributed to art galleries around the world, you can purchase them for wholesale prices. In the same building as the gallery, you can watch the artists in the process of making their spectacular works. (Open 8am-5pm daily or with advance notice.) The road to **Oenpelli** crosses a tidal river **(Cahills Crossing).** Check with the Northern Land Council about tidal information before driving. The permits to Injalak cost $12 and can be attained from the Northern Land Council in Darwin (P.O. Box 42921, Casuarina NT 0811) or in Jabiru (P.O. Box 18, Jabiru NT 0886). Allow two to four weeks for processing by mail. The permit allows you only to travel to the crafts centre. Stopping along the road or in Oenpelli is not permitted.

Sandy Creek, located on the northern shore of Arnhem Land, is a popular destination for fishing, but not much else. The drive to Sandy Creek at least a three-hour drive and is 4WD only. The cost for permits is $50 per vehicle and only 7 vehicles are allowed to enter at a time. As the road is difficult and remote, travelers heading towards the Creek should be well prepared. Permits can be attained through the Northern Land Council in Darwin or in Jabiru. Also on the Northern Shore is **Wunyo Beach,** a secluded and picturesque beach. Sunbathers and would-be swimmers beware—the beach (and Sandy Creek as well) is teeming with **salties.** The drive to Wunyo takes at least 2½ hours on a 4WD road. Permits cost $50 per vehicle and can be attained through the Northern Land Council. Neither Sandy Creek nor Wunyo Beach have facilities—travelers should bring their own water and food and be prepared to camp under the stars. Stopping on the road to Sandy Creek and Wunyo is prohibited except in emergency.

Northern Arnhem Land also is the site of Gurig National Park. The park covers 2,207 sq. km of the Cobourg Peninsula and the adjacent islands. Secluded, beautiful beaches and a variety of wildlife attract those looking for an off-the-beaten path adventure. Travelers entering the park need a **permit** from the **Australian Conservation Commission**, 1st floor, Gaymark Building, Palmerston NT 0831. (Permits $10. Three-person campsites with showers and pit toilets $4 per day, $25 per week.) The number of vehicles entering is restricted, so plan ahead.

Travelers in search of a more culturally oriented trip into Arnhem Land with less hassle involved can pay for guided tours. **Magela Tours** (tel. 8979 2114; fax 8979 2704). The day-long tours visit escarpment shelters as well as traditional hunting places and floodplains. (Adults $150, children 14 and younger $100.) **Lord of Kakadu Tours** (tel. 8979 2567 or 8979 2970; fax 8979 2035) also offers day tours of Arnhem ($140 per person) as well as multi-day tours.

■ Litchfield National Park

Although shadowed in size and popularity by the more glamorous Kakadu, **Litchfield National Park** possesses natural wonders second to none. Dramatic waterfalls and chiseled gorges combined with the spacious lure of bushland plateaus give Litchfield a unique charm. The park was established in 1986, and its 146,000 hectares encompass much of the **Tabletop Range.** Its swimming holes, walking tracks, and close proximity to Darwin bring flocks of visitors every year.

PRACTICAL INFORMATION The park is located 100km southwest of Darwin. For paved access, go south from Darwin on the **Stuart Hwy** (see p. 219) past Cox Peninsula Rd and the Manton Dam Recreation Area. Turn right on **Batchelor Rd,** 90km out of Darwin, and go toward the park through the town of Batchelor. There is also gravel road access through the Cox peninsula. *Let's Go's* distance calculations are based on the Batchelor entrance. Information is available through the **Parks and Wildlife Commission of the Northern Territory** (tel. 8999 5511; fax 8999 4558) in Darwin. Entry is free.

CAMPING Spending a night in Litchfield is highly recommended, if only for the superb stargazing. Mosquitoes, however, are fearsome predators here. Camping costs $5 per person, payable in boxes at campground entrances. **Buley Rockhole** is a quiet campground located close to the park entrance. You can wade in small pools in the nearby creek. Facilities are basic (pit toilets and picnic tables) and accessible by 2WD. Near the park entrance, **Florence Falls** is only a couple of kilometers from Buley Rockhole. Spacious camp spots, full facilities (flush toilets, showers), and access to Florence Falls make this campground appealing. **Tjaynera Falls** (Sandy Creek Falls) lies several kilometers south of the main road on tough 4WD track; look for the turn after Tolmer Falls. Road conditions discourage many visitors, but the bold will be rewarded with pleasant camping (basic facilities, Emergency Call Device). If you're looking for quiet, keep driving past **Wangi Falls.** More of a circus than a campground, Wangi is colonized not only by caravans and campers but by the persistent flow of visitors swarming to Wangi Falls. It's at the end of the main, paved road, and fills up early in the day. (Full facilities including food kiosk; open 8am-5pm daily.)

SIGHTS AND ACTIVITIES The spectacular **falls** at Litchfield are among the main attractions. Unlike many of the falls at Kakadu, those at Litchfield are spring-fed and remain throughout the year. At **Wangi** (wong-GYE), two dramatic falls plunge several meters into a large, clear pool. Besides safe, croc-free swimming, visitors can sight goannas and kookaburras that have been attracted to the area by irresponsible tourist feedings (don't do it). It's wheelchair accessible. A **walking track** starts from the lookout and winds up through the woods to the creek before the falls. Steep terrain makes this walk a 45-minute endeavor. Equally dramatic but more secluded are the **Florence Falls.** A 3.2km walk connects Florence Falls with Buley Rockhole. The walk travels through lush, tropical woods passed the creek that feeds Florence Falls. The falls and gorge are visible from a vertiginous, wheelchair-accessible lookout.

At **Tolmer Falls,** a short distance from Florence Falls, there is another steep fall plunging from a sandstone gorge. Visitors are not allowed in the gorge due to gentle ecosystems. However, you can make the requisite ooohs and ahhhs from the lookout deck (wheelchair accessible). Also at Tolmer Falls is a short path that meanders passed the pools and creek upstream from the falls. Next door is **Tjaetaba Falls,** which you can access via a walking track through monsoon forests and eucalyptus woodlands. Tjaetaba is a sacred Aboriginal site; swimming is not permitted.

The Lost City, a haunting arrangement of sandstone towers that looks like ancient ruins, is 10.5km off the main road, accessible to 4WD only. The first 9km are fairly easy going, but are followed by a steep, rocky downhill to the city. Some visitors choose to park and walk the last 1.5km. Further down on this road is **Blyth Homestead Ruins** (just what it sounds like) and **Tjaynera Falls.**

> **Living Rocks**
>
> On the way to Litchfield from Batchelor, hulking stone-like mounds of various sizes and shapes rise out of the bush. These **termite mounds,** full of eggs and nutrients, range from 50 to 100 years old. The ones with lumpy columnal structures are called **cathedral mounds.** These mounds are usually built in wooded areas and are among the largest in the world, up to 6m tall. The shorter, flatter mounds are called **magnetic mounds** because of their alignment along a north-south axis, like the needle of a compass. The termites aren't aware of the earth's magnetic fields; rather, like anyone without air conditioning in Northern Territory, they must mind their temperature. Thus, the bugs instinctively build the faces of their mounds to face the rising and setting sun. This way, the mound is warmed by the softer rays of the morning and twilight, but appears as a mere hyphen to the bright glare of midday. A short boardwalk off the Litchfield Park Rd lets you stare across a "graveyard" of these magnetic mounds without damaging the fragile ground around them.

Like the entire Top End, Litchfield is thrashed by the Wet. Flooding can shut down certain swimming areas, and the sealed main road, **Litchfield Park Rd,** from Batchelor to Wangi Falls, is often closed for several days at a time. When dry, a network of 4WD gravel roads access other areas in the park and create several potential entrance points (see p. 219). Call 8922 3394 for road conditions or turn your FM dial to 88.

■ En route to Litchfield: Batchelor

Batchelor (pop. 350) is the entry point to Litchfield along the bitumen from the east. It houses the **ranger station** (tel. 8976 0282; open M-F 8am-5pm). The station has a host of information, including track conditions. The **Batchelor Store** (tel. 8976 0045), in the transit center, supplies food and gas (open M-F 7:30am-7pm; Sa-Su 8am-7pm). Next to the store is a **post office** (tel. 8976 0020; open M-F 9am-7pm, Sa-Su 9am-2:30pm). Batchelor also has a **health clinic** (tel. 8976 0011) with a 24-hour nurse.

Batchelor boasts a college, a small stone **castle** (a 6m replica of a 600-year-old Bohemian castle built in the 1970s), and a **butterfly farm** (tel. 8976 0199) housing six species of butterflies (open daily 9am-4:30pm; adults $5.50, children $2.50). The **Caravillage Camping Park** has camping sites (sites $8; powered $20) and small cabins ($75). The **Banyan Tree Caravan Park** (tel. 8976 0330), further along the road to the park sells food and drinks (tent sites $5).

DOWN THE TRACK

Between the tropical Top End and the arid Red Centre, the Stuart Highway traverses a climatic gradient from the hilly, dense vegetation of the north to the flat, crispy desert of central Australia. The "track" was once proclaimed "the most sing-on-able road in the world." There isn't much else to do. From Katherine to Tennant Creek, the Stuart Hwy. passes through some of the emptiest and most uninspiring stretches in the outback. The people here consider their land "the Never Never," referring to the tendency residents have to never, never leave. But chances are ten to one that after canoeing down the Katherine River, bathing in the hot springs of Mataranka, or taking in the Devil's Marbles and some mining history near Tennant Creek, you *will* leave—and quite contentedly—singing "Waltzing Matilda" as you head down the Stuart Hwy in search of more blessedly populated ground.

■ Katherine

A few blocks of rugged storefronts along the Stuart Hwy cling tenaciously to life in the remote stretches of a hot, monotonous desert. Lonely Katherine lies 345km south of Darwin, 700km north of Tennant Creek, and 510km east of Kununurra, WA at the junction of the Stuart and Victoria highways. With a population of 10,700, it's the largest settlement between Darwin and Alice Springs. This provincial highway town subsists on agriculture, cattle husbandry, and mining. Katherine's Aboriginal communities, primarily Jawoyn and Dagoman, are among the most visible in the Northern Territory. In January 1998, the rough-and-tumble frontier atmosphere that normally pervades the town was replaced with rough and tumbling waters when the Katherine River rose to over 20.4m, covering much of the town in 2m of water. The flood, considered to be a once-in-500-years event, left significant damage in its wake. Through hard work and some federal aid, the plucky citizens are slowly rebuilding the town, reviving its role as a gateway to Katherine Gorge, the Top End, the Red Centre, and the Kimberley.

ORIENTATION

The Stuart Hwy goes under the guise of **Katherine Terrace** as it rumbles through town. The main blocks of this strip lie between the **transit center**, at Lindsay St, and the **Victoria Hwy,** which heads toward Western Australia. A few hundred meters south of the center, Giles St heads left toward Katherine Gorge. Parallel to Katherine Tce, First through Fourth Streets house various tourist accommodations.

PRACTICAL INFORMATION

Airport: Tindal Airport, 20km south of Katherine, is connected to an RAAF base. Airnorth (tel. 8971 7277) serves Darwin ($144) and Alice Springs ($369).

Buses: Greyhound and **McCafferty's** bus counters don't open until 20min. prior to departure. Book through **Harvey World Travel** (tel 8972 1044) in the transit center or at Traveland. Greyhound Pioneer runs to: Darwin (3hr., $45), Alice Springs (15hr., $144), Broome (19hr., $202) and Townsville (eons, $277). McCafferty's runs to Darwin ($39), Townsville ($215), and Alice Springs ($133).

Car Rentals: Territory (tel. 8972 3183) is in the transit center. **Hertz** and **Delta** (tel. 8972 2511) have offices at Knotts' Landing.

Tourist Office: Katherine Region Tourist Association (tel. 8972 2650; fax 8972 2969), on Lindsay St, south of the transit center and across the street, is more impartial than the travel desk in the transit center. Open M-F 8am-5pm, Sa-Su 10am-3pm in the Dry; M-F 8am-5pm in the Wet.

Travel Agency: Traveland, 15 Katherine Tce (tel. 8972 1344; fax 8972 2763), near Giles St. Open M-Th 9am-5pm, F 9am-6pm, Sa 10am-1pm.

Currency Exchange: Westpac, Commonwealth, and **ANZ banks** and **ATMs** are on Katherine Tce. All open M-Th 9:30am-4pm, F 9:30am-5pm.

Bookstore: Katherine's Books (tel. 8972 2530), in the Woolworths Shopping Mall, has a modest selection. Open M-F 9am-5:30pm, Sa 9am-1pm.

Pharmacy: Terrace Pharmacy (tel. 8972 1229; fax 8971 0126), at 19 Katherine Tce. Open M-F 8:30am-5:30pm, Sa 9am-noon.

Police: (tel. 8972 0111), 2km south of the tourist office on the Stuart Hwy.

Hospital: (tel. 8973 9211) on Giles St (Gorge Rd), 3km from Katherine Tce.

Post Office: (tel. 8972 1439) On the corner of Katherine Tce and Giles St. Open M-F 9am-5pm. **Postal code:** 0850.

Internet Access: Oddly enough, located inside Katherine Art Gallery (tel. 8971 1051) next to the transit center. $2 per 10min. Open daily 9am-6pm.

Phone Code: 08.

ACCOMMODATIONS

All three hostels have A/C, fans, a pool, and 10am checkout. High season is the Dry.

Kookaburra Backpackers, (tel. 8971 0257 or 1800 808 211), is on the corner of Lindsay and Third St, 3 blocks from the transit center. Every group of 8 guests shares a clean bathroom and a kitchenette overflowing with pots and pans. Relaxed social atmosphere centers around the picnic tables and the pool. Friendly and helpful mother and daughter run the hostel. Laundry, free transport to and from transit center. Reception open daily 7:30am-7:30pm. With YHA or VIP card dorms $12; twins $35. Key deposit $10. Book ahead in the high season.

Victoria Lodge, 21 Victoria Hwy (1800 808 875), a 10min. walk from Katherine Tce. Managers of this quiet hostel have used the flood as an opportunity to refurbish. Spanking clean, modern rooms have leather couches, microwave, bathroom, spacious kitchenette, and color TV. Barbecue facilities; free bus station transport. Dorms $14, weekly $85; twins $40 and doubles $45. YHA.

Palm Court Backpackers (tel. 8972 2722 or 1800 089 103; fax 8971 1443), corner of 3rd and Giles St just a block from Kookaburra. A tad musty but livable, with zany management and TV, fridge, and bath in each room. Linen, plates, and cutlery provided. Laundry facilities. Reception open daily 7am-9pm. Bunks in 8- or 4-bed dorms $12, 14; twins and doubles $45. Key deposit $10. YHA.

The Pine Tree Motel (tel. 8972 2533, fax 8972 2920), located on 3rd St across from Kookaburra's. More upscale digs for a bit more dough. Your standard motel, with clean and comfortable rooms, nice pool, and laundry facilities. Singles $78, twins $93, triple $103, quad $113.

Frontier Katherine (tel. 8972 1744; fax 8972 2790), south of town near the Stuart Hwy on Cyprus St, has camping. $8 per person; powered sites with shower $20.

Red Gum Caravan Park, 42 Victoria Hwy (tel. 8972 2239; fax 8972 2385), has sites on a noisy highway. Laundry and pool. $7 per person; 2-person powered sites $17, each additional person $5.

Knotts Crossing (tel. 8972 2511; fax 8972 2628), toward the gorge, corner of Giles and Cameron, before the hospital. Pool, barbecue. Unpowered 2-person sites $18.

FOOD

Ever the cheapest place to fill your stomach, **Woolworths** (tel. 8972 3055) stands across from the transit center (open daily 7am-10pm). For classier fare, try:

Cafe Enio's (tel. 8972 2255) located on Katherine Terrace near the intersection with the Victoria Highway. This hip, upbeat cafe and coffee bar provides a welcome respite from burgers and greasy spoons. Gleaming Gorge Salad with chicken $6; tasty fruit smoothies $4.50. Open M-Sa 9:30am-5:30pm.

Cafe on First (tel. 8971 2134), attached to the cinema. Sunny family atmosphere, with coral walls, sunflowers, and excellent focaccia sandwiches ($6). Dinner pasta bar $10. Service can be slow. Open daily 11:30am-9pm. Wheelchair accessible.

Popeye's Gourmet Food (tel. 8972 3633), on Katherine Tce near Giles St. The main event of this sailor-themed joint is the all-you-can-eat pizza buffet ($7; Su-W 6-9pm). The tomato pies will stave off scurvy, and the spacious seating is pleasant. Pies are served with salad ($7). Open M-F 9am-10pm, Sa-Su 11am-10pm.

Tommo's Bakery (tel. 8971 1155), located on the corner of 2nd and Giles. This humble bakery offers yummy bread and a sandwich bar ($2-3). The smell alone will make you hungry. Open M-F 5am-5pm, Sa 5am-1pm.

Mekhong Thai Café (tel. 8972 3170), at the junction of Stuart and Victoria Hwy. A minimalist, fluorescent-lit interior. The food is excellent, reasonably authentic, and vegetarian friendly. Mains start around $10. Open Tu-Su 6pm-10pm.

SIGHTS

The **Katherine School of the Air** (tel. 8972 2552), on Giles St about 2km from Katherine Tce, broadcasts lessons to rural schoolchildren and mistakenly identifies itself as the largest classroom in the world; that distinction belongs to the Alice Springs school (see p. 259). Still, 80 million hectares is a long way to throw a spitball. You can observe the teacher-DJs at work, but you must enter at specified times. *(Apr.-Oct. M-F 9, 10, 11am, 1, 2pm. Admission $4, children $2.)*

Three kilometers along the Victoria Hwy from the Stuart Hwy, **hot springs** bubble along the Katherine River. Though not quite Mataranka (see p. 257), the springs have safe swimming, toilets, and wheelchair access along Croker St. Katherine's numerous **art galleries** display regional Aboriginal work. The visitors center publishes *The Katherine Arts and Crafts Trail* as a guide to this cultural journey.

■ Katherine Gorge (Nitmiluk) National Park

Often eclipsed by Kakadu and Litchfield National Parks, **Katherine Gorge (Nitmiluk) National Park** offers a plethora of water and land activities. Its 292,008 hectares cover the region northeast of Katherine. Since 1989, the park has been owned by the local Jawoyn Aboriginals, who manage it jointly with the Parks and Wildlife Commission. The park's star attraction is **Katherine Gorge,** which is actually a series of 13 gorges on the Katherine River, broken by small cascades. The rocky cliffs rise dramatically from the meandering green waters of the Katherine. You can hike through gorges to view the river's luster or canoe tranquilly on it. In the Wet, the individual cascades are subsumed by a single gushing current that restricts access to the gorge.

ORIENTATION AND PRACTICAL INFORMATION

There are two entrances into the park. The northern entrance is 45km north of Katherine, and 20km further to Edith Falls. The more popular southern entrance lies 30km out of Katherine on Giles St, later called Gorge Rd. **Travel North** (tel. 8972 1044) runs buses from the hostels in Katherine several times per day ($8, children $4; book ahead). The **Nitmiluk Visitor Centre** (tel. 8972 3150), at the end of Gorge Road, is the locus for information on the park. The ranger desk (open 7am-7pm) provides information on hikes, issues camping permits, and gives a "Friendly Ranger Slideshow" (Tu, Th 7:30pm). The tourist information desk books canoes, helicopter tours, and boat cruises and is also the reception for the campground. The center also contains a small grocery store, exhibits of Jawoyn and natural history, and a bistro. The veranda outside has picnic tables with incredible views of the gorge (open dry season daily 7am-8pm; wet season 7:30am-5:30pm). A winding concrete path connects the center with another car park and the boathouse. Contact the **Parks and Wildlife Commission** (tel. 8972 1886; fax 8971 0702) in Katherine for more info on Katherine Gorge. Although some drink water straight from the river, visitors are beseeched to bring their own water and to baste themselves in sunblock.

ON THE KATHERINE RIVER

From May to September, quieter waters create a picturesque setting for canoeing, boating, and walking. **Canoeing** justifiably takes the cake in popularity; it's relaxing and allows you to check out intriguing spots on either side without taking a plunge. Paddling on the water is also more comfortable than hiking, since temperatures here are sizzling year-round. No more than 75 canoes are permitted in the gorge at a time; book several days ahead. **Nitmiluk Canoes** (tel. 8972 3150) does most rentals, although you can book through most hostels. Single-handed canoes (full-day 8am-5pm $34, half-day 8am-noon or noon-5pm $24; deposit $20) and double-handed canoes (full-day $50, half-day $37; deposit $20) are both available, and all canoes come with a waterproof safe. Most hostels can pair single travelers with a partner. Even if you hate human contact, you might want a partner, since paddling is only half the battle of the gorge tour (dragging the canoe across rocky portages is the other).

Another popular aquatic activity is **swimming,** but keep in mind that you may be sharing the space with freshwater crocs (most canoeists spot at least one). Many people like to swim near the boathouse. Those less physically motivated can enjoy the gorge through daily **boat cruises.** Flat, shaded motor vessels zoom along the gorges; at the end of each gorge, passengers hike over to a new boat on the next. The crowded arrangement makes it hard to enjoy the natural solitude of the area (dry season rates: 8hr. cruise $71; 4hr. $41; 2hr. $28). Book through Nitimik Tours. The information desk also books helicopter tours for a hefty fee.

ON TERRA FIRMA

Walking tracks in the park range from 400m to 66km. The excellent scenery provides a totally different view from canoeing, but the sun can be brutal. Bring lots of water and a wide-brimmed hat.

Day Walks

Several interesting day hikes leave from the Nitmiluk Centre. On the **Lookout Loop Trail,** a short 3.7km return walk will reward you with excellent views of the Katherine River and 17 Mile Valley. The **Windolf Trail,** 8.4km return, has views of the lower gorge as well as occasional exhibits of Aboriginal art. The **Butterfly Gorge Walk** is a 12km return walk that provides a good overview of the region, with excellent views of the expansive valley and rocky escarpment before winding through a tranquil gorge to a huge, pristine plunge pool at the end. At Edith Falls, the **Leliyn Trail,** 2.6km return, passes several swimming holes and offers awe-inspiring views.

Overnight Camping and Extended Bushwalks

The ranger info station provides detailed explanations of each long hike, including the popular **Jatbula Trail,** a five-day sojourn between Edith Falls and the Nitmiluk Visitor Centre. Topographic maps can be purchased for $5 at the Centre. Travelers planning to hike these extended trails must register with the Ranger Station at the Centre.

Overnight camping in the depths of the park is permitted ($3 per person per night, $20 deposit; register at the center). Bush-style camping areas are located along the walking tracks and at the 5th, 6th, and 9th gorges. They're graced with toilets and, usually, a water source. Fires are permitted at the walking track sites but not along the gorges. There are also trim, permanent **campgrounds** next to the Nitmiluk Centre and at Edith Falls. These can take on both tents and caravans, but only the Gorge boasts powered sites. The **Gorge Caravan Park** has tent sites ($7 per person, with power for 2 people $18; toilets, showers; more facilities than at the Falls).

The less-visited **Edith Falls** boasts an impressive system of waterfalls. They are at the end of a 20km paved access road that begins 42km north of Katherine off the Stuart Hwy. The lower pool, a short walk from the car park, is a huge, crystal-clear plunge pool with a waterfall. A walk up the Leliyn trail (see above) provides access to the smaller but equally amazing pools. There is a campground ($5 per adult, $2.50 per child) with showers, barbecue, a picnic area, and a food kiosk (open 8am-5pm).

■ Stuart Highway from Katherine to Tennant Creek

Twenty-seven kilometers south of Katherine is an unsung gem, **Cutta Cutta Caves Nature Park** (tel. 8972 1948). Meaning "many stars," the caves extend 720m through an underground labyrinth of rock columns and jagged ceilings. The tour, which is the only way to enter this underworld, is led by jovial, witty guides and proceeds through five impressive, cathedral-like chambers of the cave. Puff the Magic Dragon and Disney's Pluto appear as rock formations, while bats appear in their real-life form. Tours leave in the Dry at 9, 10, 11am, 1, 2pm ($8 adults, $4 children). The caves are closed in the Wet when the caves fill up with water.

Another 79km south, travelers enjoy what bubbles out of the ground instead of descending underneath it. Lured by clear river pools and thermal **hot springs,** bathers make their way to **Elsey National Park.** The Roper River winds through the quiet little park, creating small plunge pools. At the end of the park are the pristine **Mataranka Falls,** reachable by a 4km walk. The trail leads from 12 Mile and the Jalmurark campground. Canoes can be hired for the day at the campground (two-person canoes $7 per hour, $35 per day; one-person $5 per hour, $25 per day). The campground offers private, well maintained sites (adults $5, children $1).

Nearby lies **Mataranka Homestead.** Although hit hard by the 1998 flooding, the thermal pools still attract bathers to their 34°C waters. Be prepared to share the overused pool with a crowd, not to mention the bats that come every couple of years to nest in the surrounding trees. A new thermal spring, Bitter Springs, is expected to open in 1999 near the Mataranka Homestead. Camping at the homestead costs $7 per adult, $3.50 per child. There is a small bistro (open 7am-8pm) and a store.

Greyhound and McCafferty's routes between Katherine and Tennant Creek all stop at the **Mataranka Homestead Tourist Resort** (tel. 8975 4544; fax 8975 4580), located next to the pools (dorms $13, twins and doubles $26; non-members $15, $30). Its campground has hot showers and laundry (sites $7 per person; powered $18 for 2 people, $7 each additional person). Canoeing, fishing, and horseback riding can round off an onerous day of soaking in the clear aqua springs.

■ Tennant Creek

The discovery of gold deposits in 1930 made Tennant Creek and the **Barkly** region around it the NT's mining prima donnas. Located 506km south of Darwin on the Stuart Hwy, the town is a rare blip of urban development amid desolate desert and vast Aboriginal land. It took a while for mining here to get up to speed, but since the 1960s, the Tennant Creek area has unearthed about $4 billion worth of gold. Although there are still active mines in the area, today's outpost of 3500 people is as much a highway town as a mining center. It occupies a convenient stop-over point just south of the **Three Ways** junction. Yet, between its mining history, the living legacy of the native **Warumungu Aboriginals,** and the fascinating valley containing the **Devil's Marbles** 104km to the south, there's more to do in Tennant Creek than change buses or crash for the night.

ORIENTATION

The Stuart Hwy, called **Paterson St** in town, runs from north to south through the compact town. Several important streets cross Paterson: moving south, there's **Stuart St** (not to be confused with the erstwhile highway) and **Davidson St,** then **Peko Rd** on the east side of Paterson, and **Windley St** on the west. Continuing south is **Memorial Dr,** a truncated rib only occurring west of Paterson.

PRACTICAL INFORMATION

Tourist Office: Tennant Creek Battery Hill Regional Centre (tel. 8962 3388; fax 8962 2509). Located 1km up Pekod Rd, this new center provides informational brochures and tours, many on Battery Hill itself (see Sights, below). Open M-F 9am-5pm, Sa 9am-noon, and Su for tours. Most accommodations run shuttles here.

Currency Exchange: ANZ Bank (tel. 8962 2002), a few doors south of the transit center on Paterson St has **ATMs.** Open M-Th 9:30am-4pm, F 9:30am-5pm. **Westpac Bank,** at Paterson St and Peko Rd, has the same hours.

Buses: The **transit center,** on the west side of Paterson St, has phones, a snack bar, and public showers. **Greyhound** runs to Alice Springs (5-6hr., $78), Darwin (13hr., $101), Katherine (8-9hr., $38), and Mt. Isa (daily, $75). **McCafferty's** also runs daily to Alice Springs, Darwin, Mt. Isa and Townsville for similar prices.

Auto Club: AANT (tel. 8962 2468).

Bicycle Rental: Bridgestone Tyre (tel. 8962 2361), on the corner of Paterson and Davidson St. Bikes $10 per day, $5 half-day.

Grocery: Abundant supplies of food available at the **Tenant Creek Food Barn** on Paterson St on the South end of town. Open M-Sa 8:30am-6pm, Su 9am-6pm.

Pharmacy: Amcal Chemist (tel. 8962 2616) on Paterson St. Open M-F 9am-5:30pm, Sa 9am-12:30pm.

Internet Access: (tel. 8962 2358), at the high school library during non-school hours. Take Pekod St away from town; before Outback Caravan Park take a left. Open M-F 3-6pm, Sa 10am-6pm, Su 11am-6pm. $5 per hour. **Public library** on Pekod St has access for $2 per hour. Open M-F 10am-1pm, 2-6pm; Sa 10am-noon.

Police: (tel. 8962 4444), on Paterson St south of Peko.

Hospital: Tennant Creek Hospital (tel. 8962 4399, after hours 8962 1900) is on Schmidt St, a left turn at the end of Memorial Dr.
Emergency: Dial 000.
Post Office: (tel. 8962 2196), at the corner of Paterson St and Memorial Dr, is open M-F 9am-5pm. Postal code: 0860.
Phone Code: 08.

ACCOMMODATIONS

Safari Backpackers (tel. 8962 2207; fax 8962 3188) on Davidson St. From the transit center, walk to the end of the block and take a right on Davidson. Not much character, but clean and comfortable. Shared bath, kitchen, laundry and lounge. **Safari's Motel,** adjacent, has comfortable, quiet rooms. Reception for both is in the motel building. Dorms $14; twins and singles in hostel $38. Motel singles $69; doubles and twins $79. YHA. Book in advance.

Tourist's Rest Hostel (tel. 8962 2719; fax 8962 2718), on Leichardt St; walk south on Paterson and turn right on Windley (15min.). Spacious rooms, friendly staff. Shared bath, kitchen, pool, TV room. Free pick-up and drop-off. Offers daytrips to Devil's Marbles ($50 with accommodation). Check-out 11am. Twins, doubles, and triples $14 per person. Linen included. VIP, YHA.

Outback Caravan Park (tel. 8962 2459; fax 8962 1278), on the left side of Peko Rd, 200m from Paterson St. Stellar swimming pool, grocery, shared bath, kitchen, barbecue. Tent sites $7 per person; powered caravan sites $16 for 2 people; cabins $50-55; on-site vans $25-40.

FOOD

Near the transit center, Paterson St is lined with takeaway snack bars, from fried chicken to Chinese to Italian. **Rocky's** (tel. 8962 2049 or 8962 2522) on Paterson St provides a little old-world Italian flavor in their tasty pizzas, served in a no-frills setting. (Large $14. Takeaway and delivery. Open daily 5-10:30pm.) For a more intimate dining experience, try **Margo Miles Steakhouse** (tel. 8962 2006), across the street from the terminal next to Jackson's Bar. The antique lobby with wooden floors and old chandeliers retains a gold rush feel; the fare is more international. (Mains around $15. Open M-F noon-2pm and daily 6pm-late. Takeaway also available.) The **Dolly Pot Inn** (tel. 8962 2824), past the Safari Backpackers on Davidson St, is camouflaged with unusual decorating (barn meets squash courts), but is a family restaurant with fresh food and friendly service (mains $15; open daily 7am-late). The **Tennant Food Barn** (tel. 8962 2296), at Paterson St opposite Memorial Dr, offers the cheapest groceries.

SIGHTS

The **Battery Hill Regional Centre** (tel. 8962 3388) doubles as the tourist office and a historical sight. *(1hr. tours daily 9:30am and 5pm. Admission $12, pensioners $8, children $6.)* The location was used from 1939 as a gold stamp battery, where ore was crushed and flakes of gold extracted. Expeditions into the battery are heavy on history and the mechanics of ore processing. A replica of a mine has been newly constructed in the depths of the hill at the center, complete with authentic machinery and sound effects. A tour into the mine runs daily at 11am.

Norm's Gold and Scenic Tours (tel. 0418 891 711 or 8962 3388), besides leading the Battery Hill tours, tours other area gold-related sites. You can try your hand at panning on a two-hour Gold Fever Tour that departs weekdays at 1pm. **Ten Ant Tours** (tel. 8962 2358 or 8962 2168) features a night descent into The Dot, one of the Creek's oldest mines. *($14, children $7.)* History buffs can visit the **Tenant Creek Telegraph Reserve Station Historical Reserve** 10km north of Tenant Creek. *(Ranger talks May-Oct. F 9am-4pm on the hour.)* Built in 1872, the station was integral in the overland telegraph project. There is self-guided tour through the building. The **Parks and Wildlife Commission** (tel. 8962 4599) manages the station as well as nearby **Davenport Range National Park.**

■ Tenant Creek to Alice Springs

Most of the Red Centre's main attractions seem to be big, ancient rocks randomly appearing in the desert, and **Devil's Marbles**, 104km south of Tennant Creek next to the Stuart Hwy, is no exception. Still, these rocks rock. Science's hypothesis of 1.6 billion years of granite wind erosion is hardly a satisfying explanation for the ethereal, otherworldly effect created by the 7m-thick boulders, which stack like smooth globes in piles too numerous for the eye to see at once. The local Aboriginals' answer is that they're eggs of the rainbow serpent, and a sacred site. In any event, the Devil's Marbles is a confounding, impressive, and very photogenic wonder of nature. In many places you can see where rocks split apart or fell, and mentally try to put the puzzle back together. There is basic camping at the Marbles. (Pit toilets and barbecue only. No water. $2.50 per person fee paid at the entrance.)

The closest town is **Wavehope,** 9km south, which has petrol, food, and accommodations at a **motel** (tel. 8964 1963; single $30) or a campground (sites $4 per person; 2-person powered sites $12). The bus stops there, or may drop you at the Marbles themselves if you beg sufficiently. Alternatively, day tours make the lap from Tennant Creek. **Norm's Tours** (tel. 8962 3388; mobile tel. 0418 891 711) departs at 2:30pm and returns at 6pm for a sunset barbecue at Battery Hill.

Further down the track is more lonely road dotted with boring towns that provide basic services including gas and food. Budget accommodation of various varieties is available in **Wycliff Well** (tel. 8964 1966), **Barrow Creek** (tel. 8956 9753), **Ti-Tree** (tel. 8956 9741), and **Aelim.** The most pleasant of the four is Ti-Tree.

Sixty-nine kilometers from Alice, the **Plenty Hwy** branches to the right. Plenty of what? The answer lies 70km down the road at the **Gemtree** (tel. 8956 9855; fax 8956 9860), a private gemfield for your fossicking pleasure. There are gems for sale, gems for study, and at rather steep prices, gems for hunting. The road is sealed and the site offers campsites and indoor rooms.

THE RED CENTRE

The dry, desolate outback at the center of Australia takes its name from the color of the oxidized dust that stretches to the horizon. To many travelers, the Red Centre represents the essence of Australia. Flat lands bake perpetually under a burning sun rarely obscured by rain clouds. The gnarled vegetation is weedy and sparse, and the wildlife is locked in a constant struggle for survival with the unforgiving climate and the unbearable bush flies. Out of this stark landscape, at the geographic center of the continent, rises Uluru (Ayers Rock), a celebrated symbol of the land down under.

Alice Springs is the region's unofficial capital and the gateway to the desert beyond. The region's natural wonders include the MacDonnell Ranges, Kings Canyon, Ayers Rock, and its companion range, the Olgas, all of which do their best to penetrate the reddish monotony of central Australia. These monuments have magnetic appeal, and tourists flock to the remote Red Centre as if to an eighth wonder, prepared to brave endless distances and risk remote disasters to experience the "real" outback. ■

■ Alice Springs

Alice Springs (pop. 27,000) is the only significant human beat in the heart of Australia. A desert outpost connected to the rest of the world only by long mirage-filled highways, Alice's only significant neighbor is a big-ass rock. As if in deference to neighboring constructions of nature, architects have refrained from giving "the Alice" an obtrusive skyline. The town is nestled in a break in the MacDonnell Ranges carved by the **Todd River.** The "river" that passes through the town is usually a dry, overgrown trench of grass and sand. A spring 3km east of town, discovered in 1871 by telegraph workers, was named after Alice Todd, a foreman's wife, and became the town's namesake.

Alice had just 40 residents in 1927. Rapid growth began when the **Old Ghan railway** reached Alice from Adelaide in 1929, and was perpetuated by the sealing of the Stuart Hwy during WWII. Tourism recently eclipsed the cattle and mining industries, and the burden of 250,000 annual visitors is beginning to stress the local ecology. If the spring that is Alice's lifeline continues to fall 3m per year, residents may need to look elsewhere for water in another 30 years. Although tourism is inescapably woven into the city's identity, the streets of this oasis are often as silent in the evenings as the desert that surrounds them.

ORIENTATION

The Stuart Highway runs through Alice Springs on its way from Darwin (1490km distant) to Adelaide. Seen from the north, the **MacDonnell Ranges** form a backdrop for Alice. A break in the ranges called **Heavitree Gap** permits both the highway and the Todd River to pass south. Although usually dry, the river is an important landmark, bordering the east side of the town center. The southern outskirts of town lie beyond the Gap, as does the airport (20km south).

A compact grid of streets along the west bank of the riverbed contains central Alice Springs. **Todd St** runs parallel to the river, with a pedestrian mall, **Todd Mall,** covering two blocks between Gregory Tce and Wills Tce. Parsons St is the block in between, and intersects Todd Mall at the **Alice Plaza,** a large indoor arcade. Another major landmark on Todd St is the Melanka Lodge Complex, a block and a half south of the Gregory Tce end of Todd Mall. Further south, Todd St becomes Gap Rd and runs toward the mountains, eventually joining the Stuart Hwy at a traffic circle. The major routes to the city's outskirts are the Stuart Hwy north and south and Larapinta Drive, the extension of Stott Tce. **Anzac Hill,** a rocky rise next to Wills Tce, is the best vantage point in town.

PRACTICAL INFORMATION

Airport: Alice Springs Airport (tel. 8951 1211), 20km south of the city on the Stuart Hwy, provides domestic service only, but has tourist information, currency exchange, and car rental agencies. **Airport shuttle bus** (tel. 8953 0310) runs to central Alice (one-way $9, return $15, family $25). **Qantas** (tel. 8950 5211) has offices in the airport and in Todd Mall. Open M-F 8:30am-5pm, Sa 8:30am-noon. Destinations include Darwin (daily, $358), Yulara (1hr., $170), Cairns (2hr., $446), Sydney (3½hr., $525), Adelaide (2hr., $377), Perth (2hr., $506). Backpackers holding passports and international tickets receive a 30% discount. **Ansett** also has offices in the airport and in Todd Mall at Traveland. Discounted fares to Darwin (2hr., $353), Cairns (3hr., $441), Sydney (3½hr., $519), Adelaide (2hr., $281), Perth (3hr., $500). **Airnorth** (tel. 8952 6666) flies to destinations within NT.

Trains: Alice Railway Station (tel. 8951 6161) is a 20min. walk from central Alice. Take Stott Tce across the Stuart Hwy, where it becomes Larapinta Dr. The station is at the end of George Tce, the first right. Trains run to Adelaide ($150), but not to Darwin. Open Tu, F 8am-2:30pm. Traveland makes reservations.

Buses: Greyhound Pioneer (tel. 13 20 30) operates from Gregory Tce near Coles and runs to Darwin (18-20hr., $131), Tennant Creek (5hr., $72), Yulara (5hr., $76), Adelaide (19-20hr., $122), Townsville ($206), and Sydney ($209). A 3-day tour of Uluru and Kings Canyon is $195. Open daily 4:45am-8:30pm. **McCafferty's** (tel. 8952 3952) is on Gregory Tce, half a block toward the river from the Todd Mall, runs to Darwin (20hr., $145), Katherine (15hr., $133), Tennant Creek (6hr., $78), Townsville (26hr., $228), Yulara (6hr., $55), and Adelaide (20hr., $135). 10% discount with YHA, VIP, or ISIC. Open 5am-9pm.

Taxis: Alice Springs Taxis (tel. 8952 1877) queue on Gregory Tce near Todd Mall.

Car Rental: Territory-Thrifty (tel. 8952 9999) at the corner of Hartley St and Stott Tce has seasonal rates, often with cheap relocation deals. Economy cars $74 per day, 4WD $120. Open daily 8am-5pm. **Hertz,** 76 Hartley St (tel. 8952 2644). Economy cars $69 per day. Avis (tel. 8953 5533), at the corner of Hartley and Gregory St. **Budget** (tel. 8952 8899) on Gap Rd. All companies have counters in the airport.

Roadside Assistance: AANT (24hr. tel. 8952 1087).

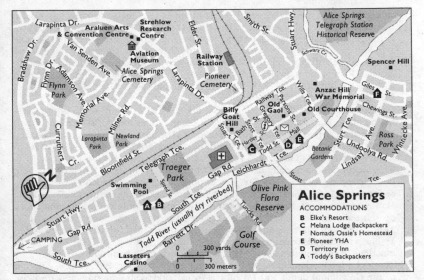

Alice Springs
ACCOMMODATIONS
B Elke's Resort
C Melana Lodge Backpackers
F Nomads Ossie's Homestead
E Pioneer YHA
D Territory Inn
A Toddy's Backpackers

Bike Rental: At various hostels. **Pioneer YHA** charges $9 per half-day, $15 per day.

Tourist Office: Central Australian Tourism Industry Association (tel. 8952 5800), at the corner of Hartley St and Gregory Tce. From the south end of Todd Mall, take Gregory Tce 1 block to Hartley. Open M-F 8:30am-5:30pm, Sa-Su 9am-4pm.

Budget Travel: Traveland (tel. 8952 7186), on Gregory Tce at the end of Todd Mall. Open M-F 9:30am-5pm, Sa 9am-noon. Most hostels have a tour desk.

Currency Exchange: Banks with **ATMs** cluster in Todd Mall. **National Australia** (tel. 8952 1611), **ANZ** (tel. 8952 1144). Both are open M-Th 9:30am-4pm, F 9:30am-5pm.

Library: (tel. 8950 0555), next to the Visitor's Center. Open M-F 9am-6pm, Sa 9am-1pm, Su 1-5pm.

Bookstore: Dymock's Booksellers (tel. 8952 9111; fax 8952 9122) next to Woolworths. Open M-F 8:30am-5:30pm, Sa 9am-5pm, Su 10am-3pm.

Hotlines: Crisis (tel. 1800 019 116). **Gayline** (tel. 8953 2844) has info for gays and lesbians in Alice and throughout NT. Leave a number; your call will be returned.

Pharmacy: Amcal Chemist (tel. 8953 0089) in Alice Plaza, by Parsons St in the Todd Mall. Open daily 8:30am-7:30pm. **Alice Springs Pharmacy** (tel. 8952 1554) near Woolworths. Open M-F 8:30am-6pm, Sa 9am-3pm, Su 10am-2pm.

Hospital: Alice Springs Hospital (tel. 8951 7777; emergency 8951 7529; ambulance 8952 2200), on Gap Rd, the continuation of Todd St south of Melanka's.

Emergency: Dial 000.

Police: (tel. 8951 8888), at Parsons and Bath St, 2 blocks from Todd Mall.

Internet Access: At the library for $2 per hour. Book well in advance. **Bizcom** (tel. 8952 9222) on Railway Terrace near K-Mart. $5 per 1/2hr. Open M-F 9am-5:30pm, Sa 9am-noon. **Torque of the Town,** 113 Todd St (tel. 8953 4755) has two terminals amidst Harvey Davidson paraphernalia. $5 per 1/2hr. Open M-F 9am-5:30 pm, Sa 9am-3pm. Many hostels have less reliable coin-op Internet hookups.

Post Office: GPO (tel. 8952 1020; fax 8953 4049), on Hartley St, a block off the Todd Mall down Parsons St. Open M-F 9am-5pm. **Postal code:** 0870.

Phone Code: 08.

ACCOMMODATIONS

The hostels of Alice are concentrated in the city center, but several quieter digs lie across the river. All listings have air-conditioned rooms and most have tour bookings.

◉**Pioneer YHA** (tel. 8952 8855; fax 8952 4144; email pioneer1@dove.net.au), on the corner of Parsons and Leichardt St, less than a block off Todd Mall from Alice Plaza entrance. Originally a deckchair cinema, this landmark was rescued from demolition a decade ago. Guests quietly relax around the pool. Cheerful coral-colored dorms, scrubbed showers, tidy kitchen, laundry facilities, free safe and luggage storage. Reception open daily 6:30am-10pm. Check-out 10am. 4- to 6-bed dorms $14, YHA nonmembers $17. One double available ($36). Linen $2. Key deposit $10. Book in advance with credit card.

Elke's Resort, 39 Gap Rd (tel. 8952 8134; fax 8952 8143), 1km south of the Greyhound office; turn right on Todd St. Elke's compensates for its distance from town by providing airport and bus station transport. The kind folks here have converted a motel into the classiest hostel in town. Each comfortable, if spartan, dorm room has its own bath, kitchenette, TV, and balcony. There's a pool. Free breakfast 6-9am. Reception open daily 6am-10pm. Check-out 10am. 6- to 8-bed dorms $16; doubles and twins $45. YHA, VIP. Key deposit $10. Linen included.

Territory Inn, Leichardt Tce (tel. 8952 2066; fax 8952 7829), in the middle of Todd Mall near Parsons St. A shampoo-included world of marble bathrooms and sport-coated receptionists. The Territory regales its guests with minibar fridges, TVs, radios, in-room phones, and daily housekeeping. Hotel-style rooms arranged around a porticoed atrium with barbecue facilities and a view of Todd Mall. Check-out 10am. A room with a double bed, a single bed, and a bathroom costs $95.

Melanka Lodge Backpackers, 94 Todd St (tel. 8952 4744; fax 8952 4587), adjacent to the Greyhound depot and 1½ blocks from Todd Mall. Free transport from airport; $3 to get to it. A huge operation, taking up a solid city block (half of which is the cleaner Motel Melanka). The complex lures tourists with a snack bar, sofa-strewn TV room, and nightclub. Reminiscent of a university dorm, complete with the party atmosphere. Pool, beach volleyball court, Internet access, free safe and luggage storage. Beds in 6- to 8-bed dorms $13, in 3- to 4-bed dorms $16; singles $30; twins and doubles $32. $1 VIP and just-off-the-bus discounts. Key deposit $10.

Toddy's Backpackers, 41 Gap Rd (tel. 8952 1322; fax 8952 1767; email sahara@ozemail.com.au), 1km from Greyhound next to Elke's. The cheapest beds in town. Two buildings flank a pool, kitchen, pool room, and contain the spartan budget annex. Courtesy bus meets most flights and buses. Free breakfast 6-8:30am; all-you-can-eat dinner ($7) starts at 7pm. Check-out 10am. 8-bed dorms $8; 6-bed dorms $12. Singles, doubles, and twins with sink and fridge $36. Linen provided Motel accommodation with TV, bathroom, and fridge available for $48. Key deposit $10.

Camping

Campsites begin just outside the town along the major thoroughfares. The **Heavitree Gap Outback Resort** (tel. 8952 4866 or 1800 896 119; fax 8952 9394) is 3km from central Alice. Follow the Stuart Hwy south, take a left on Palm Circuit. The estate has a motel, bistro, and ranging wallabies. (Sites $7 per person; 2-person powered sites $16.) **G'Day Mate Tourist Park** (tel. 8952 9589; fax 8952 2612) has two-person sites for $15 (powered $18). **MacDonnell Range Holiday Park** (tel. 8952 6111) is right down the road on Palm Ct. In the other direction on the Stuart Hwy, **Stuart Caravan Park** (tel. 8952 2547) lies 1km north of the city center on the right (sites $7 per person; 2-person powered sites $16, $6.50 per extra person).

FOOD

As a desert oasis, Alice spoils its visitors with a heap of attractive, ethnically diverse restaurants, from Chinese to Mexican to "Swiss and Indian." These are tasty but not always budget. There are several supermarkets near Todd Mall. **Woolworths** (tel. 8953 0988), the biggest and cheapest, is in the Yeperenye Plaza on Hartley St between Gregory and Parsons St (open M-Sa 7am-midnight, Su 7am-10pm). **Coles,** one block toward Bath St, is open 24 hours.

◉**Bar Doppios** (tel. 8952 6525), the Fan Arcade at the Gregory Tce end of Todd Mall. Trendy Mediterranean-style cafe. Serves tasty, inexpensive veggie fare. Relaxed atmosphere, with eclectic decorations and open windows. Scrumptious soups $5.50, falafel rolls $6, fresh salads $6. Open daily M-Sa 7:30am-9pm, Su 10am-8pm.

Red Ochre Grill (tel. 8952 2066), on Todd Mall, near the Territory Inn. The scintillating outback cuisine delves so deeply into regional ingredients that the menu literally needs its own glossary. Aboriginal artwork and didgeridoo music round out the atmosphere for an elegant, memorable meal. A fantastic array of dishes suits the vegetarian and spoils the meat-eater. The steamed vegetable appetizer ($7) is nearly a meal itself. Open daily 6:30am-9pm.

Swingers (tel. 8952 9291), just around the corner from Bar Doppios on Gregory St, pumps good alternative vibes in a spacious, colorful setting. A nice place for coffee and pastries. Soups $5, muffins $2. Open M-F 7:30am-5:30pm, Sa 7:30am-4pm.

La Casalinga (tel. 8952 4508), on Gregory Tce near the beginning of Todd Mall. Serves lots for a little. Large specialty pizzas ($14), lasagna ($8), and plenty of other pasta dishes, in a sit-down, Pizza-Hut-like restaurant without the packaged feel or the stupid roof. Open daily 5pm-1am.

Oscar's Cafe (tel. 8953 0930), in the Todd Mall next to the Cinema. Swank and sophisticated, Oscar's spoils weary-laden travelers with tangy Italian meals in a spacious, well-lit room. Mains $14-20. For a more budget-friendly experience you can enjoy the atmosphere and an excellent pastry. Open 9am-late.

SIGHTS

Most of the sights within the town center are near the Todd Mall. The **Museum of Central Australia** (tel. 8951 5335) looms directly above the Mall in the Alice Plaza. *(Open M-F 9am-5pm, Sa-Su 10am-5pm. $2.)* Primarily a natural history exhibition, the museum contains dinosaur casts and lots of stuffed animals, including a baby croc that's vertically cross-sectioned. It also showcases a run-of-the-mill collection of Aboriginal arts and crafts and rotating exhibits by local artists.

Parsons St houses a handful of historical buildings—a gaol, a museum on pioneerswomen—none of which are particularly thrilling. One attraction worthy of a rainyday visit is **Panorama Guth,** 65 Hartley St (tel. 8952 2013). *(Open M-Sa 9am-5pm; Mar.-Nov. also Su 2-5pm. $3, children $1.50.)* Take Gregory Tce a block up to Hartley from the south end of the Mall and turn left. The brainchild of Dutch artist Henk Guth, this castle-like museum displays Aboriginal artifacts and watercolors. The highlight, though, is Guth's panoramic painting of Central Australia, which towers 6m high and spans 60m in circumference, depicting Ayers Rock, the Olgas, Mt. Connor, and King's Canyon. The famous **Royal Flying Doctor Service** (tel. 8952 1129) is two blocks farther down Hartley, just past Stuart Tce and to the right on a small service lane. *(Open M-Sa*

Workin' on the Railroad

Railroad transport has never quite worked out in central Australia. Back in the days of camel transport, residents dreamed of a transcontinental track from Adelaide to Darwin. Construction began in 1878, 15 years after South Australia gained possession of the Northern Territory. Tracks were laid north from Port Augusta, and south from Darwin, but various depressions, wars, and budget problems kept the construction sporadic. The tracks never met in the middle, and the project, known as the Old Ghan in a nostalgic nod to the Afghan camels, was abandoned in 1929. Even the completed sections were rendered obsolete by an oversight: all of the states, eager to get their choo-choos chooing, had used different-sized gauges in their designs. When tracks eventually met at border towns, all cargo and people had to be transferred to a new car at the beginning of the next line. The Old Ghan's narrow gauge (1.067m), known to wash away easily in rains, was eclipsed by the newly coordinated standard gauge (1.435m) in 1971. The Ghan line that now runs from Alice to Adelaide is west of the Old Ghan tracks. The Territory government and Korean business interests have contemplated extending the line to Darwin but, as yet, it's still a dream.

9am-4pm, Su 1-4pm. Admission free; tours $3.) This building dates back to 1939 and houses a gallery of medicine, transport, and communications.

The best place to view a postcard sunset is atop **Anzac Hill,** offering a panorama of Alice Springs and the MacDonnell Ranges. Walk to Wills Tce between Bath and Hartley St; a metal arch marks the start of the "Lions Walk" from the base to the obelisk at the top (easy 10min. climb). Vehicle access is around the corner on the Stuart Hwy.

Covering Alice's more distant sights is difficult without a vehicle. The **Alice Wanderer** (tel. 8952 2111) shuttle service circles past 13 sights in the Alice area. *(Runs 9am-4pm. All-day ticket $18; start early so you can linger at sights you like.)* It departs from the Gregory Tce end of the Todd Mall. **Olive Pink Botanic Garden** (tel. 8952 2154), nestled on the opposite bank of the Todd River, is 2km from Todd Mall. *(Garden open daily 10am-6pm; visitor center open 10am-4pm. Admission by donation.)* Head south on Leichardt Tce with the river on your left, pass the traffic circle at Stott Tce, and cross the river at the next left. This is Tuncks Rd, and the Garden is ahead on the left. The desert scrub is hardly a "garden," but it's not a bad place for a picnic.

The **Alice Springs Telegraph Station,** one of the town's most popular parks, provides green grass, breezy trees, walking paths, and coin-op barbecues. *(Open Nov.-Mar. daily 8am-9pm, Apr.-Oct. 8am-7pm. Entrance to buildings $4.)* The park is 4.5km north of town on the Stuart Hwy and has a marked turn-off. This original location of the Alice Springs township rests among rolling hills. Today, actors play out a period scene around the original 19th-century buildings. Before the turn-off to the station, a sign on the Stuart Hwy points down Head St to the **School of the Air** (tel. 8951 6834; fax 8951 6835). *(Open M-Sa 8:30am-4:30pm, Su 1:30-4:30pm. $3.)* The school doubles as a visitor center where you can learn about the program and, during school hours, watch classes.

The impressive **Strehlow Research Centre** (tel. 8951 8000; fax 8951 8050), focusing on local Aboriginal communities, is on Larapinta Dr. *(Open daily 10am-5pm. Wheelchair accessible.)* From Todd St, take Stott Tce past the Stuart Hwy, where it becomes Larapinta; after a traffic circle look for Memorial Dr on the left. The center's contemporary white and packed-earth brown walls (in fact, the largest packed-earth wall in the southern hemisphere) are a metaphor for the mixture of computerized electronic technology and natural, often spiritual subject matter they enclose. The $4 admission fee (backpackers $2.50) is a pittance for the slide presentation on the earth wall, the richly designed walkways, and the 30-minute light and sound show that imitates the passing of an outback day. Next door is the **Araluen Arts and Convention Centre** (tel. 8952 5022), a prime entertainment venue that includes two painting galleries, one featuring the work of a famous Aboriginal painter Albert Namatjira. *(Open daily 10am-5pm. $2.)*

The Stuart Hwy follows the Todd River south through the Heavitree Gap. After the Gap, the first left is Palm Circuit. **Mecca Date Gardens** (tel. 8952 2425) on the right is Australia's oldest date plantation. *(Open M-F 9am-5pm, Sa 9am-1pm.)* There's not much to see, but plenty to buy: date muffins, date ice cream, date this, date that. You could even try to pick up a hot date and hang out under the shade of the date palms in the green garden. Beyond, Palm Circuit crosses a traffic circle and emerges as the Ross Hwy. The land is quite empty east of here, so it's easy to spot the **Frontier Camel Farm** (tel. 8953 0444 or 1800 806 499) 3km down the road (for a total of 8km from the town center). Alice Springs considers itself the camel capital of Australia (hey, someone's gotta be), and the Camel Museum keeps the claim alive by offering tours that include a camel ride. *(Open daily 9am-5pm. Tours $10, students $8.)*

Instead of turning on Palm Circuit, keep south on the Stuart Hwy to reach the **Transport Heritage Area** (tel. 8955 5047), 10km from the city but still one of Alice's defining sights. The access road is Norris Bell Ave. The **Old Ghan Museum** highlights the trials and tribulations of the enormous locomotive project. The **Road Transport Hall of Fame** is a spacious warehouse with a collection of vehicles from memory lane. *(Each museum open daily 9am-5pm. Admission to each $4.)*

The Largest Classroom in the World

It's Monday morning, and 140 children aged 4-13 are standing thousands of kilometers apart, yet singing their national anthem together. Forget virtual schools—the technology that carries these kids' lessons is nothing more complex than short-wave radios. The School of the Air is central Australia's educational answer to its vast geography and isolated families spread out on remote cattle stations, roadhouses, and Aboriginal lands. The program, stationed in Alice and a dozen other outback towns, brings children in contact with each other and their Alice-based teachers for three to four hours each week. Their makeshift classrooms are sheds, trailers, or rooms in their homes. A parent or appointed instructor supplements their education with an additional five to six hours of weekly schooling. The closest student to Alice is 80km away; the farthest is 1000km. Founded in 1951, the Alice School is the oldest of its kind, though Australia now has 16 such institutions. It covers 1.3 million square kilometers of land, and has thus been dubbed "the largest classroom in the world." This distinction has attracted prestigious guests, including Prince Charles, to stop by and chat with the kids.

ENTERTAINMENT

The Centralian Advocate has an entertainment section for upcoming events. The 500-seat **Araluen Theatre** (tel. 8953 3111), on Larapinta Dr, presents arthouse flicks every Sunday as well as live events (box office open daily 10am-5pm). The popular **Sounds of Starlight Theatre** (tel. 8952 8861) runs regularly a few doors down from Parsons St on the Todd Mall. (Apr.-Nov. Tu-Sa 7pm. $15, children $10.) This intense, didgeridoo-led performance—part outback education, part Pink Floyd laser light show—is accompanied by striking slides of Red Centre landscape. The **Alice Springs Cinema** (tel. 8952 4999), at the end of the Todd Mall nearest Anzac Hill, runs Hollywood movies from 10am to 9pm ($10.50, students $8, Tu $7.50).

The demon Gamblor strikes again at **Lasseters Casino** (tel. 1800 808 975 or 8950 7777), across the Todd River on Barrett Dr, a 45-minute walk or $5 taxi ride from the city center. The setting of the climax of *Priscilla, Queen of the Desert,* the casino has tinted black doors and no windows, so patrons can forget the time of day and concentrate on what really matters: the cherries in the slot machines. There's a card and board games tournament every January. (Open Su-Th 10am-3am, F-Sa 10am-4am.)

Shopping in Alice centers on tourist trap **Todd Mall,** which resounds with the didgeridoo music coming from dozens of stores. The other major shopping area is the **Yeperenye,** an indoor mall that starts roughly across from the post office on Hartley St and continues through to Bath St.

The **Desert Waterhole** at the Melanka Lodge is a casual night spot, with pool tables, a dance floor, and a DJ after 10pm (open nightly 5pm-2am). **Scotty's Tavern** in Todd Mall has a more pub-like feel, with a permanent cloud of smoke, live music almost every night, and rowdy ockers to sustain the din. (Open Su-Th 11am-midnight, F-Sa 11am-1am.) The slickest, biggest, best-known night spot is **Legends** (tel. 8953 3033), overlooking the Todd Mall from the second floor of Alice Plaza. This sprawling disco has a purple interior that belongs on a cruise ship. There's live music nightly, but the $2 drinks on Fridays are the big draw for travelers and locals. (Live band and DJ. F cover $6. Th and Sa covers are smaller and vary. Open Th-Sa 10pm-4am.) Despite the legacy of *Priscilla,* Alice is no ongoing drag show. **Swingers,** however, is a popular gay and lesbian social place (see Restaurants, above). Ask about the location of the "warehouse dance" on the first Friday of every month.

FESTIVALS AND EVENTS

September or October brings the definitive Alice Springs festival, the **Henley-on-Todd Regatta.** A good-natured mockery of the dry river, the race is in bottomless "boats" propelled Flintstones-style–by foot. The race is subject to cancellation: the river flowed in 1993. The **Honda Masters Games,** also September or October, is a friendly biennial 30-sport competition for elderly athletes, and the **Country Music Festival** is a weekend of twanging and bellowing Aussie-style. The **Corkwood Festival** in November is a folk event featuring craft booths in the day and energetic bush dancing at night. **Heritage Week** is an historical NT celebration usually held in April. The horses head out of the gates at **Pioneer Race Park** on the Stuart Hwy on the first Monday in May for the lavish **Alice Springs Cup Racing Carnival,** and on the same day the **Bangtail Muster** brings a parade and other entertainment to Alice's streets. The 7.8km walking race **King of the Mountain** sends tourists and locals to the top of Mt. Gillen (off Larapinta, west of town), also in May. On the Queen's Birthday Weekend in early June, the plucky cars of the **Finke Desert Race** traverse 240km of roadless dusty desert from Alice to the town of Finke in the south. The traditional **Alice Springs Show** and not-so-traditional **Lions Club Camel Cup** race occur in June and July. The **Alice Springs Rodeo** and the **Alice Marathon** are both held in August.

■ The MacDonnell Ranges

Alongside Ayers Rock, the Olgas, and Kings Canyon, the 460km-long MacDonnell Ranges round out the Red Centre's cast of impressive geological formations. The MacDonnells, to the east and west of Alice Springs, were formed by fault shifts that began some 600 million years ago, and once towered as high as the Himalayas. Erosion has broken the single chain of mountains into a series of ridges and valleys, 120km across at its widest point, whose multi-faceted photo-ops, recreational opportunities, historical intrigues, and biological dramas attract hardy visitors bored with one-rock tourist acts.

WEST MACDONNELLS

More popular than their eastern counterparts, the long-sculpted gorges and waterholes of the West MacDonnells shelter organic vestiges of the bygone rainforest era, scantily clad guests, and hard-core 4WD enthusiasts who know that this is where the good stuff is. Generally speaking, it grows quieter and dustier as you drive farther away from Alice, and a car is necessary to explore anything beyond the tourist-infested. Larapinta Drive heads out of Alice past the tame beginnings of the West Mac-Donnells, and Namatjira Drive veers off into deeper territory. A fulfilling loop can be made by continuing on the rest of Larapinta Drive, which passes by Finke Gorge National Park and connects with the western end of Namatjira Drive via Tylers Pass. If you're willing to brave rough, unsealed roads, hop on board the highway and choose your own adventure.

Larapinta Drive

Heading westward on Larapinta Dr from Alice Springs, the first attraction is a manmade one: **Alice Springs Desert Park** (tel. 8951 8788), a showcase of desert plants and wildlife. This recently opened quasi-zoo boasts the largest exhibit of nocturnal animals in Australia and several smaller habitat displays, but the highlight of the park is the beautiful film on the evolution of the outback landscape. The park is 6km out of Alice. (Open daily 7:30am-6pm. $12, students $6.) For a lift, call the shuttle (tel. 8952 4667; $4).

The **John Flynn Memorial Grave** rests 1km farther west on Larapinta Dr. The massive boulder resting on the grave was taken from the Devil's Marbles formation near Tennant Creek. **Mt. Gillen** serves as a backdrop for the grave. Otherwise, the grave itself is not so inspiring, but serves as the starting point for the popular 17km bike path through the bush to **Simpson's Gap.** By road, Simpson's Gap is 11km farther west on Larapinta Dr, and 8km up an access road. Erosion from millions of years of floods created this striking opening in the mountain ridges. The 2km walk from the parking lot to the gap itself might give you a glimpse of wallabies. One kilometer west of the Simpson's Gap turnoff, on the left side of Larapinta Dr, is a sight you may have seen before: the **twin ghost gums** that appear in Albert Namatjira's watercolor (hanging in Alice's Panorama Guth). Visitors and vandals have taken their toll, however, and the gums appear withered when compared to the famous painting.

Standley Chasm (tel. 8956 7440) is 21km farther on. The 80m-high fissure through the MacDonnells is owned by Aboriginals, who collect $4 at the end of the 9km access road. It took 100 million years to form, but half an hour is sufficient to traverse the rocky path, see the big crack, and return. When the sun shines directly into the crevasse at midday, the walls glow orange. (Entry permitted 7:30am-6pm.)

Namatjira Drive

Larapinta Dr forks 46km west of Alice Springs, and the right-hand path, Namatjira Dr, follows a more northerly route into the heart of West MacDonnell National Park (see below for the westward continuation of Larapinta Dr). **Ellery Creek Bighole** is 42km down Namatjira and another 2km down an access road. The 18m-deep pool in a creek through a mountain gap serves as a swimming hole when the weather's nice. A 200m path connects the parking lot to the pool. Uninspiring parking lot camping with basic facilities costs $2.50 per person. Next stop is **Serpentine Gorge,** which slithers through the mountains 11km later. An easy walk (30min. return) leads to a slim and secretive gorge which provides much beauty for little effort. A few kilometers on, **Serpentine Chalet** provides pleasant bush camping sites with no facilities. The **Ochre Pits,** 12km after that serpentine gorge, is just off the highway; a 10-minute stroll leads to walls of ochre where Aboriginals once mined paint supplies.

Another 17km brings you to sparkling **Ormiston Gorge.** With a 14m-deep permanent waterhole, popular (and crowded) basic camping facilities ($4 per person, $10 per family), and a small ranger's station, Ormiston is a veritable MacDonnells happy meal. The gorge was named by explorer Peter Warburton, who thought that the area looked a lot like his own Glen Ormiston back in Scotland. He's right, except for the gorge's dry vegetation, sand dunes, and steep orange cliffs. A 10-minute walk leads from the parking lot into the canyon-like gorge. Two beautiful 7km hikes are also available: the circuitous **Pound Walk** traverses the surrounding ridge and provides views from on high, and another circuit sneaks around the gorge through the hillside.

Across the highway a few kilometers down, the **Glen Helen Gorge** breaks grandly through the range as the **Finke River** winds its way south to the Simpson Desert. The gorge can be approached in 10 minutes from the fading **Glen Helen Lodge** (tel. 8956 7489), a one-time resort which now provides the basic gas, phones, snacks, and camping sites (sites $5 per adult, children free; powered $15 per site). The unsealed Namatjira Rd continues past Glen Helen 25km to **Redbank Gorge,** a narrow slit through mountains that shade a series of chilly pools from the warming rays of the sun. Walk 15 minutes up the creekbed and the amphitheatre of stone will tempt your toes to explore further, but carry a flotation device if you're planning to wade deeper into the gorge and float down the icy waters in style. Another way to see the West MacDonnells is to take the **Larapinta Trail,** an enormous, nearly complete hiking trail that starts at the Telegraph Station in Alice and will extend 220km west to **Mt. Razorback.** The trail connects the main attractions and is usually hiked in pieces, from one gorge to another. Before attempting these longer hikes, seek further info from the Park and Wildlife Commission (tel. 8951 8211) and notify a ranger before departing.

Larapinta Drive Revisited

For the hardy, Larapinta Dr continues west from its intersection with Namatjira Dr. The left turn 48km ahead leads an additional 18km to **Wallace Rockhole Community** (tel. 8956 7415), an Aboriginal settlement next to a natural water hole. Residents welcome tourists here, offering campgrounds (no permit required) and tours (Apr.-Sept. daily 9:30am and 1pm). Larapinta Dr continues in sealed sublimity 34km more to **Finke Gorge National Park.** This 46,000 hectare park contains the Finke River, reputedly the oldest river on the planet; some stretches date back 350 million years. The park's main attraction is **Palm Valley,** whose lush palm stands are among the least expected sights in central Australia. The last 16km along a rough creek bed to reach this wonderland valley is limited to 4WD vehicles only, and shelters the rare

Red Cabbage Palm, which once littered the lush land, but are now an outrageous anomaly amidst the desert. The 5km **Mpulungkinya Walk** traipses among the palms and returns along a raised plateau with views into the valley. A pleasant campground with toilets and barbecues is available ($5 per person), as are scenic picnic areas.

Near the turn-off to Finke Gorge is the **Hermannsburg Historical Precinct** (tel. 8956 7402). Birthplace of the Aboriginal artist Albert Namatjira, Hermannsburg confers insight into the early days of mission settlement. Namatjira's legacy lives on at a painting school. Unfortunately, the surrounding town of **Hermannsburg** is extremely unappealing. **Petrol** is available at **Larapinta Motors,** where you can also obtain the **Mereenie Tour Pass** ($2), which grants access to the unsealed **Mereenie Loop Rd.** This newly opened 200km road is accessible (with care) to all vehicles, and bisects Aboriginal land to provide the easiest route to **King's Canyon** (see p. 269).

EAST MACDONNELLS

Just beyond Heavitree Gap south of Alice, Palm Circuit branches off the Stuart Hwy and heads east. After a few kilometers, Palm Circuit becomes the **Ross Hwy** and plunges into the East MacDonnells. The East Macs are less thrilling geologically than their western counterparts, but have been populated longer and have some historical sights. The **Emily and Jessie Gaps,** 10km east of Alice, are popular picnic sites and Aboriginal sacred sites. An additional 35km drive to the east brings travelers to **Corroboree Rock Conservation Reserve,** where local Aboriginals perform ceremonies near a rock outcropping. **Trephina Gorge Nature Park,** another 23km east (plus 9km of access road), has a double gorge with quartzite cliffs, five walking tracks, and a popular swimming hole that's accessible via the Chain of Ponds Walk (1½hr.). Campsites with pit toilets but no water cost $6 per family or $2.50 per person.

The road continues east toward the **Ross River Homestead** (tel. 8956 9711), but the last 9km of road to this historic settlement is unpaved. Located a total of 88km east of Alice, Homestead is one of the most popular destinations in the East MacDonnells, offering hands-on outback activities such as camel-riding, bushwalking, and boomerang-throwing. **N'Dhala Gorge,** the site of an estimated 6000 **Aboriginal carvings,** is 11km past the Homestead on a 4WD track. A 1.5km (1hr. return) walking track leads into the gorge, and signs along the track explain what some of the petroglyphs mean. A left fork before the Homestead traverses 36km of unsealed road to the **Arltunga Historic Reserve,** the remains of central Australia's first official town. Some of the buildings of this mining outpost have been restored. Vehicles with 4WD can push on 39km to the remote **Ruby Gap Nature Park,** with rugged scenery and excellent bush camping.

The Path of Priscilla

If you want to trace the route of the *Priscilla, Queen of the Desert* drag queen caravan, you'll need a car, a feathered boa, and lots of sequins. First the drag queens went west from Sydney (p. 83), probably on Hwy. 32, to the town of Broken Hill (p. 221), where Bernadette triumphed over the pub shrew. Continuing west, they decided to hop on an unsealed back road instead of going to Port Augusta (although their left turn would not actually have put them on a northwest course toward Alice Springs). They broke down somewhere in the vast desert of South Australia, crashed the Aboriginal Corroboree, and eventually received a lift to an outback town somewhere east of Coober Pedy (p. 442). With Bob on board, Priscilla pushed on to Coober Pedy, where Felicia narrowly escaped a group of rough miners. Finally they covered the last stretch north along the Stuart Hwy. to Alice Springs (p. 259). Mitzie's reunion with his wife and their glorious drag show gig was filmed on location in Lasseters Casino, in Alice Springs (p. 265). The final scene occurs atop Kings Canyon in the Northern Territory (p. 269). For more film references, see **You, the Australian Cinema Stalker** (p. 298).

■ The Simpson Desert

South of Alice, the Stuart Hwy passes Heavitree Gap and Palm Circuit. Near the road to the airport, the **Old South Road** veers left towards the **Simpson Desert.** The track is rough, and sometimes closed after rains. Charles Sturt first explored this part of the Simpson in 1845, so bent on conquering the outback that he wouldn't rest until he returned home on his deathbed. The first worthwhile spot along this road, 39km south of Alice, is the **Ewaninga Rock Carvings,** which were etched into sandstone in ancient times. The weathered markings denote a spiritual site for modern Aboriginals, but a pleasant 30-minute stroll allows respectful visitors to view the carvings.

The Aboriginal community of **Maryvale Station,** 62km farther along the Old South Rd, marks the turn-off to **Chambers' Pillar Historical Reserve.** This sandstone formation served early travelers as a conspicuous landmark, and generations of intrepid travelers have carved initials into the rock (a practice now subject to high fines). The last 47km stretch ending at Chambers Pillar is a rough track suitable for high-clearance 4WD vehicles only. The journey is way more hard-core than the pillar itself, but the sunsets are nice. Camping at the base of the pillar costs $2.50 per person.

Rainbow Valley, another photogenic Simpson desert spot, is a jagged, U-shaped ridge standing in the desert like a Hollywood backdrop. The valley lies 21km east of the Stuart Hwy on a sandy 4WD track that begins 81km south of Alice (camping $2.50 per person). Another 51km down the Stuart, the unsealed **Ernest Giles Road** veers west towards King's Canyon; 8km past the turn-off and 5km north on an access road lie the **Henbury Meteorite Craters.** This circular ridge of mountains is the remnant of a prehistoric meteorite impact. Camping and a self-guided walk are available.

Heading further south, all that lies along the Stuart Hwy until Coober Pedy, SA are homogeneous and over-priced roadhouses, rising from endless miles of shrub.

■ Kings Canyon

Watarrka National Park contains the wayward tourist mecca of Kings Canyon, cutting deep grooves in a section of the **George Gill Mountains.** The canyon forms sheer concave walls beneath a precariously suspended rim, sheltering permanent waterholes that sustain an unusual swath of lush, tropical green. A long natural history of erosion is visible across the canyon, especially in the eccentric domes atop both sides of the precipice. The weathered surfaces of these humps appear to be natural, giant-sized stairs to the fantastic views atop. The scatter of layered domes on the flat canyon roof creates an intimidating maze that has been dubbed **Lost City.** Thankfully, the park has two well-marked paths. An easy 1km walk follows **Kings Creek** into the bottom of the canyon and then out. The more challenging 6km **Kings Canyon Walk** scales the rocky semi-steep slope, winds around the top of the canyon, and traces through much of the Lost City and along the exhilarating rail-less edge. The longer walk also descends into the **Garden of Eden,** a waterhole shaded by palm trees and the narrow canyon walls.

Water and tough hiking **footwear** are essential at Kings Canyon. There's an outhouse and an information display at the parking lot, but no other facilities at the trailhead. The long canyon walk has three emergency call boxes. The King's Canyon **Sunset Viewing** picnic area is located 1km before the main parking lot, and water, toilets, and barbecues are available. The **ranger station** is 22km east of the canyon.

There are three different ways to get to Kings Canyon from Alice Springs. The fully paved route runs south from Alice Springs to the settlement of **Erldunda,** 202km down the Stuart Hwy at its junction with the Lasseter Hwy. Travelers changing buses here may end up spending the night. To book a room or campsite at the **roadhouse,** call 8956 0984. From the junction, take the Lasseter Hwy west 112km and turn right on Luritja Rd, which goes north 168km to the Kings Canyon park entrance. Vehicles with 4WD can take a shortcut along Ernest Giles Rd, a 98km stretch of unpaved road that begins 132km south of Alice. Ernest Giles meets Luritja Rd 100km south of the park entrance. Check local road conditions before attempting this road. It's also possible to reach Kings Canyon from Alice Springs via Hermannsburg in the West Mac-Donnells by taking Larapinta Dr to the scenic **Mereenie Loop Road** which passes through Aboriginal land. The road is unsealed but accessible to all vehicles (with care). A $2 pass is required to traverse the 199km road, and can be obtained in Hermannsburg at Larapinta Motors or at the community center.

The **Kings Canyon Resort** (tel. 8956 7442; fax 8956 7410), several kilometers up the road from the canyon, is the beginning and the end of civilization in Watarrka. The compact, tourist-bus-ridden resort's major drawback is the expense. (4-bed dorms with A/C, heat, TV, and fridge $35 per person, $131 for 4. Utensils deposit $20. Shared bath and kitchen.) Dorm beds are held for Greyhound passengers; otherwise book ahead. Comfortable grassy **campsites** with flush toilets, showers, and pool are $10 per person (powered $25). Reception for all of these is open 6:30am to 9:30pm, and check-out is 10am. The resort has a **grocery store** and **fuel station** (open 7am-7pm), and a restaurant, the **Desert Oaks Cafe** (burgers $5, buffet dinner $12.50; open 5:30am-9pm). The **medical center** (tel. 8956 7807, after hours 8956 7997) can summon a Flying Doctor in an hour if necessary. **Camping** is also available at King's Creek Station, located just outside the eastern entrance to the park. Otherwise, no camping is permitted in Watarrka National Park.

■ Uluru-Kata Tjuta National Park

Dusk approachs at the Sunset Viewing Area. Tourists from all corners of the earth have assembled quietly, staring east as the sun descends at their backs. Before them unfolds a spectacle so awesome and humbling that it could occur only once—and yet it has repeated itself each day for 600 million years. Captivated spectators look on in hushed awe as the rock before them turns a brilliant, glowing red. A ripple of sighs and a burst of camera flashes moves through the throng. Here, at the junction of desert and sky, a monument to Australia's spiritual, Aboriginal past and pioneering present, is Ayers Rock.

At the core of Australia in every sense, **Ayers Rock** (known as Uluru in the language of the Anangu) is the largest single rock in the world. Oxidation of iron in the sandstone gives the rock its uniquely orange color, which turns a fiery red at sunrise and sunset. Just as old and taller still, **the Olgas** are a cluster of similar-hued domes that may have weathered from one great "superdome," many times larger than Uluru.

Together, these formations in the red dust are the defining landmarks of Uluru-Kata Tjuta National Park, a 132,500 hectare protected area 461km southwest of Alice Springs, at the very heart of the continent. Since 1985, the park has been co-managed by the National Parks Service and its traditional Anangu residents—who have occupied the desert dunes around Uluru for 22,000 years. They believe the rock is a landmark on the dreaming trails of their mythical ancestors. Europeans have only known of it since 1872, when the explorer Ernest Giles came upon it. William Gosse reached the summit in 1873 and dubbed it Ayers Rock, after the governor of South Australia. He named Mt. Olga after the Queen of Spain.

GETTING THERE AND PRACTICAL INFORMATION

To get to Uluru-Kata Tjuta by road, travel south on the Stuart Hwy 202km from Alice Springs, or north 483km from Coober Pedy, to Erldunda (see p. 269), then 254km west on the Lasseter Hwy. Long before reaching Uluru, you'll see **Mt. Connor,** a big mesa in the distance. This tricky imitation, often mistaken for Ayers Rock, has its own viewing area. The **Uluru-Kata Tjuta National Park entrance station** lies 5km past the Yulara resort village, where all visitors must purchase a five-day pass ($15). Uluru (Ayers Rock) is 14km ahead, with a turnoff 4km up that leads 42km west to Kata Tjuta (the Olgas). These roads are all paved.

The **Uluru-Kata Tjuta Cultural Centre** (tel. 8956 3138; fax 8956 3139), 1km from Uluru, is an effort by the Anangu to enlighten tourists about the natural and cultural history surrounding the rock, and includes interactive displays which explain the

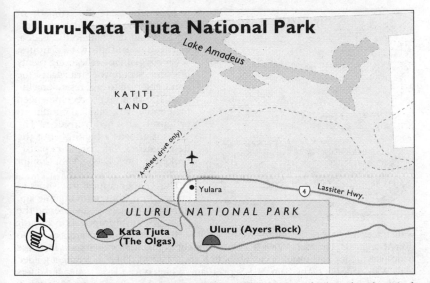

Uluru-Kata Tjuta National Park

Lake Amadeus

KATITI
LAND

4-wheel drive only)

Yulara

Lassiter Hwy.

4

ULURU NATIONAL PARK

N

Kata Tjuta
(The Olgas)

Uluru (Ayers Rock)

mythical origins of the rock and culture. The Cultural Center, built in the Aboriginal mode, is made of natural materials and contains an info booth and the Maruku Arts and Crafts shop (tel. 8956 2558) which sells high-quality Aboriginal crafts. (Open Nov.-March daily 7am-6pm; April-Oct. 7am-5:30pm. Tours M-W afternoons.) For more information, call the **information officer** at the Cultural Centre or contact the **Australian Nature Conservatory Agency** (P.O. Box 119, Yulara, NT 0872). As in the rest of the Red Centre, the **bush flies** can be unbearable in the late summer and fall. Bring mesh netting to cover your face. To avoid tour crowds, consider spending the morning at Kata Tjuta (the Olgas) and the afternoon and evening at Uluru.

The park is open daily (Dec.-Feb. 5am-9pm; Mar. 5:30am-8:30pm; Apr. 6am-8pm; May 6am-7:30pm; June-July 6:30am-7:30pm; Aug. 6am-7:30pm; Sept. 5:30am-7:30pm; Oct. 5am-8pm; Nov. 5am-8:30pm). **No camping** is permitted within the park.

ULURU (AYERS ROCK)

If the Sydney Opera House is the icon of cosmopolitan Australia, Uluru is the essence of its untamed outback. The hype is big, but Ayers Rock is bigger: 348m in height, 3.1km in length, 1.9km in width, and 9.4km around. Two-thirds of the sandstone block is actually buried, and the mass may reach an additional 3km down and 10km across. Eons of geological activity have tilted and eroded once-horizontal sedimentary layers into vertical grooves on the surface of the rock. Up close, these "grooves" become meters-long gorges, and the seemingly smooth rock walls dissolve into a rough, scaly exterior.

The strategically situated **Sunset Viewing Area,** 5km from the rock, is the place to hear the nightly oohs and aahs of awestruck travelers, punctuated by the clicking shutters of hundreds of cameras. Closer to the rock is the **Uluru-Kata Tjuat Cultural Center** and **information desk**, next door to the **Park Headquarters.** The road continues on a **paved loop** around the rock. The **main car park** and toilets are just to the left along the loop. A **Sunrise Viewing Area** lies on the opposite side of the rock, halfway around the loop.

The Anangu attach spiritual importance to the path up Ayers Rock and ask that tourists please show respect and not make the climb. However, hundreds of tourists nonetheless undertake it each day. A steady stream of would-be Sir Hillarys traversing the 1.6km return hike resembles a column of ants. A chain makes the first, and steepest part of the hike more accessible, but this is no easy jaunt; plaques memorialize

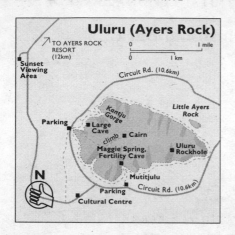

Uluru (Ayers Rock)

TO AYERS ROCK RESORT (12km)

Sunset Viewing Area

Circuit Rd. (10.6km)

Kantju Gorge

Little Ayers Rock

Parking

Large Cave

climb

Cairn

Maggie Spring, Fertility Cave

Uluru Rockhole

N

Mutitjulu

Parking

Circuit Rd. (10.6km)

Cultural Centre

0 — 1 mile
0 — 1 km

people who have died (mostly of heart attacks) while climbing Ayers Rock. Avoid climbing in the middle of the day and allow two hours. Wear **rugged footwear**, bring plenty of **water**, secure your hat against the wind, and plan to take rests along the way. The climb is not recommended for people with medical conditions or loosely attached hairpieces. The summit affords a panorama of the Red Centre's flat, barren expanse, broken by the Olgas and Mt. Connor in the distance.

The Anangu appeal to visitors to enjoy Uluru from more humble and humbling vantage-points around the base. An ambitious 9.4km **circuit walk** traces the base of the impressive rock (allow 4hr.). Signs indicate areas closed to non-Aboriginals. The **Mala Walk** is a 1km segment of this walk which leads from the main parking lot past magnificent walls to **Kantju Gorge.** There is a ranger-guided Mala Walk daily (Oct.-Apr. 8am, May-Sept. 10am) which is free, lasts 1½hr., and offers a look at Uluru from an Aboriginal perspective. Meet the ranger at the **Mala Walk** sign at the base of Uluru, near the main parking lot. A smaller parking lot to the right from the loop entrance serves the 1km **Mutitjulu Walk,** which leads to the waterhole home of the serpent **Kuniya.** Both the Mala and the Mutitjulu walks are wheelchair accessible. The educational **Liru Track** runs from the visitors center to the main car park via 2km of bush.

KATA TJUTA (THE OLGAS)

Perhaps more beautiful, if less awe-inspiring, are the 36 undulating domes scattered over an area several times the size of Uluru. Kata Tjuta ("many heads") is the second conspicuous rock formation in the Red Centre, and it seems almost as though Ayers might just be a ploy to keep tourists away from this less-touted treasure. The giant rocks nestle like eggs on the horizon and spaces between their steep walls allow entrance into their cells. The road to Kata Tjuta leaves the main road 4km after the park entrance station, passes south of the formation, and curves around to the western side. The **Dune Viewing Area,** 25km down the road, is a wheelchair accessible walk (300m) allowing relaxing views of Kata Tjuta. The **sunset viewing area** (toilets available) is just short of the starting points for two walks. The **Olga Gorge walk** is an easy 2.6km path between a pair of the most daunting domes. The dome on the right upon entering is the 546m Mt. Olga, the highest peak in the range. It takes an hour to walk to the end of the path, scan the western horizon, and return to the car park. The majestic **Valley of the Winds walk** traces an eerie 7km circuit through the outer wall of domes, into the inner sanctuary, and along the winding exit path. There are plenty of shady spots and an emergency water source at the halfway point. Bring lots of water and allow four hours. The inner circuit of the walk is closed at 11am on days hotter than 36°C, so morning jaunts are advised.

■ Yulara (Ayers Rock Resort)

Between the Rock and a dry place stands a well-sculpted community. Yulara is a municipal name that shelters employees of Ayers Rock Resort from the fact that they live on a tourist farm resembling a child's gameboard. The road that loops around Yulara curves in an effort to avoid looking pre-planned, and the town's facilities are carefully landscaped in an effort to blend into the outback. Yulara's monopoly on the

Kata Tjuta (The Olgas)

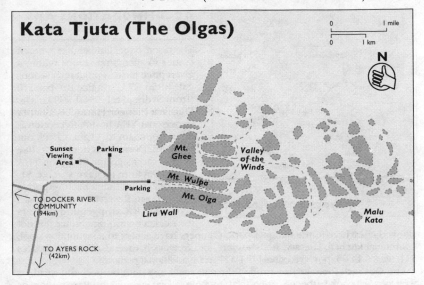

0   1 mile
0   1 km

N

Sunset
Viewing
Area ■
Parking
Mt. Ghee
Valley of the Winds

TO DOCKER RIVER COMMUNITY (194km)
Parking
Mt. Wulpa
Mt. Olga
Liru Wall
Malu Kata

TO AYERS ROCK (42km)

tourist market, however, is not as disguised; be prepared to pay hefty mark-ups on goods transported into the village, and more than a bit extra for prime real estate just 19km down the street from the world's largest monolith. That said, the resort does maintain some semblance of the outback mentality, and it offers all the service you'd expect from a high-class resort without the pompousness.

PRACTICAL INFORMATION

The so-called **Visitors Centre** (tel. 8957 7377), with a grand set of stairs rising from the road near the entrance to the village, is actually little more than a gift shop and outdated museum (open daily 8:30am-5pm). The preferred office for tourist services is the **Tourist Information Centre** (tel. 8956 2240), in the main town square shopping area, farther down on the left. This office has a keen general information counter, a list of daily conditions (temperature, sun, etc.) and desks for **Territory Rent-a-Car** (tel. 8956 2030), **Hertz** (tel. 8956 2244), **Avis** (tel. 8956 2266), and several tour agencies. (Center open daily 8:30am-8:30pm; service desks maintain shorter, variable hours.) **Connellan Airport,** to the north of town, serves **Qantas** (to Alice $170, continuing to Darwin $483, to Cairns $470, to Sydney $508; 30% discount for international backpackers), **Ansett** (to Alice $169, continuing to Darwin $473, to Cairns $464, to Sydney $502), and **Airnorth,** and has offices for the car rental agencies. A free **airport shuttle** run by AAT Kings meets all incoming flights, and also picks up from all accommodations 90 minutes before departures. **Greyhound Pioneer** departs for Alice Springs daily at 1:45pm (5½hr., $76).

Ayers Rock Resort runs a free **village shuttle** around the Resort loop (every 15min., daily 10:30am-2:30pm and 6:30pm-12:30am). This takes you past the **police** (tel. 8956 2166; **emergency** tel. 000), a 24hr. **medical center** (tel. 8956 2286; clinic open M-F 9am-noon and 2-5pm, Sa-Su 10-11am), as well as all accommodations and the **shopping center.** Many facilities are located in the town square, including an **ANZ bank** (open M-Th 9:30am-4pm, F 9:30am-5pm; 24hr. ATM). Next door is the **post office** (tel. 8956 2288; postal code 0872; open M-F 9am-6:30pm, Sa-Su 10am-2pm) and a pricey **supermarket** (open daily 8:30am-9pm) beyond. The **Mobil** station along the resort loop near the campground rents **bicycles.**

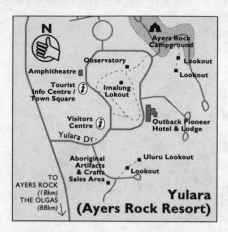

Yulara
(Ayers Rock Resort)

ACCOMMODATIONS AND FOOD

The resort offers little choice when it comes to accommodations within a given price range. For all reservations call 8956 2737 or fax 8956 2270 (from Sydney, tel. 9360 9099). The **Outback Pioneer Hotel** has a rather impersonal YHA hostel. Reception is open from 4am to 11pm. Check out by 10am. Dorm beds in barracks-like 20-bed rooms go for $22 (non-YHA $24). (Daytime luggage storage $1. Locker key and linen each require a $10 deposit. Reservations essential.) **Ayers Rock Campground** corners the market on camping, since it is not allowed elsewhere in the national park. Campers have access to a swimming pool, communal kitchen, laundry, hot showers, and free gas barbecue. (Grassy tent sites $11, ages 6-14 $5; powered sites for 1 $17, each additional person $11.)

The **Outback Pioneer** has a run-of-the-mill snack bar with burgers and salad, as well as a self-cook barbecue, open to the whole village every night. Raw meat runs from $10 for a beef burger to $17.50 for emu sausage, and includes salad, bread, corn, and baked potato. Veggie skewers available as well. This dinner is the best deal available in Yulara, apart from fixing your own meals. There's also a **Takeaway Food** counter in the shopping center which has an excellent sandwich bar (all sandwiches $6; open 9am-8pm). The restaurants listed on the back of the Resort map have Uluru-sized prices, though the **Gecko Cafe** in shopping center is mighty tasty. Creatively decorated wood-oven pizzas cost $14-18. Open 10am til late. There is also an **ice creamery, bakery,** and **supermarket** in the shopping center.

SIGHTS AND ENTERTAINMENT

Entertainment within the resort is contrived and aimed at high-budget tourists. The **Inmapiti Amphitheatre** next to the town square sets the stage every night for **Nukanaya Dreaming,** a powered-up musical and dance display of Aboriginal culture. *(Sept.-April 9pm; May-Aug. 8pm; admission $15, under 12 $7.)* The auditorium behind the Visitors Centre shows recent films *(F-Su. Admission $8, children $4.)* Call the visitors center (tel. 8957 7377) for showtimes.

The main sight, of course, is the red monolith that protrudes from the desert south of the resort. A handful of walks around town lead to lookout points. To get to the rock, you'll need a vehicle. **Sunworth Shuttles** (tel. 8956 2152) offers the most flexible transportation to the Rock (starting at $20 return) and the Olgas (starting at $35 return). Among the private tour companies, **Anangu Tours** is the only one owned by Aboriginals. Book through the Cultural Centre (tel. 8956 2123; fax 8956 3136). *(½ day tours $65-78, children $49-63. 2 tours $120, children $95. Self-drive tours $39, children $29.)* The **Greyhound Pioneer tour** grants an excellent sunset viewing and a good chance to climb the Rock, but only skims the Olgas and lacks play time near the Rock or in Yulara. Often combined with Kings Canyon, it's a compact, rushed way to see the best parts of the Red Centre. Be warned that Greyhound Tours are often full of Aussie Pass travelers, and seats may not be available on short notice.

Queensland

If the variety of the continent's attractions could be condensed into one state, the result would look something like Queensland, Australia's all-you-can-eat traveler's smorgasbord. Part rocky, part schlocky, part green, part marine, Queensland is the holiday of choice of Aussies themselves. It's the Pacific Coast that sucks most visitors in like an undertow: the endless surf beaches in the south, the Barrier Reef in the north, and the islands all along propel wave, dive, and sun enthusiasts toward the sea. For many, though, the coast is just surface skin, and the real pudding lies within—in the rainforest-drenched far north and hinterland regions and in the jewel-bedecked outback, where history, like tourism, proceeds at koala-pace. At the base of this fantasyland sits the capital city of Brisbane, big, bustling, and yet temperate in every sense of the word, an urban haven that can actually provide a relaxing break from the constant party that envelops backpackers on the well-trod path up the coast.

Queensland is beloved by travelers because, far from representing the average of Australia's natural and cultural climes, it displays the full spectrum, from the imposing reds of outback earth to the bright-hued crags of the Great Barrier Reef. Best of all, it juxtaposes these in reasonably accessible distances from one another. Make no mistake—it's a long, long trek from Brisbane up to Cairns and the northern wilderness beyond, and an equally long and far more desolate one into the central desert. Still, along the way you'll encounter charming country towns, pockets of thriving Aboriginal cultural life, and plenty of history, interspersed, of course, with miles and miles of beach. Once you make it up to the northern coast, you'll find plenty of places with urban amenities, gorgeous sea, and untrammeled wilderness within easy reach. Here, appreciating Oz at the extremes can be as simple as driving toward Cape Tribulation and watching the rainforest practically tumble into the pounding ocean.

👌 QUEENSLAND HIGHLIGHTS

- Swimming with the fishes (literally) on the vibrant **Great Barrier Reef** (anywhere; see below) or at the **Yolanga Wreck** in Townsville (see p. 345).
- Camping and 4WDing in the sandy wonderland of **Fraser Island** (see p. 318).
- Sailing by starlight in the **Whitsunday Islands** (see p. 336).
- Cultural immersion at the **Tjapukai Theatre,** near Cairns (see p. 366).
- Canoeing on the **Noosa River,** with reflections so perfect you can't see where the water begins, then relaxing at **Gagaju's** eco-campground (see p. 316).
- Taking in the galleries at the **Queensland Cultural Centre** in Brisbane, then upping the tempo for a raging night in the clubs of **Fortitude Valley** (see p. 290).
- Off-road driving in the **Cape Tribulation** rainforest (see p. 377).
- Lorikeet feedings and 'roos at play at the **Currumbin Sanctuary** (see p. 299)
- Catching the perfect wave at **Surfer's Paradise** (see p. 303).
- Looking for koalas in the wild in the lush forest of **Magnetic Island** (see p. 345).
- Relaxing with a cocktail on pristine **Mission Beach** (see p. 351).
- Making didgeridoos at the **Namoi Hills Cattle Station** in Dingo (see p. 385).

QUEENSLAND

PRACTICAL INFORMATION

The Queensland coast as far north as Cairns, plus some locations further north and in the interior, is comprehensively serviced by public transportation; the major bus lines are **Greyhound** (tel. 13 20 30) and **McCafferty's** (tel. 13 14 99), and the train line is **Queensland Rail** (tel. 13 22 32). Don't underestimate the distances involved; even within the state, many people choose to fly instead if they just want to get quickly from Brisbane to Cairns. If you've got the time for a leisurely trip, though, taking a bus up the coast allows you to stop at the innumerable great spots along the way. You'll have plenty of company; sometimes it seems like a backpacker parade. If you have a few friends to chip in for costs or you're traveling with a family, **renting a car** is, as

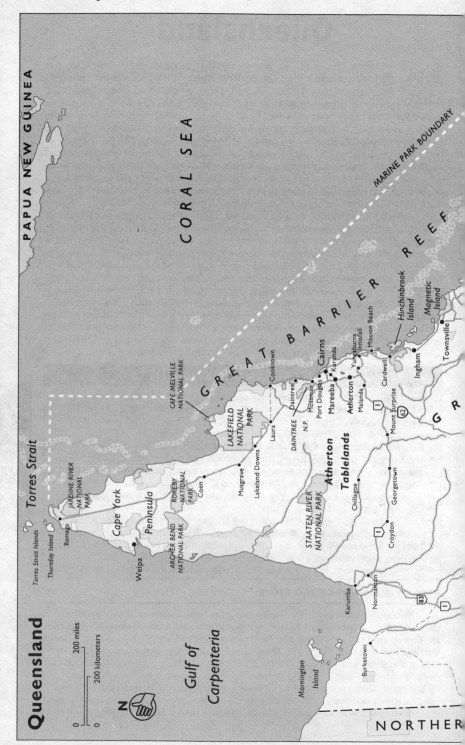

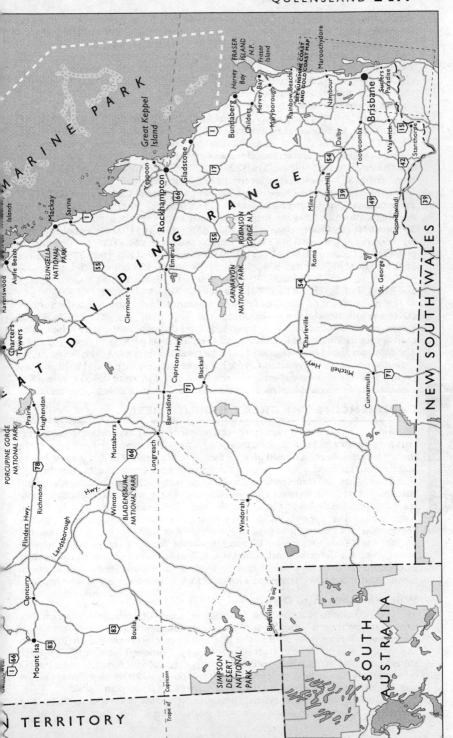

always, the option that provides the most convenience and freedom to wander off the beaten path. All the major corporations are here, plus dozens of cheaper local ones listed throughout the chapter. To tackle the area from Cooktown north through Cape York as well as some of the desert roads, you'll need **4WD.** This is pricey; it's also very tough to find an automatic transmission 4WD (try **Allcar Rentals** in Pt. Douglas, tel. 4099 4123). Roads in the tropics are especially harrowing, and often impassible, during and immediately following the **wet season** (Nov.-Apr.). It's best to call ahead for **road conditions** (24hr. tel. 3361 2406).

The central office of the **Royal Automobile Club of Queensland (RACQ)** is at 300 St. Paul's Tce, Fortitude Valley, Brisbane (tel. 3361 2444; statewide roadside service tel. 13 11 11). Affiliated with clubs worldwide, RACQ provides excellent maps, car buying or selling info, and technical services for cars and motorcycles. (Branch office 261 Queen St.; tel. 3361 2565; fax 3220 0029; both open M-F 8:30am-5:30pm. 1-yr. membership $67, overseas transfer free). See AAA in **Essentials,** p. 35, for more info.

The main office of the **Queensland Tourism and Travel Corporation (QTTC)** is in Brisbane at Level 36, Riverside Center, 123 Eagle St (tel. 3406 5400; fax 3406 5564; email qttcinfo@qttc.com.au; http://www.qttc.com.au). Their affiliate, **Tourism Tropical North Queensland** (tel. 4051 3588; fax 4051 0127, email information@tnq.org.au), is based in Cairns at Grafton and Hartley St. QTTC has branches in Sydney, 156 Castlereagh St (tel. (02) 9209 8200; fax 9209 8686), and 327-329 George St (tel. (02) 9246 7000; fax 9246 7046); Melbourne, 257 Collins St (tel. (03) 9206 4500; fax 9206 4577); Adelaide, 10 Grenfell St (tel. (08) 8401 3100; fax 8211 8841); and Perth, Shop 6, Central Park, 7 Hay St (tel. 08) 9464 3000; fax 9322 1800).

The main office of the **Queensland National Parks and Wildlife Service (QNP&WS)** is in Brisbane at 160 Ann St (tel. 3227 8187; fax 3277 8187). Branch offices are located in Cairns (tel. 4052 3096) and throughout the state. There is no entry fee for national parks in Queensland; camping costs $3.50 per person per night. The *National Parks in Queensland* pamphlet is available at any QNP&WS office.

Brother Sister and *Queensland Pride* are popular statewide gay and lesbian newspapers available at most gay-oriented venues. A free magazine called *Queensland Caravan Parks* is available at most tourist offices and is invaluable for caravanners.

EXPERIENCING THE GREAT BARRIER REEF

Whether you're a seasoned scuba diver or a neophyte who once tried on a pair of flippers for kicks in a swimming pool, there's a pretty good chance that you've got "see the Great Barrier Reef" scrawled on your mental or physical list of things to do before you die. And for good reason—the 2000km reef system, encompassing hundreds of islands and cays and thousands of smaller coral reefs, offers a marine wonderland that's easily accessible from the Queensland coast. When, where, and how to explore it are complicated decisions but important ones, since many people who don't plan sufficiently end up paying a lot for bad weather and visibility conditions or a mediocre dive site. It's important to familiarize yourself first with the types of reef and the life forms you'll see (see **Marine Life and the Great Barrier Reef,** p. 68, for an overview). *Let's Go* describes individual diving and snorkeling sites and operators throughout the book, but before making a choice, take some time to get a general sense of the options. With care and a touch of luck, your experience will be magical.

Where and When to Dive

The Great Barrier Reef is vast, and furthermore, many of Australia's very best dive sites aren't even on it—they're at more distant, smaller reefs in the **Coral Sea.** If you're a very serious diver with lots of time and money, you may want to invest in a trip for a week or two out to such sites as **Osprey, Flinders, Lihou,** or **Marion Reef,** superbly pristine spots which usually boast crystal-clear visibility. For most budget travelers, however, reaching these sites isn't an option, and it fortunately isn't necessary. There is excellent diving on the Great Barrier Reef if you plan it well.

One crucial consideration: when comparing the quality of dive sites, it's not just about what's there—it's about how well you can see it, too. Bad weather or silt deposits can turn an underwater wonderland into a turbid, murky mess. For the best **visibility,** avoid diving for a day or two after a storm and a month after a cyclone. Avoid the **wet season** altogether; the worst months are January through March, and the best are July through November. April through June bring trade winds that rock boats, but otherwise are fine for diving. Location-wise, visibility unfortunately tends to increase with distance from shore; still, you can have a very good experience close to shore even if you can only see 15m rather than 60.

Cairns is the country's most popular diving destination because of its combination of superb weather, ample supply of dive-boats, urban amenities, and excellent sites close to shore. Its **Bait Reef** is a fringe reef with nice swim-throughs. **Green Island** is a popular daytrip, but it's not as spectacular as nearby **Michaelmas Cay,** which houses tens of thousands of seabirds above water and outstanding coral color below. Further north, **Port Douglas** and **Cape Tribulation** offer similarly rich reef, but with fewer tourists to disturb the beauty. Off the shore near Cooktown, **Lizard Island** and the nearby **Cod Hole** are excellent, but can be prohibitively expensive.

Below Cairns, the ecosystem slowly changes from tropical to subtropical around the southern end of the reef. **Beaver Cay** is **Mission Beach's** most popular site, boasting numerous turtles and manta rays. Shore dives are cheap from **Magnetic Island,** but by far the best site in the Townsville region is found on the wreck of the **S.S.Yongala,** which sank 33m one year before the Titanic disaster. Today, the ship is covered in coral polyps and other sealife and is the world's premier wreck site, but its challenging currents are suitable for experienced divers only. The **Whitsunday** area has plenty of snorkeling and some island diving; most trips depart from **Airlie Beach** or are linked to several-day sailing cruises. Other locations south of the reef, like **Bundaberg,** offer extremely cheap diving, but the quality isn't as good. Still, these less-impressive destinations can be great places to find **cheap certification courses; Hervey Bay** has possibly the cheapest PADI course in the state ($149; see p. 321). **PADI** is by far the most univerally recognized form of certification.

Safety

Diving the Great Barrier Reef is exciting, but be wary of the potentially life-threatening dangers. In addition to unfriendly life forms, the major risk is **decompression sickness.** Commonly known as **"the bends,"** it results from a buildup of nitrogen in the bloodstream, generally from coming up too fast. Dive charts and tables clarify surface intervals and bottom times and should be used faithfully. Most importantly, **never dive beyond your ability.** There are plenty of fine sites you can see through **introductory** or **"resort" dives,** with trained guides and without certification. If you're certified, don't assume you're an expert—be honest with dive operators about your experience. In Queensland, you'll need a **"C-card"** or **logbook** to verify past dives.

If you're doing anything you've never done before—diving at **night** or on a **shipwreck,** for example—tell the divemaster. **Double checking airflow** and all **equipment** and pairing yourself with a **diving buddy** are essential preparations. **Medical exams** are often demanded for certified dives; you may need to update yours, which costs about $40. Finally, **don't ever go alone!** Group trips are almost always a blast, but even if you charter your own boat, make sure you're with people who know what they're doing.

If an Aussie informs you that the unidentified creature you're holding is a **nasty**—drop it. Better yet, **don't touch unfamiliar objects.** Many benign-looking creatures are poisonous, some even deadly. The most infamous nasty is the **box jellyfish,** a near-transparent creature which tends to live near the coast, particularly near river mouths or estuaries, rather than on the outer reef. Its up-to-3m tentacles contain a toxin that can kill you within three minutes; carrying a vinegar-based antivenom is wise. The wisest choice, however, is to avoid coastal diving altogether during box jellyfish season (Oct.-Apr.) and to obey all posted warnings. The **cone shell** has brightly patterned shells that look as though they would make excellent souvenirs, but the stingers inside are packed with enough venom to kill an adult human. The **stone fish** lies motionless and camouflaged against the coral, waiting for prey. If you're unlucky enough to step on its poison-filled spines, seek medical attention pronto. **Sting rays, lion fish,** and **sea snakes** are all poisonous as well, but aren't likely to attack except in retaliation. Some nasties are irritating but not deadly. If you pick up the inert **sea urchin,** you may get small pieces of its spines embedded in your skin, causing swelling and pain. A prick from the **crown of thorns,** a type of sea star, will send a low-grade poison into your bloodstream; however, its effects on the reef itself are far worse, as it feeds on coral. A recent population explosion has led to the legalization of removal of sea stars by dive boats.

Protecting the Reef

Due to their staggering biodiversity and crucial role in the marine nutrient cycle, coral reefs may be the planet's most important ecosystem. Unfortunately, they're fragile, and many of the earth's reefs have been destroyed in recent decades by reckless practices such as cyanide and dynamite fishing. While the law protects the coral of the Great Barrier Reef Marine Park from such a fate, contact by divers and snorkelers presents a subtler but still deadly threat. Follow **three simple rules** for the reef's safety and yours: first, don't touch it if you don't recognize it; second, put everything back where you found it; third, take care that all equipment is a proper distance from the reef—don't inadvertently scrape off 200 years of coral growth with your fins.

Alternatives to Diving

Diving is the ideal way to get an up-close view of the reef, but it's expensive, requires bulky, complicated equipment, and often requires time-consuming, costly training. By contrast, if you can swim, you can **snorkel.** Renting a mask and fins can be as cheap as $10 per day, somewhat more for a wetsuit. Gear is sometimes free with sailing trips or even hostel stays. Good snorkeling is often available just off the shore of islands or beaches, so you can just grab your gear and swim there unguided. Since you can't just swim down to all the good stuff, with snorkeling visibility and proximity to the surface are especially important. Other than that, the types of life you'll see—and the nasties to avoid—are similar to those encountered when diving.

Reef walking is another simple alternative that you can enjoy at low tide in areas with coral very close to the surface. Be careful not to break off pieces of the reef, though. Wear sturdy shoes, and watch out for changing tides and nasties. If you don't want to get wet at all, an even tamer choice is to view the reef through one of the ubiquitous **glass-bottom boats** that run cruises from islands or beach towns.

BRISBANE

If it weren't for Brisbane's tall office buildings and sleek commuter ferries, you might expect to see cows grazing on the city's carefully manicured lawns. Although Brisbane (pop. 1-1.5 million, according to varied estimates) is the capital of Queensland and Australia's third largest city, its recent growth has not obliterated its deliciously relaxed country-town feel, and the city seems like a ruddy-cheeked farmboy who's suddenly outgrown his britches. Originally a penal colony for recidivists, Brisbane today is neither glamorous nor industrial, but it's practical, clean, and full of energy.

🖤 BRISBANE HIGHLIGHTS

- Relaxing anywhere in the tranquil **South Bank Parklands** (see p. 291).
- An eating experience straight from a daydream at **Garuva** (see p. 289).
- Thumping techno and a funky crowd at the **Beat** in Fortitude Valley (see p. 293).
- Picnicking in the gardens at **Mt. Coot-tha Park,** then climbing to the summit for a great view of the city (see p. 291).
- Daytrip to **North Stradbroke Island** for first-rate diving and sunbathing along miles of snow-white beach (see p. 295).
- Art galleries aplenty at the **Queensland Cultural Centre** (see p. 290).

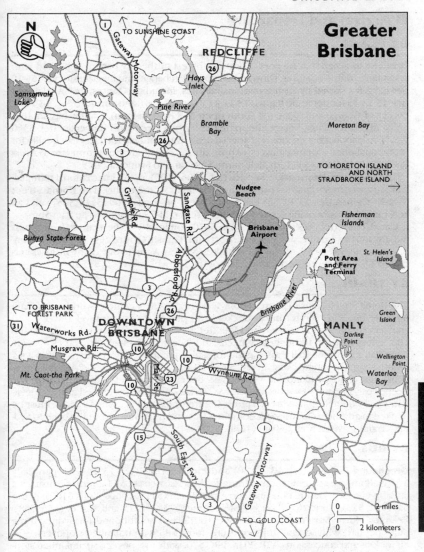

Greater Brisbane

N

TO SUNSHINE COAST

REDCLIFFE

Hays Inlet

Samsonvale Lake

Pine River

Bramble Bay

Moreton Bay

Nudgee Beach

TO MORETON ISLAND AND NORTH STRADBROKE ISLAND →

Bunya State Forest

Brisbane Airport

Fisherman Islands

St. Helen's Island

Port Area and Ferry Terminal

Green Island

TO BRISBANE FOREST PARK

Waterworks Rd.

DOWNTOWN BRISBANE

MANLY

Darling Point

Musgrave Rd.

Brisbane River

Wellington Point

Mt. Coot-tha Park

Wynnum Rd.

Waterloo Bay

Main St.

South East Fwy.

Gateway Motorway

Gympie Rd.

Sandgate Rd.

Abbotsford Rd.

Gateway Motorway

TO GOLD COAST

0   2 miles
0   2 kilometers

QUEENSLAND

The Brisbane River lends an easygoing grace to the metropolis it bisects. River transportation is simple and enjoyable; hulking ferries and slim kayaks glide between Chinatown and the South Bank Parklands, between investment banks and the trendy West End. Always a good bet for temporary employment, Brisbane earned a reputation as a tourist and holiday destination only recently, after hosting the 1988 World Expo and the 1992 Commonwealth Games. The sunny, warm climate has attracted artistic emigrés, eager to shed winter jumpers and rev up the city's cultural institutions. Today, visitors to Brisbane enjoy the gorgeous, modern Cultural Centre, 19th-century historic buildings, corner cafes, rocking nightclubs, extensive parklands, and a serene waterfront.

■ Arrival and Departure

BY PLANE

Brisbane International Airport, 17km northwest of the city center, is packed with restaurants, duty-free stores, showers, currency exchange, and luggage storage ($4-10 per day). It's served by 23 international airlines, including **Qantas,** 247 Adelaide St (tel. 13 13 13 for domestic flights, 13 12 11 international), and **Ansett** (tel. 13 13 00), corner of George and Queen St (both open M-F 8:30am-5pm). Qantas has another office in the Toowong Village Shopping Center by Queensland University (tel. 3360 2211). Ask about concessions and special deals; international travelers can qualify for 30% off full-price economy tickets. (Approximate 21-day advance return fare to Ayers Rock $545, to Cairns $377, to Melbourne $391, and to Sydney $248.)

The **Travellers Information Service** (tel. 3406 3190), in the international terminal, can answer general queries (open until last flight of the night). The **Roma Street Transit Centre** (tel. 13 12 30) has an info desk on level 2 (tel. 3211 3057) and an accommodations booking service on level 3 (open M-F 7am-6pm, Sa-Su 8am-5pm).

CoachTrans (tel. 3236 1000; fax 3236 3870), on level 3 of the Transit Centre, runs a daily **shuttle bus** between the airport and Transit Centre (every 30min. 5am-8:30pm, one-way $6.50, return $12; children $3, $5). A trip to one of the major hotels costs $7.50. A **taxi** ride between the airport and downtown costs $17-20.

BY TRAIN

The Roma Street Transit Centre, 500m west of the city's center, is Brisbane's main intercity bus and train terminal. **Lockers** ($4 per 24hr.) are on level 1 and 3, and showers are on level 2. **Queensland Rail** (tel. 3235 2222; bookings tel. 13 22 32) has 10 services that run throughout Queensland. For longer travel intineraries, Queensland Rail's **Sunshine Rail Pass** is good for a given number of travel days within a six month span. (Economy class: 14-day $267; 21-day $309; 30-day $388; Australian students and children half-price.) First class tickets include individual berths in the sleeper car, but are 50% more expensive. Tickets must be purchased at the Queensland Rail booth at Roma Street Transit Centre or Central Station. All travel must be booked in advance. **Countrylink** combines bus and train travel from Brisbane to Sydney. Trains leave daily at 7:30am (16hr., $90).

BY BUS

Greyhound Pioneer (tel. 13 20 30) and **McCafferty's** (tel. 13 14 99; open daily 6:30am-8pm) cover destinations throughout the east coast; McCafferty's is usually a little bit cheaper. Destinations include Airlie Beach ($111, concessions $100), Byron Bay ($22, $20), Cairns ($148, $134), Melbourne ($134, $121), and Sydney ($75, $68). **Premier Motor Services** (tel. 1300 368 100) leaves southbound for Sydney three times per day, with several stops en route. ($69, $88 with unlimited stopovers; 30% off for kids and concessions. VIP, YHA, ISIC $20, with 1 stopover $50, unlimited stopovers $79.) **Kirkland's Coaches** (tel. 1300 367 077) leaves a few times every day for the Gold Coast, Byron Bay, Lismore, and Ballina, among other destinations (students 20-25% off, pensioners traveling intrastate and children 50% off; to Byron Bay $26, backpackers $19). **CoachTrans** (tel. 3236 1000) leaves for the Gold Coast about every half-hour (90min., $12, children $9). **Suncoast Pacific** (tel. 3236 1901) heads to Noosa every 90 minutes ($19.50, pensioners 20% off, children 50% off).

■ Orientation

The Brisbane River hems the city and creates easily identifiable landmarks; the city's heart is cradled in the bottom of a sideways S-curve, connected to South Bank by the Victoria Bridge. The **Transit Centre** is on Roma St; a left turn out of the building and a five-minute walk down Roma St leads to the corner of Albert and Ann St and the grassy King George Square (a front lawn for the grand City Hall). Adelaide St runs along the opposite side of the square, and a block beyond is the **Queen Street Mall,** a popular, open-air pedestrian thoroughfare lined with shops and cafes. Underneath the Mall and the adjoining **Myer Centre** shopping complex is the **Queen Street Bus Station.** Seven clearly marked entrances are spread throughout the Mall. The **city center's** streets are organized by the gender of famous English figures. From Queen St moving toward the river lie Elizabeth, Charlotte, Mary, Margaret, and Alice St; from the river moving inland lie William, George, Albert, and Edward St.

Brisbane's neighborhoods radiate out from the city center. A right turn out of the transit center leads to **Petrie Terrace** and **Paddington,** both most easily reached by passing under the bridge and taking the first left up the hill. North of Boundary St is **Spring Hill,** bordered to the west by Victoria Park and 10-15 minutes from the Queen Street Mall up the steep Edward St. **Fortitude Valley** is farther east of Spring Hill and is home to Chinatown, whose ornate entrance gate lies a 20-minute walk down Ann St to Brunswick St. The nightclub-heavy Fortitude Valley is a trendy area, but contains some fairly seedy establishments—use caution when walking alone at night. A right on Brunswick St leads to **New Farm,** farther from the city center than the Valley; it officially begins at the intersection of Brunswick and Hardcourt St.

South of the river, the Victoria Bridge footpath turns into Melbourne St and heads into **South Brisbane,** crossing Boundary St six blocks later. **South Bank** is to the left of the southern end of the bridge; the intersection of Boundary and Vulture St, further on, is considered the heart of the **West End.**

■ Getting Around

BY TRAIN

Citytrain, Queensland Rail's intracity train network, has three major stations. The main transit center is at Roma St, Central Station is at Ann and Edward St, and the final station is at Brunswick St. One-zone journeys in the city area cost $1.40. One-day unlimited travel after 9am Monday to Friday is $8. (Trains run M-Th 5am-11:30pm, F 5am-1am, Sa 6am-1am, Su 6am-11pm. All tickets half-price Sa-Su.)

BY BUS

Citybus is the "all-stops" major service. Most buses depart from the **Queen Street Bus Station,** a huge underground terminal beneath the Myer Center and the Queen St Mall. Platforms are named after Australian animals, while central city stops are sorted by color. Schedules organized by suburb and bus number are posted throughout the city, particularly in the Queen St Mall. Suburban bus route schedules vary; call **TransInfo** (tel. 13 12 30) or stop by the Queen St Bus Station Info Center. Fares depend on distance and range from $1.40 to $3 (weekly $10.60-$27; children half-price). The **City Circle** bus #333 runs a loop around the central business district (M-F 7am-5:30pm; 70¢). **Cityxpress** buses, white with blue and yellow stripes, run directly from the suburbs to the city every 30 minutes. During peak hours, **Rockets** go from selected suburban stops express to the city. The **Great Circle Line,** #598 or 599, connects to major suburban shopping centers. **Nightrider** is a late-night weekend bus service servicing most major stops in 15-minute intervals (F, Sa 8pm-3am, $2).

BY CAR

Most **car rental** agencies require renters to be at least 21 years old. Expect to pay $25-$39 per day. **Ideal Rental Cars,** 63 Esker St in Pinkenba near the airport off Eagle Farm Rd (tel. 3260 2307 or 1800 065 172; fax 3260 1392), has 24-hour service and rents from $25 per day (free pick-up and delivery). **Compass Car Rentals,** 728 Main St at Kangaroo Point (tel. 3891 2614), rents new vehicles from $29. **Allcar Rentals,** 925 Ann St in Fortitude Valley (tel. 3852 1188), arranges one-way rentals between its offices in Brisbane, Cairns, Port Douglas, and Sydney from $39. **Shoestring Car Rentals,** 360 Nudgee Rd, Hendra (tel. 3268 3334), rents air-conditioned vehicles, some

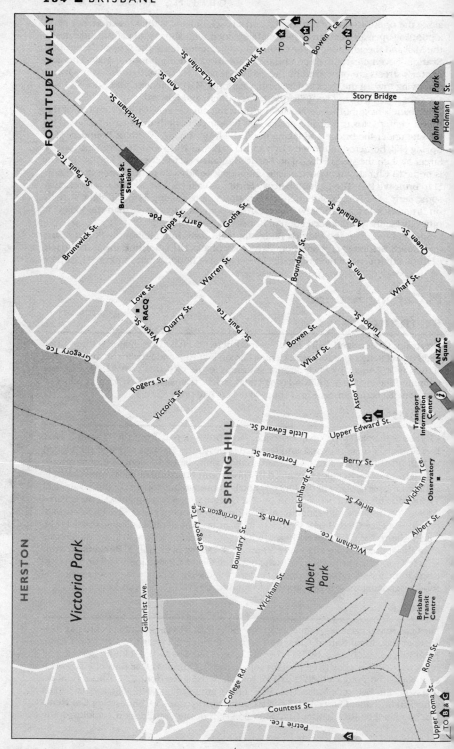

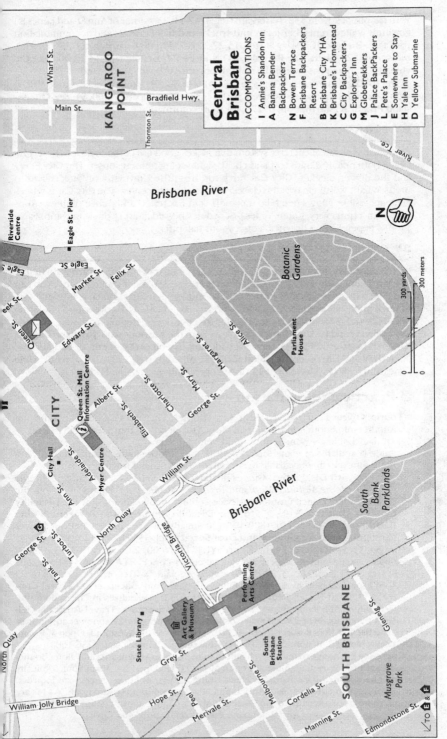

Central Brisbane

ACCOMMODATIONS
I Annie's Shandon Inn
A Banana Bender
  Backpackers
N Bowen Terrace
F Brisbane Backpackers
  Resort
B Brisbane City YHA
K Brisbane's Homestead
C City Backpackers
G Explorers Inn
M Globetrekkers
J Palace BackPackers
L Pete's Palace
E Somewhere to Stay
H Yale Inn
D Yellow Submarine

with car phones, from $32. **Allterrain** (tel. 3257 1101), corner of Ann St and James St, Fortitude Valley, rents 4x4 jeeps and trucks and has Fraser Island accommodation packages. **Budget,** 105 Mary St (tel. 13 27 27 or 3220 0699, airport tel. 3860 4466), rents from $29. **Delta Car Rentals,** 400 Nudgee Rd, Hendra (tel. 13 13 90; take Citytrain to Tomboy) has two of the only automatic 4WDs in Queensland.

The **RACQ** headquarters (tel. 3361 2444) is at 300 St. Paul's Tce, Fortitude Valley, with a branch office at 261 Queen St (tel. 3361 2565; fax 3220 0029). See **Queensland Practical Information,** p. 275, for more information.

BY FERRY

Brisbane has an excellent ferry system that makes good use of the Brisbane River, providing both practical transport and cheap sight-seeing tours at sunset. The **City Ferry** and the newer, sleeker, **City Cat** ferry run from the University of Queensland to Bretts Wharf. North Quay is the closest stop to the city center. The City Cat is wheelchair accessible, allows free bike transport, and has toilets and public phones. (Runs daily 6am-11pm every 30min. or less. Schedules posted at every dock and stop. Fares $1.40-3 depending on distance; concessions half-price.)

BY BIKE OR IN-LINE SKATES

Bicycles are a great way to see Brisbane. Local public transportation carries them free of charge, and within Brisbane City alone there are 350km of cycling paths. You can also bike to nearby sights, like Mt. Coot-tha and Stradbroke Island. The Brisbane City Council publishes a pamphlet called *Brisbane Bicycle Maps.* **Backpackers Mountain Bike Hire** (tel. 3256 0155) rents bikes for $16 per day, including maps and a helmet (free delivery and pick-up of bikes; book by 8pm the previous day). **Brisbane Bicycle,** 87 Albert St (tel. 3229 2433), carries a wide range of bikes ($9 per hr. or $20 per day; open daily and late on Friday). **Skatebiz,** 101 Albert St (tel. 3220 0157), rents in-line skates and pads ($10 for 2 hr., $12 on Su; open daily and late on Friday).

■ Practical Information

Tourist Office: Tourism Brisbane, City Hall (tel. 3221 8411). Open M-F 9am-5pm. Another info booth is in the middle of the Queen St Mall (tel. 3229 5918). Open M-Th 9am-5:30pm, F 9am-8pm, Sa 9am-5pm, Su 9am-4pm. The *Brisbane Tourism* guide is available at many tourist booths, and **InfoBrisbane,** a touch-screen computer info system, is available in several locations around town.

Travelers with Disabilities: Guides include *Access Brisbane, Accessible Brisbane Parks, Brisbane Mobility Map,* and *Brisbane Braille Trail,* all available from the Brisbane City Council customer service centers, public libraries, or the **Disability Services Unit** (tel. 3403 5796). The **Disability Information Awareness Line (DIAL)** (tel. 3224 8444 or 1800 177 120; email dial@fsaia.qld.gov.au) can answer questions, as can the **Queensland Deaf Society** (tel. 3356 8255; TTY 3856 4237).

Budget Travel Offices: Flight Centre (tel. 13 16 00; 24hr. tel. 13 31 33) has 9 offices and guarantees to beat any quoted current price. **STA Travel,** 111 Adelaide St (tel. 3221 3722; fax 3229 8435) and 5a Adelaide St (tel. 3229 2499; fax 3229 4661) specializes in backpackers. Open M-F 9am-5pm. **Backpackers Travel Centre,** 138 Albert St (tel. 3221 2225; fax 3221 3038), specializes in cheap domestic fares. Open M-F 9am-5:30pm, Sa-Su 9am-noon. **Adventure Travel Australia** (tel. 3844 0206; fax 3844 9295; email BrisbaneBackpackers@6022.aone.net.au), in Brisbane Backpackers Resort's lobby at 110 Vulture St in the West End. Open M-F 9am-12:30pm and 2:30-6pm. **YHA Travel Centre,** 154 Roma St (tel. 3236 1680).

Currency Exchange: Banks are clustered in the Queen St Mall area and along Boundary St in the West End. Most are open M-Th 9:30am-4pm, F 9:30am-5pm. Typically no charge for cash exchange, $5 for cashing traveler's checks. **American Express,** 131 Elizabeth St (tel. 3229 2729). Open M-F 9am-5:30pm, Sa 9am-noon. **ATMs** are ubiquitous, particularly in the Queen St Mall area, the transit center, and shopping centers. Most accept Australian bank cards, credit cards, and Cirrus.

Bookstores: The Queen St Mall area has a huge selection of bookstores. **Pages Bookshop** (tel. 3221 4611), in the basement at 217 Albert St, has a wide selection at good prices. **Angus and Robertson** (tel. 3229 8899) has a branch in the mall.

Library: The **State Library** (tel. 3840 7666), in the Cultural Centre. Open M-Th 10am-8pm, F-Su 10am-5pm. For free **Internet access** call 3840 7785 to book ahead. The John Oxley Library (tel. 3840 7881), on level 4, is devoted to Queensland research and history, and holds historical exhibitions throughout the year.

Public Markets: South Bank Markets (see **Sights,** p. 290); **Brunswick Markets,** Sa mornings, Brunswick St, Fortitude Valley; **Riverside Markets, all day Su,** Eagle St.

Hotlines: Brisbane Crisis Line (tel. 3252 1111). **Rape Crisis Line** (tel. 3844 4008). **Domestic Violence** (24hr. tel. 1800 811 811, TTY 1800 812 225; for men 1800 246 346, M-F 8am-10pm).

Women's Services: Women's Infolink, ground floor, 56 Mary St (tel. 1800 177 577; email infolink@thehub.com.au; http://www.qldwoman.qld.gov.au/owa).

Sexual Health Clinic: 484 Adelaide St (tel. 3227 8666).

Hospital: The Royal Brisbane Hospital, Herston Rd, Herston (tel. 3221 8083).

Emergency: Dial 000.

Police: Dial 3367 6464.

Taxi: Brisbane Cabs (tel. 3360 0000), **Yellow Cab Company** (tel. 3391 0191), and **Black and White** (tel. 13 10 08) operate 24hr. per day.

Information numbers: Weather (tel. 1190); **time** (tel. 1194); **tourist infoline** (tel. 11654); **tide times** (tel. 3224 2616); **marine report** (tel. 1182).

Directory Assistance: Local 013; Australia 0175; international 0103. **Hello Yellow** (tel. 3404 1111) has category-sorted business listings. Available daily 7am-11pm.

Post Office: GPO, 261 Queen St (tel. 3405 1434; fax 3405 1428; *Poste Restante* queries 3405 1465), half a block from the end of the mall. Check a computer to make sure you have mail before requesting collection. $6 surcharge for international money orders. Open M-F 7am-6pm. **Postal Code:** 4000; GPO code: 4001.

Internet Access: State Library (see above). **Women's Infolink** (see above). There's also a hub at 126 Adelaide St (tel. 3211 9095; info@dialup.com.au; http://www.dialup.com.au; $5 per ½hr., $9 per hr.) and a 24hr. Internet cafe at the corner of Ann and Brunswick St ($3 for ½hr., $5 per hr.). **The Hub Internet Cafe,** 125 Margaret St (tel. 3229 1119; $6 for ½hr., ISIC backpackers $5, full-time students $3).

Phone Code: 07.

■ Accommodations

Accommodations are clustered in four main areas of the city. The city center, with middle-range motels and B&Bs, has the action; South Brisbane and West End are near the cultural sights; Fortitude Valley and New Farm are trendy and alternative but not the safest areas at night; Petrie Terrace and Paddington are close to the transit center and Caxton St. Unless otherwise noted, check-out time is 10am and key deposits are $10. Linen and crockery are usually free with a deposit. Brisbane is blessed with plenty of high-quality, low-price hostels, most with TVs, videos, in-house bars, free tours of local sights, and pick-up service from the Roma Street Transit Centre.

CITY CENTER

Palace BackPackers (tel. 3211 2433, bookings tel. 1800 676 340; fax 3211 2466), corner of Ann and Edward St. 2min. walk from the Queen St. Mall. The former Salvation Army headquarters, this 5-story building is as huge as its party-central reputation. Roof access, 3-story veranda. Huge kitchen, rockin' pub, game room, Internet access. Rooms have lockers and either A/C or ceiling fans. 6- and 7-bed dorms $15; 4- and 5-bed dorms $16; 3-bed dorms $18; singles $28; doubles $38; twins $21. Weekly: $90, $96, $108, $228, $168, $126. VIP. Wheelchair accessible.

Explorers Inns, 63 Turbot St (tel. 3211 3488, reservations tel. 1800 623 288), corner of George St near the Transit Centre. Pleasant, convenient budget hotel. Rooms are compact but clean and have bathrooms, full-length mirrors, phones, minibars, small TVs, coffeemakers and mugs, clock radios, and A/C. Wheelchair-accessible units available. Non-smoking. Singles, doubles, twins $64. Deluxe (read: larger) and 4-person family rooms $84. Licensed basement restaurant; light meals $5-8.

Annie's Shandon Inn, 405 Upper Edward St, Spring Hill (tel. 3831 8684; fax 3831 3073). Like Grandma's house, complete with family snapshots. Cute, very cute. Singles $40, with bath $50; doubles or twins $50, $60; $5 each additional child, $10 each additional adult. Breakfast included. 10% discount for 7-day stay.

Yale Inner City Inn, 413 Upper Edward St (tel. 3832 1663 or 1800 773 631; fax 3832 2591), corner of Astor Tce, Spring Hill. Simple, practical budget inn. Singles $35, twins and doubles $45, triples or doubles with bath $55; breakfast included.

SOUTH BRISBANE AND THE WEST END

ⓦ**Somewhere to Stay,** 45 Brighton Rd (tel. 3846 2858; fax 3846 4584), at the corner of Franklin St, sits atop a quiet hill surrounded by vegetation. Large rooms with wooden bedframes; those in the front have a gorgeous view of the city. Beautiful, laid out like a country village. Big kitchen, cafe, garden, free bus, Monday Madness. 9:30am check-out. One wheelchair-accessible room. Prices vary based on amenities, bath, and view. 4-bed dorms $12-15; singles $20-25; doubles $30-45. YHA, VIP.

Brisbane Backpackers Resort, 110 Vulture St (tel. 3844 9956, bookings tel. 1800 626 452; fax 3844 9295), near the corner of Boundary St. Large rooms with fridge, balcony, and lockers. Each floor shares a small kitchen. Tennis court, swimming pool, sauna, and nightly movies. Travel agency in lobby. All rooms with bath. Reception open 24hr. Check-out by 9:30am. Restaurant cafe with $2.50 burgers. 6-bed dorms $16, doubles $45. YHA, VIP.

FORTITUDE VALLEY AND NEW FARM

ⓦ**Globetrekkers,** 35 Balfour St (tel. 3358 1251; email bidlake@gil.com.au). Small 100-year-old house between Brunswick St and Bowen Tce. Quiet, mellow artist's enclave, with pictures on the wall and half-finished sculptures on the porch. Wood-floored rooms are small but lovely, especially the bathrooms. Pool, kitchen. Dorms $13; doubles $30, with bath $34. Weekly $77; $196, $210. Book ahead.

Bowen Terrace, 365 Bowen Tce (tel. 3254 1575), off Brunswick St. Warm, welcoming colonial house. Only 16 beds, but worth trying to secure a room. Lounge, small kitchen, large deck. Motel-like rooms with TV, fridge, and coffee machines. Singles $15; doubles $32, with bath $40-45; weekly $95, $108, $250-$255.

Tourist Guest House, 555 Gregory Tce (tel. 3252 4171; fax 3252 2704). Homespun B&B with leisurely front porch. Wonderful rooms have TV, sink. Full cooked breakfast. Singles $35, with bath $45; doubles and twins $45, $60; triples $55, $70.

Edward Lodge, 75 Sydney St, New Farm (tel. 3254 1078). Gorgeous, modern rooms exclusively for gays and lesbians. Free breakfast served in a high-ceilinged, bright room. New, large jacuzzi and open shower. All rooms with bath. Singles $65; doubles $75. laundry $5. Book early, especially for Mardi Gras.

Brisbane's Homestead, 57 Annie St (tel. 3358 3538). Fairly quiet. Bedrooms have high ceilings and wooden bunks. Small swimming pool, kitchen, ping-pong and pool tables, Internet access, free bus service, TV room. Monday Madness drinking races. 8-bed dorms $13; twins $32, with bath $56. Weekly: $75; $175. VIP, YHA.

Pete's Palace, 515 Brunswick St (tel. 3254 1984 or 1800 808 941). Small, friendly hostel with kitchen, free transport, barbecue, and a free 300-title video library. Dorms $13, doubles and twins $15, single $25; weekly: $77, $156, $186.

PETRIE TERRACE/PADDINGTON

ⓦ**Brisbane City YHA,** 392 Upper Roma St (tel. 3236 1004; fax 3236 1947). Clean, friendly, low-key, and private. The new building is much better. Restaurant, kitchen, wonderful reading loft. Wheelchair accessible. New building: singles, doubles, twins $40, with bath $50; triples $51 (or $17 per person). Old building: 4-6 bed dorms $16, twins $36 or $18 per person; singles $28.

ⓦ**Banana Bender Backpackers,** 118 Petrie Tce (tel. 3367 1157; fax 3368 1047). Nice people, nice rooms, nice sundeck. Nice. Nightly activities. 4-bed dorms $15, twins and doubles $34; weekly $85, $200. YHA, VIP. Wheelchair accessible.

Yellow Submarine, 66 Quay St (tel. 3211 3424). A little house with lots of character, noise, and a shrine to Beatle-mania. Formerly a governor's home. Brightly painted yellow rooms, garden. Table tennis, free pizza on Sundays. 6-bed dorms $14, doubles $32; weekly: $85, $96. Book ahead, as rooms fill quickly.

■ Food

The West End has small, trendy sidewalk cafes and ethnic restaurants, particularly along Boundary St and Hardgrave Rd. Chinatown in Fortitude Valley has many small, cheap Chinese and Asian food establishments, while New Farm has trendier and more expensive eateries. The city center has a range of options.

CITY CENTER

Govinda's Vegetarian Restaurant, upstairs at 99 Elizabeth St (tel. 3210 0225). Hare Krishna owners only serve one meal a day, but its a $6 all-you-can-eat extravaganza. Open M-Sa 11:30-2:30pm, F also 5:30-8:30pm, Su 5-7pm. Su $3 feast with music.

Parrots, 93 Elizabeth St (tel. 3229 0187), serves sandwiches and 15 varieties of thick, juicy gourmet hamburgers ($9-12) that will satisfy the most voracious carnivore. Licensed. Open Tu-Th 11:30am-10:30pm, F-Sa 11:30am-11pm, Su 11:30am-9:30pm.

Gaya, upstairs at 85 Elizabeth St (tel. 3229 1424). Spare and elegant, serving Korean fare (oxleg soup $7, panfried calamari $7). Open daily 10:30am-midnight.

WEST END

Three Monkeys, 53 Mollison St, on the West End rotary off Boundary St (tel. 3844 6045). Walls bedecked with theater posters, African and Indian art, woven baskets, and statuettes. Dim lighting, jazz music. Varied, inexpensive menu includes quiche ($6), nachos ($6.50), spanakopita ($8), and a delectable choice of 15-20 cakes and cookies. The terrace out back is filled with leafy plants. Open daily 9:30am-late.

El Torito (tel. 3844 5977), on Boundary St. An inconspicuous but popular Mexican/Salvadoran joint. Can cater to vegetarians. Open M-Tu 5-10pm, W-F 11am-3pm and 5pm-10:30pm, Sa noon-3pm and 5-11pm, Su 5-9pm.

NEW FARM

⊛Moray Cafe (tel. 3254 1342), corner of Moray and Merthyr Rd. Quiet location off Brunswick, across the street from the river. Hip, popular, half-outdoor cafe with bright colors, good music, and international, veggie-friendly fare. Famous Caesar salad ($10.50). Licensed. Open daily 8:30am-late. Kitchen closes at 10pm.

Gertie's (tel. 3358 5088), corner of Brunswick and Barker St. Loud Latin and jazz music pump through the narrow interior of this cornerside cafe, but it doesn't stop the trendy yuppies from squeezing in, sipping wine, chatting, and soaking up the atmosphere. All day breakfast Sa and Su from 9am. "Happy two hours" 4-6pm. Open M-Sa 11:30am-midnight, Su 9am-late.

Rosati's at the Park, 938 Brunswick St (tel. 3358 1422). Large, contemporary, gorgeous dining room. More upscale and out-of-the-way, but worth it for the well-prepared Italian fare. Mains $10-20. Open W-Th 11:30am-11pm, F-Sa 11:30am-midnight, Su 9:30am-8pm. Kitchen closes an hour before closing.

FORTITUDE VALLEY

⊛Garuva, 174 Wickham St (tel. 3216 0124). A fantastic dining experience. You enter via a narrow passage through several doors in rooms decorated with overhanging trees and full-length mirrors. Once in, you sit on the floor as a white curtain is drawn around you. The meals, like sweet potato and bean curry or crumbed squid with coconut curry sauce, are all $8.50. Reservations essential.

Lucky's Trattoria, 683 Ann St, seems to have achieved cult status with younger members of the Valley community. Pasta dishes and vegetarian food $8-16.

Mellino's, Brunswick St Mall. A fave with famished clubbers for a late-night re-energizer or early morning pick-me-up. Cheap breakfasts, pizzas, pastas. Open 24hr.

SOUTH BANK

Sirocco (tel. 3846 1803), north South Bank Parklands. Popular, loud, and packed on Sunday, with funky lighting, outdoor seating, and Mediterranean fare. Live music and dancing on weekends; book ahead. Entrees (e.g. baby octopus with pistachio pesto) $8-13. Licensed. Open daily noon-3pm and 6-10pm.

Capt'n Snapper (tel. 3846 4036). Delicious fresh seafood and a well-stocked all-you-can-eat salad bar ($3.50 with meal). Open daily 11am-late.

Cafe San Marco (tel. 3846 4334), South Bank Parklands. Arched outside terrace has spectacular view of Captain Cook Bridge and the Brisbane skyline. Happy hour 5-6pm (cocktails $5). Mains $8-14. Open Su-Th 8am-11pm, F-Sa 8am-midnight.

Chez Laila (tel. 3846 3402), South Bank Parklands, has an outdoor deck overlooking the river and city skyline—perfect for nursing a cappuccino ($2.50). Shish kebab $11.50, vegetarian falafel plate $11. Open daily 8am-midnight.

■ Sights and Activities

MUSEUMS AND GALLERIES

On the south side of Victoria Bridge, the **Queensland Cultural Centre** (tel. 3840 7190) contains many of Brisbane's major artistic venues, including the art gallery, museum, performing arts complex, state library, and theater company. Inside, the **Queensland Art Gallery** (tel. 3840 7303; 35¢ per min. infoline tel. 0055 39373) has over 10,000 primarily Australian works spread over two levels. *(Open daily 10am-5pm. Guided 1hr. tours M-F 11am, 1, and 2pm; Sa-Su 11am, 2, and 3pm. Free admission to the permanent collections; special exhibitions $8-12.)* The gallery's licensed cafe serves coffee, cakes, and sandwiches on a terrace facing the sculpture court. 1999 exhibits include woodfired ceramics (thru Jan.), "Scary Monster" (thru Feb. 7), Whistler (Mar. 27-May 16), still-lifes (Mar. 20-May 30), and the 3rd Asia-Pacific Triennial (from Sept. on).

The **Queensland Museum** (tel. 3840 7555), spacious and brightly lit, houses dinosaur skeletons, whale models, and exhibits emphasizing cultural heritage and the environment. *(Open 10am-5pm. Free admission to regular collection; special exhibitions admission $6, concessions $4, children $2.)* A permanent exhibit devoted to Australia's most endangered species opened in July 1998. 1999 features will include a Star Trek exhibit (thru Jan.) and an Egyptian exhibit (Feb. 22-Apr. 30).

The **Queensland Office of Arts and Cultural Development** (tel. 3224 4248) publishes a pamphlet, *Brisbane Inner City Galleries,* listing names, phone numbers, and addresses of all galleries within a 15-minute walk of the city center. The collection in the **City Hall Art Gallery and Museum** in King George Square dates back to 1859, but currently focuses on Brisbane's young artists. *(Open daily 10am-5pm. Free.)* **Queensland Aboriginal Creations Shop,** 199 Elizabeth St (tel. 3224 5730), showcases Aboriginal prints, photography, and sculpture. *(Open M-F 9am-4:30pm, Sa 9am-4pm.)*

The **Sciencentre,** 110 George St (tel. 3220 0166), next to the Conrad International Hotel, has over 170 hands-on exhibits for kids to play with and parents to learn from. *(Open daily 10am-5pm. $7, concessions and children 5-15 $5, children 3-4 $2, families $24.)*

CITY TOURS

One of the best deals for a city tour is **City Sights,** offered through Brisbane Transport. *(Tickets $15, children $10, families of up to 6 $30. Tours leave at 40min. intervals daily 9am-12:20pm and 1:40pm-4:20pm.)* An open tram covers 19 cultural and historical attractions during the 80-minute loop. Tickets allow one day of unlimited access to all Council bus and ferry networks, including the City Cat, and can be purchased on the bus, from any customer service center, or at most tourist info centers.

The **City Hall** was officially opened in 1930 and earned the epithet "Million Pound Town Hall" for its outrageous building cost. The clock tower stands 92m high and has an **observation deck** with a nearly 360° view of the city. *(Deck open M-F 8:30am-4:30pm, Sa 10:30am-4:30pm for groups of 10 or more—book ahead. Free. Take the City Hall elevator to the 3rd floor.)* City Hall also has 45-minute guided **tours** (tel. 3403 4048).

For a tour of the Brisbane River, the large **Kookaburra Queen** (tel. 3221 1300) paddlewheel boat departs daily from the Eagle St Pier. A 90-minute tea cruise leaves at 10am ($20); the lunch cruise leaves at 12:45pm ($20-45, depending on menu); a Sunday afternoon tea cruise ($20) departs at 3:30pm; and nightly dinner cruises ($40 or $55) leave at 6:30pm. Book ahead.

The **Castlemaine Brewery** (tel 3361 7597), womb of Queensland's famous XXXX beer, is a 20- to 30-minute walk from the City Centre on Milton Rd. $5 will buy you a 50-minute tour and four tall ones. *(Tours M-W 11am, 1:30pm, and 4:30pm, and occasionally M at 7pm. Make bookings between 9-11am.)* Meet at the Castlemaine Perkins Visitor's Lodge on Heussler Tce behind the brewery. The **Carlton Brewhouse** (tel. 3826 5858) in Yatala, makers of VB, Foster's, and Carlton, is 30 minutes south of Brisbane. **CoachTrans** stops in Yatala on the way to the Gold Coast; buses leave daily from the Transit Centre at 9:15, 11:15am, and 1:15pm. Naturally, they offer free beer too.

PARKS, GARDENS, AND OUTDOOR ACTIVITIES

Along the South Brisbane riverbank lies the ever-popular **South Bank Parklands.** Even with construction going on around it through 1999, it's still the most relaxing spot in the city. By the new millenium, nearly three additional acres worth of tree-lined and cafe-dotted boulevards, an IMAX theatre, and trendy shops and restaurants will mark the territory; drop by before it develops an attitude. During the day, people swim in the man-made lagoon, bike, check out the "Opal World" jewelry store, play on jungle gyms, and visit the South Bank Wildlife Sanctuary (see **Wildlife,** below). There's also a well-stocked **Maritime Museum** (tel. 3844 5361). *(Open daily 9:30am-5pm. $5, concessions $4, children $2.50, family $12.50.)* On the weekends, the park center (behind the lagoon) houses a **crafts village,** replete with crafts, psychics, clothes, and massages. *(Crafts village F 5pm-10pm by lantern-light, Sa 11am-5pm, Su 9am-5pm.)*

The parklands are located just across the river to the left of the Victoria Bridge, and can be reached by foot, bus (orange B stop on Grey St), CityTrain (South Brisbane or Vulture St Stations), or ferry (terminal stop South Bank). The **Visitor Information Centre** (tel. 3867 2051, 24hr. entertainment info 3867 2020) is toward the Victoria Bridge end of the park; maps, guides, and advice are all free. *(Center open Su-Th 8am-6pm, F-Sa 8am-8pm.)* The Parklands also has phones, toilets, an ATM, a volleyball court, and, for good measure, a Nepalese Pagoda. Although there are no official gates, South Bank is "open" 5am to midnight. *(Lifeguard on duty 5am-midnight, in winter 7am-6pm.)*

Brisbane's **Botanic Gardens** (tel. 3403 7913) are a 15-minute walk from the city center. City Circle bus #333 stops at Albert or George St, near the entrance on Alice St. Visitors stroll among lily ponds, palm groves, and camellia gardens. Free **tours** (tel. 3229 1554) depart the rotunda near the Albert St entrance. *(Tours Tu-Su 11am, 1pm.)*

Brisbane's other botanic garden is **Mt. Coot-tha Park** (tel. 3403 2533), 7km from the city center, which includes a Japanese Garden, a bamboo grove, and a **planetarium** (tel. 3403 2578). *(Planetarium programs W-F 3:30 and 7:30, Sa 1:30, 3:30, and 7:30, Su 1:30 and 3:30. $8, concessions $6.50, children $4.50.)* Take public bus #39A, or 598 and 599. A 30-minute walk from the gardens leads to the Mt. Coot-tha summit, with a spectacular view of greater Brisbane. The casual **Kuta Cafe** and the fancier **Mt. Coot-tha Summit Restaurant** (tel. 3369 9922; meals $9-15) both have panoramic views.

City Heights is a two-hour tour that leaves from the City Hall City Sights bus stop at 2pm and travels to the Mt. Coot-tha lookout and the Botanical Gardens. *(Tickets $7, concessions $5, groups $15.)* The **City Nights** version leaves at 6pm, heads to Mt. Coot-tha, and then travels to the sparklingly lit South Bank and the Story Bridge. *(2hr. $15, concessions $10, groups $30. Both tours wheelchair accessible.)*

Twenty minutes from the city, **Brisbane Forest Park** (tel. 3300 4855) covers 28,500 hectares. You can picnic, camp, hike, birdwatch, cycle, and ride horses. The *Information Guide* describes more than a dozen short and half-day walks.

Brisbane has many waterways that are perfect for **canoeing.** Guides to the popular trails **Oxely Creek** and **Boondsill Wetlands** are available from libraries or tourist offices (for more info, call 3403 6757 or **Queensland Canoeing, Inc.,** at 3278 1033). Rental companies include **Wild Adventure Sports,** Edward St (tel. 3221 5747), and

Goodtime Surf and Sail, 29 Ipswich Rd, Woolloongabba (tel. 3391 8588). **Rainbow Safaris** (tel. 3396 3141; fax 3396 4941) offers canoe daytrips from $50.

WILDLIFE

The **Alma Park Zoo** (tel. 3204 6566), 30 minutes north of Brisbane, allows hands-on contact with some of its animals. *(Open daily 9am-5pm. $15, children and concessions $8.)* The zoo has walk-through kangaroo and deer enclosures, koalas, monkeys, camels, and water buffalo. Twenty acres of gardens and barbecues make it an ideal picnic spot. **Walkabout Creek Wildlife Centre,** 60 Mt. Nebo Rd, the Gap, in Brisbane Forest Park (tel. 3300 4855) has an aviary, crocs, platypuses, and strange water creatures. *(Open M-Su 9am-4:30pm, Sa 10am-4:30pm. $3.50, concessions $2.50, children $2, family $9.)*

The **Australian Woolshed** (tel. 3351 5366; fax 3351 5575) is all about sheep. The Ram Show gives a shearing demonstration, there's a wool spinning display, and you can even visit koalas, wallabies, kangaroos, and cows—some of which you can touch and feed. *($12, concessions $8, children $5.50.)* The Woolshed is located 800m from the Ferny Grove railway station in Ferny Hills, and has its own restaurant, which hosts the popular Bush Dance and Dinner weekend nights (minimum age 18).

If you prefer bugs to 'roos, the **South Bank Wildlife Sanctuary** can meet your twisted desires. *(Open daily. $8, concessions including YHA VIP, ISIC $7, children $6.)* Located in the South Bank Parklands, the Sanctuary's highlight is its fabulously motley collection of butterflies, fluttering about in a makeshift rainforest. Further on are lizards, pythons, cockroaches, and the "Spider Pit." Note: do not tap on the glass.

Rob's Rainforest Explorer Day Tours (tel. 019 496 607; email frogbus7@hotmail.com) takes you bushwalking through Mt. Glorious and Samford Valley (M and Th), Glasshouse Mountains and Kondalilla Falls (Tu and F), Lamington National Park and the Green Mountains (W), or the Natural Bridge and Springbrook National Parks (Sa). *($48, including transport, morning tea, and lunch. Occasional backpacker special $39.)*

For true ecologists, **Araucaria Ecotours** (tel. 5544 1283 or 3848 4318) offers three-day zoologist-led small-group trips through the Border Ranges and provides your own wildlife kit. *(W-F; $160, with meals $210. 2-day backpacker special Sa-Su; $50.)*

■ Entertainment and Festivals

Brisbane is full of enough theaters to satisfy any culture-craving traveler. Call the **Queensland Cultural Centre** (tel. 3840 7190) for a current schedule and info on discounts. The **Performing Arts Complex,** in the center on the south side of the river, is composed of three theaters: the **Concert Hall** hosts symphony and chamber orchestras; the 2000-seat **Lyric Theatre** sponsors large drama, musical, and ballet performances; and the 315-seat **Cremora Theater** stages more intimate productions. Whether or not you see action on stage, the theaters are gorgeous. Free guided tours of the complex leave weekdays at noon from the tour desk at the ticket sales foyer.

The **Queensland Conservatorium** (tel. 3875 6241, concert inquiries tel. 3875 6222) presents university-affiliated concerts for free or very cheap admission. **Opera Queensland** (tel. 3875 3030) produces three extravagant productions a year. For contemporary Australian theater, **La Boite** (tel. 3369 1622) offers six plays annually. The **Queensland Ballet** (tel. 3846 5266), the oldest dance group in the country, is world renowned for its neoclassical style. The **Queensland Theatre Co.** (tel. 3846 4646) offers seven or eight shows a year ($20-$45, with concessions).

The former state treasury building at the corner of Queen, Elizabeth, and George St houses a ridiculously glitzy **casino** (tel. 3306 8888), home to four restaurants, over 100 gaming tables and more than 1000 gaming machines (open 24hr.).

The **Entertainment Centre** (tel. 3265 8111, event info line 1902 241 131), on Melaleuca Dr in Boondall, is Brisbane's largest indoor complex for sports, concerts, and special events. By Citytrain, take the Shorncliffe line to Boondall Station. The **"Gabba"** (tel. 3891 5464), at Vulture and Stanley St in Woolloongabba, is Queensland's major cricket and football stadium, home of the Brisbane Lions AFL team. Take the bus to the station on the corner of Main and Stanley St.

Festivals in Brisbane include the **Queensland Winter Racing Carnival,** held each May and June, the **Biennial International Music Festival,** held in May and June of even years, and the **International Film Festival,** held each August.

■ Nightlife

Brisbane nights roll by in sweaty nightclubs, noisy pubs, and smoky jazz lounges. For a weekly rundown on the scene, check out the Wednesday or Saturday edition of the *Courier-Mail.* Other entertainment guides are *Rave, Time Off, Scene,* and *Brother Sister* (a guide to gay and lesbian entertainment and clubs), all available at the record store **Rocking Horse,** 101 Adelaide St (tel. 3229 5360), and at many local nightclubs.

For **after-hours transportation,** Brisbane Transport operates **Night Rider,** a late-night bus service on Friday and Saturday which loops between Brisbane's most popular inner city nightspots, including Caxton St, Fortitude Valley, Riverside Centre, and downtown spots like the casino. Buses begin at 8pm and run every 15 minutes until 3am (fare $2). Call **TransInfo** (tel. 13 12 30) for more information. "Monday Night Madness" is a popular inter-hostel event involving transport to clubs and drinking races.

Most clubs are open till 5am. Brisbane's mainstream night scene is centered on **Caxton St** in Petrie Terrace. **Jackass Ginger's** is the loud, purple and red, neon-pulsing, pennant-strewn club, complete with three levels of sticky dance floors, pulsing techno beats, and often a line outside the door. (No sneakers allowed.) **Caxton Hotel,** across the street, is a little more upscale (leather-soled shoes only) and is attached to an always-busy grill with "supper menus" consisting mainly of pizza crusts and nachos. **Hotel LA,** at the corner of Petrie and Caxton, is a rather typical noisy bar with rock and funk music and a slightly older clientele. **Casablanca,** across the street, has lots of stand-in-place dancing to kitschy classic rock. There are outdoor tables with occasional live music.

On the opposite side of Petrie Tce is **Metro,** a wide-open venue that seems both elegant and trashy, and appealingly so. It has the feel of a party in the living room of a mansion (well, a mansion belonging to a techno fan); there's even a fireplace. ($7 cover.) Also on Caxton St are a comedy club and a handful of pubs, including **The Irish Connection** (tel. 3368 1933), which has live bands on Wednesday, Friday, and Saturday (closes at 2am), and **East LA,** an outdoor bar with deck space and classic rock tunes.

The **gay and alternative scene,** which is arguably the principal scene in Brisbane, is concentrated in Fortitude Valley. Especially popular is the **Beat,** 677 Ann St (tel. 3252 2543), a mixed gay and straight venue whose long dance floor is lit up by disco balls. The music is a mix of techno and Saturday Night Fever fare. ($5 cover.) Upstairs is the free **Cockatoo Club,** a slightly more run-of-the-mill dance establishment. The **Zoo,** 711 Ann St (3854 1381), is an interestingly laid-back, barn-like club that offers lots of tables, fresh local music, and a funky alternative to the typical club scene. On the other side of the Mall is **The Tube,** 210 Wickham St, with three popular dance floors. **Hotel Wickham,** 308 Wickham St (tel. 3852 1301), is a popular, relaxed gay and lesbian bar by day, and a thumping, campy party by night. The **Sportsman Hotel and Bar,** 130 Leichhardt St in Spring Hill (tel. 3831 2892) is also a popular gay establishment. At the corner of Ann and Brunswick is the enormous and rocking **Empire. Options,** at the corner of Leichhardt and Little Edward is also popular with gay locals, as is the **Alliance Tavern** (corner of Boundary and Leicchardt, tel. 3832 7355). **Ric's,** on the Brunswick St Mall, is an always-crowded outdoor bar and cafe.

Backpackers religiously tread a well-known path of pubs through the week. Monday nights are spent at the **Story Bridge Hotel,** 200 Main St., Kangaroo Point (tel. 3391 2266). **Rosie's,** on Edward St. in the city center, is a new competitor, serving free drinks from 7 to 9pm. On Friday and Saturday nights, young partiers lured by cheap drinks and table dancing descend on the **Down Under Bar** at the Palace, at the corner of Ann and Edward St in the city center. The **Brunswick Hotel,** 569 Brunswick St in New Farm, has loyal followers on Fridays as well.

QUEENSLAND

MORETON BAY

The forest of masts on Manly's tranquil marina promises smooth sailing on the crystal-clear waters of Moreton Bay. Here, at the mouth of the Brisbane River, a comfortable culture thrives in perpetual slow-motion. Across the bay, North Stradbroke Island offers wonderful snorkeling, diving, and swimming, while several other islands offer even more secluded, relaxed getaways. Although the area lacks pre-packaged fun, its lack of crowds and high-rises make Moreton Bay a mellow place to unwind.

▓ Manly

Manly is a content harborside village on Moreton Bay, far removed from skyscrapers or raucous parties. The main street leads to a picturesque harbor filled with unmasted ships, and if you have your own equipment or book a tour, you can fish, sail, or scuba dive. Alternately, you can just walk for hours along the Esplanade, a foot and bike path that runs along the bay for miles and is bordered by strings of green parks. Manly is also an alternate accommodation base for exploring Brisbane or the nearby islands.

ORIENTATION AND PRACTICAL INFORMATION

Manly is easily accessible by public transportation. From Brisbane, take Citytrain on the Cleveland line (35min. from Central Station; $4.50 return). To reach Manly's **commercial district** and the **harbor,** exit the station grounds and walk out of the parking lot, straight past the small rotary, and left onto **Cambridge Parade.** Bear right so the small park is on your left, and continue to the far end of Cambridge Pde. Shops include a supermarket, bank, post office, bakery, seafood store, and butcher shop, all open daily, and several small cafes and restaurants. The **tourist office** is in the **Nautical Gift Shop** (tel. 3839 1936), next door to Moreton Bay Lodge. There's **Internet access** in **Go Video** ($5 per hr.). A brisk 30-minute walk from the harbor (facing the harbor, turn left) brings you to the center of **Wynnum by the Bay,** a nearby town.

ACCOMMODATIONS AND FOOD

Moreton Bay Lodge, 45 Cambridge Pde (tel. 3396 3020), is the best bet for back-packer-style lodging. It has impeccably clean, spacious rooms with fresh linen, a TV lounge, a functional kitchen, spotless bathrooms, and wonderfully helpful owners. (Dorms $14, weekly $91. Singles $30, with bath $35; doubles $40, $50; triples $50, $60; suite $60, $70. Key deposit $20.) A neat symmetry divides the hostel from the casual but lovely **Bay Window Cafe and Bar** (tel. 3396 3020), which has gorgeous harbor-view windows and serves coffee and thick slices of cake for $4 (meals $7-15). There's a cheaper backpackers-only menu.

Across the street, **Manly Hotel** (tel. 3396 8188) is a newly remodeled favorite of businessmen paying by company check. Wood paneling, thick patterned rugs, and leather chairs adorn the newer, small-sized rooms (doubles $90). The older section has simpler rooms (singles $35, with bath and A/C $45; doubles $45, $55). (Reception open M-Sa till 3am, Su till midnight. Live music on weekends. Restaurant attached.) **Pelican's Inn,** 143 the Esplanade, Wynnum (tel. 3396 3214), has two-bedroom units with bath, kitchen, dining area, and living room (weekly $280). Across the street is a huge saltwater wading pool, parks, and a pier extending into the bay.

Taking full advantage of its seaside locale, Moreton Bay eateries serve fish, fish, and fish. High-quality chippers run all along the Esplanade, with meals usually under $5. The **Fish Cafe** (tel. 3893 0195), at the corner of Cambridge Pde and the Esplanade in Manly, serves huge kangaroo and crocodile burgers ($4-6), fish and chips ($1.50-5), and large milkshakes ($2). The cafe terrace has lighter fare, while the front room boasts floor-to-ceiling picture windows showcasing the excellent harbor view.

SIGHTS AND ENTERTAINMENT

What Manly and Wynnum lack in nightlife they make up for in natural beauty. An hour's stroll along the Esplanade (through Wynnum, past the end of the harborwalk, through the soccer fields) leads to the **Wynnum Mangrove Boardwalk,** a 500m walk guided by informative signs. The mangroves grow in dense concentration and it's possible to see clearly their pneumatophores, specialized "breathing roots," protruding through the mud in small clumps. For the history buff, the Brisbane City Council's *Heritage Trail: Wynnum-Manly* booklet outlines a fascinating daytrip in the region.

Across the street from the Pelican's Nest is the huge **Wynnum tidal pool.** Because the muddy bay is unsuitable, people swim here instead. In the afternoons, some race model sailboats across the length. Parks with changing rooms, toilets, and barbecues run along the Esplanade. The Wynnum **public pool,** on the Esplanade, is open September to April from 8am to 7pm (admission $2, children $1.60). If sailing floats your boat, book a trip on **Solo** (tel. 3348 6100), a famous Australian ocean racing yacht (Th-Su). A daytrip ($55) includes snorkeling, swimming, sand tobogganing on Moreton Island, and water tobogganing. For free sailing, show up at noon on Wednesdays at The **Royal Queensland Sailing Club** (tel. 3396 8666). Yacht owners are always looking for temporary crew; if you are a beginner, they may teach you. **Ann's Fishing Charter** (tel. 3396 2194) operates daily offshore reef fishing trips.

■ North Stradbroke Island

A fierce cyclone in 1896 cleanly split the land mass once called Stradbroke Island. While South Stradbroke has remained relatively uninhabited, its northern neighbor is now home to 3500 people, mainly miners and their families. Many residents claim that "Straddie" is Australia's best-kept secret, and they have a valid case, what with miles of white beaches with great surf, famously blue inland lakes, and dive sites that some say compete with the Great Barrier Reef. Point Lookout, the easternmost point in Australia, is an ideal perch for whale-watching.

ORIENTATION AND PRACTICAL INFORMATION

North Stradbroke Island has three distinct townships: residential **Dunwich,** the ferry drop-off point; **Amity Point,** north of Dunwich and near great surfing beaches; and **Point Lookout,** 22km northeast of Dunwich, with two hostels. The southern end of the island is mostly lakes, swamps, national park land, and habitat reserves.

Despite its sense of isolation, North Stradbroke can be easily reached from Brisbane by public transportation. Take Citytrain to Cleveland; from there you have a couple of options. The courtesy bus **"Bessie"** will take you to the **Stradbroke Flyer** ferry (tel. 3286 1964), which departs for the island every 90 minutes between 8am and 6:30pm (also M-F 5:30am and Sept.-Apr. Su 6:30pm; $10 return). The **Stradbroke Water Taxi** (tel. 3286 2666) also provides an hourly courtesy bus to and from the train station (M-Th and Sa 6am-6pm, F 6am-7:15pm, Su 8am-6pm; $10 return). Both ferry trips are about 30 minutes each way. There is also a vehicle ferry (tel. 3286 2666) that leaves several times per day (1hr.; $45-69 return). Be sure to arrive early to load your vehicle.

The **North Stradbroke Island Bus Service** (tel. 3211 2501) runs between Point Lookout, Amity, and Dunwich 10 times per day; the tourist office carries schedules. During the day the **Stradbroke Island Taxi** (tel. 3409 9124) usually waits at the top of the hill, across from the bakery. Most **car rental** companies on the mainland will not rent vehicles to Stradbroke Island travelers because of problems with salt corrosion. The **tourist office** (tel. 3409 9555) is the yellow building with the green roof to the left and at the base of the Dunwich green. Its *What's on Where* guide is helpful. (Open M-F 8:30am-4:30pm, Sa-Su 8:30am-3:30pm.) Although there's no bank on the island, the three **post office** branches serve as **Commonwealth bank agents** and several shops have EFTPOS. Point Lookout has small **general stores,** but since most close by 6pm and are expensive, it's best to bring your own food.

ACCOMMODATIONS, FOOD, AND PUBS

The tourist office has brochures for several resorts, hotels, campgrounds, and hostels. The island has two good hostels, both in Point Lookout. **North Stradbroke Island Guesthouse** (tel. 3409 8888; fax 3409 8715) is a YHA affiliate on the left at the entrance to the Point Lookout area, close to Home Beach. Rooms are functional and tidy, with a huge shared kitchen and a game room. (Dorms $16; doubles and triples $38.) A shuttle bus departs from the Abbey Hotel, across from the Roma St Transit Center in Brisbane, and from the Brisbane City YHA (M, W, and F 2:30pm; $8). The Guesthouse has a dive centre attached to it, with equipment and lessons; book ahead.

The **Stradbroke Island Hostel**, 76 Mooloomba Rd (affectionately known as "Straddie Hostel"; tel. 3409 8679) is halfway between the Guesthouse and the end of Point Lookout. It's relaxed and much more communal than the Guesthouse, with a funky common room, a small, oldish kitchen, and purple bedrooms with ceiling fans. (Dorms $12, sectioned-off doubles $28; with deck $15, $30.)

Stradbroke Tourist Park (tel. 3409 8127) has a range of accommodations, including cabins with bath, A/C, and TV (1 person $38; weekly $239), tent sites (2 adults $10; weekly $57), and a backpackers' cabin ($10). The island also has six **campsites,** most of which have powered sites, toilets, showers, and caravan sites (around $10 per night). One of these, **Thankful Rest Caravan Park,** is near the Guesthouse.

The **Point Lookout Bowls Club** (tel. 3409 8182), a few minutes from the Guesthouse toward Point Lookout, is a popular place for cheap eats, with different specials each night. Uphill from the ferry landing at **Dunwich** is a small row of shops, including a bakery and a takeaway. Most food is in Point Lookout, clustered in the **Lookout Shopping Village** and **Centre Point Shopping Centre,** both along two main roads. The Straddie Hotel on East Coast Rd operates the **Waves Brasserie** (tel. 3409 8188; meals $5-15), which has live music on the weekends (open daily for lunch noon-2pm, dinner 5-8pm). The adjoining **Straddie Hotel Pub** is the main local hangout, and is packed on the weekends. **La Focaccia,** in the Shopping Village (tel. 3409 8778), has pizzas from $7 and filling pastas for $12. The **Laughing Buddha Cafe** (tel. 3409 8549), at the end of Mooloomba Rd, serves some of the island's best coffee and cake.

SIGHTS AND ACTIVITIES

The easiest and cheapest thing to do on North Stradbroke Island is walk—miles of unspoiled beaches, dirt roads, and seemingly unexplored bush will keep a spirited traveler busy for days. Heading toward the end of Point Lookout on the left is a "Beach Access" sign for **Frenchman's Beach,** a convenient starting point for any beach walk. Further up and near the RSL Club lies the entrance to the **Gorge Walk,** a 15-minute stroll along sea cliffs, famous for dolphin-spotting. The Gorge Walk also passes the **Blowhole,** so named because crashing waves are channeled up a narrow gorge and transformed into fountains of spray. A swimming lagoon 4.5km along the beach, past the RSL Club, makes a lovely day hike or picnic spot. On hot summer days, **Myora Springs,** the site of a one-day battle between Aboriginals and European soldiers, is a refreshing way to cool off. The tourist office also provides a trail map and guide for a rather interesting **historical walking tour** through the three townships.

The island may be best known for **scuba diving.** $35 buys an intro lesson and equipment rental from The **Stradbroke Island Scuba Center** (tel. 3409 8715; fax 3409 8588), below the Guesthouse. Daily trips to 15 sites leave at 9, 11:30am, and 2pm; there's a scuba tank for beginners to practice. *(Snorkeling $39; includes boat trip and gear.)*

For alternative adventures, **Island Boat Mine** (tel. 3409 8896) rents boats, and **Straddie Kites** (tel. 3409 8145) rents kites. The island's breezes make either a great choice. The **Eagle's Nest Ropes Course** costs $49 per half-day. *(Open Su-Tu 9am and 1pm.)* **Stradbroke Island Tours** (tel. 3409 8051) offers half-day 4WD tours of the island ($28). To tour with your own 4WD, buy a beach access permit from the tourist office. *($5 for 48hr., $10 per week.)* Local Aboriginal guides lead 90-minute walking tours along the **Goompi Trail** of Dunwich, pointing out and explaining bush tucker, bush medicine, and Aboriginal artifacts. *(M-F. $12, child $5. Call the tourist office to book.)*

■ Other Islands in Moreton Bay

The water near Brisbane is dotted with islands—Moreton, Coochiemudlo, Bribie, St. Helena, and the Bay Islands—that make popular daytrips. Cheap accommodation other than camping is sparse, but you only need a day to sample the islands' offerings: lots of pristine beach, good fishing and snorkeling, an occasional whale sighting, and some crafts. Despite **Moreton Island's** size—after Fraser, it's the largest sand island in the world—most of it is inaccessible national park, and what's left is dominated by the **Tangalooma Resort** (tel. 3258 6333), which offers day cruises with pick-up from the transit centre ($30, children $15). The **Stradbroke Flyer** (tel. 3286 1964) and the **Moreton Island Ferry** (tel. 3845 1000) also make stops at the island. Tangalooma and **Akarma** (tel. 3880 0477) each offer whale-watching cruises ($75, children $40). **Coochiemudlo Island** is a popular getaway for locals, with shops, restaurants, and occasional crafts markets. Both **Coochiemudlo Island Ferry Service** (tel. 3245 6280; 24hr. tel. 018 780 170) and the vehicle-bearing **Island Link Ferries** (tel. 0413 753 416) run regularly from Victoria Point Jetty. The **Coochie Island Bus Service** (tel. 015 113 686) will take you anywhere on the island ($1.50; tours $3.50). The Stradbroke Flyer runs here, too.

Bribie Island, closer to the Sunshine Coast and the only island accessible by car (45km north and 19km east of Brisbane), has a **tourist office** (tel. 3408 9026) just over the bridge from the mainland. Its sights are spread too far apart to be pedestrian-friendly, but vehicles give easy access to its parks, surfing, bowling, and historical sights. Bribie is separated from the mainland by **Pumicestone Passage,** a marine park teeming with mangroves, more than 350 species of birds, sea cows, turtles, and dolphins. The **Bay Islands** (in descending size order: Russell, Macleay, Lamb, Karragarra) are small, mostly uninhabited, and the definition of "getting away from it all." The islands offer picnic and barbecue facilities.

Finally, if you went to all these islands and figured out their dirty little secret—they're all pretty much the same—**St. Helena Island** offers a totally different experience. Once a violent criminals' prison akin to Álcatraz, St. Helena is no leisurely picnic spot. The **Cat-o'-Nine-Tails** vessel (tel. 3396 3994) offers day and night "tours" to the island—actors act out some of St. Helena's raunchier past over tea and scones and turn tourists into prisoners. (Day tour $30, concessions $25, children $15. Night tours available, but unsuitable for children. Cruises run from Manly about 4 days a week; call ahead for schedule and booking.) The Cat-o'-Nine-Tails also offers occasional rock-band cruises for $20. (Erratic schedule, call ahead.)

GOLD COAST

Gorgeous beaches, thumping nightclubs, excellent theme parks, and plenty of accommodations make the Gold Coast Australia's premier holiday destination. The region's permanent population of 390,000 triples to 1.2 million every summer as Australian and foreign tourists flock to the sun, sand, and parties. The term "Gold Coast" has a few possible origins, each of which addresses the its lure. Tourist officials say it's for the stretches of golden sand beaches; cynics point to high rises and tacky tinsel glitter; realists note the high concentration of visitors in their golden years, mainly in the towns north and south of pulsing Surfers Paradise. You can find personal space by the shore, but forget about it back in the grid. The little-explored but rewarding Gold Coast Hinterland, full of clean rustic towns and rainforested national parks, is a stark contrast from the unashamed artificiality of the coast. While some may find an extended stay culturally dulling, the glitz, noise, and tanning opportunities that comprise the Coast's siren song ensure that passing travelers will succumb, if only briefly, to the well-hyped thrill.

QUEENSLAND

■ Coolangatta and Tweed Heads

The twin towns of Tweeds Head, NSW and Coolangatta, Qld mark the state border and the southern end of the Gold Coast. Here, cars "watch out" for each other rather than adhere to the traffic laws of whichever state they're in at the moment, an example of the laid-back atmosphere of Coolie and Tweed. There are no tall buildings, and the beaches are sunny all day, unlike in Surfers. The Tweed-Coolangatta border is only really marked by discrepancies in daylight savings time, most notably at New Year's Eve, when eager partygoers and champagne lovers run across the street and ring in the new year twice. Not a bad place to spend the millennium eve.

ORIENTATION AND PRACTICAL INFORMATION

The state border divides the settlement down the length of **Dixon St,** which bends right into **Boundary St** and heads out onto the rounded peninsula. At the end of the peninsula is the infamous **Point Danger,** whose cliffs were responsible for the wreck of Captain Cook's ship. Some great beaches line the perimeter of Tweed Heads-Coolangatta, including the safe and sheltered **Rainbow Bay** to the north and **Flagstaff** and **Duranbah Beaches** to the southeast, the latter famous for its surfing. The main swimming beaches run along Marine Pde, Coolangatta's waterfront strip.

At the enormous, pink, spaceship-like Twin Towns Service Club, Boundary St turns into Griffith St, which passes the **Coolangatta Transit Center** (tel. 5536 1700) at the corner of Griffith and Warner St. Turn left at the club onto Tweed Heads' main drag, **Wharf St,** and walk two blocks to reach the **Tweed Heads Tourist Information Centre,** 4 Wharf St (tel. 5536 4244 or 1800 674 414; open M-F 9am-5pm, Sa 9am-3pm, Su 10am-3:30pm). Their *Tweed-Coolangatta Visitors Guide* is indispensible.

Greyhound, McCafferty's, and **Pioneer Motor Services** stop at the Coolangatta Coach Station on their Sydney-Brisbane service, but if you want to get to Surfers, you'll have to take **Coach Trans** (tel. 5588 8777), which honors McCafferty's passes and stops at the corner of Wharf and Bay St, Tweed; or **Surfside buslines** (tel. 13 12 30), which runs daily up the Gold Coast. A one-day unlimited travel pass on Surfside is $10, though you can buy sector tickets. For a **taxi,** call 5536 1144. For car rental, try **Tweed Auto Rentals** (tel. 5536 8000 or 1800 819 051; from $30), next to the tourist center, **Happy Day Car Rental,** 35 McLean St, Coolangatta (tel. 5536 8388; $20-50).

You, the Australian Cinema Stalker

Strike up the ABBA, put on your chunkiest heels, and dance your way through one of Australia's most popular movies. Fans of Australian cinema can relive the making of *Muriel's Wedding,* the 1994 Cannes Film Festival award-winner about a family living in Porpoise Spit—a pseudonym for Coolangatta. The Heslops are a real local family, and the movie's mall, motel, Chinese restaurant, and green skyscrapers are all real landmarks in the area.

Pines Mall, K.P. McGrath Dr off the Pacific Hwy, is the place to begin your whirlwind stalkfest. With judicious use of your VCR's freeze-frame button, you'll recognize the mall in the final scene. Don't bother asking the bookstore for a copy of the screenplay; they sold out long ago.

On the Beach Motel, 188 Marine Pde on Greenmount Beach, was brilliantly featured in the poignant honeymoon suite scene. True devotees will be devastated to learn that the last *Official Guest of Muriel's Wedding* T-shirt was recently sold, but the owners are eager to share in *Muriel* fanaticism. Scrutiny of the decor and swinging doors, however, reveals that the inside shots must have been filmed in a studio.

Rickshaw Room was the site of many an encounter between the family and the father's mistress. Intrepid investigation, though, uncovers a complicated chain of events: those scenes were actually filmed in the Oceanview Restaurant, on Griffith St, since converted into the Rang Mahal Indian restaurant.

or **Carter's Ampol** (tel. 5536 2806; from \$25), opposite Tweed Mall. Coolie's **post office** is across from Happy Day. **Woolworths** is in Tweed Mall on Wharf St.

ACCOMMODATIONS, FOOD, AND CLUBS

There are plenty of beds here; the cheapest are along the highway, particularly along Wharf St, where motels charge \$30 for a double.

⊛**Sunset Strip Budget Resort**, 199 Boundary St (tel. 5599 5517). Marvelous, with an enormous kitchen and outside pool. Huge, clean, nightclub-style lounges. Guests of all ages intermingle happily. Large yet incredibly cozy and personal. Thursday night \$4 barbecue. Reception open daily 7am-11pm. Singles \$30; twins or doubles \$40; triples \$60; quads \$70. Weekly: \$150; \$210; \$270; \$360.

Coolangatta YHA, 230 Coolangatta Rd (tel. 5536 7644), in Billinga. Near the airport, 3km north of Coolie. Clean, with large kitchen, laundry, pool, TV lounge. No alcohol allowed. Courtesy pick-up from bus stop with advance notice. Dorms \$14-15; twins \$16-17; families \$42-44. 7th night free. YHA nonmembers \$3 more.

Coolangatta Sands Hotel (tel. 5536 3066), at the corner of Griffith and McLean St, has decent above-pub rooms, a kitchen, and a nice porch. Overlooks noisy, bustling McLean St. Dorms \$15; singles \$20; doubles \$38.

Griffith St has a number of takeaways, including the popular **Coolangatta Pie Shop** (pies \$1-2; tel. 5536 1980; open Su-Th 5am-late, F-Sa 24hr.). The **Coolangatta Hotel** is a very popular beachside bar and bistro by the beach on Marine Pde, with karaoke on Mondays. Casino games and cheap bistro food are found in the area's big clubs, including the **Twin Towns Service Club** (tel. 5536 2277), the **Bowls Club** in both Tweed Heads (tel. 5536 3800) and South Tweed (tel. 5524 3655), and **Seagulls Rugby League Football Club** (tel. 5536 3433), on Gellan Dr in Tweed Heads West. All of these clubs (except Bowls) dispatch large roving shuttle buses for courtesy pick-up; call them for times and schedules.

SIGHTS AND ACTIVITIES

You'll trip over kangaroos, emus, and gorgeous exotic birds at the fabulous **Currumbin Sanctuary** (tel. 5534 1266), 6km north along the Pacific Hwy. See the famous lorikeet feedings (8am and 4pm daily), but be sure to duck. There's a working **chocolate factory** across the road. Entrance is free but, alas, not the chocolate.

Two companies run Tweed River cruises. **Tweed Adventure Cruises** (tel. 018 757 748) specializes in small, environmentally focused tours. *(90min. cruise \$20, children and backpackers \$15; 8 people max.)* **Tweed Endeavor Cruises** (tel. 5536 8800) leads river

Sunshine Coast & Gold Coast

N

Noosa
Nambour
Maroochydore
Caloundra
Kilcoy
Bribie Island
Caboolture
Redcliffe
Moreton Island
Esk
Moreton Bay
Brisbane
Manly
54
North Stradbroke Island
Ipswich
Beenleigh
QUEENSLAND
Southport
Surfers Paradise
Coolangatta
15
Tweed Heads
MT. WARNING N.P.
Murwillumbah
NEW SOUTH WALES
Mullumbimby
Bangalow
Byron Bay
BROKEN HEAD N.P.
Lismore
Casino
Lennox Head
Ballina

Sunshine Coast

Gold Coast

QUEENSLAND

and rainforest cruises on a 150-person double-decker vessel. *(90min. cruise W, F, and Su afternoons $22; 4hr. with barbecue lunch M, W, and F $38; 4hr. with seafood lunch T, Th $48.)*

■ Surfers Paradise

Surfers is like any good dance floor: packed, loud, and shaking, with a groove that tempts everyone around it to join in the fun. Hotel towers stand high and close together, blocking out unlucky neighbors' sunlight and creating an oddly sci-fi atmosphere of extremes. Lightbulb-framed storefronts packed along a narrow urban strip hug miles of gorgeous beach and rippling waves. A huge Australian family resort and an enormous draw for Japanese tourists, Surfers also appears on nearly every backpacker's itinerary for two reasons: sleepy days at the beach and wave-crashing nightlife. Clubs throb with techno, and 5am closing times often just transfer the parties into the street. Yeah, there's the rest of Australia—but for those content to sink into the hedonism of neon-streaked nightclubs or dazzling Pacific waters, Surfers is a self-contained Paradise.

ORIENTATION AND PRACTICAL INFORMATION

Maps of Surfers Paradise are long and narrow and reflect the fact that the entire culture is squeezed into a strip many kilometers long and just a few blocks wide between the Pacific Ocean and the **Nerang River.** Three main avenues run parallel to the shore: the **Esplanade,** which skirts the beach; the **Gold Coast Hwy,** a block over; and Ferny Ave, one more block in. Central Surfers is marked by the **Paradise Centre** pedestrian shopping mall, enclosed by the Esplanade and the highway, **Cavill Mall** to the north and **Hanlan St** to the south. The Esplanade continues north past **Main Beach** to the **Marina** and **the Spit,** the end of a peninsula of land just past Seaworld. To the south is **Broadbeach,** home to the enormous Conrad Hotel Jupiter Casino and directly across Hooker Blvd from the monolithic **Pacific Fair Shopping Centre.**

Tourist Office: Gold Coast Tourism Bureau (tel. 5538 4419; fax 5570 3259) is an outside kiosk on Cavill Mall. Their **Backpackers Information Centre** (tel. 5592 2911) arranges hostel pick-up (open daily 5am-10pm). After hours, info and a direct phone to area hostels are still available. Pick up the free booklet *Point Out.*

Intercity Buses: Surfers Paradise Bus Station, or the Transit Centre, is at the corner of Beach Rd and Remembrance Dr, 1 block west of Paradise Centre. **McCafferty's** (tel. 5538 2700) runs to Byron Bay (2hr.; 2 per day; $18) and Sydney (16hr.; 3 per day; $71, students $64). Booth open daily 7:30am-9:30pm. **Coachtrains** (tel. 5588 8777) runs frequently to Brisbane (1½hr.; 30 per day; $12). Booth open daily 5:30am-8pm. **Greyhound** (tel. 5531 6677; 24hr. tel. 13 20 30) services Brisbane (1½hr.; 6 per day; $14, students $12); Cairns (30hr.; 3 per day; $165, students $132); Byron Bay (2hr.; 3 per day; $18, students $15); Sydney (15hr.; 3 per day; $71, students $57). Booth open daily 8am-5pm. There are also **luggage storage lockers** at the bus terminal ($4 per 12hr.). Available 5am-10pm.

Local Buses: Surfside (tel. 5536 7666; info 5526 8240), the local 24hr. bus company, runs every 10min. from the back of the Pacific Fair mall to Surfers for $1.70. Unlimited 1-day passes $10, 3-day $16, 7-day $30. **CoachTrans** (tel. 5592 3488) also provides bus services. Call 13 12 30 for general local bus and train info.

Taxis: Regent Taxis (tel. 13 10 08).

Car Rental: Kangaroo Car Hire, 18-20 Orchid Ave (tel. 5592 1788). Cars from $31, with free pick-up and delivery. Accepts under-21 renters; call 5570 1300. Moped rental for 2hr. $25, 4hr. $35, full-day $50. **Thrifty** (tel. 5538 6511) rents from $29. **Betta Rent A Car,** 108 Ferny Ave (tel. 5538 5559), has new cars from $25.

Newsagent: Paradise Centre Newsagency (tel. 5570 2126). Open daily 5:30am-9pm.

Laundry: Surfers Paradise Laundrette (tel. 5592 0896), across from the bus station. Wash $3. Dry $1 per 10min. Open daily 6am-8pm.

Emergency: Dial 000.

Medical Services: The **medical center** (tel. 5539 8044) is on Trickett St. **Gold Coast Hospital** (tel. 5571 8211). **Paradise Centre Pharmacy,** Shop 230, Paradise Centre (tel. 5570 2329). Open daily M-F 8:30am-9pm, Sa-Su 9am-6pm.

Police: 68 Ferny Ave (tel. 5570 7888), opposite the Cypress Ave carpark.

Post Office: Main branch is inside the Cavill Mall. Open M-F 8:30am-5:30pm, Sa 9am-noon. **Postal Code:** 4217.

Internet: Reef Bar Cafe in lobby of **Hotel Beachcomber** (tel. 5570 1000). $3 per 15min., $10 per hr. Open 7am-10pm.

Phone Code: 07.

ACCOMMODATIONS

In Surfers, hostel owners assume the roles of camp counselors, leading the troop every day to a new regimen of activities: bungee jumping, cheap meals, and pub crawls. There are even inter-hostel competitions, except if you win, instead of an ice cream party you get a nasty hangover. Go get 'em, boys and girls. If you were never a panty raid fan and didn't come to party, either skip town or seek quieter digs at highway motels, with doubles from $30. Summer and Easter are peak season—book ahead.

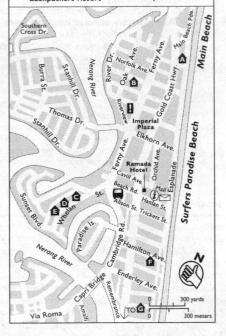

Surfers Paradise

ACCOMMODATIONS
B Cheers Backpackers
E Couple O' Days Backpackers
F Mardi Gras International Backpackers Resort
D Sleeping Inn Surfers
C Surfers Central Backpackers
G Surfers Paradise Backpackers
A Surf 'n' Sun Backpackers

Surfers Paradise Backpackers Resort, 2837 Gold Coast Hwy (tel. 5592 4677), a good 30min. walk south along the highway to the corner of Wharf Rd, in front of the Parkroyal Hotel. A miniature tennis court serves as sports arena and meeting place at this carefree, happy hostel. Many who've come for a night have become staff and stayed on for a year. Big kitchen, TV room, dorms with private bath. Everything's spotless. The games room has a new nautilus weight machine, a pool table, and a sauna ($4 per 45min). Internet access. Dorms $16; doubles $36. Weekly: $107; $125. YHA, VIP. Book 1-2 weeks in advance in summer. Beautifully kept, inexpensive self-contained apartments also available.

Sleeping Inn Surfers, 26 Whelan St (tel. 5592 4455). Immaculate and mellow, dodging the party scene. Spacious self-contained 4-person dorm units with central kitchens and small living rooms with TVs. Palm trees line the grounds. Covered outdoor common area has pool table and barbecue. Dorms $16, weekly $98; doubles $40. Singles with shared kitchen $30; doubles $37. VIP, YHA, ISIC.

Mardi Gras International Backpackers Resort, 28 Hamilton Ave (tel. 5592 5888; fax 5538 9310), the newest hostel in Surfers and a very short walk to the beach. A tad sterile, but likely to mature with age. The only hostel with a restaurant, it has hotel-like amenities and atmosphere. Spic-and-span but tiny rooms, all with a veranda. Dorms $18; doubles $22; twins $20. $2 discount on second night.

Trekkers, 22 White St (tel. 5591 5616), near Southport's Australia Fair shopping complex. Walk north from Surfers for 45min., crossing the bridge on the highway and turning left at Scarborough St in Southport, or pay $1.90 for the bus. 10-15min.

QUEENSLAND

from Main Beach. Though the distance lives up to its name, there's frequent hostel-provided transportation and a staff so friendly you won't care. Lovely outdoor pool and patio, cozy common areas, and near-nightly feedings ensure that you'll get to know everyone. Spotless rooms with private baths. Reception open daily 7am-noon and 5-7:30pm. Dorms $15; doubles $32. Weekly: $85; $190. VIP, YHA.

Surf 'n' Sun, 3323 Gold Coast Hwy (tel. 5592 2363 or 5538 7305), 4 blocks toward Southport on the corner of Ocean Ave. One block from the beach. Diminutive, with a comfortable, party-oriented atmosphere. Pool. Unrefurbished dorm rooms have bathrooms, sink, TV, and fridge. Dorms $16, weekly $98; doubles $39. VIP.

British Arms International Backpackers Resort (YHA), 70 Seaworld Dr (tel. 5571 1776 or 1800 680 269; fax 5571 1747), 30min. north of Surfers on the way to Seaworld, inside Mariner's Cove on the Spit. On the water at Fisherman's Wharf. Rooms are clean and bare. Outdoor deck, functional common room with TV, kitchen facilities. 6-bed dorms $15, weekly $96; doubles $32. VIP, YHA. Their pub, across the street, gives daily happy hour drinks and $3 meal discounts to guests.

Couple O' Days Backpackers, 18 Whelan St (tel. 5592 4200 or 1800 646 586). A little worn around the edges but with a quiet, focused atmosphere. Small kitchen, TV lounge. 6-bed dorms $12; doubles $28. Weekly: $70; $168. YHA, VIP.

Our Backpackers in Paradise, 40 Whelan St (tel. 5538 4344), 2 blocks down Whelan St off Ferny Ave. The closest hostel to the city center, but a little low on atmosphere. Staff's helpful, kitchen's large, pool's big, but the centerpiece is a car-park. A converted squash court makes for a decent recreation area. Bar, Internet access. 8- and 4-bed dorms with bath $15; doubles $36. Nomads, VIP.

FOOD

Surfers has dozens of inexpensive cafes, bistros, and Asian restaurants, and offers good deals on hotel buffet meals. **Tamal's Vegetarian Cafe** (tel. 5538 6299) on Orchid Ave has big healthy sandwiches, burgers, salads, and vegetarian meals ($4-8; open daily 8am-5:30pm). The **Cavill Ave Mall** has two all-you-can-eat Chinese restaurants with $7 meals. A couple of good seafood takeaways near the Spit on Seaworld Dr warrant a visit. **Peter's Fisherman's Markets** (tel. 5591 7747) sells fresh and cooked fish from the wharf; a fish and chips takeaway is $5 (open M-F 8:30am-8pm, Sa-Su 8am-8pm; cooked fish available noon-8pm). **Peter's Fish and Chips** (tel. 5531 0077), in Mariner's Cove on the Spit, also has $5 takeaway until 5pm and a small buffet-style seafood option.

Tedder Ave on Main Beach is jammed with slightly more expensive cafes, bistros, and bakeries. **Take Out on Tedder** (tel. 5532 0004) has big, healthy sandwiches and burgers ($5-7). **Ziggie's Café and Wine Bar** (tel. 5528 0388) has wintertime 2-for-1 lunches (Tu-Sa only; meals ordinarily $9-20). In addition, nearly every beach on the Gold Coast has a **Surf Life Saving Club (SLSC)** and an **RSL Club,** where guests can eat cheap meals and play pokies. The **Palm Beach SLSC** (tel. 5534 2180), off the highway on Jefferson Ln between Surfers and Coolangatta, has meals for $3-7, a courtesy bus, and a beautiful terrace overlooking the beach. The **RSL Club** in Southport, at the corner of Scarborough and White St, has cheap meals and $2 cooked breakfasts on the weekends. Across from the British Arms hotel, brightly colored **Frenchy's Seafood Restaurant** (tel. 5531 3030) sits right on the water. Take out fish and chips for $7 or sit down to a slightly more expensive meal (open M-S noon-3pm and 5:30-9pm, Su noon-9pm).

SIGHTS AND ACTIVITIES

A typical day at Surfers is spent lazing on the beach, raising adrenaline on thrill rides in town or at one of the nearby huge theme parks, or spending money in the enormous mall complexes. Tours visit scenery away from the coast, and a couple of museums entertain visitors on the odd rainy day or when beach burnout strikes suddenly.

Beaches, Surfing, and Water Sports

The beach stretches unbroken from the quiet **Main Beach** on the Spit peninsula to Duranbah. There is little consensus on which are the best beaches to surf, except that all are great, but none is particularly suited to the unguided novice. Nevertheless, beginners and regulars alike should do fine if they ask around first, since weather conditions significantly alter an area's quality and level of danger. The most popular beach is **Surfers North,** near the end of Staghorn Ave and just north of **Surfers Paradise,** the most central hangout off the Paradise Centre Mall and the recipient of blaring music from the local radio station during the summer. Farther south is **Broadbeach,** then **Kurrawa,** near the Pacific Fair Shopping Center. **Burleigh Heads** has a popular surfing area, though it can be mobbed and often has dangerous breaks.

Separated from the Spit by a small channel, **South Stradbroke Island** is an undeveloped 20km strip of sand. Two-person sites at Corrigee Campground cost $11 ($2 per extra person). Alternatively, it makes a lovely trip for a day or an hour, with wonderful, uncrowded surfing. The **Broadwater Ferry** (tel. 5575 8136) leaves from Fisherman's Wharf on the Spit. *(Every ½ hr. M-F 6am-1pm, Sa-Su 6am-4pm. $6 return, family $20.)*

For equipment, try the **Surfers Beach Hut** kiosk (tel. 5526 7077) on the beach end of Cavill Mall. *(Open daily 8:30am-4pm. Long boards $15 per hr., $25 per day. Short boards, in-line skates, or mountain bikes $10 per hr., $20 per day.)* They also have timed safety lockers. **Dial-A-Sports** (tel. 018 764 170) has slightly cheaper prices and free delivery and pick-up. *(Open daily 8am-7pm.)* Both companies also rent flippers and wetsuits. The **Marine Sports Club** (tel. 5526 7077) at the Surfers Beach Club House in Cavill Mall also rents and delivers equipment. **Coast to Coast Surfing School** (tel. 5536 9881) and **Surfers Paradise Surfing School** (tel. 5531 3252) have daily learn-to-surf classes. **Cable Sports World** (tel. 5537 6300) offers waterskiing ($30) bungee jumping ($69) and jet skiing ($39); buy their Gold Card for $5 and get a 25 percent discount.

Theme Parks and Thrill Rides

Dreamworld (tel. 5573 3300 or 1800 073 300), in Coomera, a 25-minute drive from Surfers, trumpets its "Tower of Terror," the tallest, fastest ride in the world. *(Park open daily 9:30am-5:30pm. $41, concessions and ages 4-13 $24; 14-day return transport pass $10.)* It shoots forward at up to 160 kph, then straight up 38 stories, and then straight down again, all in a matter of seconds. The rest of the park is an assortment of rides, an IMAX theater, a fauna reserve, and an interactive tiger attraction.

On hot summer days the whitewater flumes of **Wet 'n' Wild** water park (tel. 5573 2277) will cool you down. *(Open daily from 10am; closing times vary. $21, children $15.)* Other attractions include dry courts for volleyball and soccer, a giant 60kph speed slide, and on summer nights, a movie screen above a wave pool with new release screenings. **Seaworld,** near the Spit north of Surfers on Seaworld Dr, has lots of fish, dolphins, a very funny sea lion show, sharks, seals, some sad-looking pigeons, and a few rides. *(Open daily 10am-5pm. $41, ages 4-13 $26; or for 2 days, $61.50 and $39 respectively.)* For extra money, you can also swim with dolphins in the new Dolphin Cove.

Several companies offer **transportation** to the theme parks. The cheapest is **Surfside** (tel. 13 12 30); return transport is free if you buy the ticket on the bus. **Activetours** (tel. 5597 0344) and the **Gold Coast Tourist Shuttle** (tel. 5592 4166) also have transfers to theme parks for $12 (children $6 and $7, respectively). Book ahead.

Bungee Down Under, at Fisherman's Wharf on the Spit (tel. 5531 1103), gives you the options of hitting the water and jumping in pairs. *(Open 10am-5pm.)* There's **indoor rock climbing** for $20 in Burleigh Heads (tel. 5593 6917). Take the #7 or #25 bus from Pacific Fair. Several other **thrill rides,** including various forms of bungee jumping and virtual reality rides, share a small plot of grass borded by the Gold Coast Hwy, Ferny Ave, Palm Ave, and Cypress Ave. *(Most open daily 10am-10pm. $5-25.)*

Museums and Free Beer

The **Ripley's Believe It or Not** museum (tel. 5592 0040), in the Cavill Mall, has the usual optical illusions, magic tricks, and tales of the gross and macabre. *(Open daily 9am-11pm. $10, children $6.50; family discount 10% if you ask for it.)* The **Wax Museum,**

3049 Gold Coast Hwy (tel. 5538 3975), between Hanlan and Trickett St, has a decent collection of "famous people," fantasy figures, and, for a separate fee, a "chamber of horrors" documenting historical methods of torture. (*Open daily 10am-10pm. Admission $8.50, children $5.50, families $15.*) More traditional art, including films and a free **gallery** (tel. 5581 6520), resides at the **Gold Coast Arts Centre,** 135 Bundall Rd (tel. 5581 6800), 3km from the city center (open M-F 10am-5pm, Sa-Su 1-5pm). The **Carlton Brewery** (tel. 3826 5858), in Yatala, a 35-minute drive north of Surfers, has three tours a day ($7.50) and free tastings. CoachTrans departs Surfers at 9am and 1:40pm for the brewery.

Shopping

The massive commercial centers of Surfers Paradise elevate shopping beyond the practical. Surfers Central has many international shops, especially duty-free stores geared toward Japanese tourists. The enormous **Pacific Fair Mall** (tel. 5539 8766), on the corner of the highway and Hooker Blvd, in Broadbeach, houses over 260 stores. Some hostels, like the Resort, hand out discount vouchers which can be used for 10% off at many of the stores. Southport's **Australia Fair** is a bit smaller, yet still intimidatingly large. Many stores have sales in July, at the end of their financial year.

ENTERTAINMENT

Aside from partying and drinking, the main nighttime activity in Surfers seems to be getting the best deals on partying and drinking. Most of the hostels provide free passes and cheap meal tickets at the several clubs, and the Wednesday and Saturday night **club crawl** can be hard to avoid. Most of the clubs are around Cavill Mall, many on Orchid Ave; all are open until 5am. Bring your passport, as some clubs won't accept other forms of ID. On the crawl, a double-decker bus goes from hostel to hostel and club to club to club for $10, which includes free entry to the clubs and free drinks at the first two. An additional $8 will buy you four more drinks at **Kokoz,** the first stop, a popular club in Broadbeach by the Oasis Hotel. Then it's off to **Shooters** (tel. 5592 1144), a saloon-style club replete with bulls' heads and a pool-table area. Shooters also has $4 Thursday night dinners and free all-you-can-eat Sunday night buffets. **Cocktails and Dreams** (tel. 5592 1955) hosts the extremely popular 70s night on Tuesdays, when hostel guests painstakingly attire themselves in hostel-provided retro garb, as well as "Monday Monster Madness," a series of inter-hostel games.

The **Rose and Crown** (tel. 5531 5425), at Raptis Plaza in the Cavill Mall, has happy hour nightly until 10pm and sometimes live bands, usually grunge (W and F-Su). They give three free drinks on pub crawl nights. **Melba's,** 46 Cavill Ave (tel. 5538 7411), a more upmarket nightclub, grooves to mainstream and techno dance music on Friday and Saturday nights (dressy, 21-plus). For blues, try the **Doghouse Blues Bar & Grill** (tel. 5526 9000) in Broadbeach, a restaurant with live entertainment most nights. The **Bourbon Bar** on Caville Ave has a mix of music styles and a happy dance floor on Tuesday nights. It's popular with locals and Asian tourists. **M.P.,** or the **Meeting Place** (tel. 0411 220 284), on the first floor of the Paradise Centre, is Surfers' only **gay club.**

High rollers try their luck at **Conrad Jupiters Casino** (tel. 5592 1133 or 1800 074 144), one of Australia's largest gaming houses and a Broadbeach landmark. Over 1000 gaming machines echo with the clicks of coins and chips 24 hours a day. (Free gaming instructions Tu-Sa noon to 8pm.) **Funtasia Time Zone** in Paradise Centre (tel. 5539 9500) has a huge array of games, rides, and machines for the kiddies.

■ Gold Coast Hinterland

The area to the west of the Gold Coast, within easy reach of Surfers, Coolangatta, or Brisbane, contains an array of pleasant, laid-back towns and lovely national parks affording plenty of hiking and swimming opportunities. Several companies provide tours of the region. **Mountain Coach Company** (tel. 5524 4249) has a bus tour of **Lamington National Park, Mt. Tamborine,** the **botanic gardens,** and the famous **O'Reilly's Guesthouse.** Along the way, you'll stop for morning tea, see an army base, and visit an arrowroot mill. Tours leave Coolangatta, Burleigh, and Surfers. ($35, pick-up included, children $17.) **Scenic Hinterland Bus Tours** (tel. 5545 2030) provides a similar tour ($29 including pick-up; wheelchair accessible) to Lamington, O'Reilly's Guesthouse, and Mt. Tamborine. At O'Reilly's, you can walk above the rainforest canopy and cover yourself with crimson rosellas. These tours are popular among families and older travelers. The guesthouse gained at least part of its fame from the storybook heroism of **Bernard O'Reilly,** who single-handedly discovered and rescued two of the three survivors of the Stinson airliner crash of 1937. The bushwalking tours to Lamington and the Natural Arch are particularly popular with backpackers. Tours include a barbecue lunch with lots of wine ($23, free pick-up from hostels). Book through your hostel.

The 200 square kilometers of **Lamington National Park** are fairly easy to get to from Surfers, Coolangatta or Murwillumbah, NSW. The park's well-trod paths lead to spectacular 150m waterfalls, clear springs, and subtropical rainforest. There are two sections of the park: **Binna Burra** (ranger tel. 5533 3584) and **Green Mountains** (ranger tel. 5544 0634), each with a guesthouse and camping.

■ Tamborine National Park

If you finally want to face up to that irrational fear of lizards, check out the ones at Tamborine National Park, which preserves patches of subtropical rainforest around the Tamborine plateau. It's just an hour's drive southwest from Brisbane or west from the Gold Coast, the downside of which is the constant flow of visitors. The town of Mt. Tamborine offers Devonshire tea houses, B&Bs, and pottery shops. Luckily, most of the visitors don't venture far beyond these, and if you set out on the trails, especially on a weekday, you'll enjoy this magic place in relative solitude.

To get to the park, exit the **Pacific Hwy** (1) at Oxenford and follow the steep, twisting **Oxenford-Tamborine Rd;** you'll need to use low gear. Near the highway exit, check out the **Russel Hinze Park,** a swamp and island refuge for various water birds. As you approach the plateau, the road secretly changes its name to MacDonnell Rd. Turn right onto Long Rd, then right at the roundabout, and left at the Geissman Dr to find the **Tamborine Natural History Information Centre** (tel 5545 3200), located in Doughby Park. The enthusiastic staff provides a useful map and park routes leaflet.

Tamborine is better as a daytrip, since beds are costly. **St. Berdard's Hotel,** 101 Alpine Tce (tel 5545 1177; fax 5543 2733) is a nice enough pubstay with daily lorikeet and kookaburra feedings (singles $45, twins $70, triples $90; breakfast included). The **Cedar Creek Lodge** (tel 5545 1468; fax 5545 2707) offers affordable camping, a cafe, and a rock pool (tent sites $6 per person, powered $7). From the plateau, descend upon Cedar Creek by Tamborine Mt. Rd. From the Pacific Hwy, exit at Beneleigh and follow the Beaudesert-Beneleigh Rd to Tamborine Mt. Rd.

The 3km (1hr.) **Witches Falls Walking Track** runs along the western side of the plateau. It is stunning at points, though you'll see more backyard than rainforest at the beginning and you may blink back tears when you see some of the gutted former forest below. In addition to strangler figs, banksia, and eucalypts, you're likely to spy plenty of the park's native lizards. The **Beacon Road Track** passes the Witches Falls as well, but continues along the cliff past red cedar trees. The 4km one-way walk ends at Beacon Rd, 3km from the Witches Falls Picnic Area carpark. The **Palm Grove** section is also very interesting. You can access it via either Palm Grove Ave or Curtis Rd, which begins near the tourist office off Geissman Dr. **Jeny's Falls Circuit** (5.4km) branches off the **Palm Grove Circuit** (2.6km) and passes through several different types of vegetation.

■ Springbrook National Park

At any turn of the path at Springbrook, you may happen upon a waterfall more magnificent than the last. The cool, green rainforest is filled with natural rock pools, stranglers, rock cliffs, and overpowering views. The park has three sections: **Springbrook Plateau, Natural Bridge,** and **Mt. Cougal,** all of which are easily accessible from the

QUEENSLAND

Gold Coast and Northeast NSW. To reach Springbrook from Surfers Paradise, take the Gold Coast Hwy south and turn right onto the Nerang-Broadbeach Rd. Follow the signs for Springbrook and the Pacific Hwy; exit the Pacific Hwy at the Springbrook/ Mudgeraba turnoff. Springbrook Rd runs 22km to the park; it is steep, windy, and only one lane wide in some parts. On the way up, check out the view at the **Murwumba Lookout.** The unattended **Info Centre,** a bit farther up, has color maps of the many walks, lookouts, and camping and picnic areas. Continuing along the Springbrook Rd to the **Tallambara Picnic Area** will lead you to the fabulous **Warrie Circuit** (15km) and the **Twin Falls Circuit** (4km). The Warrie leads through rock wedge caves and behind, around, and beneath many waterfalls.

Springbrook's most popular sight is the **Natural Arch,** about 1km from the car-park, 3km north of the New South Wales border. The arch, also called Natural Bridge, is a gorgeous cavern with a waterfall created by the force of heavy boulders and con-stantly flowing water breaking through the hardened lava. At night, the cavern comes alive with bats and **glow-worms.** The 4km **Purling Brook Falls Trail,** about 17km north of the Natural Arch, is highlighted by the eerie beauty and sound of the cascad-ing Purling Brook Falls. The Springbrook **ranger** can be reached at 5533 5147. **Lodging** and **food** can be found in **Springbrook village,** about 35km east of the arch.

■ Currumbin Rock Pool & Mt. Cougal National Park

Just a half hour from the Gold Coast and tucked away in the town of Currumbin are three natural pools with cliff jumps. Signs from the Pacific Hwy between Burleigh Heads (just south of Surfers) and Coolangatta direct you to both via **Currumbin Creek Rd.** After about 10 minutes you arrive at the **Currumbin Rock Pool,** a deep freshwater pool with short cliff dives and smaller pools for lounging above and beneath short falls.

Travel another 6km along Currumbin Creek Rd to reach **Mt. Cougal National Park.** A 500m walk to **Cougal Cascades** take you into the rainforest to a **natural water slide** that only very daring folks attempt. Not much farther along the same path is another natural pool with a much higher jump than those at the Currumbin Rock Pool. **Use caution** and common sense at all of these risky attractions, and obey posted warnings.

SOUTHERN AND DARLING DOWNS

West of the Great Dividing Range lie the hills and vales of the Southern Downs, and the towns of Toowoomba, Warwick, and Stanthorpe. Travelers are likely to pass through Toowoomba only to change buses, but Warwick and Stanthorpe are located in the most fertile agricultural region of the state and are therefore popular with back-packers looking for seasonal work. Fruit-picking work is available almost year-round at a going rate of $9-10 an hour; jobs are 40 hours a week and last from two weeks to two months. Work permits are required in theory, though enforcement varies in practice. For those coming to the Downs with time to spare, Giraween and Sundown National Parks please visitors with their wildflower displays (seasonal, of course), granite outcroppings, and spectacular views. Stanthorpe is also the center of Queens-land's only wine region, the Granite Belt, and free tastings are easy to find. The high-way transects the region and crosses the border south into the New England region (see p. 185) of New South Wales.

▓ Toowoomba

Somewhere between urban sprawl and country town, Toowoomba (pop. 93,000) has the frustrations of both and the seductions of neither. Still, as home to the McCaf-ferty's bus line headquarters, it's a major transportation hub. If you do stay in Too-

Cold Enough to Freeze the Balls Off a Brass Monkey

In June, July, and August, the Darling Downs area flaunts its refreshingly chilly climate with the **Brass Monkey** season. The annual celebration has a colorful history: sailing ships used to have a brass rack, called a "monkey," to hold cannon balls. During winter, the rainwater that collected in the monkey would freeze and expand, forcing the balls off the rack. Hence the expression "cold enough to freeze the balls off a brass monkey."

woomba for longer than a bus transfer takes, you won't want to spend long in the town itself—surrounding it, the lush mountains of the Great Dividing Range beckon.

The drive to Toowoomba along the Warrego Hwy from Brisbane (100min.) is a gorgeous, windy mountain ascent. At the top, a left turn will take you to **James St** and a right to **Margaret St;** most of the town lies in the few square blocks between. The **tourist office,** 86 James St (tel. 4693 3797), is one of the prettiest buildings in town and has a useful computerized city info guide. The **post office** (tel. 4632 9888) is at the corner of Neil and Margaret St. **Commonwealth Bank** is at the corner of Russell and Ruthren. **McCafferty's Bus Terminal** is at 28-30 Neil St. (tel. 4690 9888; open daily 4am-9:15pm). Buses run frequently to Brisbane and Rockhampton.

Caravan parks are the best budget deal in Toowoomba. **Jolly Swagman Caravan Park,** 47 Kitchener St (tel. 4632 8735), is a short walk from the tourist office (tent sites $10; on-site vans $25). **Gowrie House YWCA,** 112 Mary St (tel. 4632 2642), has an extra-friendly staff and clean, simple rooms in a quiet setting a short walk from town. (Singles $20 for international travelers; doubles $35. Breakfast and train station pick-up included.) Most of Toowoomba's restaurants are around Margaret St. The **Hog's Breath Cafe,** at the corner of Neil and Bell St (tel. 4639 1400), is a typical saloon-style bar and grill with huge portions (meals $7-$20). Book ahead; it gets extremely crowded. The **High Court Cafe,** 169 Margaret St (tel. 4632 4747) combines poker and a pub with fireside gourmet elegance (meals $10-20; open late).

■ Near Toowoomba: Warwick

The second-oldest town in Queensland (pop. 25,000), **Warwick** is mainly known for its annual **rodeo**—Australia's most famous—which comes to town every October as the culminating event in the month's **Rose and Rodeo Festival.** Call the Warwick **tourist information office,** 49 Albion St (tel. 4661 3122), for more information (open M-F 9am-5pm, Sa 10am-3pm). If you need to stay, the **Kahler's Oasis Caravan Park** (tel. 4661 2874), 1km south of Warwick on the New England Hwy, has tent sites for $11, powered sites for $13, and cabins for $35-45.

In August, the **Australian Heritage Festival** (tel. 4692 2229), about 45 minutes west of Toowoomba at the Jondaryan Woodshed in Darling Downs, allows you to spend nine days reliving the pioneer days, complete with shearing and saddlemaking.

■ Stanthorpe

Easily missed on the New England Highway, Stanthorpe (pop. 10,000) is a small, rustic town that used to thrive on the tin industry. Now, its cool, crisp climate and location in the heart of Queensland's best wine country has made it a year-round destination for many Brisbane residents. The town is also an ideal base for exploring the granite formations and wildflowers of the surrounding national parks, Sundown and Girraween.

ORIENTATION AND PRACTICAL INFORMATION

Coming in from Warwick off the New England Hwy, Stanthorpe's main street, **High St,** turns into **Maryland St** as it bends south in the center of town, and then into **Wallangarra Rd** two blocks later at the Quart Pot Creek. It then merges back into the New England Hwy about 30 minutes north of Tenterfield, NSW. The **bus station** is at the corner of Maryland and Folkestone St. The **tourist office** (tel. 4681 2057) is located by the bridge at Quart Pot Creek (open M-F 8:45am-5pm, Sa 10am-1pm). At the bend on Maryland St. you'll find **ATMs** at the National and Commonwealth **banks** (open M-Th 9:30am-4pm, F 9:30am-5pm). Across the street from the banks sits the large **post office** (tel. 4681 2181; open M-F 9am-5pm). There is a large **Woolworths** grocery store in the mall at the corner of High and Lock St and a smaller **Cut Price** at 144 High St.

ACCOMMODATIONS AND FOOD

Stanthorpe has many motels, a caravan park, and over a dozen more expensive B&Bs and inns. The cheapest ($15-30 per person) and most central accommodation options are in the nearly indistinguishable pub hotels clustered on Maryland St. The rooms are clean and have sinks; most also have a TV lounge upstairs and a fireplace room downstairs. The best of the bunch is **Hotel Stanthorpe** (tel. 4681 2099), at the corner of Lock and High St. The bathrooms and hallways are a bit cleaner, the staff a bit nicer, and the price includes continental breakfast in its well-stocked kitchen. (Singles $20; doubles $40; family rooms $50.) **Top of the Town Caravan Park,** 10 High St (tel. 4681 4888), a 15-minute walk from the town center, has campsites ($7 per person) and hostel beds ($14). They arrange fruit- and vegetable-picking work and offer transport to the farms. The cheapest motel is the **Boulevard Motel,** 76 Maryland St (tel. 4681 1777), next to Quart Pot Creek. Most rooms have a TV, VCR, toaster, and fridge. (Singles from $37; doubles $42; family rooms $69.)

There are alternative accommodations on "host farms," which are actually small cattle stations, but you'll need a car to get there. Most cost $30-40 per person, but **Callemondah** (tel. 4685 6162), 58km from Stanthorpe on Texas Rd, charges just $15 per night (linen $5) to stay on the sheep and cattle station (bookings essential).

Coffee and lunch shops line the main road. The **Catholic Women's Association** on Victoria St serves cheap, light lunches (sandwiches $2-3; M-F 11am-2pm). **Lorenza's Coffeehouse,** 29 Maryland St, right next to the bank, has tasty $3-4 sandwiches and longer hours. **The Regal Cafe** on High St serves a range of traditional Aussie fare. **Il Cavallino,** next to the Central Hotel, has Italian dishes ($8-12) and excellent pizza.

GRAPES AND BERRIES

The famous Granite Belt **wineries** line either side of the New England Hwy just south (and a little north) of Stanthorpe. The tourist office has lists of wineries and tours. Unfortunately, wineries can't be reached by public transportation or on foot. **South West Safaris** (tel. 4681 3685) offers several types of 4WD tours, including a "winery to wilderness" full-day tour with pick-up from Granite Belt accommodations for $65. Another option is to travel by horse: **Red Gum Ridge** (tel. 4683 7169) gives lessons and day rides to local wineries. If you're driving, the way to the wineries is well-marked; most are close to the highway. Many are worth visiting for the stunning views as well as the wine, particularly the **Felsburg Winery** (tel. 4683 4332) in Glen Aplin. The **Heritage Estate** in Cottonvale has a beautiful interior and offers free tours. **Murray Gardens** (tel. 4681 4121) has tours for $30 ($40 with lunch).

Several farms grow berries and may be open for **berry picking** between October and April. Raspberries are in season from December to April, boysenberries in December, and strawberries from October to April. **The Bramble Patch** (tel. 4683 4205) is a beautiful berry farm, open year-round, with picnic areas 4km from the New England Hwy on Townsends Rd. They offer ample sampling of their myriad and reasonably priced berry products, including liqueurs and vinegars.

Stanthorpe has three major **festivals,** all with themes of wine and winter weather. The largest is the biennial **Apple and Grape Harvest Festival,** an extravaganza with a gala ball, rodeo, wine fiesta, and museum exhibition, held in late February or early March of 2000. The Granite Belt **Spring Wine Festival** is held during the first two weekends in October. The winter months are devoted to the **Brass Monkey** season,

QUEENSLAND

a general and ongoing Downs-wide wine-and-dine celebration of the area's (and particularly Stanthorpe's) position as the coldest region in Queensland (see p. 307).

SIGHTS

Stanthorpe's gem is the fascinating **Historical Museum** (tel. 4681 1711), 15 minutes up High St from the town center, near the showgrounds. *(Open W-F 10am-4pm, Sa 1-4pm, Su 9am-1pm.)* It's a delightful cornucopia of historical oddities: fruit fly catchers, ancient heating devices, miniature organs, and even a hand-made TV. The more sedate **Stanthorpe Regional Art Gallery** (tel. 4681 1874) is in the same building as the library, across from the Civic Center on Lock St. It features monthly exhibitions of Australian artists. *(Open M-F 10am-4pm, Sa-Su 1-4pm. Free.)* The **Sundown Observatory** (tel. 4684 1192), on Sundown Rd in Ballandean, can give you a closer look at the night sky ($5).

The 1872 discovery of tin in Quart Pot Creek marked the beginning of years of mining around Stanthorpe. The area's stones include topaz, quartz, and amethyst; rarer finds include silver, sapphires, diamonds, and gold. Today, amateurs can try their hand at **fossicking;** a license is required. **Blue Topaz Caravan Park** (tel. 4683 5279), in Severnlea, 7km south of Stanthorpe, supplies 1-month licenses for $5 (family $7).

The second Sunday of every month offers Stanthorpe's hugely popular **Market in the Mountains** (tel. 4681 1912), an arts and crafts sale held at the Civic Center.

■ National Parks near Stanthorpe

Girraween National Park is a popular destination for bushwalkers, birdwatchers, campers, and picnickers. To get there, drive 26km south on the New England Hwy, turn left at the sign, then drive 9km on a paved road. Near the NSW border, the park has an average elevation of 900m. Granite boulders, some balanced on top of each other, are interspersed among eucalypt forests and lyre birds. A 90-minute return hike takes you to the granite Pyramid, which offers a breathtakingly expansive view including the famous **Balancing Rock.** In the spring, wildflowers sprout from the bases of rocks; *girraween* means "place of flowers." The **visitors center** is at the southern end of Bold Rock Creek (open M-F 2:45-3:15pm). Nearby, there are picnic, barbecue, swimming, and rock-climbing areas. **Camping** is available in designated areas (with hot showers, toilets, and fireplaces) or in the bush. Permits are required; contact the ranger (tel. 4684 5157; open daily 2-4pm, but try calling anytime).

Sundown National Park has rugged terrain and panoramic views. To get there, drive 75km along Texas Rd from the north end of Stanthorpe and turn left at the signs for Glenlyon. Alternately, take the New England Hwy south to Tenterfield (approx. 40km) and turn right onto the Broxner Hwy; this route is longer, but the roads are wider and less harrowing. Most of the 16,000-hectare park is 600-800m above sea level, and has very different geology than neighboring parks, with a mix of sedimentary and igneous rocks that produced sharp ridges. The **Severn River** cuts the park in two. Only 4WD vehicles can reach the campsites along the river; hikers can park their cars at the entrance to the park. Campsites have pit toilets, fireplaces, and barbecue facilities. From May to September, the nights are cold but the days are warm and clear. To book campsites, contact the ranger at Glenlyon Dam Rd (tel. (067) 37 5235, daily 7am-4pm).

Two New South Wales national parks, **Bald Rock** and **Boonoo Boonoo,** are easily accessible from Stanthorpe as well. For more information, see p. 193.

SUNSHINE AND FRASER COASTS

The pastel yellow that permeates the Sunshine Coast contrasts sharply with the Gold Coast's pulsating neon. The Sunshine Coast, in many ways, is a kinder, gentler version of vacationland. The crowds are fewer, but expert surfers still dot the waves. Beaches still envelop well-established towns, and waters still greet those eager to partake in

QUEENSLAND

aquatic pleasures. Accessible national parks, like Noosa and Cooloola, replace the more artificial theme parks down the coast, and travelers content to relax are more likely to see koalas in the wild.

The largest of the islands that dot Queensland's coastal waters, sandy Fraser Island reclines under a cover of rainforest. Wild horses wander through the bush like fantastical unicorns, pausing to drink from the island's freshwater lakes, and dingoes hunt for wallabies but are happy to take off with shoes instead. On the mainland, Bundaberg is hailed as a particularly lucrative base for casual labor, and a bevy of workers' hostels have sprung up to meet the demand.

■ Maroochy

Maroochy is the general name for an area of coast encompassing the towns of Maroochydore, Alexandra Heads, and Mooloolaba. Die-hard surfers fill the beaches, and their stereotypically laid-back attitudes permeate Maroochy. **Maroochydore** is the urban center, heavily oriented toward small industry, and is located where the Maroochy River flows into the ocean. It's the main accommodation and shopping area. **Alexandra Heads** is best known for its great surfing. Its strip of small shops and cheap coffee places overlooks a safe, popular, family beach. **Mooloolaba's** largest claim to fame is its oceanarium; it's also known for its beachside nightclubs. Maroochy is a popular base for fruit-picking work, with lychee season in February, ginger in March, and strawberries from June to October ($9-10 per hr.).

ORIENTATION AND PRACTICAL INFORMATION

The main commercial strip in Maroochydore, **Sixth Avenue** runs past the huge **Sunshine Plaza** super-mall and beaches. Aerodrome Rd connects Maroochydore and Mooloolaba. Maroochy's **tourist office** (tel. 5479 1566) is located at the corner of Aerodrome Rd and South Ave. The free *Maroochy Guide* should answer most of your questions, although it's aimed more at new residents than budget travelers. The local blue-painted **Sunbus** #1 and 1A connect these areas fairly effectively. A 15-minute ride from Maroochydore's Sunshine Plaza to Mooloolaba costs $1.90 and runs every hour, with stops at Alexandra Heads and Cotton Tree. **Suncoast Pacific, Greyhound,** and **McCafferty's** all stop in Maroochydore as well.

ACCOMMODATIONS AND FOOD

The majority of Maroochy's motels line Sixth Ave in Maroochydore. Two quiet, community-oriented hostels offer lots of daily activities, including massage workshops and free use of surfboards. **Suncoast Backpackers Lodge,** 50 Parker St, parallel to Aerodrome Dr, is small, friendly, and clean, with a generous common space and kitchen. The owners offer discounts galore for trips and local service and a $5 all-you-can-eat barbecue. They also help secure fruit-picking work, and reserve one of the two dorms for early-rising laborers during the season. (Dorms $15; singles $31; twins and doubles $17-18 per person; triples $17 per person or $45 for 3. Weekly rates available. YHA, VIP. Security gate, regular bus service.) The **Cotton Tree Beachhouse,** 15 The Esplanade in Maroochydore (tel. 5443 1755), is directly across the street from the river. Though the bathrooms are tiny, the two-story house is cozy, with comfy couches, two TVs, and an excellent video collection. (Dorms $14; singles $30; twins and doubles $34.)

Maroochy has cheap, family-oriented food and several good Thai restaurants. Surf clubs are always a good bet for cheap meals. At **Friday's on the Wharf** (tel. 5444 8383), patrons who arrive between 5:30pm and 6pm on Tuesday and Thursday get 50% off any meal except seafood. (M-F lunch specials: T-bone steak $5, fish $6.) The Malibu Cafe on Cotton Tree Pde has burgers ($3-4) and a 3-course vegetarian dinner on Friday ($6.50). (Open daily 7:30am-6pm, later on F.) For health food, **Cotton Tree Health and Living,** 17 Cotton Wood Plaza, Maroochydore (tel. 5443 4700), makes four different types of beefless burgers for $4.30. *Let's Go* readers receive a 10% dis-

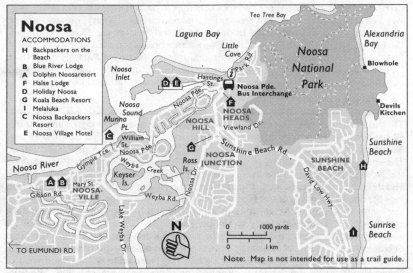

Noosa
ACCOMMODATIONS
H Backpackers on the Beach
B Blue River Lodge
A Dolphin Noosaresort
F Halse Lodge
D Holiday Noosa
G Koala Beach Resort
I Melaluka
C Noosa Backpackers Resort
E Noosa Village Motel

Note: Map is not intended for use as a trail guide.

count on vitamins and minerals. The **Surf Club** at the far end of The Esplanade in Mooloolaba is worth visiting for the $9.50 all-you-can-eat Sunday breakfast. Ask nicely for a seat with a view and you'll get floor-to-ceiling glass windows practically on the beach. (Live entertainment F-Su afternoons. Open Su-Th 10am-10pm, F 10am-midnight, Sa 10am-11pm.)

SIGHTS AND ENTERTAINMENT

Being in Maroochy means spending time near the water. There are many surf shops, but **Bad Company,** 6-8 Aerodrome Rd (tel. 5443 2457; call for current water conditions), is across the street from a good strip of beach. *(Boards $5 per hr., $15 per half-day.)* If surfing's not your thing, strap on a pair of skates and cruise alongside the river. **Maroochy Skate Biz,** 174 Alexandra Pde (tel. 5443 6111), offers free instruction and a wide range of in-line skates and bikes. *(Both $7 per hr., $15 per half-day.)* Kids and grown-ups alike will enjoy Mooloolaba's **Underwater World** (tel. 5444 2255), Australia's largest tropical oceanarium. Open daily, the oceanarium's seal presentations and interactive exhibits are great, but nothing beats the basement attraction: a moving circular walk guides you through a wrap-around clear aquarium. (Admission $18, VIP $14, concessions $11, children $9.50, family $47.) The **Mooloolaba Yacht Club** (tel. 5444 1355) offers free sailing on Wednesdays and Sundays, though no spots are guaranteed. People looking for work on sailing ships might try the Yacht Club and ask around for jobs, as many owners will exchange board for labor.

Rock On, 89 The Esplanade, Mooloolaba, is one of the busiest nightclubs with 13 TV screens, three bars, a DJ, and a dance floor. A VIP, YHA, or NOMAD card will get you free entry and a free drink (open till 3am). **Friday's on the Wharf,** Mooloolaba, is more upscale with pool tables and a $6 cover on Friday and Saturday after 9:30pm. For more down-home entertainment, join in the "American Pie" sing-along on Friday and Saturday nights at **Bullockies** steakhouse, 80 Sixth Ave, Maroochydore.

■ Noosa

Those who think of Noosa (pop. 33,000) as nothing more than a jumping-off point for Fraser Island are in danger of missing one of the Sunshine Coast's loveliest and most versatile spots. Upper-class sophisticates, Australian families, and backpackers all come to Noosa in roughly equal numbers to mingle at the gorgeous beaches and glitzy shopping areas. Some criticize Noosa for catering to upscale vacationers with carefully crafted trendiness, but the area manages to draw backpackers in droves anyway, with high quality and low prices for budget travelers. Weary, hungover backpackers may find welcome relief from the foam and tinsel of the Gold Coast, while the bush is just around the corner. The Noosa area boasts activities to suit every carefree whim, from surfing to camel-riding. **Cooloola National Park,** just north of Noosa, is a wilderness ripe for hiking, canoeing, and camping. Noosa also serves as a base for forays to the **Everglades River, Eumundi Market,** and the **Hinterlands.**

ORIENTATION

The Noosa area can be a bit confusing to navigate because its distinguishing features all have irritatingly similar names. The three main communities are Noosa Heads, Noosa Junction, and Noosaville, while Noosa National Park is a prime attraction. These areas are connected by Noosa Drive and Noosa Parade, and are located along the Noosa River, which runs into Noosa Sound and Noosa Inlet. Seriously. **Noosa Heads** is the main tourist area, and activity revolves around the sidewalk-chic **Hastings St,** one block north of the **Noosa Parade Bus Interchange.** Many trendy shops, restaurants, and upscale hotels line the street. The entrance to **Noosa National Park** is at the end of Hastings St closest to the bus interchange.

A 15-minute stroll over the hill along the wooden sidewalk ramp leads to the heart of **Noosa Junction,** Noosa's business center. The **post office, supermarket,** and string of **banks** all lie within five minutes of each other. **Noosaville** is 3km southwest of Noosa Heads, and is the departure point for most cruises to Fraser Island. The **Sunshine Beach** area is 3km east of Noosa Junction. The cluster of beachfront hostels here are best reached by car, by bus, or by foot along the beach, since the walk along the busy David Low Way takes 40 minutes. Both Sunshine Beach and nearby **Sunrise Beach** (another great moment in innovative nomenclature) are popular spots, but the total 40km stretch of sand leaves ample room for bathers to spread out.

PRACTICAL INFORMATION

Tourist Office: Noosa Visitors Centre (tel. 5474 8400; fax 5474 8222), directly across from the Noosa Heads bus interchange on Noosa Dr, in the Avis Car Rental Shop. Organizes tours of Aboriginal art. Bike rental $9 per day. Wheelchair accessible. Open daily 8am-5pm. **Tourism Noosa Information Centre** (tel. 5447 4988; fax 5474 9494; email noosat@squirrel.com.au) on Hastings St, Noosa Heads. Among the walls of brochures, *Noosa: the Guide* and *Hello Noosa* are good introductions to the town. Open M-Sa 9am-5pm.

Airport: Noosa Flying Services (tel. 5475 0187) operates out of a private airport 5km from town. For a larger regional airport, try Maroochydore or Brisbane.

Buses: Sunbus (tel. 5449 7422) offers frequent hail-and-ride service around Noosa and to Maroochydore, Mooloolaba, and Caloundra. 4 per hr. service through Tewantin, Hastings St, and Noosa Junction; 2 per hr. service through Noosa Heads, Sunshine Beach, Maroochydore, Caloundra. Transit maps and timetables available on buses and at tourist info centers. Fares $1-5; buses run 7am-8pm. **Greyhound Pioneer** (tel. 13 12 38), **McCafferty's** (tel. 3236 3033), and **Suncoast Pacific** (tel. 3236 1901) all run from Noosa south to Brisbane and north toward Rockhampton.

Taxis: Suncoast Cabs (tel. 13 10 08) provide 24hr. service.

Car Rental: Budget (tel. 5447 4588 or 13 27 27; fax 5447 2337), on Hastings St, Bay Village, guarantees the lowest price on medium- to long-term rentals. Open daily 8am-5:30pm. **Virgin** (tel. 5475 5777 or 1800 659 299), at the corner of Sunshine Beach Rd. and Berrima Row in Noosa Junction, rents from $29 per day. Bookings 7am-7pm. **Thrifty** (tel. 5447 2299) is in Noosa Junction. **Avis** (tel. 5447 4933) is on Noosa Dr, by Hastings St (open M-F 8am-5pm, Sa-Su 8am-4pm). **Henry's** (tel. 5447 3777) rents cars and 4WD from $29 per day; for airport pick-up call 5474 0198.

Money: Westpac Bank, 40 Hastings St, Noosa Heads (tel. 5447 4488). Advance on all major credit cards (with passport). Cashing less than $500 in foreign traveler's checks costs $7; over $500 is free. Wheelchair accessible. **National, Commonwealth,** and **ANZ** banks are clustered in Noosa Junction, mostly on Sunshine Beach Rd. All open M-Th 9:30am-4pm, F 9:30am-5pm.

Bookstores: Mary Ryan's, Hastings St, Bay Village (tel. 5474 5275) provides for all your beach-reading needs. Open daily 9am-5:30pm.

Sports Equipment: Sierra Mountain Bike, Hastings St (tel. 5474 8277). Bikes $12 daily. **Noosa Visitors Centre,** Hastings St (tel. 5474 8400), bikes $9 daily. **Inline Skates,** 249 Gympie Tce (tel. 5442 4344). Bikes $10 daily, skates $7 per hr.

Public Toilets: In the carpark at the entrance to Noosa National Park, off Hastings St.

Emergency: Dial 000.

Medical Services: Noosa After Hours Medical Centre, 197 Weyba Rd, Noosaville (tel. 5442 4444). Open M-F 6pm-6am, Sa noon-10pm. **Nambour Base Hospital** (tel. 5441 9600) is the closest regional hospital.

Police: on Langura St, Noosa Junction (tel. 5447 5888).

Post Office: Noosa Post Office, 79-80 Cooroy-Noosa Rd, Noosa Junction (tel. 5447 3280; fax 5447 5160). Poste Restante, **fax,** and electronic post. American Express orders for $6. Open M-F 9am-5pm. **Postal Code:** 4567.

Internet Access: Surf the net, not the waves at the **Noosanetcafe** (tel. 5474 5770); Palms Shopping Centre, Noosa Junction ($3 for 15min.).

Phone Code: 07.

ACCOMMODATIONS

Lodging in Noosa comes in three general categories: hostels, motels or hotels, and "holiday units," which include private homes. Intense competition for budget travelers keep hostel prices low and perks such as courtesy shuttle service, surfboards, on-site bars, pool tables, and free tour bookings standard. Motel and hotel rooms can top $200 on Hastings St, but are much cheaper without a beachfront view. Families and groups may find it cheaper and more convenient to rent units or homes; many agencies offer discounted weekly rates. During Christmas and school vacations, rates can double and accommodations fill; book ahead. Check-out is generally 10am. There are also several places to **camp** in the area (see **Cooloola National Park,** p. 315).

Noosa Heads

Lodging here puts you on or near busy Hastings St, close to the national park.

Halse Lodge (YHA) (tel. 5447 3377), directly opposite the Noosa Parade Bus Interchange. Perched on a small hill, this stately 115-year-old house feels relaxed and removed from Noosa's hustle, but is close to Hastings St and the national park. Common areas have wooden tables, comfy lounge chairs, and lovely wraparound porches. Attracts a quiet crowd, but close quarters and noisy doors may keep you awake. Bunks in shared cottage $15; doubles and twins $50. Breakfast included.

Koala Beach Resort, 44 Noosa Dr (tel. 5447 3355 or 1800 357 457), a 10-15min. walk from the bus interchange. Popular with surfers and die-hard partiers. Laundry, pool, and volleyball court. The adjoining **Koala Bar** has loud music, dancing, and meals for $6. Lots of live music, especially Thursday. Monday night is reserved for backpackers—bring your room key and/or passport. Friendly staff encourages group bonding and daytrips. 5-bed dorms $14; doubles $34. VIP.

Noosa Village Motel, 10 Hastings St (tel. 5447 5800; fax 5474 9282). Clean, modest rooms come with small fridge, TV, and toaster. Doubles $70-$120, depending on season. Triples and units for 5 also available.

Holiday Noosa, 12 Hastings St (tel. 5447 4011; fax 5447 3410). The Jacaranda complex includes sparsely finished studio rooms which have 2 twin beds and a small TV ($70-$105, depending on season). Suites overlook a lake and sleep 4-5 ($90-$150). Also rents expensive apartments. Discounts for weekly rentals.

Sunshine Beach

These hostels, though more worn than those in Noosa Heads, are right by the beach, but are a 20-minute walk from the Junction. By car, they're off the David Low Hwy.

Melaluka, 7 Selene St (tel. 5447 3663). Take the highway to Sunrise Beach; turn at Vernon St and make two quick rights down the hill. The clean, spacious, fully

QUEENSLAND

equipped apartments and friendly owners make up for the paint-chipped exterior. $16 per person. Free laundry. Courtesy van to town, 10min. by car.

Backpackers on the Beach, 26 Stevens St (tel. 5447 4739). Follow the signs to Sunshine Beach and turn at Parkedge Rd. Turn right on Belmore Tce, then left onto Stevens. Boogie boards, pool, and surfboard rental. 4-bed dorms with kitchen and bath $15; twin or double $34. Shared kitchen and bathroom. Separate apartments sleep 5 ($60 and up). Free laundry, courtesy vans. VIP.

Noosaville

Most of the travelers who stay in this less glamorous part of town prefer the serenity of the river to the beaches, which are a 30-minute walk away.

Noosa Backpackers Resort, 11Williams St (tel. 5449 8151). A quiet, low-key hostel driven largely by the energy and friendliness of its owners. Located on a shady side street 2min. from the river; 30min. walk to the National Park. Free courtesy van, weekly movie nights, and nightly theme dinners ($4), use of pool table, kayaks, and boogie boards. Attractive central courtyard and small, decent rooms. Lockers (bring your own locks), bar (beer $2-$2.50), open showers. Internet access. 4-bed dorms $15; doubles $34. Breakfast included. VIP and $1 weekly discounts.

Blue River Lodge, 181 Gympie Tce (tel. 5449 7564), directly across from Noosa River. Spotless units with 2 bedrooms, kitchen area, and TV $50. Book ahead.

Dolphin Noosaresort, 137 Gympie Tce (tel. 5449 7318). Clean rooms with small kitchens attached. Low-key atmosphere. Hourly trips to national park and beach. Pool, surfboards, weight machines. Dorms $15. VIP, YHA.

FOOD AND ENTERTAINMENT

Many of the restaurants on Hastings St are expensive, but with over 100 eateries in Noosa, there's plenty of great, cheap food. Most restaurants have alcohol licenses, while many smaller eateries are BYO. There are liquor stores (bottle shops) next to Angello's on Hastings St in Noosa Heads and in Noosa Junction. Restaurants frequently offer entertainment, particularly on weekend nights and Sunday afternoons. Cheaper is **Coles Supermarket** (tel. 5447 4000) off Sunshine Beach Rd on Lanyana Way, Noosa Junction (open M-F 8am-9pm, Sa 9am-5:30pm, Su 10:30am-4pm). **Bay Village Food Court,** off Hastings St, has several small eateries and vendors.

Betty's Burgers, Hastings St, Noosa Heads (tel. 5447 5639), in the Tingirana Arcade. Tucked down an alley off Hastings St, this 20-year-old establishment is one of the best deals in all Australia. Burgers served up by Betty herself range from $1-4 and make customers feel like thieves. Complimentary coffee and tea. Thirty kinds of burgers, including nine vegetarian patties. Open daily 9am-5pm (later by demand).

Topopo's, 73 Noosa Dr (tel. 5447 3700). One of the best deals in town. Generous servings of toned-down Mexican food. Nightly specials include half-price nachos (Tu) and $8.50 meals (W). Combos (easily enough for 2) run from $13.50-$25. Dine in the open air or eat in the colorfully decorated interior. Licensed.

Cafe Le Monde, Hastings St, Noosa Heads (tel. 5449 2366). A local favorite. Classy and comfortable, it's also a breakfast gathering place for local surfer celebs. Veggie-friendly. Live music 5 nights a week. Try the nachos ($8.50) or one of the 61 wines.

Noosa Reef, Noosa Dr (tel. 5447 4477), on the hill. Modern and airy, with a family atmosphere. The cafe deck has great views of the town. Parents can send their kids to the adjoining video/play room for a $7 meal while they enjoy pizza wraps, steaks, and fish and chips for $9-17.

Saltwater, 8 Hastings St, Noosa Heads (tel. 5447 2234). Sells freshly caught Noosa seafood and operates a lovely upstairs open-air restaurant, where you can sip wine under a white awning (main course $13-20). But the best bet is the $6 melt-in-your-mouth calamari, available through the take-out. Opens at 11:30am.

Noosa's hottest night spot, **Rolling Rock,** on Hastings St, Noosa Head (tel. 5447 2255), is packed with the tragically hip. Thumping techno rocks the house on Thursday nights, while Sundays feature live local bands. Beverages start around $3. (Cover

$6 after 10pm W-Su; open 9pm-3am every night, but doors close at 1:30am.) **Mocca Jam,** on Noosa Dr below the Noosa Reef Restaurant, features pool, live bands on Sundays and grunge band nights (open May-Aug W-Su 9am-3pm). The **Noosa 5 Cinema,** Noosa Junction (tel. 5447 5130, or 5447 5300 for program info), features current releases, art, and foreign films. (Admission $10.50, students and seniors $7.50, children $7. Matinee $8, students, seniors and children $6.50; Tu special $6.)

SIGHTS AND ACTIVITIES

Noosa National Park (tel. 5447 3243) is a 454-hectare area of tropical vegetation, coastal walking paths, and rare wildlife which bills itself as the most visited park in Australia. A lovely koala-strewn, 1.4km path through the woods from the Noosa information booth on Hastings St will land you at the entrance. The park is ideal for walking and jogging, though it can be dangerous at night or alone. The tourist office provides maps of five interconnected paths, ranging from 1 to 4.2km. The coastal track at sunrise (in winter around 6:30 or 7am, in summer a shocking 4:30am) is gorgeous; heat-sensitive strollers should take refuge in the inner rainforest. Bring water, particularly in the summer. The **beaches** (some nude, some gay) are on **Alexandria Bay** on the eastern side of the park. *(Picnic area, water, and toilets. Camping and dogs are prohibited, but swimming and surfing are permitted. Wheelchair accessible.)*

Noosa is crawling with tour companies. For $44 you can romp with the dolphins, courtesy of **Wildlife Tours** (tel. 014 665 183). **Camel Safaris** (tel. 5442 4402) offers two-hour camel trips down the beach for $30 or one-hour trips in the bush for $20. **Clip Clop** horse riding (tel. 5449 1254) lets you splash through lakes and trot through bush for anywhere from two hours to six days ($30 and up). Several tours to Fraser Island leave from Noosa, such as the one- to two-day tours offered through **Fraser Explorer Tours** (tel. 5447 3845) ($70, $145) and three-day camping safari with **Trailblazers Tours** (tel. 5474 1235) for $178. Thirty dollars buys a surfing lesson from **Learn to Surf** (tel. 041 787 577); full refund if you're not upright in two hours.

Everglades Water Bus Company (tel. 1800 688 045) offers a four-hour tour up the **Noosa River** ($43). **Everglades Express** (tel. 5449 9422) has half-day tours ($40). **Noosa River Tours** (tel. 5479 7362) has half-day tours with barbecue lunch ($50). Call the tourist office for more info. Many shops in Noosaville rent **canoes.**

■ Near Noosa

Cooloola National Park

Extending 50km north of Noosa up to Rainbow Beach are the sandy white coast and 64,000 hectares of forest of **Cooloola National Park.** Intrepid explorers and Sunday strollers alike will enjoy this wilderness area. The beaches are generally less populated than those in Noosa, but in summer months and holidays there's a thick blanket of tents and picnickers on the sands. From Noosa, take bus #10A to Riverlands and ride the Noosa River ferry across (ferry runs Su-Th 6am-10pm, F-Sa 6am-midnight; free, cars $4). Many people rent 4WD vehicles and drive along the coast to Rainbow Beach or the Fraser Island ferry. Drive only at low tide and during the day.

Part of the **Great Sandy Region Park,** the Cooloola National Park forests hold many natural wonders: rainforests growing from pure sand, winding waterways shaded by mangroves, and characteristic Aussie critters like kangaroos, koalas, and ground parrots. Even the plants are unusual: endangered *boroniakeysii* (pink-flowered shrubs) mingle with thin, stubborn stalks of blackbutt, while melaeluka "tea trees" dye the river a deep black. One of the best ways to enjoy the park is to canoe up to the Everglades, where the dark water creates mirror images of the riverbank.

As in any wilderness area, keep **safety** in mind and watch out for the wildlife. Sharks in the river system occasionally approach the shore. Bullrats, which are little fish with big barbs that give a nasty sting, swim alongside the stingrays, catfish, and jellyfish in the ocean. Don't swim in Lake Kinaba and use caution elsewhere. The

National Park Information Centre (tel. 5449 7364), at the Elanda Point Headquarters, 5km north of Boreen Point, offers maps, information, and advice.

Accommodations in Cooloola begin with **Gagaju** (tel. 5474 3522). Hidden in the bush 25 minutes from Noosaville, bordering the Cooloola National Park and Noosa River, it's as eco-friendly and just plain friendly a place as a campground could be ($7 per person campsite). Gagaju has an impressive recycled-wood shelter ($11 per bed) and a graffiti-decorated main tent, which holds the kitchen and "lounge" area. Lanterns, candles, and bonfires make up for the lack of electricity. (Running water, laundry facilities, and friendly management. Super-cheap canoeing from $20; kayaking, and bushwalking tours and rentals available.) The **Lake Cooroibah Holiday Park** (tel. 5447 1706; fax 5442 4452), 1.2km from the beach, has cabins, motel units, on-site tents, and campsites. Take Sunbus #10A to Riverlands, cross the river on the ferry and walk 2km up Maxmillian Rd. (Showers, laundry, barbecue, horse rides; pets allowed in camping areas, no linen supplied. Camping $4-5 per person; "billy" huts $20 for 2 people, $25 for 3, powered $4 more.)

Fig Tree Point, Harry's Hut, and the privately owned **Elanda Point** grounds are family-oriented campgrounds that provide toilets and firewood. Elanda also has electricity. The park's other 15 sites are available by booking ahead through the park headquarters. The higher the site number, the more remote the site; sites 4 and up have no facilities and are only accessible by canoe. Camping permits for all sites are $3.50 per person and are payable at the self-registration stations throughout the park and at campgrounds. At the northernmost tip of the park, **Rainbow Beach** (tel. 5486 3160) is another family-oriented campground with a trailer park, shops, and, for the truly desperate, a pub. **Freshwater** camping ground (tel. 5449 7959; reservations required) on the coast has a public phone and is a good place for bass fishing.

The Sunshine Coast Hinterland

Along the Blackall Ranges just inland of the Sunshine Coast lies a veritable smorgasbord of tourists' delights: stunning national parks, roadside crafts markets, and kitschy tourist traps, all manageable in a day's outing. The Hinterland is inaccessible via public transportation; either drive or go with a tour company. **Noosa Hinterland Tours** (tel. 5474 3366) offers moderately priced trips. Parents can enjoy a day alone with **Kids Day Out** (tel. 0414 769 305); they offer several trips daily.

Some hostels in Noosa provide return bus service to the **Eumundi Markets,** a bustling collection of chutneys and chairs, jewelry and jugs, and just about anything else on the cheap. The markets are open early Saturday mornings and close by 1pm; a kinder, gentler version appears on Wednesdays. If you're not shopped out by then, another 30 minutes or so south is the town of **Montville,** basically a couple blocks of shops and teahouses. Once known for its hippie appeal, Montville is pretty touristy, but still offers massage and herbal services for the patchouli-wearing set.

In the town of Yandina, just south of Eumundi, is the **Ginger Factory** (tel. 5446 7096) where just about everything's ginger (or ginger-friendly).The factory processes and distributes half the world's supply of the stuff. If that doesn't impress you, neither will the factory, though the huge vats of multi-colored ginger in different stages of processes are worth a look given the price (free). Otherwise, there's a train tour, a small fauna park, and lots of food and shops selling ginger products, all for moderate prices. (Open daily 9am-5pm.) Across the street is a macademia factory with free tastings of multiflavored nuts. The town of **Nambour** has a **Big Pineapple plantation** (tel. 5442 1333), a working fruit and nut plantation, with small rides, shows, and a fauna sanctuary—kids will love it (open daily 9am-5pm).

Mapleton Fall National Park and **Kondalilla Falls National Park,** both on the road south to Montville, have pleasant trails and picnic areas. The Kondalilla Falls (Aboriginal for "rushing water" are especially gorgeous. Although a 1.2km walk from the entrance to the park will technically get you to the Falls, the best views of it are sprinkled along the 2.2km circuit track that begins from there.

And finally, when in the Hinterland, be sure to try some of the roadside fruit, especially the avocados. They're everywhere, and they're the cheapest things around.

■ Bundaberg

Bundaberg is not high on the list of Australia's choice idling spots; most visitors get a coffee at the bus terminal, stretch their legs, and hop back on board. However, it is the hottest spot to put in a few weeks on the fruit-picking circuit, and hostels in town house mainly workers. The season is year-round, and the hourly wage is $8.50 after taxes. The job involves a fair amount of luck—weather, farmers, personality, what you're picking (tomatoes good, zucchinis bad)—but at the end of the day, it's all about kicking the dirt off your workboots, occasionally splurging on a bit of Bundaberg's famous rum, and saving energy for another day in the fields. Some last a day, others last months. Despite Bundy's dearth of activities, or perhaps because of it, the survivors enjoy some of the purest camaraderie on the coast.

PRACTICAL INFORMATION

Tourist Office: Tourist Information Centre (tel. 4152 2333 or 1800 060 499). Follow Bourbong St south from town about 2km toward Childers. Features an actual-size replica of Hinkler's famous airplane. Open 9am-5pm.
Parks Office: (tel. 4153 8620), on the ground floor of the "Government Office" building on Quay St. Open M-F 9am-5pm.
Trains: Train station at the corner of Bourbong and MacLean St. Ticket office open M-F 8:45am-4:30pm, Sa 9:30am-2pm and 3:30-4:30pm, Su 8:45am-2pm.
Buses: Coach's In terminal, Targo St. To get to town from the station, turn right and pass the roundabout and McDonald's to Bourbong St. Open 7am-12:30am. **S&S Travel** (tel. 4152 9700), in the terminal. Open M-F 8am-5pm, Sa 8:30-11:30am.
Hospital: (24hr. tel. 4152 1222), at the corner of Bourbong St and Tallon Bridge.
Emergency: Dial 000.
Police: (tel. 4153 9111), on Bourbong St.
Post Office: (tel. 4153 2700; fax 4151 6708), at the corner of Bourbong and Barolin St. Open M-F 8:30am-5pm, Sa 8:30am-11:45pm. **Postal Code:** 4670.
Internet Cafe: 11 Quay St (tel. 4152 5299).
Phone Code: 07.

ACCOMMODATIONS

The town's hostels slope quickly and seriously in quality, with the lowest-end places drawing in backpackers with promises of work that often fail to materialize. Ask guests at the hostel whether they have had luck finding work before you sign up for a swindle. If the managers object, it's perfectly OK to walk out. Never give your camera or passport to a hostel's management as bond on the promise that work is forthcoming. Most hostels do find work (usually within a day), provide free transport from work, have strict alcohol policies, and are equipped with walk-in refrigerators.

Bundaberg Backpackers and Travelers' Lodge (tel. 4152 2080; fax 4151 3355), across from the bus terminal at the corner of Targo and Crofton St. The optimum in comfy workers' hostels. Best of all, the proprietor's name is Bruce Willis. A/C, pick-up at the train station. Reception open daily 8am-8pm. Dorms $16; doubles $32. Weekly: $105; $190. VIP, YHA, NOMADS. Key deposit $15, linen included.
City Centre Backpackers, 216 Bourbong St (tel. 4151 3501; fax 4153 5756). Across from the train station. From the bus terminal, call for a ride. A massive maze of rooms, halls, and common areas with plenty of space to stretch out after a long day of picking. The hostel is often booked solid, a sign of the quality and cleanliness in spite of the presence of a clientele of mud-soaked backpackers. Reception open daily 5am-8pm. Dorms $15, $13 first night, $97 weekly. Doubles and units with bath and TV $16, $14 first night, $104 weekly. VIP, YHA. Key deposit $10. For a room with bath and TV, add $1. Blanket $1, linen $1.
Federal Guest House, 221 Bourbong St (tel. 4153 3711), at the Federal Hotel across from the train station. From the bus terminal, call for a pick-up. The Federal is a no-frills workers' hostel, a fun place to kick back after backbreaking labor. Attached to

a bar and cheap bistro. Reception open daily 8am-8pm. Large dorms $15; 4-bed dorms $16. Weekly: $92; $104. Key deposit $15, linen included.

Finemore Caravan Park (tel. 4151 3663; fax 4151 6399). From Bourbon St turn onto Burrum St across from the train station, then turn left at the zoo on Quay St and walk a few blocks. Open 7am-7pm. Campsites $8 (with vehicle $10); powered sites $14. Powered tents $12. Cabin for 2 with bath $38, each additional person $4.

If the hostels in Bundy are booked to the gills, consider dropping south one coach stop to the town of **Childers** (pop. 4000). The **Palace Backpackers Hostel,** 72 Churchill St (tel. 4126 2244), is big and beautiful, though the town itself is a bit boring. The owner, Jock, is happy to arrange work for guests. (Laundry facilities. Dorms $14, weekly $90. Key deposit $10, linen included, blankets $2.)

ACTIVITIES

Diving in Bundaberg is rock-bottom cheap. A carefully timed dive with **Bundaberg Aqua Scuba** (tel. 4153 5761), across from the bus terminal, will see you stepping off an incoming coach, down for a dive ($25), back for a shower at the bus terminal ($2, $5 deposit, key available at the travel agent), and on the next outgoing coach. **Salty's,** 208 Bourbong St (tel. 1800 625 476 or 4151 6422; fax 4151 4938), offers a PADI course. *($149; 4-day classes start every M, W, and F 8:30am.)* Two off-shore dives with gear cost $40 (2 reef dives $165; open M-F 8am-5pm, Sa 8am-noon, Su 8-10am). Hostels have trips to the distillery for interested guests, or ask at the information center for driving directions. Bundaberg is famous for its **sugar;** there's a sugar factory in **Fairymeed House,** a grand Queenslander in the Botanical Gardens (open daily 10am-4pm; $2). Bundaberg is also famous for Bert Hinkler, a local WWI pilot, comemmorated by the **Hinkler House Memorial Museum** (tel. 4152 0222), in the Gardens (open daily 10am-4pm; admission $2.50). But mostly, Bundaberg is famous for its **rum.** Distillery tours (tel. 4152 4077) are popular but disappointing—much is on video, and only one drink comes with the price. *(Tours daily 10am-3pm on the hour. $5)*

■ Fraser Island

Fraser Island, the world's largest sand island and a World-Heritage-listed national park, was once called "K'gari" by the indigenous Butchulla people, who rescued the shipwrecked Eliza Fraser and were shortly thereafter moved off the island and into missions. It remains one of the least tamed, yet most visited, islands off the Queensland coast. The sand dunes, beaches, and cliffs are held in place by well-rooted rain forests. Where the vegetation has been removed, the wind moves the sand, inch by inch, until places like Lake Wabby are swallowed whole by advancing dunes. The island changes its entire body decade after decade, as the hills and valleys are swept down and built up again.

If the island's topography is in constant flux, its hourglass moves one grain at a time. The trunks of the King Ferns (*Angiopteris evecta*) on Wanggoolba Creek grow 25mm in diameter every century. Botanists are still waiting for a specimen to spore, but the plants (which have been around since the birth of Mohammed) are taking their time. Hugging a tree in the hidden **Valley of Giants** is like trying to put your lips around a watermelon—the trees have grown up to 3m in diameter. Dingoes and wild horses (brumbies) roam the island, sharing the land with Bearded Dragons, the Stinkhorn Fungus, and about 250 species of bird. Sharks patrol the coast, occasionally picking off an unlucky whale on its annual migration between August and November.

GETTING THERE AND AROUND

Ferries and Barges

Kingfisher Bay Barge (tel. 4125 5511) charges pedestrians $12 (vehicles $65, $5 for additional passengers) for return trips between Riverheads and Kingfisher Bay on the island (departs daily 7:15, 9:30am, and 2pm from Riverheads; departs Kingfisher Bay

Resort at 8am, 12:30, 3:30pm). Getting out to Riverheads (30min. by car from Hervey Bay) can be tricky. Alternatively, the **Kingfisher Bay Catamaran** (tel. 4125 5511) will pick up in Hervey Bay for free, but charges between Urangan Boat Harbour (just out of town) and Kingfisher Bay. (Departs daily from Urangan 8:30am, noon, 4, 6:30, and 7pm; departs from Kingfisher at 7:40am, 9:30am, 2, and 5pm. One-way $15.) Their free shuttle will also drop off returning passengers.

If you're going over in a car, you'll need to get a vehicle permit ($30) from the QNPWS or one of its agents. **Hervey Bay City Council** (tel. 4125 0222) on Tavistock St (open M-F 9am-5pm), and **Riverheads General Store** (tel. 4125 7133), just shy of the Riverheads barge landing (open 6:30am-6pm daily), are both agents. **Camping permits** ($3.50) are also sold in these places, as well as in the convenience stores on the island. The permits are good for all campgrounds except the privately run Cathedral Beach Resort and Dilli Village, both on the east shore.

Getting from **Riverheads to Wanggoolba Creek** costs $30 each way, $5 per passenger, and departs at 9, 10:15am, and 3:30pm (booking tel. 4125 4444). **Urangan Boat Harbor to Moon Point** is the same price, departing at 8:30am and 3:30pm, but Moon Point is dangerously close to the perilous swamps of the northwest coast. The barge on the southern tip, **Rainbow Beach to Hook Point,** is $25 plus $1 per passenger (runs on demand 7am-4:30pm).

Tours

A more structured, safe, and hassle-free way to see the island is on a tour, assuming you're wiling to forego the freedom of a personal 4WD. **Kingfisher Bay** (tel. 1800 072 555) offers two- or three-day "wilderness adventures" for $75 a day, which includes food and accommodation in spacious and clean wilderness lodges with access to resort facilities (departs Tu and F). **Top Tours** (tel. 4125 3933) has day tours for $65 and two-day tours for $150 (2-day tours leave Tu, Th, and Sa). **Fraser Venture** (tel. 4125 4444) has day tours for $65. You can also sail Fraser for two days and two nights with **Stefanie Yacht Charters** (tel. 1800 650 776) for $180.

Vehicle Rental and Driving on Fraser Island

For folks who want the thrill of hurtling down a beach, without the crunch of seven or eight people to a truck, several companies rent old army 4WDs at $75 to 85 per day. Camping kits cost an additional $10-30 per day depending on how many goodies you want. Some good operators include **Safari** (tel. 1800 689 819; fax 4124 6614), and **Aussie Trax** (tel. 1800 062 275; fax 4124 4965). All of these companies will do local pick-ups. It's worth asking whether a rental agency belongs to the **Fraser Coast 4WD Hire Association,** the local self-monitoring watchdog organization.

Stepping up the price ladder, almost every hostel in Hervey Bay offers a $105 per day three-day special on a 4WD truck, including almost all necessary gear; they book both guests and non-guests. The particulars (like the maximum number of people and whether sleeping bags or accommodations are included) vary, so it's worth shopping around. A $500 bond is standard, but some may waive it with some cajoling.

Driving on Fraser gives you maximal flexibility but is only possible in a **4WD** vehicle or a well-equipped motorcycle. Inland roads, usually pothole-covered one-lane trails, wind through the forests. The **beaches** themselves are registered national highways—all normal traffic rules apply. Larger vehicles will occasionally stay on the right, however; in any case, always use your blinker to indicate which side you plan to drive on. South-going automobiles usually hang surf-side. **Beach driving is dangerous;** some drivers may be drunk, many drive recklessly, and it's almost impossible to hear oncoming traffic over the roar of the waves. You're tempting fate by driving on the beaches south of Dilli Village and Ungowa, or north of the Ngkala Rocks. The west side of the island north of Moon Point is easily mistaken for an automobile-eating swamp. The most serious danger lies in the tiny freshwater **creeks** which trickle from the hills. Even a shallow creek cuts into the sand enough to send vehicles flying off a mini-cliff—at 80 kph, that's an easy way to break an axle, bend a pin, or give everyone in the car whiplash.

Driving at **night** should be avoided since it's difficult to see the creeks. As none of the national parks' campgrounds have illuminated signs, it is nearly impossible to find an entrance in the dark. During the day, be certain to **check the tides** at a ranger's office, convenience store, or on the free Hervey Bay tourist brochure available all over the mainland city. It's generally safe to drive three hours (two hours when north of Indian Head) of either side of the low tide (a half-hour earlier than on the east coast, which is what's published for Hervey Bay).

ACCOMMODATIONS AND SIGHTS

The island hotels are prohibitively pricey, and even the beach-side huts are aimed at an upscale market. For budget travelers, the only option is **camping.**

Inland

Don't be fooled by the pleasant beige shade of Sunmap's island map; although the inland is made of sand, it is covered by rainforest and scrubby gum forest. Walking tracks zigzag around the island, connecting Central Station to Lake McKenzie (2hr.), Lake Birrabeen (1½hr.), and the closer Basin Lake (½hr.), to name a few. If you can manage to get as far as Lake McKenzie without a car, it's possible to see most of the southern sights by following the hiking trails to Central Station (6km), Lake Birrabeen (5km), Lake Boomanjin (10km), and Dilli Village (7km). There are national park campsites at Lake McKenzie, and Lake Boomanjin. As there are snakes on the island, it's wisest to tread loudly and carry a big stick.

Lake McKenzie is the most popular of the fresh-water lakes, with white sands, shady pine trees, and water of various shades of perfect blues, some totally clear. **Lake Wabby** (3½hr. by foot) is much the same, except that a towering sandblow is slowly devouring the lake as it moves along. Some visitors enjoy sliding down the dunes into the lake, but this can be disastrous for the structural integrity of both the dune and your spinal cord. Walking across the dune feels like crossing a vast desert; in fact, Fraser and nearby Cooloola National Park combined have as much sand as the Sahara. The southernmost lake, **Boomanjin,** is lined with fallen leaves. It's the largest of the lakes, and the largest of its kind in the world. Some of the lakes have tea-colored (but not flavored) water, caused by the overhanging swamp paperbarks and teatrees. There are also a number of fresh-water creeks good for swimming, especially **Eli Creek.**

The Eastern Beach

There is a *lot* of beach on Fraser Island, and most of it looks the same, bordered by raging surf, and low-lying trees announce the tentative start of island vegetation. Heading north from Eurong, patches of rocks decorate the beach. There are short bypasses at **Poyungan Rocks** and **Yidney Rocks** and a longer route around the **Indian Head** promontory. Almost at the top of passable beachland, the **Champagne Pools** (or **The Aquarium**), a collection of shallow tide pools, make prime swimming holes at low tide. Be careful of the **tides;** not only is there a danger of being stranded by high tide, but incoming waves can crash up and over the pools, causing serious injury. Other attractions along the beach are the **Coloured Sands,** or **Cathedrals,** massive sand formations of countless shades, and the **Maheno shipwreck,** the remains of a massive cruise liner that washed ashore in the early part of the century.

The **Kingfisher Bay Resort** offers a series of guided tours. The free walks are worth a look, especially the bush tucker walk, and are run on demand. Half-day tours ($45) are the best way to get to some of the more inaccessible (or impossible-to-find) places, including the **Valley of the Giants.** The resort also runs a catamaran out to Platypus Bay for whale-watching (Aug.-Oct., $65 per person). These trips are geared toward the older set; book at the **ranger station** (tel. 4120 3350; fax 4120 3413) in Kingfisher Bay Resort's Day Visitor Pavilion (open daily 8am-5:30pm). Free showers are in the resort; go to the Day Visitor Pavilion and turn right at the snack bar.

■ Hervey Bay

Hervey Bay (pronounce it HAR-vee if you don't want to be condescended to) is little more than a stepping-off point to Fraser Island, and visitors rarely feel quite like invited guests. Going through Hervey Bay is like going through customs: you must stop, however briefly, and suffer through it, before venturing into the enticing foreignness beyond. The road in winds through one-pub towns, and the closest train station is in Maryborough (although there is a shuttle bus). The whale-watching season, between August and October, draws crowds. Other than that, however, the local backpacker economy serves only to create an amenable waystation. The city lacks a real beach of its own, and "nightlife" means resting up for the following day's trip.

ORIENTATION AND PRACTICAL INFORMATION

Hervey Bay is actually a clump of suburbs, named from west to east the **Pialba, Scarness, Torquay,** and **Urangan.** Most of the action is along the **Esplanade** at the water's edge. The harbor extends all the way down the Esplanade and then around to Pulgul St, and is a superb place to pick up cheap seafood fresh from the trawlers.

Tourist Office: (tel. 4124 8741), 353 the Esplanade. Open daily 9am-5pm.

Trains: The station is outside the neighboring town of Maryborough, and a shuttle bus runs between there and Hervey Bay, leaving Hervey Bay 30min. before scheduled train departure times. There is a local bus to Hervey Bay (tel. 4123 1733; M-F 5:40am-5:25pm; Sa 7:30am, 12:15, and 4pm; $4).

Buses: McCafferty's and Greyhound are both handled by the same agent at the **Bay Bus Terminal** (tel. 4124 4402). No lockers. Most hostels send free courtesy buses to meet incoming coaches. Open M-F 7am-5pm, Sa-Su 7am-1pm.

Public Transportation: Maryborough and Hervey Bay Coaches (tel. 4121 3719) run a circuit along the Esplanade, Boat Harbour Rd, and out to the Urangan Boat Harbour. The service is hail-and-ride, with a sliding rate scale depending on how far you're going. Service every hour M-F 6am-6pm, Sa around 8am, 1, and 5pm. Schedules are found in tourist offices and most hostels.

Currency Exchange: National Bank, 415 the Esplanade (tel. 13 22 05). Commission to change traveler's checks $5, except Thomas Cook free; cash $5. Open M-Th 9:30am-4pm; F 9:30am-5pm. The **ATM** accepts V, MC, Cirrus, Plus.

Supermarket: Foodstore, 349 the Esplanade (tel. 4124 6288). Open daily 6am-10pm.

Diving: Divers Mecca, 472 the Esplanade (tel. 4125 1626; fax 4125 1833). Intro dive $80, PADI course $149. (Yes, $149—perhaps the best reason to visit Hervey Bay.)

Hospital: (tel. 4128 1444), on Long Street Pt in the suburb of Vernon.

Emergency: Dial 000.

Police: (24hr. tel. 4128 5333), on the corner of Queens Rd. and Torquay Rd.

Post Office: 3 Bryant St (tel. 4128 1047; fax 4128 2376). Head down Torquay Rd with the bay to the right; it's 10-15min. from the hostels by foot. Open M-F 8:30am-5pm, Sa 8:30-11:30am. **Postal code:** 4655.

Internet Access: Most of the booking and information centres that dot the Esplanade provide email and web access, $3-5 per 30min.

Phone Code: 07.

ACCOMMODATIONS AND FOOD

If there's one thing you can say for Hervey Bay, it's sure got its share of hostels. Most are on or next to the Esplanade, and all pick up at the coach terminal.

Friendly Hostel, 182 Torquay Rd (tel. 4124 4107). The owners are indeed friendly, and their grandparent-like demeanor indicates that guests are expected to behave as proper grandchildren. The place feels more like a B&B without the breakfast; lovely rooms (no bunks), cable TV, small reading libraries, bedside lamps, free bikes, fully supplied kitchen. A (quiet) backpacker's dream. Tours can be booked here. 3-bed dorms and twins $12 a person. Linen included.

Fraser Magic Backpackers, 369 the Esplanade (tel. 4124 3488; fax 4142 5404). A casual and friendly atmosphere with a touch of the eccentric. Clean, spacious 2- and 4-bed units with bath, kitchen, TV. No deposits. Fraser trips cost $119 but include fuel and other amenities. Reception open 7:30-11am and 2-7pm. Dorms $12; twins and doubles $15. Linen included. Laundry $1.

Colonial Backpackers (tel. 1800 818 280), corner of Boat Harbor Dr and Pulgul St in Urangan. Rustic, relaxing, and removed from the center of town, this YHA hostel sports a pond, tennis, volleyball and basketball courts, and a pool. Rooms are clean, basic, and tiny, and the common room ($10 video deposit) is next to an open kitchen—a great social scene. Laundry facilities. Reception open 6:45am-7pm and 8:30-9:30pm. 3-bed dorms $13; twins and doubles $32. Log cabin for 2 $50. Tent sites $6. Linen included. Key deposit $10. Cutlery deposit $5.

Beaches Backpackers, 195 Torquay Rd (tel. 1800 655 501). A pleasant pool-centered hostel that nicely balances partying with peacefulness. A 24hr. bar and an all-day budget bistro pull in backpackers by the busload. Internet access. 6- to 8-bed dorms with bath $13, twins $35, doubles $40. Key deposit $5, blanket $1. VIP.

Koala Backpackers, 408 the Esplanade (tel. 1800 354 535). A party hostel that looks like it's been through a few too many parties. Nice pool, daily happy hour at the pub 4:30-7pm. Laundry and pool. Reception open daily 7am-7pm. Dorms $13, doubles and twins $30. Pick up a $3 discount voucher from the Noosa or Airlie Beach Koala Hostel. Deposits for key $5, linen $5, cutlery $5. Dinner from $5.

Boomerang Backpackers Beachhouse, 335 the Esplanade (tel. 4124 3970; fax 4124 6911). An unremarkable motel reincarnated as a hostel, with laundry, pool, and hot tub. Reception open 7:30am-6:30pm. Dorms $12. Twins and doubles $30. VIP, YHA, ITC, Nomads. Key deposit $5. Linen included.

Scarness Beachfront Caravan Park, on the Esplanade near the corner of Queens Rd. (tel. 4128 1274). Minimum security municipal campground right on the water. Laundry facilities, showers, barbecue. Open 24hr. Tent sites for 2 $12; with power $14; each additional person $3.70. 7th night free.

Hervey Bay has the usual spread of fast food and chippers, with a handful of prohibitively expensive restaurants. For Japanese on a budget, try **The Black Dog Cafe,** on the Esplanade. (California roll $5, chicken teriyaki $8, green tea $2. Open 10am-3pm and 5-10pm.) **O'Riley's Pancake and Pizza Parlor,** 446 the Esplanade (tel. 4125 3100), serves, yes, pancakes ($4-6) and pizza ($15-20), and has cheap all-you-can-eat on Tuesdays. (Open M-Th 5-9:30pm, F 5-10:30pm, Sa-Su 7:30-10:30am.) The **Hervey Bay Bakery,** 432 the Esplanade (tel. 4125 1801), offers loaves ($2-3), custard tarts ($1.60), and a sublime cherry ripe slice ($1; bakery open M-F 6:30am-5pm, Sa-Su 6:30am 2pm). **Curried Away** (tel. 4124 1577) makes free delivery of Sri Lankan and Indian yummies such as pumpkin curry ($7.50), Colombo lamb ($8), and samosas (4 for $3; open late daily).

CAPRICORN AND WHITSUNDAY COASTS

From the Tropic of Capricorn, the Bruce Highway worms its way north through sugar cane fields and along the tropical coast. Between Rockhampton and Townsville, some oceanside towns have morphed into backpacker havens like Airlie Beach, while others, such as Mackay, still grimace at the sight of sandals and an unwashed t-shirt. The isolated Eungella National Park, within easy reach of Mackay, rewards its few intrepid visitors with tumbling waterfalls and elusive platypuses. The offshore islands vary in size and flavor, each with its own beaches and maze-like walking trails. Great Keppel Island, almost within sight of Rockhampton's shore, lacks roads entirely; the ferry lets passengers off on the beach. Much farther north off Airlie Beach, the Whitsundays are a blizzard of islands with rare, non-figurative Aboriginal art and the astoundingly pure Whitehaven Beach. All along the coast, there's plenty to see under the water as well, with the Great Barrier Reef close at hand.

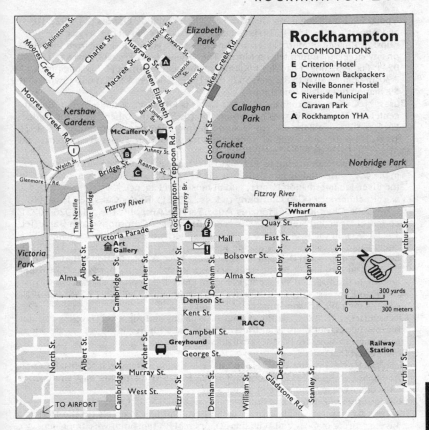

■ Rockhampton

Australia's "beef capital," Rocky sits on the Tropic of Capricorn, within easy reach of the beach escape of Great Keppel Island. The wide streets lined with over 50 National Trust buildings are a tribute to the town's prosperity, which began over 100 years ago. For the most part, it's a serious, conservative town, with its share of hair salons and saddle shops. But a few interesting activities enliven the nondescript mass and provide refuges for the wayward traveler.

ORIENTATION

Travelers arriving in Rocky from either direction are met with a bronze statue of a cow, representing the city's patron livestock. On the south side of the **Fitzroy River,** the city has an easy grid design, with most of the action near the river's edge along **Quay St. Denham St** cuts through Quay and runs to the airport; along the way, trees make unexpected cameos in the middle of the road, rising magically from the asphalt.

PRACTICAL INFORMATION

Tourist Office: Riverside Information Centre (tel. 1800 805 865 or 4922 5339), at the corner of Quay and Denham St, on the riverbank. Accommodation listings are updated regularly. Bus schedules (local and transfers to Yeppoon and the ferry terminal to Great Keppel Island). Free walking map of the city's historic sights. Open M-F 8:30am-4:30pm, Sa-Su 9am-4pm.

Airport: 6km from town, up Denham St. Carriers include **Qantas** (tel. 4922 1033) and **Ansett** (tel. 13 13 00). Taxis available curbside. No local bus service.

Trains: At the end of Murry St. From the city center go south (away from the river) on any street, then turn left on Murry. The **Queensland Travel Centre** (tel. 4932 0234; fax 4932 0627) handles bookings at the station. Open M 7:30am-5pm, Tu-F 7:30am-8pm, Sa-Su 6:15-8:25am, Su 6:15-8:15pm. Lockers $2. Taxi into town about $9. Station open daily 6am-8pm.

Buses: McCafferty's terminal (tel. 4927 2844) is just short of the bridge in the city center, off Musgrave St, which becomes Fitzroy St on the other side of the bridge. Lockers $2. Open 24hr. except Sa-Su noon-4pm. **Greyhound's** terminal (tel. 4921 1890) is on the south side of Rockhampton, on George St between Fitzroy and Archer St. Open daily 8:30am-5:30pm.

Public Transportation: Sunbus (tel. 4936 1002; fax 4936 2588) covers most corners in the city, with a sliding fare scale (usually $1.50-2). Bus schedules can be found in the Riverside Information Centre, and in most travel agencies.

Taxis: Rockhampton Cab Company (tel. 4922 7111). **Rocky Cabs** (tel. 13 10 08).

Automobile Club: RACQ: Menzies Auto Service/Ampol (24hr. tel. 4926 1022), corner of Dean and Stewart St. **Currency Exchange: Commonwealth Bank** (tel. 4922 1733), in the mall. Traveler's checks $5 fee, no fee for cash exchange. Visa checks can be cashed with no fee at **ANZ,** 214 Bolsover St (tel. 4931 7764), between Williams and Denham St. Most banks have **ATMs: National Bank,** corner of East and Denham St in the mall, accepts V, MC, Cirrus, and Plus; **Commonwealth,** in the mall, and **Westpac,** corner of Quay and Denham, also accept Cirrus.

American Express: Corner of Bolsover and Denham St (tel. 4927 6288; fax 4927 6347). Open M-F 8:30am-5pm, Sa 9-11:30am.

Library: (tel. 4931 1265), at the corner of Williams and Alma St. Travelers can not borrow books, but there is an **Internet** terminal with free email access. Bookings for 30min. sessions are possible; call ahead to get a good time.

Emergency: Dial 000.

Hospital: Rockhampton Base Hospital, on Canning St between North and Cambridge St (tel. 4931 6211, emergency room tel. 4931 6270); bus #4A south from city center will get you there in about 5min.

Police: Corner of Denham and Bolsover St (tel. 4932 1500). Open 24hr.

Internet Access: Free at the library or $6 per 30min. at **Magoo's** (in the Heritage Tavern, corner of Quay and Williams St), open M-F 11am-6pm, W-Sa 8pm-4am.

Post Office: 150 East St, between William and Derby St (tel. 4927 6566; fax 4927 6802). Fax services. **Postal Code:** 4700. Open M-F 8:30am-5:30pm.

Phone Code: 07.

ACCOMMODATIONS

Criterion Hotel (tel. 4922 1225), just south of the bridge on Quay St, is a worthwhile alternative to the relatively shabby hostel accommodations in Rocky. Grand and picturesque. Singles $21, with shower $26, plus TV and A/C $28. Twins $35. Doubles with shower (and sometimes TV, A/C) $36.

Rockhampton Youth Hostel (YHA), 60 MacFarlane St (tel. 4927 5288; fax 4922 6040), across the street and down a block to the left from the McCafferty's terminal. Or take bus #4A north from the corner of Denham and George St, and get off just after the bridge. Free airport and bus station pick-up. Good firm beds. Ask at reception for cutlery. TV room heated by a pot-bellied wood-burner. The hostel also puts together a package ($79) that includes a night in Rocky, two on Great Keppel, and return ferry ticket, including courtesy bus to and from the ferry. Reception open daily 7am-noon and 5-10pm. Dorms $15, YHA nonmembers $18; twins $36, $42. Linen included. Key deposit $5. Su barbecue $5. Bike hire $12.

Downtown Backpackers (Oxford Hotel) (tel. 4922 1837), corner of Denham and East St. From McCafferty's, walk over the bridge, turn left onto East St and walk halfway through the mall; from Greyhound it's a good bit down Denham St, at the mall. Pubstay in good downtown location. Simple rooms, relatively plush TV room. Security gate. The kitchen is less than inviting. Laundry facilities. Dorms $13.50; doubles and twins $25.

Neville Bonner Hostel, 5 Bridge St (tel. 4927 3656). From the McCafferty's bus terminal, turn right toward the bridge, then right before the bridge onto Bridge St. From Greyhound, it's a long hike down Fitzroy St, over the bridge and then your first left, or take bus #4A north from the corner of Denham and George St and get out at Bridge St. Aboriginally owned and operated; Aboriginal and Torres Strait Islander guests take priority for rooms. Unusually large motel-style rooms with private bath. Linen included. Rates run about $15-20 a night, and include 3 meals per day, plus morning and afternoon tea.

The Riverside Municipal Caravan Park (tel. 4922 3779) on Reany St just off Bridge St, north of the river (and city center). The only campground in the area, it's extraordinarily popular and only slightly inconvenient. Reception open 24hr. Tent sites $11 for 2 people, $3 each additional person; powered caravan sites $13, weekly $78; $3 for the third person. Key deposit $5 for showers and toilets.

FOOD

Cafe Neon (ΚΑφε ΝειοΝ; tel. 4922 5100), on Denham St between Bolsover and Alma St. The coziest cafe this side of Brisbane, with plush couches, teddy bears, and a trickling fountain filled with gaping carp. Upstairs is more of the same, although the floors turn hardwood and the afternoon sun seeps in. Very gay- and straight-friendly. Meals are tasty and a good deal ($7-15). Open daily 9:30am-midnight. Ring ahead to reserve your favorite sofa.

Gnomes Vegi-Tarry-In, 104 Williams St (tel. 4927 4713), near the intersection with Denison and over the train tracks. The ultimate in vegetarian hideaways, Gnomes has a roaring fireplace (winters only), wide wicker chairs, a small waterfall out back, and 2 dozen varieties of tea ($2.50-$3 a pot). Everything on the menu is vegetarian; a full meal is always $9.50. Live classical guitar music F and Sa nights. Open Tu-Th 10am-10pm, F 10am-11pm, Sa 11am-11pm.

The Wild Parrot, 66 Denham St (tel. 4921 4099), past the railroad tracks. The Parrot, with its classic Caribbean motif, is a bit of a walk for the nighttime crowd, but easy on the wallet (meals $8-11). Open Tu-F 10am-late, Sa 6am-late, Su 10am-5pm.

Cambridge Hotel, a pink building on Cambridge St. Possibly the best deal in town is the $6.90 ($8.90 on F and Sa nights) all-you-can-eat buffet, which features soup, salad, a carvery, nachos, veggies, and desserts. Open daily noon-2pm and 6-9pm.

SIGHTS AND ACTIVITIES

Rockhampton's highlights are the free **zoo** (tel. 4922 1654; open daily 8am-5pm) and **botanic gardens** (tel. 4922 1654; open daily 6am-6pm), next to each other on the south side of town. The zoo has the usual 'roos, crocs, cassowaries, and koalas (feedings 3pm), as well as a humongous geodesic dome aviary (open daily 8am-4pm) and even a pair of chimpanzees. The gardens are vast and include a fernery and a tranquil Japanese garden. They are a 10-minute ride from the city center with Sunbus on route #4A; catch it on the Denham St side of the mall (about $6 return). On the other side of town are the **Kershaw Gardens,** another sprawling floral wonder open 24 hours a day (though toilets and the carpark gates lock at 6pm). There's a waterfall barbecue area for picnics.

For more culture (or an air-conditioned refuge from the heat of summer), try the **Rockhampton Art Gallery** (tel. 4936 8248; fax 4921 1738), on Victoria Pde, has a small, stunning collection upstairs and space for touring exhibitions on the ground floor. *(Open Tu-F 10am-4pm, Sa-Su 11am-4pm. Usually free.)* Among the prints, oils, and acrylics is the unearthly *Burke in Central Australia,* by Sidney Nolan (famous for his Ned Kelly series), which captures the burning dizziness of the Red Centre.

Tucked away in the back corner of a warehouse, the **Rocky Climbing Centre,** 203 East St (tel. 4922 7800), in the Walter Reid Building next to Schwimmer's Homeopathy, is an indoor climbing club open to the public. The walls are well-studded with funky handholds, and the atmosphere lends itself to a good afternoon's fun. Casual climbing costs $10. Climbing shoes are available for hire for $6. *(Open Tu-F 4:30-9pm, Sa-Su 10am-6pm. Call ahead. Climbing $10, with harness $13. Students $7, with harness $10.)*

QUEENSLAND

Five minutes north of Rockhampton by car is the **Dreamtime Cultural Centre** (tel. 4936 1655; fax 4936 1671), providing a humble but elegant perspective on the indigenous peoples of Australia and the Torres Strait Islands. The center is set in a park with a meandering trail highlighting different medicinal and gastronomical plants of the area. (*Open daily 10am-3:30pm. Tours regularly 10:30am-1:30pm. Admission $11, students and children $5, concessions $7.50.*) **Get-about Tours** (tel. 4934 8247) has a daytrip that includes the botanic gardens and admission to the Dreamtime Centre. (*Tu and Sa departing 8:30am, $28.*) A less convenient but much cheaper alternative is the local **Sunbus** line. Route #10 north runs to the university. (*Every 30min., return $6.*)

Olsen's Capricorn Caverns (tel. 4934 2883; fax 4934 2936) is another popular spot outside of Rocky, 26km up the road from the Dreamtime Centre. There's a day tour to the caves that departs Mondays, Wednesdays, and Fridays at 9:15am ($25). Included in the price is an opportunity to take a self-guided tour through a "dry rain-forest," not the most compelling attraction of the area. Regular admission for self-drivers is $11 (students $10), including a guided tour through the spectacular caverns. No public buses run to the site. The best time to hit the caves is in December and early January, when the summer solstice does neat tricks with the cracks in the ceiling (best tour 11am). (*Open daily 9am-4pm. 1hr. tours leave every hr. Wheelchair accessible.*)

The caverns also host **Wild Caving Adventure Tours,** which allow you to spend four hours sardined in 12cm wide tunnels, navigate with the light of your helmet, and rock-climb. (*Minimum 2 people. Book at least 24hr. ahead. $40.*) Finally, **Koorana Crocodile Farm** (tel. 4934 4749), a half-hour drive east of Rockhampton along the Emu Park Rd, has a daily tour which includes watching hungry crocs shoot vertically out of the water to catch their food. (*Tours 1-2:30pm. Lunch served noon-1pm.*)

NIGHTLIFE AND ENTERTAINMENT

The nightlife in Rocky is seriously lacking, but the university students in town can give it a kick-start when nothing's happening at the student union (university parties are closed to the public). Although every pub throws some music on the jukebox at night, nothing quite compares to **Magoo's** (tel. 4927 6996) at the Heritage Tavern, on the corner of Quay and Williams St. (Th-Su live music. Happy hour 8-10pm, F 5-9pm. Open M-F 11am-6pm and W-Sa 8pm-4am. No cover.) Next door is **Flamingo,** widely accepted as the hippest nightclub in town, with multi-media sparkles. Cover is $5 after 9pm (free earlier), but the party doesn't really get started until about midnight, when you can get in free from Magoo's. Up Quay St next to the bridge is **The Criterion Hotel** (tel. 4922 1225), a great place to drink, and to drink in the history of a gorgeous period hotel with a proper beer garden out back. There's never a cover charge, live music is played Wednesday through Sunday (rock, blues, or jazz), and happy hour is limited to Wednesdays and Thursdays (5:30-6:30pm). For Rocky's **gay scene,** the only place to go is the **Grosvenor Hotel** on Alma St on weekend nights. Even then, it's pretty empty.

Rockhampton's arts venue, the elegant **Pilbeam Theatre** (tel. 4927 4111), at the corner of Victoria Promenade and Archer St, offers the occasional taste of music or theater, sometimes with student discounts (ticket office open M-F 9am-5pm, Sa 9:30am-12:30pm). Rush tickets are usually available an hour before the curtain rises. Look for a *Spotlight* event guide at the information center, or get one at the ticket office. **Rockhampton 3 Cinemas** (tel. 4922 1511), at the corner of Denham and Alma St, has Tuesday specials ($7.50; other days $9; nights and F-Sa $10.60).

■ Great Keppel Island

A trip to Great Keppel is like winning an instant vacation; it's a high-flying resort escape that miraculously falls within your budget. The butterfly-bespeckled island is mostly tracks and near-empty beaches, with fine snorkeling right off shore. And while there's budget accommodation, the island's posh resorts don't mind the odd backpacker sipping a cappuccino in style, or taking a catamaran out for a lazy afternoon.

GETTING THERE AND ORIENTATION

From the terminal in Rockhampton, **Keppel Tourist Services** (tel. 4933 6744; fax 4933 6429) runs a ferry to and from the island. (Daily 7:30, 9:15, 11:30am, and 3:30pm, plus 6pm on F. $27 return, YHA $25, children $14. Terminal open daily 7:45am-5:15pm. Departs the island daily 8:15am, 2 and 4:30pm, plus 6:40pm on F.) This is the only ferry company that plies the waters year-round; in summer others may or may not surface, depending on the local economy.

Unless you're driving or staying at the YHA in Rockhampton, which runs regular courtesy buses to the ferry, you'll need to catch a bus. **Young's Bus Service** (tel. 4922 3813) runs to the ferry from the corner of Denham and Bolsover St (M-F 7 per day, Sa-Su 3 per day; $13 return). **Rothery's Coaches** (tel. 4922 4320) offers roughly the same deal. Buy tickets from the driver. Timetables are available at the Riverside Information Centre. Free parking is available in the dusty carpark outside the ferry terminal. At the roundabout off the main road, take the second left to the underground parking lot. Follow the road down and to the left, until the ferry terminal sign blazes in front of you. The **Rosslyn Bay Inn Resort,** a two- to three-minute walk from the ferry terminal, has covered and secured car parking for $6 a day.

The ferry lets passengers out on a patch of sand called **The Spit.** The town's one main road, a brown-brick sidewalk called the **Yellow Brick Road,** runs the entire commercial strip of Great Keppel; it's a five-minute stroll.

ACCOMMODATIONS, FOOD, AND NIGHTLIFE

The budget accommodations on the island have recently been shuffled around; the YHA has moved and changed its name three times in the last year. Though most are under construction, they should be completed by early 1999. In any case, they're getting better, which is fortunate given the only other options are ridiculously expensive, and camping is not allowed anywhere on the islands.

Great Keppel Island Backpackers (tel. 1800 180 235 or 4939 8655) is friendly and laid-back. The staff takes you on boating, canoeing, fishing, and snorkeling excursions, with all gear included, as part of the deal—which happens to be the cheapest on the island. Check-out 9am. Guests get 10% off on Island Pizza. Dorms $12, first night $15. Includes linen, barbecue. Two lodges for up to 7 people each are good deals for families and groups; 2 people $90, each additional person $10.

Keppel Haven (tel. 4933 6744). Hulking green "safari tents" are the only budget accommodation the Haven provides. Each tent is half 4-bed dorm and half twin or double, divided by a partition. Check-out 9am. Very few showers and toilets. Dorms $16; twins and doubles $36, individual use $25; children $11. Linen $5, $30 deposit. Cutlery deposit $20. Reception open 7:30am-5pm.

Great Keppel Island Village, the new YHA, was still under construction when *Let's Go* went to press. 3-bed dorms $15, twins $17, family $50, more for non-YHA.

You'd do well to bring your own food. A generally overlooked deal is the **Rosslyn Bay Fisherman's Co-op** (tel. 4933 6105; open M-F 9am-5pm, Sa-Su 8:30am-5pm), on the mainland. If you have a few minutes before the ferry takes off, check out their fresh-from-the-water offerings. From the ferry terminal, take a left down the side-street, and it's a two-minute walk. Half the stuff they sell is already cooked (crabs, bugs, prawns).

Great Keppel itself has limited offerings. **The Keppel Cafe,** near the resort, looks like your basic takeaway shop, but it's the best food at the best price on the island (open 8am-9pm). At **The Shell House** (tel. 4939 1004), there are approximately one gazillion shells in the front room, where Derek cheerily serves up coffee ($1), tea ($1 a pot), and Devonshire tea ($5). It's open daily from "about early" to "not *too* late." **Island Pizza** (tel. 4939 4699) serves large pizza ($16-20) and garlic bread ($3; open Tu 6pm-late, W-Su 12:30-2pm and 6-9pm). The **Wreck Bar,** by the resort, is an ideal nightclub—spacious, with good music and a huge video screen inside featuring weekly viewings of *Melrose Place* and the *X-Files.* The beach is just outside.

ACTIVITIES

Monkey Beach is generally accepted as the best place to go **snorkeling** off the beach, a mere half-hour jaunt south from the hostels. The hike up to the **Old Homestead** and back takes a couple hours, and a trip to the unimpressive **lighthouse** twice as long. Alternately, try the hike to **Mt. Wyndham**—it's where most of the postcard photos are taken (2½hr. return). Keppel Haven's *Track Map* is ideal for bush walks; it's free at the ferry terminal on the mainland, or 50¢ on the island. A larger, prettier, but less detailed map is also widely sold on the island ($1).

For those desiring a little sport in their island adventures, the **Beach Shed** (tel. 4939 2050) has windsurfers ($8 per 30min.), jet skis ($30 per 15min.), and the old stand-by snorkel and fins ($10 per day). The **Dive Shop** (tel. 4939 5022), right next door, offers dives for the certified ($55) and the uninitiated ($80). YHA members making two dives get a 20% discount. For many visitors, however, it's enough to curl up on any one of the beaches, listen to the gentle lap of clear blue waters, and take it easy.

■ Mackay

The majority of visitors use Mackay merely as a gateway to Eungella National Park and the nearby Finch Hatton Gorge, but the city deserves a little more credit. Street mosaics, Art Deco architecture, and plenty of public gardens decorate the downtown of this easygoing and hospitable burg.

ORIENTATION AND PRACTICAL INFORMATION

Mackay sits along the southern bank of the Pioneer River. **River St** runs along the waterfront, and the town's main drag is the next parallel street to the south, **Victoria St.** Plenty of nightlife and restaurants line **Sydney** and **Wood St,** which are perpendicular to Victoria St. The **Bruce Hwy** comes into the west side of town and the exit leads to Gordon St, parallel to and just south of Victoria St.

Tourist Office: Mackay Tourism Office, 320 Nebo Rd (tel. 4952 2677; fax 4952 2034). Open M-F 8:30am-5pm, Sa-Su 9am-4pm.

Airplanes: Mackay Airport (tel. 4957 0220), about 5km from town along Milton St. No public transport, but hostels offer free pick-up and a taxi costs about $10. **Qantas** (tel. 4953 5999) and **Ansett** (tel. 4957 1574) are the major carriers.

Trains: The train station is about 5km from town. No public transport, but hostels offer free pick-ups and a taxi costs about $10. No ticket counter at the station; purchase tickets in town at any travel agent. **Queensland Rail** bookings (Brisbane tel. 13 22 32; local tel. 4952 7425). Lockers $2. Open 24hr., but only staffed daily 5:30am-8:30pm.

Buses: Mackay Bus Terminal (tel. 4951 3088; fax 4951 1009), on the corner of Milton and Gordon St. Booking desk handles bus, train, and air ticketing (V, MC). Terminal open 24hr., ticket counter open daily 7:30am-6pm. Call hostels for free pick-up.

Taxis: Mackay Taxi (24hr. tel. 13 10 08). **Taxi Transit** (tel. 4951 4990) will take you to the northern beaches (Eimeo Beach $3), but not to local destinations. Book at least 1hr. in advance; taxis leave from the Caneland Shopping Centre every hr. on the ½hr.

Car Rental: U-Drive (4957 5606) rents from $29 per day. **Thrifty** (tel. 4957 3677) and **Budget** (tel. 4951 1400) each hire from $40 per day.

Budget Travel Office: Flight Centre (tel. 4957 4844; fax 4957 4749), in the Caneland Shopping Centre. Open M-W and F 9am-5:30pm, Th 9am-9pm, Sa 9am-3pm.

Currency Exchange: Commonwealth Bank, 126 Victoria St (tel. 4953 5559; fax 4951 5592). Traveler's checks $5, no fee for cash.

American Express: 166 Victoria St (tel. 4953 5210; fax 4953 5727). Holds mail free for 1 month. Does not presently exchange traveler's checks, but plans to start that service soon. Open M-F 8:30am-5pm, Sa 8:30am-noon.

Automobile Club: RACQ, 35 Evans Ave (24hr. tel. 4957 3555).

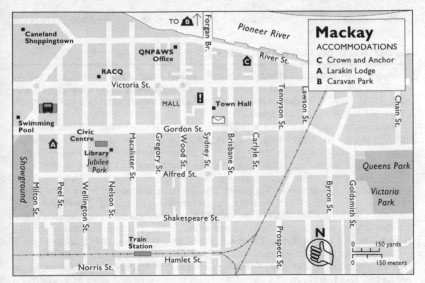

Mackay
ACCOMMODATIONS
C Crown and Anchor
A Larakin Lodge
B Caravan Park

Camping Supplies: Camping World (tel. 1800 808 783; fax 4953 1966), corner of Gregory and Alfred St. Maps, cooking supplies, tents, bush hats, and a selection of hiking gear and winter wear. Open M-F 8am-5pm, Sa 8:30am-12:30pm.

National Parks Office: River and Wood St (tel. 4951 8788). Supplies national park info, videos on the reef, and permits for the Cumberland Islands and Cape Thomason ($3.50 per person per night). Open M-F 8:30am-5pm.

Emergency: Dial 000.

Police: (24hr. tel. 4968 3444). On Sydney St, between Victoria and Gordon St.

Hotlines: Victims of Crime (24hr. tel. 1800 689 339).

Hospital: Mackay Base Hospital (24hr. tel. 4951 5211). Follow Gordon St west to the Bruce Hwy, turn right at Bridge St; it's on the left before the bridge.

Post Office: 57-59 Sydney St (tel. 4957 7333), between Victoria and Gordon St. Fax and photocopying. Also in Caneland Shopping Centre (tel. 4953 1615). Open M-W 8:30am-5:30pm, Th 8:30am-7pm, F-Sa 8:30am-noon. **Postal Code:** 4740.

Phone Code: 07.

ACCOMMODATIONS

Mackay possesses a cornucopia of accommodation options, most of which are clustered along Nebo Rd. The local YHA hostel, **Larrikin Lodge,** 32 Peel St (tel./fax 4951 3728), just 200m from the bus terminal, is a wide timber house with sloping ceilings. Its covered porch features a small pool and barbecue. (Reception open daily 7-10am and 5-10pm. Dorms $14, YHA nonmembers $15; twins and doubles $34. Linen free.) The local watering hole, the **Crown and Anchor Hotel,** 27 River St (tel. 4953 1545), at the intersection of Brisbane St, rents comfortable dorm bunks ($15), with linen, laundry (no dryer), a free Sunday barbecue, and daily lunch and dinner specials ($2). Camping in the backyard is free, but with no guarantees for the safety of your person or belongings. (Reception open 10am-10pm.)

The **Metro Motor Inn,** 34-38 Nebo Rd (tel. 4951 1811; fax 4951 1255), is one of the Nebo multitude, its rooms accoutred with TV, fridge, and phone. (Singles $46; doubles $48; family $65; two-room suite $85. 24hr. reception.) The **Pioneer Villa Motel,** 30 Nebo Rd (tel. 4951 1288; fax 4957 3647), distinguishes itself with old-school hacienda stylings. ¡Olé! (Singles $45; doubles $50; self-contained units $55. Reception open daily 9am-10pm.) **Central Caravan Park** (tel. 4957 6141), Malcomson St, just over the Jorgan Bridge, is near the city center, and offers a pool, laundry, and a kitchen. (Villa doubles $30, cabin doubles $20; sites $8, powered $10. Reception open daily 7am-8pm.)

FOOD AND ENTERTAINMENT

Mackay's many workingman's clubs located around Victoria and River St. try to draw in hungry laborers with dirt-cheap lunch and dinner specials ($2-3). For basic shopping needs, there's a **Woolworths** (tel. 4951 2288) in the Caneland Shopping Centre (open M-F 8am-9pm, Sa 8am-5pm).

The cheapest deal in town for non-fried morsels is the **Tropical Salad Bar** (tel. 4957 3116), at the corner of Victoria and Sydney St, specializing in salad sandwiches ($2-3), homemade soup with bread ($2), and generous fresh fruit platters ($3). (Open M-F 7am-4pm, Sa-Su 7am-noon). At **The Meeting House**, 53 Sydney St (tel. 4953 5835), next to the police station, oversized portions of Indonesian, Malaysian, and Singaporean pan dishes cost $5 at lunch; prepare to fight your way in for a seat (open M-F noon-2pm and 6:30-9pm, Sa 6:30-9pm; reservations accepted). **The Globe Cafe**, 36 Sydney St (tel. 4957 3913), has an open-air front and great ambience, as well as reasonable prices, good breakfasts, homemade ice cream, and four Internet terminals. (Internet access $6 per 30min. Takeaway available. BYO. Open daily 8:30am-11pm.)

The Spotted Dick, 2 Sydney St (tel. 4957 2368), is not the local herpes clinic; in fact, its wacky decor and krazy kuisine make it one of Mackay's best eateries. Good meals run $8-14, and most of the wood-fired pizzas cost less than $10. There's a happy hour every weekday (5-7pm), live music on the weekends (no cover), and krazy karaoke kontests (W-Su). (Open M-Th 10am-midnight, F-Sa 10am-2am, Su 11am-midnight.) **The Coffee Club** (tel. 4957 8294), at the corner of Wood and Victoria St, serves breakfast and killer cups o' joe. Live bands jazz up this java joint on weekends.

The cream of Mackay's decent crop of **nightlife** is **The Blue Moose** (tel. 4957 2241), on the corner of Victoria and Gregory St, where DJ-hosted party madness rages from 8pm to 3am. (Cover $5. Open W-Su.) For a rip-roarin' good time, look for the giant cow clad in country-western attire, above the entrance of **The Saloon Bar** (tel. 4957 7220) on Sydney St. Fortunately, its interior is much more hip, with high ceilings and much space for crazy dance action. (Cover $5. Open W-Su 8pm-3am.)

SIGHTS AND ACTIVITIES

For a quick overview of the town, pick up *A Heritage Walk in Mackay* from the visitors center. The **walk** begins opposite the Crown and Anchor Hotel on River St and hits all the historical and cultural hotspots. Don't miss the **Queen's Gardens,** where the lovely **Orchid Gardens** overflow with delectable flora, but be careful in the park after nightfall. *(Park open M-F 10:30-11am and 2-2:30pm, Su 2-5pm.)*

Roylen Cruises (tel. 4955 3066) shuttles between Mackay Harbor and **Brampton Island.** *(Office open M-F 8am-5pm. Departs daily 9am.)* A daytrip ($55) includes an obligatory lunch at the resort on Brampton, but you might be able to get a lower fare (without the lunch) if you wait to buy your ticket at the pier (departs daily at 9am). In addition, they run a trip out to the Barrier Reef every Monday, Wednesday, and Friday for $100 (additional diving optional—prices vary greatly). From Brampton it's possible to walk across to **Carlisle Island National Park** at low tide, but be certain to check the tides to prevent being stranded.

Reef-Gem Adventures (tel. 4959 1777) is run from Illawong Sanctuary and offers a day tour of Mackay which includes crocodile feeding, sapphire fossicking, and a city night tour. *(Tours depart daily at 1pm and return at 8pm. Free pick-up from accommodation. Adult $40, child $30.)* Abseiling with **Action Challenge** (tel. 4956 4334) is quite a rush. Half-day excursions for any level jumper cost $55 and begin at 8:30am daily, and are conducted by certified instructors.

Mackay is not known as a **diving** hotspot, but that means more pristine reef for you! Pricey charter boats are the most popular way to go, but a two-night trip on the 75ft. catamaran **Mikat** (tel. 4972 7126) includes seven day dives, one night dive, all accom-

The Leap

In 1866, the Juipera Aboriginal tribe, living in the Mackay region, made a raid on a white man's vegetable garden and killed a farmhand in the process. During the retributive counterattack, an Aboriginal woman named Kohara was cornered at the edge of a cliff holding her baby in her arms. Rather than submit to capture, Kohara laid her infant daughter on the ground and leapt to her death. In an act of reparation, Jack Barnes, the farmer whose garden was the subject of the initial raid, took the baby from the mountain and raised her as his own child. However, many, particularly Aboriginals, attributed the devastating effects of the 1918 cyclone to the vengeance of Kohara's spirit. This story was passed along firsthand in the region by Kohara's granddaughter until she died just under a decade ago.

modation, and meals for $350. Advanced courses for already certified divers are a tremendous value at $100. (These do not include reef trip.)

■ Near Mackay

Twenty minutes north of Mackay along the Bruce Hwy is the small community of **The Leap,** located at the base of a massive stone precipice. The town is most famous for the legend associated with its name (see below), but the **Leap Hotel** (tel. 4954 0993) has cheap, clean rooms (singles $15; double $25) and the beer flows daily from 10am to midnight. A few kilometers up the Bruce Hwy is the right-hand turn off to **Cape Hillsborough National Park.** Camping in the national park requires a permit ($8 per night) which can be obtained through the Mackay City Council. In town, pick up the *Cape Hillsborough Visitor Information Sheet,* which details some of the area's finest walking tracks (available at the National Parks Office in Mackay). The 1.6km **Beachcomber Cove Track** (1½hr. return) is the steepest trail but provides great views from the top of the ridge. The 1.2km **Juipera Plant Trail** is easier (1hr. return) and features a variety of catch-it-yourself bush tucker. Just next door to the Cape Hillsborough campsite is the **Cape Hillsborough Holiday Resort** (tel. 4959 0152), which offers over 7km of its own walking tracks and has a pool, restaurant, and barbecue. (Open daily 8am-7pm. Doubles $35-49; two-room beach cabins $55; tent sites $10; caravan sites $15.) Adjacent to Cape Hillsborough is one of the best northern beaches, **Smalley's Beach.** The **campsite** there has toilets and water but no showers; there's also a non-strenuous 1.5km walk from the site that leads through the Hidden Valley. Permits are issued by the **Park Ranger's office** (tel. 4954 0993; open M-Sa 10am-10pm, Su 10am-7pm). **Black's Beach** is another sweet location as is the popular **Eimeo Beach** at the end of the Cape Hillsborough turn-off.

MACKAY TO EUNGELLA

The road to Eungella heads out from the south side of Mackay, along the Bruce Hwy, through sugar cane towns with looming roadside refineries. If you're coming from the north, there's a shortcut down the sugar cane lanes; turn right at the Marian sign, just north of The Leap, and turn right (west) when you hit the main road in Marian.

Along the way is the recently relocated **Illawong Sanctuary** (tel. 4959 1777; fax 4959 1888), in Mirani, a well-maintained wildlife sanctuary sparsely populated by the usual suspects: koalas, kangaroos, crocodiles, and kookaburras. (Open daily 9:30am-5pm. Tours daily 3:30pm. Koala feedings daily 10:30am, 4:30pm; crocodile feedings at 2:30pm. Admission $10; children $5. Return bus to Mackay and ticket combo $40.)

Farther along as you come from Mackay is the **Finch Hatton Gorge.** Contact the ranger (tel. 4958 4552) for the latest on trail conditions. Walking trail maps are available for free at the QNP&WS office in Mackay. The half-hour hike up to **Firewheel Falls** is one of the most enjoyable circuits in the area with knockout floral diversity. **The Platypus Express** (tel. 4948 0999 or 4958 3359) is a shuttle service to and from Airlie Beach ($15 one-way, $30 return). **Ronnie's Palmco Kiosk** (tel. 4958 3285; open daily 9am-5pm), on the road to the gorge, is a lonely culinary outpost in the midst of the rainforest. Equally improbable are its specialties, including kickass chocolate ice cream, mango cheesecake ($4.50), sandwiches ($4-5), and fresh coffee ($2.50 a mug). A sign out front plaintively exhorts travelers, "Eat here or we'll all starve!"

Just off the dirt road to Finch Hatton Gorge is the **Platypus Bush Camp** (tel. 4958 3204 to check availability), a rugged but fabulous rainforest hostel, with rooms in elevated huts that afford great views of the adjacent creek burgeoning with platypuses, fireflies, and fruit bats. There's an open-air kitchen, a gently rocking porch swing, common area hut, and rustic but serviceable showers and toilets. (Dorm bunks $15; doubles $45; camping $5 per person. Free pick-ups from Mackay for groups of 4 or more.) Just before the range is the basic **Finch Hatton Caravan Park** (tel. 4958 3222), with a kitchen, pool, and barbecue. (Tent sites $5, caravan sites $11.)

■ Eungella National Park

Much of 49,610-hectare Eungella National Park, 84km west of Mackay and the largest national park in central Queensland, is inaccessible to the average tourist because its rainforest-covered slopes are too steep and the misty valleys too deep. What you can see is gorgeous, though. The mountains trap clouds, resulting in high precipitation, and serve as natural barriers between this park and other swaths of rainforest in Queensland. Eungella's genetic isolation have given rise to at least six entirely unique species of plants and animals. Herpetologists go hogwild over the park's diverse but endangered frog population, such as the Eungella Gastric Breeding Frog, *Rheobatrachus vitellinus.* This species of frog lays its eggs, swallows them, incubates them in its stomach, and spits out live tadpoles. More common and nowhere near as appalling, red cedars, palms, and giant ferns coat many slopes, and platypuses splash in the rushing water at the bottom of the ravines.

THE PARK

Don't let the lack of a car keep you from seeing the park. Two companies run daytrip bush safaris that are probably the best way to see the park unless you're a botany whiz. **Jungle Johnno's Bush, Beach, and Beyond Tours** (tel. 4959 1822 or 4951 1999) provides a rough-around-the-edges good time led by coal-miner-turned-tour-guide Johnno, who is knowledgeable in topics from horticulture to folklore. (Tours run Th-Su; depart 9am, return late afternoon. $50, children $30, YHA and pensioner discounts.) Cole Adams, who runs **Natural North Discovery** (tel. 4952 2677), offers tours that include full steak lunches. ($59, children $39. Combination tour to Park and Gorge for $65; 2-person minimum.) Booking on either tour may entitle you to free stays at Mackay hostels; ask about it.

The **Eungella Chalet** (tel. 4958 4509; open daily 9am-10pm) lies just outside the entrance to the park. The cafe provides a panoramic view and brews excellent coffee ($1.50). While there is fairly luxurious accommodation, budget rooms are cheap and quite comfortable. (Twin share $15; singles $20; twins and doubles $45.) Around the corner down the road to Broken River is the **Sky Window,** a 200m wheelchair-accessible trail with fantastic views, a picnic ground, and toilets.

Broken River, the park's main draw, is actually a section of river with excellent platypus-spotting, a picnic area, campground with toilets and hot showers, and an immensely knowledgeable ranger with narrow office hours (tel. 4958 4552; open daily 7-8am, 11am-noon, and 3-3:30pm). Camping permits cost $3.50 per person per night. Nine walking trails depart from Broken River.

Near the park's main bridge, the **Broken River Kiosk** (tel. 4958 4569), serves pies and sandwiches for $3 (open daily 7am-6pm). Also by Broken River is the **Hideaway Cafe** (tel. 4958 4533), a delightful international restaurant serving an array of dishes, including vegetarian options, all for under $6 (open daily 11am-late). **The Pinnacle Hotel** (tel. 4958 5207), in Eungella, is famous for scrumptious homemade pies ($3). Rooms go for $15 per person, which includes linen. (Open daily 6am-11pm.)

■ Airlie Beach

Imagine an unspoiled bay with a big grassy spot off the main road where backpackers slow down to sunbathe and watch the tides roll in and out. The islands blaze in photogenic fury at sunset, and the mountaintops of the Whitsunday Islands rise out of bottle-blue water. Airlie (AIR-lee) has become something of a port town for seafarers and island-bound divers. It was an upscale tourist destination until the pilot strike of the 1980s stalled Queensland tourism for a year and a half. The resorts became budget in a bid for survival, and backpackers flocked to them in response. Most never bothered to switch back, so Airlie is filled with generous to luxurious accommodations that you can enjoy in this little alcove of paradise.

ORIENTATION AND PRACTICAL INFORMATION

Airlie Beach's layout is simple enough. Its main street, **Shute Harbour Rd,** is where most of the hostels and restaurants are found. Picnic tables and benches line the parallel Beach Walk. Sunbathers entrench themselves along **Airlie Esplanade,** which turns left toward the bay off Shute Harbour Rd and heads into the recreation reserve.

Tourist Office: One on every street corner, but **Destination Whitsundays** (tel. 1800 644 563; fax 4649 5008), corner of Shute Harbour Rd and the Esplanade, is the most helpful. Accommodations, tour bookings, and **Internet access** ($10 per hour). Cheap camping gear hire. Open daily 7:30am-6:30pm.

Buses: Greyhound (tel. 13 20 30) and **McCafferty's** (tel. 13 14 99) drop off in the center of town within walking distance of most hostels; the YHA has courtesy pick-up. Travel offices and most hostel desks book transport. **Sampson's Bus** (tel. 4945 2377 or 1300 655 449) picks up arriving train passengers at the **rail station** in **Proserpine** ($6.50 to Airlie Beach or $8.50 to Shute Harbor).

Local Transportation: Sampson's (tel. 4945 2377) runs between Cannonvale and Shute Harbour, daily 6am-6pm, and stops in front of the post office. Fares depend on distance. **Whitsunday Taxi** (tel. 4946 4688) serves the whole area. **Airlie Beach Car and Motor Scooter Rentals** (tel. 4746 6110), on Waterson Rd, hires for $35 half-day or $45 full-day.

Marine Parks Authority Office: (tel. 4746 7022). Close to Shute Harbor on Shute Harbor Rd. Interpretive center, interactive computer programs, helpful books for sale: *Camping in Queensland* and *National Parks in Queensland* (both $5). Open M-F 8am-5pm and Sa 9am-1pm.

Currency Exchange: Commonwealth Bank, across from the bridge (tel. 4946 7433; fax 4946 7710), cashes most traveler's checks with a $15 commission. Fee for cash exchange $5. Open M-Th 9:30am-4pm, F 9:30am-5pm. There's an ANZ **ATM** next to the post office.

Emergency: Dial 000.

Police: (tel. 4948 8888), on Altman Ave in nearby Cannonvale. Open 24hr.

Medical Services: Whitsunday Medical Centre, 400 Shute Harbor Rd (24hr. tel. 4946 6275). Open M-F 9am-6pm, Sa 9am-6pm, Su 11am-6pm.

Post Office: Up the hill along Shute Harbour Rd next to McDonald's (tel. 4946 6515). Open M-F 8:30am-5:30pm, Sa 9am-12:30pm. **Postal Code:** 4802.

Phone Code: 07.

ACCOMMODATIONS

Airlie's cornucopia of budget establishments can barely keep pace with backpacker demand, so book ahead. Hostels generally provide linen, but a $10 deposit is expected for a key, unless otherwise indicated. The hostel-nightclub hybrids offer proximity to the action, but they can be lousy if you want to get a full night's sleep. The nearby Whitsunday Islands offer cheap **camping** with privacy and great views (see **Camping in the Whitsunday Islands,** p. 337).

⊛**Reef Oceania,** 147 Shute Harbour Rd (tel. 4946 6137 or 1800 800 795; fax 4946 6846), 3km from town, in Cannonvale. Sprawls luxuriously across 15 hectares of land including a lengthy stretch of private beach. Each dorm has TV, fridge, and bath. Full breakfast included. Great pool, free movies, table tennis, barbecue. Free hourly bus service (10am-late) to and from town, and courtesy bus pick-ups meet incoming buses. Dorm beds $5-10, doubles $39. 24hr. reception and security.

Backpackers by the Bay, 12 Hermitage Dr (tel./fax 4946 7267). Near town with a sweet view of the bay. Bunk-style rooms and chill atmosphere, though thin walls can make sleeping a challenge. Barbecue, laundry, saltwater pool. Courtesy bus meets incoming coaches; a shuttle runs to town 11 times per day. Dorms $13; twins or doubles $32 with VIP. Bikes $8 per half-day. Top sheet and blanket 50¢ per stay. Internet access $6 per 30min. Reception open daily 7am-7:30pm.

Whitsunday Backpackers, 13 Begley Street (tel. 4946 7376). Amenity-loaded rooms (some have tubs), pool, imperious hilltop location with killer views, and a unique pueblo feel. Hot breakfast included. Courtesy bus meets all incoming buses. Dorms $14; doubles (only 2 in the hostel) $34. VIP, YHA. Reception open daily 7am-6pm.

Koala (tel. 4946 6001; fax 4946 6761), on Shute Harbour Rd. It's closer to the beachfront and has a tiki-torch Polynesian flavor, with individual dorm huts set back from the road. Great camping ($8, $12 for 2 people). Pool, satellite TV in each room, laundry. Dorms $15. YHA. Deposits: cutlery $5; top sheet $6; blanket $20. Bar dinners from $6. Reception open daily 7:30am-7:30pm.

The Airlie Beach Hotel, 297 Shute Harbour Rd (tel. 4946 6233; fax 4946 7476). A good non-backpacker option. Old-school motel rooms equipped with TV, phone, fridge, and bath. Singles $45; doubles $55; triples $70. Reception open M-F 7:30am-7pm, Sa 7:30am-5pm, Su 7:30am-noon.

Whitsunday Wanderers (tel. 4946 6446; fax 4946 6761), on Shute Harbor Rd next to Koala. Twin rooms are a rip-off ($109), but camping is available at its caravan park. Caravan sites $18; tent sites $15. Reception open daily 7:30am-7:30pm.

Airlie Beach Motor Lodge, 6 Lamond St (tel. 4946 6418; fax 4946 5400), right off Shute Harbor Rd from Abel Point Marina. Classic motel rooms, sauna, saltwater pool, barbecue, and private balconies. Motel rooms vary with season, but start at $54 for a double and $69 for a self-contained unit. Reception open daily 7am-8pm.

Island Gateway Holiday Resort (tel. 4946 6228; fax 4946 7125), on Shute Harbor Rd 1.2km from the center of town. Very family-friendly. Cabin family rate $49, selfcontained unit family rate $59. Cabins for 2 $39, on-site vans for 2 $29. Tent sites $9, powered $17. Reception open daily 7:30am-7pm.

FOOD AND ENTERTAINMENT

Airlie Beach's eateries run the gamut from high-priced to backpacker-friendly. Some local hostels welcome the hungry and impecunious with sumptuous buffets. **Magnum's** (tel. 4946 6266) and **Beaches** (tel. 4946 6244), in the middle of Shute Harbor Rd, offer cheap dinners ($5-6), with a free glass of beer, wine, or soda if you show up early (5pm) and pick up a voucher on the street. The PA pumps music, and seating is generally at long, communal wooden tables. **Backpackers by the Bay** (tel. 4746 7267) also has a massive barbecue every Wednesday and Friday ($6.50, no vegetarian options).

Outside the hostel circuit but still well within the price range, **Chatz Brasserie** (tel. 4946 7223) has a mondo lunch special: steakburger and chips lunch special with a free beer for $5. For just $5 they'll prepare any fish you might have caught out on Whitsunday waters. Lots of crazy crap on the walls, and plenty of veggie options. (Daily happy hour 5-6:30pm. Meals served daily 11am-11pm.) Check out the **Hog's Breath Cafe,** 261 Shute Harbor Rd (tel. 4946 7894), to see the original link in a chain that now spans the Queensland coast. (Meals $7-17. Open daily for lunch 11:30am-5pm and dinner 5:30pm-late.) **Tequila Willie's,** 283 Shute Harbor Rd (tel. 4946 6644), serves damn hot Tex-Mex eats from $6.50-17, with a cheap daily specials ($6). (Internet access $6 for 30min or $10 per hr. Open daily 10:30am-11:30pm.) **Crepe Expectations,** 390 Shute Harbor Rd (tel. 4948 0400), has a punny name, self-effacing slogan ("Ugly Staff; Beautiful Food"), and divine crepes ($6) with a wide selection of meats, veggies, or fruits to fill them with. (Open daily 9am-11pm.)

Despite Airlie's young crowd, there aren't many **nightlife** options, though many restaurants host live music shows. **Tricks,** 352 Shute Harbor Rd (tel. 4946 5055), is the only actual club, and manages to whip up a great party most nights (no cover). However, **Magnum's** and **Beaches** (see **Food,** above) are the two hottest dance spots around. Each stay open till 2am on weekends and frequently merge into one big street bash. Rowdier Magnum's has been known to host mechanical-bull-riding or bucket-of-food-eating, while mellower Beaches offers live piano or a decent DJ.

ACTIVITIES AND A SIGHT

Airlie has a killer beach and a ton of ways to enjoy it. **Whitsunday Watersports** (tel. 4946 7077) is right on the beach and offers various means of navigating the ocean. *(Open daily 9am-5pm.)* They rent catamarans ($25 per hr.), water bikes ($10 per 30min.), tube ride or kneeboard ($20 per 10min.), jet skis ($25-35 per 15min.). **Salty Dog Sea Kayaking Tours** (tel./fax 4946 4634 or 1800 624 634) offers lessons, day trips (departs M, Th, F at 7am, returning 5pm, $65), and two-day, one-night trips (departs Tu, Sa at 7am, returning W, Su at 5pm, $195). The most common destination on the longer trip is nearby Newry Island. If you want to see the reefs without getting wet, try **Whitsundays All Over Yellow Sub** (tel. 4946 6900 or 1300 366 494), a semi-submergible vessel that makes coral viewing easy and painless. *($67, children $35. Dive/Cruise package $110.)*

If you want to pay money to scare your mother, check out the 61m, $49 bungee jump site at **Barrier Reef Bungy** (tel. 4946 1540; free hostel pick-ups hourly). For $70 you get a T-shirt to prove you survived, a glass of champagne, and a frameable certificate. **Whitsunday Parasail,** 283 Shute Harbor Rd, Shop 1 (tel. 4948 0000), sends you soaring 90m up behind the back of a speedboat. *($40. Free courtesy bus pick-up.)*

A public bus heads back away from the coast to **Conway National Park,** a few kilometers east of Airlie Beach. A self-guided walk lasts just over an hour and passes wrinkled fig trees, mucky mangrove swamps, and a few rare bottle trees. The **QNP&WS** office (tel. 4746 7022), located on the way to the park, has a detailed leaflet on the walk. *(Open M-F 8am-5pm, Sa 9am-1pm.)* **Fawlty Tours** (tel. 4948 0999; fax 4946 6848), offers a day tour to a local patch of rainforest for $35 (children $17) including lunch. If you're not heading much farther north it's definitely worth a look, but if Cape Tribulation is on your itinerary, don't bother. **The Barefoot Bushman's Wildlife Park** (tel. 4946 1480), on Shute Harbor Rd in Cannonvale, has the usual aviaries and koala house, as well as a nocturnal house and a cassowary breeding facility. *(Tickets $15, pensioners $10, children $7. Open daily 9am-5pm.)* There's also a giant waterslide.

The only official tourist sight in town is incontestably one of Australia's most utterly bizarre. **Vic Hislop's Shark & Whale Expo,** 13 Waterson Rd (tel. 4946 6928), is a shrine to Vic's unflaggingly zealous work to expose the "conspiracy" propagated by the "pretend conservationists" who try to save the worst denizens of the deep, the great white and tiger sharks. *(Open daily 9am-6pm. $14, children $7.)* Clippings, articles, and photographs document Vic's thankless battle to rid the coastal waters of the purported menaces. A real shark sits frozen in a block of ice for your viewing pleasure.

DIVING

The scuba scene is hot in the Whitsunday area. Dolphins, turtles, manta rays, and even small reef sharks prowl these waters. The most popular site for overnight trips are on the outer reefs which lie just beyond the major island groups, including the Bait, Hardy, and Hook Reefs. Occasionally, boats will venture to the Black or Elizabeth Reefs. Reasonable prices can be found year round.

Island Divers (tel. 4949 5650 or 1800 646 187) has a 4-day PADI class from $250. The 5-day course with 3 days on the outer reef and 8 dives is $450. A 3-day trip for certified divers includes 10 dives (optional night dive $10). $380; snorkelers $290.
Kelly Dive (tel. 4946 6122 or 1800 063 454; fax 4946 4368) offers basic tuition and 2-day trip for $275. 5-day course $545, 6-day available. 3-day trip for certified divers

$390. Special 3-day, 3-night trip for snorkelers $220 (optional intro-dives 1st $50, 2nd $40). Daytrips from $60. 2 free nights at Reef O's with any PADI class.

Oceania Dive (tel. 4946 6032 or 1800 075 035) does a 4-day course for $300 or a 5-day for $500. The *Anaconda III* sets sail twice weekly on 3-day, 3-night trips to the Elizabeth Reef and even as far as the Coral Sea (notorious for big sharks and great diving). Certified divers $420, snorkelers $350, PADI 6-day class $570.

Reefworld (tel. 4946 5111 or 1800 650 851; fax 4946 5520) is a floating behemoth built by the mega-outfit **Fantasea.** 2 days and a night aboard this watery hotel includes 2 dives and transfers for $298. Day trip $125, students/pensioners $93, children $63, and families $275 (does not include the diving cost).

Rum Runner Adventures (tel. 4946 6508 or 1800 075 120; fax 4946 5007) offers PADI certification in 4-day ($325), 5-day ($395), or 6-day ($595 including over-nights) classes. 3-day, 3-night trip to the reef $415 with a C-card; snorkelers $320.

Sea Trek (tel. 4946 5255) definitely offers the cheapest day of diving, but it's off Hook Island, not the outer reef. $29, children $20. Scuba an additional $45. Trips depart Shute Harbor at 9am and return at 5:30pm daily.

Tropical Charters (tel. 1800 677 199 or 4017 644 514) explores the *SS Yongala* wreck. Full-day trip $150, includes 2 dives and all transfers. Trips depart Tu, Th, Sa, Su at 7am and return 5:30pm. The wreck is primarily for advanced divers.

Whitsunday Diver (tel. 4946 5366) runs daytrips. Snorkelers $80, intro $40, or $120 for cruise and 2 certified dives. 3rd place in Rodale Scuba Diving's best Pacific day-boat operators. Trips depart Abel Point Marina daily at 9am, return by 5pm.

▓ Whitsunday Islands

The Whitsundays are a collection of 74 islands just off the coast of Queensland, some rising majestically from the sea, wooded and christened with creeks and waterfalls, others barely poking a tip above water. **Whitsunday Island** is the largest and most appealing in terms of camping and hiking. Other backpacker favorites include **Hook Island,** which features choice snorkeling spots and Aboriginal cave painting, **Day Dream Island, Long Island,** and the **Molle Island Group.** More creative names include Dead Dog Island and Plum Pudding Island. All of the islands and waterways belong to national parks, so their natural beauty is protected by law; keep your visit low-impact. The posh resorts on **Hayman, Hamilton,** and **Lindeman Islands** are accustomed to guests arriving by private helicopter. The water in the Whitsunday channel is usually a dazzling sapphire. It's not uncommon to see a sea turtle flapping for air in between the waves.

GETTING TO AND BETWEEN THE ISLANDS

Blues Ferries operated by **FantaSea,** departing Shute Harbor (tel. 1800 650 851 or 4946 5111; fax 4946 5520) is one of the only companies to run direct transfers with-out trying to turn each trip into a "day cruise" of the islands. Schedules are available at almost any booking office or hostel. Between three and eight ferries leave the harbor daily for Daydream ($16 return), South Molle ($16 return), and Hamilton ($38 return). Of course the multiple island daytrip is an option, and **FantaSea** has oodles of different package deals. Don't forget **Camping Connections** (see p. 337), which offers good deals to the more remote islands. **Seatrek** (tel. 4946 5255) has seven dif-ferent packages. The majority of these transfers depart 9am and return 5pm at Shute Harbor, but check schedule for time variations. **Whitsunday All Over** (tel. 1300 366 494 or 4946 6900; fax 4946 5763) ferries passengers to Daydream Island (return $24, student/pensioner $21; day or night) and to South Molle (same price). **Reef Express,** (tel. 1800 819 366 or 4946 665; fax 4946 6975) visits a different set, running daily to and from Abel Point Marina at 8:45am to Hood and Whitsunday Island in a glass-bot-tom boat. ($55, children $27.50, family $140.)

A few other non-sailing crafts do island trips. **Ocean Rafting** (tel. 4946 6848; fax 4946 1564) speeds you for $65 (departs Abel Point Marina daily at 10am). **The Whit-sunday Dreamer** (tel. 4946 6665 or 4946 6611; fax 4946 6833) chugs along to Long and Daydream Islands as well as Palm Bay Resort and Sun Lovers Reef. ($46, pensioners $40, children $38, family $120. Departs Shute 9:30am.) The **Lindemand Pacific,** (tel. 4946 5580) departs Abel Point Marina at 9am for Whitehaven and Haslewood Reef ($63). **Jade,** (tel. 4946 5299) does the old two-night/three-day sail on a catamaran, but far more expensive and exciting is their luxury air-conditioned hovercraft ($239). Call ahead to confirm departure times.

Air Whitsunday Seaplanes, (tel. 4946 9111; fax 4946 9185) buzzes the islands on a sight-seeing reef trip for $75. Flying to individual islands is costly. Helicopter tours and transfers are available from $70 from two companies: **FantaSea Flying Adventures** (tel. 4946 9102; fax 4946 8230) and **Helireef** (tel. 4946 9102; fax 4946 9107).

CAMPING AND HIKING

The island group is rich with cheap camping options. There 21 campsites on 17 different islands. The Molle group is the most popular. Before embarking, you must receive a permit from **QNP&WS.** Get them from **The Marine Parks Authority,** (tel. 4946 7022; fax 4946 7023) at the corner of Shute Harbor and Mandalay Rd. Permits cost $3.50 per night. Walk-in applications are welcome, but for small campgrounds, planning ahead is good insurance. Marine Parks also serves as an interactive interpretive center and has a nice gift shop to boot. There are several helpful titles for sale including *Camping In Queensland, National Parks in Queensland* (both $4.95), and the boater's bible, *100 Magic Miles*. Ask for brochures on island wildlife. (Open M-F 8am-5pm, Sa 9am-1pm.) With permit in hand you're ready to go, but a lot of water still stands between you and the hour's struggle to set up the tent. Ferries travel to some of the most popular destinations (see above). Or call the **Island Camping Connection** (tel. 4946 5255), which drops campers off at any of the islands (minimum of 2 campers, $35 per person, camping equipment available for hire, water containers are supplied).

Whitsunday Island

The principal draw of the Whitsunday Islands is the famed **Whitehaven Beach,** a long slip of white that resembles the foam on a cappucino. Sand flows deliciously between the towns, as pure as talcum powder. Behind the beach, a forest clings tenuously to the sand. Across the bay is another beach with the bonus of soft coral framed dramatically by the oh-so-white sand, right offshore. Whitehaven Beach runs 6km long along the western part of the island, with enough space to sunbathe in some privacy. The scene is idyllic if you can ignore the occasional helicopter that bears down, laden with grinning tourists. On the other side of the island is **Cid Harbour,** a common mooring site for the two-night boat trips. Cid Harbour houses the island's three campgrounds. The largest is **Dungong Beach** (limit 30 people), which has toilets, drinking water, sheltered picnic areas, and a walking track (1km, 40min.) that leads to the second campground, **Sawmill Beach** (limit 15 people). The same amenities are provided here, but remember to take a water supply if you're camping further south at **Joe's Beach** (limit 6 people). There is excellent **snorkeling** in the shallow waters not far from the beach.

Hook Island

The beaches on Hook have beautiful stretches of coral just off-shore, literally a stone's throw away at **Chalkies Beach** and **Blue Pearl Bay.** (Stonehaven Beach is currently going through a period of regeneration.) The chief problem with a beautiful stretch of coral, though, is that chunks of it are broken off in cyclones (or by careless snorkelers), and wash up on shore, creating a "coral beach" which is pretty enough to look at but dastardly painful to walk on.

On the south side of the island lies **Nara Inlet,** a popular spot for overnight boat trips. Visitors are greeted by a graffiti-ridden rock outcrop, desecrated by vandals (or "people with underdeveloped frontal lobes," as the local mariners' guidebook explains). Twenty minutes up the grueling path is a cave shelter used by the sea-faring Ngalandji Aboriginals, bordered on either side by middens, or piles of shells. The rare paintings inside date back to 1000 BC and may have given rise to the popular

Australian myth that a boatload of exiled Egyptians washed ashore ages ago and left hieroglyphic-like traces in various corners of Queensland. Although the story is unsubstantiated, it is true that at least one glyph in the cave is a good match for "king" in Hieroglyphic Luwian, spoken in ancient Troy. Leave it for those with overdeveloped frontal lobes to figure out.

Maureens Cove, on Hook's northern coast (limit 20 people) is a popular anchorage and nice site for really roughing it. Take a sleeping bag and plop down on the beach. Also on the island is **Stonehaven Beach** campground (limit 12 people), a popular sea kayaking site. Hook also has cheap resorts (see below), so if it looks like rain, there's a solid Plan B available.

Other Islands

Long Island is only a short journey from Airlie Beach and has just one campground at **Sandy Bay** (limit 6 people). There is a walking track (5km) which heads north toward Humpy Point, where you can relax with a frothy fruity umbrella drink at the resort. Rigorous hiking can be found on **South Molle Island. Sandy Beach** (limit 15 people) has over 15km of hiking options. The trip to the island's resort is 5km through the grasslands. Another 1km will take you to Balancing Rock. Paddle Bay, Lamond Hill, and Mount Jeffreys are other highlights along the circuit. On **North Molle Island** is the mammoth **Cackatoo Beach Campground** (limit 50 people) which is fully equipped with facilities, drinking water, and shelter and picnic grounds. Other fully equipped campsites include **Glouster Island's** Bona Bay (limit 15 people), Northern Spit on **Henning Island** (limit 40 people), and the small-secluded sites at Sea Eagle Beach on **Thomas Island** (limit 4 people), and **Armit Island** (limit 12 people), which is closed for seabird conservation from October to March. Basic grounds with simple bush camping sites are Geographer's Bay on **Tancrea Island** (limit 6 people), Burning Point (limit 12 people) and Neck Bay (limit 12 people) on **Shaw Island, Saddleback Island** (limit 6 people), Western Beach on **South Repulse Island** (limit 10 people), and the three other four-person sites of **Olden Island, Planton Island,** and **Denmon Island.**

Finally, **Boat Port** on **Lindeman Island** (limit 6 people) has some terrific walks. The **Mount Odefield walk** goes from the Airstrip Hut to the summit (3.6km). The **Loop walk** begins in the same spot but runs along the headlands to the northern beaches. This 6.3km walk is good for fruit-bat spotting. The easiest and shortest track goes to **Coconut Beach** (2.7km 1-way).

RESORTS

While it is true that some of these swanky spots are accessed by private helicopter, not everyone packs their diamonds for island stays. Several are budget accommodations. First and foremost on that list is the **Hook Island Wilderness Resort** (tel. 4946 9380; fax 4946 9470), which is definitely the best bargain in town. They offer beachfront camping ($13, child $7), clean hut-style dorms ($20, children $14), and beachfront cabins that hold up to 6 people ($60 for a double). The majority of the resort is situated just east of Matilday Bay. Guests can take part in any one of a range of activities from volleyball to goanna feeding. There is an underwater reef observatory at the end of the jetty. Transfers to the island depart daily from Shute Harbor at 9am on **Seatrek Cruises.**

A few nautical miles away is the tiny **Daydream Island,** which is considered part of the Molle group. For the most part, the resort *is* the island. **Daydream Island Resort,** (tel. 4948 8488; fax 4948 8499) has seven eating establishments, free childcare, and tons of watersport toys for hire. (Stand-by rates for twin rooms $85; add meals $123). If you prefer to spend a day at the resort without spending the money to spend the night, try **Whitsunday All Over,** which offers use of the club pool, lunch in one of the bistros, and a watersports discount (daytrip including snorkeling $37). **Club Crocodile on Long Island** (tel. 1800 075 125 or 4946 9400) offers a lodge room, transfers, and all meals (minimum stay 2 nights) for $65, or a garden room for $99.

Backpacker trips to the **Molle Island group** are growing in popularity. Many two-night sailing excursions moor off **South Molle** where guests may go ashore and use the pool, golf, or bushwalk. **The South Molle Island** Resort (tel. 1800 075 080 or 4946 9433; fax 4946 9580) offers standby rates for $90 which includes meals, transfer, and nightly entertainment. **Flames of Polynesia** is a popular but expensive Friday night floor show that combines fire dancing with a seafood buffet ($55, children $27.50). The island's watersports facility is open from 8am to 4:30pm daily and has catamarans ($10 per 30min.) and para-flying ($49). Most sailing trips in the Whitsundays offer diving and snorkeling (see **Sailing**, below).

SAILING THE ISLANDS

In choosing a ship, be picky. There are three classes of boats at play: the motor-powered, which chug along and aren't very inspiring (this includes boats that have sails but nonetheless motor everywhere); the tallships with all the rigging from yesteryear; and the proper racing yachts called "maxis," which are generally more expensive and always sexier. Travel agents may try to push the maxis (which give higher commissions), saying that the faster boats will make it to more island spots. This is hogwash. You'll have time to get everywhere you want.

To sort out the maxis, which dominate the market, try asking a few questions. How many passengers can the boat take? Are the bunks separate from the common space? Is there an opportunity to dive? Boats generally don't supply snacks or soft drinks, and if they do, they're at a mark-up. Consider bringing your own. Finally, keep in mind that it can get chilly out on the waves.

Traveling to the Whitsunday region without sailing the islands is like a trip to Venice without a glimpse of water. These islands are among some of the most beautiful in the world, and the only way to see them properly is to venture out on a sailing safari.

Daytrips

Reef Express (tel. 1800 819 366) departs 9am for Whitehaven Beach and includes snorkeling off Hook Island. $55, $90 with a pre-booked dive.

Baby J (tel. 1800 644 563) is similar to Reef Express: the beach, the snorkel, the $55.

Ocean Rafting (tel. 1800 644 563). The same thing, but in a big yellow raft. The serious downside is the ruthless 65kph wind.

The Gretel (tel. 1800 675 790 or 4946 4999), the course record-holder in the America's Cup, offers a trip to Langford reef daily from 9am-5pm. Adults $65, children $32.50. Pre-booked sail/dive combination $98. Intro dives $55, certified $45.

Maxi Ragamuffin (tel. 4946 7777; fax 4946 6941) travels to Blue Pearl Bay on Hayman Island M-W and Sa; to Whitehaven Beach and Whitsunday Island Th and Su. Departs from Shute harbor 8:45am. Adults $67, children $33.50, concessions $59. Dives $49. Pre-booked packages $101, children $75. Package trip to both islands $105, children $52.50, concessions $99, family $262.

NARI (tel. 4965 755) offers a day of sailing and snorkeling for $53, with dives $45. Pre-booked sail/dive package $63. Lunch is an additional $16.

On the Edge (tel. 4946 5433) departs from Abel Point Marina at 9am. Whitehaven trips M, W, and Sa. Trips to the northern coral reefs of Hook Island Tu, Th, F, and Su. Either trip $53. Intro dives $45. Package deals: pre-booked cruise/dive special $89; two days of sailing $95; cruise family rate $128.

Three-day, Two-night Trips

Tallarook (tel. 4946 5299; fax 4946 5294) offers a cheap trip departing Abel Point M, W, and Sa at 11am and returning M and W at 9am. $185 including dive. Further dives $30, certified $24. Night dive available.

Great Eagle (tel. 4946 5299 or 1800 677 119). Departs Abel Point Marina at 9:30am, M and F and returns 4:30pm W and Su. $195.

Freedom (tel. 4946 6922 or 1800 646 146) includes a visit to Turtle Bay. Departs Abel Point Marina W and Sa 9:30am, returns F and M 4:30pm. $220.

Summertime (tel. 4946 5299) highlights extensive bush walks at anchor sites as one of its selling points. Departs from Abel Point Marina on Th and Su at 9:30am and returns by 4:30pm on Sa and Tu. $220.

The Flying Dutchman, (tel. 1800 677 119) offers a round-trip with 8 dives. Departs Abel Point Marina W and Sa 9am, returns F and M 4pm. $299; just snorkeling $260.

Stargazer (tel. 4946 6969 or 1800 643 818). Departs Abel Point Marina M and Th 9am, returns W and Sa 4pm. $210.

The Otella (tel. 1800 635 344 or 4946 7172), carries up to 12 people to Hayman, Long, Hamilton, South Molle, and Daydream. Departs Shute Harbor W and Sa 9:30am; returns 4pm on M and F. Includes free day of sailing on the Maxi Apollo Yacht. $259.

Iceberg (tel. 4946 5299; fax 4946 5294). 50-foot racing yacht departs Abel Point Marina on Th and Su at 9:30am and returns at 4pm on Sa and Tu. $250. Also available for private charter.

Ambition (tel. 4946 6665; fax 4946 6975) carries 12 passengers. Depart Abel Point Marina Tu and F 9am, returns Th and Su 4:30pm. $250.

Extended Trips

Barefoot Cruises (tel. 4946 1777 or 1800 075 042; fax 4946 1668) offers 3-6-night excursions. The best deal is a 3-night cruise departing Abel Point Sa 1pm and Tu 12pm, returning F 10am and Tu noon. $425, 6 nights $825.

The Anaconda III (tel. 1800 075 035 or tel./fax 4946 6032) is a dive school boat offering a 3-night cruise with dives. Departs Tu and F evenings. $470.

Proublence V (tel. 1800 655 346) offers 5-day/4-night trips. Diving can be arranged. Departs Abel Point Marina Sa 9:30am, returns W 4:30pm. $550.

DIVING

Ninety-five percent of diving in this area departs from Airlie Beach (see p. 335). Boats normally venture to Bait, Hook, or Hardy reefs, which lie just beyond the largest island group. Manta Ray Bay, off Hook, is limited by two-hour mooring rules, but it's pristine and postcard perfect. A couple of trips do depart from island resorts but to get to the most bang for your buck, depart the mainland at one of the two harbors. If you are dead set on the full resort experience, a trip to Hardy Reef departs **South Molle Island Resort** (tel. 4946 9433) every day at 8:30am and returns at 5:30pm. (Adult ticket $125, child $63, family $275.) **Club Crocodile** on Long Island offers packages which are a bit more affordable. (Cruise $85; intro diving $60, certified $45. Bookings are essential.)

NORTH COAST OF QUEENSLAND

The northern Queensland coast sits at the junction of the tropical far north, the rugged frontier of the outback, and the civilized cities of the southern coastline. Waving fields and smoking mills represent the region's greatest industry, sugar cane. Townsville, Queensland's second largest city, is the economic and residential center of the area. Off its shores, Magnetic Island offers solitude and koalas in the wild. Between here and Mission Beach, white beaches glow next to crystalline water, across which the Great Barrier Reef beckons. The miles inland hide swaths of rainforest populated by birds, bugs, and bouncing 'roos, and between it all, the civilization that clings to the coast wrests its existence from the unrelenting wild.

■ Townsville

Three times larger than Cairns, Townsville (pop. 130,000) has fewer backpackers and tourist attractions than its northern neighbor. Queensland's second largest city is primarily residential and industrial. There are few scenic spots in town, save the picturesque marina near Flinders Mall and Castle Hill. The real attraction is a quick and

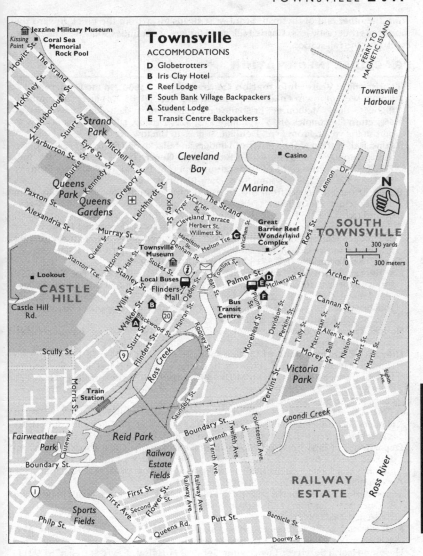

Townsville
ACCOMMODATIONS
D Globetrotters
B Iris Clay Hotel
C Reef Lodge
F South Bank Village Backpackers
A Student Lodge
E Transit Centre Backpackers

easy ferry ride to Magnetic Island, or to dive at the world-famous Yolanga wreck. But fine weather is always a plus, and Townsville averages 320 sunny days annually.

ORIENTATION

Central **Townsville** and **South Townsville** are divided by the **Ross River,** which is spanned by three bridges. Most sights and shops are north of the creek, while most hostels are on **Palmer St** on the south bank, a fifteen-minute walk over the bridge from town. **Flinders Mall** begins at the lip of the **Dean St** bridge. **Flinders St East** runs downstream with the creek to the right. From here, Flinders St West is on the left; this turns into **Charters Tower Rd** and eventually into **Ross River Rd** which leads out of town towards the **Bruce Hwy.** A left on Wickham St leads to the Anzac Memorial Park and **The Strand,** which runs along the waterfront of **Cleveland Bay.**

From the other end of the mall, **Stanley St** heads away from the creek toward the monstrous (but castle-less) **Castle Hill,** and Flinders St continues southwest along the creek past the **rail station.**

PRACTICAL INFORMATION

Tourist office: Visitor Information Centre (tel. 4721 3660), in the Flinders Mall.

Airport: West of town. An **airport shuttle bus** (tel. 4775 5544) meets all southern flights (Sydney, Melbourne, Brisbane) and runs to town daily 7am-7pm. One-way $5, return $8; couples $8, $14; family $12, $22. Driving, take Bundock St to Warburton to Eyre St. From Eyre, Denham St goes to the town center.

Trains: Rail station at the corner of Flinders and Blackwood St (tel. 4772 8288). No luggage storage. The **Queensland Rail Travel Centre** (tel. 4772 8358, 24hr. info 13 22 32) is to the right of the station. Open M-Tu and Th-F 8:30am-5pm, W 8:30am-6pm, Sa 12:45pm-4pm, Su 8:45am-12:15pm.

Buses: Arrive and depart from the Transit Centre in South Townsville, 5min. from the city center. **McCafferty's** (tel. 4772 5100) open daily 5:30am-11:30 pm. **Greyhound** (tel. 47712134 or 132030) open M-Sa 7am-7pm. Lockers $2.

Public Transportation: Sunbus (tel. 47258482) has its main terminal in the center of Flinders Mall. A 24hr. bus pass is $9. Office open M-F 7:30am-5pm. Conduct town tours in wheelchair-accessible vehicles which hold up to 10 passengers.

Taxis: Taxi Townsville (tel. 4713 1008). Has 24hr. service

Car Rental: Townsville Car Rentals, 12 Palmer St (tel. 4772 1093; fax 4721 3678). $40 with the first 100km free; scooters are $30 for 24hr. or $25 for a "daylight day" (8hr.) rental. **Can Do Rentals,** 194 Flinders St E. (tel. 4721 4766), $47 per day and 100km. Also: **Budget** (tel. 4725 2344), **Thrifty** (tel. 4772 4600), **National** (tel. 4772 5133), **Avis** (tel. 4721 2688), **Hertz** (tel. 4775 5950).

Budget Travel: mb travel (tel. 4721 3444), in the bus terminal and in Flinders Mall. Both offices wheelchair accessible and open daily 8:30am-5:30pm.

Currency Exchange: Bank of Queensland, 16 Stokes St (tel. 4772 1799) up from Flinders Mall on the left, often has the best rates with the shortest lines. $5 commission on traveler's checks. Open M-Th 9:30am-4pm, F 9:30am-5pm. The **ANZ,** 121 Sturt St (tel. 4722 3222), between Stokes and Stanley St, exchanges traveler's checks for $6.50 Visas are free of commission.

ATMs: Cirrus is accepted only at **Commonwealth Bank** (tel. 4721 1290) in Flinders Mall and **National Bank** (tel. 4750 4150), corner of Stanley and Sturt. **Plus** is accepted at National Bank and **Northern Savings** (tel. 4771 5693), Flinders Mall.

Department of Environment Information Centre, in the Great Barrier Reef Wonderland Center (tel. 4721 2399), is an excellent source of info for local marine inquiries and for all Queensland national park questions. Open M-F 9am-5pm.

Automobile Club: RACQ, 635 Sturt St (tel. 4721 2360).

Supermarket: Woolworths (tel. 4772 3200), on Sturt St between Stanley and Stoke St. Open M-F 8am-9pm, Sa 8am-5pm, Su 8:30am-1pm.

Emergency: Dial 000.

Police: Station at the corner of Sturt and Stanley St (tel. 4760 7777). Open 24hr. Also in Flinders Mall, behind the Visitor Information Centre.

Hospital/Health Services: Townsville General Hospital, 1 Eyre St (tel. 4781 9211, emergency 4781 9753). **Queensland AIDS Council** (tel. 4721 1384), corner of Flinders and Stanley, 2nd fl. Open M-F 9am-3pm. **Women's Community Health Centre,** 35 Sturt St (tel. 4771 6867), near Denham St. Open M-F 9am-3pm.

Post Office: General Post Office (tel. 4771 6133; fax 4721 1219). At the Denham St entrance to Flinders Mall. Open M-F 9am-5pm. **Postal code:** 4810.

Internet Access: Townzone Arcade, 201 Flinders St E. (tel. 4771 5780; http://www. townzone.com). Coin-op machines $1 for 6min. Open Su-W 9am-10pm, Th-Sa 9am-2am. **Transit Centre,** $2 per 10min., with 24hr. access. **Mary Who? Bookshop,** 155 Stanley St (tel. 4471 3824), on Flinders St. Open daily M-Th 9am-5pm, F-Su 9am-6pm.

Phone Code: 07

ACCOMMODATIONS

As Townsville is more of a transportation hub for backpackers than a tourist destination, its hostels are less luxurious than those elsewhere. Most accommodations are located near the transit center. Linen is usually free; expect to pay a $10 key deposit.

Globetrotters, 45 Palmer St (tel. 4771 3242; email globe@ultra.net.au). Reservations taken in cyberspace as well as over phone lines. Turn right out of the bus terminal, right again at the first intersection; the hostel is a few houses further on the right. The owners offer good deals on Magnetic Island ferry-and-hostel packages. Laundry, pool, luggage storage, Internet access, barbecue, TV, tropical garden. Gorgeous dorms $14; twins $34. VIP. Linen $1 for dorm sheet, free for twins.

Iris Clay Hostel, 261 Sturt St (tel. 4772 3649), between Blackwood and Stanley St. Aboriginally-owned and operated, the hostel is part of a national chain which gives preferential housing to Aboriginals and Torres Strait Islanders. Vacant room can go to backpackers. Laundry, TV room. Reception open 7am-9pm. By request, *Let's Go* has not published rates, but they are highly competitive. Linen and all meals included.

South Bank Village Backpackers, 35 McIlwraith St (tel. 4771 5849), near the bus terminal. Turn left out of the terminal and walk through the BP petrol station. The hostel is comprised of several scattered Queenslander stilt houses with okay rooms. Reception open 8am-noon and 2pm-8pm. Dorms $10; singles $10; doubles $20. All beds $10 per person depending upon availability.

Transit Centre Backpackers, right in the bus terminal (tel. 4721 2322 or 1800 628 836). This place has all the atmosphere of the moon. But convenient location and killer views from some of the rooms compensate for the slightly higher rates. Laundry, TV room with a view, weight room, Internet access. Wheelchair accessible. Reception open 5:30am-10pm. Dorms $14; singles $26; twins $30; doubles $32. Bikes $2 per hr., $8 per day. Cutlery deposit $5.

Reef Lodge, 4 Wickham St (tel. 4721 1112; fax 4721 1405). Decent value given the low price. Laundry, barbecue, and a courtesy bus and rail pick-ups. Lock boxes are available for valuables storage. Dorms $12; singles $28; twins $28; doubles $32.

Student Lodge (tel. 4771 6875), at the corner of Sturt and Blackwood St. The hostel only rents rooms by the week. Right in the city center. Reception open M-F 9am-4pm, Sa-Su 9am-noon. Super-clean singles $67 per week, with bath $73. Private fridges $7 per week. In-room TVs and washing machine is free (no dryer). Tenants pay an up-front $10 cleaning charge to mop and shine after they check out.

FOOD

Hidden among Townsville's panoply of steakhouses, chippers, and upscale dining extravaganzas are enough low-key budget eateries to keep a stomach happy every day of the week. Many restaurants have opened up along the newly renovated Palmer St and even more are situated on Flinders St East. One of the best is **Cactus Jack's**, 21 Palmet St (tel 47211478). Their famous margaritas are a good deal during happy hour (5-7pm) at $2.50. Try the enchiladas ($9) or the popular steak sandwich. Wednesday is $2 steak tips and chips night at the **Republic Hotel,** 31 McIlwraith St (tel. 4771 4316), diagonally across from the petrol station at the bus terminal. Early 80s music and homey local culture complement $1.80 Ned Kelly brew pots. The **Heritage Cafe and Bar,** 137 Flinders St E. (tel. 4771 2799), has a little of the Bohemian coffeehouse *je ne sais quoi*. Stuffed focaccia bread ($4-6) and some tasty chicken dishes top the menu. On Thursday after 6pm, a bucket of prawns and a beer or glass of wine costs only $7.50. **Ghekko's** (tel. 4772 5271), on the Palmer St corner of the bus terminal, is a fairly fancy restaurant run by a hospitality training school in town, so meals are super-cheap (all under $10) to make up for any imperfections in the presentation (open W-Sa 6-10pm).

Bountiful Thai, 243 Flinders St E. (tel. 4771 6338), is a small, friendly establishment that serves vegetarian dinners for $8.50-10 excellent Pad Thai and zingy red curry dishes. (Open M-F 11:30am-2pm and 6pm-late, Sa-Su 6pm-late.) Soothe morning hangovers at the **Boiling Billy,** 18 Stokes St (tel. 4771 4184), a fountain-festooned cafe with 20 varieties of coffee beans. Walk up the hill from the middle of Flinders Mall and it's on the left. Try the Coffee Game, where your $2 cuppa is free if you can guess the bean of the day. (Open M-F 7am-5pm, Sa-Su 8:30am-2pm.) **Caffe Toto,** 51 Palmer St opposite the Maritime Museum (tel 4721 1227), serves up outstanding Italian meals. Plates of pasta ($8-10) are rich and filling. Backpackers get a free beer or glass of wine with dinner. (Open Tu-F lunch and dinner and Sa-Su from 8am-late.) **The Cafe Who,** 1454 Flinders St E. has oodles of options from sandwiches to pasta, and all meals are under $10. Open M-Sa 12-3pm and 6-10pm.

NIGHTLIFE

A bank-turned-nightclub appropriately called **The Bank,** 166-173 Flinders St E., prices drinks at $2.50 until midnight; women drink free on Tuesday nights. Smart dress (jeans and a collared shirt) is the order and cover is $5. On Wednesdays there's no cover charge and your first drink is free if you show a card from your hostel. **Mad Cow,** 129 Flinders St E., features less drinking and more chewing cud; there's live music upstairs on the weekends, and never a dress code. Three pool tables here and there contribute to the calm-as-a-cow atmosphere. Cover varies, but it's rarely above $5. Sunday nights are "Cowioki" nights upstairs where contestants sing to the accompaniment of live bands. (Open M-Th 8pm-3am, F-Sa 8pm-5am, Su 7pm-1:30am).

PJ's Night Club, at Mansfield Hotel on the corner of Flinders and Knapp St, is the center of Townsville gay scene. Guys' night is on the second and fourth Thursday of every month, gals' night the first and third Thursday. Every Sunday, the club hosts a barbecue at 5pm. Cover can be up to $5. They also have weekly karaoke. **The Play Pen**, 719 Flinders St (tel. 4721 1200) is a multi-level dance party, with typical Euro, American, and techno tunes, plus live jazz every Sunday. Call ahead to check the night's events. (Open Tu and Th-Su 8pm-5am. Free until 10pm, $5 cover thereafter. In need of a little class? You can swirl and sniff all you like when testing your connoisseur skills at **Portraits Wine Bar,** 151 Flinders St E. (open 12pm-1am daily).The **Exchange Hotel** (tel. 4771 3335) specializes in beer, and lots of it. For students, pots are only $1. (Live music on Th nights. Open daily till 3am.)

SIGHTS AND ACTIVITIES

There's enough to do here to convince travelers to postpone that trip to Magnetic Island for a day. The primo sight is the **Great Barrier Reef Aquarium** (tel. 4750 0800 or 4750 0891 on weekends), in the Great Barrier Reef Wonderland at the end of Flinders St East. *(Admission $14.50, students $12.50. Open daily 9am-5pm.)* The aquarium starts at the beginning—with coral polyps that create the reef structure—and gives a full perspective on the Great Barrier Reef. There's a "venomous animals" tour led by volunteer pensioners, a wonderful touch pool full of sea cucumbers and starfish, as well as a reconstructed reef (night tours available). The Museum of Tropical Queensland has closed in anticipation for the monumental opening of **Pandora,** which will be a museum devoted to Queensland history. For a little more excitement, **Coral Sea Skydivers** (tel.4772 4889; fax 4724 4775) offers tandem dives from $217 and offers a unique course to fully license you in freefall for $400. *(Bookings are essential. Open daily.)*

For movies there's the **Townsville 5 Cinemas,** (tel. 4721 1166) at the corner of Sturt and Blackwood St. *(Tickets $8.50, students, VIP/YHA $5.50.)* The **Great Barrier Reef Marine Park Authority** (tel. 4750 0801; fax 4726 093) in the Great Barrier Reef Wonderland Complex maintains an incredible **marine life library** which includes reference books, journals, and CD-ROMs. *(Open M-Tu and Th-F 10am-noon and 2-4pm. Free.)* Seventeen kilometers south of Townsville on the Bruce Hwy, kangaroos wander at the **Billabong Sanctuary** (tel. 4778 8344; fax 4780 4569), a sprawling wildlife sanctuary with a giant pond smack in the middle (complete with a bird blind). *(Open 8am-5pm daily.)* Daily wildlife shows focus on different animal groups including informative talks on snakes and birds. **Risky Business** (tel. 4725 4571) offers exciting options, such as skysailing, rapelling, and rock climbing. *(2hr. intro climbing course $45; 1½hr. $15; 2½hr. $25.)* Horse rides are available with **Woodstock Scenic Horse Trail Rides** (tel. 4778 8888; open daily). **Bk5 Horse Hire and Trail Rides** (tel./fax 4773 3164) gallops over trails for $15 per hour on weekend or $20 per hour on weekdays. *(Open daily 9am-4pm.)*

The **Perc Tucker Regional Gallery** (tel. 4722 0289), at the Denham St entrance to the Flinders Mall; rotates exhibits throughout the year. *(Free. Open Tu, Th, and Sa 10am-5pm, F 2-9pm, Su 10am-1pm.)* **The Maritime Museum,** 42-63 Palmer St (tel. 4721 5251; fax 4721 5759) documents past sea adventures. Pieces of the U.S.S. Missouri make up one of the exhibits. *(Open M-F 10am-4pm and Sa, Su 1pm-4pm.)*

The **Townsville Omnimax Theater** (tel. 4721 1481) in the Great Barrier Reef Wonderland complex on Flinders St E shows the *Living Sea* every hour on the half hour. *(Films rotate on occasion. $9, concessions $7.50, children $4.50. Open daily 10am-5:30pm.)* The **Botanic Gardens** are comprised of three separate parks, including the **Palmetum** off University Rd (a massive collection of palm trees from all over the world) and **Anderson Park** off Wellington St (with exotic fruit trees). *(Open Su 8:30am-12:30pm.)* Flinders Mall hosts the **Cotters Market,** featuring fresh fruits, veggies, and crafts.

Many attractions near Townsville are inaccessible without a car. However, **Detour Coaches** (tel. 4721 5977) enables you to, well, take a detour. Best bets include a visit to the **Billabong Sanctuary** ($32) or dusty old **Charters Towers** ($69; see p. 389). An all-inclusive package to **Hinchinbrook Island** runs $104. *(Open daily 8:15am-5pm.)*

DIVING

Townsville's nearest access to the GBR, the Kelso Reef, is home to over 150 species of hard and soft coral and schools of brightly colored fish. These sites are on the outer reef and are fairly well preserved, but call ahead to dive companies because high winds can often obscure visibility on the more inland locations. The best diving here isn't on the reef, though. In 1911, the *S.S. Yongala* went down in the tropical waters near Townsville, and the still-intact shipwreck is considered one of the world's best wreck sites and one of Australia's best dives. Submerged in 30m of saltwater, the wreck is not for beginners; advanced certification or at least 15 logged dives are recommended. The 120m hull is the best spot. The ship is overgrown with coral and is home to a vast array of life: kingfish, batfish, and trevally are just a few of its denizens.

Coral Cat Cruises (tel. 014 444 243). 6-7 person trips (pull the people together before calling) to the *Yongala* $75.

Sun City Watersports (tel. 4771 6527) sails out to the wreck site Wednesdays and Sundays for $160. $195 includes three dives on the wreck, with one night dive. PADI and NAUI courses from $325. Departs at 5am from the Quarter Deck Marina for reef fishing trips and returns at 5pm ($125).

Mike Ball Dive Expeditions, 252 Walker St (tel. 4772 3022; fax 4721 2152). 3-day *Yolanga* trip plus night dive $399. Certification program with 6 nights of accommodation $480.

Pure Pleasure Cruises, Great Barrier Reef Wonderland on Flinders St E. (tel. 4721 3555; fax 47213590), specializes in day trips to Kelso Reef. $124, $60 more for intro dives, $30 more for non-certified. Departs Tu, W, F-Su 9am.

Pacific Dive Services, Tobruk Pool, the Strand (tel./fax 4772 6550) offers NAUI certification courses for $395 and charters for negotiable rates.

The Dive Bell, 16 Dean St (tel. 4721 1155; fax 47723119). Certification courses $350-395. *Yolanga* and Coral Sea trip prices vary seasonally. Open M-F 8am-5pm, Sa 9am-noon.

Pro-Dive, the Great Barrier Reef Wonderland complex (tel./fax 4721 1760), offers courses ($450), reef trips, and overnight stays (from $330).

Barrier Reef Dive, Cruise and Travel, Flinders Mall, (tel. 4772 5800; fax 4772 5788) organize dive trips for loners or small groups.

■ Magnetic Island

"Maggie Island?" Townsville natives will say with a shrug of the shoulders. "That's just a suburb of Townsville." But, if pressed, the source of their contempt will often

QUEENSLAND

emerge: envy. After all, it's almost always sunny on Magnetic Island. The beaches are wide and inviting, and pockets of eucalyptus trees are dotted with wild koalas. The 20km coast on the island's west side is the only inhabited area, and most of the island is national park. Transportation plans include rolling out of bed and heading into the nearest forest. On the less crowded beaches, or when young children aren't around, people bathe in the buff. Understandably, backpackers flock here in huge numbers, yet even in the peak season with the Australian school holiday crowd mixed in, there still seems to be plenty of room to stretch out in solitude.

GETTING THERE

The quickest way to Magnetic Island is with **Sunferries Magnetic Island,** 168-192 Flinders St. East (tel. 4771 3855). (20min.; 12 per day; $13 return, children $6.50, concessions $11, family $27. Reservations recommended.) **Island Adventure Ferries,** 1 the Strand, Townsville (tel. 4724 0555), does the trip seven times a day for similar fares. They can also transport you via Wildcat high-speed racing boat; including lunch on the island it's $45, and riding straight over and directly back is $30.

If you have wheels, the only way to get them across the water is on Capricorn Barge Company's **Magnetic Island Car Ferry** (tel. 4772 5422; fax 4721 3576), located all the way down Palmer St. You, your car, and up to five friends can take the hour chug to the island for $98 return. (Motorcycles $32; pedestrians and cyclists $12. Buy tickets at the terminal; call ahead to book a vehicle. Luggage can be left at no charge. Three to 5 daily departures between 7:30am-3pm, M-F 4 per day, Sa-Su 3 per day.) There's a free shuttle to the ferry; ask at the information center for details.

ORIENTATION

The island is triangular in shape, and almost all accommodations, restaurants, and activities are located along the east coast (the hypotenuse which faces Townsville). There aren't more than 20km of sealed roads and the bus system does a fine job of covering all of them. The northernmost populated area is **Horseshoe Bay. Arcadia** is the next cove of civilization, located in **Geoffrey Bay. Nelly Bay** is next and **Picnic Bay,** the island hub, sits at its southernmost point. The road continues westward (unsealed, no mokes allowed) to **West Point.**

PRACTICAL INFORMATION

Tourist Office: Information Centre (tel. 4778 5155; fax 4778 5158), next to the water taxi pier on Picnic Bay. Tour and transit bookings. Wheelchair accessible. Open M-F 7:15am-4:25pm, Sa-Su 8am-2:40pm. Luggage storage 50¢ per hr.

Public Transportation: Magnetic Island Bus Service (tel. 4778 5130; fax 4778 5380), roughly every hour Sa-Su 6:35am-11:20pm, M-F 5:30am-8pm. Stops are marked by blue signs. Tickets sold on the bus ($1.40-3.60), but the better deal is a 1-day ($9) or 2-day ($10) unlimited pass, available from any hostel or from the bus company. For stays of 5 or more days ask about the VIP pass ($6 a day). 3hr. guided tours daily 9am and 1pm ($26, children $13, family $65). Wheelchair accessible.

Taxis: Magnetic Island Taxis (tel. 4772 1555). Four cabs on the island run mainly weekend evenings. From one tip of the island to the other is $15.

Car rental: Hiring out a "moke" (an open-air, golf-cart-like auto) is super-popular, and costs $35 per day plus an additional 30¢ per km with **Moke Magnetic** (tel. 4778 5377; $60 per day deposit) and **Holiday Moke Hire** (tel. 4778 5703; $70-90 per day deposit), both at the Picnic Bay ferry pier. Open 8am-4:30pm daily.

Travel Office: Magnetic Travel (tel. 4778 5343; fax 4778 5348), in the shopping plaza at Nelly Bay. Open M-F 8:30am-5:30pm, Sa 8:30am-12:30pm.

Currency Exchange: There are **no banks** or **ATMs** on Magnetic Island. The supermarket in Nelly Bay's shopping plaza (**Cut-Price,** tel. 4778 5722, open M-F 8:30am-7pm, Sa 8:30am-5:30pm, Su 9am-2pm) will do credit card cash withdrawals (V, MC, AmEx) for $1, or free if you buy at least $10 worth of stuff first.

Medical Center: Magnetic Island Health Service Centre, in Nelly Bay (tel. 4778 5107). Open M-F 9am-11am, Sa-Su 9am-2pm.

Police: On the road out of Picnic Bay, heading to Arcadia (24hr. tel. 4778 5270). Open W and F 8:30am-2pm and M 8:30am-noon.
Emergency: Dial 000.
Post office: (tel. 4778 5118; fax 4778 5944) in Picnic Bay. Fax services. Open M-F 8:30am-5pm, Sa 9am-noon. **Postal Code:** 4819.
Phone Code: 07.

ACCOMMODATIONS

With a plethora of places to stay, Magnetic Island offers something for everyone. Camping is prohibited in the national park, and only two hostels (Geoff's and Coconuts) have campgrounds with facilities. Most backpackers buy a ferry-and-hostel combination package, usually a good deal. The two "resorts" don't have free pick-up, but other hostels do. Room prices usually include linen. Standard key deposit is $10.

Magnetic Island Tropical Resort (tel. 4778 5955; fax 4778 5601), on Yates St in Nelly Bay, is a beautiful collection of cabins of various levels of luxury. Family-oriented. A fair trek from the beach, but with lots of space and a relaxing atmosphere. Pool, hot tub, laundry, daily rainbow lorikeet feeding. Dorms are in giant, clean huts with bathrooms. Dorms $16; doubles $45. Ferry ticket with 1 night $29; with 5 nights $59. Cutlery $10. Key deposit $5.

Arcadia Holiday Resort (tel. 4778 5177), in Geoffrey Bay, is a Renaissance man's budget accommodation. Complex contains dive shops, cafes, and a nightclub, **Magnetic Mayhem** (W and Sa only). Pool, laundry, TVs in rooms. Linen available for hire. Meal hours in the resort are 7-10am for breakfast ($6.50-10), 11:30am-2pm for lunch (varies), and 6-8pm for dinner ($8-16). Reception open M-F 8am-5pm, Sa-Su 8am-4pm. Dorms $15; doubles $35; discounts for longer stays.

Centaur Guest House (tel. 4778 5668), in Geoffrey Bay. Rough around the edges, but with honest hospitality. Security is a priority here (no thefts in 9 years). The homey hostel is directly across the street from the ocean and features hardwood floors, books, board games, and a trampoline out back next to the hammocks. There's an herb garden around the side, and the full spice cabinet is at your disposal. Dorms $14; doubles and twins $34. VIP, YHA.

Dunoon (tel. 4778 5161; fax 4778 5532), just across from the Picnic Bay Mall. Divine luxury accommodation with a fantastic deal on beachfront cottages with full kitchen, dining area, living room, and immaculate bathroom ($89). Two-bedroom deluxe accommodations start at the same price; $10 per additional person. Good deal for groups. The pool is the island's best. Book as much as 2 months ahead in high season. Reception open 7:30am-7pm daily.

Coconuts (tel. 4778 5777 or 1800 065 696; fax 4778 5507), Magnetic Beach. Flush up against the ocean with kayaks and catamarans (free) and a pool for guests. Reception open daily 7am-7pm. Lunch noon-2pm, dinner 6:30pm-8pm. "Dorms" are in blue and white tents which look like a tiny fleet of starships ($16). Doubles available in run-down plastic tents ($28). Camping $6. VIP.

Hideway Budget Resort (tel. 4778 5110), in Picnic Bay. Nondescript concrete block building with scattered cabins, but quite comfy, with a nice pool. Laundry, TV, electric organ. Reception open daily 8am-7:30pm. Dorms $14; twins $16 per person; doubles $32. VIP, YHA.

Geoff's Place (tel. 4778 5577; fax 4778 5781), in Horseshoe Bay, has traditionally been the hot place to stay on the island, but a recent 11pm neighborhood curfew has curtailed the dancing and loud music (musicless bar stays open late). The hostel is the usual collection of wooden huts 5min. from the beach. Laundry, pool, tour desk. Reception open daily 8am-6pm. Dorms $14; doubles $34; campsites $6, powered $16. VIP, YHA. Meals served (dinner $6.50-8.50). Blankets $2. Cutlery $5.

FOOD AND ENTERTAINMENT

The center of gastronomical gravity is certainly **Picnic Bay,** where cafes, restaurants, and dives elbow each other next to the ferry pier; most are pretty pricey, though. The **Green Frog Cafe** (tel. 4778 5833) serves neither frogs nor flies, but has good old-fashioned sandwiches made to order ($2-4). The chicken and asparagus sandwich is delectable ($2.50). (Open daily 8:30am-5pm.) Funky **C-Shells** (tel. 4778 5959; open daily 8am-8pm) dishes out vegetarian pasta ($6), hamburgers ($5) and devilish "hot and spicy chicken chips" ($2.50). For dinner there's **Max's** (tel. 4778 5911), an open-air wicker chair restaurant with a rich view but a cheap $6.50 dinner special (open daily 11am-late). **Alla Capri** (tel. 4778 5448) has a Tuesday night all-you-can-eat pasta special for $7.50, and large pizzas are $10 on Thursday and Friday. They make good lasagna ($9) and outstanding homemade garlic bread ($4). (Open Tu-Su 6pm-late.)

The Marlin Bar (tel. 4758 1588), in Horseshoe Bay, prioritizes delicious seafood over atmosphere, and has a beachside roast on Sunday. (Mains around $10. Open M-Sa 10am-9pm, Su 10am-8pm.) **Curusoe's,** 5A the Esplanade in Picnic Bay Mall (tel. 478 5480), is much like all the chippers along the mall, but has some nice outdoor seating with an outstanding view. (All meals $6-8. Open daily 7:30am-5:30pm.) **Nelly Bay Bakery Cafe** (tel. 4758 1400), guess where, has an extensive menu specializing in baked goods. Morning croissants filled with ham and cheese or—if you're experiencing strange cravings—Vegemite, are $1.50-3. (Open daily 7:30am-late.)

The Bakery, 22 McCabe St in Geoffrey Bay (tel. 4778 5800), is tasty enough to deserve its definite article. It's always stocked with freshly made patisserie delights (open M-Sa 7am-4pm and Su 7am-3pm). **Cotter's on the Beach,** 6 Pacific Drive, Horseshoe Bay (tel. 4778 5786), is one of those rare eateries on Magnetic Island which has heaps of atmosphere. You have to shell out a bit for it, though. (Lunches and dinners $7-17. Open daily 11am-2:30pm and 6-8:30pm.)

Nelly Bay has more than its share of tempting vittles, most notably **Possum's Cafe** in the shopping plaza (tel. 4778 5409). Besides a brow-raising assortment of delectable sandwiches ($3-4) and pies that are tastier than you'd expect from a place named after roadside critters ($2.50). (Hearty, warm breakfast $6. Open M-F 8am-7pm, Sa 8am-8pm, Su 8am-3pm.) Next to Possum's is a **Cut-Price supermarket,** the largest on the island (tel. 4778 5722; open M-F 8:30am-7pm, Sa 8:30am-5:30pm, Su 9am-2pm).

There is no nightlife on Magnetic Island. However, two establishments operate under the guise. **Flamingos,** (tel. 4778 5166) in the Picnic Bay Hotel, sends courtesy buses to round up hostel guests every Friday at 11pm and lure them back to the club replete with pink velvet walls, Saturday Night Fever soundtrack, and liberal use of a fog machine. **Magnetic Mayhem** (tel. 4778 5177) in the Arcadia Resort, is less hardcore than its name suggests, although each month's theme parties sound a little wild (The Viking Party or Leather and Lace). The club promises (and occasionally delivers) "funktastic music" (cover $3-5; open W and Sa 10pm-2am).

ACTIVITIES

If you're willing to shell out more for a 15-minute thrill ride than you did for your night's accommodation, Magnetic Island has plenty of options. **Horseshoe Bay Watersports** (tel. 4758 1336) offers tube rides ($10 per 10min.), waterskiing ($25 per 15min.), paraflying ($50), catamaran ($20 per hr.), and peddle crafts ($8 per 30min.). *(Open daily 8:30am-4:30pm, weather permitting.)* **Magnetic Jet** (tel. 4778 5533) in Horseshoe Bay has jet skiing. A tour around the island on a two-seater takes a half day and includes lunch ($99). Across the street in a makeshift beach stand, **Jet Ski Hire Magnetic Island** (tel. 4758 1100) handles rental as opposed to tours. *(Singles and 2-seaters $30 per 15min., $55 per ½hr. Open Tu-Su 10am-4pm.)* **Eco Tours** (tel. 4778 5978) operates fishing trips from a van-based office by the boat ramp in Horseshoe Bay. *(Tours around the island bay $20. Fishing trips 2hr., $40; 4hr., $70.)*

Jazza, 90 Horseshoe Bay Rd (tel./fax 4778 5530), does day trips sailing around Magnetic Island. The skipper of the 42-foot vessel is a local jazz musician (hence the boat's name) who will serenade you on his trumpet as you sail. Trips include lunch and all snorkeling equipment. *(Departs daily at 10am and returns by 4pm. Maximum of 13 passengers, price does not include reef tax. $55.)* **Sun Cat** (tel. 4758 1558) in Horseshoe Bay offers a similar trip for slightly less ($49), as well as a $20 twilight cruise. Bookings may also be made through the Horseshoe General Store (tel. 4778 5080). Boomnet-riding, beach games, and snorkeling are some of the activities on this "racing yacht" (a sailboat with attitude). *(Departs 10:15am, returns 4:30pm.)*

The island's most unusual attraction comes in the form of eight camels who have made themselves very much at home in the tropics. **The Big Camel,** Lot 4 Apjohn St in Horseshoe Bay (tel. 4778 5144), can put you between the humps of the desert-bred Anwar and Sadat. *(1hr. ride $25 adult, $15 child. Departs 9:30am and 4pm. 30min. ride $15 adult, $10 child. Departs 11:30am and 1pm. Book ahead, and wear appropriate shoes.)*

Sunbird Tours, 12 Kelly St (tel. 4758 1211; fax 4758 1213), takes tourists on various walkabouts. **Walk on the Wild Side** is a bushwalk led through the World Heritage National Park (9am-noon, $25). The two-hour Sunriser ($20) or Sundowner ($25) includes tropical refreshments but is less exciting than the full-day hike to the top of Mount Cook ($70). The final package is a nature walk geared toward families with small children ($20, family rates available). **Kids Club Magnetic Island,** 5 The Grove, Nelly Bay (tel. 4778 5356), has oodles of activities geared toward little people whose parents want a solo day of touring. *(Open 8:30am-6:30am. Availability limited.)* **Bluey's Horseshoe Ranch** (tel. 4778 5109), in Horseshoe Bay, goes neighing and stomping into the bush 2 times daily (1hr. bushrides $25). The popular beach ride is sure to delight. *(2hr., 9am and 3pm, $40; or ½day $60.)*

On the pocket-money budget, **Magnetic Island Mini-Golf,** 27 Sooning St (tel. 4758 1066), has table tennis, air hockey, newly-installed lawn bowling, and, of course, mini-golf. *(Admission $5. Open M-F 9am-6pm, Sa-Su 9am-10pm, open later on demand).* **Roadrunner Scooter Hire and Magnetic Motorcycle Adventures,** Shop #4 Picnic Bay mall on the Esplanade (tel. 4778 5222) rents scooters. *(1-4hr., $20; 8am-5pm, $25; 24hr. $35. Open 8am-5pm.)* Harley sunset tours cover the island in an hour ($50).

You can visit koalas, wombats, wallabies, and red kangaroos at the **Magnetic Island Koala and Wildlife Park** (tel. 4778 5260) in Horseshoe Bay (adults $10, students/pensioners $7, children $4; open daily 9am-5pm). To see them in their natural environs, try the fantastic National Park **walking tracks.** The popular **The Forts Walk** virtually guarantees koala spotting (2km, 1½hr. return). Best koala-watching hours are between 4 and 6pm when the critters munch on the gum trees that line the path. A longer walk (6km, 2.5hr.) leads from **Picnic Bay** through wetland and mangroves to **West Point.** For a shorter jaunt with a bonus sunset panorama, try the easy walk to **Hawking Point** (600m, 30min. return; begins from the end of Picnic St in Picnic Bay).

DIVING FROM MAGNETIC ISLAND

Diving off Magnetic Island is cheap and exciting—two words that look good. A plethora of wrecks and reefs provide for multiple dives without fear of repetition. Because many dives from the island are shore dives, they do not include the expense of transport on fancy boats (which is an option too). Three dive shops operate here.

Pleasure Dives, shop 2 in the Arcadia Resort (tel./fax 4778 5788), offers incredible deals on PADI certification classes from the shore (3 days, $149; 5 days, $199). They also offer courses on the outer reef (5 days, $299) and dives at the *Yongala* wreck ($195, departs Th, only available to advanced divers).

Magnetic Island Dive Centre (tel. 4758 1399), first arcade of Picnic Bay Mall. PADI island certification classes $150 for 3, 4, or 5 days; mixed island/reef course $250. Advanced courses on the outer reef $265. Free pick-up and drop off from any island accommodation. Open daily 7:30am-5:30pm.

Pure Pleasure Cruises, Picnic Bay Jetty (tel. 4721 3555), is the largest company with the most expensive trips. Outer reef day trip $120, children $60, students and pensioners $110, family $300. This includes snorkeling only; one introductory dive is $60 extra, while two certified dives are $50.

■ Cardwell

This small village between Mission Beach and Townsville brushes up against an appealing beach that tempts wayfarers to pause and admire the surf. The town is in the middle of several large farming communities, making it an ideal place to put in a few weeks to juice up the wallet. Fruit-picking work, which pays about $10-13 per hour, can usually be arranged by owners of Cardwell's hostels.

Pacific Palms Caravan Park and Backpackers (tel. 4066 8671; fax 4066 8985), located right on the highway, offers privacy and a pool, with barbecue, laundry, and linen included. Ask the owner to call local farms about work options. (Dorms $10, twins $12, on-site caravans from $30. Tent sites $10, powered $12. Key deposit $5.) The YHA-affiliated **Kookaburra Caravan Park** (tel. 4066 8648; fax 4066 8910), on the Bruce Hwy, offers free pick-ups from the coach stop and loans out bikes, fishing gear, and crab nets. (Dorms $16, with YHA $15; doubles $32-36. Tent sites $7.50, powered $15. Reception open 7am-8pm.) The **Cardwell Beachfront Motel**, 1 Scott St (tel./fax 4066 8776), was built for relaxation, not work. Each unit is equipped with TV, A/C, washing machine, and kitchen. (Singles $50, doubles $55, twin $60. Reception open daily 8am-8pm, but tel. reservations available 24hr.)

If the giant red mudcrab in front of **Muddies**, 221 Victoria St (tel. 4066 8907), gives you seafood cravings, the atmosphere and food inside is worth sampling, though a tad pricey. (Lighter meals around $8; full meals $14-18. Open daily 11am-9pm for meals; later for drinks.) **Annie's Kitchen**, 107 Victoria St (tel. 4066 8818) makes a mean bacon and egg burger ($3.90) and an array of other sandwiches ($2-3). It's open daily for lunch and dinner. Just up the street is the **5-Star Supermarket**, 198 Victoria St (tel. 4066 8688), which despite its presumptuous name is barely large enough to qualify as a grocery store (open daily 6am-8pm).

Near the town of **Ingham**, 53km south, roars forth **Wallaman Falls**. It may be a trek, but if you're into superlatives, this is one you've got to see; at 305m, it's **Australia's largest waterfall**. Also, **Cardwell Air Charters**, 131 Bruce Hwy (tel. 4066 8468) runs scenic flights over Hinchinbrook ($69 for 40min.), the reef and islands ($95 for 1hr.), or to the **Undara Lava Tubes** ($229 for half-day, including lunch and a ground tour of the tubes). Contact pilot Margaret Prior at the Hinchinbrook ferry office.

■ Hinchinbrook Island

Cardwell is the access point for **Hinchinbrook Island** and the untrammeled wilderness of its National Park, where granite peaks loom above mangrove swamps. Outdoorsy types flock to this haven to hike and camp along the famous **Thorsborne Trail;** at least, they would flock if it weren't for the legal **limit of 40 people** allowed in this paradise at once. Book way ahead.

PRACTICAL INFORMATION A trip to Hinchinbrook is a great addition to the Queensland experience, but remember that it won't happen as a spontaneous daytrip. Instead, read up on various trail options, and you can piece together a terrific camping trip. The folks at the QNP&WS, located at the **Rainforest and Reef Centre** (tel. 4066 8601; fax 4066 8116), are anxious to help. The building is just left of the jetty where the Hinchinbrook ferries depart, on the Bruce Hwy. (Open M-F 8am-4:30pm, Sa-Su 8am-noon.) The center issues camping permits and serves as an interpretive center. A new exhibit leads visitors along an interactive boardwalk with sights and sounds of the forest contained in boxes and revealed with the push of a button. (Camping permits are $3.50 per person, per night.)

The **Hinchinbrook Ferry,** 131 Bruce Hwy (tel. 4066 8270), departs at 9am and returns at 4:30pm (one-way $45, return $69). One-way tickets are useful not just if you're planning to form a Hinchinbrook commune and never leave, but also if you want to walk the length of the island and depart from the end of the track instead of looping back. If you want to do this, **Bill Pierce** will bring you back for about the same amount one-way; ask at the office. Before leaving for the island, pick up the pamphlet on the Thornsborne Trail, which has a handy map and lots of info on camping, hiking, and wildlife.

HIKING AND CAMPING Rangers recommend spending three nights on the island. While the hike along the coastline is only 32km, rushing too much destroys the island's relaxing feel. One popular itinerary takes campers to the three main camp-sites: **Little Ramsey** the first night (6.5km), **Zoe Bay** the second (another 10.5km), and **Mulligan Falls** the third (7km further). There are seven campsites total on the islands. Take your time, but don't get too attached; there's a seven-day maximum stay on the island (sorry, the commune idea is definitely out). Mangrove panoramas abound, and there are plenty of stretches of untouched beach, although the best sand is found on the northern half of the island. The trail itself is named in honor of a local conservationist Margaret Thorsborne; if you want to help with the upkeep of the parkland, make a contribution in her name at the information center.

If you crave more rugged terrain than the coastal trail, Hinchinbrook has several impressive mountains. **Nina Peak** is the most accessible, and the only one for which a separate permit isn't required. The hike is 40 minutes each way with a great view of mangroves. The other mountains have no trails, require permits (book 1yr. in advance), and are quite challenging even for nature lovers. With even more draco-nian permitting restrictions than the island itself, the mountains receive an average of 12 trekkers per month. Still, if you're lucky enough to get permission, these are out-standing hikes. The **Mt. Straloch** hike takes you on a wild bushwalk to the island's highest point, and passes the remains of an American B-17 bomber which crashed on the island during WWII. In any event, you can't go wrong choosing a hiking agenda on Hinchinbrook, one of the most pristine areas of tropical wilderness accessible.

■ Mission Beach

Rapidly becoming a major backpacker destination, this nearly continuous stretch of beach is a placid paradise for those seeking the natural wonders of the tropical north. The town of Mission Beach is the center of the 14km strip that stretches from north-ern Bingil Bay down to Wongaling and South Mission Beach. Just off shore, the **Fam-ily Islands** are the perfect backdrop for a beach party or evening luau. Mission Beach is staggeringly beautiful and so far remains unmarred by too much tourism.

ORIENTATION AND PRACTICAL INFORMATION

The town of **Tully** lies on the Bruce Hwy north of **Cardwell** and south of **Innisfail** (see p. 354). The Mission Beach area is a ten-minute drive east of Tully, along a waterfront running almost perfectly north-to-south. **Seaview St** heads inland from Mission Beach. Not quite 200m from the beach, **Porter's Promenade** heads north toward **Bingil Bay Beach** and **Garners Beach**. Farther down Seaview, **Cassowary Dr** turns off to the south toward **Wongaling** and South Mission Beach.

The **tourist office** (tel. 4068 7099) is on Porter's Promenade just north of the Mis-sion Beach town center (open M-Sa 9am-5pm, Su 10am-2pm). Next door, the **Wet Tropics Information Centre** (tel. 4068 7179) stocks a wealth of brochures on animal life, walking tracks, and area conservation efforts (open same hours as tourist office). **McCafferty's** drops off in Mission Beach (the central area of the Mission Beach beach) and **Greyhound** calls at Wongaling Beach (near South Mission Beach) at the **unreasonably large cassowary** (a statue in the center of The Mission Beach Resort Shopping Centre).

Harvey's World Travel (tel. 4068 7187; fax 4068 2172), in the middle of Mission Beach, is a Greyhound and McCafferty ticket agent and provides foreign **currency exchange** and tour bookings. (Open M-F 8:30am-5pm; V, MC, AmEx). The only **bank** in town is **ANZ** (tel. 4068 7333; fax 4068 7431) across from Harvey's World Travel, which cashes traveler's checks ($6.50 commission, Visa free) exchanges currency ($5 commission), and accepts Visa and MC (open M-Th 9:30am-4pm, F 9:30am-5pm). The **medical centre** is on Cassowary Dr between Mission and Wongaling beaches (24hr. tel. 4068 8174; open M-F 8am-6pm). The **post office** is near Harvey's World Travel across from ANZ (tel. 4068 7200; postal code 4852; open M-F 9am-5pm).

The **Mission Beach Police Department**, half a kilometer past the ludicrously over-sized cassowary heading towards Wongaling Beach, is open 9am to 5pm daily (in theory) with a direct line to the Innisfail station for emergencies.

ACCOMMODATIONS

All hostels offer free pick-up at the bus station.

The Treehouse (tel. 4068 7137; fax 4068 7028), is perched on a hill (but not in a tree), on Bingil Bay. Sooty, the live-in burro, presides over the house, whose doors are made of interlaced bamboo. The beach is a bit of a trek (2.5km), but a free hostel courtesy bus runs the route (every 2hr.). Pool, laundry, and ultra-comfy reading space with massive pillows and newspapers from around the world. Dorms $16; doubles $40. Linen included. Camping out back $10, but discouraged. V, MC.

Mission Beach Backpackers Lodge (tel. 4068 8317; fax 4068 8616), south of Mission Beach, past Wongaling Beach. Coming from either direction, turn onto Wongaling Beach Rd at the very big cassowary; the hostel is on your left. Clean 2-story house with pool, laundry facilities, and a volleyball net out front. Dorms $16; twins $31; doubles $32. With A/C add $2. VIP. Linen included. Dinners served nearly every night ($3-5). Key deposit $5. V, MC. Mission Beach Resort, across the street, has $2 dinner specials on Tu.

Scotty's Mission Beach House (tel. 4068 8676; fax 4068 8520), farthest south and closest to the beach (follow signs for South Mission Beach). Free cocktails for guests from 6-7pm. Guests gather on the veranda, sipping and mingling next to the pool and its "topless bathing is permitted" sign with a red cross through a pair of bikini-ed breasts. Laundry facilities, TV, and shared noisy plumbing. Dorms $15 (4 available for $10 on a first-come, first-served basis, with bath $18; twins and doubles from $35).

Hibiscus Caravan Park (tel. 4068 8138; fax 4068 8778), on Cassowary Dr between Mission and Wongaling Beaches, is close to the beach and managed by a peppy family. From the Greyhound stop, walk away from the plaza toward the curve in the road; it's ahead 100m. Pool, barbecue, and a shopping plaza practically next door. Tent sites $11; with power $14; cabins for 2 $34.

FOOD

The majority of restaurants are concentrated in North Mission Beach at the village green just along Porter's Promenade. **Cut-Price,** in Mission Beach, and **Foodstore,** in Wongaling Beach behind the uncannily gargantuan cassowary, vend staples (both open daily 8am-7pm). Some cheap eats and great finds hide within Mission Beach's shopping plazas. Take a Mail & Ride bus from your hostel ($2, one-way).

The Food Brasserie (tel. 4068 7850), village green, bills itself as specializing in "Modern Cuisine." Dinners are$10-20, sandwiches $5-10. Open for lunch and dinner.

Toba, 37 Porter's Promenade, village green, serves a variety of Asian cuisine from Pad Thai to Indonesian fried noodles ($12-16.) All furniture is authentic Asian, and herbs are grown in the back yard. Open M and W-Su 6pm-late.

Mission Beach Gourmet Delicatessen (tel. 4068 7660) sits behind Friends Restaurant at the sign of the flying pig. Deli sandwiches of all varieties $3.50; a full picnic basket for 2 $25 (call ahead). Open M-F 9am-5:30pm, Sa 9am-1pm.

Friends (tel. 4068 7107), next door on the village green, is more up-market and serves seafood. Open nightly 6pm-late, closed Su. BYO.

That'll Do (tel. 4068 7300) is cheap and greasy. Burgers $3.50, fish and chips $4.50, and decent-sized ice creams $1.50. Open daily 11am-8pm.

Ma Donovan's Bakers (tel. 4068 8944), in the Wongaling Beach area to the right of the absurdly gargantuan cassowary, sells generously sized foccacia pizzas ($2.80), loaves of fresh bread ($2), and tempting "vanilla slices" ($1.20). Gluten- and yeast-free bread made to order; call ahead. Open M-F 6am-5:30pm, Sa-Su 6am-1pm.

SIGHTS AND ACTIVITIES

Mission Beach Adventure Tours (tel. 4068 8882) does calm-water canoeing trips ($65). The **Girramay Walkabout** (tel. 4068 8850) gets you out in the bush, throwing boomerangs and eating grubs (when in season). The tour ($50) includes a barbecue lunch (not just grubs). **Mission Beach Rainforest Treks** (tel. 4068 7137) leads morning ($25) and night ($15) rainforest walks. **Raging Thunder** (tel. 4030 7990) and **R 'n' R** (tel. 1800 079 039) have whitewater rafting packages ($130), and Raging Thunder also offers tamer whitewater kayaking on the Tully River ($90). Any of the hostels can book these trips, often with a 10% YHA discount. Tandem skydiving is a popular leap; try **Jump the Beach** (tel. 4050 0671), which charges $228 from 8,000 ft.

It's surprising how many terrific **walking tracks** lie within an area as sparsely populated as Mission Beach. The best overview of walking options is found in a green pamphlet called *Walking Tracks in the Mission Beach Area,* which may be attained at the Water Taxi, hostels, or the Wet Tropics Information Center. There are three separate walks within the **Licuala State Forest.** The one which begins at the car park of the Tully-Mission Beach road gives a nice view of the rainforest canopy (1.25km). The abbreviated version of this track is called **The Children's Walk** (consult the brochure *Cassowaries for Kids*). **The Cutten Brothers Walk,** constructed in 1988 as a part of the Bicentennial Celebration, snakes through Mangroves (1.5km). Longer walks include the **Bicton Hill Track** (4km, 2hr., starts 3km past the Wet Tropics Info Centre). The longest winds primarily through coastal lowlands (7km, approx. 3hr.). Finally, the **Kennedy Track** is a good sampler with mangrove views, sections of beach, and a dollop of rainforest to boot (7km, 4hr.).

In the same complex as the Wet Tropics Information Centre is the **4C,** or **Community for Coastal and Cassowary Conservation** (tel. 4068 7197), a free mini-theater of the Mission Beach area wildlife. The 4C contains giant forest dioramas, explanatory CD-ROMS, videos, and a seedling nursery.

DIVING FROM MISSION BEACH

The pristine corals and sand cays of the reefs off Mission Beach make it one of the best diving spots on the Great Barrier Reef. Divers share the virgin sites with manta rays, giant grouper, and dolphins. Only three main carriers do trips from Mission Beach. The most popular daytrip for backpackers and families is found aboard the M.V. Friendship of **Friendship Cruises,** Clump Point Jetty (tel. 4068 7262). The crew feed the giant spotted grouper affectionately named "Neptune" from the boat's side before tying off just off Beaver Cay for a great day of diving. The small boat and crew ensure personal attention, which is especially important for beginning divers taking their first plunge. (Reef trips depart daily at 8:30am and return between 5 and 5:30pm. Includes snorkeling. Adult $64, children 6 to 14 yrs. $32. First intro dive $50, second $25. First dive for certified divers $35, second $15. Bring your own lunch. Open daily 7:30am-6pm. Certification courses available upon request.

QuickCat, Clump Point Jetty (tel. 4068 7289 or 008 654 242), visits **Dunk Island** or the reef but is considerably more expensive. The island transportation is about the same as the competition. The boat is big and can accommodate many divers, so know what you want the tone of your day to be before going out. (Adult return $24, child $12. Reef cruise starts at $122 adult, $61 child, and $116 pensioner. Intro dives are a steep $65 for the first, $30 for the second; certified dive $50, $30.) For an intimate encounter with the reef, a chartered boat might be a better option. **Beach Dive Charters** (tel. 4068 7294) takes divers out to a 100-year-old shipwreck ($139), or out to the reef—prices vary greatly depending upon season and availability. The final dive centre in the area is **Mission Beach SCUBA School,** which offers PADI certification.

■ Near Mission Beach

■ The Family Islands

A daytrip to the Family Islands is perhaps the best and shortest excursion from Mission Beach. **Dunk Island,** a.k.a. the "father island," lies just off-shore. The largest of the nuclear grouping, this island is also the only tourist-accessible one. Nearby **Bedarra,** also known as "the mother," is uninhabited except for a hoity-toity resort. The "twins" are close together and only slightly farther out. The smaller land masses at the fringe of the group are the brothers, sisters, and the triplets. Big family.

To visit Dunk, take one of two boats which service the island. Those looking to maximize time on the island should opt for the **Dunk Island Express Water Taxi** (tel. 4068 8310), Banfield Parade, near Scotty's on Wongaling Beach, runs boats every 90min. from 8am-5pm. The trip takes 7 to 10 minutes and costs $22 return. The boat rests in knee-deep water for departures and arrivals so prepare to shed your shoes and wade out to catch your taxi. For lollygaggers who want to prolong their cruise over to the island, check out **Dunk Island Ferry and Cruises,** Clump Point Jetty (tel. 4068 7211; fax 4068 7447). For the same $22, the trip lasts between 30 to 45 minutes. For $9 more, you can enjoy a barbecue lunch on the island. If you would like to see Bedarra Island, a $24 package does a cruise around the island. This includes free boom net riding in the front of the boat. $49 buys you a package trip to Dunk and Bedarra, and includes lunch. Cruises depart Clump Point Jetty (1km past the village green heading toward Bingil Bay) less frequently than the water taxi.

The **Dunk Island Resort** (tel. 4068 8199) monopolizes all island activities. If the room rates ($200 and up) seem prohibitive, don't despair. Just steps from the jetty are some of the most exquisite and cheapest campsites in north Queensland (permits $3.50 per person, per night). The grounds are equipped with hot showers and limited cooking facilities, and the beach doesn't get any better than this. This isn't a well-kept secret, however, and it's small—book ahead during the high season. Try **Dunk Island Watersports** (tel. 4068 8199) or the **Dunk Island National Park Service** (tel. 4066 8601). Dunk Island Watersports also rents out a slew of water toys: jet skis, paddle skis, snorkel gear, catamarans, and motorboats.

The main attractions on Dunk, aside from the postcard beaches, are the **walking tracks** on the island's interior. The local favorite is the 10km walk circumscribing most of the island, which combines some Dunk history with diverse landscapes and a trip to the island's highest point. An easier option is the coastal hike up to Muggy Muggy Beach from the dock (1km, 1hr.).

There aren't too many choices for food on the island, but **BB's on the Beach** (tel. 4068 8199, ext. 409), next door to Watersports, is okay. It's an open-air cafe with a host of pizzas (around $9) and overpriced fish and chips ($9.50). Fancier fare, mostly seafood, is available for $20-35 at the Dunk Island Resort Restaurant.

■ Paronella Park

Just a little west of nowhere between Innisfail and Mission Beach hides the moorish castle of **Paronella Park** (tel. 4065 3225; fax 4065 3344). Built in 1911 by Spaniard Jose Paronella, this is a spot to oooh and aaah over. When the main thoroughfare was diverted in the 1960s to what is now the **Bruce Highway,** this enchanting park slipped from tourist itineraries into obscurity. New owners and rejuvenated advertising have revived tourist interest, but the crowds haven't swollen enough to mar the solitary beauty of its waterfall, Lovers Lane Palm Grove, and its Bamboo Forest surroundings. Romance is in the air—last year, 32 couples said "I do" in the castle.

If you're not tying the knot or being swept off your feet, take some time to feed the teeming fish of **Platypus Point** from the ruins of the castle's grand staircase (fish food provided). The park has been discovered by the entertainment industry and has served as the backdrop for two movies, a music video, and an international magazine's photo shoot. Allow a minimum of one hour for the self-guided tour around the grounds. The ticket cottage at the entrance provides a list of the park's horticultural highlights, some history, and even umbrellas for the mystical rainy afternoon visit. Unfortunately, this place is fairly inaccessible via public transportation. If driving, look for signs along the Bruce Highway for Paronella Park (the South Johnstone exit is the fastest). (Open daily 9am-5pm; admission $9, pensioners $7.50, children $4.50.) An adjacent caravan park (run by the park owners) blends into its surroundings. Powered sites are $14 a night, including a guided night walk of the park.

■ Innisfail

North of Mission Beach en route to Cairns lies the community of **Innisfail.** Situated on the Johnston River, this town offers few tourist attractions, but its unusual juxtaposition of architecture makes it worth a cruise down the main drag, **Edith St.** Buildings that are run down or even boarded up stand alongside day-glo Art Deco structures that seem to be plucked straight from a Hollywood set. There's an **information center** (tel. 4061 6448), along the south stretch of highway out of town (open daily 9am-5pm), and a **post office** (tel. 4061 1047), on the corner of Rankin and Edith St (open M-F 8:30am-5pm). **The Innisfail Police Department** (tel. 4061 1244), at the corner of Fitzgerald St, the Esplanade, and McGowan Dr, is open 24 hours a day. Just north of Innisfail, the road to the **Atherton Tablelands** (see p. 368) branches off inland toward Millaa Millaa.

Innisfail's main attraction, though, is the year-round casual **labor market.** The folks at **The Endeavour International Backpackers Hostel,** 31 Glady St (tel. 4061 6610; fax 4061 6003), arrange work on neighboring farms. From the rail station, follow the Bruce Hwy toward town until you reach Glady St, then turn right, and the hostel's on the left. The bus stop is between Lady and Ernest St; follow Glady down away from the park, and the hostel will be on your left. Employment listings are posted daily, and hourly wages are around $10. Pool, laundry facilities, free shuttle to work. (Rooms $15 per person per night, $75 per week if booked in advance. Key deposit $10. Linen and cutlery deposit $5. Reception open 8am-noon and 4-8pm daily.)

The Codge Lodge, 63 Rankin St (tel. 4061 8044; fax 4061 8155), is billed as a sport fishing resort, but non-fishing types need not shy away. Convenient to the town center, the lodge is hands-down the best budget accommodation in town. Hardwood floors, a beautiful pool area, and interesting decor come quite cheaply (dorm $17, single $20, double $35). Its small size increases the charm, but consider calling ahead during the high season. (Open daily 7am-10pm.) Despite some unusual taste in carpeting, **The Crown Hotel,** 25 Ernest St (tel. 4061 4722), just off the Bruce Hwy, is an excellent place to disembark after a long day's drive. In-room sinks, nice TV area, and wide verandas are some of the Hotel's positives. A sometimes rowdy pub downstairs is one of its negatives. (Singles $12, $60 per week. Doubles $20. Breakfast available from 5:30am. Open daily with 24hr. reception.) **August Moon** (tel. 4063 2211) is 8km from town on the Bruce Hwy (near the Sugar Museum). Located on nice grounds, this caravan park has the usual spectrum of accommodations. (Tent sites $10, powered sites $12, on-site caravan $24, cabin without facilities $35. Reception open daily 24hr.)

Susie's, on Edith St between Owen and Rankin St, has an all-you-can-eat Saturday breakfast buffet ($5.50). **The Tropical Beer Garden,** restaurant for the Crown Hotel on Ernest St, is what its name implies. The outdoor seating is nice, and meals range in price (prawns $6.50, full meals $10-14). (Open M-Sa 11:30am-2pm and 6-9pm.) **Roscoe's Pizza and Pasta,** 170 Edith St (tel. 4061 6888), doesn't have much atmosphere, but the food is good. Roscoe's offers home delivery as well as dine-in service (pastas $7.50-8.00, pizzas $11-$13.50). (Open daily 11:30am-2pm and 5pm-late.) **Lee's Fruit Market,** 30 Ernest St (tel. 4061 2639), has a wide array of fresh fruits and vegetables. (Open M-W and F 7:10am-6pm, Th 7:10am-8pm, Sa 7:10am-1pm.)

Just 4km from the town center along the Bruce Hwy is the **Sugar Industry Museum** (tel. 4063 2306). Highlights of the exhibit include an old steam engine and antiquated IBM mainframe that was the first computer used to keep finances and

QUEENSLAND

records within the sugar industry. Four dollars (children $2 children) will buy your entry token—depending upon your interest level in the sugar industry, dropping the shiny token in the turnstile might be the highlight. (Open M-F 9am-5pm, Sa-Su 9am-4pm). Between Innisfail and Paronella Park hides **The Cairns Crocodile Farm** (tel. 4045 2029), 10km north of Innisfail on the Bruce Hwy, one of many crocodile farms scattered along the northern coast. (Open M-Sa 9am-5pm. Afternoon feeding shows. $11, children $6, seniors $8, families $27.)

FAR NORTH QUEENSLAND

The northeast corner of the continent, from **Cairns** north into Australia's last great frontier, is nothing short of heaven for backpackers and outdoor adventurers. The **Great Barrier Reef** snakes close to shore here, luring divers with shorter boat trips and longer visits to the spectacular corals of the reef. The reef's biological diversity is complemented by that of the vast swaths of tropical rainforest, pressed up close to the Coral Sea by the craggy mountains of the **Great Dividing Range.**

As with most places in Australia, it wasn't nature but the promise of gold that first brought European settlement here, as a steady stream of prospectors advanced from Townsville to the then-tiny villages of Cairns and **Port Douglas.** The legacy of the gold rush lives on in **Cooktown,** Queensland's northernmost outpost. For the most part, divers have displaced miners in recent decades, and Cairns now caters to travelers with city comforts. Still, the more remote parts of this land remain untamed wilderness. The **Captain Cook Highway,** named after the premier European explorer of these lands, leads modern-day trailblazers north into the rainforest, which becomes impenetrably dense around **Cape Tribulation.** Wilder yet is the **Cape York** peninsula, starting beyond Cooktown and stretching all the way to the **Torres Strait,** which separates the Gulf of Carpentaria from the Coral Sea and Australia from Papua New Guinea. On Cape York, only the most rugged of tracks allow humans to venture into the ordinal landscape of hungry crocs and unforgiving bush.

■ Cairns

The last sizeable city at the corner of the great tropical outback, Cairns is both the northern end of the coastal backpacker route and the premier gateway for snorkeling and scuba diving on the Great Barrier Reef. On shore, palm-lined avenues and lush gardens blossom with color that rivals that of the reef's multifarious corals and fish. Tidal mudflats make traditional beach activities impossible, but the city's bars and parks provide plenty of diversions for travelers in between forays off the coast.

Cairns (pronounced like beer "cans") has two travel markets, one suited to the luxury tourist and the other to the backpacker. The southern end of the city is the bastion of luxury, with opal stores, opulent restaurants, and shop signs in both English and Japanese. The backpackers' ghetto is along the Esplanade. Hostels stand shoulder-to-shoulder, cheap eats await just outside the door, and the strip of green across the street encourages travelers to stop a while, swap a story, or just idle by the water's edge and watch the goliath pelicans swoop and dive.

🎯 CAIRNS HIGHLIGHTS

- Scuba diving or snorkeling among the marine wonders of the **Great Barrier Reef,** and learning about them first from **Reef Teach** (see p. 362).
- Dancing, didgeridoo music, and Aboriginal narratives at **Tjapukai** (see p. 366).
- **Rafting** on the wild whitewater of the Tully or Barron Rivers (see p. 362).
- Daytrip to the lively **Kuranda Markets,** and the views along the way there from the **Skyrail** Rainforest Cableway (see p. 368).
- The bubbly and salacious **foam party** at The Beach on Sunday night (see p. 361).
- The pure adrenaline rush of **sky-diving** (see p. 362).

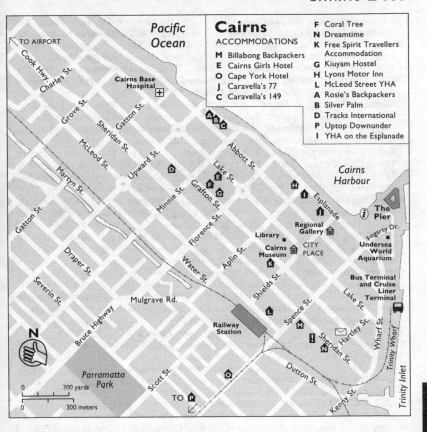

Cairns
ACCOMMODATIONS

M Billabong Backpackers
E Cairns Girls Hotel
O Cape York Hotel
J Caravella's 77
C Caravella's 149

F Coral Tree
N Dreamtime
K Free Spirit Travellers Accommodation
G Kiuyam Hostel
H Lyons Motor Inn
L McLeod Street YHA
A Rosie's Backpackers
B Silver Palm
D Tracks International
P Uptop Downunder
I YHA on the Esplanade

ORIENTATION

Cairns is tucked between undulating hills to the west and the harbor to the east, while mangrove swamps sandwich the city on the north and the south. **The Esplanade,** with its many hostels, runs along the waterfront. At its southern end is the **tourist office** and **The Pier,** which supports the Pier Marketplace. Farther south, the Esplanade becomes Wharf St. and runs past the **Trinity Wharf** and **Transit Centre.**

Shields St heads away from the Pier to **City Place,** a pedestrian mall and the destination of most intercity buses. From this intersection, **Lake St** runs parallel to the Esplanade. Continuing west, Shields St intersects first Grafton St then **Sheridan St** (called Cook Hwy north of the city). Half a block south of Shields, Grafton and Sheridan St border **Rusty's Bazaar.** The **Cairns Railway Station** is on McLeod St at Shields' terminus. **The airport** is a 10-minute drive north on the Cook Hwy from the city center. Follow signs. The **Bruce Hwy** begins two blocks to the north.

PRACTICAL INFORMATION

Tourist Office: Visitor Information Centre (tel. 4051 3588; fax 4051 0127), on the Esplanade just when it hikes a left to The Pier. From the train station, take a right onto Spence St, then turn left (away from the mountains) and walk to the end of the street. Take a left and it'll be 100m down on your right. From the bus station, head right on to Wharf St, which will curve and become the Esplanade. The office is on your right, between Spence and Shields St. Open daily 9:30am-5:30pm. **Traveller's Contact Center,** 13 Shields St in City Place (tel. 4051 4777; email adventures@adventures.com.au), is another excellent source for information and bookings. There's a lounge with email access ($5 per ½hr.). Open daily 8am-8pm.

Airport: 8km north of Cairns on Captain Cook Hwy. Signs point directly to the airport (tel. 4052 3888; fax 4052 1493). International carriers: **Air New Zealand** (tel. 1800 061 253), **Cathay Pacific** (tel. 13 17 47), **Garuda Indonesia** (tel. 008 800 873), **Japan Airlines** (tel. 4031 2700), **Malaysia Airlines** (tel. 4031 0000), **Qantas** (tel. 1800 177 767), and **Singapore Airlines** (tel. 4031 7538). Domestic carriers: **Qantas** (tel. 13 13 13), **Flight West Airlines** (tel. 13 23 92). Most hostels run a free shuttle bus pick-up service; just call from the terminal. Buses also run to town ($4.50 one-way) from just outside the terminal. **Taxis** to town are about $12.

Trains: The **rail station** is wedged between Bunda St and the new shopping mall on McLeod St. From the Esplanade, walk up Spence St and you'll find it on your right. Travel Centre Office (tel. 13 22 32) sells tickets. 10% discount with YHA card. V, MC. Open M-F 9am-5pm, Sa 9am-noon. Luggage lockers. Wheelchair accessible. The East Coast Discover Pass ($199) covers rail from Cairns to Sydney.

Buses: Terminal (open daily 6:15am-1am) at Trinity Wharf, on Wharf St. From the station, walk to the right along Wharf St toward The Pier. Here, the Esplanade begins. Leave luggage at the gift shop. **McCafferty's** (tel. 4051 5899, 24hr. tel. 13 14 99) runs buses southbound toward Brisbane (30 hr.; 5am-midnight daily; student ID discounts). **Greyhound** (24hr. tel. 13 20 30) also runs southbound. (1, 8:45am, and 3pm; VIP, YHA, and student ID discounts.)

Ferries: Quicksilver (tel. 4099 5500) runs daily to **Port Douglas** (1½hr.; 8am, return departure 5:15pm; one-way $20, return $30, 10% off with YHA card). Departs from The Pier, to the left at the end of the Esplanade. The launch is inside.

Public Transportation: Sunbus depot on Lake St in City Place. Fares $1-4; unlimited day pass $9. Routes posted at all information kiosks.

Taxis: Black and White (tel. 13 10 08) and **Taxis Australia** (tel. 13 22 27).

Car Rental: Local companies renting only between Cooktown and Townsville include **Cairns Tropical,** 140 Grafton St (24hr. tel. 4031 3995; fax 4031 4284), open daily 7:30am-6pm, and **Cairns Leisure Wheels,** 314 Sheridan St (tel. 4051 8988; fax 4051 5656). Larger companies which will rent for trips farther afield are **National,** 135 Abbott St. (tel. 4051 4600), and **Budget,** 153 Lake St (tel. 4051 9222; fax 4052 1158). 4WD is advisable for trips up to Cape Tribulation, but check with the rental company about restricted areas before you depart.

Automobile Club: Royal Automobile Club of Queensland (RACQ), 138 McLeod St (24hr. tel. 4051 6543), inside Coral Motors. Open daily 7:30am-5pm.

Budget Travel: Flight Centre, 24 Spence St (tel. 4052 1077, 24hr. info 13 31 33; fax 4051 9972), guarantees to beat any quoted price. Open M-F 9am-5pm, Sa 9am-noon. **STA Travel,** (tel. 4031 4199; fax 4031 6384), has two local branches. One in Cairns Central Shopping Centre (shop 39) and the other at 9 Shields St. Open M, Tu, and F 9am-5pm; W and Th 9am-6pm; Sa 10am-2pm.

National Parks Office: The Queensland National Parks and Wildlife Service (QNPWS), 10 McLeod St (tel. 4052 3096; fax 4051 7475). Open M-F 8:30am-4:30pm. Pick up either the *Queensland Guide to National Parks* or the *Queensland Guide to Camping.* Both are helpful tools and quite a steal at $4.95.

Maps: Absell's Map Centre, 55 Lake St (tel. 4041 2699), Andrejic's Arcade. Entrance is by Absell's News, opposite Orchid Plaza. Open M-Sa 8:30am-6pm.

Money: The best **currency exchange** rates ($3 or 1% commission) are found at the **American Express Office,** 79-87 Abbott, 2nd floor (tel. 4031 2871; fax 4031 5262), at Orchid Plaza. Mail held 30 days with no charge to card members or traveler's check holders; $3 charge for redirecting mail. Wheelchair accessible. Open M-F 8:30am-5pm, Sa 9am-noon. **ATMs** at virtually every bank accept V, MC, Cirrus.

Cairns City Public Library, 177 Lake St (tel. 4050 2404). $5 fee and $51 deposit for 4 items. Open M 10am-6pm, Tu-F 10am-7pm, Sa 10am-4pm).

Groceries: Woolworths (tel. 4051 2015), on Lake St next to City Place. M-F 8am-9pm, Sa 8am-5:30pm, Su 1-8pm.

Laundromat: The Laundry Express next to the Cairns Girls Hostel on Lake St costs $1 per 10min. to wash or dry. Open daily 6am-10pm. Most hostels offer laundry.

Emergency: Dial 000.

Police: (tel. 4030 7000 or 4031 2922; fax 4030 7144) on Sheridan St, between Spence and Hartley St. Open 24hr. **Police Beat** (tel. 4041 1178; fax 4041 1044), next to the Visitors Information Centre near the corner of Shields St and the Esplanade. Open M and Th-Su, 24hr.; Tu-W 6am-midnight.

Hospital: Cairns Base Hospital (tel. 4050 6333), on the Esplanade past the last trio of hostels (Bel-Air, Rosie's, Caravellers). 24hr. emergency department.

Hotlines: Queensland AIDS Council (tel. 4051 1028). Free confidential HIV testing.

Post Office: Cairns General Post Office (GPO) (tel. 4031 4303; fax 4051 3871) at corner of Hartley and Grafton St. *Poste Restante.* All services open M-F 9am-5pm. Another office on the 2nd floor of the Orchid Plaza (tel. 4031 2151), open M-F 9am-5:30pm, Sa 9am-12:30pm. **Postal code:** 4870.

Internet Access: The best deal in town is at **Virtual Reality Adventure Center,** located at the back of the Night Markets on the Esplanade (tel. 4041 4779). $6 per hr. Open daily 10am-11pm. **The Community Information Service Cairns** in the Tropical Arcade, at the corner of Abbott and Shields St. Open daily 9am-10pm. Most services $6 for 30min.

Phone Code: 07.

ACCOMMODATIONS

Though small, Cairns is second only to Sydney as a backpacker's destination and is consequently studded with dozens of budget hostels. Most are clustered along the Esplanade, and the more popular are booked solid during the high season. Except where noted, all have a pool, a key deposit of $10, and no curfew. Hostels generally offer coin-operated laundry, free pick-up from the bus and rail stations or the airport, and free dinner at a local pub.

Hostels

Dreamtime, 4 Terminus St (tel. 4031 6753; fax 4031 6566), just off Sheridan St, a 15min. walk from the Esplanade. A microcosm of tropical paradise, Dreamtime is, well, a dream come true. Shuttles to the Esplanade start at 7:30am and continue throughout the day upon request. Irish proprietors Steve and Kathy insist on learning guests' first names and offer more than basic amenities. Singles and doubles are cooled by ceiling fans and have refrigerators. The front office books a myriad of adventure trips, from reef diving to skydiving (8am-8pm with 24hr. phone service). Pool, barbecue, kitchen. No bunk beds. "Share Rooms" $15; doubles and twins $35. Linens, coffee, and tea included. Check-out 10am. Wheelchair accessible.

Uptop Downunder Backpackers Resort, 164 Spence St (tel. 4051 3636; fax 4052 1211). 15-min. walk from town; at night it's safer to take the quasi-regular shuttle bus outside Woolworth's on Lake St. Though an inconvenient distance from downtown, Uptop delivers in service and style. Spotless rooms are equipped with fridges. Pool tables, barbecue, and mini-cinema with nightly flicks. Dorms $15; singles $28; doubles and twins $32. VIP, YHA, student discounts. Check-out 9:30am.

Kuiyam Hostel, 162 Grafton St (tel. 4051 6466; fax 4051 6469), across from Munroe Martin Park, between Minnie and Florence St. Getting a room here is difficult, since priority goes to Aboriginal and Torres Strait Islanders. But short of living with your parents, you will never find a better deal than at Kuiyam Hostel, a member of a nationwide chain of Aboriginal-operated, government-subsidized hostels. The facilities are new and flawless, with a playground for the children and a rec room with a pool table for the adults. No tour desk. No key deposit. Singles, doubles, and family rooms are available. By request, *Let's Go* has not published rates, but they are well below the competition and include 3 meals per day.

Free Spirit Travellers Accommodation, 72 Grafton St (tel. 4051 7620). Refurbished last year and smack in the middle of town, with high ceilings and good vibes all around. TV room, kitchen, and small gym. No pool, but cheap, clean beds. Dorms $13; doubles $30. Reception open daily 7am-1:30pm and 4-10pm.

Cairns Girls Hostel, 147a Lake St (tel./fax 4051 2016), between Florence and Aplin St. A true gem (or lifeboat, as the case may be) in the morass of accommodations in Cairns, this women-only hostel has provided a safe haven for travelers for over 30 years. Gentlemen are requested to wait at the front door, and a sizeable Doberman who likes to gnaw on a stuffed bunny helps to keep order. No nunnery, though, this friendly 16-room "family" has no curfew. Guests may receive incoming calls on a specially provided line (tel. 4051 2767). Large twin rooms are cooled by ceiling fans and lit by frosted glass bulbs. Rates on a sliding scale: $15 for the first night, $12 by the fourth. Weekly: $80 for the first, $75 thereafter.

Caravella's 77 Backpacker Resort, 77-81 Esplanade (tel. 4051 2159 or 4051 2326; fax 4031 6329), between Aplin and Shields St, 10min. from the bus station. Smack in the middle of all the action, Caravella's 77 offers choice amenities. The kitchens and rooms are clean and colorful. The front desk staff is tight with all the rental and reef folks in town, and can serve as booking agents. A/C dorms $16; twins and doubles $34; luxury doubles with bath $40. Linen deposit $5. VIP. Flash your *Let's Go* and ask about a discount on your first night's stay.

Tracks International Youth Hostel, 149 Grafton St (tel./fax 4031 1474 or tel. 1800 065 464), on the corner of Minnie St. Tracks is 3 blocks from the town center or, in the opposite direction, the upper Esplanade. Shuttle services run to both locations. The rooms are newly painted, but unimpressive. Loads of great activities make up for the paucity of luxury. Guests receive free wine one night a week during the raging 70s party. Once a fortnight, the hostel goes all out with a moonlight cruise. On alternating weeks, the hostel hosts a massive barbecue, and weekly trips to Crystal Cascades and Trinity Beach are the highlight of many guests' stays. All trips free. Dorms $14, with A/C $15; singles $20; doubles and twins $28. VIP, YHA.

Rosie's Backpackers, 155 Esplanade (tel. 4051 0235; fax 4051 5191), just past Caravella's 149 at the far end of the Esplanade; a bit of a walk after a few beers. One female dorm; all others mixed. Reception controls the security gate, but keys provided. Billiards, table tennis, pinball machine, TV/VCR. Dorms $15, doubles $35.

Billabong Backpackers, 69 Spence St (tel. 4051 6946; fax 4051 6022), at the corner of Sheridan St, within spitting distance of the train station. Diagonally across from the **Underdog Pub,** the locals' drinking hole of choice. Recently renovated. Gay-friendly staff. Dorms are basic and big with 10 beds per block. Dorms $14, $15 with A/C; singles $26; doubles and twins $32. Linen provided. V, MC. Open daily 7am-12:30pm & 4-7:30pm. Check-in 7:30pm. Check-out 10:30am.

YHA on the Esplanade, 93 Esplanade (tel. 4031 1919; fax 4031 4381), on the corner of Aplin St. Extremely close to nightclubs and cheap restaurants, the YHA rooms are no-frills, clean, safe places to crash. Dorms $16; doubles and twins $36. Non-members $3 extra. No pick-up from the airport or bus station.

Caravella's 149, 149 Esplanade (tel. 4031 5680; fax 4051 4097), past the playground. Large dorm blocks are equipped with on-suite bathrooms. Dorms for women $12, mixed dorms with A/C are $16; doubles and twins $32, $34 with A/C.

The McLeod Street YHA, 20-24 McLeod St (tel. 4051 0772; fax 4031 3156) has the feel of a motel more than a hostel, with open-air hallways surrounding a pool. Clean but simple dorms have A/C and cost $16; singles $26, doubles and twins $36.

Hotels & Motels

The Cape York Hotel (tel. 4051 2008; fax 4031 0331), at Spence and Bunda St, offers comfortable rooms. Singles $30; twins and doubles $40. Weekly: singles $120 including 6 meals in the hotel pub, twins and doubles $190 with 12 meals. Open M-Sa 10am-10pm Su 11am-10pm. Reservations recommended.

The Coral Tree, 166-172 Grafton St (tel. 4031 3744; fax 4031 3064). Luxurious, moderately up-market accommodation. Pricey, but you get your money's worth. Rooms $88, suites $120. Open daily 7am-11pm with 24hr. reservations.

The Lyons Motor Inn, at the corner of Aplin St and the Esplanade (tel. 4051 2311 or 1800 079 025; fax 4031 1294) offers more affordable rooms. What these rooms lack in glamour, which is a considerable amount, they make up for twofold in view. All tower rooms have at least a partial view of the water. TVs and fridges in all rooms; two pools. Rooms in the older building from $50; those in the newer tower are generally $75 with 24hr. reservations.

The Silver Palm, 153 Esplanade (tel. 4031 6099; fax 4031 6094) has apartments behind the motel with 2 bedrooms, TV lounge, and kitchen. Affordable for families or groups. Two people $60; 4 people $90. Open daily 7am-7pm.

FOOD

Cairns bubbles with good eats, from all-night kebab and pizza stalls on the Esplanade to upscale restaurants that specialize in frying up local fauna. Coffee shops usually offer a filling **breakfast** (called "morning tea" or "Devonshire tea") for $5-6. An exceptional value is **Le Cake,** in Rusty's Bazaar, Grafton St side, with homemade croissants ($1) and fresh-pressed coffee ($2; open W-F 7am-5pm, Sa 5am-1pm, Su 6am-1pm). **Coffee Cafe,** 87 Lake St, is within earshot of the open-air concert hall and offers scones, jam, and a pot o' tea for $5 (open daily 6am-10pm). **The Bavarian Bakery** at 62 Shields St has over 30 types of breads and goodies ranging from sugary croissants to hearty veggie pastries. Open M-F 7am-6pm, Sa 7am-2pm.

Most of the smaller restaurants have a **lunch special,** but few go as cheap as **The Old Ambulance Cafe and Bistro,** 135 Grafton St (tel. 4051 0511) which serves a great quiche ($2.50) and superb iced coffee. (Open M-Th 7am-10:30pm, F 7am-11:30pm, Sa 10am-5pm.) **Tiny's Juice Bar,** at the corner of Grafton and Spence St, has a non-tiny 50 juice selections, plus sandwiches and half a dozen smoothies ($3-4). (Open M-Sa 7:30am-5pm.) **Jimmy's** (tel. 4031 6199), adjacent to the cinema on Grafton St, is a throw-back to 50s style American diners complete with jukebox, red swivel bar stools, and chrome (sandwiches $3-6; open daily 9:30am-9:30pm).

No visit to Cairns would be complete without a dinner at **Gypsy Dee's,** 41 Shields St (tel. 4051 5530), near the corner of Sheridan St. The atmosphere is thick with sultry lighting, wide wicker chairs, and strings of shells hanging as chandeliers. As if the stylized gypsy wagon just left of center stage weren't enough, this hot spot has live music every night, generous dinner portions ($10-18), and almost a dozen vegetarian entrees. In an incredible feat of engineering, the entire front of the restaurant (which otherwise looks boarded-up) folds down onto the sidewalk, providing a terrace complete with fig trees (open 6pm-2am). On the top end of things, the **Red Ochre Grill,** 43 Shields St (tel. 4051 0100), by the corner of Sheridan, combines Art Deco surroundings with good Aussie cooking. Entrees, like kangaroo sirloin or char-grilled emu, run $20 per plate, and can be washed down with anise seed tea ($3). (Open M-F for lunch noon-10pm and every night for dinner 6-10pm.)

Backpackers and locals mingle at the **Cock and Bull,** 6 Groue St (tel. 4031 1160), two blocks inland from the Esplanade. The atmosphere is relaxed and you must order and retrieve your own meals. Proportions are elephantine and extremely tasty, with numerous veggie options. (Open daily for lunch and dinner.) **Dundee's,** 29 Spence St, offers a variety of Australia's tastier fauna including kangaroo mignon ($19.50), crocodile sausages ($11.50), and the Buffalo Humpty Doo ($22.50). **La Pizza,** 93 Esplanade (tel. 4031 2646), has been open 24 hours a day for eight years. Pizzas are made fresh to order in front of you and come in small, medium, or large ($7-15). **Daeng's Thai Restaurant,** 114 Hoare St (tel. 4032 0790), may not look like much from the outside, but the owner hand-prepares each delectable dinner. Daeng's is a little hard to find—heading towards the airport on Sheridan St, take a left on James St and another left on Hoare. Daeng's is about 200m on the left. (Open daily 5-10pm.)

SIGHTS

The volunteer-run **Cairns Museum** (tel. 4051 5582), in City Place, is a low-budget masterpiece. *(Open M-Sa 10am-4pm. Admission $3, $1 children, $7 families.)* Here you'll find bits of far north Queensland history, as memorabilia of the colonial days surround two spreads of Aboriginal weaponry. There's a small exhibit on Chinese immigrants and a collection of heavy tools used to clear rainforest. When the weather turns sour, stroll over to the **Undersea World Oceanarium** (tel. 4041 1777) out in the Pier Marketplace, near the wharves. Fish feedings (10:30am, noon, 1:30, and 3pm) are interactive, since the diver is outfitted with a two-way intercom. If you book ahead you can take a 30-minute dive with the sharks. *(Oceanarium open daily 8am-8pm. Admission $10, children $6. Shark diving 3:30-8:00pm.)* If you've had enough exposure to sea life, stop by the **Cairns Regional Art Gallery** (tel. 4031 6865) at the corner of

QUEENSLAND

Abbott and Shields St. *(Admission $5.)* The gallery displays work from famous Australian artists, and adds a touch of class to any beach trip.

The **Flecker Botanic Gardens** (tel. 4050 2454) are good for a morning's lazy wander. *(Open M-F 7:30am-5:30pm, Sa-Su 8:30am-5:30pm. Free. Office open M-F 8am-5pm.)* The grounds include fern and orchid houses, a garden presenting the ways Aboriginals have traditionally used plants, a newly opened Gondwanan (evolutionary flora track) garden, and a meandering boardwalk and trail that crosses fresh and saltwater lakes. You can pick up a self-guide booklet ($2) or cassette player ($4) at the **office** next to the restaurant; the office also books guided walks ($4.50) on demand, and has a small library. Public guided walks are conducted daily at 1pm. To get to the gardens, hop the Sunbus from City Place, #1B (one-way $2.30), or drive north on Sheridan St until you can take a left onto Collins Ave. It's a hefty 10km walk from town.

From the Gardens, it's only a kilometer down Collins Ave (follow the signs after the traffic circle) to the **Royal Flying Doctor Service Visitors Centre** (tel. 4053 5687; fax 4032 1776). This is the main base for the air-ambulance of Queensland, and serves an area roughly the size of Japan. There's a great documentary depicting rescues made in remote regions of Australia, information sheets in nine languages, and lots of old radio machinery and medical equipment on display. Best of all, though, is the fully-outfitted air ambulance out back, decommissioned only six years ago. Even the flaps still flap when visitors turn the steering column. *(Guided tours every 30min. Open M-F 8:30am-5pm, Sa-Su 9am-4:30pm. Admission $5.)*

Another option from the Botanic Gardens is to walk 100m up Collins Ave toward the Bruce Hwy, to the entrance of **Mount Whitfield Environmental Park,** the last bits of rainforest in the Cairns area. The shorter Red Arrow circuit (marked by, of all things, a series of red arrows) takes about an hour, while the more rugged Blue Arrow circuit is a five-hour return trek up and around Mount Whitfield. The area is frequented by brush turkeys, and the very careful observer might find a Papuan Frogmouth bird in the brush. The Botanic Gardens office has a self-guide booklet ($3) that explains some of the Yirrganydji Aboriginal history along the trail.

ACTIVITIES AND BEACHES

Raging Thunder Adventures, 39 Lake St (tel. 4030 7990; fax 4030 7911), will put you in some of the best **whitewater** that Far North Queensland has to offer. Half-day trips on the Barron River are $70, full-day runs on the Tully $128. **Balloon rides** over the Atherton Tablelands are also available for $105. (10% discount on any package with YHA, VIP, or ISIC.) The biggest rush in Cairns comes from falling out of the sky with **Paul's Parachuting** (tel. 4051 8855; fax 4051 8266), located in the airport. Tandem jumps start at 8,000ft. ($228) and increase in price $40 every 2,000ft. up to 14,000 (plus $85 if you want pictures or a video). Paul's is widely recommended by area travel agents, who suggest you don't wait till your last day in Cairns to skydive—high winds or bad weather may leave latecomers grounded. **Sky Dive Cairns** (tel. 4035 9667; fax 4035 9658), also in the airport, has similar prices.

Despite its proximity to arguably the best diving spot in the world, Cairns lacks a beach of its own. At low tide the bay rolls back to reveal a wide expanse of mud flats, but sunbathers must make do with grassy spots in the parks or pool-side lawn chairs, and surfers will find themselves docked. Sigh. A few beaches lie north of Cairns; Sunbus #1 and 1A run to **Trinity Beach,** the favorite, from the depot in City Place (M-F every 30min., Sa-Su every hr.) Trinity Beach has nice white sand and plenty of private cove areas which keep it from feeling inundated with sunbathers.

DIVING AND SNORKELING

By far the most popular way to view Cairns is through goggles. Every day thousands of tourists suit up with masks, fins, and snorkels or air tanks and slide beneath the water's surface to experience the world's best diving on the vast 2000km of reef off the coast. The fish may not always appreciate the intrusion, but snorkelers and divers return again and again to these living waters. For the bargain price of $10, you can

Warning: Box jellyfish are serious business—a single jellyfish may have enough poison to kill three adults, and its sting usually proves deadly. They're out and about between October and May in coastal waters north of approximately Great Keppel Island. Always ask locals about them before swimming. Some beaches install jellyfish-proof nets, and some diving establishments sell jellyfish-proof wetsuits, but stay out of the water if you are at all concerned about your safety. On land, avoid **wild mangroves** when bushwalking, since **saltwater crocodiles** hide out there. The crocs can also be found in northern coastal and inland waters.

learn everything you wanted to know and more about the underwater world. **The Reef Teach,** 14 Spence St (tel./fax 4051 6882), is conducted Mondays through Saturdays at 6:15pm. This captivating 2-hour presentation by Paddy Codwell, a marine biologist who apparently doubles as a comic, is an absolutely fabulous way to learn the about the biological diversity and history of the reef. In addition to handling various coral samples, attendees will learn how to avoid doing harm to the reef or themselves. Reef Teach is terrific even for advanced divers.

Dive Boats and Shops

Knowing which dive shop to choose can be tricky and, with the bombardment of brochures and pushy booking agents, even a little daunting. It helps to decide in advance the length of trip, your level of dive experience, and in what types of marine life you are most interested. Many boats leave from the jetties each morning. You can either call ahead to book your own trip, or you can be sure that hostels will gladly book you on one of these reef-bound vessels (and gladly pocket their 25% commission). Prices fluctuate depending on season. Prices generally include a base price for the trip, which usually includes snorkeling gear; diving costs extra.

MV "Seastar II," pier B14 at the Marlin Marina (tel. 4033 0333), is quite a small operation and runs daily trips (departing 7:15 am) to the outer barrier reef. This is some of the best diving in Cairns and a bargain at $50 base including snorkeling gear. One dive $45, certified $40; 2-dive package $70. The highlight of this trip is Brookers Lagoon on Hastings Reef, but the boat also lights on Michaelmas Cay.

The Seahorse (ship mobile tel. 4018 712 042), at the Marlin Marina, is another small boat (max. 20 people) owned by a couple whose specialty is marine biology. This daily trip leaves at 9am. Snorkeling and reef cruise are the usual $55. Introductory dives $45; certified dives $25. Wetsuits $5 extra. Provides an opportunity for passengers to learn to sail while on their diving trip. Goes to nearby Upolu Cay.

Ocean Free, Radisson Pier Visitors Info Center (tel. 4041 1118; fax 4031 4361), runs a day tour out to the reef in a double master schooner, complete with a stopover on Green Island. This is a small fry operation where a basic trip is $55 (including snorkeling). Diving is another $30-45 depending upon certification.

The Falla, 8 Bradford St (tel. 4031 4361; fax 4035 2585), owns a swanky pearl luggar boat with a tight crew. Zealous divemasters are eager to help novice divers. Intro dives $30 for the first, $45 for the second.

Pro-Dive, 116 Spence St (tel. 4031 5255; fax 4051 9955; email prodive@internet-north.com.au; http://www.prodive-cairns.com.au). The most popular trip is the 5-day learn-to-dive course with the hefty price tag of $510. Three-day, 2-night trip including 9 dives for certification candidates, 11 for certified divers, costs $420. If you snorkel but don't dive, it's $350. Extended trips allow travel to more remote reefs. Short tunnel swim throughs is one highlight of Pro-Dive sites. The Reef Teach is included in dive price (medical exam $35 extra). Open daily 7:30am-6pm.

Passions of Paradise (tel. 4050 0676; fax 4051 9505) departs from finger A on the pier each morning at 8am and offers an exciting day on the Upola Cay. This boat has a young, vibrant spirit and has even been known to engage in the occasional water balloon fight with passing ships.

Deep Sea Divers Den, 319 Draper St (tel. 4031 2223; fax 4031 1210; email: info@divers.den.com), also does overnight trips to outlying ribbon reef. Two-night,

3-day packages are $330 to snorkel, or $420 for certified divers. The 4-day dive course costs $395.

Cairns Dive Centre, 121 Abbott St (tel. 4051 0294; fax 4051 7531), is generally the least expensive, with a "floating hotel" catamaran for its flagship. Introductory dives are $45, and the first certified dive is $30. These prices are added to the base price. Travels mostly to the inner reef.

Down Under Dive, 155 Sheridan St (tel. 4031 1288; fax 4031 1373; email dudive@ozemail.com.au; http://www.ozemail.com.au/~dudive), has a nifty 2-masted clipper ship with an on-board hot tub. Hastings and Saxon are the most frequented reefs. A 2-day, 1-night trip for snorkelers is $180, or $255 for certified divers. They also offer the 4-day course for beginners at $385 and the 5-day for $485. Open daily 7:30-5:30pm, taking reservations until 10pm.

Great Dive Adventures (tel. 4051 4444; fax 4031 2062) is more expensive, but with good reason. A 4-day PADI course can be taken inland for $360, $440 (including 6 dives on the outer reef), or from $600 to take lessons at the luxurious Green Island Resort. Two-day course for advanced certifications $300-400 at the resort.

Hitchhiker, Marlin Marina (tel. 4033 1711), does day-trips only and strangely recommends that their passengers be between the ages of 18-38. This youthful crew goes to the outer reef sometimes; sites vary based on weather. Reef cruise including snorkeling is $69. Introductory dives $49. Two certified dives $110.

Tusa Dive (tel. 4031 1248), corner of Aplin St and Esplanade, runs 2 boats and caters to a slightly more up-market crowd. A day of snorkeling on the outer reef is $95; with one intro dive $165, with 2 $190, with 2 certified dives $155.

SHOPPING

In a city that hides a glitzy, high-priced shopping mall in every city block, finding cheap supplies can drive you batty. The malls all sell the same selection of bush hats, T-shirts, and commercially produced handicrafts. When it comes to **Aboriginal crafts,** be cautious of purchasing boomerangs and spears that are advertised as "made by true Aboriginals." In many cases, Aboriginals surrender their culture to commercialization only grudgingly, and the white middleman takes most of the profit. The handful of Aboriginal-owned businesses that sell such artifacts are the best to patronize. **Bunna Nappi Nappe** in the Tropical Arcade is an example. **Is Aboriginal,** 44 Spruce St (tel. 4031 2912), allows customers to strip, sand, and make their own didgeridoo under the instruction of the Aboriginal staff. At $100 each ($30 more to paint), you're paying considerably less than you would in the shopping plaza. (Open M-Sa 9am-7pm, Su 10am-7pm.) For other shopping interests, there are a few options:

Rusty's Bazaar, wedged between Sheridan and Grafton St just south of Shields St, offers as good a shopping experience as Cairns has to offer. Fruit, honey, orchids, water pipes, and camera equipment are just some of the options. Show up early before the good stuff sells out. Open F 9am-7pm, Sa-Su 6:30am-1pm)

Cairns Central Shopping Centre (tel. 4041 4111), at the corner of McLeod and Aplin St. Newly opened, it's one of the nicest places to look for gifts or clothes and has a 6-screen cinema inside.

City Place, at the intersection of Shields and Lake St, is not the hub it once was, but its location and abundance of disconnected shops makes this airy center a welcome break from the engulfing mall structure of other Cairns shopping meccas.

The Night Markets, on the Pier end of the Esplanade, has cheap food and even cheaper souvenirs. Open 5pm-11pm daily.

Kaotica Secondhand, 81 Grafton St (tel. 4051 9386), near the bazaar. Backpackers flock here to unload excess belongings and pick up jeans ($20) or dresses ($20).

City Place Disposals (tel. 4051 6040), at the corner of Shields and Grafton St just north of City Place. Fine assortment of swags, buck knives, and camping gear. Open M-F 8am-5:30pm, Sa 8am-1pm.

Walker's Book Shop, 96 Lake St (tel. 4051 2410), has a section on Aboriginal history and lore, as well as bilingual children's titles, a gay literature section, and free local papers. Open M-Th 8:30am-5:30pm, F 8:30am-8pm, Sa 8:30am-4pm, Su noon-6pm.

NIGHTLIFE AND ENTERTAINMENT

Despite its widespread and well-deserved reputation as a haven for backpackers, the nightclub scene here is still a few paces behind that of other cities. An understated friction between locals and tourists has divided the bars and clubs. Some cater directly to the hostel crowd, running shuttle buses to pick up party-goers; others may turn away backpackers at the door. Still, Cairns makes up for quantity with quality, and visitors aren't likely to complain that there isn't enough to do at night. All clubs begin charging cover fees at 10pm, but if you have your hand stamped before then you can party all night for free. Also, keep an eye peeled for meal vouchers at any accommodation. Most hostels serve as liaisons for one or more of the clubs and issue dinner certificates to their guests which entitle you to either a free meal per day or at least 80% off. For the latest local word, pick up a copy of *Son of Barfly* (free) at any cafe around town. The *Pink Guide to Cairns,* available at Walker's Book Shop, 96 Lake St, details **gay-friendly** nightlife and accommodations.

The Beach (tel. 4031 3944 for free shuttle bus), at the corner of Abbott and Aplin St, hosts most of the hostels' free dinner offers and also wins top billing for nightlife. The warehouse-sized club fills 2 stories with pool tables, 3 bars, a dance floor, and a giant stage set up to look like a pirate ship. Nightly themes include Mr. Backpacker, Miss Backpacker, and Miss Lovely Legs. The infamous "foam party" commences every Sunday night at 10pm. Not suggested for the meek or modest, the party culminates in half-naked backpackers frolicking waist deep in suds. Partiers rave all night, every night, 6pm-5am.

The Chapel, level 1, 91 Esplanade (tel. 0441 4222) makes losing your religion more fun than it's ever been, with an urban feel, dim lighting, surrealistic murals, and dripping candles. Plays an eclectic mix of tunes. The Chapel is welcome relief from nightclubs crawling with zealous backpackers looking to "get wasted, man."

Johnno's Blues Bar (tel. 4031 5008), at the corner of the Esplanade and Shields St. Red hot jazz and cool blues play seven days a week in this rough-around-the-edges club. Cover charge varies greatly depending on the evening's band. The back room holds a mechanical bull for anyone who thinks he's jackeroo enough. Tuesday it's $6 jugs all night long. Open 9pm-late.

Rattle 'n' Hum (tel. 4031 3101), a block down from The Chapel, boasts hardwood, floor to ceiling, and has an open-air front with tables set up on the sidewalk, an excellent site for people-watching. Always busy, this place can get a little loud on weekends (in a good way). Open daily 11am-midnight.

The Woolshed, 24 Shields St (tel. 4031 6304 for free shuttle bus), near the City Center. Modeled after its namesake with corrugated aluminum walls and rough-cut tables, the Woolshed offers good food and a low-key environment for meeting fellow backpackers during dinner hours. There are 2 floors, 5 pool tables, and a small dance floor, but when the jam gets going, there are no qualms about dancing on the tables. Happy hour varies ($5 pitchers). Open nightly 6pm-5am.

Club Trix, 53 Spence St (tel. 4051 8223), between Grafton and McLeod St, is hard to miss with its rainbow-colored marquis. A gay bar and dance club with no dress code. Open W-Sa 9pm-late. The best shows are F-Sa; cover varies.

Gilhooley's (tel. 4051 3063), out on the pier. An old-fashioned Irish pub where Guinness flows like water. Happy hour M-F 5-7pm. Open daily 10am-1 or 2am.

If you prefer popcorn to beer, check out either the **Burch Carroll and Coyle Cinema**, 108 Grafton St (tel. 4031 1077), or the **Myer Shopping Complex Cinema** (tel. 4052 1166) on McLeod St. Ticket prices yo-yo depending on the time of day, showtime, and age, but an adult weekend fare runs $11.50 per ticket, $3-5 for popcorn.

■ Around Cairns

Before you go blind staring at the sunlight glinting off the Pacific, remind yourself that there are some inland attractions around Cairns, too. The **Atherton Tablelands** rise above the tropical forest to the southwest of Cairns, and offer a very different appeal

Oolana's Sacrifice

South of Cairns about 40km is the sugar village of Babinda, and the turn-off to Babinda Boulders, a picnic ground with a creepy story. As the story goes, there once lived a stunningly beautiful Aboriginal woman named Oolana who was slated to wed one of the elders, Waroonoo. Instead, she eloped with Dyga, a dashing young fellow from a clan that was passing through. When the lovers were caught and dragged back, Oolana leapt into the gorge rather than marry another. Supposedly, all of the loose boulders crashed down after her. Backpackers who have camped near the water's edge swear that they have heard a woman's voice calling out, as well as a didgeridoo droning through the night. More importantly, the swimming hole has a reputation for drowning men (and the occasional woman), as Oolana reaches out from the depths for her lost love.

than do the offshore reefs. The closest town in the Tablelands is **Kuranda** (see p. 368). On the road to Kuranda are a couple of slick, family-oriented tourist joints. **Rainforestation,** on the Kennedy Hwy (tel. 4093 9033; fax 4093 7578; open daily 8am-4pm), is the usual bundle of Aboriginal dancers, vicious crocs, and domesticated kangaroos. A full day's package has a hefty price tag (adult combination ticket $29), but the rainforest tour (in an army amphibious vehicle) might be worth the $11.50. The **Dreamtime Rainforest** walk is another popular choice for those who haven't much time (1hr.; $18).

Just north of Cairns and off the Cook Hwy in neighboring **Smithfield** is the national coup of Aboriginal cultural parks: **Tjapukai** (tel. 4042 9999; fax 4042 9988; http://www.tjapukai.com.au). Pronounced "JAB-a-guy," this is the most wholly rewarding, intelligently presented, and culturally fair presentation of Aboriginal myth, customs, and history in all of Queensland. Give this experience at least half a day. Highlights include the History Theatre, a slide show presenting the history of European and Aboriginal contact since Cook's landing, and the Creation Theatre, a hologram and laser light show presenting the Tjapukai's creation myth in the Tjapukai language (headsets can be tuned to any of 7 foreign languages). Next, head over a bridge and to the award-winning **Tjapukai Dance Theatre,** a clever mix of authentic dance, clear narrative, and audience participation. The "camp" behind the dance theater has on-going demonstrations of didgeridoos, fire-making, bush tucker and medicine, and boomerang- and spear-throwing. The Tjapukai community has a 51% stake in the $9 million production and most of the staff is Aboriginal. This is an excellent opportunity to experience part of the culture, with some bells and whistles added for show. (Open daily 9am-5pm. $24, children $12.) **Sunbus** (tel. 4057 7411) offers 24-hour passes which vary in price from $5.50 to $8.95 depending upon which zone you travel in. The $8.95 ticket is good for park visits.

A gem for those on working holiday, the **Palm Beach Resort** (tel. 4055 3630), off the Cook Hwy 25km north of Cairns, is near the understaffed upscale resorts in **Palm Cove.** While you're hunting for work, explore the rainforest in the backyard. The four-bed rooms are clean and beautifully furnished in wood, and linen is provided. (Dorms $10, weekly $60.) A daily shuttle bus goes into Cairns during the week.

Farther along the Cook Hwy heading north, a pair of complementary roadside attractions exist under one ownership and one system of Linnean classification. **Wild World** (tel. 4055 3669; fax 4059 1160), in Palm Cove along the Cook Hwy, 20 minutes north of Cairns, lets you get up close and personal with kangaroos and wallabies. The Koala maternity ward is a treat, and there are public crocodile feedings. The animals in cramped cages seem anything but wild, however. (Open daily 8:30am-5pm. $18, children $9). **Hartley's Creek Crocodile Farm** (tel. 4055 3576; fax 4059 1017), is 25min. north of Wild World. With the giant signs, it's hard to miss. The "crocodile attack show," where keepers taunt a croc until it eats a hand-fed chicken, begins at 3pm. At 4pm you can pet a freshwater crocodile, jaws taped shut. (Open daily 8am-5pm. Admission $13.) **Coral Coaches** (tel. 4031 7577) has regular service to the parks (5 per day). The 9:30am is the most popular for catching morning shows at Hartley's, Wild World, or Tjapukai; the 12:30pm works for afternoon shows.

If animals in cages make your stomach turn and you want to see their natural habitats, **Cape Tribulation** may be for you (see p. 377). Without your own 4WD and a lot of patience, your best bet is a tour out of Cairns. **KCT Connections** (tel. 4055 4555) is an excellent choice, with prices well below the competition. A two-day trip, including a one-night stay at either **Crocodylus (YHA)** in Cow Bay or **PK's Jungle Village** in Cape Trib, comes to $84, or $96 for the three-day, two-night package. Along the way you can stop in **Port Douglas** and **Mossman Gorge,** and they even throw in a Daintree River cruise. (24hr. reservations line. Departs Cairns around 7:30am.)

■ Near Cairns: Green and Fitzroy Islands

Green and Fitzroy Islands (technically **coral cays;** see p. 68) are each located just a stone's throw from Cairns (26 and 27km respectively), and very popular with daytrippers. Diminutive **Green Island** barely pushes above the water surface, and you can walk its perimeter in less than 15 minutes. There are no real walking tracks on the island; you can either walk the circular beach path or forge your own trail through the dense rain forest (if you can walk long enough you'll always end up back at the resort). The cheapest and quickest way to the island is with **Great Adventures** (tel. 4051 0455), which offers a 45-minute ferry. ($40; $20 for children. Departs Cairns daily at 8:30am and 10:30am and leaves Green Island at 2:30pm and 4:30pm.) Extras include diving (intro dive or 2 certified dives $8), snorkeling ($10), and rides in a dinky glass-bottom boat ($8). The sailboat **Ocean Free** (tel. 4041 1118) specializes in trips to Green Island. Travelers aboard the schooner get the chance to explore the island or dive the reef around it (intro dive $49 for one, $79 for two; certified $35 for one, $45 for two). Trips depart from Cairns daily at 9am and cost around $60. (Open 7am-10pm.) If you prefer to fly, **Aquaflight Airway** (tel. 4031 4307) has reasonably priced trips to the island ($80-100 depending on season).

Marineland Melanesia, 250 Northeast, left of the jetty, is a gallery and aquarium with stingrays in tanks and Melanesian crafts on the walls. (Open daily 8am-5pm. Admission $7, children $3.) Just off the end of the jetty is an antiquated **Marine Observatory,** from which you can observe bits of the coral reef from 1.5m below the surface ($5). The resort has a nice pool surrounded by a couple of boutiques and small cafes. Open daily from 8am to 5pm, the **dive shop** rents snorkeling gear ($8 per day) or diving equipment ($40). Instructors will be happy to outfit day-trippers and take them on an introductory dive for $70. **Michaelmas Cay,** just north of the island on the outer reef, has excellent diving as well as the site of a natural bird sanctuary. By the way, the least expensive accommodation on Green Island runs a cool $300 per person, so unless you're an antipodean Midas, forget about it.

Fitzroy Island does offer budget beds, though most people only go for a day. Great Adventures offers a cruise with diving options. ($30; children $15. 2 certified dives $75; intro dive $60; snorkel gear $10; glass-bottom boat tour $8. Departs Cairns daily at 8:30am and departs Fitzroy at 2:30 and 4:30pm.) **Sunlover Cruises** (tel. 4031 1055 or 1800 810 512) does the trip to the island for $30 (children $15) and also offers a combination of the island and Moore reef for $130 (children $65). Both cruises depart at 9:30am and return by 5pm. If you're tough as nails, try traveling to Fitzroy Island via **sea kayak** with **Raging Thunder Adventures** (tel. 4051 9588). A high-speed catamaran takes you most of the way, and is followed by three hours of reef kayaking, snorkeling, and lunch (min. age 13). The daytrip departs at 8am and returns at 5:30pm ($98), or stay in bunk accommodations at the Fitzroy Island Resort with the overnight package ($135) and get two days of kayaking. **The Fitzroy Island Resort** (tel. 4051 9588) has 24-hour reception and offers a variety of choices in shelter (bunks $28; triples $95; quads $112). Fifty **campers** are allowed on the island at a time for $10 per site (contact resort in advance for permit details). The resort has a **kiosk** which serves meals ($3-9) from 8am to 4pm. The **Rainforest Restaurant** vends more exorbitant fare ($15-40). To keep busy on the island, try a walk to the **light-**

house (5km return) which starts at a clearing adjacent to the **Reefarm**, 1km north of the resort. This giant-clam breeding center gives tours daily at 10am, 10:45am, and 1pm. ($6, children $3. Open daily 9am-5pm.) The resort's **dive shop** offers introductory diving at bargain rates ($55; $45 for certified divers), while snorkel gear costs $8.

■ Atherton Tablelands

On a high plateau inland from Cairns, the Tablelands is a rarely visited paradise of rolling creeks, lush vales, and undisturbed glens. Although much of the once-dense jungle has been cleared for agriculture, pockets of national park remain. With patience, you'll see a platypus playing at creek's edge, or hear the peculiar call of the eastern whipbird. The activity encircles **Lake Tinaroo**, three-fourths the volume of Sydney Harbour, and the forests, which contain more species of trees than Europe and North America combined. The lake is the central locus along the Tableland loop. Traveling northeast on the **Kennedy Hwy**, it's an easy 50km drive back to Cairns. Along the way lie the farming village **Mareeba** and market-centric township of **Kuranda.** Opting for a southern route back to Cairns via the **Gilles Hwy,** you'll encounter **Atherton** (the largest township but relatively uninviting), charming **Yungaburra,** and **Malanda.** The entire loop is full of variety and well worth the time, but remember to bring a sweater in the winter; at an elevation of 1000m, you'll forget you're in the tropics.

NAVIGATING THE TABLELANDS

The mountainous, lakeside roads provide drivers a mild challenge and endless verdant panoramas. The Tablelands are accessible through several alternative modes of transport, although driving provides the fullest experience. For the carless, there are two popular routes from Cairns to nearby Kuranda. The **Skyrail Rainforest Cableway** is brand new and was awarded the 1997 tourism award for best new Australian attraction. The complete trip, originating 10 minutes northwest of Cairns in Carovonica Lakes, takes 1½ hours. The skycabs stop to allow you to take quick jaunts into the rainforest on boardwalks that extend from the intermediary stations. The main station (tel. 4038 1555) lies at the end of Arara St. (Tickets $27, children $13.50. Open daily 8am-5pm.) Across the street, the **Kuranda Scenic Railway** (tel. 4052 6249 or 1800 620 342), pulls in next to the Travel Centre Office in Kuranda's railway station. The torturous journey on this rickety antique, pulled by an ancient diesel engine, comes complete with torturous commentary. (Daily from Cairns 8:30 and 9:30am, to Cairns 2 and 3:30pm. One-way: $25, children $13, concessions $15.) **White Car Coaches** (tel. 4091 1855) services all major townships on the Tablelands. (Several times daily from 25 Spence St, Cairns. One-way: Mareeba $12, Yungaburra $20.10, Atherton $16, Malanda $22.30.)

■ Kuranda

If you only have time to visit one of the Tableland townships, make it Kuranda, with a plethora of tourist-friendly activities and easy public transport access. Kuranda's famed **markets** (open W-Sa) transform the cozy village of less than a thousand into a bazaar of arts, crafts, and clothing, brimming with daytrippers from Cairns.

ACCOMMODATIONS AND FOOD Near the center of town lies the old, majestic **Kuranda Backpacker's Hostel & Accommodation (Mrs. Miller's),** 6 Arara St (tel. 4093 7355; fax 4093 7295). Massive renovations by new owners have produced a hostel that feels more like a tropical resort. In the mornings, the proprietor feeds over 50 rainbow lorikeets, a beautiful spectacle. (Kitchen, pool, laundry, bike hire, courtesy bus, BBQ, tropical garden. Open daily 8am-6pm; dorms $14, doubles $32.) Just across the street from the Skyrail and scenic railroad lies the **Kuranda Bottom Pub Hotel,** Arara St (tel. 40937 206). This tidy establishment sports a garden bar (open 11am-2pm), serving reasonably priced breakfasts and lunches. (Singles $39, doubles $49; $10 per extra person. Open M-Sa 10am-10pm; Su 10am-7pm.)

Chippers and sandwiches ($2.50-$7) are served at the **Jungle Bar** (tel. 4093 8849) towards the back of the central market building (open W-Su 9am-3pm). Locals love **Frog's,** 11 Coondoo St (tel. 4093 7405). A jam band plays Sunday nights, occasionally joined by the local dance troupe and African drummers. (Food $10-12. Open M-Sa 9:30am-4:30pm and 6-8:30pm; Su 9:30am-11:30pm.)

SIGHTS AND ACTIVITIES Even on non-market days, Kuranda offers several attractions. **Birdworld** (tel. 4093 9188), in the Heritage Markets, has a collection of 50 Australian squawkers, as well as 25 "exotic species," including the elusive canary and parakeet. *(Open daily 9am-4pm. Admission $8, children $3. Combination ticket with the Butterfly Sanctuary $16, children $6.)* The **Australian Butterfly Sanctuary** (tel. 4093 7575), next door to the Heritage Markets, bills itself as the world's largest butterfly farm, and you can walk among the grazing beauties. *(Open daily 10am-3pm. Admission $10.50, children $5. Guided tours every 15min.)* If plummeting from a tower is more your bag, try **Sky Screamers Bungy** (tel. 4041 3280). *(Jumps $39. Open daily with free transfers from hostels at 9:30am and 1:30pm; pick-up in Cairns outside Hungry Jack's.)* Convenient to the Scenic Railway and Skyrail, **River Cruise and Rainforest Tours** (tel. 4093 7476), on the Barron River just off Arara St, offers 45-minute guided riverboat rides (5 per day 10:15am-2:30pm; adults $10, children $5, families $25) and guided rainforest walks. At the bottom of the Heritage Markets sits the **Juanna** Aboriginal dance troupe, a group of 16 children who seem a bit more depressing than authentic. *(Shows daily 10:45, 11:30am, 12:15, and 1pm. Admission $12, children $8.)*

■ Lake Tinaroo and Danbulla Forest

Saturated with crater lakes and sprinkled with waterfalls, the volcanic soil of the central Tablelands sprouts massive, bizarre strangler fig trees and other mixed forest along the shores of **Lakes Tinaroo, Barrine,** and **Eacham.** The **Danbulla Forest Drive** circumscribes Lake Tinaroo, which has been dammed for hydroelectric purposes. There are no designated hikes along this route, but a free copy of the *Danbulla Forest Drive* visitor's guide lists sights along the 40-minute loop. Both Lake Eacham and Lake Barrine have walking paths for spotting birds and small, fuzzy, and not-so-fuzzy animals. The 3km Lake Circuit Track encircling Lake Eacham in Crater National Park is especially delicious. Muskrat-kangaroos and giant iguanas (water dragons) are some of the common sights along this serene, well-paved walk.

Camping in the thick of the forests is definitely the best way to get up close and personal with the Tablelands, though it can get a bit frosty on winter nights. There are no fewer than five state forest campgrounds around Lake Tinaroo (self-registration $2 per night; toilets but no showers or firewood). The locations of the campground are depicted in the visitor's guide to Danbulla; call the **Department of Natural Resources,** 83 Main St (tel. 4091 1844), in Atherton with any questions. Take care when driving along the Danbulla circuit, since most of the roads are unsealed and the dirt turns to mud when it rains.

■ Yungaburra

Tiny Yungaburra (pop. 1000; pubs 1) is smack in the middle of all the good stuff: Lake Tinaroo and the Danbulla forest to the north, waterfalls to the south, Lakes Eacham and Barrine to the east, and the volcanic hills of the Seven Sisters to the west. From Atherton, follow the Cook St sign at the main roundabout, then keep an eye out for Yungaburra signs for the next 25km. From Cairns, get on the serpentine Gillies Hwy. and head west for about 60km.

ACCOMMODATIONS AND FOOD Yungaburra's youth hostel, **On the Wallaby** (tel. 4095 2031), is utterly superb. The common area feels like a mountain hut with rough-edged wood furnishings, and a wood-burning stove, the bathrooms and showers are sided with stone and wood, and the bedrooms are clean and fresh. There's barbecue, laundry facilities, and a self-serve kitchen with a tree frog couple, Trevor and Naomi.

QUEENSLAND

(Dorms $15; twins and doubles $35; camping $8. Transport to or from Cairns $15 one-way.) Overnight tour packages from Cairns ($75, daytrips $45) include transport and lodging, a canoe trip, nightly platypus spotting, bike hire, and a waterfalls tour.

Up the Gillies Hwy by Lake Eacham is the **Lake Eacham Caravan Park** (tel. 4095 3730), with showers and laundry facilities. (Reception open daily 7am-7pm. Tent sites $9, caravan $11, powered $12.) The fee includes admission to a garden and a petting zoo, featuring Pepe the burro. Yungaburra's shops are limited but include the **Chalet Rainforest Gallery,** Gilles Hwy, (tel. 4095 2144), which sells high-quality Aboriginal goodies for prices lower than the coastal towns (open daily 9am-5pm). The **Gem Gallery and Coffee Shop** (tel. 4095 3455), has breakfast for under $2, free didgeridoo lessons after 3:30pm, and opal-cutting demonstrations throughout the day (open daily 8am-late, depending upon patronage). **Cut-Price** (tel. 4095 2177) is the local supermarket (open daily 7am-7pm). On the other end of the price spectrum is **Nick's Swiss Italian Restaurant,** Gilles Hwy (tel. 4095 3330), a regalia of hat-wearing and dancing. This kind of fun and fine cuisine ain't cheap, but while some meals run $22, pasta dishes are $9-12. (Open 10am-4pm and 6-11pm. Closed Wednesday.)

SIGHTS Just off the west side of Yungaburra (over the bridge) is a sign pointing to the **Curtain Fig Tree,** a monstrous strangler fig with hundreds of shoots forming an eerie curtain in the middle of the rainforest. The 45m tall, half-millenium-old Cathedral Fig Tree on the east stretch of the Dunbulla Forest Drive dwarfs the Curtain Fig. The second-best place for **platypus-spotting** is at the creek under the bridge into Yungaburra. There's a viewing station set up with blinders, so large groups can watch the shy critters at nightfall. Arrive at sunrise or sunset. The best place to see them, though, is off Picnic Crossing Rd, heading north, between Saylee's Strawberries and the Barron River bridge. Up past the demonic cattle crossing sign, the road dips to an Atherton Council Pump Station. There's a concrete picnic table for a late-afternoon snack, and about seven platypus families near that bend in the river.

■ Malanda and Around

Undoubtedly the dairy capital of these parts, friendly and hospitable **Malanda** produces milk consumed as far away as the Northern Territory. Not surprisingly, the town has cows, cows, and more cows, but not much else. Malanda and Yungaburra are only a short distance apart (5min. drive) so accommodations in either place should suit the same needs.

ACCOMMODATIONS A collection of other wildlife can be found 6km east of the town center at the rambling **Platypus Forest Hostel** on Topaz Rd (tel. 4096 5926), a little-known refuge for nature buffs who don't mind seeing critters both in the rough and potentially in their beds at night. Pademelons (mini-kangaroos) wander in and out of the living room and curl up in visitors' laps, platypuses hang out in the creek, possums show up in the kitchen for some sweet potato, and the swath of rainforest behind the hostel houses a colony of tree kangaroos. If you're driving yourself, call ahead for directions and to let them know they should fire up the hot tub and sauna for you. The hostel does pick-ups in Cairns as part of a one-night deal that includes a tour of the sights around Lake Tinaroo, as well as dinner and breakfast. ($55 per person; additional nights $15 per person, doubles $35; $5 per meal.) **The Malanda Hotel,** English Ave, was built in 1919 and is the largest wooden hotel in all of Australia. Attached to the hotel is one of Malanda's only pubs where you can drink beer till the cows come home, play a game of pool, or gamble on the "pokies" (slot machines). The rooms are a dingy hodgepodge of furniture, but the location is ideal.

The **Peeramon Hotel** (tel. 4096 5873), in **Peeramon** between Yungaburra and Malanda, is the oldest hotel in the Tablelands, with a real ghost to prove it. The old (*very* old) lady still floats about the place: you can see a picture of her on display in the bar, mid-air and luminescent in a group picture taken on the hotel's front steps. From Atherton, take the first paved road on the right after leaving Yungaburra; from Cairns it's the first paved left after the Lake Eacham exit off the Gillies Hwy. The newly renovated rooms upstairs are reasonably priced and well-kept. The new management recently added tiny rooms out back for $10 a night. (Live music Su from 4-8pm. Reception open daily 10am-midnight. Singles $20; doubles $40. Continental breakfast $5, cooked $7.50. Book ahead.)

FOOD AND SIGHTS The **Resto Europe,** 25 English St, (tel. 4096 6339) serves a limited lunch menu for $4-5. The cuisine is predominantly French. (Open daily 11:30an-2:30pm and 6-9:30pm.) **Granny's Country Kitchen** (tel. 4096 6506), on the main drag only two blocks from the Malanda hotel, is a no-ambiance sandwich shop where a burger, chips, and a drink come in under $5. Friday is Chinese night. (Open M-W 7am-6pm; Th and Su 7am-7pm; F 7am-9pm.) The **Five Star Fresh Market** on English Street inhabits the same block as the Malanda Hotel.

About 25km south of Malanda and just beyond the town of Millaa Millaa, the **waterfall circuit** leads past a series of spectacular swimming holes that are best visited when it's raining (fewer tourists; more water coming over the falls). From the north a sign just out of Millaa Millaa points to the falls: follow the road from waterfall to waterfall and you'll pop out on the Palmerston Hwy again. Catch the loop from the south by looking for the "Tourist Drive" sign. **Millaa Millaa Falls** is the perfect waterfall: a straight, even curtain with rocks at the bottom and a bit of green on either side. **Zillie Falls** starts off a sedate creek at the top of the falls; a path down the side follows the roaring drop, and the cascading **Ellinjaa Falls** look like liquid fireworks. Millaa Millaa is the only site with toilets, but all three provide natural showers for wading and frolicking. The **Environmental Park** adjacent to the waterfalls provides for rainforest hikes laden with all types of tropical Queensland fauna. It's wheelchair accessible.

■ Chillagoe

If it's a taste of the outback you crave, mate, Chillagoe's your place. Situated almost 200km west of Mareeba, the drive along the Burke Development Rd is half the experience on a day trip to this old mining town. Unfortunately, the dirt road demands 4WD. Lush pastoral scenes dissolve into landscapes of rust colored dirt and bolders. Wild cattle of the same dusty hue meander along the roadside, and termite mounds of all sizes dot the landscape like cemetery headstones. When you think you're desperately lost in the middle of nowhere, take heart—you're close to Chillagoe.

ACCOMMODATIONS AND FOOD The accommodation climate in Chillagoe is as arid as the land, but all basic amenities are provided. **The Chillagoe Caves Lodge,** 7 King St (tel. 4094 7106), rents camping sites ($5 adults, $2 children, plus $2 for power). To find relief from heat and critters, opt for the trailer-style backpacker single ($10), or the budget double ($30; the "full" double isn't worth the extra $20). Meals are served from a constrictive menu in the in-house restaurant (small portions $8, large $12; open daily). **The Black Cockatoo,** Tower St (tel. 4094 7168), is as basic as they come, with motel-wide barbecue Sunday evenings (doubles $32). Just a wee bit out of town is the **Chillagoe Bush Camp and Eco Lodge,** Hospital Ave (tel./fax 4094 7155), run by a couple who are eager to please backpackers. The rooms are the same brand of trailor stall, but the bunks are clean and linens are included. (Singles $15, camping $4. Kitchen available. Open daily, flexible hours.)

Chillagoe is a culinary nightmare, especially for vegetarians. If you don't eat beef or fish, your choices are essentially narrowed to one: the **Chillagoe General Store,** Queen St (tel. 4094 7100), sells groceries and fresh fruit. (Open daily 7am-6pm; knock in back if nobody's out front.) **The Post Office Hotel,** Queen St (tel. 4947 119), is neither a post office nor a hotel—discuss. This pub is open daily from 10am to midnight; the hotel might be resurrected soon. Stubbies (small beers) cost $3.

SIGHTS AND ACTIVITIES The town's main draw and entire tourism livelihood is the system of **caves.** The **Queensland National Parks and Wildlife Service** (tel. 4094 7163) runs tours through three of them. (*Open M-F 8:30am-5pm, Sa-Su 8:30am-3:30pm. Tickets for the first two are $5 adult, $3 for children and senior citizens; Royal Arch tickets are*

$7.50, $5.) The 9:30am tour explores the multi-chambered Donna Cave, the 11:30am heads to the one-room, ornate Trezkinn cave, and the 1:30pm tour of the Royal Arch cave is the easiest hike. Meanwhile, **Chillagoe Heritage Museum,** on Hill St (tel. 4094 7109), is worth the $5 entrance fee for comic relief alone. *(Open daily 8:30am-5pm.)* A one-room gallery, this charming family museum houses old bottles, cameras, and a smattering of photos with no real explanation of what you are viewing. Two posters trace the scandal-ridden political history of Chillagoe over the past century.

■ Port Douglas

The coastal road to Port Douglas, overlooking the patchwork teals and indigo waters of the sea, is as lovely as the town itself, where there are no traffic lights, the sun is always shining, and the police station closes at two for lack of crime. Welcome to Port Douglas, where the most pressing item on any agenda is relaxation on the beach.

ORIENTATION AND PRACTICAL INFORMATION

Port Douglas is 80km north of Cairns off the Captain Cook Highway (Hwy. 1). The main drag in town is **Macrossan St,** a left turn at the end of the long, palm-lined Port Douglas Road that comes into town from the highway. On the east end of Macrossan is **Four Mile Beach,** on the west the **Marina Mirage.**

Tourist Office: The **Visitors Bureau,** 12 Grant St (tel. 4099 4644; fax 4099 4645; http://www.Great-Barrier-Reef.com), off Macrossan St, has a less biased opinion than the privately owned information storefronts found on almost every corner. Soon the bureau will operate almost entirely off the Internet, but calls will still be taken in the office. Open M-F 9am-5pm.

Buses: Coral Coaches, on the corner of Grant and Warner St (tel. 4099 5351; fax 4099 4235), at the water's edge near the intersection of Wharf and Warner St, runs to Cairns daily. (Nearly hourly from 2:45 until 7pm; $16 one way plus $1 hostel pick-up charge, $30 return if used within 24hr.) Nine buses per day to Mossman ($6); $22 to the airport from Port Douglas.

Ferries: Quicksilver (tel. 4099 5500) leaves Port Douglas daily at 5:15pm for Cairns. One-way $20, return $30 per person. YHA. Departs the Marina Mirage.

Currency: All banks are open M-Th 9:30am-4pm, F 9:30am-5pm. **ANZ,** 36 Macrossan St (tel. 4099 5700; fax 4099 5679), exchanges cash for $5 commission. The ANZ **ATM** takes Visa, MC, Plus, and Cirrus. **Commonwealth Bank,** 2nd floor at the corner of Grant and Macrossan St (tel. 4099 5233), grants Visa cash advances and exchanges traveler's checks ($5 per check) and cash (no commission). The ATM takes MC and Cirrus. If headed north, keep in mind that there are **no ATMs** north of the Daintree River.

Taxis: Port Douglas Limousines (tel. 4099 5950; fax 4099 5955). To airport or Cairns $22.

Car Rental: Policies on offroading and mileage vary greatly. **Crocodile Car Rentals,** 50 Macrossan St (tel. 4099 5555; fax 4099 4114), specializes in 4WD (from $69 per day). **Network Rentals,** 5 Warner St (tel. 4099 5111; fax 4099 4423), is another option. **Allcar Rentals,** 21 Warner St (tel. 4099 4123; fax 4099 4436), rents vehicles from $39 per day, and is one of the only places in Australia that has **automatic transmission 4WD.**

Bike Rental: Port Douglas Bike Hire, 42 Macrossan St (tel. 4099 5799). Open daily 8:30am-5pm. Half-day $7; full day (24hr.) $10; week $45.

Public Toilets: On Warner St, near the parking lot behind the town hall on Macrossan, and on Wharf St, near the intersection with Macrossan. 24hr.

Book Store: Book Exchange, 12 Macrossan St, behind Star of Siam. Open M-F 10am-5pm, Sa-Su 10am-4pm. **Jungle Books,** 46 Macrossan St (tel. 4099 4203). Open M-Sa 9:30am-6pm.

Road Report: Check on all road conditions and closings (tel. 4033 6711).

Liquor Store: Central Hotel's Drive Thru Bottle Shop, 9 Macrossam St (tel. 4099 5271).Open daily 10am-10pm.

Medical Services: Medical Centre, in the Marina Mirage on the left side of the parking lot (24hr. tel. 4099 5043; fax 4099 4216). Office open M-F 8am-6pm, Sa-Su 9am-noon. The nearest **hospital** is in Mossman, on Hospital St (tel. 4098 2444).
Pharmacy: Marina Pharmacy (tel. 4099 5223) next door to the medical centre.
Emergency: Dial 000.
Police: At Macrossan and Wharf St. Open M-Th 8am-2pm. 24hr. tel. 4099 5220.
Post Office: (tel. 4099 5210; fax 4099 4584) on the corner of Macrossan and Owen St, up the hill on the left. Open M-F 9am-5pm, Sa 9am-noon. **Postal Code:** 4871.
Phone Code: 07.

ACCOMMODATIONS

Word has spread far and wide that **Port o' Call** (tel. 4099 5422; fax 4099 5495), is the fairest YHA of them all. On Port St, left off of Port Douglas Rd as you come into town, this impeccable hostel is in the most beautiful of surroundings. The hostel has a free shuttle bus to Cairns (departs M, W, Sa 8:30am; call for a 10am lift north from Cairns). (Pool, laundry. Reception open daily 7:30am-7:30pm. 4-bed dorms with bath $18 per person, $19 YHA non-members, A/C $5 more; deluxe motel rooms $60 or $84 during dry season; $5 less for rooms without TV and refrigerator. Bikes $7 half-day, $10 full day.) The hostel's bistro is open for dinner every night (6-9pm, meals $7.50-10) and swings during happy hour (5-7pm; beer $2, mixed drinks $3).

Smack in the center of town upstairs from a small shopping plaza, **Port Douglas Backpackers,** 8 Macrossan St (tel. 4099 4883; fax 4099 4827), is clean and groomed for the backpacker crowd. The place feels like an office-turned-dormitory, with fluorescent lighting and carpet tiles. The location's great, but the architecture creates an acoustic nightmare—bring earplugs. Only four somewhat mildewed showers for 50 beds, but at least there's great water pressure. There's always a movie on in the lounge. Dorms ($14) are air-conditioned and include linens.

Alternatively, pitch a tent and take a hot shower at **Kulay Caravan Park,** 24 Davidson St (tel. 4099 5449), just 100m from the beach (sites $15, powered $17, 2-person cabins $50; open daily 7am-7pm). If you've come to the far north to get away from it all and don't mind a bit of a splurge, the **Marae** (tel. 4098 4900; fax 4098 4099), a B&B 15 minutes north of Port Douglas by car, presents a peaceful, romantic escape. With mountain views and lots of wildlife around, you can relax in the salt-water pool or chat with the pet cockatoo (doubles from $80; bookings essential).

FOOD AND ENTERTAINMENT

The cheapest food is found at **Spar Market,** 6 Macrossan St (tel. 4099 5618; open daily 7am-9pm). **Port Produce Fruit and Veg Mart,** 9 Warner St (tel. 4099 4989; fax 4099 4080), has a vast selection of fruits and vegetables available at wholesale prices. Recommended tropical delights include custard apples ($3 per kilo) and ross sapote ($3.50 per kilo; mart open M-F 7am-3pm, Sa-Su 8am-noon). For the freshest produce, including the local white grapefruit, head down the Cook Hwy to **Scomazzon's Horticultural Farm,** 5km north of Mossman (open daily 7am-6pm).

EJ's Seamarkets and Take-Away, 23 Macrossan St, serves hot breakfast with bottomless coffee ($4.50) and lunch sandwiches ($2.50-4.50) daily 7am to 9pm. **On the Inlet** (tel. 4099 5255; fax 4099 5939) is obscured by the Marina Mirage—take the side street to the right. It's a perfect spot for a sunset beer ($3.50) or generous dinner of fresh seafood right off the trawler (open 11am-11pm). Happy hour (4-6pm) features the drink and seafood special, including a plate of oysters or a bucket of prawns ($10). Live music rocks on Sunday afternoon. For a quick bite, stop by **Mocha's Pies,** 16 Macrossan St (tel. 4099 5295), for a steak and kidney or cheese savory pasty ($2.60). Pies are sold daily until 3pm (or until sold out).

Ironbar Restaurant, 5 Macrossan St (tel. 4099 4776), is just across from Port Douglas Backpackers. The restaurant sponsors cane toad races every Tuesday at 9pm. Choose your own amphibian from buckets; free drinks go to the winners (the people, not the toads). The Ironbar is most popular on Saturday nights, when it serves as a venue for Port Douglas's best live music (open daily 9am-2am). The **Court House**

Hotel (tel. 4099 5181; fax 4099 4249), at the corner of Macrossan and Wharf St, has live music in the pub (Th-M nights, no cover, stubbies $3, counter meals from $5). Texan owner Michael Gabour throws the best 4th of July party this side of the Pacific, with free food and the (fire) works.

SIGHTS AND ACTIVITIES

Ben Cropp's Shipwreck Museum (tel. 4099 5858), on a low rocky precipice by the water near the corner of Wharf and Macrossan St, features incredible displays on major shipwrecks. The exhibit culminates in a re-creation of the legendary Yolanga Tomb. *(Open daily 9am-5pm. Admission $5, students $4, children $2.)* The nearby **Lower Isles Preservation Society** (tel. 4099 4573) grants camping permits for the Lower Isles ($3.50) and provides info on the marine park. Ask at the marina, to the left of the Marina Mirage, for a lift to the islands. *(Open Tu-Sa 10am-1pm.)*

Four Mile Beach, at the east end of Macrossan St, is as hard to miss as its name implies. Keep an eye out for the flags near the edge of the water, color-coded like traffic lights: don't even think about swimming on red. *(Lifeguard on duty M-Sa 9am-5pm.)*

The Rainforest Habitat (tel. 4099 3235; fax 4099 3100) has two acres, three enclosures, and over 1000 animals without cages or any discernible fear of people. The entry fee ($16) is a bit steep, but where else can you tickle a fruit bat's tummy or scratch a wallaroo behind the ears? Cockatoos and parrots mingle in the cafe, though they'll rarely offer to buy you a drink. *(Open daily 8am-5:30pm; last entry 4:30pm. Tours every 30min. Wheelchair accessible. Coral Coach departs Port Douglas depot hourly from 8am, return $2.20.)*

WATERSPORTS

Port Douglas is an excellent destination for scuba divers. The reef just off Four Mile Beach offers a diversity of marine life. The colorful coral reefs found in Cairns are just as accessible from Port Douglas, but are less crowded. Turtle Bay and Barracuda Point are highlights of the local dive sights. If you're not a diver, don't despair—there are many options for water play. Most aquatic activities launch from the Marina Mirage.

When selecting a dive or snorkel shop, ask plenty of questions. Knowing boat capacity, dive difficulty, and site destinations are important. Keep in mind companies change their destinations daily depending on weather conditions.

Discover Dive (tel. 4099 6333 fax 4099 6345), just across the street from the shipwreck museum down by the wharf. A PADI dive center which specializes in small group training. A 4-day certification coursecosts $450 including dives and equipment. The owner is specially trained to certify handicapped divers. Introductory dives without certification $165. Open daily 8:30am-6:30pm.

Haba Dive, Shop 3, Marina Mirage (tel. 4099 5254; fax 4099 5385), departs daily at 8:30am with free pick-up and lunch. Not frugal, but popular. Opal Reef is highly recommended. For beginners, who are referred to by all companies as "resort divers," depth runs 8-12m; certified dives up to 18m. Snorkeling $105. Diving with certification $145 and $30 for equipment, without certification $165.

Quicksilver Diver (tel. 4099 5050), in the Marina Mirage, offers a variety of packages. The 4-day certification course is $439; prices rise for advanced courses. Daytrips to the lower isles $128, inner reef $196, outer reef $229, with one dive and equipment included. Pre-dive helicopter transport available.

Poseidon (tel. 4099 5599; fax 4099 5070), at the end of C Jetty, Marina Mirage, has somewhat cheaper versions, also with free pick-up and lunch. Snorkeling $105; certified diving $145 for 2 dives; uncertified $175 for 1 dive, $200 for 2.

Wavelength, 20 Solander Blvd (tel. 4099 5031; fax 4099 3259), departs daily at 8:30am from the Port Douglas Slipway, to the right of the Marina Mirage. Their sweet deal is snorkeling on the outer reef (8hr., $90 includes lunch), although half-days in the Lower Isles are just $50 (no diving; max. 20 people).

QUEENSLAND

If your bag is the ocean surface and not below, check out **Port Douglas Water Sports** (tel. 019 340 335), near the beach's Warner St entrance. Mick gives 20% discounts to backpackers—just mention that you read about him in *Let's Go*—and basic instruction is thrown in free of charge. *(Catamaran rental $25 per hr., windsurfer $20 per hr., boogie board $5 per hr. Deposit $20. Open daily Nov.-March 9am-5pm.)* **Sail Away-Low Isles,** 23 Macrossan St. (tel. 4099 5070, reservations 24hr. tel. 4099 5599; fax 4099 5510), departs daily at 9:30am from berth C17, Marina Mirage. *(7hr., $85, with YHA $76.50.)* Catch their free shuttle from Cairns (7:15am) or Port Douglas (8:45am).

Hook your own catch of the day with **Trinity Sportfishing,** 18 Macrossan St (tel. 4099 5031). The barramundi, queenfish, and mangrove jack are most abundant in Port Douglas waters, and Trinity offers half-day, full-day and night trips. Half-day and night voyages take six fishers max. *($70, departs 8am, 1:30 and 6:30pm; full day $130, departs 8am.)* Enjoy a different type of serenity high above the water with **Get High Parafly,** Berth CA-Marina Mirage, (tel. 4099 6366). Parasailing is $55 solo or $80 for a couple. Couple rates are available for all activities, but single jetski prices start at $55, water skiing at $50, and "Bumpa tubes" at $25. A package including parasailing, jet skis, and bumpa tubes is $100 for one person or $150 for a couple. Call for booking or just show up at the dock on the hour between 9am and 5pm.

■ Near Port Douglas: Mossman Gorge

A few minutes up the Cook Hwy from Port Douglas is the entirely unremarkable town of **Mossman,** and its entirely remarkable natural attraction. Disgorge yourself from the idleness of quiet Port Douglas life and bushwhack through the rainforest, dodging vines along the banks of creeks, until you reach gorgeous **Mossman Gorge.** There are no crocs in the gorge, but signs warn of strong currents. Part of the Daintree National Park, the gorge is riddled with hiking paths which all originate from the visitors parking lot (follow signs). From the moment you step on any of the trails you feel engulfed by the magnificent green canopy. There are many stairs along most hikes and the flat stones on the paths are slippery. If you lose your footing, the **Mossman Hospital,** Hospital St (tel, 4098 2444), is just two minutes from the hiking area.

The best spot to get your feet wet is at **Silky Oaks** (tel. 4098 1666), a posh hunting resort downstream, located 10km outside Mossman township on the pristine Norwood Billabong. The good folks at Oaks allow the public to swim, provided one makes a purchase at the restaurant upstairs—perhaps a cappuccino ($3), sipped quietly on the canopy-height Jungle Perch Porch.

If you want to learn the secrets of the rainforest, spend an hour with an Aboriginal guide from **Kuku-Yalanji Dreamtime Tours** (tel. 4098 1305), on the road to the gorge. The tour covers traditional medicines and bush tucker, and includes tea and scone at the end. (Tours M-F at 10, 11:30am, and 2:30pm. $15, students $13.50.) The Aboriginal-owned operation has a regular shuttle to Port Douglas for pick-ups, but this service more than doubles the ticket price. **Coral Coaches** (tel. 4099 5351) run to Mossman from Port Douglas (8 per day 9:15am-6pm, $10, round-trip $18). If driving, follow Hwy 1 north from the junction to Port Douglas. Turn left at the Slippery Oaks sign (beside the roadside cemetery) and drive about 5km to the carpark.

■ Daintree

The sullen Daintree River ripples and gurgles, not from the lethargic currents, but from the teeming mass of estuarine crocodiles (salties). The people of Daintree see the fearsome predator as the town's greatest economic asset. Boatloads of camera-toting croc-hunters skim the river each day and keep half a dozen operators in business. The exit off Coast Hwy dips and turns into town, and can get flooded out. Call one of the restaurants in town to get conditions before setting out. Iridescent blue peacocks outnumber the three dozen residents who live in Daintree proper, but this tiny forest village is an excellent gateway to the rougher frontier land to the north.

There are only a handful of places to stay in town. The most comfortable is the **Red Mill House** (tel. 4098 6233) in the middle of town. There are only three double rooms available for $60 so you may want to book ahead. While munching on the complimentary continental breakfast, check out the birds from the porch. **Daintree River View Caravan Park** (tel. 4098 6119), also smack in the middle of town, rents tent sites. ($9 for 1 person, $12 for 2. Onsite vans cost $35, but if you drive your own, parking is $15. Hot showers, barbecue.) **Kenadon Homestead Cabins** (tel./fax 4098 6147) has five new cabins, each with a well-equipped kitchen, TV, double bed, and triple bunk. (Pool, linens provided, A/C, and continental breakfast. $50 for a single, $60 double plus $10 for each additional person. Open daily 7am-7pm.)

Competition is not fierce between the restaurants in Daintree, which all line Stewart St. On one side of the street is the **Daintree Village Coffee Shop and Restaurant** (tel. 4098 6173). Burgers run $6-8, the full dinner menu $10-13. (Open daily 9am-8pm.) On the other sits the more touristy **Big Barramundi** (tel. 4098 6166; same hours), which serves a large variety of sandwiches ($3-5). **Jacanas Restaurant** (tel. 4098 6146) is run in combination with the adjacent **Daintree General Store.**

Aside from visiting on an all-inclusive tour package from Port Douglas or Cairns, there are several ways to set out on the river, and all local tours can be booked from the **Daintree Tourist Information** window in the general store. The **Daintree Rainforest River Train** (tel. 1800 808 309) is immediately next to the ferry service on the Cook Hwy. (1hr. cruise departs 9:15 am and 4pm, $12; 1½hr. leaves at 10:30am, $20; 2½hr. tour $25, with varied departure times.) **Daintree Connections** runs hour-long cruises (8:15, 9:30, 10:30, 11:30am, 1:30, 2:30, and 3:30pm) for $15, from the Daintree Original's storefront in town. Both tours offer a package for $95 with pick-up in Cairns or Port Douglas. **Daintree Wildlife Safari** (tel. 4098 6125; fax 4098 6192) has a longer two-hour, wheelchair accessible tour at $40. The cheapest by far is the **Daintree River and Reef Cruise Centre** (tel. 4098 6115) on the road into Daintree (1hr. cruise $12, 1½hr. $15; binoculars included). **Chris Dahlberg** (tel. 4098 7997), runs morning bird-spotting tours which depart the Daintree jetty at 6am in the summer and 6:30am in winter (2hr., $30 per person with limited seating). **James Beitzel** (tel. 4098 6138) takes folks out fishing for the Daintree mascot, the elusive Barramundi. (4hr. trips $50, 7hrs. $90). If you prefer to remain on (and, **Wonga Beach Trail Rides** (tel. 4098 7583) offers three-hour horseback rides which go through sugar cane fields, the rainforest, and end up on the beach (3hr., 8:30am-3pm, $55 includes transport from Port Douglas).

■ Crossing the Daintree River

On the approach to the ferry crossing, large wooden signs warn that the roadway over the river is rough, wild, and potentially dangerous. They don't lie; the easy, paved roads of the Cook Hwy become dirt and eventually crushed stones and roots as the sunny savannah is lost in the shade of the rainforest canopy. Approach the crossing with caution and keep an eye out for saltwater crocs. Never feed the wildlife. And never camp by the river in this region; salties can move without a trace in knee-deep water. Ask those who know the land before getting too intimate with nature. The lands north of the river are steeped in natural beauty but laced with dangers like stinging trees and the poisonous purple cassowary plum.

On the south side of the Daintree River, passengers board the **Daintree Ferry** and are shuttled across the swirling, black, hypnotic waters toward Cape Tribulation. (Runs daily 6am-midnight. Pay the ferryman. Walk-on passengers $1, motorcycles $3, cars $7.) From the far shore, a thin road snakes through rainforest. Trees seem to lean in and leer at passing automobiles, dropping sinister vines across their roofs like a ceremonial rite of passage into this untamed jungle.

■ Cape Tribulation

The road between Daintree and Cape Tribulation is utterly fantastic. The rainforest comes crashing down to the ocean surf, and every inch is filled with living things. These days, conservationists and capitalists are locked in a heated power struggle over the future of these lush forests. The former are vying to prevent the Cape from obtaining central electricity and have plastered the area with posters reading "Don't Electrocute Our Forest." Meanwhile, businesses catering to tourists see the modernization as a perfect means to open the wilderness to a larger community of travelers. Both agree that the lands of Cape Tribulation are some of Queensland's most beautiful, but whether they will remain a virtually uninhabited jewel or become a common tourist trap remains to be seen.

The peninsula is divided into upper Daintree, Cow Bay, and Cape Tribulation although in practice everything is located on the Cape Tribulation Rd, which runs the length of the coast between ferries. **Coral Coaches** (tel. in Cairns 4031 7577; in Port Douglas 4099 5351) stops twice daily in Cow Bay (departs Cairns 7am and 3:30pm; Port Douglas 8:30am and 5:15pm). Most accommodations here are solar-powered, so don't plan to watch television, or turn on the lights, at night.

ACCOMMODATIONS

Crocodylus Village (tel. 4098 9166; fax 4098 9131) is a hostel that seems organically intertwined with the rainforest around it. Gravel paths connect the elevated cabins to the immaculate, canopied common area. Superb meals are served three times a day from one kitchen while another is open for self-catering. The amenities (pool, laundry, full bar, free bus to beach twice daily) are secondary to the surroundings: a strangler fig tree, a caged stinging plant, and the constant rustle and song from the treetops. Enjoy horseback riding ($39), a sunrise paddle trek ($35), or a guided bushwalk (3hr., $16). (Reception open daily 7:30am-5pm. Cabin rooms $16, YHA $15. Hut for 2 with bath $55, additional guests $10. Linen included. Book ahead.)

The **Daintree Manor**, just across the river at 27 Forest Creek Rd (tel./fax 4090 7041), represents the pricier end of the Cape's accommodations. With a breath-taking view, full cooked breakfast, rare 24-hour power, clean private baths, and a TV lounge with some of the only good reception within miles, you get full bang for your buck (singles $65, doubles $85). About 5km up the road is **Club Daintree** which is set off the main thoroughfare on Cape Kimberly near Snapper Island (tel./fax 4090 7501). The fabulous beachfront locale is the highlight and while deluxe cabins don't come cheap at $98, basic rooms for backpackers are available for $15, camping $8. (Open 6:30am-midnight, with pick-up packages from Cairns available.) Continuing along Cape Tribulation Rd you arrive at the slightly more populated area, not worthy of the title of township, of **Cow Bay.** Two km past the welcome sign sits The **Rainforest Retreat** (tel./fax 4098 9101) with rooms with fridges and a pool. (Dorms $15, singles $45, doubles $70. All but two rooms are dark from 10:30pm-7:30am.)

PK's Jungle Village (tel. 4098 0040; fax 4098 0006), about 500km after the "Welcome to the Cape Tribulation" sign, is more appropriately called "PK's Jungle Party." A classic example of ecotourism turned sour, nightly dance parties pale in light of the weekly theme parties, usually four-keggers. There's a restaurant and a bar, and if you miss the first daily happy hour, don't worry—there's another. Activities include volleyball, horseback riding, guided bushwalking, and bike hire (half-day $10, full day $15). (Dorms $18, with VIP $17; doubles $52.)

The **Rainforest Camp** (tel. 4098 9015) is located between Cape Tribulation and Crocodylus Village, and offers tent or campervan sites for $5 per person (laundry facilities, hot showers, barbecue). **Noah Beach Campground,** 7km south of Cape Tribulation, allows tent camping ($3.50 per person; showers and toilets; no open fires). Obtain a permit from the ranger or the QNP&WS in Cairns. **Swimming** on Noah Beach is allowed, but watch for crocodile warning placards.

FOOD

Delectable grub, including the best chili this side of Springfield, is served at the **Crocodylus Jungle Nest** (all dinners $8). **Cafe on Sea,** between Cow Bay and PK's, is right on Thorton Beach, but doesn't actually have a view of the sea. Enjoy dinner under the tented open-air dining area. (Sandwiches $5; full meals $12. Open 9am-6pm.) **Lattitude 16.21** (tel. 4098 9089), next door to The Rainforest Retreat, has a diverse menu ($3-$10; open daily 9:30am-10:30pm). **Lync Haven** (tel. 4098 9155) is by far the most amusing eating establishment on the Cape. Bozo, the resident cockatoo, welcomes guests at the door. If the staff isn't overloaded, ask to see the orphaned 'roos, which you can feed out of your hand; small donations are appreciated to help defray veterinary costs. The all-day menu includes run of the mill burgers and sandwiches ($2.50-$4) and the veggie-friendly dinner menu is expansive ($8-$16). (Open daily 7am-10pm.) **The Cow Bay General Store** (tel. 4098 9127), on Spurwood Rd just off Cape Tribulation Rd, sells groceries and is one of the northern most **gas stations** on the Cape (open 7:30am-6pm).

SIGHTS

All attractions on Cape Tribulation revolve around the wet tropics. **The Daintree Rainforest Environmental Centre** (tel./fax 4098 9171), just before Cow Bay, is an excellent reference center from which to begin. A newly built 25m tower allows for visitors to view the rainforest from above the canopy. The ticket price includes a boardwalk rainforest hike (approx. 20min.), small theatres playing wet tropic movies, and an exhibit of forest wildlife pickled in jars on the porch. *($8 for those lodging in the area, $10 from Port Douglas, $25 family. Open daily 8:30am-5pm; guided tours 2:45, 3:45pm.)* A less commercialized source of forest information is the **Bathouse**, directly past PK's on the left. The staff is all volunteer, and they will be happy to take your picture with their giant bat Rex, provided he isn't napping. The conservation society run out of this hut is responsible for two of the best boardwalk rainforest walks available on the Cape. The ½km hike near Thornton Beach is known as the Maardje (mar-ja), and the 3km Dubidgee (doob-a-gee) is just down the road from the Bathouse. All these lands belong to the Daintree National Park Service.

The **Wonga Beach** spans almost 20km along the coast and is one of Queensland's most beautiful and most deserted free beaches (watch for crocs). Speaking of watching for crocs, **Cooper Creek Wilderness Cruises** (tel. 4098 9126) will help you do just that. Highly recommended by the lodges in the know, Cooper Creek cruises explore the mangroves in search of crocodiles. *(1hr., $15 10:30, 11:30am and 1:30pm.)* They also offer creek walks and package deals which include pick up in Port Douglas. *(2hr. $12; 3hr. $16)* As with most Cape tours, book through your accommodation or call ahead, as there is no manned tourist station. **Rum Runner** (tel. 1800 686 444 or 4050 9988) is based out of Cairns but runs daily trips out to the reef off the Cape. *(Base price $80, $65 standby. Intro dives approximately $50 extra; snorkeling equipment available. Boat departs 9am from Cape Tribulation National Park Beach and returns at 3:45pm.)*

The popular two-day, one-night trip to **Snapper Island** is available at the Crocodylus Village through **Tropical Sea Kayaks** (tel. 4098 9166; fax 4098 9131) for $159. This excursion features reef walking, snorkeling, beach camping, fully prepared meals, and all equipment. If you prefer to remain on dry land, check out **Wundu Trail Rides** (tel. 4098 9156), between Lync Haven and the Rainforest Camp, to discover the coral coast on horseback. *(3hr. guided rides daily at 9:40am and 2:40pm. Call ahead or book through your lodge, as the stable is often deserted. All rides $39.)* If neither land nor sea suit your fancy, take to the air with **Cowbay Air Service** (tel. 4098 9153) just down the street from the Crocodylus Village. *($40 per person; open daily 9am-5pm. No flights in bad weather.)* Steve Terry's one-plane service accommodates up to five passengers, but he'll begrudgingly take as few as two. Trips begin once the sun is well up over the reef to ensure good lighting, and each 24-minute flight dips and soars above reef and rainforest. These flights are the most reasonably priced in Queensland.

■ Routes to Cooktown

BLOOMFIELD TRACK

The road that beats through the bush between Cape Tribulation and Cooktown is cruel on automobiles as it swerves and dips, hugging the sides of precipitously steep mountains and wading through creeks and small rivers. The surface of the road is a mess of stones and roots with the odd fallen branch or sudden pothole. When it's in "good" condition, driving the **Bloomfield Track** is about as much fun as one can legally have in a 4WD vehicle, but is it ever hard on the hiney! When it's in bad condition, the road is impassable, flooded by heavy rains. Call ahead for road conditions, and bring cash, as most places up here don't take credit.

On the southern section of the track lies **Wujal Wujal,** an Aboriginal community. The tiny village offers a **convenience store** (open M-F 8am-4:30pm) and a **service station** (open M-F 8am-5pm). Off the road are the **Bloomfield Falls,** a terrific place to relax after the hard ride. Between Wujal Wujal and Cooktown there's a dirt road, and the scenery turns to dry savannah as the mountains pull back from the coast. Along the way are small-town hotels and general stores. **The Bloomfield Inn** (tel. 4060 8174) has gas and food, but no lodging (open daily 8am-8pm; meals about $4). Fifteen minutes north, the **Ayton General Store** (tel. 4060 8125) has all the basics. (Open Tu-F 8:30am-5:30pm, Sa-Su 8:30am-4pm. **Pay phone** out front.) Just up the road, **Viv's Takeaway** (tel. 4060 8266) cooks up some tasty sandwiches and specializes in desserts made from local fruits (all meals under $10; open daily 9am-8pm).

The final road before Cooktown leads to the **Lion's Den Hotel** (tel. 4060 3911), whose rough edge is captured by its posted warning: "Keep your dogs outa the bar, and I'll keep my bullets outa your dog." (Open daily 10am-midnight, or whenever the party simmers down. Beer $3, pub grub $10 a plate.) Though the building is a tad run-down, rooms are pleasant (singles $18; doubles $25; campsites $4 per person).

INLAND TO COOKTOWN

The direct, mostly paved inland route to Cooktown is not as exciting as the coastal track, but the good road conditions allow drivers the opportunity to focus less on the next pothole and more on the fantastic views along the journey. There are a handful of interesting stop-offs. The prettiest, **Mt. Molloy,** is a 10-minute drive west of Mossman on the Peninsula Development Rd. **The Mt. Molloy National Hotel** (tel. 4094 1133) has old, basic rooms. (Open daily 7am-midnight; $20 per person.) The only pub is downstairs (open 10am-midnight). **The Mt. Molloy Cafe & Takeaway** can whip up Mexican fare or just plain sandwiches (open 7am-8pm). A **picnic area** with hiking information and public restrooms is 500m from the hotel.

Mt. Carbine lies 50km north. Once a prosperous mining town, it now consists of three roadside buildings. The **Mount Carbine Village and Caravan Park** (tel. 4094 3160; office open 8am-8:30pm) has laundry facilities, barbecue, and an untreated water supply, as well as over-priced rooms ($45) and tent sites ($12, powered $14). The **Mount Carbine Hotel** (tel. 4094 3108) is nicer. (Singles $25, doubles $40. TVs. Open M-Sa 10am-midnight, Su 10am-7pm.) Just across the street, the **Mt. Carbine Roadhouse** (tel. 4094 3043) has gas, food, and hidden backpacker lodging around back. (Bunks $10. Meals $2-7. Weekly barbecues. Open daily 6:30am-10pm.)

An hour north along a hypnotically bland road lies the **Palmer River Roadhouse** (tel. 4060 2020). It is decorated with various murals tracing the area's gold mining history. The largest depicts the Aboriginals' massacre of the Chinese and the subsequent slaying of the Aboriginals by the whites; it also features a handful of Cooktown's notorious ladies of ill repute. The roadhouse offers hot showers and camping, so long as you pay in cash. (Tent sites $5; caravan sites $10; open daily 7am-11pm.)

The **Lakeland Downs Hotel** (tel. 4060 2142) marks the end of the paved road and the last pit stop before Cooktown, 80km away. Rooms are a bit more expensive. (Singles $38, doubles $55. Lunch $8, dinner $11-12.)

QUEENSLAND

■ Cooktown

Cooktown is imbued with legends, folklore, and mystery, but you wouldn't know it by the near-deserted streets and general lack of excitement. However, just ask any resident about the history of their home, and they'll gladly shower you with Aboriginal creation myths and other fascinating tales. The Europeans arrived via Captain Cook's voyage in 1770—an event reenacted every year during June's **Discovery Weekend festival.** Sent from England to search the southern seas for *terra australis*, Cook's ship the *Endeavor* was grounded in what is now the wharf. The discovery of gold a century later at nearby Palmer's field turned the sleepy town into a port metropolis. Chinese immigrants arrived by the boatload, and prospectors filled mines outside of town. When the gold ran out, almost everyone picked up their stakes and sojourned to the southern goldfields.

The 1400 who remain today incorporate the past into the present. The train station now houses the Cooktown kindergarten class, and the legends of Mary Watson and the mystery Normanby woman interred in the Cooktown cemetery still circulate in local pubs. The tenacity of these rugged folks has created a history-rich, fun-filled place to visit, full of good old-fashioned small-town friendliness.

ORIENTATION AND PRACTICAL INFORMATION

The Cooktown Development Rd becomes **Hope St** as it runs north toward **Grassy Hill.** Two blocks to the west, **Charlotte St** contains the bulk of Cooktown's shops and services and is crossed as it runs north by Boundary, Howard, Hogg, and Walker St. Just north of Walker is **Furneaux St,** at a slight angle to the rest of the grid, and **Green St.** Beyond Green St, Charlotte becomes **Webber Esplanade** and curves along the riverside and wharf around Grassy Hill. A **lighthouse** stands atop the hill, overlooking the river to the north.

Tourist Office: None, but Barbara at **Endeavour Farms Trading Post** (see **Food,** below) is fiercely insistent on helping anyone who comes to town.

Buses: Coral Coach (tel. 4098 2600) has service between Cooktown and Cairns. **Endeavour Farms Trading Post** (see **Food,** below) is the local ticketing agent. To Cairns, by coastal route (via Cape Tribulation, Tu, Th, and Sa, 11:30am, $52), by inland route (via Mount Carbine, W, F, and Su., 2:30pm, $47).

Currency Exchange: Westpac (tel. 4069 5477), on Charlotte St, between Green and Furneaux St, charges no commission for exchanging traveler's checks or cash. Permits V, MC withdrawals. Open M-Th 9:30am-4pm, F 9:30am-5pm.

Budget Travel Office: Cooktown Travel Centre (tel. 4069 5446; fax 4069 6023), on Charlotte St next to the Anzac Park. Offers a $94 return airplane ticket to Cairns (one-way $74), flying twice daily on Transtate Air, with a 3-day advance purchase. Open M-F 8am-6pm, Sa 8am-1pm, Su 3-5pm.

Car Rental: The aptly named **Car Rental** (tel. 4069 5007; fax 4069 5834) is one of the only options this far north, and has 4WD from $90.

Taxis: Cooktown Taxis (tel. 4069 5387).

Automobile Club: RACQ, Cape York Tyres (tel. 4069 5233), at the corner of Charlotte and Furneaux St. Open M-F 7am-7pm, Sa 7:30am-7pm, Su 7:30am-6pm.

Public Toilets and Shower: At the wharf across from Cooks Landing Kiosk. Yuck.

Library: Cooktown Library (tel. 4069 5009), at the corner of Walker and Helen St Open M-F 10am-4:30pm, Sa 9am-12:30pm. Closed for lunch around 1-2pm.

Medical Center: Cooktown Hospital (tel. 4069 5433), corner of Ida St and the Cooktown Developmental Rd, on the way out of town heading south.

Emergency: Dial 000.

Police: (tel. 4069 5320), across from the wharf on Charlotte St. Staffed M-F 8am-noon and 1-4pm.

Post Office: (tel. 4069 5347), on Charlotte St across from the Sovereign Hotel. Open M-F 9am-5pm. **Postal Code:** 4871.

Phone Code: 07.

ACCOMMODATIONS AND FOOD

Pam's Place (tel. 4069 5166; fax 4069 5964), at the corner of Charlotte and Boundary St, is a hub of Cooktown. Owner Scott Orchard is a fountain of Cooktown lore. Perks include a kitchen, laundry facilities, a bar, a pool table, and a swimming pool. A bus runs each morning to the bus station and airport. (Dorms $15; singles $29; doubles $40. Linen included. Key deposit $10. Bikes $5 per day. V, MC; $1 surcharge.)

The lovely **Hillcrest Guest House** (tel. 4069 5305), on Hope St at the base of Grassy Hill, has some unusual amenities. In addition to comfortable singles ($30) and doubles ($40), Hillcrest also maintains Cooktown's only aviary and butterfly garden, both free regardless of where you're staying. There is also a pool, laundry facilities, TV, tea room, and picnic hampers for two ($10) to take to the beach. Two minutes from the wharf on Webber Esplanade, **The Seaview Motel** (tel. 4069 5377), offers more expensive but nicer accommodation ($65-$75; open daily 7am-7pm).

For a quick tasty treat, visit the **Endeavour Farms Trading Post** (tel. 4069 5723), on Charlotte St between Hogg and Howard St. Barbara, the owner, enjoys helping travelers find their way, having found Cooktown "rough as bags" herself when she first arrived. The fish and chips ($4.50) are generous. (Open daily 7:30am-7:30pm.) The main competition comes from the **Reef Cafe** (tel. 4069 5361), just down Charlotte St next to Anzac Park (hamburgers $5). **The Cooktown Bakery,** on Charlotte St, serves breakfast (most treats $1-3; open M-F 7:30am-4:30pm, Sa 7:30am-12:30pm). **The Top Pub** on Charlotte St has meals for $8-12 and beers for $2.50. The newly opened **Burragi Floating Restaurant** (tel. 4069 5956) is anchored on a dock in the wharf (mains $15-22; daily noon-2pm and 6-9pm).

The Cooks Landing Kiosk at the wharf is a fun hangout. Coffee ($2) comes with free refills and can be iced ($2.50) when the mercury gets too high. Toasted sandwiches ($2-3) are tiny but scrumptious (open daily 8am-5pm). For staples, try the **Cooktown CutPrice Supermarket** (tel. 4069 5633) on the corner of Hogg and Helen St (open daily 8am-6pm). Adjacent to the market is a popular backpacker grub stand known as **The Mad Cow Cafe** (burgers $4; open M-F 8am-4pm, Sa 9am-2pm).

SIGHTS AND ENTERTAINMENT

The best place to start in Cooktown is the **James Cook Historical Museum,** on Helen St between Walker and Furneaux St. Once an old convent, the museum is now an excellent site for separating Cooktown fact from folklore. The **Cooktown Cemetery** is on McIvor River-Cooktown Rd. Pick up a gray historical facts sheet on the cemetery at any local accommodation. The cemetery is full of legends, and its highly segregated plots are divided into sections for white, Aboriginal, and Jewish residents. The Chinese Shrine lies at the farthest left-hand corner of the cemetery, where 30,000 slaves and their possessions were buried.

The **Botanic Gardens,** off Walker St, were left to decay after the gold rush ended. Twenty years ago, the city brought the Gardens back to life; although they're far from breathtaking, there are over 150 acres of wattle in which to wander. There's a walking path out to **Finch Bay** (which can otherwise be reached by following Walker St to its end), and the trail to secluded **Cherry Tree Bay** branches out from that. Halfway to Cherry Tree Bay is **Margo's Lookout,** a boulder promontory with a superb view.

Cooktown Tours (tel./fax 4069 5125) entertains history buffs with colloquial accounts of the *Endeavor* disaster, the woolly gold rush days, and the first white settlement in Australia. *(2hr. Departs 9am. $16, children 4-14 $10. 7 people max.)* Longer tours including outlying areas are available. **Cooktown Hire Boats** (tel. 4069 5601) on the wharf rents fishing, sight-seeing, and birdwatching boats. *(4hr. $50, 8hr. $80.)*

■ Around Cooktown

Black Mountain National Park looks like a couple of burned-out hills when surveyed from the lookout off the Cooktown Developmental Rd about 35km south of Cooktown. As you draw nearer, these giant piles of black-as-night boulders take on an eerie persona. The rocks aren't actually black; lichen colors the otherwise white blocks of granite. According to the local Kukubidiji Aboriginals, there was a fight here between two Rock Wallaby brothers, Ka-Iruji and Taja-Iruji, both vying for the same Rock Python woman. The brothers threw boulders at each other, but a sudden cyclone shattered both men's pile of stones, killing them. Legend has it that one can still hear the Rock Python woman crying for her lovers. During the gold rush, Black Mountain was used for stashing quarry. Unlucky prospectors and infamous bandits have been found among the dead who've slipped between the boulders. Camping is prohibited and exploration strongly discouraged, as there are Aboriginal taboo areas and 50m chasms between sheer walls of stone. The wildlife has adapted to the hot, strange climate; this is one of the few habitats of the carnivorous Ghost Bat.

Lizard Island National Park, about 30km from the mainland, boasts dunes, bays, reef, and beaches, but it's difficult to access. The island's secluded nature has made it a hot spot for vacationing celebrities. **Marine Air Seaplanes** (tel./fax 4069 5915) in Cooktown can fly campers out to the island. ($190, with 4-person group $150 each. 15min. scenic flights $60. Routes tracing Capt. Cook's discovery also available.) Once there, they must trek 1.2km to the **Watson Bay** camping ground. **Cape Air Transport (CAT)** (tel. 4069 5007; fax 4069 5834) provides three-day camping trips including all flights and equipment ($90 per person. ½ day snorkeling trips $185).

For **divers,** hauling your equipment up here is amply rewarded with some of the reef's most spectacular sites. Whether you choose the delicate coral colonies of the island's **Blue Lagoon** to the south, or Watson Bay's **Clam Gardens,** just off the coast of the campsite, the unusually clear waters of Lizard Island are bound to impress. Lizard is also close to the world-class dive site **Cod Hole,** though trips out there are expensive. Few dive companies frequent Lizard, but charters are available and Cairns-based dive shops occasionally run promotional dives to the area.

■ Cape York

One of the last vestiges of the great Australian frontier, Cape York offers rugged, intense landscape and narrow mountain roads. Few journey all the way to the tip, but even the southern route around the Cape supplies a myriad of unique landscapes and stunning night skies. The abundant wildlife is an added bonus—packs of wild hogs, inquisitive kangaroos, and silver-crested cockatoos are common spectacles.

■ The Base of the Cape

Even if you haven't the time, the money, or the stamina for the full journey up the Cape, you can get an exciting sample of the wilderness environment within a reasonable distance of Cooktown. One good two- to three-day trip runs north 62km from lakeland along the **Peninsula Development Road** to the famed Aboriginal rock art of Split Rock, the outpost town of Laura, the town of Musgrave (2hr. north; entrance to Lakeland National Park), and then east along the rugged **Battle Camp Track** to complete the circuit. 4WD is adamantly recommended for the first two-thirds of the journey and imperative for the final leg. There's close to nothing in these towns—**Laura** (pop. 82) has the **Quickan Pub** (tel. 4060 3255; open daily 10am-midnight; beds $20, tents $5), a **post office** (open M-F 9am-5pm, lunch at noon; postal code 4871), a **police** outpost, and **medical center** (tel. 4060 3320). Limited supplies as well as fuel may be purchased next door to the pub at **The Ampol Station Laura** (tel. 4060 3238; open daily 7am-6pm). The one must-see in Laura is **Split Rock,** a series of ancient Aboriginal art sites ($3). Call the **Ang-gnarra Aboriginal Corporation** in Laura (tel. 4060 3214) with any questions.

Laura is the site of June's **Aboriginal Dance and Cultural Festival,** a huge series of concerts and workshops sponsored by **The Office of the Ang-Gnarra Aboriginals** (tel. 4094 1512; fax 4094 1276; email ang-gnarra@internetnorth.com.au; tickets $20, children $5). The office also offers tours of the rock sites. (Call ahead to book an individual guide. $50 ½-day, $100 full-day.) An hour southwest of Laura (roughly 50km,

4WD only) is the **Jowalbinna Bush Camp** (tel. 4060 3236), run by local Aboriginals. (Camping Apr.-Sept. $5 per night. Tours of rock art sites available.) Pick up a map and a cheap sandwich at the **Laura Cafe** (tel. 4060 3230; open daily 7am-10pm).

Continuing 138km north on the Peninsula Development Rd you'll see a single building off to the left—that's the town of **Musgrave,** marked by **The Musgrave Roadhouse** (tel. 4060 3229), which offers sandwiches ($2.50-4), burgers ($4-6) or full main courses ($9-11). Then it's five paces to the next room to relax with a beer and play a little pool in **The Musgrave Roadhouse Pub.** Finally, stay the night in the **Musgrave Roadhouse Lodge** (singles $25; 2 people $40; camping $5).

Tiny or not, Musgrave is the perfect juncture for exploring **Lakefield National Park.** This region of mango-lined floodlands is Queensland's second largest national park. You can strike its heart by traveling back towards Cooktown along the **Battlecamp Track,** named after a battle between miners and Aboriginals during the gold rush. During the wet season, the track is submerged in water, but in the Dry Lakefield is transformed into a bird sanctuary extravaganza. Crocodiles, feral pigs, and wallaroos are other commonly spotted critters. After entering the Battle Camp track, north of Musgrave, travel east along the track passing Lowlake, which is clearly marked.

Camping in these areas is by permit only. Permits can be obtained six to twelve weeks in advance by phoning or writing the **Old Laura Homestead Ranger Station** (tel. 4060 3271) PMB 29, Cairns Mail Centre, Qld 4870. The Ranger Station is located in the middle of the park (112km from Musgrave; open daily 8am-5pm). It's one of the few buildings on the track and a great source of information on parklands as well as a trouble-shooting center for wayward travelers. The Old Laura Homestead was once the home of pioneers but now houses parkland rangers. For those wishing to camp in the southern half of the park, you'll need a permit for the New Laura Base, while the Lakefield base requires a northern camping permit.

Cape Air Transport (tel. 4069 5007; fax 4069 5834) runs tours of the southern part of the Cape. (2-day combo trip includes 4WDing through Lakefield National Park, camping, and flight back, including meals $520 per person.)

■ The Trek to the Tip

Beyond Musgrave, the Cape's jungle becomes junglier, its heat hotter, its rough tracks rougher, and its wet season wetter. The trip all the way to the Torres Strait, which separates Australia from Papua New Guinea, is only for the hardest-of-hard-core, bornfor-the-bush traveler. Unfortunately, unless you own your own car, you can't get to the northernmost point in Australia without shelling out a lot of dough in the process. Prices vary depending upon duration of trips and modes of transportation, but all options are expensive. Rental companies who insure cars traveling to the Cape are rare (don't cheat—it'll cost you a heap more if you're in violation of the mileage limitations). **Brits Rental,** 411 Sheridan St, Cairns (tel. 4031 2360), requires a two-week minimum rental for 4WDs or campers going to the top of the peninsula. You must be at least 21 years old. (From $155 a day, not including insurance. Open daily.) You must be 26 years old to rent from **Cairns Leisure Wheels,** 314 Sheridan St (tel. 4051 8988) for such a trip (from $165 a day; 2-week min.).

Because of the this expense, **tour packages** are often the only option. Departing from Cairns, **Cape York Air,** Cairns Airport (tel. 4035 9399), is an airborne option. Retired bombardiers air-drop mail over the cape, and pilots will let passengers accompany them on their daily runs ($195-300; shorter flights also available; day tour to the Cape plus lunch W, $550). **Wilderness Challenge** (tel. 4055 6504; fax 4057 7226) offers longer combined 4WD and flying trips (8-day trip $1695; call ahead). A similar company, **Heritage Tours** (tel. 4038 2628; fax 4038 2186) is a bit cheaper if you go by land only (12-day overland safari $1450, 6-day drive/fly combo $1299; book ahead). These larger firms occasionally offer standby fares that knock $100-300 off the package price. Check with booking agents for availability. If you can scramble up as far as the Jardine River, **John Charlton's Cape York Boat Adventure** (tel. 4069 3302) can show you the rest for a very reasonable fare (1hr. sunset cruise $30 per person; full-day trips $90). In the end, visiting the Cape is a battle, whether it's against crocs (unlikely) or wallet shock (almost certain). Still, the victory is oh-so-sweet.

CENTRAL AND WESTERN QUEENSLAND

Queensland's interior has little of the charm of South Australia's and Northern Territory's outback, but it is in many ways more authentic. The land is unforgiving, water is scarce, and constant threats such as rabbit overpopulation and locusts have hardened farmers. There are no "cowboys" here: the correct title for a greenhorn is "jackeroo" (or "jilleroo," as the case may be). From the third year, workers are called stationhands, and the name "jackeroo" becomes a hard strike against pride. While outback towns can be unkind to outsiders, the people living here maintain an ethic of trust. Folks look you in the eye, and if they don't like what they see, you'll know it.

Like so much of this continent, Queensland's seemingly barren dust was found to hide lodes of all kinds of sweet stuff beneath the surface, and thus began the region's heyday. The gold rush has lost its luster, for the most part, but gem fossicking is still the backbone of towns with names like Emerald, while rich stocks of metal ore keep Mt. Isa's smelters puffing. Up by the Gulf of Carpenteria the fishing is excellent, the roads are treacherous, and a single train engine shuttles between isolated Normanton and more isolated Croydon once a week, more out of habit than demand.

Queensland's vast interior is traversed by a few highways, unsealed in patches. There are several east-west routes connecting to the coast: the **Warrego Hwy** (54) from Brisbane to Charleville; the **Capricorn** and **Landsborough Highways** (66), from Rockhampton through the Gemfields and Longreach to Mt. Isa; the **Flinders Hwy** (78), from Townsville through Charters Towers and Hughenden to Mt. Isa; and the **Gulf Development Rd** (1), from the Atherton Tablelands outside Cairns through the Gulf Savannah to Normanton. *Let's Go* has outlined the rest of this chapter to match the progression of towns, from east to west, along each of these highways, starting with the southernmost. Connecting them all, the so-called **Matilda Hwy** actually encompasses fragments of the Mitchell, Landsborough, and Capricorn Highways and the Burke Development Rd. It is the major north-south route, running from the NSW border up to Normanton.

▓ The Warrego Highway

As you head west along the Warrego Hwy from Brisbane, you'll watch the landscape slowly fade from the sharp contrasts of city lights, black pavement, and green lawns to the subdued copper hues of miles and miles of dust. After passing through the Darling Downs, you'll hit Roma and then Charleville at the junction of the Mitchell Hwy (the southern end of the Matilda Hwy). South of Charleville, the Mitchell heads through Cunnamulla and across the border to Bourke, NSW.

■ Roma

Diagonal parking spaces that face the opposite way than reason would dictate heads a list of Roma's quirky features. Though it causes senseless traffic hold-ups, the law dictates that you must park nose out, so when in Rome-a...Less irritating, if less amusing, are Roma's marvelous **bottle trees,** whose bulbous trunk is typically surrounded by colorful butterflies circling about nectar-blaring flowers. To get a taste of Roma's juxtaposition of country town charm and jackeroo grit, stop in for tea at the **Habitat,** 80 Charles St. (tel. 4622 4016), or take a stroll down **Wyndham Ave,** where bottle trees and plagues are dedicated to a WWI casualties. For rest, try the **Royal Hotel** (tel. 7622 1324), at McDowall and Hawthorne St, with a downstairs pub that gets noisy on weekends (rooms $15 per person). If you're just passing through, you can find petrol at the **BP station** on Bowen St, and numerous **banks** with **ATMs** on Wyndham St.

■ Charleville

Charleville, located at the junction of the Matilda (Mitchell) Hwy and the Warrego, is a worthwhile stop on a trip down either; it's small, but offers several interesting diversions. On one side of Sturt St, as the Mitchell Hwy is called as it passes through town, is the workshop and gallery of the **Community Development Employment Program** (CDEP; tel. 7654 3016). Enthusiastic curator Richard Clarke will demonstrate various artifacts, give a smashing didgeridoo concert, and show you the murals and painted items of local artists Gary Kinivian and Ernie Adams, all for free. (Open M-F 8am-4pm or by appointment.) In comically stark contrast to these centuries of Aboriginal cultural accomplishment stands another of Charleville's attractions, facing the CDEP across the street: the **Stiger Vortex,** a conical contraption standing 5.4m high. In 1902 Queensland meteorologist Clement L. Wragge devised these "rainmaker guns" with the hope that shooting them off would, for some reason, bring rain to end a 16-year drought. On September 6, 1902, his experiment failed.

At the end of Edward St, which runs perpendicular to Sturt St, is a base and museum of the **Royal Flying Doctor Service.** Providing medical care to remote locations, the service got its start in outback Queensland in 1928 and now has six bases around the state, plus more nationwide. The fascinating display has all sorts of history, maps, and old equipment. (Open M-F 8:30am-5pm. $2 donation requested.)

Tourist info is given at the Town Hall (tel. 7654 3037), across from the Corones Hotel on Will St. McCafferty's **buses** go to Brisbane (14hr., 1 per day, $52) and Mt. Isa (15hr., 1 per day, $92). Call the **Western Travel Service,** 94 Alfred St (tel. 4654 1268 or 4654 2018) for schedules. From the **train station,** 112 King St (tel. 4654 1591), two trains per week head to Brisbane (17hr.; $77) via Roma and Toowoomba (station open daily 6:30am-8pm). The **post office** (tel. 4654 1383) is at Will and Alfred St (open M-F 9am-5pm; postal code 4470). There's an **ATM** next door. The elegant **Corones Hotel,** 33 Will St (tel. 4654 1022) has backpacker beds ($10) and singles ($15). A dinner buffet at its restaurant costs $12, and the bar stays open til midnight.

▓ Capricorn and Landsborough Highways

The road west from Rockhampton cuts a long diagonal across Queensland's gemfields through the empty desert. Rte 66 is called the Capricorn Hwy until its junction with the Matilda at Barcaldine, then becomes the Landsborough Hwy as it passes through Longreach and Winton. It meets the Flinders Hwy at Cloncurry, two hours east of Mt. Isa.

■ Gemfields

Travelers who can't bear to pick another berry or poke another pokie may want to try their luck digging dirt a couple hours west of the coast in Queensland's Gemfields. The income is hardly steady, but potentially lucrative—an unemployed couple recently uncovered a gem worth a million dollars, and a 14-year-old matched that a few years back. Fossicking draws thousands of tourists a year to this area just off the bleak landscape stretching west along the Tropic of Capricorn, all with rolled-up sleeves and picks in hand, in quest of that elusive sapphire, amethyst, ruby, diamond, or gold that will pay for their trip westward. Usually, they leave with nothing more than snippets of sapphire and a newfound intimacy with dirt.

Tucked halfway between Rockhampton and Emerald in Dingo is the **Naomi Hills Cattle Station** (tel. 4935 9121 or 4935 9125 or 4935 9102), with budget accommodation and tour packages near the rarely visited **Blackdown Tableland,** a massive sandstone plateau jutting out of nowhere, 22km off the Capricorn Hwy. The working cattle station has beds for $13 (first night $15), and offers a $30 first-night package of dinner, continental breakfast, and a guided tour of the 130 square kilometer station complete with didgeridoo-playing, whip-cracking, and boomerang-throwing. The station also provides free mountain bike rides, an overnight horse riding campout ($70), and more expensive Aboriginal and mining tours. (Free pick-up from bus or train station in Dingo, or direct service with Oz Experience. Book ahead.)

Don't be fooled by **Emerald's** name—no emerald has ever been found there. In fact, nohing has. The town is a stepping-off point to the gemfields and a convenient stop on **McCafferty's** (tel. 4982 2755) Mt. Isa-Rockhampton route. Without a car, though, you'll have trouble getting to the prime fossicking areas (45min. away). The new **Central Inn,** 90 Clermont St (tel. 4982 0800), has rooms and breakfast for $30.

Anakie lies in the center of the prime fossicking regions, 40km west of Emerald. There's an **info center** (tel. 4985 4525) and the last **petrol** station for about 140km just off the highway, where you can buy a month-long fossicker's license ($5). Most visitors drive north 10-18km to **Sapphire** or **Rubyvale,** where they can pay $5 to wash and sort through pre-dug buckets of dirt at any of several stops along the road. For $5 more, you can dig your own dirt under the friendly scrutiny of Margaret and Sheila at the **Miner's Cottage Gem and Fossick Park** (tel. 4985 4259) in Rubyvale, though they may be selling it soon. Rubyvale is also the home of the **Miners Heritage Walk-in Mine** (tel. 4985 4444), which gives short guided tours on demand ($5), and **S'n'S** (Silk'n'Sapphires; tel. 4985 4307), which offers personalized half-day, underground, fully equipped digs ($70) and mining tours ($35). Booking and good health is essential. The **Rubyvale Caravan Park** (tel. 4985 4118) has tent sites ($8, weekly $50), van sites ($12, weekly $65), powered sites ($20, weekly $100), and cabins (2 people $40, each additional person $40, weekly $190), and a swimming pool. If you're in town in June, don't miss the biennial **wheelbarrow race** through Sapphire and Rubyvale (current record 1hr., 9min., 3sec.).

■ Barcaldine

The outpost of Barcaldine (bar-CALLED-in) is the most authentic outback town in Queensland that can be easily reached by bus (McCafferty's), train (en route to Longreach), or car. Most of the tourists who come through are among the long caravans of pensioners making their way up the Matilda Hwy, and they usually hang out in the caravan parks. The outlying population manages to keep six pubs afloat: one for every day of the week except Sunday, when everyone rolls into church.

PRACTICAL INFORMATION AND ACCOMMODATIONS Oak St is the main drag. The **tourist office** (tel. 4651 1724; fax 4651 2243) is on the highway (open daily 8:30am-12:30pm and 1:30-4:30pm). There's a **bank** (tel. 4651 1600) with an **ATM** at the corner of Ash and Beech St (open M-Th 9:30am-4pm, F 9:30am-5pm). The **train station** (open M-F 9am-5pm) prefers that tickets be booked through the central reservations desk (tel. 13 22 32). **McCafferty's** buses stop at the **BP station** (tel. 4651 1333; open daily 6:30am-9pm) at the corner of Oak and Box St. **RACQ** (tel. 4651 1337; after hours 4651 1544) is on Oak St. There's a **hospital** (tel. 4651 1311) on Oak St, **police** (tel. 4651 1322) on Ash St, and a **post office** (tel. 4651 1147; fax 4651 1120) at the corner of Ash and Beech St (open M-F 9am-5pm, Sa 9-11am; postal code 4725).

The **Artesian Hotel,** 113 Oak St (tel. 4651 1691), has mostly iron-bar poster-beds in singles ($20) and twins ($30). One double ($20) has a window that compromises privacy. **Shakespeare Hotel** (tel. 4651 1610), across from the tourist office on Oak St, boasts a beer garden and bathtubs (singles $15; twins and doubles $25). At the **Railway Hotel** (tel. 4651 1188), ping-pong is the main attraction (singles $15; twins and doubles $25). There are also two caravan parks with camping: **Homestead** (tel. 4651 1308), on Box St, and **Showgrounds Council,** on the east side of town.

SIGHTS For a tiny town, there's surprisingly much to do. The main draw is the **Australian Workers Heritage Centre** (tel. 4651 2422), a glowing tribute to Australia's civil servants marked by a giant circus tent in the middle of town. *(Open M-Sa 9am-5pm Su 10am-5pm. Admission for 1 week $7, students $5. Wheelchair accessible.)* The exhibits are sectioned off into little houses, including re-creations of a one-room school and a legislative assembly (complete with a voice-over of incessant argumentation). The highlight is the exhaustive history of Australia's Labor Party, which got its start under the now-sepulchrous ghost gum, the **Tree of Knowledge,** in the middle of town.

At the end of Pine St (off the main road, between the hospital and the cleverly named Cafe Cafe) sits **Mad Mick's Beta Farm Outback Heritage and Wildlife** (tel. 4651 1172). *(Farm open Apr.-Sept. 9:30am-noon most days, depending on Mick's whim. Admission $8, includes tea and barbecue lunch. Book ahead at info center.)* He may not be mad, but he's certainly wacky and fun, leading folks around his restored slab hut, hanging out with Ned the emu, and showing off his collection of 1000 dolls.

Artesian Country Tours (tel. 4651 2243) has an on-demand daytrip to some outlying sights, including the only local (legal) access to the **Gracevale caves** in Aramac, the oldest and largest single collection of Aboriginal rock art in Australia. The drawings date back 10,000-12,000 years and include a 60m rainbow serpent. The trip out costs a bundle ($80) but includes lunch, dinner, and a few other sights along the way (creeks, pools, and memorials of Aboriginal massacres).

■ Longreach and Around

The micropolis of Longreach is the area's major watering hole. Folks come on weekends for loud gossip and louder late-night drinking, and come Sunday jump in their souped-up utes for the long ride back to the station. People have an edge about them, earned from years of working an unforgiving earth with few modern creature comforts. The city itself is nothing flash. Most of its petrol stations close on the weekends.

The only reason to visit Longreach, but a reason which attracts flocks of pensioners throughout the year, is the **Australian Stockman's Hall of Fame and Outback Heritage Centre** (tel. 4658 2166), a massive, multi-media museum on the highway east of town. *(Open daily 9am-5pm, $15, students $12, children $7, families $35.)* Within, you'll find a brief introduction to the geological formation of the island continent astride a panel or two on the original inhabitants, then a continuation of the timeline from the hard-core early days through the issues facing the contemporary stockman.

The **information center** (tel. 4658 3555; fax 4658 3733) acts as a clearinghouse for local goings-on (open M-F 8:45am-5pm, Sa-Su 9am-1pm). Along the highway are two **ATMs.** The **library** (tel. 4658 4104) nearby has fax service and free **Internet access** (open Tu and Th, 9:30am-1pm, W and F 12:30-5pm, Sa 9am-noon). There are **police** (tel. 4658 2200) on Galah St and a **hospital** (tel. 4658 4700) on Jabiro St. **McCafferty's** (tel. 4658 1155) pulls into the center of town, while the **train station** (tel. 4658 1028) is five minutes from the center ($5 by taxi). The **post office** (tel. 4658 1887) is across the street from the info center (open M-F 9am-5pm; postal code 4730). For accommodation, try the **Lyceum Hotel** (tel. 4658 1036) all the way down the main street. (Singles $20; doubles $36. Linen included; free tea and coffee.) The **Merino Bakery** (tel. 4658 1715) sells the freshest bread in town (open M-F 4:30am-5pm, Sa 4am-noon).

Half an hour to east of Longreach is **Ilfracombe.** There's plenty of elbow room in the shire, with about 7000 acres for each of its 350 people. The **Wellshot Hotel** (tel. 4658 2106) is decorated with old bush hats and $5 notes on the ceiling (singles $25; twins and doubles $40). The Wellshot is also home to a stockmanship show, complete with whip-cracking and bull-wrestling (call ahead for times; $8). Ilfracombe's **historical museum** is actually an outdoor collection of old knick-knacks and machinery that stretches along the main road. Some local trivia: the **largest flock of sheep ever to be moved** (43,000) was shepherded here in 1886. Now you know.

■ Winton and Around

Winton is always getting the short end of the stick. By at least one method of reckoning, it's the birthplace of **Qantas,** which held its first board meeting in the Winton Club (now a Chinese restaurant), but Winton and Longreach have a perpetual tug-of-war over who has rights to the legacy, and Winton seems to end up giving ground. The town is also the site of Banjo Patterson's first performance of *Waltzing Matilda,* Australia's unofficial national anthem, but neighboring **Kynuna** is much closer to the actual billabong in the song, and *they've* got the original music score. The brand new

Waltzing Matilda Centre elaborately pays tribute to the ballad and the spirit of Australia it evokes. **Kynuna's Swagman Hall of Fame** (the circus tent on the highway with begonias growing out front) has elected only one swagman thus far, the anonymous jolly one from the song. This is kitsch like nowhere else in Queensland, a roadside attraction where it's free to step into the tent but $3 to go behind the curtain, $1 more to view Paterson's score, $8 to buy the book, and $10 for the live floor show by Richard Magoffin, a popular balladeer and arguably Australia's foremost expert on the song and its history (daily 7:30-9:30pm, includes a soup and coffee dinner).

Winton does have two up on its neighbors, though. Behind the North Gregory Hotel you'll find **Arno's Wall,** a 30m stretch of home implements and motorcycles set in concrete. The townsfolk don't really know what to do with this Arno fellow, a German immigrant and itinerant opal miner. Buy the *Mud Map* at the Qantilda for the scoop ($1). The second boon is the **Lark Quarry,** a bumpy two-hour ride south from the town center. This is dinosaur country, with an immense zigzag of footprints that's a preserved snapshot of an afternoon in prehistoric Australia when a hungry dinosaur tromped into a flock of small, two-legged lunchboxes. The meat-eater was not a *Tyrannosaurus rex,* despite the hype in Winton. Paleontologists have concluded that the little guys were coelurosaurs and ornithopods, small and lightweight dinosaurs with hollow bones, a likely forebear to the modern bird, and that the larger tracks predate the infamous carnivore by almost 50 million years.

■ The Flinders Highway

Yet another long, lonely route through the desert, the Flinders makes a straight shot from Townsville to Mount Isa. Along the way, it passes through two pseudo-outback towns, Ravenswood and Charters Towers, so near the coast that folks out in Prairie, Hughenden, and Richmond might think of them as practically Brisbane. Still, they offer a taste of the outback; further west, you'll get a healthy dose of the real thing. Don't romanticize the drive, though—it's long and boring. Towns here mean little more than a lower speed limit and a general store with a gas pump. There's no pot of gold at the end of this rainbow, either—only Mount Isa, an industrial outpost where you can stop for a breath of smoke-filled air on your way to the NT.

■ Ravenswood

Ghosts of miners shlepping from work to the century-old wooden hotels or shanty houses scattered about the fields still haunt the virtually deserted town of Ravenswood (pop. 300). If it's authentic outback you want, you'll find it here. Mining rig skeletons anchored along the only road in town complement the silhouettes of rickety windmills. Situated 125km west of Townsville on the road to Charters Towers, Ravenswood has plenty to keep wandering tourists busy on an overnight trip.

There are two hotels in town, and their pub bistros comprise the whole of the Ravenswood restaurant industry. **Macrossan St** is the only road and it features the **post office** (tel./fax 4770 2136), which doubles as the **general store.** (Open M-F 8am-6:30pm and Sa-Su 9am-1pm.) The cafe attached to the post office serves dishes for less than $10. **The Imperial Hotel** (tel. 4770 2131; fax 4770 2110) on Macrossan St retains all its old woodwork and brass fixtures. The rooms don't quite match its regal look, but are clean and affordable. (Singles $35; doubles $43; twins $45; family $55. Lunch noon-1:30pm, $3-9; dinner 6:30-7:30pm, $8-12. Reception M-F 10am-1am; Sa-Su 10am-midnight.) Very similar and very close by is the **Railway Hotel,** Macrossan St (tel. 4770 2144; fax 4770 2198; rooms $30; family rooms $40.; 24hr. reception). At the end of town, the **Showground Caravan Park** has a pool, tennis courts, hot showers, and a kitchen (sites $5).

The **old jail and courthouse** (tel. 4770 2047) near the Railway Hotel is now a museum that would be dull if it weren't for its friendly, interesting, and knowledgeable curator Woody (open W-M 10am-3pm; admission by donation). Following Macrossan St past the Imperial Hotel, take a left onto Deighton St and travel two kilometers to **White Blow,** an unusual natural quartz crystal mountain. From Macrossan St turn onto Cemetery Rd to visit the **cemetery.** Five **Heritage Trails** snake throughout the area. **Markets** are held on the first Sunday of each month in the Imperial Hotel gardens.

■ Charters Towers

South of the green Atherton Tablelands, the land dries out and old outback towns pick up. Charters Towers, 90 minutes from Townsville, is a gold rush village that's still experiencing its rush. The result is an old-country town with sweeping architecture that shows off the area's wealth, all wrapped up in a down-home attitude. Charters Towers was once the hub of Queensland, nicknamed "The World" for its 1880s cosmopolitan flair, and home to Australia's first stock market. Since those days, the city has dulled considerably, but the nickname still applies to the city's theater, an elegant complex of two cinemas and a 640-seat live theater, where the manager still comes to work every day in a vest and bow tie. The theater and cinemas are each named after one of the gold mines near town, as if to display evidence of the town's vast, hidden wealth.

ORIENTATION AND PRACTICAL INFORMATION The layout of Charters Towers seems like it was devised to befuddle newcomers; streets curve and wrap back on themselves at impossible angles. In any case, follow the signs to the Historic City Centre and keep your eyes open for the twisting directions. The city center is a simple T-intersection: government offices and "The World" theater run along Mosman St at the top, while most shops, restaurants, and banks are on the descending bar, **Gill St.**

The **tourist office** (tel. 4752 0314) is at the corner of Gill and Mosman St (open daily 9am-5pm). The **Queensland Rail Station** (tel. 4787 0201) is one block north of Gill St; a ride to Townsville costs $20. **Greyhound, McCafferty's,** and **Douglas** buses pull into the middle of town and run to Townsville for $14-17. Book at **Traveland** on Hill St (tel. 4787 2622; fax 4787 7570). Three blocks from the tourist office on Gill St are several **banks** with **ATMs.** The local **RACQ** is at **Gold City Wreckers,** 21 Dundee Ln (24hr. tel. 4787 2000). There's a **library** with free **Internet access** on Gill St, in the Old Bank of New South Wales building (tel. 4752 0338). The **hospital** (tel. 4787 1099) and **police station** (tel. 4787 1333) are both at 49-55 Gill St, while the **post office** is at 17-19 Gill St (tel. 4787 1333; open 9am-5pm; postal code 4820).

ACCOMMODATIONS The **York Street Bed and Breakfast,** 58 York St (tel. 4787 1028) is a beautiful place to stay (singles $55, doubles $65). Its lodge-style rooms equipped with TVs and fridges are less luxurious, but the price is right ($25). For cheaper accommodations, try the **Waverly Hotel,** 19 Mosman St (tel. 4787 2591; fax 4787 3988; singles $20, doubles $30). The **Charters Towers Caravan Park,** 37 Mount Leyshon Rd (tel. 4787 7944), is in a good location with a nice pool (2-person sites $10, powered $14; $5 per extra person). The **Park Motel,** 1 Mosman St (tel. 4787 1022; fax 4787 4268), is a little more upscale (singles $58; doubles $66; executive suite $63; 8-person family room $76).

FOOD The **Stock Exchange Cafe,** 76 Mosman St (tel. 4787 7954), serves uncreative but tasty cuisine including quiche ($3.80), burgers ($4.50), and lasagna ($6; open for breakfast and lunch). **The Country Bumpkin Cafe,** 14 Gill St (tel. 4787 7272), serves it up quick and cheap (open M-F 7am-4pm, Sa 8am-1pm). **Lawson's Bar and Restaurant,** 82-90 Mosman St (tel. 4787 4333; fax 4787 7230), next to the World Theater, is a classy joint for dinner, dessert, or drinks (mains $10-14; open M-F 11:30am-2:30pm and 6pm-late). The local **RSL Club** (tel. 4787 2484), on Prior St, serves a cheap buffet on weekend nights, but even regular menu meals run only $3-6 (open daily noon-2pm and 6-8:30pm). **Naturally Good,** 23 Gill St, offers vegetarian lunch options (open M-F 8am-4pm, Sa 8am-end of lunch).

QUEENSLAND

SIGHTS AND ENTERTAINMENT The big attraction in town is the largest **gold mine** in all of Queensland. Tours happen only once a week and should be booked through the tourist information center. *(W 8:30am. $12.)* Charters Towers is not a good place for individual gold fossicking; claims are protected tooth and nail, and poking around in restricted areas is an excellent way to get into heaps of trouble.

Two full-day bush safaris leave from Charters Towers. **Gold City Bush Safaris** (tel. 4787 2118) is a sight-seeing trip in an air-conditioned land cruiser. *($35-55.)* **Gold Nugget Scenic Tours** (tel. 4787 1568) departs from Caltex Service Station on Gill St. *(10am and 3pm. $15, children $5.)* **Adventure, Wildlife, and Bush Treks** (tel. 4788 1126) rides to Porcupine Gorge, the Great Basalt Wall, Dalrymple National Park, or the White Mountains. *(Departs 8am, returns 5pm. Extended trips are an option.)*

More locally, there's an **historical walking tour** which departs the tourist information center daily at 7pm, costs $6, and focuses mainly on historical stories from the town's heyday. The stock exchange contains an unarresting **mining museum** (tel. 4787 2374) which looks a lot like a garage. *(Open M-F 8:30am-1pm and 2-4:30pm, Sa-Su 9am-3pm. Admission $1.)* A block down Mosman St is the **Zara Clark Museum,** a collection of local memorabilia which includes the **flying fox money system** introduced by the city instead of the usual pounds and pence. *(Open daily 10am-3pm. Free.)*

Nightlife in Charters Towers is confined to a single nightclub, **Regent Club 96 Bar** (tel. 4787 2600) on Gill St. *(No cover. Rocking nightly until 3am.)* The **World Theatre** features ballets, operas, and plays, most of which offer student discounts. **Cor Mundi** (Information tel. 4787 4337; bookings tel. 4787 4344; fax 4787 4158) is an Aboriginal and local crafts gift shop. *(Ticket office open M-F 10am-1pm, Sa-Su 10am-noon.)* Two **cinemas** operate from the back and play mostly American films. *(Shows on W-Su nights. Tickets $8, students $6, W $5.)* On the east side of Charters Towers is a **drive-in cinema** with second-run films. *(Open W-Su. Tickets F-Su $7, W-Th $5, or $10 per carload.)* Jigsaw puzzle aficionados should check out the largest collection in Australia at the **Puzzle Palace.** *(Open Tu-Su 9am-5pm.)*

Joyflights and day tours are available through **Charters Towers Aircraft Maintenance** (tel. 4787 4147; fax 4787 2413). *(70min. flights over WWII Air Force bases, the city, and Basalt Walls is $90. ½hr. tours over the city $40.)* Drive 45 minutes on the Bruch Hwy after the Mingela turn-off to the impressive **Burdeking River Dam** (tel. 4783 0555; fax 4783 4188), which has created a lovely lake region within this dusty interior. Cattle stations nearby often hire backpackers for a couple of weeks and offer "City Slicker" holiday packages. Prices among the four stations change frequently.

■ Prairie and Hughenden

After a few hours, the road runs through a town with a pub worth a stretch and a coffee. **The Prairie Hotel** (tel. 4741 5121) was built in the same year that the typewriter was invented (1867), and both seem equally rickety and old-fashioned today. These days, there's a jukebox to enliven the nightlife, but there's only one room in the hotel (twin-share, $15 per bed). You can also camp behind the hotel (sites $8; campervans $12, with power $15), but you'll miss out on the spirit of the place, namely, the **ghost** returning to claim a gold sovereign owed him (30¢ for the story from the barmaid, but it's free to see a photo of the spook). Meals are pub grub ($8-11 per plate).

Hughenden (HYU-enden) marks the eastern edge of the **Dinosaur Highway,** which stretches a few towns west and as far south as Winton's Lark Quarry. The town itself is very, very quiet, which makes it all the more shocking to discover a completely reconstructed **Muttaburrasaurus skeleton** in the back room of the Visitor Information Centre (tel. 4741 1021; open M-F 9am-5pm). If you roll into town on the weekend, walk around back and peek through the glass door. Budget accommodation in town is limited to the ambitiously-named **Grand Hotel** (tel. 4741 1588; singles $25, twins or doubles $35; dinner specials $7-10) and the **Allan Terry Caravan Park** (tel. 4741 1190), across from the rail station. (Pool, laundry, 24hr. bus or train pick-up. Reception open M-F 7am-9pm. Tent sites $6, for 2 $9; powered $10, for 2 $13. W sausage dinner $2.)

The locals in Hughenden play on the beauty and the beast motif when selling their sights: the beast is the Muttaburrasaurus, and the beauty is nearby **Porcupine Gorge,** 60km north of town. The gorge is a bit of an oasis along the dusty trail; a clear creek past stiff chasm walls. **Adventure Wildlife and Bush Treks** (tel. 4788 11 26, or book at the caravan park) has full-day trips on demand ($55, if you drive yourself $25).

■ Richmond

West of Hughenden along the Flinders Hwy is Richmond, another very quiet town that packs an impressive paleological punch. The **Marine Fossil Museum** (tel. 4741 3429; fax 4741 3802) has the bones of cretaceous-era marine reptiles (97-130 million years old). The presentation is well-informed, easy to follow, and diverse in its offerings, and the staff of volunteers is thoroughly committed to explaining the displays in minute detail. (Open daily 8am-5pm. $3.) The **caravan park** up the street (tel. 4741 8772) is an exceptional value. A bed in the brand-new dongas ($15) includes linen and air-conditioning. The common kitchen is new, too. (Reception open 8:30am-"bedtime" for Mick, the caretaker. Tent sites $7, with power $10.)

■ Cloncurry

As you approach Mt. Isa from the east, you'll cross a few small mountains that provide a pleasant change from the monotonous plains of the outback. Mt. Isa's nearest "suburb," Cloncurry (2hr. away), isn't particularly inspiring, but it does make a good rest stop. The town has a small **Royal Flying Doctor Service Museum** that's more of a shrine to John Flynn, its founder, than an informative exhibit (M-F 7am-4pm, Sa-Su 9am-3pm; $5). The pleasant **Cloncurry Caravan Park Oasis** (tel. 4742 1313), with a pool and barbecue, will do if you can't hack the last leg to the Isa (tent sites for 1 person $7, for 2 $10; powered $12, $14). Follow the signs for the public phones to the **Post Office Hotel** (tel. 4742 1411; fax 4742 2356). The hotel is luxurious by Queensland pub standards, with a TV in each room. (Singles $25; twins and doubles $34.)

One of the more interesting phenomena of the Queensland outback is the Cloncurry Min Min. **Min-Min** is an Aboriginal name for a mysterious will-o'-the-wisp periodically spotted on the plains outside Cloncurry. Some say it is caused by luminous gases or insects, but the Aboriginals believe it is an apparition of evil spirits.

■ Mount Isa

When the subject of Mount Isa comes up, backpackers' conversations sober up and casual laughter dwindles. This is the city where hitchhikers coming in from the Northern Territory break down and buy a bus ticket. Honeymooning couples have been known to sell their campervans in the Isa and head to the airport. The city itself has the feel of an intergalactic spaceport; walking down the street, it's possible to tick off dozens of languages in overheard chitchat. Two- and three-trailer road trains crowd the outskirts of town, and in case you forgot to set your watch ahead half an hour after leaving the Northern Territory, you'll be reminded by the sounds of the 8am and 8pm underground mining blasts, part and parcel of the copper mines' 12-hour shifts. The only company to keep is the twin smokestacks that overshadow the city, constantly billowing like chain-smoking bullies. There are two reasons people come here: first, they might be copper, silver, zinc, or lead miners; second, it's the main urban outpost on the endless haul from the Queensland coast to the tropical Top End or, alternately, to the Red Centre below. So take a deep breath, try not to choke, and enjoy the amenities before commencing the dusty drive across the desert.

ORIENTATION

On the east side of the **Leichhardt River,** the center of town rises slightly near the middle. The outlying area is a mess of awkwardly angled streets, but the city center is a more manageable four-by-four grid. The **Barkly Hwy** enters from Northern Territory and runs parallel to the river until the bridge at **Miles End,** and then turns left over the water into the city center on **Grace St.** From Cloncurry in the east, the Barkly Hwy becomes Grace St as it comes into town and passes by the **Riversleigh Interpretive Centre,** a major landmark. Across from the Riversleigh Centre and up the hill is a prime lookout spot for panoramic views of Mount Isa.

PRACTICAL INFORMATION

Tourist Information: The info center at the **Riversleigh Interpretive Centre** (tel. 4749 1555; fax 4743 6296). Open M-F 8:30am-4:30pm, Sa-Su 9am-2:30pm.

Budget Travel Office: Traveland (tel. 4743 3399), next to the McCafferty's terminal. Open M-F 9am-5pm, Sa 9am-noon.

Currency Exchange: Commonwealth Bank, 23 Miles St (tel. 4743 5033). Traveler's checks or cash $5. V, MC. Open M-Th 9:30am-4pm, F 9:30am-5pm. The **ATM** takes Cirrus. **ANZ,** 16 Miles St. ATM takes V, MC, Cirrus, and Plus.

Trains: Train Station (tel. 4744 1201) on Railway Ave near Miles End, a $5 taxi ride to town or $8 to the caravan parks.

Buses: McCafferty's (tel. 4743 2006; fax 4743 3399) pulls into the west side of town, over the river. Runs to Townsville ($84), Rockhampton ($160), Darwin ($176), Alice Springs ($153). **Greyhound** (tel. 4743 6655) shares its terminal with the Riversleigh Interpretive Centre. Fares to Townsville ($84), Cairns ($122), Darwin ($176); there are ISIC discounts. Open M-F 6:30am-4pm, Sa-Su 6:30-11am.

Taxis: United Cab (tel. 13 10 08).

Automobile Club: RACQ, 13 Simpson St (tel. 4743 4300, 24hr. tel. 4743 2542).

Library: on West St (tel. 4744 4266). Open M-F 10am-6pm, Sa 9am-noon.

Laundromat: (tel. 018 121 240) at the Riversleigh Interpretive Centre. Open M-F 8:30am-5pm, Sa-Su 9:30am-2pm.

Hospital: (tel. 4744 4444), 30 Camooweal St.

Emergency: Dial 000.

Police: (tel. 4743 2222), on Isa St. Open 24hr.

Post Office: (tel. 4743 2454), at the corner of Camooweal and Isa St. From the hostel, walk downhill on Pamela St, following the road as it swivels to the right. The post office is up on the left. *Poste Restante* open M-F 8:30am-5:30pm. Post office open M-F 9am-5pm: **Postal code:** 4825.

Internet Access: Riversleigh Interpretive Centre (see **Sights,** below), the library, and the **Sweet Oasis Cafe,** 31 Miles St (tel. 4743 1555), all for $4 per 30min. More terminals at the Mt. Isa Newsagency on Miles St for $5 per 30min., $8 per hr.

Phone Code: 07.

ACCOMMODATIONS AND FOOD

Traveller's Haven (tel. 4743 0313; fax 4743 4007), at the corner of Pamela and Spence St, is the only hostel in town. Drive through town following the information signs. At the Riversleigh Interpretive Centre, drive around the left of the building and follow the road for two blocks. Unfortunately, the lack of competition has resulted in less-than-clean rooms. Free pick-ups from the coach terminals and train station are available. There's a swimming pool. (Dorms $14; singles $26; twins and doubles $34. VIP. Key deposit $5. Linen $2. Reception open daily 6:30am-1pm and 5-7pm.)

If you're prepared to camp, try **Sunset Van Park,** 14 Sunset Dr (tel. 4743 7668). Drive around the left side of the lookout and Mount Isa water tower. The road becomes Sunset Dr, and the caravan park is on the left. (Reception M-F 7:30am-10pm. Tent sites $7, for 2 $12; powered sites $10, $14. Key deposit $10.)

Food is hard to come by in Isa, but **Woolworths** is in the town center. Otherwise, try the **Buffalo Club** (tel. 4743 2365), corner of Grace and Simpson St. It offers an all-you-can-eat lunch buffet ($7.95) or $3 sandwiches if you have something reasonable to wear: collared shirt yay, sandals nay. (Open daily noon-2pm and after 6pm.) **Flamenco Coffee Shop** (tel. 4743 4569), at the top of Marian St, is a local hangout for miners, kids, and local business types, and a great place to rub shoulders with folks of many nationalities (open M-F 9:30am-6pm, Sa 9:30am-5pm, Su 9am-5pm).

SIGHTS

The most exciting thing to do in Mt. Isa the **Underground Mine Tour**—a dive into the belly of the beast. Put on the suit and the hat and ride the elevator into a winding labyrinth of tunnels as long as the Great Barrier Reef. Book as far ahead as possible via the Riversleigh Centre (tel. 4749 1555) or through the hostel. *(3hr. tour M, Tu, Th 7:30am, 11:30am, 2:30pm. $35. Min. age 16.)* The tour just...rocks.

A display of local Kalkadoon **Aboriginal artifacts** (with not-so-local Northern Territory stuff mixed in) is the **Kalkadoon Tribal Centre** (tel. 4749 1435), the vividly colored building next to the Riversleigh Centre. *(Open M-F 9am-5pm. Admission $1.)* The real reason to go are the Aboriginals, who are sometimes willing to chat, share a recipe for spinifex wax, or give directions to a local art site. Take the Lake Moondarra road northeast from Mount Isa, turn right where the telephone lines cross the road (about 3km), and continue 7km down the unsealed road. A small library at the Tribal Centre covers recent land rights issues.

Next door to the Kalkadoon Centre is the **Riversleigh Fossils Interpretive Centre** (tel. 4749 1555; fax 4743 6296), which celebrates Riversleigh Station, a fossil-rich landscape 300km northwest of Mt. Isa. *(Open M-F 8:30am-4:30pm, Sa-Su 9am-3pm. Admission $5.)* Its natural encapsulation of 30 million years of mammal evolution has earned it status as a World Heritage Site. The Centre houses a collection of animatronic models of early Australian mammals.

■ The Gulf Savannah

Though the desert is indubitably sparse, it's where many Gulf Savannahlanders go to holiday. Dotting the area between the Atherton Tablelands and the Gulf of Carpentaria along the **Gulf Developmental Rd,** which chokes the peninsula of North Queensland like a string of pearls, the Gulf region revels in its remoteness and welcomes the wayward visitor with respectful indifference. It's the outback's outback, and no matter where you're visiting from, you'll be a city slicker to folks in these parts. No Waltzing Matilda Centres here—the gulf's few tourist attractions include historic "nowhere-to-nowhere" trains, off-the-beaten-path hot springs, gorges, and lava tubes. It's the combination of nothing to do or worry about and absolutely nowhere to go that makes the Gulf an escapist fantasy—or a *true* city slicker's nightmare.

The extremely useful booklet *The Gulf Savannah: Outback by the Sea* is available at local tourist offices. Idyllic as it sounds, the sea can only be reached by one sealed road, via **Karumba,** 72km from Normaton. Here, cows and sheep are gone, and in their place are lots and lots and lots of fish, birds, and prawns. Rife with saltwater crocodiles, this area is inhospitable to human swimmers, but it's heaven for fishers and ornithologists.

PRACTICAL INFORMATION

The roads and weather of the Gulf Savannah are inhospitable during the wet season. The Dry (Apr.-Oct.) is the time to visit, though even then the road conditions can be bad. Road reports are issued regularly by the **Gulf Savannah Tourist Organization** in Cairns (tel. 4051 4658; fax 4031 3340; email glada01@internetnorth.com.au), and in local info centers, council offices, and RACQs.

The most common route through the region is the **Gulf Developmental Rd,** which links Cairns to Normanton, where it joins the north-south **Burke Developmental Rd.** Except for unsealed patches between Normanton and Croydon, these are single-lane, cattle-strewn, sealed roads. Conventional vehicles are fine on most roads during the Dry, but caravans should avoid unsealed roads. If you want to brave the Wet, 4WD is essential. Never drive the Ootann Rd connecting Mt. Surprise and Chillagoe or anywhere along the Mt. Isa-Riversleigh-Lawn Hill National Park route without 4WD.

Several tours operate from Cairns. Two, **Cool Croc** (tel. 1800 688 458) and **Wilderness Challenge** (tel. 4055 6504), leave from Cairns and arrive in Darwin, or vice versa, and are incredible ways to see the area. Cool Croc is a 5-day part-camping, part-

QUEENSLAND

hotel excursion ($415; with YHA, VIP, or ISIC $389; most meals included). You have the option of breaking up the journey; they'll provide you with a 4WD and camping equipment for $25 a day (min. 4 people), which you can use to visit **Lawn Hill National Park,** the **Riversleigh Fossil Fields,** and the fishing mecca of Karumba. Wilderness Challenge has six-, 10- and 14-day options with or without camping. Both run only during the Dry.

Stationed throughout the region are **Savannah Guides,** highly trained ranger types with specialty knowledge of their specific areas, including Lawn Hill National Park, the **Undara Lava Tubes, Cobbold Gorge,** and the **Tallaroo Hot Springs.** Bookings are essential for all tours and can be made at individual stations, most tourist info centers, or through the main office in Cairns (tel. 4031 7933; fax 4031 7939).

■ Along Route 1 from Cairns: The Eastern Gulf

Lying between the Atherton Tablelands and the Carpentaria Coast along Rte 1 (the Gulf Development Rd), **Georgetown** (pop. 3000) and **Mt. Surprise** (pop. 65) make for decent stopovers on the long trip. The towns, along with nearby **Einasleigh** and **Forsayth,** are part of the **Etheridge Goldfield** and popular with amateur fossickers. Permits can be obtained through the **Department of Mines and Energy** in Georgetown (tel. 4062 1204; fax 4062 1260), the **Goldfields Hotel** (tel. 4062 5374), the **Cobbold Gorge Camping Village** in Forsayth, or the **BP Service Station and Caravan Park** in Mt. Surprise (tel. 4062 3153). Georgetown is also the starting point for tours to **Cobbold Gorge** (tel. 4062 5470; half-day $50, shorter tours $25, camping $5). Between the towns are the **Tallaroo Hot Springs;** $8 buys a 10-minute guided tour and unlimited access to the spring-fed pool. (Open Apr.-Sept. 8am-5pm.)

The eastern Gulf's most awesome attraction is a 40-minute drive form Mt. Surprise. The **Undara Volcano** erupted 190,000 years ago, after which the cooled surface lava hardened as the rest continued to flow beneath. When the work was done—after tens of thousands of years—69 **lava tubes** remained in the middle of dense rainforest. You can visit up to nine of them with **Undara Experience** (tel. 4097 1411 or 4031 7933). (Half-day tours $58, 68 with lunch; 8:30am and 1pm daily. 2hr. tours $26; 1pm all year, additional times depending on season.) At Undara, you can stay in the tent village ($20, linen $5) or camp ($9). The **Savannahlander** train (tel. 4052 6250; fax 4052 6216) connects Mt. Surprise and Forsayth, passing through Einasleigh. (Departs Mt. Surprise M and Th 12:30pm; departs Forsayth Tu and F 7:30am.)

■ Normanton and Croydon

Normanton (pop. 1200) is the largest town in the Gulf; two-thirds of its population is Aboriginal. The town feels as preserved as its famous **Gulflander train** (tel. 4745 1307), which rests in a 30m-long, 9m-high dome station next to the info center when not journeying to nearby **Croydon.** The Gulflander was conceived as a link to the cattle industry in Cloncurry, but was quickly rerouted to Croydon upon the discovery of gold. It hasn't recorded a profit since 1907, but keeps grinding away as one of the Gulf's most popular tourist attractions. It leaves Normanton every Wednesday at 8:30am and takes a leisurely four hours to travel the 150km to Croydon, including stops and explanations along the way. The train returns from Croydon Thursday at 8:30am. ($64 return.) The Gulflander also runs two-hour trips in the dry season for $25, including tea (schedule varies; call ahead). Croyton has a **hotel** above the **Purple Pub** (tel. 4745 1324; rooms $25) and a **caravan park** (tel. 4745 1121; sites $5 per person; powered $10 or $13 for 2 people).

The population of **Croydon** increases by nearly 50 percent when the Gulflander pulls in on Wednesday afternoons. The **Club Hotel** (tel. 4745 6184) is the last remaining of the more than 122 pubs that once catered to the gold-mining community. Croydon has more history per square inch than most towns—or perhaps it only seems that way, since it's all the town has to offer the idling train passenger. Local **Chris Weirman** (tel. 4745 6125 or 4745 6185) leads walking **tours** for $5 (children free). You can pick up the pamphlet for the self-guided tour at the info center.

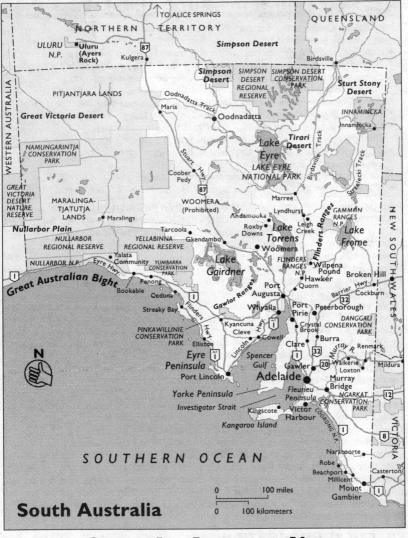

South Australia

South Australia

South Australia exists in a state of sublime schizophrenia. Alongside vast kilometers of the harshest, most uncompromising terrain on the continent, peaceful vineyards sleep lazily and a sophisticated city basks under a steady sun. Capital Adelaide is a stately, serene oasis, well-fed and well-watered by some of the best cuisine and finest wines in the country. Gracious buildings line its streets, world-class festivals crowd its boulevards, and hip cafes occupy its East End. As if in defiance, Adelaide's green parklands challenge the searing heat of the encroaching desert.

This is the driest state in Australia, but also the most urbanized, precisely because its outback is so inhospitable. In SA's gargantuan, sparsely populated top half, indigenous pitjantjatjara and colonial farmers alike subsist on land which may see rain only a few times a decade, and miners at Cooper Pedy must literally extract a living from the earth. The tenacity of these pioneers is plainly evident to the adventurous traveler who traverses the rugged Flinders Ranges or goes "back of beyond."

Some of SA's more civilized attractions ferment farther south. The majestic Murray River, Australia's largest waterway, winds through the lowlands east of Adelaide and irrigates the state's famous vineyards before emptying into the Southern Ocean. Of South Australia's seven distinct wine regions, those of Adelaide Hills are most accessible from the capital, while the Coonawarra, southeast of Adelaide, produces Australia's finest reds. Slightly more removed, the fertile valleys of the Murray River and the grassy knolls of McLaren Vale also earn recognition from connoisseurs. North toward the outback, the famous Barossa and Clare Valleys comprise the central wine regions. The gently undulating vineyards of the Eyre Peninsula lie farther northwest.

South Australia's coastline weaves a jagged path in and out of peninsulas, providing the most beach for your buck. The rolling hills and beach towns of the Fleurieu Peninsula provide quick getaways southeast of Adelaide, and access to the wildlife wonderland of Kangaroo Island. North of Adelaide the country towns of the Yorke Peninsula wind on down along a sandy coastline, and the Eyre Peninsula's juxtaposed rough surf and quiet coves reward those travelers who venture on.

South Australia is a state of extremes. Travelling here may require a swimsuit and surfboard one day, a corkscrew and distinguishing palate the next, and a spare tire and 20-gallon water jug for the upcoming stretch of road. It's a long way, physically and figuratively, from the sun-and-booze-soaked east coast backpackers' route, but those looking for an escape from that party scene love it here. Throughout SA, the local flavor rules, and the hidden sap of Australia can be tapped most sweetly by those who detour off the beaten track.

PRACTICAL INFORMATION

Almost all of SA's population is clumped in its well-watered southeastern triangle, while the vast northern rectangle of the state consists of extremely dry, sparsely inhabited outback. **Route 1,** the continuation of the Great Ocean Road, runs along the coast from Melbourne to Adelaide, continues up to Port Augusta across the Eyre Peninsula, and hugs the ocean through the Nullarbor Plain all the way into Western Australia. At Port Augusta, the lonely **Stuart Highway** branches off north towards Coober Pedy and the Northern Territory. Alternatively, the scenic **Oodnadatta Track** winds adventurously through the Flinders Ranges and skirts Lake Eyre and the remote Simpson Desert before rejoining the Stuart Hwy just past Maria.

If you don't have a car, the most practical way to see most of SA's attractions is by bus. The major national bus lines, **Greyhound Pioneer** (tel. 13 20 30) and **McCafferty's** (tel. 13 14 99) run coaches between Adelaide and Melbourne, Sydney, Alice

Springs, and Perth, stopping over at a few destinations in between. For more detailed itineraries, **Premiere Stateliner** (tel. 8415 5500) services smaller towns throughout SA. The **Wayward Bus** (tel. 8232 6646) offers more leisurely transportation tours.

For more freedom and access to attractions that are removed from the bus lines, it's best to hire your own wheels. Major **car rental** companies with branches throughout SA include **Hertz** (tel. 13 30 39), **Avis** (Adelaide tel. 8410 5727), and **Thrifty** (tel. 1800 652 008); local outfits, often with lower prices, are listed throughout this chapter. A conventional vehicle is fine for wine and beach country, but 4WD is recommended for forays into the outback. Another good option, often more practical if you're traveling alone or going to out-of-the-way places, is to book a **tour.** While the standard Oz Experience thing is pretty touristy, plenty of local organizations run excellent trips, especially in wine country and the outback. Most hostels have ample tour information and advice and can book for you, often at a discount.

The state's main tourist center, the **South Australian Tourism Commission Travel Center,** 1 King William St, Adelaide (tel. 8303 2070, bookings 8303 2033; email SthAusTour@Tourism.sa.gov.au; http://www.tourism.sa.gov.au), is a deep reservoir of information. The SATC's other major branches are located in **McLaren Vale** (tel. 8323 9455); in **Tanunda** (tel. 8563 0600 or 1800 812 662; fax 8563 0616; email hwta@dove.net.au), serving the Barossa Valley; in **Port Lincoln** (tel. 8683 3544 or 1800 629 911), serving the Eyre Peninsula; and in **Port Augusta** (tel. 8641 0793), serving the outback and Flinders Ranges.

The best way to experience SA up close and personally (besides tanking up on wine) is through its **national parks,** which showcase a cross-section of SA landscapes and are operated by the National Parks and Wildlife Service (NPWS). The **National Parks Information Center** (tel. 9204 1910) is located in the State Information Center at 77 Orenfell St in Adelaide, but for more specific information visit the headquarters of each individual park. Some offer extensive tourist information, while others are just ranger shacks with info provided on a drive-by basis. Pt. Augusta houses the **North District NPWS Office** (tel. 8548 5300), while the **Eyre District** branch (tel. 8688 3111) is in Pt. Lincoln.

Phone numbers in South Australia have recently changed. Regional phone codes are now all 08, followed by eight-digit numbers. If you have trouble making a call, use the following scheme to get the old number, and try that instead.For numbers in Kangaroo Island, see **Kangaroo Island** (p. 416).

Old Number:	New Number:	Old Number:	New Number:
(08) xx xxxx	(08) 84xx xxxx	(087) xx xxxx	(08) 87xx xxxx
(08) xxx xxxx	(08) 8xxx xxxx	(088) xx xxxx	(08) 88xx xxxx
(085) xx xxxx	(08) 85xx xxxx	(089) xx xxxx	(08) 89xx xxxx
(086) xx xxxx	(08) 86xx xxxx	(0848) y zxxx	(08) 855a bxxx

ADELAIDE

Once known only for its inordinate number of churches, Adelaide has emerged as a city with far more to offer than an uplifting Sunday sermon. The first completely planned city in Australia, in the first state not to be settled by convict labor, Adelaide was destined to be different from the other Australian capitals. The one million people who call Adelaide home take pride in the city's big leafy trees, historic buildings, and flourishing arts scene, and enjoy a big-city lifestyle that belies the lower cost of living. The long list of cultural attractions, headed by the Adelaide Festival of Arts, includes a fine symphony and chamber orchestra, numerous small, experimental theaters, and world-class galleries and museums. With more restaurants per capita than any other city in Australia, Adelaide can satisfy any palate at any budget, and then

ⓐ ADELAIDE HIGHLIGHTS

- Produce and people-watching galore at the lively **Central Markets** (see p. 408).
- Pure herbivore heaven at **Vego and Loving It!** (see p. 405).
- Unconventional accommodations at **Fuzzies Farm,** a post-industrial collective microsociety in the Adelaide Hills (see p. 410).
- Dancing and debauchery till the wee hours at pumping **Heaven II** (see p. 409).
- Spectacular views of the city from **Mt. Lofty** in the Adelaide Hills (see p. 410).
- Rollerblading in the sea breeze on the **Linear Park Bike Track** (see p. 401).
- Luxury living on the cheap at **Albert Hall** in Glenelg (see p. 403).

wash it all down with some of the country's best wines. For those who prefer a more raucous pace, the nightclubs along Hindly St, the pubs in the city center, and the cafes on Rundle St fit the hedonistic bill.

In the summer months, Adelaide's coastline becomes a temple of sun worship, with devotion to the deity reflected in the nut-brown skin of its followers. The beachfront suburb of Glenelg is a favorite late night haunt, since many of its pubs, clubs, and restaurants face the ocean. Home to the first colonists of South Australia, Glenelg is now one of Adelaide's most popular residences for families, fishermen, yuppies, and at least a gazillion seagulls. Be warned, however, that this is very much an urban hangout, and it can be difficult to find your own patch of golden sand. If sand and surf are not your first choice in outdoor activity, the gardens, playgrounds, and jogging trails in Adelaide's 668 hectares of parkland provide plenty of room to romp. Some of the most visually stunning hikes in the country can be found in the Adelaide Hills, a short drive from the city center. For information on festivals and events, pick up a copy of the *Calendar of Events for South Australia* at the SA Travel Centre.

■ Arrival and Departure

BY PLANE

The airport, 7km west of the city center, services domestic and international carriers in separate terminals. A taxi ride to the city runs $12-15. The cheapest way to get from the airport to Adelaide proper is on the **Airport to City Bus** (tel. 8381 5311), which offers drop-off at accommodations. (Shuttles M-F every 30min. 7am-9pm, Sa-Su. and holidays every 1hr.; $6 one-way, $10 return good any time.) **Trans Adelaide** public bus #270 will bring you to the airport entrance on Burbridge Rd. From there it is a 15-minute walk to the terminal. Bus #270 leaves the city from Currie St, just across from the Passenger Transport Information Centre.

Most flights in and out of Adelaide are domestic. **Qantas** (tel. 13 13 13 for domestic flights, 13 12 11 for international) travels to hubs including Sydney ($350), Brisbane ($471), Perth ($471), Melbourne ($241), Darwin ($574), and Alice Springs ($479). Qantas also oversees **ASA (**Airlines of South Australia) (tel. 8682 5688 or 1800 018 234), servicing the Eyre Peninsula, and **O'Conner** (tel. 13 13 13), servicing Mt. Gambier. **Kendell Airlines** is the major local carrier; book through Ansett (tel. 13 13 00). Its destinations include Coober Pedy ($361), Ceduna ($280), Mt. Gambier ($194), and Kangaroo Island ($90). Students 17 and under enjoy a 25% discount; seniors 40%. Fourteen-day advance tickets are cheaper. **Emu Airways** (tel. 1800 182 353) also services Kangaroo Island. Prices fluctuate and discounts may apply, so shop around.

BY BUS

Adelaide's **central bus station** is at 101-111 Franklin St. Once at the station, cross the street to the bright pink **Backpacker Travel and Transit Center** (tel. 8410 3000) for budget tour information (open M-F 9am-5pm, Sa 10am-2pm). National bus companies provide regular service to and from Adelaide at prices that generally beat rail and air travel. **Greyhound Pioneer** (tel. 13 20 30) offers service to major destinations around the country such as Sydney (22 hr., $96), Melbourne (10 hr., $45), Perth (34 hr.,

Adelaide

ACCOMMODATIONS

D Adelaide Backpacker's Hostel
C Adelaide Backpacker's Inn
A Backpack Australia
F East Park Lodge
B New World International Hostel
E YHA Hostel

600 yards

600 meters

N

Dequetteville Rd.

Hackney Rd.

Botanic Park

Botanic Plane Tree Drive

Zoological Gardens

The Botanic Garden of Adelaide & State Herbarium

Botanic Rd.

Rundle Park

Rymill Park

Bartels Rd.

Grand Prix Circuit

East Tce.

East Tce.

Victoria Racetrack

Beaumont Rd.

East Tce.

Hutt St.

Hutt St.

Hutt Rd.

F

D

Ayers House

East St.

Frome St.

Frome Rd.

Regent St.

Adult Deaf Society

Osmond Glen Rd.

South Aust. Museum

Art Gallery of South Australia

Pulteney St.

HINDMARSH SQUARE

Flinders St.

Wakefield St.

Angas St.

Carrington St.

HURTLE SQUARE

Pulteney St.

State Library

North Tce.

Rundle Rd.

Halifax St.

Gilles St.

Linley Rd.

South Tce.

Peacock Rd.

Kintore Ave.

State Info. Center

Grenfell St.

Pirie St.

Stock Exchange

Univ. of Adelaide Sports Field

Pioneer Women's Memorial Gardens

Government House

War Memorial

King William St.

Town Hall

C

King William St.

Sir Lewis Cohen Ave.

William Rd.

Elder Park

Parliament House

VICTORIA SQUARE

Veale Gardens

Pennington Gardens

The Playhouse Festival Theatre

Adelaide Casino

State Opera Theatre

Central Market

B

Whitmore Square

Montefiore Rd.

Montefiore St.

Hindley St.

Philip St.

Currie St.

LIGHT SQUARE

Waymouth St.

Morphett St.

Performing Arts Multicultural Centre

A

Morphett St.

War Memorial Drive

South Course Golf Links

Franklin St.

Grote St.

Gouger St.

Wright St.

Sturt St.

Gilbert St.

South Tce.

Gray St.

West Tce.

Adelaide Gaol

Port Rd.

Glover Ave.

Ellis Park

Burbridge Rd.

Kingston Gardens

Good-wood Rd.

Anzac Way

Edwards Park

$184), Alice Springs (20hr., $135), and many places in between. Greyhound offers a 20% discount to children, students, and pensioners, and a 10% discount to YHA members. **McCafferty's** (tel. 13 14 99), the other major bus line, offers service to destinations around Southern, Northern and Eastern Australia, including Sydney ($96), Melbourne ($45), Brisbane ($160), and Alice Springs ($135), with similar YHA discounts. **Premier Stateliner** (tel. 8415 5555 for reservations, 8415 5500 for general inquiries) offers good rates and a more detailed local itinerary around South Australia. Premier services routes north toward Port Augusta ($29), Port Lincoln ($58), and the Flinders Ranges ($52 to Wilpena) and south towards Mt. Gambier. It also offers one-to two-day tours to sights around SA including Kangaroo Island, Barossa Valley, Adelaide Hills, and the Flinders Ranges ($25-$265). For a longer journey, hop aboard the **Wayward Bus** (tel. 8232 6646) which offers tour packages from Melbourne (3 days, $170) and to Alice Springs (8 days, $640). **Oz Experience** (tel. 02 9368 1766 or 1300 300 028) also offers touring trips from Adelaide to Alice Springs (6 days, $395).

BY TRAIN

All interstate and local trains depart from the **Adelaide Rail Passenger Terminal** (tel. 13 22 32) in Keswick, 2km west of the city center. It's usually pricier than bus travel, but student fares can make train travel a good way to see the outback. Adelaide is serviced by the **Overland Train** to Melbourne (12hr., 1 per day, $50), the **Ghan** to Alice Springs (21hr., 1-2 per week, $140), the **Indian Pacific** to Perth (36hr., 2 per week, $200), and the **Speedlink** (mixture of train and bus travel) to Sydney (19hr., 1 per day; $99). Make bookings through the Keswick terminal.

■ Orientation

Adelaide is built on a coastal plain nestled between Gulf Vincent on the west and the Adelaide Hills to the northeast. The city's grid plan and surrounding **parklands** make it easy to navigate on foot or by public transport. Most major attractions are within easy walking distance of each other. Bordering the city on all four sides are the **four terraces,** creatively named North, South, East, and West. The streets running east to west are set out in a perfect grid, but are separated by **King William St,** a north-south thoroughfare, at which point their names change (Flinders becomes Franklin St, for example). Streets running north to south retain their names, and are divided only by the four smaller squares and by **Victoria Square** in the very center of the city.

Although Adelaide is a relatively peaceful city, the parklands are unsafe at night, especially near the River Torrens and in the southwest corner of the city.

■ Getting Around

BY PUBLIC TRANSPORTATION

Adelaide is serviced by public buses, trains, and one lone tram (in Glenelg) that make up an integrated public transport system called **Trans Adelaide.** A unique feature of the system is the **O-Bahn busway,** a bus that runs on concrete tracks from Adelaide city through beautiful parklands to the Tea Tree Plaza shopping center. All suburban trains depart from the **Adelaide Railway Station** (tel. 8210 1000) on North Terrace.

For information, stop into the **Passenger Transport Information Centre** (tel. 8210 1000) at the corner of King William and Currie St or pick up the free **Metroguide** brochure (open M-Sa 8am-6pm, Su 10:30am-5:30pm). You can buy a ticket when boarding buses, but for trains you must buy them beforehand. They are available at most delis, newsagents, post offices, and at the central train station. **Daytrip tickets** ($5.10) allow unlimited travel for the day. **Single tickets** used during the off-peak hours of 9am to 3pm cost $1.60, at other times $2.70, and are good for two hours from the time of validation. You must validate your ticket each time you enter a new bus or train. An option for those staying longer is the **Multitrip ticket,** good for 10 two-hour trips, which you must buy prior to boarding ($17, off-peak $10.60).

The **Beeline** is a free bus service operating in the city center. Catch it outside the Adelaide railway station on North Terrace or as it makes its way down King William St to Victoria Square, before circling back around to the train station. (Runs M 7:40am-9pm, Sa every 12 min. 8:30am-5pm, Su no service.) Another free bus service is the **Loop,** which, true to its name, makes a loop that stops at most of the major tourist attractions. Catch it at any point along its route (it runs along the North, East, and West Terraces, but only goes south as far as Grote and Wakefield St). All Loop buses are wheelchair accessible.

The best way to get to **Glenelg** from the city is the tram from Victoria Square. The ride takes approximately 30 minutes; trams leave about every 15 minutes. Tickets can be purchased on board and use the same system as Adelaide's trains and buses.

BY CAR

The **Royal Automobile Association (RAA),** 41 Hindmarsh Square (tel. 8202 4500), offers all the usual AAA services (open M-F 8:30am-5pm, Sa-Su 9am-noon; see **Getting Around By Car,** p. 34). Some of the cheaper rental companies include **Action Rent-a-Car** (tel. 8352 7044), **Delta** (tel. 13 13 90), and **Rent-a-Bug** (tel. 8234 0655). Major companies such as **Hertz** (tel. 13 30 39) and **Avis** (tel. 8410 5727) have branches at the airport. **Caudell's Explorer Self-Drive** (tel. 8410 5552; fax 8410 5556; email caudells@adelaide.on.net), opposite the bus station, offers competitively priced and reliable self-drive packages, including 4WD for outback expeditions (from $36 per day, $100 per day for 4WD Landcruiser, less for extended hire).

BY TAXI

Taxis, though pricey, become necessary when trains and buses stop running around midnight. There are **taxi stands** throughout downtown Adelaide. Some companies include **Adelaide Independent** (tel. 8234 6000) and **Access Cabs** (tel. 8234 6444), which offers wheelchair taxis. **Yellow Cab** (tel. 13 19 24) offers YHA discounts.

BY BICYCLE

Many city streets are fairly flat and have designated cycling lanes. More scenic routes include the **Linear Park Bike and Walking Track.** This 40km track provides the biking, jogging, or rollerblading enthusiast with beachside breezes and river views in the beautiful Adelaide foothills. Further info can be found at bike shops including **Linear Park Mountain Hire** (tel. 8223 6953), **Freewheelin** (tel. 8232 6860), and **Mountain Bike Hire** (tel. 8212 7800). Rental starts at $15 to 20 a day, with cheaper weekly rates. Some hostels also rent bikes to guests. Much of the shore in Glenelg has bike tracks; hire bikes from **Holdfast Cycles,** 768 Anzac Hwy, Glenelg (tel. 8294 4537).

■ Practical Information

Tourist Offices: South Australian Tourism Commission Travel Centre, 1 King William St (tel. 8303 2070, bookings 8303 2033; email SthAusTour@Tourism.sa.gov.au; http://www.tourism.sa.gov.au), directly across from Parliament House and a 2min. walk up North Tce from the central railway station. Well-informed, multilingual staff. No bookings on weekends or holidays. Wheelchair accessible. Open M and W-F 8:45am-5pm, Tu 9am-5pm, Sa-Su and holidays 9am-2pm. **State Information Centre,** 77 Grenfell St (tel. 8204 1900), is a gold mine of info on state history and government, Aboriginal history, and general tourist interests. Not a booking office for tours. The building also houses the **National Parks Information Centre** (tel. 8204 1910). **Flinders Ranges and Outback South Australia Tourism,** 142 Gawler Pl (tel. 8223 3991 or 1800 633 060; fax 8223 3995; http://www.flinders.outback.on.net; email info@flinders.outback.on.net), is the best resource for those headed to northern SA. Open M-F 9am-5pm. The **YHA Travel** office, 38 Sturt St (tel. 8231 5583) offers info on budget travel throughout Australia. Open M-F 9:30am-5pm. The small **Glenelg Tourist Office** (tel. 8294-5833) is to the right of the jetty as you face the water, within the Sandbank deli.

Get **maps** at **Mapland,** 282 Richmond Rd, Netley (tel. 8226 4946), **The Map Shop,** 16A Peel St. (tel. 8231 2033), or the **RAA** (see **Getting Around,** above).

Consulate: U.K. (tel. 8212 7280).

Money: Thomas Cook Travel Agencies, 45 Grenfell St (tel. 8212 3354), offers **currency exchange.** The main offices of Australia's largest banks are found along King William St, between North Tce and Victoria Sq. These include the **National Australia Bank,** 22 King William St (tel. 13 22 65); **Commonwealth Bank,** 96 King William St (tel. 13 22 21); **ANZ,** 81 King William St (tel. 13 13 14); **Bank of South Australia,** 97 King William St (tel. 13 13 76); and **Westpac,** 2 King William St (tel. 8210 3311). Banks open M-Th 9:30am-4pm, F 9:30am-5pm. **ATMs** are found throughout the city. Cirrus is the main network. **EFTPOS** is ubiquitous.

American Express: On Grenfell St (tel. 8212 7099). Open M-F 8:30am-5:30pm, Sa 9am-noon.

Bookstores: Europa bookshop, 238 Rundle St (tel. 8223 2289), for foreign language and travel books. **Unibooks** (tel. 8223 4366) university bookstore, on Victoria Drive just as you enter Adelaide University. **Murphy Sister's Bookshop,** 240 The Parade, Norwood (tel. 8332 7508), specializing in feminist and lesbian writing.

Library: The State Library of South Australia (tel. 8207 7200), at the corner of Kintore Ave and North Tce.

Ticket Agencies: Bass Bookings (tel. 13 12 46). 24hr. info line tel. 0055 3330.

Emergency: Dial 000.

Police Station: 1 Angas St (tel. 8207 5000).

Hotlines: Women's Information Switchboard (tel. 8223 1244). **Disability Information and Resource Centre,** 195 Gillies St (tel. 8223 7522). **Gayline** (tel. 8362 3223 or 1800 182 232).

Medical Assistance: Crisis Care Service (tel. 8272 1222). **Emergency Medical Service** (tel. 8223 0230, 8445 0230, or 8275 9911). **Emergency Dental Service** (tel. 8272 8111; open M-F 5-9pm, Sa-Su 9am-9pm). **Poison Information Center** (tel. 8267 4999). **Adelaide Medical Clinic and 24 Hour Home Visit Medical Service,** AMA House, 1st Floor 161 Ward St, North Adelaide (tel. 8267 3544, after hours 0412 829 904).

Post Office: General Post Office (GPO), corner of King William and Franklin St. Open M-F 8am-6pm, Sa 8:30am-noon. Another branch at east end of Rundle Mall, Shop 18 Citi Centre. Open M-F 8am-6pm, Sa 8:30am-noon. **Postal Code:** 5000.

Internet Access: At the **library** (see above) sign up for free 30min. time slots. Open M-W and F 9:30-8pm, Th 9:30-5pm, Sa-Su noon-5pm. Adelaide's only cybercafe is **Ngapartji,** 211 Rundle St (tel. 8232 0839).

Phone Code: 08.

■ Accommodations

ADELAIDE

If you are in Adelaide to see the city sights, sample the food and wine, or delve into the thriving cultural life, a locale in the **city center** is your best bet. Most hostels are located either in the residential southeast corner of the city or clustered around the Franklin St bus depot, and nearly all of them can be accessed from the airport (by the Airport to City Bus) or from the Keswick railway station. Those that are distant from the bus station are best reached by public transport or by arranging pick-up in advance. Book ahead, especially in summer and during the Adelaide Festival. All the listed hostels have self-catering kitchens, free tea and coffee, and 24-hour access. For more privacy than hostels, pub hotels are everywhere.

Pricier options include bed and breakfasts or motels in **North Adelaide.** This district is only a 10-minute walk from the city along Frome Rd. An additional resource is the *South Australian Short Holidays* book, available at the South Australian Tourism Commission Travel Centre. Adelaide has some beautiful heritage buildings which have been converted into B&Bs.

East Park Lodge, 341 Angas St (tel. 8223 1228; fax 8223 7772; email east-park@microtronics.com.au), facing the pink Backpacker Travel and Transit. Enter building in front of the bus station, turn right and walk down Franklin St, turn right on King William St, walk through Victoria Square and turn left on Angus St. Pick-up from the bus station available. This beautiful building is close to some of Adelaide's oldest and most coveted residences on East Terrace and fosters a quiet, mature atmosphere within its airy, newly renovated rooms. The rooftop offers a fantastic view of the city and in summer doubles as a recreation area. A/C, heating, linen free, laundry. 4-person dorms $15 a person, doubles or twins $35. VIP, YHA.

The Austral Hotel (tel. 8223 4660), on corner of Rundle and Bent St. Located on Rundle St above a super-hip pub, the Austral offers green and pink decor and big, simple rooms. It's slightly more expensive than a hostel, but for your money you get location, privacy, funkiness, and fun at your fingertips. Separate bathrooms. Many rooms have sinks and/or fireplaces. Singles $25; twins and doubles $35.

Princes Lodge Motel, 73 Lefevre Tce, North Adelaide (tel. 8267 2266; fax 8239 0787). You will probably need to catch a taxi from the bus station. The North Adelaide neighborhood is lusciously upscale, and the inadvertently retro decor is divine. Great view over the city and parks, and minutes by foot from the action on Melbourne and O'Connell Streets. Laundry facilities and recreation room. Singles $30; doubles $48-58. Continental breakfast included. Book in advance if possible.

Backpack Australia, 128 Grote St (tel. 8231 0639 or 1800 804 133; fax 8410 5881). At the bus station, with your back to the pink Backpacker Travel and Transit Centre, walk down the alley half a block to Grote St. Turn right on Grote St at the Hampshire Hotel, and the hostel is down a couple storefronts. This is fiesta central. The sociable owner loves arranging parties for guests and conveniently owns the pub next door. All the hubbub has put some wear on the rooms and furniture, but the numerous murals, plenty of hangout space, and opportunity for cheap beer make this a fun place to be. Breakfast included, other meals cheap. A/C, heating, linen supplied. Bunks $11-13; doubles $30.

YHA Hostel, 290 Gilles St (tel. 8223 6007; fax 8223 2888). Coming from the bus station, take bus #171 or #172 from King William St to the corner of Hutt and Halifax St. Gilles is the next street up from Halifax. Bus station pick-up available with advance booking. A lovely, clean, quiet and affordable hostel close to the city center and a 10min. walk from Hutt St. A/C, laundry, linen $1, travel service, Internet access. Dorms $16, with YHA $13. Try to book ahead, especially Dec.-Mar.

Adelaide Backpacker's Inn, 112 Carrington St (tel. 8223 6635 or 1800 247 725 reservations only; fax 8232 5464; email abackinn@tne.net.au; http://www.tne.net.au/abackinn). The annex across the street is newer and more comfortable than the old main building. Amiable owners serve apple pie and ice cream nightly. A/C, heating, travel center, linen supplied, laundry. Dorms $15; singles $22; twins $18 per person; doubles $44. VIP, YHA. Special winter rates.

Adelaide Backpackers Hostel, 263 Gilles St (tel. 8223 5680, reservations 1800 677 351). Down the street from the YHA. Bus station pick-up possible with advance booking. This is the oldest hostel in Adelaide, and although some of the furniture bears witness to this fact, it has a smiling proprietor, fruit trees in the yard, and a homey feel. A/C, heating, nearby public laundry. Dorms $12; doubles $28.

Adelaide Caravan Park (tel. 8363 1566), on Bruny St in Hackney, 2km east of the city. Tent sites from $18.

Windsor Gardens Caravan Park, 78 Winsdor Grove, Windsor Gardens (tel. 8261 1091). Tent sites from $12.

GLENELG

If you are visiting predominantly to soak up the sun along South Australia's coastline or visit Adelaide's outlying attractions, consider basing yourself in Glenelg, a tram ride from the city center. Not only is Glenelg relaxing, beachy, and easily accessible to the city, the airport, the coast, the Adelaide Hills, and the wine valleys, but Glenelg's two hostels are a step above anything you'll find in Adelaide.

⊛**Albert Hall,** 16 South Esplanade (tel. 8376 0488, for bookings 1800 060 488; fax and guestline 8294 1966). As you face the jetty, turn left and walk 5min. along the South Esplanade between the Grand Hotel and the beachfront until a mansion appears on your left. This, ladies and gentlemen, is your hostel. The rooms are clean and ordinary, but the surroundings are divine; marble bathrooms, a ballroom, and a beachside view make this the place to live cheap and feel like a million bucks. Limited wheelchair access, kitchen facilities, safe for valuables, laundry, free pick-up and drop-off at the airport, bus, and train station. Dorms $14, with balcony $15 (book ahead for these—it's worth it); double with view $40, double with ensuite $45. In winter, all dorms $14; twin or double $32; weekly rates available.

⊛**Glenelg Backpackers Resort,** 1-7 Mosely St (tel. 1800 066 422). Mosely St is up 1 block from the shore on your right as you walk away from the beach. Full-blown backpackers resort complex, with a licensed bar, pool tables, a stage for local bands, cafe, and games room downstairs and free tours to Adelaide and the wine valleys. Enthusiastic and well-traveled owners are attempting to build their own little corner of backpacker heaven. Perks include a spa, free mountain bikes, kitchen, laundry, free breakfast, an outdoor barbecue patio, Internet access, free linen, free pick-up and drop-off at airport, bus and train stations, and downtown. Dorms $16, singles $31, doubles $42. VIP, YHA, Nomads. Ask about winter specials.

■ Food

Adelaide has more restaurants per capita than any other city in the country. **Gouger Street,** in the city center near Victoria Square, offers good, inexpensive ethnic cuisine. **Rundle Street,** in the northeast section of the city, caters more to the young bohemian set, as students forgo lectures in nearby Adelaide University in favor of strong cups of espresso. Clusters of restaurants can also be found on the quietly cool **Hutt St** in southeast Adelaide, the upscale North Adelaide **Melbourne** and **O'Connell St,** and the flashy but cheap **Hindley St,** across King William St from Rundle St. Barbara Santich's *Apples to Zampone,* found in most major bookstores in the city, is a good guide to Adelaide's restaurants. *Dine: Eating out in SA,* edited by Ann Oliver and Nigel Hopkins, is also useful, especially if you plan to venture outside the city.

For less formal fare, bakeries, pie carts, pubs, and chippers are scattered around Adelaide. Most meat-based morsels can be found in a vegetarian form as well. For a real Aussie experience, try a late-night snack at the **"Pie Cart"** outside the Adelaide Train Station. The infamous **pie floater**—an Aussie meat pie swimming amid a thick pea soup and topped with tomato sauce—is a South Australian original. Try it with your eyes closed if you must, but you shouldn't leave Adelaide without giving it a go. The various **food halls** along Rundle Mall and at Hawkers's Corner (at the corner of Wright St) are also good for cheap and filling lunches.

GOUGER STREET

Gouger St houses the Central Market, with stall after stall of every edible imaginable and free samples to boot. The market also houses cheap cafes, which provide more ready-made eats and seating amid the bustling flow of the market. In the northeast center of the market, try **Malacca Corner** (tel. 8231 5650) for good Malaysian fare. In the southwest, **Zuma's Cafe** (tel. 8231 4410) makes a great latte, muffins in clay pots, and other savory morsels, and **The Big Table** (tel. 8212 3899) serves a generous salad for $5. One of the best of the market's numerous bakeries is **Fresh and Crusty** (tel. 8231 8999) in the Market Plaza section of the market hub. During the day, the Gouger St restaurants and cafes fill with lawyers and businessmen on lunch, but on market days and at night the street turns into a bustling, cosmopolitan center where a wonderful array of **ethnic cuisine** awaits. Korean, Malaysian, Japanese, Mongolian, and Chinese cuisines are all represented, along with traditional and modern Australian fare. Daytime meals tend to be cheaper, especially at the restaurants within the market itself. More formal Gouger St restaurants include:

Matsuri, 167 Gouger St (tel. 8231 3494). This is Adelaide's best sushi restaurant, and as with most raw, decorative fish the price is not so cheap ($20 per person). However, if you can catch this restaurant during one of its Sushi Festivals you'll enjoy a fabulous meal at half-price. Open M-F 5:30-10pm, Sa-Su 5:30-10:30pm.

Bunga Raya, 83a Gouger St (tel. 8231 7790). Dishing out authentic Malaysian noodle, rice, meat, and seafood dishes ($7-10), this simple, unassuming restaurant is more delicious than the rest of the simple, unassuming restaurants lining Gouger. Lunch specials $5. Open M-Sa 11am-3pm and daily 5-8pm.

George's Seafood Restaurant, 113-115 Gouger St (tel. 8231 4449). For seafood, the prices are reasonable ($10-18 for main dishes) and helpings are plentiful enough to share. Blends down-to-earth, family-style hospitality with world-class cuisine. Open noon-2:30pm and 5pm-9:30pm (F-Sa 10:30pm).

Noodles, 119 Gouger St (tel. 8231 8177), serves exactly that: noodles in every shape, form, and color. Big servings and reasonable prices ($7-10), with plenty of veggie options. Open Tu-F 11:30-3pm and daily 5:30-late. BYO.

RUNDLE STREET

Rundle St flows neatly on from Rundle Mall (going east, out of the city). It is *the* place to be in Adelaide, day or night, and offers an incredible range of restaurants, cafes, pubs, and holes in the wall. In summer, crowds fill overflowing cafes well into the wee hours. For good meals that won't break the budget, it's unparalleled.

◉Vego and Lovin It!, 240 Rundle St (tel. 8223 7411). Just past Mindfield bookstore and hidden up a narrow set of stairs on the 2nd floor. Listen for strains of Bing Crosby and watch for 50s tackorama decor. A huge range of vegan and vegetarian food, large portions, and delicious concoctions make this an extremely popular daytime eating spot. All ingredients are fresh each day, from the organic vegetables to the home-baked bread. The veggie burgers, entrees, sandwiches, and desserts are original and plentiful. Main dishes $5-7. Open M-F 10am-5pm.

Al Fresco's, 260 Rundle St (tel. 8223 4589). An Adelaide landmark since it opened 20 years ago, Al Fresco's serves a tempting range of Italian cakes and some of the best gelato in the city. Pick up a light meal in minutes or linger over a latte for hours. Open every day, all day, and well into the night.

Ruby's Cafe, 255b Rundle St. (tel. 8224 0365). Ruby's serves creative comfort food from chrome booths. Offers usual dishes (eggs, chicken, meat, pasta) in slightly gourmet variations and desserts such as warm toffee pudding. Main dishes $8-13, desserts $6. Open for brunch Su from 9am and for dinner daily 6:30pm-late.

Scoozi, 272 Rundle St (tel. 8232 4733). If you can put it on bread, Scoozi will put it on mouth-watering foccacia in minutes. Tempting "designer pizza" (kangaroo meat and provolone anyone?), a huge selection of antipasto, and a daunting display of cakes. Foccacia $5, pasta $8-10. Open all day and much of the night.

GLENELG

There is no shortage of food at the bay, but many beachside cafes are expensive. For an authentic day at the beach head for a chipper or a "yiros" (gyros) and falafel stand, along the shore. Since all fish and chips are not created equal, walk down Jetty Rd toward the city to **Glenelg Seafoods,** 91 Jetty Rd, for the cream of the crop. A yummy selection of Aussie baked goods can be found at **Vanderman's Homemade Cakes,** 39 Jetty Rd, with authentic finger buns, lamingtons, and green frog sponge cakes.

THE BEST OF THE REST

The rest of the city is a melange of cafes, pubs, and posh restaurants. West Terrace provides an excellent Asian food court (open M-Sa for lunch and dinner). Many downtown **pubs** offer cheap backpacker meals. Some other highlights:

◉Lizard Lounge, 172A Hutt St (tel. 8227 0210). The dim interior is mellow, but no black light wattage can disguise the punk of this place. With cow-hide booths, modern decorama, and an exciting menu, the experience is a mouthful of the utmost fun. Light snacks such as lizards rarebits (creamy melted mass of matured cheese, ale, and red pepper on crusty bread, $7), curry, gnocchi, crepe specials ($8.90), and mind-boggling desserts add to the revelry. The backyard patio and spunky owner complete this memorable night spot. Open daily 7pm-late.

The Gilbert Place Pancake House (tel. 8211 7912). Between Currie St and Hindley St on King William, turn into the alley called Gilbert Place and walk to the end. In a city that shuts down early, a sign which reads "this door will never close" is a welcome sight for hungry eyes. A 24hr. pancake house is always good, but Gilbert's fanciful creations (Jamaican Banana, Ham Steak and Pineapple, Bavarian Apple, etc. $7-9) and Tuesday all-you-can-eat specials ($5) make this place stand out.

Queen of Tarts, 178 Hutt St, (tel. 8223 1529). For unique, wholesome healthy food to take home for dinner. A wide variety of fingerfood, salads, pizzas ($3.50 a slice) sandwiches ($5), pies ($3 a slice), and cakes ($24). All natural ingredients, many vegetarian and vegan offerings. Mostly take-away, but there are a few seats.

Perryman's Bakery, 54 Tyne St, North Adelaide (tel. 8267 2766). The great pastries and "penny pies" were originally made in 1930 to sell to nearby North Adelaide primary school kids. Open M-F 8:30am-5:15pm, Sa 8:30am-12:15pm.

■ Sights and Activities

Visitors to Adelaide can indulge all of their sight-seeing cravings, from historical buildings and peaceful parks to summer festivals and outdoor adventures. Many sights and museums are located along **North Terrace,** the city's cultural boulevard. Starting at the east end, you'll pass the Botanic Gardens, the University of Adelaide, the Art Gallery, the Museum, the Central Public Library, the War Memorial, Government House, Parliament House, and Old Parliament House before finally ending up at Adelaide's historic railway station. A two-minute walk down King William St from its intersection with North Tce at Parliament House will bring you to the **Festival Centre.** Situated on the Torrens River, this is the focus of Adelaide's cultural life. Throughout the summer it holds fairs, outdoor theater events, and concerts, the majority of which are free and open to the public. Pick up a calendar of events from inside the Festival Centre complex. The **Adelaide Festival** (tel. 8216 8600) is held here in even-numbered years in late February through early March.

For guided exploration of the area, the **Adelaide Explorer,** a tram-replica bus, does a city to Glenelg touring run that takes two-and-a-half hours. Books and pamphlets outlining self-guided walking tours can be found at the SA Tourism Commission Travel Centre. **Wirra Mai** (tel. 8281 3393) runs Aboriginal Cultural Tours.

If you don't mind fighting the crowds, you may enjoy **Magic Mountain** (tel. 8294 8199), based in Glenelg. This water park is to the right of the jetty as you face the ocean. Water slides, bumper boats, and a variety of non-water parlor games are available. It can be a zoo during school holidays and peak summer months. *(Open in summer M-F 9am-10pm, Sa-Su 12:30pm-midnight; winter M-F 10am-5pm, Sa-Su 9am-10pm.)* During the summer, the smooth surf and hard sand of Glenelg's Holdfast Bay is also a great spot to try your hand at **parasailing** (tel. 0411 191 653) or **beach volleyball.**

GARDENS

Adelaide Botanic Gardens, North Tce (tel. 8228 2311), include many heritage buildings and the oldest greenhouse in Australia. Perfect spot for a picnic lunch of Adelaide's best cheese and wine purchased from the East End Markets, only a minute's walk away. Open M-F 8am-sunset, Sa-Su and holidays 9am-sunset. Free.

Adelaide Zoo, Frome Rd (tel. 8267 3255). A zoo in the middle of the city, 5min. from the University and the major city shopping district. Situated in the northern Parkland area and easily incorporated into a day's excursion of the Botanic Gardens. Open daily 9:30am-5pm. Admission $10, concessions $8, children 4-14 $5.

Bicentennial Conservatory, North Tce (tel. 8228 2311). Enter at the Botanic Gardens and follow the signs. This tropical glass house shaped like an overgrown garden slug has a computer-controlled atmosphere that simulates a tropical rainforest. Open daily 10am-4pm. Admission $2.50, concessions $1.25, families $6.

HERITAGE BUILDINGS

Even as the elegance of times past is abandoned in favor of the avant-garde scene on Rundle St and the all-night raves on Hindley, there is a movement to preserve the city's colonial architecture. Heritage buildings can no longer be torn down in the city center, and many have been restored. Some are open to the public, though hours can be limited. The numerous downtown churches and the residential areas along East Tce and in North Adelaide offer a more informal taste of Adelaide's architectural past.

Carrick Hill, 46 Carrick Hill Dr, Springfield (tel. 8379 3886). Situated in the leafy greens of Springfield, this house is built in the style of an English country manor and is surrounded by stunning gardens on 30 hectares of land. The house was imported in its entirety from an estate in the U.K., piece by painstaking piece. Tours at 11am, noon, 2, and 3pm. Open W-Su and holidays 10am-5pm.

Ayers House, 288 North Tce (tel. 8223 1234). Originally built in 1846 as a simple cottage. Sir Henry Ayers (after whom Ayers Rock is named) made expansions in 1858. Served as a government events center and later as a nurses' quarters for the Royal Adelaide Hospital. Each enormous chandelier weighs in at close to half a ton. Open Tu-F 10am-4pm, Sa-Su 1-4pm. Admission $5, concessions $3.

Beaumont House, 631 Glynburn Rd, Beaumont (tel. 8379 5301). Built around 1850, the estate has glorious, vast grounds, complete with olive groves and gardens. Admission $4, children $2. Open the first Sunday of every month 2-4:30pm.

Old Adelaide Gaol, 18 Gaol Rd, Thebarton (tel. 8231 4062). Much like all Australia's other historic gaols. Open M-F 11am-4pm; Su 11am-3:30pm; guided tours Su. Admission $5 (Su $6), concessions $4, children $3, families $15.

MUSEUMS

South Australian Museum, North Tce (tel. 8207 7500). Renowned for its comprehensive collection of Aboriginal artifacts. Most exhibits feature South Australian history—natural, indigenous, and colonial. The shop regularly features local artwork. In summer, the lawn is a great spot to soak up sun. Watch out for kids playing in the fountain lest you get soaked. Open daily 10am-5pm. Free.

Art Gallery of South Australia, North Tce (tel. 8207 7000). Showcases Australian, Asian, and European prints, paintings, sculpture, and decorative arts, with an especially good collection of Australian and South Australian 20th-century art. Houses Adelaide's most comprehensive art bookshop. Open daily 10am-5pm. Free.

The Jam Factory, Craft and Design Centre, 19 Morphett St (tel. 8410 0727). Part craft shop, part art studio, and part display case for some of the best local and interstate crafts. During opening hours, activity in the glass studio can be observed in the factory itself. The artwork is distinctly South Australian, with colors that reflect the changing hues of the local landscape. Open M-F 9am-5:30pm, Sa-Su 10am-5pm.

Tandanya-National Aboriginal Cultural Institute, 253 Grenfell St (tel. 8223 2467). This is the first major Aboriginal multi-arts complex in Australia and a good place to begin your education in South Australian and Australian indigenous culture. Exhibitions of art by Aboriginal artists change every 6 weeks. The gift shop stocks a broad range of Aboriginal arts and crafts. Guided tours and introductory talks available by appointment. Open daily 10am-5pm. Admission $4, concessions $3.

South Australian Maritime Museum, 126 Lipson St, Port Adelaide (tel. 8240 0200). This museum is spread over a number of sites at Port Adelaide, including old Bond Stores (1850s), an 1869 lighthouse, the museum wharf, and historic vessels. Open Tu-Su 10am-5pm. Admission $8, students $5, families $18.

Migration Museum (tel. 8207 7580), on Kintore Ave. Combines history, biography, and oral testimony to give insight into the patterns of immigration that have shaped South Australian society. Free admission. 1hr. guided tours $4.50. All tours must be booked. Wheelchair access. Open M-F 10am-5pm, Sa-Su and holidays 1-5pm.

The Investigator Science and Technology Centre (tel. 8410 1115), on Rose Tce, Wayville. Interactive exhibits force even the most ardent technophobes to learn and have fun. Open daily 10am-5pm. $7.50, concessions $6, ages 4-17 $5.

H.M.S. Buffalo (tel. 8294 7000), along the Patawalonga, near Wigley Reserve in Glenelg. This reconstruction of the original sailboat that brought the first colonists to South Australia is now a free museum and seafood restaurant. Open 10am-5pm.

MARKETS

⊛**Central Markets** (tel. 8203 7345), between Gouger and Grote St. The largest enclosed fresh produce market in the Southern hemisphere, with more than 250 stalls, it has a bustling, cosmopolitan atmosphere and some of the best budget cuisine in Australia. Delicacies include pickled squid, taramasalata, German breads and pastries, fresh pasta, local nuts, dried fruits, and fairy floss (the Aussie version of cotton candy). The market also contains a superb variety of inexpensive cafes and restaurants. Near closing time, the market's at its rowdiest, and you can pick up bags of leftover veggies for $1 and breads and pastries at ½-price. Parking available. Open Tu 7am-5:30pm, Th 11am-5:30pm, F 7am-9pm, Sa 7am-5pm.

East End Markets, Rundle St East (tel. 8232 5606). All that is funky in Adelaide usually ends up for sale in the 200 stalls here. Clothing, ceramics, jewelry, leather goods, and plants at good prices if you shop around. There's also an extensive produce market and a cinema complex. 2hr. free parking in carpark opposite. Open F-Su and most holidays 9am-6pm.

Orange Lane Markets (tel. 8414 1346), Orange Ln, Norwood. A mecca for the New Age, Orange Lane sells everything from antiques to crystals to curry and embodies Adelaide's version of the 60s spirit. Some bargain gifts and gloriously retro clothing can be found. Once there, stroll down Norwood Parade for good shopping outlets, Italian cafes, and excellent bakeries. Open Sa-Su and holidays 10am-5pm.

Brickworks, 36 South Rd, Torrensville, (tel. 8352 4822), refers to the markets centered in and around the old Brickworks kiln. A multitude of stalls and shops with fresh produce pottery, new-age jewelry, clothing, bikes, ceramics, arts and crafts, and a pet shop. Unique features include go-carts, sideshows, and mini golf. Parking at rear off Ashwin Parade. Open F-Su and holidays that fall on Monday, 9am-5pm.

Junction Markets (tel. 8349 4866), at the corner of Grand Junction and Prospect Rd, provide a great winter alternative, since they are in a large shed. Features mainly hardware, leather goods, plants, and sometimes live bands. There's also an international food hall and plentiful fresh produce. Open Sa-Su and holidays 9am-5pm.

Fisherman's Wharf Market (tel. 8341 2040), by the lighthouse, Port Adelaide. The market is contained within 5000 square meters of a 1940s cargo shed. Linen, glass, bric-a-brac, arts and crafts, clothing, hardware, garden supplies, and old sheet music all at bargain prices. A wide range of food and refreshments and the freshest of seafood. Open Su and holidays that fall on Monday, 8am-5pm.

Boomerang Arts and Crafts Centre, 716 Anzac Hwy, Glenelg (tel./fax 8376 3921). Though not technically a market, this Glenelg gallery has a large selection of Aboriginal art, didgeridoos, and Australian opals.

■ Nightlife and Entertainment

In this "family" city, most areas shut down promptly at 6pm, and the streets of Adelaide after dark can seem like a post-apocalyptic waste zone. If you know where to look, however, Adelaide maintains a thriving nightlife into the wee hours. The clubs along Hindley St and the hip restaurants and pubs lining Rundle, O'Connell, Hutt, and Melbourne Streets are where to find the noise. Besides a lively music and gambling scene, Adelaide has some old pubs for casual drinks and cinemas for movie buffs. To know what's on, pick up Thursday's *Advertiser,* which will include *The Guide.* Also, *Rip it Up,* an alternative entertainment newspaper, is free and available in cafes, bookstores, record stores, universities, and hostels around town. The *Adelaide Review* has some good nightlife information as well. *GT (Gay Times)* provides information on gay and lesbian events and nightlife, lists of gay-friendly establishments, and articles. It's free at **BSharp Records** on Rundle St or at the **Adelaide University Union** (in the North Tce Uni Complex).

Adelaide's two new alternative cinemas, both on Rundle St, are **The Palace East-end** (tel. 8232 3434) and **NOVA** (tel. 8223 6333). The classic art house cinema is **The**

Trak, 375 Greenhill Rd (tel. 8332 8020). **The Capri,** 141 Goodwood Rd (tel. 8272 1177), and **The Piccadily,** O'Connell St, North Adelaide (tel. 8267 1500), have good mainstream and alternative offerings. Movies run around $12 ($8 concession), and most theaters offer discount nights during the week. The Capri also has a kitschy but great **Wurlitzer Organ recital,** complete with moving parts and a trap door (Tu, F, Sa nights). Next to The Palace Eastend is an **IMAX theatre** (tel. 8227 0075) with the world's biggest screen ($12.95, $9.95 concession; $1 more for 3D shows).

Good pubs for a quiet beer include **The British,** 58 Finness St, North Adelaide (tel. 8267 2188), and **The Earl of Aberdeen,** Carrington St at Hurtle Square (tel. 8223 6433). Both are woodsy, old-style pubs with a variety of beers on tap and good pub meals. Trendier pubs are **The Exeter** (tel. 8223 2623) and **The Austral** (tel. 8223 4660), known affectionately by the locals as the "Excreter" and the "Nostril," and the **Lion Hotel** (tel. 8367 0222) on Melbourne St. All serve a colorful clientele and feature up-and-coming pub bands on weekends. Call for cover charges. If you're feeling lucky, **The Casino,** Old Railway Building, North Tce (tel. 8212 2811), provides gambling excitement and a place to hang out long after the rest of Adelaide snoozes. (Open M-F 10am-4am, Sa-Su 24hr. Smart casual dress required (collared shirt and jacket for men, no sneakers or denims). **Edinburgh Castle,** 233 Currie St (tel. 8410 1211), has a mainly gay male clientele, a pub atmosphere, beer garden, and recently refurbished interior. **Bean's Bar,** 258a Hindly St (tel. 8231 9614), has a mixed gay and lesbian clientele who save it from being simply another "daggy Aussie pub." (Women only F 6:30-9:30pm.) The pace picks up around 10:30pm Saturday and Sunday.

If you prefer dancing to pub-schmoozing, check out these **clubs:**

Heaven II, at the New Market Hotel on the corner of North and East Tce, provides a celestial vision of sorts, if your idea of the afterlife is a hedonistic mix of alcohol, dance music, lycra, and nubile 20-somethings. Opens 9pm W-Su. Lineup includes DJs, local bands, and internationally renowned acts (cover varies accordingly).

Cargo Club, 213 Hindly St (tel. 8231 2327). One of Adelaide's funkier clubs, the Cargo is a great spot for live music and funky decor. An interesting crowd swings between trendy and alternative. Cover around $6. Doors open at 10pm.

The Big Ticket, 128 Hindly St (tel. 8410 0109). Loud, packed, and lots of fun for a night of serious partying, dancing, and drinking. No cover.

The Planet, 77 Pine St (tel. 8359 2797). House music and hundreds of tightly packed, writhing young bodies imbue this hugely successful nightclub with hipness. Upstairs viewing area and downstairs lounge provide escape space. Cover $8.

Cue, 274 Rundle St, Level 1 (tel. 8223 6160). Adjacent to Scuzzi Cafe, this club is home to Adelaide's beautiful people. The bouncers are selective, so dress hip or don't even try. House music is the usual. There's pinball and pool if you don't feel cool enough to dance with the elect. No cover. Open W-Su nights.

The Synagogue, 9 Synagogue Place (tel. 8223 4233), just off the Pultney St end of Rundle St. It seems apt that a city so concerned with both the spiritual and the pleasurable should be home to a nightclub housed in the Heritage-listed and once-Orthodox Jewish synagogue. When the Jewish community decided it was time for a newer, larger complex, marketers remodeled this place into a funky dance club and live music venue, complete with its own garish 10 commandments and other semitic symbols. Open Th-Sa with varying cover.

The Mars Bar, 120 Gouger St (tel. 8231 9636). Campy surrounds and aging queens make the Mars Bar a haven for rejects from *Priscilla: Queen of the Desert.* Drag nights F and Sa. A mix of straight and gay clientele. Good for a late-night bop and a glimpse at this week's fashion *faux pas.*

■ Near Adelaide: Adelaide Hills

In a state where much of the terrain is unfriendly at best, the Adelaide Hills provide a haven of lush greenery, a suburban playground within minutes of Adelaide. As you climb toward the Mt. Lofty summit, Adelaide's lights, coastline, and green belts of parklands unfold below you. But don't just look down. Huge expanses of national parkland surround the peak, broken up by wineries, orchards, and picturesque towns from a gentler, slower past. You can browse in the numerous arts and crafts stores, sample the many family bakeries, take long, deep breaths of the fresh mountain air, and revel in the region's overwhelming sense of peace and relaxation.

GETTING THERE

Much of the Adelaide Hills is a 20- to 40-minute drive from the Adelaide city center. The main road through the Adelaide Hills is the South Eastern Freeway (Hwy 1), and town exits are clearly marked. To take **public transportation,** call the **Hills Transit Phone** (tel. 8210 1000) for routes, timetables, and fares. Bus #840 runs to Mt. Barker, #841 to Nairne, #842 and 843 to Strathalbyn, #822 to Cleland Wildlife Park, and #105 to Morialta Falls and Conservation Park. These buses leave from Currie St. Buses #163, 165, 166, and TL9 run daily from Currie St to smaller towns in the area. Other ways to get to the hills include car hire or a day tour; the latter is generally cheaper if you're not traveling in a group. **Tour Delights** (tel. 8262 6900) runs a variety of daytrips, and **Shaun's Bound-Away** offers a tour of Adelaide Hills for $43 (VIP/YHA $39). The region's main **information center** is in Hahndorf (tel. 8388 1185, see below); other tourist offices are located at Mt. Lofty's summit and in Strathylbyn.

ACCOMMODATIONS

Unfortunately, there is not a lot of budget accommodation in the Adelaide Hills. If you are planning on hiking in the hills, however, YHA maintains the **Adelaide Hills Hostel Walking Chain,** which consists of five **"limited access" hostels** along the **Heysen Trail.** They are located at Para Wirra, Norton Summit, Mt. Lofty, Mylor, and Kuitpo. Bookings must be made in advance at the YHA office, 32 Sturt St, Adelaide (tel. 8231 5583), where you will be given a key and map. Be warned: these hostels, though well-kept, only provide bare bones amenities (beds, kitchen, and bathrooms). Hikers must bring all bedding and food ($13 per night, non-members $16).

Fuzzies Farm, Colonial Dr, Norton Summit (tel. 8390 1111), provides more unconventional lodging and a glimpse at what post-industrial society might be like. Proprietors Fuzzy and Ruth believe the society of the future will be based on communal businesses (run and owned by a group, not a boss) and an ethic-driven market. Members are fed and lodged in lovely cabins overlooking the 3500 acres of beautiful bushland that make up **Morialta Conservation Park,** and all are actively involved in environmental and heritage issues, farming and management concerns, and the preservation of Aboriginal sacred sites. ($80 a week, plus chores. Meals included. Regular backpacker accommodation $29 the first night, $15 thereafter, including dinner and breakfast. Booking is essential.)

SIGHTS AND ACTIVITIES

The biggest attraction in the Adelaide Hills is **Mt. Lofty (Urebilla),** visited by 500,000 people annually. Take the South Eastern Freeway out of the city, exit at Crafers, and follow the signs. The local Aboriginal people, the Kaurna, describe Mt. Lofty and Mt. Bonython as Jureidla—"the place of the two ears." According to their tradition, the mountains are the ears of Urebilla (a benevolent ancestral being slain in battle), whose body forms the Mt. Lofty Ranges. Urebilla's feet lie north toward Clare and his head points south toward Victor Harbor. His spirit gives life to all in the plains and valley below. The summit has spectacular views of the city, as well as an extensive **Information Centre** (tel. 8370 1054; http://www.denr.sa.gov.au/nrg/mtlofty) with detailed information about the surrounding **Cleland Conservation Park,** and a restaurant-cafe (tel. 8339 2600). Mt. Lofty's original information center was destroyed by bushfires in 1983, and the new state-of-the-art center was just completed in 1997. *(Open Nov.-Mar. 10am-6pm, Apr.-Nov. 10am-4pm. Outdoor viewing plaza area open 24hr. Free.)* A popular hiking trail leaves from the summit and descends past four waterfalls, providing access to Cleland Wildlife Park along the, way.

If you've ever had a penchant for a potoroo or a yen for a yellow-footed rock wallaby, but haven't wanted to go bush to see them, **Cleland Wildlife Park** (tel. 8339

2444 or 8339 2572), also located within Cleland Conservation Park, is the perfect compromise. *(Open daily 9:30am-5pm. Admission $7, students $6, children $4.50.)* Cleland is directly below the Mt. Lofty summit, and both can be experienced in an easy day-trip from Adelaide. The short walking trail can be competed in 1½ hours, and you can wander freely among kangaroos, koalas, wallabies, emus, and waterfowl along the way. **Night walks** (tel. 8339 2444) can be arranged as well, in order to view some of the rarer (and often endangered) species of wildlife. For a more intensive hike, try the numerous trails through the broader Cleland conservation park area. Some, like the **Women's Pioneer Trail,** have local historical significance, while others, such as the **ETSA Spur Track,** are designed to display local flora and fauna.

For more wildlife, the **Warrawong Sanctuary** (tel. 8370 9422; fax 8370 8332) at Stock Rd in Mylor offers unforgettable dawn and sunset walks through the rainforest, which boasts over 50,000 native plants, as well as bettongs, wallabies, birds, the rare platypus, and southern short-nosed bandicoot. Walks cost $15 per person. To get to Warrawong, take the South Eastern Freeway, exit at the Mt. Barker Rd, when you see signs for Stirling, turn right on Longwood Rd and then left on Stock Rd (follow signs). Transportation from Adelaide is provided by **Eucalyptours** (tel. 8339 4507).

Other area attractions include **Melba's Chocolate Factory** (tel. 8389 7868; fax 8389 7977), on Henry St in Woodside. With free entry and free samples seven days per week, and deals on bags of misformed (but tasty!) candy, the factory is more pop-ular than most industrial complexes. The **biggest rocking horse in the world** is hitched along the road in Gumeracha. The 60-ft.-high red and white wooden beast actually marks the spot for **The Toy Factory** (tel. 8389 1085), open daily. Artisans make gorgeous, hand-crafted wooden toys, and the view from the horse's head is actually worth the climb. A seven-acre nature park surrounds the horse, and entrance is free.

Hahndorf

A little bit of Bavaria in Adelaide's backyard, Hahndorf is proud of its German heritage and flaunts its origins. In 1839, a group of Prussian Lutherans fled the motherland to escape religious persecution and ended up here. Just 35 minutes southeast of Ade-laide on the South Eastern Freeway, Hahndorf can be part of a larger day tour of the Adelaide Hills. The **Adelaide Hills Visitors Information Centre** is at 41 Main St (tel. 8388 1185).

The **Cedars: Hans Heysen's House,** Heysen Rd (tel. 8388 7277 or 1800 353 323), was the home of Australian artist Hans Heysen (1877-1963) and has been preserved in its original state. This landscape watercolor artist had the 1500km Heysen trail (and his own street, apparently) named after him. See where Hans ate, slept, and spilled paint as you tour his house, studio, and garden. (Open M-F and Su; admission $5; tours at 11am, 1, and 3pm.) Masterpieces of the future could be in progress at the **Hahndorf Academy** (tel. 8388 7250), on Main St. The academy includes an art gal-lery, museum, and craft shop, and much of Heysen's own stunning collection, stolen in 1995, is now back on show. (Open M-Sa 10am-5pm, Su noon-5pm).

At **Beerenberg Strawberry Farm,** Mt. Barker Rd (tel. 8388 7272; fax 8388 1108), half a kilometer through Hahndorf, you can pick your own strawberries in season (Oct.-May) or let someone else do it while you view the farm kitchen. Jams, pickles, and other innovative strawberry ideas are all on sale in the farm shop (open M-F).

If the Hansel and Gretel atmosphere of the town has you longing for some ginger-bread or hankering for a fine glass of German beer, you'll be pleased to find *gutes Essen* everywhere. Hahndorf won't let you forget where you are; almost every restau-rant includes the word "German" in its name. For a budget-oriented meal, head straight for the various (German, of course) bakeries and cafes. Some of the most authentic and tasty German cuisine can be found at the low-key **Karl's German Cof-fee House,** at the far end of Main St. **Hahndorf Gourmet Foods,** just past the info center, has loads of real German sausage links and light meals. One of the best baker-ies is the **German Cake Shop,** 2 Pine Ave (tel. 8388 7086). Try *Sacher Torte* for a sweet tooth, or *Sauerkraut* for something more substantial. (Open daily 8am-6pm.)

Mt. Barker and Strathalbyn

Both Mt. Barker and Strathalbyn are worth short visits, if only to browse in the local **arts and crafts shops** and view some of the lovely **heritage buildings** that lend character to these little settlements. But most importantly, Mt. Barker and Strathalbyn provide the back way into the Fleurieu Peninsula via car or the recently reconstructed *Southern Encounter* and *Cockle Train* **steam engines.** These vintage reproduction trains will spirit you away to the coastal towns of Goolwa and Victor Harbor (p. 414) or shuttle you between Mt. Barker and Strathalbyn (bookings tel. 8391 1223; fares: adult $15, child $8, senior $13). Strathalbyn's **tourist info center** (tel. 8536 3212) is in the old railway station at 20 South Tce (open M-F 9:30am-4pm, Sa 10am-4pm, Su 11am-4pm).

FLEURIEU PENINSULA

The Fleurieu (FLOOR-ee-oh) Peninsula has rolling hills and sweeping valleys to justify its sing-songy name. The Kauma tell the story of Tjilbruke, who carried the body of his slain nephew down the coast to Cape Jervis from where the Adelaide suburb Marion now sits. Each time that Tjilbruke stopped along the way and wept for his nephew, a spring welled up from the ground. From these tears grew the lush section of South Australia that stretches southeast from Adelaide, encompassing the hills and wineries of McLaren Vale. The Fleurieu Peninsula also boasts the small-town attractions of Victor Harbor and miles of coastline that include some of the best beaches in South Australia.

The Fleurieu regional office for the **National Parks and Wildlife Service** (tel. 8552 3677; fax 8552 3950) is at 57 Ocean St in Victor Harbor (open M-F 8:45am-5pm). If you're planning your trip in advance, the **Fleurieu Regional Booking Office** (tel. 1800 630 144) may be able to help. On dry, summer days, a complete fire ban may be in effect; call the **CFS Fire Ban Hotline** (tel. 1800 188 100). If in medical trouble, dial the **Goolwa Medical Centre** (tel. 8555 2404), call an **ambulance** (tel. 8552 2111), or, as always, dial **000** in an **emergency.** For car trouble, contact the **RAA** (tel. 8555 2009). The **police** are at 8555 2018.

■ McLaren Vale

Just 45 minutes south of Adelaide, McLaren Vale sits in the grassy inland knolls of the Fleurieu Peninsula. McLaren Vale is an idyllic, sleepy set of vineyards, where world-class wines are produced in a typically understated Australian manner. Over 45 area wineries, the majority of which are still family-owned, operate cellar door sales and grow and process their product meters from the front door. If you're a collector, buy a dozen, but if you're just an amateur, sip and smile in blissful ignorance, knowing full well that the best thing about wine tasting is that it's absolutely free.

ORIENTATION AND PRACTICAL INFORMATION

The best way to get to McLaren Vale is with a group of friends, a car, and a **designated driver.** Take the last part seriously, because the Australian police take drunk driving *extremely* seriously. It is not uncommon to find Random Breath Testing Units (commonly known as Breathos) stationed on main roads to and from wine regions. That said, drive out of Adelaide on Main South Rd. After 20-30 minutes, follow the signs for McLaren Vale, which lead to Main Rd. After you pass a row of flags proudly proclaiming the best vineyards in the region, the **McLaren Vale and Fleurieu Visitor Centre** (tel. 8323 9455) will be directly to your left. Drop in, grab a map, and off you go. The **police station** (tel. 8323 8330) and the **post office** (no. 139) are also on Main Rd.

Geographically, McLaren Vale is just east of the coast as you head south on the Fleurieu Peninsula, between Port Stanvac and Aldinga Beach. The public transportation,

Premier Coachlines (tel. 8415 5555), runs a daily bus service from Adelaide at 10am, 3:50, and 5:30pm ($5). If you take public transportation, though, getting around once in McLaren Vale will be a problem. A more practical way to avoid driving yourself is to take one of the numerous **tours** based in Adelaide. **Tour Delights** (tel. 0411 470 094) runs tours from Adelaide every Tuesday and Sunday. **Sea and Vine Tours** (tel. 8384 5151) is another good option. (Day tours cost about $45. Consult the South Australia tourist office in Adelaide for an extensive list.)

ACCOMMODATIONS, FOOD, AND FESTIVALS

The majority of accommodations are old world heritage B&Bs at new world prices. You may be best off making the region a daytrip from Adelaide. There are options, however, for the intrepid traveler willing to venture a few minutes away from the McClaren Vale township. In Willunga, down Willunga or Victor Harbor Rd from McClaren Vale, which is less strip-malled and touristy than McClaren Vale, the **Willunga Hotel** (tel. 8556 2135) on High St offers cozy, old rooms (singles $20, doubles $40; breakfast included) and generous counter meals for $6-8 at the pub downstairs.

If you desire a serious dose of farm life, the **Emu Farm** (tel. 8556 3655) on Hahn Rd is quite a spot. The inspiring owners are living out their ideals and working towards self-sufficiency on this ecologically-correct yet fun-minded farm. They'd love to teach you about their farming techniques (which include recycling precious rainwater and farming indigenous trees) or sit you down for a piece of homemade emu egg quiche. (Dorms $10.) Families are welcome, as well as courteous and interested backpackers. Outdoor adventure outings can be arranged. Call for specific directions. **Lakeside Caravan Park** (tel. 8323 9255) on Field St offers basic on-site caravans with a separate block for toilets and showers. Each van sleeps two and is clean and comfortable, although it can be chilly in winter ($32).

The cheapest way to dine is to bring a picnic and buy a good drop at a picturesque winery. Most of the wineries have picnic grounds and some, like **Andrew Garrett**, offer tables as well. The other option is to try the great selection of bakeries. The folks at **McLaren Vale Bakery**, McLaren Vale Shopping Centre on Main Rd, are the winner of the National Pie Award for their Wine Pie. Other winners include the Lamb Piquant Pie and the Chicken Champagne Pie. Down the road, the orthographically challenged **Koffee & Snax** offers bottomless honey logs with fresh cream for a mere $1.50. If you are looking for a treat and are willing to splurge, any number of the gourmet restaurants in McLaren Vale would be happy to oblige. Try **d'Arry's Verandah Restaurant** on Osborn Rd or **The Barn** (tel. 8323 8618) on Main Rd. If you're up for a *real* lunch out, the **Sallopian Inn Restaurant** (tel. 8323 8769) at the intersection of McMurtrie and Willunga Rd, is one of the most excellent restaurants in SA, and is not outrageously priced. Main dishes, which make creative use of local ingredients, hover around $20. (Open everyday except W for lunch, F and Sa for dinner.)

Although the McLaren wineries make a great trip year-round, three annual festivals are particularly exciting. **McLaren Vale's Sea and Vines Festival** is held on the long holiday weekend in June (usually the first weekend), Sunday and Monday only. With seafood at $7 a plate and wine $3 a glass, this is a good deal for fine fare. The feast is complemented by live music at each of the participating wineries. On the Sunday and Monday of the long Labor Day weekend in October, **the Continuous Picnic** comes to town. Park your car, hop on the shuttle bus that runs between the wineries, and join in an all-day feast of local produce and wines (food $7 a plate, wine $3 a glass). Finally, the **McLaren Vale Wine Bushing Festival**, on the last weekend in October, marks the arrival of the season's new whites. Organizers provide food, entertainment, arts and crafts, and a Sunday street fair complete with a 60-float parade.

WINERIES

Wirra Wirra Vineyards, McMurtrie Rd (tel. 8323 8414; fax 8323 8596). When you see the fence made entirely from giant tree trunks you'll know you've arrived; once you've tasted the "Church Block Red," you won't want to leave. Wirra Wirra has won numerous awards for both reds and whites. If you prefer red make sure you taste their Cabernet Savignon. For a dry white, try the hand-picked Riesling. The friendly, knowledgeable staff make both wine buff and wine buffoon welcome.

Dennis of McLaren Vale, Kangarilla Rd (tel. 8323 8665). Fancy a drop of hot spiced mead? Made with honey, scented with cloves, and warmed by the glass, this is a superb wine for those with a sweeter tooth. Ironically located across the road from the Andrew Garrett supercomplex, this small winery is relievingly modest and down-to-earth. Turn at the sign that reads "Horse poo $1." Make sure to fuss over Sophie, the super-friendly family dog, to ensure greater complimentary quantities of this delicious brew (the wine, that is).

Marienberg Wines, 2 Chalk Hill Rd (tel. 8323 9666; fax 8323 9600) is centered in a warm, charming cottage built in 1854. You can try over 40 of McLaren Vale's boutique wines at this center as well as a selection of Marienberg's own, including a classy 12-year-old Tawny Port.

Shottesbrooke Vineyards, Bagshaws Rd, off Kangarilla Rd (tel. 8383 0002; fax 8383 0222). This is about as small and exclusive as a winery can get—1 family, 2 vineyards, and 4 wines. But what a *great* 4. Nick Holmes, the owner, aims for "big rich reds" and "luscious whites," and he gets what he aims for.

Noon Winery, Rifle Range Rd (tel./fax 8323 8290). Specializing in reds only, this rustic winery is a great place for a barbecue (there are facilities), since the wines will complement anything from your sausage to kangaroo cutlets.

Richard Hamilton Wines, Willunga Rd, Willunga (tel. 8556 2288). A fine selection of reds and whites to choose from, earning a number of state and national prizes. Small, family-owned and run; the family cat loves a cuddle.

Andrew Garrett Wines, Kangarilla Rd (tel. 8323 8853). One of the larger wineries with a broad selection of wines and an idyllic lake setting, complete with picnic tables and a flourishing troop of ducks, swans, and other varieties of bird life. **The Opal Gem Factory** is also situated on the premises.

Haselgrove Wines, off Chalk Hill Rd (tel. 8323 8706). Haselgrove can finish off a good day's tasting with an intense Tawny Port. Strictly for port lovers (those who want a good Cab Sav should steer clear of this one).

■ Beaches West of McLaren Vale

In the summer months, the beaches west of McLaren Vale are not to be missed. To get to **Maslin Beach** (SA's only nudist beach) by car, take South Rd out of the city. Turn onto Maslin Beach Rd and follow that onto Gulf Pde—parking is at the end of this road. To get to the southern end of the beach, turn left onto Eastview Rd from Maslin Beach Rd and right onto Tuit Rd. To get to **Moana Beach** by car, turn onto Griffiths Ave from South Rd. For **Christie's Beach,** turn onto Beach Rd from South Rd and follow it until the end, or take the Esplanade from Noarlunga Beach. For **Port Noarlunga,** turn left onto Dyson Rd from South Rd, then right onto Murray Rd and left onto Saltfleet St. To hit the southern beaches via **public transportation,** take the **Noarlunga line train** from Adelaide Railway Station (North Tce) to Noarlunga. Transfer to the #741 or 742 bus at the Noarlunga Interchange for Maslin Beach or Moana Beach. For Christie's Beach, transfer to bus #741 only. For Port Noarlunga, take bus #741, 742, or 745.

■ Victor Harbor

Sheltered from the immense Southern Ocean by the sands of Encounter Bay, the small seaside town of Victor Harbor is not totally sleepy but is hardly wide awake. Despite its cheesy tourist brochures and typical beachside amusements, Victor Harbor has a genuine ocean heart. After colonial settlement, South Australia's governors chose Victor Harbor as their first summer residence. First a whaling port and later a shipping port for wool and farm produce, Victor Harbor (one of the few harbors in Australia spelled without a "u") is now a charming spot for a summer seaside frolic or a serious surf in Encounter Bay, and the perfect place for contemplative winter weekends. Prior to white settlement, the bay, the bluff, and Granite Island had great spiritual importance for the local Ngarrindjeri. Nowadays, Victor Harbor has great spiritual importance for SA retirees; retirement settlements are a booming business around town.

ORIENTATION AND PRACTICAL INFORMATION Victor Harbor is 80km from Adelaide. By car, take Main South Rd out of Adelaide and watch for signs to Victor Harbor. By bus, **Premier Roadlines** (tel. 8415 5555) provides daily service from Adelaide ($11.50). *Southern Encounter,* the historic **steam train** running from Strathalbyn and between Goolwa and Victor Harbor is an alternative means of transport. Victor Harbor is small enough to navigate on foot, but the caves and beaches are easily accessible only by car. Most attractions are around Railway Tce, the Causeway, and Ocean St. **The Visitor Information Centre,** 10 Railway Tce behind the Grosvenor Hotel, is open daily from 10am to 4pm (with extended hours in Dec. and Jan.). The local **RAA** number is 8552 1033. For **police,** call 8552 2088. The **South Coast District Hospital** (tel. 8552 1066) and **Victor Harbor Medical Clinic** (tel. 8552 1444) are both right in town.

ACCOMMODATIONS AND FOOD Book ahead for accommodation in Victor Harbor, especially Dec.-Feb., as the town overflows in summer. There are no hostels, but two of the hotels provide backpacker-style dorms. **The Anchorage,** at the corner of Coral St and Flinders Pde (tel. 8552 5970; fax 8552 1970), is right on the sea, and offers gorgeous views of the Southern Ocean. Primarily a hotel and B&B, it houses a Nomads Backpackers with a kitchen and rooms for $15 without linen or breakfast. Cozy guesthouse rooms have private sink and shower, linen, lace curtains, and hall bathroom (double $60, single $35, includes breakfast). The **Grosvenor Junction,** at the corner of Coral and Ocean St (tel. 8552 1011; fax 8552 7274), offers clean rooms and is three blocks from the shore. The Grosvenor is primarily a hotel and pub but has some rooms set aside for backpackers. ($20 per person includes continental breakfast, linen, and hall bathroom.) **Victor Harbor Council Caravan Park** (tel. 8552 1142), on the beachfront off Victoria St, near the Shell station, has unpowered sites for $12 per night, plus $4 per person in excess of two. Groups can hire a house or cottage through the **Fleurieu Booking Office** (tel. 1800 630 144).

Café Bavaria on Albert Place, next to Hotel Victor, has good coffee and sweets, and **Marg's Place** in the mall between Ocean and Stuart St offers cozy cafe fare. The **Anchorage Hotel** also has an upscale cafe with reasonable drinks and snacks.

A day at Victor Harbor is incomplete without seafood. **The Original Fish n' Chip** shop on Ocean St. has top grade—surprise—fish and chips. For those with less limited budgets or bigger appetites, the hotels provide excellent seafood at reasonable prices. The higher end of the scale is the **Hotel Victor** (tel. 8552 1288) on the seafront, by the causeway, and the lower end is the **Grosvenor** (tel. 8552 1011), on the corner of Coral and Ocean St, which is crowded with locals and offers cheap soup and a salad bar.

SIGHTS AND ACTIVITIES Little penguins win top billing on **Granite Island.** Entry onto this little island is free if you walk (a 20min. stroll from the causeway entrance) or $3 if you take the horse-drawn tram (complete with huge Clydesdales). At night, you can see the island's penguins by joining one of the **Little Penguin Sunset Walks** (tel. 8552 7555; $5). The walks generally begin at sunset and start at the bridge entrance to the island. Call for times and bookings. The **Victor Theatre** on Ocean St plays new, mainstream movies on one screen.

For smaller creatures, including koalas, nocturnal native animals, and dingoes, check out the **Urimbirra Wildlife Park** (tel. 8554 6554). *(Open 9am-5pm. Admission $6.50, children $3.50, 10% student discount.)* The wildlife park is gorgeous and is situated across from **Nangawookka Flora Park,** creating a home for thousands of varieties of native flora and fauna. Plan to spend at least a few hours here on a nice day.

Fifteen thousand people come to town each year for the 700 performers and 120 events of October's **Victor Harbor Folk Festival.** The festivities go on during the October Labor Day weekend. For info call the Folk Festival Office (tel. 8340 1069; fax

8346 8506). Accommodation and ticket info is available at 1800 630 144 or 0885 552 800.

■ Cape Jervis

Cape Jervis is the jumping-off point for the **Kangaroo Island ferry** and the **Heysen Trail** and not much else. The town itself is little more than a bunch of decrepit buildings along the shore. If you do end up here however, never fear—the surrounding mainland coastline and parks, oft ignored by those jetting off to KI and left for the more peaceful visitor, are worth exploring.

Cape Jervis Station (tel. 8598 0288 or 1800 805 288) and the **Old Cape Jervis Homestead** (tel. 8598 0233 or 1800 246 450), located adjacent to each other along the main road a few kilometers before town, can provide a pleasant holiday in themselves. Owned by the same family, the station is a homey, grandmotherly place which offers ornate in-house rooms. (Singles $50; with 4 people, $35 per person.) There's also a self-contained log cabin outside ($35 for one, $70 for group of four). Breakfast and dinner are available. The Homestead, next door, is more rustic and farmy, but also offers clean and comfortable rooms. In-house, B&B accommodations are $45 per person, but the Homestead also has shearers' quarters backpacker beds ($17.50 per person) and on-site tent and caravan sites.

Other than these more-than-pleasant options, pickings for food and bed in Cape Jervis are slim. The **Cape Jervis Hotel/Motel and Tavern** on Main St has meals and a general store, as well as uninspiring accommodation. **The Kiosk** by the ferry provides tourist information on scenic flights, ferry tickets, and accommodations, as well as typical hot-dog stand food.

If you have transportation and are up for camping in a breathtaking spot, **Deep Creek Conservation Park,** 4km northeast of Cape Jervis towards Victor Harbor, offers campgrounds with limited facilities ($10 per car) and bushcamping ($5 per car). This park offers amazing and accessible seacoast views of the **Backstairs Passage** and **Kangaroo Island,** good bushwalking, lots of wildlife, and more solitude than **Flinders Chase National Park** across the way. **Blowhole Beach,** 3 steep kilometers from Cobbler Hill picnic area, and **Deep Creek Cove,** 6.4km from Tapanappa Campground, are two spectacular walks which cross the **Heysen Trail.** Visit the **Park Headquarters** (tel. 8598 0263) for maps, information, and fees.

KANGAROO ISLAND

A popular summertime escape from the rigors of mainland life to the isolation of the Southern Ocean, Kangaroo Island (pop. 4000) is located across the Backstairs Passage from the South Australian Fleurieu Peninsula. At 156km long, it's Australia's third-largest island. With 30% of its land contained in national parks, Kangaroo Island teems with well-protected flora and fauna. The sprawling **Flinders Chase National Park** occupies the island's western corner, allowing both distinctive indigenous wildlife and endangered mainland species to thrive. Visitors enjoy strolling among snoozing sea lions or the much-hyped little penguins, past the awesome geological formations of **Remarkable Rocks, Admirals Arch,** and **Kelly Hill Caves,** or down the pleasant swimming beaches and small town streets of **Kingscote** and **Penneshaw.** The winters can be a bit lonely, but if it's solitude you seek, you'll find it here. "Nature's Pleasure Island" is pretty much left to nature as crowds slow and cooler temperatures set in.

■ Getting There and Around

Kangaroo Island is accessible by ferry and airplane, but once on the island there is **no public transportation,** and most roads are unsealed. The best options are bringing a car over on the ferry, renting a car, or signing up for a tour (none of which is particularly cheap). Relying on bike or scooter rental or walking is possible, but severely lim-

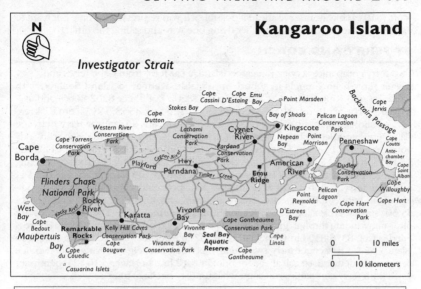

Kangaroo Island

Investigator Strait

Phone numbers on Kangaroo Island have recently changed. Regional phone codes are now all 08, followed by eight-digit numbers. If you have trouble making a call, use the following scheme to get the old number, and try that instead.

New Number:	Old Number:	New Number:	Old Number:
(08) 8553 5xxx	(0848) 35 xxxx	(08) 8553 3xxx	(0848) 23 xxxx
(08) 8553 1xxx	(0848) 31 xxxx	(08) 8553 8xxx	(0848) 28 xxxx
(08) 8559 4xxx	(0848) 94 xxxx	(08) 8553 9xxx	(0848) 29 xxxx
(08) 8559 6xxx	(0848) 96 xxxx	(08) 8559 5xxx	(0848) 97 xxxx
(08) 8559 3xxx	(0848) 93 xxxx	(08) 8553 7xxx	(0848) 33 xxxx
(08) 8553 4xxx	(0848) 21 xxxx	(08) 8559 7xxx	(0848) 37 xxxx
(08) 8553 2xxx	(0848) 22 xxxx	(08) 8559 2xxx	(0848) 36 xxxx

its access to many of the island's main attractions. **Kangaroo Island Ferry Connections** (1800 018 484 (SA only) or (08) 8553 1233) offers package tours geared towards backpackers, including round trip coach/ferry transportation from Adelaide, island tours, and overnight lodging at the Penguin Walk Hostel (2-day tours $163-$225). Tours are informative and relaxing, but may rush through the island's natural attractions. To explore at your own pace, organize your own transportation.

BY AIR

With advance purchase, flights from Adelaide (30min.) rival the ferry's cost. The **Kingscote Airport** is located 15km from the town of Kingscote and contains three airlines and two rental car agents. **Kendell Airlines** (tel. 8553 2855; fax 8553 2820) has an office at 61 Dauncey St in downtown Kingscote in addition to their terminal space. (2-3 flights per day; $45 each way if purchased 7 days in advance. Open daily 8:30am-5pm.) Kendell passengers enjoy a 10% discount on **Budget** car rental. **Albatross Airlines** (tel. 8553 2296; in Adelaide 8234 3399) provides service three times daily ($108 return, $70 children, if purchased 7 days in advance). They provide complimentary shuttle drop-off and pick-up anywhere in Kingscote. **Emu Airways** (Adelaide tel. 8234 3711; fax 8234 3747) is not as earthbound as its flightless namesake (2-5 flights per day, $120 return, if purchased 2 weeks in advance). Both Emu and Albatross limit the luggage load to 10kg checked and 3kg carry-on, charging $1 per kg thereafter. An **airport shuttle** (tel. 8553 2390) runs between the airport and Kingscote ($10 each way; reserve ahead if possible). If you're pressed for time but want to experience the ferry as well, consider flying one way and sailing the other.

BY FERRY AND COACH

Two ferry companies service Kangaroo Island: a car ferry from Cape Jervis and a passenger ferry from Glenelg in suburban Adelaide. **Kangaroo Island Sealink,** with offices at 440 King William St, Adelaide (tel. 8202 8688, fax 8202 8666) and at 7 North Terrace, Penneshaw (tel. 8553 1122; fax 8553 1207; email kiexpert@sealink.com.au; http://www/sealink.com.au), runs a large car ferry between Cape Jervis and Penneshaw, departing Cape Jervis at 9am and 6pm daily, with additional service at 10am on Saturdays and during summer holidays. (1hr.; $30, children 3-14 $15, students $24; cars $65, bicycle/surfboards $5.) Sealink also runs connecting **coach** services between Adelaide's central bus station and Cape Jervis (1¾hr., $44 including ferry, children 3-14 $22, students $34, pensioners $40; hostel pick-up possible) and between Penneshaw, American River, and Kingscote ($11, children 3-14 $5.50, students/pensioners $7, reservations recommended). The coach trips are pleasant, winding through green hillsides on country roads. **Kangaroo Island Express Ferries** (tel. 8376 8300 in Glenelg, 8212 2132 in Adelaide, 8553 0222 on Kangaroo Island) runs a passenger ferry twice daily between Glenelg and Kingscote. Service depends on demand, so call ahead for bookings. (2 hr., $43, ages 5-16 $25, pensioner $40). Both ferry companies run somewhat touristy package tours as well.

BY CAR

A vehicle is indispensable to those who want to explore Kangaroo Island's remote sights. Most roads are unsealed but in good condition; 4WD is a plus, but not necessary. Hertz-affiliate **Kangaroo Island Rental Cars** (tel. 8553 2390 or 1800 088 296; fax 8553 2878) is in Kingscote on the corner of Franklin St and Telegraph Rd, and has counters at the airport and the Kingscote Wharf. Cars at any of these locations range from manual minis ($55 per day, $336 per week) to 4WD vehicles ($120 per day; open 9am-5pm). **Budget** (tel. 8553 3133), on Commercial and Dauncey St, serves the airport and Penneshaw. (Vehicles start at $59 per day, $385 per week. Open 9am-5pm.) **Koala Car Rentals** (tel. 8553 2399) operates out of a local shop on Telegraph Rd in Kingscote. (Cars from $55 per day, $315 per week; 12-seater minibuses $150 per day, $840 per week. Open daily 9am to at least 5pm.) All rental companies offer free shuttles between the airport and Kingscote.

■ Kingscote

Kingscote (pop. 1400) bustles by Kangaroo Island standards. Most of the island's commercial services operate in the town center. Established in 1836 as the first European settlement in South Australia, this micropolis combines modern amenities with rich historical heritage and diverse native flora and fauna.

ORIENTATION AND PRACTICAL INFORMATION

Kingscote is set against the ocean, overlooking Nepean Bay. To the north, hilly farmland and steep cliffs provide stunning views of the boat harbor and the shores of Western Cove. The cliffs descend and flatten into Reeves Point and the Bay of Shoals just north of town. South of Kingscote, the cliffs are less steep, descending to sea level at the mouth of the Cygnet River, where the wide swamplands are home to a wide variety of birds. In town, Dauncy St, running parallel to the coastline, is the main drag. Although the island's formal tourist office operates in Penneshaw, tourist information is available in the back of the **Kingscote Gift Shop** (tel. 8553 2165) on Dauncey and Commercial St. For information and maps of the island's national parks, visit the **Department of Environmental and Natural Resources** headquarters (tel. 8553 2381; open M-F 9am-5pm) on Dauncey St, between Murray and Drew St. In that same block is the **post office** (open M-F 9am-5pm; postal code 5223), the **Bank SA** (with a 24hr. **ATM**) and the **police station**.

ACCOMMODATIONS AND FOOD

The only real evening dinner options in Kingscote are the overpriced and touristy **Queenscliffe** and **Ozone Hotels**. Instead, stock up at **The Veggie Patch** (tel. 8553 3151), on Dauncy St between Murray and Drew St, and improvise (open M-F 9am-5:30pm, Sa 9am-12:30pm). **Foodland supermarket** is on Commercial and Osmond St (open M-F 9am-5:30pm, Sa 9am-12:30pm).

Ellson's Seaview (tel. 8553 2030; fax 8553 2368; email ellsons@kin.on.net), on Chapman Tce and Drew St across from the ocean swimming pool, overlooking the sea. Rooms in the **guesthouse** (formerly a hostel) are cheaper and quirkier than in the adjacent motel. Rooms have fridges, soap, handbasins, tea, and coffee, and access to the oceanfront veranda, comfortable lounge, clean communal bathroom with bathtub, and email terminals (at charge). You'll feel pampered, and it's worth every penny. Single $35, double $44, triple $51, extra child 3-14 $7. Book ahead.

Kangaroo Island Central Backpackers, 19 Murray St (tel. 8553 2787; fax 8553 2694), 4 blocks west of the coast. This facility has basic dorms, a large kitchen, and a lounge. The extremely budget-conscious who don't mind spartan quarters and a run-down backyard can take advantage of bicycle rentals, cheap breakfasts, laundry facilities, and a pool table. Dorms $14, twin/double $37, triple $17 per person, family (4) $16.25 per person. VIP, YHA. Linen hire $2.

Blue Gum Cafe (tel. 8553 2089), on Dauncey St between Murray and Commercial St, serves home-cooked food with a sunny disposition. Breakfast from 7:30am (omelettes $4.50, cappucino $2) and a variety of snazzy burgers and sandwiches, including veggie options. Kangaroo burger $6.50, lentil buger $4.90, shoestring fries $2.50, fancy foccacia $7. Open M-F 7:30am-5:30pm, Sa 7:30am-1:30pm.

Rabbit Warren Bakery (tel. 8553 3299), on Dauncy St between Murray and Drew St. Just a bakery, but bakeries like this can go a long way. A wide array of donuts, pastries, rolls, buns, etc. from $1.25-$2. Open M-F 8am-5:30pm, Sa 8am-noon.

SIGHTS

Kingscote's primary historical attractions are clustered in the **Reeves Point Historical Area** on the north end of the Esplanade. Even if the sights themselves don't interest you, the walk descending from the hills to the low point of land surrounded by the water is worth it. Walking along the Esplanade from town, you'll approach **South Australia's oldest European tree,** a mulberry that was planted in 1836 and still bears fruit. Nearby, a marker commemorates **Kingscote's first post office.** At the top of the hill, you'll see a **pioneer memorial** and a view of the Bay of Shoals to your left and Nepean Bay to the right. The old **cemetery** occupies a small wooded glen overlooking the sea on the south slope of the hill.

West along Seaview Rd is the **Hope Cottage Museum** on Centenary St. *(Open daily Sept-June 2-4pm; also winter school holidays 10am-noon. $2.50, children 50¢.)* Three rooms are preserved with elegant 19th century furnishings and memorabilia. One room is reserved for historical documents, one for reading, and one as a regional museum with a wide assortment of local, historically significant holdings. Sheds outside house farm machinery and tractors spanning a century of agriculture, and an outdoor historical display chronicles sea and air transport to Kangaroo Island. If you climb to the top of the small courtyard **lighthouse,** you'll be rewarded both by the view and by the beautifully etched glass. The front lawn houses a small **heritage garden** and a **eucalypt press,** where you can watch the production of eucalypt oil (small vials sold for $3) from the Kangaroo Island narrow-leaved mallee.

A refreshing summer spot is the **John Downing Swimming Pool Reserve,** in front of the Ellson's Seaview guesthouse. This ocean pool ringed in mortared rocks has 1m diving platforms, showers, and cabanas by the shore. At dusk, the rocky coast north of the pool and all the way out to the jetty awakens with **little penguin** activity.

Though not as prominent as the Penneshaw sites, Kingscote's coastal burrows still receive a fair-sized flock. Guided tours of the burrows depart twice nightly in front of the Ozone Hotel. *(7:30 and 8:30pm in winter, 9:00 and 9:30pm in summer; $5, $3 children, $13.50 family.)* **Pelicans** take center stage at the jetty every day at 4pm when a feeding brings them together to jostle for fish.

■ Around Kingscote

South and west of Kingscote, many of Kangaroo Island's distinctive cottage industries invite the public to tour and purchase on-site. While catering to tourists, the farms are owned by locals and are interesting if you ask more than mundane questions. In Cygnet River, 12km from Kingscote, you can tour the dairy and cheese factory, sample products, and watch the sheep being milked at the **Island Pure Sheep Milking Dairy** (tel. 8553 9110) on Gum Creek Rd. In case you miss the milking (3-5pm) or dairy processing, there's a detailed video. (Open Sept.-May 10am-5pm; admission $3, under 15 $2.) South of Kingscote just off Hundred Line Rd on Willsons Rd is **Emu Ridge** (tel. 8553 8228; fax 8553 8272), a eucalyptus distillery that offers tours. Sold on-site, the mildly toxic oil is a cleanser, lubricant, topical antibiotic, and insect repellant. Distillation produces 5L of oil from a ton of leaves. (Open daily 9am-2pm. Free admission; frequent guided tours $3.) **Emu Bay,** on the other hand, is 18km northwest of Kingscote. This popular local swimming beach is accessible by sealed road. Along the foreshore, **Emu's Nest** (tel. 8553 5384) provides food and drink.

South of Emu Ridge, along Hundred Line Rd between Moores Rd and Barretts Rd, **Clifford's Honey Farm** (tel. 8553 8295) produces the honey of Ligurian bees. Island natives since 1881, they're the only pure and disease-free strain of bee in the world and produce a rich, impeccable honey. Clifford's offers tours of the hives and a variety of honey and beeswax products. (Open daily 9am-5pm; free admission; tours $2, concessions $1.) **Parndana Wildlife Park** (tel. 8553 6050), 3km west of Parndana on the Playford Hwy, offers the usual zoo selection of native and exotic fauna. Along with 'roos, tamar wallabies, and feral pigs, you'll find a few freakish domesticated animals. (Open daily 9am-5pm.)

■ Penneshaw

The sleepy, slightly run-down seaside hamlet of Penneshaw (pop. 250) perches on Kangaroo Island's northeast coast, and serves as the primary ferry arrival point from Cape Jervis on the mainland. Penneshaw's main draw, besides the ferry, is its **little penguin colony.** Each night, with curious amateur naturalists looking on, the penguins return to their burrows lining the coastline. The **Penguin Interpretive Centre,** on the shore off Middle Terrace's east end, offers the best way to see the world's smallest penguin species. Open nightly for three hours starting at dusk, it offers an informative display and interesting ranger-guided tours. (Tours 7:30 and 8:30pm in winter; 8:30 and 9:30pm during daylight savings. $5, children $3.50, families $13.50. Profits fund penguin protection efforts.) There is also a specially lit viewing boardwalk adjacent to the center. If you choose to explore the coastline yourself, please step carefully to avoid damaging penguin burrows. Stay at least 3m from the penguins, and don't shine flashlights in their eyes.

The **Kangaroo Island Gateway Visitors Centre** (tel. 8553 1185) is 1km down the road towards Kingscote from Penneshaw's ferry terminus (open M-F 9am-5pm, Sa-Su 10am-4pm). The **post office** is on Nat Thomas St between Middle Tce and North Tce (open M-F 9am-5pm, Sa 9am-11:30am; postal code 5223). For a nice meal, head up North Tce past the youth hostel to **The Old Post Office Courtyard** (tel. 8553 1063), next to the fancier **Restaurant.** In a family-friendly atmosphere, the Old Post Office offers a children's play room and reasonably priced meals including local seafood and produce. (Dinner Th-M from 5:30pm.) The **Penneshaw Supermarket** is on Middle Tce between Nat Thomas St and Bay Tce (open M-F 9am-5pm, Sa 9am-noon).

The **Penneshaw Youth Hostel (YHA),** 43 North Tce (tel. 8553 1284 or 1800 018 258; fax 8553 1295), offers functional accommodations and a heated TV lounge connected to the kitchen facilities and bathrooms. The adjoining **Blue Dolphin Cafe** offers cheap, tasty meals, a laundromat, and a souvenir shop. (Dorms $14, linen $1; YHA, VIP. Reserve several weeks in advance during summer.) One block south on the corner of Middle Tce and Bay Tce, the **Penguin Walk Hostel** (tel. 8553 1233) has converted motel units into dorm-style accommodations. Flexible room configurations and private bathrooms provide space for families or groups. The rooms are complemented by a laundry facility and a pizzeria next door. Kangaroo Island Ferry Connections operates the hostel and coordinates package tours at the adjacent office. (Dorms $14, twins and doubles $36. Linen $1; light breakfast $2.)

■ Seal Bay Conservation Park

Arguably Kangaroo Island's finest natural attraction, Seal Bay allows visitors to stroll through a colony of Australian sea lions. This is the rarest sea lion species in the world, and Kangaroo Island has 600 of the world population of 12,000. Weave your way between cows and bulls sunning on the sand, or stick to the boardwalk and watch the snoozing beasts below.

The park is on the island's southern coast, 60km along a sealed road from Kingscote. Here, an award-winning, environmentally sound **visitors center** (tel. 8553 4207) offers general information, a gift shop, toilets, and a snack bar. Although individual entry is available ($5, children $3.50, families $13.50), guided tours are an infinitely better option ($7.50, $5, $15). Tours leave every 15 to 45 minutes while the park is open, and the park rangers provide invaluable insights. A tour is included in the **Island Parks Pass** ($20, children $15, families $55), which is a good value if you plan to visit numerous national park attractions (park open 9am-4:30pm).

An elevated boardwalk crosses the dunes to the beach, while pups cavort and juveniles sunbathe underneath. Don't be deceived by their seemingly labored movement—these agile creatures can actually move twice as fast as humans on land. On their three-day hunting trips the sea lions travel up to 60km off-shore and dive up to 275m deep in search of octopus, squid, and crustaceans before returning to languish on the beach for three days. Adult males can be distinguished by their golden manes and massive size—up to 3m long and 350kg. Females are only about a third as large, and outlive bulls, sometimes reaching the ripe age of 25. Needless to say, approaching these glorious mammals (*never* come closer than 5m) provides an unforgettable experience and awesome photo op. The lions are spread out along six beaches, and many females breed and give birth in the caves on the west end of the reserve.

■ Flinders Chase National Park

Occupying the western end of the island, 17% of its total area, Flinders Chase teems with flora and fauna which are unusually accessible to visitors. Just over 105km from Kingscote (mostly along a dirt track), Flinders Chase headquarters is located at **Rocky River,** one of the few open spaces in the park, along the South Coast Rd. (Park entry $6.50 per car, $3 per motorcycle. Fee covered by Island Parks Pass: $20, children $15, families $55.) Near the park headquarters and toilet block, a **koala walk** lets visitors observe these marsupials. The koala population has swelled so large that they are now decimating eucalypt stands. Eucalypt is slightly toxic, accounting for the drowsiness of the koalas in this area. The nearby hillsides, grazed by kangaroo mobs, are covered by a thin layer of an iridescent lime green moss.

The best attractions are clustered 15-20km south of Rocky River, all along Boxer Drive. The easternmost sight, on Kirkpatrick Point, is **Remarkable Rocks.** The name could not be more apropos. The approach to the granite configuration is through bonsai-like forests of eucalypt shrubbery stunted by salt spray. As you get closer, the rocks transform from inconspicuous to surreal to, well, remarkable. The granite has been cracked into cubes by 750 million years of erosion. Ice, wind, sea, and sun have sculpted delicate details on these monoliths, flecked with orange lichen.

Five kilometers west along Boxer Dr, **Cape du Couedic** houses Kangaroo Island's finest **lighthouse.** The red-capped beacon was painstakingly constructed of hand-cut limestone between 1907 and 1909. It still emits a beam which can be seen 100km out to sea. Just south of the lighthouse, a footpath winds to the edge of Cape du Couedic. In the distance, the two Casuarinas Islands are visibly bombarded by the vigorous Southern Ocean surf. These two reserves are uninhabited, except for colonies of New Zealand fur seals. More common than the Australian sea lions, 15,000 fur seals reside on Kangaroo Island. Descending the steps, one approaches the **Admirals Arch** and the adjacent seal breeding area. While the seals quietly bask on the rocks, a splendid surf crashes around them, framing the Admirals Arch. The arch is actually an eroded limestone cave whose attenuated stalactites remain, framing the setting sun.

Camping fees in four locations in Flinders Chase and two locations in Cape Gantheume are $5 per car (up to 5 people, $2 each additional person) except in Rocky River ($12 per car). Contact the local park offices (tel. 8553 2381 in Kingscote, or in person at Rocky River) for information. You can also rent a rustic cabin at one of Flinders Chase's three light stations. ($30 per adult, $5 child. Minimum charge $90 at Cape du Couedic, $60 at Cape Borda and Cape Willoughby. Linen $10 per person per stay.) Contact Flinders Chase National Park (tel. 8559 7235) for bookings. Reserve well in advance, especially during holidays.

SOUTHEAST OF THE MURRAY RIVER

The majestic Murray River winds west from the Great Dividing Range. Fed by a watershed that spans most of New South Wales and portions of Victoria, the largest waterway in Australia slices through the southeast corner of South Australia and empties into the Southern Ocean. Fruit, especially wine grapes, flourishes along the irrigated river basin, while the **Coorong,** a 145km stretch of coastal lagoons, supports over 240 species of native birdlife. The towns near the Victoria border can be associated with geographic regions within that state. The area around Naracoorte is an extension of the agricultural Wimmera district (see p. 544) and Mount Gambier continues the themes of Victoria's southwest coast (see p. 528).

■ Naracoorte

The best part of Naracoorte is underground. The small town, roughly 125km west of Horsham, Victoria on the Wimmera Highway, and 100km north of Mount Gambier along the Riddoch Hwy, is utterly forgettable save for its nearby conglomeration of eerily gorgeous caves, recently designated a World Heritage site. While the town itself doesn't warrant much attention or even have any particularly good budget accommodation, it's well worth a stop to see these subterranean natural masterpieces.

It's fitting that the town center in such a nondescript hamlet is described by the intersection of **Jones** and **Smith** streets, where there's a large park surrounded by banks with **ATMs, newsagents,** a **pharmacy,** and a **supermarket** (open M-F 8:30am-8pm, Sa 8:30am-5pm, Su 9:30am-5pm). The **public library,** on the east side of the park, has three terminals for free **internet access** (open M 10am-5pm, Tu, W, F 9:30am-5pm, Th 10am-8pm, Sa 8:30am-noon). There's a **Tourist Information Centre** (tel. 1800 244 421) west of town on MacDonnell Rd. The **bus depot** is on Rolland St, just off Smith St, but V/Line does not service Naracoorte. There is a **post office** at 23 Ormerod St. (open M-F 9am-5pm; fax 8762 2021; postal code 5271).

When you get to Naracoorte, drive 12km south of town, to the **Naracoorte Caves Conservation Park,** a well-marked 4km west off the Riddoch Hwy. Four caves are available for touring and a fifth is rigged with television cameras for remote viewing. The **Alexandra Cave** features five chambers full of delicate calcite stalagmites, stalactites, straws, and flowstone. Bizarre cave crickets also call Alexandra home. When food grows scarce, the crickets remove their own legs to eat instead. **Blanche Cave** lacks these delicate decorations and limping crickets, but has immense columns and windows caused by a partial collapse of the roof. Back in the 1850s, before the days of conservation, the local landlord used the cave for lavish parties, and the wooden furniture remains inside.

Now the most famous of the caves, the **Victoria Fossil Cave,** discovered in 1969, contains the remains of nearly 100 different species of Pleistocene fauna from 2 million to 10,000 years ago. Buried under silt after dying in the cave, the animals' fossils provide important clues to how the Australian marsupial megafauna were affected by the arrival of humans. Now-extinct species found here include a giant boa-like snake, marsupial "lions," hippo-sized wombats, and gigantic leaf-eating kangaroos. Every spring, hundreds of thousands of bent-wing bats descend on the Naracoorte caves to breed. **Bat Cave** provides perfect nursery conditions. Infrared bat-cameras have been installed to allow tourists to view the bats without disturbing the breeding grounds. **Wet Cave** isn't quite as spectacular as the others, but it's pretty good, and it's the only cave you can see without a tour guide.

Excellent guided **cave tours** are available from 9:30am to 4pm daily. Tours of Alexandra Cave, at 9:30am and 1:15pm, cost $5 (concessions $3.50); the Victoria Fossil Cave, at 10:15am and 2pm, cost $7.50 ($5); Blanche Cave, at 3:30pm, cost $6 ($5); viewings of the Bat Cave (only in warm months), at 11:30am, cost $7.50 ($5); and self-guided tours of Wet Cave $3 ($2). Day passes to all of the guided caves cost $22.50. More strenuous "adventure caving" guided tours (tel. 8762 2340) must be booked ahead of time. These tours most closely approximate the joy and peril of genuine cave exploration. Pricing depends on the number of people and the tour particulars.

A few kilometers farther along the Riddoch Hwy, south of the caves turnoff, a 7km access road leads west to **Bool Lagoon,** a major stopover point for many species of birds on transcontinental migrations. Boardwalks, walking tracks, and information posts allow you to appreciate the many acres of wetland and appreciate the colorful and weird-looking birds in comfort ($5 per car, concessions $4) Back in town is the **Sheep's Back** (tel. 8762 1518), on MacDonnell St, a museum filled with four stories of the history and culture of sheep and shepherds in southeast Australia. Even if the topic sounds as soporific as counting sheep, you may be surprised by how interesting the museum is; it's earned state and national awards. Not for the weak of constitution, it brings every ignominious shearing and grotty disease of the woolly beast to odiferous life ($5, concessions $3; open 10am-4pm).

Two mirror-image hotels face each other across Naracoorte's town center. The **Kincraig Hotel,** 168 Smith St (tel. 8762 2200), is slightly costlier and slightly better, offering high-ceilinged rooms with sinks and teapots (shared bath; $25 single, $40 double). Its doppelganger, the **Naracoorte Hotel-Motel,** 73 Ormerod St (tel. 8762 2400), has basic shared-bath accommodation for $24 single, $43 double. **Camping** is available both at Bool Lagoon and at Naracoorte Caves Conservation Park ($15 per car, $8 per motorcycle, or $4 per person for groups of 6 or more). The Naracoorte sites feature laundry and BBQ facilities, showers, and toilets. The Bool Lagoon sites are more primitive, and you must bring your own water. Get **permits** at the Conservation Park ticket office or the permit kiosk at Bool Lagoon (open daily 10am-3pm). **Maddie's Cafe** (tel. 8762 3953), on Goodchild Place at the corner of Smith St, is a friendly spot for light fare and strong coffee (open M-F 9am-5pm). **Dragon Village,** 8 MacDonnell St (tel. 8762 1919), cooks up spicy chili chicken and other Chinese takeaway dishes for under $10 (open daily 11:30am-2:30pm and 5-10:30pm).

▓ Mount Gambier

In an obsidian palace deep below the Wimmera, beneath Mount Gambier's famed **Blue Lake,** a disgruntled deity lives in permanent exile. The Lake King originally lived with his fellow gods in divine bliss, but betrayed them during a conflict long since forgotten, and was banished. The lake's mercurial hues reflect his shifting moods; it's a shimmering sapphire during summer, but fades to slate gray in colder months.

For historical and cultural precision, it should be noted that *Let's Go* completely made this story up. (And you wonder how "local legends" get started.) Still, it's as good an explanation as any for Blue Lake's mysteriously shifting color, a phenomenon which has continuously baffled scientists. The lake is Mount Gambier's only big drawing card (well, besides being named Australia's Tidiest Town in 1991), but its caves and lively downtown lined with Victorian balconies are worth a spin, too. Plus, as the largest town in the area (pop. 21,000), Mount Gambier makes a good base when exploring nearby wineries or the caves of Naracoorte.

PRACTICAL INFORMATION, ACCOMMODATIONS, AND FOOD The main commercial area lies at the intersection of Bay and Commercial St, where you'll find **pharmacies, markets,** and a ton of **banks** (banks open M-Th 9:30am-4pm, F 9:30am-5pm; **ATMs** open 24hr.). Across the park that lies on the other side of the town hall from the intersection of Bay and Commercial St is the **Civic Center,** where you'll find **public toilets** and a **library** (tel. 8721 2540; open M, W, F 9am-6pm, Tu 9am-5pm, Th 9am-8pm, Sa 9-11:30am) with in-demand but free **Internet access** that should be booked ahead. The local **post office** has recently moved to 30 Helen St (open M-F 9:30am-5pm; postal code 5290). **V/Line** buses stop at the Shell Blue Lake service station at 100 Commercial St West. Buses run northwest to Adelaide ($39, concessions $19) and east to Melbourne ($48, concessions $24), via the Victorian cities of Heywood, Portland, Port Fairy, Warrnambool, and Geelong.

Throw a rock on Commercial St East and you'll hit one of a million motels where you can get a basic room with bath for $30-40. There are some less expensive options, too, the best of which is the dimorphous **Federal Hotel-Motel,** 112 Commercial St East (tel. 8723 1099), half of which consists of cozy shared-bath rooms with TV and fabulously effective space heaters. (Singles $17; doubles $30. Hearty pub lunch specials $4-5.) The **Blue Lake Motel,** 1 Kennedy Ave (tel. 8725 5211; fax 8725 5410), off the Jubilee Hwy East, has converted motel rooms into cramped but clean hostel bunkrooms. The motel lobby serves as a pleasant lounge area, complete with a fireplace, TV, and **Internet access** (bunks $12 per person; breakfast $5; linen $1.50; laundry $3.50, Internet $2 for 10min.). The **Central Caravan Park,** 6 Krummel St (tel./fax 8725 4427), just east of the central business district, is centrally located; there's faces a laundromat and features a barbecue. (Tent sites $8; powered sites $12; on-site caravans $25; cabins $28-38.)

Commercial St is packed with chip shops and takeaway joints, supermarkets and greengrocers. Fully licensed **Cafe Luna,** 82 Commercial St West (tel. 8725 4887), vends victuals in a glossy, caffè-Roma setting (entrees $10-12), and has a coffee bar featuring a truly superior cappuccino ($2; open Su-Th 7:30am-midnight, F-Sa 7:30am-1:30am). The **Pepper Pot Cafe,** 41 Commercial Rd East (tel. 8724 9220), across the street from the town hall, serves a scrumptious breakfast ($8) and has two **Internet** terminals ($10 per hour, min. charge $2.50; open M-F 8:30am-5pm, Sa-Su 8:30am-3pm). The **Aquarium Cafe,** just south of Commercial on Wehl St, serves Mexican food with a conspicuously Australian interpretation, as well as "monster burgers," whose name refers to their considerable size rather than the animal from which they're fashioned. True to its name, the cafe boasts an aquarium in the back room (open W-Sa 4:30pm-1am, Su 4:30-10pm).

A number of pubs congregate in the town center. The one on the first floor of the **Mount Gambier Hotel,** 2 Commerical St West (tel. 8725 0611), bleeds old-school class, with high wooden ceilings and a prime scoping vantage point on the second-floor balcony. There are also pool tables and video games, as well as live bands and dancing Thursday through Saturday nights (alas, only till midnight).

SIGHTS The first European to sight Mount Gambier and the surrounding areas was Lieutenant James Grant, sailing the brig *Lady Nelson* in 1800. A replica of this historic ship now graces the **Lady Nelson Visitor and Discovery Centre** (tel. 8724 9750 or

1800 087 187; fax 8723 2833), on Jubilee Highway East. *($6, seniors $5, students and children $2.50; open 9am-4:15pm.)* The center highlights the area's history, Aboriginal life, botany, and curious geological phenomena. The self-guided tour has its Disney-landish spots (accordingly, it's great for kids), but is definitely worthwhile. Particularly impressive is the ghostly hologram of missionary Christina Smith.

Bay Rd leads south through the center of town to spots that overlook Blue Lake and its resident demons or whatever the hell makes it change color all the time. Back in the center of town, there are two caves. The **Cave Gardens,** at Bay Rd and Watson Tce, were once the original water source for the town, and have been made the centerpiece of the town square park, replete with flowering vegetation and thin trickling waterfalls. The flooded **Engelbrecht Cave,** located on Jubilee Hwy West between Victoria Tce and Ehret St, is a popular spot for **cave divers.** *(Open daily noon-3pm. Tours on the hr. $4, children $2.)* Two of the cave's chambers have been opened for viewing. There is a third nifty hole in the ground on Jubilee Hwy East known as the Umpher-ston Sinkhole. This one is carpeted with trees, ivy, and flowers, has barbecue and picnic facilities, and is dramatically lit at night, when possums scarf up food offered by irresponsible tourists.

CENTRAL WINE REGIONS

Early colonial settlers migrated to the rolling valleys of SA with visions of the pastoral plantation life dancing in their heads—they just had to figure out what to plant in their pastures. Hitting upon the magical grape, farmers converted to the religion of the vine with missionary zeal. Indeed, the gods have blessed SA with many sanctuaries and soil that is perfectly pH balanced. Regular worship is encouraged, with cellar door sales and tastings occurring daily in most regions. For the observant, the ritual is sure to provide an unending source of spiritual nourishment.

TOURS Numerous companies offer multi-winery tours of one or several days. They generally average $40 per day, but "gourmet tours" add a hefty charge for meals. Some companies run winter (June-Sept.) specials, some have backpacker discounts, and prices fluctuate. The **SA Travel Centre,** 1 King William St (tel. 8212 1505), in Adelaide, has information. The best deals for run-of-the-mill coach tours (which may be touristy, but tend to be taken more seriously by wineries, who offer more copious samples) can be found with **Premier** (tel. 8415 5566) and **Tour Delights** (tel. 8366 0550). **Groovy Grape** (tel. 8395 4422) offers laid-back, more personalized tours of the Barossa Valley that cater to the backpacker crowd ($39)—"they're not just tours, they're groovy days out!" Some other alternatives include **E&K Mini Tours** (tel. 8365 3816), **Prime Mini Tours** (tel. 8293 4900), **Mac's Winery Tours** (tel. 8362 7328), and **Freewheelin' Cycle Tours** (tel. 8232 6860).

The **Barossa Valley** is closer to Adelaide than the other wine regions, and its wineries are more numerous and consolidated. The **Barossa Adelaide Passenger Service** (tel. 8564 3022) runs a bus to and from Adelaide, and **Barossa Valley Taxis** (tel. 8563 3600) can transport you for a price. Bikes can be hired from the **Bunkhaus** (tel. 8562 2260) in Nuriootpa ($10 per day) or the **Zinfandel Tea Rooms** (tel. 8563 2822) in Tanunda for a few dollars more. **Car hire** (with a designated driver) is strongly recommended for those bent on a serious wine tour; too many wineries are in out-of-the-way places to do a fulfilling circuit by public bus or on a whirlwind tour.

■ Barossa Valley

Arguably Australia's most famous wine region, the Barossa Valley offers a variety of wines to suit all palates and budgets. Taste all the wine you want at no cost whatsoever, or begin your own wine cellar for as little as $8 a bottle. In between sips, there's plenty of time to explore the townships and their individual quirky attractions.

ORIENTATION AND PRACTICAL INFORMATION

The Barossa is comprised of several townships. Approaching from Adelaide via **Gawler,** the first town you will enter is **Lyndoch** (LIN-dock). After Lyndoch, the **Barossa Valley Highway** enters **Tanunda** and changes its name to **Murray St.** It then continues on to **Nuriootpa** (noor-ee-OOT-pah) and proceeds east to **Angaston. Williamstown** lies south of Lyndoch. Alternatively, you may choose to bypass Gawler and take the **Sturt Hwy** from Adelaide, which enters the Barossa at Nuriootpa. The towns are small enough to navigate easily, but for individual wineries it is best to pick up a wineries map from the Tanunda tourist office.

> **Tourist Office: Barossa Wine and Tourism Association,** 66-68 Murray St, Tanunda (tel. 8563 0600 or 1800 812 662; fax 8563 0616; email bwta@dove.net.au). Open M-F 9am-5pm, Sa-Su 10am-4pm.
>
> **Buses: Barossa Adelaide Passenger Service** (tel. 8564 3022) sends buses to Barossa from Adelaide on M-F 9am, 1 and 5:45pm, Sa 9am and 5:45pm, Su 5:45pm. One-way fares to: Lyndoch $7.90, Tanunda $9.70, Nuriootpa $10.50, and Angaston $11.50. Buses leave Angaston for Adelaide M-F 6:25, 9am and 3:25pm, Sa 7:05am and 3:25pm, Su 3:25pm.
>
> **Taxi: Barossa Valley Taxi Service,** Tanunda (tel. 8563 3600).
>
> **Royal Automobile Association:** Offices in Gawler (tel. 8522 2478), Tanunda (tel. 8563 2123 or 018 811 118), and Williamstown (tel. 8524 6268).
>
> **Bike Hire: Barossa Bunkhaus,** Nuriootpa (tel. 8562 2260), or **Zinfandel Tea Rooms,** Tanunda (tel. 8563 2822). The Barossa Valley isn't terribly compact and the summer (Dec.-Mar.) is the only time it can manageably be covered by bike.
>
> **Emergency:** Dial 000.
>
> **Police:** In Gawler (tel. 8522 1088); in Nuriootpa (tel. 8560 9020); in Williamstown (tel. 8524 6288).
>
> **Hospitals:** Doctors can be contacted in Angaston (tel. 8564 2266; hospital tel. 8564 2062), Gawler (hospital tel. 8521 2000), Nuriootpa (tel. 8562 2444), and Tanunda (tel. 8563 2777; hospital tel. 8563 2398).
>
> **Post Offices:** In **Gawler** on Tod St, in **Lyndoch** on the Barossa Valley Hwy, and in **Williamstown** on Queens St. The post offices in **Tanunda**, **Nurioopta,** and **Angaston** are all on Murray St (the main road).

ACCOMMODATIONS

Although the Barossa is easily covered as a daytrip from Adelaide, you won't want to make the drive back if you've spent the day getting plastered. Turn your visit into a leisurely stay so you can sample more of the local ambrosia.

> **The Bunkhaus Travelers' Hostel** (tel. 8562 2260), before the turnoff to Angaston on the Barossa Valley Way from Tanunda to Nuriootpa. The best value in the Barossa, this clean, comfortable hostel overlooks gorgeous vineyards. Great location for those touring by bike (mountain bikes $8 per day for guests). Dorms $11. Quilt included, but bring your own sheets. The nearby, 4-person **Shiraz Cottage,** with a kitchen, barbecue, pool, laundry, and TV, can also be rented ($35).
>
> **Barossa Valley Hotel,** 41 Murray St, Angaston (tel. 8564 2014). Basic, clean, and comfortable rooms, with shared bathrooms for $20, breakfast included. The pub downstairs has inexpensive food for the other meals.
>
> **The Tanunda Hotel,** 51 Murray St, Tanunda (tel. 8563 2030; fax 8563 2165). This slightly posher pub-style hotel offers comfortable rooms, a central location, and a family atmosphere. Shared-bathroom rooms $44 single, $50 double, $10 per extra person; self-contained rooms $10 more.
>
> **Sandy Creek YHA,** at Sandy Creek, 2km from Lyndoch. This limited-access hostel has beautiful rooms; bring your own linen and food. Bunks $10. You get the key from the YHA South Australia office, 38 Sturt St, Adelaide (tel. 8251 5583).

SOUTH AUSTRALIA

FOOD

Food is a high priority in the Barossa, and the most sumptuous display of this obsession is the Barossa Classic Gourmet Festival, during which wineries accompany their wares with gourmet feasts. There are some fantastic (though pricey) restaurants for moments of complete self-indulgence; **The Wild Olive** (8562 1286), on Pheasant Farm Rd in Nurioopta, is the best around. Otherwise, turn to the unusual assortment of cafes and bakeries.

Cafe Lanzerac, 109 Murray St, Tanunda (tel. 8563 0322), is one of the best medium-priced cafes around. Gourmet bistro food includes coffee, baked goods, wood-fired pizzas, pasta, salads, and wine. Slick but unpretentious decor. Pesto linguini $8.50, crepes with citrus syrup and fresh cream $7.50. Open daily 8am til late.

Lyndoch Bakery (tel. 8524 4422), on Barossa Valley Way, Lyndoch. Another great German bakery with big wooden doors, a wood stove, and wholesome, homemade bread, danishes, tortes, and sandwiches. The attached restaurant has fine German lunches at reasonable prices. Open Tu-Su 9am-5:30pm.

Apex Bakery, 4 Bilyara Rd, Tanunda (tel. 8563 2483), at Elizabeth St and Bilyara Rd, just off the main road. This insignificant-looking little bakery is much better on the inside. Family owners use wood-fired ovens to bake up the best goods in town.

Linkes Nuriootpa Bakery and Tearooms, 40 Murray St, Nuriootpa (tel. 8562 1129). Huge variety of hot foods and cakes, including a famous cheese pastry. Eat takeaway to avoid the table charge. Open M-F 8am-5:30pm, Sa-Su 8am-1:30pm.

Angas Park Fruit Company, 3 Murray St, Angaston (tel. 8564 2052; fax 8564 2686). After dinner, treat yourself to something sweet. Angas Park markets fruits *glacé*, dried fruit confectionery, nuts, chocolates, honey, and other preserves. All South Australian and all delicious. Yum! Open M-Sa 9am-5pm, Su 11am-5pm.

WINERIES

The complete tour of over 40 wineries requires Bacchanalian spirit, Herculean effort, and Gargantuan ability to hold your liquor. Most wineries are open daily from 10am to 4pm for free tastings and sales. Those walking or biking can head out of Tanunda, beginning at **Basedow Wines** (tel. 8563 3666) on Murray St. Follow the loop starting at **Richmond Grove Barossa Winery** (tel. 8563 2204), on Para Rd, Tanunda, around to **Peter Lehmann Wines** (tel. 8563 2500), **Langmeil Winery** (tel. 8563 2595), and **Veritas Winery** (tel. 8563 2330). The walking and tasting will take at least a couple of hours, and on a nice day, you'll get scenic views all around.

The additional mobility afforded by a **car** allows you to be a little more selective. As your party drives between these excellent wineries, remember to keep a **designated driver** absolutely sober. Roads are not in top condition, and Barossa Valley's police are diligent and unforgiving when it comes to drunk driving, and often form blockades and pull over everyone who passes by for breathalyzer tests.

Saltram Wine Estate (tel. 8564 3355), Nuriootpa Rd, Angaston. Saltram's Semillon is the stuff from which dreams are made—smooth, fruity, and fabulously decadent. A little plate of delicious nibbles from the estate restaurants ($1) will whet your palate as you wade your way through liters of pure joy.

Kellermeister (tel. 8524 4303), Barossa Valley Way, Lyndoch. Perched upon a hill with a panoramic vista, this family-owned winery sells their distinctive, time-tested blends only from the cellar door. The Sable, a chocolate port, is a highlight.

Grant Burge Wines (tel. 8563 3700), Barossa Valley Way, Tanunda. One of the larger Barossa wineries, Grant Burge has an extensive range of fine reds and whites. Linger at this lovely estate to absorb them all.

Kaesler Wines (tel. 8562 2711), Barossa Valley Way, Nuriootpa. Set in an old stable, this cozy winery has a Tawny Port that will have you reeling with visions of musty English parlors and cigar-smoking aristocrats. Perfect on a chilly winter afternoon.

Seppeltsfield Winery (tel. 8568 6200), in Seppeltsfield; continue on Murray Rd through Nuriootpa, turn left on Stonewall Rd, and then right on Seppeltsfield Rd. Wares range from a century-old tawny port (not for tasting, however) to a unique sparkling red shiraz. The real reason to visit, or at least drive by, is the grand 1850s estate of Joseph Seppelt, one of the first vintners in the valley. The magnificent old mansions, the family mausoleum, and the roads lined with date palms seem plucked from a Caribbean wonderland. (When business turned bad during the 1930s depression, Seppelt employees were commissioned to plant the date palms rather than being laid off.)

SIGHTS AND FESTIVALS

Designated drivers, take heart: not every attraction in the Barossa will get you drunk. Behind its ramshackle exterior, the **Mechanical Music Museum** (tel. 8524 4014), on the Barossa Valley Hwy in Lyndoch, hides musical wonders you never dreamed possible. Tom, the guide, likes to pull visitors' legs (metaphorically). Take his own advice: "if you don't have a sense of humor, don't come in." *(Open daily 9am-5pm; admission $5.)* The **Story Book Cottage and Whacky Wood** (tel. 8563 2910), Oak St, Tanunda, offers animal feeding and a cutesiness that kids will enjoy. The **Whispering Wall** in Williamstown is a free, man-made wonder—you can gossip with a friend on the other side of the dam, 200m away.

As if you needed an excuse to drink, festivals abound. The **International Barossa Music Festival** is held every October. The **Oom-Pah Festival,** in February, is a German celebration with food stalls, music, entertainment, and, of course, wine. The **Barossa Balloon Regatta** is held in May in Nuriootpa. The **Barossa Vintage Festival**, Australia's foremost wine event, begins on Easter Monday (Apr. 5-11, 1999).

■ Clare

In limbo between Adelaide and the South Australian outback, Clare and its neighbor, Burra, constitute the last outposts of civilization. The **Clare Valley,** running from Auburn up to Clare along the Main North Road, is one more wine area with a dozen vineyards and the attendant revelry. Take advantage of this last bastion—feast on genuine Aussie fare, sip wine, snoop around heritage buildings, and embrace decadence. In short, eat, drink, and be merry, for tomorrow the desert awaits.

If you're driving from Adelaide (136km south of Clare), take Main North Rd, which runs through the town center and past most of the wineries. The **Clare Valley Tourist Information Centre** (tel. 8842 2131) is on 229 Main North Rd, in the town hall. **Commonwealth, ANZ,** and **Bank SA** all have branches (and **ATMs**) along North Main Rd. Rather than drive drunk from the out-of-the-way wineries, call a **taxi** (tel. 018 847 000). There's a **police station** (tel. 8842 2711), a **hospital** (tel. 8842 2500; ambulance 8842 1224), and an **RAA** (tel. 8842 2172). In late May on the Adelaide Cup Weekend, Clare celebrates the **Clare Valley Gourmet Weekend.**

Bungaree Station (tel. 8842 2677; fax 8842 3004) lies 12km north of Clare along Main North Rd. This secluded village was established in 1841 as a sheep station, and has been restored to its original appearance. Historical tours are offered. Lodging is available in self-contained, cozy cottages (adults $40, children $25; $10 per night discount for multiple-night stays), or in the stark shearer's quarters (BYO linen and food; $15 per adult, $11 per child; $3 multi-night discount). The accommodations may be rustic, but they are comfortable and it's all in the spirit of the place.

A central location in Clare and clean, standard rooms make **Taminga Hotel** (tel. 8842 2808) on Main St a good choice for those without their own transport (singles $20, doubles $30). Slightly nicer, the **Clare Hotel** (tel. 8842 2816), also on Main St, has ensuite motel rooms (single $40, doubles $45) and basic hotel singles for $16.

Clare offers a good selection of bakeries and cafes, but for a heartier feed, you'll have to grab a counter meal in a hotel. **Bebas Coffee Lounge** (tel. 8842 2917), opposite the post office on Main St, has homemade soup, sandwiches, cakes, and superfrothy cappucinos. The generous Devonshire tea will suffice for supper. **Price's Traditional Bakery** (tel. 8842 2473), north of the post office, has pies, pastries, and sausage rolls; try the honey log with fresh cream ($1.50). The **Taminga Hotel** (tel. 8842 2808), on Main St, serves the town's best counter meals. Generous portions and fresh ingredients (daily special $5). 70s decor. The **Chaff Mill Country Kitchen** on Main St (tel. 8842 3055) has fresh homestyle meals (open 7:30am-late).

■ Wineries of the Clare Valley

The wineries that draw travelers to Clare dot the main thoroughfare from Auburn north to central Clare. A car is required to fully sample the fruit of these vineyards. Signs to the wineries tend to be very poor and opening times change frequently; it is essential to pick up a guide to the wineries at Clare's tourist office.

Sevenhill Cellars (tel. 8843 4222), in Sevenhill, 6km South of Clare, had its beginnings in sacramental wine made by and for the brothers of the adjoining St. Aloysius church. Seven Jesuit brothers have continued the 145-year tradition of winemaking here by producing a fine array of red, white, and fortified wines.

Leasingham Wines, 7 Dominic St, in Clare (tel. 8842 2785). Given the quality of the reds here, it's easy to see why Leasingham is a perennial medal-winner. The appeal is rounded out by lovely surroundings and friendly service.

Taylor's Wines (tel. 8849 2008), on Mintaro Rd in Auburn. The "Southern Gateway" to the Clare Valley, Taylor's is a family-owned-and-operated winery which produces lovely, cool whites and hearty reds.

Jim Barry Wines (tel. 8842 2261), just north of Clare. This vineyard has one of the best views in the valley. On a nice day, take a picnic and buy a bottle of fine white wine from the cellar door for an afternoon of indulgence.

■ Burra

Thirty minutes north of Clare and 156km north of Adelaide, this old mining town boasts plenty of heritage buildings, and plays up its copper roots for tourists. Some people choose to stay in Burra to access the vineyards of the Clare Valley; the town itself is not exactly a thrill a minute. From Adelaide, pass through Clare and then take the right fork at the end of Main North Rd to Burra. The southern half of Burra, starting at the intersection of Market and Commercial St, has most of the tourist services. The **Burra Tourist Information Office** (tel. 8892 2154) is in Market Square.

Accommodation in Burra is not so pleasant and not so cheap. Proprietors seem to be taking advantage of the fact that on this road to and from nowhere, people will sleep anywhere. The **Paxton Square Cottages** (tel. 8892 2622) on Kingston St are former mining quarters that have been converted into self-contained, clean but uninspiring cottages. (Singles start at $25, doubles $35; proceeds go to historical preservation.) The **Burra Hotel** has singles for $30, including breakfast.

For food, head to Market Square, at the intersection of Market and Commercial St. The **Burra Country Pantry** proffers freshly baked treats at pleasing prices. **Water's Burra Baker** has delectable Cornish pastries (fresh pies $1.50), many of them vegetarian. At the **Commercial Hotel,** $2.50 will get you soup and a fresh roll, $5 a generous, tasty counter meal. There is not always a vegetarian option on the menu.

To see the town history, buy the "Burra Passport" ($20 per car) at the tourist office, which grants discounts to local museums and comes with the booklet *Discovering Historic Burra.* The **Mangdata Gold Mine Tours** (tel. 8892 2573 or mobile tel. 019 692 981), 23km east of Burra, offers a guided tour of the old government battery and an underground tour of the mine (admission $5; call ahead to book). The **Martindale Hall** (tel. 8843 9088), in Mintaro off the road between Burra and Clare, was featured in the film *Picnic at Hanging Rock.* The mansion is now a B&B, where you can almost hear the laughter and see the flashes of muslin as the schoolgirls in the film glide gracefully by.

■ Peterborough

Nestled within sight of the Flinders, Peterborough is the first frontier town along the drive north into the Flinders from Clare and Burra. You wouldn't want to vacation here, but it's a worthwhile place to stop for a short break or a night's stay.

Peterborough offers basic amenities; there is a **Bank SA** branch and a **post office** on Main St, and a police station on Jervais St. The **Peterborough Tourist Office** (tel. 8651 2708) is located in an old railroad car on Main St. There is a basic **Budget Travellers' Hostel** (tel. 8651 2711) on Railway Tce, behind the rail station (single $20, 3-bed dorm $14, 4-bed dorm $12). There are also a few pub hotels on Main St. The **Railway Hotel** (tel. 8651 2427) isn't bad (rooms $20). The **Peterborough Hotel** (tel. 8651 2006), also on Main St, offers more basic rooms for $16. Both hotels have ensuite motel rooms available at higher prices.

For food, there are the usual options. **Sue's Place** (tel. 8651 3166) has homebaked goods ($1), light food, coffee, and spunky animal placemats. The **Peterborough Cafe** is a basic deli and takeaway. The **Railway Hotel** serves up fine pub food. Peterborough tries hard to market its historical attractions, but most are of dubious interest. **Magnetic Hill** is a must-see, however, for those with the time and the giggles. Get detailed directions from the tourist office, drive to Magnetic Hill (between Peterborough and Ororoo), park your vehicle in neutral and watch as it rolls *up* the hill!

YORKE PENINSULA

On this peninsula west of Adelaide, rolling farmland is punctuated by sandy coves, and sheer cliffs plunge into sheltered bays of the Southern Ocean. The northern half of the Yorke primarily features copper mining history. The towns of **Kadina, Moonta,** and **Wallaroo** comprise the **Copper Triangle,** about a 90-minute drive from Adelaide's center. These towns offer the most to see and do, with beach access for when you get tired of mining lore. Many travelers head further south, however, for the spectacular ocean views, pleasant surfing beaches, and gorgeous camping of **Innes National Park.** The Yorke's southern tip is an additional two hours past the Copper Triangle, between the Spencer Gulf to the west and the Gulf of St. Vincent to the east.

■ The Copper Triangle

A trio of old mining towns, **Kadina, Wallaroo,** and **Moonta** sprang up as a result of discoveries of large copper deposits in the 1860s. The nightlife isn't as hopping as it may have been during the miners' heyday, but these settlements retain some of the feel of SA's colonial days. They're also a convenient stop on the way to destinations farther south on the Yorke Peninsula.

ORIENTATION AND PRACTICAL INFORMATION

Though they may be triplets, these towns are not identical. Kadina is the most metropolitan, offering modern conveniences including the peninsula's only **ATMs,** a movie theater, a large supermarket, and 24hr. **RAA** services (tel. 8821 1111). Limited **tourist information** is available on weekdays in the **Council Office** on Taylor St. **Internet access** is available at the **public library** (tel. 8821 2704), on Graves St, for $5 an hour.

Moonta is the most history-oriented town, playing its Cornish and mining heritage to the hilt. The **Moonta Station Visitor Centre** (tel. 8825 1891), on Kadina Rd in the old railway station, is a newly restored office which serves the entire Yorke Peninsula (open 9am-5pm daily). Wallaroo is the sleepiest and most relaxing of the trio, and the only one located ocean-side. For the vacationer in retreat, Wallaroo is the best place to sleep in a nice bed and wake up with the smell of the sea at your window. **Tourist information** is available in the **post office** on Owen Tce on weekdays, and at the **Sonbern Lodge** on John Tce on weekends.

The **Premier Bus Company** (tel. 8415 5555) runs daily to Kadina, Wallaroo, and Moonta, as well as the satellite coastal towns of Port Hughes and Moonta Bay (one-way $15.30, ages 5-15 $7). There are **post offices** in all three towns, and **hospitals** in Moonta (tel. 8825 2146) and Wallaroo (tel. 8823 2100).

ACCOMMODATIONS

Sonbern Lodge Motel (tel. 8823 2291), on John Tce in Wallaroo, is just how your rich, kooky grandmother's house would be, if you had one. The wood is deep brown, the 2nd-floor porch peeks out at the sea, and the pool table and old velvet chairs should be layered in the dust of ages (but aren't, thanks to the attentive management). Linen, tea, coffee, TV lounge. Licensed dining room. Motel rooms out back are more modern and more expensive but still charming. Singles in the main lodge $24, doubles $38. Ensuite rooms $35, $55. Family deals available.

Akeringa (tel. 8821 4033), on Pine Flat Rd in Bute, 20km northeast of Kadina. It's a piggery, but that's a good thing. For 10 years, friendly Roslyn and Neil Paterson have had backpackers mucking out the pens, feeding the chooks (chickens), harvesting grain, and generally making a fair dinkum Aussie farm tick. No payment but a long day's sweat is expected in return for comfortable accommodations and meat-heavy meals. Work clothes provided. 4-day minimum. Book ahead so transport can be arranged. Busiest in June, Sept., and Dec.

Ashhurst Farm House, near Akeringa, is also owned by the Patersons and set in a secluded corner of the farm. The price of a stay includes supplies for a hearty farm breakfast, including eggs and jams produced on the premises. $80 for two people, or midweek $30 for two people not including breakfast. Call Akeringa to book.

The Weerona Hotel (tel. 8823 2008), on John Tce in Wallaroo. Nice oceanfront location. Comfy rooms and decent meals downstairs. Singles $22; doubles $32.

The Royal Hotel (tel. 8825 2108), on Blanche Tce in Moomba. The Royal has everything a real Aussie pub hotel needs—beer, and lots of it. It also has friendly management, clean rooms, and tasty counter meals. The beds could be firmer, but are fairly comfortable. Singles $25; doubles $40. Light breakfast included.

The Wombat Hotel (tel. 8821 1108), on Taylor St in Kadina. Clean, basic, cheap pub accommodation. Singles with shared bath $19. Light breakfast included.

FOOD

The Yorke Peninsula is famous for its Cornish cuisine, especially the humble Cornish pasty (about $1.50), so have two and curb your appetite without blowing your budget. **Price's Bakeries** are found in all three of the Copper Triangle towns, but even better are the assorted local bakeries. The best is the **Jetty Road Bakehouse** (tel. 8823 3600), on Jetty Rd in Wallaroo, with hearty pies and delicate, doughy doughnuts. Mmm, doughnuts…is there anything they can't do? The **Cornish Kitchen** in Moonta, diagonally opposite the Commercial Hotel, is famous for Cornish pastries. **Skinner's Jetty Fish Cafe** (tel. 8823 3455), on Jetty Rd in Wallaroo, serves fresh seafood at cozy tables overlooking the jetty. At sunset, the view and Skinner's special sauce are a gorgeous combo. (Lunch specials $6, dinner $7. Open daily 10am-8pm.)

For an authentic Australian dinner you can't beat the local hotels. A generous main dish of fish, chicken, veal "parma," prawns, calamari, or (once in a while) a vegetarian concoction is accompanied by chips and an all-you-can-eat salad bar. Occasional specials (generally Th-Sa) are $5. Most hotel kitchens close around 8pm, so don't be fashionably late. For the freshest seafood, friendliest service, and most authentic Australian decor (read: brown vinyl), go to **The Royal,** on Ryan St, Moonta.

SIGHTS

The **Moonta Museum** (tel. 8825 1988 or 8825 2588) pays tribute to the Cornish immigrants who once mined copper here. *(Open Tu-Sa 1:30-4pm, Su and school and public holidays 11am-4pm.)* In the schoolhouse to the rear is the **Family History Resource Centre** (open W and Su 1-4pm), the **Miner's Cottage** (open W, Sa, and Su 1:30-4pm), and the **Tourist Railway** (departs museum hourly). Across the road, the **Old Sweet**

Shop (tel. 8825 1988) is a dentist's nightmare. The **Wallaroo Heritage and Nautical Museum** (tel. 8823 2843 or 8823 2366), in the Old Post Office on Jetty Rd, is filled with memorabilia from the romantic days of the shipping industry. *(Open W 10:30am-4pm; Sa, Su, and school holidays 2-4pm; public holidays 10am-4pm. Admission $2.50, concessions $2, children 50¢.)*

The **Kadina Heritage Museum** (tel. 8821 2721 or 8821 1083), situated in a miner's cottage, examines the history of the Matta Mine from Kadina's point of view. *(Open W and Sa-Su 2-4:30pm. Admission $4, under 5 free.)* It's 2km south of the Kadina post office on Matta Rd and can be accessed from the Kadina-Moonta Rd or from Russell St. For something a bit more eccentric, go to the privately owned **Banking and Currency Museum,** 3 Groves St, Kadina (tel. 8821 2906). *(Open Su-Th 10am-5pm. Admission $3, ages 5-17 $1.)* Take Mick's free guided tour through this tribute to tender. With money lining everything from the walls to the doors, only the most die-hard socialists will fail to be impressed. Tours of the **Wheal Hughes Copper Mine,** located on the outskirts of Moonta, on Wallaroo Rd, venture underground to display the workings of this real-life mine (hard hats and batter lamps provided). *(Tours 90min. $12, concessions $10. No children under 6.)* Tickets must be purchased at the Moonta Station Visitor Information Centre on Kadina Rd (tel. 8825 1891 or 8825 1892).

■ Southern Yorke Peninsula

If surf, sand, and sun are your major reasons for visiting the Yorke Peninsula, either coast will do the trick. The road down the east coast follows the shoreline more closely than the west coast road, but both areas offer beautiful swimming beaches, good snorkeling and diving facilities, and excellent surf. The remote Innes National Park is the most idyllic spot for any of these activities.

ORIENTATION AND PRACTICAL INFORMATION The southern half of the peninsula is served by the **Yorke Peninsula Passenger Service** (tel. 1800 625 099), which runs daily from Adelaide to **Yorketown** ($25). Buses go no further than Warooka, west of Yorketown. Stenhouse Bay is more than 50km distant, requiring a car for any measure of flexibility in exploring the park. **Minlaton** qualifies as the main inland town just because it has a **tourist office** in the Harvest Corner Information and Craft Co-op, 59 Main St. (tel. 8853 2600; open M-F 10am-5:30pm, Sa-Su 10am-4pm), the **RAA** (tel. 8853 2243), a **hospital** (tel. 8853 2200), and **police** (tel. 8853 2100). The town of **Port Vincent** lies along the east coast.

Farther south, the peninsula dog-legs west. **Innes National Park** (tel. 8854 4040) is located at the southwestern extreme. The **tourist office** and park entrance is in **Stenhouse Bay,** along the southern coast, at the **Innes Park Trading Post** (tel. 8854 4066; open daily). This hamlet has the **RAA** (tel. 8854 5138), a **hospital** (tel. 8852 1200), and **police** (tel. 8852 1100).

Less official information on surfing and fishing, as well as last-minute **petrol** and provisions, are available at the **Marion Bay General Store** a few kilometers before Innes Park. The park's main road is sealed and suitable for conventional vehicles.

ACCOMMODATIONS AND FOOD The **Tuckerway** (tel./fax 8853 7285) in Port Vincent provides a simple but clean place to lay your head. To get there, follow the road along the east coast of the peninsula from Port Wakefield through Port Clinton, Pine Point, and Port Julia. Take the Port Vincent turn-off down the gulf. Linen is not provided but there are kitchen facilities and the beach is 10 minutes away. Beds in barracks-like dorms cost $8 (YHA nonmembers $9).

"Beds" in the southern peninsula are usually sleeping bags, best used in **Innes National Park.** Numerous coastal **campsites** are overseen by the national park office in Stenhouse Bay. To camp, self-register at the office just inside the entrance. No bookings are required for tent sites, but you must camp in designated areas; the brochures at the office will help you choose the site. Sites at **Pondalowie Bay** have water and toilets ($12 per vehicle). **Casuarina** is in a restricted-access area ($15 per site, per vehicle; $5 key deposit). All other camping areas cost $5 per night per vehicle.

Several **lodges and huts** provide rustic shelter in Inneston, a historic mining village within the park. It is crucial to book ahead; call the national park office (tel. 8854 4040; fax 8854 4072). Some have solar-heated water, full kitchens, and flush toilets. Others just have four walls. The lodges usually sleep four to 12 people ($22-50 per night). These are perfect for families and groups looking for a rustic getaway.

In most of the southern peninsula, you're destined to chippers or hotel counter meals at mealtime. Fortunately, the fish here is fabulous. For exceptional butterfish, whiting, and garfish, don't miss **Gum Flat Deli, Fish n' Chips** on Main St in Minlaton. Go authentic with the takeaway wrapped in paper, head for the nearest beach, and eat some of the freshest seafood in Australia with an ocean view for less than $5.

BEACHES AND INNES NATIONAL PARK Beaches line both coasts of the penin-sula. Most are ideal for swimming, but a few are dangerous; speak with the folks at the Kadina tourist office before taking the plunge. They also distribute the free book-let *Walk the Yorke* to those interested in coastal walks. Innes National Park is a fantas-tic spot for surfing, diving, snorkeling, whale-watching, and fishing. Approximately 10,000 hectares were set aside as national parkland in 1970 to encourage the repop-ulation of the rare Great Western Whipbird. You may not catch sight of these rather shy creatures, but the sculptured, rocky headlands and crashing Southern Ocean waves should suffice. **The Innes Park Trading Post** in Stenhouse Bay (see **Practical Information,** above) has detailed information on which areas are safe for swimming and surfing.

EYRE PENINSULA

In the driest state on the driest continent on Earth, the Eyre Peninsula provides a wel-come belt of lush countryside, sandy white coves, and pounding, fish-filled surf—all uncrowded and removed from anything resembling urban bustle. A popular vacation spot for South Australian residents in the know, the population burgeons during vaca-tion times. The peninsula covers a huge area stretching nearly 1000km from **Port Augusta** and **Whyalla** in the east to the border with Western Australia. Projecting into the Southern Ocean and circumscribed to the north by the **Gawler Ranges,** the main, genuinely peninsular part of the Eyre is traversed by two main routes. The inland **Eyre Highway** runs 468km from Whyalla west to **Ceduna.** The coastal triangu-lar route, via the **Lincoln Hwy** and **Flinders Hwy,** takes 763km to connect the same two towns. West of Ceduna, the peninsula eases into the mainland as the road to WA sets out across the vast, desolate **Nullarbor Plain.**

The eastern side of the peninsula offers quirky coastal towns with sheltered bays, good swimming areas, and vast stretches of white sand. At the tip, **Port Lincoln** rests by the calm waters of Boston Bay, while farther west the rugged coastline bears the full force of the Southern Ocean's pounding surf. The **Great Australian Bight,** along Eyre's west coast, is known for some of the roughest waves in the world and some of the best surfing. Eyre's appeal lies in its remote inlets and expansive national parks. Even if the towns don't hold your attention themselves, they provide good bases for exploring mile after mile of spectacular, isolated coastline.

■ Port Augusta

Port Augusta sells itself as the "Crossroads of Australia," and there is an element of truth to this—many travelers pass through Port Augusta on their way north into the outback and on to Ayers Rock, south along the coast of the Eyre Peninsula, or west straight across the Nullarbor toward Perth. Port Augusta may not rate highly in excite-ment, but it can provide a comfortable bed, a good meal, a gigantic supermarket, and some modern conveniences to ease you into the next leg of your journey.

ORIENTATION AND PRACTICAL INFORMATION Port Augusta lies on the northernmost shore of **Spencer Gulf** at the eastern endpoint of the Eyre Peninsula. If you're just passing through from Adelaide, stick to the highway, which becomes **Victoria Parade.** This then becomes Hwy 1 to the peninsula and sprouts Hwy 87 heading north to Coober Pedy. The city center focuses around **Commercial Rd,** with the other main streets forming a surrounding grid. One-way streets abound irritatingly here. The **Port Augusta Tourist Information Office,** in Wadlata Outback Centre, 41 Flinders Tce (tel. 8641 0793), is open daily from 9am to 5:30pm. The North District Office of the **National Parks and Wildlife Service** (tel. 8548 5300) is also in town. This NPWS office deals with areas north of Hwy 1 (the Flinders Ranges and outback). The NPWS office in Port Lincoln oversees the Eyre Peninsula.

The **bus station** is on Mackay St downtown. **Stateliner** (tel. 8642 5055) runs buses to and from towns around South Australia, including Adelaide (4hr., 3-5 per day), and to Whyalla (1hr., 2-5 per day), Port Lincoln (4½hr., 2 per day), and Quorn (35min., 3 times per week). **Greyhound Pioneer** (tel. 13 20 30) runs to Port Augusta en route to locations around Australia (Coober Pedy, Alice Springs, Sydney, Melbourne, Perth, and Darwin). Call or check schedules posted at the station for exact times. There is also coin-operated **Internet access** at the bus station. **The Ghan railway** (tel. 13 22 32) also stops in Port Augusta between Adelaide and Alice Springs. **Budget,** 16 Young St (tel. 8642 6040), rents vehicles. The **RAA** (tel. 8641 1044) and **police** (tel. 8648 5020) provide assistance. The **post office, banks,** and **ATMs** are located on Commercial Rd.

ACCOMMODATIONS AND FOOD **Port Augusta Backpackers,** 17 Trent Rd (tel. 8641 1063), is just off the highway and before the town center coming from Adelaide. A brisk walk from the town center, this quiet, relaxing ranch house isn't the fanciest, but it'll do (beds $14, YHA nonmembers $15). The **Flinders Hotel Motel,** 39 Commercial Rd (tel. 8642 2544), offers backpacker accommodation ($14 including linen). There is a fridge for guests, but no kitchen. Good counter meals are served downstairs. The **Great Northern Hotel** (tel. 8642 2522) offers single rooms with breakfast ($25, extra person $5; linen provided). To get to the **Hotel Augusta,** on the waterfront at 1 Loudon Rd, continue along the highway from Adelaide, cross to Westside Beach, turn left onto Caboona Rd, and then left onto Loudon. Clean, comfortable singles or doubles cost $35; linen is provided.

All the hotels downtown offer inexpensive, hearty meals; the **Flinders Hotel Motel** has the most invigorating menu and atmosphere. The cozy **Ozzie's Coffee Lounge** and the more gourmet **Hot Pepper Cafe,** both on Commercial Rd, offer inviting soup, sandwich, coffee and baker items. Port Augusta's two downtown **supermarkets, Coles** in the Gateway Shopping Center and **Woolworths** in the Gulf Arcade, both have a humungous selection and are open long hours.

SIGHTS **Wadlata Outback Center,** 41 Flinders Tce (tel. 8642 4511), offers a hands-on outback exhibit on the geological evolution of the Flinders Range. Displays also address Aboriginal Dreaming and early colonial exploration. *(Admission to Interpretive Centre $6, children $3.50.)* The **School of the Air,** 59 Power Circle (tel. 8642 2077), provides radio-based primary education for remote communities. *(Tours daily at 10am, $2.)* See **The Largest Classroom in the World,** p. 265, for more information. Isolated outback townships also rely on the **Royal Flying Doctor Service,** 4 Vincent St (tel. 8642 2044), which provides medical service from 14 bases throughout Australia. *(Open M-F 10am-3pm.)* The **Australian Arid Lands Botanic Garden** (tel. 8641 1049), 1.4km north of Port Augusta on the Stuart Hwy, offers 80 hectares of walking tracks through arid-zone environments and views of the Flinders. *(Open M-F 9am-5:30pm, Sa-Su 10am-4pm. Free.)*

■ Whyalla

Gateway to the Eyre Peninsula, Whyalla (pop. 25,000) is South Australia's second largest city. A commercial mining port, Whyalla's economy has declined over the last decade, and the place now has more mini-malls than charm. The town doesn't have much to offer apart from modern amenities and a general sense of civilization, such as it is, that will be missed on a trek across the rugged terrain farther west.

ORIENTATION AND PRACTICAL INFORMATION The town is large enough to warrant picking up a good map at the tourist office. Whyalla is divided into five major suburbs. **Whyalla** proper is to the northeast and is the oldest, nicest part of the city; **Whyalla Playford** is southeast, **Whyalla Stuart** southwest, **Whyalla Jenkins** northwest, and **Whyalla Norrie** central.

The **Whyalla Tourist Centre** (tel. 8645 7900 or 1800 088 589) is on the Lincoln Hwy as you enter Whyalla from the north next to the mammoth ship *Whyalla* (open M-F 8:45am-5:10pm, Sa 9am-4pm, Su 10am-4pm). There are plenty of **banks** and **ATMs** in town, and an **RAA** office (tel. 8645 7257). **Stateliner** (tel. 8645 9673 in Whyalla, 8415 5555 in Adelaide) runs from Adelaide to Whyalla (3-5 per day) and returns to Adelaide (4 per day, 2 on Sa) via Port Pirie and Port Augusta. To get around, catch **Whyalla City Transport** (tel. 8645 7257; timetables available at the tourist center), or call **Des's Cabs** (tel. 13 13 23). **Westland Shopping Centre,** on the corner of McDouall Stuart Ave and Nicolson Ave in Whyalla Norrie, might be considered the city's hub and contains the **post office.**

ACCOMMODATIONS AND FOOD The pink **Hotel Spencer,** 1 Forsyth Ave in the city plaza (tel. 8645 8411), offers pub accommodation, with a clean bed, shared bath, and courteous management (singles $25; twins $30). The run-of-the-mill **Lord Gowrie Hotel,** on Gowrie Ave (tel. 8645 8955), has singles for $25 and slightly more expensive doubles for $40. **Hillview Caravan Park** (tel. 8645 9357), is off the Lincoln Hwy 6km south of Whyalla (tent sites $10, powered $13; 2-person on-site caravans $25). For food, head to the **city plaza** in Whyalla proper, where plenty of hotels and restaurants are located. **Foreshore Cafeteria** at Foreshore Beach, Whyalla, offers a lovely view of the sea. The **Westland Shopping Centre** has an extensive food court.

SIGHTS AND ATTRACTIONS The Lincoln Hwy runs by several points of interest. North of the city, the **Whyalla Maritime Museum** is housed in the mammoth *HMAS Whyalla*, the first ship built in the Whyalla Shipyard in 1941. *(Tours depart at 11am, noon, 1, 2, and 3pm. Book through the tourist office.)* Heading west on the highway, you'll pass **Whyalla Wildlife and Reptile Sanctuary** (tel. 8645 7044). A diverse display of fauna, both native and imported, lies along a lush, 1km walking trail. *(Open daily 10am-dusk. Admission $5.)* To see the **Whyalla Steelworks,** book a coach tour through the tourist office. *(2hr. M, W, and Sa 9:30am. $8.)*

■ From Whyalla to Port Lincoln

Heading down Hwy 1 along the west coast, you'll find a few dots of civilization tucked away in the flatness. At the least they provide colorful signs and gas stations; at the most, **Cowell, Arno Bay, Port Neill,** or **Tumble Bay** (as you head south) could be a quiet seaside town to crash for the night. All four towns have pub hotels with food and $20 single rooms (doubles $30) and caravan parks. **Port Neill** appears just when the drive starts to get more beautiful than monotonous, and if you can't wait to get in the water, the town has a nice **swimming beach.**

Cowell offers one of the safest and best fishing areas in South Australia **(Franklin Harbor),** a thriving oyster industry, and Australia's only commercial jade mining operation. The livelier of the town's two hotels is the **Franklin Harbour Hotel** (tel. 8629 2015), at the end of Main St by the jetty. The pub downstairs serves up the freshest of fish and a plate of unopened oysters for $5. One kilometer south of town on Smith Rd, **Schultz Farm Bed and Breakfast** offers extremely comfortable and homey rooms, mothering included. There's a fluffy carpet, copious linen, a quandong (traditional SA fruit) orchard in the backyard, and handmade jade jewelry for sale. ($45 for 2, $5 senior discount, $50 per family. Home-cooked breakfast included.)

SOUTH AUSTRALIA

■ Port Lincoln

At the southern tip of the Eyre Peninsula sits breezy Port Lincoln, a bustling coastal town that spreads nets for tourists as well as fish. Port Lincoln is a frequent port-of-call for vacationers, as both a stopover en route to the more remote attractions of the Eyre Peninsula, and a decent destination for those who like urban beach culture.

ORIENTATION AND PRACTICAL INFORMATION Nestled along **Boston Bay,** the town peers out toward the Southern Ocean. The main drag is **Tasman Terrace,** where the major hotels, pubs, cafes, and tourist shops are to be found. Farther in, **Liverpool Street** provides good grocery and department store shopping. Port Lincoln is small enough to walk around comfortably, but a car is advantageous for reaching the more secluded beaches in the vicinity.

The **Port Lincoln Visitor Information Centre,** 66 Tasman Tce (tel. 8683 3544 or 1800 629 911), is open daily 9am to 5pm. There are several **banks** and **ATMs** in town. The **airport** is served by **Kendell Airlines** (tel. 8231 9567; to Adelaide $80 with 14-day advance purchase) and **ASA** (tel. 8682 5688 in Port Lincoln, or 1800 018 234 or book through Qantas 13 13 13; to Adelaide $90, $75 advance purchase). Other services include the **RAA** (tel. 8682 3501), **Budget Rent-a-Car** (tel. 8684 3668), the **police** (tel. 8688 3020), and the **hospital** (tel. 8683 2200).

ACCOMMODATIONS AND FOOD Hostel-less Port Lincoln has a handful of pub accommodations along the main drag. **Lincoln Hotel** (tel. 8682 1277), at the beginning of Tasman Tce as you enter town from Whyalla, has clean, cozy rooms, if you ignore the peeling paint, and an ocean view if you're lucky (singles $20, doubles $35; with bath $5 more). The **Pier Hotel** (tel. 8682 1322), at the center of Tasman Tce, incorporates stunning views of the ocean (if you ask) with show-biz decor and amenities including private bath, front bar, dining room, and bar (singles $30, doubles $40). **Kirtan Point Caravan Park** (tel. 8682 2537), just off Gawler Tce, has a lovely setting by Shelley Beach near the town center (unpowered sites $5; cabins from $22).

For a cheap counter meal, the hotels offer competing "special" nights, where a hearty feed can be as low as $6. Seafood dishes are especially recommended in this area. **Paragon Cafe,** on Tasman Tce (tel. 8682 1442), has a view of the deep blues and greens of Boston Bay. A toasted fruit bun, butter, and a good cappucino will set you back a mere $2.50. Service is friendly and fast. The **Flix Cafe,** in the Flinders Theatre at 3 Hallet Place, offers more than popcorn: interesting dishes and sandwiches ($5-6), decadent desserts, and good coffee.

SIGHTS AND ACTIVITIES Port Lincoln is home to South Australia's bizarre **Tunarama Festival** (on the Australia Day long weekend in late Jan.), during which fish are elevated well above sea level in the highly competitive **tuna-throwing** events. Hey, whatever floats your boat. The rest of the year, you can view these fish in Boston Bay from the safety of a platform at the **Tuna Farm** (tel. 8682 2425). To see more exciting sea life, contact **Dangerous Reef Tours** (tel. 8682 2425), which includes an underwater viewing platform on Dangerous Reef, a well-known breeding spot of the infamous great white shark. You'll also see some friendlier sea creatures such as sea lions and seals. Book through the tourist office ($25).

A daytrip from Lincoln affords plenty of time to take in the gorgeous sea views of **Lincoln National Park.** Cliffs and sheltered beaches surrounded by small islands make this area a haven for sand- and nature-lovers. Camping is possible, but access to grounds can be difficult without 4WD. For further information, call the Eyre District office of the **NPWS,** 75 Liverpool St (tel. 8688 3111), or ask at the tourist center.

At the south of the park lies **Memory Cove Wilderness Area,** a restricted-access area where rare plants and animals live largely undisturbed in an impossibly pristine coastal landscape. Fifteen vehicles per day are allowed entry; to book a Memory Cove Pass and pick up a precious key, contact the Port Lincoln Visitor Center. *(Pass $5 per vehicle, $15 per night, plus a refundable $10 key deposit. 4WD recommended.)*

■ From Port Lincoln to Ceduna

The Flinders Hwy heads northwest from Port Lincoln to the remote outpost of Ceduna. This road is largely more of the same flat, mallee-scrubbed, but unpeopled land, but there are some blips of interest. The journey peaks early; a mere 47km from Lincoln toward Ceduna, you'll find the lazy **Coffin Bay**. The town itself provides little—except a crowd if you happen there during summer vacation when its population swells. **Coffin Bay National Park** is the big attraction, and rightfully so. This peninsular park is a remote beach heaven; surfers, fisherpeople, beachwalkers, picnickers, and pelicans co-exist peacefully amongst the dunes and sheltered bays. Most areas are accessible only with 4WD, but the worthwhile **Yangie Bay** and **Point Avoid** can be reached in conventional vehicles. Entry permits are available at the ranger station at the park ($5 per vehicle). **Bush camping** is allowed in specified areas only. **Maps** are available at the ranger station or Port Lincoln Tourist Office.

Fast forward 250km more toward Ceduna and you reach the idyllic **Streaky Bay**, a town which manages to be appealing to visitors without being touristy. And don't worry, the bay was named such because there was seaweed floating around—there's nothing funny in the water. **Tourist information** is dispensed at the **Shell** roadhouse on Alfred Tce (tel. 8626 1008). Besides offering the usual town services and an ocean view, Streaky Bay has pleasant accommodation in two forms. **Labatt House** (tel. 8626 1126) on Alfred Tce is an airy, beachside house with turquoise seascape murals. It offers bunkbed and double-bed backpacker-style digs. ($10 per night. Check in at the Shell roadhouse across the street.) The recently refurbished **Streaky Bay Community Hotel Motel** (tel. 8626 1008; fax 8626 1630), also on Alfred Tce, is tastefully fancy and heartily comfortable. The complex includes a restaurant, a pub with counter meals, and a gaming lounge. (Singles $25, doubles $30; ensuite singles $48, doubles $57, triples $69. Family units available.) The motel rooms are more expensive, and more ordinary.

■ Ceduna and Beyond

At the far west corner of the triangular Eyre circuit, the Flinders Highway meets up with the more direct and dull Eyre Highway and rolls into **Ceduna,** a lonely settlement which is civilization's last watering hole before the westward track across the Nullarbor Plain toward Perth. Ceduna provides the basic beds, beans, and booze, plus a few nice beaches. The second-most profitable port in South Australia is the **Venard,** a giant complex 2km southwest of Ceduna on the peninsula past Murat Bay. **Decres Bay,** 12km from town, is a good swimming beach, and a little farther on is **Laura Bay,** a tranquil beach within the **Wittelbee Conservation Park.** Get maps and directions from the tourist office, or follow the signs heading southeast from town.

The **Ceduna Gateway Tourist Office** (tel. 8625 2780 or 1800 639 413), 58 Poynton St, has loads of detailed info about local and regional areas and the Nullarbor Plain (open M-F 9am-5:30pm, Sa 9am-11:30am). At the same desk and telephone number is **Traveland Ceduna,** with info on **plane travel. Stateliner** (tel. 8415 5555 in Adelaide or 8642 5055 in Port Augusta) runs buses daily to Ceduna via Port Augusta, and **Greyhound Pioneer** (tel. 13 20 30) also passes through daily en route to Perth. **Police** (tel. 8628 7020), **hospital** (tel. 8625 2404), and **taxis** (tel. 8625 2964) are at your service.

Right next to the **bus station** on Kuhlmann St is **Ceduna Greenacres Backpackers** (tel. 8625 3811), a typical hostel with muraled concrete walls, a messy yard, and a free home-cooked dinner. (Dorms $15, twins or doubles $30; linen provided.) The **Ceduna Community Hotel Motel** (tel. 8625 2008), on O'Loughlin Tce along the waterfront, is owned by Best Western, and even its hotel rooms are motel-ish. But the rooms are comfy, with all the furnishings (tea, coffee, sink, biscuits, fridge, color TV), and the motel has a pub with meals and gaming room. (Singles $25, doubles $29; $10 more for self-contained rooms.)

Past Ceduna, Hwy 1 continues west through the **Nullarbor Plain.** It's a longer, lonelier road than you can possibly imagine, and there are very few places to get petrol, food, or water along the way (see **Crossing the Nullarbor,** p. 612, for more information). Only the most self-destructive of outlaws would drive this route by choice, but if you've already done it and you're arriving from the west (congratulations—now seek professional help for road-induced shellshock), you can receive your certificate of completion at the Ceduna tourist office.

FLINDERS RANGES AND OUTBACK

As you head north into South Australia's famed **Flinders Ranges,** the Australian outback surpasses legend and becomes dirt real. The endless hills of colored dust and sagebrush, with the road threading through them like a dribble, make all the trite sayings come true. Humans become minuscule in the face of the land, the sky never ends, the colors deepen with the setting sun as intense russets, blazing oranges, and soft purples emerge and darken before the burning sun reclaims the land with its unrelenting glare.

The Flinders Ranges begin at the northern end of the **Gulf of St. Vincent** and continue 400km into South Australia's vast northern outback. Within the Ranges, the southernmost national park is **Mt. Remarkable** (15,632 hectares). The **Flinders Ranges National Park** (92,746 hectares) comprises a large portion of the central Ranges, including **Brachina Gorge** and **Wilpena Pound.** The **Gammon Ranges National Park** (128,228 hectares) contains much of the rugged wilderness of the northern Ranges. If you're planning to hike in the central Ranges, **Quorn** is the best base. Of course, camping is always an option, especially in the north.

North of the Flinders, a moisture-deprived basin has created the salt flats of **Lake Torrens** and **Lake Eyre.** Much of the sparsely populated outback beyond is encompassed by the **Desert Parks** nature reserve. The **Oodnadatta Track** is a rough 4WD circuit carving through this area. Most people who travel through northern SA, however, are interested in getting through it as soon as possible en route to the more touristed loci of the Red Centre, including Ayers Rock and Alice Springs in the Northern Territory. The **Stuart Highway,** which slices the continent in half from Port Augusta up to Darwin, is the quickest and, for the most part, the only option. The road passes through the outback outpost of **Coober Pedy** on its way to the NT.

A car allows flexibility in traveling this region, but with many roads unsealed, 4WD is essential if you plan to diverge from the Stuart Hwy. Keep in mind that this region, although arid, is subject to **flash flooding.** Before setting out it is always a good idea to check road conditions on the **Northern Road Conditions Hotline** (tel. 11633). Towns are few and far between, so fill your tank whenever you strike **petrol.** Carry plenty of water for long drives as well (both for drinking and for your car). Also note that **banking services** are extremely limited in these parts. Only Cooper Pedy has an **ATM,** although Quorn has EFTPOS. Carry ample cash and traveler's checks.

■ Mt. Remarkable National Park

Between Adelaide and Port Augusta, somewhat near the otherwise uninviting industrial town of **Port Pirie,** rises **Mt. Remarkable National Park,** showcasing the southern Flinders Ranges. While this park doesn't have the remoteness or big wonders of its northern counterparts, it is only a couple of hours from Adelaide, has its own quiet splendor, and is perfect for laid-back bushwalking and camping. The **park headquarters** are at **Mambray Creek,** 45km north of Port Pirie on Hwy 1. Here you can find an information and pay station with trail maps, a campground, and access to a variety of bushwalks through canyons or ridges. Park fees apply ($5 per vehicle for day use and $5 per night to camp). The scenic **Alligator Gorge** section of the park is accessible via **Wilmington** in the north, on the Main North Rd between Clare and Port Augusta. **Mt. Remarkable** itself can be approached from a trail 3km north of **Melrose,** along the Main North Rd south of Wilmington (4hr. hike). Bush camping is prohibited in

Hidden Gorge, Alligator Gorge, and within a 2.5km radius of the Alligator/Mambray Creek junction, but with a good map in tow, you'll find tons of space elsewhere.

■ Quorn

Quorn, smack in the middle of the Central Flinders Ranges, is the quintessential Australian outback town. Charming simplicity and straightforward inhabitants create a relaxing atmosphere in which to take in the beauty of the Flinders Ranges. Quorn boasts friendly pubs, yarn-spinning bushmen, and down-home country hospitality without the saccharine edge. It's often ignored by those heading to famous national parks up north, but Quorn is the best *town* around (though that may not be saying much) and serves as a good jumping-off point for daytrips or journeys further north.

ORIENTATION AND PRACTICAL INFORMATION

Quorn lies 40km north of Rte 1 on Hwy 47. The town has a simple grid pattern, with **Railway Terrace** as its main thoroughfare and the rest of the roads cooperating to form a compact, square town center. A 15-minute walk around central Quorn will familiarize you suitably. Be careful when venturing further afield, however—the Flinders are a bit more difficult to negotiate than these quiet streets.

The **Quorn Tourist Information Office,** on 7th St (tel. 8648 6419 or 8648 6031), is open daily from 10am to 4pm. **National Australia Bank** is on Railway Tce (open M-Tu, and Th-F noon-4pm). There are **no ATMs** in Quorn. For road conditions, call the **Northern Roads Conditions Hotline** (tel. 11 63 33). **Stateliner** (tel. 8415 5555) runs to Quorn from Port Augusta (30min., 1 per day Su, W, and F; returns to Port Augusta Th, F, and Su) and continues through Hawker to Wilpena Pound. Call for exact times and pick-up information. The **Andu Lodge** (tel./fax 8648 6655; mobile 0417 830 533) provides a **travel service** which is cheaper and more flexible than the bus. By arrangement, they'll pick up or drop off at any time in Port Augusta, Wilpena Pound, Devil's Peak, or Dutchman's Stern ($6, Wilpena $14). The **post office** (postal code 5433) is also on Railway Tce and has **public phones** outside.

ACCOMMODATIONS AND FOOD

Andu Lodge, 12 1st St (tel./fax 8648 6655; mobile 0417 830 533). An excellent base for a Flinders holiday, the Lodge feels smaller than its 56 beds. The warm and wise owner is extremely helpful in planning hikes. You can rent a mountain bike, play with the dog, or try his musical instruments (the owner's, not the dog's). Clean rooms, well-equipped kitchen, TV/VCR, Internet access. The chickens outside alleviate the need for an alarm clock. Dorms $14; doubles $38; twins $18 per person; single $28; family $65. Breakfast $3.

The Transcontinental Hotel (tel. 8648 6076), on Railway Tce. The best of Quorn's four hotels, with good, clean pub accommodation. The bar below is a great place to chill out and meet locals. Shout the owner a beer and sit back for an entertaining tale. Singles $29; doubles $49; family $48.

If not the cheapest places to bed down, Quorn's four hotels at least serve inexpensive **counter meals.** On "special" nights, a schnitzel, chips, and salad may be just $4.50. Hotel bars are good places to meet locals, particularly the **Transcontinental** on Railway Tce, where the whole town gathers for raucous drinking, $4.95 dinner specials, and schnitzel night every Wednesday. The **Quandong Cafe and Bakery,** on 1st St, is a cozy place to meet the quilting club for tea or to ingest some wholesome food to settle your stomach after last night at the pub (pies $4, sandwiches $3.50).

SIGHTS AND TOURS

To see the rugged ranges without scuffing your shoes, book a ride on the **Pichi Richi Railway** (for bookings call 8400 2205 interstate or 131 246 local), a scenic heritage train that travels through the stark grandeur of the Flinders. *(2hr.; $22 adult, $11 child, $19 concession, $55 family.)* If a more manufactured aesthetic appeals to you, check out

Quornucopia, 17 Railway Tce (tel. 8648 6282). *(Open 9am-6pm.)* Aussie kitsch—from frill-necked lizard magnets to koala tissue box covers—floods this hippie-friendly store. Quornucopia also arranges accommodations and tours for visitors.

The **Wallaby Tracks Adventure Tours** (tel. 1800 639 433, or call Andu Lodge), based in Andu Lodge, runs sweet adventure tours which allow intrepid but vehicle-less travelers to see the sights and have fun along the way. The best is the three-day, three-night Mountain Safari, which includes bushwalks, famous sights, bush camping, and Aboriginal art sites ($270 from Adelaide), but shorter, cheaper tours are offered too. Tours are also offered by **Andu Backpacker Lodge** (tel. 8648 6655) and **Flinders Ranges-Adelaide Stepover Tours** (tel. 1800 658 866; based in Adelaide).

Quorn is a great base for bushwalking in the Flinders Ranges. **Devil's Peak,** 11km from town on the Richmond Valley Rd, offers a fantastic view at the top of a steep, stony climb (2-2½hr. return; closed during Nov.-Apr. fire ban). Other recommended hiking areas include the **Buckaringa Sanctuary,** 32km from Quorn, and **Warren Gorge,** 22km down Yarra Vale Rd. There's also **Waukerie Falls,** but don't take the name literally; the falls, 16km from Quorn on the Richmond Valley Rd, are usually dry. Get directions and hiking tips from Mick at the Andu Lodge. There is **camping** (no facilities) in Warren Gorge, a beautiful spot owned by the town of Quorn.

■ Hawker

Hawker, lacking the charm of Quorn, provides little more than utilitarian proximity to **Wilpena Pound.** The town itself is quite impossible to get lost in, with a simple grid pattern centered around the intersection of **Wilpena Rd** and **Graddock St.** The **information booth** is on your left as you enter town from the south. Or contact **Hawker Motors** at the corner of Wilpena and Graddock St (tel. 8648 4014; fax 8648 4283). Hawker houses the Far North District Office for the **NPWS** (tel. 8648 4244).

The only budget beds in Hawker are at the **Hawker Hotel** (tel. 8648 4102). It's across the road from the Old Ghan Railway Station as you enter Hawker from Quorn. Beds are firm and facilities are clean. (Singles $25; doubles from $35.) For inexpensive light meals, friendly service, and Hawker's only espresso, check out the **Sightseers Cafe** (tel. 8648 4101), opposite the information booth (open 7:30am-6:30pm).

Hawker Shopping Centre on Wilpena Rd is a typical country general store with everything from Mars bars to monkey wrenches, good for last-minute supplies and on-the-road snacks. **Gloede's General Store** at the corner of Graddock St and Wilpena Rd has an extremely well-stocked camping supplies section. As this is the last bit of civilization before Wilpena, campers are well advised to stock up here before heading out. The **Old Ghan Restaurant and Gallery** in the Old Ghan Railway Station has mediocre art and expensive food; the historic building itself is the reason to visit. Rail buffs may be intrigued by this former home of the legendary Ghan train line. (Open Th-Su 11:30am-3pm and 6pm-late.)

■ Near Hawker: Parachilna

Just outside of Flinders Ranges National Park, 89km from Hawker on Hwy 83, Parachilna is a tiny blip of a town, but worth knowing about. The newly renovated **Prairie Hotel** (tel. 8648 4895; fax 8648 4606; email ab@flinders.outback.on.net) is beyond most budgets (doubles $120), but offers cabin and ATCOS (eco-unit) accommodation ($20-50 per person, depending on number of people). It may be worth a look around this original, ecosensitive resort, or at least a splurge on the best gourmet Australian bush tucker you'll eat at the scrumptious restaurant: apple and celery soup with blue cheese croutons ($5.50); spinach, feta, and pumpkin triangle ($6); feral grill ('roo, camel, venison, goat; $16). If all this decadence busts your budget, but you want a stunning view of the Flinders, the **Old Parachilna School** (tel. 8648 4676) down the street offers $12 dorm beds, kitchen and barbecue facilities, and a common room.

■ Wilpena Pound and the Flinders Ranges National Park

A highlight of the **Flinders Ranges National Park,** Wilpena is the stuff of legends. Of deep spiritual significance for local Aboriginal people, Wilpena inspired secret ceremonial ritual and was a source of a rich Dreaming heritage. To the traveler it offers spectacular views, challenging hikes, a glimpse into Aboriginal and geological history, and a calm serenity unmatched in the rest of the park's 94,500 hectares. Tread carefully and you may spot rosellas, galahs, and even the occasional emu. The **Wilpena Pound Resort** (tel. 8648 0004) serves as the park entrance and headquarters. The resort operates a general store, gas station, pub, visitor center, and campground as well as an upmarket hotel. Check in at the **Wilpena Pound Visitor Center** (tel. 8648 0004), which houses the National Park Office, for info on bushwalking, sight-seeing, or camping. **Camping** is the only budget accommodation option in Wilpena Pound. Camping in the park costs $5 per night per vehicle; at **Wilpena Campground,** which is newly and tastefully refurbished with central picnic tables and showers, it costs $10.50 per night plus a $5 park entrance fee. A day-use pass is $5 per vehicle.

To explore the Pound, you must sweat or spend a bit. There are no cars allowed. Ask the ranger at the visitor center for bushwalking advice and directions. Walking trails begin nearby, and any walk in Wilpena is worth it. A short, picturesque walk runs along the **Heysen Trail** to Pound Gap, while the slightly more strenuous **Wangara Hill walk** (2hr. return) affords wonderful views of the Pound. A high-intensity scrambling climb for serious hikers is the trail to **St. Mary's Peak.** All trails are clearly marked in blue. If you plan to attempt a longer walk, advise the ranger of your plans, the direction you will be walking in, and your expected time of return. There are also 4WD tours (half-day $55), scenic flights (20min. from $50), and guided walks (1hr. $5) into the Pound. Information is available at the visitors center.

Outside but near Wilpena Pound, the park offers more accessible attractions. **Sacred Canyon,** a site of ancient Aboriginal significance and ceremonial painting, is reached via an unsealed road which leaves the main road 4km before Wilpena Pound Resort. At **Arkaroo Rock,** accessible via a short walking trail 14km before Wilpena Pound (look for signs), Aboriginal ochre paintings decorate hillside caves. The drive through **Barchina Gorge** provides a self-guided tour of the area's spectacular geological history. Most tours through the Flinders Ranges stop by Wilpena Pound. You can also take the **Stateliner bus** (tel. 8415 5555) from Adelaide (7hr.; Th, F, and Su; $52).

■ Northern Flinders Ranges

Adventuresome travelers with strong legs for hiking, a strong car for driving, and a strong psyche for dealing with isolation will find much challenge and beauty in the rugged, remote terrain that stretches north past Flinders Ranges National Park toward the central deserts. These areas are less touristed and an even longer distance on the other side of anywhere than the southern Flinders, so bring a traveling companion if possible, plenty of supplies, and a healthy dose of grit.

■ Between Flinders Ranges National Park and Gammon Ranges National Park

These destinations are separated by a couple hundred kilometers, but the Flinders continue unbounded. If you continue beyond Flinders Ranges, be warned that you are entering the hinterland, and it's good to know that there is a full service gas station (open 8am-8pm) and supermarket in **Leigh Creek.** Other than these services, this company-built mining town and "Tidy Town" winner in 1990 has little to offer tourists. Stop in **Copley,** just past Leigh Creek, to visit **Tulloch's Bush Bakery and Quandong Cafe** (tel. 8675 2683), an extremely yummy and gourmet aberration which offers a pleasant garden seating area, cakes ($4), pies ($2.60), cappucino

($2.80), and light meals (salads $4.50, sandwiches and lasagna $5-7), served with amazingly attentive care. (Open M-F 8:30am-5pm, Sa 9:30am-4pm, Su 10:30am-4pm.)

■ Gammon Ranges National Park

This is where Australia gets serious. **The Gammons** are more craggy, more exotic, more stunning, and more isolated than the southern Flinders, and possibly than anything you've ever seen. It may be absolutely, fantastically worth it, but think hard before braving the Gammons, and come prepared. The Gammons are only accessible by **unsealed 4WD track,** and are far from services. Carry extra water, extra fuel, a spare tire, a jack, and rope at all times. Wilderness experience is advisable.

Check in at the **Balcanoona Ranger Station** (tel. 8648 4829), where the friendly rangers can give local and updated advice on bush camping and bushwalking. Water available. Park fee is $5 per vehicle per night. Many sights are reached via unmarked trails, climbing, and scrambling. A good guide to bushwalking in the Gammons is *A Walking Guide to the Northern Flinders Ranges* by Adrian Heard. If you're game and prepared, the Gammons are utterly unlike anywhere else in the world.

■ Arkaroola-Mt. Painter Wildlife Sanctuary

Big-shot Australian scientist **Reg Stubbs** spent years studying fossils in the Northern Flinders, and made millions in the oil business before establishing the **Arkaroola Resort.** Though it seems to have gone downhill in recent years, the resort blends nicely into its surroundings and provides a smattering of precious amenities (showers, general store, restaurant, gas) and a range of accommodation options (twin share cabins $29, shearers quarters $10 per person, camping $10 per site). Arkaroola offers a world-famous **Ridgetop Tour** ($55 adult, $35 children), taken in specially constructed 4WD vehicles that allow spectacular panoramic views. For information and reservations, call the Arkaroola Travel Center (in Adelaide, tel. 8212 1366) or the resort directly (tel. 8648 4848). Stubbs also established **Mt. Painter Sanctuary,** to the east and adjacent to Gammon Ranges National Park. The place is now a rugged outback wonderland. Mt. Painter Sanctuary can be explored on unsealed roads, 4WD tracks, and walking trails.

■ Coober Pedy

Be advised that the outback town of Coober Pedy is a mining settlement. This means several things, not the least of which is that there are mineshafts everywhere. When signs indicate that an area is restricted or unsafe you should take them extremely literally. Coober Pedy also has a reputation for roughness. It is not a good idea for lone travelers, particularly females, to wander aimlessly late at night.

This renowned subterranean outpost digs a hole in the ground for road-weary travelers along the seemingly unending Stuart Hwy on its lonely journey from Port Augusta towards Alice Springs. More than a stop-over point, this town is a bastion of opal frenzy, desolate scenery, and outback peculiarity. "Coober Pedy" means "white man's hole in the ground," and alludes to the form of this settlement and to the economy which sustains it. Its inhabitants are here for what is *in* the ground, not what's on it: they mine opals by day and sleep in the comfort of their underground dwellings by night, escaping severe summer heat and winter chill. The town is punctured by mine shafts, and layered in dust, debris, and miners' willpower. Coober Pedy's creative resolve to carve a niche in the "boringest" of lands forces a second look at what the outback offers in its details and opens up secrets of the surrounding area that would otherwise go unexplored. .

ORIENTATION AND PRACTICAL INFORMATION

Coober Pedy may seem disconcertingly invisible until you realize that half of the town is underground. The town layout, however, is quite simple. The turn-off from the Stuart Hwy (Hwy 87) leads into **Hutchinson St,** home to both backpacker hostels, the **tourist office** (tel. 8672 5298), and the **post office** (tel. 8672 5062; postal code 5723) in the miners' store. **Westpac Bank,** also on Hutchinson St, has an **ATM.** Coober Pedy has **police** (tel. 8672 5056) and the **RAA** (tel. 8672 5230). For car rental, compare **Coober Pedy Vehicle Hire,** (tel. 8672 5688; fax 8672 5198) on Hutchinson St and **Desert Cave** (tel. 8672 5688). Despite a bad reputation, Cooper Pedy hosts a number of **gay-friendly** establishments. **Underground Books** (tel. 8672 5558), on Post Office Hill Rd, has a queer fiction section. The management is a mine of information on the area and general travel information. Ask about gay accommodations, but don't expect anything budget.

ACCOMMODATIONS, CAMPING, AND FOOD

Radeka's Backpacker's Inn (tel. 8672 5233), at the corner of Hutchinson and Oliver St. For truly underground living you can't beat Radeka's. Clean and comfortable, if a little claustrophobic, this maze of underground "caves" comes complete with its own dungeon. A great place to meet other backpackers. Linen provided, kitchen, pool table, underground bar. Dorms $14, doubles $38, YHA/VIP/ITC.

Joe's Backpacker's (tel. 8672 5163 or 1800 631 758; fax 8672 5821), attached to the Budget Motel on Hutchinson St. If the couple behind the counter look familiar, perhaps you saw them in *Priscilla,* carting a kangaroo carcass across the outback by jeep. In the film, Joe and Maria refused to give the stranded drag queens a lift. In real life, they're a good bit more friendly. The motel is a bit crusty, but the hostel has clean dorms, kitchen, and tv lounge. $14: VIP.

Camping: Riba's (tel. 8672 5614), on William Creek Rd. Turn off 4km before Hutchinson St coming from Port Augusta. Riba's has aboveground and subterranean campsites for $12, including a free, hot underground shower.

Opal attracts treasure-hunters from the world over, and this is reflected in its diverse array of food: Greek, Chinese, Italian, and Aussie cuisines are readily available but rarely cheap. The budget-conscious are best off cooking. If you splurge, take a Greek counter meal at **Tom and Mary's Taverna** (tel. 8672 5622), on Hutchinson St. **John's Pizza Bar II,** (tel. 8672 5561) also on Hutchinson St, makes a mean pizza. The Last Resort Cafe, adjacent to Underground Books on Post Office Hill Rd, serves good swiss-influenced cafe cuisine—the only real cozy coffee lounge in town.

SIGHTS AND ATTRACTIONS

Organized tours are a decent way to see Coober Pedy's fascinating mining and geological sights, if you're willing to pay about $25. Some of the best operators are **Rodeka's Desert Breakaway Tours** (tel. 8672 5223), **Desert Cave Tours** (tel. 8672 5688), and **Discovery Tours** (tel. 8672 5028). Another novel tour is the **Mail Run** (tel. 1800 069 911), which will take you on a 12-hour adventure to the remote outback communities of William Creek, Oodnadatta, and numerous cattle stations, lookouts, and other points of interest along the way ($60; lunch not included). If you've got wheels, drive yourself to the **Breakaways Reserve,** about 50km from Coober Pedy. These colorful, flat-topped mesas which broke away from the Stuart Range. This is amazing but harsh country that would be hard to brave without Coober Pedy right there. Pick up the map (50¢) from Undergound Books, take ample water, make sure your car is in good condition, and explore a 70km return loop (roughly 2hr. drive) through to the Breakaways, where scenes from *Mad Max Beyond Thunderdome* and *Priscilla: Queen of the Desert* were filmed, on to the **Dog Fence** (a 2m high wire fence that stretches 5300km across 3 states), over the aptly named **Moon Plain,** and then back to town.

SOUTH AUSTRALIA

Tasmania

With Australia lying empty in a far corner of the Empire, England seemed to have a perfect solution for its 18th-century prison overflow problem. Parliament members happily sent their rabble across the ocean, washed their hands, and went to tea. But lawlessness was still a huge problem in the new prison colony, and penal officials in New South Wales decided to ship the troublemakers away once again. Australia was already at the end of the earth, but Tasmania was at the end of Australia. The British considered assignment to the wild little island, then known as Van Diemen's Land, to be the worst punishment available, reserved for the most heartless recidivists.

Silly Poms. What was thought to be an inhospitable, weatherbeaten rock was in fact the lushest corner of the continent. Still, the penal settlements established in the gorgeous areas near Hobart and Strahan were brutal indeed. Furthermore, the native Aboriginal populations were decimated by the new colony through the invasion of their lands and even outright genocide. During this century, Tasmanians have tried to forget their state's ugly history, embracing a conservative, Anglophilic ethos with power and social status monopolized by a small elite. Today, this pervasive conservatism is juxtaposed with a fervent, fascinating strain of radicalism. Tassie has been critical to the emergence of the Australian conservation movement, an early landmark of which was the struggle against the proposed Franklin Dam in Lake Pedder in the early 1980s. The world's first Green party has been in part of the state's governing coalition twice in the past decade. Tasmanian Aboriginals—who had not been completely annihilated, despite what most Australians are taught—were behind the pre-*Mabo* nationwide push for Aboriginal sovereignty (see **Land Rights,** p. 57).

Many visitors to Australia don't make it down under down under, but it is well worth the time and money required to detour through Tassie. A third of the state is preserved as wilderness, protecting the last great temperate rainforest on the globe. Bushwalkers from around the planet come to Tasmania's mountainous interior to explore the Overland Track, the premier hiking trail in the southern hemisphere. The uninhabited west coast bears the brunt of the Southern Ocean's fury, but the storms rarely push past the mountains, so the east coast and midlands are quite pleasant year-round. Tiny holiday villages, filled with prosperous fishing fleets and vacationing families, speckle the shore. In the southeast, capital Hobart, Australia's second-oldest city, is pleasantly mired in its own history. Rolling farmland stretches north from Hobart to Launceston, Tasmania's second city and northern hub. The Cradle Mountain World Heritage Area and central plateau regions are easily accessible from Launceston, and any point on the island is within a day's drive. Those on a mission can see much of the island in just a few days, but those who lose themselves in the wilderness and history may never be able to get enough of Tasmania.

TASMANIA HIGHLIGHTS

- Hiking the spectacular ridges of the world-famous **Overland Track** (see p. 482).
- Sunset framed by granite peaks and still water at **Wineglass Bay** (see p. 470).
- Macabre tales of the convict days on a **ghost tour** at Port Arthur (see p. 455).
- Picnic in the gardens of **Cataract Gorge Reserve** in Launceston (see p. 462).
- Sampling the sweet wares of Hobart's **Cadbury Chocolate Factory** (see p. 451).
- Splashing in a waterhole after hiking the **Apsley River gorge** (see p. 470).
- Wallabies and kangaroos on a safari in **Mt. William National Park** (see p. 468).

PRACTICAL INFORMATION

Tasmania has three principal gateways: Hobart (by air), Launceston (by **Devilcat** ferry or air), and Devonport (by **Spirit of Tasmania** overnight ferry or air). The state then comfortably divides into south, northeast, and northwest zones as the respective domains of the gateway cities. This chapter is arranged accordingly.

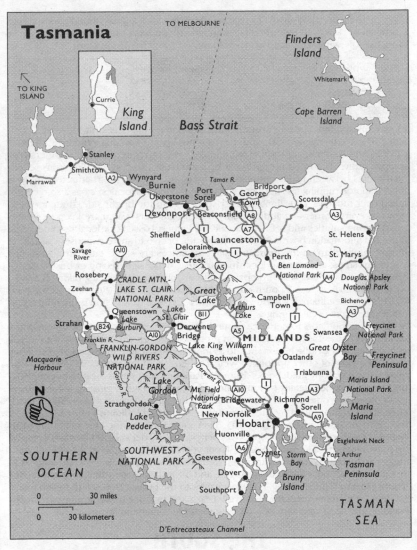

Tasmania

TO MELBOURNE

Flinders Island

Whitemark

TO KING ISLAND

Currie

King Island

Bass Strait

Cape Barren Island

Stanley

Smithton

Marrawah

A2 Wynyard

Burnie

Ulverstone

Devonport

Port Sorell

Tamar R.

Bridport

George Town

A8

Beaconsfield

Scottsdale

A3

Sheffield

Deloraine

Launceston

A7

St. Helens

Savage River

A10

Mole Creek

A5

Perth

Ben Lomond National Park

St. Marys

Roseberry

Zeehan

CRADLE MTN.-LAKE ST. CLAIR NATIONAL PARK

Great Lake

Campbell Town

A4

Douglas Apsley National Park

Bicheno

A3

Strahan

B24

Queenstown

Lake Burbury

A10

Lake St. Clair

B11

Arthurs Lake

A5

MIDLANDS

Swansea

Freycinet National Park

Franklin R.

FRANKLIN-GORDON WILD RIVERS NATIONAL PARK

Derwent Bridge

Lake King William

Bothwell

Oatlands

Great Oyster Bay

Freycinet Peninsula

Macquarie Harbour

Gordon R.

Lake Gordon

Mt. Field National Park

Derwent R.

A10

Triabunna

Maria Island National Park

N

Strathgordon

Bridgewater

Richmond

A3

Sorell

Maria Island

Lake Pedder

New Norfolk

Hobart

A9

Huonville

Eaglehawk Neck

Port Arthur

SOUTHERN OCEAN

SOUTHWEST NATIONAL PARK

Geeveston

A6

Cygnet

Storm Bay

Tasman Peninsula

Dover

Bruny Island

TASMAN SEA

Southport

0   30 miles

0   30 kilometers

D'Entrecasteaux Channel

The Tasmanian Visitor Information network has offices and agencies in towns throughout the state and travel centers in **Melbourne,** 256 Collins St (tel. 03 9206 7922); **Sydney,** 149 King St (tel. 02 202 2022); **Brisbane,** 40 Queen St (tel. 07 3405 4122); **Adelaide,** 32 King William St (tel 08 400 5522); and **Canberra,** 165-7 City Walk (tel. 06 209 2122). Their free bimonthly newsprint magazine **Travelways** lists up-to-date details on accommodations, transport, tours, and so forth. Their colorful **Visitors Map of Tasmania** is the best map available. Many towns have a bank, while in some the supermarket or news agency operates as a limited "bank agent," but almost none have **ATMs. EFTPOS** is ubiquitous but only accepts Australian plastic— if you have a foreign card, get cash before leaving the gateway cities. The city libraries have Internet terminals, but bookings are essential; don't expect same-day access.

The good news for budget travelers in Tasmania is that you won't have to break the bank to find a place to lay your head. Campsites, hostels, and other affordable accom-

Phone numbers in Tasmania have recently changed. Regional phone codes are now all 03, followed by eight-digit numbers. If you have trouble making a call, use the following scheme to get the old number, and try that instead.

Old Number:	New Number:
(002) xx xxxx	(03) 62xx xxxx
(003) xx xxxx	(03) 63xx xxxx
(004) xx xxxx	(03) 64xx xxxx

modations abound. **Getting around Tasmania** on a budget is a bit more of a challenge. There is no rail network, and the main bus lines, **Tasmania Wilderness Travel (TWT)** and **Redline,** are expensive, limited, and infrequent; many travelers feel trapped rather than freed after purchasing a multi-day bus pass. (Redline runs scheduled routes between major population centers, while TWT is structured more as a hiker's shuttle running less frequent service to wilderness locales; it has also recently taken over much of **Tigerline's** former service.) On the bright side, there are residents in every corner—including many hostel managers—who are keen to fill the gap, offering shuttles and tours on a call-and-request basis. Seek local recommendations and information boards. With a companion or two to share expenses, car hire is more popular than on the mainland, since distances are short, most attractions are not at bus stops, and you can lock up extra gear while sight-seeing or bushwalking. The gateway cites have small companies offering cheaper, older cars. Biking is a satisfying alternative, especially on the more accessible east coast. *Bicycling Tasmania,* by Terry and Beedham, is a good guide; **Rent-a-Cycle** in Launceston is the only rental outfit catering to cycle touring.

There's an outdoors experience around every corner in Tasmania, from backyard bandicoots to the Tasmanian Trail. You probably can't go wrong. Travelers are often exhorted to visit **Cradle Mountain** and **Wineglass Bay.** These places are magical, but there are plenty of other options as well. The gazette of bushwalks would last a lifetime. Several walking guidebooks, National Park brochures, and local visitor information boards provide details beyond our highlight coverage. Tasmania's 16 national parks, covering some 20% of the state, are a locus of wilderness and wildlife experience. They are managed by the **Tasmanian Parks and Wildlife Service** (tel. 6233 6191; http://www.parks.tas.gov.au). There are uniform fees for entry into the National Parks, payable as a day pass ($3 per person, $9 per vehicle), a holiday pass of up to two months ($12 per person, $30 per vehicle), or an annual pass ($42 per vehicle). State forests and reserves are often free. The **Backpackers Barn** in **Devonport** is an excellent resource for hiking gear hire and information, as is the **Launceston City Youth Hostel.** While nobody in Hobart caters to the budget traveler, there are many outdoor equipment stores there as well. Learn and practice **minimum impact bushwalking,** and keep wildlife wild—feeding them does them no favors.

THE SOUTH

Anchored by capital Hobart, a beautiful city of good food and good people, the southern end of Australia welcomes travelers to its towns, forests, and coast. Ninety minutes east of Hobart lies historic Port Arthur, the most significant remaining testament to Tassie's colonial history; 90 minutes west lies the beginning of the vast untrammeled expanse of the South-West World Heritage Area. In between, amid the hop vines of the Derwent Valley and the apple orchards of the D'Entrecasteaux Channel, flourish the homes of people who know a good life when they see it.

TASMANIA

Map labels:

Warwick St.
TO **E**
Aberdeen St.
Aquatic Centre (A3)
Queens Domain
Patrick St.
Edward St.
Edward Brooker Ave.
Penitentiary Chapel & Criminal Courts
Brisbane St.
Campbell St.
Brooker Ave.
Tigerline
Tasman Hwy.
Distillery and Museum
N
Elizabeth St.
Melville St.
C
Theatre Royal
Macquarie St.
R.A.C.T.
Bathurst St.
B
Argyle St.
Davey St.
0   150 yards
0   150 meters
Murray St.
Liverpool St.
Elizabeth Mall
Library
YHA Office
Collins Buses
Tasmanian Museum and Art Gallery
Macquarie Wharf
Hobart
ACCOMMODATIONS
A Central City Backpackers
B New Sydney Hotel
C Ocean Child Hotel
D Transit Centre Backpackers
E Adelphi Court YHA

Metro
Cat & Fiddle Arcade
A
Centrepoint Arcade
Franklin Square
St. Davids Cathedral
Town Hall
Constitution Dock
Franklin Wharf
Elizabeth St. Pier
Sullivan's Cove
Morrison St.
FERRY TO BELLERIVE
Harrington St.
Royal Tennis Club
Parliament House
Parliament Square
Princes Wharf
Redline
D
Macquarie St.
Barrack St.
Davey St.
Sandy Bay Rd.
St. Davids Park
Gladstone St.
Salamanca Place
Salamanca Market
Kelly's Steps
Castray Esplanade
Princes Park
Molle St.
Hampden Rd.
BATTERY POINT
Kelly St.
Runnymede St.
River Derwent
Anglesea Barracks
(A6)
(B68)

■ Hobart

A comforting hub for the island state, Hobart holds forth around the sheltered mouth of the Derwent River, obedient at the feet of moody Mt. Wellington. It is an old city by Australian standards, founded on February 21, 1804 by Lieutenant David Collins at Sullivan's Cove. Tens of thousands of convicts were imported to Hobart Town, most from urban areas of Great Britain. Today, many reminders of the city's penal past can be found throughout the region. Since convict days, the capital's fortunes have mirrored the state's. Mining wealth helped it establish itself as a city, but as a small fish in the federated Australian pond, Hobart has never grown large or complex. The river and the mountain remain dominant natural spirits. Hobart's social strata is transparent to the visitor: the conservative establishment, the quietly creative intelligentsia, the disaffected, black-clad alterna-teens. But in the last week of every year, the whole city still manages an exciting unity, hosting finish-line festivities for the classic Sydney-to-Hobart and Melbourne-to-Hobart yacht races.

@ HOBART HIGHLIGHTS

- Seeing mountains halfway across Tassie from windy **Mt. Wellington** (see p. 452).
- The sweet taste of sinfulness at the **Cadbury Chocolate Factory** (see p. 453).
- Perusing the Saturday morning market at **Salamanca Place** (see p. 452).
- Scrumptious veggie feast washed down with lassi at **Zanskar Cafe** (see p. 451).
- The **Cascade Brewery.** Beer. 'Nuff said. (See p. 453.)

TASMANIA

ARRIVAL AND DEPARTURE

There is no passenger rail service anywhere in Tasmania, and ferry service from the mainland connects only to the north. Consequently, air and road are the only two means of transport in and out of Hobart.

By Plane

Hobart Airport is 18km east of Hobart on Highway A3. **Ansett** (tel. 13 13 00) and **Qantas** (tel. 13 13 13) fly to Melbourne four times daily ($130-260) and to Sydney once daily ($178-376). International flights must make connections in Melbourne. Fares change frequently, but are cheaper with advance booking. International travelers can often get better deals; bring your passport and international ticket when arranging flights. Call to book the **Airporter Bus** (tel. 0419 382 240 or 0419 383 462) for transport to and from the city for $8.50 (bikes $8.50).

By Bus

Hobart's main **bus depot** is at 199 Collins St. **Redline Coaches** runs several times per day to Launceston (2½hr., $19) and Oatlands (1hr., $10.60) with connections to Devonport ($32.30). Sunday through Friday, one coach a day runs to Swansea (3½hr., $20), St. Helens (4¼hr., $26), St. Marys (3½hr., $22.50), Bicheno (4¼hr.) and the highway turn-off to Coles Bay (4hr.). **Tasmanian Wilderness Travel** (tel. 6334 4442; fax 6334 2029; email info@taswildtravel.com.au; http://www.tassie.net.au/wildtour) offers special bushwalking packages for Overland Trackers and other hikers. They also have regular service to smaller towns around Tasmania, including most of what was until recently **Tigerline** service. Several coaches per week run to Richmond (40min., $4), Triabunna (2-2½hr., $12-16.50), Sorell (20min., $4), Swansea (2¼hr., $16.50), the Coles Bay turn-off (3hr., $20), Bicheno (3hr., $20), St. Helens (4hr., $30), New Norfolk (40min., $4.50), Lake St. Clair (3¼hr., $29), Queenstown (5hr., $36), and Strahan (requires transfer, $42). Service to other areas is seasonal. From April to November, they run to Mt. Field National Park (1¼hr., $25) and Lake St. Clair (4¼hr., $29). From November to March, they run to Scotts Peak and Southwest hiking trails (3½hr.; $47) and south to Lone River (4hr., $45) and Cockle Creek (4¾hr., $45).

ORIENTATION

The central business district is on the western bank of the **Derwent River,** with most tourist attractions and services clustered downtown in a grid around the **Elizabeth Street Mall**, just behind the wharves of Sullivan's Cove. Just south of the Cove lies Battery Point, one of the oldest sections of the city, choked with antique shops and cottages. The northern border of Battery Pt is defined by **Salamanca Place,** a row of old Georgian sandstone warehouses that have been restored and renovated as galleries, shops, and restaurants. **Franklin Wharf,** adjacent to Salamanca Place, is the departure point for the many cruises and tours that operate in the harbor. Hobart is backed by the **Wellington Range,** which affords fine views from Mt. Nelson, to the south, or the larger Mt. Wellington, about 7km west of the central Hobart. The city proper can be navigated on foot, while public buses run to the outer reaches of the suburbs.

Beyond the Queen's Domain north of downtown, the **Tasman Bridge** spans the Derwent River. There, the Tasman Highway (A3) heads east to the Tasman Peninsula and the sun coast, both easy daytrips. Brooker Ave leads north out of the city up the Derwent Valley, becoming Rte 1 to Launceston, and connecting to the A10 for points west. Davey St leaves downtown southwards as the A6, heading toward the Huon Valley, Bruny Island, and the southern wilderness beyond.

PRACTICAL INFORMATION

Local Transportation: Metro city buses (tel. 13 22 01) run throughout Hobart and the suburbs. Service daily 6am-midnight. Fares $1.20-2.80; purchase on board.

"Day Rover" tickets ($3.10) allow unlimited travel M-F 9am-4:30pm and after 6pm, all day on weekends. **The Metro Shop,** 18 Elizabeth St, has timetables.

Car Rental: Autorent Hertz, 122 Harrington St (tel. 6237 1111), from $44 per day. **Thrifty,** 11-17 Argyle St (tel. 6234 1341; airport tel. 6248 5678), from $57. At **Rent-A-Bug,** 105 Murray St (tel. 6231 0300; fax 6231 5017; email rentabug@south-com.com.au), VW Beetles from $25 per day are a very popular option. **Range,** 136 Harrington St (tel. 6231 0678), rents from $30 per day, including minibuses and campervans. **Advance,** 221 Harrington St (tel. 6224 0822).

Automobile Club: RACT, at the corner of Murray and Patrick St (tel. 6232 6300). Open M-F 8:45am-5pm.

Bikes: McBain Cycles, 132 Bathurst St (tel. 6234 7594; fax 6234 7176) for parts and repairs. Open M-F 9am-5:30pm, Sa 9am-noon. **Brakeout** (tel. 6227 9516) cycle rental from $20 a day. $30 includes lift to the top of Mt. Wellington.

Tourist Office: Hobart Tasmanian Travel and Information Centre, 20 Davey St (tel. 6230 8233), 200m inland on the corner of Davey and Elizabeth St. Accommodation bookings ($2), organized tours and walks, travel arrangements and itineraries. Open M-F 8:30am-5:15pm, Sa-Su 9am-4pm (winter Su 9am-1pm).

Budget Travel Office: YHA's Tasmanian Headquarters, 28 Criterion St, 2nd floor (tel. 6234 9617; fax 6234 7422), between Bathurst and Liverpool St. Travel insurance, passport photos, tickets, and travel advice, in addition to YHA memberships and hostel bookings. Open M-F 9am-5pm.

Currency Exchange: Mobs of banks, most with **ATMs,** crowd in and around the Elizabeth St Mall. **ANZ** (tel. 13 13 14), 40 Elizabeth St and 154 Liverpool St. **Commonwealth,** 81 Elizabeth St (tel. 6238 0560). **Westpac** has branches at 66 Murray St (tel. 6224 8577) and 38 Elizabeth St (tel. 6230 4142). All open M-Th 9:30am-4pm, F 9:30am-5pm. **National Australian Bank,** 76 Liverpool St (tel. 6234 2977).

American Express: 74a Liverpool St (tel. 6234 3711). Open M-F 9am-5pm.

Bookstores: Hobart Bookshop, 22 Salamanca Square (tel. 6234 9654). Richly, carefully stocked shelves of new and secondhand books. Open M-F 9am-6pm, Sa-Su 9am-5pm. **Angus & Robertson,** 96 Collins St (tel. 6234 4288). Large and mainstream, including good Tasmania travel coverage. Open M-F 8:30am-6pm, Sa 9am-5pm. **The Wilderness Shop,** Shop 8 Galleria, 33 Salamanca Pl (tel. 6234 9370). Volunteer staff sell books, clothes, postcards, and wonderful Dombrovskis posters for $14. Profits to protect Tasmanian wilderness. Open M-F 9:15am-5:30pm, Sa 9:15am-3:30pm, Su 11am-4:30pm. **Tasmanian Map Centre,** 96 Elizabeth St (tel. 6231 9043; fax 6231 9053; email maptas@netspace.net.au; http://www.ontas.com.au/map-supplies), is a travel-related book and map store.

Library: At the corner of Bathurst and Murray St (tel. 6233 7462). Open M-Th 9:30am-6pm, F 9:30am-8pm, Sa 9:30am-12:30pm.

Ticket Agents: Centretainment (tel. 6234 5998).

Market: There is a very popular craft and produce market in Salamanca Place on Saturdays from early morning until about 3pm (tel. 6233 7529).

Laundromat: Machine Laundry/Cafe, 12 Salamanca Sq (tel. 6224 9922), behind Salamanca Pl; enter through Fruit Market or Wooby's Lane. Very new, overly hip joint that combines delicious cakes, coffee, and front-loading washing machines ($3). What will they think of next? Open M-Tu 8am-6pm, W-Sa 8am-9pm, Su 9am-6pm.

Outdoor Equipment: Retailers line Elizabeth St north of the mall. **Snowgum,** 104 Elizabeth St (tel. 6234 7877), sells climbing and kayaking gear. Open M-F 9am-5:30pm; Sa 9am-2pm. **Hobart Indoor Climbing Gym,** 7 Wilson St, N. Hobart (tel. 6234 9544; email jayhawk@ozemail.com.au), has equipment and lessons.

Fishing Equipment: Information and equipment available at the **Compleat Angler,** 142 Elizabeth St (tel. 6234 3791).

Emergency: Dial 000.

Police: 37-43 Liverpool St (tel. 6230 2111). **Lost and found** tel. 6230 2277.

Pharmacy: Corby's Everyday Pharmacy, 170 Macquarie St (tel. 6223 3044). Open daily 8am-10pm.

Hospital: Royal Hobart Hospital, 48 Liverpool St (tel. 6222 8308; fax 6231 2043).

Post Office: At the corner of Elizabeth and Macquarie St (tel. 6220 7351; fax 6234 9387). Open M-F 9am-5pm. **Postal Code:** 7000.

TASMANIA

Internet and Fax: The **library** has free, heavily booked Internet access. **Trumpnet,** 117 Harrington St (tel. 6231 2820). $5 for 30min. on the Net. Open M-F 9am-5pm. **The Xerox Shop,** 118 Bathurst St (tel. 6234 8466; fax 6234 8903), has drop-in copying and fax services. Open M-F 8:30am-5:30pm.

Phone Code: 03.

ACCOMMODATIONS

Many of the pubs downtown have rooms to let, and two backpackers are in the middle of the city; the YHA is in North Hobart.

New Sydney Hotel, 87 Bathurst St (tel. 6234 4516), a few blocks northwest of the central business district along Elizabeth St. Cozy rooms are well-maintained despite their age, and the bathrooms are spotless. TV lounge, full kitchen. Popular pub downstairs serves hearty meals noon-2pm and 6-8pm; it plays loud music, but shuts down by midnight. 7-night max. stay. Dorms $12; doubles $35. Key deposit $10.

Adelphi Court YHA, 17 Stoke St, New Town (tel. 6228 4829; fax 6278 2047). Take a bus from Argyle St to stop 8A, just opposite the hostel, or take a bus from the terminus on Elizabeth St to stop 13. Built like a motel around a pleasant courtyard. The mothership of the YHA Tasmania fleet; a good place to find out who's been where, and who's going there next. The space heaters are next to useless. Large kitchen, comfy common area with games, grocery kiosk, wash basins in rooms. Reception can book tours, coach tickets, and other YHA accommodations (open 8am-8pm). Dorms $13; twins $36; singles with bathroom $45; doubles $47. YHA nonmembers $3 more. Breakfast: continental $5, cooked $8. Bikes $12 per half-day, $20 for 1 day, $15 per day for 2 or more days, with a $30 deposit.

Transit Centre Backpackers, 199 Collins St (tel./fax 6231 2400), above the Redline depot. Drab bus station setting, but extremely comfortable. Can get cold in the winter, though the huge common rooms are woodstove-warmed. Free storage. Coin-op laundry. No alcohol; free coffee and tea. Dorms $13. Linen $4.

Central City Backpackers, 138 Collins St (tel. 6224 2404), on the 2nd floor through the Imperial Arcade. A large hive of a hostel with industrial common areas and a great location. Efficiently run, the atmoshpere is a bit withdrawn, but not entirely unfriendly. No smoking. Coin-op laundry and Internet. Reception open daily 8am-10pm. 6-bed dorms $12; 4-bed dorms $16; singles $30; twins $38; doubles $38. Sleepsheet $2, towels $1. Key deposit $5. Sleeping bags allowed. No credit cards.

Ocean Child Hotel, 86 Argyle St (tel. 6234 6730; fax 6234 9306), a short walk from the city center. This nautical pub is being modernized to provide up-to-date amenities while retaining its wood-paneled charm. The upstairs rooms can be a bit dark, but everything is kept neat and tidy. Guests cook in the full kitchen or take a 25% discount on pub meals. Live music W-Sa is usually some sort of jazz or folk that isn't likely to keep people awake, even those in the audience. Pub has a good selection of beer. Dorms $12, with doona and towel $15; doubles $30. Coin-op laundry.

Sandy Bay Caravan Park, 1 Peel St (tel. 6225 1264), next to the casino off Sandy Bay Rd. The only caravan park near the city center. Large, clean cinderblock amenities including a reasonable camp kitchen. Sites $7 per person; powered sites for 2 $16. Caravans for 2 $35; self-contained cabins for 2 $55.

FOOD

Hobart has a variety of good bargains. Beyond our listings below, you can pillage the central business district for takeaway and chips, or head to the pubs for lunch and dinner. There are supermarkets in the northern and southern suburbs; closer to town look for **Jim's Shopping Oasis,** 190 Davey St (tel. 6223 1090), or **Ralph's Festival,** 189 Campbell St (tel. 6234 8077; open daily 8am-7pm). Stop for food at the 24-hour **Food Stop** on Elizabeth St, a few blocks north of Bathurst St. The Saturday **Salamanca Market** has excellent deals on local produce, honey, and cheese. Stalls sell Mutsu apples, which grow to the size of an infant's head, among other appetizing fruits. Good value restaurants cluster on Elizabeth St a kilometer or two from the mall.

TASMANIA

Restaurants

Vanny's, 181 Liverpool St (tel. 6234 1457). The Cambodian fare is as excellent as the price. Meals $5-7.50; lunch special $3.50. Open M-F 11:30am-3pm, daily 5-9:30pm.

Mure's, Victoria Dock (tel. 6231 2121). A complete seafood complex. The sea-level **Bistro** serves fish and chips ($6.50). Open daily 11am-9pm. The **Upper Deck** restaurant has lunch (11:30am-4:30pm) and winter dinner specials ($11.50). At starboard, **Orizoro** (tel. 6231 1790) makes super-fresh, totally raw sushi ($5-9). Open M-Sa noon-2:30pm, 6-9:30pm. You can cook for yourself at **Fishmongers.** Open daily 7am-6pm. **Polar Parlor** has ice cream and other desserts. Open daily 8am-9pm.

Little Bali, 84a Harrington St (tel. 6234 3426). Tiny yellow dining room, bright with wide-eyed Indonesian masks and flying animals. Good, quick, cheap meals (small $5, large $7). Open M-F 11:30am-3pm and daily 5-8pm.

Little Salama, 82a Harrington St (tel. 6234 9383). Tweedledum to Bali's Tweedledee next door. Huge grilled kebab $5—if you can possibly fit a second, it's only $2. Open lunch M-F 11:30am-2:30pm and daily 5-9pm.

A Taste of Asia, 358 Elizabeth St (tel. 6236 9191). A favorite with locals, with quirky "Asian inspired" cuisine. Small but innovative menu. The large plates ($8) are a great deal. BYO. Open M-Th noon-8pm, F noon-9pm, Sa 4-9pm.

Trattoria Casablanca, 213 Elizabeth St (tel. 6234 9900). A shrine to its namesake movie, this pasta and pizza joint is staggeringly popular; book ahead on weekends. Standard pastas $7-10, funkier pizzas (small $7, medium $11-16). Open till midnight.

Steve's Kebab House, 127 Liverpool St (tel. 6231 6000). Other locations around the city. The best Turkish fast food in Hobart. International kebabs are a specialty: Yankee-doodle kebabs with mustard and ketchup, Aussie kebabs with a fried egg and sauce, and tasty vegetarian falafel. Fresh fruit and vegetable juices. Almost everything is less than $5. Open Su-Th till 10pm.

Noah's Foods, on Constitution Dock (tel. 6231 9444). Noah's is the tastiest and least greasy fish shop on Constitution Dock—it's not even all fried. The fresh food is the best, and the specials are often a good choice. Open daily 11am-7:30pm.

Megasnax, 30 Criterion St (tel./fax 6231 0225). Coffee shop with tasty, nutritious food that provide a great break from meat pies. Hot dishes change daily and always include a veggie option. The homemade soup is a highlight. Open M-F 7am-5pm.

Cafes

Zanskar Cafe, 39 Barrack St, near Goulburn St (tel. 6231 3983). The plain exterior hides yellow walls, loving woodwork, and contented stained-glass trees that cradle a den of teas, lassi, breads, organic soups, and great vegetarian and vegan dishes (meals $5-8.50). Caters to special diet needs. Open M-F 9am-9pm, Sa-Su 2-9pm.

Retro Cafe, on Salamanca Pl, corner of Montpelier Retreat. Lots of regulars enjoy cosmopolitan atmosphere and excellent coffee. On Sat, there's great people-watching at the Salamanca Market. Stay up-to-date by checking out their events posters. Open M-F 8am-6pm, Sa 8:30am-6pm, Su 9am-6pm.

Muffin Munchies, 138 Collins St (tel. 6224 2520), in the Imperial Arcade. Excellent muffins ($1.50) are the highlight, especially the spinach and cheese and the sugar-free multi-grain. 2-for-1 muffin special 5-5:30pm. Great coffee. Open daily 7:30am-5:30pm, with a stall at the Salamanca Market on Saturdays.

Drifters, Shop 9 The Galleria, Salamanca Pl, just uphill from Cafe Retro (tel. 6224 3244). Good homemade soups ($4.50), foccacia ($6), and all-day breakfast ($2-5).

Kaos Kafe, 237 Elizabeth St (tel. 6231 5699), is strewn with *objets d'art* and cool floor tiles. Bring your clip-on ponytail for this trendy eatery. Abundant choices include foccacia, sandwiches, nachos, and salads (all $5-10). Open M-F noon-midnight, Sa 10am-midnight, Su 10am-10pm.

SIGHTS

Mt. Nelson, just south of central Hobart, offers sweeping views of Hobart and the Derwent estuary. A signal station at the top, part of the chain that connected Port Arthur to the capital, is today equipped with a tea house (open daily). The road to the

TASMANIA

top is open daily from 9am to 9pm. Take the Mt. Nelson bus to its terminus. **Mt. Wellington,** several kilometers west of Hobart, is even more impressive, reaching a height of 1270m. *(Observation shelter open 8am-4:30pm.)* The top is barren, extremely windy, cold, and often snowy. On a clear day, you can see the peaks of half the state. The road to the top closes occasionally due to snow and ice. **Fern Tree,** on the lower foothills of the mountain, is a lovely picnic and barbecue area with walking tracks up the slope. For track details, get the *Mt. Wellington Day Walk Map* from the Travel and Information Centre. By bus, take the Fern Tree service to stop 27.

Back at ground level, many of Hobart's convict-era buildings have survived into modern times. **Battery Point** is particularly well-preserved, and a stroll through the narrow streets is very enjoyable. The Travel and Information Centre has maps with historical notes. **Narryna,** 103 Hampden Rd (tel. 6234 2791), is a stately Georgian house set in a meticulous old world garden. *(Open Aug.-June Tu-F 10:30am-5pm, Sa-Su 2-5pm).* Built in 1836 by Andrew Haig, the house today contains Australia's oldest folk museum, with household goods, furniture, clothing, and other pioneer artifacts.

Just behind the Esplanade on the edge of Battery Point, the pleasant green space of **Princes Park** was the site of the Mulgrave Battery, the gun emplacement after which the point is named. The 1818 signal station, right on the Esplanade, is the oldest building on Battery Point. It was later converted to relay messages between Hobart and the surrounding country as far away as Port Arthur. There are many galleries and antique shops scattered around the Point.

North of Battery Point, **Salamanca Place** is a famous row of old sandstone warehouses now used as galleries, restaurants, cafes, shops, and the backdrop to the **outdoor market** on Saturdays. Around the bend in the cove, the **Elizabeth, Brooke,** and **Murray Piers** harbor most of Hobart's large vessels. Look for the Antarctic Research Expedition's giant orange icebreaker, *Aurora Australis*. **Constitution** and **Victoria Dock** are thronged with fishmongers and marine restaurants. Several companies run **harbor cruises** from this area. **Roche O'May Ferries** (tel. 6223 1914) sails from the

---

Mmm...Tastes Like Chicken

The case of Alexander Pearce provides a glimpse of the prison colony system at its macabre nadir. An Irishman transported to Tasmania for stealing six pair of shoes in 1819, he escaped with seven other prisoners from Macquarie Harbor on September 20, 1822. The group set out through an uncharted section of forbidding wilderness. They wandered for days, lost and starving, until one night Pearce broached the topic of cannibalism. In their famished delirium, the group assented and soon debate ensued as to who would be the first to go. Pearce cut the discussion short when he summarily killed a compatriot, warmed his heart and liver over the fire and consumed them with a gusto that shocked the rest of the group (though by the next morning they were all feasting on human flesh). The journey only got harder, and eventually Pearce killed and ate all his fellow travelers, sustaining himself for months on their meat.

When finally captured, Pearce volunteered his gruesome story to the reverend of Hobart, who firmly refused to believe what he thought was an outrageous lie told to cover for the other absconders. Thus, Pearce received nothing more than the standard punishment for escapers, a return to hard labor at Macquarie. His long-term jailbreak made him a hero among his fellow convicts, who also didn't believe the cannibalism story, and simply wanted to join him in his next escape. Eventually, a young convict named William Cox convinced Pearce to abscond with him. Sure enough, their escape was successful—and Cox was lunch only a few days later. When captured, Pearce still had pieces of Cox's flesh with him, and this time convinced the authorities that he had been cannibalizing his compatriots all along. Mortified, the officials executed Pearce and made his body available for scientific experimentation (considered the ultimate posthumous ignominy). His skull was acquired by a then-famous phrenologist, and it is still on display today at the Academy of Natural Sciences in Philadelphia, USA.

TASMANIA

Brooke St Pier to the Wrest Point Casino on the east bank; trips are available with meals or without. The **Lady Nelson** gives river cruises in a more historical context (tel. 6272 2823 or 6234 3348). Popular combination cruises visit the **Cadbury Chocolate Factory** (see below); try contacting **Cruise Company** (tel. 6234 9294) or **M.V. Emmalisa** (tel. 6223 5893), or call **Cadbury** (tel. 1800 627 367) itself.

The pleasant area just inland from the wharves features two large parks; **Parliament Square** is the broad green in front of the Parliament House, and **St. David's Park,** featuring huge trees and a gazebo on a gently sloping hillside, is one block to the west. St. David's also has a cathedral at the corner of Murray and Macquarie St which is worth a gander. A bizarre, ancestral form of tennis lingers on at the **Royal Tennis Club,** 45 Davey St (tel. 6231 1781), adjacent to the park. The club contains one of the few Royal courts in the southern hemisphere.

The **Tasmanian Museum and Art Gallery** (tel. 6235 0777), on the corner of Argyle and Macquarie St, has fine displays exploring Tasmania's early convict history, unique ecology, and artistic heritage. *(Free guided tours leave from the bookshop W-Su 2:30pm. Open daily 10am-5pm. Museum and gallery free.)* The modern Australian art section is particularly strong. The adjacent Bond Store houses a dynamic selection of temporary exhibits. The **Penitentiary Chapel and Criminal Courts** (tel. 6223 5200), on the corner of Brisbane and Campbell St, is one of the oldest, best-preserved buildings in Tasmania, and an excellent example of Georgian ecclesiastical architecture. *(Guided tours available M-F 10am-2:30pm, Sa-Su 2-5pm. Ghost tours daily 8pm.)* The buildings house the southern regional offices of the National Trust. The **Maritime Museum** (tel. 6223 5082) is on Secheron Rd. *(Open daily 10am-4:30pm. Admission $4.)* Concentrating on local shipping and whaling, this crowded museum is filled to the gunwales with model boats, ancient photographs, and crusty relics of times gone by.

The **Royal Tasmanian Botanical Gardens** (tel. 6234 6299), north of the city near the Tasman Bridge, are the second oldest in Australia, founded in 1818. *(Free admission.)* With 13 hectares and 6000 species, this is the largest public collection of Tasmanian plants in the world, and of conifers in the southern hemisphere. Take any bus to the eastern shore and get off at stop 4 before the bridge, or take the X3-G express to Bridgewater, which stops at the main gate. Further north in Glenorchy, the **Tasmanian Transport Museum,** on Anfield St (tel. 6272 7721), has lots of train-related relics. *(Open Sept.-Apr. Sa-Su 1-5pm; May-Aug. Sa-Su 1-4:30pm. Admission $3, children $1.50. Train rides 1st and 3rd Su each month.)*

Risdon Cove (tel. 6243 8830), on the east bank of the Derwent at Risdon Vale, is the site of Tasmania's first settlement in 1802. *(Open daily 9:30am-4:30pm.)* The location was then deemed foolish and the colony was moved across the river to Sullivans Cove. The government returned the site to the Aboriginal community in 1995.

One of Hobart's most popular attractions is the **Cadbury Chocolate Factory** (tel. 6249 0333 or 1800 627 367; fax 6249 0334), in Claremont. *(Tours M-F 5 per day. Tickets $10, students $7, children $5. Advanced bookings required.)* Tours examine packaging, mixing, shaping, and coating machines, and chocolate tasting features prominently. Take the Claremont service to the factory, or make it a cruise stop (see above).

If you prefer death by beer rather than chocolate, visit the **Cascade Brewery** (tel. 6224 1144), built in 1832 by a Mr. Degraves, who drew up the plans while in prison for debt default. *(Tours 1½hr. Tickets $7.50, students and seniors $5, children $1.50. Free beer at the end. Book ahead M-F.)* The oldest brewery in Australia, it produces 800 stubbies per every minute. Take the Strickland Ave bus service to stop 17.

See the fabulous beasts that roam the island's wilderness up close at the **Bonorong Wildlife Park** (tel. 6268 1184; fax 6268 1811), north of Hobart in Brighton. *(Open daily 9am-5pm. Admission $7, children $3.50.)* Devils (Tasmanian, that is), koalas, quolls, and wombats live in enclosures, while 'roos bounce where they will. Every visitor gets a bag of kangaroo feed, which the mannerless brutes will eat right out of your hand. Food for humans is also available. Devil feeding time is particularly interesting and noisy. Take the Brighton bus all the way to the end.

South of Hobart in Kingston, the **Australian Antarctic Division** (tel. 6232 3524) organizes the Australian National Antarctic Research Expeditions (ANARE). *(Su-F 5 per* *day. $2.50.)* The Division maintains a small museum on the Australian role in the exploration of the earth's most forbidding frontier. The exhibit is well worth the effort of getting there; take Tigerline Coaches from St. David's Cathedral on Murray St.

NIGHTLIFE AND ENTERTAINMENT

Hobart is often mocked for its lukewarm nightlife, but with an open mind, one can find things to do. This isn't the place to find a world-class club scene on par with that of Melbourne or Sydney, however. Big-name acts rarely bother to go to Tasmania, but the crowds are gigantic and wildly appreciative when they do.

Pubs, Clubs, and Music

The main dance clubs are **Club Surreal,** 86 Sandy Bay Rd (tel. 6223 3655), and **'round Midnight,** 39 Salamanca Pl (tel. 6223 2491), with fluctuating standards of dress and behavior. Cover is usually $5 to $8. Most pubs downtown have music on weekends.

⊛**The New Sydney Hotel,** 87 Bathurst St (tel. 6234 4516), is an extremely popular Irish pub with live music Tu-Su, mainly cover bands. On Sa afternoons, there are open Irish jam sessions. Margaritas, in a dubious Irish tradition, are the most popular beverage. Meals available noon-2pm and 6-8pm ($6-15). Closes at midnight.

Joe's Garage, 145 Elizabeth St (tel. 6234 3501; fax 6234 3502). Half-pub, half-auto parts store, 100% shrine to all things automotive, serving honest drinks to honest folks at honest prices. Industrial aesthetic, with engine block tables and license plates on the walls. The restaurant next door has Cadillac tailfin booths and a Beatles corner with a papier-maché yellow submarine. Closes at midnight.

The Shamrock Hotel, 195 Liverpool St (tel. 6234 3892), is the local footy pub, with posters and pictures of the game's heroes. Very uncrowded. Open M-Tu 11am-10pm, W-Th 11am-midnight, F 10am-4am, Sa 10:30am-4am, Su noon-8pm.

Cafe Who, 251 Liverpool St (tel. 6231 2744; fax 6231 5241), is the place for both aging and youthful hipsters. The modern, abstract architecture distinguishes the place from its surroundings and complements the very modern cuisine ($8-15). Local and big-name acts appear regularly; genres include jazz, world, and dance music. Open Tu-Th 4:30pm-midnight, F-Sa 4:30pm-late.

Cinema, Theater, and the Casino

The giant **Village Cinema** complex, 181 Collins St (tel. 6234 7288), screens Hollywood's best a few months after U.S. releases. The art house cinema is the **State,** 375 Elizabeth St (tel. 6234 6318), with avant-whatever fare in glitzy facilities (tickets $9, students $6.50; W $6). **The Theatre Royal,** 31 Campbell St (tel. 6233 2299, outside Hobart 1800 650 277), the oldest theater in Australia, produces reliably good shows. More experimental fare is produced in the **Salamanca Theatre,** 79 Salamanca Pl (tel. 6234 8561), with several spaces around the city. Fun with strings attached is available at the **Terrapin Puppet Theatre,** 77 Salamanca Pl (tel. 6223 6834).

The **Wrest Point Hotel** in Sandy Bay, the oldest casino in Australia, caters to Hobart gamblers 24 hours a day. The emphasis is on pokies and other electronic games, but there are a few real gaming tables. The on-site nightclub, **Blackjacks Showroom,** is free, except when it books live acts.

■ Near Hobart: Richmond

Richmond is a pretty, compact 1870s village gracefully preserved as a historic and tourist site. It's less than a half-hour drive from Hobart to the northeast (the road branches north off the A9 after 10km), and thus is a popular daytrip. **Tasmanian Wilderness Travel** runs weekdays to Hobart (30min., $4.10) and the East Coast, including the towns of Triabunna (1¼hr., $7) and Swansea (1¾hr., $11.40).

Superlative-collectors can pass a pleasant afternoon looking at old things: the oldest state school still in use in Australia (built in 1834 on Torrens St), the oldest bridge still

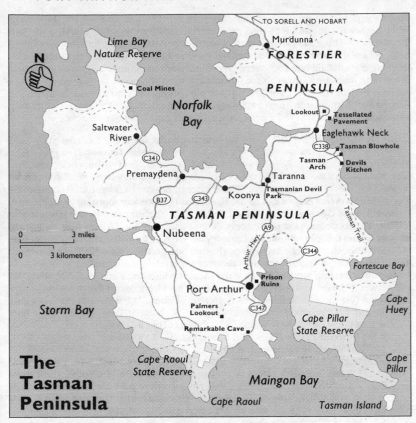

The Tasman Peninsula

in use in Australia (built by convict labor in 1823), and the oldest Catholic Church still in use in Australia (built in 1837 just over the bridge), to name but three.

The **Richmond Gaol** (tel. 6260 2127) requires a more serious visit. Built in 1825, the Gaol confined a generation of convicts, Aboriginals, and bushrangers; its history is colored with tales of escapes. It has remained unaltered after being closed and you can pace the same floorboards convicts paced, stand in the same corner where they were flogged, and lean against the same coat of paint they stared at in the darkness of solitary confinement. It's an eerie but intimate counterpoint to the expansive Port Arthur ruins. (Open daily 9am-5pm. Admission $4, children $1.50.) The wares on offer behind the sandstone storefront may be beyond your means, but they're good for a browse. Enjoy some leading lights of **Tasmanian art** in **Sadler's Court Gallery,** 48 Bridge St (open daily 9:30am-5pm summer, 10am-5pm winter), or step into **Sweets and Treats** next door just for the smell (open daily 10am-5pm).

The **Richmond Bakery** behind Sadlers court on Edward St serves pastries and decent coffee; a salad roll on fresh bread is $3.50. **Richmond Cabin and Tourist Park,** 48 Middle Tea Tree Rd (tel. 6260 2192), is a quality campground with a heated indoor swimming pool. (Tent sites $7 per person, powered $16; on-site vans $38.)

■ Port Arthur and the Tasman Peninsula

The Tasman Peninsula is very nearly the Tasman Island, barely connected to the mainland at **Eaglehawk Neck.** When the British were looking for a place to dump recidivists, this narrow access, coupled with a reasonable climate and a safe harbor, made the peninsula a natural choice. Beginning in 1830, convicts were shipped to **Port Arthur** for offenses including murder, "gross filthiness," and "skulking without permission." The inmates were put to work, and Port Arthur eventually became a self-contained, sustainable settlement that exported timber, leather, and church bells. Many fine sandstone buildings were erected through the convicts' labor; the ruins of these structures are Tasmania's most popular tourist attraction, with 250,000 visitors touring the site annually. Further historic and prehistoric fascinations wait off the beaten Port Arthur path. The Tasman coastline, the edge of the world, is particularly astounding. From the top of a peak, or the tip of a cape, try to get a view.

PRACTICAL INFORMATION The lone scheduled bus service out here is still called "Tigerline," but is now owned by **Tasmanian Wilderness Travel** (tel. 6334 4442). Buses depart from the Coach House, 23 Safety Cove Rd., Port Arthur (M-F 6am, 2hr., $11.50), running through Eaglehawk Neck about 15 minutes later. Bookings can be made with the YHA management. The owner of Seaview Lodge (see Accommodations, below) drives his bus out to the Hobart and back every morning as well.

Port Arthur General Store (tel. 6250 2220), by the entrance to the Historic Site on the A9, has petrol, post office services, and takeaway food (open daily 8am-7pm, in winter 8am-6:30pm). **Peninsula Laundry Services** (tel. 6250 2900) next door takes $2 coins only. By the Eaglehawk Neck Historic Site on the A9, the **Officers Mess** (tel. 6250 3635) has basic groceries and takeaway (open daily 8am-8pm).

The uninteresting town of **Sorell** is the main service center and last ATM along the A9 between Hobart and the Tasman Peninsula; it's also a useful stop en route to the Sun Coast (via the A3). Redline runs to Hobart (45min., M-F 9 per day, Sa 2 per day, $3.30), and TWT returns from Hobart (40min., W, F, Su 5:30pm, $4.10). TWT runs up the East Coast (W, F, Su 8:50am) to Triabunna (1hr., $7), Swansea (2hr., $11.20), Coles Bay turn-off (2½hr., $14.60), Bicheno (2¼, $15.40) and St. Helens ($3¾, $24.20). The **Westpac bank,** with **ATM,** is at 36 Cole St, right at the junction of the A3 and A9 (open M-Th 9:30am-4pm, F 9:30am-5pm). **Chemmont,** 31 Garden St (tel. 6265 1195; 24hr. line 6265 1888), is a pharmacy (open daily 9am-8pm). The expansive **Purity Supermarket** (tel. 6265 1204) has a carpark off Cole St and reasonably priced gas (open M-W 8am-6pm, Th-F 8am-9pm, Sa 8am-6pm). The **post office** is at ˙9 Garden St (tel. 5265 2911; fax 6265 1195; open daily 9am-8pm).

ACCOMMODATIONS Of the several "seaviews" in the state, the **Seaview Lodge** (tel. 6250 2766), 6km west of Tarana, perhaps best deserves its name. Their spectacular site is 1½km up the dirt Nubeena Back Rd, signposted on the B37. Lively local hosts can help you decide where you'd like to go, and their colorful bus can probably take you there, including a daily shuttle to Port Arthur. (Dorms $15. Laundry $2. Guest bike hire $15 per day.) The **Port Arthur YHA** (tel. 6250 2311) sits mere yards from the historic ruins. The pleasant wooden cottage has rambling rooms, a resident goat named Socrates, and a resident ghost named Alice. The pot-belly stove is an essential companion on winter nights. (Dorms $12; YHA nonmembers $15.)

The **Port Arthur Garden Point Caravan Park** (tel. 6250 2340; fax 6250 2509) has dorm bunkhouses ($13), cabins ($50-65), and tent sites ($11, powered $13) in a wooded setting filled with noisy birds. (Peak season cabins $60-75, tent sites $12-14.) **Eaglehawk Neck Backpackers,** 94 Old Jetty Rd (tel. 6250 3248), offers two self-contained weatherboard beach huts on their florid, ramshackle acre, minutes from the water and the Neck. The friendly owners are experienced, passionate local walkers, and they rent bikes ($5 per day) and a canoe. (Fresh vegetables in season; full recycling facilities; no smoking. Singles $12; limited tent space $6 per person.)

PORT ARTHUR SIGHTS The **Port Arthur Historic Site** (tel. 6250 2363; http://www.portarthur.org.au) is the most striking reminder of Australia's convict heritage. *(Open daily 8:30am-8:30pm, but most buildings close at 5pm. Admission $13, after 4:30pm $6.50. Buy admission stickers and Ghost Tour tickets from the YHA manager.)* Penal colonies for repeat offenders were also set up at Sarah Island near Strahan and at **Maria Island** just northeast of Hobart, but both of these have since been razed, leaving Port Arthur as the final remnant of this troubled time. The model prison, lunatic asylum, hospital, and church are on display alongside some private residences. Guided **tours** of the grounds, included in the price of admission, are a good way to explore the site (meet at the visitor center; bookings not required). The **Historic Ghost Tour** runs nightly at 6:30 and 8:30pm; $10 buys nearly two hours of spooky stories and creepy shadows. Many of the buildings are floodlit at night for a spectacular effect. Allow four hours to explore the site. A cruise around the harbor to inspect the **Isle of the Dead,** the colony's cemetery, and **Point Puer,** the convict boys' colony, is included in the price of admission; book at the visitor center. Cruises that land on the Isle of the Dead can also be arranged for $5.

The colony was under martial administration from its founding in 1830 until 1854, when civilian governors took over. The military period gave the colony a fearsome reputation for physical hardship and cruelty. For years, Port Arthur was feared throughout the empire as the foulest hell-hole in the British penal system. The **cat o' nine tails** was a whip made of nine strands of nautical cord, each with nine knots, soaked in sea water to make the tails stiff and salty. Far from discouraging repeat offenses, in most cases this treatment engendered a hatred of authority and strengthened the outlaw mentality. Eventually, the whip was abandoned in favor of more subtle torments, and a separate prison was built at Port Arthur in the late 1840s.

On Sunday, April 28, 1996, a gunman killed 35 people in Port Arthur historic site and township. The shock to Tasmania and Australia as a whole will last a long time; it has triggered recent gun law reform. Reading on the tragedy and its aftermath is available in any Tasmanian bookstore; please be respectful by not asking Port Arthur staff.

AROUND THE TASMAN PENINSULA The **Tasmanian Devil Park Wildlife Reserve Centre** (tel. 6250 3230; fax 6250 3406), in Taranna, is one of the best wildlife parks around, rehabilitating injured or orphaned critters. Over 25 species are housed in large, unobtrusive enclosures on spacious grounds. Many of the animals are returned to the wild after a short period, while others are long-term residents or have been bred in captivity. The center runs a variety of **wilderness tours,** ranging from a few hours to several days in length. It offers the best value for your animal-watching dollar, and you needn't feel guilty about supporting animal imprisonment. The Tasmanian devils are fed each day at 10 and 11am.

Next door are the assuredly secure pens of the new **World Tiger Snake Centre.** Promising medical research and an eerie addiction to walking around in a pit full of one of the world's deadliest serpents has inspired the dedicated tiger snake farmers to maintain over 1000 individuals on site. *(Both attractions open daily 9am-5pm. Devil Park $11, children $3.50; combined ticket $16, children $8.)*

The east coast of the Peninsula offers stunning clifftop **hiking trails.** From the **Devils Kitchen** carpark at the end of C338 (unsealed road) near Eaglehawk Neck, short hikes reach **Cash's Lookout, Waterfall Bay, Camp Falls,** and **Yatnell's Hill.** An overnight hike of the **Tasman Trail** south to Fortescue Bay can be breathtaking. **Fortescue Bay State Forest,** at the end of the unsealed C344 east of Port Arthur, offers primitive camping for $6 per person. **Cape Huoy** is three hours return from the camp, and features **The Candlestick, The Needle,** and **The Lanterns,** dolerite spires enjoyed by rock climbers. Heading south from Forescue Bay, **Cape Pillar** is a long but highly praised two-day round-trip to the edge of the world. A detailed walking guide is recommended.

Curses—Foiled Again

On May 17, 1832, Port Arthur escapee George "Billy" Hunt tried to cross Eaglehawk Neck, which was protected by guard stations and a line of savage dogs. He attempted to disguise himself by donning a kangaroo skin and hopping through the blockade. The guards bought the act—and started shooting at him; kangaroo meat was an important supplement to their rations. Mr. Hunt threw off the skin, crying "It's only me, Billy Hunt!"

■ D'Entrecasteaux Channel

The channels, islands, and caves south of Hobart were first charted by the Frenchman Bruni D'Entrecasteaux in 1792, more than a decade before the first English settlement in the area. The **Huon River** flows gently through the valley, feeding fertile soil and a cool, misty climate perfect for berries, pears, and apples. The spit of land between the Huon River and the D'Entrecasteaux Channel teems with antiques, crafts, cottages, and vineyards, all in a tranquil pastoral setting. The hamlet of **Cygnet** is a good base for exploring the area, while **Bruny Island** is practically deserted and well worth a look. South of the Huon River, the pastoral English landscapes drop away, and the Van Diemen's Land wilderness looms. Here **Geeveston** and the **Lone River** area are launchpads to the great wildlands of the southwest.

■ Cygnet and the Huon Valley

Located near the mouth of the Nicholls Rivulet on Port Cygnet, Cygnet's main attributes are peace and quiet, but most of the Huon Valley's attractions are just a few minutes from the town. **Hobart Coaches** buses from Hobart stop on weekdays at the Shell Garage on the corner of Mary St and the Channel Hwy. **Mary St** houses the **Trust Bank** (tel. 6295 1682; open M-F 9am-12:15pm, 1pm-5pm); **post office** (tel. 6295 1400; **postal code** 7112; open M-F; 9am-5pm); **newsagent** with limited ANZ banking capability (tel./fax 6295 1500; open M-Th 7am-6pm, F 7am-7pm, Sa 8am-5pm); **laundry,** beside the newsagent ($1.40 a load); and a **supermarket** (tel. 6295 1530; open daily 7:30am-9:30pm). The **Red Velvet Lounge** (tel. 6295 0466), a cafe and art gallery, serves breakfast, vegetarian dishes, and hot drinks galore. Seat yourself in the dining room, cafe, garden, verandah, or hallway. (Meals $3-8; open daily 10am-6pm and beyond.)

The **Huon Valley (Balfes Hill) YHA & Backpackers** (tel./fax 6295 1551), just north of Cygnet in **Cradoc,** is the best bet for a budget bed in the valley. The hostel caters to the flocks of eager workers that come to pick fruit, train vines, and prune orchards between November and May, helping to find employment and providing transportation for $10 a week. Workers and loafers alike enjoy the video lounge, pool and ping-pong tables, big kitchen, and twin rooms. Basic groceries and meals can be arranged. Moderately priced bus trips to Hobart, points in the valley, and the wilderness to the southwest are also available. (No smoking. Beds $12, weekly $75.)

The **Talune Wildlife Park** (tel. 6295 1775; fax 6295 0818; email wombat@south-com.com.au), 6km south of Cygnet on the road to Gordon, houses wombats, devils, and roaming bands of 'roos and wallabies. Some of the enclosures are a bit ramshackle, but the animals look healthy. (Open daily 9:30am-5pm. Admission $7, children $2.50, families $16.50.) Just outside of Cygnet on Nicholls Rivulet, the **Deepings Woodturner** (tel. 6295 1398; fax 6295 0498) transforms native timbers into beautiful carved goods. You can watch and buy. (Open M-Sa 9am-5pm, Su noon-5pm.)

This region of Tasmania is locally famous for its cool-climate wines, many of which are available at the **Hartzview Vineyard and Wine Centre** (tel./fax 6295 1623) in Gardner's Bay. In addition to its own blends, Hartzview sells those of smaller area vineyards without cellar-door sales of their own. (Open daily 9am-5pm.)

■ Bruny Island

Bruny Island was the first bit of land Abel Tasman glimpsed when he "discovered" Tasmania in 1642. The island has seen more than its share of famous explorers since. Captain Cook and his understudy Captain Bligh (of *Bounty* fame) both visited the island and believed it to be part of the mainland. This assumption was shattered when D'Entrecasteaux sailed through the channel that bears his name in 1792. In the glory days of bay whaling, the island's shores teemed with whalers, but with the end of the great creatures came the end of industry on Bruny. Half-hearted attempts to mine coal failed, so the few remaining inhabitants fell back on timber and agriculture;

this pastoral lifestyle continues today. The island offers visitors dramatic coastal scenery, remnants of its exploratory past, and plenty of space.

PRACTICAL INFORMATION A **tourist information center** is across the channel in **Kettering** (tel. 6267 4494; fax 6267 4266; open daily 9am-5pm). Bicycles can be rented here (or at the YHA on the island); sea kayaks next door. The **ferry terminal** is adjacent to the information center (boats run roughly every hr. M-Sa 7am-6pm, F 7am-7:30pm, Su 8am-6:30pm). The crossing takes about 15 minutes. (Automobiles $18, motorcycles $11, bicycles $3, pedestrians free.) There is no public transportation on the island. **Buses** to Hobart leave from the Kettering General Store (tel. 6267 4413) several times per day on weekdays (45min., $5).

ACCOMMODATIONS The **Bruny Island YHA** (tel. 6293 1265), in Lumeah, Adventure Bay, is a superb hostel offering comfortable beds in a friendly setting. Run by a young couple and their boisterous brood, Lumeah has spacious wooden dorms and huge common areas, as well as a brick fireplace that is well appreciated on stormy winter nights. The managers will organize sea kayaking, camel trekking, and bushwalking. (Dorms $13, YHA non-members $15; doubles $40. Bike hire $12 per day, tandem bikes $15.)

The **Adventure Bay Holiday Villages** (tel. 6293 1270), in Adventure Bay, has an array of cabins and caravans that can be economical for groups of three or more, as well as excellent tent sites ($10, powered $13). The block is decorated with bleached whalebones and holds coin-op showers. Many of the island's state reserves also offer camping. **Cloudy Bay** (on the southern part of the island), **Neck Beach** (on the spit between North and South Bruny, just north of Adventure Bay), **Jetty Beach** (near the lighthouse, accessible by kayak), and **Partridge Island** (off the southern cape, accessible by boat only) all offer free primitive sites with pit toilets, no water, and unreliable firewood.

SIGHTS AND RECREATION The **Bligh Museum** (tel. 6293 1117), in Adventure Bay, contains marine photos and memorabilia concentrating on Captain Cook and the much-maligned Captain Bligh. (*Open daily 10am-3pm. Admission $4, concessions $3, children $2.*) It's fascinating if you're interested in Pacific exploration. **Cloudy Bay** has excellent surf, while **Jetty Beach** has more sheltered waters suitable for kids. Both fairy penguins and shearwaters (muttonbirds) roost on the Neck, the thin strip of land that connects North and South Bruny Islands. The Neck has fine views from the top and has been fitted with a long staircase, called **Truganini's Steps** after the last full-blooded Tasmanian Aboriginal woman, who was a Bruny Islander. A ranger stationed at the **Labillardiere State Reserve** (tel. 6298 3229) can provide info on the many coastal recreation opportunities on Bruny, including the popular daytrip destination **Cape Bruny Lighthouse**. The lighthouse was built by convicts between 1836 and 1838. Hiking there through the coastal heath of the Labillardiere Reserve takes about seven hours return.

■ Far South: Gateways to Wilderness

Below Huonville, the A6 continues south along the D'Entrecasteaux Channel toward the bottom of the bottom of the world. About 25km along, **Geeveston** proclaims itself the gateway to the southwest wilderness. The west bank of the Huon River, long a stomping ground of the timber industry, is now the edge of a **World Heritage wilderness area** and a major conservation battleground. It's an amazing region. **Tasmanian Wilderness Travel** (tel. 6334 4442) runs to the region from Hobart three days a week, stopping in Lone River (2½hr., $45) and Cockle Creek (3¼hr., $45).

The Geeveston **Visitor Information** (tel. 6297 1836) is in the Forest and Heritage Centre on Church St (open daily 9:30am-5pm, in winter 10am-4:30pm). Church St houses a **post office** that's also an arts, crafts and video store (tel. 6297 1102; open daily 9am-8pm; **postal code** 7116), a **pharmacy** (open M-F 9am-5:30pm), and a **supermarket** (open Sa-Th 9am-6pm, F 9am-7pm). The managers of the post office have just opened a budget accommodation: the **Geeveston Forest House** (tel./fax 6297 1102), just off Church St, boasts real spring mattresses and no bunks. Ask at the post office for access. (Single $12. Free laundry.)

The **Lone River YHA** (tel. 6298 3163), 40km south of Geeveston, is an institution. "The doing place" has a minivan to truck people off to all their doings (bike hire $10 per day; canoes $6 per half-day). The loungey common space is plastered with photos, charts, and maps detailing the **Cockle Creek** walks, the **thermal spring** jaunt, the **Mystery Creek Cave** system, the **Ida Bay** rail trip, and the **Lone River** canoe runs. Lone River celebrates each full moon with fresh fish and music; other festivals are cooked up as inspired. (Bunks $10.) **Camping** options abound in the region, with free sites at the **Tahune Forest Reserve** and **Arve River Picnic Area** west of Geeveston, **Hastings Forest** west of Dover, and Cockle Creek. About 90 minutes driving from Lone River is the **Hastings/Newdegate Cave,** dripping with gorgeous dolomite formations (last tour at 4pm; $10, children $5.) The admission price includes entry to nearby **hot springs.**

Cockle Creek, a 25-minute drive south of Lone River, is the trailhead for the **South Coast Walk.** The first leg out to South Cape Bay is an easy four-hour return walk for a taste of the National Park. This is **Australia's southernmost tip.** Be prepared for all weather, even in summer. Most people hiking the full track fly into **Melaleuca** and hike out in six to nine days. For info on flights, contact **Par-Avion Wilderness Tours,** Cambridge Airport, Hobart (tel. 6248 5390; fax 6248 5117; email paravion@tassie.net.au).

■ Derwent Valley and the Southwest

The **Derwent River** flows down into Hobart from the northwest and empties into the Tasman Sea. From the coast, the A10 highway traces the river toward its source in the heavily forested interior wilderness. The river divides the South zone of Tasmania from the agricultural Midlands region to the north (see p. 473). To the south of the Derwent Valley lies the great expanse of **Southwest National Park,** whose mountains and forests stretch down to the Southern ocean, and in which the vast **Lake Gordon** and **Lake Pedder** shine like diamonds in the rough.

■ New Norfolk

A cool, misty valley enfolds the small town of New Norfolk, 25km northwest of Hobart on the Derwent River. The climate is perfect for growing hops, and regional cultivators harvest up to 45 tons per day. The well-maintained **Oast House** (tel. 6261 1030), on Hobart Rd, was once used to dry the harvest. New Norfolk's biggest tourist attraction today, Oast House contains a hop museum, hop gallery, and hophouse cafe (open W-Su 9am-5pm). A few of the town's old 19th-century buildings have been preserved, including the church of St. Matthew and the Bush Inn. Historical walking tour maps are sold for $1 by the **Derwent Valley Council** (tel. 6261 0700), on Circle St (open M-F 8:15am-5pm). The Council can also provide info on other tourist attractions in the area. **Tasmanian Wilderness Travel** (tel. 6334 4442) has service on Tuesdays, Thursdays, Saturdays, and Sundays to Hobart (40min., $4.50), Lake St. Clair (2½hr., $25.40), and Queenstown (4¾hr., $31.70), with connections to Strahan and Launceston.

The only budget accommodation in town is the **New Norfolk Esplanade Caravan Park** (tel. 6261 1269), down by the river. (Coin-op showers and laundry. Unpowered sites for 2 people $8, additional adults $5; powered sites for 2 $12, $10. Use of the amenities block $3; a keycard for the gate requires a $7 deposit.)

Devil-Jet Jet Boats (tel. 6261 3460; fax 6261 1743) operate daily on the Derwent River near New Norfolk. Bookings for the 30-minute cruises ($40, students $30) can be made at the Bush Inn on the Lyell Hwy or by phone. The prop-less jet boats can shoot through rigorous rapids without getting stuck on rocks.

■ Mt. Field National Park

Founded in 1916, Mt. Field is one of Tasmania's oldest national parks, just an hour from Hobart. **Russell Falls** has long been the favorite destination, but there's more to see here, too. The park can be divided into two distinct areas. The lower slopes near the park entrance have picnic and barbecue facilities, a **visitor kiosk** (tel. 6288 1477), and short, easy walks to Russell Falls and other rainforest attractions. On the upper slopes, the alpine moorland around **Lake Dobson** features Mt. Field's primitive **ski** facilities, glassy highland lakes, and large network of extended bushwalks. The **Pandani Grove** nature walk circles Lake Dobson and provides a good introduction to the unusual plant life. Swamp gum (*Eucalyptus regnans*), the tallest flowering plant in the world, and the man fern, which can live to be 800 years old, both thrive in the lower levels. Maps are available at the kiosk at the bottom of the hill.

The upper Lake Dobson area is reached by a tortuous 16km unsealed road, sometimes impassable in winter. A gradual change from rainforest to heath can be observed while winding up the mountain. The ski area is a 30-minute hike from the Lake Dobson carpark. During the ski season, **buses** leave for the skifields from the kiosk at 9 and 10:15am ($8 round-trip). A discovery tour bus runs from the same spot at 10:15am (in summer daily, off season Tu-Th; $15). For bus information, call 6334 4442. **Tasmanian Wilderness Travel** (tel. 6334 4442) runs buses to Hobart (1¾hr.; Dec.-Mar. daily, Apr.-Nov. Tu, Th; $25), Lake St. Clair (2½hr., Dec.-Mar. daily, $25), and Scott's Peak in the Southwest National Park (3hr.; Nov.-Mar. only; $40). The **Mt. Field Information Line** (tel. 6288 1319) has a recording on ski and road conditions.

The snow cover is seldom very good, and the lifts servicing the ski fields are quite ancient, but the ski kiosk rents skis and sells food and lift tickets. The National Park Office administers three very rustic **cabins** near Lake Dobson. Each six-person cabin comes with mattresses, a wood heater, firewood, and cold water ($10, concessions $8, children $5; $20 min. per night). Bookings must be made at least a week in advance (tel. 6288 1149). The visitor kiosk also runs a campground near the park entrance. The **campsites** are equipped with excellent showers and bathrooms, as well as coin-operated laundry machines. (Sites $5 per person, students $2.50; powered $7, $3.) Just outside the national park on Garden River Rd, **Mt. Field YHA** (tel. 6288 1369) provides basic beds within earshot of the park's falls. The bathrooms could be cleaner and the mattresses thicker, but the location can't be beat. (No smoking or drinking. Bunks $12, YHA non-members $15. Sleep sheets $1.)

■ Southwest National Park

Beyond Mt. Field National Park, the B61 highway strikes out to the vast lakes **Gordon** and **Pedder,** and the hamlet of **Strathgordon.** The beautiful lakes are the centerpiece of Southwest National Park, which encompasses the entire southeastern corner of Tasmania. The lakes are currently the subject of huge conservation battles. There is neither gas nor powered campsites beyond Maydena, but there are many basic camping areas, some with tank water, and stunning lookouts all along the road. Hikers head down the unsealed C607 to **Scott's Peak Dam** for treks to **Mt. Anne** or the **Arthur Range**. National Park fees apply (there is a gate at Maydena). For info contact **Southwest National Park** (tel. 6288 1283) or the **Mt. Field Park Office** (tel. 6288 1149). In the summer, Tasmanian Wilderness Travel (tel. 6334 4442) runs from Scott's Peak back to civilization, stopping at Mt. Field National Park (3hr., $40) and Hobart (3¾hr., $47).

THE NORTHEAST

Tasmania's Northeast is blessed with a sunny disposition. Folks here grow up listening to Melbourne radio, drinking Boag's beer, and disdaining the political antics of the South. The midlands offer wool, the north coast wine, and the sun-coast water, all a

TASMANIA

gently civilized counterpoint to the state's famed wilderness. The priceless coastal pockets of Mount William, Freycinet, and Maria Island National Parks are worlds away from the mountainous World Heritage Areas of the south and west. In the middle of miles of flatness, Ben Lomond rises to survey the entire region; its ski slopes provide a bit of winter fun. Self-confident Launceston bustles at the head of it all and the heart of Tassie, a mere three hours' drive from anywhere in the state.

■ Launceston

Built where the North and South Esk rivers join to form the Tamar, Launceston (LON-seh-ston) is Tasmania's second-largest city and Australia's third-oldest, founded in 1805. The intense historic rivalry between Hobart and Launceston has decreased only slightly, and now manifests itself most clearly in beer loyalty: Boags is the ale of choice in the north, Cascade in the south. Launcestonians are a friendly bunch and welcome visitors to their city, but the town's attractions are quickly exhausted, especially with world-famous wilderness right on its doorstep.

ORIENTATION

Launceston is built on a very regular grid of familiar colonial names. The main pedestrian mall is on **Brisbane St,** between Charles and St. John St. The town is best explored by foot, since most attractions are within four blocks of the mall; all the one-way streets make it tough to drive anyway. The city center is bounded on the north by the **North Esk River** and on the west by the **South Esk,** which flows through the Cataract Gorge. Shaped like an amphitheater, Launceston slopes steadily uphill from the North Esk and downtown area, a handy navigational aid. From here, the A8 runs north to George Town, Hwy 1 heads south to Hobart through the Midlands and west to Deloraine and Devonport, and the A3 snakes east through Scottsdale to St. Helens and the east coast.

PRACTICAL INFORMATION

Tourist Office: (tel. 6331 3133), on the corner of St. John and Paterson St. Offers a walking tour M-F 9:45am. Open M-F 9am-5pm, Sa 9am-3pm, Su 9am-noon.

Airplanes: Launceston Airport, south of Launceston. **Airporter Bus,** 112 George St (tel. 6331 5755), provides airport shuttles timed to meet flights ($7). Will pick up from accommodations if you call ahead. **Ansett** (tel. 13 13 00) and **Qantas** (tel. 13 13 13) run flights to state capitals via Melbourne. To Melbourne $196, to Sydney $286.

Buses: Redline (tel. 6331 3233) has a depot at 112 George St. Buses run 3-6 times per day to Oatlands (1¼hr., $13.80), Hobart (2½hr., $19), Burnie (2½hr., $18), Deloraine (45min., $6.70), and Devonport (1½hr., $13.30). There's less frequent service to George Town (45min., Su-F 1-3 per day, $7), Scottsdale (1½hr., Su-F 2-3 per day, $9), Winnakeah (3hr., M-F, $14.30), St. Mary's (2hr., $15), and St. Helen's (2¾hr., Su-F 1-2 per day, $18.80). **Tasmanian Wilderness Travel,** 101 George St (tel. 6334 4447; fax 6334 2029), has buses west on Tuesdays, Thursdays, and Saturdays to Cradle Mountain Lodge (3hr., $36.50) and Queenstown (6½hr., $43.10) with connections to Strahan ($49). They also run 3-7 times per week to Dove Lake at Cradle Mountain (4¾hr., $43.50), Lake St. Clair (2½hr., $45) and Bicheno (2½hr., $19).

Local Transportation: Run by **Metro,** 168 Wellington St (tel. 6336 5888; fax 6336 5899; hotline 13 22 01). Most buses run 7am-7pm. Fares $1-3.

Taxis: Central Cabs (tel. 6331 3555 or 13 10 08). Fare to airport $17.

Car Rental: Hertz, 58 Paterson St (tel. 6335 1111), from $37 per day. **Advance Car Rentals,** 32 Cameron St (tel. 6391 8000), from $39 per day. **Budget,** 138 George St (tel. 6334 5533, airport tel. 6391 8566), from $38 per day. **Economy,** 27 William St (tel. 6334 3299), from $28 per day.

Bike Rental: Rent-a-Cycle Tasmania, 36 Thistle St West (tel. 6344 9779), in Launceston City Youth Hostel. Bikes $15 per day. Extended tours with repair kit, clothing, instruction $6 and up per day. Open hostel hours. **Rik Sloane Cycles,** 10-

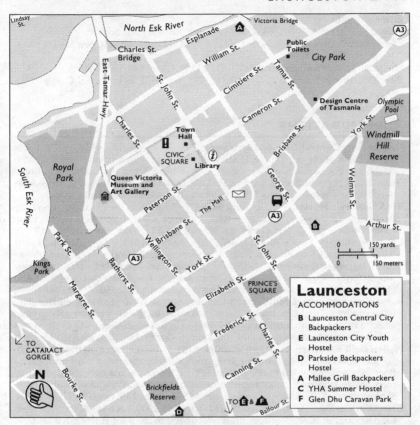

Launceston

ACCOMMODATIONS

B Launceston Central City Backpackers
E Launceston City Youth Hostel
D Parkside Backpackers Hostel
A Mallee Grill Backpackers
C YHA Summer Hostel
F Glen Dhu Caravan Park

14 Paterson St (tel. 6331 9414 or 6331 9482; fax 6334 4476). $20 per day. Open M-F 8:30am-5:30pm, Sa 8am-2pm.

Currency Exchange: Commonwealth Bank, 97 Brisbane St (tel. 13 22 21). Open M-Th 9:30am-4pm, F 9:30am-5pm. **Trust Bank,** 79 St. John (tel. 6336 6444), open M-Th 9:30am-4pm, F 9:30am-5pm. **Thomas Cook,** 85B George St (tel. 6334 6304). Open M-F 9am-5:15pm, Sa 9am-noon. The mall features **ATMs** of every stripe.

Hiking Equipment: Allgoods (tel. 6331 3644), at York and St. John St. Huge, inexpensive, and comprehensive, including army surplus. Basic equipment hire at their Tent City annex, 60 Elizabeth St. Open M-F 9am-5:30pm, Sa 9am-4pm. **Paddy Palin,** 110 George St (tel. 6331 4240). Good source of info on local hiking and climbing. Open M-F 8:30am-6pm (winter 9am-5:30pm), Sa 9am-3pm. **Launceston City Youth Hostel** (see **Rent-a-Cycle,** above), also has a wide range of gear.

Bookstore: Birchalls (tel 6331 3011), in the Brisbane St mall. Australia's oldest bookshop. Wide selection, especially field guides and histories of Tasmania. Open M-Th 8:30am-5:30pm, F 8:30am-9pm, Sa 8:30am-5pm, Su 10am-4pm. **Wilderness Shop,** 174 Charles St (tel. 6334 2499), has outdoors books, postcards, and gifts. Proceeds used for wilderness protection. Open M-F 9:30am-5:30pm, Sa 10am-1pm.

Library: 1 Civic Square (tel./fax 6336 2625). Open M-Th 9:30am-6pm, F 9:30am-9pm, Sa 9:30am-12:30pm. Free **Internet access.**

Ticket Agency: Fortune's Newsagency, 68 Charles St, (tel. 6334 3033).

Automobile Club: RACT (tel. 6335 5633, 24hr. help tel. 13 11 11), at the corner of York and Macquarie St. Open M-F 8:45am-5pm.

Public Laundry: 341a Wellington St (tel. 6344 5418), in the district of Glen Dhu. Open daily 6am-11pm.

Emergency: Dial 000.
Police: On Cimitiere St (tel. 6336 3701). Enter through Civic Square.
Pharmacy: Centre Pharmacy (tel. 6331 7777), 84 Brisbane St. Open M-Sa 8:30am-10pm, Su 9am-10pm.
Hospital: Launceston General (tel. 6332 7111), Charles St, uphill block.
Post Office: 107 Brisbane St (tel. 6331 9477; fax 6331 844). **Postal Code:** 7250. Open M-F 9am-5:30pm, Sa 9:30am-1pm.
Phone Code: 03.

ACCOMMODATIONS

Launceston Central City Backpackers, 173 George St (tel. 6334 2327), a few blocks south of the city center. Homey and spotless, with a comfy common room couch and giant bean bag. The lounge is well-heated, but the kitchen and bunk-rooms can get cold during the winter. During the summer, they use Parkside as overflow (see below). Dorms $14; doubles $30. Book ahead, even in winter.

YHA Summer Hostel, 132 Elizabeth St (tel. 6334 4505). Open Dec.-Jan. only; student dorm during school year. Arranged in apartments with two twin rooms, bathroom, kitchen, and lounge. Generous, if unlovely. $14, YHA nonmembers $17.

Launceston City Youth Hostel, 36 Thistle St (tel. 6344 9779), near the Coats Patons building off Wellington. Built in an old wool mill's imposing canteen. Bunks line long, spare dorm rooms, ideal for large groups and no-frills travelers. Four blocks further from downtown than other hostels. Guests get discount bike hire ($10 per day). Closed and quiet from midnight. Dorms $12; $30 for 3 nights.

Parkside Backpackers Hostel, 103 Canning St (tel. 6331 4615). Open Dec.-Jan. only; run by Central City Backpackers. Near the Brickfields Reserve. Has trouble shaking off the institutional blur of its day job as a student dorm, but lively guests and experienced management add some verve. Dorms $14; doubles $30.

Mallee Grill Backpackers, 1 Tamar St (tel. 6331 4513). Entrance off the Esplanade. Sometimes called by its former name, Andy's Backpack. Rooms are on the 2nd floor of a well-renovated hotel, with new blue bunks packed tight. Minimal common space, kitchenette. Restaurant downstairs. All rooms use same shared bath. Sardine dorms $12; more spacious singles $25; doubles $35; twins $45.

Glen Dhu Caravan Park, 94 Glen Dhu St (tel. 6344 2600; fax 6343 1764). The best-located caravan park, 20min. from downtown. Spacious lot surrounded by blossoming trees. Free barbecue, hot, clean showers, cozy campers' kitchen, coin-op laundry. 2-person sites $8, powered $15; caravans $32; cabins $45-52.

FOOD

Launceston has several tasty options. For groceries, **Grand Central Super Store** (tel. 6331 9422), on Wellington between Frederick and Canning St, is open 24 hours.

The Happy Pumpkin, 117 Charles St (tel. 6334 2985). More than a great name, this place serves delicious chicken and vegetable dishes, coffee, and pastries. Most dishes $3-5. Open M-F 9am-5pm, Sa 11am-3pm. For a bit more pump than Pumpkin, the same management offers Mexican food next door. Burritos and tacos $5-7.

Josey's, 195a Charles St (tel. 6334 9833). A Greek-inspired takeaway a cut above the ubiquitous souvlaki bar. Good veggie options, and the homemade Greek pastry is a treat. Multicultural night every 2 weeks. Open Su-Th 9am-9pm, F-Sa 9am-11pm.

Cafe Gazebo, 135 George St (tel. 6331 0110). Late hours, convenient location, and the best food in town, usually with some mid-priced dishes. Divine pasta, plenty of veggie options. They're busy for a reason. Mains $9-18. Open daily 10:30am-late.

Elaia, 238-240 Charles St (tel. 6331 3307), second block south of Princes Square. Great Mediterranean cafe decor and classy food. Very busy F and Sa dinner, and prices may rise out of budget range, but the focaccia and salad ($7.50) makes a lovely light meal. Alternatively, just buy the gourmet ingredients from the deli counter. Veggie-friendly. Open M-Th 9am-6:30pm, F-Sa 9am-9pm, Su 10am-6pm.

O'Keefe's Hotel, 124 George St (tel. 6331 4015). Meals ($6-16) range from wallaby salad to sushi. Live music F-Su evenings. Open daily noon-2pm and 5:30pm-late.

SIGHTS

The most spectacular sight in Launceston is the handiwork of the South Esk River: the **Cataract Gorge Reserve** (tel. 6337 1288), about a 20-minute walk from York St toward the Kings Bridge. Don't expect pristine wilderness—the First Basin of the gorge has been a favorite watering hole since the town's settlement, and now boasts peacocks, an exotic tree garden, a restaurant, and a free swimming pool. For a less-manicured experience, walking tracks run on either side of the river; some climb to the gorge's rim for excellent views of the river and cataracts. The gorge circuit is a leisurely two-hour walk. The **Duck Reach Power Station** (open daily dawn to dusk), at the far end of the gorge, and the **Band Rotunda** (open M-F 9am-4pm, Sa-Su 9am-4:30pm), near the far end of the Alexandra Bridge, provide info on the gorge.

If hiking doesn't do it for you, try **Cable Hang Gliding** (tel. 13 27 88) above the Trevallyn Dam Quarry. It's not as much fun as the real thing, but you're much less likely to leave a crater in the ground. *(Open May-Nov. daily 10am-4pm, Dec.-Apr. 10am-5pm. $10.)* The longest single-span **chairlift** on the globe runs across the First Basin (tel. 6331 5915). *(Open Dec.-May daily 9am-4:30pm, June-Aug. Sa-Su 9am-4:30pm. Rides $5.)*

The Queen Victoria Museum and Art Gallery, at the corner of Cameron and Wellington St (tel. 6331 6777), houses an impressive natural history display that focuses on Tasmania's wildlife and a popular science section that seeks to explain mining and other industrial phenomena. *(Open M-Sa 10am-5pm, Su 2-5pm. Free.)* The upstairs gallery has some interesting sculpture and innovative textile art. Guided gallery tours run Saturdays and Sundays at 2:30pm. The **Launceston Planetarium** is part of the complex. *(Shows Tu-F 3pm, Sa 2 and 3pm.)*

Launceston is blessed with an abundant supply of parks, most built on former rubbish sites. **Brickfields Reserve,** on the corner of Frederick and Bathurst St, boasts grand elms, while the white oaks of **Princes Square,** at Elizabeth and St. John St, are planted in honor of various Victorian-era jubilees and royal weddings and also once shaded the audiences of public hangings. The **Heritage Forest,** 2km up Invermay Rd north of the North Esk River, has horse and bike tracks, barbecue facilities, and a nature trail. **City Park,** at Tamar and Brisbane St, harbors a war memorial, a 150-year-old wisteria, good public toilets, and an enclosure teeming with Japanese macaque monkeys. It also houses the **City Park Radio Station** (tel. 6334 3344), with a small radio museum on the ground floor. *(Museum open Tu-Th and F 10am-3pm. Free.)*

The Design Centre of Tasmania, on the corner of Tamar and Brisbane St (tel. 6331 5506; fax 6331 5662), was founded in 1976 to showcase Tasmanian crafts. *(Open M-F 10am-6pm, Sa 10am-1pm, Su 2pm-5pm. Free.)* Historic walks depart from the visitor information center Monday through Friday at 9:45am (about 1hr., $10). Bookings are preferred (tel. 6331 3679). **Tamar River Cruises** (tel. 6334 9900; fax 6334 9911) is another leisure option. *(Lunch cruises daily $46, concessions $40, children $23. Dinner buffet cruises W and F-Su $55, $49.50, $27.50.)* The **Tamar Seaplane** (tel. 6334 9922) offers 20-minute ($50) and one-hour ($100) flights.

ENTERTAINMENT

Many of the pubs downtown have live music on the weekends; the best and most popular is **Irish Murphy's,** 211 Brisbane St (tel. 6331 4440; fax 6334 5503). The decor is true to its name, but it's not as overdone as many Aussie Irish bars. (Pints of Guinness $5. Open Su-W noon-midnight, Th-Sa noon-late.) The hip **Cucina Simpatica** cafe (tel. 6334 3177), by the Brickfields at 57 Frederick St, hosts live jazz on Sunday afternoons (open daily 10am-late). **The Royal Oak** (tel. 6331 5346), on the corner of Tamar and Brisbane St, also has live music on the weekends. **The Princess Theatre** on Brisbane St hosts orchestral and other musical events. Brisbane St also has a **Village Cinema** which shows first-run Hollywood films.

TASMANIA

■ North Coast

Tasmania's pleasant northeast coast is a tame, settled area, with beaches dotted by small fishing and port towns. The Bass Strait waters are calmer than their counterparts in the west and south, and so is the way of life of the mellow folk who live and visit here.

■ George Town

The coastal port of George Town perches on the Bass Strait 50km northeast of Launceston. The settlement was named by Lachlan Macquarie in 1811, after King George III (of American Revolution infamy). A complement of navigational aids was built to keep ships safe. A lighthouse powered by 25 whale-oil lanterns was built by the famous colonial architect John Lee Archer in 1833. A pair of leading lights, miniature lighthouses used for short-range navigation, were constructed in 1882 to combat the treacherous Hebe Reef. These measures were not completely effective, however. As recently as 1995, the *Iron Baron* wrecked on the reef, spilling countless liters of oil into the sea. The hulk was eventually towed away and scuttled near Flinders Island.

There is no reliable budget accommodation in George Town, but **Redline** has regular bus services to Launceston, making daytrips easy. **Buses** depart Pinos Gift and Hardware, 21 Elizabeth St (tel. 6382 1484), for Launceston (45min.; M-F 3 per day, Su 1 per day; $7). The **post office** is at 78 Macquarie St (postal code 7253), near the **bank** and the **police** station (tel. 6382 4040).

The town's colorful seafaring history has been preserved in the **Pilot Station Maritime Museum** in **Low Head,** just north of the town. Established in 1805, it's the oldest continuously operating facility of its kind in Australia, and contains thoughtful displays on marine-related topics including communication, navigation, and shipbuilding. (Open daily 8am-late. Admission $2, kids and concessions $1.) **Fairy penguins** use some of the beaches around George Town and Low Head as rookeries during the spring.

■ Bridport

Bridport lies along a sweep of sheltered beach at the estuarine mouth of the **Great Forester River.** Beach and heath walks abound, as do many of the joys you might hope for in an estuary: birds to spot, oysters to dig, beach cricket to play. A bit off the bus-beaten path, Bridport is a good base for exploring the Northeast by car, with a touch more warmth and a lot more beach than Launceston has.

The volunteer staff at the information center, **Bridport 2000 Plus** in the Main St shops, are friendly and helpful. **Stan's Coach Service** (tel. 6356 1662) ferries passengers on his twice-daily 30-minute mail run from Scottsdale to Bridport, meeting Redline coaches from Launceston and Derby at the Scottsdale Newspower newsagency and departing for Bridport at 10:30am and 6pm. Bridport has **no bank** and **no ATM;** the major shops accept EFTPOS, but only with Australian plastic. **Tubbies** supermarket on Main St (tel. 6356 1282) houses a **post office** desk (open daily 7am-7pm).

The **Bridport Seaside Lodge,** 47 Main St (tel. 6356 1585), is a budget traveler's dream. The kitchen and common room are vast, as are the views of the estuary and the beach. Friendly managers Rob and Mary Williams can point out walks and oyster digs right from your breakfast table, and you have the benefit of their bikes, canoes, and home brew. Rob works in Launceston and may be able to offer a ride. (Dorms $13; double $30.) **Bridport Caravan Park** (tel. 5356 1227), on Bentley St, has sites along a full mile of beach (sites $9.50, powered $12.50). Beyond the usual takeaway, pizza, and pub fare, several Main St shops offer delectably fresh fish and chips. The **Bridport Hotel** (tel. 5356 1114), next to Tubbies, has half-price scallops on Wednesday nights (open for lunch daily noon-2pm; dinner Su-F 6-8:30pm).

Bridport isn't exactly brimming with sights, but pleasant walks abound. A 20-minute shoreline stroll north from the Main St bridge, past the old pier, takes you to

WE GIVE YOU THE WORLD...AT A DISCOUNT

LET'S GO®

TRAVEL

LET'S GO

Euro pean 1999 Railpasses

Eurailpass Unlimited travel in and among all 17 countries: **Austria, Belgium, Denmark, Finland, France, Germany, Greece, Holland, Hungary, Italy, Luxembourg, Norway, Portugal, Republic of Ireland, Spain, Sweden, and Switzerland.**

	15 days	21 days	1 month	2 months	3 months	10 days	15 days
First Class	*c o n s e c u t i v e*		*d a y s*			*in two months*	
1 Passenger	$554	$718	$890	$1260	$1558	$654	$862
2 or More Passengers	$470	$610	$756	$1072	$1324	$556	$732
Youthpass (Second Class)							
Passengers under 26	$388	$499	$623	$882	$1089	$458	$599

Europass Travel in the five Europass countries: **France, Germany, Italy, Spain, and Switzerland.** Up to two of the four associate regions (Austria and Hungary; Benelux (Belgium, Netherlands, and Luxembourg); Greece; Portugal) may be added.

	5 days	6 days	8 days	10 days	15 days	first	second
First Class	*in two*		*m o n t h s*			*associate country*	
1 Passenger	$348	$368	$448	$528	$728	+$60	+$40
2 to 5 Passengers traveling together	$296	$314	$382	$450	$620	+$52	+$34
Youthpass (Second Class)							
Passengers under 26	$233	$253	$313	$363	$513	+$45	+$33

Pass Protection For an additional $10, insure any railpass against theft or loss.

Discounts _with_ _the purchase of a railpass_
- $30 off a World Journey backpack
- $20 off a Continental Journey backpack
- Any _Let's Go_ Guide for 1/2 Price
- Free 2-3 Week Domestic Shipping

Call about Eurostar—the Channel Tunnel Train—and other country-specific passes.

Airfares & Special Promotions

Call for information on and availability of standard airline tickets, student, teacher, and youth discounted airfares, as well as other special promotions.

Publications & More

Let's Go Travel Guides— The Bible of the Budget Traveler

USA • India and Nepal • Southeast Asia	22.99
Australia • Eastern Europe • Europe	21.99
Britain & Ireland • Central America • France • Germany • Israel & Egypt • Italy • Mexico • Spain & Portugal	19.99
Alaska & The Pacific Northwest • Austria & Switzerland • California & Hawaii • Ecuador & The Galapagos Islands • Greece • Ireland	18.99
South Africa • Turkey	17.99
New York City • New Zealand • London • Paris • Rome • Washington D.C.	15.99

Let's Go Map Guides

Know your destination inside and out!
Great to accompany your Eurailpass.

Amsterdam, Berlin, Boston, Chicago, Florence, London, Los Angeles, Madrid, New Orleans, New York, Paris, Rome, San Francisco, Washington D.C.   **8.95**

Michelin Maps

Czech/Slovak Republics • Europe • France • Germany • Germany/Austria /Benelux • Great Britain & Ireland • Greece • Italy • Poland • Scandinavia & Finland • Spain & Portugal **10.95**

LET'S GO® Order Form

Last Name*   First Name*   Home and Day Phone Number*
(very important)

Street*   (Sorry, we cannot ship to Post Office Boxes)

City*   State*   Zip Code*

Citizenship‡§◻   School/College§   Date of Birth‡§   Date of Travel*
(Country)

Qty	Description	Color	Unit Price	Total Price

Shipping and Handling

2-3 Week Domestic Shipping	
Merchandise value under $30	$4
Merchandise value $30-$100	$6
Merchandise value over $100	$8
2-3 Day Domestic Shipping	
Merchandise value under $30	$14
Merchandise value $30-$100	$16
Merchandise value over $100	$18
Overnight Domestic Shipping	
Merchandise value under $30	$24
Merchandise value $30-$100	$26
Merchandise value over $100	$28
All International Shipping	$30

Total Purchase Price

Shipping and Handling   +

MA Residents add 5% sales tax on gear and books   +

TOTAL

◻ Mastercard   ◻ Visa

Cardholder name:

Card number:

Expiration date:

When ordering an International ID Card, please include:
1. Proof of birthdate (copy of passport, birth certificate, or driver's license).
2. One picture (1.5" x 2") signed on the reverse side.
3. (ISIC/ITIC only) Proof of current student/teacher status (letter from registrar or administrator, proof of tuition, or copy of student/faculty ID card. FULL-TIME only).

* Required for all orders
‡ Required in addition for each Hostelling Membership
§ Required in addition for each International ID Card
◻ Required in addition for each railpass

Prices are in US dollars and subject to change.

Make check or money order payable to:
Let's Go Travel
17 Holyoke Street
Cambridge, MA 02138
(617) 495-9649

1-800-5LETSGO

Hours: Mon.-Fri., 10am-6pm ET

(social studies)

Use **AT&T Direct**^{SM} Service
when you're out exploring the world.

On your next journey bring along an

AT&T Direct[SM] **Service** wallet guide. It's a list of

access numbers you need to call home fast and clear

from around the world, using an AT&T Calling Card or credit card.

What an amazing culture we live in.

For a list of **AT&T Access Numbers,** take the attached wallet guide.

It's all within  your reach.

www.att.com/traveler

For your calling convenience tear off and take with you!

AT&T Direct℠ Service

WALLET GUIDE

Inside you'll find simple instructions on how to use AT&T Direct Service to place calling card or collect calls from outside the U.S.

All you need are the AT&T Access Numbers when you travel outside the U.S., because you can access us quickly and easily from virtually anywhere in the world. And if you need any further help, there's always an AT&T English-speaking Operator available to assist you.

www.att.com/traveler

Calling From Specially Marked Telephones

Throughout the world, there are specially marked phones that connect you to AT&T Direct℠ Service. Simply look for the AT&T logo. In the following countries, access to AT&T Direct Service is *only* available from these phones: Ethiopia, Mongolia, Nigeria, Seychelles Islands.

Public phones in Europe displaying the red 3C symbol also give you quick and easy access to AT&T Direct Service. Just lift the handset and dial **✱60** (in France dial M60) and you'll be connected to AT&T.

Pay phones in the United Kingdom displaying the New World symbol provide easy access to AT&T. Simply lift the handset and press the pre-programmed button marked AT&T.

NEW WORLD

Customer Care

If you have any questions, call 800 331-1140, Ext. 707.

When outside the U.S., dial the AT&T Access Number for the country *you are in* and ask the AT&T Operator for Customer Care.

108-25   © AT&T 6/98

Printed in the U.S.A. on recycled paper.

To Call the U.S. and Other Countries Using Your AT&T Calling Card* or credit card∞, Follow These Steps:

1. Make sure you have an outside line. (From a hotel room, follow the hotel's instructions to get an outside line, as if you were placing a local call.)

2. If you want to call a country other than the U.S., make sure the country *you are in* is highlighted in blue on the chart like this:

3. Enter the AT&T Access Number listed in the chart for the country *you are in.*

4. When prompted, enter the telephone number you are calling as follows:

- For calls to the U.S., dial the Area Code (no need to dial 1 before the Area Code) + 7-digit number.

- For calls to other countries,† enter (01 + the Country Code, City Code, and Local Number.

5. After the tone, enter your AT&T Calling Card* or credit card number (not the international number). If you need help or wish to call the U.S. collect, hold for an AT&T Operator.

* You may also use your AT&T Corporate Card, AT&T Universal Card, or most U.S. local phone company cards.

† The cost of calls to countries other than the U.S. consists of basic connection rates plus an additional charge based on the country you are calling.

∞ Credit card billing subject to availability.

Special Features

Just dial the AT&T Access Number for the country *you are in* and follow the instructions listed below.

- To call U.S. 800 numbers: Enter the 800 number you are calling. (Note: Based upon the 800 number dialed, calls may be toll-free or AT&T Direct℠ Service charges may apply for the duration of the call; some numbers may be restricted.)

- To set up conference calls: Dial AT&T TeleConference Services at 800 232-1234. (Note: One conferee must be in the U.S.)

- To access language interpreters: Dial AT&T Language Line® Services at 408 648-5871.

- To record and deliver messages: Dial #123 if you get a busy signal or no answer, or dial AT&T True Messages® Service at 800 562-6275.

Here's a time-saving tip for placing additional calls: When you finish your conversation, or if there is a busy signal or no answer, don't hang up – press # and wait for the voice prompt or an AT&T Operator.

AT&T Access Numbers

(Refer to footnotes before dialing.) From the countries highlighted in blue below, like this [ ], you can make calls to the U.S. location in the world; and from all the countries listed, you can make calls to virtually any

Albania ●	00-800-0010
American Samoa	633-2-USA
Angola	0199
Anguilla +	1-800-872-2881
Antigua +	1-800-872-2881
(Public Card Phones)	#1
Argentina ▲	0-800-54-288
Armenia ●▲	8♦10111
Aruba	800-8000
Australia	1-800-881-011
Austria ○	022-903-011
Bahamas	1-800-872-2881
Bahrain	800-001
Bahrain ↑	800-000
Barbados ♦	1-800-872-2881
Belarus ✕,—	8♦800101
Belgium ●	0-800-100-10
Belize ▲	811
(From Hotels Only)	555
Benin ●	102
Bermuda +	1-800-872-2881
Bolivia ●	0-800-1112
Bosnia ▲	00-800-0010
Brazil	000-8010
British V.I. +	1-800-872-2881
Brunei ●	800-1111
Bulgaria ■ ▲	00-800-0010
Cambodia ✳	1-800-881-001
Canada	1 800 CALL ATT
Cape Verde Islands ●	112
Cayman Islands +	1-800-872-2881
Chile	022-903-011 or 800-800-288
China, PRC ▲	800-800-311
(Easter Island)	800-800-311
Colombia	980-11-0010
Cook Island	09-111
Costa Rica	0-800-0-114-114
Croatia ▲	0191
Cyprus	080-90010
Czech Rep. ▲	00-42-000-101
Denmark	8001-0010
Dominica +	1-800-872-2881
Dom. Rep. ✱,□	1-800-872-2881
Ecuador ▲	999-119
Egypt ● (Cairo)	510-0200
(Outside Cairo)	02-510-0200
El Salvador ○	800-1785
Estonia	8-00-800-1001
Fiji	004-890-1001
Finland	9800-100-10
France	0800 99 00 11
French Antilles	0800 99 00 11
French Guiana	0800 99 00 11
Gabon ●	00♦001
Gambia ●	00111
Georgia ▲	8♦0288
Germany	0130-0010
Ghana	0191
Gibraltar	8800
Greece ●	00-800-1311
Grenada +	1-800-872-2881
Guadeloupe + (Marie Galante)	0800 99 00 11
Guam	1 800 CALL ATT
Guantanamo Bay ↑ (Cuba)	935
Guatemala ○, ✱	99-99-190
Guyana ✱	165
Haiti	183
Honduras	800-0-123
Hong Kong	800-96-1111
Hungary ●	00♦800-01111
Iceland	800 9001
India ✱,▶	000-117
Indonesia ↦	001-801-10
Ireland ✓	1-800-550-000
Israel	1-800-94-94-949
Italy ●	172-1011
Ivory Coast ●	00-111-11
Jamaica ○	1-800-872-2881
Jamaica □	872
Japan KDD ●	005-39-111
Japan IDC ● ,▲	0066-55-111
Kazakhstan ●	8♦800-121-4321
Korea ●²	00729-911 or 0030-911
Korea ↑	550-HOME or 550-2USA
Kuwait	800-288
Latvia (Riga)	7007007
(Outside Riga)	8♦27007007
Lebanon ○ (Beirut)	426-801
(Outside Beirut)	01-426-801
Liechtenstein ●	0-800-89-0011
Lithuania ✱,—	8♦196
Luxembourg †	0-800-0111
Macao	0800-111
Macedonia, F.Y.R. of ●, ○	99-800-4288
Malaysia ○	1800-80-0011
Malta	0800-890-110
Marshall Isl.	1 800 CALL ATT
Mauritius	73120
Mexico ▽¹	01-800-288-2872
Micronesia	288
Monaco ●	800-90-288
Montserrat	1-800-872-2881
Morocco	002-11-0011
Netherlands Antilles ☼	001-800-872-2881
Netherlands ●	0800-022-9111
New Zealand	000-911
Nicaragua	174
Norway	800-190-11
Pakistan ▲	00-800-10011
Palau	02288
Panama (Canal Zone)	109
Papua New Guinea	0507-12880
Paraguay ▲,▲	008-11-800
Peru ●	0-800-50000
Philippines ●	105-11
Poland	0♦0-800-111-1111
Portugal ●	05017-1-288
Qatar	0800-011-77
Reunion Isl.	0800 99 0011
Romania ●	01-800-4288
Romania ↑	01-801-0151
Russia ●,▲ (Moscow)	755-5042
(Outside Moscow)	8-095-755-5042
Russia ●,▲ (St. Petersburg)	325-5042
(Outside St. Petersburg)	8-812-325-5042
St. Kitts/Nevis & St. Lucia +	1-800-872-2881
St. Pierre & Miquelon	0800 99 0011
St. Vincent ▲	1-800-872-2881
Saipan ▲	1 800 CALL ATT
San Marino ●	172-1011
Saudi Arabia ◇	1-800-10
Senegal	3072
Sierra Leone	1100
Singapore ■	800-0111-111
Slovakia ▲	00-42-100-101
Solomon Isl.	0811
So. Africa	0-800-99-0123
Spain	900-99-00-11
Sri Lanka ■	430-430
Sudan	800-001
Suriname △	156
Sweden	020-795-611
Switzerland ●	0-800-890011
Syria	0-801
Taiwan	0080-10288-0
Thailand ◁	001-999-111-11
Trinidad/Tob.	1-800-872-2881
Turkey ●	00-800-12277
Turks & Caicos +,■	01-800-872-2881
Uganda	800-001
Ukraine ▲	8♦100-11
U.A. Emirates ●	800-121
U.K. ▲,✦	0800-89-0011 or 0500-89-0011
U.S. ▼	1 800 CALL ATT
Uruguay	000-410
Uzbekistan 8 ♦	641-744-0010
Venezuela	800-11-120
Vietnam ●	1-201-0288
Yemen	00 800 101
Zambia	00-899
Zimbabwe ▲	110-98990

● Public phones require coin or card deposit. 2 Press end button. ▶ Additional charges apply when calling outside of Moscow. ■ AT&T Direct℠ calls cannot be placed to this country from outside the U.S. ✳ Available from public phones in Phnom Penh and Siem Reap only. ✕ Not available from public phones. ✤ From St. Maarten or phones at Bobby's Marina, use 1-800-872-2881.

◇ From this country, AT&T Direct℠ calls terminate to designated countries only. ◆ From U.S. Military Bases only. ▽ Not yet available from all areas. ✱ Select hotels. ● May not be available from every phone/payphone. † Collect calling from public phones. ▶ Available from phones with international calling capabilities or from most Public Calling Centers. ✓ From Northern Ireland use U.K. access code.

✱ Collect only. ○ Public phones require local coin payment through the call duration. ◆ Await second dial tone. ▽ When calling from public phones, use phones marked "Lantalor". † If call does not complete, use 001-462-4240. ● Available from public phones only. ◀ Public phones and select hotels. ◁ When calling from public phones use phones marked Lenso.

□ Calling Card calls available from select hotels. ✦ Use phones allowing international access. ▼ Including Puerto Rico and the U.S. Virgin Islands. ▼AT&T Direct℠ Service only in Da Nang, Ho Chi Minh City and Quang Ninh. ✤ If call does not complete, use 0800-013-0011. ● AT&T Direct℠ calls available from telephone calling centers in Hanoi and post offices in Da Nang, Ho Chi Minh City and Quang Ninh. ✤ If call does not complete, use 0800-013-0011.

AT&T

Mermaids Pool, a swimming hole whose delicate juxtaposition of ocean, beach, bush, and granite conjures a hint of its namesake. A much longer walk (4hr. return) to East Sandy Point leads to huge dunes, great views, and wildflowers in the spring. Bridport is the Tasmanian port for the ferry service to **Flinders Island,** including **Strezelecki National Park.** The **ferry** (tel. 6356 1753) departs at high tide on its six-hour journey to the island town of **Lady Barron** ($70 return; bicycle $14 extra).

■ Scottsdale

Scottsdale, about 45km northeast of Launceston along the A3, is nothing special, but it's the main service center for the region. Visitor information is in the **Lyric Theatre** (tel. 6352 3095), on King St, as the highway is known in town. The street also houses **Commonwealth, ANZ, Westpac,** and **Trust** banks (all open M-Th 9:30am-4pm, F 9:30 am-5pm). King St also has a **Roelf Vos** supermarket and the **post office** (tel. 6352 2719; open M-F 9am-5pm). The only budget accommodation option is the **North-East Caravan and Camping Park,** 37 Ringarooma Rd (tel. 6352 2017), just downhill from the town center on the A3 toward St. Helens (2-person sites $7.50; powered $10). The **Gemini Coffee Shop** (tel. 6352 2938) offers good takeaway and sit-down fare, including veggie options (sandwiches $2.50; grill and salad $7; open M-F 9am-5pm, Sa-Su 10am-2pm). **Redline** buses leave from the **Newspower** newsagency (tel. 6352 2413) on King St and head to Launceston (1¼hr., M-Su, $9); Winnaleah (1½hr., M-F 10:30am, $6.70), with connections on Suncoast Coaches to St. Helens; and Bridgeport (20min., school days only, 5:20pm). **Stan's Coach Services** (tel. 6356 1662) meets buses from Launceston to take passengers on to Bridgeport (30min.; M-F 10:30am and 6pm).

■ The A3 East of Scottsdale

The road from Scottsdale east to St. Helens and the Suncoast takes just an hour or two, but you could easily spend a couple of days enjoying the pleasant, often stunning parks, hiking trails, and lookouts along the way. The first notable feature lies 45 minutes from Scottsdale: the **Mt. Victoria Forest Reserve.** From the A3, follow signs south to Ringarooma; the last 8km before the carpark are gravel road. **Ralph Falls** are a 10-minute walk from the carpark, and lush **Caches Canyon** lies another half-hour beyond. The hike up Mt. Victoria itself requires stamina and bushwalking experience, as it includes some rock scrambles and fast-changing weather. Your reward is a melange of Tasmanian ecosystems and a panorama of the whole northeast, from Ben Lomond in the south to Flinders Island in the north. Not bad.

A bit further along, the **Winnaleah YHA,** 524 Racecourse Rd (tel. 6354 2152), offers the only hostel between Bridport and St. Helens. It's 6km up a side road from the tiny town of **Winnaleah;** follow the green YHA signs. The hostel doubles as a commercial dairy farm in a storybook rolling-fields-and-wooded-hills setting, and guests are welcome but not required to help with the milking. (Beds $10, YHA nonmembers $12, children $5.) Redline West connects to Scottsdale (1½hr.; M-F 2pm; $6.70) and to Launceston (2¾hr., $14.30), while Suncoast Coach Service has service to St. Helens (M-F at noon).

The **Weldborough Pass Scenic Reserve,** just beyond **Weldborough,** offers a magical rainforest walk right by the highway. The 15-minute circuit weaves beneath huge, otherworldly tree ferns and myrtle beeches. Along the way, the story of Gondwanaland is related by signs that are more than a little loopy. Don't miss Grandma Myrtle!

About 30 minutes north of St. Helens, **The St. Columba Falls Hotel** (tel. 6373 6121) epitomizes the Aussie pub in an Aussie location. In the middle of a paddock in **Pyengana,** the pub recalls a time before pokies, and before pubs had to be Irish or Western to attract customers. There's good beer and excellent counter meals ($8-14). The grave of **Piggy Boo,** the infamous **beer-drinking pig,** lies by the driveway as stern warning to other debaucherous porcines: in Australia, you're supposed to drink like a whale, not like a hog. (Pub open M-Sa from 11am, Su from noon. Food served noon-2pm and 6:30-8:30pm.) Accommodation is a good deal (singles $20; doubles $30).

The beautiful **St. Columba Falls,** the highest falls in Tasmania, are just down the road; a five-minute drive along unsealed road leads to a 10-minute gully walk.

■ Mt. William National Park

More of a hill than a mountain, Mt. William nevertheless is the protector of a quiet stretch of coast in the sunny northeast corner. The park around it is one of the state's premier animal-spotting locales. The gentle 180m peak has wide views over a flat, sandy region and across the water to the **Furneaux Islands,** which once provided a bridge between Tassie and the mainland. The group of Aboriginals who lived here for 36,000 years until European settlement enjoyed abundant food of possum, kangaroo, and shellfish; their shell middens pile deep throughout the park's dunes. Grassland wildlife abounds in the park's pasture lands once cleared by European settlers.

The major reason to visit Mt. William is the chance to safari through ground thick with marsupials. At dusk, if you have your eyes open, you'll see Forester kangaroos, which stand chest-high, and you're likely to spy plenty of smaller Tasmanian pad-melon and common wombats. Even with your eyes closed, you'll still probably see thigh-high Bennett's wallabies. Those actually looking can see echidnas during the day and, with a good flashlight, brushtail possums, spotted-tail quolls, and Tasmanian devils after dark; the eagle-eyed might glimpse the rare New Holland mouse. Then there are all the birds. **Drive carefully** through the park—your car doesn't think the little beasties are as cute as you do.

Mt. William is a relatively isolated, primitive national park. There are no shops, petrol, telephones, flush toilets, or fresh water, so come prepared. A supply of **drinking water** is essential. **Firewood** is available for a donation at the north entrance to the park. In an emergency, call the **ranger** (tel. 6357 2108 or 6357 2147) at the north entrance. There is no scheduled bus service to the park; it's about a 90-minute drive from Scottsdale or St. Helens. The **access roads,** unsealed but well-maintained, are signposted from **Gladstone.** The more popular north entrance is by the hamlet of **Poole;** the south entrance is by **Ansons Bay.** (The direct route north from St. Helens to Ansons Bay is an extremely rough dirt track; take the access roads instead.)

Both ends of the park offer ample coastal **camping** and hiking. The north end, along **Stumpy's Bay,** has four campsites: sites 1 and 3 have bore water pumps, site 4 has a picnic shelter with free gas barbecues, and generators and boats are restricted to site 3. The northern access road leads to **Forester Kangaroo Drive,** which loops through some of the best grassland viewing, and the trailhead for the **Mt. William walk** (1hr. return, moderate climbing). Beach walks abound; the track from Stumpys Bay site 4 south to **Cobler Rocks** is rewarding (2hr. return).

■ The Suncoast

If Tasmania is a huge serpent, the east coast is its soft underbelly. The weather is mild, the natives are mild-mannered, and the mild waters produce mild-tasting fish. A mountainous interior shelters the east coast from the storms that regularly pound the west. The docile climate, combined with tracts of arable land, has led to fairly thick settlement by Tasmanian standards. By mainland standards, however, the area remains quiet year-round and grows positively hushed in the winter. Most of the settlements rely on agriculture or maintain the image of popular summer holiday spots for fresh- and saltwater fishing, swimming, and just loafing in the sunshine.

Most of the east coast towns are serviced by bus, but winter schedules are often restrictive. There are currently **no ATMs** between Sorell and St. Helens.

■ St. Helens

St. Helens is the northernmost of the vacation villages that dot the east coast. The settlement began as a land grant around Georges Bay in the 1830s, with most of its income coming from timber and fishing. The discovery of tin in the Blue Tier to the west prompted rapid population growth during the 1870s. By the 1890s, the decreased price of tin made mining unprofitable, and the town reverted to harvesting the sea. Plentiful and interesting information on the area's history is offered by the **St. Helen's History Room,** 59 Cecilia St (tel. 6376 1744). They also have **Internet access,** used by schoolchildren during the week but otherwise open to the public. (Open M-F 9am-4pm, Sa 9am-1pm, Su 11am-2pm. Admission $4, children $2.)

The **St. Helens Visitor Information Centre** (tel. 6376 1329) is at 20 Cecilia St (open M-F 9am-5pm). **Redline** (tel. 6376 1182) buses run to Hobart (4hr.; M, W, F; $26), St. Mary's (40min., Su-F, $3.80), and Launceston (2½hr., Su-F, $19). **Tasmanian Wilderness Travel** (tel. 6334 4442) runs to Bicheno (1hr., M-F 2pm, $8), the highway turn-off for Coles Bay (1¼hr., $9-10), Swansea (1¾hr., $11), and points south including Hobart (4hr., $30). **Trust Bank,** 18 Cecilia St (tel. 6376 1111), has an **ATM,** a rarity on the east coast (open M-F 9am-5pm). **East Lines,** 28 Cecilia St (tel. 6376 1720), rents a huge variety of sporting goods, including golf clubs and fishing tackle. (Bikes $5 per hour, $20 per day; $50 deposit. Open M-F 9am-5pm.) The **post office** is at 46 Cecilia St (tel. 6376 1255; fax 6376 1099; open M-F 9am-5pm; **postal code** 7216).

The **St. Helens Caravan Park** (tel. 6376 1290; fax 6376 1514) is 1km from the town center on Penelope St, just off the Tasman Hwy on the southeast side of the bridge. There is a campers' kitchen and a kiddie playroom along with the standard amenities. (2-person sites $13, powered $14-15, with private bath $18. On-site caravans $30-35. Cabins $40-55. Summer prices higher.) The **St. Helens YHA,** 5 Cameron St (tel. 6376 1661), off Quail St, has beautiful views of Georges Bay through enormous windows, but the bunks are mere foam (dorms $12, YHA nonmembers $15; book ahead in summer). Cheap and healthy eats are available at the **Deli,** 22 Cecilia St (tel. 6376 1649), whose offerings are essentially coffee lounge fare without the grease (open M-F 7:30am-5pm, summer M-Su 7am-9pm).

Points of interest include the state recreation areas of **Humbug Point** and **St. Helens Point.** Humbug Point offers better-than-humbug walks and views, while St. Helens Point has decent fishing and good surf at **Beerbarrel Beach.** North of Humbug Point, the **Bay of Fires Coastal Reserve** rounds out the roster of peculiar place names with its long beaches and primitive campsites.

■ Bicheno

The Gulch of Bicheno's Esplanade sheltered sealers and whalers in the early days, and when coal was discovered in the region, **Waub's Bay** became the natural port. Like the rest of the Suncoast, however, Bicheno has long since left its industrial beginnings behind in favor of fishing and tourism. With postcard penguins on hand and pin-up national parks **(Freycinet and Douglas-Apsley)** within an easy daytrip, Bicheno is deservedly a stop on many Tassie itineraries. Redline has service from Sundays through Fridays to the Coles Bay highway turn-off (10min., $3.20) and Swansea (40min., $6.40), with connections to Hobart (5hr.) and Launceston (2¾hr., $21). Tasmanian Wilderness Travel runs three times per week to Launceston (2½hr., $19), St. Helens (1hr., $7.90), the Coles Bay turn-off (5min., $2), Swansea (10min., $4.30), Triabunna (1½hr., $8.80), and Hobart (3hr., $20-30). **Bicheno Coach Service** (tel. 6257 0293) runs daily to Coles Bay and Freycinet National Park, including connections from the Coles Bay turn-off.

The **Tourist Information Centre** (tel. 6375 1333) is a hut right in the elbow of the A3 in the center of Bicheno. It runs nightly **penguin-spotting** tours in summer ($12), hires mountain bikes ($15 per day), charters glass-bottom boat and fishing jaunts, and sells surf gear and boogie boards. The **newsagency** (tel. 6375 1181) across the highway from the Information Centre is an agent for **Trust Bank** (open M-Sa 7:30am-6pm, Su 8am-5pm). The **Value-Plus** supermarket (tel. 6375 1388; open daily 7:30am-6pm) and the **post office** (tel. 6375 1244; open M-F 9am-5pm) are also at the A3 elbow.

The **Bicheno Hostel,** 11 Morrison St (tel. 6375 1651), lies off the A3 behind a little white church. It's comfortable and well-designed, with individual bed curtains, quality board games, and a slate-floored bathroom. (Bunks $13.) The three-minute walk up the nearby hill to **Lookout Rock** is a great start to a Bicheno visit, no matter where you're staying. **Bicheno YHA** (tel. 6375 1293) is 3km north of the town center on the A3; look for a blue YHA sign. This classic Australian beach shack has a view past a line of oaks to the surf beyond, and penguins nest behind the washing machine. The facilities are a bit cramped and aging, but the location is unbeatable. (Bunks $11.)

The **Waubs Harbour Backpackers Hostel** (tel. 6375 1117) is a new building in the large grounds of the **Bicheno Cabin and Tourist Park,** at 4 Champ St immediately behind the info center. The hostel is clean and quiet but lacks personality (bunks $14). The campground is packed in the summer (2-person site $11, powered $13; on-site vans $30, summer $40). The park also has **mini-golf** ($2). **Food** in Bicheno is run-of-the-mill, with two pubs and a takeaway that are easy to find.

■ Douglas-Apsley National Park

Douglas-Apsley is a national park's national park. It lacks the poster appeal of a coast or mountain or rainforest, but protects an otherwise sorely neglected native community: the dry eucalypt forest. By the time the ecological importance of dry forest was recognized, the Douglas-Apsley region was the last significant unlogged stand in Tasmania. Its recent elevation to national park status signifies the greening of Tassie politics. Furthermore, the park provides ample hiking and swimming opportunities in the midst of a rich, diverse, and unusual ecosystem.

The popular southern (Apsley River) end of the park is only a 15-minute drive from **Bicheno,** which acts as the service center since the park itself has no shops, telephones, or fresh water apart from the river. The southern access road leaves the A3 5km north of Bicheno and heads west along 7km of gravel road. There is no scheduled bus service into the park, but the **Bicheno Coach Service** (tel. 6257 0293) or **Tasmanian Wilderness Travel** (tel. 6334 4442) can arrange a minibus. There are free primitive **campsites** and pit toilets near the carports, and additional campsites by the Apsley waterhole. The **ranger** can be reached at 6375 1236.

The **Apsley waterhole** is a deep pool in the middle of the stony bed of the rarely-running Apsley River. It makes a magic splash on a warm summer day, and is just a 10-minute walk from the southern carpark. A lookout over the park sits right above the waterhole. A three-hour walking loop to the **Apsley River gorge** follows a track from the north side of the waterhole. It includes moderate climbing and some rock scrambling down the dry riverbed. The **Leeaberra Track** runs the length of the park. It's a three-day walk through all the fascinating eco-tones between the Douglas and Apsley rivers, designed for experienced bushwalkers with a map and a compass.

Signs along the lookout walk introduce several of the major tree species in the park, such as the blue gum, black wattle, and native (edible!) cherry. Rarer residents protected by the park include the black Tasmanian ironbark, the South Esk Pine, and several highly endangered *Epacrial* heath species. Springtime offers beautiful wildflower displays. Gravely endangered animals surviving in the park include the Tasmanian bettong and the southern grayling fish in the Douglas River.

■ Freycinet Peninsula

Show us a promotional brochure of Tasmania without a picture of **Wineglass Bay,** and we'll show you a tacky cartoon devil in convict clothes. The endlessly photogenic bay is found in **Freycinet National Park,** as is the picturesque calm of **Great Oyster Bay** and the beautiful pink granite **Hazards,** all in a pleasant coastal clime. Just three hours' drive from both Hobart and Launceston, it's as popular as it is pretty. Coles Bay is the service center for Freycinet—get what you need there. For information, stop at the **visitors kiosk** (tel. 6257 0107) near the park entrance. National park fees apply, and passes are valid. Excellent **campsites** with wood, water, and basic toilets are available. (Unpowered sites $5, concessions $4, children $2.50; powered sites $6, concessions $5, children $3.) Register and pay fees at the visitor kiosk.

Bicheno Coaches (tel. 6257 0293) run to the park daily from the Coles Bay highway turn-off en route to Bicheno; at the turn-off, you can connect with Tasmanian

Wilderness Travel and Redline services to all other destinations. Shuttles run daily from the hostel to the park's walking tracks. There is no fresh water on the day hikes—bring your own. The Mt. Amos track is a taxing climb, but pays off with spectacular views. The one-hour return walk to Wineglass Bay Lookout is the classic choice; an alternative is a half-day loop by Wineglass Bay and Hazards Beach. A hike around the whole peninsula takes two or three days. Excellent beaches just north of the park include the **Friendly Beaches** and the **Lagoon Beaches Coastal Reserve.** The coastal reserve has broad, soft sand beaches with shallow lagoons full of black swans. There are free primitive campsites.

■ Coles Bay

The well-equipped town of **Coles Bay** is the gateway and service center for **Freycinet National Park.** Its safe and sunny shelter in the lap of **Great Oyster Bay** satisfies many summer holiday-makers. There are two centers of commerce and information. The **4 Square Supermarket,** on Garnet Ave (tel. 6257 0109), houses the **tourist information office** and the **post office,** as well as offering limited banking, petrol, bike hire ($15 per day), and boat hire (dinghy $25 first hr., $5 each additional hr., fishing gear $4). (Open daily 8am-9pm in summer, 8am-6pm winter.) **Tasmanian Wilderness Travel** (tel. 6334 4442) and **Redline** (tel. 6231 3233) buses run as close as the turn-off for Coles Bay on the A3; from there, take **Bicheno Coaches** (tel. 6257 0293), which connects to town, the park, and Bicheno.

At the western end of the Esplanade is the YHA-affiliated **Iluka Holiday Center** (tel. 6257 0115; fax 6257 0384), a hotel boasting a large kitchen, TV room, and convenient access to the bakery and beach. (Bunks $13 members, $15 non-members, twins and doubles $40. On-site vans and units $35 for two; tent sites $10, $12 with power.)

Freycinet Backpackers is part of the **Coles Bay Caravan Park** (tel. 6257 0100; fax 6257 0270), 3km north of town off the Coles Bay Main Road, or an easy walk around Muir's Beach from the Iluka shops. The long horseshoe of dim bunkrooms can feel lonely but offers great kitchen and common space for large groups (bunks $14). Unlike most hostels, each double-bunk has its own little room. The Caravan Park has ample good tent sites nestled under the peppermints ($11 for two).

■ Swansea

Swansea is a calm, settled town on a calming, settling bay. Indeed, the old-school architecture attests to the longevity of that settlement. The Council Chambers and Community Center are gentle 1860 timber buildings, and the brick edifice of Morris' General Store has been run by the same family since 1838. Swansea offers fine swimming **beaches** and swimming holes, and temperate weather for enjoying them.

Swansea's most unusual attraction is the **Black Wattle Bark Mill,** 96 Tasman Hwy, the only **bark crusher** in Australia. In days gone by, bark was stripped from wattle trees, dried in bundles, and ground to a powder to make "vegetable tonic," a solution used in the tanning of hides. The machine has been faithfully restored along with a number of tools and contraptions from the area's past. A classier effort at social history, the **Mill Museum** (tel. 6257 8382; fax 6257 8485; email barkmill@vision.net.au) chronicles the routines and ecologies and changing technologies of Swansea workers from early settlement through 1960, complete with the slap and chuff of a working original bark mill (open daily 9am-5pm; complex admission $5, children $2.75). The adjacent wine and wool center operates as the Swansea tourist information center.

The **post office** at Arnoll and Franklin St (tel. 6257 8170) offers limited banking services (open M-F 9am-5pm; postal code 7190). **Redline** (tel. 6257 8118) runs buses every morning except Saturday to Bicheno (40min., $6.40), Hobart (4¼hr.), and Launceston (2hr., $17). **Tasmanian Wilderness Travel** (tel. 6334 4442) runs Wednesdays, Fridays, and Sundays at 10:45am to Bicheno (40min., $4.30) and St. Helens (1¾hr., $11), and has twice-daily service to Triabunna (50min., $5) and Hobart (2¼hr., $16.50).

Other services line **Franklin St,** the main drag. These include a **newsagent** (tel. 6257 8212; open daily 7:30am-5:30pm), **pharmacy** (tel. 6257 8167; emergency 6257 8014; open M-F 9am-530pm, Sa 9am-12pm), and **Valu-Plus Supermarket** (tel. 6257 8101; open M-F 9am-5:30pm, Sa-Su 9am-4:30pm). The **police** (tel. 6257 8044), are one block back on Nayes St. **The Op Shop,** 38 Franklin St, fills another fine old building with used clothes and books (open Tu, Th, and F 9:30am-12pm and 2-4pm; Sa 9:30am-12pm).

The budget accommodation option is the **Swansea YHA,** 5 Franklin St (tel. 6257 8367). This old, beachy hostel boasts a well-equipped kitchen, a piano in the common room, and rude metal bunks. Hand-washing tubs replace laundry machines. (Dorms $11, YHA non-members $14.) There is a caravan park at either end of town. Both are on the beach, and have full amenities with coin-op laundries. The **Swansea-Kenmore Cabin and Tourist Park,** 2 Bridge St (tel. 6257 8148; fax 6257 8554), has limited tenting options and a spa-sauna ($7 for two). (Unpowered sites $10-12, powered $15; on-site caravans $30-35; cabins $45 winter, $60 summer.) The **Swansea Caravan Park,** on Shaw St (tel. 6257 8177; fax 6257 8511), is less landscaped and has more tent space and air hockey to boot. (Sites $12, powered $16; cabins $40 winter, $50 summer.)

■ Triabunna

Triabunna (try-a-BU-na) is a tiny town where you can stock up on food before heading out to **Maria Island.** The **Triabunna Caravan Park,** 6 Vicary St (tel. 6257 3575), has shady, grassy tent sites. The toilet and shower block is small but well-scrubbed. (Unpowered sites $10, powered $12.) The **Triabunna YHA,** 12 Spencer St (tel. 6257 3439), is off Amelia St, 1km from the town center across the bridge. A pack of friendly dogs patrols this ramshackle domicile. The manager grows and cooks great organic food. (Dorms $12, YHA non-members $15; doubles $28.) The **Valu-Plus Supermarket** (tel. 6257 3227) is on Vicary St (open M-F 7:30am-6pm, Sa-Su 8am-6pm).

For a restful, harmonious experience, head to the **Girraween Gardens and Tearoom,** 4 Henry St (tel./fax 6257 3458), in "downtown" Triabunna. Light meals are served in a peaceful grove, and you can tour the award-winning gardens for $2. (Free with the purchase of food; most items are less than $7. Open daily 9:30am-4:30pm.) **Tasmanian Wilderness Travel** (tel. 6334 4442) runs on Wednesdays, Fridays, and Sundays to Swansea (50min., $5), Bicheno (1½hr., $8.80), and St. Helens (2½hr., $17.10), and Hobart (1¾hr., $11.70); they also connect to the Eastcoaster Island Ferry (5min.).

■ Maria Island National Park

Maria (muh-RYE-uh) Island has housed penal colonies, cement industries, whalers, and farmers. When these all passed on, only an empty, desolate rock was left. Today, the island national park is almost devoid of civilization. The ruins of the settlement at **Darlington** are the main attraction, along with the abundant wildlife and isolation. There are no shops or facilities save a **ranger station** (tel. 6257 1420), which has a public telephone and distributes maps and brochures. To get beyond the ferry wharf at Darlington, walk or bring a mountain bike. The old Darlington prison has been renovated into **dorms** with toilets and laundry, but there are no showers or hot water. Hey, nobody said prison life was easy. Bookings must be made with the ranger before arrival ($8 adults, $4 children, $20 family). There are three **campsites** on the island. The first is in Darlington, with ample grassy space ($4 adults, $2 children, $10 family). The French's Farm camping area is 11km south down the main gravel road, and includes an empty weatherproof farmhouse, a pit toilet, and rainwater tanks. The Encampment Cove camping area is another 2km down a side road near French's Farm, with a small bunkhouse and a pit toilet. National park fees apply. Exotic birds abound, from the huge, shy albatross to the gravely endangered forty-spotted pardalote.

Maria can be reached via the **Eastcoaster Express** catamaran, which leaves the Eastcoaster Resort. (3-4 times daily; daytrip fare $17, children $10; overnight fare $20, children $13. Bikes, kayaks, and other large cargo items $3.) The **Eastcoaster Resort** (tel. 6257 1589) is midway between Triabunna and Orford, a 20-minute drive from either town. Take the turn for "Louisville Pt./Maria Island Ferry" off the A3.

■ Central East

The pocket of the Northeast away from the coast is mostly open plains, broken up by the ski mountains of Ben Lomond National Park. The agricultural Midlands roll their way across the heart of the state toward the Derwent Valley in the south.

■ Ben Lomond National Park

Tasmania's premier ski resort, **Ben Lomond National Park** (tel. 6390 6279; recorded conditions line 190 229 0530) is about 60km from Launceston. "Premier" is all relative: the lifts are nothing to brag about, the slopes are less challenging than those at resorts on the mainland, and there's less natural snow and no mechanical snowmaking. Still, if you're in Tassie and you need to ski, this is where to go. Park entry costs $12 per car for the first day (additional days $6). **Ski rental** costs $36 per day (snowboards $55 plus deposit $100). Lift tickets run $20-28 for adults and $10-15 for students; beginner lift/lesson/equipment packages are available. During ski season, **Tasmanian Wilderness Travel** (tel. 6334 4442) provides daily service from Launceston (round-trip $29) or from the base of the mountain (round-trip $5), in addition to package deals. If driving your own vehicle, rent chains at the base ($15, plus $5 for fitting).

■ The Midlands

The fertile, rolling hills between Hobart and Launceston were originally settled as garrison towns to keep watch over the colony's convicts. The English settlers decided to make the midcountry of Tasmania look more like the midcountry back home, planting a wealth of English plants and building hedges and narrow lanes. The spirit of the Midlands is exemplified by the small town of **Oatlands,** a bit closer to Hobart than Launceston. There are no oats anywhere near the place, but the current theory is that Macquarie was nostalgic for Scotland when he named the place. A walk down High St takes you past a great number of old stone stores, cottages, and government buildings that have been recycled as antique galleries or cafes.

The town's showpiece building is the **Callington Mill,** opened in 1837. At peak capacity, the mill could grind up to one ton of grain every hour, but the introduction of the steam engine rendered it obsolete by the turn of the century. Even without its 25m sails, the mill is an impressive sight. (Open daily 9am-5pm. $2.) If you're staying

---

A Day in the Life: The Hunter

Aboriginals crossed over to Tasmania from mainland Australia during the last ice age, about 30,000 years ago. When the ice caps melted, the peninsula connecting Tasmania to the continent flooded with water, isolating these first colonists. For 30 millennia, Tasmanian Aboriginal culture thrived. These peoples pursued a semi-nomadic existence, following seasonal food supplies within a well-established home range. Fire was used to drive game out of the bush onto the spears of waiting hunters, and the periodic burning of vegetation shaped the terrain throughout the island. Although stones were used as tools, they used no stone-tipped weapons or implements. Instead, spears were fashioned entirely from wood, hardened in fire and sharpened with stone tools. The result was a highly effective weapon that could be thrown with deadly force and precision at a range of 60m. Analysis has revealed that these ancient Aboriginal spears had the same aerodynamics as today's Olympic javelins, with similar weight distribution.

overnight in Oatlands, don't miss the **Ghost Tour,** given every night at 8pm. The guide dons period dress and knows all there is to know about the area and its potential spectral inhabitants. (2hr., $8. Meet at the Callington Mill, rain or stars.)

One of the gems of the Midlands is the **Oatlands YHA,** 9 Wellington St (tel. 6254 1320). This tiny building is full of trinkets and curiosities sent back by the hordes of weary travelers who have come to regard this hostel as a second home. Beds in the tiny bunkrooms cost $11. **Tigerline** has buses to Launceston (2hr., daily, $13) and Hobart (1¼hr., daily, $10). **Redline** coaches run to Hobart (1½hr., daily, $10.60) and Launceston (1½hr., daily, $13.80). The **Oatlands post office** is on High St. (tel. 6254 1160; open M-F 9am-1pm and 2-5pm; postal code 7120). **Redline** (tel. 6231 3233) runs three to five times per day to Hobart (1¼hr., $10.60) and Launceston (1¼hr., $13.80).

THE NORTHWEST

The ferry brings most Tasmanian visitors first to the Northwest, and after a week hiking the Overland Track and two more running the Franklin River, many find it takes a while to leave. World Heritage wilderness is the big draw, punctuated by seaports on the northwest coast and mining towns along the highways out west. As you scoot around the A10 or join the pilgrims thronging to Cradle Mountain, take note of the layered worlds around you: Aboriginal homeland, fierce wilderness, ecotourism jackpot, mining motherlode, colonial convict myth and memory. The currents that dominate Tasmania's recent history and identity play out their drama here in the starkest relief.

▓ Devonport

Many people come to Tasmania in search of untouched wildlands, unspoiled rivers, and unending mountains. Many people also arrive in Devonport, which proves a bit of a shock; a grim waterfront, dominated by a cluster of gigantic grey silos, greets passengers arriving on the Spirit of Tasmania ferry. Still, the city is a useful gateway to the rest of the state, furnishing information outlets and numerous transportation options. It is also the major hub of the otherwise sparsely populated Northwest Zone, and quality budget accommodations ensure that any time you spend here before moving on will be comfortable, if not aesthetically rewarding.

ORIENTATION

The port of Devonport is the mouth of the **Mersey River,** and the ferry terminal is on its eastern bank. The city center lies on the western bank, with **Formby Street** at the river's edge, the **Rooke Street Mall** a block behind, each intersected by **Best Street** and **Stewart Street** running away from the river. Almost everything you might need in town lies within a block of these four streets. North of this center square, Formby St becomes **Victoria Parade,** which becomes **Bluff Road,** leading out to **Mersey Bluff** and **Bluff Beach** at the western head of the river. Devonport is bounded to the west by the **Don River** and to the south by the **Bass Highway** (Rte 1), which offers the only bridge across the Mersey. **Burnie** is 40 minutes west on Rte 1, and **Deloraine** is 30 minutes southeast. From Deloraine, **Launceston** is 30 minutes east and **Hobart** is three hours south. The drive to **Cradle National Park** takes 1½ hours.

PRACTICAL INFORMATION

Tourist Information: The official **Tasmanian Travel and Information Centre,** 5 Best St (tel. 6424 4466; fax 6424 8476), in the Devonport Showcase next to the McDonalds off Formby Rd, can book accommodations and bus, air, and auto transport. Open daily 9am-5pm. **The Backpackers' Barn,** 10-12 Edwards St (tel. 6424 3628; fax 6423 1119), specializes in orienting prospective bushwalkers, with equipment, maps, and plentiful advice. It's a good place to meet other hikers. Open M-F 9am-6pm, Sa 9am-noon.

Airplanes: The **Devonport Airport** is 6km east of the city center on the Bass Hwy. **Kendell** (tel. 6424 1411 or 13 13 00) and Qantas-affiliated **Southern Australia** (tel. 13 13 13) operate flights 3-4 times per day to Melbourne (1hr., $105-185; book well ahead for cheaper rates). The airport shuttle bus (tel. 018 142 692) meets all flights and delivers passengers anywhere in town for $5.

Buses: Redline Coaches, 9 Edward St (tel. 6424 5100), runs daily buses to Hobart (5hr., $32); Launceston (1¼hr., $13), with connections to points east and south; and Burnie (40min., $7), with connections to Wynyard ($9.60) and Stanley ($17.50). **Tasmanian Wilderness Travel** (tel. 6334 4442; fax 6334 2029) buses leave several times a week from the Redline Terminal or the Visitor Centre on Best St, bound for Cradle Mountain (3hr, $30); Cradle Mountain Lodge (1½hr., $24); and Queenstown (5hr., $30), with connections to Strahan ($36).

Ferries: The **Spirit of Tasmania** arrives from Melbourne on Tu, Th, and Sa (8:30am), and departs for Melbourne on the same days at 6pm. The overnight ferry passage includes dinner, breakfast, and hostel-style accommodation on the lowest decks of the ship. (Dec.-Jan. $130; Feb.-Mar. and Oct.-Nov. $110; Apr.-Sept. $103. Cars $30.) There is a free shuttle service from the ferry dock to the town center. It is essential to book ahead at the info center or by calling 13 20 10.

Car Rental: Major companies with counters at the airport and ferry terminals include **Hertz** (tel. 6424 1013), **Avis** (tel. 6427 9797), **Budget** (tel. 6424 7088), and **Thrifty** (tel. 6427 9119). **Advance** (tel. 6424 8885 or 1800 030 118) and **Rent a Bug** (tel. 6427 9034) often have better prices than the bigger chains.

Automobile Club: Royal Automobile Club of Tasmania (RACT), 5 Steele St (tel. 6421 1933), is open M-F 8:30am-5pm.

Currency Exchange: Commonwealth Bank, 20 Rooke St (tel. 13 22 21), and **ANZ,** 150C William St (tel. 6423 1300), are both open M-Th 9:30am-4pm, F 9:30am-5pm. **Trust Bank,** Rooke St Mall (tel. 13 18 28), is open M-F 9am-5pm. **ATMs** of every stripe are in the Rooke St Mall, between Best and Steel St.

American Express: Pat Young Travel (tel. 6424 7699), in Day's Building on Best St, Rooms 7-8. Offers AmEx travel, not financial, services. Open M-F 9am-5pm.

Bookstores: Angus & Robertson's, 43 Rooke St (tel. 6424 2022), open M-F 9am-5:30pm, Sa 9am-3pm. **The Wilderness Shop,** 26 Stewart St (tel. 6424 7393), open M-F 9:30am-5pm, Sa 9:30am-2pm. **Dead Tree,** 9 Steele St (tel. 6423 6334), sells used books.

Library: 21 Oldaker St (tel 6424 4255). Open M-Tu 9:30am-5:30pm, W-Th 9:30am-6pm, F 9am-9pm, Sa 9:30am-12:30pm.

Public Toilets: In the carpark adjacent to the Rooke St Mall. **Public showers** are available at the Backpackers Barn for $2.

Emergency: Dial 000.

Police: 17 Oldaker St (tel. 6421 7511).

Pharmacy: Fourways, 155 William St (tel. 6424 4233). Open 9am-9pm.

Post Office: 88 Formby St (tel. 6424 8282; fax 6424 7658). Open M-F 9am-5pm. **Postal Code:** 7310.

Internet Access: At the library (see above). Bookings essential.

Phone Code: 03.

ACCOMMODATIONS AND FOOD

Tasman House Backpackers, 114 Tasman St (tel. 6423 2335; fax 6423 2340). From Formby Rd on the river, go west along Steele St, turn left at William St, then right onto Tasman St. Once a hospital, the facilities have a pronounced institutional flavor, but family owners add a personal touch. Huge lounge, kitchen, and dining areas kept toasty by an immense wood stove, but the dorms can get chilly. Fresh bread and produce provided sometimes; potluck dinners for special occasions. Beds are a bit short for tall folks. The owners also operate tours and bushwalking trips. Dorms $12; doubles $28, with bath $35. VIP. Free storage.

Tamahere Hotel, 34 Best St (tel. 6424 1898), near the city center. Rooms are clean if a bit cramped; each has its own heater. Fully stocked kitchen and lounge. Lively pub downstairs has counter meals, pokies, pool, darts, and beer. Check in at the affiliated Backpackers Barn just down the street or with the pub. Dorm beds $10.

MacWright House-Devonport YHA, 115 Middle Rd (tel. 6424 5696), past Home Hill, just south of the Bass Hwy about 2km from town center. Very basic, aging facilities. No alcohol. Dorms closed 10am-5pm. Dorms $9, YHA nonmembers $12.

Mersey Bluff Caravan Park (tel. 6424 8655), on Bluff Rd, on the Mersey Bluff headland, about 1.5km from the city center. A well-equipped caravan park in an interesting spot on the Bluffs. Kitchen, barbecue, clean showers, and coin-op laundry. Tent sites $6.50, powered $15; on-site caravans $40; cabins $50.

Abel Tasman Caravan Park, 6 Wright St (tel. 6427 8794), on the east bank of the Mersey. Very convenient to the ferry terminal, located next to the East Devonport Beach. Two-person tent sites $10, powered $14; on-site caravans $35; cabins $56.

The **Rooke Street Mall** is packed with takeaways, chippers, hotel counter meals, and multinational fast food outposts. **The Kitchen Cappuccino Bar,** 2A Stewart St (tel. 6424 1129), is one of the better coffee lounges downtown (open M-F 9am-4pm). **The Family Hotel** (tel. 6424 1601), on Formby St, has excellent counter fare with a rotating schedule of half-price specials on the trinity of Tasmanian tucker: schnitzel, steak, and seafood (around $6; open M-Th). **Renusha's Indian Restaurant,** 157 Rooke St (tel. 6424 2293), stocks a good variety of veggie and meat dishes ($10-12), eat-in or takeaway. **Paul's Pizza Bar,** 21 King St (tel. 6424 3307), delivers for free (open daily 6pm-late). Large **Coles** and **Roelf Vos** supermarkets anchor Best St downtown.

SIGHTS AND ENTERTAINMENT

Tiagarra (tel. 6424 8250 or 6427 9037; fax 6427 0506), on Mersey Bluff near the lighthouse, is an interpretive center that explores 30,000 years of Tasmanian Aboriginal history. *(Open daily 8:30am-5pm. Guided tours every 30min. Admission $3, concessions $2.)* Detailed displays explain Aboriginal hunting methods, tool manufacture, and the genocide resulting from European settlement. The bluffs around the center bear many signs of Aboriginal occupation, including **rock engravings** visible (though sometimes inconspicuous) via a short walking track from the visitor center.

The **Devonport Maritime Museum,** on Gloucester Ave just off Bluff Rd, preserves a decidedly less ancient history. *(Open Apr.-Sept. Tu-Su 10am-4pm, Oct.-Mar. Tu-Su 10am-4:30pm. Admission $2, children 40¢.)* Mainly a collection of old photographs and model boats, the museum focuses on local lore, with a good archive of family history. Housed in an old church, the **Devonport Gallery,** 45-47 Stewart St (tel. 6424 8296), showcases the best of Tasmanian arts and crafts, concentrating on paintings, ceramics, and glass. *(Open M-Sa 10am-5pm, Su 2-5pm. Free.)* The gallery also hosts occasional cultural events and workshops. To the west of Devonport proper, in the small hamlet of **Don,** the **Don River Railway** (tel. 6424 6335) offers steam train rides to and from **Coles Beach,** a few kilometers away, and a small display of historical train equipment. *(Daily 10am-4pm on the hr. $7, children $4, pensioners $5. Display only $4.)*

At night, **Spurs,** 18-22 King St (tel. 6424 7851), has a country-western American theme, video games, and pool tables that attract a young, casual crowd. *(Open W-Su 4pm-1:30am. Live music F-Sa.)* Next door, the **Warehouse** is a weekend dance club with big name acts. *(Open F until 3am, $5 cover; open Sa until 4am, $6 cover.)* **Devonport Village Cinema,** 9 Stewart St (tel. 6424 4622), shows first-run movies.

■ Near Devonport

The **Leven Canyon Reserve,** southwest of the city near Nietta, boasts a lookout with stunning views of Leven Gorge. To get there, take the Bass Hwy west, then the B15 south to Nietta, then route 128 to the Canyon. A bit to the north, buried under farmland, lie the **Gunns Plains Caves** (tel. 6429 1388). In addition to the usual geological wonderland one finds underground, these caves boast a creek that houses platypuses and up-to-4kg freshwater crayfish. (Tours daily on the hr. 10am-4pm; $8, children $4.)

The **Asbestos Range National Park** is a small coastal reserve between Devonport and Launceston, popular with local weekenders as well as travelers. Its principal merit is convenience: it's close to towns, swimming, fishing, and walking tracks. **Camping** is abundant, and wildlife even more so. The latter is its stellar aspect—if you need to see a wild wombat before you can leave the state, come to Asbestos.

The park is accessible by car only, via three gravel-road entrances. The westernmost, with **Springlawn** and **Baker's Beach,** has the most to offer; take the C740, which heads north from the B71 between Devonport and Exeter. Springlawn (ranger tel. 6428 6277) has camping, toilets and a public telephone, but no other services. Two other camping areas are 3km further down the road on the beach by **Baker Point.** (All camping $4, $2 children; firewood included.) The 20-minute Springlawn nature walk heads scrub and lagoon ecosystems rife with wallabies and birds. Another hour of moderate climbing leads to **Archer's Knob.** A hike to **Badger's Beach,** about halfway along the park's coast, takes seven to eight hours return.

■ Deloraine

Set in the foothills of the western Tiers and ensconced in the agricultural Meander Valley, Deloraine functions as a perfect base for exploration of the World Heritage Wilderness to the southwest. Nearby **Mole Creek** has some of the most spectacular caves in Australia: **Marakoopa** and **King Solomon's Cave.** Cave **tours** (tel. 6363 5182; fax 6363 5122) run several times a day. (Each cave $6; children and concessions $4.)

The **Deloraine Visitor Information Centre,** 98 Emu Bay Rd (tel. 6362 2046), is open from 9:30am to 4pm daily. **Trust Bank** is at 24 Emu Bay Rd (tel. 13 18 28; open M-Th 9:30am-4pm, F 9:30am-5pm). **Redline** (tel. 6362 2046) has three to four coaches per day to Launceston (45min., $6.70), Devonport (1hr., $9), and Burnie (1¼hr., $14.20). **Tasmanian Wilderness Travel** (tel. 6334 4442; fax 6334 2029) has coaches to Cradle Mountain (4hr.; Apr.-Oct. Tu, Th, Sa, Su; daily Nov.-Mar.; $40). All coaches depart from the visitors center. The **police** (tel. 6363 4004) are at Westbury Pl. The **post office** is at 10 Emu Bay Rd (tel. 6362 216; fax 6362 3244; open M-F 9am-5pm; **postal code** 7304).

The **Deloraine Highview Lodge YHA,** 8 Blake St (tel. 6362 2996), is the best hostel around, with fine mountain views and comfy bunks. Day tours and activities can be arranged through the hostel, and bikes can be hired for $15 per day. (Bunks $12, YHA nonmembers $15). **The Apex Caravan Park** (tel. 6362 2345), down by the river on West Pde, is pleasant, green, and tidy (sites $8, powered $10).

Marsupials from Hell

It doesn't spin around faster than you can see it, and it's rarely seen in convict stripes. Still, the Tasmanian devil is a remarkable creature. These marsupials are rarely more than 45cm high and aren't built for speed, being far more adept at climbing than at running. Their jet-black coats are occasionally marked with white bands or spots. The maw is the most striking feature, full of jagged teeth and usually open wide. The powerful jaws can crush bones up to 7.5cm in diameter and allow the devil to eat almost anything. Devils are entirely carnivorous, hunting small mammals as well as scavenging carrion. Once common throughout Australia, they were driven off the mainland by dingoes; however, they thrive in Tasmania to the point of being considered a pest in some areas. While devils' attacks on humans are limited to the occasional theft of souls, they do sometimes kill farm animals. They are also extremely noisy, particularly when feeding, and are very irritating when they take up residence under people's houses. Despite their abundance, you won't often see the nocturnal, secretive critters in the wild; your best hope for spotting one is to try a wildlife park.

■ Cradle Mountain

If you haven't seen a picture of mystic Cradle Mountain rising above quiet Lake Dove, you must not be in Tasmania yet. The mountain is Tassie's most famous natural landmark, visited by hundreds of thousands every year. The area is Tasmania's highest Alpine region, a complex glacial fabric of tarns, creeks, and crags that shelter pockets of the state's unique biotic jewels: sweet-sapped cider gum woodlands, rainforest of king billy and celery top pine, carpets of cushion plants. Supposedly long-dead species including the freshwater crayfish, mountain shrimp, and velvet worm have been found alive and kicking around Cradle Mountain. *Nothofagus gunnii,* the state's only native deciduous tree, thrives along the mountain's skirt, and thousands throng in late April and May to see the fiery colors of its turning leaves. Naturalist Gustav Weindorf, an early champion of the area's importance, described Cradle Mountain as the place "where there is no time and nothing matters."

Cradle Valley is the trailhead for the **Overland Track,** Tasmania's most prominent walk, traversing the length of the **Cradle Mountain-Lake St. Clair National Park** (see **Lake St. Clair,** p. 481). The National Park is the northernmost end of the Cradle Mountain wilderness area, which is a World Heritage site. Its heavy tourist load is a burden on the environment, so keep your visit eco-friendly. Regular national park fees apply (pay at the gate). The large **Visitors Centre** (tel. 6492 1110; fax 6492 1120) features informative displays with suggestions for day hikes, as well as an excellent shop (open daily 8am-5pm). A 7km gravel road connects the center to Dove Lake and Cradle Mountain itself. **Maxwell's** shuttle bus (tel. 6492 1431) makes frequent unscheduled runs between the campground, the visitor's center ($2), and Dove Lake ($7), and offers service throughout the northwest region; call for customized arrangements. **Tasmanian Wilderness Travel** (tel. 6334 4442) sends buses to two points in the park several days a week. Cradle Mountain Lodge receives buses from Devonport (1½hr., $23.50); Launceston (2¾hr., $36.50); and Queenstown (3¼hr., $17.60), with connections from Strahan (5hr., $23.20) and Lake St. Clair (5¾hr., $35). Dove Lake Lodge receives buses from Devonport (2¾hr., $30) and Launceston (4¼hr., $43.50).

ACCOMMODATIONS AND FOOD On the entrance road, 2km outside the park, the **Cradle Mountain Tourist Park** (tel. 6492 1395; fax 6492 1438) provides bunk rooms, tent sites, and beautiful amenities in an ideal location. (Tent sites $7 per person, in winter $5. Basic bunks $20; in winter $16.) Inside the park, the **Waldheim Cabins,** run by the Visitor's Centre and named after the lodge built by Weindorf, offer rustic group lodgings—no electricity, but good spirit (approximately $25 per adult). **Food** options are limited; it's wise to bring your own supplies. There is a cheap, unremarkable restaurant and takeaway joint opposite the tourist park. For a splurge on a tasty meal, try **Cradle Mountain Lodge,** by the Visitor's Centre at the park entrance.

BUSHWALKS The Cradle Mountain Area has a web of trails which combine to form innumerable potential walks. Check out the trail map ($3) at the visitor's centre. The two-hour walk around **Dove Lake** is an environmentally friendly track suitable for almost anyone and worth every step. The first stage of the **Overland Track,** and its side trails offer more arduous climbs; the ascent of Cradle Mountain is a difficult day hike from Waldheim or Lake Dove. A trail map and walker registration are advised for any walks longer than two hours. According to park statistics, it rains 275 days a year—dress accordingly. Trails around the Visitors Centre and the Cradle Mountain Lodge explore more sheltered habitats, and include a wheelchair-accessible rainforest walk and the pretty **Pencil Pine Falls.**

■ The Western Wilderness

At the upper end of the Derwent Valley, the A10 crosses the Derwent Bridge and winds past Lake St. Clair and the Franklin River toward Tasmania's west coast. Much of the interior has been set aside to preserve the dense temperate rainforest that dominates the terrain and borders the road on either side. The western coastline of Tasmania is among the most desolate, uncivilized areas in Australia. Twenty thousand kilometers of Indian Ocean separate the shore from the nearest landmass and periodically send violent storms crashing against the formidable coastline. Strahan, the only coastal settlement of any size between Hazard Bay in the northwest and Recherche Bay south of Hobart, is hardly a sprawling metropolis.

The first communities in the area supported themselves by exploiting thick stands of old-growth timber. Soon after logging began, prospectors began searching the hills and creeks for gold, hoping to strike it rich like their Victorian comrades. Alas, they never reached the end of the rainbow, and many hapless diggers departed bankrupt. Eventually, explorers less blinded by gold lust discovered mountains of tin, silver, and copper just beneath the surface. Still, natural resources are finite, and when the lode ran out, the end was at hand for many of the ramshackle mining communities. The logging industry too fell on harder days, which is good news for the forest; today, vast tracts of the West are as wild and pristine as they were when the first settlers arrived.

■ Strahan

Strahan is built on the vast **Macquarie Harbour,** the only sheltered cove on the west coast. Once the management locus for nearby **Sarah Island's** prison for recidivist convicts, it then became an important port for minerals and timber in the days before roads and railways. As these industries declined and overland transport routes were established, the port's main industry shifted from shipping to fishing. Strahan has a few interesting historical attractions, but is best known as a gateway to the **Franklin-Gordon Wild Rivers National Park** World Heritage Area and the rest of the southwest wilderness. Franklin-Gordon is accessible only by bushwalk or boat.

PRACTICAL INFORMATION AND PERFORMANCES The **Strahan Visitor's Centre** (tel. 6471 7622; fax 6471 7533) on the Esplanade is run by a theater company, an unlikely but tremendously successful association. (Open daily Nov.-Apr. 10am-8pm; May-Oct. 10am-6pm.) The permanent exhibit entitled "West Coast Reflections" is a classy, rather postmodern production of several of Tasmania's artistic gurus, combining fragments of local stories, voices, and images. If you can't bring yourself to gush over another historical collection or shining mountain lake, here is welcome respite from standard Tassie fare ($4.50, concession $3, children free). Another creative production at the Visitor's Centre, the local play *The Ship That Never Was* explores convict history (daily at 5:30pm; adults $10, concession $7.50, children $5).

The **Strahan World Heritage Area Visitor Centre** (tel. 6471 7122), a branch office of the Parks and Wildlife Service, is located in the historic customs house. (Open M-F 9am-noon and 1-5pm.) They dispense info on local wildlife and history and sell passes to national parks (vehicles $9 per day; pedestrians $3). The *Strahan Foreshore Historic Walkway* pamphlet outlines a 2.5km path that visits many of Strahan's old buildings. **Tasmanian Wilderness Travel** (tel. 6334 4442; fax 6334 2029) runs buses several times a week to Queenstown (1hr., $5.60), Lake St. Clair (3hr., $22.50), Hobart (6hr., $42), Cradle Mt. (4¼hr., $23), Devonport (5¼hr., $36), and Launceston (6¼hr., $49). The **police station** (tel. 6471 8000) is on Beach St. The Strahan **post office** (tel. 6471 7171) is attached to the Customs House (open M-F 9am-5:30pm; **postal code** 7468).

ACCOMMODATIONS AND FOOD The only good budget accommodation is the **Strahan YHA** (tel. 6471 7255) on Harvey St, one block inland. This complex of cabins furnishes bunkbed dorms and large communal areas, and has a resident platypus. (Dorms $13, YHA nonmembers $16; bike hire $20 per day.) YHA's daytime reception is in **Strahan Central** (tel. 6471 7612), a posh cafe and crafts store with tasty coffee, on the corner of Herald St and the Esplanade (open 8am-late). The best fish option is **Strahan Fresh Seafood** (tel. 6471 7209) on the Esplanade opposite Garden River Cruises (open M-F noon-3pm and 5:30-7:30pm).

WALKS AND CRUISES Wildlife abounds on the pleasant walking track to **Hogarth Falls,** just a few kilometers from central Strahan. The path follows **Botanical Creek,** which is home to all manner of aquatic Tasmanian critters, including the elusive platypus. The Hogarth Track is accessed through People's Park; just follow the dirt road to the track. Just north of town, **Ocean Beach** stretches from Macquarie Head in the south to Trial Harbour, over 30km to the north. It's the longest beach in Tasmania and one of the wildest, with brooding surf and windy dunes. Open seas across the Indian and Atlantic Oceans all the way to South America create massive swells; swimming can be unsafe. Beginning in late September, thousands of **mutton-birds** descend on the beach after flying 15,000km from their Arctic summer homes.

Many Strahan visitors try a cruise up the **Gordon River.** A multitude of cruises of various lengths operate from the wharf in central Strahan ($40-60). A typical tour with **Gordon River Cruises** (tel. 6471 7187 or 6471 7281; fax 6471 7317) runs across Macquarie Harbour and up the Gordon to the Heritage Landing, home to a 2,000-year-old huon pine that managed to survive decades of intensive logging. Tours also access **Sarah Island,** a penal colony for secondary offenders from 1822 until 1833. Known as one of the darkest pits in the British penal system, convicts on the island were forced to wade chest-deep in the harbor's freezing water, pushing giant huon pine logs. Today, all of Sarah Island's buildings have been reduced to sign-posted ruins. Costlier but more exciting views of the area are provided by **Strahan Wilderness Air** (tel. 6471 7280; fax 6471 7303); an 80-minute flight over the harbour and river costs around $99.

■ Queenstown

In 1883, **Mick and Bill McDonough,** also mysteriously known as the **Cooney Brothers,** discovered a large outcropping of copper-rich rock, later termed (for an equally mysterious reason) the **Iron Blow.** The Blow was mined for gold alone for many years, though each ton of rock yielded just two ounces of the precious metal. The **Mount Lyell Gold Mining Company** formed in 1888, but redirected its efforts toward copper in 1891. This was a wise decision, for millions of pounds of copper had already slipped away during the relatively poor gold mining days. The company built a smelter to process the copper ore on site, wreaking environmental havoc. Nearly every large tree in the surrounding hills was felled to feed the smelter, young growth was killed by the thick yellow sulphur haze released during the pyritic processing, and the exposed topsoil was washed into the Queen River by heavy rainfall. This rainfall supports incredibly lush forest in areas not ravaged by mining, so the town (pop. 3000 and falling) currently resembles lunar wasteland in the midst of dense vegetation.

Information is available from the **Queenstown Parks and Wildlife Service** (tel. 6471 2511; open M-F 8am-4pm). **Trust Bank** (tel. 13 1828; fax 6471 1958; open M-F 9am-5pm), one of few banks in the region, is at Orr and Sticht St. The **police** station is at 2 Sticht St (tel. 6471 3020). The **post office** is at 32 Orr St (tel. 6471 1782; fax 6471 2381; open M-F 9am-5pm, **postal code** 7467). **Tasmanian Wilderness Travel** runs several times a week to Lake St. Clair (1¾hr., $17.20), Hobart (4¾hr., $36), Strahan (45min., $5.60), Cradle Mt. (3hr., $17.60), Devonport (4hr., $30), and Launceston (5¼hr., $43).

The **Empire Hotel,** 2 Orr St (tel. 6471 1772), retains some of the glory of its heyday as a miners' pub. A grand wooden staircase leads up to clean accommodations. Meals are available downstairs, while minimal kitchen facilities are upstairs, adjacent to the avocado-green lounge room. (Singles $20; doubles $35, twin $35, ensuite $45.)

The **Mt. Lyell Mine** still chugs along, with tours exploring the working areas. Underground tours leave from the offices at 1 Driffield St (tel. 6471 2388; fax 6471 2222). Daily surface tours visit the old open-cut mines and other relics of the past. (Surface tours Oct.-Apr. 9:15am, 2:30pm, and 4:30pm; May-Sept. 9:15am and 4pm; 1hr.; $11, under 16 $6.50.) Underground tours are more thorough but quite pricey (M-F 8:30am and 1:30pm; 3½hr; $48). Bookings are essential. The old Iron Blow open-cut mine, just off the Lyell Hwy near **Gomanston,** offers broad views of surrounding barren hills and of the water-filled crater that was once a mine. The **Galley Museum** (tel. 6471 1483) has early mining artifacts and an impressive collection of photos, along with a less impressive display of ladies' underpants. (Open Oct.-Mar. M-F 10am-5:30pm, Sa-Su 1-5:30pm; Apr.-Sept. 10am-12:30pm and 1:30-4:30pm. Admission $3, concessions $2.)

■ Franklin-Gordon Wild Rivers National Park

The **Lyell Highway** (A10), connecting Queenstown to Derwent Bridge, cuts through the Franklin-Gordon Wild Rivers National Park, at the heart of the **Tasmanian Wilderness World Heritage Area,** which is otherwise roadless for miles and miles to the north and south. The highway follows the original hard-won road first laid only 70 years ago, which itself followed the harder-won **Linda Track,** cut in 1883 to finally connect the wild and isolated west with the east. Several stops along the highway allow casual visitors to get a taste of the wildlands. To use any of these facilities, purchase a National Parks Pass. The 10-minute **Nelson Falls Nature Trail,** hidden in wet rainforest 28km east of Queenstown, leads to a lovely cataract.

There is a **campsite** and picnic area on the west bank of the **Collingwood River** where the highway crosses the river 48km east of Queenstown; the access road leaves the north side of the highway 100m west of the bridge. **Donaghys Hill Lookout,** 52km east of Queenstown, is accessed by a 40-minute return track and boasts panoramic views of the Franklin River Valley and **Frenchman's Cap,** its principal peak. The hike to the top and back is a strenuous 4- to 5-day venture. **The Franklin River Nature Trail,** 62km east of Queenstown, is a well-maintained track through rainforest with interpretive markers that ponder the meaning of the wilderness.

Roadside lookouts at **Surprise Valley** and **King William Saddle** (67km and 72km east of Queenstown, respectively) offer views of the eastern side of the wilderness area. The saddle marks a major divide of Tasmania. To the west, a 2.5m annual rainfall flows into the Franklin-Gordon rivers, through wet rainforest, and out to Macquarie Harbor. The land to the east is much dryer eucalypt woodland, whose water trickles into the Derwent River and out through Hobart into the Tasman Sea.

■ Lake St. Clair

Half of the headline act of the **Cradle Mountain-Lake St. Clair National Park,** Lake St. Clair is Australia's deepest lake as well as the source of the Derwent River. Its Aboriginal name is Leeawuleena ("sleeping water"), and many find the place exceptionally calm, a serene juxtaposition of mountain, wood, and water. The lake anchors the southern end of the famous **Overland Track** (see below) with Cradle Mountain at its northern terminus. There are also a number of day hikes and a few family-friendly nature trails in the vicinity of the lake.

Cynthia Bay, at the southern end of the lake, is accessible via a 5km access road that leaves the Lyell Hwy just west of Derwent Bridge. There, the park's **visitors center** (tel. 6289 1172; fax 6289 1227) has excellent displays on wildlife and European and Aboriginal inhabitants of the area. A spooky hologram of a group of Tasmanian tigers dominates the exhibit (open daily 8am-5pm). The **ranger's office** offers maps and information on local trails. **Register your party** here for any extended walks, especially the Overland Track. Next door, the **general store** (tel. 6289 1137; fax 6289 1250) provides a variety of services. **Fishing** equipment costs $15 per day ($15 deposit). The store's **ferry** runs the length of the lake from the Cynthia Bay jetty daily at 9am, 12:30, and 3:30pm, subject to demand and winter weather. It stops at Echo Point ($12) and Narcissus Bay ($15) at the far side. A round-trip cruise with commentary is also available (1½hr., $20); bookings are essential.

The general store also runs **campsites** ($5 per person, powered $6). **Hostel bunks** are comfortable enough but overpriced at $20. The other accommodation option is the barn-sized **Derwent Bridge Wilderness Hotel** (tel. 6289 1144; fax 6289 1173), on the Lyell Hwy opposite the Lake St Clair access road. It's worth a visit at least for a

---

Cold Kills

Many people come to Tasmania to hike the endless, untamed wilderness. Tourist brochures emphasize the splendor and majesty of the island's mountains and forests, encouraging tourists with little bushwalking experience to brave the wild with little idea of what they are doing. Make no mistake: Tasmania's wilderness is still wild, and can kill the unwary given half a chance. The greatest hazard in the wilderness is the unruly weather that can shift from zephyr to gale in a heartbeat. Even in the summertime, when the weather is hot, carry warm and waterproof clothing to protect yourself from hypothermia, a lowering of the body's core temperature that can be fatal. With a little planning, you can prevent hypothermia in the first place. Do not attempt bushwalks without the proper equipment and experience. Ask the locals about what kind of weather and track conditions to expect. Wear wool or fiber pile clothing, including gloves and a hat. Wet cotton, especially jeans, is deadly. For details on symptoms and treatment of hypothermia, see **Essentials,** p. 17. The Parks and Wildlife Service will advise on gear.

---

post-hike pint and some fire-warmed lounge relaxation. Backpacker rooms are small modular units detached from the main hotel building (all singles $20, in winter $15). The hotel serves hearty, plain meals at reasonable prices.

Walking tracks radiate from **Watersmeet,** 20 minutes from Cynthia Bay. The **Woodlands Nature Walk, Platypus Bay Trail,** and **Rainforest Bower** are short, easy, and excellent. Longer hikes head west to **Forgotten** and **Shadow Lakes** (4hr. return) or up steep, weather-beaten **Mt. Rufus** (7hr. return from Cynthia Bay). If you take the ferry out in the morning, the lakeside hike back to Cynthia Bay from Narcissus Bay takes five hours; it's three hours from Echo Point.

Tasmanian Wilderness Travel (tel. 6334 4442) buses depart several times a week from the hotel, and head to Hobart (3hr., $29), Queenstown (1¾hr., $17), with connections to Strahan (3hr., $22.50); and Launceton (3½hr., Dec.-Mar. only, $45).

■ The Overland Track

Stretching 80km through World Heritage wilderness, the Overland Track connects **Cradle Mountain** and **Lake St. Clair** and is Australia's most famous trail. Every year, approximately 3000 attempt the track, most taking five to eight days to complete the journey. Even in the dead of winter an average of 50 are on the track at any given time. Some purists contend that the Track has become a highway; still, its grandeur cannot be denied, as it traverses an astonishing array of landscapes and ecosystems. If you're feeling strong, numerous side trails will tempt you, including the ascent of the state's tallest peak, **Mt. Ossa** (1617m). Anyway, the frequently miserable weather filters out travelers without a truly rugged spirit.

The heavy traffic can have disastrous impacts on the path's fragile alpine ecosystems, so it is crucial to observe minimum-impact bushwalking practices. The Track huts fill easily, so hikers must carry **tents.** If you are planning to walk the track, write to the rangers to request an information kit at **Parks and Wildlife Service,** Cradle Mountain Visitor Centre, P.O. Box 20, Sheffield TAS 7306 (tel. 6492 1110; fax 6492 1120). The Track itself can be undertaken from either the Cradle Mountain end (see p. 478) or Lake St. Clair (see above); it costs $12 for a national park permit.

■ The Northwest Coast

West of Devonport, the A2 highway traces the northern coast of Tasmania. A2 passes through **Ulverston** and Burnie before reaching the junction where A10 branches south toward Queenstown, Zeehan, and Strahan. From Burnie, A2 continues northwest past Wynyard and **Rocky Cape National Park** to **Smithton** and nearby Stanley.

The area's major transport hub is **Burnie,** a dull industrial town. **Redline,** 117 Wilson St (tel. 6431 3233), connects Burnie to Devonport (40min., 4-8 per day, $7), Deloraine (1¼hr., 3-4 per day, $14), Launceston (2¾hr., 3-4 per day, $18), Stanley

(1½hr., M-Sa 1-2 per day, $9), and Wynyard (20min., M-Sa 1-2 per day, $2.50). The **Tasmanian Travel and Information Centre** (tel. 6434 6111; open M-F 9am-5pm, Sa 9am-noon) is in the Civic Centre complex. An **ANZ Bank** with an **ATM** is on the corner of Wilson and Cattley St (tel. 6430 4311). The only budget accommodation is the **Treasure Island Caravan Park,** 253 Bass Hwy (tel. 6431 1925; fax 6431 1753), with an indoor pool, laundry, and barbecue facilities. (Tent sites $10, powered $14; caravans $36; cabins $54.)

Known (to itself) as Tulip Town, **Wynyard** is a charming tiny town with many green areas and tulip festivals each spring. **Southern Australia** and **Kendell** both operate flights from the **Wynyard airport** to Melbourne (several daily $93-168, call 6431 2166 for airport information). **Badger's Skybus** (tel. 0419 501 115) meets every flight to shuttle folk to town ($7). Wynard has a **YHA** at 36 Dodgin St (tel. 6442 2013), convenient to the airport (dorms $12, YHA nonmembers $14), and a **caravan park** right off the highway (sites $10, powered $13). The **Table Cape** is a striking volcanic promontory right outside Wynyard. Covered in a mosaic of farmland, the cape has a lighthouse and arresting views of the coastline.

In the extreme northwest of the state, Stanley is one of the oldest European settlements, colonized by the Van Diemen's Land company in the 1840s. Stanley is built at the base of the **Nut,** a huge volcanic plateau first seen by a European, Matthew Flinders, in December 1798. Flinders described it as a "cliffy round lump in form resembling a Christmas cake." Stanley is just a small, quiet town, thick with tea rooms, craft shops, and little else. But the Nut is well worth seeing, and the townspeople couldn't be nicer. The best way to see the Nut is to make the short, sweet climb yourself, but there's a chairlift to cart the less-ambitious to the top (open 10am-4pm; return $6, children $4). If you can't even be bothered to walk around at the top, take a **Nut Buggy tour** (tel. 6458 1312; $5; closed in winter). The top of the Nut is windy and can be bitterly cold; dress appropriately. Fine views in all directions reward those who brave the climb and the wind. A small **post office** and **general store** is on 11-13 Church St. (open 9am-12:30pm and 1:30-5pm). The **Stanley Caravan Park** (tel. 6458 1266), on the waterfront at Wharf Rd, doubles as a **YHA hostel.** (Office open 8am-8pm. Twins or doubles $12, YHA nonmembers $14. Tent sites $9.50, powered $12.)

TASMANIA

Victoria

Victoria may be mainland Australia's smallest state, but it's blessed with far more than its share of fantastic attractions of the cultural, natural, and historical varieties. Its environment runs the gamut from the dry and empty western plains of the Mallee to the inviting wineries along the fertile banks of the Murray River, from the ski resorts of the Victorian Alps to the forested parks of the Gippsland coast. The capital of the state and the cultural center of the nation, sleek and sophisticated Melbourne over-flows with stained glass and elaborate iron latticework. Its multifarious districts offer verdant gardens, eclectic ethnic neighborhoods, seaside strips, and student haunts. And because Victoria is compact and has a well-developed infrastructure, its attractions lie within easy reach of one another and of Melbourne.

Victoria's most distinctive attractions are found on the coast. West of Melbourne, which perches conveniently in the center, the breathtaking Great Ocean Road winds its way alongside the roaring Southern Ocean. Hand-cut between 1919 and 1931 from the limestone cliffs, the road passes surfing beaches, coastal getaways, temper-ate rainforests, and geological wonders, including the Twelve Apostles rock forma-tion, which pokes precariously from the sea like ancient fingers. East of the capital, the coastline unfolds past Phillip Island's penguin colony and the beach resorts of the Mornington Peninsula, heading into Gippsland. Here, crashing waves collide with granite outcroppings to form the sandy beaches at the edge of the renowned Wilsons Promontory National Park. East Gippsland's Riviera climate and resort beaches slowly give way to stony, sandy tidal estuaries teeming with birds and fish.

Most of the state's interior is remarkable less for its natural grandeur than for its his-torical significance. The mid-19th century gold rush flooded central Victoria with seekers of the sweet stuff. When the ore waned, a host of charming, elegant country towns were left in its wake, today preserved in tourist-oriented nostalgia. Later, leg-endary bushranger Ned Kelly had a plan to stick it to the man in his wanderings throughout the Hume Corridor. Today, this area is a fertile land of wineries nestled in the shadow of Australia's ski mecca, the High Country. The 20th century brought extensive agricultural and commercial development, including several massive hydroelectric public works projects that continue to impact the state's ecosystems. Still, Victoria's physical beauty remains, tempered by a refined sensibility and cosmo-politan flair that add a touch of class to Australia's down-to-earth grit.

🐨 VICTORIA HIGHLIGHTS

- The **12 Apostles.** Touristy? Yes. Spectacular? Definitely. (See p. 527.)
- A day or a lifetime at the **Taggerty Bush Settlement** for a first-hand experience with Australian fauna, pioneer history, and Aboriginal culture (see p. 558).
- Going sports-mad with the local **footy** fans at Melbourne's MCG (see p. 513).
- Phillip Island's penguins are great and all, but we prefer dusk feedings at the **Koala Conservation Centre** followed by sunset over the **Nobbies** (see p. 519).
- Melbourne's delectable, diverse, and de-groovy **restaurants.** (See p. 501.)
- Learning about the Koori people at the **Brambuk Cultural Centre** (see p. 549).
- Echuca's marvelously kitschy **World in Wax Museum** and its just-plain-marvel-ous **National Holden Motor Museum** (see p. 551).
- Ghoulish night tours of the **Old Melbourne Gaol** (see p. 508).
- Sunrise at **Wilsons Promontory's** wind-swept lighthouse (see p. 569).

PRACTICAL INFORMATION

The **Victoria Visitor Information Centre** (tel. 9658 9036 or 9658 9524; fax 9654 1054; nationwide 24hr. info line 13 12 42), in the Melbourne Town Hall at the corner of Little Collins and Swanston St, offers oodles of maps and information on accommo-dations, attractions, and tours throughout the state. It also houses **AUSRES** (tel. 13

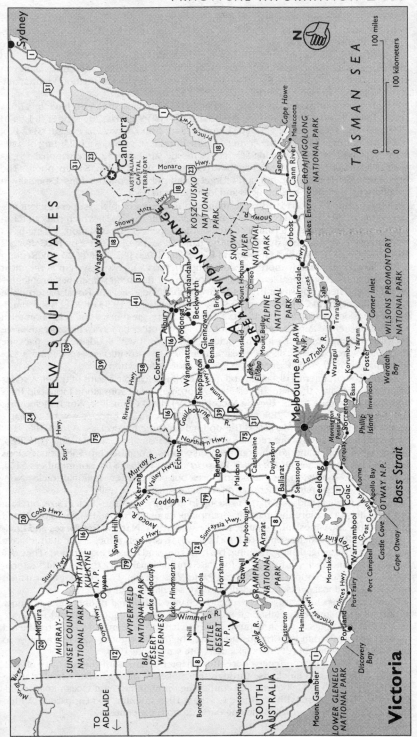

VICTORIA

10 66), an independent, private booking service that arranges tours and transport across Australia. (Open M-F 8:30am-5:30pm, S-Su and public holidays 9am-5pm.) **Information Victoria,** 356 Collins St, Melbourne (tel. 1300 366 356), has an exhaustive range of publications on travel throughout the state. There are excellent maps and atlases, parks information, and specialty guides on stuff like biking and bushwalking on the ground floor. (Open M-F 8:30am-5:30pm.) There's also an Information Victoria outlet in Sydney at 403 George St (tel. (02) 9299 2288 or 13 28 42).

The three major Australian hostel chains (YHA, Nomads, and VIP) have locations throughout Victoria. **Youth Hostels Association (YHA) Victoria,** 205 King St (tel. 9670 7991; fax 9670 9840; email yha@c031.aone.net.au; http://www.yha.org.au; GPO Box 4793, Melbourne, 3001), on the corner of Little Bourke St, provides a full listing of statewide YHA hostels and a booking service (domestic surcharge $2, international $5), as well as an attached budget travel agency. (Open M-F 9am-5:30pm, Sa 9am-noon.) The hostel network is excellent, but don't forget about pub accommodations. Especially in small towns, they offer bargain beds and local flavor to boot.

Getting around Victoria is a breeze thanks to the very complete, super-efficient system of intrastate trains and buses known as **V/Line** (tel. 13 22 32), which runs an information center in its main terminal at Melbourne's Spencer Street Station. V/Line has a few interstate options, but more complete national service is offered by **McCafferty's Bus Lines** (tel. 13 14 99) and **Greyhound Pioneer** (tel. 9663 3299 or 13 20 30). Renting a car allows considerably more freedom, and Victoria's highway system is the most extensive and easily navigable in the country. To cut down on sometimes prohibitive rental costs, check ride-share boards at any hostel. The excellent **Royal Automobile Club of Victoria (RACV),** 360 Bourke St, Melbourne (tel. 13 19 55 or 9642 5566; emergency roadside assistance 13 11 11; fax 9642 5040), has great maps and sells short-term travelers' insurance. Members of automobile clubs in other countries may already have reciprocal membership. To join in Victoria, the basic RACV Roadside Care package (including 4 free service calls each year and limited free towing) costs $47, plus a $28 first-time-joiner's fee. See **Essentials,** p. 35, for more information.

Victoria's short internal distances and make **cycling** a feasible means of travel. A series of byways crisscross the state, traversing its more remote regions along mountain trails and abandoned train tracks. **Bicycle Victoria (BV),** 19 O'Connell St, North Melbourne (tel. 9328 3000; fax 9328 2288; email bicyclevic@bv.com.au; http://www.bv.com.au), across from the Victoria Market, is the optimal resource for cyclists. (Open M-F 9am-5pm.) Members can procure recreation maps, theft insurance, and national park info, and can join groups and go on organized bike tours. (Membership $38; concessions $32.) BV also publishes *Discovering Victoria's Bike Paths* ($14; nonmembers $17), which focuses mostly on the Melbourne area but covers a few regional tracks. Nonmembers can pick up free brochures on the state's many bike trails.

Victoria's national and state parks make up in diversity what they lack in size, offering opportunities to explore the majestic Grampians mountain range, expanses of blasted Mallee scrub, and Gippsland's strange marine wilderness. **Natural Resources and Environment (NRE),** 8 Nicholson St (tel. 9412 4745), East Melbourne, is the authoritative resource for camping, fishing, hunting, bushwalking, and coastal exploration. They distribute maps and visitor information for state and national parks throughout Victoria. (Open M-F 8:30am-5:30pm.) You can call **Parks Victoria** (tel. 13 19 63) for information on state and national parks, but they don't have a walk-in location.

Phone numbers in Victoria have recently changed. Regional phone codes are now almost all 03, followed by eight-digit numbers. The last two digits of the old area code are the first two digits of the new number. If you have trouble making a call, try the old number instead (within Victoria, just add a zero before the eight digits). Towns close to the New South Wales border may take that state's area code (02).

Like most visitor's experiences here, this chapter begins with the hub city of Melbourne. It then moves clockwise through the spokes of the Victorian wheel, starting with the area south of Melbourne and continuing through the Great Ocean Road, Goldfields, the Mallee, Murray River, Hume Corridor, High Country, and Gippsland. Within each region, towns are ordered moving outward from the center.

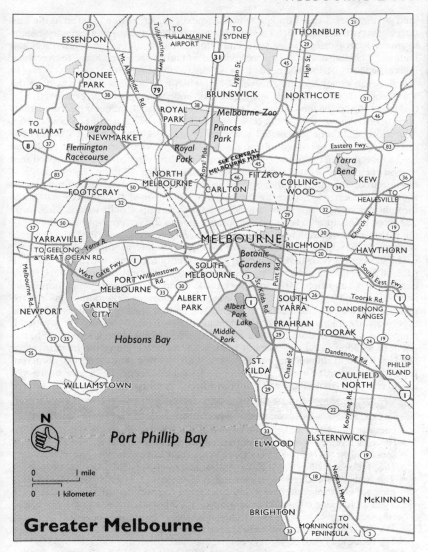

Greater Melbourne

MELBOURNE

The capital of Victoria and Australia's second-largest city, Melbourne is frequently thought of more as an ideal place to live than a great place to visit. This is half true; as Melburnians themselves are likely to tell you, there are countless reasons why this metropolis deserves the oft-touted designation as the World's Most Liveable City it earned in 1990. But Melbourne's bad rap as a travel destination stems from its lack of a singular, Kodak-moment icon like the Sydney Opera House or Ayers Rock. Instead, the city is a sleek and stylish cosmopolitan collage of sights and sounds. Both ultramodern skyscrapers and ornate neogothic edifices line its wide streets, and the rumble of the green-and-gold trams that run down them is penetrated now and then by the roar of a hundred thousand sports nuts at the MCG. You might spend one hour window-shopping at Southbank's chic boutiques, and the next comparing ripe fruits amid the bustling clamor of the Queen Victoria Market. Students enjoying late-night caffeine sessions in smoky Fitzroy cafes coexist with clubhoppers raging till 6am in South Yarra and Prahran. Sprawling over 6200 square kilometers of urban space and home to over three million denizens, Melbourne needs to be savored, not just seen.

It all began rather inauspiciously in 1825, when John Batman sailed a skiff up the Yarra, got stuck on a sandbank, and uttered the understatement of the century: that he had found the "place for a village." Then named Batmania, the diminutive burg had its phenomenal growth spurt at the onset of the Victorian Gold Rush three decades later. "Marvelous Melbourne" celebrated its coming-of-age in 1880 by hosting the World Exhibition, which attracted over a million people. When the Victorian economy crashed in the 1890s following a series of bank failures, Melbourne's infrastructure collapsed, and its fetid open sewers earned it the nickname "Marvelous Smellbourne." By the early part of the 20th century, though, things were up and running again, and Melbourne posed a legitimate challenge to Sydney for the honor of being named Australia's capital. While the Canberra compromise ultimately deprived both metropoli of this status, Melbourne was more than happy to serve as temporary home to the government until the Parliament House was completed. The city's 20th-century apex was the 1956 Olympic Games, which brought Melbourne's love for sport to an international audience.

The subsequent years have seen even more population growth, with a stronger international flavor than ever before; most of the recent immigrants hail from China, Southeast Asia, Italy, and Greece (Melbourne has the world's third-largest Greek population after Athens and Thessaloniki). Today, Melbourne's various neighborhoods—the frenetic Central City, alternafunky Fitzroy, Italianate Carlton, mellow, seaside St. Kilda, and more—invite exploration and lie within minutes of each other via tram. The weather is temperate, though beware frequent rainstorms; most of the time, it's great for beachgoing or walking along the Yarra at night with the reflection of the banana-yellow Flinders St Station shimmering on the water. With picturesque waterfronts, numerous parks, famous sporting events, and a world-class cultural scene, Melbourne invites visitors to relax and enjoy all the attractions of a large city with none of the hype.

⬛ MELBOURNE HIGHLIGHTS

- Footy at the **MCG,** the epitome of Melbourne's sports obsession (see p. 507).
- Fitzroy's stylish, inventive, and popular **Vegie Bar** (see p. 502).
- Spooky night tours bring to life **Old Melbourne Gaol's** grim past (see p. 508).
- The **National Gallery of Victoria,** Australia's premier art collection (see p. 509).
- The hourly **Waltzing Matilda** display in Melbourne Central's glass atrium—a moment of national sentiment within a temple to consumerism (see p. 506).
- Vendors hawking tremendous bargains on food and Australiana in the massive, labyrinthine rows of stalls at the **Queen Victoria Market** (see p. 508).
- The Art Deco elegance and huge screen at **Astor Cinema,** St. Kilda (see p. 512).
- The **Moomba Festival:** 11 days of raw, unbridled pandemonium (see p. 514).
- **Cycling** the scenic waterfront of the Yarra River and Port Philip Bay (see p. 514).

■ Getting There

BY PLANE

Boomerang-shaped **Tullamarine International Airport,** 22km northwest of Melbourne, has three terminals. The central terminal houses all international arrivals and departures. The first floor serves **United Airlines** (tel. 9335 1133), **Cathay Pacific** (tel. 13 17 47), **Singapore Airlines** (tel. 9339 3344, reservations 13 10 11), Ansett Airlines, and Qantas. The two major domestic carriers lie on each side of the international terminal: **Qantas** (tel. 13 12 11) to the left and **Ansett** (tel. 9399 5290) to the right. Each flies to all Australian capitals at least once daily, and have similar fares. Return fares with three weeks' advance purchase include: Adelaide $241, Alice Springs $558, Brisbane

$391, Cairns $591, Canberra $222, Darwin $723, Hobart $207, Perth $581, Sydney $230. Stand-by fares may be cheaper.

Travellers Information (tel. 9297 1805; fax 9297 1051), directly in front of arriving international passengers as they exit, books same-day accommodations, provides maps and brochures, and has a useful backpacker bulletin board. Lockers ($4-8 per day) are located on either end of the international terminal.

Skybus (tel. 9335 2811; fax 9338 5075) provides ground transport to Melbourne's city center. It stops at the YHA Queensberry and at the Spencer Street bus and train station downtown. The bus departs from the station for the airport at a quarter past and a quarter to the hour, and from the **Melbourne Transit Centre,** 58 Franklin St, every half-hour. (One-way $9, return $16.) Taxis (tel. 13 10 08) to the city center cost $28 and take approximately 30 minutes. **Car rental** companies are clustered to the left when exiting international arrivals (see Getting Around, below).

BY BUS AND TRAIN

Spencer Street Station (tel. 9619 2300 or 9619 2587), on Spencer where it intersects Bourke St, is the main intercity bus and train station (open daily 7am-9pm). **V/Line** (tel. 13 22 32) runs service to Adelaide (11hr.; daily; $58), Albury (3-3½hr.; M-F 5 per day; $38), Ballarat (2hr.; M-F 12 per day, Sa-Su 6 per day; $13), Bendigo (2hr.; M-F 12 per day; $20), Bright (4½hr.; Sa-Th 1 per day, F 2 per day; $38), Canberra (8½hr.; daily; $47), Echuca (3-4hr.; M-Sa 4 per day, Su 3 per day; $26), Geelong (1hr.; 14 per day; $8.40), and Sydney via Albury (11hr.; 2 per day; $90, $54). **McCafferty's,** located in the barrel-shaped coach station just north of the main station, offers bus service to most major Australian cities. YHA-discounted one-way tickets will take you to Adelaide ($40), Alice Springs ($162), Ayers Rock ($162), Brisbane ($117), Cairns ($247), Canberra ($41), Darwin ($292), and Sydney ($45). **Melbourne Transit Centre,** 58 Franklin St, near Elizabeth St and the brown Qantas tower, is the main terminal for Skybus, Ansett Airlines, and **Greyhound Pioneer** (tel. 9663 3299 or 13 20 30), which has daily service to Adelaide ($50), Brisbane ($117), Canberra ($41), and Sydney ($45). All rates listed are high season, and most decrease in winter.

■ Getting Around

BY PUBLIC TRANSPORTATION

Melbourne's superb public transportation system, the **Met,** is comprised of light-rail trains, buses, and trams. **Tram** routes criss-cross the metropolitan area and are the most useful for navigating the city and its proximate outskirts. Running every three to 12 minutes, they're usually quite punctual but aren't as quite so fast as modern subways. The burgundy-and-gold **City Circle Tram** circumnavigates the central business district, provides running commentary on the city's sights and history, and is totally free. Many Melbournians hop on all the trams without paying, since you don't actually have to show your pass to ride them—but if an inspector decides to make a spot check and you're without a valid ticket, expect a very hefty fine ($50-150). The bus and light-rail train systems are mostly for commuters going to farther-afield residential areas, and you can't board without a valid Metcard. There are **train stops** at **Melbourne Center, Parliament, Flinders St,** and **Spencer St,** though the main rail hub is the banana-colored **Flinders St Station** at the southern foot of Swanston StSwanston St, identifiable by its big clock.

The entire network criss-crosses the metropolitan area, comprising a total of three Met zones, though you'll only be in Zone 1 unless you travel out to a distant suburb. **Tickets** within Zone 1 can be used on any of the three types of transportation, and are valid for unlimited travel for a two-hour period ($2.20), the day ($4.30), the week ($18.60), or the month ($69.50). Student rates are half-price; you qualify if you have a valid Australian university I.D. (ISIC cards or international university I.D.s are not accepted). Only two-hour tickets can be purchased on board trams and buses; if you're going to be in town for a week or month, the longer-term passes save a lot of time and

Meat Market ■

Queensberry St.

Errol St.

Chetwynd St.

Howard St.

Peel St.

Queen St.

Elizabeth St.

Flemington Road

Royal Parade

Pelham St.

Leicester St.

Ⓐ

Ⓑ

Ⓒ

Ⓓ

Ⓔ

Queen Victoria Market

Franklin St. Bus Terminal

Victoria St.

King St.

Hawke St.

Roden St.

Spencer St.

Rosslyn St.

Dudley St.

Adderley St.

Flagstaff Gardens

Franklin St.

A'Beckett St.

La Trobe St.

Little Lonsdale St.

Lonsdale St.

Little Bourke St.

Bourke St.

Little Collins St.

Collins St.

Flinders Lane

Flinders St.

Ⓕ

Ⓖ

Roy Melbourn Institute Technolo

State Library

Melbourne Central

THE GREE PRECINC

CHIN

City Centre Arcade

✉ GPO

Mall

Swanston Walk

ⓘ

St. Paul's ✝

William St.

King St.

Queen St.

Elizabeth St.

🚌

YHA Travel ■

Spencer St.

Spencer St. Station

Rail Freight Terminal

⌂ King St.

Rialto Towers

CITY CENTRE

North Wharf Rd.

World Trade Centre ■

Yarra River

Enterprize Park

Yarra River

Flinders St. Station

Southbank Promenade

Polly Woodside Maritime Museum 🏛

Museum Rd.

ⓘ

TO ⌂
↓

Melbourne Casino

Whiteman St.

Kings Way

Queensbridge

Clarendon St.

SOUTH MELBOURNE

City Rd.

Southbank Blvd.

Sturt St.

Concert Hall

Theatre

National Gallery 🏛

St. Kilda Rd.

Queen Victori Garde

TO SHRINE & LA TROBE COTTA

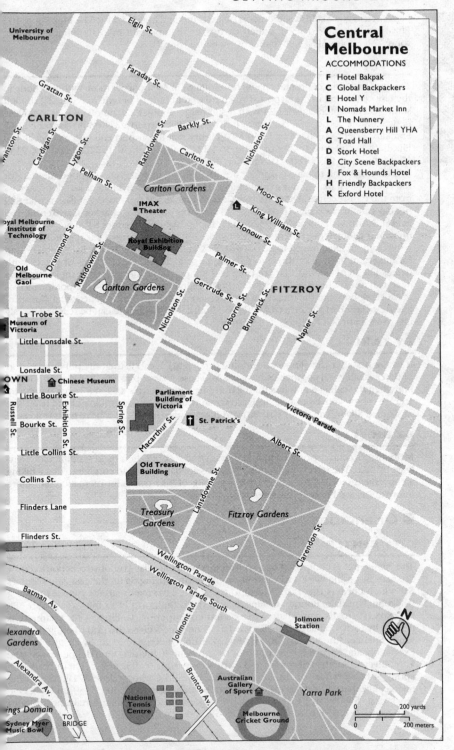

Central Melbourne

ACCOMMODATIONS

F   Hotel Bakpak
C   Global Backpackers
E   Hotel Y
I   Nomads Market Inn
L   The Nunnery
A   Queensberry Hill YHA
G   Toad Hall
D   Stork Hotel
B   City Scene Backpackers
J   Fox & Hounds Hotel
H   Friendly Backpackers
K   Exford Hotel

VICTORIA

hassle. Tickets are sold at stations, on board trams and buses, and at **The Met Shop,** 103 Elizabeth St (tel. 13 16 38), which carries an all-important map showing every Met route. (Met hours M-Sa 5am-midnight, Su 8am-11pm.)

BY CAR

The usual national car rental chains have offices in Melbourne, most with locations in the city center and in the airport. They tend to rent only to people over age 25, though some accept renters ages 21-24 with a surcharge. **Budget's** main office is at 398 Elizabeth St on the corner of A'beckett St (tel. 9203 4844; airport 9241 6366). **Hertz** is at 97 Franklin St (tel. 9663 6244 or 13 30 39). **Thrifty** is at the airport and near Budget at 390 Elizabeth St (tel. 9663 5200 or 1300 367 2277; airport 9330 1522; airport fax 9335 1706). **Avis** (tel. 9338 1800) is at the airport.

Local firms tend to have cheaper rates, though if you're traveling around the state or the country you may find it inconvenient that they don't have lots of locations. Across from the transit center, **Delta Rent-a-Car,** 85 Franklin St (tel. 9662 2366), starts at $29 per day (minimum rental 10 days, age 23 and over only). **Backpacker Car Rental,** 169 Peel St, North Melbourne (tel. 9329 4411; fax 9329 4422), charges $100 per week with unlimited kilometers in the metropolitan area. Backpacker has a car re-purchase plan where cars are guaranteed to be bought back at set rates after 12 weeks, a good option for long-term visitors or those too young to rent. There are also tons of places with names like Rent-a-Bomb that are only half joking about the quality of their cars. The deals can run as cheap as $10 per day, but weigh the savings against the potential costs of breaking down in the middle of nowhere in a foreign country. The **Royal Automobile Association of Victoria (RACV),** 360 Bourke St, Melbourne can be reached by calling 13 19 55 or 9642 5566 (see p. 484).

BY TAXI

If you're out after the Met stops running (midnight), a cab is the only public transport option available. All companies have a $2.60 base charge plus 96¢ per km, or 33¢ per km when the cab is going less than 21km per hour. There's a $1 surcharge when you arrange cab pick-up by phone, and also when you ride between midnight and 6am. The misnamed **Silver Top** (tel. 13 10 08) and **Black Cabs** (tel. 13 22 27) are both yellow.

BY BICYCLE

Melbourne's central city is compact, though traffic congestion makes it difficult to navigate by bike. The streets in the outer suburbs are flat and broad enough to make biking a convenient transit option, and there are loads of bike tracks for recreation. For more information, see **Melbourne Recreation,** p. 464.

■ Orientation

CITY CENTER

The city center is composed of a well-arranged rectangular grid of streets bordered by **Spencer St** on the west, **LaTrobe St** on the north, **Spring St** on the east, and **Flinders St** (which borders the Yarra River) to the south. Five major streets run east to west (LaTrobe, Lonsdale, Bourke, Collins, Flinders). To the north of all but LaTrobe are "little" streets—roads named after their southern superior (Collins St, for example, is flanked by Little Collins St and Flinders Ln). Nine streets cross this grid running north to south: Spencer (the westernmost), King, William, Queen, Elizabeth, Swanston, Russell, Exhibition, and Spring. Spencer St runs by the primary bus and train depot, bridges the Yarra River to South Melbourne, and carries trams #48, 75, 95, and 96. On the east end, Spring St borders Parliament and both Treasury and Carlton Gardens. Directly in the middle, **Elizabeth St** carries major northbound tram lines (#19, 50, 57, 59, and 68). One block east, **Swanston St** is a pedestrian walk but also carries important north-south tram routes (#1, 3, 5, 6, 8, 16, 22, 25, 64, 67, and 72).

The east end of the city contains most restaurants and sights. **Bourke St Mall** (a ɔedestrian stretch of Bourke St between Swanston and Elizabeth St, traversed by trams Ͻ5 and 96) marks the heart of the city and swarms with people every day. The triangle st north of the city center bordered by LaTrobe, Queen, and Victoria St borders North ɪelbourne's Queen Victoria Market and is a hive of budget accommodations, while ɪst Melbourne contains the spectacular **Fitzroy Gardens** as well as Victoria's sporting ɪrine, the **Melbourne Cricket Ground.**

ɪTZROY

ʇam #11 runs the length of **Brunswick St,** the main artery of Fitzroy that marks Mel-ɔurne's bohemian district. Fitzroy is a shopping mecca whether you're looking for ɛw or used clothes, music, or books, and has Melbourne's best cafe society and excel-nt restaurants of all stripes. While it's packed with style and populated with "ferals" ɪustralians' term for the nose-ring crowd), Fitzroy is blessedly low on attitude, and its ʇablishments house a healthy mix of freaks, families, and everyone in between. The ɔcks of Johnston St between Brunswick and **Nicholson St** comprise the Latin Quar-ɪr, with lots of Iberian stores, restaurants, tapas bars, and dance clubs.

ARLTON

ɔominated by Italiana, Carlton begins at Nicholson St and extends through the Carlton ɪrdens and west to the **University of Melbourne.** Its primary thoroughfare is **Lygon t,** where upmarket Italian bistros, cheaper gelaterias and pasticcerias, and a smattering ʹ ethnic and eclectic food cater to a crowd comprised of crusty old Mediterranean ɔes and college students alike. Public transportation doesn't go all the way to Lygon . Either take a tram up Swanston St (these include #1, 3, 5, 6, 8, 16, 22, 25, 64, 67,and ϩ) and head east along Queensberry or Faraday St or take #96 up Nicholson St and ɪad west along Faraday St.

ɪORTH MELBOURNE

orth Melbourne is a pleasant mix of bungalows, flats, refurbished residences, and ɛighborhood shops and eateries, all within easy striking distance of the city center. ɔrming its eastern edge, **Elizabeth St** heads north from the city center and passes the ʼueen Victoria Market with its abundant, inexpensive food stocks and wares; travel ʼest along Victoria St (traversed by tram #57) to find lots of cool budget eateries. Will-ɪm St heads north from the city center past Flagstaff Gardens and becomes **Peel St.** ɛel and Elizabeth intersect near the University of Melbourne with Elizabeth continuing ɔrthwest under the name **Flemington Rd** (along which tram #55 continues to run), ɪtimately leading to the **Melbourne Zoo.** At this intersection Peel St becomes **Royal ɪrade,** which borders the University of Melbourne.

ɔUTH MELBOURNE

ʰe Yarra divides Melbourne into the more working-class suburbs of the north and the ɪncier ones to the south. South Melbourne, west of **St. Kilda Rd** and stretching south ɔm the **West Gate Freeway** to Albert Park, is an exception. More blue-collar than ɪljacent communities, this neighborhood has some great accommodations, restau-ɪnts, and nightspots along its main drag, Commercial Rd. It's also a quick strike to the ɪrk, the Royal Botanical Gardens, the city center, or the beach at Port Phillip Bay.

West of South Melbourne along Port Phillip Bay are three of Melbourne's quietest, ɪost posh suburbs. **Port Melbourne** is the most commercial and least impressive. Fer-ɪes to Tasmania depart from **Station Pier,** at the terminus of tram #109. Bay St (known ; City Rd closer to the CBD), marks the division between Port Melbourne and more ɪrbane **Albert Park,** an upscale residential neighborhood with stately bungalows along ɪe seaside. **Middle Park,** just south of Albert Park and Kerferd Rd, is a mellow bayside ɔmmunity, less showy and more livable than its northern neighbor.

ST. KILDA

Though it's a bit removed to the southeast of the city center (and officially in the city of Port Phillip), St. Kilda is a budget hotspot with excellent accommodations and eateries. Trams #16 and 96 bring people to St. Kilda from the city center's Flinders St and Spencer St Stations, respectively. The former travels along **St. Kilda Rd,** and passes Melbourne's two largest green spaces, the Royal Botanic Gardens and Albert Park, en route. At **St. Kilda Junction,** St. Kilda Rd intersects Fitzroy St, which runs west toward the beach where it curves south to follow the waterfront and becomes the Esplanade. **Barkly St** runs south from the junction toward the beach, completing a triangle with Fitzroy St and the Esplanade. A half-kilometer toward the beach from St. Kilda Junction, **Grey St** links Fitzroy and Barkly St, and is the focus of St. Kilda's budget accommodations. The last street that branches south from Fitzroy St before it turns into the Esplanade is Acland St, one of Melbourne's many excellent cafe districts, distinguished by its superlative old-time cake shops.

SOUTH YARRA AND PRAHRAN

South Yarra and Prahran span the area enclosed by the Yarra to the north, St Kilda Rd to the west, Dandenong Rd to the south, and Williams St to the east. Commercial Rd, the focus of gay Melbourne, runs east-west, separating South Yarra from its southern neighbor, Prahran. The district's main drag is **Chapel St;** the section of the boulevard that lies in South Yarra is the commercial incarnation of the fancy suburbs south of the river. On sunny Sundays, the beautiful people come here to shop for Prada and Versace and to snipe about the catty salesgirls in sleek, pricey sidewalk bistros. Chapel St gets a little more down-to-earth south of Commercial Rd in Prahran, which is closer in spirit to St. Kilda. **Greville St** branches west from Chapel and is a den for secondhand clothing, record stores, and bizarre restaurants. Trams #78 and 79 run slowly down Chapel St. By tram from Flinders St Station, #8 travels below the Botanical Gardens, then along Toorak Rd to its intersection with Chapel St, while #5 and #64 head south along St Kilda Rd, and then go east along Dandenong Rd to Chapel. The quickest way to get to the area from the central city, though, is to hop a train and take it to South Yarra, Prahran, or Windsor Stations, each of which lies only a few blocks west of Chapel St.

■ Practical Information

TOURIST AND TRAVEL INFORMATION

Victorian Tourist Office: Victoria Visitor Information Centre and **AUSRES,** Melbourne Town Hall, at Little Collins and Swanston St (tel. 9658 9036 or 9658 9524; fax 9654 1054; 24hr info line 13 12 42). Open M-F 8:30am-5:30pm, Sa-Su and public holidays 9am-5pm. **Information Victoria,** Collins St. (See p. 484 for more info.)

Melbourne Tourist Office: City Experience Center (tel. 9658 9955), Melbourne Town Hall, at Little Collins and Swanston St. Features interactive virtual tours of the city and free Internet access (15min. max). Their website (http://www.melbourne.org) is also excellent and up to date. Open M-F 9am-7pm, Sa-Su and public holidays 10am-5pm. In the same building, the **Melbourne Greeter Service** is great—and free!—way to get acquainted with the city, with 3-4hr. tours tailored to your personal interests and given in six languages. Arrange one by filling out a brief application 3 days in advance; you can also do this via email (greeter@mebourne.vic.gov.au). There are also info booths scattered throughout the city, at **Queen Victoria Market** (open Tu, Th 9am-2pm, F 9am-4pm, Sa-Su and public holidays 10am-4pm); **Bourke St Mall** (open M-Th 9am-5pm, F 9am-7pm, Sa 10am-4pm, Su and public holidays 11am-4pm); **Flinders St Station** (open M-Th 9am-5pm, F 9am-6pm, Sa 10am-4pm, Su and public holidays 11am-4pm).

Disabled and Elderly Travelers Information: Travellers Aid, 169 Swanston St, 2nd fl (tel. 9654 2600; fax 9654 1926), by the corner of Bourke St. Provides information, cafe, showers, and toilets, and rents strollers. The disabled access center is open M-F 9am-5pm and Sa-Su 11am-4pm; the building is open M-F 8am-9pm. A cafe, lounge, lockers, showers, and disability access service at **Spencer St Station** also lend a helping hand. Open M-F 7:30am-7:30pm.

Outdoors Information: Natural Resources and Environment (NRE), 8 Nicholson St, (tel. 9412 4745), East Melbourne. Scads of info about everything relating to the outdoors, including obtaining various licenses. Lots of maps. Open M-F 8:30am-5:30pm. You can call **Parks Victoria** (tel. 13 19 63) for info on state and national parks, but they don't have a walk-in location.

Budget Travel: YHA Victoria, 205 King St (tel. 9670 7991; fax 9670 9840; email yha@c031.aone.net.au; http://www.yha.org.au; postal address: GPO Box 4793, Melbourne, 3001), on the corner of Little Bourke St. Provides a full listing of YHA hostels and a booking service (domestic surcharge $2, international $5). Attached budget travel agency. Open M-F 9am-5:30pm, Sa 9am-noon. **Backpackers Travel Centre,** Shop 19, Centre Place, 258 Flinders Ln (tel. 9654 8477; fax 9650 3290; email info@backpackerstravel.net.au), has a staff that's been there and done that. They offer lots of cheap tour packages and can help plan itineraries around Australia and New Zealand. **STA Travel's Victorian headquarters** are at 222 Faraday St, Carlton (tel. 9349 2411; fax 9349 2537), and there are branches all over the city center, including 208 Swanston St (tel. 9639 0599; fax 9639 0831).

Consulates: Melbourne's range from Austria to Vanuatu. Some of our personal favorites include: **Canada,** 123 Camberwell Rd, Hawthorne East (tel. 9811 9999). **France,** 492 St. Kilda Rd, Melbourne (tel. 9820 0921). **Germany,** 480 Punt Rd, South Yarra (tel. 9828 6888). Open M-F 9am-noon. **Great Britain,** 90 Collins St, Level 19, Melbourne (tel. 9650 4155). Open M-F 9am-4:30pm. **Japan,** 360 Elizabeth St, 45th fl, Melbourne (tel. 9639 3244). Open M-F 10am-12:30pm and 2-4:30pm. **New Zealand,** 60 Albert Rd, South Melbourne (tel. 9696 0399). Open by appointment only. Visa applications available outside the door. **United States,** 553 St. Kilda Rd, level 6, Melbourne (tel. 9526 5900). Open M-F 10am-noon and 2-3pm.

FINANCIAL SERVICES

Currency Exchange: All banks will exchange money during regular operating hours (M-Th 9:30am-4pm, F 9:30am-5pm). The currency exchange at 190 Collins St (tel. 9654 2768) is open 8am-8:40pm daily. **Thomas Cook Foreign Exchange,** 330 Collins St (tel. 9602 3811; fax 9606 0560), at the corner of Elizabeth St. No commission when exchanging Thomas Cook traveler's checks. Other checks and cash exchange face 1% commission ($4 minimum). Open M-F 8:45am-5:15pm, Sa 9am-4pm. Several banks have offices at the airport.

American Express Travel Office, 233 Collins St (tel. 9633 6333), and inside the GPO at the corner of Elizabeth and Bourke St (tel. 9203 3001). Buys all traveler's checks commission-free and provides free letter service (no packages) to holders of AmEx cards or traveler's checks. Wire transfers are available. Open M-F 8:15am-5:30pm, Sa 10am-1pm.

ATMs: ANZ, Commonwealth Bank, and **Westpac** accept V, MC, AmEx, Cirrus, and Plus. Their 24hr. outlets swarm like locusts all over the city.

EMERGENCY AND SOCIAL SERVICES

Lost Property: In Melbourne Town Hall, Swanston St (tel. 9658 9463, Sa-Su 9658 9774).

Bookstores: Reader's Feast (tel. 9662 4699; http://www.readersfeast.com.au), in the basement of the Midtown Plaza at the corner of Bourke and Swanston St, has the latest fiction, some great staff picks, and a good travel section if you need another copy of *Let's Go: Australia 1999* or ten. **The Foreign Language Bookshop,** 259 Collins St (tel. 1800 350 990 or 9654 2883; fax 9650 7664) stocks books in over 90 languages, including dictionaries, travel guides and books, and software.

Library: State Library of Victoria, 382 Swanston St (tel. 9669 9888), on the corner of LaTrobe St. Several slow, crowded Internet terminals (see **Internet Access,** below). Open M 1-9pm, Tu and Th-Su 10am-6pm, W 10am-9pm.

Ticket Agency: Ticketek (tel. 13 28 49 or 1800 062 849; fax 9639 3499), and **Bass** (tel. 13 28 49), for sports, performances, and other events. Student and senior discounts. $3 charge for booking by phone. Both open M-Sa 9am-9pm, Su 10am-7pm.

Halftix (recorded info tel. 9650 9420), Bourke St Mall opposite Myer Department Store, sells half-price tickets on performance day only and often sells out by 2pm.

Public toilets: Two on Elizabeth St, in front of the GPO and opposite the Queen Victoria Market. Also on the south side of Melbourne Town Hall along Little Collins St near the intersection with Swanston St.

Information Lines: Weather (tel. 0055 26177). **Swimming and surfing conditions** (tel. 9628 5777, ext. 5). **Time** (tel. 0055 14888).

Newsagent: Transit News, Shop 211, Melbourne Central (tel. 9662 2411), at Swanston and La Trobe St opposite the State Library, has reams of magazines and newspapers from around the globe. Open M-Th 7:30am-6:40pm, F 7:30am-9pm, Sa 8:30am-5:30pm, Su noon-4pm.

Employment Assistance: Backpacker's Resource Centre (BRC; tel. 1800 154 664), in the lobby of Hotel Bakpak (see **Accommodations,** p. 496). For a $20 registration fee, they guarantee work, usually within a week, as well as lifts to most jobs and help with work clothes. Melbourne's biggest daily paper, *The Age,* has an extensive classifieds section that comes out on Saturdays and can be accessed online at http://www.theage.com.au.

Translating and Interpreting Service (tel. 13 14 50; TTY 9657 8130). Operates 24hr. and offers assistance in over 100 languages.

Emergency: Dial 000.

Police: 637 Flinders St (tel. 9247 6666).

Crisis Lines: Victims Assistance and Referral Hotline (tel. 9603 9707 or 1800 819 817). **Centre Against Sexual Assault** (tel. 9344 2210). **Lifeline Counseling Service** (tel. 13 11 14). **Dental Emergency Service** (tel. 9341 0345). **Poisons Information Service** (tel. 13 11 26). **Alcohol and Drug Counselling Service** (tel. 9416 1818). **Emergency Surf Life Saving House Victoria** (tel. 9534 8400).

Pharmacy: The Block Pharmacy, Shops 7 and 8, The Block Arcade, 282 Collins St (tel. 9650 6688; fax 9654 1799), has a "naturopath" on hand for all you starry-eyed New Age zealots. Open M-F 7am-5:30pm, Sa 8:30am-12:30pm.

Hospital: Access Medical Centre, 349 Elizabeth St (tel. 9642 1266), opposite Melbourne Central. **Central Medical Centre,** Qantas House, 114 William St, 3rd fl (tel. 9670 3871), at Little Collins St, has a travelers' vaccination clinic.

POST AND COMMUNICATION

Post Office: Melbourne's General Post Office (GPO) (tel. 13 13 18 or 9203 3044), at the corner of Elizabeth and Bourke St, does mail in style, with vaulted ceilings and carpeted floors. Wire transfer service, phone books, stationery shop, and AmEx office with currency exchange. **Poste Restante** is at counter 19. Open M-F 8:15am-5:30pm, Sa 10am-1pm. **Postal Code:** 3000. Post Australia has an office at the airport (tel. 9338 3865) with full fax, photocopy, and **Poste Restante** services. Open M-F 9am-5pm, Sa-Su 10am-4pm; address is Melbourne Airport, Vic 3045.

Internet Access: There are eight free terminals at the **State Library** (see Emergency and Social Services, above), but they're slow and crowded and you can only book for 30min. at a time. **Melbourne Internet,** Shop 133A, Melbourne Central, 300 Lonsdale St (tel. 9663 8410; http://www.melbint.com.au), has ten slick terminals hooked up with superfly 64k ISDN connections, and you can get wired on cappuccino, too. $10 per hr. Open M-Th 9am-6pm, F 9am-7pm, Sa 10am-5:30pm, Su 10am-5pm. **Cyberia,** 19 Carlisle St, St. Kilda (tel. 9534 6221), has fast modems for only $1 per 10min. ($2 minimum charge) and serves free tea and coffee if you surf for an hour or more. Open 10:30am-8pm.

Phone Code: 03.

■ Accommodations

As a population and party center that's second only to Sydney as a gateway to Oz, Melbourne supports a vast number of budget accommodations to host its booming backpacker population. The two biggest hostel hives are St Kilda and the triangle just north of the city center enclosed by LaTrobe, Peel, and Victoria St, each of which offer places to stay for all styles and price ranges. The mostly YHA-affiliated hostels in North Melbourne tend to be a quieter and more sedate, popular with at least as many school groups and elderly travelers as 20-something backpackers, while the accommodations in the central city are as gritty and boisterous as they are conveniently located. South Yarra and Prahran lie farther afield but are preferred by those who enjoy the proximity to these districts' profusion of shopping and nightlife.

Availability drops during the high season (summer, roughly Nov.-Feb.), when most accommodations raise their prices a tad ($2-4). The more popular hostels tend to be booked solid during these periods (and are also in demand during school holidays, from June-Aug.), so be sure to book as far in advance as possible. Unless explicitly noted otherwise, all accommodations have a common room with TV, hall baths, 24-hour access, and no chore requirements, offer parking, or have wheelchair access. An increasingly popular form of deposit is the requirement of an international passport in lieu of cash. This policy, which has been adopted by many of Melbourne's major hostels, can be inconvenient, though you can generally get your passport back for the evening should you need it for ID purposes. Laundry, when available, costs $2 per wash or dry.

CENTRAL CITY

The Friendly Backpacker, 197 King St (tel. 1800 671 115 or 9670 1111; fax 9670 9911), a block east of Spencer St station at the corner of Little Bourke St. The Friendly B lives up to its name with a cheery atmosphere and loads of local scene info. Small lounges on each of four floors; no central lounge. Big kitchen. Sparsely decorated but brand-new digs range from intimate 4-person bungalows to massive barracks that sleep 16. Bunks $15; winter weekly rate $90. Linen and doona included. Towel rental $2. Wheelchair-accessible suites available.

Exford Hotel, 199 Russell St (tel 9663 2697; fax 9663 2248), at the corner of Little Bourke St, in Chinatown. A little worn around the edges, but very welcoming and comfortable. A few rooms offer sweeping views of the Chinatown gates. TV lounge, laundry, kitchen. Locals and travelers party in the lively hotel pub till the wee hours. Bunks in 4-, 6-, or 10-person dorms $11-15; doubles and twins $39-45.

Fox and Hounds Hotel, 356 Flinders St (tel 9629 5943; fax 9629 5090), at Queen St. Unadorned, unimpressive rooms above a workers' pub aren't much to look at, but they're the cheapest ones around. Big downstairs lounge has three TVs, pool table ($1), video games, and cheap drink specials Sa night ($1 pots, $2 mixed drinks). Passport required for key deposit. Reasonably clean bathrooms, bunks in spartan barracks. Decent pub meals discounted for residents ($4.50). Bunks $10; weekly $75, in summer $85. Doubles and twins $15, $50, $70.

JUST NORTH OF THE CITY CENTER

Walk uphill past La Trobe St on Elizabeth St, or take tram #57 or #55.

⊕Hotel Bakpak, 167 Franklin St (tel. 9329 7525; fax 9326 7667), between Elizabeth and Queen St. This cavernous 6-level facility can sleep up to 500 and is well on its way to becoming the pulsing, party-hearty nerve center for Melbourne's backpacker scene. Dubious wall murals and a blaring intercom don't do much for atmosphere, but no one beats Bakpak's cornucopia of amenities, which include a travel agency, employment service, basement "Roo Bar," cafe, laundry, backpack-size lockers ($2), Internet access ($2 per 8min), several lounges, budget travel agency, fitness center, small movie theater, and sparsely-appointed kitchenette. Lots of parties in the Roo Bar offer amazingly cheap drinks and provide a great way to meet fellow travelers. No smoking. Passport required for key deposit. Spare but spruce 10- to 16-bed barracks $15; smaller dorms $18; doubles and twins $45-50. VIP discount in winter. V, MC.

Toad Hall, 441 Elizabeth St (tel. 9600 9010; fax 9600 9013), between A'beckett and Franklin St. A classier, more sedate cut above the frenetic backpacker scene, Toad Hall's appealing Victorian structure combines the intimacy of a B&B with the conveniences and attentive staff of a large inn. Large, newly furnished dorm rooms, airy kitchen, patio, basement den with TV, VCR, and stereo, central heating, in-room tea-or coffee-makers. Reception open 7am-10pm. Dorms $17; singles $30; twins $45; doubles $50. VIP. Linen $3, parking $5, laundry $4. Reservations recommended a week in advance. V, MC.

Hotel Y, 489 Elizabeth St (tel. 9329 5188 or 1800 249 124; fax 9329 1469), between Thierry and Franklin St, less than a block from the transit center. Winner of Australian Tourism awards 2 years running, the Y has the feel of a luxury hotel with stellar rooms, a swimming pool, sparkling laundry and kitchen, TV lounge, and the sleek, Cafe Y. The bathroom tiles, designed by Deb Halpern, the creator of Melbourne's Ophelia statue, have even photographed for architectural journals. Y would one want anything more? 24hr. reception. Dorms with bath $25; singles $70; doubles $80; triples $90; quads $100. 10% discount for all YMCA or YWCA members. No vacancies for back-scrubbers. Book 2 weeks ahead; credit card deposit required, refundable only with 48hr. cancellation notice. V, MC, AmEx.

Stork Hotel, 504 Elizabeth St (tel. 9663 6237; fax 9663 8895), at the corner of Thierry St. The Stork dates back to the days of the Victorian gold rush, when it was the last stop on the line between the Port Melbourne and the Goldfields. It remains a genial gathering place for travelers, retaining its history without seeming worn. Impeccably clean, mostly twin-share rooms have gleaming hardwood floors and entirely modern furnishings. The ground-floor pub (see **Bars and Pubs,** p. 517) closes early in deference to its guests. $17.50 and up per person.

Global Backpackers, 238 Victoria St (tel. 9328 3728; fax 9329 8966), across from Victoria Market, just past Elizabeth St. This 100-year-old building is guarded by Henry, a friendly pit bull. Recent paint jobs have spruced up the once-raggedy rooms. Guests get into the adjacent Public Bar (see **Bars and Pubs,** p. 517) free and get cheap drinks. Dorms $13-16; singles $25; doubles $35. Key deposit $10.

FITZROY

🕮**The Nunnery,** 116 Nicholson St (tel. 9419 8637, 1800 032 635; fax 9417 7736; nunnery@bakpak.com), at stop 13 on tram #96, two blocks west of Brunswick St. Housed in the former convent of the Daughters of Mercy, this heavenly hostel amply justifies its prices with a chill, personable atmosphere and cheerfully distinctive decor. New carpets line halls that are snazzily decorated with an incongruous mix of religious paraphernalia and psychedelia. Breezy wooden deck with barbecue, two kitchens, a gorgeous TV lounge, rooms with balconies overlooking Carlton Gardens, and the "trip room," for planning your next vacation and surfing the Internet ($2 per 8min.). Staff coordinates tons of activities. Bunks in large dorms $18; in small dorms $20; twins and doubles $55-60. VIP. Weekly rates are available in summer. V, MC.

NORTH MELBOURNE

Residential North Melbourne is quieter and more relaxed than the city center, and though its accommodations are quite a hike from downtown, it's made accessible by tram #57 from Elizabeth St and tram #55 from Williams St.

Queensberry Hill YHA, 76-86 Howard St (tel. 9329 8599; fax 9326 8427). Take tram #55 from Williams St in the city center to stop 11 on Queensberry St, turn left and go 2 blocks west to Howard St. This YHA grand dame overflows with 314 bunks on 3 colorful floors, glistening communal bathrooms, and tons of amenities in a nearly new, highly functional facility. Perks include free parking, free use of mountain bikes, rooftop patio with barbecue and sweeping view of city, travel agency, designated quiet reading room, huge kitchen, bistro, weekly movies, pool tables, video games, Internet access, currency exchange, photocopy and fax service. Dorms $17, YHA nonmembers $20; children age 7-17 $13, $16; under 7 free. Doubles $55, $61; single $45, $48; family $63, $69. Doubles, singles, and family rooms come with linen and towels and can have ensuite bath for $10 extra. 2-week max. stay. Book ahead in summer. Wheelchair accessible. V, MC.

Chapman Gardens YHA Hostel, 76 Chapman St (tel. 9328 3595; fax 9329 7863). Take tram #57, get off at stop 18, turn right on Chapman St. The hostel is on the left side. The C-Gardens' landscaped estate and pleasant gazebo are in a quiet, tree-lined residential neighborhood and feature clean, softly lit, centrally heated rooms (mostly twins). Continental breakfast sold in the kitchen. TVs in the dining area and various lounges. Free bike use and parking. Dorms $15, YHA nonmembers $18; doubles $44,

$50. Weekly: $91, $106; $210, $252. Linen $2. Key deposit $10. Reception open 7:30am-noon and 3-10pm. Book 1 week ahead in summer. V, MC.

City Scene Backpackers, 361 Queensberry St (tel. 9348 9525). Take tram #57 to stop 7 (Queen Victoria Market), walk north up Elizabeth St, and turn left onto Queensberry St. New, small hostel in a quiet neighborhood. Rooms are sparsely appointed but immaculate. Friendly atmosphere. Bunk in 4-person dorms $15 per night, $98 per week; twin rooms $34, $220; double rooms $36, $224. Linen included.

SOUTH MELBOURNE

Less frequented by backpackers than hostel hives like St. Kilda, South Melbourne is low-key and residential, with access to more active spots via trams #12, 95, and 96. Both establishments are near the South Melbourne tram stop; exit the tram station heading east and proceed one block to the intersection of Cecil and Coventry St.

Nomads Market Inn, 115 Cecil St (tel. 9690 2220; fax 9690 2544; email nomads@dove.mtx.net.au). A free beer or coffee will greet you when you enter these excellent budget digs. Downstairs lounge boasts warm fireplace, TV, and tons of cushy couches and bean bags. Sunny, spacious rooms with comfortable beds. Bathrooms and small kitchen are quite clean. Free breakfast. Weekly barbecue on the outdoor deck with spa. Small pub has billiards and very cheap drinks, particularly during happy hour (7-8pm; pots $1, pints $2, spirits $3). Internet access $5 per hr. No smoking. Call for free bus station pick-up. Dorms $12-20; doubles and twins $40-60. Weekly: $75-100; $228-300. Linen included.

George Hotel, 139 Cecil St (tel 9699 9928), at Coventry St. Homey pub accommodation in an old neighborhood hotel. Rooms are bright and very clean, with comfy old oak-frame beds. Good laundry facilities but small, poorly stocked kitchen. Small, well-heated TV lounge. Locals gather in adjacent pub to down VB and play the horses. Bunk in 4-person room $20, singles $30, doubles or twins $60. Family rooms available; discounts on longer stays.

MIDDLE PARK

◉**Middle Park Hotel,** 102 Canterbury Rd (tel. 9690 1882; fax 9645 8928), directly across from the Middle Park stop on trams #95 and 96. Beautiful budget accommodation in a restored 1890s building with high ceilings, wide hallways, clean, pleasant rooms, small kitchen, TV lounge, and large terrazzo bathrooms. Everything's spotless. No heating, though thick doonas are provided. No smoking. Staff can provide assistance with job placement. Nightclub, upscale bistro, and casual neighborhood bar with excellent pub meals ($7-12) downstairs. Dorms $15; doubles and twins $40. Seventh night free.

ST. KILDA

St. Kilda is backpacker heaven, with excellent budget digs mostly centered around Grey St. Though removed from the city center, it's easily accessed by tram (stop 133 on lines #16 and 96). The beach, restaurants, and lively nightlife are in easy reach.

◉**Olembia,** 96 Barkly St (tel. 9537 1412; fax 9537 1600). Tucked behind a small canopy near the intersection with Grey St, Olembia provides serene budget accommodation with a touch of real class that sets it apart from the rest of the party-obsessed backpacker scene. Extremely helpful staff, snug TV/VCR lounge with crackling fireplace, well-equipped kitchen, spacious dining room. Ornate, high-ceilinged rooms are impeccably clean, as are the bathrooms. No smoking. Free parking. Bike hire $12 per day. Reception 7am-1pm, 4-8pm. Bunks $17; singles $35; doubles and twins $50. Book ahead in summer.

Enfield House, 2 Enfield St (tel. 9534 8159; fax 9534 5579). Take tram #16 or 96 to stop 30 by Fitzroy and Grey St. Walk half a block down Grey, turn on Jackson St, then onto Enfield St. Housed in a sprawling mansion, Enfield packs in the amenities and peppers them with groovy, mellow atmosphere: there's a chill TV lounge, rooftop deck, big well-stocked kitchen, garden sitting area, laundry room, and scads of info on local and national backpacker happenings. Daily events include trips to the footy and occasional extravagant parties. The rooms are nothing special, but are basically clean. Courtesy bus, train, and airport pick-up. No smoking. Bunks $16; twins $40-45. Weekly: $100; $250. VIP.

Kookaburra Backpackers, 56 Jackson St (tel 9534 5457, fax 9534 8854), is inconspicuously located; from the roundabout at Fitzroy and Grey St, head up Grey and take the first right. Kookaburra's will be three doors down on the right. This small nook offers as much intimacy and coziness as its backpacker neighbors do size and party atmosphere. Two lounges, porch with barbecue. Dorms sleep 4-6 people. Bunks $14-16; twins and doubles $34-40 per person. Weekly discounts. Linen provided. Reception open 8:30am-noon and 5:30-7:30pm.

Leopard House, 27 Grey St (tel. 9534 1200). Stately old two-story greystone house was recently converted into a small backpacker but retains its homey atmosphere, with a personable staff and plenty of snug, well-equipped common areas. Pleasant outdoor deck with free barbecue. Free airport pick-up. Linen provided. Passport required for deposit. Dorm bunks in spare but clean rooms $14; twins and doubles (available in winter only) $19 per person, weekly $125.

The Ritz for Backpackers, 169 Fitzroy St (tel. 9525 3501; fax 9525 3863). Tram #16 stops at the front door (stop 132). The name may contrast with the minimalist aesthetic, but the Ritz offers a full range of amenities: TV lounges, plush couches, and a spacious, well-supplied kitchen. Don't come here if you don't want to party. There's traffic noise at night and the bands at the Ritz Bar downstairs rattle the first floor silly on weekends; fortunately, free earplugs are provided. Rooms have space heaters. Tons of activities; drink specials at the Ritz Bar. Smoking restricted to central lounge. Free pancake breakfast M-F. Internet access $2 per 8min. Dorms $12-14, weekly $85; doubles and twins $34-36, $200-220. VIP. Doona $2. Reception 7am-10pm. Reservations required in early Mar. during the Grand Prix.

Coffee Palace Backpackers Hotel, 24 Grey St (tel. 9534 5283; fax 9593 9166), a block off Fitzroy St. The Coffee Palace gang downs java by day, VB by night, and then sleeps it all off in worn but livable digs, though the recently renovated deluxe rooms on the top floor are somewhat better. Really popular, but only with party types who don't mind the grungy atmosphere and lax approach to rules. Nightly events include 70s dance, wine and cheese night, billiards tourney. Dorms $14-16, deluxe dorms $16; unrenovated doubles and twins $35-40, deluxe doubles and twins $50. VIP. Linen included. 24hr. reception.

Oslo Hotel, 38 Grey St (tel 9525 4498; fax 9527 9186). Lacks a backpacker scene or stylish vibe, but offers clean and extremely quiet accommodation. No guests after 10pm. Spic 'n' span communal baths and balconies overlooking Port Philip Bay. Dorm rooms are placed off central common areas with fridge, couches, and ensuite bath ($12-15, weekly $70-84). Lots of doubles and triples, many recently remodeled, make the Oslo ideal for families and couples ($15-22 per person, weekly $90-110).

SOUTH YARRA & PRAHRAN

Chapel St Backpackers, 22 Chapel St (tel 9533 6855; fax 9533 6866), on tram routes #78 and 79, Prahran. Conveniently located just a stumble from Melbourne's best nightlife, this small hostel is clean and new. Small bunk rooms and doubles mostly have ensuite baths. Internet access $6 per hour. Diminutive but well-stocked kitchen offers free breakfast. Female-only dorms available. Free luggage storage, safe for valuables, mail holding service, and very friendly staff. Bunks in 4-6 person dorm $15-20; double or twin $45-50. Check-out at noon.

Claremont B&B, 189 Toorak Rd (tel 9826 8000, 9826 8222; fax 9827 8652), South Yarra. One block east of the South Yarra train station, and directly on tram route #8. A stylish budget B&B set in an elegantly refurbished 1886 Victorian building. Central staircase with mahogany banisters is brilliantly lit by stained-glass skylight. High-ceilinged hallways lead to rooms with hardwood floors, wrought-iron beds, and TVs. Spotless hall baths boast gleaming modern facilities. Laundry facilities. Continental breakfast in spacious kitchen served M-F 6:30am-9:30pm, Sa-Su 7:30am-10:30pm. Singles $46, doubles $58, additional person $10, weekly $235, $295, $60.

Lord's Lodge, 204 Punt Rd (tel 9510 5658), Prahran. Take tram #3, 5, 6, 16, 64, or 67 south along St Kilda Rd to stop #26 and walk east 2 blocks along Moubray St, or take the train to Prahran Station and head west for about 6 blocks along Greville St to Punt Rd. Very mellow hostel whose ornate interior is accented by corniced archways and stained glass. Rooms are basic but clean, and some include fridge. Excellent, very warm lounge with TV, books, and squishy couches. Pleasant outdoor patio with barbecue. You can pitch tents out back in summer when demand for rooms is high. Rooms in 8-bed separate-sex dorms $15. Doubles and twins $45. Weekly discounts. Office hours M-Sa 8:30-11:30 and 5-6pm, Su 8:30-11:30am.

■ Food

Melbourne boasts an array of restaurants dazzling in both diversity and number, from steamy Chinatown holes-in-the-wall to Fitzroy café *couture* to Carlton Italian cuisine to South Yarra sidewalk bistros to St Kilda's backpacker-targeted eateries to everything else and then some. The city's restaurants constitute a scene in themselves; on most nights, Melburnians pack into their favorite restaurants until closing time (which is whenever the proprietors feel like shutting the doors). And if you like to quaff spirits with your dinner, be familiar with Victoria's byzantine liquor licensing laws, which sort restaurants into a number of categories: "licensed" ones sell liquor, "BYO" means you can bring your own, and there are some restaurants that are "licensed-BYO" that permit both as well as more limited versions like "BYO wine only," which is painfully self-explanatory. Now stop reading and go eat something.

CITY CENTER

Amid the bustling urban jungle of Melbourne's CBD lurk what seem like a million fantastic eateries, hidden away in labyrinthine corridors or diminutive crannies between high-rise office buildings. Most are Asian, including Chinese, Japanese, Indian, Nepalese, Sri Lankan, Malaysian, Indonesian, and Vietnamese. The neon-pulsing focal point is **Chinatown,** the stretch of Little Bourke St hemmed in by colorful red gates between Swanston St and Exhibition St. At the **Midtown Plaza,** on Swanston St between Bourke and Little Bourke St, you can get a quick, filling sushi or noodle-soup meal for around $5. Blink and you'll miss the **Greek Precinct,** on Lonsdale St between Swanston and Russell St. It consists of only 12 or so Hellenic restaurants and tavernas, but the baklava is divine. Many of the city's coolest cafes, most with an Italian twist, call the CBD home as well; they often lurk in narrow arcades (such as the Block Arcade, between Collins and Little Collins St) that snake through the city blocks. Above all, the city center rewards the adventurous gourmet; wander around with only your nose and palate as a guide and you're sure to find a culinary treasure.

■**Porta Via,** 277G Little Collins St (tel. 9654 3100). Follow the narrow passageway off the south side of the street and you'll happen upon this den of haute style, a low-lit nook that counts among its incongruous decor abstract art and statuettes of the Michelin Man. Light modern Italian fare includes a range of salads and sandwiches as well as breakfast (try the salmon omelette or overflowing fruit bowl) and killer coffee. Full meals $7-9. Coffee takeaway window too. Open M-F 7am-6pm, Sa 8am-5pm.

■**Pho' Hien Vuong,** 242 Swanston St (tel. 9662 3813). Their specialty is *pho',* a Vietnamese noodle soup served in all shapes and sizes. The more adventurous can get soup with beef balls, bone marrow, or chicken livers, but there are less exotic versions as well as vegetarian-friendly ones. A mere $5-6 will get you a massive, steaming tureen of the stuff. Mmm...good pho' your soul. Open daily 11:30am-9:30pm.

■**Shark Fin,** 131-135 Little Bourke St (tel. 9663 1555), Chinatown. A standout distinguished by elegant decor and truly superior cuisine. A tad pricey, but you get what you pay for; portions are huge and served with the perfect amount of delicately spiced sauce. Open 11:30am-3pm and 5:30-11pm, except Su opens 11am.

Antipodes, 195 Lonsdale St (tel. 9663 4760), Greek Precinct. Greek fare done with a classy, nouvelle cuisine flair. The *sagunaki,* cheese pan-fried on sauteed spinach ($6.50), looks almost too good to eat. They have the old Hellenic standards too, such as tangy mousaka ($11.50), and *rizogalo* (rice pudding) for dessert ($5.50). There's a snazzy bar if you just want to drop in for an ouzo shot or ten. Open M-F 10:30am-11pm, Sa-Su 5:30pm-late.

Curry Bowl, shop 41, Myer House Arcade, 250 Elizabeth St (tel. 9639 0868). Sri Lankan and South Indian fare served hot, fresh, and quickly, especially to the loyal hordes of suits who crowd in at lunchtime. Steaming plates of curry are piled high. A "small" will feed even the hungriest backpacker. Many veggie options include lentil and pumpkin curries. All meals $4-6. Open M-F 9:30am-5:30pm, Sa 10:30am-3:30pm.

Krank Kafe, 273 Swanston St (tel. 9663 8199). Vervy, nervy, swervy cafe that hosts one of the most cutting-edge caffeine scenes in town. Interior gleams with chrome, but the atmosphere is easy-going rather than attitude-heavy. Light brekkie comes with free bottomless cup of rich Italian coffee. Avocado vinaigrette or chicken satay salad makes for a full meal ($7-9), and there's an entire range of meaty options as well ($8-15). Open M-Th 8am-8pm, F 8am-1am, Sa 10am-6pm, Su sometimes.

Nudel Bar, 76 Bourke St (tel. 9662 9100). Sleek interior glows with neon and the aura of Melbourne's beautiful people. It's easier to get a seat downstairs, but the upstairs dining room overlooks Bourke St's club-and-restaurant scene. Every imaginative, flavor-packed meal is noodle-based, whether in salad, cold, wet, in broth, as pasta, or wokked. The Mee Goreng or roast duck noodles are house specialties. Veggie-friendly. All dishes about $13. Open Su-Th 11am-11pm, F-Sa 11am-midnight.

Wrapt Cuisine, 422 Collins St (tel. 9640 0689). Fresh, cheap, authentic Japanese sushi rolls ($1.60) and Aussie variations (smoked 'roo roll $2.50). Four or 5 wraps make a hearty lunch. Three varieties of miso soup ($2.50). Plenty of veggie and low-fat options. Open M-Tu 11:30am-3:30pm, W 11am-4pm, Th-F 11am-5pm. Another location at 392 Bourke St (tel. 9670 4414).

Charles Dickens Tavern, at the foot of the Block Arcade, off Collins St. A hoary, underground Anglophile pub. You may think "English cuisine" is an oxymoron, but you'll be proved wrong by the Tasmanian smoked salmon whirls and a beef Wellington that'll make you want to raise a glass of John Bull Ale (pints $4) and break out into a chorus of *Rule Britannia* on the spot. Plus, it's a kick to order bangers 'n' mash. Open 10am-late.

Fast Eddy's Cafe, 32 Bourke St (tel. 9662 3551). A fave-rave with the late-night crowd for its 24hr. food service every damn day of the year. Filling faux-American diner fare: omelettes, burgers, steaks and milkshakes (meals $8-15). Bad if you're on a diet, perfect if you're a night-owl who loves good food, good times, and a whole lotta craziness on the walls.

FITZROY

The heart of Melbourne's bohemian scene and cafe society lies here, along Brunswick St between Gertrude and Princes St. Particularly on sunny weekend days, hippies, post-hippies, ferals, and freaks of all ilks (and some more conventional types) frequent the countless artsy coffeehouses and eateries. The area gets progressively posher as you go south along Brunswick, closer to the city. The stretch of Johnston St just west of Brunswick St is Melbourne's Latin Quarter, with Latin dance clubs, Iberian grocers, and several great tapas bars.

Vegie Bar, 380 Brunswick St (tel. 9417 6935). A converted warehouse where Fitzroy's large meat-averse population gathers to chow guilt-free. They promise "food for the body and soul" and serve it up in heaping portions. Smoothies $3-4, mains all under $8.50. The Mee Goreng (egg noodles with fried potatoes, veggies and tofu in spiced satay sauce; $7) is delectable, but the rich mushroom risotto is the all-star ($7). Fully licensed, and gets very crowded and lively even on weeknights. Lots of vegan and wheat-free options. Open Su-Th 9am-11pm, F-Sa 9am-midnight.

Retro Cafe, 413 Brunswick St (tel. 9419 9103). While not particularly retro in design (though boasting a mesmerizing indoor waterfall), this somewhat upmarket eatery is nothing if not eclectic. An intriguing fusion of Southeast Asian, modern Italian and nouveau Australian influences; the kangaroo filet ($14.50) hops with flavor, as does the house specialty, lamb shank ($15). Lots of veggie pastas and stir-fries. Sunday breakfast here is a Fitzroy tradition, with buckwheat pancakes ($6) and the "Famous

Retro Breakie": bacon, poached eggs, toast, mushrooms, tomato, and avocado, all slathered in rich hollandaise. Open daily 8am-late.

Black Cat Cafe, 252 Brunswick St (tel. 9419 6230). The Cat is hugely popular, as much for its vibrant environs as its cuisine. Bedecked with an inscrutably varied array of objets d'art, many feline in theme. Basic cafe fare (salads $4-6, sandwiches $5-7) with occasional innovative specials. Things get more bar-like as the evening wears on. Ivy-strewn outdoor garden terrace. Open daily 9am-1am.

Carmen Bar, 74 Johnston St (tel. 9417 4794). Locally beloved tapas bar, the cream of Fitzroy's small Latin Quarter. All kinds of tapas ($5-7), from the familiar (tortilla, a Spanish omelette) to the adventurous (*angulas al ajillo,* baby eels in garlic). Tantaliz-ing sangria flows freely (glass $4, jug $14). Flamenco dancers perform Th-Sa begin-ning around 11pm, and occasionally brave sangria-fueled patrons will join them onstage. Minimum food charge $14 per person F-Sa. Open Tu-Su 6pm-late.

Nyala, 113 Brunswick St (tel. 9419 9128). Nyala's menu spans the continent of Africa. Start off with a selection of delicious dips, such as deberja, a combination of egg-plant, chili, garlic, and yogurt ($6). Mains tend to be meaty, though Futari ($11.50), a Tanzanian selection of mixed vegetables, is meat-free. The house specialty is Domeda ($13.50), a Gambian lamb dish in a spicy, herby sauce. Don't miss the after-dinner specialty, rich, strong Ethiopian coffee ($2). Open M-Sa 6pm-late.

Provincial Hotel (tel. 9417 2228), corner of Brunswick and Johnston St. A landmark in the heart of Fitzroy, housing three different establishments. The Hotel itself has slightly pricey bar food but cheap focaccia and antipasti ($3-6) and light snacks ($1.50-2). By night, it's a popular meeting place for a quiet drink. The adjacent **Cafe Provincial** has French-Italian fare. Despite the misleading huge hamburger sculpture over its entrance, the **Ruby Cafe** blends Eurasian, Malaysian, Indian and Chinese influences to create cheap, inventive curries and noodle dishes ($7-8). It's all open Su-W 11am-11pm, Th-Sa 11am-1am.

Gypsy Bar, 334 Brunswick St (tel. 9419 0548). Where staff at the other hipster joints on Brunswick St go on their days off—the epitome of the stylish, laid-back, somewhat attitude-laden Fitzroy eatery. For breakfast, step up to the aptly-named "Gutbuster": 2 poached eggs, bacon, tomato, toast, avocado, mushrooms, and hash browns ($10.50). While most mains lie beyond budget range, excellent pastas and risottos run $8-12. Heaping portion of dreamy tiramisu $7. The fully licensed Gypsy morphs into a mellow, buzzing bar by night. Open 7am-late (licensed til 3am).

Rhumbarala's, 342 Brunswick St (tel. 9417 5652). Bold, geometric swaths of color and bright plastic furnishings create an aesthetic that lies somewhere between Mark Rothko and McDonald's, but the space is light and airy, the staff friendly, and the eclectic menu first-rate. The dip platter has enough smoked salmon, tzatziki, olives, and warm flatbread for a full meal ($8), and the bruschetta ($4) is a flaky, flavorful delight. Excellent breakfasts and wood-fired pizzas ($6-9). A mellow scene develops around the fully licensed bar by night. Open 8am-1am.

Jasper's Caffeine Dealers, 267 Brunswick St (tel. 9416 0921). Devoted to the love of all things caffeinated, Jasper's vends exquisite portions of the life-giving liquid as well as light cakes and biscuits (cookies), which you can enjoy on their narrow outdoor terrace. Open M-F 7am-9pm, Sa 7am-6pm, Su 9am-5pm.

CARLTON

The best known street in Carlton is **Lygon St,** Melbourne's Little Italy, where tons of Italian pizzerias, cafes, and gelaterias line the five-block stretch between Queensberry St to the south and Elgin St to the north. Despite Carlton's proximity to the University of Melbourne and its attendant student traffic, most of the Italian eateries are out of the budget range. There are, however, a fair number of affordable non-Italian places, and a few cafes where you can get a cheap pasta that's still *delicioso.*

Tiamo, 305 Lygon St (tel. 9347 0911). Diminutive but elegant modern Italian joint, good for a full meal or a cappuccino. All mains, such as chicken alla diavolo and veal Romana (each $12), include fresh vegetables. Cheap breakfasts ($6), tasty apple stru-del ($5.50). *"Ti amo"* means "I love you" in Italian, and perhaps you'll fall in love with this place. If you did, you'd be utterly desperate, however. It's just a restaurant—get a grip. Open M-Th 9:30am-10pm, F-Sa 9:30am-10:30pm.

Jive, 131 Lygon St (tel. 9347 6666). Very popular with the Uni crowd, Jive's walls are splashed with big bold color and its sound system reverberates with American soul tunes. The food is basic, but good and cheap: bargain brekkie, Asian noodles, and pizza in all kinds of varieties. Nothing's more than $12, and most is much less. It's fully licensed, and the upstairs bar gets funky on weekends. Open daily 8am-3am.

Caffe lo Bello, 275 Lygon St (tel. 9347 1562). A gelateria, pasticceria, and rosticceria to die for. In fact, they do serve a cake called "Death by Chocolate," which will not in fact kill you but rather make you feel as though you have just eaten a very rich, delicious piece of chocolate cake. The New Orleans Mud Cake is also not deadly and is quite delicious (slices of either $2.30). Tart, fruity gelati is a lighter treat and does not carry any real death risk ($3). A sidewalk patio allows you to enjoy the thrill of cheating the Grim Reaper *al fresco.* Open M-Th 6:45am-6pm, F-Sa 6:45am-midnight, Su 7:45am-7pm.

Calalou Carribbean Cafe, 108 Lygon St (tel. 9650 8787). What it's doing in the Italian district is anyone's guess, but this chill joint revives the cool atmosphere and hot cuisine of the West Indies. The Phulowric, batter balls with spicy mango sauce, will tantalize your tongue ($6), while the jerk chicken can be made hot enough to induce hallucination ($12.50). Delectable Caribbean-style curries $9-15. Open 6pm-late.

NORTH MELBOURNE

The Queen Victoria Market (QVM; see **Sights,** p. 508) serves as the focal point of culinary North Melbourne. In fact, much of the city congregates here, where you can get all the fresh ingredients you need to cook up a fabulous dinner cheaply. The surrounding area is home to some fine eateries as well.

⊛**La Porchetta,** 302-308 Victoria St (tel. 9326 9884), across from the Queen Victoria Market. Hundreds of tantalizing wood-fired pizzas served daily (small $4.80, medium $6.20, large $8). When you've received the check, you'll think they've undercharged you; you may want to cry out "For the love of all that's holy, charge me more for this godly manna." Suppress the urge; the absurdly low prices are in fact accurate. Merely pay due homage to Carl, the patron saint of backpackers. BYO wine only. Open Su-Th 11am-midnight, F-Sa 11am-1am.

The White Lotus, 185 Victoria St (tel. 9326 6040). Entirely vegan menu follows the Buddhist tenets of Tien Tao, or "way to heaven," and all meals are prepared without meat, meat products, or even onions or garlic. Carnivores will be placated by the presence of excellent imitation meat dishes, like mock abalone and goose made from soy and wheat gluten or the sizzling, spicy Mongolian "beef." Meals $7-12. BYO. Open M-F noon-2:30pm and 5:30-11pm, Sa-Su 5:30-11pm.

The Traveller's Cafe, 229 Victoria St (tel. 9328 1118). Seasoned traveler owners have festooned the walls with pictures and kitsch from around the globe. The menu is similarly cosmopolitan, ranging from Hokkien noodles to eggs Manhattan ($6-10). Salads and sandwiches $4-6. Full juice and coffee bar. $1 discount with an international passport. Open M-F 7:30am-4:30pm, Sa-Su 9:30am-4:30pm.

The Queen Vic (tel. 9320 5822), in the Queen Victoria Market. The food court is a repository of excellent budget fare, mostly made from fresh goods sold next door. **Victoria Fish** serves unusually delectable beer-battered fish 'n' chips ($7-8) as well as wine. **Afghan** purveys charcoal-grilled treats like souvlaki and doner kabob ($6) and many vegetarian dips such as baba ghanoush and tzatziki ($4-6). The **Consciousness Cafe** has light, healthy salads and sandwiches that you can design from an array of fresh toppings ($4-6).

ST. KILDA

With all the hipness of South Yarra and Chapel St but far less pretense, St. Kilda offers diverse and exciting menus with prices aimed at the district's large backpacker contingent. The result is budget food nirvana. Fitzroy St is a tad more upscale and has some fancier bistros, while Acland St, locally legendary for its divine cake shops, also has a menagerie of great bistros of all ethnic stripes. Try the Espy kitchen for quick and cheap but very good pub meals (see **Entertainment,** p. 512).

Veg Out Time, 63a Fitzroy St, shop 8 (tel. 9534 0077). It's all about "positive eating" here, whatever the hell that means. Still, the vegetarian and vegan fare is damn fine and cheap. Tofu and veggie stir-fries with delectable sauces, 14 varieties of curry, lots of spicy noodle dishes (all $6). Small eating area; takeaway's a better option with Albert Park across the street. Open M-Sa 4:30-10:30pm, Su noon-10pm.

Chichio's, 109 Fitzroy St (tel. 9534 9439). Vast Italian menu offering pasta, seafood, salads, grilled meats, and wood-fired pizzas. Special menu for backpackers is a budget feast: extra large pizza or pasta and pesto focaccia, Italian salad, and wine or soft drink (serves 2; $7.50, $10 for seafood pizza or pasta). "Small" means large and "large" means enormous. Great lasagna ($7.50). Fully licensed.

Greasy Joe's, 68 Acland St (tel. 9525 3755). Joe's friendly staff and cheap (if, indeed, greasy) diner food make this place a St. Kilda institution. Breakfast ($4-10) is served all day, though the house specialty is the burger in all its glory. Get it naked for $6.50 or go for the works (chicken, beef, bacon, and all the toppings; $10.50). Lots of salad options ($6.50-9). Full bar with pub-priced drinks create a festive atmosphere. Window counter and outside patio offer super people-watching. Open daily 7am-1am.

Monarch Cake Shop, 103 Acland St (tel. 9534 2972). The oldest cake shop on Acland St (est. 1934) and still the best. All-star desserts are chocolate kugelhof, Polish cheesecake, and tartalicious plum cake. Slices $2.50. Open daily 7am-9pm.

Jin's Place, 89B Fitzroy St (tel. 9534 1488). Sleek and sparkling hole-in-the-wall serves Melbourne's cheapest and best raw fish. There are lots of other options too, such as Korean-style pizza, tofu steak, tsukune (tasty mushroom turnovers), spicy chicken kimchi rice, and green tea ice cream. It's all perfectly fresh, and nothing costs over $5. Open daily 7:30am-7pm. Also in Richmond at 60 Bridge Rd (tel. 9428 8383).

The Coffee Machine, 191 Acland St (tel. 9525 5166). This machine is actually a full cafe and manufactures some of the finest breakfasts on either side of the Yarra, served all day. Gargantuan serving of pancakes with apple-cinnamon and berry compote $8. Many consider the coffee the best in Melbourne. Rich lasagna lunch comes with salad ($7). Bloody marys $6, imported beers $4.50. Open 8am-6pm.

Vibe, 138 Acland St (tel. 9537 0911). Trendy nouveau-Oz eclecticism characterizes the menu as well as the decorative stylings. Tandoori burger is a cross-cultural treat ($9). Italian options include a range of risottos: vegetarian, seafood, and chicken mushroom ($9-11.50). All-day breakfast; toast, bacon, tomato and eggs $6. Free coffee with all breakfasts before noon. Open M-Th 10am-6pm, F 10am-10:30pm, Sa 9am-10:30pm, Su 9am-7pm.

SOUTH YARRA AND PRAHRAN

Sleek, pricey South Yarra's aggressively markets itself as the place to see and bee seen, and its mod-Oz bistros with sidewalk seating see their share of preening black-clad fashion mavens after a day of shopping in Chapel St's boutiques. There are some excellent budget options, though, particularly south of Commercial St in more down-to-earth Prahran. The ubiquitous coffee bars are a wallet-friendly way to sample the scene (cappuccino around $2.20). Check out the Prahran Market, on Commercial Rd at Izett St, for cheap, fresh produce, meat, and ethnic foodstuffs sold *al fresco.*

Gratzi, 534 Chapel St (tel. 9824 0099). Slick, artsy decor belies the low prices of the mod-Italian. Breakfast is served all day; try the weird yet tasty Greek yogurt, a creamy, honey-flavored concoction with muesli and strawberries ($6). Crepes ($4.50-7) bulge with anything from fresh fruit to roasted eggplant, ham, cheese, and tomato, and you can design your own. Open 8am-6pm.

Candy Bar, 162 Greville St (tel. 9529 6566). Hyper-cool eatery by day, with ice-blue walls, 2 otherworldly fireplaces wrought with warped designs, and a remarkably homogenous crowd of black-clad hipsters. The eats are quintessentially mod-Oz. Excellent Caesar salad $9, wok-tossed bean thread noodles with calimari and Asian vegetables $11. Daily specials $9-15. On weekends it morphs into a hyper-cool dance club, Late Night Candy (no cover). Open Su-Th 11am-10pm, F-Sa 11am-5am.

That Little Noodle Place, 565 Chapel St (tel. 9827 3148). The name says it all: noodles, done in a ton of Asian varieties. Design your own from a selection of all kinds of meat, veggies, and sauce. The Bum Bo Xao is a specialty, incorporating beef, peanuts, vegetables, and garlic fish sauce on a bed of rice vermicelli. All noodle dishes $8.50. Amazingly cheap cappuccino ($1.50). Open 11:30am-11pm.

Saigon Rose, 206 Chapel St (tel. 9510 9651). Vast menu boasts 134 different Southeast Asian dishes and mad cheap noodles ($6-8). Lots of seafood specialties, including 10 different types of squid. Saigon Rose salted prawns are a much-beloved local specialty ($12). Vegetarians have tons of options at well; just be sure to ask for something without seafood, since they don't consider that "meat." Open M-Th 11am-10pm, F 11am-11pm, Sa 11am-3pm and 5-11pm, Su 5-10pm.

■ Sights

CITY CENTER

The **Rialto Towers,** 525 Collins St, between King and Williams St, rise high above the city center. At 253m, they constitute Melbourne's tallest building and the tallest office building in the Southern Hemisphere. The 55th floor observation deck provides spectacular 360° views of the city and surrounds, it's a great place to start your tour and get your geographical bearings. The Rialtovision Theatre plays a 20-minute film, *Melbourne, the Living City* (to distinguish it from all those cities populated entirely by perambulatory corpses) that highlights Victoria's tourist spots in dramatic, wide-angle shots. *(Open daily 10am-late. Film every ½hr. Film and deck admission $7.50, concessions $5.)* You can get a less impressive but entirely free view of the city on the other end of Collins where it intersects Exhibition St, at the **Hotel Sofitel.** Ascend to the 35th floor and peer out the bathroom windows to eyeball the Melbourne skyline.

Four blocks east, **St. Paul's Cathedral** presides over the corner of Flinders St and Swanston St, diagonally opposite Flinders St Station. *(Open daily 7am-6pm. Enter on the Swanston St side.)* The Anglican cathedral impresses not in its scale but in its degree of intricately wrought detail. The floor tiling is exquisite, both the simpler patterns throughout the nave and the more intricate mosaics near the altar. The beautifully stenciled pipes of the 19th-century Lewis organ are also worth a look. The Anzac Christmas painting depicts soldiers as shepherds at the Adoration of Christ.

The pagoda gates at the corner of Swanston and Little Bourke St indicate your arrival in **Chinatown,** a two-block stretch of Asian restaurants, groceries, and bars that was first settled by Chinese immigrants during the 1870s. One and a half blocks farther east, the **Chinese Museum,** 22 Cohen Place (tel. 9662 2888), provides an excellent overview of the role of Chinese immigrants in Australia's history. *($5, concessions $3. Open Su-F 10am-4:30pm, Sa noon-4:30pm.)* The ground floor houses Dai Loong (Great Dragon), the **biggest imperial dragon in the world** (not the longest, which is in Bendigo), a staple of Melbourne's Moomba festival, and so huge that he has to be wound around the entire floor and through the basement. The third floor is the best, providing an honest look at ethnic discrimination as well as the contributions that Chinese merchants, war veterans, and sportsmen have made to the country.

At the northern end of Swanston St is the **Melbourne Central** megamall, which houses some of Australia's swankiest boutiques and cafes alongside tourist shops selling cheesy koala-and-kangaroo merchandise at outrageous prices. In the central atrium of the mall stands the 50m-tall Coop's Shot Tower, built in 1889-90, then Melbourne's highest structure. Today it houses shops and is enclosed by a soaring 20-story, 490-ton glass cone, an iconic feature of Melbourne's skyline. A huge fob watch dangles in the atrium in front of the Shot Tower and has an automated Waltzing Matilda display that drops down on the hour.

Across Swanston St from Melbourne Central is the **State Library of Victoria** (tel. 9669 9824; http://www.slv.gov.au), which offers a great space to read or work plus all manner of international newspapers. *(Open M 1-9pm, Tu and Th-Su 10am-6pm, W 10am-9pm. Closed public holidays. Free tours M-F 2pm.)* It's worth a visit just to marvel at the spectacular interior design. The first floor is the most impressive, with the Domed Reading

Room, an octagonal space that soars 35m high; the Queen's Hall, which has small art exhibitions; and a series of murals above the foyer depicting Australian soldiers campaigning in Palestine and on the Western Front. Formerly the home of the Museum of Victoria, it will hold a fraction of the permanent collection of the National Gallery of Victoria after mid-1999 while the gallery undergoes renovations (see p. 509).

At the eastern edge of the city center's grid, the **Parliament of Victoria** (tel. 9651 8568), where Bourke St meets Spring St, is a stout, pillared 19th-century edifice every bit as stolid and imposing as a seat of government should be. *(Free tours when Parliament is not in session 10am, 11am, noon, 2pm, 3pm, and 3:45pm.)* The **Old Treasury Building** resides 2½ blocks south on Spring St and contains an excellent museum chronicling Melbourne's history. *(Open M-F 9am-5pm, Sa-Su 10am-4pm. $5, concessions $3, young children free.)* The intelligent, informative displays have a lighter side, one odd juxtaposition finds an orangutan's skeleton opposite a death mask of Ned Kelly, and there are some great stories about the idiosyncrasies of the city's early history. The gold vaults in the basement were built to prevent an epidemic of theft that plagued the Treasury during the Victorian Gold Rush; by themselves they're not much to see, but free guided tours, which run daily at 1 and 3pm, bring the site to life.

Head east through the modest Treasury Gardens and across the street to reach the much more impressive **Fitzroy Gardens.** *(Open daily 9am-5pm. $3, concessions $2, ages 5-15 $1.50.)* These gardens, originally laid out in the shape of the Union Jack, bloom with tropical flora all year round. On the south end is **Cook's Cottage,** a small stone home constructed by Captain James Cook's family in England in 1755 and moved to Melbourne in 1934 to celebrate the city's centennial. Cook never actually reached the site and may not even have spent time in this house, but it's a well-preserved domicile filled with period stuff. Next door is the **Conservatory,** a refreshing, colorfully stocked greenhouse that blooms with seasonal assortments of plants and flowers. *(Open daily 9am-5pm. Free.)* A little way east lies the **Sinclair Gallery** (tel. 9419 4677), in the bantam hovel once occupied by James Sinclair, founding horticulturalist of the Fitzroy Gardens. *(Open 9am-5pm. 1hr. tours M 10:30am and 2:30pm; book ahead. $5, concessions $3.)* Today the gallery houses a collection of sleek Australian-made crafts in a variety of media. Insightful historical and horticultural tours start at the north end of the conservatory. Just west of the gardens' northwest corner on Cathedral Place sits **St. Patrick's Cathedral,** a beautiful product of Gothic revival replete with all manner of grotesque gargoyles. Just inside the door lies the baptismal font, which houses a fine example of 17th-century religious narrative painting, *The Finding of the Child Jesus in the Temple.* The cathedral is most spectacular by night, when its 106m spires are illuminated by floodlights.

Southeast of the Fitzroy Gardens across Wellington Pde lie **Yarra Park** and the **Melbourne Cricket Ground** (MCG; tel. 9657 8893; fax 9650 6750). *(MCG admission $9.50, concessions $6, family $25. Tours run on all non-event days hourly 10am-3pm. Accessible via trams #48 and 75.)* Originally built for the 1956 Summer Olympics, the 90,000-seat arena functions as the sanctum sanctorum of Melbourne's robust sporting life. It houses Aussie Rules Football every weekend in winter, including the Grand Final in late July. There are also, of course, cricket contests, highlighted by test matches between Australia and strong competitors from England, Pakistan, and the West Indies. The best way to see the stadium is to take a guided tour, which offers unique insight into MCG's history and allow you to step inside the player's changing rooms, the **Melbourne Cricket Club Museum,** and onto the hallowed turf itself. Entertaining guides make the one-hour tour well worth the price tag even if you don't have the slightest idea what the hell a wicket, over, or googlie are. **AFL games** are also a must; tickets cost only about $13 and allow you to experience firsthand an essential aspect of Melburnian culture. Be sure to order a meat pie and beer, and if you don't get the rules (which are really quite simple; see **Sports,** p. 65), just cheer along with the passionate fans. Berating the referees as loudly as possible is always a good move.

Located on the north side of the MCG, the **Australian Gallery of Sport and Olympic Museum** (tel. 9657 8879; fax 9654 1387) further celebrates Australia's love for sport. *(Admission included with MCG tour. Open daily 10am-4pm.)* The venue houses the **Australian Cricket Hall of Fame,** which requires some understanding to appreciate; the **Olympic**

Museum, which traces the Games' history back to 1896, with a focus on Australian achievements and the '56 Melbourne contest; and a gallery with rotating exhibits. Across the railroad tracks to the west sits the ultramodern **National Tennis Centre,** now called **Melbourne Park.** The stadium's retractable domed roof shelters the **Australian Open** Grand Slam every January. Former champions' photos line the inside walls, and you can follow in their footsteps by playing on the famous courts for a hefty fee.

NORTH OF THE CITY CENTER

The **Carlton Gardens** beckon north of the city center on Spring St and Victoria Pde. Spanning three city blocks, the verdant gardens are criss-crossed with pathways and feature some spectacular fountains. They also frame the **Exhibition Hall,** which is currently undergoing renovation to house the **Museum of Victoria.** Expected to open by early 2000, what should be a new and greatly improved museum—formerly situated behind the state library—will feature natural history displays, a children's museum, an Aboriginal center, and an IMAX cinema (already operational) with the **world's largest movie screen.**

The **Old Melbourne Gaol** (tel. 9663 7228), on Russell St just north of La Trobe, offers a fascinating slice of Melbourne history that's not to be missed. *($7, concessions $5, children $4, families $21. Open daily 9:30am-4:30pm. Night tours W, Su 7:30pm sharp; $17, children $10, families $39. Bookings essential for night tours; call Ticketmaster at 13 61 00.)* The stalwart prison was completed in 1864 and housed a total of 50,000 prisoners in its 84 years. Upon entering the main structure, you'll see three levels of cells tightly packed together and linked by iron catwalks. The tiny cells each house small displays about everything from the history and specifications of the Gaol to fascinating stories about **Ned Kelly's gang,** though the creepiest display is the "murderer's row of the 1800s," featuring the stories and death masks of the most notorious criminals executed here. Kelly was Australia's most infamous bushranger. He was hanged in the gaol, and the trap door and scaffold are still here, as is the suit of armor that he wore in his final shoot-out with police. Wonderfully spooky evening tours of the gaol led by professional actors provide a chillingly vivid sense of how horrible it was. Or sate your thirst with a Ned Kelly soda in the gift shop on your way out and be thankful you've escaped—no criminal ever did.

The modernizing development that brought the rest of Melbourne into the 20th century passed over **Queen Victoria Market** (tours tel. 9320 5822; http://www.qvm.com.au) on Victoria St between Queen and Peel St. *(Open Tu, Th 6:30am-2pm, F 6am-6pm, Sa 6am-3pm, Su 9am-4pm. Tours depart from 69 Victoria St, near the intersection with Elizabeth St. Tours Tu and Th-Sa. Food tour departs 10am; $18. History tour departs 10:30am; $12. Parking in south margin non-market days 1hr. free, market days $4 per day.)* It remains an old-fashioned open-air market, vibrant with the buzz of hundreds of vendors "spruiking" (hawking) their wares and the thousands of Melburnians who pack in for excellent bargains on produce, dairy products, and meat. Sundays see the market at its

To Dance upon Nothing

During the days of "The System" (Britain's euphemism for its prison colonies), countless prisoners were put to death by hanging. In fact, hangings were so common that a peculiar set of traditions and superstitions grew up around them. A doctor was required to be present at every hanging so that an on-the-spot autopsy could be performed immediately afterward. Astonishingly enough, the cause of death was always determined to be "hanging." Colorful euphemisms for hanging included "to dance upon nothing," "to be in deadly suspense," and "to have a hearty choke [artichoke] and caper sauce for breakfast," a reference to the gagging and leg-twitching that overtook victims. And according to Anglican theology of the time, a hanged prisoner was not entitled to a Christian burial. Instead, he was placed in the ground at an anonymous site, in an upright position, so that he was not symbolically "laid to rest." If the burial site was in a prison yard, as it usually was, the corpses were buried facing the walls so they would look on the barriers of their captivity for eternity.

frenetic best. Don't be afraid to bargain with the vendors; good deals can turn into amazing ones after noon, when sellers are anxious to empty their stock. Walking tours explore the market's history and cultural importance, and include plenty to eat.

A few blocks north at the northern terminus of Howard St, the **Metro! craft center,** 42 Courtney St (tel. 9329 9966), houses all kinds of local art and crafts in a converted meat market building. *(Open Tu-Su 10am-5pm. Free.)* Many of the artists use the space as a studio as well, allowing visitors to see works in progress. Recent shows have highlighted edible art and the art of Australian tourist souvenirs.

North of the University of Melbourne is the world-class **Melbourne Zoo** (tel. 9285 9300; fax 9285 9350; http://www.zoo.org.au) on Elliott Ave. *(Open daily 9am-5pm. $13, concessions $10, kids 6-14 $7, families up to 4 children $38. Wheelchair accessible. Strollers and wheelchairs available for hire. Free tours by appointment. Take tram #55 to the zoo stop.)* Many sections are expertly recreated native habitats that allow visitors to view animals much as they live in the wild. The African Rainforest, with its pygmy hippos, arboreal monkeys, and gorillas, is first-rate. A darkened platypus area lets you watch the bizarre monotreme swim about. The Great Flight Aviary has birds zooming overhead, while the residents of the butterfly house may even land on you. A new exhibit due to open in October 1998 will massively increase the space for Australian fauna and promises to be an excellent place to view kangaroos, koalas, dinky-headed emus, and their kin.

SOUTH OF THE YARRA RIVER

Across the Yarra from the west end of the city center lies the **Melbourne Exhibition Centre,** home to a thousand boring trade shows. Of considerably more interest is the adjacent **Polly Woodside Maritime Museum** (tel. 9699 9760), on Lorimer St East. *($7, concessions and children $4, family $15. Open 10am-4pm.)* It won't convert you to a grizzled sailor if you hate the sea and all that's in it, but if you have a nautical bent it'll shiver your timbers with a wealth of displays about maritime history, culture, and exploration in the Southern Hemisphere.

The riverside walk that begins across Clarendon St from the Exhibition Centre is **Southbank,** with an upmarket shopping and sidewalk-dining scene. It's most crowded on sunny Sundays, when an odd mix of skater kids, toned health nuts, and the Armani-clad gather here to relax, show off, and conspicuously consume. The area extends along the Yarra for two very long city blocks, and while you could easily squander your entire budget here within a day, you can window-shop, people-watch, and get some great views of the Flinders St Station and the city skyline for free. There are also some cool fountains where water performs more tricks than you thought possible, as well as two of Melbourne's most famous icons: a four-story-high Victoria Bitter sign, and the strange, Y-shaped sculpture *Ophelia*, by Deb Halpern, replete with big eyes, two noses, and a fat-lipped smile.

At the east end of Southbank, just across the river from Flinders St Station, the strange gold spire of the **Melbourne Concert Hall** indicates the presence of the **Victorian Arts Centre.** Aside from putting on world-class performances (see **Entertainment,** p. 512), the complex houses the **Performing Arts Museum** (tel. 9281 8000; http://www.arts-centre.net.au/pam), which showcases shoes, outfits, and photos that chronicle the history of Australian live arts. *(Open M-Sa 9am-11pm, Su 10am-5pm. Free.)*

On the next block south, the rectangular, slate-gray building ringed by sculpture and fountains is the **National Gallery of Victoria,** 180 St. Kilda Rd (tel. 9208 0356; http://www.ngv.vic.gov.au). *(Open 10am-5pm. Admission free. Temporary exhibitions $6-10, concessionsconcessions $4-7. 2nd floor closed M.)* Constructed in 1968, the National Gallery houses what is generally regarded as the finest art collection in the southern hemisphere. A mesmerizing waterfall concealing a glass wall marks the entrance, and the gallery encircles an open-air sculpture garden. The ground floor houses a large collection of Australian paintings. On the first floor is the Access Gallery, featuring local work relating to community issues, and the Asian Gallery, filled with funerary art and Buddhist religious sculpture offset by pithy Zen sayings. The second floor gallery displays changing exhibitions of traditional and contemporary Aboriginal art. European paintings span from the Renaissance to modern masters. Notable selections include an intricate 16th-century

Flemish carved retable of the Passion of Christ and Picasso's *Weeping Woman,* stolen in the late 80s and eventually found in a locker at Flinders St Station. Don't miss the huge, ornate gold candelabra dubbed "The Centerpiece of Melbourne." There are a number of modern works on the second floor as well, including a meditative Rothko, *Untitled Red,* and Chuck Close's large-scale etching, *Self-Portrait.* Temporary exhibitions are generally excellent, often highlighting Australia's cutting edge recent work, and there are also thematic shows featuring the work of major artists. After June 1999, the National Gallery location at St. Kilda Rd will close for renovations and a fraction of the permanent collection will temporarily move to the State Library of Victoria. *(Hours and admission fees for temporary location yet to be determined; call the NGV or check the web for details. For info about the State Library, see Practical Information, p. 494.)*

Continuing south, the **Royal Botanical Gardens** (tel. 9252 2300), stretch along St. Kilda Rd east to the Yarra and south to Domain Rd. *(Open daily Nov.-March 7:30am-8:30pm, Apr.-Oct. 7:30am-5:30pm. Free. Free tours depart Gate F Tu-F 11am and 2pm, Su 11am. Wheelchair accessible.)* Over 49,000 plants fill the 36 acres. The gardens first opened in 1845, and the extensive array of mature species reflects 150 years of care and development. Stately palms unique to Melbourne share the soil with twisting oaks, rainforest plants, possums and wallabies, and even a pavilion of roses. A number of walking tracks highlight endemic flora; the **Australian Rainforest Walk** is right inside Gate F and provides an overview of wetlands vegetation from Tasmania to Queensland. There's also a steamy **rainforest glasshouse** (open 10am-4:30pm), and lake where you can have tea and feed ducks and geese. The **National Herbarium and the Garden Shop** (open 10am-5pm) are located at Gate F in the southeast corner and sell souvenirs and disperse free maps of the gardens. Special events, such as outdoor film screenings, take place on summer evenings

The small cottage by Gate F is the **LaTrobe Cottage,** Melbourne's first government building. *(Open M, W, Sa, and Su 11am-4pm. $2.)* The modest homestead was erected for Melbourne's first governor, Charles Joseph LaTrobe, who occupied it from 1839 to 1854. It's now fully restored and stocked with pioneer artifacts, including many original pieces. Just south of the Garden Shop and National Herbarium on Dallas Brooks Dr, the **Australian Centre for Contemporary Art** displays rotating exhibits of avant-garde, multimedia work. *(Open Tu-F 11am-5pm, Sa-Su 2-5pm. Free.)*

Occupying an adjacent hill to the southwest is Melbourne's **Shrine of Remembrance,** an imposing temple with columns and a ziggurat roof. *(Open 10am-5pm. Free, though a $2 donation is requested.)* The main structure commemorates fallen soldiers from WWI, with later veterans honored by an adjacent monument. Ascend to the shrine's balcony for spectacular views of the Melbourne skyline. From here the **eternal flame**—lit by Queen Elizabeth II in 1954—and Australia's **national flag** are visible. The flag is lowered each evening at precisely 5pm to the sounds of a bugle call. Inside the shrine, the central space is crowned by a stepped skylight which on November 11th at 11am (the time of the WWI armistice) a beam is precisely designed so that sunlight shines onto the word "love" in the central inscription, "Greater Love Hath No Man." Don't worry about missing this: the effect is simulated every half hour with artificial light, after which volunteer guides give excellent talks about the site's history and significance. At the back, you can read about Anzac Day—April 25th—which commemorates the bloody battle of Gallipoli that Australian and New Zealand troops fought, and lost, during WWI. You can venture down into the crypt and view the colorful division flags and memorial statue.

North of the shrine, in the Kings Domain garden, picnickers lounge on blankets at the **Sidney Myer Music Bowl** (tel. 9281 8360). This open-air concert bowl features concerts in the summer months and a small ice-skating rink during the winter. *(Rink open April 5-Oct. 5 M-Tu 10am-4:30pm, W-Sa 10am-4:30pm and 6-10pm, Su 10am-6pm. Skating $8, under 15 $7, families of four $25; prices include skate hire. Enter at the rear of the stage.)* The **Victoria Gardens** lie just north and west of the music bowl, dotted with statuary, palms, and ponds with the National Gallery providing a dramatic backdrop. To the east past the Botanic Gardens you'll reach the **Como House** (tel. 9827 2500), an elegant Victo-

Public Art in Melbourne

Part of Melbourne's oft-cited livability is the attention to detail in its public spaces. In addition to Neogothic architecture and verdant parks, much of the central city is scattered with sculptures and statues. Best-known is Deb Halpern's *Ophelia*, in the midst of Southbank, the fat-lipped, multi-colored, Y-shaped visage that has become one of the city's most prominent icons. On the pavement in front of Halpern's work, look for the ephemeral drawings of Bev Isaac, a chalk colorist who fashions multichrome representations of scenes from folk and fairy tales that remain until they are washed away by the elements. North along Swanston St in front of the State Library of Victoria, a stone cornice with part of the word "library" protrudes from the pavement. This work of Petroneous Sponk seems to suggest either a library rising from or sinking back into the earth; either way, it's pretty weird. Perhaps the most popular of the sculptures is the group of three businessmen cast in bronze standing at the corner of Swanston and Collins St. Their emaciated frames and wild-eyed expressions inspire amusement in most onlookers, though the work was originally underwritten by the government of Nauru and meant to reflect the greed and spiritual impoverishment of the Australian businessmen who plundered the tiny Polynesian country's natural resources. This is only a partial list, though—anywhere you go in Melbourne, art may lurk just around the corner. Beware art!!!

rian mansion built in an Italian villa style. *(Open daily 10am-5pm. Take Tram #8 from Swanston St to stop 33 on Toorak Rd.)*

ST KILDA

Bayside St Kilda lies just far enough away from the city to be relaxed, but close enough to maintain a live—if mellow—vibe. There aren't a lot of tourist sights per se, but the offbeat shops, gorgeous sandy shoreline, and comfortably mixed population of freaks and straights are indeed a sight to behold. St. Kilda Beach is easily accessed by any number of trams (see **Orientation,** p. 492), and swarms with swimmers and sun-worshippers during summer. The **Esplanade** along the length of the strand is a great place for rollerblading and jogging. The entrance gate of **Luna Park** (tel. 9525 5033), on the Lower Esplanade, is a St. Kilda icon, shaped like a grotesque, mammoth face. Venture through its mouth to find classic carnival rides, including a rollercoaster, ferris wheel, and tunnel of terror. *(Admission free. Ride tickets $1; most rides require 3 tickets.)* **Albert Park,** the southern extension of Melbourne's vast park system that lies south of the Yarra, is opposite Fitzroy St, where you'll find ample green space with free barbecues and groups of kids playing footy.

The **Jewish Museum of Australia,** 26 Alma Rd (tel. 9534 0083; http://www.vicnet.net.au/~jmuseum), east of St Kilda Rd by stop 32 on tram lines #3 or #67, outlines the Jewish experience down under from the time of the first fleet. *(Open Tu-Th 10am-4pm and Su 11am-5pm. $5, concessions $3. Tours of the adjacent synagogue are free with admission and take place T-Th 12:30pm and Su 12:30 and 3pm.)* The Belief and Ritual Gallery provides a thorough overview of the religion's basic tenets, including a painfully detailed French woodcut of a circumcision ceremony. There are also rotating displays featuring art and Judaica. Chatty guides add colorful personal insights.

FARTHER AFIELD

The Museum of Victoria's **ScienceWorks,** 2 Spotswood St (tel. 9392 4800; http://www.mov.vic.gov.au/sw.html), 5km from downtown in the suburb of Spotswood, is a big hit with kids, who pack in droves during weekends and school holidays. *(Open 10am-4:30pm. $8, children $4, lots of family discounts.)* The displays are designed to trick children into learning via fun and cheekiness (two words: fake feces). There's an engaging section about surviving in the bitter cold of Antarctica, and Sports Works affords the opportunity to engage in simulated competition against Olympians. (Don't try too hard;

you will lose, and the kids will laugh at you for taking it too seriously.) Take the Werribee or Williamstown line from Flinders St Station, get off at Spotswood, and follow the ample signs; the walk takes about 15 minutes.

The **Museum of Modern Art at Heide,** 7 Templestown Rd (tel. 9850 1500), in the northern suburb of Bulleen, was a meeting place for artists, writers, and poets during the emergence of Australian modernism in the 1930s and 40s. It has since been converted into an excellent venue for contemporary Australian and international art. The collection traces the emergence of Australia's avant-garde from the 1930s, and features work by Charles Blackman, Authur Boyd, Joy Hester, and Sidney Nolan. There are also rotating exhibitions of cutting-edge art from international makers. Perhaps most impressive is the 5-hectare sculpture park, which combines art and nature spectacularly with sculpture, roses and magnolias, and views of the stately Yarra River. The museum lies about 20 minutes from the city center; catch a train to Heidelberg Station (Hurstbridge line) from Flinders St Station and then take National Bus 291.

■ Entertainment

Melbourne prides itself on its style and cultural savvy, and nowhere is this more evident than in its excellent entertainment scene. The range of options can seem overwhelming; there are world-class performances at the Victorian Arts Centre, edgy experimental drama in Carlton and Fitzroy, the popular dramas and musicals of the moment, and a panoply of independent and avant-garde cinema. The definitive site for performance events is http://melbourne.citysearch.com.au.

FILM

Melbourne has long been the center of Australia's independent film scene, and there are tons of old theaters throughout the city that screen artsy and experimental fare as well as old cinema classics. The URL of choice among the arthouse crowd is http://www.urbancinefile.com.au, which features flip reviews of the latest stuff. The annual **Melbourne International Film Festival** (see **Special Events,** p. 514) showcases the year's indie hits. Plenty of theaters in the city center show mainstream first-run movies as well; **Hoyt's Cinema Centre,** 140 Bourke St (tel. 9663 3303), has a bar in the lobby if the flick isn't entertaining enough. **Movieline** (tel. 13 34 56) has recorded info on show times and locations as well as a ticketing service. At the theater, try a "choc-top," the chocolate-dipped ice-cream cone that's a staple of Melbourne moviegoing ($2-3).

⑧Astor Theatre (tel. 9510 1414), corner of Chapel St and Dandenong Rd, St. Kilda. Spectacular Art Deco theatre originally built in 1936 that still bears many of its original furnishings and all of its stately beauty. Excellent film quality and sound system, with a screen 19m wide and 9m high. 1100 seats on 2 levels. Mostly repertory and reissues. Special events held include the **St. Kilda Film Festival** (see **Seasonal Events,** p. 514). $10, concessions $9, children $8; book of 10 tickets $70.

Cinema Nova, 380 Lygon St (tel. 9347 5331), in Lygon Court, Carlton. Five theaters, with luxuriously comfortable seats and indie and foreign fare. $11, backpackers $8.50, students $7, under 15 $6. Privilege cards ($10) entitle bearers to $7 admission.

The Kino, 45 Collins St (tel. 9650 2100), downstairs in the Collins Place complex, City. Quality independent and foreign films on 3 screens where all the seats provide good views. $11, students $8.50, pensioners and children under 16 $6.50. M special $7 all day. Yearly Kino Cinecard ($10) entitles bearer to $7 admission.

IMAX, Melbourne Museum (tel. 9663 5454), Rathdowne St, Carlton. The world's biggest movie screen, dwarfing even the standard IMAX format, located in a massive subterranean theater. Shows are short on content but more than make up for it with astounding visuals—some even offer 3D action viewed through space-age liquid crystal glasses. $14, children $10, concessions $11; 3D shows $1 extra.

PERFORMING ARTS

First-rate dance and classical music goes down at Southbank's Victorian Arts Centre, while major Broadway musicals visit Melbourne's big central city venues. There are plenty of more offbeat, smaller performances farther afield, particularly in Carlton and Fitzroy. Book for larger shows through **Ticketek**, or try **Halftix** for half-price same day tickets (see **Tickets**, p. 495); for smaller ones, call the theater companies directly. The **Victorian Arts Centre**, 100 St. Kilda Rd (tel 9281 8000; fax 9281 8282; http://www.artscentre.net.au), is hard to miss—right across the Yarra from Flinders St Station, it's topped off by a spire that looks as though it's had a net cast over it. It houses three venues: the **State Theatre** for major dramatic, operatic, and dance performances; the **Melbourne Concert Hall,** for symphonies; and the **Playhouse**, for recent dramatic hits. (Tickets range from $25-55. Box office open M-Sa 9am-9pm.)

Regent Theatre (tel. 9820 0239), Little Collins St between Swanston and Russell St. Dazzlingly ornate. Hosts big-name touring shows, especially musicals. Tickets $15-40.

The Forum (tel. 9299 9700), corner of Russell and Flinders St, City. Looks like an Arabian palace and Florentine villa combined, with a few gargoyles thrown in. Big-budget dance and drama. Frequent cabarets provide a bawdier show. Tickets $10-35.

Universal Theatre, 19 Victoria St, Fitzroy (tel. 9419 3777; email universal@bsgn.net). Mixed theatrical bag somewhere between the mainstream and the wacked-out fringe, including comedy, experimental stuff, serious drama. Tickets $15-27.

La Mama, 205 Faraday, Carlton (info tel. 9347 6948, bookings 9347 6142), obscured down an alleyway and behind a parking lot. Features new Australian drama in diminutive, black-box space. Similar cutting-edge work is performed at the affiliated **Carlton Courthouse Theatre**, just around the corner in the old courthouse building, 349 Drummond St, across from the police station. Tickets $11-16, concessions $7-10.

National Theatre (tel. 9534 0221), corner of Barkly and Carlisle St, St. Kilda. Offbeat, cosmopolitan fare, including modern dance and "world music." Tickets $10-30.

Last Laugh, 380 Lygon St (tel 9419 8600), Carlton. Melbourne's biggest comedy club scene, with big-name international jokesters. Ticket prices $5-25, depending on the act and whether it's a weekend.

GAMBLING

The Australian penchant for "having a flutter" (betting) reaches its neon-lit apotheosis at **Melbourne's Crown Casino,** 8 Whiteman St (tel. 9292 8888), at the western end of South Bank. It houses the most gaming tables of any casino in the world, plus five-star accommodations, luxury shopping, Elvis impersonators, fog-filled, laser-lit jumping fountains, and a perennially packed Planet Hollywood. The Crown is a little slice of Las Vegas down under. Minimum bets are around $5, though the more cautious can start at the less cutthroat "how to play" tables. (Open 24hr.)

RECREATION

Melburnians refer to themselves as "sports mad," but it's a good insanity, one that causes fans of footy (Aussie Rules Football), cricket, tennis, and horse racing to skip work or school, get decked out in the costumery of their favorite side, and cheer themselves hoarse. Their main asylum is the **Melbourne Cricket Ground**, adjacent to the world-class **National Tennis Centre** (now called **Melbourne Park;** see p. 508). The lunacy peaks at various yearly events: the **Australian Open,** a Grand Slam tennis event, in late January; the **AFL Grand Final** in late September; the **Melbourne Cup,** a "horse race that stops a nation," in early November; and cricket's **Boxing Day Test Match** in late December. See **Seasonal Events,** below, for more information.

Melbourne's passion for sport is not limited to spectator events. City streets and parks are packed with joggers, skaters, and footy players. Best for **running** is the newly refurbished, crushed gravel tan track that circles the Royal Botanic Gardens. Other great routes include the pedestrian paths along the Yarra, the Port Phillip/St. Kilda shore, and the Albert Park Lake. All of these wide, flat spaces make for excellent **rollerblading** as well. **City Skate,** Wednesday at 9pm, draws local bladers together at the Victorian Arts Centre near the waterfall; folks convene and break into smaller groups based on preferred route and skill level. You can rent equipment at the **Skate Warehouse,** 354 Lonsdale St (tel. 9602 3633; $7.50 per hr, $12.50 per ½ day, $17.50 per day). **Skateboarders** should check out the public **skate park** at the corner of Swanston and Lonsdale St next to the State Library, which has a decent selection of half-pipes and such.

An extensive **bike trail** runs along the Yarra, and others loop through Albert Park and Middle Park, along the Port Phillip beaches, and around North Melbourne's gardens. Southern Melbourne's flat bayside roads make for low-impact, scenic cycling. Bike shops include **Hire A Bicycle** (tel. 9429 0000), on Yarra Bank beside Princes Bridge (open 10am-5pm, weather permitting), and **Fitzroy Cycles,** 224 Swanston St (tel. 9639 3511; open M-Th 9am-6pm, F 9am-7pm, Sa 9am-5pm). Rates are around $28-35 per day and include helmets and locks. Many hostels rent bikes for little or no charge. **Bicycle Victoria (BV),** 19 O'Connell St (tel. 9328 3000; fax 9328 2288; http://www.bv.com.au; bicyclevic@bv.com.au), has scads of info (see **Victoria Practical Information,** p. 484).

The **Melbourne City Baths,** 420 Swanston St (tel. 9663 5888), on the corner of Franklin St north and east of the city center, offer two excellent pools, sauna, spa, squash courts, and an exercise gym in a restored Neoclassical building. (Open M-F 6am-10pm, Sa-Su 8am-6pm. Pool $2.80; sauna and spa $6.50. Student discounts on long-term memberships.) Take the kiddies to **Putters** mini-golf course (tel 9662 9733), on Lonsdale St near its intersection with Swanston ($5, family $6). There's a bar on the premises where you can drown your sorrows after losing to a five-year-old.

SEASONAL EVENTS

Melburnians love to create excuses for citywide street parties any time of the year. Below are the city's major events, but there are too many to list. For a complete seasonal guide, grab a free copy of *Melbourne Events* at any tourist office, or look under "Festivals and Events" at http://www.melbourne.org.

Australian Open (tel. 9286 1234), late Jan. One of the world's elite four Grand Slam tennis events, held at Melbourne Park's hard courts.

Midsumma Gay and Lesbian Festival (tel. 9525 4746), late Jan. to early Feb. Three weeks of homosexual hijinks ranging from the erotic (a "Mr. Leather Victoria" contest) to the educational (a Same-Sex Partners Rights workshop), with lots of parades, dance parties, and general licentious pandemonium.

Moomba (tel. 9699 4022), mid-March. Named after the Aboriginal word for "party," Moomba is basically a non-stop 11-day fête amid food, performances, and events.

International Flower and Garden Show (tel. 959 4400), 1st week of April. A floral spectacular. Royal Exhibition Building and Carlton Gardens, Carlton.

International Comedy Festival (tel. 9417 7711), April. Huge 3-week international and Aussie laff-fest, beginning on April Fools Day. Over 1000 gut-busting performances.

St Kilda Film Festival (tel. 9209 6699 or 9209 6327), last week of April. The country's finest short films: documentary, experimental, comedy. Astor Cinema, St Kilda.

Anzac Day Parade (tel. 9650 5050), April 25. ANZAC vets gather for a Commemoration March that heads south through town and ends at the Shrine of Remembrance.

International Film Festival (tel. 9417 2011), last week of July-first week of Aug. The cream of the international cinematic crop, plus top-level local work. Held at various swish performance venues throughout the city. Book way ahead for tickets.

Autumn Moon Lantern Festival (tel. 9662 2888), 3rd week of Sept. Celebrates the fall harvest in a tradition that dates back to the Tang Dynasty. Chinatown.

Melbourne Festival (tel. 9866 8866), late Oct. A 3-week cultural celebration bringing together many of the world's best known actors, writers, and dancers for more than 400 performances, workshops, shows, and parties in 30 different venues.

Melbourne Fringe Festival (tel. 9534 0722), 1st 2 weeks of Oct. Street parades, performance art, and parties celebrate Fitzroy's general zaniness. Brunswick St, Fitzroy.

Spring Racing Carnival (tel. 9258 4666), 1st week of Nov. The Australian love for horse racing reaches a fever pitch during this event, punctuated by the Melbourne Cup. Flemington Racecourse.

Melbourne Boxing Day Test Match (tel. 9657 8893), last week of Dec. More than 100,000 cricket fans pack into the MCG to root for the boys in green and gold against top cricketers from around the world.

■ Nightlife

Melbourne pulses with a world-class nightlife scene. Only a handful of venues play the standard bass-heavy club remixes of familiar mainstream dance hits. Most feature DJs (some of whom have international followings) who spin funky, mind-bending original selections of techno, house and deep house, trance, drum 'n' bass, jungle, garage, and breakbeats. You probably won't recognize any of it, but it's eminently danceable. Tons of retro nights feature 70s and 80s faves, with a crowd bedecked in campy period wear. Covers are ubiquitous and range up to $15, but you get your money's worth—few clubs close earlier than 3am.

There are three main areas for **nightclubs.** Downtown tends to be straighter (as in less gay and more mainstream), though you'll find a little bit of everything. South Yarra and Prahran have the trendiest venues as well as the best **gay scene.** Though most clubs in the area are gay-friendly, predominantly gay places are concentrated along Commercial Rd. Fitzroy and St. Kilda are more casual, tending toward grungy music shows and charging the cheapest covers. Venues, genres, and cover charges change with bewildering rapidity. To keep up, read *In Press* and, to a lesser extent, *Beat* magazines, both of which are free, released every Wednesday, and have exhaustive weekly listings. For music shows, the best coverage is in The Age's *Entertainment Guide* (*EG*) or the Herald-Sun's *Gig Guide,* both of which come out in their respective Friday papers.

There is a blurry but important distinction between **bars** and **pubs** in Melbourne. The bars tend to be a bit more chill but no less slick than their nightclub cousins; they don't have covers, though. Drinks are expensive (beer bottles $3.50-4, wine and mixed drinks $4-5), and wine and spirits are the intoxicants of choice; many bars don't have beer taps at all. Most pubs, on the other hand, charge less for drinks (half-pint pots $2-2.50, pints $4-5, mixed drinks $3-4), are loud and raucous, and have live entertainment on weekends (cover $3-8), making the distinction between pub and club somewhat blurry as well. So might your mind be after a night of hitting local watering holes, as most of them try to lure backpackers with cheap drink specials (pots as low as $1-1.50) and often keep taps flowing until early in the morning, or even 24 hours.

NIGHTCLUBS

City Center

Ⓧ**Inflation,** 60 King St (tel. 9614 6122). Hands-down the biggest backpacker nightclub scene in the city center, probably in all Melbourne. Tu: *huge* backpacker party, with free 1-liter buckets of beer from 9-10pm and 11pm-midnight on the ground floor and hardcore techno party in the basement. F: live funk-reggae band; Sa morning: Recovery, an early morning party for ragers who have stayed up all night, beginning at 6am. Sa night: 3 levels of utter dance craziness: R&B in the basement, retro on the ground floor, and mainstream techno upstairs. $1 beer pots Sat 6-10pm. Cover $6-10.

Ⓧ**Scubar,** 383 Lonsdale St (tel. 9670 2400). Shagadelic, baby! Prototype for the space-age bachelor pad, this downstairs venue is befitted with groovalicious furniture, mohair wall coverings, a translucent bar, and a big ceiling aquarium with tropical fish. Most active F-Sa, with live bands early on and DJs spinning trancy beats later on. Stays mellow but fun after other bars shut down. Tapas bar serves light food. Cover $7-10.

Metro, 20-30 Bourke St (tel. 9663 4288). The largest club in the southern hemisphere. A younger (18-21), straight crowd packs in on weekends for a major scope-and-scam scene. Four bars and 3 floors of dance action; the ground floor's the most frenetic, with fog, flashing lights, and a video screen that spotlights the smoothest movers. Th: alternative-grunge night; F: house beats; Sa: mainstream dance hits. Cover $7-12.

Club 383, 383 Lonsdale St (tel. 9670 6575). The central city's big alternative venue. Pool tables and a big dance floor on the first floor, a more intimate dance area and black-lit lounge areas on the second, and plenty of bars everywhere. A large video screen plays squeaky-clean 1950s-era films to contrast with the jaded 90s nihilism of the music. Friday is a more lighthearted 80s scene, Saturday a darker industrial mood with Marilyn Manson T-shirts aplenty. Cover $5-10.

South Yarra & Prahran

Revolver, 229 Chapel St, 1st floor (tel. 9529 1117). The most happening alternative club in the city, with a mixed crowd of slick, black-clad clubgoers and edgy, multiply-pierced skate-punk types. U2 and Massive Attack hung out here every night during their recent tours through Melbourne. Performance/dance area frequented by all manner of alternative bands on weekends; a DJ takes over around midnight for groovy late-night dance action. The lounge is calmer, with pool, campy pinball machines, and retro furniture. Lines are long (especially Sa) and you have to look stylin' to get in. Cover $5-15.

Chasers, 386 Chapel St (tel. 9827 6615). Massive complex of nighttime revelry with 2 stories, 6 bars, and a vast dance floor offset by various smaller spaces to lounge and chill. W: alterna-hits in the main arena, retro alternative and electronica in the other rooms, cheap drinks all around ($3 VB and $2 "bourbon bonanza"). Sa: "Enter the Dragon," resplendent with sultry Asiatic accoutrements; progressive dance and house. Su: disco and new wave from the 70s and 80s in the main arena, 90s house and garage elsewhere. Dress casual but sharp, especially on weekends. Cover $5-15.

Dome, 19 Commercial Rd (tel. 9529 8966). Melbourne's most popular and expensive nightclub, the place to be seen (particularly on Sa night). Hordes of would-be patrons wait outside for hours. The main arena is a vast, crowded, sweaty vortex of dance action—mostly straight but very gay-friendly—packed with groovers who remove more clothing as the night wears on. Operates F-Sa only. Cover $12-15. If you can snag an invite from *Beat* or *In Press* or from a local music store, you'll get a few bucks discount and, more importantly, you'll get in. If you can't, show up early or don't bother. Dress sharp. Open 10pm-way late.

Diva, 153 Commercial Rd (tel 9824 2800). Chill, down-to-earth, very popular gay bar (straight-friendly) with tons of theme nights and drink specials. Th: drag night with $1.50 beer pots and sassy shows from 10:30pm. F: a steamy selection of the latest dance hits and bar shows featuring male exotic dancers. Sa: acid-tongued queen Lucy Loosebox presides a very popular retro show (from 9:30pm). Su: more drag! Happy hour Tu-Su 6-8pm (everything $3). No cover, ever.

Three Faces, 143 Commercial Rd (tel. 9826 0933). Styled as the "total venue," this is Melbourne's slickest, hippest gay club (straight-friendly). The top floor is a chill cocktail lounge where sassy queens strut their stuff, and patrons cruise, play pool, and scope the dance floor from a circular balcony. The bottom floor is all about bodies grinding to serious techno beats and bass-heavy remixes of gay anthems. Th: killer queens Paris, Zowie, and Rita perform at 11:30pm and 1am. F: exotic male dancers downstairs, drag shows upstairs. Sa: club faves in the main dance area, the lovely and talented Tabitha Turlington upstairs (no cover before 11pm). Cover $5.

Lizard Lounge, Union Hotel, 90 Chapel St (tel 9510 4396). A refreshingly unpretentious place where young hipsters boogie to psychedelic and alternative pop hits from the late 60s to the present. Welcoming to anyone and any style. Two bars and small but very groovy dance floor. Th-Su only. Cover $5-6 F-Sa nights.

Fitzroy

Night Cat, 141 Johnston St (tel. 9417 0090). Deeply cool, swankily elegant, and heaps of fun, this velvety den draws a slightly older set (20s and 30s) F-Su nights for live acid jazz. Uni students and 20somethings populate the dance-funk scene Th night. The predominantly red interior recalls *Twin Peaks,* with lamps that look like they were stolen from a motel in 1963, twinkling faux-chandeliers, massive mirrors, and comfy leather chairs. Open 8pm-1am.

Binary Bar, Brunswick St (tel. 9419 7374; http://www.binary.net.au). Recently named "best Internet cafe in Australia" by *internet.au* magazine, the Binary is that and so much more. They serve drinks, sell snacks and food, make coffee, screen films, host DJ dance nights, showcase musical acts (Th live ambient and acid jazz), have a pool table, offer open-mic poetry nights (W), and provide free Internet access in terminals set into the bar, so you can surf while you imbibe. Open 3pm-1am.

St Kilda

Sunset Strip, 16 Grey St (9534 9205). Much-beloved haunt in the heart of St K's backpacker district with wildly varied—and just plain wild—theme nights. Hard-core industrial DJ nights, "funk 'n' flat-out retro," mellow jazz trios, and outrageous drag acts. $1 beer specials draw backpackers like alcoholic flies. Usually rages till 5am.

Mansion, 83 Queens Rd (tel. 9521 1711). Seriously weird, in a weirdly serious way. F: hard, psychedelic trance, industrial acid, and kaleidoscopic electro-rhythms as well as a trippy, chill lounge serving energy drinks, chai, and erotic-exotic foods. Su: an anything-goes S&M/fetish night (think whips and chains, and you've got about a tenth of it). Licensed till 7am, and the party frequently goes that late. Cover $10-12, sometimes cheaper if you bring an ad from *In Press* or *Beat*.

The Ritz, 169 Fitzroy St (tel. 9534 1287). Not as swank as its name, but loads of fun. Th: Car Wash, billed as the "mother of all discos." Backpackers are lured with $1 pots and $2 spirits from 9-11pm, and prices only go up $1 the rest of the night. F: a variety of live bands. Sa: Latin night, with samba, salsa, and general spicy lasciviousness. Sometimes a cover ($5-7).

BARS AND PUBS

City Center

◉**Up Top Cocktail Bar,** 163 Russell St., 1st fl. (tel. 9663 8990). Enter via the alleyway off Russell St. The vanguard of the *Swingers* aesthetic's first tentative forays down under. Smallish lounge decked out with disco ball, brocade-framed mirrors, and other lounge-daddy accoutrements. Popular enough for lines to form on weekends. Excellent music, with live jazz, trip-hop, or jungle beats nightly. Mixed drinks from $4, beer from $3.50, snacks from $2. Open 4pm-4am.

◉**Rue Bebelons,** 267 Little Lonsdale St (tel. 9663 1700). There's no sign outside; you have to be in the know. The consummate Melburnian bar, relaxed and understatedly stylish, with an excellent selection of wines ($2.50) and spirits ($4-5). The deep house music and dim lighting create the ideal atmosphere for a silent, brooding solitary drink or an intimate tête-a-tête. Open 11am-3am.

Young and Jackson, 1 Swanston St (tel. 9650 3884). Classic Melbourne spot, with a quiet, low-key atmosphere. Downstairs section across from Flinders St Station gets a bit rowdy, especially on weekends when the post-footy crowd stops by. Around the corner of Swanston and upstairs is the section known as Chloe's Bar, after the subject of the titillating painting of a nude 14-year-old girl that was unveiled at the Melbourne Exhibition of 1880. It caused a great stir at the time, which was later surpassed when its maker, French painter Jules Lefebvre, ditched Chloe for her sister, and the distraught model killed herself by drinking a cocktail of match heads and champagne. The painting now hangs upstairs at Y&J, which is the classier and more sedate portion of the bar, though it's prowled by pool sharks. Generally open till midnight.

The Dark Horse, 407 Swanston St (tel. 9639 2619). The spare decor in this subterranean grotto creates an unpretentious space to enjoy their naughtily named drinks ($5), which include the "slippery nipple" (White Sambuca and Bailey's) and others that can't be printed in a family-friendly travel guide. Open 10am-late.

Stadium, 125 Flinders Ln (tel 9654 3622). Drunker than a sailor on shore leave and hornier than a cat in heat, the crowd here parties past the point of heartiness, to the very brink of heart attack. Stadium's frat-boy and girl patrons get sloshed with cheap drinks and then descends into a dance-till-you-drop Dionysian frenzy as the jukebox blasts club classics. 2 for 1 drinks F 5-7pm and Sa 7-9pm. Cover $8-10. Open til 2am.

Fitzroy

◉**Labour in Vain,** 197 Brunswick St (tel. 9417 5955). The name of this pre-gold rush era hotel laments the back-breaking work of the early settlers and convicts; today, it's been remodeled to celebrate their hard-drinkin' after-work antics. Strewn with artifacts from the period, it's part watering hole, part history museum. The ale's mighty nice, the folks are friendly, and there's a pool table ($1) and good-quality pub meals ($10-15). Open M-Sa 1:30pm-1am, Su 1:30pm-11pm.

Bar Open, 317 Brunswick St (tel. 9415 9601). Edgy urban chic tempered by a solid dose of post-hippie haziness. Portraits of the Queen Mum abound, offset by minimalist black barstools and a baffling sign that reads "Tofu and Drinks." They charge pub prices for beer, but fancy cocktails run $6.50. Upstairs Th-Sa houses an eclectic mix of international fusion acts, earnest folk singers, and soulful blues bands. No cover. Open M-W 5pm-late, Th-F 4pm-late, Sa-Su 1pm-late.

Evelyn Hotel, 351 Brunswick St (tel. 9419 5500). A pub that serves as a major music venue for local, national and international acts. Genres range heavy metal to jazz to trip-hop. Best acts generally Th and Sa. Cover $3-10 depending on the show. Open Su-W 10am-1:30am, Th-Sa 10am-3am.

Punters Club, 376 Brunswick St (tel. 9417 3006). Music-oriented pub with live indie acts every night. Weekends usually have the best acts. Band schedule is posted outside the pub. Cover $3-10. Open noon-late, licensed till 3am.

Rush Bar, 272 Brunswick St (tel. 9419 8058). Part bar, part exhibition space where Fitzroy hipsters mingle and imbibe amid artwork. Ornate second-floor lounge has squishy overstuffed couches and affords an view of Brunswick St. Ask the friendly, spacey staff for the Cascade, a Tasmanian brew that packs a kick. Coffee bar and restaurant by day, serving tasty chow till 11pm. Open 11am-late, licensed till 3am.

St Kilda

⊛Esplanade Hotel, 11 Upper Esplanade (tel. 9534 0211). Multifaceted seaside hotel. Lounge bar serves tasty pub meals ($8-15) and has live music at night; no cover, though drink prices rise slightly when a band's on. The ornate Gershwin Room, which once housed sumptuous fêtes for the Melburnian elite, now has live bands and comedy nights (cover up to $8 depending on act). The gritty public bar has no cover and cheap beer; happy hour 4-7pm.

⊛Greyhound Hotel, 1 Brighton St (tel. 9534 4189). Tripartite entertainment factory with numerous levels of debauchery. Two public bars: one gay, one straight, both tolerant and friendly. The band room hosts a series of theme nights. M: Metronome, a mixed bag of open-mike hopefuls ranging from gentle, starry-eyed folk singers to self-flagellating performance artists. T-Th: local bands who generally improve in quality as the week wears on. F: headliner bands. Sa: fab drag show. Su: the self-explanatory "Kooky Karaoke." Cover $3-20. Open M-Sa till 1am, Su till 11:30pm.

Prince of Wales, 29 Fitzroy St (tel. 9536 1177). Longstanding local haunt has recently come under new management and lost the grit in favor of a sleeker feel. There's a live band or a DJ every night; some are quite famous, all are pretty damn good. M nights are a backpacker haven with $1 beer pots. Cover $5-35.

North Melbourne

The Public Bar, 238 Victoria St (tel. 9329 6522). Its walls scattered with shards of broken mirrors, morose narrative murals, and other detritus of the urban wasteland, the Public is particularly popular with ferals, though it draws all kinds of folks. The music line-up is solid, with local alternative/grunge bands every weekend night and some weekdays as well. Cover $5. Open late.

The Stork Hotel, 504 Elizabeth St (tel. 9663 6237). Backpacker-friendly pub where grizzled locals rub elbows with travelers in a lounge warmed by a roaring fire. Events include reggae bands and all-night happy hour (M) and live 70s bands (Th). Unusually cheap drinks: $2 pots and $3 spirits, plus lots of specials. Open till 1am.

■ Around Melbourne

About 30 minutes west of Melbourne along the Princes Hwy lies the mansion at **Werribee Park** (tel. 9741 2444 or 13 19 63), K Road, replete with sculptured gardens, imposing billiard room, and expansive nursery wing. (Open M-F 10am-4pm, Sa-Su 10am-5pm. Admission $8. Various thematic tours available. Wheelchair accessible.) It was built between 1874 and 1877 by a Scottish sheep tycoon determined to move beyond his working-class heritage. The estate fell into disrepair after the owner's death and was taken over by a monastery. Since being purchased by the Victorian government, it's become a popular tourist stop. Just behind the mansion on K Rd, Victoria's **Open Range Zoo** (tel. 9731 1311) invites you to go on safari among animals from the grasslands of Australia, Africa, and Asia. (Open daily 9am-5pm. 1hr. safaris M-F every 30-60min. 10:30am-3:40pm, Sa-Su every 20-30min. 10am-3:40pm. Admission $14, ages 3-

14 $7, families $38.) To explore on your own, take the 30-minute walking trails; a tour of the park takes about three hours.

Another open-air zoo, the **Healesville Sanctuary,** lies in the Yarra Valley. (Open daily 9am-5pm. $14, students $10.50, children $7, families up to 6 $38.) Its minimum-security environs keep the Aussie menagerie steps from visitors. In the platypus habitat, you can walk through the enclosure where the weirdass monotremes splash in waterfalls. The zookeepers oversee close-up encounters with the animals between 11am and 3:30pm; check signs for display times. There's a bistro, snack bar, and gift shop. From Melbourne, take the Met's light rail to Lilydale, then take bus #685.

Oz is all about unique geological formations, and the Melbourne area boasts one of its own: the **Organ Pipes National Park,** just off the Calder Hwy (Hwy 79), 20km northwest of Melbourne. Although the 6m metamorphic landmarks look more like french fries than organ pipes, they're still a good daytrip or stop en route to the central Goldfields. Plus, french fries taste good. To reach the pipes, walk 15 minutes down the gulch. In addition to the organ pipes, look for the **Rosette Rock,** which resembles a flowing stone frozen in time (10min. down the path). The park is also a laboratory for environmental restoration and has been largely repopulated with native plants and trees since the early 1970s, when weeds concealed the pipes. The park has picnic and barbecue facilities, is wheelchair accessible, and charges no entrance fee.

Yes, **Hanging Rock National Park** is more than just a movie. The unique rock formations featured in the well-known *Picnic at Hanging Rock* are nearly as curious as the protagonists' fate. Entering from Calder Hwy, follow the signs and enter at the south gate on South Rock Rd. In addition to the rocks, tennis, barbecue facilities, and fishing await. (Open daily dawn-dusk. Admission $2.50, $5 per car, $2 per motorcycle.)

PORT PHILLIP AND WESTERNPORT BAYS

Two semicircular stretches of bayside land curve south from Melbourne to circumscribe Port Phillip and Westernport Bays: the Bellarine Peninsula to the east and the Mornington Peninsula to the west. This was the site of the first white settlement in Victoria (near Sorrento, see p. 521), a squalid effort that failed within a few years. By the later 19th century, however, its spectactular bay views and sunny, temperate climate made it the site of choice for summer homes of the goldfield-spawned nouveau riche. With the exception of Phillip Island and its way-popular fairy penguins, this area remains largely a haunt of the hoity-toity, a fact that deters most backpackers. Too bad—there are plenty of budget oppotunities here that allow everyone to enjoy the awesome scenery, sandy beaches, excellent surfing, and outdoorsy fun.

Phillip Island

Thanks to a massive ad campaign, Phillip Island has become synonymous with the endearing fairy penguins that inhabit its southwest corner and scamper back to their burrows nightly in a "Penguin Parade." The parade's massive popularity—it's second only to Ayers Rock as an Australian tourist attraction—frequently overshadows the island's many other attractions. Koalas, wombats, and seals call Phillip Island home, and you can spot them in the wild on one of a number of excellent nature walks or visit the island's two excellent new wildlife centers. The large breakers that crash against the island's southern shore draw countless surfers in summer, and Phillip Island's rolling, pastoral hills and gorgeous views of vivid blue Bass Strait waters provide ample reason to relax for a few days here, whether or not you see any penguins.

PRACTICAL INFORMATION Phillip Island lies across a narrow strait from San Remo, 120km southeast of Melbourne. Numerous backpacker-oriented tours take groups to the island daily. The best is the **Duck Truck tour,** which includes transfer to and from Melbourne, up to three nights at the Amaroo Park Hostel, a guided tour of the Penguin Parade and the whole island, meals, and half-day of bike use ($84, $75 with YHA or VIP discounts). By car, Phillip Island is just two hours from Melbourne; take the Princes Hwy (1), then the South Gippsland Hwy, and finally the Phillip Island Tourist Rd (Hwy 186). This road leads straight to **Cowes,** Phillip Island's biggest township. **V/Line** serves Cowes from Melbourne (3hr., 1 per day, $13.40). To purchase V/Line tickets in town, head to either Cowes Travel or Going Places Travel, on the main drag, Thompson Ave.

Once on Phillip Island, you'll see the **Phillip Island Information Service** (tel. 5956 7447, email piic@compcom.com.au; open daily 9am-5pm), just over the bridge. Buy Penguin Parade tix here to avoid long queues. You can also tune your dial to 87.6 FM for sunny tourist radio, or go to http://www.phillipisland.com. The **Cowes Post Office** is at 73-79 Thompson Ave (open M-F 9am-5pm; **postal code:** 3922), and directly across the street is the fully licensed IGA Island **supermarket.**

ACCOMMODATION AND FOOD The best budget lodging on Phillip Island is the **Amaroo Park Hostel,** 97 Church St, Cowes (tel. 5952 2548), 400m west of the post office. The common room has rich wooden furniture, piano (with occasional impromptu performances), pool table, and a snazzy pub with cheap drinks; there's also an outdoor veranda with barbecue. The friendly staff runs all kinds of tours; ask them for a sheet listing local restaurants and services that give discounts to backpackers. Twelve-bunk barracks have single-sex options, and there are several doubles as well. (Bunks $14, YHA nonmembers $17; doubles $32, $38. Pick-up available from Melbourne Tu, F only, around 1pm.) The **Parkside Cafe,** 72 Chapel St (tel. 5952 2951), serves up fresh, homemade, delectable chow, and wicked cheap. There's a wide variety of gourmet burgers and sandwiches ($3-5), and lots of veggie options. (Coffee and cake $2.50; open 8am-4:30pm.) For more upmarket eats, sample the offerings of **Cafe Terrazzo,** 5 Thompson Ave (tel. 5952 3773). The whimsically painted bistro offers a fine range of pasta and wood-fired pizza (open nightly until 9pm).

ACTIVITIES AND WILDLIFE Phillip Island's tourist magnet is the **Little Penguin Parade,** on display at the Phillip Island Nature Park. Each night the penguins return to their burrows from the day's fishing expedition to attend to their hungry chicks. Most visitors come with tour bus companies, but if you're on your own, follow the street signs to the carpark and **visitors center** (tel. 5956 8300; fax 5956 8394; http://www.penguins.org.au). This facility provides extensive information about the penguins, including interactive exhibits on their life cycle and diet and windowed burrows where you can observe their behavior. *(Open daily 10am-about 10pm. Tickets $9.50, children $7, family of 2 adults and up to 4 kids $24.50; included in group tour prices.)*

An elevated boardwalk provides beach access from the visitors center and allows you to watch the penguins burrow after they arrive on shore. There are two observation areas. A smaller, unlit area to your right offers less-touristed viewing, although fewer birds enter by this route. Most people await the penguins from the large grandstand along the main boardwalk. To grab a good seat, arrive by sunset, equipped with warm clothing and something soft to pad your seat. Head straight for the sand and sit beneath the cord if space is available. The best vantage points are closest to the central tunnel area. Once seated, you'll wait 30 to 60 minutes for the penguins to arrive. Their parade generally lasts nearly an hour. Flash photography isn't allowed, so you must either pick up 1600-speed film or get photos from the gift shop. The number of penguins can vary nightly from a handful to over 1000. Everything's wheelchair-accessible.

Although the penguins are Phillip Island's main draw, several other notable species make cameos. On the island's western extreme past the penguin parade, Australia's largest colony of **New Zealand fur seals** lives just off shore from the **Nobbies** rock formation. A boardwalk wraps around the Nobbies, enabling you to take in the beautiful eroded hills and crashing sea (open 7:30am to dusk). The **Seal Rocks Sea Life Centre** (tel. 1300 367 325) enhances the zoological experience dramatically. *($15, children and students $12; open 10am-dusk.)* Displays on local marine life include a real-time video feed of the seals, information about the Great White Shark (the largest ever was caught here a few years back), and a Disneyesque boat ride past animated displays tracing the area's history of seal hunting and conservation. The **Koala Conservation Centre** (tel. 5956

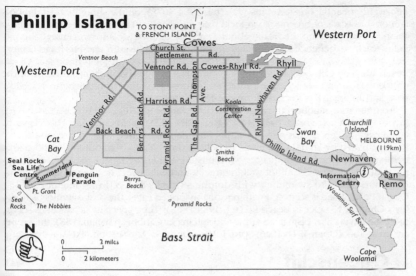

Phillip Island

TO STONY POINT & FRENCH ISLAND

Cowes

Western Port

Western Port

Ventnor Beach

Church St.
Settlement Rd.

Ventnor Rd. Cowes-Rhyll Rd.

Rhyll

Ventnor Rd.

Harrison Rd.

Berry's Beach Rd.

Koala
Conservation
Center

Rhyll-Newhaven Rd.

*Cat
Bay*

Back Beach Rd.

Pyramid Rock Rd.

The Gap Rd.

Thompson Ave.

Smiths
Beach

Swan
Bay

Churchill
Island

TO
MELBOURNE
(119km)

Seal Rocks
Sea Life
Centre

Summerland

Penguin
Parade

Berrys
Beach

Phillip Island Rd.

Newhaven

Information
Centre ⓘ

San
Remo

Pt. Grant

Seal
Rocks   The Nobbies

Pyramid Rocks

Woolamai Surf Beach

N

0   1 miles
0   2 kilometers

Bass Strait

Cape
Woolamai

8691) on Phillip Island Rd, between the Cowes, is an excellent sanctuary housing 23 koalas in eucalypt canopies. *(Open daily 10am-6pm. Admission $5, children $2, families $12.)* The torpid marsupials are most active at feeding time, 90 minutes before dusk. An elevated platform permits closer inspection of the koalas in their natural habitat.

Throughout the year—but particularly in summer—Phillip Island offers great outdoor recreation. Surfers swarm to the island's southern coast; ask the staff at the information center for the *Surfing Guide to Phillip Island,* with information about all the island's 15 surfing beaches. **Island Surfboards,** 147 Thompson Ave (tel. 5952 3443), can set you up with equipment and provide excellent instruction (2hr. lesson $20). Bushwalking trails crisscross the island, ranging from casual to hard; the info center's pamphlet *Discover Phillip Island Nature Park* covers it all.

▨ Mornington Peninsula

South of Melbourne and St. Kilda, a thick spit of land projects out and around the eastern and southern edges of Port Phillip Bay. As Melbourne suburbs give way to summer beach resort communities, the distinct atmosphere of the Mornington Peninsula becomes apparent. A wine-producing region with excellent bushwalks, the peninsula almost fuses with the Bellarine Peninsula, which flanks Port Phillip Bay to the west. It is possible to cross the strait between the peninsulas by ferry.

SORRENTO From the tip of the Mornington Peninsula, sunny Sorrento beckons visitors to relax among its old sandstone buildings. Though it's dotted with the beachside resorts of the wealthy, the town is friendly to the budget traveler. From Melbourne, take a **train** to Frankston (1hr.; every 15min.), then bus #788 to stop 18 (6 per day, 1½hr., $6.60). If you're coming from the Great Ocean Road, you can reach Sorrento via **ferry** from Queenscliff, on the Bellarine Peninsula (1hr.; 9 per day, 6 in winter; $7 per person, $36 per vehicle with 2 people). Along Sorrento's main drag, **Ocean Beach Road,** you'll find a **National Bank ATM, markets, and a post office** (16 Ocean Beach Rd; open M-F 9am-5pm; postal code 3943).

The town's main attraction is its bottle-blue bay, which is popular for surfing, swimming, and sailing in summer. The most popular area is **Back Beach,** which is free and open to the public, though there's a parking fee ($2-4). Numerous companies operate boat trips to sight **dolphins,** and some even let you down into the water to swim alongside the cagey, squeaky creatures. Bells Hostel can advise on the best trips, and the

information center on St. Aubins Way (tel. 5984 5678), on the shore next to the boat launch, has scads of brochures on local tour companies. The first white settlement in Victoria took place on the beach about 5km east of Sorrento's town center. The pioneers' rocky experience is chronicled in the **Sorrento Museum and Heritage Gallery** (tel. 5984 0255), just outside the roundabout at the corner of Melbourne and Ocean Beach Rd. The gallery's historical paraphernalia includes boomerangs, totems of the indigenous Kulin people, cigar cutters and camisoles dating from Sorrento's wealthy past, and an original water cask from the 1803 settlement.

From the roundabout at the inland end of Ocean Beach Rd, head up Osset St and follow the YHA signs to reach **Bells Hostel** (tel. 5984 4323), on Miranda Rd. This YHA-affiliated backpackers retreat provides a tidy kitchen and inviting sofas in a wood-paneled lodge warmed by an old-fashioned pot-bellied stove. There's an outdoor patio with a barbecue and spruce dorm quarters with ensuite baths. The hostel operators can transport you to the area's beautiful walking tracks, and will secure discounts on everything from horse rides to swimming with dolphins (bunks $14, YHA nonmembers $17). Ocean Beach Road is scattered with reasonably priced cafes, the best of which is **Buckley's Chance,** 174 Ocean Beach Rd (tel. 5984 2888). Their specialty is pancakes served in exotic flavors like Tasmanian apple and sultana or Caribbean banana ($8); the crepes are great, too. (Open M-Th 10am-8pm, F 10am-9pm, Sa 9am-9:30pm, Su 9am-9pm.)

■ Queenscliff

The posh hamlet of Queenscliff perches perilously on the easternmost tip of the **Bellarine Peninsula,** 120km southwest of Melbourne, attached to the mainland by a thin spit of ti-tree covered land. Queenscliff underwent a series of incarnations during its first few turbulent years, first as a major fishing village, then as an important military outpost, and finally as a resort village for Victoria's elite. The last of these stuck, and the area was nicknamed "the Queen of the South," and the "playground of the gentry." It's unfortunate that this reputation has scared away most wallet-conscious travelers, since a few hidden gems make it possible to stay here as cheaply as anywhere and have a rare and fantastic experience of resort living to boot.

While most of the accommodations in Queenscliff are stratospherically expensive, the newly YHA-affiliated **Queenscliff Inn B&B,** 59 Hesse St (tel. 5258 4600), has a hostel wing that offers an elegant but affordable taste of the town's luxury. Set in a red brick 1906 Edwardian building, the Inn is centered around its gorgeous drawing room where there's an open fire, free coffee and tea, and mulled wine in the winter. A delectable complimentary breakfast is served at 8:30am, and there's a communal kitchen for other meals. (Bunks $15; single $15; doubles $50; family rooms around $70 depending on number of guests. Linen included.) The grand old **Queenscliff Hotel,** presiding regally over the bay and replete with stained glass and intricately patterned tiles, served as a summer resort for hoity-toity Victorians since the town's earliest days. You probably can't afford the rooms or the main dining room, but the casual hotel bar **Mietta'** provides a chance to pretend you can. The smoked salmon sandwich is light and fresh ($5.50), salads are crisp and delicious ($3.50), and the grilled fillet of steak is the best of them all ($13.50).

While not officially on the **Great Ocean Road,** Queenscliff is a distinctive and characterful place to start off a drive there; head down the Mornington Peninsula along Hwy 3 to Sorrento and take the ferry across the bay (see **Sorrento,** p. 521). If you have a little time in town for a great adventure, contact **Sea-All Charters,** 26 Santa Monica Blvd (tel. 5258 3889), which conducts snorkeling tours to the middle of the bay where you can swim with a colony of playful Australian fur seals and, conditions permitting, wild dolphins. The four-hour, environmentally conscious tours include all equipment as well as light refreshments. ($50, children $40. Depart at 1pm.)

■ Geelong

Geelong (ja-LONG), an hour southwest of Melbourne on the Princes Hwy (Hwy 1) at the western end of Port Philip Bay, is an important transportation hub for the **Great Ocean Road** and points west. While most people just pass through, it's a pleasant, if not particularly exciting, place to spend a few hours, with a gorgeous bayside district punctuated by the Cunningham Pier. If you have a little while to wait for a train, **Johnston Park,** just across the street from the V/Line station, has lots of green space and shady trees. If you've got a little longer, head east along Brougham St to the corner of Moorabool to the **National Wool Museum,** in a historic bluestone wool store. The topic may seem pedestrian, but it's surprisingly fascinating, with live weaving demonstrations as well as interactive displays illustrating the centrality of the wool industry in Australian history and folklore. (Open daily 10am-5pm. $7, concessions $5.80, children $3.50.) The building also houses the **tourist information center** (tel. 5222 2900), with info about Geelong and Victoria as a whole (open daily 9am-5pm).

Impressive woolliness notwithstanding, the **V/Line Station** (tel. 13 22 32), on Brougham St, remains Geelong's most important building to most travelers. Trains run to Melbourne ($8.40), Ballarat ($9.60), Bendigo ($28.40), and Warrnambool ($23.80). The **post office,** 99 Moorabool St, is near the museum (open M-F 9am-5:30pm, Sa 9am-noon; postal code 3220). Several **banks** with **ATMs** line Moorabool and Malop St (banks open M-Th 9:30am-4pm, F 9:30am-5pm).

For accommodations, trek south out of the V/Line station down Fensick St for two blocks, then turn right (west) on Ryrie St, which will eventually turn into Aberdeen, signalling the beginning of Geelong's accommodation district. There are tons of motels and B&Bs here, but the best of the bunch is **Irish Murphy's,** 30 Aberdeen St (tel. 5221 4335; fax 5223 3055). Located above a great Celtic pub, Murphy's has small but clean kitchen facilities, renovated bathrooms, and a deck with fab views of the bay. (Bunks $14, $17 with doona and towel; twins $17 per person, including linen and towel; doubles $40, including linen and towel.) Guinness pints are $4 during happy hour (daily 9-10pm, F also 5-7pm), and live Irish bands perform W-Su nights, stopping at 1am in deference to guests. The **Riverglen Caravan Park,** 75 Barrabool Rd (tel. 5243 5505), 5km southwest of Geelong center, in Belmont, is the cream of the campervan crop, with sites for only $8.

Diagonally across Johnston Park, at the corner of Gheringhap and Lt Melop St, the **Courthouse Cafe** (tel. 5229 3470) is a cool spot for a quick coffee or full meal right near the train station. The outstanding salads ($4) are loaded with fresh ingredients, you can dine al fresco on their wooden deck, and there's free Internet access (open M-F 10am-6pm). **Gilligan's,** 100 Western Beach Rd (tel. 5222 3200), has the best fish 'n' chips in town. The daily special gets you two pieces of fresh fish, fries, and a soft drink for $5 (open M and W-Th 11am-7:30pm, F-Su 11am-8pm). At **Smorgy's** restaurant, at the end of Cunningham Pier, you can sip fancy cocktails and ogle sweeping views of placid, blue Corio Bay (open Su-Th 10am-10:30pm, F-Sa 10am-midnight).

GREAT OCEAN ROAD

The entire serene and spectacular southwestern coast of Victoria, from Torquay east to Portland, is encompassed by the Great Ocean Road (GOR) region, though the road itself is just the 200km stretch that links Torquay to Warrnambool before being absorbed by the Princes Highway. The Victoria government, in tribute to Australians who died in World War I, commissioned the coastal highway with the intention of creating one of the world's greatest drives. By all accounts, they succeeded, carving a route that winds between misty temperate rainforests and the unearthly pillars, stone arches, and gorges sculpted by the Southern Ocean.

The 73km stretch from Anglesea to Apollo Bay is particularly striking, as the moist ocean winds confront the brooding forest barrier of the **Otway Ranges.** The resulting cool, rainy climate nurtures tree ferns, large pines, waterfalls, and a range of fauna, all of which surround the extensive network of walking trails traversing the park.

Heading west, the first part of the Great Ocean Road is called the **Surf Coast,** stretching from Torquay to Lorne. Surfers here must equip themselves with wetsuits to stay warm, while bathers find the friendliest swimming areas by the larger towns. After Apollo Bay, the hub of the Otways, the drive turns inland across Cape Otway, rejoining the shoreline at the **Shipwreck Coast.** Here, unrelenting winds, unpredictable offshore climes, and inconvenient limestone formations turned the region into a graveyard for 19th-century vessels. Near Pt. Campbell lie the famous **Twelve Apostles** rock formations and the wreckage site of the *Loch Ard.* Moving further west, a handful of attractions make the drive worthwhile: right whales off **Warrnambool,** mutton birds in **Pt. Fairy,** and estuary fishing in **Lower Glenelg National Park.**

GETTING AROUND THE GREAT OCEAN ROAD

If you're lucky enough to have a **car** to explore the Great Ocean Road, you're, well, lucky, as public transport won't get you everywhere you probably want to go. **Bicycling** along the highway is a possibility, but make sure your legs are in shape for it: the hilly topography between Torquay and Lorne provides better exercise than any Stairmaster. Public transportation from Melbourne via **V/Line** (13 22 32) requires a pitstop in Geelong, where you can board buses heading to points west (Torquay and Lorne, M-F 4 per day, Sa-Su 2 per day; Apollo Bay M-F 3 per day, Sa-Su 2 per day). On Fridays throughout the year and Mondays in December and January, the "coast link" V/Line bus services Lorne, Apollo Bay, Pt. Campbell, and Warrnambool, with brief stops in tourist lookouts along the Shipwreck Coast. **Bellarine Transit** (tel. 5223 2111) sends approximately 3 buses a day from Geelong to Torquay.

Several **bus tours** from Melbourne to Adelaide allow travelers to take their time sampling the southwest coast, with layovers en route. **Oz Experience** (tel. (02) 9368 1766; fax (02) 9368 0908), based in New South Wales, runs from Melbourne to Adelaide, allowing you to hop on and off for up to six months, for $147 (5% discount for YHA members). **Wayward Bus** (tel. 1800 882 823 or (08) 8232 6646; fax (08) 8232 1455), based in South Australia, operates a three-day adventure with more structure; $160 pays for lunches, planned pitstops, and accommodations. Short day and overnight trips that cover lots of ground quickly are also very popular. **Let's Go Bush Tours** (cool name! No affiliation, though) gives you dinner, breakfast, and accommodation plus a loaded itinerary for $85 (tours Jan.-July M, W, and Sa; Aug.-Dec. Sa only). **Otway Discovery Tours** guarantees a koala sighting in its one-day, pack-your-own-lunch tour ($50). The two-day **Natural Discoveries Ecotour** (tel. 9629 3848) limits its groups to 9 persons who accompany a guide in a 4X4 vehicle; a rainforest-by-night tour and log cabin accommodations are highlights (Tu, Th, Sa; $135 includes breakfast, dinner, and overnight stay). **Autopia Tours** (tel. 9326 5536) organizes one- to three-day tours ($50-125).

Several useful publications on the Great Ocean Road are available at tourist offices and bookstores throughout Victoria. The free glossy *The Great Ocean Road* provides factual information, but not much advice. The National Park Service's *Map Guide: SouthWest* has reliable maps and sample short-term itineraries. *Great Ocean Road: A Traveller's Guide* is another option.

■ Torquay

Wave seekers and beach bums who feel like you've wandered a little too far south from Byron Bay, take heart: there's great surfing to be found in Victoria, and Torquay, at the eastern end of the Great Ocean Road, is the center of the action. Among the excellent sites is world-famous **Bell's Beach,** home to the longest-running **pro surfing** competition, the **Rip Curl Pro Classic,** held every Easter.

ORIENTATION AND PRACTICAL INFORMATION Most commercial activity takes place along the Surfcoast Highway, a continuation of the Great Ocean Road, or just off the highway on Gilbert St, a well-marked shopping district. There, you'll find ATMs and several food options. **Tourist information** is available behind the towering Quicksilver World headquarters at the Surfcoast Plaza. **V/Line buses** (13 22 32) leave from outside the Barnell Caravan Park by the Nomad's hostel for Geelong (M-F 4 per day, weekends 2 per day) and points west. **Bellarine Transit** (5223 2111) provides additional bus transport to Geelong.

ACCOMMODATIONS AND FOOD Book two weeks in advance for the Easter surfing competition and a day ahead the rest of the year for a bed at **Nomad's Bell's Beach Backpackers**, 51-53 Surf Coast Hwy (tel. 5261 7070; fax 5261 3879) a brand-new hostel with a pronounced surfing mood set by posters, Nintendo, cushy sofas, and magazines. This brightly painted bungalow-style bunkhouse offers new mattresses and immaculate bathrooms, lockers, linen, bikes, tea, coffee, and good vibrations. Transport from Melbourne can be arranged (dorms $17; doubles $40). If Nomad's is booked, travel 20min. south to the **Anglesea Backpackers** (see **Torquay to Lorne,** p. 525), or to Fairhaven's **Surf Coast Backpackers,** 5 Covan Ave. (tel. 5289 6886; M-F $12, Sa-Su $15). Hordes of surfers with the munchies provide a large market for the pizza and nacho joints which dominate Torquay's food scene. The **FoodWorks** supermarket on Gilbert St (open daily 7am-midnight), and **Spooner's,** a cheap and tasty cafe between Nomad's and Quicksilver, are healthier choices.

SURF, SAND, AND SHOPPING Peak season for surfing spans from March to August. The reef breaks at **Bell's Beach** attract the top professional surfers for the Rip Curl Classic at Easter. It's a 10-minute drive from town, a half-hour bike ride, or an hour walk along the **Surf Coast Walk,** which winds past some stunning cliff views and terminates at Airey's inlet. The walk passes **Jan Juc,** the second-best surfing site around and also safe for swimmers. For more proximate swimming, cross the highway from Nomad's and continue straight ahead for 10 minutes to **Cozy Corner, Torquay Front Beach,** or **Fisherman's Beach.**

The colossal **Rip Curl World Headquarters** (tel. 5261 0000) presides over a string of surfer retailers and a pair of secondhand shops around the corner; most operate daily 9am to 5pm. Behind Rip Curl the worthwhile **Surfworld** (tel. 5261 4606) has a hall of fame of Australia's most venerated surfers, as well as interactive displays on wave physics, different kinds of breaks, and surfing history. *(Open daily 10am-4pm. $6, concessions and Nomads patrons $4.)*

■ Torquay to Lorne

The turnoff to **Point Addis** appears abruptly about 5km out of Torquay. The point offers some of the most outstanding views of Victoria's western coastline, serrated by silty clay and gray cliffs. Choppy winds usually preclude beach swimming in this area. Between Point Addis and the highway is the beginning of the recently cleared **Koorie Walk,** which leads through the **Ironbark Basin Reserve.** Displays along the walk elucidate the ways of life of the Koorie Aboriginals who once inhabited the area. Red ironbarks and peregrine falcons are natural highlights; the park recommends visiting in the early morning or late afternoon.

If you've somehow managed to avoid seeing **kangaroos in** the wild so far, Anglesea will correct that problem, as a very large troupe of them lives on the golf course just a kilometer from the main road. (Kangaroos are rarely seen in checkered polyester pants, however.) From the town center, pass the rotary and the bridge and turn right on Noble St. **Anglesea Backpackers** is also on Noble St, just ½km up (tel. 5263 2664; dorms $15). An uninspiring **information caravan** is by the river in the car park.

■ Lorne

The resort town of Lorne enjoys an admirable location, flanked by a popular surf and swim beach and a temperate rainforest. The National Parks Service has routed several manageable walking tracks through the **Angahook-Lorne State Park,** a 21,000 hectare reserve known for its waterfalls and bird variety. The Great Ocean Road morphs briefly into the Mountjoy Parade as it passes through town.

Buses depart daily from the Commonwealth Bank on Mountjoy Pde. to Geelong (1½hr, $10.90) and Melbourne (2½hr, $21.30). Buses to Apollo Bay leave on Saturday and Sunday only (1hr, $4.80). **Banks** with ATMs are also in the complex (Open M-Th 9:30am-4pm, F 9:30am-5pm). **Ridgeway's supermarket** (tel. 5289 1645) is just across the Erskine River on the Melbourne side of town at 1 Great Ocean Road. The **post office** (tel./fax 5289 1405) is nearby in the Cumberland Resort complex on the southwest end of Mountjoy (open M-F 9am-5pm).

The idyllic **Great Ocean Backpackers** (tel. 5289 1809) is on Erskine Ave, which leaves the main road between the supermarket and the bridge as you approach town from the Melbourne direction. The facility is a colony of wood cabins set on a hillside in the midst of the forest. A chorus of birds performs at dusk, followed by the arrival of possums for a feeding on the kitchen patio. The staff knows every walk in the park, and will even give you a lift to the trailhead of a one-way walk. Book in advance, especially in high season. (Free linen and laundry. Dorms $15, YHA non-members $17. Christmas through January, $23-27.) **Campgrounds** without amenities are available inside the park (tel. 5289 1732; $6 fee paid to a roving ranger). Or travel 10km west to the beautiful riverside **Cumberland River Camping Reserve.** (tel. 5289 1790; $10 per site or $66 weekly; cabins $35-45).

■ Near Lorne: Angahook-Lorne State Park

The two most popular stops in Lorne's forest reserve are **Teddy's Lookout,** a sweeping view of the countryside, and **Erskine Falls.** Teddy's is a half-hour walk from Lorne; walk up Bay St and turn left on George St. Erskine Falls is for the more industrious, requiring a fairly steep three-hour climb with several river crossings along the way. Feeling wimpy? The walk only takes five minutes if you first drive for 15 minutes via William St and Erskine Falls Rd. Various simple tracks begin at the **Sheoak Picnic Area,** an hour walk or 15-minute drive up Allenvale Rd from Lorne; off the main road, take the first right after the bridge and turn off the rotary after circling 270 degrees. **Lower Kalimna Falls** (1hr. round trip) takes you beneath a waterfall, which you can see from above if you take the walk entitled **Upper Kalimna Falls** (1½hr.). Along Allendale Rd, inside the park, you can visit **Qdos** (tel. 5289 1989), an art studio and gallery of humorous and bizarre pieces. (Open Th-Tu 10am-dark).

If you're into guided tours, try **Otway Ocean Tours** (tel./fax 5232 1081), which offers 4WD trips through forest and hinterland ($50). **Otwild Adventures** (tel. 5289 1740 or 5236 2119) runs rock climbing, canoeing, and bushwalking tours of varying lengths. You can paddle with a platypus in a rainforest.

■ Apollo Bay

Apollo Bay is the gateway to **Otway National Park** and **Cape Otway** to the west. Lobstering is the primary industry, although many sea creatures are hauled in. The Otway Ranges, one of the highest rainfall areas in the country, provide a lush, hilly backdrop for Apollo Bay, a slightly upscale resort town. Culinary options benefit from traces of international influence. **Triplet Falls,** near Laver's Hill, is a three-tiered waterfall reached by taking Beach Forest Rd from Lavers Hill, turning right onto Phillips Rd, then following signs on unsealed roads. Picnic tables and barbecue are available.

At night, **glow-worms** emerge to slither through the verdant undergrowth. To see the light, try your luck in most parts of Otway National Park, or take a tour and be led right to them. Tours leave from **Willow Bryn** (tel. 5237 6791 or 5237 6493) at the end of the Barham Valley Rd., north of Apollo Bay on the road to Paradise. Tours begin at dusk every night. ($5, children $2).

The **Tourist Information Centre** (tel. 5237 6529; fax 5237 6194) is on the Great Ocean Road. The staff will book accommodations and arrange tours (open daily 9am-5pm). **Buses** leave Apollo Bay from the **Westpac bank** on Collingwood St. There are daily buses to Lorne (1hr., $4.80), Geelong (2½hr., $17.50), and Melbourne (3½hr., $20.60). Buses to other points along the GOR operate on Fridays only. The town has a **post office** (open M-F 9am-5pm, postal code 3233), and a Rite-Way licensed **supermarket** (open M-Su 9am-6pm), also on the highway.

Pisces Caravan Park (tel. 5237 6749; fax 5237 6326), on the east side of town on the GOR, has powered and unpowered sites, cabins, and bunks. (Dorms $12, YHA nonmembers $15; sites $12 and up. Barbecue, laundry, playground, kitchen.) **Apollo Bay Backpackers** 47 Montrose St (tel. 5237 7360 or (04) 1932 2595), is another option, but closes during winter (dorms $15). **Surfside Backpackers** (tel. 5237 7263) at GOR and Gambier St, has dorms ($15) and doubles ($35-45). The **Wholefood Shop,** 139 GOR (tel. 5237 6995), will leave you wholly satisfied, with options ranging from samosas ($1.40) to latte ($2). (Open daily 8:30am-6pm; coffee till 7pm.)

■ Around Apollo Bay: The Otways

The Otways stretch 60km west of Apollo Bay and encompass three major parks: **Otway National Park, Otway State Forest,** and **Melba Gully State Park.** Within the cool, temperate rainforest, myrtle beech trees will shade you while tree ferns dominate the eye-level scenery, occasionally animated by swamp wallabies, ring-tailed possums, and gray kangaroos. Misty waterfalls cascade down the steep hillsides to form clear creeks in the valleys, sometimes diffusing into marshy bottomlands. **Mait's Rest** walk is one of the best known walks in Victoria; beginning 17km west of Apollo Bay along the GOR, it's a 30-minute self-guided intro to the temperate rainforest.

Shortly after Mait's Rest along the GOR is the turnoff for the **Cape Otway Lightstation,** built in 1848 on the terminus of Cape Otway as a beacon for ships attempting the western approach to Bass Strait. The lighthouse stands on the southernmost spit of land along the entire approach, and can now be seen through a guided tour (tel. 9237 9240). The hour-long tours provide interesting historical information and magnificent views. (Tours every 30min. 9:30am-4:30pm. $6.)

Maps of the Otways' many well-marked walks are available at the Apollo Bay Tourist Information Centre (see above) or at the **Apollo Bay National Parks Office** (tel. 5237 6889). Several companies offer guided tours, including **Otway Eco-Guides** (tel. 5237 7240), which has an interesting "Bushfoods and Medicine" walk (2½hr., $20).

There are three recommended **camping** areas in Otway National Park. In summer, you may pitch at **Blanket Bay;** follow Lighthouse Road, then watch signs for a left turn (tel. 5237 6889; sites $8), The **Aire River West** camping area is reached from the GOR another 5km west by way of the Horden Vale turn-off. The Aire River is suitable for swimming, and three walks emanate from the grounds. For **surfing,** check out **Johanna Beach,** which also has a free camping area, though swimming is ill-advised. Take the sealed Johanna Rd from the GOR.

■ Port Campbell

Port Campbell, the only safe harbor from Apollo Bay to Warrnambool, is a sleepy fishing village on one of the nastiest yet most picturesque coastlines in the world. This most treacherous stretch of the **Shipwreck Coast** has claimed hundreds of lives and was once feared by mariners around the world. The town provides a good base for diving, fishing, or scenic boat charters. It also holds the headquarters of the **Port Campbell National Park,** which preserves many of the strange and wondrous rock formations that shivered the timbers of so many ships. The **Twelve Apostles** (formerly known as the Sow and Piglets, and today including just seven disciples) is the most famous of the formations, though many others are just as interesting. Be sure to stop off at Gibson Steps, just before the Twelve Apostles, where you can descend to the beach and view a stack from sea level. The **Razorback,** for example, is a long spine of rock, perforated in many places and serrated along the top. The Bay of Martyrs and Bay of Islands have many tall columns of rock which, like some of the Apostles, occasionally tumble into the sea.

> ### Why London Bridge Fell Down
> The bizarre rock formations you see around you didn't spring up overnight, but they are a relatively recent geological phenomenon. Pt. Campbell National Park is founded upon layers of soft limestone which have amassed from marine animal remains. Over thousands of years, the wind, seawater, and rain have eroded the softer strata, leaving only the firmer, more resistant rock that has spelled the demise of hundreds of ships. The wind plays a critical role, as gusts destroy coastal vegetation and expose the shoreline to the erosive force of the tides. In the process of forming the Twelve Apostles, for example, waves curling into the sides of jutting cliffs bored tunnels, which in turn left archways. These archways eventually collapsed, leaving the solitary stacks that still stand. The London Bridge formation displays an intermediate stage of this erosion process. It was once conjoined with a second arch that linked it to the mainland. In 1990 the other arch collapsed—leaving two tourists stranded—explaining why it is no longer really a bridge. So before you climb carelessly about, remember: Peter may have been called the Rock, but *these* Apostles represent only the shakiest of foundations.

The **National Park Information Centre** (tel. 5598 6382), on the corner of Morris and Tregea St, is one block from the GOR (open daily 9am-5pm). The Port Campbell **Discovery Walk** shows off many of the town's extraordinary natural features. The gentle 2.5km circuit begins at the cliff base at the western end of the beach, or at the car park west of the bay. Obtain brochures at the Information Centre, along with a map to supplement the numerous signposts. The **post office** (postal code 3269) is in the superb **General Store,** on the GOR. The small **Shipwreck Museum** (tel. 5598 6463) along the highway is mostly a gift shop, but also does bookings for **Port Campbell Boat Charters** (tel. 5590 6411), which offers crafts for diving, fishing, or sight-seeing expeditions. (Open 9am-5pm. Admission $4.) A **scuba** and marine center (tel. 5598 6499) is next to the General Store.

The **YHA Hostel** (tel./fax 5598 6305), just down the road from the museum at 18 Tregea St, was recently renovated and features a marvelous, large kitchen, a lounge with a wood stove, coin-operated laundry, and small showers. Very popular with tour buses and other groups, so be sure to book ahead during the summer. (Bunks $12, $15 for YHA non-members; $5 key deposit.) There is a **caravan park** (tel. 5598 6492)with barbecues, showers, and laundry next to the national park information center on Morris St (sites $13, powered $16).

■ Warrnambool

Warrnambool is the self-proclaimed capital of the Shipwreck Coast. The city may lack the historical charm of towns further west, but in this remote region urban amenities are priceless. Plus, from May to October, you can see southern right whales without even leaving the docks. The whales combine with the usual sand and surf to make Warrnambool a popular holiday destination.

ORIENTATION AND PRACTICAL INFORMATION

The city is built around the Princes Hwy (called **Raglan Parade** in town) and envelops Warrnambool Bay (a.k.a. Lady Bay). The bay is bounded by the Merri River on the west and the Hopkins River on the east. The **Warrnambool Visitor Information Centre,** 600 Raglan Pde (tel. 5564 7837; fax 5561 2133), provides excellent free maps of the district and city, marked with points of interest (open daily 9am-5pm). The **West Coast Railway Station** is just north of Lake Pertrobe on Merri St. There are rail links with Geelong (2½hr., $23.80) and Melbourne (3½hr., $33.20; both destinations M-F 3 per day; Sa-Su 2per day). **V/Line buses** depart from South Western Roadways on Raglan Pde. and head to: Ballarat (2½hr., M-F 1 per day, $17.50); Mount Gambier (2½hr., daily, $26.10); Portland (1½hr., daily, $11.90); and Port Fairy (30min., M-F, $4.20). **Coast Link** to the eastern towns on the Great Ocean Road runs only on Fridays (also M Dec.- Jan.).

Bank offices can be found at 140 Karoit St (open M-Th 9:30am-4pm, F 9:30am-5pm), and another ATM on the corner of Laura and Liebig St. For police call 5562 1111. The post office is on the corner of Timor and Gilles St (open M-F 8:45am-5pm; postal code 3280).The APCO service station, 485 Raglan Pde, is a 24-hour gas station and Hertz car rental center ($65 per day and up).

ACCOMMODATIONS AND FOOD

In summer, book ahead. **Great Ocean Road Backpackers,** 17 Stanley St (tel. 5562 4874), has comfortable dorm beds and excellent extras. Arriving from the Melbourne direction, turn left on Danyan St, continue onto Petrobe St (60° around the rotary), and go right onto Stanley St. A courtesy bus runs to and from town every 20 minutes on weekend nights. The management runs free and discounted tours to Tower Hill and points on the GOR. The front room is BYO-licensed, and can get noisy on summer weekends, but the back bunkrooms are quiet. (Dorms $15; key deposit $10. Free barbecue, lockers, linen, enormous kitchen, and cable TV.) The **Stuffed Backpacker,** 52 Kepler St (tel. 5562 2459), is in the middle of town, just off the Ragland Pde. It's a no-nonsense, no-frills establishment with clean showers, ample parking, small kitchen and lounge with a fireplace and TV, and a *laissez-faire* attitude (bunks $14; toast and coffee included; key deposit $5). Just down the street, the **Western Hotel Motel,** 45 Kepler St (tel. 5562 2011; fax 5562 4324), has 30 beds spread among 15 rooms, offering more privacy than the other budget options (dorms $12; singles $15). There's a **pub** on the ground floor (counter meals $5-6; breakfast $2).

For midnight munchies, the **Coles supermarket** (tel. 5561 2957) on Lava St is always open. **Fishtales,** 63-65 Liebig St, specializes in fish, vegetarian pasta, and Asian food (most dishes under $10; open daily 8am-8pm; BYO; eat in or takeaway).

SIGHTS AND ACTIVITIES

The most popular thing to do in Warrnambool is to watch whales. This has spawned many cetacean-themed gift shops and an entire tourism sub-industry. The information center has booklets on the continuously tracked **southern right whales.** Every winter in late May or June, a population of whales stops just off **Logans Beach,** to the east of Warrnambool Bay, to give birth to their calves. They stay until September or October, when they return to the Antarctic to break their five-month fast. Viewing platforms have been built above the beach to protect the delicate dune vegetation, and tourists gather to watch the beasts roll, blow, and breach. These right whales used to be hunted in large numbers all along the Victorian coastline, but have now been protected for several decades. Whale watching is much more fun if you have some sort of visual amplification (binoculars, telescope, or a nice telephoto lens). A common error is to look too far out to sea; the whales often swim very close to shore. A right whale is easily distinguished by its lack of a dorsal fin, the peculiar shape of its head and jaw, and its unique V-shaped spout.

Warrnambool's other great tourist attraction is the **Flagstaff Hill Maritime Museum** (tel. 5564 7841), on Merri St. *(Open daily 9am-5pm. Lighthouse open 11am-5am. Admission $9.50. Concessions $8. Children $4.50.)* The museum, a re-creation of a late 19th-century coastal village, includes a few original edifices as well as artifacts from wrecked ships, including the fabulous Schomberg Diamond. The **Loch Ard peacock,** taken from the wreck of the *Loch Ard* in 1878, is located in the Public Hall. Only two people survived the wreck, but this giant ceramic fowl escaped with only slight beak damage. It shouldn't take more than a few hours to wander the grounds, but admission includes a second day. A series of interesting video presentations is shown in the **Interpretation Centre** (at the entrance complex); schedules are available from the front desk.

On the road between Warrnambool and Port Fairy, the main attraction is the **Tower Hill State Game Reserve,** situated in a volcanic crater. The reserve swarms with koalas, kangaroos, emus, possums, echidnas, and Cape Barren geese. It is possible to drive right through the crater, but to really get a good look at the wildlife, try one of the many walking paths around the reserve.

■ Port Fairy

In 1826, by the best reckoning, **Captain James Wishart** of the cutter *Fairy* first sailed into the mouth of the River Moyne in search of potable water. Neither wish nor art produced great water, but the commemoration of his voyage did give the 1843 port settlement a permanent Tinkerbell complex. From the 1850s to the 1880s, Pt. Fairy was the busiest Australian port outside Sydney, loading ships with wool headed for Mother England. Activity has slowed considerably since. More than 50 old buildings have been preserved by the National Trust, giving Pt. Fairy a distinctive O.K. Corral sort of feel. A booklet with historical details and a walking tour map of many of these buildings is available from the **Tourist Information Centre** (tel. 5568 2682) on Bank St (open daily 9am-5pm). Occasionally, members of the Port Fairy Historical Society conduct tours of the buildings; inquire at the visitor information center.

Like most of Victoria's southwestern coast, Port Fairy claims its share of shipwrecks. A total of 30 boats were lost near Port Fairy, and six of them can be observed along the **Shipwreck Walk.** To mitigate future disasters, a lifeboat station and rocket house were built in 1873 and 1888, respectively. Tours of the station are available on most Sundays. Book at the information center.

A lighthouse still stands on **Griffith's Island,** the site of the old whaling station. The short-tailed shearwater, known as **mutton birds** because early colonists fed on them during starvation years, colonize the island from the end of September to April. Their nesting rituals, visible just after dusk from a viewing platform and at the less crowded **Pea Soup Colony** down the road, are a popular spectatle. Every year, thousands of birds fly back and forth over the Pacific, spending eight months of the year on the island. After the 15,000km flight to North America the birds rest briefly, then fly right back. If you are resourceful, you can arrange a visit to **Lady Julia Percy Island,** 19km out in the Bass Strait, where seals, fairy penguins, and peregrine falcons dwell. Try **Mulloka Cruises** (tel. 5568 1790 or 1852 9827), which stations at the harbor.

For budget accommodation, try the **YHA Hostel,** 8 Cox St (tel. 5568 2468). The hostel is in a house built by Port Fairy's first official settler, William Rutledge (the "King of Port Fairy"), and includes TV and a communal kitchen. Sleeping bags are not permitted on the mattresses, as the owners fear vermin from the backcountry. It is essential to book well ahead for March, when the hostel fills completely. (Beds $13, YHA nonmembers $16.) In fact, almost every bed on the Shipwreck Coast is hired out in March, during the **Port Fairy Folk Festival.** Call 5568 2227 for festival information and order tickets many months in advance to avoid disappointment.

Port Fairy's whaling days are long gone, but there is still a large fishing fleet. Fresh crayfish and abalone can be bought along the **Fisherman's Wharf** on the Moyne. The

---

Wanted: Sunken 16th-Century Portuguese Ship
Reward: $250,000

In 1522, **Cristovao de Mendonca,** a Portuguese adventurer, may have sailed a mahogany caravel along the east coast of Australia and mapped much of the coastline. Thus, some historians argue that the Portuguese were in fact the first Europeans to discover Australia. But thanks to 16th-century diplomatic arguments and the Lisbon earthquake of 1755, the Portuguese records are lost forever. A French map of a southern land called Java la Grande was published in Dieppe in 1547, but since many of the names appear in Portuguese, some think that the French map was actually plagiarized from de Mendonca's original charts. But de Mendonca lost more than his potential claim to the first map of Australia; his mahogany ship crashed on the coast somewhere between Warrnambool and Port Fairy. Since the first sighting of the wreck in 1836, many claim to have spied it, but the constantly shifting coastline has kept it obscured and it has drifted into legend. So when walking this stretch of coastline, keep alert, and perhaps the legend will be verified. The ship's finder, after all, can collect the $250,000 reward still posted by authorities in Warrnambool.

town has recently become an artists' haven, and has therefore developed a lively **cafe** scene; the town center is thick with them. Don't miss the **Kitehouse,** 27 Cox St (tel. 5568 2782), which sells any kind of kite or wind sock a windy day deserves, rents **bicycles,** and provides tours and tourist information.

Buses leave from Bank St near the info center and head to Warrnambool (3 per day, $4.20), Melbourne (daily, $35.40), Geelong (daily, $28.40), and Portland (3 per day, $8.40). The **bank** at 51 Sackville St has an **ATM,** with a **supermarket** next door. The **post office** is at 25 Sackville St (open M-F 9am-5pm; postal code 3284).

■ Near Port Fairy: Mt. Eccles National Park

Some 20,000 years ago, igneous activity formed Mt. Eccles, and the volcanic turbulence continued until about 7000 years ago. Because the volcano is so young, many of its topographical features are in excellent condition, not yet muted by the forces of weather, vegetation, and time. Although not particularly astonishing, **Lake Surprise** is pleasant for strolling around and swimming in—though if the volcano decided to erupt again, any swimmers would be quickly boiled alive, since the lake fills the three largest of Eccles' craters. Maybe that's the surprise.

The point of entry to the park is **Macarthur,** which is about 40km north of Port Fairy and 30km south of **Hamilton.** The latter township is on the Hamilton Hwy, which runs west from Geelong. Within the park, well-marked walking tracks lead to several interesting relics of the mountain's volcanic past. The **lava cave** was formed as the top skin of a lava flow hardened into rock. The liquid stone then flowed out from underneath this roof, forming the broad cavity present today. A small section of roof has collapsed, allowing visitors to explore the pitch-black interior of the cave. At the **lava canal,** the entire roof has collapsed, leaving a trench of igneous rock.

Thick **manna gum woods** cover parts of the slope, providing habitat for elusive, crabby **koalas,** who are most active in the evening. About 50 years ago, the northwest slope of the mountain was quarried for scoria (the porous volcanic rock that makes up much of the slope). Thankfully, this destructive land use was put to an end when the area was declared a national park in 1960. The **Crater Rim Nature Walk** includes all of these topographical features, and is detailed in a pamphlet available from the **tourist information center** (tel. 5576 1338). The center's rangers can also provide camping permits and information about the bushland surrounding the park.

■ Portland

Maritime history buffs may take pleasure in Portland's storied past; most travelers will focus more on the beds and parking spaces that make it a hub for the **Great South West Walk, Discovery Bay National Park,** and **Lower Glenelg National Park.** The area was a base for whalers, sealers, escaped convicts, and other colorful characters before the Henty brothers and their sheep enterprise permanently settled it in 1834.

PRACTICAL INFORMATION The **Portland Visitor Information Centre** (tel. 5523 2671; fax 5521 7287), located near the waterfront on the corner of Bentinch and Cliff St, can provide maps of **historic building walking tours** (free port tours depart information center Sa 1 and 2 pm; open daily 9am-5pm). The information center is also the trailhead for the popular **Great South West Walk.** The **Natural Resources and Environment (NRE)** information center midway up Julia St, which runs down to the port, is another useful resource (open M-F 9am-4:30pm). **Commonwealth Bank** has offices on the corner of Henty and Percy St (open M-Th 9:30am-4pm, F 9:30am-5pm). **ATMs** are at 90 Percy St. Two **V/Line buses** per day connect Portland to Port Fairy (1hr., $8.40) and Warrnambool (1½hr., $11.90). On Fridays (plus M Dec.-Jan.), buses run to Port Campbell (2½hr., $21.30), Apollo Bay (4hr., $33.20), and Lorne (5hr., $37.80). There is a **post office** at 108 Percy St (open M-F 9am-5pm; postal code 3305).

ACCOMMODATIONS AND FOOD The **Garden Hotel** (tel. 5523 1121), 63 Bentinck St, provides good budget accommodation close to the info center and waterfront. The pub downstairs is complete with an electronic gambling den (bed and breakfast $20). Most hotels provide standard-issue counter meals for around $5. **Sunstream** (tel. 5523 4895), 49 Julia St, is a healthy choice with bins of oddities inside, and tasty lentil burger with salad roll-ups (sandwiches $4-5; open M-F 9am-5pm; Sa 9am-1pm).

ACTIVITIES   Although fairly reliable today, the port was in olden times a death trap, and many ships came to grief in or near the Portland Harbor. Many of these are memorialized along yet another **Historic Shipwreck Trail,** which begins at Moonlight Head and stretches to the South Australian border (brochures available at the information center). Shipwrecks, kelp forests, and delicate corals make the waters near Portland a delight for **snorkelers and divers.** Many shops offer equipment and instruction. Try **Duck Dive Scuba,** 57 Bentinck St (tel./fax 5523 5617). For a very different kind of tour, check out the **gigantic aluminum smelter** (tours tel. 9923 2071) cunningly landscaped to soften the aesthetic blow delivered by metal-processing plants. This "Smelter in the Park" is a great example of environmentally conscious design.

Starting and ending at Portland's information center, the looping, 250km **Great South West Walk** rambles along the coast, then doubles back through the **Lower Glenelg National Park.** The walk traverses a variety of terrains and provides a grand introduction to the wildlands of southwest Victoria. Daytrips can access sections as short as 8km. Detailed maps and guided tours are available at the Portland visitor information center. For safety, register with the center staff before setting out.

A few kilometers west of Portland at Cape Bridgewater, the Great South West Walk passes through a robust cliff trail leading to a **seal colony.** A little farther along (by road; it's quite a walk by the path), the **"petrified forest"** looms. True petrification involves direct replacement of vegetable matter with mineral, while this is a rock formation that formed in the cavities left behind when the trees rotted away. Nevertheless, it creates an eerie effect and is well worth a look. At the foot of the sea cliffs, pockets of stone have been weathered by the waves, forming channels that direct the incoming swells high into the air and cause loud booming sounds. These **blowholes** can be spectacular if the tidal and meteorological conditions are right. Or they can, well...blow. The salt mist often blows ashore, stunting the growth of beach vegetation. The area is currently undergoing rabbit-baiting and revegetation campaigns.

■ West of Portland: Lower Glenelg and Discovery Bay National Parks

Covering nearly 36,000 hectares, these two parks preserve a variety of terrain, including forests, heath, rivers, swamps, dunes, and cliffs, supporting diverse plant and animal life. As Victoria gives way to South Australia, the characteristic eastern species are supplanted by western ones. **Nelson** is the nearest base for exploring these parks; the town is about 30km southeast of Mt. Gambier, just inside Victoria. **Portland** is much larger, and provides easy access from the east.

Lower Glenelg National Park

Limestone dominates the topography of the Lower Glenelg National Park, and for 15km near the mouth of the river, the flowing water has cut a deep gorge, with banks as high as 50m. Many caves have been formed by percolating rainwater or underground watercourses. The largest and most spectacular of these (and the only ones open to the public) are the **Princess Margaret Rose Caves** (tel. (08) 8738 4171), located 2km east of the South Australian border and about 15km south of the Princes Hwy, where a short bush walk begins as well. (Cave tours 5-7 times daily except Fridays in winter; $4.20, children $1.60.) The caves area also features a few nature walks, a large, wooded picnic area with barbecue, and limited camping facilities (both tent sites and on-site caravans). Camping arrangements must be made before 5pm with the ranger at the Caves Information Center. The Glenelg estuary, the longest in Victoria, is one of the prime fishing spots in the country, populated by mulloway, bream, mullet, salmon trout, and perch. Boats and gear can be rented in Nelson.

The **Glenelg River** is usually calm, deep, and wide, making it ideal for tranquil **canoeing.** Four days of paddling can bring you all the way from Dartmoor, on the Princes Hwy, to the mouth of the river at Nelson. This 75km stretch of river supports 11 campsites along the way, most of which cannot be reached by automobile. Permits are required and can be obtained at the Department of Conservation, at the **Forests and Lands Information Center** (tel. (08) 8738 4051), on Forest Rd in Nelson. This office can also answer questions about river conditions and canoe rental. If you are short on time, you needn't canoe the entire 75km stretch, since there are numerous boat landings along the way. The **National Park Office** (tel. (08) 8738 4051) operates on Forest Rd, inside the park.

Discovery Bay Coastal Park

Discovery Bay Coastal Park stretches 55km from Portland to the South Australia border. Fickle weather patterns make it very important to plan carefully for your adventures in the park's long seashore, dunes, marshes, and lakes. Red emu markers point the way along the **Great South West Walk.** There's plentiful surf fishing at **Nobles Rocks,** 7km from Nelson. Connecting the sea to freshwater lakes and swamps are mobile dunes up to 20m high; be sure to stay on the marked walking tracks. An extensive lakes system welcomes fishing, swimming, boating, and close-up views of pelicans, swans, and ducks. Look for (from east to west) **Bridgewater Lakes,** reached by the road from Portland; **Swan Lake,** up a steep gravel road off the Portland-Nelson Rd; and **Long Swamp,** a 3km walk from Nobles Rocks.

GOLDFIELDS

In 1851, the first year of Victorian statehood and just two years after the California gold rush, gold was discovered in the unassuming burg of Clunes. A year later, the London *Times* reported that 50,000 diggers had already converged on Victoria's goldfields. And to the chagrin of Victorians who had taken pride in the fact that free persons had settled in Victoria before convicts had, ex-convicts from Van Diemen's Land floated over as well. Gold was to prove the great equalizer of classes, as convicts hardened by years of manual labor dug up ore more efficiently than their effete bourgeois counterparts, and the silk-clad, genteel landed gentry soon found themselves having to rub elbows with an unpedigreed nouveau riche. The established classes did not allow this social shakeup willingly, forcing the government to invoke mining taxes and grog prohibition, factors which ultimately led to the brief and bloody Eureka Rebellion of 1854. The Victorian prospectors eventually extracted more ore than even the Californian '49ers, but by the end of the 19th century, the mines were largely exhausted, and most of the boom towns withered away to ghost towns. A few, such as Ballarat and Bendigo, remain substantial cities, and others, such as Castlemaine and Maldon, have been preserved as historical relics. These remaining cities and townships of the Goldfields region, occupying the central area of western Victoria, afford travelers the opportunity to enjoy the recreated gold rush spectacles, a handful of wineries, and the hurly-burly frontier spirit that grew out of this short wave of settlement but went so far in shaping Victoria's—and Australia's—national character.

■ Ballarat

Victoria's largest inland city (pop. 83,000), Ballarat is the self-appointed capital of the Goldfields. The most important of the boom towns during the gold rush, it clings to its gracious 1850s image. Although the gold is long gone, much of the 19th-century architecture has been preserved, and the city's golden past has been parlayed into a bustling tourist trade. Huge, elegant Victorian buildings line the main street, and more than 60 buildings in town have been recognized for historical architecture by the National Trust. But the main attraction is Sovereign Hill, a reconstructed gold town built around a mine. The town has also gained fame among gardeners for its begonias. Ballarat is a favorite for schools, churches, and other groups looking for an educational holiday.

It was here in Ballarat, which lies an hour northwest of Melbourne by the Western Highway, that Australia had its closest brush with civil war in the early morning hours of December 3, 1854. An uprising over miners' rights ended in a bloody 15-minute clash, which came to be known as the Eureka Rebellion and remains an emblem of Australian populism. Ballarat retains the memory of this event by billing itself "the birthplace of the Australian spirit."

ORIENTATION

Ballarat straddles the Western Highway, which is called **Sturt St** as it runs through town. The **train station** is a few blocks north of Sturt on the cross street **Lydiard St.** From the station, turn left on Lydiard and cross **Mair Street** to get to Sturt St. The **tourist center** is a couple of blocks east of Lydiard on the corner of Sturt and Albert St. Just past the tourist office, Sturt becomes **Bridge Mall,** a pedestrian mall with shops, restaurants, and a large supermarket complex. Local buses congregate out front. To the east of the mall, the Western Highway becomes **Victoria St. Main Rd** curves off Victoria St to the south; this becomes **Geelong Rd,** where you will see signs for Sovereign Hill to the west. **Eureka St** branches off Main Rd to the east, leading to the **Eureka Stockade** and a caravan park and swimming pool.

PRACTICAL INFORMATION

Tourist Information Centre: Corner of Sturt and Albert St (tel. 5332 2694 or 1800 648 450; fax 5332 7977; email tourismb@netconnect.com.au). From the V/Line station, walk south along Lydiard St to Sturt St, turn left, and walk east to the corner of Albert St. Blue signs point the way. Maps $1. Open daily 9am-5pm.

Trains and Buses: V/Line (tel. 13 22 32) operates passenger trains and coaches from Ballarat Station at 202 Lydiard St N (tel. 5333 4660), to Melbourne (1hr., $26.00), and Daylesford (½hr., 1 per day, $8.40).

Local Buses: For information, call 5331 7777. Most routes depart from the Bridge Mall at the eastern end of Sturt St. For Ballarat Station, take bus #2. For Sovereign Hill, take bus #9 or #10. For the Botanical Gardens and Lake Wendouree, take bus #9 or #15. Services typically run every 30-35min., less frequently on weekends. Student discounts. Full bus schedules are available at the Tourist Information Centre.

Taxis: Ballarat Taxis (tel. 13 10 08) operates 24hr. Service from the city center to Sovereign Hill is about $4.50. Up to 5 people can share a cab.

Currency Exchange: There are many banks and **ATMs** along Sturt St. National is at 329 Sturt St (tel. 5331 1700). Open M-Th 9:30am-4pm, F 9:30am-5pm.

American Express: 37 Sturt St (tel. 5331 1144). Offers a range of travel services, but does not hold mail. Specializes in Qantas bookings. Open M-F 9am-5pm.

Laundromat: 711 Sturt St (tel. 5333 6746). Wash $2, dry $1. Open 6am-10pm.

Public Toilets: On either end of the Bridge Mall at the eastern end of Sturt St.

Hospital: St. John of God, 101 Drummond St (tel. 5331 6677). **Ambulance:** tel. 5311 4400.

Bookstore: Book City, on Sturt St, is open M-F 9am-7pm, Sa-Su 10am-5pm.

Swimming Pool: Outdoor pool on Eureka St (tel 5331 2820) reserves 2 lanes for lap swimmers. Open Sept.-May M-F 7am-7pm, Sa-Su 9am-7pm.

Emergency: tel. 000.

Police: (tel. 5337 7222). On Camp St, across Sturt St from the tourist center.

Post Office: (tel. 5331 4744; fax 5331 7642), on the corner of Lydiard and Sturt St. Poste Restante and **fax** services. Open M.-F 9am-5pm. **Postal Code:** 3350.

Phone Code: 03.

ACCOMMODATIONS

Ballarat's accommodations market is aimed more at Melburnian families on weekend trips than at international backpackers. If you happen to strike it rich while in Gold

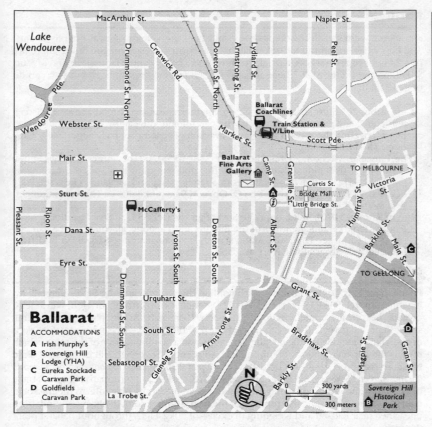

Country, try one of the palatial bed and breakfasts on Lydiard St. Hapless diggers will have to make do with one of several cheaper options.

Sovereign Hill Lodge (YHA) (tel. 5331 1944; fax 5333 5861), on Magpie St. Follow signs to Sovereign Hill, which this hostel overlooks, then to the lodge from Geelong Rd, a continuation of Main St. Take bus #9 or #10 from Sturt St to Sovereign Hill. The buildings retain an 1850s style, but have recently been refinished and are in excellent condition. Amenities include a full kitchen, pool, TV lounges, ping-pong tables, and a bar with good prices (VB $2). Issues tickets for all Sovereign Hill events. 24hr. reception. Checkout 10am. The old military barracks have been converted into dorms ($18, $16 with YHA). Breakfast $4. Book ahead for holidays or weekends, especially between Christmas and New Year's. V, MC, AmEx.

Irish Murphy's, 26 Sturt St (tel. 5331 4091; fax 5331 2289), just downhill from the tourist office. Above a relatively authentic Irish pub, clean doubles come with free tea, coffee, and live music Th-Sa nights. $14 per person, $17 with a cozy comforter.

Ballarat Goldfields Holiday Park, 108 Clayton St (tel. 5332 7888; fax 5332 4244), 300m from Sovereign Hill. Follow the signs to Sovereign Hill from downtown. Pricey new cabins, kitchens, recreation rooms, and tent sites. $9 for individuals, $14 per couple, $16 with power; $5 refundable key deposit.

Eureka Stockade Caravan Park (tel. 5331 2281,) on Stawell St, off Eureka St. Basic caravan park next to a large water slide/mini-golf compound. Facilities include barbecue, laundry, and access to an Olympic-sized pool. Reception staffed daily 8am-7pm. Tent sites $11, powered $13, on-site caravans $25-45 per couple. V, MC.

FOOD

Sturt St is lined with fish and chips shops, milk bars, and other takeaway establishments. The best **cafes** are up the hill, especially at the corner of Dawson and Sturt. There are two 24-hour **supermarkets,** a produce shop, and a bakery at the far eastern end of Sturt St behind the Bridge Mall. There are also several fast-food restaurants, but you can do better than that.

Cafe Bibo, 205 Sturt St (tel. 5331 1255). Mediterranean snack food and pasta. Excellent coffee and cakes reward those who can tolerate the campy magazine advertisements covering the walls. Takeaway is available. Focaccia $6. BYO. Open Su-W 8am-6pm, Th-Sa 8am-midnight.

The Pancake Kitchen, 2 Grenville St (tel. 5331 6555), on the corner of Lewis St in a restored 1870s building. Bottomless coffee and pancakes in assorted incarnations ($1.50-12). The bottom floor features an open fireplace and a gigantic chess set. Fully licensed, or 80¢ corkage fee for BYO. Open M 9am-midnight, Tu-Th 10am-midnight, F-Su 7:30am-1am.

Inn of Khong, 519 Main Rd, opposite Sovereign Hill (tel. 5331 4088). The dining room features large ceramic figurines of the Buddha and a generic, all-you-can-eat Asian buffet ($9). Chinese, Thai, and Malaysian dishes, most under $10. BYO and fully licensed. Takeaway and delivery available.

SIGHTS

People have long come to Ballarat with gold on their minds, and the **Sovereign Hill** living museum (tel. 5331 1944; fax 5331 1528), while it won't make you rich, will at least provide historical commemoration. *(Open daily 10am-5pm.)* Actors playing miners mill about in period garb, and you can marvel as a $50,000 gold ingot is poured before your eyes. Exhibits include candle-making, smelting, and a 40-minute tour of the mine which reveals the harsh conditions of mining life. Adjacent to Sovereign Hill is the small **Gold Museum** (tel. 5331 1944) on Bradshaw St. *(Open 9:30am-5:20pm. Combined admission to the museum and Sovereign Hill is $17.50, students $13, children $9.)* Informative displays trace the function and importance of gold from the slave pits of the pharaohs to the microcircuitry of today. There are also replicas of the two largest gold nuggets ever found, both unearthed near Ballarat and weighing in excess of 60kg. Signs throughout Ballarat point the way.

The remains of the **Eureka Stockade** are propped up on Eureka St. The flimsy stockade commemorates the miners' resistance in the Eureka Rebellion of 1854. State forces easily suppressed the uprising, but the general discontent eventually led to important reforms in Australian government. The fallen rebels are commemorated by an impressive bluestone memorial.

The Eureka rebels fought under the Southern Cross flag, the remains of which are at the **Ballarat Fine Art Gallery** (tel. 5331 5622), 40 Lydiard St, north of Sturt St. *(Open daily 10:30am-5pm. Guided tours available. Admission $4.)* For many years, foreign dignitaries who visited Ballarat were presented with pieces of the flag. Unfortunately, the tradition has left this symbol of Australia's patriotism tattered. The gallery also houses a fine collection of regional artwork.

The **Ballarat Wildlife Park** (tel. 5333 5933) is located on the corner of Fussel and York St. *(Open daily 9am-5:30pm. Guided tours at 11am. Admission $10, students $7.50, children under 15 $4.50.)* Take York St off Main Rd midway between Sovereign Hill and Eureka St. The park's 15 hectares of open bush are home to some of Australia's diverse fauna, including flesh-rending saltwater crocodiles and Tasmanian devils, and less imposing emus, goannas, wombats, koalas, and free-roaming 'roos.

Less wild but just as entertaining is the **Great Southern Woolshed** (tel. 5334 7877), located several kilometers east of Ballarat toward Melbourne on the Western Highway. *(Open daily 9:30am-5pm. Admission $9, students $7, children $4.)* A shrine to the sheep industry (Australia has the world's largest), this gigantic shed is insulated with several inches of wool and is thus cool in summer and warm in winter. Cheer for rams on parade, buy wool souvenirs, and witness the speed and skill of the modern shearer as one lamb is

One for All and All for Gold

When miners first started working the Ballarat goldfields, the pickings were easy. Alluvial gold, weathered from upstream rocks, was visible to the naked eye in riverbeds and could be mined with nothing more than a shovel and pan. As the easy gold ran out, prospectors began searching for buried riverbeds that might contain gold covered by accumulated deposits. Miners formed small collectives and pooled their resources since individuals could not afford the necessary equipment. By 1854, deep lead mining had largely replaced surface methods. As mines went deeper the cost of the supportive timbers and other equipment needed for their maintenance rose, and profitability declined. Once the majority of the deep leads had been exploited, miners turned to quartz reef mining, a capital-intensive method that extracted gold from quartz ore. Much of this mining occurred below the water table, so massive steam-driven pumps were required to keep the miners from drowning. As with most mining operations, this proved extremely dangerous, and roughly two miners lost their lives each week. WWI marked the end of such intensive mining.

unceremoniously stripped. Don't leave before experiencing the **Waltzing Matilda 3D holographic historical diorama.**

Portions of Ballarat retain their gold rush charm and are excellent for evening walks. **Lydiard St** in particular is famous for its Victorian streetscape. Several companies offer guided tours of Ballarat's historic areas. Try **Timeless Tours** (tel. 5342 0652) or **Golden Heritage Walks** (tel. 5333 1632). The **Botanical Gardens** next to Lake Wendouree are also popular with joggers and cyclists. The annual **Ballarat Begonia Festival,** held in early March, is an open-air fair featuring arts and crafts.

For evening entertainment, the **Bridge Mall** at the east end of Sturt St fills with pedestrians and street musicians on weekends. Numerous hotels and pubs serve as venues for live bands. Popular with locals, the **Provincial Hotel** at 121 Lydiard St features pool and video entertainment. At 13 Lydiard St, the historic **Her Majesty's Theatre** (tel. 5333 5888) presents live drama nightly. *(Tickets available through Majestix.)* **Blood on the Southern Cross** (tel. 5333 5777), a dazzling 80-minute sound and light show, is a must-see. It first introduces viewers to life on Sovereign Hill and then tells the bitter tale of the Eureka Rebellion. *(M-Sa, plus Su during holiday periods. Bookings are essential, and require credit cards with less than 2 weeks notice. Admission $20.50, full-time Australian students $15.50, under 15 $10.50.)*

■ Near Ballarat: Vineyards

Most vineyards in the Ballarat wine region began production in the 1980s. With cool climate chardonnays increasingly in the mode among connoisseurs, it's regarded as an up-and-coming area. Expect a warm reception at these young vineyards, as every traveler is seen as a potential customer. Pick up the glossy *Wine Regions of Victoria* pamphlet in state and local tourist offices. In addition to wineries, the **Enfield State Park** is nearby, 25 minutes south of Ballarat on the Colac-Ballarat Rd. Mining relics are scattered here, as are 61 species of orchids and all the typical fauna. Spring wildflower season is the best time to visit.

Dulcinea Vineyard

Owner and regional promoter Rod Stott says his philosophy is "I believe in education." This means he will be on sight to answer all your questions, urging you to roam through his small cellar and the vineyard, tasting his delectable blends as you go. The delicate, fruity 1996 gold-medal Chardonnay is first-rate. Take the Glenelg Hwy 15 minutes south from Ballarat. *(Open daily 9am-5pm; bottles $15-15; tasting free.)*

St. Anne's Vineyards

St. Anne's (tel. 5368 7209) is 22km from Ballarat and 77km from Melbourne off the Western Hwy. Free tastings are available in a cool, cobwebbed wooden cottage. A peppery red shiraz and tawny port head the list. *(Open M-F 9am-5pm, Sa-Su 10am-5pm.)*

■ Daylesford and Hepburn Springs

Feeling disharmonious? Picking up negative vibrations? Energies out of alignment? If so, the twin townships of Daylesford and Hepburn Springs could be the answer. This region contains the largest concentration of mineral springs in Australia. The springs have been in use since before European settlement, but the scores of guest cottages and B&Bs have sprung up recently, as New Age culture has infused these quiet communities with healing crystals, essences, oils, and aromatherapy. Stressed Melburnians frequent these hillside retreats and the associated gourmet and specialty shops all year. The spa complex is in Hepburn Springs, while most of the restaurants and services are in Daylesford. Victorian tourist offices distribute the free pamphlet *Macedon Ranges and Spa Country*.

ORIENTATION AND PRACTICAL INFORMATION

Daylesford is 107km northwest of Melbourne and 45km northeast of Ballarat. **V/Line buses** depart for Melbourne (4 per day M-F, 2 per day Sa, 1 per day Su; $11.90) and Ballarat (3 per day, $8.40) from **Little's Garage** at 45 Vincent St, in the heart of Daylesford. The **Tourist Information Centre** (tel. 5348 1339) is located several blocks south of the garage and has a listing of local accommodations and information on masseurs, healers, and other indulgences (open daily 9am-5pm). Next door, find the **post office** at 86 Vincent St (tel. 5348 2101; **fax** service available; open M-F 9am-5pm; postal code 3460). **Public phones** are located outside the post office. ANZ and Commonwealth **banks** are both on Vincent St, and the latter has an **ATM** across from Little's Garage. **Hepburn Springs** is about 2km north of Daylesford. Buses run between the two towns throughout the week ($1.50), but it is an easy, pleasant walk.

ACCOMMODATIONS AND FOOD

Most of the area's lovely guest cottages and B&Bs will set you back $80-100 per night. The **Hepburn Springs Caravan Park** (tel. 5348 2297) is considerably cheaper, and closer to the springs (tent sites $8, with power $10). **Continental House,** 9 Lone Pine Ave (tel. 5348 2005), described by some of its patrons as a living work of art, hides behind a dense 5m hedge just a few hundred meters from the spa. Refresh yourself at this strictly vegetarian, strictly relaxed guesthouse with large, tranquil common areas (singles $18, doubles $40, call ahead for reservations). The Continental House's resident eatery, the **Strange Fruit Cafe,** provides biodynamically and organically sound meals for guests on Saturday nights or when the place is busy.

Other spiritually enlightened aliments are found at **Naturally Fine Foods,** 59-61 Vincent St (tel. 5348 3109), which sells mountainous veggie burgers ($6), veggie pies and cakes, and bulk dried goods. **The Food Gallery,** 77 Vincent St (tel. 5348 1077) caters to both carnivores and herbivores. The Rite-Way **supermarket** is open daily 8am to 5pm.

SIGHTS AND ENTERTAINMENT

Most visitors come to Hepburn Springs seeking the curative properties of its waters. The **Hepburn Spa Resort** (tel. 5348 2034; fax 5348 1167), next to the springs, provides the works. Services are pricey, but spring waters are free.

The highlight of Daylesford center is the **Pantechnicon Art Gallery,** 34 Vincent St, which rotates its highly varied contemporary exhibits. *(Open F-M 11am-5pm.)* In Daylesford, the **Wombat Hill Botanical Gardens** are pleasant for strolling, while the **Pioneer Memorial** tower on top of the hill affords views of the rolling countryside. The excellent **Convent Gallery** (tel. 5348 3211) occupies the side of the hill and showcases local artwork. *(Open 10am-6pm. Admission $3.)* The 19th-century convent has been beautifully restored as a gallery and landscaped with lush, terraced gardens.

The **Hepburn Regional Park** surrounds much of Daylesford and Hepburn Springs and lures tourists with its excellent walking trails and picnic areas. Some relics of the gold rush days are visible, but others are less so—take care to avoid plunging into an abandoned shaft. Trail maps are available at the tourist information center.

■ Castlemaine

Castlemaine, 120km northwest of Melbourne in the central goldfields, peaked early as a boom town in the heady days of the gold rush. Since then, it's faded into a sleepy, provincial burg with only a single street light. But while it can't offer the bustle of goldfield neighbors Bendigo or Ballarat, it does have some good—if mellow—drawing points: the blossoming of fantastic polychromatic gardens in spring, a surprisingly vital arts scene, and an unhurried, altogether unpretentious atmosphere.

ORIENTATION AND PRACTICAL INFORMATION To get to Castlemaine, take a bus from Melbourne's Spencer St Station (9 depart daily). From Castlemaine, **V/Line** has bus and train service to Melbourne ($14.80), Bendigo ($4.20), Maldon ($2.40), Ballarat ($13.40), and Maryborough ($6). By car, take Hwy 79 (Calder Hwy) to Elphinstone, then Hwy 122 (Pyrenees Hwy) to Castlemaine—plenty of signs will guide you. **V/Line** originates from the **railway station** (open M-F 6am-8pm, Sa 7am-3pm, Su 9:30am-7:30pm) at the north end of Kennedy St and faces the town center.

Kennedy, Barker, Hargraves, and Urquhart Streets run north to south, and Templeton, Lyttleton, Mostyn, and Forest Streets run east to west. Barker St is the main drag, and its intersection with Mostyn St forms the corner of a big park that marks the town center. The **tourist office** (tel. 5470 6200) is a kiosk located on the Pyrenees Hwy just a block from where it becomes Forest St. (Open M-F 10am-4pm, Sa-Su and holidays 9am-5pm; lists of accommodations posted outside for after-hours perusal.) There's also a town map at the corner of Barker and Lyttleton St. Castlemaine's **post office** is at 202 Barker St (open M-F 9am-5pm). **Internet access** is available at the public library (tel. 5443 5100; open M, Tu, and Th 10am-6pm, W and F 10am-8pm, Sa 9am-noon).

ACCOMMODATIONS AND FOOD It's tough to grab a cheap bed in Castlemaine; you'll fare better in less expensive Maryborough (44km west) or Melbourne. However, if you've got money to spare, and you don't mind human agony being converted into novelty accommodation, incarcerate yourself in the **Old Castlemaine Gaol** (tel. 5470 5311; fax 5470 5097), on Bowden St, atop the hill to the west of the railroad station. The 1861 jail held inmates until 1990, when it was renovated as a well-heated and ventilated B&B. The iron catwalks and small cells of the gaol have been preserved, and the latter, now carpeted, contain 130 bunks that allow guests to slumber in the slammer. Dungeons, once the site of horrific torture, now house a wine bar and lounge with billiards and TV. If you're not staying here, it's worth taking a self-guided tour anyway ($4). (F-Su nights only. $45 for bunk and continental breakfast, $65 with dinner. Reserve 1 month in advance if possible.)

A simpler accommodation is the clean, quiet **Botanic Gardens Caravan Park** (tel. 5472 1125), with laundry facilities, toilets, a 50m pool, picnic, and barbecue. (Tent sites $8.50 single, $10 double. Powered caravan sites $10 single, $11.50 double. On-site caravans $26 single, $31 double. Cabins with bathrooms but no linen $40 single, $45 double. Limited wheelchair access.) The **Commercial Hotel,** 16 Hargreaves St (tel. 54 721 173), rents rooms above the pub for $30 per night ($45 double).

Chippers, cafes, and markets run the length of Barker and Mostyn St. **Capone's Pizzeria,** 50 Hargraves St (tel. 5470 5705), relives the memory of the bloodthirsty American crime lord through fancifully named Italian cuisine, such as the "Forgery Fritatta." The less inventively monikered deep-dish pizzas are better, though. (Meals under $10. Open M-Th 11:30am-6pm, F-Sa noon-9pm, Su noon-6pm.) The **Screaming Carrot Cafe,** 16 Lyttleton St (tel. 5470 6555), dishes out alterna-food such as tempeh burgers and the coy "herby nut loaf." For a delectably sweet treat, pick up a can of Barnes' Castlemaine Rock ($3.20 per tin), a golden-colored peppermint candy that has been made in town since the 1850s.

SIGHTS AND ACTIVITIES The Castlemaine **Botanic Gardens,** six blocks north of the railway station at the end of Kennedy St, is one of Australia's best assemblages of flora, with cypress trees, rose bushes, a central pond and barbecue. The biennial **Garden Festival** celebrates the blossoming of the city in November of odd years, alternating with the Castlemaine **Arts Festival,** held in even years. Both festivals attract visitors from all over Victoria. The **Castlemaine Art Gallery and Historic Museum,** 12 Lyttleton St (tel. 5472 2292), between Kennedy and Barker St, is located in a sleek, white 1931 Art Deco edifice. The interior is equally elegant, framing a strong collection of Australian art that focuses on late-18th-century landscapes. *(Open M-F 10am-5pm, Sa-Su noon-5pm.)* The newly renovated **Castlemaine Market Complex,** on Mostyn St between Barker and Hargraves, is a historic market and pleasant courtyard that offers local wares and shady resting spots. Occasional shows feature local artistic and horticultural feats and are free and open to the public.

▓ Maldon

If you stand at the intersection of Main and High Streets in the center of Maldon, surrounded by musty 19th-century buildings with corrugated iron roofs and hand-painted wooded signs, you can close your eyes and almost see old Bloke McCarty, a crusty old prospector, stumbling through the dusty streets with a rusty pan in one hand and a whiskey bottle in the other. Open them again, and you may be disappointed to see yuppified tourists clutching cameras and mineral water. Still, if history's your thing (and if it isn't, why are you in the Goldfields?), Maldon, approximately 20km northwest of Castlemaine, is a necessary stop on your itinerary. It presents the best preserved and most extensive array of gold rush era buildings in the state. The array of tea rooms, country collectible shops, and blacksmiths cater mostly to a somewhat upmarket weekend crowd; some attractions close during the week, so plan accordingly.

ORIENTATION AND PRACTICAL INFORMATION As you reach town, the highway splits into High St (left) and Main St (right). The superb **Visitors Information Centre** (tel. 5475 2569) on High St, in the tan brick building, is an invaluable resource (open daily 10am-4pm). Although Maldon lacks ATMs, the **bank** at 59 High St will **exchange currency** (open M, W, and Th 11am-4pm, F 11am-5pm). To get to Maldon, take the **V/ Line** from Castlemaine (tel. 13 22 32; M-F 2 per day; $2.40, students $1.50). The **post office** is north of the Visitors Centre on High St (open M-F 9am-5pm, Sa 8:30-11am; postal code 3463).

ACCOMMODATION AND FOOD Maldon's B&Bs can be pricey but may be worth a splurge for visitors enamored with the period feel and small town atmosphere. The **Maldon Caravan and Camping Park** (tel. 5475 2344) on Hospital St, northwest along High St, has toilets and barbecue facilities. (Tent sites $5 per person; on-site caravans $29 for 2; cabins $43 for 2. Multiple night discounts.) Behind Main St, the **Derby Hill Accommodation Centre** (tel. 5475 2033) on Phoenix St provides weekend lodging in a funky and functional wood and concrete youth camp. Units include a TV, linens, and a kitchenette. (Singles $35; doubles $60. F-Su only.) The **Historic Bakery** on High St is all the rage but lacks space (meat pies $2). The **supermarket** on High St is open weekdays till 6pm, weekends till 1pm.

SIGHTS AND ACTIVITIES Adjacent to the visitor center, amateur historians may enjoy the **Maldon Museum and Archives** (tel. 5475 1633), which displays local artifacts from the 1850s to the early 20th century. *(Open M-F 1:30-4pm, Sa-Su 1:30-5pm. Admission $2, children 50¢, families $5.)* On Main St, the original **Tarrangower Times** building (tel. 5475 2256) lets you tour the old print machinery and take home souvenirs. For a bird's-eye view of Maldon—and, on a clear day, more than 50km in all directions—follow

High St north to the signs for **Mt. Tarrangower,** which rises 570m above sea level from the geographic center of Victoria. The windblown iron **lookout tower** enables daring souls to ascend an additional 24m. Astonishingly enough, there's a mine you can visit: go south of Maldon, toward Newstead off the Pyrenees Hwy, to **Carman's Tunnel Goldmine** (tel. 5475 2667; open Sa-Su 1:30-4pm). The **Vintage Railway steam train** (tel. 5475 1427), off Hornsby St, north along Main St, runs the 8km trip to Muckleford. *(Two trips W, 3 Su. Return $9, students $7, ages 4-15 $5, families $25.)* **Seasonal highlights** in Maldon include its colorful Easter festivities and the annual influx of musicians and performers for the early November Folk Festival.

■ Maryborough

Zippy, modernized Maryborough contrasts pleasantly with its sleepy central goldfield neighbors. The town's most impressive attraction, the **Maryborough Railway Station,** is a stately Victorian structure somewhat out of place in the suburban bustle. Famous for **Mark Twain's** remark that Maryborough was a railway station with a town attached, the station now serves as the **Central Goldfields Tourist Centre** (tel. 5460 4511; open daily 10am-6pm). Inside, there's an adjoining antique emporium and cafe. **V/Line** (tel. 13 22 32) departs for Melbourne from the car park behind the building on Clarendon St (5 per day, 1hr., $8.60) and Castlemaine (3 per day, 1hr., $5.80). Tickets can be purchased at **Hoober's Meals/Tahiti Coffee Lounge** (tel. 5461 1527) on High St. The **post office** (open M-F 9am-5pm; postal code 3465) is on Campbell St behind the Bull and Mouth Hotel.

Maryborough offers numerous inexpensive accommodations for those interested in visiting nearby Maldon (33km), Castlemaine (43km), and gold prospecting areas. The **Bull and Mouth Hotel** (tel. 5461 1002) on High and Nolan St offers no-nonsense, practical accommodations above the pub. The clean, high-ceilinged rooms come with electric blankets and closets. Mark Twain stayed here during his Maryborough visit. (Singles $18, with bath $25; doubles $30, $37. V, MC.)

■ Bendigo

Bendigo, like almost all the towns in the Victorian goldfields, sprung into existence in the 1850s when scads of miners flooded in, lured by the promise of some of Australia's most lucrative mines. But while many of its neighbors were tossed from prosperity to obscurity by the boom and bust cycle, Bendigo endured. This was due to the longevity of its gold output (25 million ounces of gold were removed from the area between 1851 and 1954) as well as its status as town of choice for many gold magnates. These same magnates used their early gold fortunes to indulge their Victorian fancy, creating public buildings in grandiose Gothic style and forging wide thoroughfares with names like Pall Mall and Charing Cross. These signs of its wealthy past imbue Bendigo with a certain Anglophilic nostalgia, but its continuing status as a major regional social and economic center lends it a vitality that many of its gold-rush relic neighbors lack. Neither too touristy nor too bland, Bendigo is a fun and laid-back place to visit, offering authentic historical charm in an indisputably modern setting.

ORIENTATION

Bendigo is a combination of wide, well-planned streets and winding gold gullies originally packed down by the trampings of diggers' feet. Most points of interest are near the city center, bounded on the south and east by the railroad tracks and on the north by Rosalind Park. The **Calder Highway** (which leads eventually to Melbourne) runs into the center of town, and then veers north and heads to Mildura. At Charing Cross, **High St** (the stretch of Calder Hwy in town) becomes **Pall Mall,** which eventually turns into McRae St. **Rosalind Park** is to the north of this thoroughfare, while **Hargreaves St** runs parallel to the south. **Mitchell St** runs perpendicular to High and Hargreaves, heading south toward the transit center.

PRACTICAL INFORMATION

Tourist Office: 51-67 Pall Mall (tel. 5444 4445, fax 5444 4447, email tourism@bendigo.vic.gov.au, http://www.bendigo.com.au). Located in the ornate Victorian gothic post office building (no longer a post office). Slick, rather cheesy interactive computer displays tell Bendigo's story. Immaculate public restrooms located in back of the building. Open daily 9am-5pm.

Currency Exchange: National Bank, on the corner of Queen and Mitchell St, is open M-Th 9:30am-4pm, F 9:30am-5pm. ANZ bank is at the corner of Pall Mall and Williamson St. Both have 24hr ATMs.

Trains and Buses: Transit Center is in the Market Place Discovery Centre at the south end of Mitchell St. Recorded information is available (tel. 190 2210 857), and reservations can be made statewide (tel. 13 22 32), or at the Regional Center in Bendigo (tel. 5440 2765). You can purchase bus tickets on board if there are empty seats. Once-daily rail and/or coach service goes to Ballarat (Su-F, 2 1/2hr, $17.50), Geelong (M-F, 3 1/2hr, $28.40), Adelaide (8 1/2hr, $49), Mildura (1 per day, 6hr, $45.50), and Swan Hill (1 per day, 2 1/2hr., $22.60). Bookings M-F 5:35am-8pm, Sa 6:50am-6:45pm, Su 7:05am-7pm.

Car Rental: Budget, 150 High St (tel. 5442 2766; fax 5441 5859). **Thrifty,** 29-31 Myers St. (tel. 5441 6448).

Post Office: Corner of Hargreaves and Williamson streets. Open M-F 9am-5pm, Sat 9am-1pm.

Laundromat: View Street Laundry, 41 View St (tel. 5441 8877), next to Rosalind Park.Open daily 6am-9pm.

Public Library: 259 Hargreaves St. (tel. 5443 5100, fax 5441 2247). Books, magazines, and free **internet access.** Call ahead to book internet time if you can, but there are usually free terminals. Open M,W,F 9:30am-8:30pm, Tu,Th 9:30am-6pm, Sa 9am-noon.

Police: Dial 5440 2555. **Ambulance:** Dial 114400.

Emergency: Dial 000.

Phone Code: 03.

ACCOMMODATIONS

The strip of High St (Calder Hwy, or Hwy 79) that runs south of town is loaded with motels, most of which are cookie-cutter links in a corporate chain, though there are some cute indie ones that haven't been made over since the 1960s and look it. You can usually grab a room in one of the latter for around $30-40, but none of them beat the **Central City Caravan Park,** 362 High St (tel./fax 5443 6937), next to the Subaru dealership, about 2.5km south of the Alexandra Fountain. This former YHA affiliate still offers hostel beds; there are two sets of bunks in each of six small rooms, and the owners rarely put more than one party in a room. Bathrooms and a small kitchen are in separate buildings (barbecue and pool available; bunks or shaded sites $12).

Most of the fancy hotels downtown will eviscerate your wallet, but there are a few provide a good deal with an old-school gold-rush feel—pub accommodations are a good bet. Best of these is the centrally located **Old Crown Hotel,** 238 Hargreaves St (tel. 5441 6888), which rents out no-nonsense rooms with squishy, comfortable beds on its second floor (the first floor houses a homey pub; see Entertainment, below). Rooms (all with shared bath) come as cheap as $30, and include a light continental breakfast. To book a room, talk to the bartender.

FOOD

The strong Asian presence in Bendigo, whose history dates to the gold rush migrant labor days, is heralded by numerous Chinese restaurants, whose product is heavily Australianized. There are many good ones to choose from; the **Imperial Palace Food Court,** 2 High St (tel. 5443 4329), is fully licensed, delivers for free, and has freshly prepared lunchboxes ($4.50; V, MC). Most main dishes cost less than $10 (open M-Sa 11am-2pm, also Su-Th 5-10pm and F-Sa 5-11:30pm). Next door, **Jojoe's,** 4 High St (tel. 5441 4471), is fully licensed and has slightly more expensive eclectic cuisine (entrees

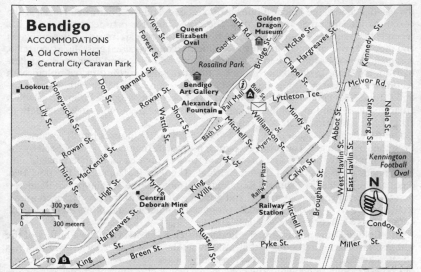

Bendigo
ACCOMMODATIONS
A Old Crown Hotel
B Central City Caravan Park

open daily 5pm "'til late"). For cheap and tasty takeaway, check out the **Turkish Kitchen,** 289 Lyttleton Tce (tel. 5441 1556), with dips, salads, kebabs, and pastries. Almost everything is less than $5 (no seating; open M-Sa 11am-9pm).

Hargreaves Mall, the pedestrian mall along Hargreaves St between Williamson and Mitchell, is a haven for cheap eats. Bendigo's own **Gillies Famous Pies** make a mean steak-and-kidney pie; their window is at the corner of Hargreaves Mall and Williamson St. The **Loaded Dog** doesn't refer to a pooch that's had too many Victoria Bitters; it's an excellent hot dog joint with a vast selection of gourmet sausages and toppings. Try the delectable weisswurst or, if you don't eat meat, the veggie dogs (lunch special: dog and coke $3.70). Across the west end of the mall, **Pure & Natural,** 28 Mitchell St, lets you make your own health-conscious sandwiches, with organic ingredients like avocado, cashews, pineapple, and bell pepper; there are some carnivorous options as well.

Cafe au Lait, 20 Mitchell St (tel. 5443 5126) is a classy, glassy hangout, popular with Bendigo's beautiful people. They serve an array of bizarrely named caffeine beverages ($2-3)—even regular coffee is cryptically termed a "long dark"—and solid breakfast chow in the $5 range. There is a **Safeway Supermarket** in the Bendigo Marketplace, next to the train station off Mitchell St. The nearby **Bendigo Health Foods,** 70 Mitchell St, is an organic green grocer with all kinds of fresh produce.

SIGHTS AND ENTERTAINMENT

The **Alexandra Fountain,** at Charing Cross, where High St turns into Pall Mall, is a massive stone piece over 25 feet high, adorned with fanciful horses and lions' heads which delicately vomit streams of water over the outstretched arms of topless maidens. It's most impressive at night when illuminated by floodlights. Northwest of the fountain rises the slope of **Rosalind Park,** a vast expanse of greenery scattered with winding pathways, statues (including a particularly unflattering likeness of Queen Victoria), and trees. You could easily spend an hour or three getting lost here, but don't miss the incline on the park's west end, where a steep path leads up past a waterfall to an observation tower. Fashioned from a device used to extract miners from caves, the tower is hundreds of feet tall and resembles a gargantuan 3-dimensional trapezoid made out of red steel girders. If you can brave the vertiginous climb to the top, your prize will be sweeping views of Bendigo and the surrounding gold country.

The late-Victorian feel of Bendigo's architecture is most pronounced along **Pall Mall** (pronounced "Pell Mell"), which is littered with more neo-Gothic touches than you can shake a spire at. The best exemplars are the **old post office building** (which now houses the visitors center, see Practical Information, above) and the **Shamrock Hotel,** at the corner of Williamson St and Pall Mall. The hotel, built for prospectors in 1897, has recently been redone in period style down to the last stone archway. Be nice and quiet and they'll let you can sneak into the lobby, decked out in stained glass, hoary portraits, and mahogany banisters. The iron-latticed balcony on the second floor overlooks Bendigo's main drag. Lazy folk are in luck – you can take a tram tour, complete with recorded commentary, using the once-state-of-the-art, restored 19th century tram system (1hr., $7.50, concessions $7, children $4). In keeping with the efforts to establish an antipodean London, double-decker buses also tour the town's major attractions (1hr., $7, concessions $6.50, children $4).

The **Bendigo Art Gallery,** 42 View St (tel. 5443 4991), houses mostly local works from the gold rush era. You won't recognize most of the names or be impressed by the technical mastery, but the assemblage nevertheless provides a nuanced insight into local political development (Theodore King's The First Parliamentary Election, Bendigo) and social history (Thomas Kennington's Homeless). It's a glimpse of Bendigo's past that's vastly more honest, rich, and gripping than any of the pre-packaged tourist stuff. The gallery shop deals in locally produced handicrafts and prints (admission $2, concessions $1; free guided tours daily 2pm).

The **Golden Dragon Museum,** 5-9 Bridge St (tel. 5441 5044), offers a history of the Chinese population in Bendigo that unfortunately glosses over the racism that has affected local Chinese-Australian relations. Still, it's a solid overview of the significance of Chinese culture in Bendigo. The collection's highlight is the fantastically ornate Sun Loong, the **longest imperial dragon in the world,** a ceremonial dragon that's still in full effect during the big parade that punctuates the annual **Bendigo Easter Fair.** Adjacent to the museum are the recently completed and tranquil **Classical Chinese Gardens.** (Museum and garden open daily 9:30am-5pm; museum and garden admission $6, children $3. Garden alone $2, children 50¢.)

The **Central Deborah Mine,** 76 Violet St, was the last mine to operate commercially in Bendigo. Although no longer a commercial mine, it is still operational. Tours take visitors 61m down to the second level where mining history and techniques are explained and, in some cases, demonstrated. On the surface, much of the original processing equipment has been preserved and displayed, including a gigantic, evil-looking stamper battery (mine tours start at 9:30am daily and cost $15, concessions $13, children $7.50). Combined mine/tram tickets cost $20, concessions $18, children $10. The whole Central Deborah tourist empire is open daily from 9am to 5pm.

Pubs are everywhere, usually marked by the ubiquitous "Carlton Draught" sign, advertising the local brew of choice. Most are tame local hangouts which close around midnight or 1am. The **Old Crown,** 284 Hargreaves St, is a neighborhood haunt filled with families by day and burly locals at night. On weekends, it's open later than most pubs (2-3am) and there's live music (cover $2). Thursdays and Saturdays are big for Bendigo's nightclubs (Fridays tend to be rather tame). On the corner of Hargreaves and Williamson streets you'll find three stories of after-hours madness. The bottom floor houses **Jack Daniel's Cafe,** a basic pub, with late-night food, billiards, and the occasional band (no cover). The upper floors comprise the glitz-o-rama **Eclipse** with two DJs – Top 40 on the second floor, dance remixes of club classics on the second. It's open to all ages before 11pm; if you're over 20, you'll enjoy it more when the hordes of teenagers depart (cover $2-5, open 'til 5am). **Studio 54,** 2b Queen St, strives hard to match the legendary debauchery of its New York City namesake; in fact, it's a warehousish two-story dance venue where Bendigo's 20-somethings cruise and dance their pants off to house and watered-down hip-hop remixes (open 'til 5am; cover $2 before midnight, $5 after).

THE MALLEE

West of the Goldfields, inland Victoria rises among the rugged peaks of Grampians National Park before slowly settling into an immense plain that stretches to the southeast of South Australia and north into New South Wales. The Mallee draws its name from the plant that populates its blasted plains, the *mallee eucalypt,* a hardy water-hoarding tree that thrives in the semi-arid environment. This flat expanse is often taken for wasteland by the uninformed observer, but the region is actually extremely productive agricultural land, full of sheep, cattle stations, and vineyards. The Mallee's many lakes and waterways teem with fish and attract a steady stream of anglers. Agricultural pressure, increasing salinity, and the introduction of alien species like goats, cats, and bees, are steadily eroding the once vast areas of mallee scrub. Unlike the oft-lamented clearing of rainforest, the destruction of this seemingly desolate habitat has proceeded without much public outcry. The region extends north of the Grampians to Little Desert National Park, a sanctuary for threatened species of flora and fauna. The river-wrought region west of Little Desert is sometimes known referred to as the Wimmera. It stretches just over the border of South Australia, the Coonawarra region boasts some of Australia's most-lauded vineyards, and the Naracoorte cave system and Bool Lagoon arc of interest to naturalists the world over. These sites, as well as the South Australia towns of Naracoorte (see p. 422) and Mount Gambier (see p. 423), are traditionally considered part of the Wimmera.

■ Ararat

In 1857, a party of 700 Chinese miners discovered gold at the **Canton Lead,** causing a massive influx of people—20,000 in two weeks—and spawned the settlement that would become Ararat. Today, the tiny hamlet lies at the intersection of the Western and Pyrenees highways. There's little here to justify any sort of detour, but its site makes Ararat ideal as a stopover on the way to, or a base camp for, trips to the **Grampians (Gariwerd) National Forest** (25km to the east, see p. 546).

PRACTICAL INFORMATION Barkly St, the strip of the Western Hwy that runs through town, is Ararat's main drag. The **tourist information center** (tel. 5352 2096; fax 5392 1695), located in Town Hall Square on Barkly, can provide information on any of the town's attractions and recreational opportunities (open M-Sa 9am-5pm, Su 10:30am-3pm). The **post office** is at 93 Barkly St (postal code 3377; open M-F 9am-5pm). 24hr ATMs are scattered up and down Barkly. **V/Line buses** to and from Ararat stop at the BP Station at 10 Ingor St. Buses run to Ballarat (4 per day, $10.90), Stawell (2 per day, $3.30), Melbourne (4 per day, $26.10), and other points in western Victoria.V/Line **trains** haul into town at the station off High St. The **Ararat Municipal Library** (tel. 5352 1722) sits at the intersection of Barkly and Queen St (open M-W 10:30am-5:30pm, Th-F 10:30am-7pm, Sa 10am-noon).

ACCOMMODATIONS AND FOOD Ararat's best accommodation is the **Ararat Hotel,** 130 Barkly St (tel. 5352 2477), whose imperious Art Deco facade dominates Barkly St. The small rooms are impeccably tidy, and there's a balcony with barbecue facilities as well as an elegant TV lounge where they serve breakfast. ($25 single, $30 double, includes delectable continental breakfast). You can scare up a good deal at the **Grampians Hotel,** 157 Barkly St (tel. 5352 2393), which lets single private rooms with shared baths for $20, doubles $30. The three-story hotel is definitely aging, but the bathrooms are clean, and renovations are coming soon. (Ghosts included at no extra charge; see graybox below). The **Acacia Caravan Park,** 6 Acacia Ave (tel. 5352 2994) sits just west of town, 1km from the post office. A lot of noise intrudes from the adjacent train tracks, but with two-person tent sites for $14, it's the cheapest deal in town, and there's a barbecue kiosk and heated pool for the kiddies.

Barkly St is loaded with takeaway fish 'n' chips joints and pubs, each of which serve meals for $5-10. **Robinson Foodworks,** 102 Barkly St, is a fully-licensed grocer with decent coffee and takeaway food. For a quick bite (basic breakfasts $6) before a long bus ride, try the friendly **Mt. Langi Ghiron Roadhouse,** adjoining the BP on Ingor St.

SIGHTS AND ENTERTAINMENT Built in the 1860s, the infamous **J-Ward** (tel. 5352 3621) served as Ararat's gaol until taken over by the Lunacy Department in 1887 and made into a prison for the criminally insane. *(Tours M-Sa 11am, Su 11am, noon, 1, 2, 3pm.)*

The Ghost of the Grampians

Though you wouldn't know it now, the Grampians Hotel was once a five-star establishment during the heady days of the Australian gold rush, housing ore millionaires and other hoity-toity types who passed through town. It was also the site of several mysterious deaths, most notably that of a tall, robust prospector from Holland by the name of Jorge. After striking gold at the nearby Canton lead, Jorge made merry (got wasted) at the hotel pub, and was last seen alive climbing the stairs to his ill-fated room, notorious number 51. The next morning, Jorge was found dead at the base of the stairs, and all the gold in his room had gone missing. His killer seemed to have gotten away clean and was never found out, but in the years that followed, hotel guests and workers began to suspect that Jorge's restless soul still roamed the halls at night. There have been countless reports of guests (especially in number 51) waking up to the sounds of footsteps at night only to find no trace of a person; some have even claimed that they were pursued down the halls and stairs of the Grampians by phantom footfalls. Disturbances range from the ephemeral (uncanny sensations of being watched) to the unmistakable (barstools being violently overturned by an unseen hand). You can still stay at the Grampians, if you don't mind the hint of a preternatural presence—just be sure to steer clear of room 51.

It served in this capacity until 1991, when its creepy innards were opened to the public. The 90-minute tours tend to drone on, but are worth it to see the morbid circumstances suffered by inmates, and hear some of the Ward's more macabre legends—e.g., no frost forms over the courtyard gravesites of three hanged prisoners, even when the rest of the area is thick with ice. The **Alexandra Gardens,** across Girdlestone from J-Ward, bloom with orchids and are an excellent place to regain sanity. The **Langi Morgala Museum** (tel. 5354 2544; from Aboriginal words meaning "home of yesterday"), on the corner of Queen and Barkly St, appears at first glance to be nothing more than a big warehouse filled with junk, but upon closer inspection provides a fascinating look at Ararat's history. *(Open Sa and Su 1-4pm or by arrangement. Admission $2, children 50¢.)* Pay extra attention to the old daguerreotypes and Aboriginal implements. The **Ararat Gallery,** on Vincent St between High and Barkly streets (tel. 5352 2836), specializes in modern arts and crafts, especially textiles, woven sculpture, and fiber arts. Rotating exhibits of local work supplement the permanent exhibits. ($2, children 50¢. Open M-F 11am-4pm, Su noon-4pm).

There is a 50m, heated indoor pool at the **YMCA** near the intersection of Queen and High St, which also has spa and sauna facilities as well as squash and basketball courts. *(Open to the public M-F 6am-9pm, Sa-Su 2-6pm. Admission $3.)* The **Ararat Entertainment Center** (tel. 5352 2616) is across the street and screens mainstream Hollywood movies about six months after their USA releases.

■ Grampians (Gariwerd) National Park

Millions of years ago, what is today the Grampians mountain range lay under a shallow sea. Through geological heat and pressure over the span of millennia, the sandy bottom of this primeval ocean solidified into 6000m-thick slabs of sandstone. Tectonic disturbances then tilted and jostled the sandstone beds to form the jagged peaks we observe today, all of which will eventually be ground back into sand by the merciless wind and rain. But don't worry—you still have plenty of time to enjoy the 167,000-hectare park, located 260km west of Melbourne and 400km east of Adelaide, which feature breathtaking ranges, wild beasts, rare birds (nearly 200 species), a springtime carpet of technicolor wildflowers, and 80% of the Aboriginal rock art sites in Victoria.

PRACTICAL INFORMATION The most convenient point of entry is on the eastern edge of the park at **Halls Gap.** This is the park's only town, and it's a small one (consisting only of a small strip of stores on Dunkeld Rd near its intersection with Grampians

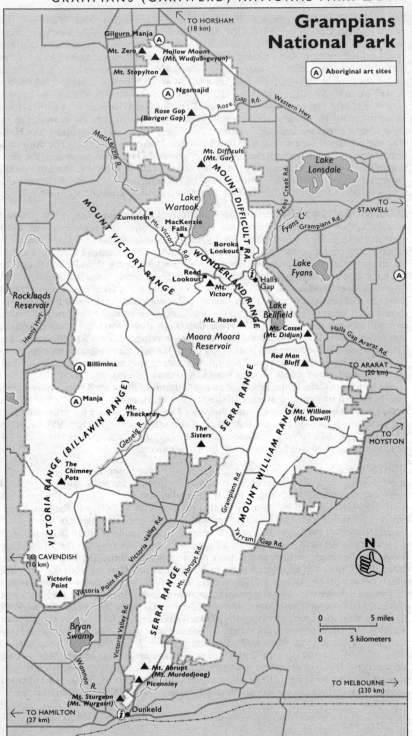

Grampians National Park

(A) Aboriginal art sites

TO HORSHAM
(18 km)

Gilgurn Manja
(A)
Mt. Zero ▲
Hollow Mount
(Mt. Wudjub-guyan) ▲
Mt. Stapylton ▲
(A) Ngamajid ▲
Rose Gap
(Barigar Gap) ▲
Rose Gap Rd.
Western Hwy.

Mt. Difficult
(Mt. Gar) ▲

Lake
Lonsdale

MOUNT DIFFICULT RA.

Lake
Wartook

Fyans Creek Rd.

TO
STAWELL

Zumstein
MacKenzie
Falls
Mt. Victory Rd.

Fyans Ct.
Grampians Rd.

Boroka
Lookout

WONDERLAND RANGE

Lake
Fyans

Reed
Lookout ▲
Mt.
Victory ▲

(i) Halls
Gap

(A)

MOUNT VICTORY RANGE

Lake
Bellfield

Mt. Rosea ▲

Mt. Cassel
(Mt. Didjun) ▲

Halls Gap Ararat Rd.

Rocklands
Reservoir

Moora Moora
Reservoir

Red Man
Bluff

TO ARARAT
(20 km)

Henty Hwy.

(A) Billimina

(A) Manja
Mt.
Thackeray ▲

SERRA RANGE

Mt. William
(Mt. Duwil) ▲

MOUNT WILLIAM RANGE

TO
MOYSTON

The
Sisters ▲

Glenelg R.

VICTORIA RANGE (BILLAWIN RANGE)

The Chimney
Pots ▲

Grampians Rd.

TO CAVENDISH
(10 km)

Victoria
Point ▲

Victoria Point Rd.

Victoria Valley Rd.

Mt. Abrupt Rd.

SERRA RANGE

Yarram Gap Rd.

N

0   5 miles

0   5 kilometers

Bryan
Swamp

Wannon

Mt. Abrupt
(Mt. Murdadjoog) ▲
Picanniny ▲

Victoria Valley Rd.

TO MELBOURNE →
(230 km)

R.

Mt. Sturgeon
(Mt. Wurgarri) ▲

(i) Dunkeld

TO HAMILTON
(27 km)

Rd), but has all the basic amenities, and is near most of the park's points of interest. The park's **Visitors Centre** (tel. 5356 4381, fax 5356 4446; open daily 9am-4:45pm; donations appreciated) sits 2.5km south of Halls Gap's town center on Dunkeld Rd, and has excellent information about Grampians flora, fauna, and history, as well as a helpful staff of rangers (specialized walking/hiking maps $3). V/Line **buses** leave across from the newsagent in Halls Gap (M-F at 1:30pm, Sa at 12:50pm, and Su at 4:20pm) for Stawell (45min., $7.30), Ararat (1hr., $10.90), Ballarat (2½hr., $23.80), and Melbourne (4½hr., $37.80). The **newsagent** (open daily 7am-7pm) also has plenty of general tourist information. The local **post office** is hidden in the unimaginatively named "Coffee Shop," but it's well-marked with "Australia Post" signs (open M-F 9am-5pm). The **Halls Gap supermarket** (open daily 8am-9pm) is a good place to stock up. The approach from the north passes through the almost-empty town of **Horsham,** situated at the junction of the Western and Henty Hwy, roughly 80km north of the park. From the south, the town of Dunkeld, on the Glenelg Hwy, right on the border of the park, provides access via Mt. Abrupt Rd. From the east, the closest town is **Stawell,** 26km away.

ACCOMMODATIONS AND FOOD There are 16 major **camping** areas in the national park, all with toilets and fireplaces. All sites are first-come, first-served, and campers must pay a $8.30 fee (up to 6 people or 1 vehicle; additional vehicles $3.20). The fee is payable through self-service permits, available at the Visitors Centre and at most camping areas. Bush camping costs the same, but is forbidden in the Wonderland Range, in the Lake Wartook watershed, and in any other areas demarcated accordingly. The **Brambuk Backpackers** (tel. 5356 4250) is on Dunkeld Rd in Halls Gap directly across from the Visitors Centre. Large lounge areas, patio with barbecue, ensuite bathrooms, rooms with heaters, fridges, and radios, and friendly staff make this the best value around ($15 per person; linen $2). **Halls Gap YHA** (tel. 5356 6221), less than 1km down Grampians Rd, is a passable alternative with dorm beds for $13 (nonmembers $16) and provides bedding and laundry facilities, though they require residents to do chores. The **Halls Gap Caravan Park** offers nothing special, but at least it's conveniently located (powered site $16 for two, $18 in peak season).

The **Brambuk Cafe,** in the Brambuk Living Cultural Centre (see **Sights,** below), specializes in bush tucker, such as emu kabobs ($5) and kangaroo burgers ($7). Halls Gap's town center has a handful of eateries. **Ralphy's Family Restaurant** has takeaway fare, but eat-in meals include free unlimited use of the salad and veggie bar (BYO; entrees $7.50-12; open daily 7am-7pm). **Golden Dynasty** has Chinese and Malay fare in the $9-12 range (open W-M noon-2pm and 5-9pm, Tu 5-9pm only).

SIGHTS Although extremely rugged, Grampians is a very user-friendly national park; most of its highlights can be reached via relatively easy walking trails, without the need to overnight in the bush. It's thus a fave with families and nature lovers of the less-hardcore variety. The strip of **Mt. Victory Rd** that runs through Halls Gap to the park's eastern end is loaded with phenomena that will impress even the staunchest urbanite. Ascend to the **Boroka Lookout,** a 5km drive up the steep grade of Mt. Difficult, to catch spectacular views of the verdant Fyans Valley stretching out beneath the Mt. William Range, whose rough, wrinkly slopes have been aptly named the Elephant's Hide. The **Balconies,** The Grampians' predominant icon, lie about 1km up from the car park which lies just off Mt. Victory Rd. The mostly flat approach takes about 20 minutes; it's well worth it to see the sweeping panoramas as well as the Balconies themselves, a pair of parallel slabs of sandstone jutting out over the steep sides of Mt. Victory. If you don't kill yourself on the steep, slippery path to **MacKenzie Falls,** which begins just off Lake Wartook Rd, you'll see one of Victoria's—and perhaps Australia's—most spectacular waterfalls, a cacophonic 35-ft. wall of crashing water. A new, wheelchair-accessible approach was recently opened. **Zumstein recreation area,** west of Lake Wartook on Mt. Victory Rd, comes complete with picnic and barbecue facilities, and is extremely popular because it crawls with kangaroos. Many tourists feed the 'roos, but informed and eco-friendly *Let's Go* readers know that human food can harm the little beasties.

Tourists pack Mt. Victory Rd and its attendant sights, but many of the less-peopled attractions are worth a visit too. The **Wonderland Range,** off Mt Victory Rd in the heart of the park, is an excellent daytrip. Several easy walks lead to serene waterfalls, curious rock formations, and the occasional hookah-smoking caterpillar. To the south, **Victoria Valley** is carpeted with redgum woodlands, and is home to numerous emu and kangaroo. **Glenisla,** at the park's western border, contains some of its best Aboriginal art sites, while hardcore hikers might want to tackle **Mt. William,** at the park's extreme eastern end, which has a steep track up to the Gramps' highest peak (1168m). **Action Adventures** (tel. 5356 4540) run a series of tours, with night biking ($20), rock climbing ($55), and canoeing ($20) options.

Be sure not to miss the **Brambuk Living Cultural Centre** (tel. 5356 4381; fax 5356 4455), adjacent to the Visitors Centre in Halls Gap, which has a small but excellent series of displays on the culture and history of the Koori, southwest Victoria's native people. Two videotaped documentaries run constantly and provide unflinching insight, and there's a gift shop with aboriginal crafts. The building's loopy, curvy roof design was inspired by the Dreaming myths of the Koori. *(Open 10am-5pm. Free.)*

■ Little Desert National Park

The Little Desert is not, in fact, a desert. The park's 132,000 hectares are covered with vegetation, some quite lush and verdant, and the average rainfall is a decidedly non-arid 5m per year. By far, though, most tracts of the park are classic Mallee territory, the kind that bear some visual similarity to a true desert: rough flatlands scattered with vegetation (such as the aptly named "stringybark") grown scraggly and warped from constant battle against rocky soil and periodic bushfires. The harsh Malleeland won't wow you with spectacular natural wonders, but its strange, uniquely Australian habitat is great for bushwalking and camping, and possesses a tough, compelling beauty all its own.

PRACTICAL INFORMATION The Little Desert is best approached from **Nhill** (pronounced nil), north of the central block of parkland, or from **Dimboola,** on the Wimmera River in the east. There are **Department of Conservation and Natural Resources** offices in Nhill, 6 Victoria St (tel. 5391 1275), and Horsham, 21 McLachlan St (tel. 5381 1255), with information, but the best place to go is the **ranger station** (tel. 5389 1204) on Nursery Rd in **Wail.** There are **tourist information centers** in Nhill (on Goldsworthy Park, along Victoria St) and **Dimboola,** 119 Lloyd St (tel. 5389 1290; both open W-M 9am-5pm). Each dispenses information on the entire region; you can also call the **Victoria Parks Hotline** (tel. 13 19 63).

The **post offices** in Dimboola, 61 Lloyd St (tel. 5389 1542; open M-F 9am-5pm; postal code 3414), and Nhill, 98 Nelson St (open M-F 8:30am-5pm; postal code 3418), each have **fax** service. **Commonwealth Bank,** 13 Victoria St (open M-Th 9:30am-4pm, F 9:30am-6pm), Nhill, has an **ATM.** Nhill's **public library,** on Clarence St, provides free **Internet access** (Tu 1:30-5:30pm, W 2-6pm, Th 12:30-5:30pm, F 1:30-5:30pm and 7-8pm). **Buses** depart Nhill from the station opposite **Rintoule's Travel Service,** 27 Victoria St (tel. 5391 1421), twice daily for Dimboola (20min., $4.20), Horsham (50min., $8.40), Stawell (2hr., $19), Ararat (2½hr., $23.20), Ballarat (4½hr., $35.40), Melbourne (6hr., $43.90), and other points. (For trips from Dimboola, subtract $4.20 from the fare and 30min. from the time. Dimboola's station is at the corner of Lochiel and Hindmarsh St.) Timetables are available at the station, from Rintoule's or **V/Line** (tel. 13 22 32).

CAMPING, ACCOMMODATIONS, AND FOOD There are two **camping areas** in the National Park, one just south of **Kiata,** a small hamlet on the Western Hwy between Nhill and Dimboola, and the other at **Horseshoe Bend** just south of Dimboola. Both campgrounds have fireplaces, tables, and toilets. The $7.50 fee is payable at any of the ranger stations, or in the pay receptacles at the campsites. Bush camping is permitted in the western and central blocks only and must be vehicle-based.

The **Little Desert Lodge,** 26 Brougham St (tel. 5391 5232 or 5391 1714), 16km south of Nhill's town center, is run by Malleefowl expert Whimpey Reichelt and provides

VICTORIA

No Small Feat

Most birds sit on their eggs and use the heat of their bodies to warm their unborn young. But Malleefowl, members of the family Megapodiiae (meaning "great footed") have come up with a way to save on baby-sitting and still get out of the nest. These cousins of the pheasant mate for life and then use their great feet to build a mound out of dirt, sticks, and tree litter, in which the female deposits her eggs. Each mound takes weeks or months to build, but once completed it garners its warmth from the sun and the fermentation of the litter in which the eggs are buried. Over the next few months, the parents tend and repair the natural incubators. By changing the depth of the sand and litter layers, the Malleefowl can control the temperature of the eggs. In studies of the Malleefowl hatching cycle, researchers have found that the temperature of a mound's interior varies by fewer than two degrees over a span of several months. Once the eggs hatch, the chicks dig themselves out of their nurseries and are immediately on their own, receiving no assistance from their parents. These hatchlings are nearly mature and can fly within a few hours.

---

both accommodations and an excellent introduction to Mallee wildlife. The lodge has comfortable bunk beds ($16; $30 including linen; breakfast included), as well as camp-sites in the lush surrounding bush for $9 (with power $11.50; call a few weeks ahead for availability). The **Commercial Hotel** at Victoria and Nelson St, Nhill, lacks that authentic desert feel but is still a great deal. The classic late-19th-century hotel is replete with ornate wrought-iron balconies, and lets tidy rooms with sparkling shared baths for $20 (single occupancy, includes continental breakfast).

The Little Desert Lodge also functions as a fully licensed restaurant. **Nhill's Coffee Shop,** 24 Victoria St (tel. 5391 1467), provides a welcome respite to ubiquitous pub meals, with a full coffee arsenal and fresh, inventive sandwiches—the Chicken Waldorf features chicken, walnuts, and apple with a creamy herbed mayo (open M-F 8am-6pm). The **Tuckerbag Supermarket** is on Lochiel St in Dimboola (M-Th 9am-5:30pm, F 9am-6pm, Sa-Su 9am-12:30pm).

SIGHTS AND ACTIVITIES Little Desert's unique Mallee ecology is best explored on foot, although 4WD drivers can usually use the rough, unpaved roads (often closed in winter) to reach remote corners. An excellent 30-minute introductory walk leads to the lookout on **Pomponderoo Hill,** and shows off typical Little Desert terrain and biota. Go through the gate marked "Gateway to Little Desert" at Dimboola (not the official park entrance), turn left immediately after crossing the Wimmera River bridge, and go south, following the "National Park" signs; the trailhead is 1km past the actual park entrance.

Other **self-guided walks** begin at the campground south of Kiata and at the Gymbouen Rd south of Nhill. The truly hard-core may wish to take on the 84km **Desert Discovery Walk,** a 1-4 day trek across the eastern section of the park and can be tackled in parts or all at once, depending on what you think you're made of. Detailed brochures on all the walks are available at the **Little Desert Lodge,** ranger stations, and tourist information centers. The Little Desert Lodge runs half ($25), three-quarter ($40), and full-day ($50) Land Rover tours deep into the heart of the park. If the desert hasn't quenched your thirst to eyeball wildlife, the **Malleefowl Aviary** at the Little Desert Lodge guarantees up-close views of the fowl, sugar-gliders, and other scrub denizens. *(Open daily 9:30am-4:30pm; $4, children $2).*

MURRAY RIVER

Australia's longest river, the Murray rambles along the New South Wales-Victoria border for 2600km before meeting the sea in South Australia's Encounter Bay. The river became an essential transportation artery in the late 19th century, its waters plied by giant freight-toting paddlesteamers. But extensive rail and road networks rendered these boats obsolete by the end of the 1930s and they have since been reincarnated as tourist attractions. Today the river feeds a productive agriculture of vegetables and fruits (including wine grapes) through a complex irrigation system. It's also a favorite spot for picnicking, water sports, and fishing, drawing travelers for a day or a week of relaxation along the grand old Murray's banks.

■ Echuca

As the closest point to Melbourne along the Murray, Echuca was once Australia's largest inland port, a clearinghouse for the wool and agricultural products of southern New South Wales. A massive redgum wharf was built to accommodate the paddlesteamers and barges, and a lively array of hotels, brothels, and breweries was built to accommodate the men who sailed them. Although river traffic declined in the late 1800s, many boats have been preserved, and Echuca now possesses the world's largest flotilla of side-wheel paddlesteamers—its major industry is nostalgia. Old-time facades dominate its main streets, and a late-19th-century feel still pervades the town. Despite its exterior, however, Echuca has the bustle of an entirely modern city, and its tourist industry avoids the theme-park hokiness of other historic river towns, making this the best place to immerse yourself in the Murray riverboat culture.

ORIENTATION AND PRACTICAL INFORMATION

Echuca lies about 200km north of Melbourne, at the intersection of two highways, the **Murray River Valley** and **Northern Hwy,** and two rivers, the **Campaspe** (north-south) and the **Murray** (east-west). Echuca's main drags are **Hare** and **High St,** parallel roads that run from the Murray to the Murray Valley Hwy. Hare has more of the area's retail shops and businesses, while High has more accommodations, restaurants, and tourist attractions. The **Visitor Information Centre,** 2 Heygarth St (tel. 5480 7555 or 1800 804 446; fax 5482 6413), is on the Echuca side of the Echuca-Moama bridge. The staff can assist in booking accommodation. (Open daily 9am-5pm.) The visitor center also houses the **bus depot.** The **Echuca Branch Library,** at the corner of Heygarth and High St right across from McDonald's, offers free **Internet access** (M, Tu, Th, F 10am-5:30pm, W 1-9pm, Sa 10am-1pm, Su 2-4pm). **V/Line** runs coaches to Melbourne (3½ hr., 4-6 per day, $26.10), Bendigo (2hr., 1-3 per day, $6), Kerang (1 ¼hr.; M, W, Th, Su, 1 per day; $10.90), Swan Hill (2hr.; M, W, Th, Su; $17.50), and Mildura (6hr.; M, W, Th, Sa; $33.20). Summon **Echuca-Moama taxis** by calling 1800 339 616 or 5482 2700. The **post office** is on the corner of Hare and Anstruther St (open M-F 9am-5pm; postal code 3564). **ANZ** and **Commonwealth banks** with **ATMs** are diagonally across from the post office on Hare St (both banks open M-Th 9:30am-4pm, F 9:30am-5pm).

ACCOMMODATIONS

Echuca's accommodation scene consists mostly of luxury riverside B&Bs and pricey motels, but there are a few budget options, including the centrally located **Echuca Hotel,** 571 High St (tel. 5482 1087, fax 5480 2275), across from the port and within walking distance of all the restaurants and museums. The rooms have seen a few years, but they come with sinks and heaters, and are eminently livable. (Shared-bath single $25, includes continental breakfast.) The **Echuca Gardens Hostel (YHA),** 103 Mitchell St (tel. 5480 6522), is farther afield, about 1.5km from the wharf. The pleasant garden courtyard is filled with fountains and fruit trees. There is a small kitchen, a cozy, well-appointed lounge, and a communal atmosphere, with the owner's kids and dogs running about. (Dorms from $15. Office open 8-9:30am and 5-8pm.)

The other budget option near town is the **Echuca Caravan Park** (tel. 5482 2157) on Crofton St. This gigantic, park-like facility is run by the local government, and due to its idyllic location right on the Murray, it's choked with campervans, especially on long weekends and holidays. Tent sites ($13) are shaded and grassy. (5-person cabins with bathroom $55; on-site caravans $40.)

VICTORIA

FOOD AND ENTERTAINMENT

The standard Australian array of chip shops, grub-serving pubs, and fast-food joints line High St, and there are some more upmarket riverfront spots on the Murray Esplanade. The **Heritage Food House,** 591 High St (tel. 5480 2163), serves up great breakfast featuring the house specialty, fluffy buttermilk pancakes. The Heritage Special matches up to any appetite, with eggs, bacon, sausage, tomatoes, and a heaping stack of flapjacks with maple syrup, all for $8. All meals are made with fresh local ingredients, and in good weather afternoon tea is served on the backyard patio. (Open 7am-5pm.) **River Palace,** 614 High St (tel. 5482 3182), offers over 100 Szechuan and Malay dishes for dine-in or take-away. For a splurge well worth the extra cash, visit **Giorgio's On the Port,** 527 High St (tel. 5482 6117), which is not actually on the port, but serves awesome Italian fare nevertheless. There are many varieties of wood-fired pizza ($12-15) and delectable pastas, including the fiery penne picante ($14-15, large appetizer portions $10-11). For light fare or a killer cappuccino, head to **Murray Provender,** 568 High St (tel. 5482 5295), which offers caffeine, cakes, cookies, and even bagels with lox (open Tu-Sa 10am-4:30pm, Su 10:30am-4:30pm).

The numerous pubs on High and Hare St are peopled by friendly locals who are more than willing to shout you into a state of drunken oblivion. A younger crowd chills at the **Atomic Pool Bar Cafe,** 207 Darling St (tel. 5480 2227), a slick entertainment complex with food, coffee, pool tables, drinks galore, and DJ tunes, with occasional live bands on weekends. (Open M-F noon-late, Sa noon-1am, Su noon-11pm.)

SIGHTS

The main attraction in Echuca is the **historic port** (tel. 5482 4248; fax 5482 6951), which consists of the wharf and several historic buildings. *($7, concessions $5.50, children $5.)* The wharf itself, built in 1865 of local redgum, has three levels to accommodate the changing river conditions, with a steam-driven sawmill on the top level. Blacksmith and woodturning shops sell handmade wares. Several old hotels are on display as well. The **Star Hotel** is equipped with a secret underground tunnel that allowed drinkers to escape police raids after the place was de-licensed in 1897, and the **Bridge Hotel,** Echuca's first, boasts a carefully preserved suite and gallery upstairs. The other end of the port is marked by the old **Customs House,** 2 Lesley St, where tariffs were exacted from passing watercraft when the Echuca was the commercial hub of the Murray. Today, the Customs House building houses **Murray Esplanade Cellars,** which exacts a tariff of zero dollars for sampling its excellent wines and spirits. *(Open 9am-6pm.)* There's also a small display of historical artifacts that seem much more interesting after a few glasses of tawny port.

Several paddlesteamers still ply the waters off the old port, and are now open to the public for leisurely cruises. A variety of cruises are available, some of which last up to two days and nights if you're willing to shell out a few hundred clams. Tickets for the much more budget-tolerable 1- to 2-hour cruises are available at the **main port ticket office,** 101 Murray Esplanade (tel. 5482 4248). *($12, students $10, children $5. Package deals including port tour and 1hr. cruise $16, students $14, children $9; cruises daily at 10:15, 11:30am, 1, 2:15, and 3:30pm.)*

For car-lovers or anyone who's interested in a fascinating perspective on an iconic slice of Australiana, the **National Holden Motor Museum,** 7-11 Warren St (tel./fax 5480 2033), is a must-see. *(Open 9am-5pm. $5, concessions $4, children $2.50.)* It showcases "Australia's Own" automobile, the GM-affiliated Holden, with over 40 lovingly restored models. It spotlights not only the car, but also Australia's love for it, and through the Holden ads and a hilarious video retrospective, you get a vivid sense of Australian popular culture from the late 1940s to the present.

Although not particularly relevant to the history of the Murray, the **World in Wax Museum,** near the port at 630 High St (tel. 5482 3630), provides a fun, kitschy departure from the standard, serious historical thing. Figures include dignitaries both foreign and domestic, arranged by era and disposition (amusingly, Stalin, Hitler, Castro, and Churchill share a case). Other displays include Mao Tse-Tung, Princess Di, and Dolly

Parton. The "sect d'horreur" contains likenesses of Count Dracula and Alfred Hitchcock, as well as a set of wax miniatures chronicling torture devices throughout the ages. *(Open daily 9am-5:30pm. $6, students $5.)* Adjacent to the port, **Sharp's Magic Movie House and Penny Arcade** (tel. 5482 2361; fax 5480 1881) houses Australia's largest collection of working penny arcade machines. Also on display is an array of antique cinematic equipment, along with continuous screenings of old newsreels, comedy shorts, and historical documentaries. *(Open daily 9am-5pm. $10, concessions $8, children $6, which includes the movies and some pennies for the arcade machines.)*

■ Near Echuca: Barmah State Park and State Forest

The **Barmah State Park and State Forest** is the largest redgum forest in Victoria. Located 27km from Echuca, the forest is well-endowed with roads and walking tracks, but rain and high water levels can render many of them impassable. The **Dharnya Centre** (tel. 5869 3302; fax 5869 3249), on Sand Ridge Rd near the park entrance, 5km north of the township of Barmah, can provide info on road conditions and should be visited before venturing into the bottomlands (open daily 10:30am-4pm). **Camping** is free and abundant in the park, and fishing is excellent. When water levels are high enough, the wetlands can be explored by boat. **Kingfisher Wetland Cruises** (tel. 5869 3399; fax 5869 3388) offers two-hour trips (M, W, Th, and Su 12:30pm; $15, children $10). **Gondwana Canoe Hire** (tel. 5869 3347), on Moira Lakes Rd on the way to the park entrance from Barmah, provides canoes for private trips (rental $15 per hr., ½-day $25, full day $40, 2 days $70). Note that dry conditions may make canoeing the park impossible. There is no public transport to Barmah. Tour companies will make a trip into Echuca to pick up a group of 6 or more; ask at the youth hostel about ride-sharing.

▓ Kerang

The tiny township of **Kerang**, between Echuca and Swan Hill, boasts a ratio of about 1000 birds for every human. The entire area comprises one of Australia's most important wetland reserves for avian life; one of the most fecund areas is **Middle Lake**, a rookery for huge flocks of ibis, with a shelter to allow visitors to view the birds without disturbing them. The **Kerang Caravan Park** (tel. 5452 1161) lies 300m west of town, right along the Loddon River, on Riverwood Dr (unpowered sites $11; on-site caravans $30; cabins $42). The **Old Water Tower**, right on the Murray Valley Hwy on the edge of town, houses a visitor information center and a small but cool museum. It's well worth the $1 admission to climb the four-story tower, which holds old shells and fossils, a trippy fluorescent rock display with black light, and a circular lookout over Kerang's wetlands and its attendant flocks of fowl. The **Gunbower Creek,** a few kilometers east of Kerang, is another popular area for bird-watching and swamp-rambling. To see the wetland in air-conditioned style, book a cruise on the **Wetlander** (tel. 5453 3000; fax 5453 2697), off Koondrook-Cohuna Rd on Orr's Rd (also called Southern Rd). Two-hour cruises leave daily (except Th) at 2pm. ($17, concessions $15, children $9. Tours run Aug. 15-May 15.)

▓ Swan Hill

Swan Hill, located on the Murray River about 340km northwest of Melbourne, has little to do with swans or hills. It is a tranquil rural town, ideal for families, caravaners, and anybody else who values peace over energy. Swan Hill's range of activities matches its tenor of life; the area is thick with nurseries, craft shops, tea rooms, wineries, and other serene pastimes. This part of the Murray has great fishing and is good for water sports. Cruising down the river on rented houseboats is popular, especially with seniors.

PRACTICAL INFORMATION Swan Hill's civic activity centers on the strip of Campbell St between Rutherford and McCallum St. The **Swan Hill Development and Information Centre**, 306 Campbell St (tel. 5032 3033 or 1800 625 373; fax 5032 3032), is one block west of the river (open 9am-5pm). **National and ANZ banks,** each with 24-hour **ATMs,** face one another at the intersection of Campbell and McCallum St (open M-Th 9:30am-4pm, F 9:30am-5pm). Swan Hill is the northern terminus of **passenger rail service** to Melbourne; trains leave daily (4½hr., $42.10). The station is on Curlewis St, between McCrae and Rutherford St, near the Giant Murray Cod. Coach service is available to points along the Murray: Mildura (3 hr.; daily; $28.40), Echuca (2hr.; Tu, W, F, Su; $17.50), Shepparton (4¼hr.; Tu, W, F, Su; $28.40), and Albury-Wodonga (7hr.; daily; $38.50). Swan Hill's **public library,** 6 McCrae St, has two terminals for free **Internet access.** (Open Tu, Th, F 10am-5:30pm, W 10am-5:30pm and 7-8:30pm, Sa 10am-noon.) The **Swan Hill District Hospital** (tel. 5432 1111) is on Splatt St, and the **RACV** (tel. 5433 1555) is at 7 Pritchard St. The **post office** is at 164 Campbell St (open M-F 9am-5pm; postal code 3585).

ACCOMMODATIONS AND FOOD The **White Swan Hotel** (tel. 5032 2761), 182 Campbell St, is a one-stop food/entertainment/budget lodging multiplex. Downstairs, there's a pub with hearty, mostly carnivorous fare (lunch specials $6-7, dinner specials $10-11); a public bar for the serious drinker; and, in the back, **Hustlers Saloon,** which draws a younger crowd on weekends, especially Fridays, when it features live bands. Cheap hotel accommodations lie upstairs, with clean, spare rooms, somewhat murky but basically serviceable bathrooms, and a TV lounge with comfy couches and fridge. Early sleepers be warned, the downstairs saloon rocks on till 3am on weekends. The White Swan offers breakfast from 7-9am for guests, and there's also **Bartalotta's Bakery,** two doors down at 178 Campbell St, servers-up of standard morning fare and stiff cappuccinos (open M-F 7am-6pm, Sa-Su 7am-2pm). The **Swan Pasta Inn** provides respite from standard Aussie cuisine with a selection of pizzas and pasta dishes, as well as icy-good gelati. (Open M-F 9:30am-9pm, Sa 10am-1:30pm and 4:30-10pm, Su 4:30-9pm.) Alternative cheap accommodation can be had at **Riverside Caravan Park,** 1 Monash Dr (tel. and fax 5032 1494), on the river adjacent to the Pioneer Settlement. The office doubles as a small grocery, and 3-wheeled "daisy bikes" are available for hire ($6 per ½hr., $10 per hr.). Squadrons of noisy parrots and waterbirds awaken guests in the morning. (2-person sites $13; barbecue, swimming pool.)

SIGHTS The **Horseshoe Bend Pioneer Settlement** (tel. 5032 1093; fax 5032 1096), on Horseshoe Bend, is the oldest outdoor museum in Australia. *(Open daily 8:30am-5pm.)* The settlement's seven acres are jam-packed with original buildings and old-time equipment. A full century (1830-1930) of the history of frontier agricultural settlement is represented. The period-costumed employees of some shops perform uproarious street theater at regular intervals. Paddle-steamers cruise the river along the banks of the settlement, and nighttime in the park brings the **Mallee Heritage Sound and Light Show,** a family-friendly, if slightly cheesy, extravaganza. *(Settlement admission $13, concessions $9, children $6.50. River cruises 10:30am and 2:30pm daily; $8.50, concessions $6.50, children $4.50. Sound and light show $8.50, concessions $6.50; children $4.50. Package tickets for all 3 $30, concessions $22, children $15.50.)*

Smaller than the Pioneer Settlement, but much more provocative and engaging, is the **Swan Hill Art Gallery** (tel. 5032 9744; http://www.swanhill.vic.gov.au/artgal/), housed in a mud-brick structure right next door. *(Admission $3, concessions $2; open M-F 10am-5pm, Sa-Su 11am-5pm.)* Three galleries showcase local work and contemporary artists on a rotating basis. There's a permanent collection of Australian art from throughout the 20th century as well as concerts, films, and lectures. Swan Hill is also proud of its excellent **fishing.** That pride has metastasized into the **Giant Murray Cod,** quite possibly the largest Murray Cod in the world, towering over its living brethren. The statue measures 6m by 11m by 6m, and was originally built as a prop for the movie *Eight Ball.* It now guards the northern end of the rail station on Curlewis St, complete with a placard featuring a mawkish paean to the noble fish.

■ Mildura

Mildura, with its wide, palm-lined streets and bustling riverside wharf, is an oasis in dry Mallee country. The area, in the extreme northwest corner of Victoria, was settled in 1887 by the Chaffey brothers, Canadians who had established irrigation communities in California and repeated their successes here. The cleverly harnessed waters of the Murray support thriving citrus groves and make Mildura one of Australia's most productive fruit-growing areas. It's also one of the sunniest parts of Australia, and were it not for the massive irrigation system, the landscape would be as arid as the outback that stretches north and west to the horizon. Enjoy it while you're here; Mildura is the last bastion of green foliage for a long, long time.

ORIENTATION AND PRACTICAL INFORMATION

Mildura was thoroughly planned before being built, and is laid out in a grid on the southern bank of the Murray. The **Mildura Visitor Information and Booking Centre,** 180-190 Deakin Ave (tel. 5021 4424, booking desk tel. 1800 039 043), is housed in the brand-spanking new Alfred Deakin Centre; look for the silvery tornado sculpture out front. Inside, you'll find glossy, informative exhibits (a free 10min. video runs on the half-hour and provides a good intro to local history), a cafe, and library (tel. 5023 5011) with free **Internet access.** (Info center open M-F 9am-5:30pm, Sa-Su and public holidays 9am-5pm; library open Su-M 1-5pm, Tu-F 10am-7pm, Sa 10am-2pm.) There is an **ANZ bank** (tel. 5023 9200) on the corner of Eighth and Deakin St with a 24hr. **ATM** (bank open M-Th 9:30am-4pm, F 9:30am-5pm).

The **railway station and bus depot** is on Seventh St, near the river. From Deakin Ave, turn left onto Seventh. (Booking office open M-F 7am-6pm and 9pm-10pm, Sa 7:30pm-midnight, Su 7:30-11am, 1-2pm, and 10-11pm.) **V/Line** runs three buses daily to Melbourne (6½hr.; $52), via Swan Hill (3hr.; $28.40) and Bendigo (5hr.; $45.50). There's also service to Echuca (Tu, W, F, Su; 5hr.; $33.20) and Broken Hill (W, F; $37). **Sunraysia Transit** has daily buses to Adelaide ($35) and Sydney ($74). If you have a YHA membership, you should be eligible for substantial transit discounts. **Mildura Associated taxis** are on call 24 hours (tel. 5023 0033). The **police station** (tel. 5023 9555) is on Madden St, between Eighth and Ninth St. The Mildura Private Hospital (tel. 5022 2611) is located at 220 Thirteenth St. The Mildura **post office** is on the corner of Eighth and Orange Ave (open M-F 9am-5pm; postal code 3500).

ACCOMMODATIONS AND FOOD

The best place to stay in Mildura is the YHA-affiliated **Rosemont Guest House,** 154 Madden Ave (tel./fax 5023 1535), one block east of Deakin Ave off Eleventh St. A traditional guest house with fragrant gardens and a swimming pool, Rosemont combines hostel and B&B-style rooms. Coffee and tea are free, kitchens are available, and generous breakfasts are available for $3. Most of the hostel beds are singles or twin share ($15, weekly $90; YHA nonmembers $3 more per night). Two-person suites with TV, fridge, and full breakfast go as low as $42. The affable manager can book tours of the outback and nearby national parks (no commission, often with a YHA discount), and provides job search assistance during the fruit-picking seasons (best time of year is Feb.-March). If there's no room at the Rosemont, a livable alternative is **Mildura International Backpackers,** 5 Cedar Ave (tel. 5021 0133), one block east of Deakin Ave between Eleventh and Twelfth St, a bare-bones hostel designed with the migrant worker in mind. Rooms are basic and the demeanor of the place is very proletarian. This is the place for information from experienced pickers. The place remains friendly despite its functionality, and it has a full kitchen, laundry, barbecue facilities, ping-pong, and cable TV (beds $13; weekly $80).

Mildura offers more than your typical country city when it comes to food. The **Mildura Workingman's Club** (tel. 5023 0531), on Deakin Ave just north of the YHA hostel, is a private club that also operates a public bistro serving large portions of carnocentric fare in a classic Aussie atmosphere (most meals around $10; open noon-

2pm and 6-8pm). The **Langtree Avenue Mall,** one block west of Deakin between Eighth and Ninth, is lined with supercheap takeaway joints, while the strip of Langtree just north, between Seventh and Eighth St, is a veritable international foodfest. The eateries span the price range and encompass Thai, Mexican, Chinese, Turkish, and Italian cuisines, among many others. **Taco Bill's,** 36 Langtree Ave (tel. 5023 6204), does a very respectable rendition of south-of-the-border fare, especially considering how far south of the U.S.-Mexico border it is. Part restaurant, part cantina, they serve mescal tequila in your own personal mini-bottle ($10) and provide a certificate of merit if you swallow the worm (open daily from 6pm). The **Club Langtree Cafe,** 32 Langtree Ave (tel. 5023 2336), is open late and serves Greek-inspired pasta and tasty souvlaki (open M-F 9am-3pm). **Fisher's Supermarket** is at 10th St and Deakin Ave.

SIGHTS AND ENTERTAINMENT

Mildura is the base camp for a variety of tours into the outback and associated national parks. Commercial operators abound, and information on most is available at the visitor center. **Mallee Outback Experiences** (tel. 5021 1621) has charismatic, extremely well-informed guides who operate daytrips to **Mungo National Park** (see **Mungo National Park,** p. 224; tours W, Sa; $45, concessions $43, families $100), along the Chaffey Trail, highlighting the early history of the Mildura Settlement (Th only; $40, concessions $38, families $100), and to the Hattah Kulkyne National Park lakes system (F only; $45, concessions $43, families $100). **Harry Nanya Tours** (tel. 5027 2076), from half a day to one day, focus on ancient and recent Aboriginal history and the Dreaming as it relates to local sites. **Junction Tours** (tel. 5027 4309, mobile tel. 018 596 438; http://www.ruralnet.net.au/junction) goes to Mungo (W, F, Su; $38), leads a nature and history tour (F $38) and runs a longer outback tour to Broken Hill (3 days and 2 nights of camping for $240). Ride a bit easier with **Mildura Freedom Harley Rides** (tel. 5021 2876), also available for weddings.

The **P.S. Melbourne,** one of Australia's last steam-powered watercrafts, departs daily at 10:50am and 1:50pm for a two-hour cruise through historic Lock 11 ($16). The paddlewheeler **Rathbury,** built in 1881, conducts longer cruises to local wineries (Th at 10:30am, $34). Call 5023 2200 for bookings.

Remnants of Mildura's early development into an irrigation community are strung along the banks of the Murray. The **Old Mildura Homestead,** on Cureton Ave west of the railway station on the river, features relics from the area's earliest settlement. (Open daily 9am-6pm. $2, concessions $1.) If you drop by at the right time, you can see live woodturners plying their trade in the woodshed (Tu, Th 11am-3pm). Down the road lies the grandiose **Rio Vista mansion,** built in 1889 by W. B. Chaffey, which has been preserved with its original furnishings. (Open M-F 9am-5pm, Sa-Su 1-5pm. $2, concessions $1.) The mansion adjoins the **Mildura Art Gallery,** which has a decent permanent collection highlighted by Degas' chunky-but-funky *Femme a la baignoire se coiffant,* and rotating exhibits of work from Australia's avant-garde, such as it is. Seven kilometers southeast of town off 11th St, the **Psyche Bend Pumping Station** houses the restored steam pumps that kept Mildura alive and growing in the early days. Nearby **King's Billabong** is a bird-filled wetland reserve. (Station open Tu, Th 1-4pm, Su 10am-1pm. $2, families $5.)

If you've always wanted to learn how to tell good fruit from bad, **Orange World** (tel 5023 5197) beckons you to the "land of the living orange," more commonly known as the town of **Buronga,** about 8km north of Mildura on the Silver City Hwy, across the NSW border. Orange World offers free tastings and tours of its panoply of fruit. (Open Su-F 9am-4pm. Tours 10:30am, 2:30pm. $6, concessions $5, children $3.)

A few nightclubs are at 8th and Langtree St. The **Sandbar** (tel. 5021 2181) warms even the chilliest of winter nights with its tropical motif. Live music starts at 10:30 or 11pm. (Open Tu-Sa until 3am. No cover.) Down the street, at the corner of Lime and 8th St, **Star Bar** (tel. 5023 4199) has billiards and a cool second-floor verandah, and attracts some of the area's better bands and more suspect live acts (tickets $10-20) on Friday nights. On Saturdays, there's DJ-inspired dance action (open until 3am). The **Mildura Film Festival** brings the best in foreign and independent films to the edge of the outback. (Third weekend in June; call 9531 8016 or 5021 4424 for info.)

HUME CORRIDOR

The Hume Highway links Melbourne and Sydney, shuttling visitors along 872km of open road through relatively unspectacular scenery. However, intrepid travelers who venture an hour or two off the Hume will be rewarded with world-class wineries, dusty, unassuming hamlets, and quietly inviting country towns. Don't blink or you'll miss Glenrowan and Ned Kelly's Last Stand. Stray a bit more from the highway, and you can snowboard or ski on Mt. Buller's excellent powdery slopes. The culturally inclined can cruise through Wangaratta to catch it renowned November Jazz Festival, or if you're in more of a party mood check out the wineries of the nearby Rutherglen Valley. Sun worshippers can laze away the days by heading west along the Murray Valley Highway to fish, swim, or snooze on the Murray's banks in Yarrawonga and Cobram. Those in a hurry can simply cover the whole stretch in nine or ten hours. Across the Murray River, the Hume continues north into New South Wales (see Albury-Wodonga, p. 211).

■ Marysville

A precocious small town only an hour and a half northeast of Melbourne, Marysville is best known as the closest town (20km) to cross-country ski mecca **Lake Mountain.** Lake Mountain has 31km of regularly groomed trails (entry fee $17, trail fee $5). Back in Marysville, **Lake Mountain Ski Hire** (tel. 5963 3444) rents skis ($16), skates ($25), toboggans ($5-8), and chains ($10). (Open M-F 8am-6pm, Sa-Su 8am-6:30pm.) Chains are required for the drive up Lake Mountain during the winter. Other ski hires in town offer identical rates.

Also near Marysville, **Steavenson Falls** lie 4km down Falls Rd. These soaring cataracts are illuminated at night, when you can take a starlit stroll past huge ferns, eucalypts, and stringybark trees. Several lush, hilly bushwalks lead off the path to the falls. There's a half-hour ascent to the top of a nearby peak with a view of the falls, and a 40-minute trail downhill through the town. In the town itself, **Bruno's Art & Sculpture Garden,** 51 Falls Rd (tel. 5963 3513), has beautiful gardens and an extensive collection of paintings, collages, and sculptures that is both whimsical and powerfully expressive. (Gallery open F-Su and holidays 10am-5pm. Garden open daily 9am-5pm. Gallery and garden $3, garden alone $1.)

While the area's best lodging lies 10km up the road at Taggerty's YHA-affiliated Australian Bush Settlement (see below), the **Marysville Caravan Park** (tel. 5963 3443) on Buxton Rd is bucolically situated by the Steavenson River on the edge of the town center. There are powered sites as well as bunkhouse accommodation and grassy spaces with camp fires and barbecues (bunkhouses, from $38, must be rented in full). No disrespect to Mentos, but **Marysville Country Bakery** (tel. 5963 3477), at the corner of Murchison St and Pack Rd, is the real "freshmaker". They bake delectable breads and desserts daily; you can get day-old loaves for about $1.20. They also purvey sandwiches ($3-4) and over 20 varieties of pies and pasties ($1.75-2.60), the best of which is the Bushman's Pie with chunky steak, celery, onion, carrot, peas, tomato, and potato ($2.60). (Open 7am-6pm.)

The **Mystic Mountains Visitor Information Centre** (tel. 5963 4567), on Marysville's main thoroughfare, **Murchison St,** posts Lake Mountain snow reports and road conditions, arranges accommodations, and posts a list of available places to stay (open 10am-5pm). **V/Line buses** depart daily for Melbourne (2¾hr., $10.90) and for Eildon (1hr., $4.80) from the bus stop across from the **general store** at 4 Murchison St. The store also functions as the V/Line ticketing agent, has EFTPOS, and vends foodstuffs as well as hot soup, sandwiches, and snacks ($2-3). (Open 7am-7pm.) By car, take the Maroondah Hwy (Hwy 34) to Hwy 172, which continues to Lake Mountain. The Marysville **post office,** at the intersection of Murchison St and Pack Rd, vends crafts along with the standard post office stuff and has a **Commonwealth Bank** outlet (open M-F 9am-5pm, Sa 9-11am; post code: 3779).

■ Taggerty

The **Taggerty Australian Bush Settlement** (tel. 5774 7378; fax 5774 7442) provides a splendorous stay for a one-night guest or a several-month visitor. This 30-hectare, YHA-affiliated farm by the Cathedral Range National Park simulates an early pioneer village but lies just off the Maroondah Hwy. The remarkable host, Bronwyn Rayner, has operated Taggerty for 20 years and built it into a combination B&B, hostel, campsite, working farm, classroom, museum, and youth development facility. Rayner cultivates an organic vegetable garden and cares for a variety of unwanted, misfit, or orphaned animals ranging from sheep and horses to wombats and kangaroos. Guests and visitors can interact with the animals, and the working farm and bush settlement serves as a backdrop for educational programs run for special-needs and at-risk kids. Taggerty houses an extensive collection of 19th-century bush memorabilia, including costumes, carriages, and even an 1853 Norwegian slab hut.

Taggerty gives guests an authentic bush adventure, integrating the experiences and traditions of both Aboriginals and white settlers. Rayner's work to provide these experiences has been the subject of several TV specials. Accommodations come in four degrees of comfort and privacy (beds $15-30). Richly decorated with a blend of antiques and contemporary furnishings, the homestead bungalow was House Beautiful's 1990 Home of the Year and Design of the Year. In the lodge, cozy environs and hostel-style bunks offer a more familiar setting for socializing with other backpackers. The cabins, set a bit further uphill, are bunk-style lodgings offering modern conveniences. Finally, there are several waterproof canvas tent sites with mattressed. All lodgings come with excellent kitchen and toilet facilities in-room or nearby.

All guests may range along the extensive property. For reasonable prices, guests can take advantage of a board plan or bush activities, with longer trips and more involved excursions offered for groups of six or more. The four-day tour is a fantastic bargain and an unforgettable experience; it includes all meals (including real bush tucker), bushwalks, a tour through Marysville, trout fishing, visits to the animal nurture center, and learning about local Aboriginal culture. ($215; $195 with YHA; return bus ticket to Taggerty $24.) The Bush Settlement usually has vacancies, but takes reservations (V, MC). It's 104km east of Melbourne on the Maroondah Hwy. (Hwy. 34), 4km after Buxton. It is accessible by **V/Line** from Melbourne to Alexandra or Eildon; ask to stop at Taggerty YHA at the 104km marker. For a closer look at Taggerty, read *Don't Pat the Wombat* by Elizabeth Honey, Children's Book Council of Australia Book of the Year 1997.

■ Mansfield

With few attractions of its own, Mansfield's *raison d'etre* is its convenient location at the foot of Mt. Buller, allowing tourists to stop and rent skis and chains before making the 45km ascent to Victoria's most popular ski resort. The **Mansfield Visitors Centre** (tel. 5775 1464; fax 5775 2518; infocent@mansfield.net.au) lies at the west end of **High St,** the town's main drag (open 9am-5pm). Heading east into town, you'll find oodles of **ski rental places** and a few **ATMs.** The **Mansfield Passenger Terminal,** 137 High St (tel. 5775 2606), is the **V/Line** agent, with service to Melbourne (3hr., 2 per day, $26.10) and Mt. Buller (1hr., 6 per day, one-way $19, return $31.20). Bus travelers receive a 10% discount on rentals at Ski Center Mansfield.

Law requires all vehicles heading to Mt. Buller to carry chains from June 8 (Queen's Birthday) until October 1. You can leave them in the trunk, but be aware that there are spot checks and hefty fines. **Ski Centre Mansfield,** 131 High St (tel. 1800 647 754 or 5775 2859), and its affiliate, **PJ's Ski Hire,** a few doors down, rent chains ($12) and offer a wide range of ski paraphernalia. (Open in season M-Th 6am-7pm, F 6am-midnight, Sa-Su 6am-7pm or later.) Stock up on food at the **IGA Supermarket,** 47 High St (open M-W 8am-6pm, Th 8am-7pm, F 8am-8pm, Sa 8am-5pm, Su 10am-5pm), or **Mansfield Fruit Palace,** 68 High St, which has lots of fresh fruit and pre-made salads (open M-F 8am-6pm, Sa 8am-2pm). The **post office,** 90 High St, is located just west of the intersection with Highett St, offers fax service and public phones (open M-Sa 9am-5pm; postal code

3722). **Internet access** is free at the Mansfield **public library,** at the corner of High and Collopy St, though their one terminal is frequently busy; another alternative is **Mansfield Internet and Computers,** 12 High St (tel. 5775 3066), which has lighting-fast ISDN lines ($5 per ½hr.). There's no Internet access on Mt. Buller, so get your email fix here.

The best budget beds are at the **Mansfield Travellers Lodge,** 112-116 High St (tel. 5775 1800; fax 5775 2396). This restored, rustic building has high cedar ceilings and brickwork, and provides spacious, well-lit dorms with central heating. Sturdy metal bunks come with linen, quilts, and reading lights, and spotless hallway bathrooms. (Dorms Su-Th $15, F-Sa $20; weekly $84; YHA.) For a bit more privacy, check out the newly constructed triples with shared adjoining bathrooms (Su-Th $70, F-Sa $75), or spring for large motel-style family rooms (Su-Th $105, F-Sa $120). Reserve at least 2 weeks in advance for weekends and 1 week for weekdays, during high ski season. The **Delatite Hotel** (tel. 5775 2004), at the corner of High and Highett St, rents out clean, spacious rooms above its popular pub. Shared bathrooms are sparkling, and all rooms have washbasins and access to the 2nd-floor balcony ($25 per person, includes continental breakfast). **Buckley's Chance,** 141 High St (tel. 5775 1277), is budget-food nirvana: quick eats low on price, high on quality. The pancakes are a local fave, and the burgers are delicious too. (BYO. Open 6:30am-9:30pm, 10% discount for guests at Mansfield Travellers Lodge.) **Come 'n' Get Stuffed,** 50 High St (tel. 5775 1955), complements its cheeky name with stucco walls festooned with abstract art and a wine bar featuring the fruit of local vines. The food's got as much attitude as the venue; in addition to the standard carnivorous fare, there are veggie-friendly pastas and wood-fired pizzas, such as the Red Earth, topped with pumpkin, capsicum, roasted vegetables, and onion chutney ($10.50).

■ Mt. Buller

Victoria's largest and most popular ski resort, **Mt. Buller** is a three-hour drive from Melbourne. Skiers from the northern hemisphere shouldn't expect the Rockies or the Alps, as Buller's terrain and steepness, 400m vertical drop, and 1.5m average snowfall may seem middling by comparison. Still, it's a mecca for Aussie skiers and snowboarders from the Queen's Birthday (June 8) through early October. Expect crowds on weekends and public holidays during the height of the season, mid-July through late August. Intermediate slopes predominate, though several expert trails are sprinkled in; beginning skiers will have plenty to choose from too, as well as numerous lesson packages. The lift capacity, including several detachable quads, is excellent. Après-ski options include a fairly hip nightlife scene, and some budget accommodations despite the resort's chichi elegance. The slopes can be fun without snow, too; mountain biking is all the rage in the summer.

PRACTICAL INFORMATION AND SKIING Buses to Mt. Buller depart from Melbourne's Spencer St Station (3hr.; 2 per day; $89.80 round-trip includes resort entry fees) or from Mansfield (1hr.; 6 per day; $19, $31.20 return). If traveling by car, bring snow chains (it's the law) and take Hwy 164 east to Mt. Buller. (Daily car admission $17 per day, overnight fee $6 per night F-Sa, $3 per night Su-Th). Free parking is available on the side of the mountain, but then you have to get to the village; day visitors or anyone without luggage can take a free shuttle, but overnight visitors must take a taxi ($8.50 each way). Beware: these daily charges add up fast—a one-night stay can cost up to $40, not including lodging, skiing, food, or anything else except pure rip-off charges. Consider taking the bus, especially if you're staying awhile.

Buses pull into the **Cow Camp Plaza,** right in the center of Mt. Buller village. The village is the hub of accommodation, food, and ski services. The Cow Camp also houses **Auski ski hire** (though renting in Mansfield is cheaper; see p. 558), lockers, payphones, restaurants, and bathrooms. Directly across from the plaza is the **information tower** (tel. 5777 6052; fax 5777 6027; http://www.skibuller.com.au), with maps of the resort and slopes, as well as information on work and long-term accommodations opportunities (open 8am-6pm during ski season, erratic hours in summer). The **lift ticket office** lies across the village center from the plaza and info tower. (Tickets $60 for 1 day, $114 for 2 days, $264 for 5 days; ages 6-14 $30, $57, $132; children under 6 free.) Call the **Buller Report** (tel. 5533 3333), for the latest snow conditions, or tune into 93.7 FM. Mt. Buller's **post office** is at the foot of Summit Rd, across from the Cow Camp Plaza (open daily 8:30am-5pm; postal code 3723).

ACCOMMODATIONS AND FOOD Mt. **Buller YHA Hostel Lodge** (tel. 5777 6181) is the least expensive lodging on the mountain. Located in the heart of the village, the lodge has blessedly well-heated dorms, and piles three blankets on each bed anyway. TV lounge, kitchens, and ski lockers are available (lockers $3). ($45, non-YHA $49; Sept.-June 29 $36, $40. Linen $3. Check-in 8-10am and 5-10pm.) Reserve at least two weeks in advance for July weekdays, one month in advance for July weekends and August weekdays, and two months in advance for August weekends.

Next door to the YHA in the Village Center, the **Kooroora Hotel** (tel. 5777 6050; fax 5777 6202) offers more intimate 4-person dorms with baths. Guests get free breakfast in the fully licensed bistro pub, which hosts late-night entertainment. Video games and a restaurant round out the amenities, along with a 10% discount for guests' ski hire on-site. (M-Th $60, F-Su $70, weekly $340. Breakfast included. Reservations require a deposit and should be made months in advance.)

The Cow Camp Plaza houses several upstairs eateries. The **Pancake Parlour** is done up in faux-1890s style and serves up mean pancakes in crazy varieties like Hot Bavarian Apple and Jamaican Banana ($5.40-8.30). The same area is home to the **Skiosk,** whose coolest feature is, alas, its punny name, and serves basic snack bar and take-away fare (open 8am-9pm ski season, 9am-5pm off-season). A small **market** lies across Summit Rd from the lift ticket office, with pricey food, a paucity of fresh produce, and a small snack bar. Upstairs on the opposite side of the Cow Camp, **Cafe Moguls** (tel. 5777 6882) is slightly more upmarket, offering mostly hearty meat-and-potatoes fare. Its desserts are a standout, especially the decadent Black Forest Belgian Waffle ($7.50). Moguls also competes with the **Kooroora's pub** for best nightlife on the mountain. Both places rage into the wee hours; Kooroora has more live cover bands, while Moguls has dance parties with Melbourne DJs.

MOUNTAIN BIKING In the summer, mountain biking is the thing to do at Buller. It's oriented toward downhillers, with a plethora of tracks and lift access to the top. Lifts operate daily from December 20 to the end of January, then on long weekends and public holidays until Easter. Before taking bikes up the lift, which you can do during **"expression sessions"** (9:30am-12:30pm and 1:30pm-4:30pm), a lesson is required. Group lessons plus two sessions cost $55, or $75 with bike and helmet hire. Lift passes, if you've already been trained, cost $30 for one session or $35 for two in one day. Pricier private lessons are also available. Cheaper biking sans chairlift is available; ask the resort staff for advice and a trail map. Bike and helmet hire ranges from $15 per hour to $45 per day for front suspension; more for dual suspension. **Raw NRG** (tel. 5777 6887; fax 5777 6890), Mt. Buller's biking center, has more information.

■ Glenrowan

A small stop off the Hume Highway (Hwy 31) between Benalla and Wangaratta, Glenrowan owes its fame entirely to the notorious bushranger Ned Kelly and the authorities who finally corralled him here. Upon entering the town, visitors are greeted by the 6m Kelly statue, clad in the armor mask he wore on that fateful day. The primary attraction is the $2.5 million animatronic tourist extravaganza, **Ned Kelly's Last Stand,** located at the **Glenrowan Tourist Centre** (tel. 5766 2367) a corny, cultish narrative presentation in which Ned's outlaw exploits are presented in a self-described "40 minutes of rip-snorting action." (Every 30min., 9:30am-4:30pm and 7:30-8pm; $15, ages 5-15 $8.) Next door, the **Ned Kelly Memorial Museum and Homestead** offers a small shack in gold prospector style as a re-creation of Kelly's headquarters. A sprawling gift shop has Kelly kitsch galore (museum admission $2, kids 50¢).

Ned Kelly: Outlaw and Hero

Born in Beveridge in 1855, Edward "Ned" Kelly gained a reputation as Australia's foremost outlaw and, for many, its most colorful hero. The son of a convicted thief, Kelly, along with the other boys in his clan, began claiming unbranded horses at an early age. He served his first jail time at 14, but became a serious horse thief only after teaming up with his father-in-law George King in 1874. Over the next nine years, Kelly and his small gang terrorized the countryside between Beechworth and Benalla, an area now known as Kelly Country. Constantly running from the law, they shot officers when confronted, took townspeople hostage, and robbed two banks. An autobiographical manifesto written by Kelly and handed to a teller at one heist can today be viewed at the Melbourne Public Library (see p. 495). The document, intended to give Kelly's side of his much-contested story, was never published during his lifetime nor examined during his trial. The Kelly gang made its last stand at the Glenrowan Inn on Monday, June 28, 1880. That day, Ned Kelly, wearing a 44kg suit of armor fashioned from melted (and stolen) plows and an overcoat, walked steadily toward a wave of shooting policemen. The officers, finally realizing his deceit, shot at Kelly's exposed legs. Kelly was brought to Melbourne and hanged on November 11, 1880, in the Melbourne Gaol, at the age of 25. The jail (see p. 506) displays his death mask, his famous armor, and the gallows on which he met his end. Ned Kelly's legendary status looms large in Australia, and an excellent account of his life and feats can be found at http://www.netspace.net.au/~bradwebb/.

■ Wangaratta

With expansive brick sidewalks and 19th century edifices, Wangaratta is a quiet rural crossroads along the Hume Hwy, which runs north into New South Wales. Set among fields of snow in winter, Wangaratta has a wealth of budget accommodations and some good eateries that make it both a convenient stop on the way north through the Hume Corridor and a natural base for exploring Victoria's alpine country.

ORIENTATION AND PRACTICAL INFORMATION For information on Wangaratta and the surrounding snowfields, tune to 88FM or spin by the **Wangaratta Visitor's Centre** (tel. 5721 5711), located on the Hume Hwy (Tone Rd), 1km southwest of the city center (open 9am-5pm). Tone Rd is called **Murphy St** downtown, and intersects Ford, Ely, Reid, and Faithfull St as you proceed north. **ATMs** are clustered on Murphy between Reid and Faithfull, and **Willoughby's Camping World,** 106 Murphy, vends all the camping gear you'll ever need. **V/Line** runs from the station on Docker St (tel. 5721 3641; Docker is called Ford St downtown) to Bright (1½hr, daily, $9.60), Melbourne (3½hr, 5 per day, $28.40), and Albury-Wodonga (1hr, 5 per day, $9.60). Free **Internet access** is available at the **public library,** 62 Ovens St (open M, Tu, Th, F 9:30am-6pm, W 1-6pm, Sa 9am-noon). The **post office** is at the intersection of Murphy and Ely St (open M-F 9am-5pm; **postal code** 3677).

ACCOMMODATIONS AND FOOD The **Grand Central Hotel** (tel. 5721 3705), on Murphy just north of Reid St, offers centrally located digs. Although the heated rooms are a tad dark, they each have a clean bathroom. The hotel is above a lively sports bar and tavern with a delectable lunch buffet ($5; rooms $20). The **Royal Victoria Hotel Motel** (tel. 5721 5455), on Faithfull St just north of Murphy St, offers basic lodging with linens and hand basins in small rooms (singles $15; doubles $30; $4 pub meals), and the downstairs pub is an R&B venue on weekend nights. Book all beds well in advance for early November's jazz festival.

Safeway supermarket, on Ovens St between Reid and Ford St, is open daily 7am to midnight. The **Scribbler's Cafe,** 66 Reid St (tel. 5721 3945), which gets its name from the local artwork that festoons its walls, serves all-natural, budget-friendly fare for breakfast, lunch, and dinner. **Vespa's Cafe** (tel. 5722 4392), at Reid and Ovens St, has an excellent, eclectic menu in a jazzy, Mediterranean bistro setting, and a bar specializing in local wine. (Dinner $11-15, lunch $5-7.50 noon-2:30pm. Open daily noon-10pm.)

SIGHTS AND ACTIVITIES Wangaratta's Heritage Trail provides an overview of the town's architecture and history; pick up info at the tourist office. Aircraft enthusiasts should jet 7km down Greta Rd to **Air World** (tel. 5721 8788), an aviation museum housing over 40 vintage aircraft. *(Open daily 9am-5pm. $6, ages 6-15 $4, families $12.50. Wheelchair accessible.)* Forays into nearby wine country yield Bacchanalian fun. **Milawa,** to the east, is dotted with vineyards; the **Brown Brothers Winery** (tel. 5720 5547) is one of the best. Wangaratta's renowned **jazz festival,** the first weekend of November, ranks among Australia's best (tel. 1800 803 944; http://www.Wangaratta.Jazz.org.au).

■ Rutherglen

Rutherglen, at the heart of Victoria's most renowned wine region, is an excellent base for touring the surrounding wineries. The Murray Valley Hwy, called Main St in Rutherglen, runs from Yarrawonga (45km west) through Rutherglen to Albury (50km east). The **tourist office** (tel. 6032 9166 or 1800 622 871), located in the Jolimont Centre on the corner of Drummon and Main St, down the hill from the city center, is the place to go for winery literature and maps. The tourist office also rents slightly suspect bicycles ($10 half-day, $15 full day; open daily 9am-5pm). A Commonwealth Bank **ATM** is on the corner of Murray and High St. Back down Murray St is the **post office** (open M-F 9am-5pm; **postal code** 3685). Note that the **phone code for the region is 02**, not 03.

The **V/Line** leaves Rutherglen for Melbourne (3½hr.; M, W, and F 6:35am; $33.20). To make more V/Line connections while school is in session (and finally reach that long-suppressed dream of being the cool kid in the back of the bus), take the Wangaratta-bound school bus from the post office at about 8am. Pay the driver upon boarding. **Kelly's Bus Service** (tel. 0419 244 897) shuttles to Albury-Wodonga at 9:30am on weekdays from the BP station west of the city center ($3). V/Line tickets can be purchased at the **McNamara's Country Store** (tel. 6032 9533; open M-F 8am-5:30pm, Sa 8:30am-noon) across from the post office. General transport inquiries can be made here as well. **Grapevine Getaways** (tel. 6023 2599) runs a tour from Albury to several wineries. Tours start from $30 and run daily at 9:30am; advance bookings are essential. For visitors who can't spare the time to see the wineries but want a souvenir, the **Walkabout Cellar** (tel. 6032 9784) next to the Victoria Hotel sells all of the local labels (open M-F 9am-5pm, Sa 9am-1pm, Su 10am-1pm).

The only truly budget accommodation in town is the **Star Hotel** (tel. 6032 9625), on the corner of Main and High St. Although a bit worn and dim, these rooms are an adequate place to crash after a day of tastings. (Singles $15, doubles $30.) Nicer motel rooms outside range from $30-49. The **Victoria Hotel,** 90 Main St (tel. 6032 7022), across from the post office, provides excellent lodging in a beautifully restored building that has been classified by the National Trust. Rooms contain lovely period desks and beds. The paneled ceiling and preserved fixture bases are thoroughly authentic. Amenities include fans, space heaters, electric blankets, and complimentary breakfast. (Singles $35; doubles $58. Reserve in advance during school holidays and major wine festivals.) A **Foodtown Supermarket,** 95 Main St (tel. 6032 9232) has plenty of provisions. (Open M-W 7:30am-6pm, Th-F 7:30am-8pm, Sa 7:30am-1pm, Su 8:30am-noon.)

■ Rutherglen Wineries

Choosing from among these excellent wineries can be quite difficult. If you only have time to visit one, make it **All Saints Estate** (tel. 6033 1922), east of Rutherglen via Corowa Rd, then north on All Saints Rd. This experience matches most people's romantic visions of what wineries should look like. Towering elms line the driveway as visitors approach the striking red brick castle, and a sculptured rose garden with a central fountain borders the parking lot. The most tourist-oriented of the wineries, All Saints welcomes visitors to its **Cellar Door** (open M-Sa 9am-5:30pm, Su 10am-5:30pm) for free tastings, and provides succulent and expensive lunches at its **Terrace Restaurant** (reservations imperative on weekends). A marked, self-guided tour leads past immaculate gardens, huge display casks, and a playground. A peek into the well-preserved **Chinese Dormitory and Gardens** on the grounds gives a sense of the early laborers' living conditions. Adjacent to the parking lot, the **North East Victoria Winemakers Hall of Fame** is an informative display of the region's leading figures and wineries.

    Campbells Winery (tel. 6032 9458), located just west of the visitors center on the Murray Valley Hwy, is a fully functional winery with an open house policy. Visitors can take the self-guided tour or wander and observe grapes being gathered and crushed and wine being bottled. Picnic tables out front are perfect for a BYO lunch. (Open M-Sa 9am-5pm, Su 10am-5pm.) For the best in fortified wines, connoisseurs should stop by **Morris Wines** (tel. 6026 7303), east of Rutherglen and north of the Murray Valley Hwy on Mia Mia Rd. The muscats are among the world's finest. The best place to find an affordable lunch and affable family winemakers is at **Gehring Estate Winery** (tel. 6026 7296), farthest east out of town on the Murray Valley Hwy (open M-Sa 9am-5pm, Su 10am-5pm). Gehring's claims to be Victoria's oldest winery, but they don't focus much on tours, selling most of their wine only at the cellar door. Lunch is served in the small restaurant out back (Tu-Su and public holidays noon-3pm).

    For those traveling by car, the *Rutherglen Touring Guide* is an indispensible map available at the visitors center. Navigating the area by bike is made easier by picking up a free *Muscat Trail Map,* also available at the tourist office. For a campier tour, take a horse-drawn stagecoach from **Poachers Paradise Hotel** (tel. 6032 9502) at 1pm daily, tours three wineries in two hours, and only costs $10 per person (under 15 $5). Reserve in advance. If 1pm tour is fully booked, a 10am tour may operate in addition.

HIGH COUNTRY

Victoria's High Country, tucked between the Murray River and Gippsland's thick coastal forest, strikes an unexpected counterpoint to the standard Australian sights like Surfer's Paradise or the Red Centre. Here, ancient forests display dazzling fall colors and rambling valleys nurture spring flowers that shame Crayola. In winter, Mt Hotham and Falls Creek offer the continent's best skiing, centered around the charming sub-Alpine village of Bright. And while people flock to the coast in summer, there's a ton to do here too, where Mt. Buffalo's gorgeous soaring peaks and warm thermal winds support some of the world's best paragliding in addition to eco-adventures like abseiling and mountain biking. For those who prefer tamer pleasures, the small town of Beechworth boasts a terrific concentration of gold rush era Australiana. All vehicles heading into the mountains must carry chains from June 8 (Queen's Birthday) until October 1.

▓ Beechworth

This robust, upscale country town preserves a large number of gold-rush era stone masonry buildings amid a slew of elegant boutiques, antique shops, and galleries. One attraction for tourists is the supporting role Beechworth played in the life of the infamous criminal Ned Kelly.

PRACTICAL INFORMATION The **Visitors Information Centre** (tel. 5728 3233) is located in beautifully preserved Shire Hall on Ford St, Beechworth's main north-south street (open daily 9am-5pm). Camp St forms the major cross street in the middle of town. Clustered together along Ford St near the amain intersection with Camp St are a Commercial Bank **ATM,** a **laundromat** (open daily 7am-9pm), a **Foodtown market** (tel. 5729 1055; open M-F 8:30am-5:30pm, Sa 8:30am-5pm, Su 10am-5pm), and the **post office** (open M-F 9am-5pm; **postal code** 3747). The **V/Line bus** stop is on Camp St, just west of Ford St, and tickets should be purchased at **Beechworth Animal World,** 32 Camp St (tel. 5728 1374; open M-F 9am-5:30pm, Sa 9am-4pm, Su 11am-4pm). Buses run to Melbourne (3½hr., 2-3 per day, $33); Sydney via Albury (1 per day, $84); and Wangaratta (30min., 2-3 per day, $5.40).

ACCOMMODATIONS AND FOOD Beechworth overflows with B&Bs. The visitors center can help you select one based on price (starting at $45 per double), theme, or amenities. A reasonable hotel-style accommodation with B&B charm is the **Hibernian Hotel** (tel. 5728 1070) on Camp St on the corner of Loch St, one block west of the town center. The well-appointed rooms boast tasteful, eclectic country decor, while the cozy, book-filled lounge and the garden invite guests to sit back and relax. (Singles $30; doubles or twins $45. Breakfast $5-10.) A larger, similarly styled pub hotel is the **Tanswells Commercial Hotel** (tel. 5728 1480). Glorious central heating and cooling fills the rooms, which are decked out in Victorian-era decor. Friday and Saturday nights are noisy until late. (Singles Su-Th $30, F-Sa $40; doubles Su-Th $45, F-Sa $60; family rooms Su-Th $60, F-Sa $80. Breakfast included.)

The award-winning **Beechworth Bakery** (tel. 5728 1132), on Camp St, should simply not be missed by those who prize anything leavened. Boothed seating and stools in the sunny cafe-style bakery provide a convenient niche from which to sip a mug of chocaccino ($2.45) or devour a grilled focaccia sandwich ($5.50; open daily 6am-7pm).

SIGHTS AND ACTIVITIES The bushranger **Ned Kelly** was first tried and jailed in Beechworth, detained in a cell you can still visit behind Shire Hall (admission by donation). Three trials later, proceedings against Kelly for the killing of constables Lonigan and Scanlon in the infamous Glenrowan siege commenced here before moving to Melbourne in search of an impartial jury. Inside the **Beechworth Historic Court House,** 94 Ford St (tel. 5728 2721), you can marvel at how well the courtroom has been preserved in its original 19th century condition, right down to the dock where Ned Kelly stood during his trials. *(Open daily 10am-4pm. Admission $2, concessions $1, family $4.)*

Directly behind the information center, on Loch St, the **Burke Museum** (tel./fax 5728 1420) displays all the gold-rush era artifacts you ever wanted to see, plus some interesting exhibits of Aboriginal culture. *(Open daily 10:30am-3:30pm. $5, children $3, families $14.)* Robert O'Hara Burke, the museum's namesake, was a popular local police superintendent who made up half of the ill-fated Burke and Wills expedition which set out to explore central Australia. Behind the stained glass window sits a row of period shops whose lively displays simulate 1860s bustle with an amusement park feel.

One block north and three blocks west of the town center is the site of **M.B. Historic Cellars,** 29 Last St (tel. 5728 1304). The friendly folks at this 100-year-old brewery produce non-alcoholic cordials in 14 authentic turn-of-the-century flavors, taking us all back to the world before Coca-Cola. Next door, up-and-running old-style blacksmith operations complete the effect. *(Site open daily 10am-4pm. Tours free.)*

Beechworth **cemetery,** located north of the town center on Cemetery Rd, houses the **Chinese Burning Towers.** The towers, which resemble giant firecrackers, and the simple headstones are all that remain of the gold rush era Chinese presence in Beechworth. Chinese miners once outnumbered whites five to one, but their segregated, diminutive, and tightly packed grave sites testify to the discrimination they faced.

■ Near Beechworth: Yackandandah

A small, friendly gold rush town with a funny name, Yackandandah, or "Yack," offers a less touristy and less expensive getaway in Victoria's rugged northeast country than better-known Beechworth. From Beechworth (23km) or Wodonga (27km), Hwy C315 leads to a turn-off for Yackandandah. In town, shops and services can be found on High St. The staff at the **Yackandandah Visitors Information Centre** (tel. 6027 1988), on High St in the Athenaeum building, are eager to point you to their town's gems (open daily 10am-4pm). Craft shops, fragrant tea rooms, and historic buildings give the town its character. There are **no ATMs** in Yackandandah. The **post office** is located on High St (open M-F 9am-5pm; **postal code** 3749). The **phone code is 02,** not 03.

Although a night in the nearby town of Albury-Wodonga is probably preferable, the **Yackandandah Hotel** (tel. 6027 1210) on High St and Isaacs Ave, makes a good alternative to Beechworth's pricier digs ($20; reception at bar 11am-8pm). For excellent breakfasts or lunches, try the sandwiches, pies, and loaves from **The Yackandandah Bakery** (tel. 6027 1549), on High St. For those with a car and a sweet tooth, it's worth a trip out to the award-winning **Vienna Patisserie Chalet** (tel. 6027 1477), 7km north towards Wodondga from downtown, at the Allan's Flat turn-off, where an Austrian couple decked out in traditional garb serve an ever-changing menu of delicious tortes and strudels. (Open daily 10am-6pm, but closed during July.)

Just down the road from the Patisserie, slightly closer to town, is **Schmidt's Strawberry Winery** (tel. 6027 1454) at the Allan's Flat turn-off. The Schmidts made wine for generations, and began strawberry production and winemaking in 1968. They produce dry and semi-sweet wines, popular with spicy food, and sweet, tasty dessert wines ($12.50 each, all 3 varieties for $29). A luscious strawberry liqueur is also available for $20. (Open for sales and tastings daily 9am-5pm.)

With over 9000 plants and 20 varieties of lavender cultivated, **The Lavender Patch** (tel. 6027 1603), 5km west of Yackandandah on Beechworth Rd (called High St in the town center), soothes and delights the senses. Natural lavender products including soaps and potpourri can be purchased in the shop, and the hosts encourage guests to roam the aromatic hillside. (Open daily 9am-5:30pm. Free.) To relive the gold rush firsthand, take a goldmine tour with **Yack Track Tours** (tel. 6027 1757), 2 Kars St, who will provide torches, hardhats, and commentary for your one-hour tour through an underground gold tunnel. (Adults $7, children 12 and under $4, family $20. Tours leave Sa-Su and holidays at 10:30am, noon, 1:30, and 3:30pm; by appointment during the week.)

■ Mt. Buffalo National Park

The sheer rock faces of Mt. Buffalo rise up imposingly alongside the Ovens Hwy (Great Alpine Rd), signaling the site of a rich sub-alpine ecosystem that offers numerous outdoor adventure opportunities throughout the year. Though the mountain's craggy walls look intimidating from a distance, the ski slopes that draw people here in winter are gentle. If you're a serious skier or looking for nightlife, you'd be better off elsewhere; for families and beginners, though, this is a great value in a friendly environment. In summer, the park blooms with all kinds of water sports, as well as abseiling, rock climbing, mountain biking, hang gliding, and bushwalking.

PRACTICAL INFORMATION AND ACCOMMODATIONS Entrance to the national park is just off the Great Alpine Rd roundabout by Porepunkah, 5km north of Bright and 320km from Melbourne. The $7 per-car entrance fee is waived for guests of either mountaintop lodging, and is sometimes waived altogether in the off-season. The **park office** (tel. 5755 1466) provides maps and tour information (open sporadically, mostly weekday mornings and afternoons).

The clean, simple lines of the main lounge and bistro at the **Mt. Buffalo Lodge** (tel. 5755 1988), 7km along the main road from the visitors center, overlook the slopes (meals $2.50-10). Inside, a ski shop and ski hire serve visitors for both cross-country and downhill skiing, while guests have access to laundry facilities, towels, games room, and TV/VCR lounge. Dorms have basic bunks, storage, shared facilities, and coffee and tea service. (Bunks in Aug. $30; July and Sept. $25; Oct.-June $18.) Motel units have bath, veranda, and cheery decor ($79, $109 during ski season). Three meals are included for all rooms. Ask the staff about job opportunities.

Excellent unpowered **campgrounds** lie beside Lake Catani, 1km south of the park office. Some are caravan-accessible, and there are toilets, water, hot showers, and laundry nearby. Bookings can be made through the information office. (Campground closed May-Oct. Sites $10-14 for up to four people, additional people $2.70.)

SKIING, SIGHTS, AND ACTIVITIES Mt. Buffalo's slopes cater almost entirely to beginner and intermediate skiers, and its atmosphere is heavily family-oriented. **Lift passes** are available for the **Cresta Valley site** adjacent to the Mt Buffalo Lodge, and the price is a steal. *(Morning $25, afternoon $29, full day $34; ages 7-16 $14, $16, $19; under 7 $5, $7, $10. Lift ticket and intro lesson package $35; children under 15 $24.)*

The drive up to Mt. Buffalo is one of its most dramatic ascents, as **waterfalls** snake over the craggy face of the mountain. There are some spectacular lookout points as well as numerous walking tracks, the most challenging of which is aptly titled "The Big Walk," and spans much of the ascent to the summit. After entering the park, the winding mountain road passes through dense eucalypt forests that hold over 400 plant species and 90km of walking tracks. A left turn just before the park office leads toward the Mt. Buffalo Chalet and Bent's Lookout. This stunning view provides a panoramic sweep across the Buckland Valley, with Australia's tallest peak, Mt. Kosciusko, visible on clear days. In the carpark, brilliantly colored crimson rosellas display uncanny intelligence and will land on you to feed if you entice them with snacks. Abseilers descend and hang gliders launch from all along the rock face.

Driving south past the park office toward the Tatra Inn, you'll see numerous marked **walking trails.** Opposite the office, the tremendous view from the Monolith rock outcropping is definitely worth the short walk. A kilometer further along, **Lake Catani** serves as a hub for summer water sports and winter ice skating. Farther south, you'll pass **Dingo Dell,** the first Australian ski run with a chairlift. Past Dingo Dell, an excellent short walk leads to the **Cathedral,** a granite peak that juts sharply above the snowplain.

Mt. Buffalo doesn't shut down when the skiing stops; its warm-weather activities are at least as popular as its winter ones. **Abseilers** (rapellers) go over the edge near Bent's Lookout year-round. **Rock climbing, caving,** and rugged mountaineering expeditions led by certified instructors are run through the **Mt. Buffalo Chalet Activities Center** (tel. 5755 1500), and can be coordinated through Bright's hostels (half-day $50, full day $100). Prices include meals, transport, and equipment. The area is also a hub of paragliding and mountain biking (see below), though tamer, cheaper activities like bushwalking and fly-fishing are also big. **Wild Wilderness photography tours** ($22 for 2hr.) offer full-day wilderness art excursions ($39).

■ Bright

Bright is an apt name for this alpine community, whose radiant natural beauty is complemented by glowing hospitality and adventure. With excellent budget accommodations and proximity to wineries, snowfields, and larger cities, Bright serves as a popular base for skiing in the surrounding Australian alpine country during winter, and in summer people flock here to take advantage of local bushwalking, paragliding, abseiling, and other eco-tourism opportunities. Bright is located 79km southeast of Wangaratta along the **Ovens Highway (Great Alpine Rd).**

ORIENTATION AND PRACTICAL INFORMATION The **Bright Visitors Centre,** 119 Gavan St (tel. 5755 2275 or 1800 500 117; fax 5750 1655; open daily 9am-5pm), sells **V/ Line** and **Rail Australia** tickets to Melbourne (4½hr., 1 per day, $37.80), Mt. Beauty (30min.; M, F; $5), Wangaratta (1½hr.; daily; $9.60), and Albury-Wodonga (2hr.; daily; $18.20). Buses depart from the post office. The town center is marked by a roundabout with a high Art Deco clock tower, where **Barnard** and **Anderson** (each of which connect to **Gavan St,** as the **Great Alpine Rd** is known in town) meet **Camp, Ireland,** and **Burke St.** There's an **ANZ bank** with a 24-hour **ATM** on Gavan St, while the **post office** is on Ireland St (open M-F 9am-5pm; postal code 3741).

ACCOMMODATIONS AND FOOD The more centrally located of Bright's two backpacker accommodations is VIP-affiliated **Bright Hikers Backpackers Hostel,** 4 Ireland St, 2nd floor (tel. 5750 1244; fax 5750 1246; email gwhite@netc.net.au), located across from the post office. Two comfy common rooms have great lounge furniture, pool, ping-pong, a video library, and multifarious international incarnations of Monopoly. Kitchens, dorms, and bathrooms are sparklingly clean; extras include laundry, safe for valuables, and Internet access. (Dorms with 4-6 beds $15. Weekly: $84. Internet $10 per hour, $2.50 per 10min. Linen rental $2.50; lockers 50¢; mountain bikes $3 per hr.,

$12 per day; breakfast $4-5.50.) Both Hikers and the YHA Lodge book local adventure activities on a discount basis.

One block east of the information center, off Cherry Lane lies the creekside **Bright YHA Lodge** (tel. 5750 1180; fax 5750 1186; email yhalodge@bright.albury.net.au). The hostel has clean four-bunk rooms with storage lockers, adjoining shared bathrooms. The central kitchen, dining room, and TV lounge feature a roaring fireplace. (Dorms $16, nonmembers $19. Weekly: $105, $126. Wheelchair accessible. Linen rental $2.) Adjacent **Bright Caravan Park** (tel. 5755 1141; fax 5750 1077) has shaded sites ideal for summer campers. (During school holidays, long weekends, and ski season, sites $15, powered $18. Weekly: $105, $126. Off-season sites $12, $15. Weekly: $72, $90. Cabins $50-60 per double.) Reserve in advance during peak seasons.

Bright is blessed with quite a few good restaurants. **Alps,** 94 Gavan St (tel. 5755 1526), has Mexican and Italian fare, including excellent wood-fired pizza of all varieties, such as the delicious Americano, with pepperoni, onion, and heaps of extra cheese. The **Liquid Am-bar** (tel. 5755 2318) lies on the upper end of the budget range but has truly memorable eclectic cuisine, such as the prawn and avocado salad ($12), in a sleek setting. It serves exotic cocktails as well; try the "Am-bar Illusion," a combination of countless delectable liquors which packs a heavy kick that's well worth the $8.50 price tag (open M-S from 5pm, Su from 6pm). The **Alpine Hotel** (tel. 5755 1366) is about the only place in town open for breakfast and also has a lively bar that gets a little crazy on weekend nights when local bands perform. The **Riteway supermarket** is on Ireland St (open M-F 8am-7pm, Sa 8am-5pm, Su 9am-2pm).

SIGHTS AND ACTIVITIES While it's merely a base for winter skiing in neighboring Mt. Hotham, Falls Creek, and Mt. Buffalo, Bright stands alone as the undisputed regional king of summer adventure activities. At the center of town, **Bright Ski Centre,** 22 Ireland St (tel. 5755 1093; fax 5750 1093), offers ski gear, apparel, and snow chains. Every set of rented skis comes with a ski rack. (Per day rentals: skis, boots, and poles $23, under 15 $16; snowboards and boots $45; toboggans $8; chains $18. V, MC, AmEx. Multi-day rentals discounted. Open Sa-Th 7am-7pm, F 7am-2am.)

The valleys surrounding Bright boast warm thermal air currents ideal for hang-gliding and paragliding; the area was home to the 1986 World Championships. **Alpine Paragliding,** 6 Alpine St (tel. 5755 1753; email alpnpara@netc.net.au; http:// www.netc.net.au/alpnpara/), next to Bright Hikers, offers tandem paraglides ($95). These flights are guaranteed to last 10-15 minutes, and often extend longer. Wimpier and cheaper vicarious thrills can be found by watching the gliders soar en masse; take the bus to the launching point (round-trip $8). The local ranges are ideal for mountain biking during warm, dry weather; **Mountain Thunder Bike Tours** (tel. 1800 500 117 or 5755 2275) offers full- and half-day trips that include thrilling descents ($45-80; summer only). **Adventure Guides Australia** (tel. 5728 1804) conducts abseiling (similar to rappelling; half-day $42), night caving ($48), rock climbing (full day $95), and bushwalking and camping excursions. Their top-notch staff overflows with advice and encouragement. All adventure activities are year-round, though they're subject to weather and are much more sporadic in winter. Group bookings are encouraged.

If you're feeling lucky, try panning for gold in local rivulets, which have not yet been exhausted of their ore. **Bright Gold Panning Tours** (tel. 5750 1494) operates tours that range from a half-day to a week; they guarantee you'll get at least a flake of the shiny stuff (tours from $20). Five minutes south of Bright along the Great Alpine Rd, the **Wandiligong Maze and Garden Cafe** (tel. 5750 1311; open W-Su 10am-5pm) is a delightful hedge maze (admission $5, children $2).

■ Falls Creek

Just an hour's drive uphill from Bright along a road with sweeping views of the Victorian Alpine country, **Falls Creek Ski Resort** (tel. 5754 4718 or 1800 033 079; fax 5754 4287; http://www.skifallscreek.com.au) lifts guests as high as 1780m. The ample snowfall, both natural and man-made, is a selling point, as are the 19 chairlifts serving 90 trails and the resort's partnership with nearby Mt. Hotham. Intermediate runs predominate, but 17% and 23% of the runs are suited for beginners or advanced skiers, respectively. There's a 2.2km beginner run, while some open-bowl powder skiing as well as narrow tree-lined trails are more appropriate for advanced skiers. Shredders will appreciate the snowboarding terrain park, which includes a halfpipe and a varying set of obstacles. Lift tickets allow unlimited use of both Falls Creek and Mt. Hotham resort lifts (see p. 568), as well as cross-country loops. (Resort entry $19 per day, $25 overnight; this doesn't cover lifts. 1-day lift tickets $61, under 15 $32, families of 4 $165. 1-day lift and lesson package $83, under 15 $57. Discounts for advance purchase.)

Activity at Falls Creek is concentrated at the eastern and western edges of the village. The **Falls Creek Information Centre** (tel. 5758 3490) sits at the northern end of Bogong High Plains Road, just inside the park entrance, and offers information on lessons, lift packages, and accommodations (open 8:30am-5pm). Uphill on Slalom St is the **Wombat Cafe** (tel. 5758 3666), which houses the **post office** (open M-F 9am-5pm; postal code 3699), a mini-market downstairs, and an inexpensive snack bar upstairs. The **Frying Pan Inn,** 4 Village Bowl Circle (tel. 5758 3390; fax 5758 3416), at the western end of the village, rents bunks in dorms for $35-68 (weekdays on the margin of the season are cheapest). It's the Inn place to be on weekends, when there are live bands, dance parties, and plenty of drink specials to fuel the debauchery. There are **ski rental places** everywhere, but it's cheaper to get equipment in Bright (see p. 566). An active summer resort as well, Falls Creek offers bushwalking, horseback riding, tennis, and water sports. The **Food, Wine, and Wildflower Festival** showcases gourmet cuisine and locally-produced vino amid blooming flora during the second week of January.

■ Mt. Hotham

With Victoria's highest average snowfall depth, 13 lifts (including 8 quads), and a strong partnership with nearby Falls Creek, Mount Hotham is Australia's intermediate and advanced skiing and snowboarding headquarters. Located 1½ hours from Bright along the Great Alpine Rd, the slopes are more challenging than Australia usually offers, with short but steep double black diamonds cutting through the trees in the "Extreme Skiing Zone." Beginner skiing is more limited, though the usual array of lessons is available.

PRACTICAL INFORMATION In the tradition of great ski resorts the world over, Hotham's not cheap. There's a fee just to enter the resort, not covering lift tickets, payable at the tollbooth on the Great Alpine Road (cars $19, $25 per night, $100 season pass). If you're just driving through without skiing, it's free, but you have to get a special transport ticket. From the north, Mt. Hotham is accessible for most of the winter on a winding sealed road. Entrance from Omeo to the south is safer and more reliable, but inconvenient for those based in Melbourne or Sydney.

To get to Mt. Hotham by **bus,** depart from Melbourne's Spencer St Station ($65), Wangaratta Railway Station ($50), or Bright's post office ($16). Contact **Trekset Tours** (tel. 9370 9055 or 1800 659 009; fax 9372 0689) to book. Drivers heading for Omeo and parts south can rent mandatory snow chains from **Hoy's Ski Hire** in Harrietville or **Mt. Hotham Roadside** (tel. 5759 2622) for $20 with a $30 deposit. These can be returned to Burke's in **Omeo** on the south side of Mt. Hotham.

The resort's lodges cluster to its south, with ski lifts and services farther north. A tractor transports folks for free around the resort. The **information center** (tel. 5759 3550 or 1800 354 555; http://www.hotham-fallscreek.com.au) is on the first floor of the tourist shelter and administration building, just north of the Corral carpark. Directly across the street, Hotham Central houses a **ski school office,** helicopter, and the **Swindlers Valley Brand Bistro,** which overlooks the slopes and sells **lift tickets,** valid both here and at Falls Creek. (Full-day ticket $61, children $32. Lift and lesson packages start at $83 per day, children $57.) Student "extreme" packages (ages 15-18) provide discounts on lift and lessons. Tickets for round-trip helicopter rides to Falls Creek are $49.

ACCOMMODATIONS AND FOOD Lodging on Mt. Hotham is pricey, and Bright's excellent hostels offer an inexpensive alternative. Those interested in ski lodge accommodations should contact the **Mount Hotham Accommodation Service** (tel. 5759 3636 or 1800 032 061; fax 5759 3111; http://www.mt-hotham-accommodation.com.au), who can sometimes place you in a club lodge for as low as $35 from late July to mid-September, or $20 in the off-peak season. In the summer, Hotham is relatively quiet, with nature trails and a few shops and lodgings open for visitors. From mid-October to Queen's Birthday in June, resort admission is free.

On the south side of both the resort and the Big D chair lift sits **Big D,** a complex housing a ski boutique as well as the **Isobar** (tel. 5759 3066), a trendy joint with cheap, tasty food for dine-in or take-away. This is also the place for beginner ski lessons and **night skiing** (Tu, Th, Sa 6:30-10pm). Next door is **The General** (tel. 5759 3532), a general store with a mini-market, pub, and mailbox. The excellent 11km **cross-country track** to Dinner Plain begins just beyond the store. The **Swindler's Balcony Bar & Restaurant** (tel. 5759 4421), downstairs at Hotham Central, serves hearty lunches and dinners by its open fireplace; the bar is an après-ski hotspot with live music on weekends.

GIPPSLAND

As you flip through your scrapbook collage from your trip to Australia, the cutout newsprint headline "Victorian Wilderness" catches your eye. It's the beginning of a few pages on Gippsland, the southernmost area of the mainland. The first page is filled with photographs of **Wilsons Promontory,** one of Australia's most famous parks: gum trees filled with crimson rosellas and cockatoos, a wallaby loose on the heathland, a lighthouse framed against the Southern Ocean, and you, worn out but triumphant after a two-day hike. Turning the page, you see overlapping images that challenge your memory. A photograph of misty rainforest encroaches upon salty coastal marshlands, fern trees and sea snails; along the top, there's a panoramic shot of the yellow sand and cool green surf of Ninety Mile Beach.

A passage from *Man from Snowy River* by Banjo Patterson introduces a smattering of pictures from **Snowy River National Park;** here you look truly exhausted, at the top of a lookout over a rugged, pine-lined gorge. The last page, covering the **Gippsland Lakes** (a.k.a. Victorian Riviera, at the far east), almost repeats the start. Again, rainforest images overlap with ocean and peninsular scrubland, highlighted by one lucky shot of a solitary penguin by the estuaries of desolate **Cape Conran**.

The Gippsland region covers the coast and hinterland east of Melbourne and south of the Victorian Alps, all the way to New South Wales. The area from Melbourne to the Gippsland Lakes is called **South Gippsland;** the rest, **East Gippsland.** Leaving Melbourne, the Southeast Hwy passes into the South Gippsland Hwy. The Princes Hwy takes an inland route just below the High Country, and meets the South Gippsland Hwy at **Sale.** From there the Princes Hwy takes over, moving along the coast of East Gippsland until it crosses into NSW. A **car** is recommended for exploring the region. Almost all important roads are sealed, and many dirt tracks are 2WD-accessible. **Greyhound, Oz Experience,** and **V/Line buses** cover some of the territory.

■ Wilsons Promontory National Park

Whether it's a first echidna sighting in the woodlands or the 360° view of granite headlands from Mt. Orbost, chances are you'll leave Wilsons Promontory with some unforgettable experiences. One of the world's most unspoiled and diverse natural reserves, **the Prom** is one of Australia's most famous parks. Four hundred thousand visitors come to experience its wonders each year. Tidal flats and marshland meet clusters of heath and towering gum forests. Rich fern gullies follow the contours of the land. This diversity of flora creates habitats for a plethora of native marsupials and bird life. Protruding like a beard to form the continent's southernmost extreme, Wilsons Prom consists of 49,000 hectares of parkland and an additional 8300 marine hectares off the mesmerizing granite coastline. Declared a UNESCO World Biosphere Reserve, the Prom is off limits to both public transportation and human settlement.

Still, travelers remain undeterred, and ever since George Bass first spotted its coastline in 1798, the area has been anything but a secret. In the early days of Australia's settlement, sealers and whalers exploited the waters offshore of the Prom. The emigration booms of the Gold Rush (1850s) and Federation (1900s) brought an active forestry industry, as timber was needed to support new development elsewhere in Victoria. During World War II, the government sealed off the Prom for commando training. Meanwhile, the park's geological history has taken some turns too. At various points, the peninsula was an island; it's now connected to the mainland by parallel sandy ridges. At one time, these ridges extended south to Tasmania, allowing for the spread of unusual flora and fauna.

Restricted access to the park creates a dilemma for its many visitors. Only one 30km sealed road accesses the Prom's western extremity, ending at Tidal River, a mass of caravans, dust, and flip-flop sandals that does little justice to the park's natural splendor. You should consider an overnight hike or daytrips from this area. If you don't have access to a car, the only other transportation to the Prom is via the daily Postie to and from Foster (see below). For more **information** on Wilsons Promontory, call 1800 350 552, or see the handy website for Victoria's parks (http://www.dce.vic.gov.au/parks/).

FOSTER: GATEWAY TO WILSONS PROMONTORY

If you are traveling by the daily **V/Line bus** (tel. 13 22 32) from Melbourne (M-F 4:30pm, Sa 6:40pm, Su 5:35pm, 2¾hr., $21.30; returns M-Sa 7:49am, Su 3:20pm), the current schedule requires that you spend the night in Foster before shuttling down to the Prom. Don't fret—Foster welcomes its role as a way station and treats backpackers with an earnest small-town warmth.

The **Prom Postie** (tel 5682 6614) runs mail and passengers down to the park once daily (departs M-F 9:30am, Su 1:30pm; returns to Foster M-F 12:30pm, Su 2:30pm; return $20). The proprietors of the **Little Mud Hut (YHA),** 17 Pioneer St (tel. 5682 2614), have been running the Postie for a decade; they will be sailing the world in 1999 but assure that an adequate substitute will be found. As you arrive from the South Gippsland Hwy to the rotary at the post office, turn right onto Main St, then left onto Ridge Rd, then right onto Pioneer St, and there you are. This miniature hostel has tiny cabin rooms with simple, homespun amenities. Nine beds, all in heated rooms, and an outdoor stove and kitchen area complement a TV lounge where you can sip tea and coffee as you await your trip to the Prom. Beds cost $15, doubles $34. Reserve a couple of days in advance during peak season.

Main St has it all. **Tourist information** is available inside the Stockyard Gallery at the end of Main St toward Wilsons (tel. 5682 1125; open daily 10am-4pm; off-season Th-Su 10am-4pm). The dynamite **post office** (tel. 5682 2597) has won awards, and deservedly so (postal code 3960; open M-F 9am-5pm, Sa 9am-1pm). The two **supermarkets** are open daily, as are the two excellent **bakeries** (sandwiches around $2.50) and the **pub,** which fills with locals from 6:30 to 10:30pm and stays open till around midnight.

PARK ACCESS AND TOURIST INFORMATION

The 25km **Foster Promontory Rd** snakes toward the national park passing through the town of Yanakie along the way. Speed limits are strictly enforced along the route. The entrance to the park is nearly 10km past **Yanakie** (entry $7 per car; free if you have arranged for accommodations at Tidal River, but not for outstation campers). Once you've entered the park, the 37km **Wilsons Promontory Rd** weaves south along the park's western edge to **Tidal River.**

Visitors who wish to stay overnight, obtain a fishing license, or need a map should continue 30 km to the **Tidal River Information Centre** (tel. 5680 9555 or 1800 350 552; fax 5680 9516; winter hours Tu-Th 8am-7:30pm, F-Sa 8am-9pm; summer Su-Th 8am-9pm, F-Sa 8am-10pm) at the end of the main road. Here, visitors can obtain maps of the park, trail guides, updates on weather conditions, and information about the

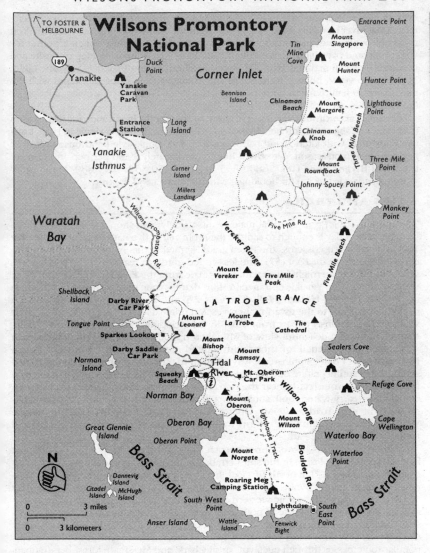

Wilsons Promontory National Park

Prom's geology and teeming plant and animal populations. All visitors must register their intentions to bushwalk and camp so that park officials will be on the lookout should things go awry. Tidal River also has the last toilets, pay phones, snack machines, and mini-market you'll see before setting off into the bush. Outside the information centre is a 24-hour Blue Box for contacting a ranger. The park, including outstation campsites, is patrolled at all hours.

ACCOMMODATIONS

Securing a place to spend the night at the Prom during the summer months is notoriously difficult, and Victorian residents lottery for spots. High-season rates apply from September through April, during school holidays, and on long weekends. To camp for an extended period at Tidal River in summer, you must enter a mid-year lottery. However, in high season the park reserves last-minute campsites for non-residents of Victoria at Tidal River (2 nights max; $14.50 per night for 1-3 people plus one vehicle). You need not book in advance for outstation camping, but you must obtain a permit for your group and pay nightly fees (adults $4, students $2). At **Roaring Meg** campsite and northern sites you may stay two nights, but at all others you may only stay one night. You may, however, bounce from site to site, though this must be registered with the info centre. At bathrooms at outstation sites, the park has ceased to provide toilet paper (go figure). No sites are powered.

For **roofed accommodation,** reserve three to six months in advance for high season (Oct.-Apr.). (**Cabins** with kitchen, living room, bathroom, $105 per single or twin. **Lorikee Flats** units with kitchen and bathroom $75, $45. Bunk-style **lighthouse units** $32 per person, $26 off-season. 4- to 6-bed **huts** approximately $9.50 per person.) Contact the **Tidal River Office** (tel. 5680 9555 or 1800 350 552; fax 5680 9516; email wprom@parks.vic.gov.au) for bookings, which require a $50 deposit.

WALKS AND TRAILS

To experience the Prom's natural majesty most richly, you should tackle a few bushwalking trails. A day is enough to sample the Prom; allow five days to savor it. The over 100km of trails that crisscross the Prom are described in the information center's *Discovering the Prom on Foot* ($7). The less-visited northern reaches of the park are traversed mostly by overnight hikes which originate from the **Five Mile Track Car Park,** the first left after the Yanakie entrance. A short detour along the Five Mile Track leads to the **Miller's Landing Nature Walk.** The easy 2.5km (2hr. return) walk leads through banksia woodlands to the dwarf mangroves and mudflats of Corner Inlet. Seven short walks (1-2km at most) depart from Tidal River, including **Whale Rock** (1km, 30min. round trip), with a delightful view of Mt. Oberon; **Loo-ern Track** (1km, 25min. each way), specially designed for those with limited mobility; and the **Squeaky Beach Nature Walk** (1.8km, 30min. each way). This third track winds through dunes, coastal scrub, and beautiful granite outcroppings. Look for wombats in the scrub, and once on the beach, slide your feet to hear the remarkably uniform white-grained sand squeak. On all hikes, carry water, food, sunblock, a hat, and insect repellent. A road branches off from the main road to the Mt. Oberon Car Park, where the **Mt. Oberon Nature Walk** begins. The 6.4km (2hr. return) walk leads to one of the best sunrise spots and panoramic views in the park.

For more ambitious hikers, three spectacular day hikes cover some of the most beloved spots in the Prom. In the southern half of the park, **Tongue Point Track** starts from Darby Saddle 6.7km north of Tidal River and proceeds past two sweeping lookouts to a small granite peninsula with a stunning view of the coast. The **Oberon Bay Track** (6km) follows the scenic western coastline along yellow sand beaches from Norman Bay to Norman Point, site of both Oberon Bay and Little Oberon Bay. In the opposite direction, departing from the Mt. Oberon car park east of Tidal River, the **Sealers Cove Track** (19.5km) takes you across nearly every environment in the Prom. This popular route passes through eucalypt, stringy bark, and Messmate forest before opening into a grassy area 3km from the car park. From here it descends into Sealers Swamp and through fern gullies en route to the striking **Sealers Cove.**

The two **overnight hikes** in the south are absolutely worth the time and extra preparation, as they allow hikers to savor the multitude of terrains and spectacular, secluded spots. The most popular two- to three-day hike sweeps 36km around the eastern coastal areas along well-maintained trails, to Sealers Cove, Refuge Cove, and Waterloo Bay. Camping facilities and pit toilets line the trail. To slip off the beaten path for a truly invigorating experience, try the **Lighthouse Trail** (33km return). Departing the Mt. Oberon car park, head south past the Halfway Hut through stands of eucalypts. From here a rugged walking trail through tea tree groves, temperate rainforest, and windblown plateaus proceeds past Roaring Meg before making a final steep descent along the old telegraph line. The fury of gale and surf combine with the majestic 1858 vintage lighthouse (tel. 5680 8529) to frame an unparalleled bushwalk.

■ Yarram and Tarra-Bulga National Park

The three most outstanding features of Yarram are friendliness, outrageously good baked food, and proximity to the **Tarra-Bulga National Park**. By the time you leave Yarram you will have seen the densest rainforest in Victoria and will have "G'day" firmly rooted in your traveling lingo.

The South Gippsland Hwy is called Commercial Rd as it passes through Yarram. In the old Court House, at Commercial Rd and Rogers St, you will find the **Tourist Information Centre** (tel. 5182 6553; open daily 10am-4pm). The **post office** (tel. 5182 5109) is a block away on the same side of Commercial Rd (postal code 3971; open M-F 9am-5pm). There are **banks** and **ATMs** galore. The **pharmacy,** 199 Commercial Rd (tel. 5182 5109), is open Monday through Saturday 8am-4:30pm. Take a dive into the **swimming pool,** on Greenwich St off Commercial St on the Melbourne end of town (open in summer M-F 6am-6pm, Sa-Su 10am-6pm; adults $2.50, students $1.70). The **Toppa Coffee Lounge** (tel. 5182 6066) on Commercial Rd sells **V/Line** tickets to Melbourne (3½hr.; 1 per day; $26.10, students $13.04) via Foster (50 min.).

The **Yarram Club Hotel,** 271 Commercial Rd (tel. 5182 5027; fax 5182 5490), is a no-frills budget hotel attached to a pub, bottle shop, and bottling center (singles $15, doubles $25). The **Yarram Bakery** (tel. 5182 5488) is next to the **Post Office** and sells delicious cinnamon buns, lemon cakes, meat pies, and pizza rolls (sandwiches $2.50; open M-F 6:30am-6pm, Sa 6:30am-3pm, Su 7am-4pm). The grandiose **Federal Coffee Palace,** 305 Commercial Rd (tel. 5182 6464), serves coffee, snacks, meals, and desserts in a nouveau-something interior (BYO; lunch menu sandwiches $2 and up; open W-Th 10am-10pm, F-Sa 10am-midnight, Su 10am-6pm). The **Strands Festival IGA** supermarket (tel. 5182 6033) is inside the Yarram Plaza mall (open M-F 8am-6pm, Sa 8am-1pm).

Tarra-Bulga National Park

To access the rainforest from the South Gippsland Hwy, take either the **Tarra Valley Rd** through (surprise!) the Tarra Valley, or the **Balook Yarram Rd** (unsealed), which passes through the Bulga Forest. You may end up taking both roads, since both connect to the perpendicular **Grand Ridge Rd,** forming a great loop through the forest. The ascent through the **Tarra Valley,** along a narrow and windy 25km stretch of sealed road, passes through lush fern and eucalypts, with occasional patches of yellow wildflowers. Walking trails begin about 20km up the road at the Tarra Valley picnic ground. The **Tarra Valley Rainforest Walk** (1.2km) leads to **Cyathea Falls.** Several kilometers before the picnic area lie the superb **Tarra Falls,** just by the road.

At the junction of the Grand Ridge Rd and the Balook Yarram Rd is the **Tarra Bulga Visitor Centre** (tel 5196 6166), which keeps limited hours that attest to the lack of tourist traffic through the park (Sa-Su and school holidays 10am-4pm). From here begins the **Fern Gully Nature Walk** (½km), which leads to Corrigan's Suspension Bridge, a fine overlook of a gully housing birds, wallabies, bats, and bush rats.

Tarra-Bulga fills a section of the **Strzelecki Ranges** (also see Morwell State Park), named after the neurotic Polish explorer Count **Paul Strzelecki.** During his 1840 expedition from New South Wales to the Victoria coast, the Count insisted on maintaining a direct line through any and all terrain by using a compass, sextant, and chronometer. His Aboriginal guide, **Charlie Tarra,** saved the expedition from starvation. The Tarra Valley is named for him; *Bulg* is an Aboriginal word for mountain.

There is no bush camping in the park, but there are two **caravan parks** along the Tarra Valley Rd inside the forest. The **Nageela Tourist Park,** 1369 Tarra Valley Rd (tel. 5186 1216), is lower in elevation (sites $12-14 per pair; cabins $27). A bit higher up is the **Tarra Valley Caravan Park,** 1385 Tarra Valley Rd (tel. 5186 1283; sites $10-12 per pair; vans $25 per pair). Visit the Yarram Information Centre for more information on walks and driving tracks.

> **Legends of the Gunai: Gippsland's Aboriginal History**
>
> For at least 18,000 years, the Gunai (or Kurnai) Aboriginal people have inhabited Gippsland. According to legend, Borun, "the Pelican," was the first Gunai. He descended from the northwest mountains carrying his canoe on his head. As he crossed the Tribal River by Wayput (now **Sale**), a tapping noise began to follow him. Finally, he reached the ocean inlet, still bothered by the incessant tapping. When he put down the canoe, Borun found sitting in it the woman he would wed: Tuk, "the Musk Duck," who would become the mother of all Gunai people.
>
> Since then, the five clans descended from Borun and Tuk have met occasionally for ceremonies, trade, and feasts, and sometimes battled amongst one another. In order to discourage their children from disobeying tribal laws, the Gunai told them fables. One explains the fallen link between Tasmania and the mainland (at Wilsons Promontory). One day, the story goes, two children at play removed a sacred object from the land and brought it back to their mother. Thereupon, the ground rapidly crumbled into the sea, breaking up families and drowning many Gunai. For more information on Aboriginal history and current issues, visit the **Ramahyuck Aboriginal Corporation** in Sale (see p. 574).

■ Port Albert and Gellions Run

Were you the kid on the playground who was taunted into eating worms? Did you secretly develop a fondness for these invertebrates that were your only friends? You, and anyone with zoological interests, can check out the common worm's much rarer cousins in the salt marsh and mangrove of **Gellions Run,** a section of the **Nooramunga Marine and Coastal Park** near **Port Albert.** The marine sediments support a wonderland of marine worms, sand fleas, burrowing crabs, mollusks, burrowing sea anemones, and other jelly-like translucent creatures. The marsh begins abruptly beside the road; strong winds have ripped away a foot of the flat sand to reveal soil and roots. Marine birds such as black swans, pacific gulls, reef herons, and ibis frequent the scenery. To get to Gellions Run, take the dirt road marked "No Through Road" that branches off from the rotary just outside the Pt. Albert wharf area. Look for the anchor on the rotary island and take the nearest road, unsealed but adequate for conventional vehicles.

Port Albert itself is a classic, rugged fishing village, once the only port in Eastern Victoria. The wind is powerful, the sky grey, the water green, and the waves choppy. You can rent fishing equipment and charter boats (tel. 5183 2394 or 0419 003 384) or fish from the pier. If you like to eat fish but not to catch them, drop by the wharf, where fishermen transfer the catch from the boat to the batter to the oil and wrap it all (except the boat) in brown paper in a matter of minutes ($2.50 and up; open daily till 7:30pm).

Port Albert is approximately 50km east of Foster and 15km south of Yarram, off the South Gippsland Hwy (Rte 180). The portside **Pt. Albert Hotel** (tel. 5183 2212; fax 5183 2429), on Wharf St, claims to be the oldest licensed hotel in Victoria, and why not believe them ($15 per person).

■ Sale

The East Gippsland Hwy and the Princes Hwy meet at Sale, which is the beginning point of the **Bataluk Cultural Trail.** The trail starts at the important **Ramahyuck Aboriginal Corporation** information office, 117 Foster St (tel. 5143 1644; open M-F 9am-5pm). Here you can acquire a color brochure that details and maps out the trail, which marks significant Aboriginal sites in Gippsland and also relates several legends of the Koorie people. The first sight marked on the Bataluk trail is a wetlands walk from **Lake Guthridge,** off Foster St, to the **Sale Common** state game refuge and along its boardwalk. To drive to Sale Common, look for the small sign marked "Wetland Boardwalk," south of town off the South Gippsland Hwy.

The town of Sale itself has little to see. There is a **Tourist Information Centre** (tel. 5144 1108) on the Princes Hwy west of town, before the highway turns into Foster St (open daily 9am-5pm). **V/Line buses** (tel 5144 2042) leave from Gippsland Center Mall near Cunninghame and Desaily St, and travel to Melbourne, Bairnsdale, Lakes Entrance, Canberra, and Sydney. Should you miss your connection or otherwise feel compelled to stay overnight in Sale, check out the **Sale Caravan Park** (tel. 5144 1366), next to the tourist office on the Princes Hwy (sites $12-15 per pair, vans $28).

■ Bairnsdale

Every town has its virtues, and Bairnsdale's is that it's near the **Mitchell River National Park.** Only a few locations in the town itself merit a stop if you are passing through. The colorful brick and stone **Court House,** on Nicholson St parallel to Main St, is worth visiting, as are the **Main Street Gardens,** a great picnicking area running the length of town. Bairnsdale is a stop along the Bataluk Cultural Trail. The **Krowathunkoolong Museum,** 37-53 Dalmahoy St (tel. 5152 1891) inside the Gippsland Aboriginal Cooperative, displays shields, boomerangs, bark canoes, and contemporary artwork of the Koorie people (open M-F 9am-5pm; $3, children $2).

If you can avoid the enormous suction power that Bairnsdale's McDonald's seems to exercise, visit its neighbor, the **Tourist Information Centre,** 240 Main St (tel. 5152 3444 or 1800 637 060; open daily 9am-5pm). The knowledgeable staff runs one of three Parks Victoria central information networks, the others of which are in Orbort and Lakes Entrance. The **post office** is at Nicholson and Baily St (open M-F 9am-5pm; postal code 3875). For **bike and scuba gear rental,** visit Marriott's Cycles, 209 Main St (5152 3783), opposite McDonald's. Bairnsdale has a **train station with no trains,** though there are plenty of **V/Line buses,** on MacLeod St, across from the tourist office and a straight shot town Pyke St. Buses run to Melbourne (4hr., M-F 3 per day, Sa-Su 1 per day) via Sale (1 hr.), to Lake's Entrance (30min., daily), and to Canberra.

At the **Bairnsdale Backpackers,** 119 MacLeod St (tel 5152 5097), you may use a sleeping bag, and the rate covers breakfast. It's 75 paces from the train station. ($15 per night; kitchen available; lounge free 5pm-midnight.) The food scene is dominated by fast food with a few cafes sprinkled in. Go to **Safeway** (tel. 5152 3262), behind Main St on the McDonald's side, for groceries (open daily 7am-midnight).

■ Near Bairnsdale: Mitchell River National Park

The **Mitchell River** flows from the alpine high country down to the Gippsland Lakes, bisecting 11,900 hectares of rainforest that comprise the park. In addition to visiting the several gorges and the high cliff looming over the river, most daytrippers venture into the park to pay respect to the **Den of Nargun.** Gunai legend describes Nargun as a giant stone female creature who destroyed intruders with their own spears or boomerangs. Elders told children that she abducted kids who strayed from camp. The cave is said to have been used for initiation ceremonies for women.

To reach the park, take the Dargo Rd to the Mitchell Dam Rd. For the Den of Nargun, turn right at the Waller Rd and take Nargun Rd from there. The 3km (1hr. round trip) includes the impressive Bluff lookout. Canoeing, rafting, and hiking through the **Mitchell River Gorge** is the best way to see the park's splendors, like the giant kanooka trees flying out of the water and the lush, fern-filled gullies.

There are two places to **camp** in the park. One ground is at the far north end of the park, near Angusville, reached by taking the sealed Mitchell Dam Rd off the Dargo Rd (pit toilets, river water only). There's also a campsite at Billy Goat Bend, accessible by walking only. Information is available at the Bairnesdale Parks Victoria info center.

■ Lakes Entrance

Lakes Entrance is the implicit capital of the Gippsland Lakes region, and it provides a good place to stay while you explore. But if you seek either tranquility or adventure, you should get the hell out of town from sunup till sundown. Nearby, you'll find all the beach and fishing space you could ask for; there's much to see in this network of saltwater lakes and small wilderness islands. In the summer, the town quickly uglifies with campervans and lawn chairs; book accommodations well in advance. In the off-season, the town itself is more pleasant; it's still an eyesore, but it's not overcrowded.

ORIENTATION AND PRACTICAL INFORMATION

The **Princes Hwy** is called the **Esplanade** in town, and becomes a waterfront strip full of unattractive shops and services. The **Lakes Entrance Visitors Centre** (tel. 5155 1966) is at the western end of the Esplanade, at the intersection of Marine Pde, where boat hire firms are moored (visitors center open daily 9am-5pm). This is one of three **Parks Victoria** offices in East Gippsland, which means they have plentiful regional information. A few blocks east is the **post office,** 217 Esplanade (tel. 5155 1809; open M-F 9am-5pm, and Sa 9am-noon in summer; postal code 3909). This part of town houses most **banks** and **ATMs,** such as **National Bank** at 299-301 Esplanade. **V/Line buses** leave from near the post office, heading to Narooma, NSW (1 per day) and Melbourne (5hr., 3 per day, $40) via Bairnsdale (30min., $7.30). **Greyhound** serves Lakes Entrance, albeit in the middle of the night; call **Esplanade Travel** (tel. 5155 2404) for reservations and schedules. The **crime rate** in Lakes Entrance is high for the region; don't camp illegally, as night prowlers may pillage your belongings.

ACCOMMODATIONS

Riviera Backpackers (YHA), 5 Clarkes Rd (tel. 5155 2444; fax 5155 4558), just off the Esplanade at the eastern end of town. Ask the bus to stop near the hostel, although hostel staff will pick you up at the station if you call in advance. This excellent motel-style YHA earns high marks for its sparkling new facilities and off-street parking. Large lounge with TV, a solar-heated pool, and pool table. Laundry facilities, kitchen, free linen, and safe storage. 24hr. reception. Heated and fan-cooled dorms, twins, and doubles all $13 per person with or without YHA (weekly $78). V, MC, AmEx, DC. Book well ahead for Dec.-Jan.

Echo Beach Holiday Park (tel. 5155 2238; fax 5155 3110), on Church St, which is parallel to the Esplanade. This 4-star park has a kitchen, barbecue, laundry, spa, TV, and billiards. Office open daily 8am-10pm. High season rates: powered sites $24, cabins $80-100. Half-price off-season. Book at least 1 week in advance for tent sites.

Lakes Main Caravan Park (tel. 5155 2365), 2 blocks north of the YHA, is more spartan, but is an option if the others are booked. Dorms $10, during Christmas holiday $15. Tent sites $5 per person, $1 extra to use the kitchen; powered sites $6 per person; mobile homes $30, $55. V, MC, Bancard.

FOOD

Restaurants and takeaway shops dot the Esplanade. Highlights include:

Riviera Natural Farm Ice Cream Parlor (tel. 5155 2972), opposite the footbridge on the Esplanade. Award-winning farm-produced ice cream in 35 flavors. Generous portions $1.80-4. Open daily 9am-5pm, or "late" in summer.

Lakes Charcoal Chicken, 21a Myer St (tel. 5155 2603), will give you a quarter chicken, peas, roasted potatoes, potato salad, a newspaper to read, and a table outdoors for $5. Open daily 8:30am-7:30pm.

Aldo's Pinocchio Inn, 569 Esplanade (tel. 5155 2565), offers a great all-you-can-eat pizza and pasta dinner ($10, children $5). They're open late.

SIGHTS AND ACTIVITIES

For a perfect view of the island patchwork of the Gippsland Lakes, stop off or hike up to the **Kalimna Lookouts,** above town at the western end. The lake's biggest attraction is its expansive beachfront. To reach the **Ninety Mile Beach,** cross the footbridge opposite Myer St. From the snack bar and toilet area, a one-hour (one-way) walking track follows the coast to the man-made entrance that was dug out to make this into a recreational area. You can catch **water taxis** from the entrance. Most simply **hire boats** at reasonable rates from one of the various jetties along the Marine Pde. Rates are standard. *(6-8 passenger half-cabins $20 first hr., $15 thereafter. 12 passenger barbecue boat $25 per hr. plus fuel;. Canoes $8 per hr.)* Try **Portride Boat Hire** (tel. 5155 3832), generally open during daylight hours. There's a beach and fishing at **Green Light** at **Drews Jetty. Barrier Landing** is the western strip of land created by the entrance. Only accessible by boat, the landing puts you by a lake beach, surf beach, great fishing, and sometimes seals and dolphins that you can feed. If you dig sitting around with a rod and reel, call the **Mulloway,** 70 Marine Pde (tel. 014 943 154), for three-hour trips that provide all equipment and bait. *(Trips 9am-noon and 1-4pm. $25.)* Pick up the guide *Fishing On and Around the Gippsland Lakes* at the tourist office.

The **Corque Winery Cruises** (tel. 5155 1508) offer a chance to tour the lakes and sample vintages from the Wyanga Park Winery. *(2-4hr. tours including morning tea or lunch $18-28.)* Cruises also stop to tour the old Signal Station overlooking the Bass Strait and include free tastings, a main course, and a glass of wine at Henry's Winery Cafe. If you're more ambitious, visit **Victor Hire Boats** (tel. 5155 1888), on the north arm behind Glenara Motel, and be your own skipper for the day. An interesting rainy-day stop is the **Griffith Sea Shell Museum** (tel. 5155 1538), just east of Centrepoint on the Esplanade. *(Open daily 9am-noon and 2-5pm; in winter 10am-noon and 2-4pm.)* Browse an extensive collection of shell displays and shells for sale.

■ Metung

Perhaps it is the uniformity of structure and color in the architecture, or maybe the stylishly oblique plane of the condos with their sunstreaked sliding doors opening onto a blue lake. Or it may just be that you don't see the cars, hidden in covered lots, nor many people, for that matter. Whatever the reason, Metung is the most tastefully planned, least chaotic, and wealthiest community on the Lakes. To reach Metung from Lakes Entrance, take the Metung Rd off the Princes Hwy at Swann Reach (15min.) rather than the first road signposted for Metung.

To hire a boat, visit **Bull's Cruises** (tel. 5156 2208) at the docks. (Open M-F 8:30pm-5pm, Sa-Su 8:45am-4:45pm. 3m inboard with half-cabin $20 first hr., $10 per hr. thereafter.) Most people take a boat out to the beaches and wilderness islands, though children enjoy the closer-by **Back Beach. Rotamah Island,** a bird observatory managed by the Royal Australian Ornithologists Union (tel. 5156 6398), is a full-day trek. You may be able to arrange accommodation on the island. At Metung, in the waters by the yacht club, is **Legend Rock,** the last standing of three rocks that, according to Gunai Aboriginal lore, were hunters turned to stone for not sharing their spoils. The knowledgeable owner of **EK** (tel./fax 5156 2600) at Metung is a valuable source of advice and rents biking, camping, and snorkeling equipment.

The only budget option is the **Metung Tourist Park** (tel./fax 5156 2306), at Mairburn and Stirling Rd, a right off Metung Rd. Reserve way ahead for the Christmas holidays. (Kitchen, barbecue, laundry. Cabins $40-55. Sites $14. Higher in high season.)

■ Buchan

In the heart of Gippsland, Buchan (rhymes with "truckin"), is known for its spectacular caves. Just 58km north of Lakes Entrance and 53km northeast of Bruthen, Buchan can be used as a regional hub. Since **no public transport** serves Buchan, most backpackers arrive on the **Oz Experience** bus (tel. 1300 300 028), bound for Melbourne or Sydney. South of the Buchan Caves, the small town center contains a **general store** (open 8:30am-5:30pm) with basic food and **tourist information.** Across the street, more visitor info can be found at the **post office** (open M-F 9am-5pm; postal code 3885).

The **Buchan Lodge** on Saleyard Rd (tel. 5155 9421), just north of the town center, provides decent budget accommodation in a building beautifully constructed with natural timbers. The lodge's large dorm rooms teem with Oz Experience backpackers. The grand central lodge houses a dining area and a well-equipped kitchen. Guests are invited to swim, take tube rides, or watch for platypuses in the Buchan River. (Beds with bath $15, breakfast included; dinner $5. Book ahead.)

The **Buchan Caves** is a 260-hectare reserve just across the Buchan River. These limestone caves outshine the omnipresent 'roos. Numerous campsites make the park an excellent stop. As you enter the park, the **visitors information center** (tel. 5155 9441), on the left, reserves campsites and sells refreshments and tickets for cave tours (open 9am-3pm in peak season; latecomers can pay in the morning). The two big caves, **Fairy Cave** and **Royal Cave**, are open for guided tours (1hr., departing each hour 10am-3pm.; $10, children $5, families $25).

Detours Eco-Adventures (tel. 5155 9264) runs a wide range of outdoor activities from the Buchan Lodge and other locations. Try your hand at abseiling, horseback riding, or bushwalking, or place your bets on a mystery trip.

■ Snowy River National Park

Shrouded in mythic Australiana, Snowy River National Park surrounds the once mighty **Snowy River** with rugged, jagged hills dressed in green. This is some of the most extreme wilderness in Australia. The Snowy itself is great for rafting, canoeing, and swimming. The cleanest approach to the park is the Buchan-Gelantipy Road, which passes through **Gelantipy** (1hr.) before reaching a split—the right fork, McKillop Rd, leads to the park (1hr.), while the left leads along the Jindabyne Rd. You can also approach from the northeast through **Jindabyne,** NSW (see p. 204).

HIKING One of the most fantastic and least known lookouts in the park is just 5km from the Little River Bridge at the park entrance. **Hanging Rock,** or World's End, juts out over a 400m valley with a 270° view of the countryside. Take the Milky Creek Track from the bridge, turn left at Rocky River Ridge Track, then left at Hanging Rock Track. The rock is a 5- to 10-minute downward climb. Returning to McKillop Rd, 1km further into the park lies the 400-million-year-old **Little River Gorge,** the steepest gorge in Victoria (500m). A 400m trail leads down to the gorge from the car park.

Another 25km drive (1hr.) along steep, serpentine dirt track brings you to **McKillop's Bridge,** where the Deddick River and the Snowy meet. This road should only be tackled by competent, careful drivers, but is suitable for 2WD. The original bridge rose 22m above the Snowy, but on the day before the scheduled opening, the great river showed the bridge who was boss by flooding it out. The current bridge soars 30m above the luxuriously warm and clear waters. There is a landing for entering the river with canoes and rafts. The 18km **Silver Mining Track** and the 30-minute **Snowy River Track** leave the area. Damming for hydroelectricity has cut water flow to 5% of its original levels. Even so, the rugged beauty depicted in the legendary film *The Man From Snowy River* (actually filmed in **Mansfield,** p. 558) can still be appreciated from campsites based at MacKillop Bridge and along paths that depart from the kiosk and traverse the full range of the park. **Whitewater rafting, canoeing,** and **kayaking** are quite popular, water levels permitting. You may camp away from designated sites in the park. Those with extra time for a slow but beautiful drive can complete a circuit to **Bonang** or **Orbost** by continuing on the gravel Bonang Gelantipy Rd as it skirts the park's eastern edge.

ACCOMMODATIONS A great way to explore the Snowy and experience life in the high country is to stay a couple of days at the **Karoonda Park YHA** (tel. 5155 0220), on the Buchan-Gelantipy Rd 1½ hours from the Princes Hwy. The main highlights on this family farm are the adventure activities and the gravy-laden feasts. A swimming pool, billiards, ping pong, and tennis court are at your disposal. Useful hands can stay on longer as farm workers. Guided activities include overnight rafting trips (seasonal; $110, backpackers $75), overnight horseback trips ($110, backpackers $75), day rides ($15 per hour), abseiling (intro $10, full 40m $25), and indoor rock climbing ($4). Accommodations are cabin units with shared kitchen, toilet, shower, and bunk rooms ($15, YHA nonmembers $18). Backpackers pay $25 for full room and board; others pay $45. Motel units with fridge and bathroom cost $25 per person.

Farther north along the dirt track en route to Suggan Buggan and Jindabyne, NSW is the tranquil mountain retreat of **Candlebark Cottage** (tel. 5155 0263), at "Springs" along the Snowy River-Jindabyne Rd. Adjacent to Alpine National Park in a picturesque country valley, the heated cottage contains a double bed and six loft bunks. It's an ideal base for bushwalking, trout fishing, or exploring the surroundings. The owners can arrange activities, meals, and tours within their property and the surrounding national parks. The on-site Eagle Loft Gallery exhibits an excellent range of country artisanry. ($40 for 2 people, $15 for each additional person; weekly $300.)

■ Orbost and Around

Parks Victoria chose the improbable site of Orbost to plant its all-senses-activating **Rainforest Centre** (tel. 5161 1375), on Lochiel St just off the Princes Hwy and 60km northeast of Lakes Entrance (open M-F 9am-5pm). Displays and reference materials compare the different kinds of forests found in Australia and the world. A large-screen audiovisual show explores the history and geology of the rainforests of Victoria. Two paths outside the center snake through manicured rainforest. One walk teaches aboriginal plant use, while the other awakens your senses to the colors, textures, and sounds of the bush. The center supplies information on the national parks of East Gippsland. Orbost can be reached by **V/Line bus** from Melbourne (5hr., 1 per day).

Two of Victoria's overlooked gems lie an hour outside of Orbost. Errinundra National Park (to the north) is a significant patch of rainforest, while Cape Conran (to the southeast) is suited for bathers, birdwatchers, bushwalkers, wildflower lovers, and anyone seeking space and solitude. To reach either reserve, you must stray boldly from the main tourist circuit—a move you won't regret.

Errinundra National Park
Normally, cool rainforests like the Errinundra are dominated by ancient myrtle beeches, as in the Otway Ranges of southwestern Victoria. Here, however, black olive berry and cinnamon-scented sassafrass cover the forest floor. You can approach the forest by the winding Bonang Hwy either from the north (from Snowy River) or from the Princes Hwy just east of Orbost. The Errinundra Rd is the best entryway, though, leaving Bemm River 54km east of Orbost and turning into the Gunmark Rd as you pass through the Errinundra Plateau. Some of the best walking areas leave Gunmark Rd. The **Goonmirk Rocks** track leads through mountain plum pines, silver wattle and, in springtime, the red flowers of the Gippsland waratah. The longer **Coast Range** track shows off the forest's unique features. You can **camp** at **Ada River,** along the Errinandra Rd at the south end of the park (toilets available). Another campground is at **Goongerah,** at the west end of the park off the Bonang Hwy. Pick up a map and the *Guide to Walks and Tours* on the Errinundra Plateau at the Orbost Rainforest Centre (tel. 5161 1375). In winter, many park roads become impassable.

Cape Conran
Cape Conran offers a solitary and rugged melange of dunes, heath, wetlands, swamps, and woods. One of the most peaceful spots in all of Victoria is **French's Crossing,** where the Snowy River meets the sea. Two thin strips of land divide the murky river's end from its shallow estuary and the breaks of the Bass Strait. The bird variety here is astounding; pelicans, herons, and swamp hens abound. The **Marlo-Cape Conran Rd** passes French's Crossing, about 6km west of the actual cape, just east of **Marlo.** Even closer to Cape Conran, along the Marlo-Cape Conran Rd, is **Point Ricardo,** a desolate beach with outstanding scenery; wildflowers lead you down the path from the carpark.

To reach Cape Conran from the Princes Hwy, take the Cape Conran-Cabbage Tree Rd and do not take the right fork to Marlo. The road is mostly unsealed but more than adequate, and ends at the Marlo-Cape Conran Rd. Go right for Pt. Ricardo and French's Crossing, and for the **Brubang Caravan Park** (tel. 5154 8219), which is embedded in the forest and has a pool, barbecue, and tennis court (sites $10-14, vans $26-38).

Go left once on the Cape to reach the **East Cape,** where you'll find **Sailor's Grave,** the safest swimming beach in the area, despite the morbid name. From here begins the 2.5km Cape Conran Nature Trail (45min. each way) and shorter walks. The Cape is fantastic for sighting nectar feeding birds like honeyeaters and lorikeets. The quiet and natural **Banksia Bluff Camping Area** (tel. 5154 8438), near East Cape along a dirt road emanating from the Marlo-Cape Conran Rd, offers campsites for about $12 per day. A van from the Marlo supermarket swings by with **food** from time to time. Book eons in advance for Christmas through January. The campground is just south of the **Yeerung River,** popular for fishing. Here commences the **Dock Inlet Walk** (15km), a six to eight hour round-trip walk. Because of occasional **flooding,** you should check with rangers (tel. 5154 8438) before setting out.

■ Croajingolong National Park

Tickling Victoria's eastern coastline from the New South Wales border to Sydenham Inlet, Croajingolong (crow-uh-ZHING-a-long) National Park provides visitors with a rich diversity of environments. This rarely visited national park extends nearly 100km and covers 87,500 hectares. Despite having been recognized by UNESCO as a World Biosphere Reserve, Croajingolong remains a largely undiscovered gem.

ORIENTATION AND PRACTICAL INFORMATION

East of Lakes Entrance, the coast of Victoria becomes a seemingly endless stretch of wilderness punctuated by secluded lakes and estuarine inlets. The **Princes Hwy** surrenders the coast to this length of wild and retreats 10 to 20km inland. The highway passes through **Cann River** and **Genoa** before crossing the border into New South Wales. From Cann River, you can take the Tambook Road south into the western regions of the park, or else take the Cann River Hwy (23), which heads north past Mt. Coopracambra and into New South Wales toward Cooma (see p. 203) and Canberra (see p. 70).

The park is most accessible from the east, via the town of **Mallacoota.** Public transportation misses Mallacoota, approaching only as close as Genoa, 23km north on the Princes Hwy. Visitors should arrange transport with a tour provider before arriving in Genoa if they can't find another way to get there. Once in Mallacoota, you'll approach the town center along Maurice Ave, which possesses a **Tuckerbag market** (open daily 8:30am-6:30pm) and a **post office** (open M-F 9am-5pm, Sa 9am-noon). The YHA **Mallacoota Wilderness Lodge** (tel. 5158 0455), also on Maurice Ave, is a good choice for budget lodging, with an excellent waterfront location (dorms $13; doubles and twins $30). Book in advance for peak times.

The best way to navigate the park from Mallacoota is with **Journey Beyond Eco-Adventures** (tel. 5158 0166; fax 5158 0090), on Lincoln Lane opposite the YHA hostel. The staff coordinates activities from sea kayaking and bushwalking to 4WD adventures and evening spotlight walks. Their price for a full day's activity hovers around $100, including equipment, transport, top-notch guides, and nourishment. For maps, bookings, and general info on Croajingolong National Park, visit a **Department of Conservation and Natural Resources** (DNCR) center either in Cann River (tel. 5158 6351) or Mallacoota (tel. 5158 0219). Campsites should be booked weeks in advance for the summer school holidays. Remember to bring firewood, food, and water.

BUSHWALKS AND SIGHTS

Before exploring Croajingolong, contact the DCNR (tel. 5158 0219), on the corner of Allan and Buckland Dr in Mallacoota, and inform them of your plans.

Western Croajingolong: Approach from the Princes Highway

Heading south from Cann River along the **Tamboon Rd** will bring you to three camping areas in Croajingolong's western half. The **Mueller River Camping Area** is 15km down Tamboon Rd. and then 24km left down Point Hicks Rd. From here a left turn on to Bald Hills Track leads to the campsite, just 1km away. Twelve walk-in and drive-in sites along the Mueller Inlet and Sandy Beach share two pit toilets. Nearby on Point Hicks Rd, 1km closer to the beach, the 47-site **Thurra River Camping Area** offers similar facilities. Swimming and canoeing are popular at both locations. A short walk to the **Point Hicks Lighthouse,** erected in 1888, is a terrific outing.

On the Princes Hwy about 12km west of Genoa and 17km east of Cann River, West Wingan Road turns off south toward the wild coast. A drive on West Wingan leads visitors 34km south to **Wingan Inlet Camping Area.** All 24 sites have access to pit toilets, fresh water, picnic tables, and a small boat launch. The **Wingan Nature Walk** skirts the inlet and leads to the beach, Lake Elusive, Rame Head, and Easby Creek. The fishing is excellent, but you must purchase a **license** from the Cann River DCNR.

Eastern Croajingolong: Approach from Mallacoota

The easternmost extreme of Croajingolong boasts a richly diverse environment. From the New South Wales border west past Lake Barracoota, the **Cape Howe Wilderness Area** is comprised of craggy red granite shores, tidal rivers, temperate rainforest, eucalypt forest, and sweeping sand dunes. From the east end of Bottom Lake in the Mallacoota Inlet, the **Lake View Track** heads northeast, intersects the **Barracoota Track** (which heads southeast), and terminates at Lake Barracoota. Unlike the tidal estuaries which surround it, **Lake Barracoota,** Australia's second largest freshwater lake, stores freshwater less than 1km from the edge of the sea. Pick up the brochure *Discovering Mallacoota Inlet* for more detailed information.

Although not a part of Croajingolong, **Gabo Island** juts out to the south of the Cape Howe Wilderness Area. Connected to the mainland until the isthmus eroded away at the turn of the century, Gabo Island's vibrant, exotic red granite composes Victoria's easternmost isle. Quarried from the island in a Herculean feat of 1862, the **lighthouse** (Australia's second-tallest at 47.5m) continues to steer ships clear of the coast. Gabo Island also houses the world's largest colony of **Little Penguins,** with over 40,000 adult birds. Access to Gabo Island can be coordinated by boat, kayak, or plane.

West from Mallacoota, the **Centre Track** is a decent unsealed road leading to the **Shipwreck Creek Camping Area** and its five campsites, pit toilets, fireplaces, and fresh water. The camping area is a 45-minute drive from Mallacoota, near the beachfront forest and rock outcroppings nearby. You can also sea kayak into the Creek's tidal basin. The surf beach can be quite rough in places, but the inlet by the creek is ideal for water play. Tracks facilitate exploration of the heath from Mallacoota to Seal Creek.

Western Australia

To say that Western Australia is immense is something of an understatement. The water pipes that stretch from Perth to Kalgoorlie are the length of England. The state boundaries enclose an area three-and-a-half times the size of Texas and could contain the Netherlands 70 times over. You can drive for hours along the desert roads without seeing another car. Yet most visitors, like most Westralians, never see more than a fraction of it. Of the state's 1.7 million people, 1.3 million live in the Perth area, and most of the rest are close to the coast, among the vineyards of the southwest or along the surf-pounded capes of the northwest. Perth, WA's capital, is a modern city complete with shiny skyscrapers, four universities, and—in the words of the American consulate—"the kind of weather that California thinks it has."

From cute quokkas in the south to camels and saltwater crocs in the north, WA is home to a range of uniquely Australian wildlife. The state's interior is covered with miles and miles of desert, spinifex grass, and sandy plains, but to tourists, WA is best known for wildflowers and woods. Between August and November, 8000 flower species bloom in carpets in the Pilbara and along the coast south from Exmouth into the Great Southern. Southwestern WA is the domain of old-growth forests. Among the world's largest trees, the majestic karri reaches heights of 80m and stand in defiance of the state's thriving wood-chipping industry. In the north, the desert gives way to the rugged tropical vegetation of the Kimberley. Though drenched by monsoons during the wet season, this region is gorgeous, if inaccessible, from April to November. A few rough roads carve through the huge expanses of rainforest, unearthly rock formations, and spectacular waterfalls that cascade into the Indian Ocean.

Sheer isolation reinforces Westralians' independent nature. In 1933, a state referendum revealed a two-to-one preference to separate from the Commonwealth of Australia. Secession never became a political reality, but the self-sufficient spirit that bred the movement remains a subtle undercurrent. While many proud Westralians depend on heavy industry for their livelihood, a growing number are fighting for the protection of their state's natural resources. Ecotourism and promotion of natural attractions have begun to edge out the fishing and animal husbandry industries; tourists certainly prefer swimming with the dolphins at Monkey Mia to visiting the massive open-pit mines of the outback. But resource exploitation is unlikely to cease, and the continuing debate suggests that sometimes a state just can't be large enough.

WESTERN AUSTRALIA HIGHLIGHTS

- Sunset camel rides down miles of sand on **Cable Beach,** Broome (see p. 628).
- Gazing down on a lush canopy of giant redtingle from the **Valley of the Giants Treetop Walk** near Walpole (see p. 603).
- Testing your **windsurfing** skills against the gales at Geraldton (see p. p. 614).
- Wading in the dark at **Tunnel Creek** in the Kimberley (see p. 633).
- Springtime **wildflowers,** anywhere, especially along the rigorous climb to Bluff Peak in **Stirling Range National Park** (see p. 605).
- Swimming with whale sharks at **Ningaloo Reef,** Exmouth (see p. 620).
- Picnicking with a view over the Swan River from **Kings Park,** Perth (see p. 592).
- Sipping local wine after a long day exploring **Margaret River's** caves (see p. 599).
- The unearthly shape of the **Pinnacles** rising from desert-like dunes (see p. 613).
- Spying on dolphins from the wind-beaten cliffs of **Rottnest Island** (see p. 595).

PRACTICAL INFORMATION

The **Western Australia Tourist Centre** (tel. 9483 1111 or 1300 361 351; fax 9481 0190) is headquartered in Perth, and has all manner of maps and brochures; it's the retail office of the **Western Australia Tourist Commission.** The Perth headquarters of **YHA Western Australia** is at 236 William St, Northbridge 6003 (tel. 9227 5122 or

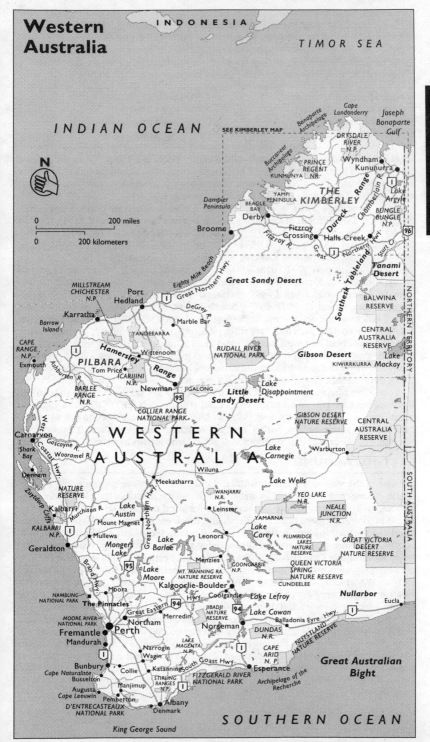

Western Australia

INDONESIA

TIMOR SEA

INDIAN OCEAN

SEE KIMBERLEY MAP

Cape Londonderry

Joseph Bonaparte Gulf

Bonaparte Archipelago

DRYSDALE RIVER N.P.

Wyndham
Kununurra

PRINCE REGENT NR.

KUNMUNYA

Buccaneer Archipelago

YAMPI PENINSULA

THE KIMBERLEY

Durack Range

Chamberlain R.

Lake Argyle

BUNGLE BUNGLE N.P.

Dampier Peninsula

BEAGLE BAY

Derby

Broome

Fitzroy Crossing

Halls Creek

Fitzroy R.

Great Northern Hwy.

Southesk Tableland Hwy.

Sturt Cr.

Tanami Desert

N

0   200 miles

0   200 kilometers

Eighty Mile Beach

Great Sandy Desert

BALWINA RESERVE

MILLSTREAM CHICHESTER N.P.

Port Hedland

Karratha

DeGrey R.

Marble Bar

CENTRAL AUSTRALIA RESERVE

Barrow Island

YANDEEARRA

Lake Mackay

CAPE RANGE N.P.

Exmouth

Hamersley

Wittenoom

PILBARA

Tom Price

KARIJINI N.P.

Range

Newman

JIGALONG

RUDALL RIVER NATIONAL PARK

KIWIRRKURRA

Gibson Desert

Ashburton R.

BARLEE RANGE N.R.

Little Sandy Desert

Lake Disappointment

GIBSON DESERT NATURE RESERVE

CENTRAL AUSTRALIA RESERVE

COLLIER RANGE NATIONAL PARK

Carnarvon

WESTERN

Gascoyne R.

Wooramel R.

AUSTRALIA

Lake Carnegie

Warburton

Shark Bay

Denham

Wiluna

Lake Wells

NATURE RESERVE

Zuytdorp Cliffs

Meekatharra

WANJARRI N.R.

YEO LAKE N.R.

Kalbarri

Murchison R.

Lake Austin

Leinster

YAMARNA

NEALE JUNCTION N.R.

KALBARRI N.P.

Mount Magnet

Lake Carey

Geraldton

Mullewa

Mongers Lake

Leonora

PLUMRIDGE LAKES NATURE RESERVE

GREAT VICTORIA DESERT NATURE RESERVE

Great Northern Hwy.

Lake Barlee

Brand Hwy.

Menzies

GOONGARRIE N.P.

QUEEN VICTORIA SPRING NATURE RESERVE

NAMBUNG NATIONAL PARK

Lake Moore

MT. MANNING RA. NATURE RESERVE

Kalgoorlie-Boulder

CUNDEELEE

Moora

Coolgardie

Lake Lefroy

Nullarbor

The Pinnacles

Great Eastern

Hwy.

JIBADJI NATURE RESERVE

Eucla

MOORE RIVER NATIONAL PARK

Merredin

Northam

Lake Cowan

Balladonia

Eyre Hwy.

Fremantle

Perth

Norseman

DUNDAS N.R.

NUYTSLAND NATURE RESERVE

Mandurah

Narrogin

LAKE MAGENTA N.R.

CAPE ARID N.P.

Bunbury

Wagin

Cape Naturaliste

Collie

Katanning

South Coast Hwy.

Esperance

Great Australian Bight

Busselton

STIRLING RANGES N.P.

FITZGERALD RIVER NATIONAL PARK

Archipelago of the Recherche

Augusta

Manjimup

Cape Leeuwin

Pemberton

D'ENTRECASTEAUX NATIONAL PARK

Albany

Denmark

SOUTHERN OCEAN

King George Sound

NORTHERN TERRITORY

SOUTH AUSTRALIA

Phone numbers in Western Australia have recently changed. Regional phone codes are now all 08, followed by eight-digit numbers. If you have trouble making a call, use the following scheme to get the old number, and try that instead. For all numbers with a three-digit phone code followed by six digits, the last two digits of the code become the first digits of the new eight-digit number.

New Number:	Old Number:
(09) xxx xxxx (Perth)	(08) 9xxx xxxx
(090) xx xxxx	(08) 90xx xxxx
(099) xx xxxx	(08) 99xx xxxx

1800 811 420; fax 9227 5123), and sells voucher packets good at YHAs nationwide (10 nights $145, 20 nights $270). All YHA hostels can book ahead for you at any other YHA in the state. The *Westside Observer* newspaper, available at news agents statewide, is a good resource for **gay and lesbian travelers.**

WA's 63 **national parks,** as well as its state forests and marine parks, are administered by the **Department of Conservation and Land Management (CALM).** CALM's headquarters are in the Perth area; it has a **Customer Service Centre,** 50 Hayman Rd, Como 6152 (tel. 9334 0333; fax 9334 0498; open M-F 8am-5pm) and a **"WA Naturally" Outdoor Information Centre,** 47 Henry St, Fremantle 6160 (tel. 9430 8600; fax 9430 8699; open W-M 10am-5:30pm). Regional branch offices are scattered throughout the state, most notably: **Kimberley,** in Kununurra (tel. 9168 0200); **Pilbara,** in Karratha (tel. 9143 1488); **Midwest,** in Geraldton (tel. 9921 5955); **Goldfields,** in Kalgoorlie (tel. 9021 2677); **South Coast,** in Albany (tel. 9842 4500); and several offices in the **Southwest,** including Manjimup (tel. 9771 7948) and Bunbury (tel. 9725 4300). **Day park fees** vary from park to park, but are usually nominal, as are **camping fees. National park passes,** valid in all national parks for various lengths of time, are available from all CALM branches and most tourist offices. CALM publishes a range of maps and bushwalking publications, available at all offices. For more info, check their website (http://www.calm.wa.gov.au).

In the more remote parts of WA, **ATMs** are rare. Don't get sucked into indentured servitude because you forgot to get extra cash 100km back. **EFTPOS** is ubiquitous at petrol stations, supermarkets, and pubs; you can use the machines to get $100-200 cash back on your purchase with a Visa, Mastercard, or most bankcards. Some small town tourist bureaus and post offices will act as bank agents in a pinch.

GETTING AROUND

Because of the size of Western Australia, the distances between attractions, and the dearth of long-haul transportation, many travelers—even budget travelers—**buy a car** for long visits. A thriving gray market exists for used cars, 4WDs, and campervans, fueled by hostel message boards in Perth and the *West Australian* classified section. **Used car dealerships** line Beaufort St several kilometers north of Northbridge, outside Perth. Before putting money down, have the car checked by a mechanic. The **Royal Automobile Club (RAC),** 228 Adelaide Tce, Perth (tel. 9421 4444), at the corner of Hill St, offers inspections for members (1yr. membership $80; inspections from $80). As WA's branch of AAA, RAC also provides roadside assistance. Some unscrupulous car dealers prey on backpackers and don't honor the warranty after you've bought a lemon. Be wary and do your homework before making the investment.

If you plan to make a long **drive through the desert,** keep plenty of water and petrol on hand, in addition to a spare tire and fanbelt. Winter and early spring are the safest times of year to drive the Great Northern Hwy because temperatures are lower and traffic more frequent. Throughout WA, you'll share the highway with **road trains,** massive tractor-trailers. Give them plenty of space and take care when overtaking (or if they overtake you)—it's clear who will emerge the loser in any tangle with these beasts.

WESTERN AUSTRALIA

With the exception of the Kalgoorlie stop on the Indian Pacific line, passenger **rail** service is essentially non-existent. **Greyhound Pioneer** (tel. 13 20 30) is the only **bus** company that runs north of Geraldton. The seasonal Greyhound timetable book, available at bus stations and tourist bureaus, is indispensable. Try to book at least a day ahead; space may be limited, and the bus might not even stop unless the driver knows you're waiting. If you plan on a lot of bus travel, Greyhound has a number of passes that can save you serious money. South of Perth and Kalgoorlie, Greyhound service ends and **South West Coach Lines, Westrail,** and **EasyRider** take over.

It is possible to tour portions of Western Australia by **bicycle.** Consider the amount of space and weight that water will take up, and start getting in shape well ahead of time. In northern WA, it's not advisable to bike in the hotter, wetter months. Advise regional police and, in the north and outback, the **Royal Flying Doctor Service** of your itinerary. The **Ministry of Sport and Recreation** (tel. 9387 9700) has more info.

Let's Go does not recommend **hitchhiking,** but some people do it. Particularly in northern and eastern WA, there is so little traffic that you really could get stuck in the middle of nowhere. Hitchers report that roadhouses are the best places to find rides, though some aren't too amenable to backpackers hanging around. A more reliable way to pick up a ride is to check **hostel message boards.** It's generally not tough to find someone willing to give you a lift in return for petrol expenses.

Perth offers a bewildering range of guided group **tours** around the city and throughout the state. Tours aren't for everyone, and their quality is mixed. Tourist officials, travel agents, and hostel managers can help you narrow down the options. Half-day tours taking in Perth and the suburbs start around $25, while marathon day-trips to the Pinnacles begin around $70. Standard prices for four- to five-day tours through the Southwest are around $350. This sum will also get you north to Monkey Mia, Kalbarri, and the Pinnacles. Longer, pricier tours are also available, and some tours operate one-way only (e.g. from Perth to Broome or vice versa).

PERTH

Spread out like a picnic by the tranquil, lake-like Swan River and the eternal surf of the Indian Ocean, everything in Perth is as easily done outdoors as in, in sandals as in shoes. Rumor has it that WA spurns daylight saving time so that business executives can get in a quick surf before work. This mellow attitude is a point of pride for many Perthites, as is their city's status as the world's most isolated capital. (Adelaide, the nearest state capital, is at least a two-day drive away.)

But isolation does not mean desolation. WA's capital, home to 88% of the state's population, is an extreme example of Australian demography. Business booms of the 80s and 90s injected fresh funds into the city, which now bristles with new skyscrapers and condominiums. The growth is easy to understand, given the clean air, accessible beaches, gorgeous sunsets, and mild climate. Yet as central Perth grows, some nostalgic residents point to Fremantle, the city's port and the other focus of Perth's energy, as the example to emulate. Funds flowing into "Freo" have been spent on historic, restorative facelifts rather than skyline lifts. In between Freo and the city center lie parks, sails, beaches, and plenty of souls content to share with visitors the lifestyle

🖐 PERTH HIGHLIGHTS

- Bike paths, wildflowers, and a vista of the Swan River in **Kings Park** (see p. 592).
- Catching the perfect breaks in the challenging surf of **Trigg Beach** (see p. 593).
- A ghostly, macabre candlelight tour of **Fremantle Prison** (see p. 594).
- Biking and whale-watching on a daytrip to relaxing **Rottnest Island** (see p. 595).
- Grooving to DJ tunes at the **nightclubs** of Northbridge (see p. 595).
- A **ferry ride** around Perth Harbour with a view of the city skyline (see p. 594).
- Perusing the funky and the scrumptious at the **Fremantle Markets** (see p. 594).

that their city is famous for. If you've made the effort to cross the kilometers to Perth, you'll be more than welcome: pick your patch of sand and join the picnic.

■ Arrival and Departure

BY PLANE

Qantas (tel. 13 13 13) and **Ansett** (tel. 13 13 00) fly daily between Perth and Sydney (4½hr.). For trips within the state, try Ansett, Qantas, or regional carrier **SkyWest.** Qantas' **Airlink** network offers direct flights between Perth, Karratha, Port Hedland, Tom Price, Broome, and Kalgoorlie. Local tourist flights around the Perth region fly from **Jandakot Airport,** south of the city; air traffic into and out of the region arrives and departs at **Perth Airport,** east of the city. The terminals are small and easy to navigate, but the international terminal is several kilometers away from the domestic terminals. Keep this in mind if you're planning a connection.

Getting to and from the Perth Airport is a bit vexing. **TransPerth buses** #200, 201, 202, 208, and 209 run between the domestic terminals and St. Georges Tce. in the city center (35min., every 40-50min.). The bus from Perth to the airport leaves from the north side of St. George Tce, stop 39, just west of William St. An **Airport City Shuttle** bus with more room for luggage runs frequently to a number of stops in Perth from both the domestic ($7) and international ($9) terminals. Travelers can also book trips to the airport, with pick-up from accommodations. A **taxi** to or from the airport costs around $25-30. The **Fremantle Airport Shuttle** (tel. 9383 4115) goes to both Perth Airport terminals. The shuttle departs from the Fremantle Railway Station; pick-ups at Fremantle accommodations can be arranged (runs daily every 2hr., 6am-10pm; $12).

BY TRAIN

Intercity trains run from the **East Perth Terminal** on West Pde., a 20-minute walk northeast from the Perth tourist center. **Westrail** (tel. 9326 2244, 9326 2813) has service to Kalgoorlie (M-Sa 8:45am, M, W, and F 5:15pm, Su 4:15pm, 8hr., $49) and to Bunbury (daily 9:30am and 5:45pm, 2hr., $18). The **Indian Pacific** runs to Sydney (M and F 1:35pm, 65hr., $389).

BY BUS

Westrail (tel. 9326 2244) runs buses from the East Perth Terminal to Albany (2 per day, 8hr., $35), Esperance (1-2 per day, 10hr., $53), Geraldton (1-2 per day, 6-8hr., $37), and Kalbarri (M, W, and F 8:30am, 8hr., $59). **Greyhound** (tel. 13 20 30), also at the East Perth Terminal, runs to Kalgoorlie (daily 6:30am, 8hr., $85), Adelaide (daily 6:30am, 13hr., $191), and Port Hedland (daily 10:30am and W, F, and Su 3:30pm, 21hr., $163) via Geraldton (3¾hr., $38), Cervantes (3hr., $68, including the Pinnacles), Kalbarri (7½hr., $70), Monkey Mia (10hr., $115), Carnarvon (12hr., $103), and Exmouth (16½hr., $176) continuing to Broome (32hr., $220) and Darwin (59½hr., $393). **Southwest Coach Lines** (tel. 9324 2333) departs from the **Perth City Bus Port,** Mounts Bay Rd, and runs to Bunbury (daily 9am, 1:30, and 5:45pm, 2½hr., $16), and Margaret River (daily 1:30pm, also Sa-Su and public holidays 9am, 5hr., $23).

BY CAR

To get to the southwest coast, take the Kwinana Freeway (Hwy 2) from the west side of Perth and follow the signs for Hwy 1. To head east to Kalgoorlie, take Riverside Dr. (Hwy 5) to the Great Eastern Hwy (Hwy 1, then National 94). To head north to Geraldton, follow the Great Eastern until Midland, change to the Great Northern Hwy (National 95), and then take the Brand Hwy (Hwy 1) at Muchea. To head toward Meekatharra or Newman, follow the Great Northern, and take lots of water and fuel.

One of the cheapest **car rental** agencies is **Bayswater,** 160 Adelaide Tce (tel. 9325 1000) or 13 Queen Victoria Ave, Fremantle (tel. 9430 5300), which rents to drivers

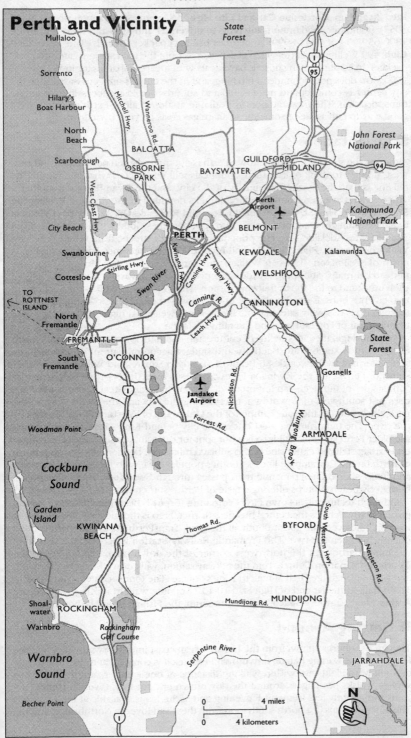

Perth and Vicinity

aged 20 and up. **Cottlesloe Car and Lite Hire,** 2 Servetus St, Swanbourne (tel. 9383 3057), is another good option, and rents to drivers 21 and up. **Atlas Rent-a-Car** (tel. 1800 659 999 or 9444 8999) sometimes has backpacker specials. The **Travellers' Club,** 499 Wellington St (tel. 9226 0660), across from the train station, caters to backpackers. In addition, many hostels have deals with local companies for lower rates.

Let's Go does not recommend **hitching,** and in the city it's unneccessary, since the city center is compact and most sights and suburbs are easily accessible by public transportation. The message boards available at almost all of Perth's hostels are a good way to find a ride or someone to share gas costs on your own drive.

■ Orientation

Although the street grid of downtown Perth is not quite aligned north-south and east-west, it helps to think of it as such, and locals will understand what you mean. The rail line is then the northern boundary of the city, and the **Swan River** the southern. The east-west avenues from the railroad tracks downhill to the river are **Wellington St, Murray St, Hay St, Saint Georges Tce,** and **Riverside Dr.** As they pass **Victoria Square** heading east out of the city, Murray St becomes Goderich St and St. Georges Tce becomes Adelaide Tce. The principal north-south streets, from west to east, are **William, Barrack, Pier, Victoria,** and **Hill St.** Victoria becomes Lord St as it heads north of Wellington. Between William and Barrack St, Hay and Murray St become **pedestrian malls.** Shopping arcades and overhead walkways connect the malls to each other and to the **Perth Railway Station.** The **Wellington St Bus Station,** one of two city bus hubs, is one block west of the railway station, across William St. Downtown Perth is relatively safe, but much of it is not well-lit. At night, it's probably wise to steer clear of Forrest Place and the railway station.

Northbridge, the city's nexus of culture and nightlife, is a two-minute walk north of the railway station. Most activity and budget accommodation is clustered in a square formed by Newcastle St, Beaufort St, Russel Square, and William St. Directly south of Perth city, the Kwinana Freeway passes over the Narrows Bridge to the "other side" of the river—an important distinction to locals. Great, green **Kings Park** rises just southwest of downtown, overlooking the city and the Swan. Beyond the park, the beautiful sandstone campus of the **University of Western Australia** rises by the river. The train running west out of the city behind King's Park passes through the older Perth suburbs. **Subiaco** is a hot spot for cafes and cuisine, and offers weekend market stalls on either side of the Subiaco train stop. **Leederville,** one stop north of Perth on the Currambine line, is another popular area, with plenty of pubs, cafes, and funky shops. The Fremantle train passes through **Swanbourne** and **Cottlesloe,** both lively beach suburbs offering a taste of Perth's surf culture.

Although technically its own city, **Fremantle (Freo)** is best thought of as a part of greater Perth. Perth is the central business district, Freo is the laid-back, lucrative fishing port, and everyone goes to both all the time. TransPerth buses and trains run frequently between the two. The Fremantle **Railway Station** is across the street from the Inner Harbour in the northwest corner of the downtown area. To get to the **Tourist Information Centre** from the railway station, walk down Market St, turn left, and walk through the High St mall to King's Square. The tourist center stands next to Town Hall. At the far end of High St, a 10- to 12-minute walk from King's Square, are **Arthur Head, Bathers Beach,** and, to the south, the **Fishing Boat Harbour.**

■ Getting Around

Though its suburbs sprawl from the Indian Ocean coast into the Swan Valley and the foothills of the Darling Range, downtown Perth itself is compact and easy to navigate on foot. Most sights are within walking distance of one another, and the **CAT bus service** whisks passengers around the downtown grid for free. (Every 5-10min. M-F 7am-6pm; slightly less frequent F evening and Sa-Su. Maps available at bus stations.) The blue CAT runs in a north-south loop from the Swan River to Northbridge, and the

Central Perth

ACCOMMODATIONS

B Britannia International
E Coolibah Lodge
A Globe Backpackers
I Hay St. Backpackers
C Northbridge YHA
G North Lodge Central City Backpackers
D Ozi Fun Inn
H Rainbow Lodge Backpackers
F The Shiralee

Swan River

Trinity Ave.

Gloucester Park Trotting Ground

W.A.C.A. Oval

Nelson Ave.

Hale St.

Nelson Queens Gardens

Plain St.

Waterloo Cr.

East Perth Cemetery

East Perth Terminal

Summers St.

East Pde.

Kensington St.

Brown St.

EAST PERTH

Royal St.

Haig Park

Wittenoom St.

Wickham St.

Bronte St.

Royal St.

Bennett St.

Claisebrook Station

PERTH

Bulwer St.

Lord St.

Perth Oval

Brewer St.

Pier St.

Brisbane St.

Edward St.

Parry St.

Stirling St.

Beaufort St.

Short St.

McIver Station

Moore St.

Lord St.

Hill St.

Wellington St.

Wellington Square

Goderich St.

Hay St.

Royal Automobile Club

Adelaide Tce.

Hill St.

Langley Park

Victoria Ave.

Newcastle St.

Monger St.

Robinson Ave.

Brisbane St.

TO E F

William St.

Forbes Rd.

Aberdeen St.

James St.

CITY

Perth Cultural Centre

Art Gallery of W.A.

Roe St.

Perth Station

St. Mary's Cathedral

Victoria Square

Murray St.

Pier St.

St. Georges Tce.

Irwin St.

Concert Hall

PERTH

Government House

Stirling Gardens

Town Hall

Barrack St.

NORTHBRIDGE

Stuart St.

Palmerston St.

Lake St.

Francis St.

James St.

Roe St.

Cinema Paradiso

Bus Station

Wellington St.

Murray St.

Hay St.

King St.

Centreway Arc.

William St.

Pedestrian Mall

City Arc.

Piccadilly Arc.

Carillon

Forrest Pl.

Trinity Arc.

Plaza Arc.

St. Martins

Sherwood

London Ct.

Howard St.

The Esplanade

The Esplanade

Ferry Terminal

Barrack Square

Transperth City Busport

Fitzgerald St.

Milligan St.

Murray St.

Hay St.

St. Georges Tce.

Mill St.

Bay Road

Mounts

Riverside Dr.

Swan River

Harvest Tce.

Parliament House

300 yards

300 meters

N

red CAT runs east-west from Outram St in West Perth to Horation St in East Perth. The weekend CAT, a modified blue loop, runs till 1am Friday and Saturday.

The **TransPerth** network of **buses, trains,** and **ferries** connects to more outlying areas. Schedules and information are available weekdays at the **Perth City Bus Port,** west of the Esplanade along Mounts Bay Rd. Information is also available at the **Wellington Street Bus Station** just west of William St. The system is divided into eight **fare zones;** a two-zone ride costs $2.30 and will get you from the city center to the airport or to Fremantle (day pass $6, discounts on multi-ride cards). **All-day passes** ($5.50) and **multi-ride cards** are available at TransPerth InfoCentre machines and newsagents and can save you up to 25%. Save your **ticket stub**—it can be used to transfer between bus, train, and ferry services. Speedy, carpeted trains also connect the city center with Fremantle, City Beach, and the suburbs.

It's also easy to get around by **taxi;** a taxi ride between the airport and Northbridge costs between $25 and $30. **Bikes** are also a good option; the tourist office hands out terrific free maps of rides in and around the city. Call **Bikewest,** 441 Murray St (tel. 9320 9301; email bikewest@transport.wa.gov.au), for more information.

■ Practical Information

Many shops and services have extended hours on Thursday for "late shopping night" and frequently stay open later Friday nights as well. Standard business hours on Saturday are from 9 or 10am to 5 or 6pm and on Sunday from noon to 5 or 6pm.

Tourist Office: (tel. 1300 361 351). Across the street from the Railway Station near the GPO. Crowded office with busy staff. Plenty of maps and brochures. Free bus and tour booking. Opens year-round M-Sa 8:30am, Su 10am. Closes May-July M-Th 5pm, F 6pm, Sa 4:30pm, Su 3pm; Aug.-Apr. M-Th 6pm, F 7pm, Sa-Su 5pm.

Budget Travel: Student UniTravel, 513 Wellington St (tel. 9321 8330), across from the Railway Station. Friendly staff caters to backpackers. Free info and booking tours, free Internet. Open M-F 8:30am-6pm, Sa 10am-2pm. Next door, the **Travellers' Club,** 499 Wellington St (tel. 9226-0660), is also good. Internet access $6 per hour, first 15min. free. Open M-F 9am-5:30pm, Sa 10am-4pm.

Consulates: Britain, 77 St. Georges Tce (tel. 9221 5400); **Canada,** 267 St. Georges Tce (tel. 9322 7930); **Ireland** (tel. 9385 8247); **Japan,** 221 St. Georges Tce (tel. 9321 7816), **United States,** 16 St. Georges Tce (tel. 9231 9400; fax 9231 9444).

ATMs: Everywhere, especially on William St in Northbridge and on Hay St in the mall area between Barrack and William St. Most machines accept Cirrus and PLUS.

American Express: At 645 Hay St (Hay Street Mall) in London Court (tel. 9221 0777). Foreign exchange open M-F 8:30am-5:30pm, Sa 9am-noon.

Library: The Alexander Library Building (tel. 9427 3111), at the north end of the Perth Cultural Centre, has limited **Internet access** and an excellent selection of international newspapers and magazines. Wheelchair accessible. Open M-Th 9am-9:45pm, F 9am-5:30pm, Sa-Su 10am-5:30pm.

Public Toilets and Showers: Around the Hay St Malls, generally on level B1.

Hotlines: Sexual Assault referral center (24hr. tel. 9340 1828). **Crisis Line** (tel. 1800 199 008). **Domestic Violence Hotline** (tel. 9325 1111).

Hospital: Royal Perth Hospital (tel. 9224 2244), north side of Victoria Sq, near Lord St. **Fremantle Hospital** (tel. 9431 3333), South Tce and Alma St.

Emergency: Dial 000.

Police: tel. 9222 1111; Fremantle tel. 9336 3333.

Post Office: General Post Office (GPO) (tel. 9237 5460; fax 9322 7862), west side of Forrest Pl. *Poste Restante* pick-up M-F only. Open M-F 8am-5:30pm, Sa 9am-12.30pm, Su noon-4pm. Branch offices: Frances St in Northbridge; several along Hay St and St. George Tce. Generally open M-F 9am-5pm. **Postal Code:** 6000. **Fremantle GPO,** 13 Market St (tel. 9313 1318). Open M-Sa 8:30am-5pm.

Phone Code: 08.

■ Accommodations

Perth is crammed to the brim with accommodations of all sorts, from basic back-packer joints to pricey luxury affairs. Booking ahead is wise, especially during the summer. The heaviest concentrations of hostels are in Northbridge and the city center. If you are in town for more than a few weeks, check the classified section of the *West Australian* for listings of rooms and flats to let, which can be cheaper than hostels. All of the hostels listed below offer free luggage storage, on-site laundry facilities, and kitchens with food storage space. There are no lock-out times, though it's a good idea to call ahead with your estimated time of arrival to ensure that someone will be there to greet you.

The Coolibah Lodge, 194 Brisbane St, Northbridge (tel. 9328 9958). Formerly Rory's Backpackers. Pristine rooms in a beautifully remodelled colonial home. Wood rafters, brick construction, and leafy courtyard with barbecue adds charm. Free pick-up, email, and laundry. A/C. Dorms $15, $85 weekly; singles $26; doubles $37, $39 with fridge. YHA, VIP.

Rainbow Lodge Backpackers, 133 Summers St, Northbridge (tel. 9227 1818; mobile 24hr. 1792 7529). East of the Perth Oval, cross Lord St to Summers St. A hike from the town center, but 3min. from the intercity railway station. Colorful, airy, and very clean, with friendly management. Two tidy kitchens, Internet access. Reception open 8am-9pm. Free bus and train station pick-up. Dorms $13, weekly $80; twins $16 per person, $95; singles $20, $120. Breakfast included. YHA, VIP, *Let's Go* discounts $1. Winter rates negotiable.

The Shiralee, 107 Brisbane St, Northbridge (tel. 9227 7448). Mellow and relaxed, with a pioneer ambience. Patio looks out on a quiet neighborhood. Friendly and clean, beautiful glass showers, A/C, nice kitchen. Free airport and bus pick-ups. Dorms $15, weekly $90; twins $40, $220; triples $16, $100. No singles. YHA, VIP.

Britannia International, 253 William St, Northbridge (tel. 9328 6121; fax 9227 9784), between Aberdeen and Francis St. Large, clean, and efficient. Credit-card-run Internet access ($5 per hr.) and travel agent in reception area; office open 24hr. No smoking. Dorms $14; singles $20; doubles $40 first night, $35 after that. Family rooms for 4 $60. non-YHA $3 more. Book ahead in summer. Some rooms wheelchair accessible.

North Lodge Central City Backpackers, 225 Beaufort St, Northbridge (tel. 9227 7588; fax 9386 9065), half a block from Newcastle St. Beautiful, well-kept old house with 25 backpackers' beds and great self-contained flats catering to a quiet international crowd. Super-friendly management. Call ahead for free airport, train, or bus pick-up. 24hr. check-in. Check-out 9:30am, but you can use the facilities for the rest of the day. Dorms $13. Singles $25; twins $32; flats $25 per person. Weekly: dorms $80, with the option to skip days. Linen included.

Hay St Backpackers, 266-268 Hay St, East Perth (tel./fax 9221 9880). Clean and freshly painted rooms with heat and A/C. Internet access, two kitchens, pool table, small swimming pool. Knowledgeable staff will help arrange tours. Office open 8:30am-10pm, call ahead for arrival at other times. Dorms $15-16, weekly $98-105; with bath $17, $112; doubles $36, $238; with bath $45, $299.

Ozi Inn, 282 Newcastle St, Northbridge (tel. 9328 1222), is clean, comfortable, and friendly. All rooms have heat and A/C. Free airport shuttle and bus/train pick-up. Basic bunks $12. Slightly nicer rooms $15, $90 weekly. Doubles $36. YHA, VIP.

Northbridge YHA, 46 Francis St, Northbridge (tel. 9328 7794). Basic, somewhat cramped rooms in a massive building. Internet access ($6 per hr.). Office open 7am-10pm. Dorms $15, $85 weekly; twins $35; doubles $41. YHA, VIP.

Nomads Globe Backpackers, 497 Wellington St (tel. 9321 4080), across from the train station. Half hostel, half hotel. Huge and a tad institutional with fluorescent lights, but convenient and popular. Singles and doubles have fridges. Office open 8am-midnight. Dorms $14; weekly $80, $69 with Nomads card. Twins $19; $110, $95. Singles $25; $150, $120. Doubles $38; $240, $205. Breakfast included.

FREMANTLE

⊛**YHA Fremantle Backpackers Inn Freo,** 11 Pakenham St (tel. 9431 7065; fax 9336 7106). From the train station, turn right onto Phillimore St, then left onto Pakenham. Plush carpeting, carved wood. Relaxed atmosphere and a quiet, international crowd. Dorms $14; singles $20; doubles $32. YHA nonmembers $15; $22; $35. 7th night free. Reception open 7am-11:30pm, 24hr. check-in available.

Old Firestation Backpackers, 18 Phillimore St (tel. (04) 1996 6066; fax 9319 1414). Turn right from the train station into Phillimore. Friendly management and a lively crowd of both short- and long-term guests. Basic rooms, off-street parking. Dorms $14 for the first night, $12 after that; doubles/twins $35. Book ahead in summer. Reception open daily 8am-6pm, 24hr. check-in available.

■ Food

Perth is chock-full of great restaurants. Cheap, tasty eats abound, particularly on weekdays, when there are terrific lunch and dinner specials. Northbridge is the best place to head for ethnic food ranging from Italian to Malaysian, Lebanese to Spanish. Subiaco, Claremont, and Freo also have their share of fun restaurants and cafes.

Chef Han's Cafe, at the corner of Francis and William St, is popular among backpackers and has heaps of vegetarian-friendly noodle and stir-fries for around $6 (open daily 11am-10pm). The busy Hare Krishna **Food For Life** cafeteria, 200 William St, serves mild, vegetarian Indian food to a fascinating cross-section of Perthites and travelers. All-you-can-eat lunch (M-F noon-2:30pm) costs $5 (concessions $4). Next door, **Il Padrino** (tel. 9227 9065) has tasty $6 pasta and half-price pizza lunchtime specials (M-F noon-3pm). **Giuseppe Corsica Pastries,** at the corner of Lake and Aberdien St, has a forty-year history as the heart of Little Italy in Northbridge. You'll pay little more here for a tartlet or Neapolitan pastry than you would for a lamington or hedgehog slice elsewhere. (Open M-F 8am-5:30pm, Sa 8am-noon.)

For a less formal meal, try one of the city's **food halls,** where you'll find booths vending international fare. The **Northbridge Pavilion Food Hall,** on the corner of Lake and James St, has Japanese, Indian, Italian, and more (open W, Th, Su 11am-midnight, F-Sa 11am-3am). The Hay St Mall houses the **Downunder Food Hall** and the **Carillon Arcade Food Hall** (both open M-Sa). The food halls at the **Fremantle** and **Subiaco** markets are also good values, though they're mobbed on weekends.

A number of pubs and clubs in town cater specifically to Perth's backpacker set, taming the hungry crowds with free meals and drink specials. They're not very veggie-friendly, though. The determined can find free food almost every night. On Monday night, the **Aberdeen Hotel** on Aberdeen St, near Lake St, is the place to go, while on Tuesday and Thursday, the **hip-e-club** on Newcastle St in Leederville hosts a lively crowd that shimmies to Bee Gees tunes while downing free drinks and food. **The Good, the Bad, and the Ugly,** across the street from the Aberdeen, serves up free barbecue and Mexican fare on Thursday and Sunday, and on Wednesday nights **The Post Office,** on the corner of Aberdeen St and Parker St, delivers.

Coles, SupaValu, and **Foodland** are Perth's major **supermarket** chains. For cheap, quality, imported bulk pasta, cereals, and deli foods, elbow your way through the crowds into **Kakulas Brothers Wholesale Importers,** 185 William St (open M-F 8am-5:30pm, Sa 8am-12:30pm). In Fremantle, **Kakulas Sister** emulates her Perthite sibs on the corner of Market and Leake St (open M-F 9am-5:30pm, Sa 9am-2pm).

■ Sights

If you do nothing else in Perth, visit **Kings Park.** Its 400 hectares are criss-crossed with foot and bike paths and nature trails, and on sunny days its picnic lawns and playgrounds echo with the sounds of children. On weekdays it's less crowded, and offers a bit of urban wilderness perfect for a quiet afternoon. Perched atop **Mt. Eliza,** the park offers a great view of the Swan River and city below. The park is home to hundreds of plant and animal species and blooms with wildflowers in the spring;

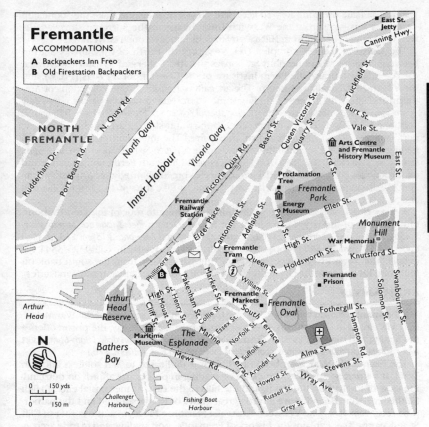

there's a **Wildflower Festival** in September. There's ample **parking** within the park. By foot, head west from the city center up St. George's Tce and bear left as it becomes Malcom St and heads to the roundabout at the north end of the park. Alternatively, head to the Swan River and turn right, following signs as the walking path passes under the freeway.

Atop the Mt. Eliza Escarpment, you'll find a **memorial** to WA soldiers killed in overseas battles during WWI. Try whispering at one end of its long, granite bench. The Fraser Ave **Information Centre,** across from the memorial, hands out maps of the park, rents bikes, and arranges guided tours. South of the memorial, the excellent **Western Australian Botanic Garden** is home to over 1700 native species. Free tours depart from the karrilog opposite the war memorial. *(Tours daily 10am; also 2pm W and Su July-Oct.)*

Perth wouldn't be Perth without its assortment of **beaches. Cottlesloe Beach,** on the Fremantle train line, is a popular family spot with safe swimming. **City Beach** is another good swimming spot, while **Scarborough** has bigger surfing waves; its crowds of twenty-somethings make for excellent people-watching. **Trigg Beach,** just north of Scarborough, is another surfers' dream, but the waves can get a bit rough for swimming. Bare it all if you dare at **Swanbourne Beach,** also on the Freo train.

For a closer look at sea life of a different sort, check out the aquariums at **Underwater World** (tel. 9447 7500), north of Perth along the West Coast Hwy at Hillary's Harbour. Fish galore, guided marine biology tours, and daily dolphin feedings make the trek well worthwhile. *(Open daily 9am-5pm. $15.50, concessions $12.50, kids $7.50, families $39.)* You can watch the dolphin show for nothing by walking along the rocky sea-wall just outside the complex. To get there on public transport, take the Soondalup Train and bus #423 from the Warwich Interchange to the Sorrento stop. Whale-watching cruises depart from Hillary's from September through November.

The **Cultural Centre** complex (tel. 9492 6600), north of the railway station between William St and Beaufort St, houses the **Art Gallery of Western Australia,** the **Alexander Library,** the **Perth Institute of the Contemporary Arts (PICA),** and the **Western Australian Museum.** The art gallery houses several collections of Aus-tralian and international arts, including some interesting Aboriginal pieces. *(Open daily 10am-5pm. Free admission, except to rotating special collections. Free guided tours T-Th and Su 1pm, and F 12:30pm.)* PICA shows contemporary and student art and hosts evening performances. *(Open Tu-Su 11am-8pm. Usually free.)* The museum (tel. 9328 4411) has good exhibits on WA's natural history and culture. *(Open Su-F 10:30am-5pm, Sa 1-5pm. Free.)* The **Zoo** (tel. 9367 7985), on Labouchere Rd in South Perth, houses native and exotic animals and conducts endangered species breeding programs. *(Open daily 9am-5pm.)* Walk across the river from the city center, or take the #36 bus from William St and St. George's Tce.

A **ferry ride** from Perth or Freo, including a 20-minute tour of the Freo Harbour, offers a view of the city skyline from the Swan. *(Departs Pier 3, Barrack St Jetty, daily 9:45am and 2pm. Departs East St Jetty, Fremantle, daily at 11am and 3:15pm. $13, children under 14 $9, families $40.)* More elaborate cruises are available; call 9325 3341 for details. The Swan River offers freshwater fun, particularly from the south bank off Mill Point Rd opposite the city center, where you can hire catamaran and windsurfes.

FREMANTLE

The **Fremantle Prison** (tel. 9430 7177), off Hampton Rd just south of the War Memo-rial, was closed in 1991 shortly after a dramatic prison riot. Today, the prison offers a fascinating and macabre look at Australia's penal history. *(Open daily 10am-6pm. Tours every 30min., last tour 5pm; spooky candlelight tours W and F at 7:30pm. $10.)*

The **Fremantle War Memorial** on High St is dedicated to WA soldiers killed in WWI. It's a perfect spot for picnicking or reading in peace, and affords an outstand-ing view of the harbor, the town, and the hills to the east. At the coastal end of High St, the limestone **Roundhouse** affords great views of Rottnest Island and the harbor. *(Open daily 9am-6pm.)* The **Western Australia Maritime Museum** at the corner of Cliff St and Marine Tce, explains the history of Fremantle, port trading, and marine archae-ology. *(Open daily 10:30am-5pm. Admission by donation, with charges for special exhibits.)*

The excellent **Fremantle markets** (tel. 9335 2515), on the corner of South Tce and Henderson St, are a treasure trove for everything from antique coins to tie-dyed velvet pants. Cheap, fresh veggies abound; prices hit rock bottom around closing time on Sunday. *(Open F 9am-9pm, Sa 9am-5pm, Su and holidays 10am-5pm.)*

Escape from Fremantle

Although its colonial keepers regarded Fremantle Prison as escape-proof, one man managed not only to escape but to dramatically embarrass British authori-ties in the process. John Boyle O'Reilly and six of his comrades were sentenced to imprisonment at Fremantle for their role in the 1868 Fenian uprising in Ire-land. O'Reilly broke out of the prison and hitched a ride to North America aboard a whaling ship. He moved to Boston, where the Irish-American commu-nity raised money for him to outfit a new ship, the *Catalpu.* O'Reilly then sailed for Australia to rescue his brethren. When British ships fired on the *Catalpu* off Fremantle, O'Reilly raised the American flag and reminded his attackers that they were in international waters, whereupon his aggressors grudgingly backed off. O'Reilly made his rendezvous with his fellow Fenians and returned to Boston.

■ Entertainment

There's always something to do in Perth. The city has heaps of good pubs, clubs, and cafes, with laid-back, friendly crowds. Much of Perth's nightlife scene is centered in Northbridge. Everything's open much later on weekend nights than during the week; on slow Sunday evenings, some places shut their doors as early as 7pm. The free entertainment weekly *XPress* has the lowdown on what's happening around town.

For drinking, try the pricey but tasty house brews at **The Brass Monkey** on the corner of James and William St in Northbridge. The **Universal Bar,** 221 William St, Northbridge, has *sake,* live jazz, and a hipper-than-thou crowd. Big-name acts tend to hit the **Metropolis Club,** with locations at 146 Roe St in Perth and 58 South Tce in Fremantle. On Thursday, creatively pierced crowd flocks to **The Loft,** 104 Murray St, for Goth Night; on Sunday a cleaner-cut set grooves to Wham! and Madonna. **O₂,** 139 James St, Northbridge, keeps clubbers breathing easy with dance tunes, plenty of smoke, and flashing lights. For live music, try heading to the suburbs. **The Breakwater Tavern,** at Hillary's Boat Harbor, generally hosts local bands Wednesday through Sunday, as do the **Swanbourne Hotel,** Swanbourne, and **Indi Bar and Bistro,** Scarborough. The live afternoon "Sunday Session" at the **Cott,** 104 Marine Pde, Cottlesloe, is good fun.

Fremantle is another good nightlife destination. South Tce, also known as "Cappuccino Strip," is lined with cafes open late, and is an excellent people-watching spot. The **Sail and Anchor** is a British-style pub with good house brews, and **Mojo's Pub,** 237 Queen Victoria St, North Freo, has tasty pub grub, dancing, and live music.

Perth is a reasonably **gay- and lesbian-friendly** city. Same-sex couples don't attract much attention in most of city's popular nightspots, and there are a few gay clubs and pubs. The *Westside Observer,* a gay and lesbian newspaper, is a good source of info on local goings-on ($1 at newsagents, free in some businesses). The cheery owner of the intelligently stocked **Arcane Bookshop** (tel. 9328 5023; email arcbooks@highway1.com.au) is a font of info and publications on Perth's gay scene (open M-Th 10am-5:30pm, F 10am-7pm, Sa 10am-5pm, Su 10am-4pm). **Connections Nightclub,** 81 James St, Northbridge (tel. 9328 1870), is a very popular gay-owned club, with DJ-spun dance, house, and techno beats (Tu-Su 10pm-6am; men only Tu night). The **Court Hotel,** 50 Beaufort St, Northbridge (tel. 9328 5292), near the corner of James St, is another hotspot, with off-the-wall theme nights like "bears' night"—for big hairy men and their fans (open M-Sa 11am-late, Su 3pm-9 or 10pm). Catch one of the periodic **drag shows** at the **Rainbow Connection Cafe** if you can; you won't be disappointed.

■ Near Perth

Although a car facilitates daytrips around Perth, TransPerth bus service is fairly comprehensive, if not always frequent or easy to understand. Don't be daunted: it's worthwhile figuring out the timetables to see some of the neighboring country. The adventurous will find that many sights are accessible with a bike and a bit of effort.

■ Rottnest Island

Called a "rat's nest" by Dutch explorers who mistook the island's wallabies (quokkas) for giant rats, Rottnest Island is a hunk of limestone about 19km (40min. by ferry) off the coast near Fremantle. The island was originally settled in 1830 by farmers but was turned into a prison for Aboriginals in 1838. It also served at various times as a boys' reformatory, a coastal defense installation, and a wartime internment camp. The prison wasn't closed until 1903, and many stone buildings erected by the prisoners remain. Today, the island is a class-A nature reserve, and tourists and locals flock there daily to cycle, swim, snorkel, surf, and relax in the fresh air away from the city. The quokkas, Rottnest's unofficial mascot, roam about the island unafraid of humans.

Watch out if you're carrying any food—quokkas have voracious appetites. Feeding the critters is prohibited, though, as it's quite harmful to their health.

PRACTICAL INFORMATION The **Visitors Centre** (tel. 9372 9752) is in Thompsons Bay, directly in front of the ferry jetty (open daily 8am-5pm). It provides information on accommodations and bus tours of the island. Courtesy buses depart from the Visitors Centre roughly every hour and head to Geordie Bay, Kingstown, and the airport (8:15, 8:45, 9:45am, then every hr.). The **Bayseeker Bus** is a better way to get around the island; friendly drivers make the 45-minute loop roughly every hour from 9am to 4:30pm, chatting about the island's history and ecology along the way. Hop off whenever you like and catch a later bus back (day ticket $5). An **ATM** is across from the grocery store in the shopping area.

Three companies offer **ferry service** to Rottnest from Perth, Fremantle, and Hillary's. The cheapest is **Oceanic Cruises** (tel. 9325 1191 or 9430 5127), which departs daily from Pier 2 of the Barrack St Jetty (8:45 and 10am; same-day return $40, kids $14) and from the East St Jetty, Fremantle (9:45 and 11:45am; $27, $10). (Extended stay $5 more. Free pick-up from Perth hotels and Freo train station.) **Rottnest Express** (tel. 9225 6406) has several daily departures from Victoria Quay, Fremantle (same-day return $32, kids under 12 $10; extended stay $5 more). **Boat Torque** (tel. 9221 5844) leaves North Freo at 10 and 11:30am daily ($30). For extended trips in the summer, proof of pre-booked accommodation may be required. All three ferries offer $5 YHA/VIP discounts.

ACCOMMODATIONS AND FOOD There's plenty of accommodation on Rottnest, but you should book ahead in the summer. The **Rottnest Youth Hostel** (tel. 9372 9780; fax 9292 5141) is on Bickley Point, a 20-minute walk from the Visitors Centre at Kingstown. Facing the center, head left and follow the YHA signs. The hostel has a kitchen, laundry, and luggage storage facilities inside old army barracks. (Dorms $16, doubles $38; YHA nonmembers $19, $44. Linen $4. Meals cost around $6. Office open 8am-5:30pm; later check-in by prior arrangement. Check-out 10am. Wheelchair accessible.) Those traveling in a group may find the **Rottnest Island Authority** (tel. 9432 9111) a better deal. Units range from basic bungalows with outdoor toilets to posh cottages with spectacular bay views. Rates vary according to season and length of stay; four people can stay in a simple bungalow for a week in summer for around $8 per night each, even less in winter. (Book ahead. Check-out 9am.) **Camping** is also available (tent sites $5 per person, children $2.50), as are **cabins;** phone for details.

It's a good idea to bring picnic supplies to the island even for a daytrip; though the Thompsons Bay settlement has a **bakery** and a **grocery store,** both in the pedestrian mall behind the tourist center, prices are considerably higher than on the mainland.

ACTIVITIES The best way to see Rottnest is by bike. There are very few cars on the island, and biking along the gently hilly coastline is sheer pleasure. **Rottnest Island Bike Hire** (tel. 9292 5105) has a wide selection and meets incoming ferries. *(1-speed $13 per day; 18-speed $18. Locks and required helmets included.)* Pick up a map in the Visitors Centre, or simply explore on your own. The beaches become emptier as you head away from the settled areas—go far enough and you may have the luxury of a cove all to yourself. **Narrow Neck** and **Parker Point** offer good fishing, while **Ricey Beach** is a popular swimming, surfing, and diving spot. **Whales** and **dolphins** are frequently seen from the windy, breathtaking cliffs at **West End.** The island houses 20 established osprey nests that may be spotted on rocks and outcrops along the coast.

Ocean currents moving south from the tropics bring warm water and multifarious fish to the waters off Rottnest, creating a great spot for **diving** and **snorkeling.** The **Environmental Office** near the visitor's center has maps of "snorkel trails" in the island's bays, and the **Dive, Ski & Surf Shop** (tel. 9292 5167) has tours and equipment rentals. Rottnest is also a **surfing** hotspot, hosting three competitions each year. An annual daring **swim** for the super-fit runs to Rottnest from Cottlesoe Beach in town.

■ The Darling Range, York, and the Avon Valley

Heading east from Perth, the city's suburbs gradually give way to the gently rolling orchards and verdant forest of the **Darling Range,** also called **Perth Hills.** Take the M1 train from Perth to Midland, then buses #317-320 or 327-330 from Midland Station. **John Forrest National Park** offers miles of shaded hiking trails, a colorful **wildflower** season, and kangaroos, parrots, and kookaburras galore. **Lake Leschenaultia** affords peaceful swimming, canoeing, barbecues, and walking trails. Come mid-week and book ahead for **camping** (tel. 9572 4248; $5 plus $3 per person).

Undulating hills, misty dales, and wildflower-studded fields make the **Avon Valley,** 100km east and somewhat north of Perth, a great place for a drive or a bicycle ride. WA's first inland settlement, **York** is home to a host of restored historical buildings. The **tourist bureau** (tel. 9641 4301) is in the Town Hall on Avon Tce (open M-F 9:30am-5pm, Sa-Su 10am-5pm). The **1885 Railway Station Museum and Tea Gardens** is a weekends-only affair (open Sa-Su 11am-4pm). York is host to a multitude of festivals; the **jazz festival** (tel. 9641 1366) at the end of September is especially popular. The **Old York Gaol and Courthouse** complex, with buildings dating from the 1840s to 1900, is also open to the public (open M-F 11am-3pm, Sa-Su 10am-4pm; $3).

SOUTHWEST

The Indian Ocean coast of Southwest Australia is experiencing a boom in both tourism and year-round residency. This winery region features a mild climate of wet winters and dry summers, the world's greatest variety of wildflowers, and beautiful dunes. And it's primed for visitors. Many of the hostels, caravan parks, and even vineyards in the area are less than five years old. Land prices are rising and large commercial wine makers are moving in. Meanwhile, cattle and sheep stations—the latter long profitable as a source of Merino wool—are being pushed out. The Department of Conservation and Land Management (CALM) is struggling to set limits on beachfront development and combat the destructive effects of tourism on the environment.

Mother Nature has been kind to Australia's Southwest; the region's spectacular scenery and mild climate make it a favorite destination for travelers from around the globe. Hikers rave about the **Stirling** and **Porongurup Ranges,** and many surfers swear by the Southwest's gorgeous beaches and pounding waves. Bushwalking in the region's karri and jarrah forests is a unique experience, and few visitors leave the Southwest without having gone on a whale- or dolphin-watching cruise. The Mediterranean climate is ideal for vineyards, and the region has witnessed a recent explosion in commercial wine-making. It's worth a trip just to tour these wineries and try your tongue at some tasting.

The easiest way to see the region is by car. Many sights are well off the bus routes, and public transportation in many of the region's towns is either nonexistent or inadequate. Tours can be arranged to many sights, but costs can be quite high. Nevertheless, several options exist for the auto-less. Some travellers use the **Easy Rider Backpackers** bus (tel. 9226 0307; 24-hr. notice for pick-up). A three-month pass ($139) covers bus service among most regional hostels. (Southbound buses leave Perth Tu, F, and Su, and W in peak season; buses return to Perth M, W, and Sa, and Th in peak season.)

Another option is Westrail's 28 day **Southern Discovery Pass** ($119). This pass allows for bus and train travel to most southern and eastern destinations including the Southwest, Albany, Esperance, and Kalgoorlie. Most travelers tend to follow a similar circuit south from Perth along the coast, east through the Great Southern, and north into the Goldfields, before driving west back to Perth. Drivers unfamiliar with Australia's roads may prefer this direction of travel as well, since they'll begin with well-traveled highways around Margaret River before heading out into the interior and Goldfields. Those traveling without a car will find it much easier to arrange rides when traveling this route. Check hostel bulletin boards for rideshare options. *Let's Go* does not, however, recommend hitching. If the stark and desolate interior holds little appeal to you, driving south and then back north along the coast is another option.

■ Perth to Margaret River

The scenic three-hour drive south of Perth toward Margaret River is lined with forests, farms, cattle stations, and the occasional (and decidedly unattractive) limestone quarry. It's a pleasant drive, with forested picnic areas at frequent intervals. From Victoria Square in Perth, drive south on Victoria Ave to Riverside Dr and head west. Follow the signs for Hwy 2 Southbound and stay on Hwy 2 until the exit for Hwy 1.

About 100km south of Perth is **Yalgorup National Park,** a right-hand turn-off marked by a sign 500m up the road. The park is a popular summer weekend destination among Perth residents and features tent sites, nature reserves, miles of dunes, and a forest of jarrah and tuart trees with peppermint undergrowth. Its beaches make for good bird-watching in the fall and winter (Oct.-Mar.), but during the summer, speedboats and jet skis tend to scare off the wildlife. The best stopover point en route to Margaret River is **Bunbury,** which boasts great dolphin-viewing, though little other excitement.

■ Bunbury

Two hours south of Perth, **Bunbury** (pop. 30,000) boasts the snazzy **Dolphin Discovery Centre** (tel. (097) 913-088), on Koombana Drive. Swim and snorkel with **dolphins** or keep dry and check out the center's theater and interactive exhibits. (Admission free; film $2. Open Oct.-Apr. daily 8am-5pm; May-Sept. 8:30am-4:30pm.) **Dolphin-sighting tours** depart daily from the Centre; call the Centre or **Naturalist Charters** (tel. 9755 2276 or 018 938 056) to reserve a space (1½ hr.; $15, children $10, concessions $12).

If you're heading south by train, Bunbury is 3km from **Wollaston,** the southern terminus of WA's **train** network. Transit buses will honor a train ticket stub for a free lift to Bunbury. **South West Coachlines** runs daily bus service to Perth (2½ hr.; departs 8:45am, 2:30pm, 6:30pm; $16). **Transit buses** circle the city (M-Sa, $1.60). The buses run regularly (M-F 7am-6pm, Sa 7am-2:30pm). Bunbury's **tourist office** (tel. 9721 7922) is conveniently located next door (open M-F 8:30am-5pm, Sa 9am-5pm, Su 9:30am-4:30pm). **Internet access** is at the **Bunbury Internet Cafe** (tel. 9791 1257), which is also next door to the bus station ($5 per 30min.). Bunbury's main drag is **Victoria St.** The **post office,** several **banks,** and a handful of cafes and restaurants share the strip with boutiques and art shops. The **police** reside on Wittenoom St at Stephen St (just up the block from the post office), and the **hospital** is at Parkfield and Edward St.

The quiet and tidy **Bunbury YHA** (tel. 9791 2621) is at the corner of Stirling and Moore St (dorms $14, YHA nonmembers $17; family rooms from $38; Internet access). The **Wander Inn,** 16 Clifton St (tel. 9721 3242), is a bit busier, with a pool and ping-pong (dorms $15; singles and doubles $18 per person; YHA, VIP). Both hostels rent bikes and can arrange **dolphin tours, bushwalking, kayaking,** and so forth. The shopping center behind the tourist office features two **supermarkets. Dewsons** is slightly cheaper for staples, but **Coles** is bigger (both open M-Sa 8:30am-6pm).

■ Bunbury to Margaret River

Small towns dot the coast as one heads southwest toward Margaret River. **Busselton** is dull, but offers budget accommodation if need be. **Yallingup** is well-known for its excellent surf and hosts a number of surfing competitions throughout the year. Another worthwhile attraction is the limestone **Yallingup Cave,** also known as Ngilgi's Cave, from an Aboriginal legend about two battling spirits. A number of **hiking trails** from 7-11km in length begin at the caves and the stark **Cape Naturaliste Lighthouse** (lighthouse open Tu-Su 9:30am-4pm). **Dunsborough** is another popular holiday destination for Perth residents, mainly because of its sandy beaches and somewhat more sheltered swimming. Or arrange it yourself by calling **Dive and Adventure Sports** (tel. 097 553 299 or 097 521 2888) for diving and snorkeling lessons and charters. For whale-watching tours, call **Naturaliste Charters** (tel. 9755 2276). Tours depart daily from the Boat Ramp on Geographe Bay Rd at 11am (3hr., $35 adults, $15 kids under 12). The **Dunsborough YHA,** 285 Geographe Bay Rd (tel. 9755 3107), is located right on the beach—follow the signs from Caves Rd. (Standard dorms $15 YHA, 18 without; doubles $36 YHA, $42 without; family rooms from $50 YHA, $60 without; dorm beds $16 with VIP card.) Bikes, canoes and windsurfers can be rented; the hostel managers will help arrange tours and whale watching.

 contains map labels: Cape Naturaliste, Lighthouse, Geographe Bay, N, Sugarloaf Rock, Dunsborough, Yallingup, Ngilgi Cave, Busselton, Vasse, TO BUNBURY AND PERTH, Cape Clairault, Caves Rd, INDIAN OCEAN, Bussell Hwy, Treeton Estate, Cowaramup Bay, Cowaramup, Cowaramup Point, Gracetown, Margaret River, Prevelly Park/Surf Point, Leeuwin Estate, Mammoth Cave, Lake Cave, Cape Freycinet, Leeuwin Naturaliste National Park, Bussell Hwy, TO PEMBERTON, Lookout, Boranup Maze, Brockman Hwy, Hamelin Bay, Karridale, 0 5 miles, 0 5 kilometers, Cape Hamelin, Jewel Cave, Far Southwest, Augusta, Lighthouse, Cape Leeuwin, Flinders Bay

■ Margaret River

Nestled between expansive vineyards, towering karri and jarrah forests, and the rolling surf of the Indian Ocean, Margaret River (pop. 2000) is a small easy-going community of winemakers, artisans, surfers, and thirty-something would-be hippies. The laid-back attitude of locals is contagious; most visitors find that it's best to take a few days to relax in this area. "Margaret's" (as it's known) also makes a convenient base from which to explore much of the southwestern coast; Cape Leeuwin and Cape Naturaliste are each about 40 minutes from town by car. Margaret River can be reached by heading south from Busselton on **Bussell Hwy** (Hwy 10) or by the more scenic but slower **Caves Rd.** Both make for a nice drive through bush and karri forest as well as a thicket of prize-winning vineyards.

PRACTICAL INFORMATION The **Bussell Highway** serves as Margaret River's main drag. The **South West Coachlines bus stop** in Margaret River is on the Bussell Hwy, across the street from the **tourist office** (tel. 9757 2911; open daily 9am-5pm) and the **supermarket** and liquor store. The **post office** is one block east, up Wilmott Ave, and the **police** station lies just behind it. There is a **hospital** on Farrelly St, near Wallcliffe Rd two blocks west of the Bussell Hwy.

ACCOMMODATIONS Margaret's accommodates flocks of tourists in its three hostels and numerous hotels and bed and breakfasts. Though hostels are the cheapest option, the area's B&Bs can be a sweet deal for those traveling in pairs or larger groups. Though tough to reach without a car, the **Surf Point Lodge** (tel. 9757 1777), on Riedle Dr, 10km north of town towards Prevelly, is the area's newest and spiffiest hostel. Perks include clean, spacious rooms, a pool table, satellite TV, barbecue facilities, bikes ($12 per day), and boogie boards ($10 per day). (Dorms $19 winter, $20 summer. Doubles $45 winter, $55 summer, private bath $4 extra. Linens included. Free pick-up from bus terminal upon arrangement. Book ahead in summer.) The friendly **Margaret River Lodge** (tel. 9757 9532) lies 1½km southwest of the Bustle Hwy along Wallcliffe Rd and is owned by folks who are full of ideas about local sights. (Dorm beds $15. Singles $25; doubles $35. YHA, VIP, Nomads, ISIC. Showers and toilets outside. Bike and bodyboard rentals available. Swimming pool, pool table. Free pick-up.) The **Wallcliffe Lodge** (tel. 9757 2699), off Wallcliffe Rd a few kilometers out of town near the cemetery and golf course, is an immaculate B&B. It's very comfortable, and toasty warm in the winter. (Singles $45; doubles $65, with private bath $85. Hearty hot breakfast included.)

FOOD Margaret River's restaurants are good but pricey. Many are BYO, perfect for enjoying the fruit of the local vineyards. The **Arc of Iris** (tel. 9757 3112), in town on the Bussell Hwy near Wallcliffe Rd, serves up tasty specials in a funky, laid-back atmosphere. Local artwork and mismatched cutlery give the place heaps of character. (Appetizers $4-6, entrees $7-18. BYO. Open for lunch W-Sa noon-3pm, dinner W-M 6pm-late.) **Goodfellas Cafe Woodfire Pizza**, 97 Bussell Hwy (tel. 9757 3184), offers huge bowls of pasta ($14-15), salads ($7.50), and exotic pizzas ($10-15 small, $15-20 large). Try the fiery Inferno (with chili sauce, onions and jalapeños) if you dare—but have that jug of cold beer ready! The **Sea Garden Cafe** (tel. 9757 3074), at Prevelly Park about 9km out of town, is a friendly local favorite, and worth the short drive if you have a car. The gnocchi with Tasmanian salmon ($14) is divine. (BYO. Open daily 8:30am-10:30pm.)

SIGHTS AND ENTERTAINMENT Several wineries are accessible by bike or foot from town. **Chateau Xanadu** (tel. 9757 2581; email chxanadu@netserv.net.au), 3km southwest of town on Terry Rd, is run by friendly folk offering free tastings daily from 10am to 5pm. Just behind Xanadu, the **Cape Mentell** winery (tel. 9757 3266), just off Walcliffe Rd, also offers free tastings in a slightly stuffier atmosphere. *(Open daily 10am-4:30pm.)* The **Eagles Heritage Raptor Wilderness Centre** (tel. 9757 2960) is nearby on Boodjidup Rd. *(Free flight displays daily 11am, 11:30pm. Wheelchair accessible. $7, $5 seniors, $3 kids, $17 family.)* Australia's largest collection of birds of prey, it's dedicated to education, rehabilitation of injured birds, and breeding projects.

Biking in and around Margaret's is quite nice; area maps are available for free in the tourist office. Margaret's **beaches** and **surf** are a major tourist draw. Packs of grommets (young surfers) learn the ropes in the relatively tame surf at **Rivermouth;** more experienced surfies delight in the mammoth waves off **Surf Point** at **Prevelly Beach.** **Conto's Beach,** with its white sand and dramatic scenery, is another fine spot.

A young crowd boozes it up at the **Settler's Tavern,** 97 Bussell Hwy (tel. 9757 2398). The tavern also serves grub and hosts occasional live bands.

■ Around Margaret River

Caves Road south of Margaret's is one of the area's most spectacular drives. Winding through the karri forests of **Leeuwin-Naturaliste National Park,** the road passes hundreds of hidden **caves,** though only four are open to the public. It's difficult to get there without a car; a taxi from Margaret's to **Mammoth Cave** costs about $25 each way, or hostels can usually help arrange transport. The **Cave Works Eco Centre** (tel. 9757 7411), at Lake Cave about 15km south of Margaret's, offers interpretive exhibits. *(Open daily 9am-5pm. Admission $5, children $3.)* The caves themselves are much more interesting; and admission to any of the cave tours includes admission to the interpretive center. Tours of **Lake Cave** depart the center regularly. *(Every ½hr. 9:30am-3:30pm. In winter every hr. 55min. $12 adult, $5 kids.)* The first chamber of Mammoth Cave, about 2km north of Lake Cave, is wheelchair accessible. *(Tours every hr. 9am-3pm. 45min. $10, children $5. Plans are in the works to make Mammoth Cave self-guiding by the end of 1998.)* The highly recommended **Jewel Cave** and **Moondyre Cave** are about 25km further south. *(Tours at Jewell Cave every half hr. 9:30am-3:30pm; in winter* *every hr. 1hr. $12, children $5. Moondyre Cave tours 2pm daily. $25 adults, $18 kids. 2½hr.)* The **Grand Pass** covers all the caves ($28, children $12).

Follow the gravel road (Canto Rd) 5km past Lake Cave to get to **Conto Spring** and **Merchant Rock,** a stunning spot with violently crashing waves and well-weathered trees. The road down can be rough on a 2WD. About 25km south of Margaret's on the left side of Caves Rd is the **Boranup Maze,** a shrub labyrinth that loses its lushness in winter ($2, children $1). Just south of the maze a right turn off Caves Rd leads to the **Boranup Lookout,** a windy spot with views out to the Indian Ocean.

Local champ Josh Dalmateer's **Surf Academy** (tel. 08 9757 1850) gives two-hour lessons. (Private lessons $55; group lessons $25 per person. Equipment included.)

Tours

Several companies can organize half- or full-day tours of wineries and other local sights. One of the most popular is the **Cave and Canoe Bushtucker Tour** (tel. 9757 9084 or 9757 2911). In four hours, this tour packs in a canoe adventure on Margaret River, a tasting of bushfood, a cave visit, and a quick guided walk through the bush. (Tours daily in summer, 4 per week in winter. Departs at 10am from kangaroo sign at Rivermouth Beach, Prevelly Park, off Walcliffe Rd. $25, children under 15 $15.) Also popular are **Boranup Eco Walks** tours (tel. 9757 7576), guided walks through karri and jarrah forest. Book ahead; personalized walks may be arranged. (Daytime walks 2½-3hr. $12, children under 15 $8. Night walks 1½ hr.; in summer $10, $6.) **Highlight Tours** (tel. 9757 3395) run tours which depart daily from the car park at the tourist bureau. Morning tours depart at 8:45am to visit Lake Cave, the Boranup Forest, Redgate Beach and a local berry farm. Afternoon tours depart at 1:15pm to visit the **Margaret River Regional Wine Center,** a cheese farm, a vineyard, a brewery, and a historic home site (4hr., $30). More info can be found in the tourist office.

Another well-regarded company, **Margaret River Tour Company** (tel. 041 991 7166) will arrange similar sight-seeing, winery tours, and surfing trips. (Half-day tour $40, full day $60. Free pick-up at accommodations.) **Milesaving tours** (tel. 1800 818 102) offers similar tours at similar prices; call for details. Trevor McGowan's **Adventure In Margaret River** (tel. 9757 2104 or 0419 927 160) arranges **abseiling, climbing and caving** for the thrill-seeking (½day $60; full day $80 adults, $65 kids under 16).

■ Augusta

About 45km south of Margaret River lies Augusta, a small, pleasant community at Australia's southwestern tip. It's a good base for exploring the surrounding area and (in season) cruising the bay and ocean on a whale-watching tour. Nine kilometers south of the town is **Cape Leeuwin,** Australia's most southwestern point, and the spot where the Indian and Southern Oceans meet. A **lighthouse** built in 1895 stands guard over the spot (tours available daily 9am-4pm).

Whales can often be spotted off the coast June-Sept., and almost every spot in town provides excellent views of Flinders Bay. **Naturaliste Charters** (tel. 9755 2276) runs whale-watching tours from Augusta in the winter, departing daily at 11am (3hr.; $35, children $15). The best lodging deal in town is the sparkling clean **Baywater Manor Resort,** alias the **Augusta YHA,** 88 Blackwood Ave (tel. 9758 1290, fax 9758 1291). The brick rooms with jarrah wood accents are homey, and the owners arrange whale-watching and sight-seeing tours. (Dorms $15; doubles $38, with bath $48. YHA nonmembers $3 more. Linen included; bike and car hire available. Wheelchair accessible.) If you can't get a bed in town at the Baywater Manor, the **Hamelin Bay Caravan Park** (tel. 9758 5540) has unpowered sites (Oct.-June $14; July-Sept. $10). Booking in advance for summer months is advised.

The **Gull Rock Cafe,** 100 Blackwood Ave (tel. 9758 1513), serves tasty breakfasts and lunch fare (burgers around $5, soup $4.50) and pricier, more elaborate dinners on Friday and Saturday nights (seafood curry, $15). (Open daily 8:30am-4pm, F-Sa 6pm-late.) Across the street, the **Augusta Bakery** and the **Augusta Cafe** offer baked

Protecting Their Own

The towering karri trees of WA's southwest fear fire like any other trees, but they also once served to fight flames. Rangers the world over erect fire towers to catch signs of forest fire as early as possible, but those in WA decided to construct cabins in the tops of the trees themselves. Rather than attempt to build 60m-tall observation towers up to the lofty canopy from the forest floor, the rangers drove pegs into the karri trunks so that they could climb to these treetop dwellings. From here, the fearless (and vertigo-resistant) firefighters remained vigilant from the 1930s to 1970s, when they switched to aircraft. Today, the towers are open to visitors. Tremendous views reward those who can muster the courage to ascend a mammoth eucalypt. The highest such treehouse, at 75m, is in the **Bicentennial Tree** in Warren National Park.

goods and simple meals (open M-F 8am-5pm, Sa-Su until 4pm; cafe also open Sa nights for dinner).

Along Blackwood Ave you'll find a **news agency, fruit market,** and **grocery store** on the left, and the **tourist office** and **post office** on the right. About 12km north of Augusta at the southern tip of Caves Rd lies **Hamelin Bay,** the site of 11 shipwrecks since 1882 and home to a passel of semi-tame stingrays. Independent scuba and snorkeling outings to the four visible wrecks are welcome, but you'll need to hire a boat.

■ Pemberton

The eastern spur of Hwy 10 runs from Karridale, north of Augusta, out to Pemberton, a good 90-minute drive. Watch the signs—an easily missed right turn about 40km from Karridale leads to the last 69km stretch to Pemberton. As the surrounding denuded hills attest, tiny Pemberton is first and foremost a timber town. Logging trucks rumble at a steady rate along the **Vasse Hwy,** the town's main drag, and Pemberton is home to the largest hardwood sawmill in the southern hemisphere. Fortunately, much of the area's spectacular karri forest has been designated as national parkland and remains safe.

The **Karri Visitors Centre,** Pemberton's **tourist bureau** (tel. 9776 1133), located in the town's old school building, has information on the surrounding forest, showers and toilets for campers, a pioneer museum, and a Karri "Discovery Centre" with a talking plastic frog (Discovery Centre $2, children $1, family $5). Karri trees are unique to southwestern WA, and a walk or hike through the forest is very worthwhile. The tourist bureau sells useful bushwalking guides. (Open daily 9am-5pm.)

The **Gloucester Tree,** one of the tallest fire lookouts in the world, is a prime attraction in Pemberton. Steel dowels wind 61m up the trunk to the platform, from which the bravehearted get a breathtaking view of the forest canopy and distant sand dunes. Miles of walking trails crisscross the surrounding **Gloucester National Park.** Scenic rail tours of the area may be booked in the tourist office or by phone (tel. 9776 1322). (Tours 1¾-5½ hr. Prices start at $12, kids $6.) Head up Ellis St and follow the signs.

West of Pemberton on the road to Augusta is **Beedelup National Park,** home to the **Beedelup Falls** and a karri tree with a hole cut in its middle that you can walk through. Roads inside the park are not paved past the highway, and can be rough on vehicles without 4WD. The ascent to the falls is quite dangerous after dark.

Pemberton has two hostels, neither of which is very appealing. The **Warren Lodge** (tel. 9776 1105), located in town on the highway, is the cleaner and more centrally located of the two (dorm beds $14, doubles $38). *Let's Go* does not recommend **Pemberton YHA Pimela Chalets** (tel. 9776 1153), unless you have no other option. In town, the cheery **Rug 'n' Joe's Cafe** (tel. 9776 1411) offers bottomless mugs of tea and great coffee. (Burgers $5, lasagna $8.50. Open W-M 8am till late.)

GREAT SOUTHERN

Stretching from the karri and tingle forests of Pemberton and Walpole, through the rugged Porongurup and Stirling Ranges, to the vast scrubland at the beginning of the Nullarbor Plain, the Great Southern region possesses an expansive beauty. The character of the land and people changes as one follows the South Western Hwy (Hwy 1) east. Albany functions as a sort of urban hub for the sparsely populated southern coast, and by the time you reach Esperance, Perth's cosmopolitan strivings seem a world away.

The largely agricultural Great Southern is home to a number of respected vineyards, many of which offer complimentary wine-tastings. Tourism is another key money-maker, peaking in the spring wildflower season and in the summer, when the beaches around Denmark, Albany, and Esperance draw tourists like flies to honey. Winters in the Great Southern can be chilly and wet, so bring a good jacket.

■ Denmark

Located 66km east of Walpole along the South Coast Highway, Denmark is green, squeaky clean, and proud of it. Though originally a timber town, Denmark rapidly exhausted its trees and has since turned into quite an earth-friendly place. Today the town has a thriving organic farming scene and won the 1998 national "Tidy Town" title for its appearance and progressive environmental policies. Denmark has more organic produce shops, health food stores, and whole grain bakeries than you'd expect to find in a town of its size, and town folks are a friendly, crunchy lot.

Denmark's coastline is impressive, and has spots for good fishing, surfing, boating and swimming. The tourist office gives out a good map of the area and has info on **West Cape Howe, William Bay** and **Walpole-Nonalup National Parks.** Hikes for all skill levels abound, and the extensive **Bibbulmun Track** runs along the coast.

Strickland St, Denmark's main thoroughfare, intersects the **South Coast Highway.** Heading east, turn right on Strickland to reach the **tourist office** (tel. 9848 2055) and adjacent bus stop (open daily except Christmas, 9am-5pm). **Westrail buses** run to Perth (5½hr., $41.50) and Albany (40min., $6) once daily; the tourist office does bookings and has schedules. The **post office** is across the street and the **hospital** is at the north end of Strickland. The **police station** (tel. 9848 1311) is west of Strickland St along the south side of the highway. The volunteer-run **Denmark Environment Centre** (tel. 9848 1644; fax 9848 1248) is also on Strickland St and has an herbarium, a small library, and plenty of information on the local community and national environmental issues, as well as a neat gift shop. The town holds four **market days** each year, with live music: one at Easter, two in January, and one in late December.

The **Wilson Inlet Holiday Park** (tel. 9848 1267) is in a beautiful spot 4km down Ocean Beach Rd right on the inlet. (Rooms in unheated, somewhat dingy cabins $12; on slow days you might get one of the nicer brick houses for the same price.) In town, the **Denmark Unit Hotel** (tel. 9848 2206) rents dim, institutional rooms. (Singles with shared bath $25, doubles $40; with bathroom, TV, and phone singles $50, doubles $70.) Strickland St has several good cafes and bakeries, and on weekends and in summer there's live music in a courtyard known as "the Spot." The **Denmark Bakery** has tasty cakes and breads (open in summer daily 7am-6pm; in winter M-Sa 7am-5pm). Denmark has a solid **arts and crafts** scene, with wares for sale at a number of shops around Strickland St. The **Festival of Classics,** held each November, spotlights local talent in a series of classical music and drama performances. Denmark is also home to several **wineries;** ask at the tourist office about tastings.

■ Walpole

Tiny and friendly, Walpole (pop. 450) is experiencing a tourism boom because of its proximity to **Walpole-Nornalup National Park** and the recently constructed **Valley**

of the Giants Tree Top Walk 14km out of town. The friendly, volunteer-run **tourist bureau** (tel. 9840 1111), on the north side of the highway, hands out information on the surrounding tingle and karri forest and the beautiful coast of Walpole and Nornalup Inlets, and sells Tree Top Walk tickets (open daily 9am-4pm, 5pm in holiday season). Walpole's **post office** and **grocery store** can be found across the street, along with a handful of shops and balcony cafes.

The **Top Deck Cafe** (tel 9840 1344) serves coffee and lunch (spinach pie and salad $6.50; hours vary). The newly renovated **Tingle All Over** (tel. 9840 1041), boasts clean accommodations, a barbecue, free tea and coffee, and a spiffy new paint job. The technicolor shag rugs in some of the rooms might, indeed, make you tingle. All rooms have sinks, but showers are a short walk outdoors. (Singles $22, twins $34, family rooms $16 per person.) The **Dingo Flat YHA** (tel. 9840 8073) is a good 18km out of town at the edge of Walpole-Nornalup National Park. Although the views of the surrounding fields and forest are spectacular, the hostel itself is quite run-down. Follow the signs from the Valley of the Giants Tree Top Walk. (Singles $12, children $6; tent sites $6. No linens.)

By far the park's biggest draw is the **Tree Top Walk** (tel. 9840 8263), a 600m metal catwalk passing through the canopy of tingle trees as high as 40m above the forest floor. It's wheelchair accessible, with wheelchairs available on-site. (Open Mar.-Nov. daily 9am-5pm; Dec.-Feb. 8am-6pm. $5, children $2, families $12. Last admission 45min. before closing.) The free **Ancient Empire** boardwalk is a short, pleasant walk departing from the Tree Top Walk info center and passing through a grove of giant redtingle, which can reach 16m in circumference (no wheelchair access).

Fifteen kilometers east of Walpole is the right turn down Conspicuous Beach Rd leading to **Conspicuous Cliff,** a popular stretch of beach with an information board, picnic space, and public restrooms. About 6km east of town is the left-hand turn-off to the **Giant Tingle Tree,** 24m in diameter and the largest known living eucalypt in the world. Walpole is also famous for its diversity of **wildflowers,** including more than 90 species of orchids; prime viewing runs between August and November.

■ Mt. Barker

Mt. Barker (pop. 1500), 47km north of Albany along the Albany Highway, is the sleepy gateway to the floral paradise of **Porongurup National Park.** There are a number of **wineries** in the area; ask the tourist office about free tastings. **The Porongurup Range** is the oldest volcanic formation in the world. To get there from town, follow Lowood Rd north and turn right on Albany Hwy, then turn left on Porongurup Rd (tourist drive 252). Two of the most popular hikes are the short but very photogenic **Castle Rock** walk and the slightly longer **Tree in the Rock.** Both are accessible by right-hand turns from Porongurup Rd. Hundreds of varieties of **wildflowers,** many endemic, have been identified in Porongurup and the nearby **Stirling Range National Park.** Peak viewing times are September through November.

Most lodging and restaurants are located along the Albany Hwy and the Muir Hwy, which becomes Langton Rd as it enters town. The **tourist office** (tel 9851 1163) is in the old train station on the Albany Highway (open M-F 9am-5pm, Sa 9am-3pm, Su 10am-3pm). The **hospital** is on Langton Rd a few blocks west of the Albany Hwy, and the **police** are at the corner of Montem and Mt. Barker St. **Westrail buses** run to Perth and Albany once daily; ask the tourist office for schedules and fares.

The **Boronia Cafe and Guest House** (tel. 9851 1275) has pleasant, inexpensive rooms with shared clean bath, kitchen, and laundry facilities (singles $29, doubles $40; price includes breakfast). About 20km down Porongurup Rd on the right is the homey, family-run **Porongurup Shop and Tearoom** (tel. 9853 1110; fax 9853 1116), which offers backpackers accommodations for $14 per night (no linen). Rooms are clean and some are quite spacious, and guests are free to putter in the vegetable garden and play with the family's pet wallaby. (Two course meals available for $7.)

The town's most appealing restaurant is the spiffy **Indulgences Cafe and Restaurant,** 17 Lowood Rd (tel. 9851 2233), which serves up quality coffee, breakfasts, and lunches (sandwiches $3.50) inside a beautifully remodelled old building—in previous lives a bank, a surgery ward, and a hair salon. Friendly owner Phil may give you a tour if you ask. (Open daily 9am-9:30pm, and Th-Sa for posh dinners till late.) **Tippet's Diner** (tel. 9851 2151) on Lowood Rd serves more basic pub grub (nachos $6, veggie burgers $5; open daily 9am-5pm). For groceries, head to **Supa Valu** on Lowood Rd.

■ Stirling Range National Park

The **Stirling Range National Park** should not be missed. The contrast between the rugged, rocky 1000m peaks and the surrounding valleys and farmland is striking, and the drive from Albany is undoubtedly the Great Southern region's most scenic route. Chester Pass Rd cuts through the park; the surrounding bush is home to thousands of 'roos and other critters, so drive carefully, particularly after dark.

To take in the spectacular scenery and the park's impressive **wildflowers** (nearly 1600 identified species), try any of the worthwhile hikes. One of the most popular is the 3.1km ascent to **Bluff Knoll,** the highest peak in Southwestern Western Australia. Known to local Aboriginals as Bullah Meual (Great Many Face Hill) for its mercurial climate and face-like appearance, the knoll has been rated as one of Australia's top 25 climbs. Experienced hikers can make the moderately strenuous ascent in a little over an hour. A rockier, less manicured 2km trail ascends to **Toolbrunup,** the Range's second-highest peak. The Stirling Range is the only place in Western Australia which regularly sees **snow,** and high winds and rain are common near the top. Bring food, water, and warm clothing. **Passes** for park entry may be purchased at the Bluff Knoll Cafe. (Day pass $8 per car; 4-week holiday pass valid at all of Western Australia's parks $20 per car.) Though a **shuttle** to Bluff Knoll from the Stirling Range Retreat may be arranged ($10), the best way to see the area is by car. **Car rental** is easily arranged in Albany through a number of rental agencies or through either of the hostels in town (around $35 per day with 100km limit, $45 per day with unlimited km).

Dreamers of impossible dreams will enjoy the craziest landmark in these parts, 11km north along Chester Pass Rd. **The Lily** (tel. 9827 9205), a five-story replica of a 16th-century Dutch windmill, is the largest traditional windmill ever built in Australia. (Open Tu-Su 10am-5pm; call ahead for tours. Cafe serves inexpensive lunch and tea and $26 3-course dinner.) Along Chester Pass Rd, 90km north of Albany, the **Bluff Knoll Cafe** serves standard fare (open daily 8am-9pm).

Across the street from the cafe (turn left from the main road), **Stirling Range Retreat** (tel. 9827 9229; fax 9827 9224) offers comfortable, inexpensive, and immaculate accommodations with a swimming pool just across the road from the turn-off to Bluff Knoll. (Cozy, well-heated trailers with beds and stove $25 for one person, $30 for two or three. Spacious 3-6 person cabins with kitchens Sept.-Nov. $59; Dec.-Aug. $48.) Friendly owners Ayleen and Tony Sands offer seasonal slide shows and guided nature walks ($2-5). Book well in advance for the wildflower season (Sept.-Nov.).

■ Albany

Established in 1826, Albany was the first colonial settlement in what is now WA. Albany is proud of its history; the tourist office has information on the dozens of buildings of historic interest. Though surrounded by gorgeous, uncrowded beaches, the city itself is the commercial center of the Great Southern region. Albany offers all of the conveniences—and annoyances—of a small city, with plenty of shops and cafes, but also increasing traffic and congestion, making **Stirling Range** or **Porongurup** perhaps a better choice for an overnight stay.

PRACTICAL INFORMATION Albany's main drag is **York St.** The **tourist office** (tel. 9841 1088) is in the Old Railway Station, just east of the Southern end of York St near Stirling Tce (open M-F 8:15am-5:30pm, Sa 9am-5pm, Su 8:30am-5pm). The railway station is not operative, but there is **bus** transportation to Albany, coordinated by the tourist office. The **Westrail** (tel. 9813 1053) *Southerner* bus departs daily for Perth (6 hr.) and *The Bays* bus heads to Esperance (6 hr., M and Th). **Hitchhikers** usually wait by the "Big Roundabout" on the Albany Hwy, 2km west of the north end of York St. The two hostels in town have a steady stream of travelers sharing rides, though Let's Go does not recommend hitching. Louie's Bus Service provides **city transport** (M-Sa; tourist office has schedules), but it's not hard to get around Albany on foot.

The regional **hospital** (tel. 9892 2222) is on Hardie Rd, a few kilometers northeast of the city center. The **police station** (24hr. tel. 9841 0555) is on Sterling Tce one block west of York St, on the right. **ATMs** are on York St. Check email on the computer (yep, there's only one) at **Comtech Corporation** (tel. 9842 2503), 107 Lockyer Ave ($10 per hr.). The **post office** (open 8:30am-5pm) is at York St and Peels Place.

ACCOMMODATIONS AND FOOD Albany has two hostels near the center of town. The **Albany Backpackers** (tel 9842 5255), on Spencer St just around the corner from Stirling Tce and one block east of York St, is the more appealing. Psychedelic murals enliven many of the hostel's rooms, and a cheery atmosphere prevails. The hostel also offers bike and movie rental, and between June and September has a deal with the Esperance Backpackers: stay two nights between the two and the third is free. (Dorms $15; doubles $35. Linen included. VIP, ISIC, YHA. Reception open 8am-10pm.) The hostel also arranges day-long tours of local sights for $25.

The **Albany Bayview YHA,** 49 Duke St (tel. 9842 3388), two blocks west of York St, lacks the panache of the Albany Backpackers but is another decent choice. The hostel also rents bikes, boogie boards, and cars ($45 per day). (Dorms $14; twins $34. Linen included. VIP, YHA.) The **Discovery Inn Guest House** (tel. 9842 5535), 9 Middleton Rd, near Middleton Beach a few kilometers from downtown, offers a comfortable, inexpensive alternative to the hostels. Clean, quiet rooms with heaters and electric blankets make for a peaceful night's sleep. (Singles $35, $25 in winter; doubles $55, $40. Rates include filling, hot breakfast.) Somewhat pricey restaurants and cafes can be found along the main drags. For **groceries,** head east on Albany Hwy to the **Coles** supermarket, about 100m from York St. **Foodland,** at the bottom of York, is open daily until 9pm but is more expensive. **French Hot Bread,** next door to Coles, offers cheap bread and tasty pastries (open M-F 6am-6pm, Sa-Su 6am-4pm).

SIGHTS AND ENTERTAINMENT Albany has the dubious distinction of being home to the world's largest whaling museum. **Whaleworld** (tel. 9844 4021) on Frenchman Bay Rd past the Gap and Blowholes, inside Australia's last whaling station, pays homage to the industry's bloody history, which ceased in 1978. *(Open daily 9am-5pm except Christmas; adults $5, seniors $4, kids $2-4.)* If live whales are more your speed, check out a whale watching tour in the winter. Several tour outfits run cruises; **Southern Ocean Charters** (tel. 015 423 434) has daily departures ($22).

Apart from whales, Albany's most impressive sights are the **Gap and Natural Bridge,** a rock formation in the shape of a bridge 24m above the crashing waves. The nearby **Blowholes** are impressive only in rough weather. Take care on the rocks—it's a long drop to the water below. Both of these sights are located in **Torndirrup National Park,** about 20km south of town along Frenchman Bay Rd Free. In town, **Dog Rock** on Middleton St looks somewhat like a Labrador's head; it can be as hard to see as a Magic Eye sailboat hologram, and the end result is less exciting. Just outside of town along Middleton Rd lies the protected **Middleton Beach,** a lovely expanse of clean white sand perfect for swimming. The **Middleton Bay Scenic Path** is a great walk from the beach out to Emu Point and Oyster Harbor.

Albany has a **movie theatre** (tel. 9842 2210), on the Albany Hwy 4km from downtown. *($6.50 M-Tu and before 5 pm W-F; $9.50 otherwise; $6.50 children.)* The **Earl of Spencer Inn** on Dulce St is an English-style pub popular among backpackers. The **1912 Club,** around the harbor end of York St, is open weekends only. In the summer, **Legends Bar at Middleton Beach** is hopping. The **Town Hall Theatre** (tel. 9841 1661), at York and Grey St, hosts plays, musicals, and public meetings.

■ South Coast Highway East of Albany

Although considered part of the Great Southern, the terrain around Esperance is different from that of the rest of the region. Along the South Coast Hwy east of Albany, karri forests give way to brush. Do not disregard road trains; you may be approaching them at a combined speed of 240kph. It's wise to fuel up in Albany before hitting the road—petrol stations appear only every 50-75km or so. **Terramuhgup** and **Ravensthorpe** are small towns en route with roadhouses and a cafe or two. The highway is low and fast, but take care: 'roos abound and the entire 500km stretch to Esperance is subject to high crosswinds and winter flooding.

About halfway between Albany and Esperance lies the enormous **Fitzgerald River National Park,** an excellent spot for bushwalking. The park is home to thousands of species of plants and wildflowers which bloom year-round, though spring (Sept.-Nov.) is the best time for viewing. **Whales** are often seen off the coast, and **Mt. Madden, Mt. Short,** and **Mt. Desmond** offer excellent views. The park can be tricky to access without **4WD,** but this remoteness makes for plenty of peace and quiet once you've made it there. The **Ravensthorpe/Hopetown Tourist Bureau** (tel. 9838 1277) periodically publishes a newsprint guide to the area; check the tourist offices in Albany or Esperance or call for a copy. The park can be accessed via **Bremer Bay** or **Hopetown** or via one of several unsealed roads running south from the South Coast Highway. To get to Bremer Bay from the South Coast Highway, turn right onto Bremer Bay Rd about 120km east of Albany, then travel 65km east. Hopetown is a bit more of a drive, 50km south of Ravensthorpe. **Westrail** buses (tel. 9838 3180 or 9838 1024) run daily between Albany and Esperance, stopping in Ravensthorpe en route (connecting service to Hopetown M, Tu, W, and F). In the area, **police** may be phoned at 9838 1004; the **hospital** at 9838 1006. **EFTPOS** is available at most petrol stations and at the **Hopetown general store** (tel. 9838 3052).

■ Esperance

Though blessed with a spectacular bay and some of the best beaches and diving Australia has to offer, Esperance (pop 10,000) is quite far from Perth, Albany, or even Kalgoorlie, and isn't as much of a year-round destination as other spots along the southwest coast. Come summer, though, the town is hopping, as tourists flock to the area to swim, fish, dive, and explore nearby **Stokes, Cape Le Grand,** and **Cape Arid National Parks.** Tourism and agriculture are the area's lifeblood; vast fields of oats and barley carpet the earth just inland from white sand beaches which stretch for miles. Esperance itself is a pleasant, though rather ordinary small town—the key to enjoying your stay here is to get out into the surrounding natural splendor.

ORIENTATION AND PRACTICAL INFORMATION The **Esplanade** flanks the bay, and **Dempster St** snakes along roughly parallel to it for several kilometers. The **tourist office** (tel. 9071 2330) is inside an old train station in the museum village near the center of town on Dempster St (open M-F 8:45am-5pm, Sa-Su and holidays 9am-5pm). **Hitchhikers** report luck at the north end of Dempster St and in the suburb of Castletown further north. *Let's Go* does not recommend hitching. Arriving by **car** from the west, the South Coast Hwy (Monjingup Rd) intersects Harbour Rd, which runs south into town. **Buses** (tel. 9013 2232) stop near the tourist office, and run to Albany (6hr.; Tu, F, Sa 8am; $45.90) and Kalgoorlie (5hr.; W, F 11am, Su 3:15pm; $33.50). The **post office** (tel. 9071 1470) is located at the corner of Dempster and Andrew St. The **police** (tel. 9071 1900) are half a block away on Dempster St. **Banks** with **ATMs** accepting Cirrus and Plus cards lie along Andrew St and the block of Dempster St immediately to the north. Several **car rental** companies have offices in town.

ACCOMMODATIONS, CAMPING, AND FOOD The colorful **Esperance YHA Blue Waters Lodge,** 299 Goldfields Rd (tel./fax 9071 1040), right on Esperance Bay, is hands-down the best place to stay in town. Formerly a hospital in Queensland, the entire building was transported to Esperance, reassembled, and spruced up. The hostel is a 15-minute walk from the city center along the harbor bike path, and free bus station pick-up and drop-off is available. (Pool table, ping-pong, book exchange. Dorm beds $14, YHA non-members $17; twins $32; family rooms $40.)

There is good **camping** in Cape Le Grand National Park, 60km east of town, and on **Woody Island** in Esperance Bay. (Entry to each park $8 per car per day.) For up-to-the-minute info on camping, contact CALM at 92 Dempster St (tel. 9071 3733).

Savory's Country Cuisine, 120 Dempster St (tel. 9071 3663), has cheap takeaway and a small dining area. (Fish and chips $5, soups $2.50, lasagna and veggies $8. Open M-F 8am-late, Sa-Su 5pm-late.) **Carusoe's** (tel. 9071 771), at Centrepoint Arcade on Dempster St, has inexpensive Mexican, Italian, and standard food-hall fare (open daily 7:30am-11pm). Among Andrew St's bakeries, the burgeoning chain **French Hot Bread** offers the best prices on lamingtons, doughnuts and, of course, hot french bread (open M-F 6am-6pm, Sa-Su 6am-4pm). A **supermarket** (open M-Sa) is in the shopping center along Pink Lake Rd, one block west of Dempster St.

ENTERTAINMENT AND ACTIVITIES Drivers or bikers with strong legs should try the 38km loop along the **Great Ocean Drive,** which snakes along the coast and the algae-tinged **Pink Lake,** affording spectacular views and numerous places to pull over and stare. The tourist office provides a decent map, and the road is clearly marked. Take care if you're on a bike—the road gets quite narrow and curvy in some spots. To begin the drive, start at the southern end of Dempster Rd and turn right onto Great Ocean Dr. Check out the experimental power-generating **wind farms** at **Salmon Beach** and **Ten Mile Lagoon,** which are open to the public.

In town, **sea lions** frolic on the big tanker jetty; they know where the big fish are. Rent fishing tackle in town or borrow it from Esperance Backpackers. **Merivale Farm** (tel. 9075 9020), 25km east of Esperance along Merivale Rd, serves lush desserts and coffees. (Open in summer Sa-M and W-Th 10am-5pm.) **Cape Le Grand National Park** lies 60km east of Esperance and should not be missed. Take Goldfields Rd north to Fisheries Rd, turn right onto Marivale Rd. and right again onto Cape Le Grand Rd. The road into the park is muddy and narrow at times but is accessible to most vehicles. For transportation to the park, ask at Esperance Backpackers on Emily St before 10am (tours leave by 11am). Once in the park, try the gentle ascent at **Frenchman Peak** (3km return; less than 1hr. climb). At the top, phenomenal natural topology allows for completely sheltered views of coast and sea. Down the road, **Lucky Bay** offers incredible white sands, some surf, and 'roos, but beware of riptides, undertows, and quicksand.

The **diving** in and around Esperance is quite good. **Sanko Harvest,** the second largest wreck dive in the world, is a popular spot. Ask the tourist office or hostels about the dive charters operated by several outfits in town.

GOLDFIELDS

A few hundred kilometers east of Perth, a handful of goldmining towns cling tenaciously to an existence in the middle of WA's desert. Since 1903, water has been piped into the region and signs everywhere warn against wastage. People seeking employment follow this trickle toward **Kalgoorlie,** the center of the local mining industry. Although there are a handful of sights in the area, Kal is a long way from anything and not much of a destination in itself. If you're heading west to Perth from Eyre, you're probably better off circumventing this area and heading south instead. The coastal towns along the scenic South Coast Highway make for a much better trip.

■ Great Eastern Highway

The drive from Perth to Kalgoorie along the Great Eastern Highway is long (nearly 600km) and uneventful. The first hour heading east from Perth winds through the city's suburbs and the **Swan River Valley,** then up a steep slope into the **Darling**

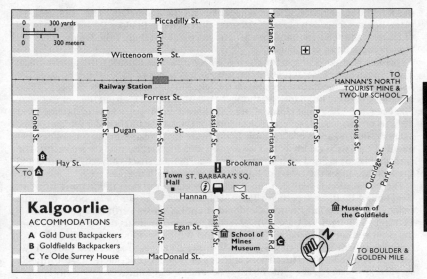

Kalgoorlie

ACCOMMODATIONS

A Gold Dust Backpackers
B Goldfields Backpackers
C Ye Olde Surrey House

Range; you may encounter nasty **traffic** near the city. Road trains rule this highway; beware of wide loads bearing machinery, farm equipment, and even buildings on the truck bed. The last hard stretch between the tiny town of **Southern Cross** (really no more than a wide spot in the highway) and **Coolgardie** is 200km of very rough road through the middle of nowhere. This part of the highway is poorly maintained, and even the truckers hate it. Fuel up when you can (in Southern Cross and Coolgardie)—it's a long way to the next petrol station.

Merredin (pop. 3700) is the largest town on the Great Eastern between Coolgardie and Perth. The friendly **Shell Merredin Roadhouse** makes a good pit stop, with tasty, inexpensive home-cooked meals and takeaway (open daily 7am-10pm).

Coolgardie has exceedingly little to offer the average traveler. It's a dusty, empty, vaguely unsettling frontier town that serves mainly as a residential satellite for the families of miners working in Kalgoorlie. The main street (the 94 Hwy, known as Bayley St in town) houses a **tourist office, post office,** and **police station,** on your right when driving toward Perth. If you must spend the night in Coolgardie, the **Denver City Hotel** (tel. 9026 6031) on Bayley St has simple, unheated rooms for $25. The noise from the rather unfriendly pub downstairs may keep you up. At the west end of town, the **Caltex Roadhouse** (tel. 9026 6049) rents clean rooms for $50. There are no **ATMs** in town, but most roadhouses have EFTPOS.

■ Kalgoorlie-Boulder

The twin towns of Kalgoorlie and Boulder (total pop. 30,000) cling together as if to escape the isolation of the surrounding outback. Their reason for existence is simple—more than a century after panning began here, the region's gold mines are still going strong. These days, folks don't come to town hoping to stumble upon a lode, stake a claim, and strike it rich. Mammoth mining interests run the show, and the work is dirty, the hours long, and the pay low. Nevertheless, workers flood the area and its hostels, creating an atmosphere that backpackers may find a bit gritty.

ORIENTATION AND PRACTICAL INFORMATION

The main commercial boulevard in Kalgoorlie is **Hannan St,** where the Great Eastern Hwy (the continuation of National 95 from Coolgardie) ends at the Goldfield Hwy. Hannan St runs parallel to Hay St and perpendicular to Lionel St, Wilson St, and **Boul-**

der Rd. The residential district of Boulder lies several kilometers to the southeast. To reach Boulder from downtown Kalgoorlie, turn right on Boulder Rd at the north end of Hannan and follow it into **Lane St.** The once-rich ground of the **Golden Mile** is a few kilometers east of Boulder.

Heading north on Hannan St between Wilson St and Boulder Rd, the **tourist office,** 250 Hannan St (tel. 9021 1966), is on the left just south of St. Barbara's Square. The **post office** is a little further on, also on the left. The **police station** (tel. 9021 9777) is one block east, on Brookman St, through St. Barbara's Square from the tourist office. The **Kalgoorlie Regional Hospital** (tel. 9080 5888; 24hr. sexual assault hotline 9091 1922) is on Maritana St, several blocks north of Hannan St and Boulder Rd. The police maintain that no areas of Kalgoorlie-Boulder are particularly unsafe for visitors, but much of the city is poorly lit and it's a good idea to exercise caution after dark. The dimly-lit **Hay St** is lined with tawdry, neon-adorned tin shacks advertising sauna and spa services, and is the center of Kal's notorious red-light district.

The **bus station** is between the tourist office and the post office on Hannan St. **Greyhound Pioneer** departs for Perth daily at 10:15am (8hr., $75, book at tourist office). From the tourist office, **Goldfields Express** serves Perth (8hr.; M, W, and F 11:10pm; $65, with YHA $58.50). **Westrail Prospector** trains depart for Perth from the **train station** on the corner of Forrest and Wilson St (8hr., M-Sa 8:15am, $49.30, concession with Westrail card $24.65). Westrail also runs to Esperance (5hr.; M, W, and F at 5pm; $33.50). The **airport** is south of Boulder off Gatacre St. **Automobile services** are clustered along the highway several blocks southwest of the city center.

ACCOMMODATIONS, FOOD, AND PUBS

Most of the low-cost accommodation in Kalgoorlie is geared toward visitors who have come to town to work and are looking to stay several weeks or months. Some hostels will only rent rooms by the week. The two hostels on Hay St are smack in the middle of Kal's red-light district and tend to be noisy and full of miners.

> **Goldfields Backpackers,** 166 Hay St (tel. 9091 1482, mobile 017 110 001), near the intersection of Hay and Lionel St. Shared kitchen, swimming pool, lounge, and laundry. Call the cell phone if nobody's at reception. Dorms $14, doubles $17 per person with YHA. Linen included. **Hay Street Homestay,** 164 Hay St (same phone), has longer-term accommodations in a former brothel. $100 per week.
>
> **Gold Dust Backpackers,** 192 Hay St (tel. 9091 3737). Clean and neat, though the cinderblock construction isn't pretty. Dorms $14, doubles $17 per person. YHA nonmembers $2 more. Linen included. Internet access $8 per hour. Management offers day-long tours of local sights for $15. Wheelchair accessible.
>
> **Ye Olde Surrey House,** 9 Boulder Rd (tel. 9021 1340). Head east on Maritana St until it becomes Boulder Rd. Cramped but carpeted, with a fridge in each room. Communal kitchen, 24hr. check-in. Dorms $20; twins $25 per person; singles $30. Good weekly rates (singles $140). Linen included. Wheelchair accessible.

There are two **supermarkets** near the center of town. **Woolworths,** at the corner of Wilson and Hay St, has a better selection of fruits and breads and better prices than **Coles,** near St. Barbara's Square (both open M-Sa until about 5:30pm). **French Hot Bread** is cheap and tasty, just around the corner from Woolworths (open daily 6am-6pm). Cafes line Hannau St, and many open early or close later to serve the miners.

Kal is a hard-working, hard-drinking town. Many pubs cluster around Hannau St in the city center. **Paddy's Ale House** on Hannau St is a popular choice. For an inexpensive meat-and-potatoes dinner, locals recommend the **Star and Garter,** 497 Hannan St, on the left heading south (roast $8, food available daily 6-9pm; pub open late).

SIGHTS AND ACTIVITIES

Hannans North Tourist Mine (tel. 9091 4074), a right turn off the Goldfields Hwy 2km north of Hannan St, offers demonstrations of gold panning and underground mining techniques. *(Open Aug.-Dec. daily 9am-5pm, off season 9am-4pm, closed M and Th.*

Engineering a Tragedy

Ask any WA local for the story of the Kalgoorlie pipeline, and you'll likely hear a popular Westralian yarn. The tale concerns an engineer who claimed he could build a conduit which would carry water from Perth all the way to Kalgoorlie. Since Kalgoorlie is over 500km away from Perth and 400m higher in elevation, no one believed that it could be done, but he insisted, and finally someone gave him the money to try. The local legend relates that after he designed and built this huge pipeline, the engineer went to Kalgoorlie and turned on the tap. When nothing happened, the broken man shot himself in the head. No one bothered to turn off the tap, and about an hour later, water flowed out of the pipe and into Kalgoorlie. This is a myth, but the real story of the engineer's death is tragic as well. After proposing the project in 1898, C. Y. O'Connor, frustrated by delays in construction and plagued by faithless critics, took his own life in 1902, one year before his visionary pipeline became a successful reality.

Admission $15, children $7.50, families up to 6 $38. Underground tour not wheelchair accessible.) The gold pouring and drilling demonstrations are worthwhile, but watching gold panning is almost as boring as doing it. Take ear plugs for the underground demonstration. The **Museum of the Goldfields** (tel. 9021 8533), at the north end of Hannan St on the right, has small exhibits on the history and ecology of the Goldfields region. *(Open daily 10am-4:30pm. Requested donation $2.)* The **Super Pit** is an immense open-pit working mine, the largest hole in the Southern Hemisphere. *(Open daily 6am-6pm except when closed for further blasting. Free.)* If something compels you to see this monstrous scar, head to the lookout just outside of town, turn towards Boulder on the Goldfield's Highway, then turn left at the sign for the pit. The **Goldfields Aboriginal Art Gallery**, 222 Dugan St (tel. 9021 1710), displays local art and artifacts. *(Open M-F 9am-5pm, irregular hours Sa and Su.)* If you're bored, there's **bowling** at **Goldfields Ten Pin** (tel. 9021 5533) on Lionel St in Boulder. *(Open daily 9am-late.)*

To explore the area beyond the towns, take a drive or walk along the old railway. The woodlines mark the limits of the clear-cutting that took place in the early part of this century; the forest has not yet fully recovered. Some sheep stations allow visitors; ask at the tourist office. Several outfits offer bush tours; Aboriginal guide **Jeff Stokes** (tel. 9093 3745) runs day tours ($70) and camping trips ($150 per night) focusing on Aboriginal culture and native plants and animals. **Goldrush tours** (tel. 9021 2954) offers half and full-day tours ($25-65). **Geoff Smith** (tel. 9021 2669) also arranges bush tours according to clients interests. *(Tours from $50 per vehicle per day plus fuel.)*

WORKING IN KAL

Though the main reason that people come to Kal is to work, it's not as easy as you might expect to find a job. Many mining companies will only hire employees with previous mining experience, and all require safety training and certification, which takes time and costs money. It can be done, if you're prepared to spend the time and effort to make it work. The two hostels in town are a good source of info on jobs.

■ Norseman

A one-horse town even today, Norseman owes its existence to one particular horse who lived over a century ago. As the story goes, an equine named "Hardy Norseman" was tethered in the area overnight. Restless, he pawed the ground, revealing a chunk of gold in the process. Prospectors quickly rushed to the area, and the town was founded. Today, Norseman serves more as a waystation than a destination. For travelers heading north from Esperance, Norseman is the first encounter with the Goldfields. For those heading east from Coolgardie across the desolate Nullarbor Plain, it is the last taste of civilization (except for roadhouses, which are a civilization all their own) for over 1000km. South of town, **Lookout Point** provides a good spot from which to observe the workings of the Central Norseman Gold Corporation.

The **tourist office** (tel. 9039 1071) on Robert St, one block east on the highway between Sinclair and Richardson St, has information about Norseman and traveling the Eyre Highway (open daily 9am-5pm). Next to the office is a small park, one of the few green spots in town (open daily 8am-6pm with public showers and picnic tables). There are no ATMs in town, but the service stations permit **ATM withdrawals** at the cash register. A **police station** is located at the corner of Prinsep and Ramsey St. The **hospital** is at the west end of Talbot St.

The charming, family-run **Lodge 101** (tel. 9039 1541) on Prinsep St offers comfortable accommodations. Single and double room rates include a continental breakfast, and backpackers can also use a small kitchen. (Dorms $15; singles and doubles $25 per person.) Farther north on Prinsep St is the **Gateway Caravan Park** (tel. 9039 1500). (2-person on-site caravans $25. Spiffier cabins with refrigerator and stove $37. Bunks sometimes available for $12. Linen $4. Free space heaters available in the office.) Norseman's **food** options are limited. The **Supa Valu** (tel. 9039 1032), 89 Robert St, has groceries (open M-F 8:30am-6pm, Sa 8:30am-5pm, Su and holidays 9:30am-1pm), as does the smaller **Coventry's General Store** (tel. 9039 1038) at 78 Prinsep St. (open M-Sa 6am-8:30pm, Su 8am-8pm). The **BP 24-hour Travelstop** offers a diner, convenience store, and **petrol**. Hitchhikers can sometimes be seen loitering here.

■ Crossing the Nullarbor

The **Eyre Highway,** running between Norseman and Adelaide across the **Nullarbor Plain,** is a grueling desert haul by car or bus; via **Greyhound,** it's 34 hours. Driving the Eyre is not something to be taken lightly. The Nullarbor is very sparsely populated, and has no natural fresh water supply. In summer, temperatures reach well over 100°F, and in winter dark falls before 6pm and the thermometer regularly hits freezing. While the road is more heavily traveled than some highways up north, the distance between roadhouses can approach 200km. Bring along bottled water, plenty of gas, warm clothing, and blankets just in case. Drive at a safe speed, and watch for wildlife on the road. The coast along the Nullarbor is spectacular, and the vast unpopulated stretches make for excellent stargazing far from the lights of civilization. **Southern right whales** are often visible off the coast in winter; **birdwatching** can be quite good as well. **90 Mile Straight,** the longest completely straight stretch of highway in Australia and possibly the world, begins just west of Cocklebiddy.

The Eyre passes through national parks and Aboriginal land; permits are often required for bushcamping. The 5614km **dingo exclusion fence,** running from Queensland to the Great Australian Bight, crosses the Eyre east of **Yalata.** The Department of Agriculture takes **quarantine laws** quite seriously; be prepared for inspection at the WA/SA border. It's illegal to transport most fruit, vegetables, and plants from state to state, and fines can be high. The **tourist office** in Norseman has a host of helpful info on the Eyre. When you reach **Ceduna** at the eastern corner of SA's **Eyre Peninsula,** pick up a Nullarbor certificate of completion at the tourist office (see p. 437).

MIDLANDS AND BATAVIA COAST

Renowned as much for the seas of bright color that blanket the region during the autumn wildflower season as for its beautiful coast, this region depends on fishing, agriculture, and tourism to earn its keep. The Branch Hwy marches north from Perth a few dozen kilometers inland from the coastline of the Indian Ocean, while the wheat-growing Midlands extend for hundreds of kilometers to the east. The Batavia Coast stretches from just north of the Pinnacles up as far as the red cliffs of Kalbarri, and takes its name from the most famous of the many shipwrecks that litter its waters. A handful of small fishing towns dots the shore, and there's good swimming all along. While swarms of tourists descend upon the Midlands during wildflower season, Geraldton's high season is the summer when the windsurfing is at its best, and Kalbarri's is the winter.

■ Along the Coast North of Perth

The major route north from Perth toward Gascoyne River is Hwy 1, known along this stretch as the **Brand Hwy** and peppered with service stations. Leaving Perth, take Riverside Dr (Hwy 5) east and follow the signs for the Great Northern Hwy. The Brand Hwy splits from the Great Northern almost an hour north of Perth. The **Wanneroo Rd,** which continues from Charles St northwest of the Northbridge district of Perth, hugs the coast but goes only as far north as Lancelin. To see the **Pinnacles** (see p. 613) en route north or south requires a detour of more than an hour each way from the Brand Hwy, which runs well inland of Cervantes.

About 300km north of Perth, 22km north of the tiny town of **Eneabba,** and smack in the midst of millions of wildflowers, lies the **Western Flora Caravan and Tourist Park** (tel. 9955 2030). Friendly owners Allan and Lorraine know all about the local flora and fauna, and host slide shows and daily wildflower walks at 4:30pm. (Basic bunks with shared kitchen $12, linen $6 extra. On-site vans with cooking facilities $25 for 2 people, linen $10 extra. Huge mud brick chalets $55 for 2 people, linen included.) Wildflowers are at their peak from July to January. The park also sells cheap **petrol,** with a look at a pet emu and wallaby included at no charge.

■ Lancelin

Considered by many to be the **windsurfing** capital of Australia, Lancelin (pop. 700) is a small fishing village about 120km north of Perth. The windsurfing season runs roughly from October through March each year, with the famed **Ledge Point Sailboard Classic** taking place each January. During the rest of the year, the sheltered waters of Lancelin Bay make for excellent, safe **swimming. 4WD vehicles are** allowed on the beach, and it's possible to drive along the dunes up the coast to **Cervantes;** still, even Land Rovers can get stuck in the soft, wet sand. **Lancelin Surfsports** (tel. 9655 1441), in the shops at 127 Gingin Rd, rents scuba, snorkeling, sandboarding, and surfing equipment. A one-hour windsurfing lesson costs $20.

There is no public transportation to Lancelin. **Coastal Coachlines** (tel. 9652 1036) runs buses from Perth's Wellington St Bus Station to nearby Regans Ford (2hr., M and F 4:30pm, $16), but you've still got to get yourself the last few kilometers. The easiest way to reach Lancelin is by car; from Perth, take Bulwer St to Charles St, which becomes Hwy 60 (the Wanneroo Rd). As you pass through **Wanneroo,** note the pine tree plantations. Pines are not native to the area, but they're lower-maintenance than eucalypts, since they are self-pruning and do not shed their bark. While these trees are ideal for timber and paper, they also use much more water than indigenous species, and their presence has significantly lowered the water table north of Perth.

The sparkling, well-run **YHA Lancelin Lodge** (tel. 9655 2020; fax 9655 2021; email lanlodge@iinet.net.au) has a comfy lounge, free bikes, and a lovely kitchen. (Office open daily 8am-10pm, check-in 24hr. Check-out 10am, flexible in winter. Dorms $15, weekly $90; doubles $40, $240. Family rooms $50. Wheelchair accessible.)

■ Nanbung National Park: The Pinnacles

As hyped as EuroDisney, the so-called **Pinnacles Desert,** located in **Nanbung National Park,** is nevertheless worth a visit, possessing an eerie, ethereal beauty. Despite the moniker, the park isn't a desert, but a sand dune with thousands of wind-eroded limestone pillars, some up to 4m tall. Dutch sailors sighting the jagged outcrops from the sea mistook them for the ruins of an ancient city. To avoid the crowds and to see the Pinnacles in the best light, come in the early morning or evening.

The park is a good 250km north of Perth. **Jurien Bus Lines** runs service to nearby **Cervantes,** and there are also a plethora of one-day and overnight tour packages. It's also accessible by car. Allow an hour for the drive west to Cervantes from the left turn off the Brand Hwy, about 20km north of the Cataby Roadhouse. **Camping** is not allowed in the park, but there are picnic areas and a beach at **Hangover Bay,** a few kilometers from the Pinnacles site. The last stretch of road before the Pinnacles is unsealed, and there's a $8 vehicle fee to drive the sandy loop through the site. Do not get caught out on the driving loop after dark—it's challenging enough when the jagged rocks are actually visible. The road is usually passable with 2WD, but gets a bit rough in spots. You can check on conditions in Cervantes.

■ Near Nanbung: Cervantes

Cervantes is a tiny, pleasant fishing village whose main attraction to travelers is its location 2km west of the turn-off for the Pinnacles. There's good swimming in town when it's warm. The friendly **Pinnacles Beach Backpackers,** 91 Seville St (tel. 9652 7377; fax 9652 7318), is at the end of Seville at the intersection with Barcelona St, just before the road turns to dirt and heads to Thirsty Point. The hostel has 24-hour check-in, is wheelchair accessible, and offers beds in four- or eight-bed dorms for $15. **Happyday Tours** buses (tel. 9652 7244) run daily between the Greyhound stop at the Brand Hwy turn-off and the Cervantes **post office** (open M-F 9am-5pm).

▓ Geraldton

For a town sprawled along the stunning Indian Ocean, Geraldton (pop. 24,000) pays surprisingly little attention to its coastline. Most restaurants, shops, or hotels in town actually face away from the nearby beach. Somehow, though, this attitude is fitting for this "crayfish capital of the world." Though windsurfers eager to test their skill in the strong southerly winds flock to Geraldton every summer, the city relies more on its busy port, fishing, mining, and agriculture than on tourism for its survival. There are a handful of worthwhile sights in and around town, though, and quality budget accommodations and pleasant surroundings make Geraldton a good place to stop for a day or two on your way north to Kalbani or Carnarron or south to Perth.

ORIENTATION AND PRACTICAL INFORMATION

If you're arriving by car from the Brand Hwy, head straight through the rotary up **Cathedral Ave** to get to the town center. The town's main drag, **Chapman Rd,** and the shop-lined **Marine Tce** both run roughly parallel to the coast and intersect Cathedral Ave. The **tourist office** (tel. 9921 3999) is located inside the massive **Bill Sewall Complex** at the corner of Bayly St and Chapman Rd, about 1km north of Cathedral Ave. The tourist office can book bus tickets, local tours, and accommodations. (Open M-F 8:30am-5pm, Sa and holidays 9am-4:30pm, Su 9:30am-4:30pm.) **Greyhound** buses stop at the tourist bureau, **Westrail** buses at the railway station across the street. **Police** (tel. 9964 1511) await at the station on the corner of Chapman Rd and Forrest St, a couple of blocks north of Cathedral Ave. The **Geraldton Regional Hospital** (tel. 9956 2222) is on Shenton St one block southwest of Cathedral Ave. The **post office** is on Durlacher St near the corner of Chapman Rd (open M-F 8:30am-5pm).

ACCOMMODATIONS AND FOOD

⊛**Geraldton YHA Foreshore Backpackers,** 172 Marine Tce (tel. 9921 3275), 1 block southwest of Cathedral Ave. Cozy rooms, homey atmosphere, super-friendly owners, shiny wood floors, pool table, parking. Dorms $13; singles $18; twins $33; family $33 for 2 adults, $5 per child. YHA nonmembers $2-3 more. Linen included.

Batavia Backpackers (tel. 9964 3001/fax 9964 3611), next to the tourist office inside the Bill Sewall Complex. This former hospital and jail has a predictable institutional feeling, with metal bunk beds. Still, pleasant balconies, tennis courts, pool table, and an interesting mural liven up the place. Check-out 10am. Dorm beds $14; singles $18; twins $32. Linen included. YHA, VIP. Wheelchair accessible.

Chapman Valley Farm Backpackers (tel. 9920 5034), 30km northeast of town, rents out beds in a rustic cabin on a working sheep and wheat farm. Perks include horseback riding for experienced riders and a pet lamb. Free pick-up from bus station with 2 night stay. Bring food—there are no shops or restaurants nearby. No linen. $10, weekly $60. Call ahead for directions; the drive is gorgeous.

The **Sun City Food Hall,** 56 Durlacher St (tel. 9964 2313), near the post office, has Indian, Italian, Mexican, and Chinese booths with meals for $5-6 (open Su-M and W-Sa 11:30am-2pm and 5-9pm). **Tanti's Restaurant,** 174 Marine Tce (tel. 9964 2311), next to the YHA, serves excellent Thai food. Takeaway is available, or you can eat in the restaurant under gilt pictures of royalty. (Veggie pad thai $7, with pork $8. Open M-Sa 5:30-10pm and for lunch, with $8 3-course specials, Th-F 11am-2pm.) As ever, **Woolworths** has cheap groceries (open M-F 8am-6pm, Th 8am-9pm, Sa 8am-5pm).

SIGHTS AND ACTIVITIES

Most people come to Geraldton for one reason: **windsurfing.** The best conditions are in October, November, March, and April, though it can be good year-round; you'll need a wetsuit in winter. Bring your own gear or rent it at the **Geraldton Surf Company,** 164 Chapman Rd (tel. 9964 5533), which also has a host of info about good windsurfing locations around Geraldton. **Point Moore** is the windiest spot in the area and is not for the inexperienced. **St. George's Beach** has tamer breezes. In the town itself, **Back Beach** is the main surfing beach, and also has reasonably good swimming.

The **Geraldton Regional Museum** and **Maritime Museum** (tel. 9921 5080), on Marine Tce a couple of blocks southwest of Cathedral Ave, have exhibits on the natural and cultural history of Geraldton and the mid-west, including dusty artifacts from several shipwrecks offshore. *(Open M-Sa 10am-5pm, Su 1-5pm. Free.)* The **Geraldton Art Gallery** (tel. 9921 6811), at the corner of Chapman Rd and Durlacher St, hosts a variety of traveling exhibits, some of which are quite good. *(Open Tu-Sa 10am-5pm. Su-M 1:30pm-4:30pm.)* You can catch a fairly recent flick or some local live theater at **Queen's Park Theatre** (tel. 9956 6690), on Cathedral Ave at Maitland St ($8, kids $7).

About 60km off the coast of Geraldton lie the spectacular, protected **Abrolhos Islands,** center of Geraldton's rock lobster industry and home to a variety of corals and tropical fish far south of their normal range. The waters surrounding the Abrolhos are notoriously treacherous, and dozens of shipwrecks litter the ocean floor. Getting to the islands is tough even today. The only way to make the short trip is by plane or on a diving or fishing charter, none of which are cheap. Check with the tourist bureau for details and expect to pay upwards of $150 for even a short visit.

■ Kalbarri

Originally home to Australia's earliest known European settlers, two Dutch settlers marooned just south of town for their role in the Bataria mutiny, Kalbarri (pop. 1500) is a vacation hotspot for both Australian and international tourists. Pensioners and backpackers alike flock to this tiny town for its mild winter climate and spectacular natural surroundings. During rock lobster season (Nov.-June), crayfishing boats bob in the calm waters of the mouth of the **Marchison River;** during most of the rest of the year, vacationers stroll along the beaches and about town. The main reason to come here, though, is to hike in the wonderland of **Kalbarri National Park.**

ORIENTATION AND PRACTICAL INFORMATION

The access road from the North West Coastal Hwy connects to Grey St, which skirts the coast and runs to the town center. The **tourist bureau** (tel. 9937 1104 or 1800 639 468) is south of Woods St (open daily 9am-5pm). The **Department of Conservation and Land Management (CALM)** number is 9937 1140. The **police** (tel. 9937 1006) are on Porter St. To reach a **doctor,** call 9937 1159 (after hours 9937 1174). The **post office** is at Grey and Porter St (open M-F 8:30am-5:30pm, Sa 8:30am-12:30pm). The **pharmacy** (24hr. tel. 9937 1026) is next door. **Greyhound buses** to Ajana for connections to Perth and Carnarvon (M, Th, and Sa 8am) and **Westrail** service to Perth (Tu, Th, and Sa 6:15am) both depart from the tourist bureau, which does booking for Westrail.

ACCOMMODATIONS AND FOOD

Though Kalbarri has tons of accommodations, it's a good idea to book ahead, especially during winter school holidays.

YHA Rock Lobster Lodge, 52 Mortimer St (tel. 9937 1430; fax 9937 1563). From the tourist bureau, turn right on Grey St, then right on Woods St. Clean, basic rooms, swimming pool, barbecue, free use of snorkel gear and boogie boards. Knowledgeable managers can book tours and advise on area sights. Dorms $14; singles $22; doubles $34. YHA nonmembers $2 more. 7th night free. Same managers run the **Pelican's Nest** next door. Flats have fans, kitchen, bathroom, and TV. 2 people $45, each additional person $10. During school holidays, prices rise $20 and units may only be booked by the week. 7th night free; linen included. 24-hour check-in; office open 8am-8pm. 10am check-out.

Kalbarri Palm Resort, 8 Porter St (tel. 9937 2333; fax 9937 1324). Clean, no-nonsense suites, some with kitchens. Nightly cinema in hotel restaurant; dinner and a fairly recent movie around $12. Family rooms $75, during school holidays $85.

Murchison Park Caravan Park (tel. 9937 1005; fax 9937 1415), at the corner of Grey and Wood St. Central and cheap—book ahead. On-site campervans $35.

Kalbarri Hot Bread Shop (tel. 9937 1017), in the shopping center across from the post office, sells excellent, cheap bread, pies, and pasties. **Finlay's Fresh Fish BBQ** (tel. 9937 1260), on Magee Crescent, serves up tasty seafood dishes in an old tin ice shed and is a local fave (meals around $10; open daily 5:30-8:30pm). From the tourist bureau, turn left onto Grey St, left on Porter, right on Walker, and right onto Magee. The town has two somewhat pricey supermarkets: **Foodland,** in the Ampol station on Grey St at the north end of town (open daily 7am-6pm), and **Kalbarri Supermarket** near the post office (open M-F 8:30am-5:45pm, Sa-Su 8:30am-12:30pm).

SIGHTS

The town of Kalbarri is dwarfed by the 183,000 hectares of wilderness which surround it. The dramatic oceanside cliffs and red river gorges of **Kalbarri National Park** are well worth exploring. The park's unsealed roads are generally in good condition and 2WD-accessible, though check with **CALM** (tel. 9937 1140) or the tourist bureau for updated road info, particularly after heavy rains. Admission to the inland river gorge area costs $8 per vehicle; the machine doesn't accept bills, so bring $1 and $2 coins. Alternatively, pick up a **four-week pass** to all national parks at the tourist bureau ($20). From the left turn 11km east of town along the Ajana-Kalbarri Rd, it's a 25km drive to all the good stuff. The park is easily explored by car; otherwise, book one of the myriad **tours** available at the hostel or the tourist bureau. **Kalbarri Safari Tours** (tel. 9937 1011) runs a popular day trek along Z Bend. *(Departs T, F and Su. $50.)* **Kalbarri Adventure Tours** (tel. 9937 1677) runs a worthwhile day-long "Canoe the Gorges" trip. *(Departs Tu, Th, Sa and Su. $45.)* No pets are allowed in the park.

Scenic lookouts over the Merchison River at **The Loop** and **Z Bend** afford great photo ops. Bring plenty of water and food for the six-hour hike through the gorges at the Loop. The trail is unmarked, but the best circuit heads east along the clifftop from **Nature's Window** to the first river bank, then down along the ledges and floodplain at water level. Keep the river to your right. Along the coast, the banded sandstone and limestone cliffs have been worn into fantastic formations by 400 million years of harsh weather and, in some places, worms. The four-hour, 8km cliffside hike from **Eagle Gorge** to the **Natural Bridge** is recommended, though don't get too close to the edge. The oddly-named **Pot Alley** is another particularly nice spot.

The **Abrolhos Islands** (see p. 615) are visible by airplane. **Kalbarri Air Charters** (tel. 9937 1130), next to the tourist bureau, runs tours to the islands and several other locations including Monkey Mia ($29-149). Plant lovers will appreciate the herbarium and nature trail at the **Kalbarri Wildflower Centre** (tel. 9937 1229) on the North West Coastal Hwy, 1km before Kalbarri. *(Open June-Nov. daily 9am-5pm. $3, kids under 15 free. Free bus service daily around 10am from tourist bureau. Guided walks daily 10:30am.)*

OUTBACK COAST AND GASCOYNE REGION

With its safe swimming, spectacular diving and snorkeling, and lively marine life, the Outback Coast stretches from Shark Bay and its dolphins in the south to the whale sharks and corals of the Ningaloo Marine Park in the north. Though the region sees plenty of visitors year-round, winter is peak season, when caravanning Perthites park themselves along the sunny coast to wait out the cold weather down south.

Of the major coastal destinations between Perth and Exmouth, only Geraldton and Carnarvon are actually along Hwy 1. Kalbarri, Shark Bay, and Exmouth all require significant detours. The routes from the highway to the coast are all paved, but service stops are up to 160km apart, and the roads become hillier and narrower. Keep your eyes peeled for wandering 'roos, emus, sheep, and cattle in the road. Heading north from Kalbarri or south from Carnarvon, you'll pass a roadhouse at **Overlander** (tel. 9942 5916; open 24hr.), marking the turn-off for Shark Bay. It's a 129km drive northwest along the Peron Peninsula to **Denham,** then another 24km to the **Monkey Mia Reserve.** The road to Coral Bay and Exmouth splits from the North West Coastal Hwy 350km north of the Overlander just past the 24-hour **Minilya Roadhouse.** Turn left to head to Exmouth, 217km to the north. Hwy 1 continues toward **Port Hedland.**

■ Shark Bay

Shark Bay, WA's much-touted World Heritage area, was the site of the earliest recorded European landing in Australia. In 1616, Dutch Explorer Dirk Hartog came ashore at Cape Inscription on the island that now bears his name, leaving an inscribed pewter commemorative plate. Today, Shark Bay is known mainly for the dolphins at **Monkey Mia,** tranquil shell beaches, and the "living fossils" (stromatolites) at **Hamelin Pool.** The land around Shark Bay is roughly W-shaped; the western peninsula is home to the striking **Zuytdorp Cliffs** and a salt mine, and is accessible only by 4WD. The eastern peninsula, boasting Monkey Mia, **Francois Peron National Park,** and the tiny town of **Denham,** is much more heavily touristed. The best way to see the area is by car or on a tour; bus service is inconvenient and infrequent, and taking in all of the sights requires traveling quite a long distance.

■ Denham

With around 500 permanent residents, the westernmost town in Australia is just a speck on the Peron Peninsula, looking out across the Freycinet Reach toward Useless Inlet and Dirk Hartog Island. The main street, Knight Tce, runs parallel to the town's narrow beach. Although a row of shiny new halogen streetlamps whispers "growth," Denham is, for now, still just a place to stay overnight on a visit to Monkey Mia.

The **bus,** a Shark Bay Tours coach contracted by Greyhound, stops at the **Shell station.** (Departs for the Overlander Roadhouse M, Th, and Sa 5:20am and 6:15pm; returns to Denham same days 8:45am and 11:20pm.) Although Denham is warm year-round, fierce winds can make it unpleasant to stand outside, and the Shell station is not open when the early bus departs. The **tourist bureau,** 71 Knight Tce (tel. 9948 1253), is a few doors down from the Shell station (open daily 8am-6pm). Its main function seems to be selling T-shirts, but the friendly staff also hands out brochures and maps and books bus tickets to Monkey Mia ($8; ask for a lift at the hostel first). A few doors down, **CALM,** 67 Knight Tce (tel. 9948 1208), also has maps and info on the Francois Peron National Park, Hamelin Pool Reserve, and Shark Bay Marine Park.

The **police station** (tel. 9948 1201) is on the corner of Hughes and Durlacher St. The **post office** is two doors down from the tourist bureau (enter through the newsagent). **Tradewinds Supermarket** (tel. 9948 1147) is at the BP Station (open daily 6:30am-7:30pm). The **Loaves and Fish Bakery** (tel. 9948 1442), next to the Shell station on Knight Tce, has excellent, cheap pasties and sweets (open M-F 8:30am-5pm, Sa 8:30am-2pm).

Caravan parks fill up months ahead for the winter school holidays. The **YHA Denham Bay Lodge** (tel. 9948 1278 or 1800 812 780; fax 9948 1031) is on Knight Tce 100m south of the bus stop. Bunks in small, co-ed rooms are $12. Late check-out is available for those catching the evening bus.

■ Monkey Mia

All along the coast, the debate rages over Monkey Mia (MY-uh) and its **dolphins.** The Indian bottlenose dolphins really do come right up to visitors' knees, eat fish, and click as obliging (and numerous) tourists scratch their flanks. Some think Monkey Mia provides an unparalleled opportunity to interact with intelligent, sociable cetaceans and that such interaction highlights the need for marine environmental protection. Others find it a contrived, exploitative, and downright tacky show. Regardless, the site is one of WA's biggest tourist attractions, and though a visit to Monkey Mia requires a detour of over 300km from the NW Coastal Hwy, most travelers end up making the trip.

One-day access to the site is $5; $8 buys a two-week pass, although it only takes an hour or two to "do" Monkey Mia. Four-week all-park passes also apply ($20). Feeding times vary, but generally there are three feedings between 8am and 1pm. The reserve is also home to an information center with videos and talks, a swimming beach, a short walking trail, and aggressive pelicans. The **Monkey Mia Dolphin Resort** (tel. 9948 1320) has basic backpacker's beds ($12 per night; linen $10 extra).

■ Hamelin Pool

About 100km south of Denham and 27km west from the Overlander Road House along the Denham-Hamelin Rd lies the striking Hamelin Pool, with its crisp white shell beach and eerie "living fossils." The latter are **stromatolites,** formed over thousands of years by microbes whose lineage dates back 3.5 billion years, making them the oldest known form of life on Earth. Though nothing more than a mess of oddly shaped rocky lumps at first glance, the Hamelin Pool Reserve stromatolites are one of two living colonies in the world. A short boardwalk extending into the pool's crystal clear, salty waters allows for a closer look at some fine specimens.

Back on shore, a short walking trail winds along the beach and through a small quarry where chunks of sedimentary shell "rocks" were cut and used to construct many of the area's early buildings. There's also an old telegraph station, tearoom, and small shop. **Camping** is available (tel. 9942 5905; sites $10, powered $12). Fifty kilometers north of the turn-off to the Hamelin Pool along the Denham-Hamelin Rd is the turnoff for **Shell Beach,** a dazzling 60km expanse of billions of tiny white shells, up to 10m deep. Bring something to sit on if you intend to do any sunbathing (ouch!).

▒ Carnarvon

The main reason most people come to Carnarvon (pop. 7000) is to find work. The area's banana plantations and commercial fishing operations need labor especially during the winter picking season, though work, like almost everything else in the area, tends to dry up during the summer months. The town beach is unimpressive, and though the pedestrian footbridge across the Gascoyne River is splendid, on the far side it becomes a dilapidated, muddy path. Even the bars are rowdy and uninspiring. Ask travelers here how long they've been in town and chances are good you'll

---

Mosquito-borne Diseases

From Carnarvon northward, those annoying bites from mosquitoes ("mozzies") can also be dangerous. In this region, certain species of mosquito can transmit the Ross River and Barmah Forest viruses, as well as encephalitis. The viruses cause low-level somatic problems such as joint ache and fatigue, but are self-limiting and not contagious. Symptoms usually arise within two weeks after transmission and may last intermittently for months. Less common but more serious is Australian encephalitis. Carriers breed annually north of Port Hedland between February and April. Very wet summers can produce a risk as far south as Kalbarri. The incubation time for this kind of encephalitis is at least five days. The disease can be fatal—seek diagnosis if you suffer headaches, neck stiffness, or nausea that do not seem to be caused by dehydration. The Health Department of Western Australia recommends wearing long, loose clothing and using topical DEET to fend off bites. Try to avoid long periods outdoors at dawn and at dusk.

---

hear "too long." A few sights highlighted below will ease your stay, but for the most part, Carnarvon is still a place to make a buck, then get the hell out.

ORIENTATION AND PRACTICAL INFORMATION A big yellow plastic banana welcomes visitors to Carnarvon as they head into town along Robinson St from the North West Coastal Hwy. The center of Carnarvon is **Robinson St** between **Babbage Island Rd** and **Olivia Tce.** The friendly **tourist bureau,** 11 Robinson St (tel. 9941 1146), in the Carnarvon Civic Centre at the corner of Stuart St, dispenses brochures and maps aplenty (open M-F 8:30am-5pm, Sa-Su 9am-noon and 1-4pm). **Greyhound buses** depart from the tourist bureau bound for Perth (daily 3:45 pm and M, Th, and Sa 7:25pm) and for Broome and Darwin (daily 10:25pm). Several **banks** with **ATMs** are located on Robinson St. The **police station** (tel. 9941 1444) is next door. The **regional hospital** is two blocks down Francis St (ambulance tel. 9941 1555). The **post office** is on Stuart St across from the Civic Centre (open M-F 9am-5pm). **Woolworths,** on Robinson St two blocks from the tourist bureau, has cheap food and is centrally located (open Su-W and F-Sa 8am-8pm, Th 8am-9pm).

ACCOMMODATIONS YHA **Carnarvon Backpackers,** 50 Olivia Tce (tel. 1800 642 622 or 9941 1095), lies just around the corner from the tourist office; leaving the office, turn right, walk to the end of Robinson St, and turn left onto Olivia. The friendly management has heaps of info on jobs and will even drop you off and pick you up from work. An assortment of dorms, kitchens, and bathrooms spreads over several buildings, some of which have seen better days. (Free seasonal fruits and veggies, barbecue, off-street parking, A/C, free canoe use. Dorms $13, YHA nonmembers $14; weekly $80, $85. Doubles $34, $36; $200, $215. Family rooms available at double rate plus $10 per extra person.) Carnarvon has more than its share of caravan parks. The **Carnarvon Tourist Centre Caravan Park,** 90 Robinson St (tel. 9941 1438), five blocks down Robinson St to the left from the tourist office, has friendly management and clean ablution blocks. (Sites $11, powered $14; spiffy cabins for 4-6 people $45. Check-in 7:30am-8:30pm; check-out 10am. Book ahead in winter.)

Finding the Tunes

For lone drivers, music can be critical to staying alert and comfortable. If you run out of tapes or lack a tape deck, try 666 AM kHz. "Triple-six" may never be your favorite radio station, but it's the only one in the region (unless you like listening to the pre-recorded message on tourist radio, 88 FM). The mix is vociferously eclectic—don't be surprised to hear the Beach Boys, Midnight Oil, the Supremes, and Flock of Seagulls all in the same hour, in addition to the latest alternapop. Interruptions are frequent but fascinating; listen for the Carnarvon market report to hear how bananas, mangoes, and paw-paws are trading.

SIGHTS The coast toward **Pelican Point** is nice, and the bike ride down Babbage Island Rd to get there offers a glimpse at mangroves. The **lighthouse keeper's cottage,** near the one-mile jetty, houses a small museum run by the town historian. *(Open daily 10am-noon and 2-4pm.)* **The Blowholes,** 73km north of town, boasts water jets that reach as high as 20m in choppy weather, and a lovely beach 1km south. To get there, go 24km north on the North West Coastal Hwy and turn left at the sign. About 40km farther north is the visible wreck of the huge **Korean Star,** victim of the May 1988 cyclone Herbie. Look, but don't touch—climbing on the wreck is dangerous.

A drive or bike ride through the outskirts of town is worthwhile—the back roads are jammed with banana and mango plantations. Fresh fruit and veggies are plentiful and cheap. **Munro's Banana Plantation** (tel. 9941 8104), 10km east of town on South River Rd, grows all sorts of fruit and serves excellent homemade baked goods and, improbably, mango beef nachos in a lush tropical garden. Try the mango smoothie ($3.50) or scones with cream and jam ($2.25). *(Open Su-F 10am-4pm. Tours daily 11am; $2, family $4.)* **Westoby Banana Plantation** (tel. 9941 8003), on Robinson St just past the big banana at the edge of town, is similar. *(Open W-M, tours 11am and 2pm.)*

■ Coral Bay

Coral Bay is a popular stopover en route to Exmouth, 160km north. The town itself is little more than a glorified caravan park, but the beautiful beach is a good spot for snorkeling and swimming. The friendly **Bayview Coral Bay Backpackers** (tel. 9942 5932) has small doubles and twins, with linen, a barbecue, and a hot tub ($15 per person). The resort also has cabins and self-contained duplexes and chalets which can be a good deal for groups of three or more. (24hr. check-in with prior booking, or pick up a key until 10pm at the Reef Cafe. Book ahead in winter.)

On the right side of the road, as you head into town, the shopping complex houses a small **supermarket** that also functions as the **tourist bureau** (tel. 9942 5988; open daily 7:30am-7pm), **bakery** (open daily 7am-5pm), **post office** (open M-F 9am-5pm), and **dive shop.** The **Ningaloo Reef** is over 250km long, starting south of Coral Bay and stretching north around the Northwest Cape and back into Exmouth Gulf. Several outfits run coral-viewing glass-bottom boat trips (2hr. trips start around $20), and the **Ningaloo Reef Dive Centre** runs one-day "resort course" trips ($95). For PADI or advanced courses, it's better to head to Exmouth, where there are better facilities and a hospital for your dive medical. The Perth-Exmouth **Greyhound bus** heads from Coral Bay to Exmouth (W, F, and Su at noon); to Perth (M, Th, and Sa at 4:20pm).

■ Exmouth

The scuba diving epicenter of the west coast, this is the place to swim with giant, easygoing whale sharks. The wonders of the colorful Ningaloo Reef are complemented on land by the dry, dramatically beautiful Cape Range National Park. The beach is further from town than at other spots along the coast, but for diving or fishing, it can't be beat.

PRACTICAL INFORMATION Most action takes place around **Maidstone Crescent,** which intersects **Murat Rd** (the highway) at both ends. The **tourist bureau** (tel. 9949 1176) is on Payne St near the north end of Maidstone Crescent (open daily 8:30am-9pm). The **CALM office** next door has more detailed info on Cape Range. The shopping center just off Maidstone Crescent houses a **pharmacy,** two **supermarkets,** and a busy bakery. The **police station** (tel. 9949 2444) is just south of the shopping center, on the corner of Bennet St. Next door is the **post office** (open M-F 9am-5pm). The **hospital** (tel. 9949 1001) is two blocks west, on Lyon St near Fyfe St. **Challenge Bank,** on Learmouth St around the corner from the shopping center, is home to Exmouth's one **ATM.**

ACCOMMODATIONS Fierce competition between Exmouth's hostels has led hostel owners to offer backpackers lots of freebies, including free bike hire, barbecues, swimming pools, and A/C. Many of the dive shops in town have deals with hostels: take a dive course, get discounted accommodation. **Exmouth Base Lodge** (tel. 1800 241 474 or 9949 1474; fax 9949 1440) is 5km north of town inside the refurbished old naval base. All rooms are twins and have comfortable beds and free linen. The bathrooms and kitchens are spotless, and you get free use of the base pool, tennis courts, and gym. (Rooms $14. VIP. Free transport to town and bus station.)

YHA Pete's Exmouth Backpackers (tel. 9949 1101; fax 9949 1402), at Truscott Crescent halfway between town and the beach, is always hopping. The small cabins vary greatly in quality; ask to see yours first. (Dorms $15; singles $18; twins $36; tent sites $7. Chalets for 6 from $55. Free linen and bus service to Bundegi 4 times per week.) **The Exmouth Excape Backpackers** (tel. 1800 655 156 or 9949 1201; fax 9949 1680) is closely linked with the mammoth Exmouth Diving Centre; both are across the street from the tourist bureau. It has basic two- and four-bed dorms with A/C and free linen. The kitchen and bathrooms are small, but guests enjoy the use of the adjacent Potshot Hotel's pool and spa. (Dorms $14; doubles $16 per person. Check-in 8am-8pm.) **Camping** is permitted in designated sites within Cape Range National Park ($8), but don't camp elsewhere—fines are high, and rangers patrol.

DIVING AND SIGHTS Most people come to Exmouth to see the impressive **Ningaloo Reef,** and the town is full of dive shops catering to all experience levels. Introductory PADI courses cost around $250, take four or five days, and include at least four ocean dives. Shop around before choosing a dive shop; though all have certified instructors and good equipment, class size and quality of instruction vary tremendously. **Coral Coast Dive** (tel. 9949 1004), at the naval base, has intro and advanced courses with a maximum class size of six. **WAGS Diving** (tel. 9949 2661) also has a maximum class size of six, offers a free video of your course, and has free videos about the reef Monday, Thursday, and Saturday at 7:30pm. **Ningaloo Deep** (tel. 9949 1663) has pricey but fun live-aboard diving trips. **Village Dive** (tel. 9949 1101) and **Exmouth Dive Centre** (tel. 1800 655 156) have exclusive rights to diving on the old navy pier.

Several operators run tours of the Exmouth area and Cape Range National Park. **Ningaloo Ecology Cruises** (tel. 9949 2255) and **Ningaloo Coral Explorer** (tel. 9949 2424) both offer snorkeling and coral-viewing tours on glass-bottom boats. *(1hr. tours from $20. 2hr. snorkeling trips from $30, backpackers $25, children $10.)* **Ningaloo Safari Tours** (tel. 9949 1550) has a day-long tour that's worth its price, which includes snorkeling at Turquoise Bay, a boat cruise up Yardie Creek, and a 4WD trek over the top of the Cape Range ($110, children under 10 $80). **West Coast Safaris** (tel. 9949 1625), **West Treks Safaris** (tel. 9949 2659), and **Exmouth Ecotours** (tel. 9949 2809) offer similar tours at similar rates; ask the tourist bureau for the skinny.

Boasting rugged limestone cliffs, canyons, and gorges, **Cape Range National Park** lies 39km from Exmouth. **Ningaloo Marine Park** begins 14km from town. The solar-powered **Milyering Visitor Centre,** 52km from Exmouth, is open daily 10am to 4pm and hands out maps and info on the parks. A 4WD is the best vehicle for exploring the area, but a 2WD will get you as far as **Turquoise Bay,** a popular snorkeling spot. (National Park entry $8 per car. No water available. No dogs or guns.) If you don't have a car, try the Cape's excellent shuttle service, which stops at the lighthouse, Yardic Creek, Turquoise Bay, Mangrove Bay, the Milyering Visitor Centre, and Tantabiddi Reef. (Adults $20, YHA, VIP, and pensioners $18, children $10; includes park entry and snorkel gear.) Check with the tourist bureau for details.

THE PILBARA

Red dust and iron ore are the stuff the Pilbara is made of. Miles of flat, hot coastal plain are populated by a handful of mining and port towns. The region has a tropical

---

Heat Kills

Winter in the northwest is a season of dry heat, and you may not realize you are dehydrated until the onset of constipation or a massive headache. By the time you feel thirsty, you're a couple liters low. Drink several liters of water every day to stave off heat stroke. Take a water break every hour during a daytime drive. Undiluted fruit juice, available in 250mL bottles at roadhouses and supermarkets, will help keep sugar and vitamin C levels high.

---

climate: wet in the summer, dry in the winter, and hot year-round. The dramatic Hammersley Ranges add spice to the otherwise monotonous landscape. Its roads are surrounded by prickly spinifex grass and gum trees, and is often festooned with kangaroo carcasses. Heat, floods, cyclones, winds, and mosquito-bourne disease are just some of the impediments to settlement in the region. But despite all this, the Pilbara is a compelling destination for the seasoned traveler. Take the time to visit the gorges of Karijini National Park, the Aboriginal rock carvings of the Burrup Peninsula, and the historical towns and sheltered beaches of Roebourne and Point Samson, and you may be pleasantly surprised by the treasures hidden in this scrubland.

■ Karijini National Park

With its spectacular scenery and variety of excellent hikes and bushwalks, Karijini National Park is a highlight of any trip. It is, quite simply, awesome. Homeland to the **Banjima, Innawonga,** and **Kurrama** Aboriginal people, the park takes its name from their traditional name for the **Hamersley Range.** At over 2.5 billion years and counting, Karijini's dramatic mountains and gorges are among the oldest land forms on earth. Originally an ancient sea floor, the area is decorated by colorful bands of sedimentary rock which formed over millions of years, now easily visible in the cliff faces of the massive gorges that slice through the Range.

The Karijini is easily reached from both Tom Price and the Great Northern Hwy; a recently completed access road bisects the park south of the gorges. The park's northern entrances, through Yampire Gorge and Wittenoom, are not recommended. Both are both severely contaminated by asbestos, inhalation of which can cause cancer and death (see **Hold Your Breath,** p. 623); what's more, the road through Yampire Gorge is in extreme disrepair. The other park roads are unsealed but quite well-kept and 2WD-accessible. The one-day park fee is $8 per car. **Camping** is permitted only in designated areas near Weano Gorge, Joffre Falls, and Fortescue Falls (sites $5).

CALM publishes a map of Karijini with information on the park's varied walking trails. Vehicle-accessible lookouts provide plenty of photo ops, and there are hikes suitable for all experience levels. At **Dales Gorge** the short, steep trail down to **Fortescue Falls** and the **Circular Pool** is quite nice (3hr. return). The falls at **Joffre Gorge** are usually dry, but become quite impressive after a good rain. At **Weano Gorge,** a steep, winding track leads down into the imaginatively named **Handrail Pool;** hang on tight as you make your way down unless you fancy a dip in the chilly pool below. From the junction of four gorges (Weano, Red, Hancock, and Joffre), you can look down to the crumbled rock outcropping where the old lookout used to be.

Carry plenty of **water,** as tanks are scarce and the summer heat (and flies) are oppressive. **Petrol** and supplies are available west of the park in **Tom Price** and at the **Auski Roadhouse** to the northeast. **Maps,** updates on **road conditions,** and **weather** forecasts can be found at area tourist bureaus, including Tom Price, Karratha Roeburne, and Port Hedland, as well as at Karijini's **visitor center** near Fortescue Falls. The temporary visitor's center is open only April through November, but a new, year-round center 6km up the road should be up and running by late 1998 or early 1999. For more info, contact **CALM** (tel. 9189 8157) in Tom Price.

■ Tom Price

At 747m above sea level, Tom Price is head and shoulders higher than any other town in the state. While calling it WA's "top town" is a bit of an exaggeration, Tom Price is very pleasant, and it's an ideal base to explore **Karijini National Park.** Named after an American mineral surveyor, the town gained its independence from the Hamersley Iron Company in 1988 and since then has worked to turn itself into a popular destination. Though iron ore is still the town's lifeblood, these efforts have paid off, and Tom Price is slowly making a name for itself on the tourist map of Western Australia.

ORIENTATION AND PRACTICAL INFORMATION Tom Price lies about 300km east of the Nanutarra Roadhouse. From the Northwest Coastal Hwy, head east on Hwy 136 just north of Nanutarra. The well-maintained, paved road passes through some spectacular country, but no services are available until **Parabudroo,** 276km away, so gas up before you go. After about 220km, the road forks. Both ways are scenic, 2WD-accessible except after heavy rain, and arrive at Tom Price; the left fork is 70km shorter but unsealed. Once in town, the very friendly **tourist bureau** (tel. 9188 1112) on Central Rd has maps and information on Karijini, local accommodations, and tours. (Open M-F 8:30am-5pm, Sa 9am-noon, sometimes later; May-Oct. also Su 9am-noon.) Across the street, the shopping center complex houses the **post office** (open M-F 9am-5pm), a **chemist,** a **supermarket** (open M-Sa 8am-8:30pm, Su 8am-6pm), and a **bank** with an **ATM.** The **police** (tel. 9189 1334) are a few doors down from the tourist bureau, and the **hospital** (tel. 9189 1199) is around the corner on Mine Rd.

ACCOMMODATIONS AND SIGHTS The best beds in town are at the **Tom Price Caravan Park** (tel. 9189 1515), which is 4km west of town and has grassy tent sites, on-site vans, posh chalets, and villas. They plan to install backpackers accommodation by summer 1999. Sparkling ablution blocks and a swimming pool help beat the summer heat. (Campsites $7 per person, powered $17 per site. On-site vans $40 for 2 people. Chalets and villas $75-90 for 2 people, $10-15 per additional person up to 8.) On the northeastern corner of Karijini, and just before the dusty turnoff to Wittenoom, the **Auski Roadhouse** (tel 9176 6988) has accommodations with linen but no cooking facilities other than a barbecue (singles $40; doubles $45).

Hold Your Breath

About 40km west of the Auski Roadhouse lies the erstwhile town of Wittenoom. A 1937 asbestos boom led to the 1947 incorporation of the town as a home for miners. Asbestos tailings, the waste product of the milling process, were used extensively as landfill in town, and the road from Wittenoom through Wittenoom Gorge past the old asbestos mine is actually paved with the stuff. Despite the early warnings of health researchers, asbestos mining continued until 1966 when the mine and mill were closed down. Residents of Wittenoom continue to pay the price. Many have contracted mesothelioma, which is always fatal, from inhaling airborne asbestos fibers. More than thirty years after the mine and mill were shut, government officials still warn against travel to the area.

Despite all of this, and seemingly in the face of reason, a handful of diehard Wittenoomans continue to hang on. For 20 years, the state has been buying buildings in Wittenoom and demolishing them, and funding the relocation of residents. With the failure of carrots, the government found some hefty sticks, ordering the shut-off of water, electricity, and phone service to the 25 or so remaining residents on January 1, 1997. But the determined holdouts arranged a private deed with Telstra for phone service, and a court challenge has kept power and water flowing. Though area tourist bureaus refuse to distribute information about Wittenoom or even to give directions, a handful of still-healthy residents push Wittenoom as a destination, trying to preserve the memory of the town that Western Australia would like to forget.

The main attraction near Tom Price is **Karijini National Park**. The park is easily explored by car; rentals are available in Tom Price. Pick up a map in town. Alternatively, try a tour. Two outfits shuttle visitors through the park. **Design-A-Tour** (tel. 9188 1670) has daytrips daily (May-Oct.) from Tom Price and Auski Roadhouse ($80, children 6-11 $40) and two-day camping trips departing each Saturday (Mar.-Nov.) from Tom Price for $230. **Lestok Tours** (tel. 9189 2032) daytrips depart from the Tom Price Caravan Park and the tourist bureau ($70, children 5-14 $35).

The hike up **Mt. Nameless** (1128m above sea level) from behind the caravan park is steep and rocky (3hr. return). 4WDs can also make the trip up, but the going can be a bit hairy at times. The 90-minute **Mine Tour** through the Hamersley Iron Open Cut mine offers visitors an up-close look at Tom Price's reason for existing. ($12, children under 14 $6. Departs tourist bureau daily 8am; book at tourist bureau.)

■ Millstream Chichester National Park

Once a watering hole for weary Afghan camel drivers, Millstream is a lush green oasis in the midst of thousands of acres of rock and dry, rolling, spinifex-covered hills. Date, cotton, and Millstream palms, Indian water ferns, and water lilies thrive in and around the park's freshwater pool, and the surrounding wetlands support a diverse range of insects, birds, and mammals, including the elusive black flying fox and fruit bats. The **Millstream Homestead,** near the southwest corner of the park, was originally a family home and later a tavern, and now is the park's **visitor info center,** with displays on local flora and fauna, early settler life, and the culture of the Yinjibarndi Aboriginals (open daily 8:30am-4:30pm). **Snappy Gum Safaris** (1800 094 811) runs tours of Millstream from Karratha, Dampier, or Roebourne ($70, pensioner $68, children under 12 $25). The nearby **Chinderwarriner Pool** was once an important campsite for visitors attending tribal meetings. Another spot worth visiting is the **Python Pool**, about 25km to the north along the Wittenoom Roebourne Rd. The **Cameleers Trail** uphill from the pool is a nice, short walk with a rewarding view at the top.

Camping is permitted in the park only at the designated sites of **Crossingpool, Deep Reach Pool,** and **Snake Creek** (sites $5). The **park entrance fee** is $8 per car. The turnoff to Millstream-Chichester is 28km east of Roebourne, 175km southwest of Port Headland on the North West Coastal Hwy; then head 60km south along the unsealed but well-maintained Roebourne-Wittenoom Rd. You can also take the winding, unsealed rail service road owned and maintained by Hamersley Iron. You need a free permit to travel this road; ask at the security gate at the 7-Mile Yard between Karratha and Dampar (staffed 24hr.), or in Tom Price. The park has **no petrol.**

■ Karratha

The commercial and administrative center of the Pilbara, Karratha (pop. 9000) developed in the late 1960s and early 70s as a home to workers on the massive Hamersley Iron ore export project; today, it houses WA's largest shopping center north of Perth. Travelers often find casual labor around town and on the trawlers and prawn boats operating offshore. Karratha also makes a good base from which to explore the nearby Burrup Peninsula, the Dampier Archipelago, Roebourne, and Pt. Samson and their environs, and Millstream-Chichester National Park.

ORIENTATION AND PRACTICAL INFORMATION Most of Karratha's services are clustered in the town center, bounded by Warambie Rd to the north, Searipple Rd to the east, Welcome Rd to the south, and Balmoral Rd to the west. The **tourist bureau** (tel. 9144 4600) is about 1km south of the town center on Karratha Rd. (Open Mar.-Oct. M-F 8:30am-5pm, Sa-Su 9am-4pm; Nov.-Feb. M-F 8:30am-5pm, Sa 9am-noon.) **Greyhound buses** leave daily from the Shell station at the corner of Searipple Rd and Welcome Rd (northbound 7:30am, southbound 8:30pm; book at the tourist bureau). The **police** (tel. 9144 2233) are on the corner of Welcome and Balmoral Rd, and the **Nickol Bay Hospital** (tel. 9144 0330; ambulance tel. 9144 1222) is on Millstream Rd west of the town center. The hefty Karratha City **Shopping Centre** (tel. 9185 4288) takes up most of a block on Welcome Rd and Sharp Ave. Inside you'll find Coles, Woolworths, and KMart, as well as a **chemist, travel agent,** and all sorts of other goodies. (Most shops open M-W and F 9am-5:30pm, Th 9am-9pm, Sa 8:30am-5pm, Su 10am-2pm.) The **post office** is next to the shopping complex (open M-F 9am-5pm).

ACCOMMODATIONS AND SIGHTS The **Karratha Backpackers,** 110 Wellard Wat (tel. 9144 4904), has new, super-friendly management, not to mention comfortable beds and a well-stocked kitchen, free bus pick-up and drop-off, and the cheapest Internet access in the northwest ($6 per hr.; singles $30, twins $40, dorms $15). Catch a flick under the southern sky at the **Karratha Drive-In** (tel. 9144 2212; movies run F-Su at 7:30pm; $8 per person; $25 per family; $5 seniors). The **Jaburara Heritage trail** begins from the carpark at the tourist bureau. This 3.5km walk passes by some fascinating Aboriginal carvings and offers good views of Karratha and its environs. The annual **Fe-NaCl-NG festival,** named after the area's major natural resources (iron, salt, and natural gas), is held in early August and includes fair food and carnival rides guaranteed to please. Check with the tourist bureau for dates.

■ Near Karratha

The nearby **Burrup Peninsula** was once the site of thriving Aboriginal communities, and their legacy remains in over 10,000 rock carvings. The Burrup is also home to a handful of safe **swimming beaches,** and a drive out to the peninsula makes a good daytrip from Karratha. To get there, head towards Dampier on the Dampier Rd and after about 15km turn right on the gravel Burrup Rd, which runs 5km to the shell beach at **Hearson's Cove.** About 1km before the beach, a dirt track heading right will take you into **Deep Gorge,** a small canyon housing hundreds of petroglyphs.

Dampier is a pleasant town with a handful of shops and services and a popular swimming area just off the Esplanade. The industrial giants of the area, the **Northwest Shelf Natural Gas Project** and the **Hamersley Iron Port Facility,** do their best to attract tourists to their complexes. The NW Shelf project has a **visitor's center** at the end of the Burrup Rd, about 10km from the turn-off from the Karratha-Dampier Rd (open Apr.-Oct. M-F 10am-4pm; Nov.-Mar. M-F 10am-1pm). "Hamertours" run regularly (Apr.-Nov. M-F 9am; Dec.-Mar. M and Th 9am; $5, concessions $3; book ahead at Karatha tourist bureau). The Karratha tourist bureau has info on how to get access to and camp in the **Dampier Archipelago.** The 42 islands are fringed by coral reefs and the ocean floor is littered with shipwrecks, making for excellent diving, snorkeling, and fishing.

■ Roebourne, Cossack, and Pt. Sampson

The oldest existing town in the Pilbara and once a thriving capital of the northwest, **Roebourne** today is a shadow of its former self. The Roebourne **tourist bureau** (tel. 9182 1060), inside the old gaol, has a host of information on Roebourne and nearby Cossack and Point Samson (open Apr.-Oct. M-F 8:30am-5pm, Sa-Su 9am-4pm; Nov.-Mar. M-F 9am-3pm, Sa 9am-noon). There are **police** (tel. 9182 1133) and a **hospital** (tel. 9182 1004). A number of restored historical buildings stand sentinel over Roebourne's empty streets.

The history of European-Aboriginal contact in the area is chilling—kidnapping and forced labor were common practice as countless Aboriginals were rounded up and forced to work as agricultural laborers and pearl divers. Those who tried to escape were thrown in the gaol. The museum inside the gaol includes a number of upsetting photos of the shackled Aboriginal inmates. It's a spooky place, and some Aboriginals today believe that the site is haunted.

Twelve kilometers north of Roeburn lies historic **Cossack,** the first port to be established in the Northwest and once the center of a thriving pearling industry. Originally named Tien Tsin in honor of its first settlers, the town's prosperity was short-lived, and only a handful of people live there today. Some of its old buildings have been restored, and continued restoration is planned. Tourists trickle into the town to wander through its abandoned streets and fish from lawnchairs along the site of the old jetty; you can also hire a dinghy (tel. 9182 1190). There are no groceries in Cossack, but the **Cossack Tearooms,** in the old Customs House, have coffee, cakes, and light lunches (open daily 8am-5:30pm, and from Apr.-Oct. Su for dinner 6-8pm). **Settler's Beach** is a sandy beach with safe swimming and Aboriginal carvings can be found in the surrounding cliff faces. There's one **hostel** (tel. 9182 1190) with 30 beds inside the old police barracks. The building dates back to 1897, but the facilities are modern and clean, with tidy fan-cooled rooms, laundry, TV, and a nice sitting area. (Beds $15; rooms for 2-5 $35. Free pick-up from the daily Roebourne bus. BYO linen.)

A further 10km north on the main road lies busy little **Point Samson.** Its **beach** is good for swimming and fishing and is home to some awesome sedimentary rock formations. Just around the point lies **Honeymoon Cove,** whose potential seclusion is often disturbed by crowds of families enjoying the calm swimming and snorkeling. **Moby's Kitchen,** at the point, serves some of the Northwest's best fish and chips (open M-Th 11am-2pm and 5-8:30pm, F 11am-2pm and 5-9pm, Sa, Su, and holidays 11am-9pm). The **Trawler's Tavern** upstairs has cold beer and a relaxing view from the balcony. Free three-hour tours of Cossack and **Wickham,** site of Robe River Iron's ore operation, are run by the company from mid-April to early November (M-W and F). Tours depart from and may be arranged at the Roebourne tourist bureau.

■ Port Hedland

Industry is definitely king in Port Hedland: salt mines, refineries, shipping docks, and red dust rule the skyline of this narrow city sandwiched between the Indian Ocean and the Great Northern Hwy. Though the city gets its share of visitors, most either come to work or just pass through on their way to more pleasant spots.

Most of the action takes place around the intersection of **Wedge St** and **Richardson St.** The port itself is just a stone's throw to the north, across Richardson. The **tourist bureau,** 13 Wedge St (tel. 9173 1711), near the corner of Anderson St has public bathrooms and a phone. (Open M-F 8:30am-5pm, Sa 8:30am-12:30 pm; May-Oct. also Sa 1:30-3:30pm, Su noon-4pm.) The **post office** is across the street (open M-F 9am-5pm). Several **banks** with **ATMs** cluster around this area. The **police** (tel. 9173 1444) are nearby on Anderson St. The **hospital** (tel. 9158 1666) is a few blocks to the east on Sutherland near the corner of Howe; this is also the corner where **Greyhound buses** bound for Perth (3:10pm), Broome, and Darwin (both 10:15am) stop. Port Hedland's **international airport** is 13km out of town. The **shopping center,** 3km from Wedge St east along Wilson, has a **supermarket** and a **pharmacy.** The **South Hedland shopping centre** on Throssell Rd in South Hedland is the area's biggest, accessible only by car or Port Hedland's infrequent **bus service.**

Port Hedland's **accommodation** leaves much to be desired. Hordes of laborers drive prices for even the dingiest joints through the roof. The two places in town with backpacker accommodation are very friendly, if basic. **Port Hedland Backpackers,** 20 Richardson St (tel. 9173 3282), is the town's main hostel. Turn right onto Richardson at the end of Wedge St. The basic rooms have fans; some have A/C. There's laundry, a kitchen, and a nice enclosed patio area. (Bunks $14, twins $32. YHA nonmembers $15, $34. Linen included; $10 cutlery deposit. Limited wheelchair access. Check-in 8am-10pm. Check-out 10am.) The hostel also runs tours of **Karijini National Park** (departs M noon, 2 nights, $220). The **Harbour Lodge** (tel. 9173 2996) at 11 Edgar St around the corner from the tourist bureau, has a handful of backpacker beds in a room with a fridge and much-needed fan and A/C. Bring earplugs—the walls are thin, and the noise in the adjoining kitchen and lounge starts up in the morning almost before the roosters outside do. There's a well-equipped kitchen and free linen and towels, but no laundry facilities. (Dorm beds $15, doubles $40.)

The **Pretty Pool,** a massive tidal mudflat which extends for miles at low tide, is a popular shell-collecting and swimming spot, but wear shoes, as toxic rockfish lurk in

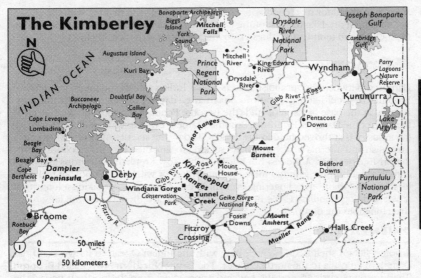

The Kimberley

rocky areas. The pool is about 7km from the tourist bureau; from Wedge St turn left Dr about 5km later. Turn right onto Styles Rd and follow the signs to the pool. In the summer, several species of **sea turtles** may be seen in local waters; the Pretty Pool, **Cooke Point,** and **Cemetery Beach** are good places to look. If you're lucky, you might spot newly hatched babies making their way to sea from November to April. The Port Hedland base of the **Royal Flying Doctor Service,** on Richardson St opposite the boat ramp, can be visited from 11am to noon and 1 to 2pm.

■ Port Hedland to Broome

Six hundred kilometers of empty Great Northern Highway separate Port Hedland and Broome. It's nearly 300km between the Sandfire Roadhouse and the Roebuck Roadhouse outside Broome, so it is essential to carry extra fuel and plenty of water along this stretch. A strong headwind can cut fuel efficiency terribly. Try not to make the drive alone. Many travelers head from Port Hedland to Broome, and there's only one backpackers' hostel in Port Hedland, so it's not difficult to find traveling companions. By bus, the trip takes seven hours. The desert is full of strange driving perils. It's bad enough to hit a cow, but the potential for disaster inherent in colliding with a camel is best left to the imagination.

THE KIMBERLEY

Pressed between the Indian Ocean and the Great Sandy Desert, the Kimberley's 320,000 square kilometers of rough, raw tropical bush are broken only by unpredictable rivers, magnificent boulder-stacked cliffs, and tiny pockets of settlement. Only rugged souls venture past the beach mecca of **Broome,** but those who do are rewarded by a wilderness experience they won't soon forget. Occupying the entire northern end of Western Australia, the Kimberley is accessible from the rest of the state by flights to Broome or via a long, lonely desert highway from Port Hedland, and from the Northern Territory via Routes 1 and 96, which branch off the Stuart Highway. Within the region, the only major paved route is the **Great Northern Highway.** Most other roads, including the **Gibb River Road** and its offshoots in the northern Kimberley, are unsealed 4WD tracks. Flooded rivers during the monsoonal Wet (Nov.-Mar.) often close these roads altogether; the East Kimberley is wetter than the

West. Call ahead for road conditions (tel. 1800 013 314) and register with the police before setting off. Like the rest of the tropics, the Kimberley's high season is the Dry (Apr.-Oct.), and temperature doesn't vary nearly as much as precipitation.

■ Broome

Harbored between the turquoise waters of the Indian Ocean and green mangroves, Broome may feel like the Land of Canaan after days of driving through the dust. Located at the base of a spit of land (the Broome Peninsula) projecting west, itself at the base of the Dampier Peninsula, Broome's fame grew as a result of the active pearling industry that thrived here in the 1880's. Today, the serene town of 9000 attracts Australian and international vacationers seeking to sink their toes in the cool sands of the pristine beaches. A modest but bustling Chinatown replete with shops and cafes complement Broome's untrammeled natural splendor with a cosmopolitan feel. Visitors may find themselves lingering over their iced cappuccino or taking a long stroll down seemingly endless Cable Beach, reluctant to leave the oasis for the long roads stretching into the desert.

ORIENTATION

Broome sits on sheltered Roebuck Bay, with the Indian Ocean to its west and the Dampier Peninsula to the north and east. The **Great Northern Hwy,** called **Broome Road** in town, curls around the bay and approaches from the north. It passes the **tourist office** and becomes **Hamersley St** at its intersection with **Napier Tce.** This corner is **Chinatown,** the oldest part of Broome and the closest thing it has to a center. A block south of Napier, Frederick St heads west toward **Cable Beach** on the other side of the peninsula. East of Broome, the Great Northern Hwy enters the Kimberley proper and commences its grueling haul toward kununurra and the Northern Territory beyond.

PRACTICAL INFORMATION

Tourist Office: Broome Tourist Bureau (tel. 9192 2222), well marked on Broome Rd at the corner of Bagot St. Open M-F 8:30am-5pm, Sa-Su 9am-4pm.

Airport: Broome International Airport (tel. 9193 5455) is most easily accessed by taking a right from Frederick onto Coghlan St, then a left on McPherson Rd. Ansett flies from Broome to Sydney ($710), Perth ($419), Melbourne ($850), Brisbane ($536), and Darwin ($279), among other destinations. Qantas flies to Darwin ($385), Perth ($531) and Melbourne ($890). All prices are return fare.

Buses: Greyhound Pioneer, on Hamersley St a few blocks south of Napier Tce. To Perth ($234), Alice Springs ($313), and Darwin ($202). 10% YHA discount.

Public Transportation: Town Bus (tel. 9193 6000) has two shuttle lines that circle Broome hourly. Covers Chinatown, Cable Beach, Gantheaume Point, and the port. Blueline runs daily 7:10am-6:15pm. **Redline Service** runs daily 9:15am-3:15pm. Fares $2.50; day pass $8, $4 children. Timetable available at the tourist office.

Taxis: Broome Taxis (tel. 9192 1133). **Roebuck Taxis** (tel. 1800 812 441).

Car Rental: Broome Discount Car Hire (tel. 9192 3100), 100m from the airport on Macpherson St. **Broome Car Rentals** (tel. 9192 2210 or 1800 676 725), in Chinatown. **Woody's 4WD Hire** (tel. 9192 1791), on Dampier Tce. **Hertz** (tel. 9192 1428), on Frederick St.

Budget Travel: Harvey World Travel (tel. 9193 5599) in Paspaley Shopping Centre, Chinatown, is the broker for Qantas. Open M-F 8:30am-5:30pm, Sa 9am-3pm. **Traveland** (tel. 9192 2000), also in Paspaley. Open M-F 8am-5pm, Sa 9-noon.

Currency Exchange: ANZ Bank (tel. 9193 5096), behind Paspaley Shops on Carnarvon St. Open M-Th 9:30am-4pm, F 9:30am-5pm. **Commonwealth Bank** (tel. 9192 1103), on Hamersley a block north of Greyhound.

Bike Rental: Broome Bikes Cycle Hire (tel. 0417 177 489), on the corner of Hamersley and Stewart St. Day hire $9-17. Deposit required.

Markets: Thursday Night Market, at Paspaley Shopping Centre, 5pm-8pm. The busier **Courthouse Market** is near the Courthouse on Hamersley St Sa 8am-1pm.

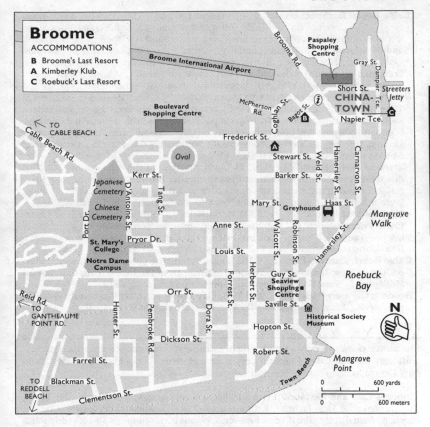

Broome
ACCOMMODATIONS
B Broome's Last Resort
A Kimberley Klub
C Roebuck's Last Resort

Broome International Airport

Paspaley Shopping Centre

Gray St.

Short St. Streeters Jetty

CHINA-TOWN

Napier Tce.

TO CABLE BEACH

Cable Beach Rd.

Boulevard Shopping Centre

McPherson Rd.

Coghlan St.

Bagot St.

Broome Rd.

Dampier Tce.

Frederick St.

Stewart St.

Barker St.

Weld St.

Hamersley St.

Carnarvon St.

Oval

Kerr St.

Japanese Cemetery

Chinese Cemetery

D'Antoine St.

Tang St.

Mary St.

Greyhound

Haas St.

Mangrove Walk

St. Mary's College

Notre Dame Campus

Pryor Dr.

Anne St.

Walcott St.

Robinson St.

Hamersley St.

Louis St.

Port Dr.

Reid Rd.
TO GANTHEAUME POINT RD.

Orr St.

Forrest St.

Herbert St.

Dora St.

Guy St. Seaview Shopping Centre

Saville St.

Roebuck Bay

Historical Society Museum

N

Hunter St.

Pembroke Rd.

Dickson St.

Hopton St.

Robert St.

Farrell St.

TO REDDELL BEACH

Blackman St.

Clementson St.

Town Beach

Mangrove Point

0   600 yards
0   600 meters

WESTERN AUSTRALIA

Books: Recycled Books, in Paspaley Shopping Centre. Open M-Sa from 9:30am.
Pharmacy: Chinatown Pharmacy (tel. 9192 1399), in Paspaley Shopping Centre.
  Open M-F 8:30am-5:30pm, Sa 8:30am-2pm.
Hospital: Broome District Hospital (tel. 9192 1401) on Robinson St. Turn left off
  Frederick St and it's on the right.
Police: At the corner of Frederick and Carnarvon St.
Emergency: 000
Post Office: Australia Post (tel. 9192 1020) in Paspaley Shopping Centre. Open M-F
  9am-5pm. **Postal Code** 6725.
Internet Access: Telecentre (tel. 9193 7153), on Dampier Tce near the intersection
  with Napier Tce. Open M-F 9am-4:30pm, Sa 9am-1pm. Also at the **Kimberley Klub**
  (see accommodations below) for $5 per ½hr.
Phone Code: 08.

ACCOMMODATIONS

✪Kimberley Klub (tel. 9192 3233), on Frederick St opposite Coghlan St a couple of
  blocks from Hamersley St. This spanking new hostel has successfully inserted a bit
  of luxury into budget travel. Social and family-friendly, with a sparkling pool, spacious modern kitchen, rec room with ping-pong and billiards, open-air TV den and
  sand volleyball court, licensed poolside bar/cafe (a bit noisy at night). Timber
  decks, veranda, pink corrugated steel architecture. Coin operated A/C. Free Greyhound pick-up. Reception 24hr. Dorms $14; quads $16 per person; doubles and
  twins $45. Nomads discount. Book way ahead in the high season.

Cable Beach Backpackers (tel. 9193 5511 or 1800 655 011; fax 9193 5532; email meyo@tpgi.com.au), on Lullfitz Dr 400m east of main Cable Beach facilities. Bowing to Broome's sun culture, the hostel centers around the open pool, courtyard, and the nearby beach. Kitchen, laundry, recreation area with billiards and tiny basketball court. Free shuttle runs to town 5 times daily; discounts on town bus rides. Free pick-up from Greyhound and airport. Pushbike hire $5 per ½-day. 4-bed dorms $15; twins $40. YHA, VIP. Reservations essential in the high season.

Broome's Last Resort (tel. 9193 5000 or 1800 801 918; fax 9193 6033), on Bagot St 100m past the tourist office. Recently refurbished, this lively hostel caters to a social crowd. Patrons enjoy the tropical pool by day and the in-house bar by night. Wooden walkways and blue paint create a shady treehouse feel. Laundry, open-air kitchen, free luggage storage, coin-op A/C. Wednesday theme nights. Dorm rooms $13-15; twins and doubles $38. YHA, VIP.

Harmony Bed & Breakfast (tel. 9193 7439), 5km out of town on Broome Rd. This quiet, homey B&B provides retreat from the noisier hostel scene. Though not luxurious, the rooms are clean and comfortable and the atmosphere is relaxed. Pool, patio, full breakfast. Singles $46; doubles $70. Book ahead in high season.

Roebucks Last Resort (tel. 9192 1183), on Napier Tce past Carnarvon St in Chinatown. Prime location and the cheapest beds in town compensate for a lackluster interior. Laundry, kitchen, pool, bus discount to Cable Beach, pick-up from bus station. Dorms with shared bath $12; doubles and twins with bath $40. YHA.

Cable Beach Caravan Park (tel. 9192 2066), behind the Cable Beach Resort, a short path away from the coast. Turn onto Lullfitz St from the beach road, then left on Millington St. Sites $7.50 per person; 2-person powered sites $18.

Broome Caravan Park (tel. 9192 1776), 5km out of town on Broome Rd. Sites $6 per person; 2-person powered sites $14. On-site caravans $55.

FOOD

Chinatown possesses only a smattering of Chinese restaurants, but the area is packed with tasty outdoor cafes. Coles grocery store (tel. 9193 6299), in the Papsaley Shopping Centre, is open 8am to 8:30pm daily.

🍸**Blooms Cafe and Restaurant** (tel. 9193 6366), on Carnarvon St near Napier Tce in Chinatown. A local favorite, with a relaxed yet sophisticated demeanor. Colored chalkboard displays the diverse and scrumptious menu (dinners $9-15, sandwiches $7-9). Mango smoothie $3.80. Open 7:30am-late.

Old Zoo Cafe (tel. 9193 6200), near Cable Beach on Lullfitz St. Chic atmosphere, excellent food. Salty sea air and golden sunlight stream through the windows. Chicken chickpea salad $14, more adventurous "Wild Willie" $24. Book ahead for dinner in high season. Open 7am-4pm daily, Th-Su dinner from 6pm.

Fong Sam's Cafe (tel. 9192 1030), on Carnarvon St across from the Cinema. Another sunny street cafe catering to the throngs of tanned visitors with a large menu. The salads (Italian $5) are a tasty, lighter alternative to the pre-made sandwiches. Delectable pies and pastries galore. Open daily 7am-5pm.

Sheba Lane Garden (tel. 9193 6036), on Napier Tce. A variety of Asian cuisine served in a simple bungalow. Dinners from $17; lunches $9. Open daily 6pm-late.

Murray's Pearler (tel. 9192 2049), a block down Dampier Tce near Napier Tce. Palate-pleasing Asian fare served on intimate white-clothed tables. Enjoy the quiet atmosphere while feasting on chicken with black bean sauce ($11.50) or King Prawn with mango ($14.50). Open daily 6-10pm.

SIGHTS

Travelers flock to Broome for **Cable Beach.** Here, 22km of light blue waters lap against the pearly white sand, and rolling green lawns tumble down to the edge of the beach. From town, follow Frederick St to a right on Cable Beach Rd; take another right on Ocean Dr and a left that hops onto another piece of Cable Beach Rd. Signs mark the way, or follow the stream of barefoot bodies. The beach is wheelchair-accessible. If the drive to Broome didn't quell your desire for all things desert-ish, you can take a camel ride on the beach. **Ships of the Desert** (tel. 9192 2222) has morning, afternoon, sunset, and twilight tours (1hr., $25). **Broome Camel Safaris** (tel. 041 991 6101) runs half hour tours for $15. For a groovy night experience, **Astro Tours** (tel. 9193 5362) gives tours and explanations of the night sky. *($30 per person.)*

Not surprisingly, beach-happy Broome offers a range of water sports. **Surf Academy** (tel. 041 895 8264) offers two-hour lessons in the tame waves of Cable Beach. *($55 per person, $25 apiece for 2-14 persons.)* **Windrider Safari Tours** (tel. 015 010 772) caters to the backpacker scene with a two-day sailing cruise geared towards breeze and beer ($175). Parasailing, jet skiing, and tubing operators work from Cable Beach.

Broome Crocodile Park (tel. 9192 1489) lies 200m from the beach access on Cable Beach Rd. *(Feedings W-Su 3pm. Guided tours M-Tu 3pm. Open M-F 10am-5pm, Sa-Su 2-5pm. $12, concessions $9, children $6, families $28.)* A maze of separate pens holds in over 1500 aggressive salties. Their distant relatives once trampled all over the area; one set of **dinosaur footprints** is preserved in the rocks at **Gantheaume Point**, the western tip of the Broome Peninsula about 4km from Cable Beach. The 120-million-year-old prints surface at low tide and can be difficult to find. A plaster replica is at the top of the cliff.

Chinatown bustles with shops, cafes, and tourists. The **Sun Pictures Outdoor Cinema** (tel. 9192 3738 for tickets; movie hotline 9192 1077) on Carnarvon St claims to be the oldest operating outdoor film theater in the world. It spun its first reel in 1916 and spins the newest flicks every night. *(Admission $10, concessions $8, children $6, families $28.)* Seven blocks south of Chinatown is the **Broome Historical Society** (tel. 9192 2075), which traces the heritage of Broome from the war to racial tensions to the pearling industry. *(Open May-Nov. M-F 10am-4pm, Sa-Su 10am-1pm; Dec.-May daily 10am-1pm. Admission $3, pensioners $2, children 50¢)* On the way to Chinatown, just south of the junction of Cable Beach Rd and Frederick St, the **Japanese Cemetery's** impressive field of black marble and gray stone slates bears testimony to the hundreds of divers who lost their lives in the pearling industry.

Town Beach is farther south on the Roebuck Bay shore. Here, for three consecutive days each month from March to October, Broome's massive 10m tide is so low that the exposed mudflats stretch for miles, reflecting shimmering moonlight. The city celebrates this phenomenon with the **Staircase to the Moon market** at the tourist office. Check the office for days. At the lowest tides, the waters off Town Beach uncover the skeletons of flying boats sunk in WWII. **Reddell Beach**, the southern shore of the Broome Peninsula, is covered with rocky outcroppings and red cliffs.

The **Broome Bird Observatory** (tel. 9193 5600) lies 8km outside of town on Broome Rd, and is an excellent place to spy migratory birds. *(Open Tu-Su 8am-noon and 2-5:30pm.)* The **Willie Creek Pearl Farm** (tel. 9193 6000), 38km north of Broome, is the only pearling operation that welcomes public inspection. The farm runs transport back and forth daily from its showroom on Lullfitz Dr near Cable Beach. *(Coach tour $45, children $23. Self-drive tour $17.50, children $9.)* If you're driving, check on road conditions during the Wet and call ahead for directions.

Plenty of **tours** of the area are available if you're willing to spend the cash. The priciest are **scenic flights**, some of which range all the way to Mitchell Falls and the Buccaneer Archipelago. Try **King Leopold Air** (tel. 9193 7155; $75 for ½hr. flights over Cable Beach) or **Broome Aviation** (tel. 9192 1369; extended flights $260-400). **Land tours** are costly too, but at least provide a day or five of exploration; if you lack a strong 4WD, they may be your only way to see the remote and rugged terrain of the Kimberley. **Pearl Farm Tours** (tel. 1800 636 802 or 9193 7267) runs daytrips to the pristine beaches north of Broome. *(M, W, and F; $125.)* **Over the Top Adventures** (tel. 9192 3977) offers one- and two-day tours to the Dampier Peninsula ($175; $275) as well as to Windjana Gorge and Tunnel Creek ($150; $275). Their five-day trip includes stops along the Gibb River Road as well as Winjana and Tunnel Creek ($720). **West Kimberley Tours** (tel. 9193 1442) has cheaper daytrips to Windjana Gorge and Tunnel Creek. *(Tu, Th, and Sa; $80.)* Several companies offer extensive trips into the Kimberley via the Gibb River Road. Check with the visitor's center in Broome or Kununurra.

WESTERN AUSTRALIA

ENTERTAINMENT AND FESTIVALS

Like Baywatch's lifeguards, Broome's beaches and clubs seduce the weak-willed into brief affairs. A backpackers-only bar is run out of the Roebuck's complex and borrows the name **Rattle 'n' Hum** from a semi-infamous Darwin establishment. Other party-seeking backpackers must be the draw; this dingy billiards bar has less atmosphere than Mars. (Drinks about $4-6. Open Su-W 9:30am-midnight, Th-Sa till 1am. Happy hour daily noon-2pm and 5-6pm.) **Nippon Inn** (tel. 9192 1941), on Dampier Tce across from Murray's Pearler restaurant, is Broome's only nightclub, replete with purple walls and techno beats. When the other bars wind down around midnight, Nippon starts humming. (Open 9am-late.) At Cable Beach, people flock to the **Divers Camp Tavern,** a bar and bistro that gets drunken and jovial on weekends.

Horse racing is big in June and especially in July when the town starts hopping for the **Broome Cup.** Mid-April features the aquatic **Rotary Dragon Boat Classic.** The end of May boasts the bigger **Broome Firing Arts Festival,** when the aesthetically inclined display their stuff. Much of the art is Aboriginal. The late August **Shinju Matsuri Festival** celebrates the natural aesthetic of the pearl. In late November, the **Mango Festival** pays homage to the harvest and includes a Mardi Gras celebration.

■ The Dampier Peninsula

To the north of Broome, miles of pristine white beaches stretch along the coast of the Dampier Peninsula. Travelers who venture down the 4WD-only access road earn striking views of the Indian Ocean. **James Price Point,** with its famed contrast of red cliffs and white beaches, and **Quandong Point** are two popular destinations. Ask the tourist center for road and weather conditions and tide charts before you leave. Allow at least two days to visit; the roads are long and slow.

The peninsula is also home to several Aboriginal communities, once the sites of Catholic missions, who welcome travelers interested in history and cultural life. Each charges a $5 entrance fee, and each is closed on Sunday. **Beagle Bay** (tel. 9192 4913), 118km up a rough 4WD track, is home to the Beagle Bay Church, built in 1918 and boasting a mother of pearl shell altar. There is petrol, but no accommodation or camping. Visitors must contact the tourist office on arrival. Fifty kilometers further north, the mellow coastal waters of the **Middle Lagoon** (tel. 9192 4002) offer swimming, snorkéling, and fishing. There are campsites ($10, powered $12), beach shelters ($30 for 2 nights), and beach cabins ($80 for four nights). Neither fuel nor groceries are available.

The highlight of **Lombadina** (tel. 9192 4936), 200km from Broome, is the **old mission church** that combines corrugated iron and paperbark in a bizarre architectural feat. Aboriginal crafts are available for sale. There's accommodation, fuel, and groceries. The end of the peninsula, **Kooljaman** (Cape Leveque tel. 9192 4970), is 220km from Broome and offers swimming, fishing, diving, and accommodation.

■ Derby

Dirt reigns in Derby, which is surrounded by extensive mudflats, 220km east of Broome at the brink of the **Great Sandy Desert.** Derby has the highest tide fluctuation in the southern hemisphere; the waters of King George Sound can rise and fall as much as 10m in a few hours. The town itself, a friendly community of 5000, was the first to be established in the Kimberley, in 1883.

The 14m berth of the **Prison Boab Tree,** 8km south of town, served as a natural slammer for Aboriginal prisoners in the 19th century. **Myall's Bore,** adjacent to the tree, is the longest trough in the southern hemisphere (120m), capable of quenching the thirst of 1000 cattle at once. More recent claims to fame include the regional headquarters for the **Royal Flying Doctor Service** (tel. 9191 1211) and the **School of the Air** (tel. 9193 1006). Both offer free tours. (Doctor Service tours M-F 11, 11:30am, 2, and 2:30pm. School of the Air tours during school term only, M-F 8 and 10am.)

Derby's **tourist office** (tel. 9191 1426) has varied hours (year-round M-F 8:30am-4:30pm, Sa 9am-1pm; additional hours Apr.-Sept. Su 9am-1pm; July Sa-Su till 4pm). There is a **hospital** (tel. 9193 1246 ambulance, 9193 3214 outpatient), a **police station** (tel. 9191 1144), a **post office** (open M-F 9am-5pm), and an **ANZ bank** with an **ATM** next to the post office (bank open M-Th 9:30am-4pm, F 9:30am-5pm). There are several **grocery stores,** including the mammoth **Woolworths** (tel. 9191 1055) at the junction of the Derby Hwy and Loch St (open M-W and F 8am-6pm, Th 8am-8pm, Sa 8am-5pm, and Su 10am-4pm). **Accommodations** fill up quickly in the Dry and should be booked in advance. The **West Kimberley Lodge** (tel. 9191 1031), at the corner of Sutherland and Stanwell St, is the best budget accommodation in town, offering clean and quiet rooms with kitchen and laundry facilities (singles $35, twins $45, suites $65). The **Boab Inn** (tel. 9191 1044) has motel-style accommodation (singles $60, twins $75, doubles $75, family $105). The **Kimberley Lodge Caravan Park** (tel. 9193 1055) overlooks a stretch of mudflats (sites $6 per person; powered $9).

■ Gibb River Road: Derby to Kununurra

Eight kilometers south of Derby, a rugged 4WD track begins its severe haul eastward into the Kimberley. The Gibb River Road is not for the faint of heart (or of car). This "shortcut" to Kununurra is for the serious traveler with a sense of adventure. The trip presses through the most rugged reaches of the Australian wilderness, especially if you take some long detours from the road itself to take in the remote and spectacular sights of the continent's far northwestern corner.

Windjana Gorge can be reached either from the Great Western Hwy (turn onto a gravel road 40km west of Fitzroy Crossing and travel 107km north) or from the Gibb River Road, along a gravel road 146km from Derby. This 3.5km crevasse in the limestone landscape looms as high as 100m over the Lennard River and is part of the 350-million-year-old Devonian Reef. The hordes of freshwater crocs that laze carelessly in the sun are the gorge's main attraction, but swimming is allowed for the brave. An 8km return walk skirts the river to the right, past the sheer walls of the gorge. **Campsites** with toilets, water, and showers are available at the Gorge ($7, children $1).

A little over 40km south of Windjana is **Tunnel Creek,** where a stream winds through dark passages of limestone. During the Dry, the creek is shallow, and wading through the thigh-deep water in the pitch-dark tunnel is a thrill. The walk is over 1km return; upon reaching the daylight on the other side, people simply turn around and head back through. A flashlight and shoes are essential. **Bungoolee Tours** (9191 5355) provides a full day tour of both Windjana Gorge and Tunnel Creek, leaving at 7am from Fitzroy Crossing ($85, children $50).

Farther east, the Gibb River Rd bumps past a 100m chain of cascades at **Bell Creek Gorge,** and then runs on to **Mt. Barnett.** Up to this point, all roadways are harsh but passable for sedans, but 4WD is necessary to push eastward. On the way, the unforgiving **Kalumburu Road** branches north toward the remote **Mitchell Falls,** a four-cataract waterfall plunging into the Indian Ocean and one of the most isolated yet spectacular sights in the Kimberley. These roads are accessible only from April to October when the weather permits. The unsealed tracks can be tough on your car and on your psyche; passengers venturing through should have plenty of water and food, at least two **spare tires,** and a hearty helping of grit and self-sufficiency. Most local tourist offices sell a copy of the *Travellers Guide to the Gibb River and Kalumburu Roads* which has information on distances and road conditions ($2). Travelers should **register with tourist offices** at either end before starting the journey, and renting a walkie-talkie, CB radio, or cell phone isn't a bad idea for the most remote stretches, as traffic is scarce and you could get stuck for a while. Conditions on the more rugged parts vary depending on the severity of the most recent wet season; check with tourist offices ahead of time.

■ Fitzroy Crossing

Fitzroy Crossing sits near the **Fitzroy River,** which, while a sandy stream in the Dry, is one of the world's largest rivers during the Wet. Fitzroy's small-town appeal is not enough to attract visitors, who mostly pass through on their way to nearby **Geike Gorge, Tunnel Creek,** and **Windjana Gorge.** There is a **tourist center** (tel. 9191 5355) on the west side of town that distributes maps and information on the gorges (open M-F 9am-5pm, Sa-Su 9am-4pm). The Greyhound bus stops here daily. Next door is the **supermarket** (open M-F 8:30am-5:30pm, Sa 8:30am-12:30pm, Su 9am-noon). There is a **hospital** (tel. 9191 5001) and a **police station** (tel. 9191 5000). The **post office** (tel. 9191 5060) is north on Forrest Rd (open M-F 9am-5pm).

A community unto itself, the **Fitzroy River Lodge** (tel. 9191 5141 or 1800 355 226) offers a range of accommodation. Motel rooms soar above $100, but powered camping sites cost $8 per person. **Darlngunaya Backpackers** (tel. 9191 5140) is 4km from town on the way to Geike Gorge; take Forrest Rd and turn right on Russ Rd. Situated in the historic post office, it offers a soothing atmosphere, with high ceilings, wood floors, porches, a spacious kitchen, and laundry (dorms $15, tent sites $7).

Geike Gorge (GEEK-ee), 18km from town, is the most popular attraction nearby. Carving through the streaked limestone rock, the Fitzroy meanders (or rages, depending on the time of year) along this wide gorge. Ninety-minute boat tours leave at 8am, 11am, and 3pm, motoring up the quiet gorge for views of freshwater crocs and birdlife. Boat tickets go on sale 20 minutes prior to departure at the gorge station. A 3km return reef walk rambles between the rock wall of the gorge and the river. There are toilets and water but no camping at the Gorge.

■ Halls Creek

Halls Creek's brief heyday was during the short-lived gold rush of 1885. Today it's a low-key venue for the steady trickle of travelers en route between **Bungle Bungle National Park** and **Broome.** This pocket of civilization is 288km east of Fitzroy Crossing, along the Great Northern Hwy at the edge of the Great Sandy Desert. The **tourist center** (tel. 9168 6262) is on the west side of town (open M-F 8am-4:30pm, Sa 9am-1pm). When the center is closed, the map-and-info board in the town park suffices. Halls Creek has **police** (tel. 9168 6000), a **hospital** (tel. 9168 6003), and a **post office** (tel. 9168 6111; open M-F 9am-5pm). **Stop 'n Shop** (tel. 9168 6186) offers groceries (open M-F 8am-6pm, Sa 8am-noon, Su 9am-noon) and **Shell** (tel. 9168 6060) sells petrol (open daily 6am-10pm). While most travelers stop in Halls Creek just long enough to fill the gas tank, accommodations do exist. The **Shell Roadhouse** has backpacker-style beds and hotel rooms for $15, as does the **Kimberley Hotel/Motel** (tel. 9168 6101).

In addition to Bungle Bungle, Halls Creek acts as a somewhat distant base for trips to another natural spectacle: the **Wolfe Creek Meteorite Crater,** which is 150km south of town. It's the second-largest such site in the world. Also near Halls Creek, a distinct quartz formation called **China Wall** towers 6km north of town. The **Caroline Pool, Sawpit Gorge,** and **Palm Springs** also lure leisurely visitors with swimming in the gorges (Palm Springs and Caroline Pool) and short walking tracks (Sawpit Gorge).

■ The Bungle Bungles (Purnululu National Park)

The distinct sandstone forms of the Bungles were created 360-370 million years ago, and Aboriginals have settled the area for over 20,000 years. To the non-Aboriginal population, however, this natural wonderland, covering 45,000 hectares in the eastern Kimberley, was unknown until the 1980s. Though the secret is out, the granting of national park status in 1987 ensured that the area would continue to be wild and spectacular. Huge mounds tower 200m above the surrounding land, which contains sheer edges, canyons, and gorges cut by seasonal rivulets. The effect is a bumpy, curvy massif resembling an egg-carton cushion. Millions of years of rain eroded the fragile limestone of this ancient plateau, sculpting it into thousands of smooth, free-standing sandstone towers bedecked by vivid orange silica and black lichen.

Many travelers choose to avoid the tough tracks into the Park and view the natural spectacle from above. **Alligator Airways** (tel. 9168 1333) offers tours of the Bungles which leave from Kununurra (see below) as does **SlingAir Heliwork** (tel. 9169 1300 or 1800 095 500) which runs flights from Kununurra and Turkey Creek. To enter the Bungles by vehicle requires a 4WD, supplies, and chutzpah. The 4WD-only **Spring Creek Track** (from Halls Creek 109km north, 4hr.; from Kununurra 250km south, 5hr.) turns eastward from the Great Northern Hwy and runs 55km to the Bungles. The track is rough; two spare tires and extra water are highly recommended.

In the park, the Track passes the **ranger station** (self-registered 7-day admission $8, children $1) and comes to a three-way intersection. To the left, 7km away, is the **Kurrajong camping area,** with tent sites, water, toilets, and firewood. To the right, 13km farther, is the similar **Walardi campground.** ($7 per adult, children $1.) The ranger station is staffed only during the Dry, and the park closes January through March.

A handful of **walking tracks** meander along the edge of the massif and into its colossal crevasses. The most popular, reasonably easy hike is through Cathedral Gorge, starting from a carpark 25km south of the ranger station (2km return). The **Piccaninny Gorge hike** (30km) requires more stamina and a night in the bush. Register with the rangers before setting out from the same lot. The fairly easy **Echidna Chasm walk** (2km return) starts 21km north of the ranger base. In the same vicinity, the more challenging **Froghole** (1.4km return) and **Mini Palms** (3km) gorge walks leave from a second carpark.

Several companies offer day and overnight trips that can be a good but pricey way to experience the remote area. **East Kimberley Tours** (tel. 9168 1711 or 1800 804 005) offers a three-day safari (June-Aug. $435, otherwise $395). **Desert Inn 4WD Adventure** (tel. 9169 1257 or 1800 805 010) offers a similar trip for $390. More expensive trips include other Kimberley attractions as well. Most trips into the Bungles depart from Kununurra. If you're rushed, **East Kimberley Tours** (tel. 9168 2213 or 1800 682 213) offers a daytrip into the Kimberley that departs from Turkey Creek and costs $125.

Turkey Creek (or Warmun) is the last town north of the Spring Creek Track turn-off. Less than 100km from the park, it can serve as a stopover for those driving from Kununurra. The **Turkey Creek Roadhouse** (tel. 9168 7882; fax 9168 7925; reception open daily 6:30am-6:30pm) offers a variety of accommodations. (Dorms $17.50; singles $30. Tent sites $5 per person. Caravan sites $10, with power $15.)

■ Kununurra

Five hundred kilometers west of Katherine, NT, and past countless desert mirages stands the little oasis of Kununurra, the eastern entry point to the Kimberley. The name means "big waters," appropriate for a town that accesses the Ord River and grew tremendously during the effort to reroute that river for a massive irrigation project. Extensive parks and lawns create a pleasant, relaxed atmosphere for farm workers and travelers alike. Kununurra's main appeal is its proximity (a relative term in this expansive country) to dramatic and rugged destinations like **Bungle Bungle, Lake Argyle, Windjana Gorge,** and the **Gibb River Road.**

ORIENTATION AND PRACTICAL INFORMATION

Kununurra (cun-ah-NOR-ah) is a small town with just a few main roads. Messmate Way turns off the Victoria Hwy at a 24-hour fuel station and heads to the center of town, where it crosses Konkerberry Drive at a traffic circle and ends at Coolibah Drive. Most points of interest lie along either Konkerberry or Coolibah.

Buses: Greyhound Pioneer runs daily to Broome ($137), Darwin ($102), and Alice Springs ($201). Buses stop across from the tourist office.
Taxis: Spuds Taxis (tel. 9168 2553).
Cars: Territory (tel. 9169 1911), **Budget** (tel. 9168 2033), **Avis** (tel. 9169 1258).
Tourist Office: Tourist Bureau (tel. 9168 1177; fax 9168 2598) on Coolibah Dr, 100m off Messmate. Open M-Th 8am-5pm, F-Sa 8:30am-5pm, Su 9am-4pm.
Budget Travel: Traveland (tel. 9168 1888), in the Kununurra Shopping Centre. Open M-F 8am-5:30pm, Sa 8:30am-12:30pm. **Harvey World Travel** (tel. 9168 3331), on CottonTree between Konkerberry and Coolibah. Open M-F 8:30am-5:30pm, Sa 8:30am-noon.
Banks: Commonwealth Bank (tel. 9169 1511), at Cotton Tree and Coolibah Dr, has an **ATM**. Open M-Th 9:30am-4pm, F 9:30am-5pm.
Pharmacy: Amcal Chemist (tel. 9168 1111), in the Kununurra Shopping Center on Konkberry Dr. Open M-F 9am-5:30pm, Sa 9am-1pm.
Police: tel. 9169 1122.
Hospital: tel. 9168 1522.
Post Office: (tel. 9168 1072), across from the tourist office. Check information computer to see if you have mail waiting. Open M-F 9am-5pm. **Postal Code:** 6743.
Internet Access: Telecentre (tel. 9169 1868), around the corner from the tourist office. Open M, W-Th 2-6pm, Tu, F 9am-1pm. **Hobbit's Computers,** 1093 Konkerberry Dr (tel. 9169 1053; ½hr. minimum). Open M-F 9am-5pm. Both $5 per ½hr.
Phone Code: 08.

ACCOMMODATIONS:

There are two competing backpacker lodges in Kununurra, both small enough to necessitate reservations in the high season (Apr.-Oct.).

Kununurra Backpackers, 111 Nutwood Circle (tel. 9169 1998; fax 9168 3998), is a 10min. walk from the tourist office. Follow Konkerberry away from the highway; take a right on Nutwood and follow the signs. Located in a quiet neighborhood, with well-lit rooms, A/C, pool, laundry, kitchen. Linen available upon request. Dorms $15, triples $15 per person, twins $18 per person, doubles $38. Free transport from tourist office and bus station. $10 key deposit.
Desert Oasis (tel. 9168 2702 or 1800 805 010), 2 blocks from the shopping center. Take Konkerberry Dr to Trustania St, where a sign points to the lodge near the corner. Performs decorating miracles with scrap metal and the color purple. Pool patio, shaded lounge areas, spacious kitchen, laundry, and a purple bus. Rooms are a bit dark and cell-like. Dorm beds $14, doubles $40. Plate and cutlery deposit $10.
Duncan House Bed & Breakfast, 167 Coolibah Dr (tel. 9168 2436). For a price, there's luxury even in the outback. Well-decorated, comfy rooms; tasty breakfasts. Friendly owner and atmosphere. Singles $85, doubles $95. Children $15 extra.
Town Caravan Park (tel. 9168 1763), behind the Hotel Kununurra just off Konkerberry Dr on Bloodwood, offers proximity to town but not much privacy. Crowded sites $6, powered $9.50. Laundry facilities.
Kimberley Holiday Park (tel. 9168 1280), just west of Messmate Way on the Victoria Hwy, has spacious sites, pool, laundry. Two-person sites $14; powered $16.
Ivanhoe Village (tel. 9169 1995), at the intersection of Coolibah Dr and Ivanhoe Rd. Two-person campsites $14; powered $17.

FOOD

Kununurra's scenery may be spectacular, but the food is nothing to write home about. The best option for the palate and the wallet may be the grocery stores: head to **Coles** (tel. 9168 2711) in the Shopping Center (open daily 7am-10pm), or **Tuckerbox** (tel. 9168 1100), on the corner of White Gum and Konkerberry Dr (open M-F 8am-1pm). However, the **Hot Gossip Cafe** (tel. 9169 1377), on Konkerberry Dr, serves conventional fare (continental breakfast $5, burgers galore $5-6) in a petite mirrored room with wicker chairs. At dinner, a tasty Chinese menu is added (chow mein $10.50). (Open M-Sa 8am-9pm, Su 5:30pm-9pm.) **Kimberley Cottage Coffee Shop** (tel. 9169 1696), located between Coolibah and Konkerberry on Papuana St, is simplicity at its best. This quiet little haven surpasses its arts and crafts facade, offering the best sandwiches in town ($3). The hummus, chicken, and avocado sandwich is a highlight. (Open M-F 8:30am-4:30pm, Sa 8:30-noon.) For juicy tidbits missed at the Hot Gossip Cafe, try **Rumours Patisserie** (tel. 9168 2071). This 50s-style burger and milkshake joint satiates the ravenous crowds at the Kununurra Shopping Center. Expect standard burgers ($4-6) and sandwiches ($3), but not peace and quiet. **Gulliver's Tavern** (tel. 9168 1666), on Konkerberry Dr at Cotton Tree, is the town's main pub and serves counter meals (open M-Th noon-11pm, F noon-midnight, Sa noon-11pm, Su 1-9pm).

SIGHTS

Kelly's Knob, an impressive rock peak at the north end of town, offers some perspective on the stunning geography around Kununurra; the sunset up here is fantastic. Take Konkerberry Dr to the end; turn left on Ironwood, right on Speargrass, and right again at the path to the peak. It's a trek to the top, but that's why the view is so good. **Hidden Valley (Mirima) National Park** (tel. 9168 8200), 4km east of town, gives an enticing sample of the bumpy sandstone formations in the Bungle Bungle range to the south (see p. 634). *(Ranger-led walks M, W, and F 9am; Tu, Th 3:30pm.)* Three short paths wind past the 360-million-year-old formations. The **Didbagirring trail** is 800m return and ascends a steep hill for a fantastic lookout. You can circumvent the $8 vehicle entrance fee by parking outside the park and walking.

The **Ord River Diversion Dam** is the result of the irrigation project that gave the Kununurra region its current topography. Finished in 1963, the 335m-long dam holds back the Ord River to create **Lake Kununurra.** The lake irrigates the land and provides a sanctuary for an estimated 7000 freshwater crocs. The Victoria Hwy passes by the lake and over the dam to cross the Ord River 7km west of town. The PackSaddle Plains and the Ivanhoe Plains together are the **Ord River Irrigation Area.** Backpackers can find work at these farms, which grow bananas, melons, chickpeas, and dozens of other crops. Several farms invite visitors to taste and purchase the fruits of this labor.

Several companies offer **scenic flights** over the Lake on the way to Bungle Bungle (see p. 634). **Alligator Airways** (tel. 9168 1333) offers flights over the lake and the Kununurra area (40min., $85) and longer flights over Bungle Bungle (135min., $150). Both plane and helicopter flights are available with **Slingair Heliwork** (tel. 9168 1129 or 1800 095 500; 2hr. flights $150).

■ Near Kununurra: Lake Argyle

Lake Argyle, 72km southeast of Kununurra, is a byproduct of the Ord River Irrigation Project. In 1972, waters filled the dusty region with a building of a second dike, the **Rod River Top Dam.** Created as a backup reservoir, the Lake is the largest freshwater body in the southern hemisphere; at 70km long, it could hold 55 Sydney Harbours at full capacity. The means may have been artificial, but the ends are still beautiful, as glimmering waters lap at the base of ancient orange hills.

Most people daytrip here from Kununurra and bring a picnic. If you want to stay here, though, the **Lake Argyle Tourist Village** is 35km east of Kununurra on the Victoria Highway and another 35km down a marked access road. The Village is home to Lake Argyle Cruise (see below), as well as a caravan park, motel, and restaurant. There's a **campground** with showers and laundry (sites $6; powered $9.50). If you want a roof, try the motel (tel. 9168 7360; singles $65, doubles $75). The restaurant serves standard fare (breakfast 7am-9am, lunch 11am-1:30pm, tea 5:30pm-7:30pm).

There are several ways to enjoy Lake Argyle. Cruise ships meander through the expansive waters, providing travelers with glimpses of the region and its wildlife. **Lake Argyle Cruise** (tel. 9168 2682) offers a two-hour morning cruise with a focus on wildlife ($27 adults, $13.50 children, $42 with pick-up in Kununurra), a two-hour sunset cruise ($35 adult, $17.50 children, $50 with pick-up in Kununurra), and a six-hour cruise that tours much of the distant mountains and remote islands ($90). These tours run from May to September. **Triple J Tours** (tel. 9168 1177) provides cruises of the Lake and the Ord River. *($85 adult, $45 children.)* One popular tour includes a bus trip down to the Lake and a cruise ride back up the Ord River to Kununurra.

Kimberley Canoeing Experience (tel. 1800 805 010) offers two- to three-day self-guided tours that depart the Lake Argyle Dam and meander down the Ord River, stopping at established camps. *(Tours cost $120 and up. Cooking and camping gear included.)*

■ Wyndham and Around

The tiny port town of Wyndham lies 100km north of Kununurra, wedged between the **Bastion Range,** the tidal waters of the **Cambridge Gulf,** and expansive mudflats. The village hasn't changed much since its early days over a century ago. The few stores and handful of locals remain unfazed by the influx of day-visitors and a quiet, almost ghost-town feeling pervades the town. The **Five River Lookout,** several kilometers from town up a steep winding road, offers an excellent view of the Gulf and the surrounding region. The **Wyndham Zoological Gardens and Crocodile Park** (tel. 9161 1124) offers views of the ferocious locals of the Gulf region. (Open 8:30am-4pm. Daily crock feedings 11am.) Also near the wharf, on Barytes Rd 4km from town, is the **Wyndham Historical Society and Museum,** whose displays include articles about the Japanese bombing in WWII. (Open daily 10am-3pm. $2, students 50¢.)

Wyndham has a **grocery store** (tel. 9161 1018; open M-F 7am-6pm, Sa 7am-1pm, Su 8am-1pm), a **post office** (tel. 9161 124; open M-F 9am-5pm, Sa 9am-2:30pm, Su noon-3pm), and a **tourist center** at the Mobile Station (tel. 9161 1201; open M-F 9am-5pm, Sa 9am-noon). A **caravan park** at the end of town boasts a 2000-year-old boab tree (sites $6, powered $9). The **Wyndham Hotel** (tel. 9161 1003) offers singles ($60), twins, and doubles ($80 for either).

Further from Wyndham's sleepy center are a variety of sites accessible with car. Fifty-two kilometers south of Wyndham and 58km north of Kununurra is the turn-off for the **Gibb River Road** (see p. 633). Twenty kilometers up this rugged road and 2km down an access road lies **Emma Gorge,** yet another impressive gorge complete with plunge pool. Just north of the Gibb River Road lies a turn-off for a 1km access road to **The Grotto.** This secluded gorge has 140 steps descending down a rocky ledge to a hidden pool below where you can swim near a waterfall, with nothing but the hush of the gorge and the splash of the cascade to keep you company.

Appendix

■ Holidays and Festivals

Banks, museums, and other public buildings are often closed or operate with reduced hours on the following **public holidays,** which fall on weekdays. During **school holidays,** many Australians go on vacation, and accommodations fill up, often increasing prices. Public transportation may run on weekend schedules during school holidays. There are variations between schools and regions, but the school holidays are typically from Christmas through most of January, Easter Week (the Thursday before through the Friday after), and in early July and early October.

Cities and towns across Australia hold countless festivals and crafts fairs throughout the year, with most taking place during the summer months (Dec.- Feb.). Ask the local tourist offices for more information on festivals. The **Mardi Gras Parade** in Sydney, Australia's biggest gay and lesbian festival, will be held on February 27 in 1999.

PUBLIC HOLIDAYS 1999

January 1	New Year's Day
January 26	Australia Day
April 1	Maundy Thursday (Thursday before Easter)
April 2	Good Friday (Friday before Easter)
April 4	Easter
April 25	Anzac Day
December 25	Christmas
December 26	Boxing Day

■ Road Distances in Kilometers

Adelaide								
1530	**Alice**							
2119	2990	**Brisbane**						
3524	2411	1717	**Cairns**					
1201	2731	1265	2664	**Canberra**				
3020	1490	3414	2835	3977	**Darwin**			
731	2261	1673	3078	656	4391	**Melbourne**		
2708	3626	4457	5862	3909	4268	3439	**Perth**	
1424	2822	980	2697	285	4821	879	4000	**Sydney**

■ Time Zones

The following table should help you convert time between different Australian states, New York City, London, and Greenwich Mean Time. Unfortunately, you can't just memorize one time difference for the year—daylight savings time makes everything complicated, especially since some Australian states use it and some don't. To use the following table, **imagine it is noon, Greenwich Mean Time (GMT),** and then look at what time it would be in the two cities you are comparing, take the difference between

At Noon, Greenwich Mean Time (GMT)	last Sunday in Oct. to last Sunday in Mar.	last Sunday in March to first Sunday in Oct.	first Sunday in Oct. to last Sunday in Oct.
ACT	11pm	10pm	10pm
New South Wales	11pm	10pm	10pm
Northern Territory	9:30pm	9:30pm	9:30pm
Queensland	10pm	10pm	10pm
South Australia	10:30pm	9:30pm	9:30pm
Tasmania	11pm	10pm	11pm
Victoria	11pm	10pm	10pm
Western Australia	8pm	8pm	8pm
New York City	7am	8am	8am
London	noon	1pm	1pm

them, and then apply it to whatever the real time is. (GMT is an international standard time; unlike the rest of England, it's not affected by daylight savings.) Remember that the **date** is affected too—Australia is ahead of the Western Hemisphere, so Monday evening in New York is Tuesday morning in Sydney.

■ Measurements

1 inch = 25 millimeters (mm)	1mm = 0.04 inches (in.)
1 foot = 0.30 meters (m)	1m = 3.33 feet (ft.)
1 yard = 0.91m	1m = 1.1 yards (yd.)
1 mile = 1.61kilometers (km)	1km = 0.62 miles (mi.)
1 ounce = 25 grams (g)	1g = 0.04 ounces (oz.)
1 pound = 0.45 kilograms (kg)	1kg = 2.22 pounds (lb.)
1 quart = 0.94 liters (L)	1L = 1.06 quarts (qt.)

■ Glossary of 'Strine

'Strine is 'stralian for "Australian." The first trick to speaking Australian slang is to abbreviate everything: **Oz** for Australia, **brekkie** for breakfast, **cuppa** for cup of coffee, **sammy** for sandwich. Some words aren't as easy to guess, and nothing is sacred: **abo** is Aboriginal, **reffo** is refugee, **rezo** is a residential college. The term **pommie,** meaning English person, has a debatable origin. Some say it comes from "pomegranate," referring to stereotypically rosy cheeks, while others point to the acronym worn on the early convicts' uniforms: POHME, or Prisoners Of Her Majesty in Exile. The second, less ubiquitous aspect of Aussie slang is **rhyming. Noahs** are sharks (shark rhymes with ark, Noah built an ark), while **I'm on the dog** means "I'm on the phone" (bone rhymes with phone, and then the whole dog-bone thing). Get it? American travelers may be disturbed to be called **seppos,** for good reason: Yanks rhymes with tanks, and the worst kind of tanks are septic tanks. Ouch!

Australian **pronunciation** is harder to learn than the lingo—with Aboriginal words especially, but even with English-derived proper nouns it can seem inexplicable. Americans and Canadians generally have particular difficulties, as much of 'strine has distinctly Anglo origins. Smile, and don't be embarrassed—yes, you're a tourist, but in Australia that's not such a mark of shame. One rule to note: when Australians spell a word out or pronounce a number, they always use the expression "double" (or "triple"), as in the phone number "nine-three-double-seven-five-triple-one" (9377 5111).

ablution block: shower/toilet block at a campground
abseil: rappel
ace: awesome
ANZAC: Australia-New Zealand Army Corps
ANZAC biscuits: honey-oat cookies
arvo: afternoon
Aussie: Australian (pronounced Ozzie— thus, Australia is Oz)
backpackers: hostel
barbie: barbecue
bathers: bathing suit/swimsuit
belt bag: fanny pack (don't say "fanny" in Oz: it's a crude word for a part of the female anatomy)
billabong: a watering hole
biscuit: cookie
bitumen: a rough black asphalt used to pave roads (BICH-uh-min)
bludger: moocher, grifter, lazy person
bluey: someone with red hair (seriously)
bonnet: hood of a car
book: make reservations
boot: trunk of a car
bottle shop: liquor store
brekkie: breakfast
bush: wilderness
bush tucker: traditional Aboriginal wild foods
bushwalking: hiking
busk: play music on the street for money

BYO: bring your own alcohol (at some restaurants, wine only)
campervan: mobile home, RV
caravan: trailer, like a cab-less campervan
carpark: parking lot
chips: thick french fries, usually served with vinegar and salt
chippers: fish and chips or fish and chips shops
chook: chicken
coldie: a cold beer
concession: discount; usually applies to students, seniors, or children, sometimes only to Australian students and pensioners
cordial: concentrated fruit juice
dag: one who is daggy (usage is common, often benevolent)
daggy: unfashionable, unhip, goofy, silly
damper: traditionally unleavened bread
Devonshire tea: tea and scones, often served in the late afternoon
doona, duvet: comforter, feather blanket
dramas: problems. "No dramas" is interchangeable with "no worries."
drier than a dead dingo's donger: very thirsty
dummy: pacifier (for infants)
ensuite: with bath

entree: appetizer ("main" is a main dish)
esky: a cooler (originally from the brand name Eskimo)
excess: deductible (as in car insurance)
fair dinkum: genuine, authentic
fairy floss: cotton candy
feral: wild, grunge-style (a common slang term)
flash: fancy, snazzy
flat out like a lizard drinking: doing nothing
flat white: coffee with hot milk and a touch of foam
free call: toll-free call
franger: condom (colloquial, somewhat crude)
fossicking: gem-hunting and gold-sifting
g'day: hello
glasshouse: greenhouse
ground floor: American first floor ("first floor" is second floor, etc.)
hire: to rent
hoon: loud-mouth, show-off
icy-pole: popsicle (sweet frozen treat on a stick)
jersey: sweater, sweatshirt
jackaroo: stationhand-in-training
jillaroo: female jackaroo
jumper: see jersey
keen: term of respect ("a keen surfer")
Kiwi: New Zealander
licensed: legally serves alcohol

lollies: candies
magic: really wonderful, special: "that beach is magic"
mate: friend, buddy (used broadly)
milk bar: convenience store
moke: an open-air, golf-cartesque vehicle
mozzie: mosquito
nappy: diaper
newsagent: newsstand/convenience store
no worries: sure, fine, or "you're welcome"
ocker: hick, Crocodile Dundeetype
odds and sods: odds and ends
off like a bucket of prawns in the sun: leaving like lightning
ordinary: bad. An "ordinary" road is full of potholes.
Oz: Australia
pavlova: a creamy meringue dessert garnished with fruit
pensioner: senior citizen (someone on a pension)
petrol: gasoline
piss: beer (usually)
pissed: drunk (usually)
pokies: gambling machines
powerpoint: outlet (also electrical hookup for tents or caravans)

pram: stroller (for a baby)
prawn: jumbo shrimp
pub: pub. Never, never "bar." Pub.
push bike: bicycle
return: round-trip
'roo: as in kangaroo
roundabout: traffic rotary
rubber: eraser
sandgroper: a West Australian (also Westralian)
sauce: Usually tomato sauce. Aussie's closest equivalent to ketchup.
serviette: napkin
sheila: slang for a woman
shout: buy a drink or round of drinks for others. Also a noun, as in an evening's worth of everyone buying rounds for each other.
side: team
singlet: tank top or undershirt
skivvie: turtleneck sweater
sang or sanger: sausage
spider: ice cream float or nasty arachnid (use context clues here)
squiz: a look (to take a squiz at something)
stone the crows!: an expression of surprise
'strine: Aussie dialect (from Australian au-STRINE)

swimmers: swimsuit
suss: figure out, sort out
ta: short for thank you—usually muttered under breath. Rhymes with la.
TAB: shop to place bets, sometimes in pubs
TAFE: Technical and Further Education. Community adult education; cooking schools often produce fabulous budget meals.
takeaway: food to go, takeout
Tassie: Tasmania (TAZ-zie)
torch: flashlight
touch wood: knock on wood**r**
ack suit: sweat suit, jogging suit
tucker: food.
uni: university (YOU-nee)
unsealed: unpaved roads, usually gravel, sometimes dirt
ute: utility vehicle, pick-up truck
upmarket: upscale, expensive
Vegemite: yeast-extract spread for toast and sandwiches
walkabout: to spontaneously set off across the countryside
wanker: jerk (very rude term)
XXXX: pronounced four-ex, a brand of beer
yakka: hard work
yute: see ute
zed: Z (American "zee")

APPENDIX

■ Beer Terminology

Nothing's more Australian than beer, and accordingly, the language used for it has an Aussie twist too. Because of the hot climate, Australian pubs generally eschew the British pint in favor of smaller portions which stay cold till you're done. Thus, size is a major variable in the argot of ale. If you're too drunk to think of the proper terms, ordering by size, in ounces, usually works. On the mainland, try a "5," "7," "10," or "15." In Tasmania, order using the numbers "6," "8," "10," or "20."

Beer: 7 oz. in Qld and Vic; 15 oz. in NSW; 10 oz. elsewhere	**Middy:** 285mL (10 oz.), used in NSW and SA
Bludger: a weak drinker who can't finish a full cycle of shouts	**Pint:** 425mL (15 oz.) in SA, smaller than the British or American pint
Butcher: 200mL (7 oz.) in SA	**Pony:** 140mL (5 oz.)
Darwin Stubbie: 1.25L bottle in NT	**Pot:** 285mL (10 oz.) in Qld and Vic
Glass: 200mL (7 oz.) in Qld and Vic	**Real Pint:** 560mL (20 oz.); used in SA or Tas to get a proper glass of beer
Handle: 10 oz. glass with a handle	**Schooner:** 425mL (15 oz.) in NSW; 285mL (10 oz.) in SA
Jug: pitcher	**Shout:** a round of drinks, or to buy a round of drinks. Standard pub custom.
Long neck: 750mL bottle	**Stubbie:** 375mL bottle **Tinny:** 375mL can

Index

Researcher-Writers

David Collins *Tasmania*

After four years of fun and a summer blessing our office with his charms, Dave's homecoming to native Australia was triumphant. Dave's love for all things green shone through in his delightfully clear, colorful writing. Wild and woolly Tasmania was his perfect venue, and his perceptive copy not only captured the glory of its wilderness but also lent insight into the complex web of its history and politics. Dave was also a font of useful ideas for itinerary design and book organization. The tangible enthusiasm for Tassie that pervaded each of his copybatches kept us eagerly awaiting the next; he didn't disappoint. Thanks, Dave, and enjoy home; we miss you.

David Fagundes *Victoria, Far East SA, Far West NSW*

Grizzled veteran David came from his Rough Guides stint back into the warm embrace of Ma Let's Go, and he couldn't have done her prouder. Combining impeccable research with deliciously witty prose, he earned more superlatives than we have in our index. His demanding itinerary through parts of three states didn't faze him, nor did a melted engine or a gaol that was a little darker than he expected. And then there was Melbourne, a city with which David seemed to form an instant ionic bond, its cosmopolitan whirlwind perfectly matched to his boundless energy. On his return from Oz, David came to the office to provide days of crunch-time assistance. We already knew you were the bomb, DF, but we thank you, and so do the clowns.

Robert Fuller *Brisbane, Southern and Outback Queensland*

Eternally patient with an ever-lengthening itinerary, Rob plunged into Queensland with a zest that carried over into his vibrant, evocative, thoroughly researched copy. Even spicier was his marginalia, which brightened our sunlight-starved office pod with frequent laughter and an occasional raised eyebrow or three. From happening upon a non-family-friendly kangaroo exhibit at a zoo, to cruising the outback using part of his car as a sail, to testing a new career in paleontology, Rob always had an eye for the adventurous, the salacious, and the just-plain-hilarious. Sand ruled Rob's life almost as much as applesauce did, from the rigors of life on Fraser Island to the endless push across the desert. Thanks for a stellar job, Rob, and long live Jell-O.

Derek Glanz *Great Ocean Road and Gippsland, Vic;*
Northern NSW, Outback Queensland

We knew the man could rip a line drive, but it turned out he could rip up Australia too. Covering an unbelievably strenuous itinerary from western Victoria to Queensland, Derek was the hardest of hard-core; he did everything, and did everything well. His prose was eloquent and funny, written with an experienced editor's insight and a flair for botany, ornithology, history, and Austin Powers. Derek thrived on the challenge of adding new coverage, and revealed his tree-huggin' tendencies with his penchant for national parks. Returning from his Australian summer in time to help the other researchers get prepared, he also showed off some sweet dance moves and mad softball skills. Roar, mighty Cougrzz, roarrrr.

Lillian Gutwein *Sydney, Northern NSW*

Ever-thoughtful Lilly took on the task of keeping her editors sane and happy, deluging us with postcards, candy, and kitschy souvenirs. In between the care packages, she also supplied us with clear and perceptive copy, complete with always-upbeat marginalia that kept us laughing. Lilly strapped on her 'pack, put on her dancing shoes, and immersed herself in North Coast beach culture. Despite the ever-present lure of the sand and surf, she chugged along through her itinerary and produced incredibly comprehensive research along the way. Considerate, cheery, careful, and competent, Lilly was a great asset to the guide and a pleasure to have on the bookteam.

Bryan Leach
Sydney, the ACT, Southern NSW

With pluck and impressive stamina, Bryan completed a breakneck itinerary without once skimping on coverage or attention to detail. He lived it up in Sydney and loved it, but wasn't too spoiled by the big city to appreciate the small-town charms of the Central West or the serene beauty of the South Coast. Bryan kept us entertained with stories of his encounters with Kings Cross denizens, and kept us totally satisfied with his quality writing and research. His communicativeness and desire for feedback were much appreciated, as were his dry wit and cutting honesty. Bryan had a love affair with Australia from the get-go, and it lived up to all expectations; so did he.

Kathleen Peggar
Western Australia

Kathleen's ankle may have been hobbled, but her spirit was unfettered. A seasoned Let's Go vet fresh out of college and ready for adventure, she found it in spades in the wind and surf all the way around the Westralian coast. Less savory parts of the interior brought more challenges, but Kathleen met them all unflinchingly and returned to the coast with a crunched-up car but a healthy dose of spunk and energy. Her clear and insightful prose was a pleasure to read, and her wide-ranging, fine-tuned research brought vitality and depth to our coverage of Perth and the rest of WA. Her earth-friendly sensibilities gave our orange book a green tint, while her no-worries attitude tickled us pink. A bedrock of reliability and a lot of fun besides, Kathleen was ace.

Amy Piper
Northern Queensland

Braving dangers from mud-drenched roads to renegade *a cappella* singers, Amy dove into Queensland's north coast without a second thought and returned with markedly shorter hair, a zillion great stories, and a job excellently done. Equally at home in the Cape York jungle as on a Whitsunday sailboat, 3000m above ground as 10m under the ocean, Amy was unfazed by anything. She flooded us with cheerful, highly descriptive prose backed up by voluminous research and accompanied by ever-witty cover pages and journal entries. Our super new diving coverage can be credited to her love for things marine. Always ready to jump into a new escapade, Amy kept us laughing and brought to our office a bit of the spirit of tropical paradise.

Sarah Thomas
The Northern Territory and the Kimberley, WA

Enthusiastic, funny, and utterly unflappable, veteran R-W Sarah seemed as comfortable in the wilderness as your average wallaby. With expert driving skills and deft use of posterboard, she took on some of Australia's roughest roads and most remote terrain with aplomb. Whether it was the darkness of Tunnel Creek, a "road" resembling a river, or a harrowing boat ride, Sarah braved every danger and inconvenience with a sharp sense of humor and a can-do attitude. Her always-thorough copy captured the excitement, beauty, and spirituality of the bush, while her phone calls, complete with hilarious storytelling, brightened each week. She came, she saw, and she conquered the tropics, the desert, and all of our hearts.

Georgia Young
South Australia, the Red Centre

Locked and empty hostels, blowouts on rough roads, and inexplicable desert downpours might have held a lesser R-W back, but they were no match for Georgia's verve and dedication. Nature-girl Georgia thrived in the Flinders and the MacDonnells, lent her wine-country-native conneisseurism to the Clare Valley and McLaren Vale, and set out with determination to resolve the mystery of the bakeries. A stellar researcher, she seemed to have an innate knack for the job. Her prose bordered on poetry, with descriptions so hauntingly evocative that, despite our instinctive need to edit, we often couldn't bring ourselves to alter a word. Plus, damned if we wouldn't all kill for her handwriting. A stray golf ball might have laid her low for a bit, but nothing could keep her down—Georgia was unstoppable.

Acknowledgments

A rousing hurrah to Nic, our favorite dag (in the most affectionate sense), a font of wisdom, helpfulness, and masking tape. To David and Jen, for invaluable crunch-time assistance. To Allison and Ben, who paved the way. To the whole Jungle Down Under crew, for greenery and good times, and to Rapunzel for her locks. To Marina, our intern, for her Westralian insight. To Prince and Madonna, for inspiration. To Derek, Matt, and Dan, for maps; Production, the unsung heroes; Anne, MEs, receptionists, typists, proofers, and the entire office gang, for a great summer.—**Team Oz**

The maddest of props to Kristin and Eli, for a stellar job through all the craziness and the fun: office nights, beach days, happy hours, and all. To Carl, David, Ron, Liz, and the clowns, for poker, weekend trips, and chili; to Aaron and Dave, for Flav-O-Ice and keepin' it real at 10 Homer; and to Alex, for all of the above. To Jen, Kirsten, and Kira, for swing dancing and years of coolgirldom. To the LG family, for a fantastic summer. To Mom, Dad, Karin, Lisa, and Erika, with love, for everything.—**SBS**

Thanks to Sonja for her guidance, energy, and friendship. To Eli for his integrity, storytimes, and for making it all fun. To both for their understanding and support. To Anne, for biodots and good advice. To Nic, Allison, Monica, Heath, and the rest of the crew for help and a LG summer. To EKR, ALRS, JAK, J&A, and the Cambridge/Somerville city line. To Alice, Kate, and Caty. To JAN. To Mom, Dad, Sarah, Karenna, Drew, and Albert for making everything worthwhile. —**KCG**

Thanks to Mom, Dad, Mark, Beth, and the rest of the family for always listening. To Sonja for her tireless efforts and witty banter, and Kristin, for her vitality and understanding. To Nic, David, Allison, the research crew, and everyone else who contributed. To Robert, Sarah, and Beth, with fondest memories of Australia. To Mateo, T.J., and Pierce, with love.—**Eli**

Editor	Sonja B. Starr
Associate Editor	Kristin C. Gore
Associate Editor	Eli Ceryak
Managing Editor	Nicolas R. Rapold
Publishing Director	Caroline R. Sherman
Publishing Director	Anna C. Portnoy
Production Manager	Dan Visel
Production Associate	Maryanthe Malliaris
Cartography Manager	Derek McKee
Design Manager	Bentsion Harder
Editorial Manager	M. Allison Arwady
Editorial Manager	Lisa M. Nosal
Financial Manager	Monica Eileen Eav
Personnel Manager	Nicolas R. Rapold
Publicity Manager	Alexander Z. Speier
New Media Manager	Måns O. Larsson
Map Editors	Matthew R. Daniels, Dan Luskin
Production Assistant	Heath Ritchie
Office Coordinators	Tom Moore
Director of Advertising Sales	Gene Plotkin
Associate Sales Executives	Colleen Gaard, Mateo Jaramillo, Alexandra Price
President	Catherine J. Turco
General Manager	Richard Olken
Assistant General Manager	Anne E. Chisholm

Thanks to Our Readers...

Mano Aaron, CA; Jean-Marc Abela, CAN; George Adams, NH; Bob & Susan Adams, GA; Deborah Adeyanju, NY; Rita Alexander, MI; Shani Amory-Claxton, NY; Kate Anderson, AUS; Lindsey Anderson, ENG; Viki Anderson, NY; Ray Andrews, JPN; Robin J. Andrus, NJ; L. Asurmendi, CA; Anthony Atkinson, ENG; Deborah Bacek, GA; Jeffrey Bagdade, MI; Mark Baker, UK; Mary Baker, TN; Jeff Barkoff, PA; Regina Barsanti, NY; Ethan Beeler, MA; Damao Bell, CA; Rya Ben-Shir, IL; Susan Bennerstrom, WA; Marla Benton, CAN; Matthew Berenson, OR; Walter Bergstrom, OR; Caryl Bird, ENG; Charlotte Blanc, NY; Jeremy Boley, EL SAL; Oliver Bradley, GER; A.Braurstein, CO; Philip R. Brazil, WA; Henrik Brockdorff, DMK; Tony Bronco, NJ; Eileen Brouillard, SC; Mary Brown, ENG; Tom Brown, CA; Elizabeth Buckius, CO; Sue Buckley, UK; Christine Burer, SWITZ; Norman Butler, MO; Brett Carroll, WA; Susan Caswell, ISR; Carlos Cersosimo, ITA; Barbara Crary Chase, WA; Stella Cherry Carbost, SCOT; Oi Ling Cheung, HK; Simon Chinn, ENG; Charles Cho, AUS; Carolyn R. Christie, AUS; Emma Church, ENG; Kelley Coblentz, IN; Cathy Cohan, PA; Phyllis Cole, TX; Karina Collins, SWITZ; Michael Cox, CA; Mike Craig, MD; Rene Crusto, LA; Claudine D'Anjou, CAN; Lizz Daniels, CAN; Simon Davies, SCOT; Samantha Davis, AUS; Leah Davis, TX; Stephanie Dickman, MN; Philipp Dittrich,GER; Tim Donovan, NH; Reed Drew, OR; Wendy Duncan, SCOT; Melissa Dunlap, VA; P.A. Emery, UK; GCL Emery, SAF; Louise Evans, AUS; Christine Farr, AUS; David Fattel, NJ; Vivian Feen, MD; David Ferraro, SPN; Sue Ferrick, CO; Philip Fielden, UK; Nancy Fintel, FL; Jody Finver, FL; D. Ross Fisher, CAN; Abigail Flack, IL; Elizabeth Foster, NY; Bonnie Fritz, CAN; J. Fuson, OR; Michael K. Gasuad, NV; Raad German, TX; Mark Gilbert, NY; Betsy Gilliland, CA; Ana Goshko, NY; Patrick Goyenneche, CAN; David Greene, NY; Jennifer Griffin, ENG; Janet & Jeremy Griffith, ENG; Nanci Guartofierro, NY; Denise Guillemette, MA; Ilona Haayer, HON; Joseph Habboushe, PA; John Haddon, CA; Ladislav Hanka, MI; Michael Hanke, CA; Avital Harari, TX; Channing Hardy, KY; Patrick Harris, NY; Denise Hasher, PA; Jackie Hattorl, UK; Guthrie Hebenstreit, ROM; Therase Hill, AUS; Denise Hines, NJ; Cheryl Horne, ENG; Julie Howell, IL; Naomi Hsu, NJ; Mark Hudgkinson, ENG; Brenda Humphrey, NC; Kelly Hunt, NY; Daman Irby, AUT; Bill Irwin, NY; Andrea B. Jackson, PA; John Jacobsen, FL; Pat Johanson, MD; Russell Jones, FL; J. Jones, AUS; Sharon Jones, MI; Craig Jones, CA; Wayne Jones, ENG; Jamie Kagan, NJ; Mirko Kaiser, GER; Scott Kauffman, NY; John Keanie, NIRE; Barbara Keary, FL; Jamie Kehoe, AUS; Alistair Kernick, SAF; Daihi Kielle, SWITZ; John Knutsen, CA; Rebecca Koepke, NY; Jeannine Kolb, ME; Elze Kollen, NETH; Lorne Korman, CAN; Robin Kortright, CAN; Isel Krinsky, CAN; George Landers, ENG; Jodie Lanthois, AUS; Roger Latzgo, PA; A. Lavery, AZ; Joan Lea, ENG; Lorraine Lee, NY; Phoebe Leed, MA; Tammy Leeper, CA; Paul Lejeune, ENG; Yee-Leng Leong, CA; Sam Levene, CAN; Robin Levin, PA; Christianna Lewis, PA; Ernesto Licata, ITA; Wolfgang Lischtansky, AUT; Michelle Little, UK; Dee Littrell, CA; Maria Lobosco, UK; Netii Ross, ITA; Didier Look, CAN; Alice Lorenzotti, MA; David Love, PA; Briege Mac Donagh, IRE; Brooke Madigan, NY; Helen Maltby, FL; Shyama Marchesi, ITA; Domenico Maria, ITA; Natasha Markovic, AUS; Edward Marshall, ECU; Rachel Marshall, TX; Kate Maynard, UK; Agnes McCann, IRE; Susan McGowan, NY; Brandi McGunigal, CAN; Neville McLean, NZ; Marty McLendon, MS; Matthew Melko, OH; Barry Mendelson, CA; Eric Middendorf, OH; Nancy Mike, AZ; Coren Milbury, NH; Margaret Mill, NY; David H. Miller, TX; Ralph Miller, NV; Susan Miller, CO; Larry Moeller, MI; Richard Moore, ENG; Anne & Andrea Mosher, MA; J. L. Mourne, TX; Athanassios Moustakas, GER; Laurel Naversen, ENG; Suzanne Neil, IA; Deborah Nickles, PA; Pieter & Agnes Noels, BEL; Werner Norr, GER; Ruth J. Nye, ENG; Heidi O'Brien, WA; Sherry O'Cain, SC; Aibhan O'Connor, IRE; Kevin O'Connor, CA; Margaret O'Rielly, IRE; Daniel O'Rourke, CA; Krissy Oechslin, OH; Johan Oelofse, SAF; Quinn Okamoto, CA; Juan Ramon Olaizola, SPN; Laura Onorato, NM; Bill Orkin, IL; K. Owusu-Agyenang, UK; Anne Paananen, SWD; Jenine Padget, AUS; Frank Pado, TX; G. Pajkich, Washington, DC; J. Parker, CA; Marian Parnat, AUS; Sandra Swift Parrino, NY; Iris Patten, NY; M. Pavini, CT; David Pawielski, MN; Jenny Pawson, ENG; Colin Peak, AUS; Marius Penderis, ENG; Jo-an Peters, AZ; Barbara Phillips, NY; Romain Picard, Washington, DC; Pati Pike, ENG; Mark Pollock, SWITZ; Minnie Adele Potter, FL; Martin Potter, ENG; Claudia Praetel, ENG; Bill Press, Washington, DC; David Prince, NC; Andrea Pronko, OH; C. Robert Pryor, OH; Phu Quy, VTNM; Adrian Rainbow, ENG; John Raven, AUS; Lynn Reddringer, VA; John Rennie, NZ; Ruth B.Robinson, FL; John & Adelaida Romagnoli, CA; Eva Romano, FRA; Mark A. Roscoe, NETH; Yolanda & Jason Ross, CAN; Sharee Rowe, ENG; W. Suzanne Rowell, NY; Vic Roych, AZ; John Russell, ENG; Jennifer Ruth, OK; William Sabino, NJ; Hideki Saito, JPN; Frank Schaer, HUN; Jeff Schultz, WI; Floretta Seeland-Connally, IL; Colette Shoulders, FRA; Shireen Sills, ITA; Virginia Simon, AUS; Beth Simon, NY; Gary Simpson, AUS; Barbara & Allen Sisarsky, GA; Alon Siton, ISR; Kathy Skeie, CA; Robyn Skillecorn, AUS; Erik & Kathy Skon, MN; Stine Skorpen, NOR; Philip Smart, CAN; Colin Smit, ENG; Kenneth Smith, DE; Caleb Smith, CA; Geoffrey Smith, TX; John Snyder, NC; Kathrin Speidel, GER; Lani Steele, PHIL; Julie Stelbratch, PA; Margaret Stires, TN; Donald Stumpf, NY; Samuel Suffern, TN; Michael Swerdlow, ENG; Brian Talley, TX; Serene-Marie Terrell, NY; B. Larry Thilson, CAN; J. Pelham Thomas, NC; Wright Thompson, ITA; Christine Timm, NY; Melinda Tong, HK; M. Tritica, AUS; Mark Trop, FL; Chris Troxel, AZ; Rozana Tsiknaki, GRC; Lois Turner, NZ; Nicole Virgil, IL; Blondie Vucich, CO; Wendy Wan, SAF; Carrie & Simon Wedgwood, ENG; Frederick Weibgen, NJ; Richard Weil, MN; Alan Weissberg, OH; Ryan Wells, OH; Jill Wester, GER; Clinton White, AL; Gael White, CAN; Melanie Whitfield, SCOT; Bryn Williams, CAN; Amanda Williams, CAN; Wendy Willis, AUS; Sasha Wilson, NY; Kendra Wilson, CA; Olivia Wiseman, ENG; Gerry Wood, CAN; Kelly Wooten, ENG; Robert Worsley, ENG; C.A.Wright, ENG; Caroline Wright, ENG; Mary H. Yuhasz, CO; Margaret Zimmerman, WA.

"A crash course that could lead to a summer job— or a terrific party." —*Boston Globe*

With **THE OFFICIAL HARVARD STUDENT AGENCIES BARTENDING COURSE**, you could find yourself mixing drinks professionally and earning great money, or at least, giving fabulous cocktail parties!

- Over 300 recipes for the most asked-for drinks— including a section on popular nonalcoholic beverages
- Tips on finding top-paying bartending jobs
- How to remember hundreds of recipes
- How to serve drinks and handle customers with aplomb

ALSO AVAILABLE FROM ST. MARTIN'S PRESS

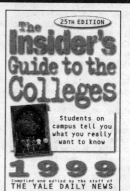

The only college guide written by college students is now better than ever with...

- Profiles of more than 300 schools in the U.S. and Canada, focusing on academics, housing and food, social life, student activities, and the campus and vicinity
- Insider tips on the application and admissions process
- Up-to-date statistics on tuition, acceptance rates, average test scores and more
- Plus: a College Finder, which picks the right schools in dozens of categories

 VISIT THE BEST BET ON THE NET FOR TEENS

's Go 1999 Reader Questionnaire ★

Please fill this out and return it to **Let's Go, St. Martin's Press,** 175 Fifth Ave., New York, NY 10010-7848. All respondents will receive a free subscription to **The Yellowjacket,** the Let's Go Newsletter. You can find a more extensive version of this survey on the web at http://www.letsgo.com.

Name: _____

Address: _____

City: _____ **State:** _____ **Zip/Postal Code:** _____

Email: _____ **Which book(s) did you use?** _____

How old are you? under 19   19-24   25-34   35-44   45-54   55 or over

Are you (circle one)   in high school   in college   in graduate school
   employed   retired   between jobs

Have you used Let's Go before? yes no   **Would you use it again?** yes no

How did you first hear about Let's Go? friend   store clerk   television
   bookstore display   advertisement/promotion   review   other

Why did you choose Let's Go (circle up to two)? reputation budget focus
   price   writing style   annual updating   other: _____

Which other guides have you used, if any? Fodor's   Footprint Handbooks
   Frommer's $-a-day   Lonely Planet   Moon Guides   Rick Steve's
   Rough Guides   UpClose   other: _____

Which guide do you prefer?

Please rank each of the following parts of Let's Go 1 to 5 (1=needs improvement, 5=perfect). packaging/cover   practical information   accommodations   food   cultural introduction   sights   practical introduction ("Essentials")   directions   entertainment   gay/lesbian information   maps   other: _____

How would you like to see the books improved? (continue on separate page, if necessary) _____

_____

How long was your trip?   one week   two weeks   three weeks
   one month   two months or more

Which countries did you visit? _____

What was your average daily budget, not including flights? _____

Have you traveled extensively before? yes no

Do you buy a separate map when you visit a foreign city? yes no

Have you used a Let's Go Map Guide? yes no

If you have, would you recommend them to others? yes no

Have you visited Let's Go's website? yes no

What would you like to see included on Let's Go's website? _____

What percentage of your trip planning did you do on the Web? _____

Would you use a Let's Go: recreational (e.g. skiing) guide gay/lesbian guide
   adventure/trekking guide   phrasebook   general travel information guide

Which of the following destinations do you hope to visit in the next three to five years (circle one)? Canada   Argentina   Perú   Kenya   Middle East
   Caribbean   Scandinavia   other: _____

Where did you buy your guidebook?   Internet   independent bookstore
   chain bookstore   college bookstore   travel store   other: _____